MOON HANDBOOKS®

ARGENTINA

FIRST EDITION

WAYNE BERNHARDSON

Ⓐ AVALON TRAVEL

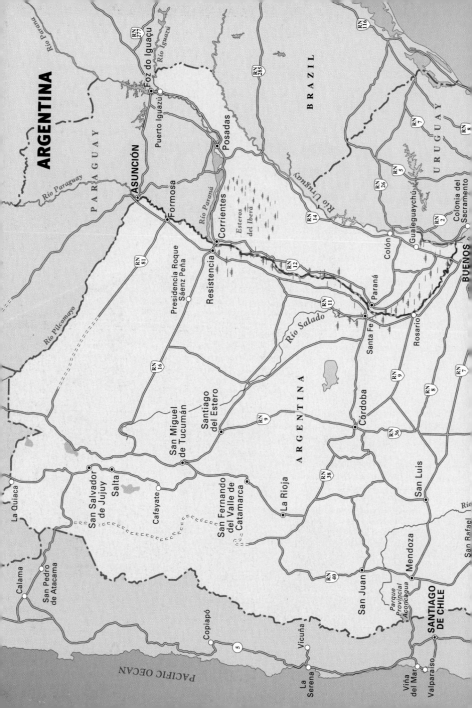

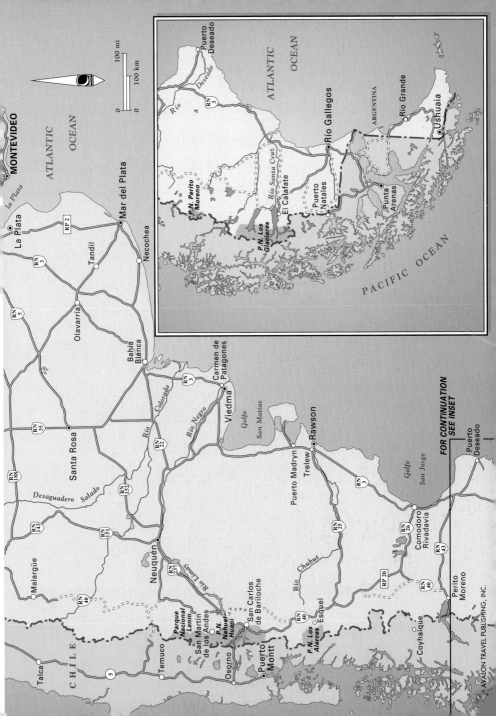

CONTENTS

Discover Argentina

Explore Argentina

Buenos Aires and Vicinity 32

The Pampas 118

MAPS

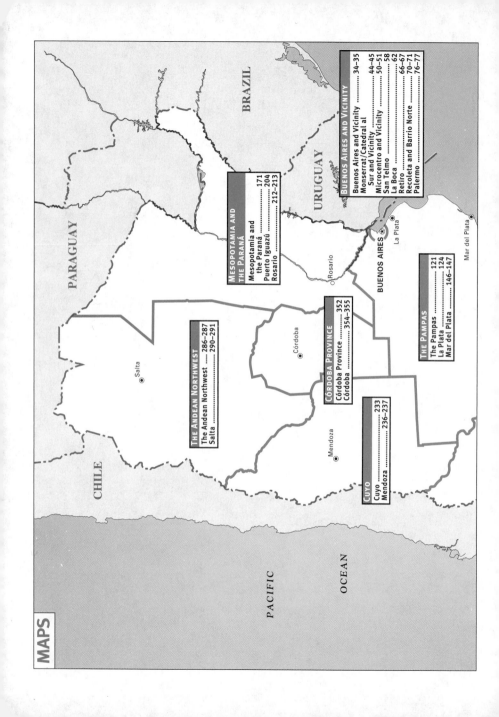

PARAGUAY

CHILE

BRAZIL

URUGUAY

PACIFIC OCEAN

Salta

Mendoza

Córdoba

Rosario

BUENOS AIRES

La Plata

Mar del Plata

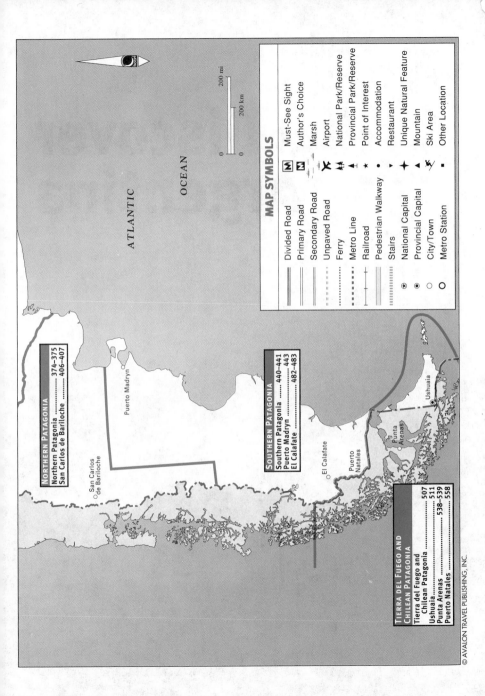

ATLANTIC

OCEAN

NORTHERN PATAGONIA

Northern Patagonia 374–375
San Carlos de Bariloche 406–407

Puerto Madryn

San Carlos
de Bariloche

SOUTHERN PATAGONIA

Southern Patagonia 440–441
Puerto Madryn 443
El Calafate 482–483

El Calafate

Puerto
Natales

Ushuaia

Punta
Arenas

**TIERRA DEL FUEGO AND
CHILEAN PATAGONIA**

Tierra del Fuego and
  Chilean Patagonia 507
Ushuaia 511
Punta Arenas 538–539
Puerto Natales 558

MAP SYMBOLS

⬒ Divided Road	M̄ Must-See Sight	
⬒ Primary Road	★̄ Author's Choice	
⬒ Secondary Road	⌇ Marsh	
⋯ Unpaved Road	✈ Airport	
⋯ Ferry	♦ National Park/Reserve	
▪▪ Metro Line	★ Provincial Park/Reserve	
┼ Railroad	• Point of Interest	
▮ Pedestrian Walkway	▸ Accommodation	
▮▮ Stairs	◂ Restaurant	
⊛ National Capital	✗ Unique Natural Feature	
◉ Provincial Capital	◂ Mountain	
○ City/Town	✗ Ski Area	
○ Metro Station	▪ Other Location	

0 ——— 200 mi

0 ——— 200 km

© AVALON TRAVEL PUBLISHING, INC.

Discover
Argentina

Nestled where the South American continent tapers to its tip, pointing toward Antarctica, Argentina is a country of superlatives and extremes. In the region known as the Southern Cone for its shape on the map, it's a geographical jewel even if it owes its very name—deriving from the Latin root for silver—to Spanish settlers' misguided hopes of finding precious metals.

As the world's eighth-largest country, slightly smaller than India, Argentina's diversity can satisfy almost any interest. Its capital, Buenos Aires, is famous for the tango and has the highest international profile of any South American city. The first city on the continent to exceed a million inhabitants, its European-immigrant vitality has survived repeated crises to remain a cultural as well as political capital.

For some visitors, Buenos Aires alone is enough, but it's also the port of entry to some of the greatest sights in the Americas. The Río de la Plata, which empties into the South Atlantic here, is longer than the Mississippi; to the west, the gaucho homeland of the flat green pampas stretches beyond the horizon. To the north, the legendary Iguazú Falls are half again the height of Niagara and nearly four times wider. Along the western border with Chile, higher than Denali in Alaska, the Andean summit of Cerro Aconcagua is "The Roof of the Americas."

Among its staggering landscapes, Argentina counts ten UNESCO World Biosphere Reserves and seven World Heritage Sites, including Iguazú and the ruins-rich polychrome canyon of the Quebrada de Humahuaca, linked to the highlands of Peru and Bolivia. In the southern region of Patagonia, there's the wildlife-packed Atlantic coastline of Península Valdés, the aboriginal rock art of Cueva de las Manos (Cave of Hands), and the Glaciar Moreno, a grinding river of ice that's a feast for the eyes *and* the ears.

Argentine paleontologists have put the desert parks of Ischigualasto and Talampaya on the map with groundbreaking fossil research. Dinosaur-hunters have made other major advances both in the arid north, whose bright sedimentary landscapes recall the southwestern United States, and on the vast Patagonian steppes.

Península Valdés, for that matter, is only one of many wildlife reserves on a seemingly endless South Atlantic shoreline. Northernmost Patagonia's forested lake district reminds visitors of the European Alps, and only New Zealand, Norway, and the Alaskan panhandle can match archipelagic Tierra del Fuego's sub-Antarctic wildlands.

However, Argentina's not all nature. In the shadow of Aconcagua, the Cuyo region is wine country, and Mendoza is one of South America's most livable cities. The cities of Rosario and Córdoba—the latter's colonial Jesuit heritage is also a UNESCO site—are cultural as well as economic forces in Argentina.

For many years, relatively few braved travel to a country that suffered one of the most brutal and arbitrary military dictatorships on a continent that was infamous for them. In the 20-plus years since the return to constitutional government, though, international travel has steadily increased even through hard economic times, and it's now an almost ideal place to travel. By North American or European standards, it's also affordable—even cheap.

When planning any trip to Argentina, don't overlook the fact that this is the world's eighth-largest country. Unless your trip is an open-ended overland excursion, this means choosing among numerous options both as to destinations and means of transportation.

Buenos Aires, South America's premier urban destination, is compact and easy to travel around, but visiting other high-profile destinations like Mesopotamia's Iguazú Falls and southern Patagonia's Moreno Glacier require either two- to three-hour flights or 15- to 30-hour bus trips. Driving (though not recommended in Buenos Aires) is an option, but for most visitors this will mean a rental car from a provincial airport or city.

In a country of Argentina's size and diversity, there's an infinity of itineraries, depending on each traveler's time and interests. The ones suggested in this book can be mixed and matched to create an individualized experience. The assumption is that, for most readers, Argentina is a relatively remote destination that few will visit for less than a week or ten days. Most of those who spend a shorter period will be in and around Buenos Aires, for which *Moon Handbooks Buenos Aires* can provide more detail. That book is also suitable for extended visits to the capital.

While primarily about Argentina, this book overlaps substantial sections of southernmost Chile. There's a reason for this—more than any other part of the two countries, the Argentine provinces of Santa Cruz and Tierra del Fuego, and the Chilean region of Magallanes, form an almost seamless region. International borders seem only an inconvenience, and foreigners in particular rarely visit Santa Cruz's Parque Nacional Los Glaciares without also seeing Chile's Parque Nacional Torres del Paine and, as often as not, Magallanes' regional capital of Punta Arenas (Chile) along with Tierra del Fuego's capital of Ushuaia (Argentina).

By jet, Argentina is about eight hours from Miami, 10 hours from New York, and 15 hours from Los Angeles—close enough for short-term visitors focused on special interests in specific regions. Since Argentine standard time is only two hours ahead of New York and three hours behind Western Europe, even jet lag is only a minor issue.

WHEN TO GO

The fact that the Southern Hemisphere's seasons are opposite those of the Northern Hemisphere, where most foreign visitors live, adds to Argentina's appeal. Still, it remains a year-round destination, where urban exploration, winter skiing, and desert trekking are all possible.

Buenos Aires's urban appeal is largely independent of the seasons, but some visitors—and many Argentines, for that matter—would rather avoid the capital's hot, sticky summer; business travelers should avoid January and February in particular. Activities like the theater and special events, most notably the increasingly popular Festival Buenos Aires Tango, resume near the end of February as the *porteños* of BA return from summer holidays. The spring months of September, October, and November may be the most comfortable, but the relatively mild winter sees some stretches of warm, brilliant weather.

Because Argentina extends from the southern edge of the tropics to the sub-Antarctic in Tierra del Fuego, seasonality can vary according to latitude, but also with altitude. Neither is an issue in the pampas, but the summer months of January and February can be uncomfortably crowded at beach resorts like Mar del Plata.

Subtropical Iguazú is an impressive sight at any season, but summers there are even hotter, wetter, and stickier than in Buenos Aires. It can get crowded, too, when Argentines take their winter holidays in late July and early August. Nearby Corrientes's wildlife-rich Iberá wetlands never get really crowded, but the summer heat and humidity can be trying.

In the northwestern Andean highlands, summer is the rainy season. Though that may mean only an afternoon thundershower, occasional downpours can cause flash floods and cut off roads, reducing access to areas of interest; at the highest altitudes, it can even mean snowstorms. Winter's warm, dry days, by contrast, can be ideal for exploring the backcountry, though nights get cold at higher elevations.

Cuyo's wineries are open at any season, but March's Festival de la Vendimia (wine harvest festival) makes that the ideal time to visit the provincial capital of Mendoza. Summer is the time for mountaineering on Aconcagua, while winter is ski season at Las Leñas and other provincial resorts. For fossil fanatics, destinations like San Juan's Parque Provincial Ischigualasto, La Rioja's nearby Parque Nacional Talampaya, and San Luis's Parque Nacional Las Quijadas can get dangerously hot in summer, but the rest of the year is ideal.

Patagonia and its lake district are traditional summer destinations, with places like Bariloche as busy as the beaches of Buenos Aires Province, but it's also a magnet for fly-fishing enthusiasts from October to April, and the heart of Argentina's ski industry from June to August.

Elsewhere in Patagonia, the season is lengthening, especially among foreign visitors. El Calafate, gateway to the Moreno Glacier, was once a January–February destination, but now many services stay open October to April, and even for July winter holidays. Patagonia's Península Valdés is a special case that depends on South Atlantic wildlife—the right whale's arrival in July brings the first tourists, and they keep coming along with the influx of elephant seals, orcas, and penguins until the end of March.

As an extension of Patagonia, Tierra del Fuego is still primarily a summer destination, though it also has a ski season. The city of Ushuaia is the South American gateway to Antarctica, where the spring breakup of pack ice determines the season.

WHAT TO TAKE

LUGGAGE

What sort of luggage you bring depends on what sort of trip you're planning, for how long, and where you're planning to go. For shoestring travelers planning months in Argentina and perhaps neighboring countries as well, for instance, a spacious but lightweight backpack is the best choice; a small daypack for local excursions is also a good idea.

Even for nonbackpackers, light luggage is advisable, even though traveling on airplanes, shuttles, and taxis can be logistically simpler than buses alone—door-to-door service is the rule. Even then, a small daypack for excursions is convenient.

Small but sturdy lightweight locks are advisable for all sorts of luggage, if only to discourage temptation.

CLOTHING

A good rule of thumb is to bring appropriately seasonal clothing for comparable northern-hemisphere latitudes. Buenos Aires's climate is mild in spring and autumn, hot and humid in summer, and cool but not cold in winter. Humidity and winter winds can make it feel colder than absolute temperatures might suggest, but frost is almost unheard-of. For summer, then, light cottons are the rule, while a sweater and perhaps a light jacket suffice for the shoulder seasons. A warm (but not polar-strength) jacket and rain gear are advisable for winter.

Much depends, of course, on what sort of activities you will be undertaking—for opera at the Teatro Colón, for instance, formal clothing is obligatory. Likewise, individuals conducting business in the capital will dress as they would in New York or London, with suit and tie for men and similarly appropriate clothing for women. A compact umbrella is a good idea at any time of year.

Travel elsewhere in the country may require different attire, though appropriate seasonality is still the rule. In the high altitudes of the Andean northwest or Cuyo, or the high latitudes of Patagonia, warm clothing is essential; in southernmost Patagonia and Tierra del Fuego, additional wet-weather gear is imperative, especially for hikers.

ODDS AND ENDS

Since public toilets sometimes lack toilet paper, travelers should always carry some, even though it's readily available within the country. Some budget hotels have thin walls and squeaky floors, so earplugs can be useful.

Leg pouches and money belts are good options for securing cash, travelers checks, and important documents. A compact pair of binoculars is a good idea for bird-watchers and others who enjoy wildlife and the landscape.

Physiographically, culturally, and economically, Argentina divides into several more or less discrete vernacular regions, which coincide fairly conveniently with provincial boundaries.

BUENOS AIRES AND VICINITY

Since the devaluation of 2002, South America's highest-profile capital has become a bargain destination that's reason enough to visit the country—many visitors spend weeks or even months enjoying its first-rate accommodations, innovative cuisine, all-night entertainment, non-stop shopping, and matchless cultural resources. Despite its international sophistication, it's also a city of intimate neighborhoods where no one is truly anonymous. The nearby suburbs offer rewarding excursions, most notably the myriad channels of the Paraná Delta.

THE PAMPAS

Beneath seemingly endless horizons, the grassy plains of the pampas were the original gaucho country, now occupied by sprawling cattle ranches that often open their doors to paying guests. In the south, low mountain ranges diversify the landscape before giving way to an inviting Atlantic coastline that's the prime vacation destination for Argentines themselves.

The country's most densely populated region, the pampas are also the most productive in terms of agriculture and industry. More than a third of Argentina's population lives in Gran Buenos Aires (Greater Buenos Aires, including the federal capital); together, the capital and Buenos Aires Province hold nearly half the country's inhabitants.

Geographically speaking, the pampas divide into the humid pampas (most of Buenos Aires Province along with some parts of Santa Fe and Córdoba) and the arid pampas (the most westerly parts of Buenos Aires Province and the entire province of La Pampa). Coverage in this book includes the two main pampas provinces, Buenos Aires and La Pampa, only.

MESOPOTAMIA AND THE PARANÁ

One of the world's great river systems supports two of the continent's most spectacular attractions: the world-famous Iguazú Falls and the isolated, almost unknown wetlands of the Esteros del Iberá. The region can also boast landmark historical Jesuit missions that extend into Brazil and Paraguay.

North of Buenos Aires, between the Río Paraná and the Río Uruguay, the humid agricultural provinces of Entre Ríos, Corrientes, and Misiones form a mix of rolling lowlands, marshes and rounded mountains that stretch north to the Paraguayan and Brazilian borders. On the Paraná's right bank, Santa Fe is one of the country's most prosperous provinces, thanks to its fertile alluvial soils, abundant rainfall, and the industrial port city of Rosario—also one of the country's cultural centers.

Beyond Santa Fe, the northwestern Paraná provinces of Chaco and Formosa belong to the Gran Chaco, a brutally hot lowland that extends west into Salta and Santiago del Estero Provinces, where it's much drier. In this book, Salta and Santiago del Estero are covered in the Andean Northwest chapter.

CUYO

If the pampas are Argentina's breadbasket, the Cuyo provinces of Mendoza, San Juan, and San Luis are its wine barrel—about three quarters of the country's wine production comes from the irrigated vineyards on the eastern Andean slope, and exports are increasing. Visitors can spend days or even weeks hopping from winery to winery.

In colonial times, Cuyo fell under Chilean administration, but the same snows that blocked winter communications over the Andes—helping forge a distinct regional identity—now welcome skiers. The snow never vanishes from 6,959-meter Cerro Aconcagua, the "Roof of the Americas" and the Western Hemisphere's highest point, drawing climbers and hikers from around the globe.

Economically, Mendoza is also an energy storehouse, as much of the country's petroleum and natural gas originates here.

THE ANDEAN NORTHWEST

In colonial times, the densely populated northwest was the River Plate's link to the Viceroyalty of Peru and to Spain, and its palpable indigenous and colonial landmarks—set among incomparable mountain and desert scenery—are the region's strongest assets. Cities like Salta, San Salvador de Jujuy, La Rioja, Catamarca, and Santiago del Estero were thriving when Buenos Aires was a hardship post; not until well after independence did they reverse their orientation toward the Atlantic.

In addition to its historic and scenic appeal, the Northwest can claim a unique, underappreciated status as a wine region. The areas around Cafayate can boast distinctive high-altitude wines, including what most consider to be Argentina's top Torrontés, but La Rioja's Chilecito also has notable vineyards and wineries.

CÓRDOBA PROVINCE

Córdoba's cultural primacy, dating from its early history as a Jesuit ecclesiastical and educational center, has set it apart from Argentina's other provinces. The Jesuit legacy is palpable in the capital and scattered throughout the rest of the province, whose rolling mountainous backcountry is one of the country's favorite year-round playgrounds.

Traditionally, the capital—widely considered Argentina's "second city"—is also an industrial powerhouse.

PATAGONIA

Beyond the Río Colorado, which flows southeast from the Chilean border to the Atlantic Ocean, continental Patagonia consists of Neuquén, Río Negro, Chubut, and Santa Cruz Provinces. For purposes of this book, Patagonia subdivides into Northern Patagonia, comprising Neuquén and Río Negro, plus northwesterly parts of Chubut that correspond to the so-called "lake district" along the Chilean border; and Southern Patagonia, the remainder of Chubut and all of Santa Cruz Province.

While most of Argentine Patagonia is desert steppe, the densely wooded sector near the Chilean border boasts numerous national parks. Centered around the city of San Carlos de Bariloche, this is the country's conventional holiday destination, but activities-oriented travel, including hiking, climbing, rafting and kayaking, and fly-fishing, has grown rapidly over the past decade. At select locations, ski resorts take advantage of the heavy winter snowpack.

For more than three centuries, northern Patagonia was a zone of conflict where Araucanian (Mapuche) Indians kept both Spanish and Argentine forces and settlers off guard, before finally bowing to Argentine sovereignty in the late 19th century. While marginalized economically, the Mapuche play an increasingly visible role in regional politics through their persistent land claims.

All the way south to the Chilean border, southern Patagonia's Atlantic coastline is a scenic cornucopia of whales, seals, penguins, and other wildlife. The southern province of Santa Cruz is famous for the dramatic Moreno Glacier, a crackling outlier of the Campo de Hielo Sur, the southern Patagonian ice sheet.

Most of the region's population is urban, but the rural economy supports everything from subsistence plots to extensive grazing of cattle and sheep.

TIERRA DEL FUEGO AND CHILEAN PATAGONIA

Across the Strait of Magellan from the continent, Chile and Argentina share the scenic grandeur of the sub-Antarctic Isla Grande de Tierra del Fuego, where Ushuaia is the world's southernmost city. Across the Beagle Channel, Chile's Puerto Williams is the last major settlement north of Antarctica. The region's biggest draw, though, is the igneous spires of Chile's Parque Nacional Torres del Paine.

Most of the areas of Chilean Patagonia covered in this book consist of jagged mountains and islands set among inland seas that bear the brunt of Pacific storms; copious quantities of rain and snow feed surging rivers and the sprawling glaciers of the Chilean side of the Campo de Hielo Sur, the southern continental ice field that extends into Argentina's Santa Cruz Province. In much of the region, nearly pristine woodlands still cover the mountainsides. The only significant city is the regional capital of Punta Arenas, though the town of Puerto Natales is a gateway to Torres del Paine.

For first-time visitors, the big sights are Buenos Aires, Iguazú Falls, and Patagonia's Moreno Glacier. Since most will arrive in Buenos Aires, this simplifies logistics, but great distances mean that flying to Iguazú and Patagonia is unavoidable.

Fortunately, El Calafate's new airport has eliminated the tedious, time-consuming transfer from Río Gallegos to the Moreno Glacier. If you have just seven nights in Argentina, figure at least two nights in Buenos Aires (at the beginning and end), two nights in Iguazú, and three at El Calafate, gateway to the glacier. With two or three extra days, you could spend more time in the capital, take an excursion to the Fitz Roy Sector of Parque Nacional Los Glaciares, or perhaps stay at an *estancia* near Buenos Aires or El Calafate.

If you can manage a two-week trip, you'll have greater flexibility in itineraries, though the long distances can still mean airport time, and returning to the hub airport at Buenos Aires may be unavoidable. Possible extensions include Puerto Madryn for the wildlife of Península Valdés, Bariloche as a base for numerous excursions in the northern Patagonian "lake district," and the "uttermost part of the earth" at Ushuaia, the world's southernmost city in Tierra del Fuego.

From Iguazú, a few additional days could include the colonial Jesuit missions, but also the wildlife-rich wetlands of Corrientes Province's underrated Esteros del Iberá (in many ways, more appealing than Iguazú itself). Other worthwhile options could include the northwestern city of Salta, an ideal base for a variety of excursions including the Quebrada de Humahuaca or the Quebrada de Cafayate (also a wine district), and the Cuyo wine region in and around Mendoza.

DAY 1

Arrive at Aeropuerto Internacional Ministro Pistarini (Ezeiza) and transfer to a Buenos Aires hotel, with the afternoon free for sightseeing.

DAY 2

Catch an early morning flight to Puerto Iguazú, with the afternoon at the falls; if the timing's right, take the full-moon tour.

Garganta del Diablo, Parque Nacional Iguazú

DAY 7

Strenuous full-day hike to Laguna de los Tres, with stupendous views of Cerro Fitz Roy. Evening return to El Calafate.

DAY 8

Spend a relaxing day at an *estancia* like the rustic Estancia Nibepo Aike or the more luxurious Hostería Alta Vista, on Estancia Anita.

Estancia Anita's Hostería Alta Vista

DAY 3

Take an excursion to the Brazilian side of the falls or, alternatively, hike the rainforest on the Argentine side. Or, visit the historic Jesuit mission at San Ignacio.

DAY 4

A morning flight back to Buenos Aires and on to El Calafate will take most of the day. Make an evening excursion to a nearby *estancia* for an *asado*.

DAY 5

Full-day excursion to the Moreno Glacier, Parque Nacional Los Glaciares.

DAY 6

Overland by bus or rental car to the Fitz Roy Sector of Parque Nacional Los Glaciares, with accommodations at the settlement of El Chaltén. With an early arrival time and good weather, you'll have time for a swift hike to view the glaciated needle of Cerro Torre.

DAY 9

Return flight to Buenos Aires, with afternoon and evening free for sightseeing and perhaps a tango floor show.

DAY 10

Morning and afternoon free for exploring Buenos Aires before an evening departure.

Spending three whole weeks in Argentina really opens the doors, either to see some of the prime destinations in a more thorough and leisurely way, or to add destinations and sights where logistics are more complex. Near Buenos Aires, for instance, it's easier to add worthwhile second-tier destinations like the Paraná Delta, the gaucho capital of San Antonio de Areco, the river port of Rosario, the Sierras of Buenos Aires Province, or the South Atlantic beaches in and around Mar del Plata. It's even possible to hop across the River Plate to the World Heritage Site of Colonia, Uruguay.

One of the best areas to spend extra time, though, would be the northwest, where you'll find truly off-the-beaten-track sights like the Jujuy provincial village of Iruya, the cloud forest national parks of the *yungas*, and the stunning desert highlands in and around Cachi. Cities such as Córdoba and Tucumán, with their colonial heritage and scenic nearby Sierras, are other possible extensions.

While Cuyo is Argentina's wine cask, its backcountry can boast some of the world's highest mountains, topped by 6,959-meter Cerro Aconcagua. A month's not long enough to climb Aconcagua while seeing or doing anything else—acclimatizing to the altitude takes at least a week—but it would be possible to trek to base camp and back. That sort of time could also be used to visit paleontological parks like San Luis Province's Parque Nacional Las Quijadas, San Juan's Parque Provincial Ischigualasto, and nearby La Rioja's Parque Nacional Talampaya.

It's Patagonia, though, where the extra time can help conquer distance and rough roads to permit extended hiking in the northern lake district or the Fitz Roy Sector of Los Glaciares, excursions to dinosaur sites in Neuquén Province, archaeological sites like the Cueva de las Manos, and side trips like Chile's magnificent Parque Nacional Torres del Paine.

DAY 1

Arrive at Aeropuerto Internacional Ministro Pistarini (Ezeiza) and transfer to a Buenos Aires hotel, with the afternoon free for sightseeing.

DAY 2

Early morning flight to Puerto Iguazú, with the

afternoon at the falls; if the timing's right, take the full-moon tour.

San Ignacio Miní

taking most of the day. Time permitting, visit a working *estancia* near El Calafate for an *asado*.

DAY 7
Full-day excursion to the Moreno Glacier, Parque Nacional Los Glaciares.

DAY 8
Overland by bus or rental car to the Fitz Roy Sector of Parque Nacional Los Glaciares, with accommodations at the settlement of El Chaltén. Depending on arrival time, you might squeeze in a swift hike to view Cerro Torre's glaciated needle.

DAY 9
Strenuous full-day hike to Laguna de los Tres, with stupendous views of Cerro Fitz Roy. Evening return to El Calafate.

DAY 10
Morning flight to Ushuaia, capital of Tierra del Fuego, followed by a wildlife-viewing excursion on the legendary Beagle Channel.

DAY 11
Full-day excursion to Parque Nacional Tierra del Fuego, with options for multiple short hikes. Be sure not to miss Museo Marítimo de Ushuaia, Ushuaia's misleadingly named prison museum.

DAY 3
Excursion to the Brazilian side of the falls; alternatively, hike the rainforest on the Argentine side or visit the historic Jesuit mission at San Ignacio.

DAY 4
Overland by bus to Posadas, capital of Misiones Province, and by hired jeep with driver to Colonia Carlos Pellegrini, in the Esteros del Iberá wetlands.

DAY 5
Full-day excursion among the floating islands of the Iberá marshes to see their wealth of subtropical wildlife.

DAY 6
Overland transfer to the provincial capital of Corrientes, then fly to El Calafate via Buenos Aires,

DAY 12
Morning flight to Trelew and transfer to Puerto Madryn, with an afternoon visit to the city's Ecocentro environmental museum. You should still have time for sunning on the beach or more active pursuits like diving or windsurfing.

DAY 13
Full-day excursion by tour bus or rental car to Península Valdés where, depending on the season, there'll be penguins, orcas, or right whales. Many other species—rheas, guanacos, and sea lions, for instance—are present all year.

© WAYNE BERNHARDSON

Magellanic penguin

with the afternoon free to view its colonial monuments.

DAY 16
Full day tour of the altiplano high steppe; in the winter dry season, take the "Train to the Clouds."

DAY 17
Excursion to archaeological sites and colonial monuments of the Quebrada de Humahuaca, a World Heritage Site in Jujuy Province. Spend the night in Purmamarca or Tilcara.

DAY 18
Morning tour to Iruya, a remote and stunningly scenic Andean village, with an afternoon return to Salta.

DAY 19
Return flight to Buenos Aires, with the afternoon and evening free for sightseeing and perhaps a tango floor show.

DAY 14
Full-day excursion to the gigantic Magellanic penguin colony at Punta Tombo, south of Trelew. On the way back, visit Trelew's state-of-the-art paleontology museum and take Welsh tea at Gaiman.

DAY 15
Return flight to Buenos Aires and on to the city of

DAY 20
Overland excursion to the gaucho capital of San Antonio de Areco or ferry across the River Plate to the World Heritage Site of Colonia, Uruguay.

DAY 21
Full day for exploring Buenos Aires before an evening departure.

Buenos Aires is the starting point—and the flashpoint—of Argentine history. Time has transformed, but not erased, the colonial quarters of Monserrat and San Telmo, but it's the epic of independence, the era of immigration and excess, the populism of the Peróns, and the ruthless 1976–83 dictatorship that helped create contemporary Argentina. Just to sample the historical sites and museums touching on these topics would require three days of intensive sightseeing, and at least a week would be desirable. Add a few days on the nearby pampas to appreciate the gaucho tradition.

What is now northwestern Argentina was only an outlier of the fabled Inka empire, but there are plenty of pre-Inka archaeological sites in Jujuy's Quebrada de Humahuaca, the highlands of Salta and other Andean provinces, and Córdoba and its Sierras. In colonial times, this was the country's most densely populated region, with chapels and churches to prove it, and many of these monuments played key roles in the independence campaign and its intrigues. Serious students of history will spend no less than a week here, and preferably at least two.

History plays second fiddle to nature in Mesopotamia, at least at Iguazú, but the remains of the Jesuit missions tell an epic story in their own right. In early independence times, this was the land of provincial warlords like Justo José de Urquiza, who built an extravagant palace in Entre Ríos. Figure on a couple of days to appreciate the missions, before or after seeing Iguazú. Some of the best-preserved ruins are in Paraguay, just over the border from the Argentine city of Posadas.

Earthquakes have leveled many Cuyo landmarks, but the legacy of José de San Martín, who crossed the cordillera to Chile with his Army of the Andes, endures at various sites in Mendoza, San Juan, and the Andean backcountry. The history of mountaineering, of course, is a topic in its own right in the highest peaks of the Andes.

In European terms, most of Patagonia's history is relatively recent, but Magellan's epic voyage of 1520 passed the winter at Puerto San Julián on the South Atlantic coast, and Darwin visited many locations from Buenos Aires Province to the tip of Tierra del Fuego—an itinerary British author Toby Green tried to trace on horseback in *Saddled with Darwin*. This, though, is for visitors with enough time and patience to view the landscape with 16th- or 19th-century eyes.

Until the late 19th century, Patagonia was Mapuche territory, and indigenous people are still a palpable presence in parts of Neuquén, Río Negro, and Chubut. Easily reached from Bariloche, northern Chubut was the South American hideout of Butch Cassidy and the Sundance Kid; many pilgrims pay homage to their crumbling cabin near Cholila.

Tierra del Fuego and Chilean Patagonia have a common history tied to the early European explorations, the travels of Darwin and Fitzroy and subsequent missionization, the California Gold Rush, and the opulence of immigrant wool barons. Some of the continent's greatest fortunes started here, and their founders left monuments to themselves around the Chilean city of Punta Arenas and scattered across the steppes. Spending several days or a week here would be easy.

DAY 4

Overland to the landmark Jesuit mission at San Ignacio and smaller ruined missions en route, with an overnight at the city of Posadas. From Posadas, time permitting, take an excursion across the Paraguayan border to the well-preserved missions of Trinidad and Jesús.

DAY 5

Return flight to Buenos Aires and on to the colonial city of Salta, with the afternoon free to visit the city's colonial churches, monuments, and museums.

DAY 6

Full-day tour of the altiplano high steppe; in the winter dry season, take the "Train to the Clouds."

DAY 7

Excursion to the archaeological sites and colonial monuments of the Quebrada de Humahuaca, a World Heritage Site in Jujuy Province. Stay overnight in Purmamarca or Tilcara.

DAY 1

Arrive at Aeropuerto Internacional Ministro Pistarini (Ezeizà) and transfer to a Buenos Aires hotel. Afternoon sightseeing at main historic sites like the Plaza de Mayo, the Casa Rosada presidential palace, and the Congreso Nacional.

DAY 8

Morning tour to the remote and stunningly scenic Andean village of Iruya, returning to Salta in the afternoon.

DAY 2

Full-day city tour, including the colonial neighborhood of San Telmo, the colorful immigrant barrio of La Boca, and upscale Retiro.

DAY 9

Departure by rental car for the town of Cafayate via the colorful desert canyon of the Quebrada de Cafayate, with a side trip to the pre-Columbian ruins of Quilmes. Taste Cafayate's unique white wine, Torrontés, at any of several local bodegas.

DAY 3

Early morning flight to Puerto Iguazú, with the afternoon at the falls; if the timing's right, take the full-moon tour.

DAY 10
Return loop to Salta via the scenic Andean village of Cachi and Parque Nacional Los Cardones.

DAY 11
Return flight to Buenos Aires, with afternoon visits to the historical cemeteries at Recoleta and Chacarita. In the evening, take in a tango floor show.

DAY 12
An overland excursion to the pilgrimage center of Luján, Argentina's single most important religious site, and the gaucho capital of San Antonio de Areco.

DAY 13
Ferry across the River Plate to the World Heritage Site of Colonia, Uruguay.

DAY 14
Take the morning and afternoon for exploring Buenos Aires, including Palermo's José Hernández gaucho museum and Eva Perón museum, before an evening departure.

Construction of the Basílica Nuestra Señora de Luján began in the 1880s.

© WAYNE BERNHARDSON

Early Argentine art is derivative, but Buenos Aires is the heart of a vigorous contemporary painting, sculpture, and multimedia scene. Its numerous art museums—including the state-of-the-art MALBA—and galleries could occupy art lovers for weeks on end. There are also folk art traditions like the urban craft of *filete*, a sort of calligraphic sign painting on display at the Feria de San Pedro Telmo in Plaza Dorrego.

Buenos Aires still displays a variety of architectural traditions, though there are only a handful of late colonial constructions around the Plaza de Mayo. The city really came into its own around the turn of the 20th century, when Francophile architects erected mansard-crested *palacetes* for oligarchic families, and the wealth of the pampas funded grandiose public buildings like the Congreso Nacional. Modern landmarks include the MALBA, but there are also vernacular traditions like the brightly painted, metal-clad houses of La Boca.

Argentina's finest colonial art and architecture survives in the northwest, on an axis that runs south from Jujuy and Salta through Tucumán and Córdoba. Several chapels and churches are de facto galleries of ecclesiastical art from the colonial tradition of Bolivia and Peru, including the distinctively indigenous Cuzco school. Like Buenos Aires, the region has a tradition in its adobe buildings, sometimes embellished with details like Moorish arches that use cardón cactus timber for support.

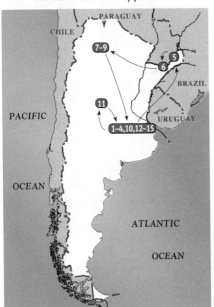

Contrasting with Mesopotamia's verdant subtropical vegetation, bright red sandstone blocks distinguish Mesopotamia's colonial Jesuit missions; indigenous Guaraní artisans crafted the elaborate adornments.

DAY 1

Arrive at Aeropuerto Internacional Ministro Pistarini (Ezeiza) and transfer to a Buenos Aires hotel. Visit main historic sites like the Plaza de Mayo, the Casa Rosada presidential palace, and the Congreso Nacional.

DAY 2

Take in a full-day's sightseeing including colonial San Telmo (home to Buenos Aires's finest *filete* and the Museo de Arte Moderno) and the architecture of the barrio of La Boca (also home to the Museo Quinquela Martín and the Fundación Proa).

DAYS 3–4

Visit the Francophile mansions of Retiro, Recoleta, and Palermo, key art museums (Museo Nacional de Bellas Artes, Museo de Arte Decorativo, Museo Sívori, and especially Museo de Arte Latinoamericano Buenos Aires—MALBA), and private galleries in Retiro and Recoleta.

DAY 5

Morning flight to Puerto Iguazú, with afternoon visit to the falls. If the timing's right, return for the evening full-moon tour.

DAY 6

Overland to the historic Jesuit mission at San Ignacio and other ruined missions en route, with an overnight at the city of Posadas. From Posadas, time permitting, take an excursion across the Paraguayan border to the well-preserved missions of Trinidad and Jesús.

DAY 7

Return flight to Buenos Aires, continuing to the colonial city of Salta. Visit the city's key colonial churches, monuments, and museums.

DAY 8

Take an excursion to the archaeological sites and colonial monuments of the Quebrada de Humahuaca, a World Heritage Site in nearby Jujuy Province. Stay overnight in Purmamarca or in Tilcara, site of several notable provincial art museums.

DAY 9

Return to Salta, continuing to Cafayate, the pre-Columbian ruins of Quilmes, and the museums at Santa María. Overnight in Cafayate.

DAY 10

Overland to Cachi, visiting several colonial churches and Cachi's archaeological museum, returning to Salta via Parque Nacional Los Cardones and the scenic Quebrada de Escoipe. Catch a return flight to Buenos Aires.

© WAYNE BERNHARDSON

ruins of Quilmes

DAY 11

Morning flight to Córdoba, with afternoon visit to Jesuit constructions at Manzana de las Luces, part of a UNESCO World Heritage Site, and the Jesuit ruins and museum at Alta Gracia.

DAY 12

Return flight to Buenos Aires. Afternoon visit to Belgrano art museums including Museo Yrurtia, Museo Larreta, and Museo Badii.

DAY 13

Full-day excursion to the gaucho capital of San Antonio de Areco, home to many artists and artisans. Or, ferry across the River Plate to the World Heritage Site of Colonia, Uruguay, a walled city that's one of the Southern Cone's best-preserved colonial sites.

DAY 14

Full-day excursion to La Plata, the Buenos Aires provincial capital created as a planned city in the late 19th century. Known for its European-style architecture, La Plata also has notable murals.

DAY 15

Full day for exploring Buenos Aires, including the Museo de Arte Moderno, before an evening departure.

Visitors who can't make it out of Buenos Aires will find numerous wine bars where they can sample the country's best, and restaurants around the country carry a broad selection.

But true aficionados should spend at least a week in and around Mendoza—a region that's making it easy to sample its production—but that's not nearly enough to visit all the 100-plus wineries around the provincial capital. The vineyards of San Rafael, two hours to the south, and San Juan, two hours north, are also worth trying.

In the Andean northwest, the vineyards of Cafayate (Salta Province) and Chilecito (La Rioja Province) produce distinctive high-altitude wines. While the wineries are not so numerous, they are interesting enough to justify at least two or three days in the area.

Before recent developments in New Zealand, the Río Negro Valley of northern Patagonia boasted of producing the world's most southerly wines (around 39° S latitude). Wine tourism here, though, is in its infancy.

Plaza de Mayo, the Casa Rosada presidential palace, and the Congreso Nacional.

DAY 2

Full-day city tour including the colonial neighborhood of San Telmo, the colorful immigrant barrio of La Boca, and the northern barrio of Retiro. Evening visit to a lively wine bar before dinner.

DAY 3

Morning flight to the provincial capital of Mendoza, center of Argentina's largest wine-producing region. Afternoon visit to wineries of Maipú, in the city's eastern suburbs.

DAY 4

Day tour to wineries of Luján de Cuyo, in the city's southern suburbs. Have dinner at the Dionisio Wine Bar in its fashionable Chacras de Coria neighborhood before returning to Mendoza.

DAY 1

Arrive at Aeropuerto Internacional Ministro Pistarini (Ezeiza) and transfer to a Buenos Aires hotel. In the afternoon, visit central historic sites like the

DAY 5

Take a breather from the wineries, with a tour or rental car excursion up the valley of the Río Mendoza, offering views of Cerro Aconcagua (the

© WAYNE BERNHARDSON

Competitively priced, quality Argentine wines are gaining ground in the international market.

Western Hemisphere's highest summit). Or, check out the view from the statue of **Cristo Redentor**, a peace monument on the Chilean border near Las Cuevas. Dinner at **1884**, adjacent to Mendoza's **Escorihuela** winery.

DAY 6

Excursion to the provincial capital of **San Juan,** home to several lesser-known wineries, with a side trip to the offbeat **Difunta Correa** shrine.

DAY 7

Travel to high-altitude wineries of the **Valle de Uco,** southwest of Mendoza, with special attention to the state-of-the art **Bodegas Salentein**. Overnight at **San Rafael.**

DAY 8

Full-day tour of San Rafael wineries, returning to Mendoza in the afternoon.

DAY 9

Morning flight to Buenos Aires and on to the city of **Salta,** with an afternoon city tour.

DAY 10

By bus or rental car via the scenic desert canyon of the Quebrada de Cafayate, make your way to the town of **Cafayate,** home to the finest vintages of the white varietal Torrontés. Visit wineries and take a side trip to nearby pre-Columbian ruins at **Quilmes,** in Tucumán Province.

DAY 11

Visit additional wineries near Cafayate and travel overland to the picturesque desert village of **Cachi** for an overnight.

DAY 12

Return to Salta via **Parque Nacional Los Cardones** and the precipitously scenic **Quebrada de Escoipe.**

DAY 13

Return flight to **Buenos Aires,** with the afternoon and evening free for sightseeing and perhaps a tango floor show.

DAY 14

Full day for sightseeing in Buenos Aires before an evening departure.

In its nearly three million square kilometers, Argentina can offer an astonishing diversity of natural environments, starting with the Río Paraná Delta barely half an hour from downtown Buenos Aires. Ascending the Paraná and the Uruguay Rivers, several national parks have similar concentrations of birds and aquatic life, but the real can't-miss is the Esteros del Iberá marshes, in Corrientes Province, where the colorful subtropical birds, reptiles, and mammals are reason enough to visit Argentina for a week or more. For wildlife-watching, the famous Iguazú Falls finish a distant second.

To the south and west, the Atlantic coastline and marshy grasslands of Buenos Aires Province are home to shorebirds and many other species that will be new to visitors from the Northern Hemisphere.

The cradle of biological diversity is the front-range *yungas* cloud forest of the northwest, but the rugged Andean terrain creates micro-environments that range from red desert canyons to scrubby high puna, where the condor soars over dormant volcanic cones. In the winter dry season, itineraries are easy to stick to, but the wet summer can disrupt overland transportation.

In the Cuyo provinces, the highlights are the desert paleontological parks at Ischigualasto, Talampaya, and Las Quijadas, worth several days. Northern Patagonia has its own paleontological circuits in and around the city of Neuquén, an accessible excursion from the lake district, and in and around the city of Trelew, near Puerto Madryn and the wildlife mecca of Península Valdés.

Nearly the entire Patagonian coastline abounds in wildlife like elephant seals, penguins, and sea lions, but the great distances require time and money to see them—public transportation is fine along the main highway, but poor off it. The same is true of the Patagonian steppes, home to the llama-like guanaco and the ostrich-like rhea, and the forests of the southern Andes beyond the main tourist clusters. In terms of its natural assets, Tierra del Fuego is a southern extension of Patagonia.

caiman, Esteros del Iberá, Corrientes Province

DAY 1

Arrive at Aeropuerto Internacional Ministro Pistarini (Ezeiza) and transfer to a **Buenos Aires** hotel. Visit main historic sites.

DAY 2

Take a full-day tour to the riverside suburb of **Tigre** and the Río Paraná Delta, including the island of **Martín García** near the Uruguayan border.

DAY 3

Early morning flight to **Puerto Iguazú**, with the afternoon at the falls; if the timing's right, take the full-moon tour.

DAY 4

Overland transfer and overnight at **Yacutinga Lodge**, a distinctive accommodation on a private nature reserve east of Puerto Iguazú.

DAY 5

Return to Puerto Iguazú and, time permitting, take an excursion to the Brazilian side of the falls.

DAY 6

Overland to the city of **Posadas,** with a stop at the landmark Jesuit mission at **San Ignacio**. Continue on to **Colonia Carlos Pellegrini**, in the Esteros del Iberá wetlands, by 4WD vehicle with driver.

DAY 7

Full-day wildlife-viewing excursion among the floating islands of the **Esteros del Iberá**.

DAY 8

Travel overland to the provincial capital of **Corrientes** to catch a flight back to Buenos Aires and on to the colonial city of **Salta**.

DAY 9

Overland loop, by rental car, from Salta up the Quebrada del Toro to the altiplano at **San Antonio de los Cobres,** stopping at enormous salt flats, and then descending to **Purmamarca** or **Tilcara** for the night.

DAY 10

Excursion to the archaeological sites and colonial monuments of the **Quebrada de Humahuaca**, a

World Heritage Site in Jujuy Province. Return to Salta.

DAY 11
Full-day excursion to the *yungas* cloud forests of **Parque Nacional El Rey**.

DAY 12
Depart by rental car for the town of **Cafayate** via the colorful desert canyon of the Quebrada de Cafayate, with a side trip to the pre-Columbian ruins of **Quilmes**. Taste Cafayate's unique white wine, Torrontés, at any of several local bodegas.

DAY 13
Return loop to Salta via the scenic village of **Cachi**, **Parque Nacional Los Cardones**, and the precipitous canyon known as the **Quebrada de Escoipe**.

DAY 14
Morning flight to Buenos Aires, continuing to **San Carlos de Bariloche**. Late-afternoon excursion to Circuito Chico, in **Parque Nacional Nahuel Huapi**.

DAY 15
Day trip by bus or rental car to **Villa la Angostura**; boat excursion to **Parque Nacional Los Arrayanes**, returning by footpath to Villa la Angostura.

El Bolsón and Parque Nacional Lago Puelo, from Cerro Piltriquitrón

© WAYNE BERNHARDSON

DAY 16
Travel by bus or rental car to **El Bolsón**, with a

visit to its Feria Artesanal for organic beer and grazing at various food stands. Take an afternoon excursion to nearby **Parque Nacional Lago Puelo** or, with an early enough start, hike to the summit of **Cerro Piltriquitrón** for spectacular views of the Andes along the Chilean border, to the west.

DAY 17
Bus or rental car to the city of **Esquel**, gateway to Parque Nacional Los Alerces and its millennial *alerce* forests. Spend the afternoon at the ski area of **La Hoya**, where the chairlift carries hikers to the trailheads in summer.

DAY 18
Boat excursion (Circuito Lacustre) at **Parque Nacional Los Alerces**, with an overnight at the park's landmark **Hotel Futalaufquen** or in more modest accommodations, including camping.

DAY 19
Return to San Carlos de Bariloche, stopping at Butch Cassidy's former cabin, with a detour to **Parque Nacional Nahuel Huapi**'s Ventisquero Negro (Black Glacier).

DAY 20
Return flight to **Buenos Aires**, with the afternoon and evening free for sightseeing and perhaps a tango floor show.

DAY 21
Full day for exploring Buenos Aires before an evening departure.

Because of Argentina's vast distances, overland travel tends to be for those with plenty of time. Most routes are well-served by reasonably priced public transportation, but those who can afford a vehicle can usually travel more efficiently and stop to see appealing second-tier sights.

On the otherwise featureless pampas of southern Buenos Aires Province, the most interesting itinerary would be a loop from Tandil and its Sierras east to the coastal resorts of Pinamar and Villa Gesell, south to Mar del Plata, and east to Necochea and the Sierra de la Ventana, north of Bahía Blanca. Either Tandil or Mar del Plata would make an ideal base for a week or more; Bahía Blanca is the provincial gateway to coastal Patagonia.

Mesopotamia and the Paraná offer several routes north. The shortest route to Iguazú is RN 14 along the Río Uruguay, passing the Carnaval city of Gualeguaychú, the palm savannas of Parque Nacional El Palmar, the quaint riverside city of Colón, and national hero José de San Martín's birthplace at Yapeyú. A northwesterly tangent leads to the Iberá wetlands. Traffic statistics, though, prove that this is one of Argentina's most dangerous highways.

An alternative would be to travel northeast from Buenos Aires to Rosario, where a new bridge crosses the Paraná to Victoria, and north to Paraná (passing the gallery forests of Parque Nacional Pre-Delta) and Iberá before continuing to Iguazú. By bus, these routes could take one to several days or more, depending on stops en route.

For long-distance travelers, an increasingly popular route crosses the Chaco to link Salta with the cultural oasis of Resistencia, the provincial capital of Corrientes, Iberá, Posadas, and Iguazú. In addition to can't-miss Iberá and Iguazú, the trans-Chaco RN 16 could also include a short detour to the dense thorn forests of Parque Nacional Chaco.

In the northwest, the artery of access is RN 9, which runs north from Córdoba through Tucumán, Salta, and especially Jujuy, where it climbs the Quebrada de Humahuaca. Except for the Quebrada, though, the real interest lies in detours to the foothills, steppes, and summits of the Andes. Culturally closer to the Andean highlands than the pampas pasturelands, this has the country's richest concentration of pre-Columbian and colonial monuments, and could easily absorb two weeks to two months.

Parallel to RN 9, the mother of all Argentine roads is RN 40, from the Bolivian border in Jujuy to the Chilean border in Patagonia's Santa Cruz Province. Some northwestern segments of this celebrated highway are almost impassable, while others would be smooth enough for lowriders. In the Cuyo provinces, RN 40 is the axis of the wine country that stretches from San Juan south to Mendoza and San Rafael.

It's in Patagonia, though, that RN 40 has acquired an international reputation as *the* adventurous alternative between the northern lakes and southern glaciers. Only in the last few years has there been any semi-regular public transportation between Perito Moreno and El Calafate, and there's still not any between Perito Moreno and Río Mayo, though there are overland "expeditions" from Bariloche. For the foreseeable future, any trip south of Río Mayo will seem like an expedition, and travelers need to be prepared for several days—or weeks, if they want to explore off the main route—of rugged travel.

As late as the 1980s, coastal RN 3, the Patagonian road that leads from Buenos Aires to the tip of Tierra del Fuego, was nearly as rugged as RN 40 is now. Today, it's almost entirely paved, with regular public transportation, but it still glows with the charisma of the world's southernmost highway. To grasp the vastness that so impressed the first Europeans, and to view prodigious concentrations of wildlife, "Ruta Tres" is still a matchless route.

Explore Argentina

Buenos Aires and Vicinity

Cosmopolitan Buenos Aires, South America's highest-profile capital, has undergone extraordinary changes since its shaky origins as a Spanish imperial backwater. Massive post-independence immigration changed what was once a cozy "Gran Aldea" (Great Village) into the first Latin American city to have a million inhabitants; increasing prosperity transformed it into a "Paris of the South" with broad avenues, colossal monuments, and mansard-capped mansions.

For much of the 20th century, though, Buenos Aires underwent a steady decline, interrupted by spectacular spurts of growth and even more spectacular economic and political disasters. Yet somehow, like its melancholy signature music and dance of the tango, it has retained its identity and mystique.

Despite Buenos Aires's cosmopolitan outlook, many of its inhabitants, known as *porteños* ("residents of the port"), still identify strongly with their own barrios or neighborhoods in the Gran

ust-Sees

Look for to find the sights and activities you can't miss and for the best dining and lodging.

Plaza de Mayo: Buenos Aires's historic center is ground zero for public life in Argentina (page 46).

Café Tortoni: For nearly a century and a half, the Avenida de Mayo's traditional gathering place has been an island of stability in a tumultuous ocean of political, social, and economic upheaval. It often plays host to artists, writers, singers, dancers, and visiting royalty and diplomats (page 49).

Galerías Pacífico: Even non-shoppers will appreciate the vision with which 1990s developers adapted this historic Microcentro building, on the Florida pedestrian mall, to contemporary commerce. The stunning murals in the cupola can be enjoyed on your own or with a guide (page 53).

Teatro Colón: The continent's most important performing arts venue retains its style and dignity. Simply enjoy the beautiful Italian Renaissance design or take in a world-class performance (page 54).

Plaza Dorrego: Antique vendors and spirited performers clog San Telmo's principal plaza and surrounding streets every Sunday (page 60).

Cementerio de la Recoleta: For both the living and the dead, the barrio of Recoleta is the capital's prestige address. In the cemetery, you can visit the graves of Eva Perón and the Argentine elite (page 74). Those that failed to qualify for Recoleta, like Evita's husband, Juan Perón, repose at the more egalitarian **Cementerio de la Chacarita,** across town.

MALBA: For decades, even during dictatorships, Argentina has had a thriving modern art scene, but the striking Museo de Arte Latinoamericano Buenos Aires in Palermo has given it a new focal point (page 80).

Museo Eva Perón: Promoted by Evita's partisans, Argentina's first museum dedicated to a woman is as notable for what it omits as for what it includes (page 81).

Museo Argentino de Ciencias Naturales: In the decidedly untouristed barrio of Caballito, this improving museum houses exhibits that shed light on the impressive Argentine dinosaur discoveries of recent decades (page 83).

Isla Martín García: Just off the Uruguayan coast, its bedrock rising out of the River Plate's muddy waters, this historic island is an absorbing and tranquil getaway from Buenos Aires's bustle. Get there from **Tigre,** only half an hour north of Buenos Aires (page 115).

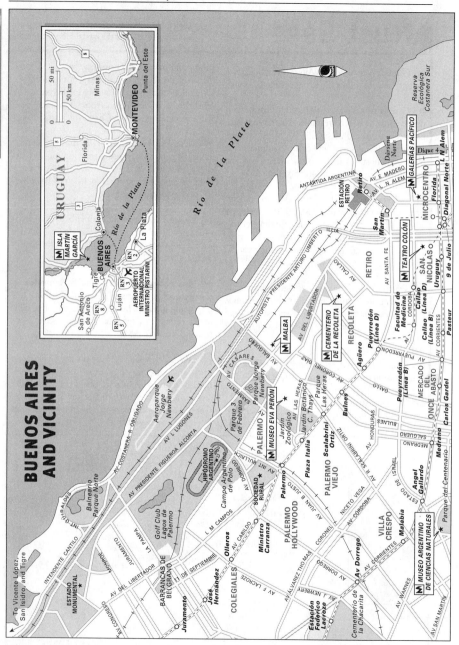

BUENOS AIRES AND VICINITY

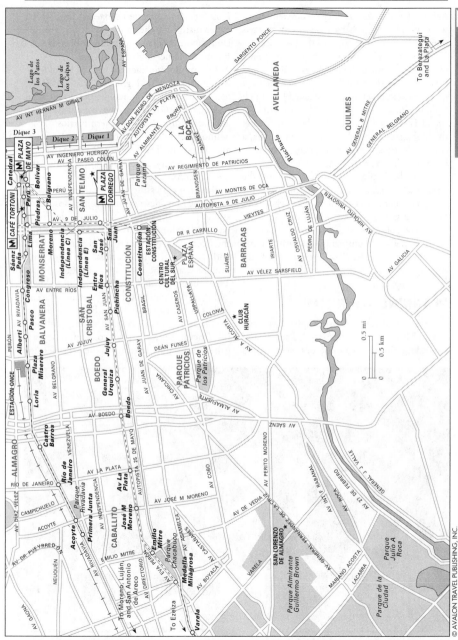

Aldea. Like New Yorkers, they are often brash, assertive people, with a characteristic accent that sets them apart from the people of the provinces.

When *porteños* tire of the city, there are plenty of nearby escapes in Buenos Aires Province and beyond. The closest are the intricate channels of the Río Paraná Delta, easily reached by launch from the increasingly fashionable northern suburb of Tigre, itself easily reached by train. One of the highlights is the island of Martín García, a colonial fortress and onetime prison camp with historic architecture and nature trails.

All in all, despite Argentina's problems, the River Plate's megalopolis still has much to offer the urban explorer in a city that, as the cliché about New York says, never sleeps. For diverse interests, it's one of the most underrated destinations on an underrated continent—notwithstanding the 2002 crisis, *Travel & Leisure* named it Latin America's top tourist city.

PLANNING YOUR TIME

Buenos Aires deserves as much time as you can give it. Those planning an extended stay in and around the city, say two weeks or longer, should look for *Moon Handbooks Buenos Aires,* which is exhaustive on the capital itself but also includes more detail on excursions in Buenos Aires Province and neighboring Uruguay.

At a minimum, though, visitors should figure on three days for highlights like the Plaza de Mayo, the adjacent sights like the presidential palace and cathedral, and the Avenida de Mayo and Café Tortoni; the southern barrios of San Telmo (preferably on a Sunday) and La Boca; and the famous Teatro Colón, Recoleta (with its famous cemetery), and Palermo (including the new Latin American art museum).

But that's pressing it, and at least a week would be more desirable for seeing those same sights more thoroughly, at a more leisurely pace, and taking in additional highlights like the Puerto Madero waterfront, Palermo's parks and traditional fine arts museum, Chacarita cemetery, and the Río Paraná Delta at Tigre. That, though, would permit only limited partaking of BA's rapidly evolving restaurant scene in Recoleta, Palermo Soho, Palermo Hollywood, and Las Cañitas; the vibrant cultural life (including numerous contemporary art galleries and unconventional theater offerings

sidewalk dining in Las Cañitas

like those of La Boca's Catalinas Sur group); BA's hyperactive nightlife; and even compulsive shopping at Galerías Pacífico and other recycled landmarks.

No matter how much time you spend in Buenos Aires, there's always more to see and do.

HISTORY

Buenos Aires's origins are, in some ways, as murky as the muddy Río de la Plata. Everyone agrees that bands of Querandí hunter-gatherers roamed the river's southern banks, but their encampments of *toldos* (tents of animal skins) shifted with the availability of game, fish, and other resources. No Querandí settlement could reasonably be called a city, a town, or even a village.

Buenos Aires proper dates from January 1536, when Pedro de Mendoza's expedition landed on its shores, but his short-lived colony withered in the face of supply shortages and Querandí opposition. Traditionally, Argentine histories place Mendoza's settlement on the barrancas (natural levees) of present-day Parque Lezama, but *porteño* author Federico Kirbus has concluded that the first Buenos Aires may have been some distance up what is now the Paraná Delta, closer to the provincial town of Escobar. While the evidence is circumstantial rather than definitive, it's an intriguing hypothesis.

While Mendoza's initial effort failed, Juan de Garay refounded Buenos Aires on a southbound expedition from the successful Spanish settlement in Asunción, Paraguay, in 1580. Garay himself died at the hands of the Querandí, but the settlement he established—peopled by *mancebos de la tierra* (offspring of Spaniards and Guaraní Indians)—survived.

On the muddy river banks, the location had little to recommend it as a port, but this was largely irrelevant—the new Buenos Aires was subordinate to Asunción, which was in turn subordinate to the Viceroyalty of Lima and the Spanish capital of Madrid via a long, indirect overland and maritime route. It took nearly two centuries for Buenos Aires, a backwater of Spain's American empire, to match Lima's viceregal status.

Colonial Buenos Aires

The Mendoza expedition had one lasting legacy: the escaped herds of horses and cattle that, left to proliferate on the lush pampas pastures, soon transformed the Buenos Aires backcountry into a fenceless feral-cattle ranch. The presence of horses and cattle, nearly free for the taking, spawned the gaucho culture for which Argentina became famous. Durable hides were the primary product; beef had little value because it was perishable.

Buenos Aires had no easily accessible markets, though, because low-value hides were too bulky to justify shipment to Spain via Lima and Panama. But they could support a vigorous contraband trade with British and Portuguese vessels in the Paraná Delta's secluded channels, and Spain acknowledged Buenos Aires's growing significance by making it capital, in 1776, of the newly created Virreinato del Río de la Plata (Viceroyalty of the River Plate).

The city's population, only about 500 by the early 17th century, grew slowly at first. By 1655, it was barely 4,000, and it took nearly a century to reach 10,000, in 1744. By the time of the new viceroyalty, though, the numbers exceeded 24,000, and nearly doubled again by the early 19th century. As Madrid loosened its control, the livestock economy opened to European commerce and expanded with the development of *saladeros* (meat-salting plants). The improving economy and growing population, which previously consisted of peninsular Spaniards, criollos ("creoles," or American-born Spaniards), small numbers of *indígenas* (Indians), and mestizos (the offspring of Spaniards and *indígenas*), soon included African slaves.

Republican Argentina and Buenos Aires

While the *porteños* resisted the British invasions of 1806 and 1807, those invasions undercut Spain's authority in the Americas and paved the way for the end of Spanish rule in the Revolution of May 1810. The movement reached its climax in 1816, when delegates of the Provincias Unidas del Río de la Plata (United Provinces of the River Plate) issued a formal declaration of independence, but the loose confederation only papered over differences between provincial "Federalist" caudillos and the cosmopolitan "Unitarists" of Buenos Aires.

In Buenos Aires, the largest of the provinces, Federalist caudillo Juan Manuel de Rosas took command and ruled from 1829 until his overthrow in 1852. Ironically enough, the ruthless and opportunistic Rosas did more than anyone else to ensure the primacy of the city which, nevertheless, did not become the country's capital until 1880.

By the time Rosas took power, Buenos Aires's population had grown to nearly 60,000; in 1855, only a few years after he left, it reached 99,000. In 1833 Charles Darwin was impressed with the city's size and orderliness:

> *Every street is at right angles to the one it crosses, and the parallel ones being equidistant, the houses are collected into solid squares of equal dimensions, which are called quadras. On the other hand the houses themselves are hollow squares; all the rooms opening into a neat little courtyard. They are generally only one story high, with flat roofs, which are fitted with seats, and are much frequented by the inhabitants in summer. In the centre of the town is the Plaza, where the public offices, fortress, cathedral, &c., stand. Here also, the old viceroys, before the revolution had their palaces. The general assemblage of buildings possesses considerable architectural beauty, although none individually can boast of any.*

Rosas' dictatorial rule, obstinate isolationism and continual military adventures discouraged immigration, but his defeat at the battle of Caseros, in 1853, opened the country to immigration and economic diversification. For the city, still a provincial rather than a national capital, this meant explosive growth—its population more than doubled, to 230,000, by 1875. Shortly thereafter, in 1880, when the other provinces forced the federalization of Buenos Aires, irate provincial authorities shifted their own capital to the new city of La Plata, but the newly designated federal capital continued to

grow. By the early 20th century, it became the first Latin American city with more than a million inhabitants.

The Porteños Get a Port

Unfortunately for a fast-growing city of *porteños,* Buenos Aires was a poor natural port. Its muddy river banks and shallow waters made loading and unloading slow, laborious, expensive, and even hazardous, as freighters had to anchor in deep water and transfer their cargo to shallow-draft lighters. Before it could become a great commercial port, Buenos Aires had to speed up a process that took months rather than weeks for the average steamship.

Engineer Luis Huergo offered the simplest and most economical solution, to provide better access to existing port facilities in the southern barrios of La Boca and Barracas. As so often happens, though, political influence trumped practical expertise, as the congress approved downtown businessman Eduardo Madero's vague plan to transform the mudflats into a series of deep water *diques* (basins) immediately east of the central Plaza de Mayo.

Approved in 1882, Puerto Madero took 16 years to complete, came in well over budget, caused a scandal because of shady land dealings, and, finally, even proved inadequate for the growing port traffic. Only improvements at La Boca and the 1926 opening of Retiro's Puerto Nuevo (New Port) finally resolved the problem, but port costs remained high.

From Gran Aldea to Cosmopolitan Capital

Federalization gave the city a new mayor—Torcuato de Alvear, appointed by President Julio Argentino Roca—and Alvear immediately imposed his vision on the newly designated capital. Instead of the traditionally intimate *Gran Aldea* (Great Village), Buenos Aires was to become a city of monuments, a cosmopolitan showpiece symbolizing Argentina's integration with the wider world. Where single-story houses once lined narrow colonial streets, broad boulevards like the Avenida de Mayo soon linked majestic public buildings like the Casa Rosada presidential

© WAYNE BERNHARDSON

the fountain at Plaza del Congreso

palace and the Congreso Nacional, the federal legislature.

Newly landscaped spaces like the Plaza de Mayo, Plaza del Congreso, and Plaza San Martín, not to mention the conversion of Rosas's former Palermo estate into parklands, reflected the aspirations—or pretensions—of an ambitious country. Some, though, castigated Alvear for favoring upper-class barrios such as Recoleta, Palermo, and Belgrano over struggling immigrant neighborhoods like San Telmo and La Boca.

As immigrants streamed into Buenos Aires from Spain, Italy, Britain, Russia, and other European countries, such differential treatment exacerbated growing social tensions. In 1913, Buenos Aires became the first South American city to open a subway system, beneath the Avenida de Mayo, but in poorer neighborhoods large families squeezed into *conventillos* (tenements) and struggled on subsistence wages. The gap between rich and poor frequently exploded into open conflict—in 1909, following police repression of a May Day demonstration, anarchist immigrant Simón Radowitzky killed police chief Ramón Falcón with a bomb, and in 1919, Pres-

ident Hipólito Yrigoyen ordered the army to crush a metalworkers' strike during what is now recalled as *La Semana Trágica* (The Tragic Week).

Yrigoyen, ironically enough, pardoned Radowitzky a decade later, and his was the first administration to suffer one of the repeated military coups that plagued the country for most of the 20th century. The military dictatorship that followed him continued the policy of obliterating narrow colonial streets to create broad thoroughfares like Corrientes, Córdoba, and Santa Fe, all parallel to Avenida de Mayo, and the crosstown boulevard Avenida 9 de Julio. Despite public deference to working-class interests, the populist Perón regimes of the 1940s and 1950s splurged on pharaonic works projects, heavy and heavily subsidized industry, and unsustainable social spending that squandered the country's post–World War II surpluses.

The Dirty War and Its Aftermath

As Gran Buenos Aires grew and sprawled, encompassing ever more distant suburbs, the capital and its vicinity became home to more than a third of the country's population; by 1970, it had more than eight million inhabitants. Continued political instability, though, emerged into almost open warfare until 1976, when the military ousted the inept President Isabel Perón (Juan Perón's widow) in a bloodless coup that became the most systematic and bloodiest reign of terror in Argentine history.

One rationale for taking power was the corruption of civilian politicians, but the military and their civilian collaborators were just as adept in diverting international loans to demolish vibrant but neglected neighborhoods and create colossal public works like freeways that went nowhere. Much of the money, of course, found its way into offshore bank accounts.

Following the return to constitutional government in 1983, Argentina underwent several years of hyperinflation in which the Radical government of President Raúl Alfonsín squandered an enormous amount of good will. President Carlos Menem's succeeding Peronist government, at the direction of Economy Minister Domingo Cavallo, brought a decade of economic stability during which foreign investment flowed into Argentina, and Buenos Aires was one of the main beneficiaries. The financial and service sectors flourished, and ambitious urban renewal projects like the transformation of Puerto Madero into a fashionable riverfront of lofts and restaurants, gave *porteños* a sense of optimism through most of the 1990s. There was a dark side to the boom, though, in the form of "crony capitalism" in which associates of the president enriched themselves through favorable privatization contracts.

Even before the partial debt default of late 2001, the economy contracted and *porteños* began to suffer. After the resignation of Menem's hapless successor Fernando de la Rúa, in December, the country had a series of caretaker presidents until the election of Néstor Kirchner in May of 2003.

As the economy stagnated and unemployment rose, homelessness also rose and scavengers became a common sight even in prosperous barrios like Palermo and Belgrano. Strikes, strident pickets blocking bridges and highways, and frustration with politicians and institutions like the International Monetary Fund (IMF) contributed to the feeling of *bronca* (aggravation). Yet somehow the city, with its blend of neighborhood integrity, cosmopolitan sophistication, and rich cultural life, continued to function.

Buenos Aires

Visitors to Buenos Aires often conflate the city, internationally known for the spectacle of Perón and Evita, with Argentina—even though provincial Argentines vociferously protest, "Buenos Aires is *not* Argentina." Likewise, residents of the city's 47 barrios might even protest that their own neighborhoods are too closely identified with the national capital and its political notoriety.

That's because each "Baires" neighborhood has a distinctive personality. The compact, densely built "Microcentro" boasts the major shopping and theater districts, as well as the capital's Wall Street in "La City." Immediately to the south, in the barrio of Monserrat, the Avenida de Mayo is the city's civic axis, the site of spectacle and debacle in Argentina's tumultuous 20th century politics. Monserrat gives way to the cobbled colonial streets of San Telmo, with its tango bars and famous flea market at Plaza Dorrego. Farther south is the working-class outpost of La Boca, also an artists' colony known for the Caminito, its colorful curving pedestrian mall.

Northern neighborhoods like Retiro and Recoleta are more elegant and even opulent, so much so that many affluent Argentines have elected to spend eternity at the Cementerio de la Recoleta, one of the world's most exclusive graveyards. Beyond Recoleta, the parks of Palermo were once the province of 19th-century despot Juan Manuel de Rosas, but much of the barrio itself has become a middle- to upper-middle-class area with some of the city's finest dining and wildest night life. North of Palermo, the woodsy barrio of Bel-

ORGANIZED TOURS

Some of BA's best guided tours are available through the municipal tourist office on Saturday and Sunday, often but not always with English-speaking guides. The *Buenos Aires Herald*'s Friday getOut! section and *Clarín*'s event section both contain listings, but the complete schedule also appears in *Viva Bue,* a monthly giveaway guide. In case of rain, the tours are canceled.

For conventional tours of the capital and vicinity, including the Microcentro, Recoleta and Palermo, and San Telmo and La Boca, the usual choices are **Buenos Aires Tour** (Lavalle 1444, Oficina 10, tel. 011/4371-2304, buenosairestour@sinectis.com.ar) and **Buenos Aires Visión** (Esmeralda 356, 8th floor, tel. 011/4394-4682, bavision@ssdnet .com.ar, www.buenosaires-vision.com.ar).

Several city operators provide thematically oriented tours, with English-speaking and other guides available. Though primarily oriented toward outdoor activities, **Lihué Expediciones** (Paraguay 880, 7th floor, Retiro, tel./fax 011/5031-0070, viajes@lihue-expeditions.com.ar) also offers walking tours focused on literary figures like Jorge Luis Borges and Julio Cortázar.

Borges's widow, María Kodama, leads free-of-charge, fortnightly Borgesian tours, sponsored by municipal tourism authorities and her own **Fundación Internacional Jorge Luis Borges** (Anchorena 1660, tel. 011/4822-8340); phone for schedules.

Travel Line Argentina (Esmeralda 770, 10th floor, Oficina B, tel. 011/4393-9000, fax 011/4394-3929, info@travelline.com.ar, www.travelline.com.ar) conducts specialty excursions such as its "Evita Tour," which takes in the CGT labor headquarters, Luna Park Stadium, the Perón and Duarte residences, and other locales associated with her era.

grano is a mostly residential area that sometimes fancies itself not just a suburb or separate city, but a republic in itself—and it was in fact briefly Argentina's capital.

ORIENTATION

Gran Buenos Aires (Greater Buenos Aires) is a sprawling metropolitan area that takes in large parts of surrounding Buenos Aires Province. The Ciudad Autónoma de Buenos Aires (Autonomous City of Buenos Aires), also known as the Capital Federal, lies within the boundaries formed by the Río de la Plata, its tributary the Riachuelo, and the ring roads of Avenida General Paz and Avenida 27 de Febrero.

Buenos Aires's 47 barrios give a major megalopolis a neighborhood ambience. Its historic center is the barrio of **Monserrat** (also known as Catedral al Sur, "South of the Cathedral"), whose Plaza de Mayo is ground zero in Argentine public life. To the immediate north, part of the barrio of San Nicolás, the **Microcentro** (also known as Catedral al Norte, "North of the Cathedral") is the city's commercial hub, including the financial district. To the east, stretching north-south along the river, redeveloped **Puerto Madero** is the city's newest barrio.

South of Monserrat, **San Telmo** is a tourist-friendly Bohemian blend of the colonial barrio, peopled with artists and musicians, with a scattering of old-money families and more than a scattering of *conventillos* (tenements) abandoned by old money. To the southeast, the immigrant working-class barrio of **La Boca** has never been prosperous, but it has a colorful history, an extravagantly colorful vernacular architecture, and a palpable sense of community.

West of Monserrat and San Nicolás, the barrio of **Balvanera** subdivides into several smaller neighborhoods including Congreso (home to the Argentine legislature), Once (the largely Jewish garment district), and the Abasto (which gave the city tango legend Carlos Gardel).

Across Avenida Córdoba, once-elegant **Retiro** marks a transition to the upper-middle-class residential barrios to the north and northwest. Immediately to the northwest, **Recoleta** retains that elegance near its legendary necropolis, the Cementerio de la Recoleta. Barrio Norte, a mostly residential area that overlaps Retiro and Recoleta, is an imprecise real estate concept rather than a barrio per se.

Beyond Recoleta, Avenida Santa Fe, Avenida Las Heras, and Avenida del Libertador lead to the open spaces of **Palermo**. One of the city's most rapidly changing areas, the city's largest barrio subdivides into several smaller but distinct units: the embassy row of Palermo Chico, between Avenida del Libertador and the river; the residential and nightlife zone of Palermo Viejo, across Avenida Santa Fe, which further subdivides into "Palermo Soho" and "Palermo Hollywood"; and Las Cañitas, on the Belgrano border.

Once a separate city, **Belgrano** prizes its residential identity, but its leafy streets also host an assortment of museums and other cultural resources. More outlying barrios have scattered points of tourist interest, including museums, parks, and ferias.

MONSERRAT/CATEDRAL AL SUR AND VICINITY

In 1580, Juan de Garay reestablished Pedro de Mendoza's failed settlement on what is now the **Plaza de Mayo,** whose name derives from the date of the Revolution of 1810, but its fame comes from the massive and spectacular demonstrations that have taken place here in support and protest of the Peróns, the Falklands/Malvinas war, and other political causes.

Monserrat also encompasses substantial parts of the **Congreso** neighborhood to the west. Its southern border with San Telmo is a more subtle transition on the ground itself—some businesses technically within Monserrat's boundaries identify with tourist-friendly San Telmo.

Most major civic institutions surround the Plaza de Mayo, which has experienced major transformations since colonial times. The barrio's axis is the **Avenida de Mayo,** the city's first major boulevard, which links the **Casa Rosada** presidential palace (1873–1898) with the **Congreso Nacional** (National Congress, 1906); the

broad perpendicular Avenida 9 de Julio splits Monserrat in half.

At the plaza's northwest corner, the imposing **Catedral Metropolitana** dates from 1827. At the southwest corner, construction of the Avenida de Mayo required demolition of part of the colonial **Cabildo de Buenos Aires** (1725–1765), but a representative segment of the building remains.

At the northeast corner, renowned architect Alejandro Bustillo designed the **Banco de la Nación** (1939) on the original site of the Teatro Colón, the opera house that moved to Plaza Lavalle in the early 20th century; if the economy were as solid as this neoclassical construction, Argentina would be a global economic power.

Across the Plaza, immediately south of the Casa Rosada, the marble facade of the **Ministerio de Economía** (Economy Ministry) still bears marks from navy planes that strafed it and other public buildings in the 1955 "Revolución Libertadora" that sent Juan Domingo Perón into exile.

As the Avenida de Mayo obliterated several city blocks in 1894 to become Buenos Aires's first boulevard at 30 meters wide, it experienced a major building boom with several surviving landmarks. First among them, perhaps, is the **Café Tortoni** (Avenida de Mayo 825), a *porteño* institution since 1858. Reopened in 1994 after nearly being destroyed by fire in 1979, the **Teatro Avenida** (Avenida de Mayo 1212) is second only to the Teatro Colón as a classical music and dance performance venue.

One of the avenue's literal landmarks is Mario Palanti's marvelously detailed **Pasaje Barolo** (1923), a recently restored office building topped by a high-powered rotating semaphore visible from Montevideo's Palacio Salvo (the work of the same architect). In 1923, when Argentine heavyweight Luis Angel Firpo fought Jack Dempsey in New York, the Barolo erroneously announced a Firpo victory with a green light from the tower.

At the west end of the avenue, the **Plaza de los dos Congresos** (1904), a frequent site for political demonstrations, faces the **Congreso Nacional** (1908), home to Argentina's notoriously dysfunctional national legislature. The Plaza itself houses the **Monumento a los Dos Congresos,** commemorating the meetings in Buenos Aires (1813) and Tucumán (1816) which achieved the country's independence. Two Belgians, sculptor Jules Lagae and architect Eugene D'Huique, created the monument, which reflects Argentina's geography: the easterly fountain symbolizes the Atlantic Ocean, while its granite stairways signify the Andes mountains that form the western border with Chile.

South of the Plaza de Mayo, Monserrat's major landmarks are nearly all colonial, though most have undergone major modifications. The most significant is the **Manzana de las Luces,** comprising several ecclesiastical and educational institutions occupying an entire block bounded by Alsina, Bolívar, Moreno, and Perú.

At opposite corners of Alsina and Defensa are the **Capilla San Roque** (1759), a colonial chapel, and the **Farmacia de la Estrella** (1900), a classic apothecary with magnificent woodwork and health-oriented ceiling murals. The Farmacia's exterior windows display materials from the upstairs **Museo de la Ciudad,** which specializes in themes dealing with the city proper and elements of everyday life, including architecture, floor tiles, furniture, and postcards.

A block to the south, the **Museo Etnográfico Juan B. Ambrosetti** (Moreno 350) has become one of the country's best anthropological museums. From the roof of the **Casa de la Defensa,** *porteños* poured boiling oil on British invaders in 1806–7; the building now houses the **Museo Nacional del Grabado** (Defensa 372, tel. 011/4345-5300, museodelgrabado@yahoo .com, 2–6 P.M. daily except Sat., admission free Sun.), which displays high-quality works by Argentine engravers.

Half a block south, at the corner of Avenida Belgrano, the 18th-century **Iglesia y Convento de Santo Domingo** shares grounds with the Instituto Nacional Belgraniano, a patriotic research institute that contains the grave of General Manuel Belgrano, a soldier of questionable competence who at least distinguished himself by designing the Argentine flag.

Two blocks south, at Defensa and México, the erstwhile **Casa de la Moneda** (National Mint, 1877) houses the army's **Instituto de Estudios Históricos del Ejército** (Army Institute of Historical Studies). Within a couple of years, though, this handsome 10,000-square-meter building is due to become a contemporary science museum.

© WAYNE BERNHARDSON

Plaza de Mayo and Casa Rosada

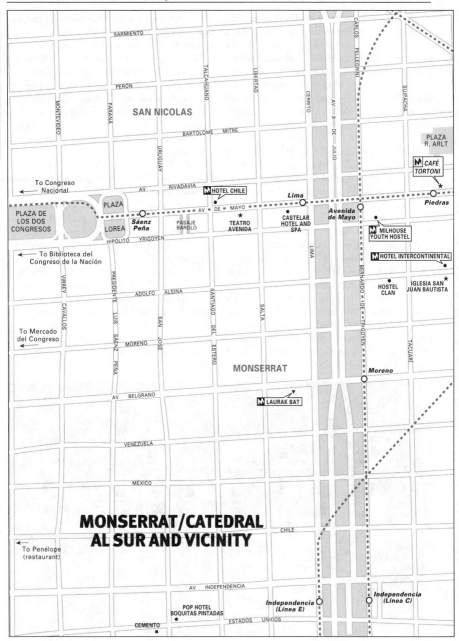

MONSERRAT/CATEDRAL
AL SUR AND VICINITY

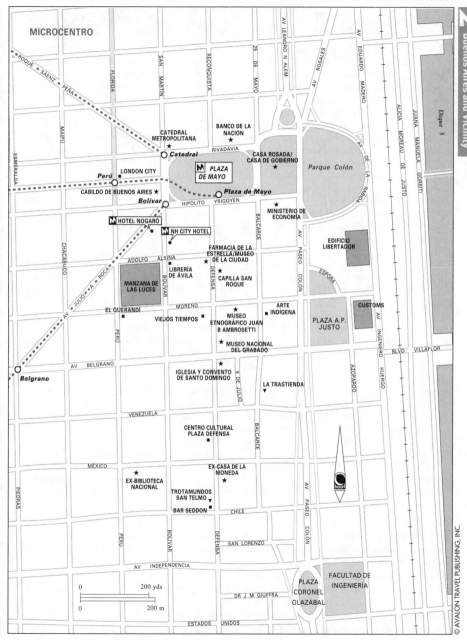

MICROCENTRO

ROQUE · SÁENZ · PEÑA

AV LEANDRO N ALEM

AV ROSALES

EDUARDO MADERO

ALICIA MOREAU DE JUSTO

JUANA MANUELA GORRITI

Dique 3

FLORIDA
SAN MARTIN
RECONQUISTA
25 DE MAYO

MAIPU

ESMERALDA

CATEDRAL METROPOLITANA ★

BANCO DE LA NACIÓN ★

RIVADAVIA

Catedral

CASA ROSADA/ CASA DE GOBIERNO ★

Parque Colón

AV DE LA RÁBIDA

Perú   LONDON CITY

M PLAZA DE MAYO

CABILDO DE BUENOS AIRES ★

Bolívar

Plaza de Mayo

HIPÓLITO   YRIGOYEN

MINISTERIO DE ECONOMÍA ■

M HOTEL NOGARÓ

BALCARCE

AV PASEO COLÓN

EDIFICIO LIBERTADOR

CHACABUCO

M NH CITY HOTEL

ADOLFO   ALSINA

FARMACIA DE LA ESTRELLA/MUSEO DE LA CIUDAD ★

LIBRERÍA DE ÁVILA ■

CAPILLA SAN ROQUE ★

MANZANA DE LAS LUCES

BOLIVAR
DEFENSA

MORENO

ARTE INDÍGENA ■

ESPORA

CUSTOMS

AV JULIO · A · ROCA

EL QUERANDÍ ■

VIEJOS TIEMPOS ■

MUSEO ETNOGRÁFICO JUAN B AMBROSETTI ■

PLAZA A.P. JUSTO

AV INGENIERO

MUSEO NACIONAL DEL GRABADO ★

PERU

AV   BELGRANO

IGLESIA Y CONVENTO DE SANTO DOMINGO ★

S DE JULIO

LA TRASTIENDA ▼

BLVD   VILLAFLOR

AZOPARDO

HUERGO

Belgrano

VENEZUELA

CENTRO CULTURAL PLAZA DEFENSA ■

BALCARCE

MÉXICO

EX-BIBLIOTECA NACIONAL ★

EX-CASA DE LA MONEDA ★

PIEDRAS

TROTAMUNDOS SAN TELMO ▼

AV PASEO COLÓN

BAR SEDDON ■

CHILE

PERU

BOLIVAR

DEFENSA

SAN LORENZO

MOON

AV   INDEPENDENCIA

0   200 yds

0   200 m

DR J M GIUFFRA

PLAZA CORONEL OLAZÁBAL

FACULTAD DE INGENIERÍA

ESTADOS   UNIDOS

UNDERGROUND CULTURE

In his short story "Text in a Notebook," Julio Cortázar imagines a life of pallid people who never leave the Subte system—"their existence and their circulation like leucocytes." Filmmaker Gustavo Mosquera went even farther in his 1996 movie *Moebius,* which depicts a Subte train and its passengers in an endless loop beneath the city.

In reality, there is an underground culture in the city's subways, but nothing quite so enigmatic as Cortázar and Mosquera concocted. Beginning in the 1930s, builders embellished Subte stations with tiled ceramic murals; more recently, the private operator Metrovías has begun to restore some of these faded glories and, at the same, commission new ones and even construct minimuseums with rotating or permanent art and history exhibits at newer stations.

Every Sunday at 2 P.M., a group of three guides that goes by the name Flor de Buenos Aires (tel. 15/4049-3337) offers a two-hour tour of various Subte stations on the A, C, and D lines, which takes in a broad sample of murals. The starting point is Pasaje Roverano, on the 500 block of Avenida de Mayo, a short distance from Línea A's Estación Perú. Advance reservations are advisable for these tours, which cost US$1.50 pp and include an annotated map of the network's main murals.

The Subte, then, provides a means to see both classic and contemporary Argentine art on the move. Visitors who prefer their own means can use the following details to orient themselves to this artistic legacy.

Línea A

Buenos Aires's oldest subway line, originally the Compañía de Tranvías Anglo Argentina (Anglo-Argentine Tramway Company) or Línea Anglo (Anglo Line), is its least decorated, though its classic wooden cars are works of art in their own right.

Línea B

Línea B, though it has some of the system's newest and most comfortable cars, is also short on decoration. As of writing, though, the Uruguay station was undergoing a thematic remodel to display the history of Argentine cinema; for some years, the Abasto district's remodeled Carlos Gardel station has featured a ceramic mural of an *Orquesta Típica* (Typical Orchestra) on its northern platform.

Línea C

Imported Spanish tiles adorn the so-called Línea de los Españoles (Spanish Line, 1934) with Iberian scenes, but more-recent additions provide some balance. The most venerable pieces are a series of ceramic *Paisajes de España,* depicting landscapes from Lérida, Segovia, Sevilla, and other locales at Avenida de Mayo, Independencia, Lavalle, and Moreno stations.

The line is also notable for its Moorish masonry and elegant friezes, such as the ceramic coats of arms at San Juan station, the decorative dragon at Moreno station, and the Arabic script, also at Moreno station, of the aphorism "there is no greater victor than God."

Since 1998, reproductions of three of *gauchesco* caricaturist Florencio Molina Campos's paintings line the western platform of Constitución station: *El de Laj Once y Sais,* depicting gauchos awaiting a train in the pampas; *Pa' Nuevos Hori-*

Ⓝ Plaza de Mayo

Colloquially known as the Plaza de Protestas for its frequent, large, and often contentious political demonstrations, the Plaza de Mayo has often played center stage in Argentine history. Juan and Eva Perón, in particular, used it for spectacle, convoking hundreds of thousands of the fervent *descamisados* (shirtless ones) who comprised their underclass disciples.

Internationally, though, the plaza became notorious for some of the smallest gatherings ever to take place there. During the late 1970s, a handful of Argentine mothers marched silently every Thursday afternoon to demand the return of their adult children kidnapped by the armed forces and paramilitary gangs. Most of the disappeared died at the hands of their captors but, in the absence of a complete accounting, the Madres

zontes, showing a gaucho family on a horsecart loaded with personal belongings, bound for a new *estancia;* and *Beyaquiando Juerte,* a gaucho breaking a new mount. Molina Campos titled his pieces in gaucho dialect.

Línea D

In contrast to the Iberian-themed murals of Línea C, most of those on Línea D are more strictly nationalist, dealing with Argentine landscapes, legends, tradition, and native customs by artists like Léonie Matthis de Villar, Rodolfo Franco, and Alfredo Guido. As the line opened in 1937, this change of focus may reflect events of the Spanish Civil War and the military regime then ruling in Argentina. The exception is Palermo station, whose ceramic vestibule mural resembles those of Línea C's *Paisajes de España.*

On the north platform of Catedral station, *Buenos Aires 1936* reflects the construction of the modern city, with its subways and skyscrapers. In the same station, the ceramic *Buenos Aires 1830* displays the city of early republican times.

Ceramic murals at the Facultad de Medicina station offer insight into provincial cities with *Rosario 1836, Santa Fe 1836,* and *Rosario 1938.* Agüero station's *Camino a Córdoba del Tucumán* shows the rigors of travel between provincial capitals in the 19th century.

Bulnes station's *Las Leyendas del País de la Selva* (Legends of the Forests) has a folkloric focus, while *Arqueología Diaguita* portrays northwestern Argentina's archaeological heritage. Scalabrini Ortiz's *Evocaciones de Salta* depicts the far-northwestern province.

Among the best works on this line are the Plaza Italia station's *La Descarga de los Convoyes,* a series of port scenes based on sketches by Benito Quinquela Martín, which cover the platforms themselves.

The spacious, well-lighted new stations on the Línea D extension—José Hernández, Juramento, and Congreso de Tucumán—all feature custom-made display cases with rotating exhibits of historical and cultural artifacts, and artwork such as sculptures.

Línea E

Opened in 1944, Línea E reflects even more nationalistic times, coinciding with the rise of Juan and Evita Perón. Estación San José is the only station to celebrate the country's scenic treasures, *Las Cataratas del Iguazú* (Iguazú Falls) and *Los Lagos del Sur* (The Southern Lake District).

Estación Entre Ríos, though, glorifies *La Conquista del Desierto,* General Julio Argentino Roca's genocidal 19th-century campaign against the Patagonian Indians, and the *Fundación de Pueblos en la Pampa,* the founding of the towns that displaced the indigenes.

Estación Jujuy represents its namesake province and people in *Jujuy, Sus Riquezas Naturales* (Jujuy's Natural Riches) and *Los Gauchos Norteños* (the Northern Gauchos). Estación General Urquiza portrays the triumphs of the provincial warlord who overthrew the dictator Rosas in a reproduction of Cándido López's *La Batalla de Caseros* and *La Entrada Triunfal del General Urquiza en Buenos Aires* (General Urquiza's Triumphant Entry into Buenos Aires).

de la Plaza de Mayo still parade every Thursday at 3:30 P.M. around the **Pirámide de Mayo,** the plaza's small central obelisk.

Ironically enough, emotional throngs cheered the 1976–83 dictatorship here following the April 1982 occupation of the British-ruled Falkland Islands. As the war went badly, though, the crowds turned on General Leopoldo Galtieri's de facto government, and the military collapse

brought a quick return to constitutional government.

Most recently, following Argentina's economic meltdown of December 2001, the Plaza de Mayo witnessed major protests and a police riot that killed several demonstrators and brought about the resignation of the honest but indecisive President Fernando de la Rúa. In the interim, contentious demonstrations have taken place, both by leftist groups who deplore the so-called "model" ostensibly imposed by international lending agencies, and bank depositors outraged at *corralito* banking restrictions that limited access to their savings.

Catedral Metropolitana

At Avenida Rivadavia and San Martín, the capital's cathedral occupies the site of the original colonial church designated by Juan de Garay in 1580. It opened in 1836 in its present form; Joseph Dubourdieu's 1862 bas reliefs on the triangular pediment symbolically compare the biblical reconciliation of Joseph and his brothers with the results of the battle of Pavón, in which Buenos Aires forces under Bartolomé Mitre defeated caudillo Justo José Urquiza.

Even more significantly for Argentines, a separate chapel contains the **Mausoleo del General José de San Martín,** the burial site of the country's independence hero. Disillusioned with post-independence turmoil, San Martín spent the rest of his life in exile in Boulogne-sur-Mer, France, where he died in 1850; his remains returned to Argentina in 1880, after President Nicolás Avellaneda ordered construction of this elaborate tomb, marked by an eternal flame.

Museo del Cabildo

The Plaza's only remaining colonial structure, the Cabildo was a combination town council and prison, and the site where criollo patriots deposed Spanish viceroy Baltasar Hidalgo de Cisneros in 1810. The present structure preserves part of the *recova* (arcade) that once ran the width of the plaza.

The museum itself is thin on content—a few maps, paintings and photographs of the plaza and its surroundings, along with a portrait gallery from the British invasions of 1806–07 and the Revolution of May 1810. The real star is the building, part of which survived 19th-century mayor Torcuato de Alvear's wrecking ball, which opened the route of the Avenida de Mayo to connect the Casa Rosada with the Congreso.

The Museo del Cabildo (Bolívar 65, tel. 011/4343-4387, US$.35) is open 11:30 A.M.– 6 P.M. Wednesday–Friday, 2–6 P.M. Saturday, and 3–7 P.M. Sunday. The interior has a small *confitería,* and occasionally hosts live music events.

Casa Rosada

For better or worse, the presidential palace, facing the Plaza de Mayo and also known as Casa de Gobierno Nacional, has been the site of contentious political spectacle, the place where Perón and Evita summoned the cheering masses who later jeered the ruthless military dictatorship after the Falklands War in 1982. Most recently, it witnessed the shooting of demonstrators by federal police under the inept De la Rúa administration in December of 2001. The building owes its distinctive pinkish hue to President Domingo F. Sarmiento, who proposed the blend of Federalist red and Unitarist white to symbolize reconciliation between the two violently opposed factions of 19th-century politics.

The Casa Rosada was not originally a single building; in 1884, Italian architect Francesco Tamburini merged the original Casa de Gobierno with the former Correo Central (Central Post Office) to create the present, somewhat asymmetrical structure. On the east side, facing Parque Colón, pedestrians can view the excavated ruins of the colonial **Fuerte Viejo** (fortress) and early customs headquarters (buried beneath landfill during port improvements in the 1890s).

In the basement, entered from the south side on Hipólito Yrigoyen, the **Museo de la Casa de Gobierno** contains memorabilia from Argentine presidents but, unfortunately, its charter prohibits inclusion of material any more recent than 30 years ago (and does not even require it to be that timely). Visitors can, however, stroll among the colonial catacombs visible from the pedestrian mall outside.

The Museo de la Casa de Gobierno (Hipólito Yrigoyen 219, tel. 011/4344-3804, info@museo. gov.ar, www.museo.gov.ar, free) is open 10 A.M.– 6 P.M. weekdays, 2–6 P.M. Sunday only. Guided tours, free of charge, take place at 11 A.M. and 4 P.M. weekdays, at 3 and 4:30 P.M. Sunday.

Guided tours of the Casa Rosada itself take place weekdays at 5 P.M. These are free, but make reservations at the museum at least two hours ahead of time, and show identification.

Manzana de las Luces

Ever since the mid-17th century, when the Jesuit order established itself on the block bounded by the present-day streets of Bolívar, Moreno, Perú, and Alsina, Monserrat has been a hub of the capital's intellectual life. While the Jesuits were the most intellectual of all monastic orders, they were also the most commercial, and the two surviving buildings of the **Procuraduría,** fronting on Alsina, stored products from their widespread missions.

The Jesuit structures, which also housed missionized Indians who came to Buenos Aires from the provinces, contained a number of defensive tunnels. After the Jesuits' expulsion from the Americas in 1767, the buildings served as the Protomedicato, which regulated medical practice in the city. Following independence, they served a variety of purposes ranging from the public library to a medical school and various university departments. After 1974, the Comisión Nacional de la Manzana de Las Luces attempted to salvage the historical buildings for cultural purposes, opening the tunnels to the public and restoring part of the "Universidad" lettering along the Perú facade.

The **Iglesia San Ignacio** (1722) replaced an earlier structure of the same name. Expelled in 1767, the Jesuits returned in 1836, at the invitation of dictator Juan Manuel de Rosas; in 1955, at the instigation of Juan Perón, mobs trashed the building, but it has since been restored.

The church has one common wall with the **Colegio Nacional de Buenos Aires** (1908), the country's most prestigious and competitive secondary school, taught by top university faculty. Another notable feature of the complex is the re-created **Sala de Representantes,** the province's first legislature.

The **Instituto de Investigaciones Históricas de la Manzana de las Luces Doctor Jorge E. Garrido** (Perú 272, tel. 011/4331-8167, int. 129, www.manzana.fwd.com.ar) conducts a series of guided tours for US$1 pp, Monday at 1 P.M., weekdays at 3 P.M., and weekends at 3, 4:30 and 6 P.M.

Museo Etnográfico

Affiliated with the Universidad de Buenos Aires, the city's ethnographic museum has first-rate archaeological, ethnographic and ethnohistorical material on Argentina's Andean Northwest (on the periphery of the great civilizations of highland Peru), the Mapuche of northern Patagonia, and the archipelago of Tierra del Fuego. Well-organized, with good narration in Spanish only, it does a lot with what it has—and what it has is pretty good.

The Museo Etnográfico Juan B. Ambrosetti (Moreno 350, tel. 011/4331-7788, US$.35, free for retirees) is open 2:30–6:30 P.M. Wednesday–Sunday. There are guided tours Saturday and Sunday at 3 P.M. (19th-century Tierra del Fuego), 4 P.M. (Northwestern Argentine archaeology) and 5 P.M. (the Pampas and Patagonia, 19th century).

Museo de la Ciudad

Upstairs in the same building as the remarkable Farmacia La Estrella, the city museum specializes in themes dealing with the city proper and elements of everyday life, including architecture, floor tiles, furniture, and postcards; the pharmacy's exterior windows have been turned into display cases.

Except in February, when it's closed, the Museo de la Ciudad (Defensa 219, tel. 011/4343-2123 or 011/4331-9855, US$.35, free Wed.) is open 11 A.M.–7 P.M. weekdays, 3–7 P.M. Sunday.

Café Tortoni

One of the most fiercely if quietly traditional places in town, Café Tortoni has made no concessions to the 21st century and only a few to the 20th: upholstered chairs and marble tables stand among sturdy columns beneath a ceiling punctuated by stained-glass light fixtures, the wallpaper looks original between the surrounding stained wooden trim, and walls are decorated with pictures, portraits, and *filete,* the traditional calligraphy of *porteño* sign painters. Past patrons acknowledged on the walls include tango singer Carlos Gardel, La Boca painter Benito Quinquela Martín, dramatists Luigi Pirandello and Federico García Lorca, and pianist Arthur Rubinstein; more recently, the Tortoni has hosted King Juan Carlos I of Spain and Hilary Rodham Clinton.

The original entrance was on Rivadavia, on the north side of the building, but Torcuato de Alvear's creation of Avenida de Mayo forced it to reorient itself. One of BA's can't-miss sights, for drinks or tango or just a coffee, its current address is Avenida de Mayo 825.

Iglesia y Convento de Santo Domingo

Since late colonial times, the mid-18th-century Dominican church (also known as the Iglesia de Nuestra Señora del Rosario) at Avenida Belgrano

and Defensa has witnessed some of Argentine history's most dramatic events. It still contains banners captured by Viceroy Santiago Liniers from the Highlanders Regiment No. 71 during the initial British invasion of 1806, and the facade and left-side tower still show combat damage from the British occupation the following year. On the east side, near the entrance to the church, an eternal flame burns near sculptor Héctor Ximenes's **Mausoleo de Belgrano** (1903), the burial site of Argentina's second-greatest hero; by most accounts, Belgrano was an indifferent soldier, but he did design the Argentine flag.

Following independence, President Bernardino Rivadavia secularized the church, turning it into a natural history museum and one of its towers into an astronomical observatory. In 1955, during the overthrow of Juan Perón, anticlerical Peronists set it afire.

MICROCENTRO AND VICINITY

Formally known as San Nicolás, the area bounded by Avenida Córdoba on the north, Avenida Eduardo Madero on the east, Avenida Rivadavia on the south, and Avenida Callao to the west, encompasses much of the city's traditional financial, commercial, and entertainment centers. The area between Avenida 9 de Julio and the riverfront, immediately north of the Plaza de Mayo, is commonly called the Microcentro and, on occasion, Catedral al Norte. Calle San Martín, with its concentration of banks and exchange houses between Avenida Rivadavia and Avenida Corrientes, is the main axis of the financial district, La City.

Named for Argentina's independence day, **Avenida 9 de Julio** literally separates the Microcentro from the rest of the barrio—only a

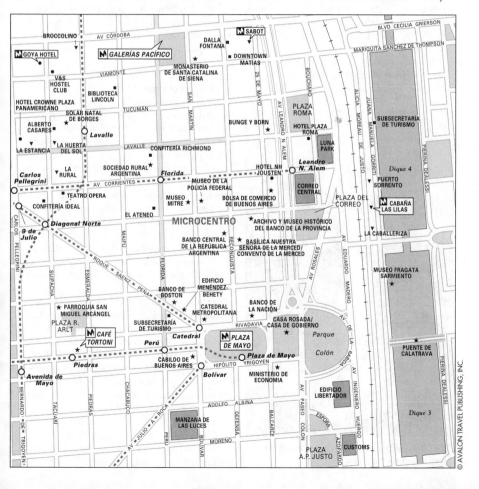

world-class sprinter could safely cross 16 lanes of seemingly suicidal drivers fudging the green light. Fortunately for pedestrian safety, there are several traffic islands, as well as subterranean passageways.

One of the Microcentro's foci is the north-south **Calle Florida,** a pedestrian mall that first became a *peatonal* in the early 20th century, but for only a couple of hours each day. On being completely closed to automobile traffic, it became the city's smartest shopping area, but it's much less fashionable than it once was, with one major exception: the restored **Galerías Pacífico,** an architectural and historical landmark that occupies nearly an entire block also bounded by Avenida Córdoba, San Martín, and Viamonte.

Originally a private residence, the headquarters of the **Sociedad Rural Argentina** (1910), Florida 460, house an organization that has voiced the in-

terests of large-scale landowners—many Argentines would say "the oligarchy"—since 1866. Other oligarchs included the financial and commercial house of **Bunge y Born,** with headquarters at 25 de Mayo 501.

East-west **Avenida Corrientes,** the traditional axis of *porteño* nightlife, has recently taken a back seat to trendier areas like Puerto Madero and Palermo; several cinemas have closed and, while some traditional cafés and restaurants have survived beneath gaudy illuminated signs, others seem to be hanging by a thread. The once-vibrant cinema district along the Lavalle pedestrian walkway has seen an influx of bingo parlors, evangelical churches blaring amplified hymns, and raucous video arcades, but a recent municipal initiative will attempt to control the worst excesses.

At the foot of Corrientes, occupying an entire block also bounded by Avenida Leandro N. Alem, Bouchard, and Sarmiento, the **Correo Central** (central post office, 1928) is a Beaux Arts landmark whose original architect, Norberto Maillart, based his design on New York City's General Post Office.

At the south end of Florida and San Martín, in La City, angry bank depositors expressed their *bronca* with graffiti on the corrugated aluminum that covered the windows of financial institutions after the events of late 2001 and early 2002. Even sturdy, secure buildings such as the elegant Spanish Renaissance **Banco de Boston** (1924), at the intersection with Diagonal Roque Sáenz Peña, suffered defacement at the hands of *corralito* protestors.

Argentina's central bank, the Italianate **Banco Central de la República Argentina,** has identical facades on the 200 blocks of San Martín and Reconquista. Its **Museo Numismático Dr. José E. Uriburu** (Reconquista 266, tel. 011/4393-0021, 10 A.M.–3 P.M. weekdays only, free), offers insights on the country's volatile economic history. The federal police guards require identification from those climbing to the first-floor museum.

The nearby **Museo Mitre** (San Martín 366, tel. 011/4394-8240, museomitre@ciudad.com .ar, 1–6 P.M. weekdays, 2–6 P.M. Sun., US$.50) was the home of Bartolomé Mitre (1821–1906),

© WAYNE BERNHARDSON

The Obelisco is a major landmark along the broad Avenida 9 de Julio.

Argentina's first president under the Constitution of 1853 and founder of the venerable daily *La Nación.*

At the intersection of Avenida 9 de Julio and Corrientes, the 67.5-meter **Obelisco** (Obelisk, 1936) is a city symbol erected for the 400th anniversary of Pedro de Mendoza's initial encampment of the banks of the Río de la Plata. From the Obelisco, the Diagonal Roque Sáenz Peña ends at **Plaza Lavalle,** which stretches north for three woodsy blocks along Talcahuano and Libertad between Lavalle and Avenida Córdoba.

On the west side of Plaza Lavalle, the **Palacio de Justicia** (commonly known as Tribunales or Law Courts, 1904) has lent its colloquial name to the neighborhood. Ever Monday since 1994, the capital's Jewish community gathers at 9:53 A.M. for a moment of silence to protest judicial inaction on the bombing of the Asociación Mutualista Israelita Argentina (AMIA), which took place on July 18 of that year.

Across the plaza is the **Teatro Colón** (1908), the stately opera house (Libertad 621). To its north, fronting on Libertad and protected by bulky concrete planter boxes, architect Alejandro Enquín's **Templo de la Congregación Israelita** (1932) is the capital's largest synagogue. It also holds the small but impressive **Museo Judío Dr. Salvador Kibrick** (Libertad 769, tel. 011/4374-7955); Tuesday and Thursday, from 3:30–5:30 P.M., it offers guided tours (US$5 pp) in Spanish, English, and Hebrew. Identification is obligatory; do not photograph this or any other Jewish community site without express permission.

Galerías Pacífico

As Calle Florida developed into an elegant shopping district in the late 19th century, Francisco Seeber and Emilio Bunge were the main shareholders in the proposed Bon Marché Argentino, inspired by Milan's Galleria Vittorio Emmanuele II. Unfortunately for Seeber and Bunge, their French investors backed out, but

© WAYNE BERNHARDSON

Galerías Pacífico—recycled railroad offices transformed into upscale shopping center

Seeber resurrected the project by 1894 as the Galería Florida.

One of the tallest and broadest buildings of its era, with a double basement and four upper stories, it covered an entire city block bounded by Florida, Avenida Córdoba, San Martín, and Viamonte. In 1908, though, the British-run rail company Ferrocarril de Buenos Aires al Pacífico acquired the sector fronting on Córdoba for its business offices; within two years, it controlled the rest of the building. It later passed into the hands of Ferrocarriles Argentinos, the state railroad enterprise created when Juan Perón nationalized the sector in 1948.

Meanwhile, in 1945, Argentine artists gave the cupola its most dramatic feature: some 450 square meters of murals including Lino Spilimbergo's *El Dominio de las Fuerzas Naturales* (the Dominion of Natural Forces), Demetrio Urruchúa's *La Fraternidad* (Brotherhood), Juan Carlos Castagnino's *La Vida Doméstica* (Domestic Life), Manuel Colmeiro's *La Pareja Humana* (The Human Couple), and Antonio Berni's *El Amor* (Love). Linked to famous Mexican muralist Davíd Alfaro Siqueiros through Spilimbergo, all belonged to the socially conscious Nuevo Realismo (New Realism) movement; the murals have twice been restored, in 1968 under Berni's direction and then again by an Argentine-Mexican group in 1991.

For most of the 1980s the Galerías languished until, in 1992, the murals became a highlight of a transformation into one of the capital's most fashionable shopping centers—appropriately enough, its original purpose. Well worth a visit even for nonshoppers, the tastefully modernized Galerías offers guided tours Wednesdays at 6:30 P.M. from the central information desk at street level. On the basement level, it has a high-quality food court and the city's best public toilets.

Teatro Colón

Possibly the continent's most important performing arts venue, the ornate Teatro Colón (1908) is approaching its centenary down but far from out in the face of economic crisis. Unable to pay for top-tier international opera, ballet, and symphonic performers because of devaluation, it still manages to present first-rate local talent in opera, ballet, symphony, and occasionally in more popular idioms.

Argentine lyric theater dates from the early 19th century, immediately after the Revolution of May 1810, with the first European artists arriving in the 1820s. The original Teatro Colón, at the northeast corner of the Plaza de Mayo, seated 2,500 people and opened with Verdi's *La Traviata* in 1857. As the earlier theater became the Banco de la Nación, authorities chose a site on the country's first-ever railway station for the new facility. Italian architect Francesco Tamburini was responsible for the original Italian Renaissance design.

Occupying a lot of more than 8,000 square meters, with floor space of nearly 38,000 meters on seven levels, the Colón opened with a performance of Verdi's *Aída*. Seating 2,478 patrons, with standing room for another 700, it's one of the country's most ornate buildings, its **Gran Hall** outfitted with Verona and Carrara marble, its **Salón de los Bustos** studded with busts of famous figures from European classical music, and its **Salón Dorado** (Golden Salon) modeled on palaces like Paris's Versailles and Vienna's Schoenbrunn.

The main theater itself follows lines of French and Italian classics, with world-class acoustics; a rotating disc makes it possible to change scenes rapidly. The orchestra accommodates up to 120 musicians. Seating ranges from comfortably upholstered rows to luxury boxes, including a presidential box with its own phone line to the Casa Rosada, and a separate exit. Presidential command performances take place on the winter patriotic holidays of May 25 and July 9.

Since the Colón's opening, notable performers have included the composers Richard Strauss, Igor Stravinsky, Camille Saint-Saëns, Manuel de Falla, and Aaron Copland; conductors Otto Klemperer, Wilhelm Furtwaengler, Herbert von Karajan, Arturo Toscanini, and Zubin Mehta; singers Enrico Caruso, Lily Pons, Ezio Pinza, María Callas, José Carreras, Frederika von Stade, Kiri Te Kanawa, Plácido Domingo, and Luciano Pavarotti; dancers Anna Pavlova, Vaslav Nijinsky, Rudolf Nureyev,

FOREIGN FILMS ON AND IN BUENOS AIRES

Foreign filmmakers have found Buenos Aires both visually and thematically appealing. Argentine-born but British-based, Martin Donovan made the cult thriller *Apartment Zero* (1989), which brilliantly and even humorously portrays *porteño* life—its depiction of busybody neighbors in a Buenos Aires apartment building is priceless—even as it deals with Dirty War savagery. British actor Colin Firth plays the protagonist, an Anglo-Argentine cinema manager.

The worst of the worst is Alan Parker's kitschy version of the already kitschy musical *Evita* (1996). Filmed partly in Buenos Aires but also in Budapest, it was most noteworthy for the controversy it caused with Peronist politicians obsessed with Evita's legacy, and the highly publicized meeting between Madonna and a flagrantly lecherous President Carlos Menem.

Nearly as bad, though, is British director Sally Potter's narcissistic *The Tango Lesson* (1997). For a better representation of the tango, despite a weak story line, see Puerto Rican director Marcos Zurinaga's *Tango Bar* (1988); Zurinaga worked with his compatriot, the late Raúl Juliá, and a cast and crew of Argentines including bandoneonist Rubén Juárez and singer Valeria Lynch.

It's only incidental, but the hero of Dutch director Paul Verhoeven's *Starship Troopers* (1997), a hilarious adaptation of Robert Heinlein's sci-fi novel, is a *porteño*. In the process, Buenos Aires gets vaporized by alien bugs.

American actor/director Robert Duvall, a frequent visitor and fervent tango aficionado, filmed the thriller *Assassination Tango* (2003) on location in the city. British director Christopher Hampton filmed the movie version of Lawrence Thornton's novel *Imagining Argentina*, with Emma Thompson and Antonio Banderas, in Buenos Aires and in the provinces.

In what could be the definitive *porteño* film, American actor/director John Malkovich has floated the idea of turning novelist Ernesto Sábato's complex psychological novel *On Heroes and Tombs* into a movie.

Margot Fonteyn, and Mikhail Barishnikov; and choreographer George Balanchine.

Foreign dance companies that have appeared include the Ballet de Montecarlo, London's Festival Ballet, the Opera Privée de París, the Ballet de la Opera de París, and the Ballet de la Opera de Berlín; orchestras include the New York Philharmonic, the London Philharmonic, and the Washington Philharmonic. Soloists include Arthur Rubinstein, Pablo Casals, Yehudi Menuhim, Mstislav Rostropovich, Isaac Stern, Itzhak Perlman, Yo-Yo Ma, Andrés Segovia, and Anne Sofie Mutter. At times, though, the administration has let its hair down to accommodate performers like politically conscious folksinger Mercedes Sosa, the *porteño* rhythm-and-blues unit Memphis La Blusera, and rock guitarist-songwriter Luis Alberto Spinetta.

The Teatro Colón (Libertad 621, tel. 011/4378-7344, boleteria@teatrocolon.org.ar, www.teatrocolon.org.ar) presents some 200 events per annum, in a season that runs from May to No-

vember; the ticket office is open 10 A.M.–8 P.M. Thursday–Saturday, 10 A.M.–5 P.M. Sunday, and 5 P.M. until the beginning of the performance (if there is one) Monday. While the main entrance is on Libertad, tours enter from the Viamonte side.

Guided tours, always available in Spanish and English but sometimes in French, German, and Portuguese, take place at 11 A.M. and 3 P.M. weekdays, and 9, 10, and 11 A.M. and noon Saturdays. For reservations, contact the Teatro Colón (Viamonte 1168, tel. 011/4378-7132, visitas@teatrocolon.org.ar, US$3 for nonresident adults, US$1.50 for Argentine residents, US$.75 for children up to age 10); tours last 50 minutes and go behind the scenes as well.

PUERTO MADERO

Born amidst 19th-century corruption and designated a separate barrio in 1991, modern Puerto Madero is an attempt to reclaim the riverfront,

Puente de Calatrava, Puerto Madero

which languished off-limits during the military dictatorship of 1976–83. Comparable in some ways to Baltimore's Inner Harbor and London's Docklands, it has recycled several of the handsome brick warehouses around its four large *diques* (basins, one of which has become a yacht harbor) into stylish lofts, offices, restaurants, bars, and cinemas. One measure of its success may be that director Fabián Bielinsky used the promenade for a uniquely entertaining chase scene in his con-man film *Nine Queens.*

Built on landfill east of the river's barrancas, what is now Puerto Madero expanded during the dictatorship as the military dumped the debris from its massive public works projects east and southeast of the *diques.* Ironically enough, as native plants and animals colonized this expanse of rubble and rubbish, it became the **Reserva Ecológica Costanera Sur** (Avenida Tristán Achával Rodríguez 1550, tel. 4893-1597/1588), now a popular destination for Sunday outings, cyclists, and joggers—not to mention a cruising area for the capital's homosexuals. Hours are 8 A.M.–7 P.M. daily except Monday; there are guided tours weekends and holidays at 10 A.M. and 3 P.M., and moonlight

tours at 8:30 P.M. on given Fridays—by previous Monday's reservation only.

Sequentially numbered from south to north, the rectangular basins stretch from Retiro in the north to La Boca in the south. Dique No. 3 holds a 450-berth yacht harbor; its **Museo Fragata Sarmiento** (tel. 011/4334-9386, 9 A.M.–9 P.M. daily, US$.35, children under 5 free), an early-20th-century naval training vessel, is now a national historical monument.

The newest feature along the basins is the **Puente de Calatrava,** a modernistic pedestrian suspension bridge whose center section rotates to allow vessels to pass between Dique No. 3 and Dique No. 2. Permanently anchored at the southernmost Dique No. 1, the **Buque Museo A.R.A. Corbeta Uruguay** (tel. 011/4314-1090, 9 A.M.–9 P.M. weekdays, 10 A.M.–9 P.M. weekends, US$.35) rescued Norwegian explorers Carl Skottsberg and Otto Nordenskjöld from Antarctica in 1903. Dating from 1874, it's the oldest Argentine vessel still afloat.

Toward the north end of the barrio, the **Hotel de Inmigrantes** (Avenida Antártida 1355) was Argentina's Ellis Island for European immigrants. From 1911 until 1953, Old World arrivals could

immigration museum is off to a good start with sample family histories and panels showing the evolution of immigration and the treatment of new arrivals.

At present, the only areas open to the public are the reception area and the dining room; the upstairs dormitories are undergoing restoration. Part of the dining room provides access to a computerized archive on 3.7 million immigrants from 60 countries, who arrived by boat after 1882.

The Museo Nacional de la Inmigración (Avenida Argentina 1355, tel. 011/4317-0285, US$1) is open 10 A.M.–5 P.M. weekdays, 11 A.M.–6 P.M. weekends. Genealogical consultations cost US$1 each.

SAN TELMO AND VICINITY

San Telmo, with its narrow colonial streets, antique shops, and street fairs, is a favorite among Argentines and foreigners alike. Six blocks south of the Plaza de Mayo, bounded by Chile on the north, Piedras to the west, Puerto Madero to the east, and Avenida Brasil, Parque Lezama, and Avenida Caseros to the south, it's also one of the city's best walkers' neighborhoods—especially on Sunday, when most of Calle Defensa is closed to motor vehicles.

After yellow fever drove elite families to higher ground in northern barrios like Palermo and Belgrano in the 1870s, San Telmo became an area where impoverished immigrant families could find a foothold in its *conventillos,* abandoned mansions where large families filled small spaces—often a single room. Today, though, it's a mixed neighborhood where *conventillos* still exist but young professionals have also recycled crumbling apartment buildings and even industrial sites into stylish lofts. It's also the barrio most closely identified with tango, at least of the high-priced spectacle with professional dancers.

While colonial Spanish law dictated a city plan with rectangular blocks of equal size, in practice things were not quite so regular. North-south **Calle Balcarce,** for instance, doglegs several times between Chile and Estados Unidos, crossing

© WAYNE BERNHARDSON

The old warehouses along the Puerto Madero waterfront have been redeveloped into upscale lofts and restaurants.

spend three nights here before heading into the great Argentine unknown.

Several original cranes remain in place along the west side of the basins, where British engineers designed the handsome but practical red brick *depósitos* (warehouses), now recycled into bars, restaurants, and entertainment venues, as well as apartments and offices. Work on the east-side buildings has been slower to progress, especially during the economic crisis, but the riverfront is finally making a contribution to Buenos Aires's livability.

Museo Nacional de la Inmigración

Building on lessons from earlier mistakes, Buenos Aires's reception facility for immigrants, called Hotel de Inmigrantes, was by all accounts an exemplary institution when it opened in 1911. While definitely a work in progress, the current

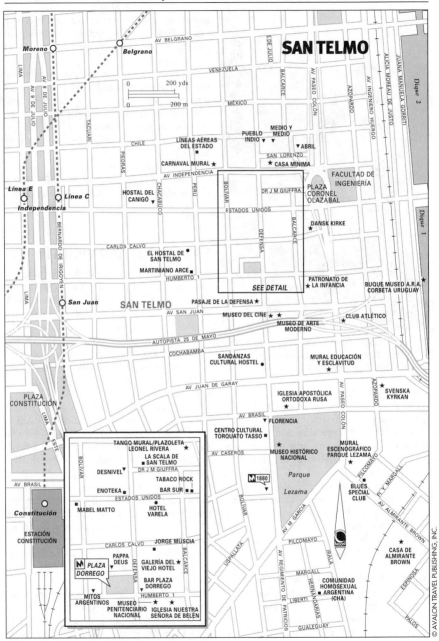

SAN TELMO

AV BELGRANO

Moreno

Belgrano

VENEZUELA

0   200 yds
0   200 m

MÉXICO

MEDIO Y
MEDIO

PUEBLO
INDIO ▼

▼ ABRIL

CHILE

LÍNEAS AÉREAS
DEL ESTADO

SAN LORENZO

CARNAVAL MURAL ★

★ CASA MÍNIMA

AV INDEPENDENCIA

FACULTAD DE
INGENIERÍA

Línea E

Línea C

HOSTAL DEL
CANIGÓ ▼

DR J M GIUFFRA

PLAZA
CORONEL
OLAZÁBAL

Independencia

ESTADOS UNIDOS

DANSK KIRKE
★

CARLOS CALVO

EL HOSTAL DE
SAN TELMO ●

MARTINIANO ARCE ■

HUMBERTO 1

PATRONATO DE
★ LA INFANCIA

BUQUE MUSEO A.R.A.
CORBETA URUGUAY

San Juan

SAN TELMO

PASAJE DE LA DEFENSA ★

SEE DETAIL

AV SAN JUAN

MUSEO DEL CINE ★ ★

CLUB ATLÉTICO

MUSEO DE ARTE
MODERNO

AUTOPISTA 25 DE MAYO

COCHABAMBA

SANDANZAS
CULTURAL HOSTEL ●

MURAL EDUCACIÓN
Y ESCLAVITUD

AV JUAN DE GARAY

PLAZA
CONSTITUCIÓN

IGLESIA APOSTÓLICA
ORTODOXA RUSA
★

SVENSKA
★ KYRKAN

AV BRASIL

▼ FLORENCIA

CENTRO CULTURAL
TORQUATO TASSO ■

MURAL
ESCENOGRÁFICO
PARQUE LEZAMA

AV CASEROS

MUSEO HISTÓRICO
NACIONAL

Constitución

M 1880
▼

Parque

BLUES
SPECIAL
CLUB

AV BRASIL

Lezama

ESTACIÓN
CONSTITUCIÓN

CASA DE
ALMIRANTE
BROWN ★

COMUNIDAD
HOMOSEXUAL
★ ARGENTINA
(CHA)

Detail inset

TANGO MURAL/PLAZOLETA
LEONEL RIVERA ★

LA SCALA DE
■ SAN TELMO

DR J M GIUFFRA

DESNIVEL ▼

TABACO ROCK

ENOTEKA ▼

BAR SUR ■ ■

ESTADOS UNIDOS

MABEL MATTO ■

HOTEL
VARELA

CARLOS CALVO

JORGE MUSCIA

PLAZA
DORREGO

PAPPA
DEUS

GALERÍA DEL ★
VIEJO HOTEL

BAR PLAZA
DORREGO

HUMBERTO 1

MITOS
ARGENTINOS

MUSEO
PENITENCIARIO
NACIONAL

IGLESIA NUESTRA
SEÑORA DE BELÉN

© AVALON TRAVEL PUBLISHING, INC.

the cobblestone alleyways of **Pasaje San Lorenzo**
and **Pasaje Giuffra.** The **Casa Mínima** (Pasaje
San Lorenzo 380) takes the *casa chorizo* (sausage
house) style to an extreme: the width of this two-
story colonial house, given to a freed slave by his
former owner, is barely greater than the an average adult male's armspread.

To the east, on Paseo Colón's **Plaza Coronel
Olazábal,** Rogelio Yrurtia's massive sculpture
Canto al Trabajo (Ode to Labor), a tribute to
hard-working pioneers, is a welcome antidote to
pompously heroic monuments elsewhere in the
city. On the plaza's east side, the Universidad de
Buenos Aires's neoclassic **Facultad de Ingeniería**
originally housed the Fundación Eva Perón, established by Evita herself to aid the poor—and
her own political ambitions.

San Telmo's heart, though, is **Plaza Dorrego**
(Defensa and Humberto Primo), site of the colorfully hectic weekend flea market. Antique shops
line both sides of Defensa, north and south from
the plaza.

Half a block east of Plaza Dorrego, dating from
1750, stands the colonial **Iglesia Nuestra Señora
de Belén** (Humberto Primo 340); its convent
became a women's prison after independence and
is now the **Museo Penitenciario Nacional Antonio Ballvé** (Humberto Primo 378, tel. 4362-
0099, Tues. and Fri. 2–6 P.M., Sun. 2–7 P.M.,
US$.35), an improving penal museum.

San Telmo is a neighborhood where the up-
wardly and downwardly mobile mix. Dating
from 1880, the **Pasaje de la Defensa** (Defensa
1179) originally belonged to a single wealthy
family but housed upward of 30 families before
being recycled as a shopping gallery. The **Galería
del Viejo Hotel** (Balcarce 1053) is a similar
cluster of workshops, studios, shops, and a
bar/restaurant around a courtyard; until its present incarnation around 1980, though, it served
at various times as a hotel, hospital, *conventillo,*
and even an *albergue transitorio* (a by-the-hour
hotel). Nearby, until recent evictions, the former **Patronato de la Infancia** (Balcarce 1170)
was still a *conventillo*—appropriately enough a
one-time orphanage.

In a cavernous recycled warehouse, the **Museo
de Arte Moderno** (Avenida San Juan 350, tel.

© WAYNE BERNHARDSON

San Telmo's Casa Mínima, barely two meters
wide, was reportedly a gift from a slaveholder
to his freed slave.

4361-1121, US$.35, free Wed.) showcases ab-
stract works of contemporary Argentine artists
like Antonio Berni, León Ferrari, and Kenneth
Kemble. Hours are 10 A.M.–8 P.M. Tuesday–Saturday, 11 A.M.–8 P.M. Sunday, though it's closed
in January. Guided tours take place Tuesday,
Wednesday, Friday, and Sunday at 5 P.M.

In new quarters around the corner, the **Museo
del Cine Pablo A. Ducrós Hicken** (Defensa
1220, tel. 011/4361-2462, museodelcine@aba-
conet.com.ar, 10 A.M.–6 P.M. weekdays, 3–6:30 P.M.
Sun.) devotes special exhibits to director María
Luisa Bemberg, actress Niní Marshall, and sex-
pot Isabel Sarli, and has a small cinema that
shows Argentine classics for free (no subtitles,
though). The upper floor is devoted to Argentine films since the 1970s, from the years of

early turmoil through the Proceso, the return to constitutional government and increasing liberty of expression.

One of the barrio's more unsettling sights, on Paseo Colón beneath the Autopista 25 de Mayo (the freeway to Ezeiza), the so-called **Club Atlético** is a grisly archaeological dig whose basement cells belonged to a building used as a torture center during the 1976–83 military dictatorship before being demolished to build the road.

At the corner of Defensa and Avenida Brasil, a graffiti-covered statue of Pedro de Mendoza guards the entrance to **Parque Lezama,** where Mendoza ostensibly founded the city in 1536. It is also the site of the **Museo Histórico Nacional,** the national history museum. On the south side of the park, architect Alejandro Christopherson designed the turquoise-colored onion domes and stained-glass windows of the **Iglesia Apostólica Ortodoxa Rusa** (Russian Orthodox Church, 1904), Avenida Brasil 315, built with materials imported from St. Petersburg.

© WAYNE BERNHARDSON

Gaucho souvenirs are on the docket at Sunday's Feria de San Pedro Telmo, on Plaza Dorrego.

Plaza Dorrego

Six days a week, Plaza Dorrego is a nearly silent shady square where *porteños* sip *cortados* and nibble lunches from nearby cafés. On weekends, though, when authorities close Defensa between Avenida San Juan and Avenida Independencia, it swarms with Argentine and foreign visitors who stroll among dozens of antiques stalls at the **Feria de San Pedro Telmo,** the most famous and colorful of the capital's numerous street fairs. Items range from antique soda siphons to brightly painted *filete* plaques with *piropos* (aphorisms), oversized antique radios, and many other items.

The plaza and surrounding site streets also fill with street performers like the ponytailed Pedro Benavente ("El Indio"), a smooth *tanguero* (dancer) who, with various female partners, entrances locals and tourists alike—even though his music comes from a boom box. Up and down Defensa there are also live tango musicians and other dancers, not to mention puppet theaters, hurdy-gurdy men with parrots, and a glut of *estatuas vivas* (living statues or costumed mimes, some original and others trite). One favorite, though, is the trio of fresh-off-the-boat immigrants who, at the drop of a coin, jabber in the Italian-Spanish pidgin *cocoliche,* which has had such an influence on the Argentine language since the late 19th century.

The Feria de San Pedro Telmo takes place every Sunday, starting around 9–10 A.M. and continuing into late afternoon. Even with all the antique and crafts stands, there's room to enjoy lunch and the show from the sidewalk cafés and balconies overlooking the plaza.

Parque Lezama

The presumptive but improbable site of Pedro de Mendoza's founding of the city, famed landscape architect Carlos Thays's Parque Lezama is an irregular quadrilateral on the banks above the old rivercourse, which has long been covered by landfill. Shaded by mature palms and other exotic trees and studded with monuments, it's the place where aging *porteños* play chess, working-class families have weekend picnics, and a Sunday crafts fair stretches along Calle Defensa to Avenida San Juan.

On the capital's southern edge in colonial times, the property came into the hands of Carlos Ridgley Horne and then Gregorio Lezama, whose widow sold it to the city in 1884. Horne built the Italianate mansion (1846) that is now the **Museo Histórico Nacional,** the national history museum; at the northwest entrance, Juan Carlos Oliva Navarro sculpted the **Monumento a Don Pedro Mendoza** (1937) to mark the 400th anniversary of Buenos Aires's original founding—a year too late.

Museo Histórico Nacional

From the permanent exhibits at Parque Lezama's national history museum, it's hard to tell that Argentina lived through the 20th century, let alone made it to the 21st. Mostly chronological, it offers a token account of pre-Columbian Argentina and a brief description of the founding of Spanish cities; its most vivid exhibits are the meticulous 19th-century illustrations of Buenos Aires and the surrounding pampas by Royal Navy purser Emeric Essex Vidal.

Politically, it offers a perfunctory account of independence and the 19th-century caudillos (provincial warlords), with a stereotypical nod to the gaucho. Its low point is a chauvinistic version of the so-called Conquista del Desierto (Conquest of the Desert), which expanded the country's Patagonian frontier at the expense of the Mapuche in the late 19th century.

One entire salon is devoted to the maturation of the iconic independence hero José de San Martín, but a superficial narrative of the conservative republic of the 19th century—consisting mostly of presidential portraits—ends abruptly with the deposed Hipólito Yrigoyen, victim of the country's first modern military coup in 1930. There is nothing on Juan Domingo Perón, his equally charismatic wife Eva, the 1970s Dirty War, the 1980s democratic restoration, or the failed boom of the 1990s.

Despite its shortcomings, the building itself is a well-kept landmark whose subterranean gallery hosts special exhibits and occasional weekend concerts. The Museo Histórico (Defensa 1600, tel. 011/4307-1182, US$.35) is open 11 A.M.– 6 P.M. Tuesday–Friday, 2–7 P.M. Saturday, and 1–7 P.M. Sunday. There are guided tours at 3:30 P.M. Saturday and Sunday.

LA BOCA

On the west bank of the twisting Riachuelo, the working-class barrio of La Boca owes its origins to mid-19th century French Basque and Genovese immigrants who settled here to man packing plants and warehouses during the export-beef boom. Perhaps more than any other neighborhood in the city, it remains a community, symbolized by fervent—most would say fanatical—identification with the Boca Juniors soccer team.

La Boca is, literally, the city's most colorful neighborhood, thanks to the brightly painted houses with corrugated zinc siding that line the pedestrian **Caminito** and other streets. Initially at least, these bright colors came from marine paints salvaged from ships in the harbor.

Still one of the country's most polluted waterways, the **Riachuelo** is undergoing a visible cleanup, as authorities are gradually removing the corroded hulks that oozed contamination along the landmark meander known as the **Vuelta de Rocha.** A new high **Malecón** (levee), with improved lighting, a bicycle path, and incipient landscaping, has made the riverside more appealing, but it's still not for sensitive noses. Historically, La Boca has been vulnerable to floods—many residents still keep rowboats— and there remain many elevated sidewalks.

Socially and politically, La Boca has a reputation for disorder and anarchy, but it is also an artists' colony, thanks to the late Benito Quinquela Martín, who sympathetically portrayed its hard-working inhabitants in his oils. *Porteños* may still claim that the barrio is dangerous, but anyone with basic street smarts should be able to visit without incident. Still, some visitors prefer guided tours, which often start at the Caminito.

La Boca's real gateway, though, is Avenida Almirante Brown, at the southeast corner of Parque Lezama. There, the barrio's Catalinas del Sur theater group has erected the **Mural Escenográfico**

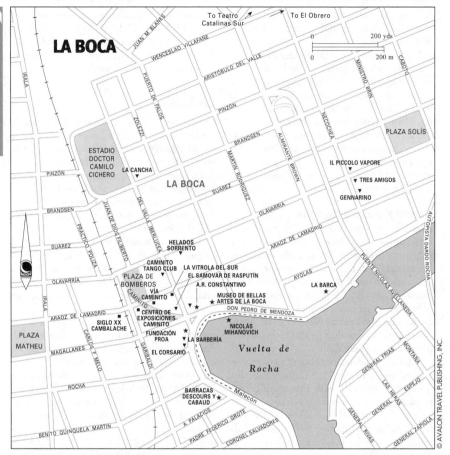

LA BOCA

To Teatro
Catalinas Sur

To El Obrero

LA BOCA

ESTADIO
DOCTOR
CAMILO
CICHERO

LA CANCHA

PLAZA SOLÍS

IL PICCOLO VAPORE

TRES AMIGOS

GENNARINO

HELADOS
SORRENTO

CAMINITO
TANGO CLUB
PLAZA DE
BOMBEROS
VÍA
CAMINITO

LA VITROLA DEL SUR
EL SAMOVAR DE RASPUTÍN

A.R. CONSTANTINO

MUSEO DE BELLAS
ARTES DE LA BOCA

LA BARCA

CENTRO DE
EXPOSICIONES
CAMINITO

SIGLO XX
CAMBALACHE

FUNDACIÓN
PROA

NICOLÁS
MIHANOVICH

LA BARBERÍA

PLAZA
MATHEU

EL CORSARIO

Vuelta de

Rocha

BARRACAS
DESCOURS Y
CABAUD

Malecón

© AVALON TRAVEL PUBLISHING, INC.

Parque Lezama, a three-dimensional mural depicting community life through colorful caricatures. Only a block east of the avenue, the parallel **Calle Necochea** houses a traditional cluster of gaudy and raucous cantinas that once were brothels, but this area's tourist appeal is declining.

From the foot of the avenue, where it intersects Avenida Pedro de Mendoza at the Riachuelo, the remaining massive girders of the former **Puente Nicolás Avellaneda** (1940), towering above the river, are a civil engineering landmark; the current namesake bridge, parallel to it, is a concrete construction that leads into the capital's major industrial suburb.

The starting point for most visits remains the cobbled, curving **Caminito,** once the terminus of a rail line and now a pedestrian mall where artists display their watercolors on weekends and, sometimes, on weekdays. Taking its name from a popular tango, the Caminito may once again sing with the sound of the rails, as a new tourist train to the **Plaza de Bomberos** (Firemen's Plaza) is due to connect to Puerto Madero.

On either side of the Caminito, along Avenida Pedro de Mendoza, several landmarks lend character to the neighborhood. Immediately to the east, high relief sculptures stand out above the display window of the ship chandler **A.R. Con-**

stantino. A short distance farther east stands the **Museo de Bellas Artes de La Boca Benito Quinquela Martín,** in the artist's former studio.

One block farther, the former restaurant **La Barca** retains a batch of Vicente Walter's well-preserved bas reliefs on nautical themes.

Immediately south of the Caminito, the cavernous **Fundación Proa** (Avenida Pedro de Mendoza 1929, tel. 011/4303-0909, info@proa.org, www.proa.org, 11 A.M.–7 P.M. daily except Mon.) is an ultramodern display space that showcases abstract and figurative works by Argentine and international artists. On weekends there are guided tours in Spanish only. Admission costs US$1 for adults, US$.35 for children and seniors, but children under age 12 accompanied by an adult do not pay.

For residents, though, the barrio's key landmark is the **Estadio Doctor Camilo Cichero,** better known by its nickname **La Bombonera,** at the corner of Brandsen and Del Valle Iberlucea; murals of barrio life cover the walls along the Brandsen side of the stadium. It is now home to the appropriately named **Museo de la Pasión Boquense** (Museum of Boca's Passion), which integrates the history of the soccer team with its role in the community.

Numerous *colectivos* either pass through or end their routes at La Boca, most notably the No. 86 from Congreso, but also No. 29 (from Belgrano and Palermo), No. 33 (from Retiro), No. 64 (from Belgrano, Palermo and Congreso), and No. 152 (from Belgrano, Palermo, and Retiro).

Museo de Bellas Artes

Boca's very own artist-in-residence, Benito Quinquela Martín (1890–1977), was an orphan who became a son of his barrio, living and painting in the building that is now a homage to his life and work promoting the community. His well-lighted studio displays his oils of working-class life (Quinquela himself labored as a stevedore before devoting himself to painting). There is also a collection of brightly painted bowsprits that reflects the barrio's maritime orientation, and a selection of works by other notable Argentine painters, including Antonio Berni, Raquel Forner, Eduardo Sívori, and Lino Spilimbergo.

The Museo de Bellas Artes de la Boca Benito Quinquela Martín (Pedro de Mendoza 1835, tel. 011/4301-1080, US$.35) is open daily except Monday, 10 A.M.–5:45 P.M.

Museo de la Pasión Boquense

In the catacombs of La Bombonera, Boca's newest museum is a thunderous interactive homage to the barrio's passion for soccer and its role in the community. Professionally organized, this state-of-the-art facility's 1,800 square meters includes photographs of almost every individual who ever played for the team; it also includes roster cards, trophies and even a photograph of Eva Perón in a blue-and-gold Boca jersey. The ultimate icon and idol of Boca, though, remains retired striker Diego Maradona who, despite his drug problems and other erratic behavior, can seemingly do no wrong in front of his fans.

Interactive video timelines attempt to integrate local, national, and international events—even the Dirty War that the military dictatorship waged as Argentina hosted the World Cup in 1978—with those in the sporting world. In the end, though, it tests the patience on non–soccer fans except for its depiction of the barrio.

The Museo de la Pasión Boquense (Brandsen 805, tel. 011/4362-1100, www.museoboquense .com, 10 A.M.–7 P.M. daily) charges US$2.50 pp, or US$4.50 pp with a guided tour including the stadium.

BALVANERA (ONCE AND THE ABASTO)

West of Avenida Callao and Entre Ríos, Balvanera's most conspicuous sights are major public buildings like the **Congreso Nacional,** which faces the Plaza de los Dos Congresos, and architectural landmarks like the sadly neglected **Confitería del Molino,** at the corner of Avenida Callao and Avenida Rivadavia. At the other extreme is the magnificently preserved **Palacio de las Aguas Corrientes,** the former city waterworks, at the northern end of the barrio.

Rarely mentioned by its official name, Balvanera subsumes several smaller neighborhoods with scattered points of interest: the bustling area commonly known as Congreso overlaps Monserrat and San Nicolás, while the Once and Abasto neighborhoods have their own distinctive identities.

Once, roughly bounded by Avenida Córdoba, Junín, Avenida Rivadavia, and Avenida Pueyrredón, is the city's garment district; it takes its colloquial name from the **Estación 11 de Septiembre,** the station for the westbound Ferrocarril Sarmiento. It is one of the most densely populated parts of town, with little green space, but its **Plaza Miserere** and **Plaza 1° de Mayo** are at least undergoing renovation.

Ethnically, Once is the capital's most conspicuously Jewish enclave, where men and boys in yarmulkes, and even Orthodox Jews with their suits and beards, are common sights, especially east of Pueyrredón between Córdoba and Corrientes. There are several Jewish schools, noteworthy for the heavy concrete security posts outside them—Once was a victim of the unsolved terrorist bombing of the **Asociación Mutualista Israelita Argentina (AMIA)** (Pasteur 633), which killed 87 people in 1994.

West of Once, Abasto was the home of tango legend Carlos Gardel, whose restored residence is now the **Museo Casa Carlos Gardel** (Jean Jaurés 735, tel. 011/4964-2071, 11 A.M. to 6 P.M. weekdays except Tues., US$1, free Wed.), a tango museum off to an auspicious start.

During Gardel's time, the magnificent **Mercado del Abasto** (1893), bounded by Avenida Corrientes, Anchorena, Agüero and Lavalle, was a wholesale produce market that fell into disrepair before its rescue as a modern shopping center by international financier George Soros in the late 1990s.

Immediately east of the Mercado de Abasto, the **Pasaje Carlos Gardel,** a block-long pedestrian mall, attempts to capitalize on Gardel's legacy, but most of its storefronts remain vacant, except for the restored **Chanta Cuatro,** where Gardel often lunched. San Juan sculptor Mariano Pagés created the larger-than-life-size bronze statue of Gardel, **El Morocho del Abasto,** 2.4 meters high and weighing 300 kg, but it's less impressive than the singer's tomb at Chacarita.

Palacio del Congreso Nacional

Balvanera's largest landmark, the neoclassical Congreso Nacional, was one of the last major public works projects undertaken before Francophile architecture became the norm. The Italianate building faces the Plaza de los Dos Congresos and, in the distance, the Casa Rosada presidential palace.

Argentines view their legislators with skeptical and even cynical eyes, and the Congreso has always given them good reason. Progressive mayor Torcuato de Alvear chose the site in 1888; the Italian Vittorio Meano won a controversial international design competition, but the project overshot the budget and Meano, following a congressional inquiry, died mysteriously by a gunshot from his maid in 1904.

The Palacio de las Aguas Corrientes, the onetime city waterworks also known as Obras Sanitarias, is one of the capital's most striking buildings.

Functional by 1906, the building didn't receive its final touches until 1946. Its 80-meter-high bronze cupola still bears marks from the 1930 military coup against Hipólito Yrigoyen. Presidents who have died in office, such as Perón, have lain in state here, as did his wife Evita in 1952.

Phone at least an hour ahead for guided tours of the Senado (upper house, Hipólito Yrigoyen 1849, tel. 011/4959-3000, int. 3855), which take place Monday, Tuesday, Thursday, and Friday at 11 A.M., 5 P.M., and 7 P.M. in Spanish; for English and French speakers, there are tours at 11 A.M. and 4 P.M. on the same days.

Guided visits to the Cámara de Diputados (lower house, Avenida Rivadavia 1864, tel. 011/4370-7532, ceremonial@hcdn.gov.ar) take place Monday, Tuesday, Wednesday, and Friday at 11 A.M. and 5 P.M., in Spanish only. There is also a congressional website (www.congreso.gov.ar), with separate entries for each house.

Palacio de las Aguas Corrientes

Perhaps the capital's most photogenic building, the former city waterworks (1894) glistens with 170,000 rust-colored tiles and 130,000 enameled bricks imported from Britain, crowned by a Parisian mansard. Filling an entire city block, the extravagant exterior conceals a utilitarian interior of 12 metallic tanks that held more than 60 million liters of potable water supply for the growing city.

Swedish architect Karl Nystromer conceived the building, popularly known as Obras Sanitarias, whose tanks became superfluous as engineers developed subterranean tunnels for moving water through the city. Since its privatization in the 1990s, the building houses offices and the small but interesting **Museo del Patrimonio Aguas Argentinas** (tel. 011/6319-1104), a waterworks museum open 9 A.M.–noon weekdays only. The storage tanks now hold the archives of city maps and plans that were created in conjunction with the waterworks.

The Palacio's official street address is Riobamba 750, but the museum entrance is on the Rivadavia side; follow the arrows to the elevator, which takes you to the first floor.

RETIRO

Retiro commonly describes the area surrounding **Plaza San Martín,** but takes in all the terrain north of Avenida Córdoba, also bounded by Uruguay, Montevideo, Avenida Presidente Ramón S. Castillo, San Martín, and Avenida Eduard Madero. It also overlaps the sector known as Barrio Norte—not a true barrio but a vague designation that's more a real estate contrivance.

Retiro (literally, a retreat) was home to an isolated 17th-century monastery, but the word itself does not appear formally until 1691, when Spanish Governor Agustín de Robles built a house on the barranca (terrace) where Plaza San Martín now sits, above the river. In late colonial times, it was home to a slave market, bullring, and cavalry barracks, but after

© WAYNE BERNHARDSON

The extravagant facade of Retiro's Centro Naval reflects the military's traditional sense of privilege.

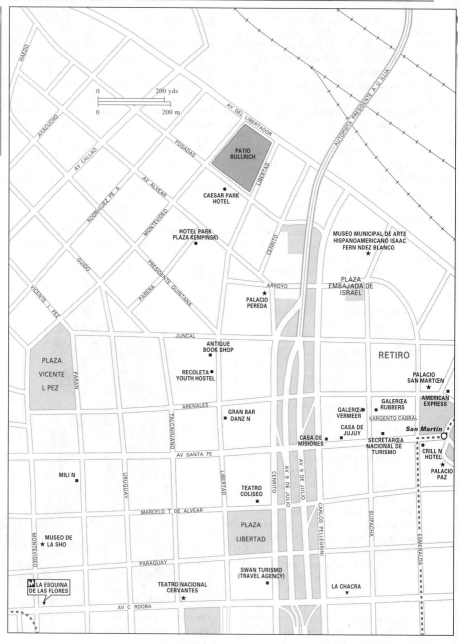

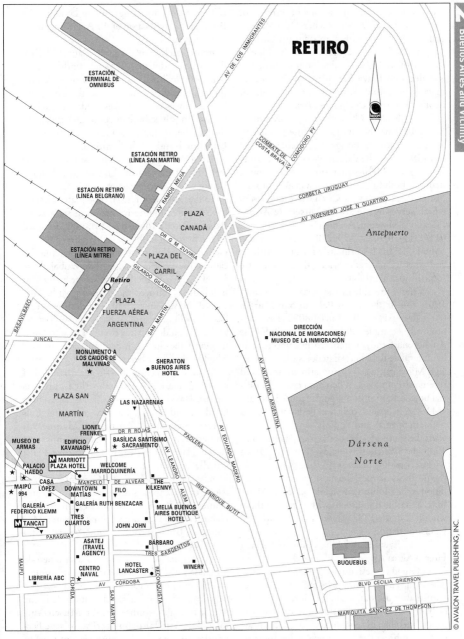

Buenos Aires and Vicinity

RETIRO

ESTACIÓN TERMINAL DE OMNIBUS

ESTACIÓN RETIRO (LÍNEA SAN MARTÍN)

ESTACIÓN RETIRO (LÍNEA BELGRANO)

ESTACIÓN RETIRO (LÍNEA MITRE)

AV DE LOS INMIGRANTES

COMBATE DE COSTA BRAVA AV COMODORO PY

CORBETA URUGUAY

AV INGENIERO JOSE N QUARTINO

Antepuerto

PLAZA CANADÁ

PLAZA DEL CARRIL

AV RAMOS MEJÍA

DR G M ZUVIRÍA

GILARDO GILARDI

Retiro

PLAZA FUERZA AÉREA ARGENTINA

SAN MARTÍN

JUNCAL

BASAVILBASO

MONUMENTO A LOS CAIDOS DE MALVINAS

SHERATON BUENOS AIRES HOTEL

DIRECCIÓN NACIONAL DE MIGRACIONES/ MUSEO DE LA INMIGRACIÓN

AV ANTÁRTIDA ARGENTINA

Dársena Norte

PLAZA SAN MARTÍN

LAS NAZARENAS

FLORIDA

LIONEL FRENKEL

DR R ROJAS

BASÍLICA SANTÍSIMO SACRAMENTO

PAOLERA

MUSEO DE ARMAS

EDIFICIO KAVANAGH

MARRIOTT PLAZA HOTEL

WELCOME MARROQUINERÍA

MARCELO T DE ALVEAR

AV EDUARDO MADERO

PALACIO HAEDO

CASA LÓPEZ

DOWNTOWN MATÍAS

FILO

THE KILKENNY

AV LEANDRO N ALEM

ING ENRIQUE BUTTY

MAIPÚ 994

GALERÍA FEDERICO KLEMM

GALERÍA RUTH BENZACAR

MELIÁ BUENOS AIRES BOUTIQUE HOTEL

TRES CUARTOS

JOHN JOHN

TANCAT

PARAGUAY

MAIPÚ

ASATEJ (TRAVEL AGENCY)

BÁRBARO

TRES SARGENTOS

BUQUEBUS

LIBRERÍA ABC

CENTRO NAVAL

HOTEL LANCASTER

WINERY

RECONQUISTA

FLORIDA

SAN MARTÍN

AV CÓRDOBA

BLVD CECILIA GRIERSON

MARIQUITA SÁNCHEZ DE THOMPSON

independence it became a zone of quintas, or country houses. By 1862, General San Martín's equestrian statue marked its definitive urbanization and, on the centenary of the Liberator's birth in 1878, Robles' original property was declared **Plaza San Martín.** Progressive mayor Torcuato de Alvear was responsible for turning it into a large public park.

From the late 19th century, the surrounding streets became the city's most elite residential area. The most extravagant residence, dating from 1909, was the **Palacio Paz** (Avenida Santa Fe 750), a 12,000-square-meter Francophile mansion built for *La Prensa* newspaper founder Jose C. Paz. It is now the **Círculo Militar,** part of which serves as the army's **Museo de Armas** (Weapons Museum, Avenida Santa Fe 702, tel. 011/4311-1070, int. 179, 2:30–7 P.M. weekdays only, US$.70). It's primarily for gun fetishists and other weapons aficionados, though there are some historical exhibits.

On the north side of the plaza, dating from 1905, the Art Nouveau **Palacio San Martín** (Arenales 761, tel. 011/4819-8092, free) was originally a complex of three houses built for the Anchorena family. Purchased in 1936 for the Ministerio de Relaciones Exteriores y Culto (Foreign Ministry), it serves primarily protocol and ceremonial purposes. When not needed for official functions, it's open for guided tours Thursday at 11 A.M. in Spanish only, and Friday at 3, 4, and 5 P.M. in Spanish and English.

At the southeast edge of the plaza, dating from 1935, the **Edificio Kavanagh** (Florida 1035) is a 33-story building that was BA's first skyscraper. At the northeast corner, the most recent major addition is the **Monumento a los Caídos de Malvinas,** a marble monument with names of those who died in the 1982 war with Britain over the Falkland Islands.

Across Avenida del Libertador, the **Plaza Fuerza Aérea Argentina, Plaza del Carril,** and **Plaza Canadá** are extensions of Plaza San Martín. The former, once known as Plaza Britania, was renamed after the war, when the air force was the only branch of the Argentine military that performed credibly; its centerpiece, though, is still architect Ambrose Poynter's **Torre de los Ingleses**

(1916), a clock tower resembling London's Big Ben that was a donation of the Anglo-Argentine community.

Immediately across Avenida Ramos Mejía is the **Estación Retiro** (1915), a recently restored relic of the railroad era, where British-operated trains linked the capital to Argentina's northern and northwestern provinces. Today, though, it receives mostly suburban commuter trains. To the northeast, long-distance buses from the **Estación Terminal de Ómnibus** (1982) have replaced the long-distance trains; much of the area immediately north of the bus terminal is a dubious *villa miseria* (shantytown).

To the northwest, foreign diplomatic missions have acquired impressive mansions such as the **Palacio Pereda** (Arroyo 1130), now occupied by the Brazilian Embassy. In March of 2002, Israeli ambassadors from all over Latin America came to the dedication of the **Plaza Embajada de Israel** (Arroyo and Suipacha), where a 1992 car bomb blast destroyed the embassy that had occupied the site since 1950. The destroyed embassy's outlines are still visible on the wall of the building next door, while twenty-two trees commemorate the diplomatic personnel and passersby who lost their lives here.

South of Plaza San Martín are a handful of other landmarks, most notably the Beaux Arts **Centro Naval** (Naval Center, 1914) at Avenida Córdoba and Florida. Literary great Jorge Luis Borges resided in an apartment at **Maipú 994,** immediately south of the weapons museum. Across Avenida 9 de Julio, opposite Plaza Lavalle at the corner of Libertad, the Plateresque **Teatro Nacional Cervantes** (1921) is one of the capital's most important theater venues; state-run, it also houses the **Museo Nacional del Teatro** (National Theater Museum, tel. 011/4815-8883, int. 195, 10 A.M.–6 P.M. weekdays).

Prosperous Retiro is a barrio where people purchase rather than make art, and its numerous contemporary galleries around Plaza San Martín are almost all worth a look. It is the site of one major museum, the **Museo Municipal de Arte Hispanoamericano Isaac Fernández Blanco.** At the southwestern edge of the barrio, a block north of the Cervantes, the **Museo de la Shoá** (Montevideo 919, tel. 011/4811-3537, info_fmh@fibertel.com.ar, www.fmh.org.ar, US$.35) is a small but professional Holocaust museum with an Argentine focus. Hours are 10 A.M.–7 P.M. Monday–Thursday, 10 A.M.–5 P.M. Friday. Note that even when the museum is open, the heavy metal door is closed for security purposes, and the friendly but muscular young men at the entrance provide additional deterrence.

Museo Municipal de Arte Hispanoamericano

Housing the colonial and independence-era art collections of its namesake founder, the municipal art museum contains an impressive array of Spanish- and Portuguese-American religious painting and statuary, as well as exquisite silverwork and furniture. It occupies the Palacio Noel, an equally impressive neocolonial residence built for city mayor Carlos Noel by his brother Martín in 1921. With its nods to Andalucía, Arequipa (Perú), and especially Lima for its balconies, the house was an overdue antidote to the fashionable Francophile architecture of the time.

The Museo Municipal de Arte Hispanoamericano Isaac Fernández Blanco (Suipacha 1422, tel. 011/4327-0272 or 011/4327/0228, www.buenosaires.gov.ar/areas/cultura/museos/, US$.35, free Thurs.) is open 2–7 P.M. daily except Monday, when it's closed, and holidays, when hours are 3–7 P.M. only. Guided tours take place at 4 P.M. Saturday and Sunday, but the museum may close in January and/or February.

RECOLETA AND BARRIO NORTE

Recoleta, where the line between vigorous excess and serene but opulent eternity is a thin one, is one of Buenos Aires's most touristed barrios. In everyday usage, Recoleta means the area in and around the celebrated **Cementerio de la Recoleta** (Recoleta Cemetery), but the barrio proper is a sprawling area bounded by Montevideo, Avenida Córdoba, Avenida Coronel Díaz, Avenida General Las Heras, and the Belgrano railway line.

© WAYNE BERNHARDSON

Recoleta's Biblioteca Nacional (National Library) occupies the site of the demolished presidential residence.

One of the city's prime dining and nightlife zones, Recoleta also encompasses much of Barrio Norte, a mostly residential area of vague boundaries that extends westward from Retiro and north into Palermo. Barrio Norte is more a real estate concept than a barrio proper, but one which is widely used by both its residents and those of other parts of the capital.

Once a bucolic outlier of the capital, Recoleta urbanized rapidly when upper-class *porteños* fled low-lying San Telmo after the yellow fever outbreaks of the 1870s. Originally the site of a Franciscan convent, it is internationally known for the Cementerio de la Recoleta (1822), whose elaborate crypts and mausoleums cost more than many, if not most, *porteño* houses. Historically, it shelters the remains of the elite (the exception being Eva Perón, of inappropriately humble origins). Flanking the cemetery is the Jesuit-built **Iglesia de Nuestra Señora de Pilar** (1732), a Baroque church.

Surrounding much of the church and cemetery are sizable green spaces including **Plaza**

Intendente Alvear and **Plaza Francia,** the latter home to a growing Sunday crafts fair; there are also street performers and a legion of *paseaperros* (professional dog walkers), some with a dozen or more canines each under their control. On the southeastern corner, along Robert M. Ortiz, are some of Buenos Aires's most traditionally exclusive cafés, most notably **La Biela** and **Café de la Paix.**

Alongside the church is the **Centro Cultural Ciudad de Buenos Aires,** one of the capital's most important cultural centers with an interactive museum, exhibition halls, and a full events calendar. Facing Plaza Francia, the **Museo Nacional de Bellas Artes** (1933) is the national fine arts museum, described in detail later. Several other plazas stretch northwest of the museum, along Avenida del Libertador toward Palermo.

The **Palais de Glais,** a former skating rink, now houses the **Salas Nacionales de Cultura** (Posadas 1725, tel. 011/4804-1163, 1–8 P.M. weekdays, 3–8 P.M. weekends, admission depends on the program), a museum with a steady calendar of artistic and historical exhibitions, plus cultural and commercial events (for the current schedule, visit www.artesur.com/links/palais.htm).

Recoleta's other landmarks and attractions are scattered around the barrio. A block west of the cemetery, the neo-Gothic **Facultad de Ingeniería** occupies an entire block fronting on Avenida Las Heras between Azcuénaga and Cantilo. Four blocks farther north, architect Clorindo Testa's **Biblioteca Nacional** (Agüero 2502, tel. 011/4806-4729, www.bibnal.edu.ar, 10 A.M.–9 P.M. weekdays and noon–9 P.M. weekends) is a concrete monolith on the grounds of the former presidential palace; the last head of state to actually live there was Juan Domingo Perón, along with his wife Evita. The website has a regularly updated calendar of events.

Well to the west, lending its name to this part of Barrio Norte, the Universidad de Buenos Aires's **Facultad de Medicina** (Paraguay 2155) contains two museums. Named for Argentina's 1947 Nobel Prize winner, the **Museo Houssay de Ciencia de Tecnología** (tel. 011/5950-9500, int. 2102, www.fmed.uba.ar/depto/histomed/houssay.htm, noon–4 P.M. weekdays only when classes are in

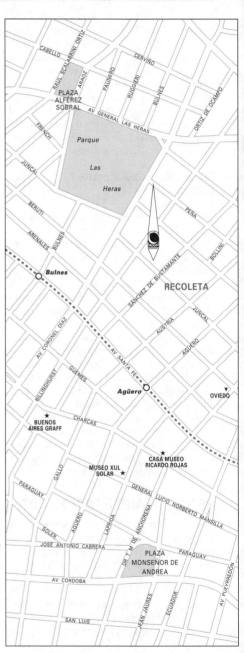

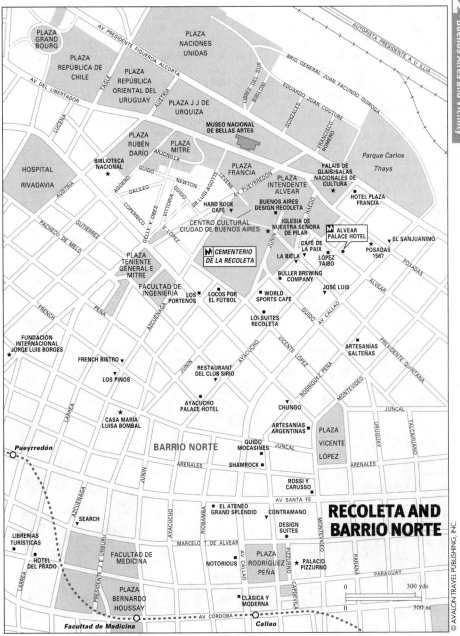

session) is a small but engaging museum of educational and experimental equipment, instruments and documents relating to Argentine medicine. The morbidly intriguing **Museo de Anatomía José Luis Martínez,** which displays every possible human organ pickled in formaldehyde, keeps the same hours; admission is free (UBA med students, by the way, are notorious for pranks and practical jokes with stray body parts).

Barrio Norte's western sector boasts a substantial literary and artistic tradition. Jorge Luis Borges' widow María Kodama established the **Fundación Internacional Jorge Luis Borges** (Anchorena 1660, tel. 011/4822-8340), which has begun a series of Borges-focused tours of the city. Writer Ricardo Rojas (1882–1957), who showed greater respect for South America's indigenous civilizations than perhaps any other Argentine literary figure, lived at the **Casa Museo Ricardo Rojas** (Charcas 2837, tel. 011/4824-4039, 10 A.M.–5 P.M. weekdays, 1–5 P.M. Sat., 10 A.M.–2 P.M. Sun.), and his house's architecture conveys that respect. Admission costs US$.35 pp for guided tours conducted by motivated, congenial personnel.

The innovative paintings of Borges's close friend Alejandro Schulz Solari are on display at the **Museo Xul Solar** (Laprida 1212). For equally spontaneous but more contemporary work, check out the elaborate spray-can street art by **Buenos Aires Graff** (www.bagraff.com), covering the walls from the corner of Charcas and Sánchez de Bustamante.

Centro Cultural Ciudad de Buenos Aires

In the 1980s, architects Clorindo Testa, Jacques Bedel, and Luis Benedit turned the 18th-century Franciscan convent alongside the Iglesia Nuestra Señora del Pilar into one of Buenos Aires's major cultural centers; it now boasts exhibition halls, a cinema, and an auditorium that's one of the most important sites for February and March's Festival Buenos Aires Tango. In addition, outside the center proper, the architects added the **Plaza del Pilar,** a stylish arcade housing the upscale Buenos Aires Design shopping mall and a gaggle of sidewalk restaurants and cafés.

Interestingly enough, immediately after Argentine independence, General Manuel Belgrano

Iglesia de Nuestra Señora de Pilar

© WAYNE BERNHARDSON

EVITA ON TOUR

Eva Perón became famous for her visit to Europe in 1947 when, as representative of an Argentina that emerged from WWII as an economic powerhouse, she helped legitimize a shaky Franco regime in Spain and, despite missteps, impressed other war-ravaged European countries with Argentina's potential. But even her death, five years later, did not stop her from touring.

Millions of *porteños* said adios to Evita in a funeral cortege that took hours to make its way up Avenida de Mayo from the Casa Rosada to the Congreso Nacional, where her corpse lay in state. She then found a temporary resting place at the headquarters of the Confederación General del Trabajo (CGT), the Peronist trade union, where the shadowy Spanish physician Pedro Ara gave the body a mummification treatment worthy of Lenin in preparation for a monument to honor her legacy.

Evita remained at the CGT until 1955, when the vociferously anti-Peronist General Pedro Aramburu took power and ordered her removal. Eventually, after a series of whistle stops that included the office of an officer who apparently became infatuated with the mummy, Aramburu shipped her into exile at an anonymous grave near Milan, Italy—even as a cadaver, Evita's presence was a symbolic reminder of Peronism's durability.

Despite banning the party, Aramburu had reason to worry. For many years, Argentines dared not even speak Perón's name, while the former strongman lived in luxury near Madrid. In 1970, though, as Argentine politics came undone in an era of revolutionary ferment, the left-wing Montoneros guerrillas kidnapped Aramburu and demanded to know Evita's whereabouts.

When Aramburu refused to answer, they executed him and issued a public statement that they would hold the retired general's body hostage until Evita was returned to "the people." A common slogan of the time was "Si Evita viviera, sería Montonera" (If Evita were alive, she would be a Montonera); Perón himself, though, detested the leftists even as he cynically encouraged their activism to assist his return to power.

The police found Aramburu's body before the proposed post-mortem prisoner swap could take place, but a notary to whom Aramburu had confided came forward with information as to Evita's whereabouts. In September 1971, Perón was stunned when a truck bearing Evita's casket and corpse arrived at his Madrid residence; remarried to dancer María Estela (Isabelita) Martínez, he neither expected nor wanted any such thing. His bizarre spiritualist adviser José López Rega, though, used the opportunity to try to transfer Evita's essence into Isabelita's body, as the mummy remained in the attic.

Perón returned to popular acclaim in 1973—leaving Evita in Madrid—and was soon elected president with Isabelita as his vice president. Meanwhile, the Montoneros once again kidnapped Aramburu—from his crypt in Recoleta cemetery—until Evita's return.

Angry but increasingly ill and senile, Perón died the following year, but now president Isabelita brought Evita's corpse on a charter flight from Madrid to the presidential residence at Olivos, just north of the capital. It stayed there until March 1976, when General Jorge Rafael Videla's military junta overthrew Perón's living legacy.

At Cementerio de la Recoleta, Evita finally achieved the respectability that she envied and resented during her rise to power. Though she was an illegitimate child who went by her mother's Basque surname Ibarguren, she landed in the family crypt of her father Juan Duarte, a provincial landowner—only a short walk from the tomb of Aramburu.

Even that may not end Evita's wanderings. In mid-2002, there were rumors of yet another move—to San Telmo's Franciscan convent at Defensa and Alsina (ironically enough, set afire by Peronist mobs in 1955, but it's also the burial place of her confessor Pedro Errecart). Another possibility is Juan Perón's *quinta* (country house) in the northern suburb of San Vicente, where a new mausoleum would reunite the two (Perón presently rests at Chacarita cemetery).

Isabelita, for her part, has indicated her agreement in moving the caudillo's remains to San Vicente; maintaining her close relationship with Evita, she's even willing to see the Peronist icon lie alongside her late husband. The major objection, it seems, is that Isabelita, former caretaker president Eduardo Duhalde, and other Peronist politicians like the idea better than the Duarte heirs do.

established an art school on the site. Thereafter, though, it served as a beggars' prison until reformist mayor Torcuato de Alvear cleaned up the site in the 1880s; Italian architect Juan Buschiazzo turned the chapel into an auditorium and transformed adjacent walls and terraces into an Italianate style. Until its 1980s remodel, it served as a retirement home.

Other facilities include the **Museo Participativo de Ciencias** (tel. 011/4807-3260, 9 A.M.–4 P.M., 3–8 P.M. weekends and holidays), a participatory science museum for children; and a **Microcine** with repertory film cycles.

The Centro Cultural Ciudad de Buenos Aires (Junín 1930, tel. 011/4803-1040, www.centroculturalrecoleta.org) is open 2–9 P.M. weekdays except Monday, and 10 A.M.–9 P.M. weekends and holidays. Admission is free except for the Museo Participativo, which costs US$2 pp for those age five or older. There are also charges for some film programs.

Museo Xul Solar

Despite his blindness, Jorge Luis Borges left vivid descriptions of the paintings of his friend Alejandro Schulz Solari, better known as Xul Solar. Obsessed with architecture and the occult, Xul Solar (1897–1963) was an abstract artist who produced vivid oils and watercolors. During his lifetime, he showed his work in Buenos Aires, Brasil, France, and Italy; after his death, it also appeared in Miami, New York, London, Madrid, Stockholm, and other European cities.

The Xul Solar museum displays a large assortment of his work, mostly smallish watercolors, in utilitarian surroundings with plasterboard walls and relatively dim light that contrast dramatically with the painter's intense colors. It also shows personal effects, such as postcards directed to famous writers like Nietzsche.

The Museo Xul Solar (Laprida 1212, tel. 011/4824-3302, xulsolar@ciudad.com.ar, www.xulsolar.org.ar) is open noon–8 P.M. weekdays only, and it's closed in January and February. Admission is US$1 except for children under age 12 and retired persons, who pay only US$.35.

Cementerio de la Recoleta

For the living and dead alike, Recoleta is Buenos Aires's most prestigious address. The roster of residents within its walls represents wealth and power as surely as the inhabitants of surrounding Francophile mansions and luxury apartment towers hoard their assets in overseas bank accounts. Arguably, the cemetery is even more exclusive than the neighborhood—enough cash can buy an impressive residence, but not a surname like Alvear, Anchorena, Mitre, Pueyrredón, or Sarmiento.

Seen from the air, the cemetery seems exactly what it is—an orderly necropolis of narrow alleyways lined by ornate mausoleums and crypts that mimic the architectural styles of the city's early 20th-century *belle epoque*. Crisscrossed by a few wide diagonals, but with little greenery, it's a densely *de*populated area that receives hordes of Argentine and foreign tourists during opening hours.

Many, if not most, go to visit the crypt of Eva Perón, who overcame her humble origins with a relentless ambition that brought her to the pinnacle of political power with her husband, General and President Juan Perón, before her painful death from cancer in 1952. Even Juan Perón, who lived until 1974 but spent most of his post-Evita years in exile, failed to qualify for Recoleta; he lies across town in the Cementerio de la Chacarita.

There were other ways into Recoleta, however. One unlikely resident is boxer Luis Angel Firpo (1894–1960), the "wild bull of the Pampas," who nearly defeated Jack Dempsey for the world heavyweight championship in New York in 1923. Firpo, though, had pull—one of his sponsors was Félix Bunge, a powerful landowner whose family owns some of the cemetery's most ornate constructions.

Endless economic crises, though, have had an impact on one of the world's grandest graveyards. Even casual visitors will notice that many mausoleums have fallen into disrepair, as once-moneyed families can no longer afford their maintenance. Municipal authorities, recognizing its importance to tourism, have intensified overdue repairs to sidewalks and the most significant sculptures, but still face budget problems.

Cementerio de la Recoleta, Buenos Aires's world-famous cemetery

The Cementerio de la Recoleta (Junín 1790, tel. 011/4803-1594, 7 A.M.–6 P.M. daily) is the site for many guided on-demand tours through travel agencies; the municipal tourist office sponsors occasional free weekend tours.

Museo Nacional de Bellas Artes

Argentina's traditional fine arts museum mixes works by well-known European artists such as Degas, El Greco, Goya, Kandinsky, Klee, Monet, Picasso, Renoir, Rodin, Tintoretto, Toulouse-Lautrec, and Van Gogh with their Argentine counterparts including Antonio Berni, Cándido López, Ernesto de la Cárcova, Raquel Forner, Benito Quinquela Martín, Prilidiano Pueyrredón, and Lino Spilimbergo.

In total, it houses about 11,000 oils, watercolors, sketches, engravings, tapestries, and sculptures. Among the most interesting works are those of López, who recreated the history of the war with Paraguay (1864–70) in a series of detailed oils despite losing his right arm to a grenade.

Oddly enough, architect Julio Dormald designed the 1870s building, in a prime location on the north side of Avenida del Libertador, as a pumphouse and filter plant for the city waterworks; renowned architect Alejandro Bustillo adapted it to its current purpose in the early 1930s.

The Museo Nacional de Bellas Artes (Avenida del Libertador 1473, tel. 011/4803-0802, info@mnba.org.ar, www.mnba.org.ar, free) is open weekdays except Monday from 12:30–7:30 P.M.; weekend hours start at 9:30 A.M. Guided tours take place Tuesday–Friday at 4 and 6 P.M., and weekends at 5 and 6 P.M.

PALERMO

Buenos Aires's largest barrio, Palermo enjoys the city's widest open spaces thanks to 19th-century dictator Juan Manuel de Rosas, whose private estate stretched almost from Recoleta all the way to Belgrano, between present-day Avenida del Libertador and the Río de la Plata. Beaten at the battle of Caseros by rival caudillo Justo José de Urquiza, a onetime confederate from Entre Ríos Province, Rosas spent the rest of his life in British exile. The property passed into the public domain and, ironically enough, the sprawling **Parque 3 de Febrero** takes its name from the date of Rosas's defeat in 1852.

Even apart from its parkland, Palermo is a large and diverse barrio. Formally, its boundaries zigzag along La Pampa, Avenida Figueroa Alcorta, Avenida Cabildo, Avenida Dorrego, Avenida Córdoba, Avenida Coronel Díaz, Avenida Las Heras, the tracks of the Ferrocarril Belgrano, Salguero, and the Avenida Costanera Rafael Obligado.

Once part of the capital's unsavory *arrabales* (margins), its street corners populated by stylish but capricious *malevos* (bullies) immortalized in the short stories of Jorge Luis Borges, Palermo hasn't entirely superseded that reputation—in some areas, poorly lighted streets can still make visitors uneasy. Yet it also has exclusive neighborhoods such as **Barrio Parque,** also known as **Palermo Chico,** across Avenida del Libertador immediately north of Recoleta.

Home to many embassies and single-family mansions, Barrio Parque boasts some of Buenos Aires's highest property values. One of its landmarks is the **Instituto Nacional Sanmartiniano,** housing the research institute on national hero José de San Martín's life, on **Plaza Grand Bourg.** Built to mimic San Martín's home-in-exile in Boulogne sur Mer, France—but a third larger—it no longer serves as a museum.

Barrio Parque has several other museums, however, including the gaucho-oriented **Museo de Motivos Argentinos José Hernández** (Avenida del Libertador 2373). Dating from 1918, the Beaux Arts **Palacio Errázuriz** (Avenida del Libertador 1902) is a former private residence that contains the **Museo Nacional de Arte Decorativo.** The new kid on the block, though, is the state-of-the-art **Museo de Arte Latinoamericano de Buenos Aires** (Malba, Avenida Figueroa Alcorta 3415), which concentrates on contemporary Latin American art.

Across Avenida del Libertador, the **Botánico** is an upper-middle-class neighborhood that takes its name from the **Jardín Botánico Carlos Thays** (Avenida Santa Fe 3951, 8 A.M.–

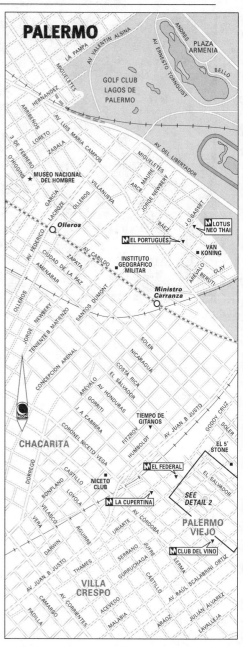

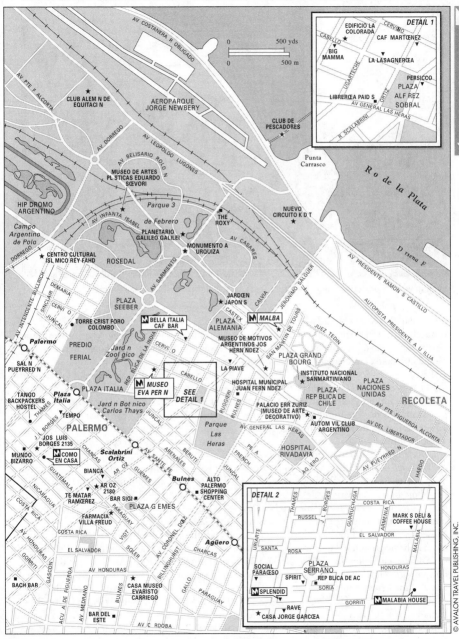

© AVALON TRAVEL PUBLISHING, INC.

Even in winter, *porteños* enjoy the outdoor scene at Palermo Viejo's Plaza Serrano.

6. P.M. daily), a lovely botanical garden unfortunately infested with feral cats. Opposite nearby Plaza Italia, the rejuvenated **Jardín Zoológico** (Avenida Las Heras s/n, tel. 011/4806-7412; 10 A.M.–6 P.M. weekdays, 10 A.M.–6:30 P.M. weekends) is an ideal outing for visitors with children. Admission costs US$1.50 per adult, but it's free for children under age 13; retired and disabled people enter free Tuesday–Friday.

Once a neighborhood of imposing *palacetes,* the Botánico is still affluent but no longer so exclusive as when, in 1948, Eva Perón enraged the neighbors by appropriating one of those mansions to create the **Hogar de Tránsito No. 2,** a home for single mothers that now houses the **Museo Eva Perón** (Lafinur 2988). For a glimpse of what the neighborhood used to look like, visit the **Edificio La Colorada** (Cabello 3791), a 24-unit imported brick building that housed executives of the British-run railways.

South of Parque Las Heras and across Avenida Santa Fe, one of Palermo's main traffic arteries, **Alto Palermo** is a densely built area that has given its name to one of the city's major shopping centers. The real center of action, though, is slightly northwest at **Palermo Viejo,** where **Plaza Serrano** (also known as **Plaza Cortázar**) is a major axis of *porteño* nightlife.

Palermo Viejo further subdivides into **Palermo Soho,** a trendy term to describe the area south of Avenida Juan B. Justo, and the more northerly **Palermo Hollywood,** where many *porteño* television and radio producers have located their facilities. Shaded by sycamores, many of Palermo Viejo's streets still contain lowrise *casas chorizos* (sausage houses) on deep narrow lots. One of the most interesting private residences is the **Casa Jorge García** (Gorriti 5142), whose garage facade features Martiniano Arce's *filete* caricatures of the García family.

North of the Zoológico, the Sociedad Rural Argentina has rented out the historic **Predio Ferial** (ex-Sociedad Rural Argentina) as the site of events ranging from traditional livestock shows to book fairs. The area's most conspicuous new landmark is the controversial **Centro Cultural Islámico Rey Fahd** (Avenida Bullrich 55, tel. 011/4899-1144), built with Saudi money on land acquired from the Menem administration.

It's open for guided tours only, Friday noon–1 P.M. and Sunday 11 A.M.–1 P.M.

At the northern end of the barrio, overlapping Belgrano, **Las Cañitas** is a new gastronomic and nightlife area challenging Palermo Viejo among *porteño* partygoers.

Parque Tres de Febrero

Argentine elites got their revenge on José Manuel de Rosas with the creation of Parque Tres de Febrero. Not only does the equestrian **Monumento a Urquiza,** at Avenida Sarmiento and Avenida Figueroa Alcorta, commemorate Rosas's conqueror at the battle of Caseros, but Unitarist President Domingo F. Sarmiento's name graces one of the park's main avenues. Sarmiento, Rosas's implacable enemy, oversaw the estate's transformation during his presidency (1868–1874); in the late 19th century, a Rodin statue of Sarmiento even went up on the site of Rosas's bedroom after the dicator's Roman-style villa had been dynamited.

In the early 20th century, noting the Sunday spectacle of horse-drawn carriages and motorcars, British diplomat James Bryce remarked that "Nowhere in the world does one get a stronger impression of exuberant wealth and extravagance." Today, though, the park is a more democratic destination, where the automobiles move slowly and picnickers, walkers, joggers, in-line skaters, and cyclists can enjoy its verdant serenity.

That doesn't mean, though, that Palermo's "culture wars" are over. In early 2003, Peronist city councilman Mario O'Donnell proposed changing Avenida Sarmiento's name to honor Rosas, a move that drew howls of opposition from Sarmiento's descendents. For the moment, though, Sarmiento's position is secure.

The park's sights include the **Jardín Japonés** (Japanese Gardens, Avenida Casares and Avenida Adolfo Berro); the **Rosedal** (Rose Garden, Avenida Iraola and Avenida Presidente Pedro Montt); the **Museo de Artes Plásticas Eduardo Sívori** (Avenida Infanta Isabel 555, tel. 011/4772-5628, noon–6 P.M. daily except Mon.), a fine painting and sculpture museum; the **Hipódromo Argentino** (racetrack) at Avenida del Libertador and Avenida Dorrego; and the

Campo Argentino de Polo (polo grounds) directly across Avenida del Libertador.

Jardín Japonés

An oasis of calm in the city's rush, Buenos Aires's Japanese garden opened in 1967, when Crown Prince Akihito and Princess Michiko visited Argentina. Argentina has a small but well-established Japanese community in the capital and the suburban community of Escobar.

Administratively part of the Jardín Botánico, the Jardín Japonés enjoys far better maintenance and, because there's chicken wire between the exterior hedges and the interior fence, it's full of chirping birds rather than feral cats. Like Japanese gardens elsewhere, it mimics nature in its large koi pond, waterfall, and "isle of the gods," but also culture in features like its pier, lighthouse, and "bridge of fortune." In addition, the garden contains a **Monumento al Sudor del Inmigrante Japonés** (Monument to the Effort of the Japanese Immigrant), erected during the military dictatorship of 1976–83—and still bearing the name of dictator Jorge Rafael Videla as "president."

The Jardín Japonés (Avenida Casares and Avenida Adolfo Berro, tel. 011/4801-4922, www.jardinjapones.com.ar, 10 A.M.–6 P.M. daily) charges US$.70 for adults, US$.35 for children; there are guided tours at 3 and 4 P.M. Saturdays.

Museo de Motivos Argentinos

It's tempting to call this the "museum of irony": Argentina's most self-consciously gaucho-oriented institution sits in the middle of one of the country's most urbane, affluent, and cosmopolitan neighborhoods, also home to many international diplomatic missions. Named for the author of the *gauchesco* epic poem *Martín Fierro,* it specializes in rural Argentiniana.

Even more ironically, land-owning oligarch Félix Bunge built the derivative French-Italianate residence with marble staircases and other extravagant features. Originally named for the Carlos Daws family who donated its contents, it became the Museo de Motivos Populares Argentinos (Museum of Argentine Popular Motifs) José Hernández until the 1976–83 dictatorship deleted the ostensibly inflammatory word

THE PORTEÑO PSYCHE

In May of 2002, the daily *Clarín* posed the online forum question "Do you think winning the World Cup would improve Argentines' self-esteem?", while an editorial bore the title "Chocolate Is Not an Antidepressant," and another piece argued the pros and cons of sofa-based psychoanalysis. Meanwhile, the *Buenos Aires Herald* carried classified ads for "post-modern psychotherapy with a family focus," and the 2002 Festival Buenos Aires Tango included a session on *Tango de Autoayuda* (Self-help Tango) by Mexico-based Argentine Liliana Felipe.

New Yorkers may boast about their therapists, but *porteños* can more than match them—in Buenos Aires, psychoanalysis and other therapies are not for the upper and upper middle classes alone. During registration at the Universidad de Buenos Aires medical school, a proliferation of flyers offers psychoanalysis and psychotherapy with UBA professionals—the first session free—for individuals, couples, and groups.

To a degree, the current obsession with therapy may be a function of the economic crisis, and even the *corralito* banking restrictions have been interpreted in this context. According to an early 2002 interview by National Public Radio's Martin Kaste, a Freudian psychiatrist made the case that "money has a certain symbolic equivalence to the penis. People put their money in the bank, but at the moment they want to withdraw it they lose their money, so this produces a castration anxiety."

Another commented that "sexual desire has also been caught in the *corralito*—men worry about lack of desire and premature ejaculation, and women are unable to have orgasms." In a different context, angry real estate brokers picketed the residence of caretaker President Eduardo Duhalde (himself a former realtor), but not in hope of any relief for a frozen real estate market. Rather, remarked one of the protestors, "This turned into our therapy, a place to set our anguish free."

Therapy, though, is not just a function of the times; it has a long history in Buenos Aires, beginning with the arrival of Jewish refugees from Europe in the 1930s. Mariano Ben

"popular" (which in this context means "people's") from the official name. Thus, perhaps, it could justify depictions of gentry like the Martínez de Hoz family—one of whose scions was the regime's economy minister—as representatives of a bucolic open-range lifestyle.

That said, the museum has many worthwhile items, ranging from magnificent silverwork and vicuña textiles created by contemporary Argentine artisans to pre-Columbian pottery, indigenous crafts and even a typical *pulpería* or rural store. Translations of Hernández's famous poem, some in Asian and Eastern European languages, occupy a prominent site.

The Museo de Motivos Argentinos José Hernández (Avenida del Libertador 2373, tel. 011/4803-2384, www.naya.org.ar/mujose, 1–7 P.M. Wed.–Sun.) charges US$.35 except Sunday, when it's free. It's normally closed in February.

Museo Nacional de Arte Decorativo

Matías Errázuriz Ortúzar and his widow Josefina de Alvear de Errázuriz lived less than 20 years in the ornate four-story Beaux Arts building (1918) that now houses the national museum of decorative art. Its inventory consists of 4,000 items from the family's own collections, ranging from Roman sculptures to contemporary silverwork, but mostly Asian and European pieces from the 17th to 19th centuries. Man items are anonymous; the best-known artists are Europeans like Manet and Rodin.

The Museo Nacional de Arte Decorativo (Avenida del Libertador 1902, tel. 011/4802-6606, www.mnad.org.ar, 2–7 P.M. daily, US$.70, free Tues.) offers guided tours Wednesday, Thursday, and Friday at 4:30 P.M., by appointment.

MALBA

The Museo de Arte Latinoamericano de Buenos

Plotkin has chronicled this history in *Freud in the Pampas: The Emergence and Development of a Psychoanalytic Culture in Argentina* (Stanford University Press, 2001); he has also followed up with *Argentina on the Couch: Psychiatry, State and Society, 1880 to the Present* (Albuquerque, NM: Dialogo, 2003).

Many of BA's thousands of shrinks practice in Palermo's so-called Villa Freud, an area bounded by Avenida Santa Fe, Avenida Las Heras, Avenida Scalabrini Ortiz, and Avenida Coronel Díaz. Many area businesses play on this reputation, including the Bar Sigi (Salguero and Charcas), and patients can top off their medications at Farmacia Villa Freud (Paraguay and Medrano). One online magazine specializes in listings for professional office rentals. Even acting classes are often exercises in therapy.

Several institutions contribute to the capital's therapeutic ambience. The **Asociación Psicoanalítica Argentina** (Rodríguez Peña 1674, tel. 011/4812-3518, apainfo@pccp.com.ar, www.apa.org.ar) organized a month-long exhibition on *Psychoanalysis, Culture and Crisis* at the Microcentro's Centro Cultural Borges. Buenos Aires's **Museo de Psicología** (Avenida Independencia 3063, 3rd floor) is open 9 A.M.–2 P.M. weekdays.

The locus of Villa Freud, though, is the bookstore **Librería Paidós,** in the Galería Las Heras (Avenida Las Heras 3741, tel. 011/4801-2860, info@libreriapaidos.com, www.libreria paidos.com.ar). Other bookstores are closing, but Paidós opened a Barrio Norte branch (Avenida Santa Fe 1685, tel. 011/4812-6685).

If *porteños* and other Argentines continue to feel the need for therapy, their Chilean neighbors may have had the last word. In the midst of the 2002 crisis, a satirical Santiago newspaper published a short note under the headline "New Foundation, Argentines Anonymous, Created." According to the article, "A group whose members hope to rehabilitate themselves from their nationality met yesterday for the first time. At the beginning, each one must announce his name and then continue, 'I am an Argentine.'"

Aires, Buenos Aires's most deluxe museum, is a striking steel-and-glass structure dedicated exclusively to Latin American art, rather than the European-oriented contents of many—if not most—Argentine collections. Designed by Córdoba architects Gastón Atelman, Martín Fourcade, and Alfredo Tapia, the building devotes one entire floor to the private collection of Argentine businessman Eduardo F. Constantini, the motivating force behind the museum's creation; the second floor offers special exhibitions.

The most prominent artists on display are the Mexicans Frida Kahlo and Diego Rivera, but there are also works by Antonio Berni, the Chilean Robert Matta, the Uruguayan Pedro Figari, and others. Given the current crisis, it plans to focus on contemporary Argentine art, both in terms of its own exhibitions and those it sends abroad, rather than importing megabucks items from overseas.

The Museo de Arte Latinoamericano de Buenos Aires (Avenida Figueroa Alcorta 3415, tel. 011/4808 6500, www.malba.org, US$1.10, free Wed.) is open Monday, Thursday, and Friday noon–8 P.M., Wednesday noon–9 P.M., and weekends 10–8 P.M.

Museo Eva Perón

At her most combative, to the shock and disgust of neighbors, Eva Perón chose the upscale Botánico for the **Hogar de Tránsito No. 2,** a shelter for single mothers from the provinces. Even more galling, her Fundación de Ayuda Social María Eva Duarte de Perón took over an imposing three-story mansion to house the transients in their transition to the capital.

Since Evita's death in 1952, middle-class multistory apartment blocks have mostly replaced the elegant single-family houses and distinctive apartment buildings that once housed the

Palermo's new Museo Eva Perón occupies the former Hogar de Tránsito No. 2, established by Evita to house homeless single mothers from the provinces.

porteño elite (many of whom have since moved to exclusive northern suburbs). Fifty years later, on the July 26th anniversary of her death—supporting Tomás Eloy Martínez's contention that Argentines are "cadaver cultists"—Evita's great-niece María Carolina Rodríguez officially opened the museum to "to spread the life, work and ideology of María Eva Duarte de Perón."

What it largely lacks is a critical perspective that would make it possible, again in Rodríguez's words, "to understand who this woman was in the 1940s and 1950s, who made such a difference in the lives of Argentines"—a goal not necessarily consistent with her other stated aims. Rather than a balanced account of her life, the museum's initial stage is a professionally presented chronological homage that mostly sidesteps the issue of personality cults that typified both Evita and her charismatic husband.

The Museo Eva Perón (Lafinur 2988, tel. 011/4807-9433, ievaperon@uol.com.ar, 10 A.M.–8 P.M. daily except Mon.) has a museum store

with a fine selection of Evita souvenirs, and there's a café-restaurant as well.

BELGRANO

Linked to central Buenos Aires by Subte, bus, and train, Belgrano remains a barrio apart. In fact, before becoming a barrio of the capital, it was a separate city and then, briefly in the 1880s, the country's capital. It is bordered on the south by Palermo, on the west by Colegiales and Villa Ortúzar, on the north by Coghland and Núñez, and on the east by the Río de la Plata. The actual line zigzags among many streets; the major thoroughfares are Avenida Cabildo, the northward extension of Avenida Santa Fe; Avenida Luis María Campos; and Avenida del Libertador.

Only a block off Cabildo, **Plaza General Manuel Belgrano** hosts a fine Sunday crafts market; immediately to its east, at Vuelta de Obligado 2042, the landmark **Iglesia de la Inmaculada Concepción** (1865), colloquially known as **La Redonda** for its circular floor plan, figures prominently in Ernesto Sabato's psychological novel *On Heroes and Tombs*.

North of the plaza, the **Museo de Arte Español Enrique Larreta** (Juramento 2291, tel. 011/4783-2640, museolarreta@infovia.com.ar, 2–7:45 P.M. daily except Tues.) reflects the interest of the Hispanophile novelist who built it, but also hosts special exhibitions, such as the 2002 display of regional costumes given to Evita Perón during her 1947 tour of Spain—at a time when the Franco dictatorship was desperately seeking legitimacy after World War II. It's set among impressive Andalusian gardens, which include a theater. Admission costs US$.35, but is free on Thursdays. There are guided tours Sunday at 4 and 6 P.M. Like many other museums, it usually closes in January.

When Belgrano was briefly Argentina's capital, both the executive and legislative branches met at what is now the **Museo Histórico Sarmiento** (Cuba 2079, tel. 011/4783-7555, museosarmiento @fibertel.com.ar, 2–7 P.M. Tues.–Fri. and 3–7 P.M. Sun.), honoring President Domingo F. Sarmiento. Though Sarmiento never lived here, immediately east of the plaza the exhibits contain many of his personal possessions and a model of his provincial San Juan birthplace; it also chronicles the near–civil war of the 1880s that resulted in the federalization of Buenos Aires. Admission costs US$.35, but is free Thursdays. Guided tours take place Sunday at 4 P.M.

A few blocks northwest of the plaza, **Museo Casa de Yrurtia** (O'Higgins 2390, tel. 011/ 4781-0385, www.casleo.secyt.gov.ar/index.htm, US$.35) was the residence of sculptor Rogelio Yrurtia (1879–1950), creator of San Telmo's noteworthy *Canto al Trabajo* and other works that challenged the traditional pomposity of *porteño* public art. Hours Tuesday–Friday and Sunday from 3–7 P.M. Guided tours, at no additional expense, take place Tuesday–Friday at 3 P.M. and Sunday at 4 P.M.

The famous landscape architect Charles Thays turned **Barrancas de Belgrano,** on the river terrace three blocks east of Plaza Belgrano, into a shady public park; it now includes a fenced dog run, where *paseaperros* can take their charges for off-leash romps. Just across from the park, the **Museo Libero Badii** (11 de Septiembre 1990, tel. 011/4783-3819, 10 A.M.–6 P.M. weekdays only, free) exhibits the work of one of the country's most innovative sculptors. Ring the bell for entry.

Across the tracks from the Barrancas, along Arribeños north of Juramento, Belgrano's **Barrio Chino** (Chinatown) grew rapidly in the 1990s but has languished in recent hard times. The number of Chinese restaurants and other businesses, though, remains higher than it was a decade ago—Belgrano residents who need *feng shui* consultants can find them here.

OUTER BARRIOS

Beyond its most touristed barrios, Buenos Aires has a variety of worthwhile sights that range from the relatively mundane to the morbid. Some are less easily accessible by Subte, but have regular *colectivo* (city bus) service.

M Museo Argentino de Ciencias Naturales

Once on the city's outskirts, the barrio of Caballito

gets fairly few tourists, but its largest open space, heavily used **Parque Centenario,** is a good area for visitors to see an unadorned but gradually gentrifying neighborhood that's popular with urban homesteaders. The park's natural history museum, housing one of the country's largest and best maintained natural history collections, veers between the traditional stuff-in-glass-cases approach and more sophisticated exhibits that provide ecological, historical, and cultural context. Dating from 1937, its equally impressive quarters are only a third the size of the original grandiose project, but include decorative details such as bas-relief spider webs around the main entrance, and sculpted owls flanking the upper windows.

The main floor contains exhibits on geology and, paleontology (including a reconstruction of the massive Patagonian specimens *Giganotosaurus carolini,* the world largest carnivorous dinosaur, and the herbaceous *Argentinosaurus huinculensis,* whose neck alone measures about 12 meters. The second floor stresses mostly South American mammals (including marine mammals), comparative anatomy, amphibians and reptiles, birds, arthropods, and botany.

The Museo Argentino de Ciencias Naturales Bernardino Rivadavia (Angel Gallardo 490, tel./fax 011/4982-1154, www.macn.secyt.gov.ar, US$.60 for visitors seven and older) is open 2–7 P.M. daily. It's about equidistant from the Malabia and Angel Gallardo stations on Subte Línea B.

Cementerio de la Chacarita and Vicinity

Buenos Aires's second cemetery may be more affordable than Recoleta, but eternity at the **Cementerio de la Chacarita** can still mean notoriety. Its residents include many high-profile Argentines in fields ranging from entertainment to religion and politics—and the lines between these categories are not always obvious.

The most universally beloved is tango singer Carlos Gardel, who died in a plane crash in Colombia in 1935. Hundreds of admirers from around the globe have left plaques on the tomb, many thanking him for miracles, and every June 26 they jam the streets of Chacarita—

laid out like a small city—to pay homage. As often as not, the right hand of his bronze statue holds a lighted cigarette, and a red carnation adorns his lapel.

In terms of devotion, probably only Spanish-born faith-healer-to-the-aristocracy Madre María Salomé can match Gardel; on the 2nd of most months—she died October 2, 1928—her tomb is covered in white carnations. Other famous figures entombed here include aviator Jorge Newbery, for whom the city airport is named, killed in a plane crash in 1914; tango musicians Aníbal "Pichuco" Troilo and Osvaldo Pugliese; poet Alfonsina Storni; La Boca painter Benito Quinquela Martín; and theater and film comedian Luis Sandrini.

Certainly the most famous, though, is Juan Domingo Perón, whose vaulted remains lie across town from wife Evita's Recoleta tomb. His remains are incomplete, though—in June 1987, stealthy vandals entered the crypt, amputating and stealing the caudillo's hands in a crime that has never been solved. Anti-Peronists speculated, despite lack of evidence, that the thieves sought Perón's fingerprints for access to supposed Swiss bank accounts.

The Cementerio de la Chacarita (Guzmán 680, tel. 011/4553-9338, 7 A.M.–6 P.M. daily) covers 95 blocks with a total of 12,000 burial vaults, 100,000 gravesites, and 350,000 niches. It's only a short walk from Estación Federico Lacroze, presently the terminus of Subte Línea B (which is being extended to the northeast).

In addition to Chacarita, there are two contiguous but formally separate cemeteries: the **Cementerio Alemán** (German Cemetery, Avenida Elcano 4530, tel. 011/4553-3206), and the **Cementerio Británico** (British Cemetery, Avenida Elcano 4568, tel. 011/4554-0092). Both keep identical hours to Chacarita.

The Británico is more diverse, with tombs belonging to Armenian, Greek, Irish, Jewish, and many other immigrant nationalities. The Anglo-Argentine Lucas Bridges, son of pioneer Anglican missionaries in Tierra del Fuego and author of the classic Fuegian memoir *The Uttermost Part of the Earth,* was buried here after dying at sea en route from Ushuaia to Buenos Aires. The Alemán

features a large but politically neutral monument to Germany's World War II dead—no German or German-Argentine wants to be publicly associated with the Third Reich.

ENTERTAINMENT

In terms of entertainment, Buenos Aires is a 24-hour city with as much to offer as New York or London. Argentines in general and *porteños* in particular are night people—discos and dance clubs, for instance, may not even *open* until 1 A.M. or so, and they stay open until dawn. Not everything takes place at those hours, though.

All the Buenos Aires dailies have thorough event listings, especially in their end-of-the-week supplements. For tickets to events at many major venues, contact Ticketek, tel. 011/4323-7200, www.ticketek.com.ar). The company adds a US$1 service charge to most tickets. It has a Microcentro outlet at El Ateneo (Florida 340), in Barrio Norte at Lee-Chi (Avenida Santa Fe 1670); in Retiro at Patio Bullrich (Avenida del Libertador 740); and in Palermo Chico at Shopping Alto Palermo (Avenida Santa Fe 3253).

For discount tickets to certain events, including tango shows, cinemas, and live theater, try carteleras, agencies with last-minute specials. Among them are **Cartelera Espectáculos** (Lavalle 742, tel. 011/4322-1559); **Cartelera Baires,** (Avenida Corrientes 1382, Local 24, tel. 4372-5058, www.entradascondescuento.com); and **Cartelera Vea Más** (Avenida Corrientes 1660, tel. 011/6320-5319, Local 2).

Cafés

No single place embodies tradition better than Monserrat's historic **Café Tortoni** (Avenida de Mayo 825, tel. 011/4342-4328, www.cafetortoni.com.ar). Most tourists come for coffee and croissants, but there's live tango and the bar serves good mixed drinks (US$5) accompanied by a sizable *tabla* of sliced salami, paté, cheese, and olives that easily feeds two people; separately, drinks cost only about US$2.

The worn-about-the-edges **Confitería Ideal** (Suipacha 384, tel. 011/4326-0521) is one of

THEATER IN THE CAPITAL

Despite Argentina's countless economic crises, Buenos Aires remains the theater capital of the continent. The district's traditional heart is Avenida Corrientes, between Avenida 9 de Julio and Avenida Callao, but many venues are showing the effects of economic hardship. Avenida de Mayo and many Microcentro side streets are also home to important theaters, many of them historic.

Winter is the main season, but events can take place at any time of year. For discount tickets, check *carteleras* or online ticket-purchasing services. All major *porteño* newspapers, including *Ámbito Financiero, Buenos Aires Herald, Clarín, La Nación,* and *Página 12,* provide extensive listings and schedules.

The single most notable facility is the **Teatro General San Martín,** (Avenida Corrientes 1530, tel. 011/4371-0111, teatrosanmartin@tsm.data-markets.com.ar, www.teatrosanmartin.com.ar), a multipurpose complex that lacks architectural merit but compensates with its diverse offerings. Covering more than 30,000 square meters, this utilitarian building (1961) has three main auditoria, a cinema, exhibition halls, and other facilities that draw up to a million visitors per year. Students with international ID cards get 50 percent discounts for most shows, and there are many free events as well.

Other major theater venues include the following, all in or near the Microcentro unless otherwise indicated:

Multiteatro: Avenida Corrientes 1283, tel. 011/4382-9140

Sala Pablo Neruda: Avenida Corrientes 1660, tel. 011/4370-5388

Teatro Avenida: Avenida de Mayo 1212, Monserrat, tel. 011/4381-3193

Teatro La Carbonera: Balcarce 868, San Telmo, tel. 011/4362-2651

Teatro Nacional Cervantes: Libertad 815, tel. 011/4815-8883, www.teatrocervantes.gov.ar

Teatro Payró: San Martín 766, tel. 011/4312-5922

Teatro Presidente Alvear: Avenida Corrientes 1659, tel. 011/4374-6076

There are several smaller and less conventional "off-Corrientes" venues, some of which might be called microtheaters—**Teatro El Vitral** (Rodríguez Peña 344, tel. 011/4371-0948) can seat only about 40 people in front of each of its three small stages. **LiberArte** (Avenida Corrientes 1555, tel. 011/4375-2341) is a politically and socially conscious bookstore that also offers weekend theater programs.

The **Centro Latinoamericano de Creación e Investigación Teatral,** (Bolívar 825 in San Telmo, tel. 011/4361-8358, correo@celcit.org.ar, www.celcit.org.ar) is an innovative theater and educational institution that produces plays by top Latin American dramatists.

San Telmo's **Teatro Margarita Xirgu** (Chacabuco 863/875, tel. 011/4300-2448, info@complejomxirgu.com.ar, www.complejomxirgu.com.ar) is the performing arts arm of the Casal de Catalunya cultural center (tel. 011/4300-5252). Catalan refugees from Francisco Franco's Spanish dictatorship founded the center.

Before his death in 1977, La Boca artist and promoter Benito Quinquela Martín donated the building that serves as headquarters for La Boca's **Teatro de la Ribera** (Pedro de Mendoza 1821, tel. 011/4302-8866). Their barrio compatriots **Teatro Catalinas Sur** (Benito Pérez Galdós 93, tel. 011/4300-5707, catalinasur@arnet.com.ar, www.catalinasur.com.ar) form one of the capital's most entertaining and creative companies, and it's worthwhile even for those who don't know a word of Spanish.

Some companies lack regular venues in the strictest sense—they may appear spontaneously or rent theaters to put on their productions. Less-conventional groups to watch for include **Teatreros Ambulantes Los Calandracas** (California 1732, Barracas, tel. 011/4302-6285, loscalandracas@hotmail.com); **Teatro Callejero La Runfla;** the puppet theater **Diablomundo,** from the Gran Buenos Aires suburb of Temperley; and **Casita de la Selva** (La Selva 4022, Vélez Sarsfield). These groups often take to the streets, performing in parks and other public venues, but the **Grupo Teatral Escena Subterránea** (tel. 011/4777-8599) takes its show beneath the streets—performing in Subte trains and stations.

the Microcentro's most traditional settings for coffee and croissants. Despite its worn upholstery and cracked floor tiles, the Ideal served as a set for Madonna's *Evita* debacle, and it hosts tango events.

By contrast, the elegant **Confitería Richmond** (Florida 468, tel. 011/4322-1341), one of Jorge Luis Borges's favorites, looks as good as the day it opened. Prices are higher here, though, and the service can be a little distracted.

Recoleta's **La Biela** (Avenida Quintana 596/600, tel. 011/4804-0449) is a classic breakfast spot, but even after devaluation it remains a relatively pricey place to eat. In good weather, try the patio, beneath the palm and palo borracho trees, and the giant *gomero* or *ombú*, which needs wooden beams to prop up its sprawling branches. It's slightly more expensive to eat outside, though, and the outdoor service can be inconsistent.

Bars and Clubs

The distinction between cafés and bars is more a continuum than a dichotomy. Some of the more stylish (or pretentious) bars often go by the English word pub, pronounced as in English, though many call themselves Irish.

Relocated to Monserrat after the demolition of its classic Microcentro locale, **Bar Seddon** (Defensa 695) has made a successful transition to the capital's oldest neighborhood. Behind its streetside restaurant, **La Trastienda** (Balcarce 460, tel. 011/4342-7650) has recycled a Monserrat warehouse into an attractive theater that hosts both live music and drama.

Downtown Matías (Reconquista 701, tel. 011/4311-0327) is the Microcentro branch of BA's oldest Irish-style pub; drinks are mostly in the US$2–3 range, with pub lunches for about US$3. There is live music in various styles, including Celtic, depending on the night, and a 7–11 P.M. happy hour.

In new quarters, the artsy **Foro Gandhi** (Avenida Corrientes 1743, tel. 011/4374-7501) is a hybrid bookstore/coffeehouse/cultural center whose offerings include films, poetry readings, tango shows, and theater.

San Telmo's **Bar Plaza Dorrego** (Defensa 1098, tel. 011/4361-0141) makes an ideal break

from Sunday flea-marketeering or for a beer on its namesake plaza any other day. **Enoteka** (Defensa 891, tel. 011/4363-0011) is a wine-by-the-glass and tapas bar with a wide variety of Argentine and foreign vintages.

Cemento (Estados Unidos 1234) is a cavernous warehouse that hosts *rock nacional* groups on the way up. Often threatened with closure, it somehow keeps hanging on. **Tabaco Rock** (Estados Unidos 265) is a tiny venue featuring live rock bands.

A restaurant by day, La Boca's **El Samovar de Rasputín** (Del Valle Iberlucea 1251, tel. 011/4302-3190) is a lively blues-and-rock venue on weekends. Opposite Parque Lezama, the **Blues Special Club** (Almirante Brown 102, tel. 011/4854-2338) traditionally flies in performers from Chicago and other blues hotbeds in the States.

Congreso's **Celta Bar** (Sarmiento 1702, tel. 011/4371-7338) makes great pizza, serves good drinks, and has hip live entertainment.

BA's ultimate sports bar is the Abasto's **Café Bar Banderín** (Guardia Vieja 3601, tel. 011/4862-7757). Decorated with soccer pennants dating decades back, it recalls the era when *porteños* argued about rather than gawked at *fútbol*. There's TV now, but the mid-1950s atmosphere endures.

Retiro's **Bárbaro** (Tres Sargentos 415, tel. 011/4311-6856) takes its punning name from a *lunfardo* (Buenos Aires street slang) term roughly translatable as "cool." And it is, but unpretentiously so. Typical of British/Irish-style pubs is **John John** (Reconquista 924), which has reasonably priced drinks and an "erotic happy hour" Wednesdays. Nearby, **The Kilkenny** (Marcelo T. de Alvear 399, tel. 011/4312-7291, noon–6 A.M.) hosts a 7–9 P.M. happy hour, and has Irish beers on tap, plenty of whiskey, and live bands around midnight. Intimate **Dadá** (San Martín 941, tel. 011/4314-4787) has a devoted following.

Bordering Barrio Norte **Milión** (Paraná 1048, tel. 011/4815-9925) is a tapas bar occupying three stories of a magnificent 1913 mansion; minimally altered for its current use, it offers garden, patio, and interior seating. There's a 6–9 P.M. happy hour, for beer only, on weekdays; it keeps late hours except on Sunday night, when it closes at 1 A.M. Restaurant entrees cost US$3.50–6.

The nearby **Gran Bar Danzón** (Libertad 1161, tel. 011/4811-1108) is a sophisticated wine bar that doubles as a restaurant, with a fine sushi special at happy hour (7–9 P.M.), though the sushi chef takes Mondays off. Drinkers can lounge on the comfy chairs and sofas, or at the long bar; the dining area is separate. The music could be better and the volume lower, but the staff is cordial and the wine selection impressive.

Sometimes derided as a pickup bar, Recoleta's **Shamrock** (Rodríguez Peña 1220, tel. 011/4812-3584) is the Barrio Norte version of an Irish pub. **Buller Brewing Company** (Presidente Ramón Ortiz 1827, tel. 011/4808-9061) is a brew pub that produces seven different types of beer served with tapas, seafood, and pizza.

In the Village Recoleta complex, **Locos por el Fútbol** (Vicente López 2000) has gigantic, larger-than-life-size screens for soccer matches. The nearby **World Sports Café** (Junín 1745, tel. 011/4807-5444) is not so overwhelming. The **Hard Rock Café** (Avenida Pueyrredón 2501, 011/4807-7625, noon–3 A.M. daily) is the barrio branch of the worldwide hamburger and rock 'n' roll–memorabilia chain.

Los Porteños (Avenida Las Heras 2100, tel. 011/4809-3548) is a corner bar that holds only about 70 people for live blues, with an exceptional house band on Friday and Saturday (Latin music) for a US$1 cover charge; drinks are reasonably priced, there's a decent bar-food menu, friendly staff, and an unpretentious crowd with a good age mix. The air quality is better than at most *porteño* bars.

Fronting on Plaza Serrano, Palermo Soho's **República de Acá** (Serrano 1549, tel. 011/4581-0278) is a combination comedy club, karaoke bar, and relatively expensive Internet café. Toward Plaza Italia, **Mundo Bizarro** (Guatemala 4802, tel. 011/4773-1967) is a self-consciously hip bar with erotic décor. It attracts a youthful crowd with deafening techno. The trendy **El 5° Stone** (Thames and Nicaragua, tel. 011/4832-4961) has live and recorded rock music. On

weekends, the **Salón Pueyrredón** (Avenida Santa Fe 4560) showcases alt-punk in a place that looks like it was rented just for the occasion.

One of the city's most intimate entertainment venues, the **Club del Vino** (Cabrera 4737, tel. 011/4833-0048) is a restaurant, a wine bar, and a theater seating up to 150 persons for live tango and folkoric music. Prices for shows vary but start around US$3, and the air quality's not bad by *porteño* standards.

Palermo Hollywood's **Niceto Club** (Niceto Vega 5510, tel. 011/4779-6396) has become one of the area's top live music venues over the last several years; it's open Thursday, Friday, and Saturday nights. The offerings cover many styles of music.

Beneath a rickety railroad bridge in Parque Tres de Febrero, drawing performers of the caliber of Charly García, **The Roxy** (Avenida Sarmiento and Avenida Casares, tel. 011/4899-0314, www.theroxybsas.com.ar) is rowdy and sweaty but not violent—just what rock 'n' roll is supposed to be. Overhead trains shake the building and the roof leaks in heavy rain.

In Las Cañitas, **Van Koning** (Báez 325, tel. 011/4772-9909) is a Netherlands-style pub that capitalizes on the Argentine fixation with all things Dutch since the country acquired its own royalty with the marriage of Máxima Zorreguieta to Crown Prince William in 2002. Dutch expats gather here the first Wednesday of every month.

Jazz

Clásica y Moderna (Avenida Callao 892, tel. 011/4812-8707) is a complex hybrid bookstore/café/live jazz venue that's occupied the same Barrio Norte location since 1938. Performers here have included Susana Rinaldi, Mercedes Sosa, and Liza Minelli. It's open 8 A.M.–2 A.M. daily except Friday and Saturday, when it stays open until 4 A.M.; regulars seem to get better service than strangers.

Differing slightly in concept is the nearby **Notorious** (Avenida Callao 966, tel. 011/4815-8473), a combination bar, CD store (listen to what interests you), and live music venue. It's normally open 8 A.M.–midnight daily except

Sundays and holidays, when it opens at 11 A.M.; live music shows go later.

Primarily a restaurant—and a very fine one—Palermo Viejo's **Splendid** (Gorriti 5099, tel. 011/4833-4477) also offers live jazz Thursday and Saturday around 10 P.M. In Palermo Hollywood, check the schedule at **Tiempo de Gitanos** (El Salvador 5575, tel. 011/4776-6143), a bar/restaurant serving an eclectic mix of Spanish and Middle Eastern dishes. Dinner shows cost about US$12 pp.

Tango and Milonga

Many but not all tango venues are in the southerly barrios of Monserrat and San Telmo, with a few elsewhere and in outlying barrios. Professional shows range from simple, low-priced programs to truly extravagant productions at high, sometimes excessive cost. *Milongas,* of course, are participatory bargains for those who want to learn.

Monserrat's legendary **Café Tortoni** (Avenida de Mayo 825, tel. 011/4342-4328, www.cafetortoni.com.ar) hosts live song-and-dance shows at its Sala Alfonsina Storni, separated from the main part of the café, for around US$4 pp plus drinks and food. Dating from 1920, the elegant **El Querandí** (Perú 302, tel. 011/5199-1770, querandi@querandi .com.ar, www.querandi.com.ar) is another classic; for US$35 pp, the nightly dinner (starting at 8:30 P.M.) and show (starting at 10:30 P.M.) is toward the upper end of the scale.

San Telmo's **Bar Sur** (Estados Unidos 299, tel. 011/4362-6086, info@bar-sur.com.ar, www .bar-sur.com.ar) is a relatively spontaneous and informal venue open late every night except Sunday. The US$6 charge pp includes unlimited pizza, but drinks are additional. **Mitos Argentinos** (Humberto Primo 489, tel. 011/4362-7810) has a Sunday afternoon tango show 2–5 P.M., which coincides with the nearby Feria de San Pedro Telmo on Plaza Dorrego. Both male and female tango singers are accompanied by live guitar and/or recorded music, and dancers perform to recorded music. There is no charge in addition to the food and drink, which are reasonable.

One of San Telmo's classic venues, occupying a late-18th-century building **El Viejo Almacén** (Balcarce and Avenida Independencia, tel. 011/4307-6689, valmacen@infovia.com.ar, www.viejo-almacen.com.ar) charges US$19 pp for the show alone, US$27 pp including dinner at its restaurant, directly across the street.

Literally in the shadow of the redeveloped Mercado del Abasto, part of a municipal project to sustain the legacy of the "Morocho del Abasto" in his old neighborhood, the **Esquina Carlos Gardel** (Carlos Gardel 3200, tel./fax 011/4867-6363, info@esquinacarlosgardel.com.ar, www.es-quinacarlosgardel.com.ar) has nightly shows from US$23 (show only) to US$32 (with dinner).

Named for the great songwriter, the **Esquina Homero Manzi** (Avenida San Juan 3601, tel. 011/4957-8488, info@esquinahomeromanzi .com.ar, www.esquinahomeromanzi.com.ar) was once part of the *arrabales* (outskirts) in the barrio

Café Tortoni and the Academia Nacional del Tango

© WAYNE BERNHARDSON

CINEMAS

Buenos Aires's traditional commercial-cinema district is in the Microcentro along the Lavalle pedestrian mall, west of Florida, and along Avenida Corrientes and Avenida Santa Fe. In addition, there are multiplexes in the shopping malls of Puerto Madero, Retiro, and Palermo, and clusters in outer barrios like Belgrano.

Most cinemas offer half-price discounts Tuesday and Wednesday, and sometimes for afternoon shows on other days. On Friday and Saturday nights there is usually a *trasnoche* (midnight or later) showing, but even on weeknights there may be shows as late as 11 P.M.

Alto Palermo 1-2: Avenida Santa Fe 3251, Palermo, tel. 011/4827-8362

Atlas Lavalle: Lavalle 869, tel. 011/4322-1936

Atlas Santa Fe 1-2: Avenida Santa Fe 2015, Barrio Norte, tel. 011/4823-7878

Belgrano Multiplex: Obligado at Mendoza, Belgrano, tel. 011/4783-2186

Cinemark 8 Puerto Madero: Avenida Alicia Moreau de Justo 1960, tel. 011/4315-3008

Cinemark 10 Palermo: Beruti 3399, Palermo, tel. 011/4827-9500

Complejo Cine Lorca 1-2: Avenida Corrientes 1428, tel. 011/4371-5017

Electric: Lavalle 836, tel. 011/4322-1846

Galerías Pacífico 1-2: Florida 753, tel. 011/6556-5357

Gaumont 1-3: Rivadavia 1635, tel. 011/4371-3050

General Paz 1-6: Avenida Cabildo 2702, Belgrano, tel. 011/4781-1412

Los Angeles 1-3: Avenida Corrientes 1770, tel. 011/4372-2405

Metro 1-3: Cerrito 570, tel. 011/4382-4219

Monumental 1-4: Lavalle 780, tel. 011/4393-9008

Paseo Alcorta 1-4: Figueroa Alcorta at Salguero, Palermo, tel. 011/4806-5665

Patio Bullrich 1-6: Avenida del Libertador 750, Barrio Norte, tel. 011/4816-3801

Premier 1-3: Avenida Corrientes 1565, tel. 011/4374-2113

Savoy 1-4: Avenida Cabildo 2829, Belgrano, tel. 011/4781-6500

Showcase Cinemas: Monroe 1655, Belgrano, tel. 011/4786-3232

Solar de la Abadía 1-2: Luis María Campos at Maure, Belgrano, tel. 011/4778-5181

Village Recoleta: Vicente López at Junín, Recoleta, tel. 011/4810-4446 or 4810-6843

Art Houses

Independent films or reprises of commercial films are generally show at smaller venues scattered around town. Tuesday and Wednesday discounts may also be available.

A particularly welcome revival is the Cinemateca Hebráica, which was closed for several years after the terrorist bombings against the Israeli embassy and the AMIA.

Centro Cultural Ricardo Rojas: Avenida Corrientes 2038, tel. 011/4954-8352

Cine Club Tea: Aráoz 1460, Palermo, tel. 011/4832-2646

Cinemateca Hebráica: Sarmiento 2255, tel. 011/4952-5986

Complejo del Cine Argentino Tita Merello: Suipacha 442, tel. 011/4322-1185

Cosmos: Avenida Corrientes 2046, tel. 011/4953-5405

Sala Leopoldo Lugones: Avenida Corrientes 1530, tel. 0800/333-5254

of Boedo. Dinner starts at 9 P.M. nightly; the show commences at 10 P.M.

In the southern barrio of Nueva Pompeya, **El Chino** (Beazley 3566, tel. 011/4911-0215), has become a tourist hangout for its rugged authenticity. Inexpensive shows and live music take place Friday and Saturday nights only; arrive well before midnight for a table, though the music doesn't start until later. The food is working-class Argentine.

For those who want to dance instead of watch, or who want to learn, the best options are neighborhood *milongas*. Organized events charge US$2–3 with live orchestra, less with recorded music. For classes, a good clearinghouse is Monserrat's **Academia Nacional del Tango** (Avenida de Mayo 833, tel. 011/4345-6968, www.sectur.gov.ar/cultura/ant/ant.htm). For the truly committed, it even offers a three-year degree in tango.

Upstairs at Confitería Ideal, **A Toda Milonga** (Suipacha 384, tel. 011/4729-6390, osvaldo_marrapodi@yahoo.com, www.domart.com.ar/marrapoditango, US$1.50) takes place every Thursday 3–10 P.M. Instructor Osvaldo Marrapodi also offers Tuesday lessons, 3:30–6:30 P.M. and 6:30–9:30 P.M., and individual lessons by arrangement.

Another central location is **El Sótano** (Perón 1372, tel. 011/4854-5647, US$1.50), whose orchestra-accompanied *milonga* takes place Thursday at 11 P.M.

San Telmo's highly regarded **Centro Cultural Torquato Tasso** (Defensa 1575, tel. 011/4307-6506, admission US$1.50 except Sun., when it's nominal) offers shows Friday and Saturday night at 11 P.M. (with a live orchestra) and Sunday (with recorded music). Instruction is also available.

In the barrio of San Cristóbal, **Club Gricel** (La Rioja 1180, tel. 011/4957-7157) offers live orchestra *milongas* Friday at 11 P.M. and Saturday at 10:30 P.M. (US$1.50). Sunday, at 9:30 P.M., there's a cheaper event with recorded music.

Classical

The classical music and opera season lasts March–November but peaks in winter, from June through August. For nearly a century, the capital's premier classical music locale has been the **Teatro Colón** (Libertad 621, tel./fax 4011/378-7344, boleteria@teatrocolon.org.ar, www.teatrocolon.org.ar), though the recent economic crisis has meant increasing reliance on Argentines rather than high-profile foreigners.

Other classical venues include the Microcentro's **Teatro Opera** (Avenida Corrientes 860, tel. 011/4326-1225); Monserrat's **Teatro Avenida** (Avenida de Mayo 1212, tel. 011/4381-0662); and Retiro's **Teatro Coliseo** (M.T. de Alvear 1125, tel. 011/4807-1277, www.fundacioncoliseum.com.ar/teatro.htm).

La Scala de San Telmo (Pasaje Giuffra 371, tel. 011/4362-1187 or 011/4813-5741, scala@lascala.com.ar, www.lascala.com.ar) is an intimate high-culture performing arts venue, focused on theater and classical music, but with occasional folkloric indulgences.

Cultural Centers

Buenos Aires has a multitude of municipal, national, and international cultural centers, offering entertainment, events, dance and language classes, and many other activities.

Adjacent to the Galerías Pacífico, the **Centro Cultural Borges** (Viamonte and San Martín, tel. 011/5555-5359, ccbor@tournet.com.ar, US$.70) features permanent exhibits on Argentina's most famous literary figure, as well as rotating fine arts exhibitions and performing arts events. Hours are 10 A.M.–9 P.M. daily except Sunday, when it opens at noon.

Balvanera's increasingly important **Centro Cultural Ricardo Rojas** (Avenida Corrientes 2038, tel. 011/4954-5521, rojas@rec.uba.ar, www.rojas.uba.ar) has regular theater programs as well as exhibitions, classes, and workshops in theater, dance, tango, art, language, photography, and the like.

Monserrat's **Centro Cultural Plaza Defensa** (Defensa 535, tel. 011/4342-8610, plazadefensa@buenosaires.gov.ar) is a neighborhood cultural center that hosts small-scale events. Occupying a colonial-style house in Barracas, the **Centro Cultural del Sur** (Avenida Caseros 1750, tel.

011/4306-0301) hosts some of the Festival Buenos Aires Tango's biggest events.

Recoleta's **Centro Cultural Ciudad de Buenos Aires** (Junín 1930, tel. 011/4803-1040, www.centroculturalrecoleta.org) is one of the city's outstanding cultural venues, with many free or inexpensive events. It's open 2–9 P.M. Tuesday–Friday, 10 A.M.–9 P.M. weekends and holidays; there are guided visits (tel. 011/4803-4057) Wednesday at 6 P.M. and Saturday at 3 and 5 P.M.

Gay Venues

Buenos Aires has a vigorous gay scene, centered mostly around Recoleta, Barrio Norte, and Palermo Viejo, with a handful of venues scattered elsewhere. Lots of gay men hang out on Avenida Santa Fe between Callao and Pueyrredón, a good area to meet people and learn the latest. The widely available monthly publication *La Otra Guía* has extensive listings of gay-oriented and gay-friendly businesses.

The capital's gay venues are mostly tolerant and even inclusive of non-homosexuals. When non-Argentine heterosexual women tire of Argentine machismo, they sometimes even prefer gay bars for dancing, but Argentine *machistas* are catching on to this.

Search (Azcuénaga 1007, tel. 011/4824-0932) is a well-established Barrio Norte gay bar open daily with live entertainment, while **Contramano** (Rodríguez Peña 1082) is a disco open nightly except Monday and Tuesday. In Balvanera/Once, **Angel's** (Viamonte 2168) is a gay-male bar that's open Thursday–Sunday after midnight.

Open Thursday–Sunday, Palermo Viejo's **Bar del Este** (Bulnes 1250, tel. 011/4864-4056, bardeleste@sinectis.com.ar) is popular for dancing and drag shows; Saturday is the biggest night. Actively welcoming people of any orientation, it's comfortable, with contemporary style and lighting, and serves strong drinks at moderate prices.

Palermo Soho's **Bach Bar** (Cabrera 4390) is a predominantly lesbian locale that doesn't advertise the fact—there's no sign outside—but there's usually a crowd. It's open nightly except Monday from about 11 P.M.

EVENTS

Buenos Aires observes all the typical national holidays and quite a few special events on top of that. The summer months of January and February, when most *porteños* leave on vacation, are generally quiet; things pick up after school starts in early March.

Dates for the pre-Lenten **Carnaval** (Carnival), in February or March, vary from year to year; while unlikely ever to match Brazilian festivities, Carnaval is enjoying a revival, with the performances of barrio *murgas* (street musicians and dancers) rather than elaborate downtown events. Unlike Brazil, celebrations take place on weekends rather than during the entire week.

Though it began in 1998 on Gardel's birthday of December 11, the increasingly important

CELEBRATING THE TANGO

Despite its recency—the first event took place only in 1997—the **Festival Buenos Aires Tango** (tel. 0800/3378-4825, informacion@festivaldetango.com.ar, www.festivaldetango.com.ar) has become one of the city's signature special events. Lasting several weeks between mid-February and early March, this celebration of music, song, and dance ranges from the very traditional and conservative to the imaginative and even daring.

Shortly after its creation, the festival moved from December to February and March to follow Brazilian Carnaval, but it is not strictly a tourist-oriented affair; it is also widely accepted and anticipated by a demanding *porteño* public. Unlike Brazilian Carnaval, it's not a mass spectacle, but rather a decentralized series of performances at relatively small, even intimate, venues around the capital. As such, it offers opportunities to see and hear not just established artists, but also developing performers.

Most of the funding for the city-sponsored festival goes to pay the artists, and admission is either free or inexpensive; however, tickets are usually available on a first-come, first-served basis on the day of the performance.

Festival Buenos Aires Tango (www.festivaldetango.com.ar) now follows Brazilian Carnaval in late February and early March. Over several weeks, it includes dance competitions and free music/dance events at venues like the Centro Cultural San Martín, Centro Cultural Recoleta, and Centro Cultural del Sur, where calendars are available.

April's annual three-week book fair, the **Feria del Libro** (www.el-libro.com.ar) has been a fixture on the *porteño* literary scene for nearly three decades. Most but not all exhibitors are from Latin America. It has recently moved from Recoleta to Palermo's Predio Ferial (Cerviño 4474, Avenida Sarmiento 2704, tel. 011/4777-5500, US$1).

Toward the end of April, the **Festival Internacional de Cine Independiente** (International Independent Film Festivals) proved a success even during the economic crisis of 2002, its fourth year. Featuring independent movies from every continent, it takes place at various cinemas around town.

For more than a decade now, mid-May's **Feria de Galerías Arte BA** shows work from dozens of Buenos Aires art galleries. Like the Feria del Libro, it takes place at Palermo's Predio Ferial.

Though not an official holiday, June 24 commemorates the **Día de la Muerte de Carlos Gardel,** the anniversary of the singer's death in an aviation accident in Medellín, Colombia. Pilgrims crowd the Cementerio de la Chacarita to pay tribute, and there are also tango events.

For more than a century, the Sociedad Rural Argentina's **Exposición Internacional de Ganadería, Agricultura y Industria Internacional,** the annual agricultural exhibition at Palermo's Predio Ferial, has been one of the capital's biggest events. It takes place during the July winter holidays.

Though the Festival Buenos Aires Tango has moved to late February and early March, the city still closes the street near the Central Cultural San Martín on December 11, Gardel's birthday, for the **Milonga de Calle Corrientes,** dancing to live and recorded music.

SHOPPING

Buenos Aires's main shopping areas are the Microcentro, along the Florida pedestrian mall toward Retiro; Retiro (especially around Plaza San Martín and along Avenida Santa Fe); Recoleta, near the cemetery; and the tree-lined streets of Palermo Viejo, where stylish shops sit between the newest restaurants and bars. Street markets take place in San Telmo, Recoleta, and Belgrano.

Shopping Centers

Over the past decade-plus, many older buildings have been recycled into upscale malls good for one-stop shopping. The most notable is the Microcentro's magnificent **Galerías Pacífico** (Florida and Córdoba, tel. 011/5555-5100).

Once a livestock auction house, Retiro's **Patio Bullrich** (Avenida del Libertador 750, tel. 4814-7400/7500) has become a palatial 24,000-square-meter commercial space with nearly 70 shops, plus restaurants and cinemas, on four levels.

Several other places are under the same management as Patio Bullrich, most notably the **Buenos Aires Design Recoleta** (Avenida Pueyrredón 2501, tel. 011/5777-6000), a 3,000-square-meter complex of shops and restaurants, on two levels, alongside the cultural center and cemetery. As its name suggests, it focuses on design and interior decoration.

Antiques

Sunday's outdoor **Feria de San Pedro Telmo,** one of the city's biggest tourist attractions, fills Plaza Dorrego with antiques and bric-a-brac. There are also many antique dealers in commercial galleries with small streetside frontage, including **Galería Cecil** (Defensa 845); **Galería French** (Defensa 1070); and **Galería de la Defensa** (Defensa 1179).

Art Galleries

Buenos Aires has a thriving modern-art scene, with the most innovative galleries in Retiro and Recoleta. Retiro's **Galería Ruth Benzacar**

FERIAS OF BUENOS AIRES

For sightseers and spontaneous shoppers alike, Buenos Aires's diverse ferias (street fairs) are one of the city's greatest pleasures. Easily the most prominent is Sunday's standout **Feria de San Pedro Telmo**, which fills Plaza Dorrego and surrounding streets—authorities close Calle Defensa to vehicle traffic—with booths full of antiques, *filete* paintings, and other crafts. There are professional tango musicians and dancers, and dozens more street performers range from the embarrassingly mundane to the truly innovative. Lasting roughly 10 A.M.–5 P.M., it also offers sidewalk cafés and nearby upscale antique shops.

So successful is the Feria de San Pedro Telmo that, gradually, it's aided the now-thriving **Feria Parque Lezama**, a Sunday crafts fair that's gradually spread north from its namesake park up Calle Defensa and under the freeway; only the broad Avenida San Juan has been able to stop it. Parque Lezama itself now gets Sunday street performers, though not so many as Plaza Dorrego.

In La Boca, the **Feria Artesanal Plazoleta Vuelta de Rocha** (Avenida Pedro de Mendoza and Puerto de Palos) takes place weekends and holidays 10 A.M.–6 P.M.; along the length of the nearby Caminito, painters, illustrators and sculptors sell their works in the **Feria del Caminito,** open 10 A.M.–6 P.M. daily.

© WAYNE BERNHARDSON

Filete, the traditional *porteño* sign-painting art, makes for popular souvenirs at Sunday's Feria de San Pedro Telmo, on Plaza Dorrego.

After San Telmo, the most frequented tourist feria is probably Recoleta's crafts-oriented **Feria Plaza Intendente Alvear.** Immediately northeast of the Centro Cultural Recoleta, also strong on street performers, it's begun to stretch south along Junín; hours are 9 A.M.–7 P.M. weekends and holidays.

On weekends and holidays, crafts stalls cover most of Belgrano's main square at the easygoing **Feria Artesanal Plaza General Manuel Belgrano** (Juramento and Cuba). Hours are 9 A.M.–7 P.M. or even later (when it's better). When it rains, the stalls are well-sheltered with tarps.

(underground at Florida 1000, tel. 011/4313-8480, www.ruthbenzacar.com) showcases some of the capital's and the country's most avant-garde artists.

Galería Rubbers (Suipacha 1175, tel. 011/4393-6010, www.rubbers.com.ar) is an excellent contemporary gallery that has a Barrio Norte branch in the Ateneo Gran Splendid (Avenida Santa Fe 1860, 2nd and 3rd floors). **Galería Vermeer** (Suipacha 1168, tel./fax 011/4393-5102, www.galeriavermeer.com.ar) is not quite so up-to-date but is still a good one.

Also visit **Galería Federico Klemm** (downstairs at Marcelo T. de Alvear 636, tel. 011/4312-2058, www.fundacionfjklemm.org).

Bookstores

Bookstores are where Buenos Aires shopping really shines; they are as much—or more—cultural as commercial institutions, and they take that role seriously.

Buenos Aires's signature bookstore is the Microcentro branch of **El Ateneo** (Florida 340, tel. 011/4325-6801, www.tematika.com.ar), which has a huge selection of Argentine history, literature, and coffee-table souvenir books, plus a good selection of domestic travel titles (it is also a publishing house).

The most elegant outlet, though, is the affiliated **El Ateneo Grand Splendid** (Avenida Santa Fe 1880, Barrio Norte, tel. 011/4813-6052). Opened in December 2000, it occupies a recycled cinema that deserves a visit simply to see its seamless transformation—the stage is a café, the opera-style boxes contain chairs for readers, and bookshelves line the curving walls of the upper levels from floor to ceiling. It also has a good selection of music.

In a noteworthy Art Deco building, Monserrat's **Librería de Ávila** (Adolfo Alsina 500, tel. 011/4311-8989, www.libreriadeavila.servisur.com) is a classic book dealer that specializes in history, ethnology, travel literature, tango, folklore, and the like; it also hosts book presentations and even musical events, and has a café.

Excellent independent stores include **Zivals** (Avenida Callao 395, Congreso, tel. 011/4371-7500, www.zivals.com); **LiberArte** (Avenida Corrientes 1555, tel. 011/4375-2341), a leftish bookseller that also offers weekend theater programs; and **Librería ABC** (Avenida Córdoba 685, Retiro, tel. 011/4314-8106), which has English-language books and books about Argentina.

Librería Platero (Talcahuano 485, Tribunales, tel. 011/4382-2215, fax 011/4382-3896, www.libreriaplatero.com.ar), may be the city's best specialist bookstore, with an enormous stock of new and out-of-print books (the latter in the basement stacks). It does good trade with overseas academics and libraries.

Retiro's **Antique Book Shop** (Libertad 1236, tel. 011/4815-0658, breitfel@interprov.com) carries a good but expensive selection on Argentine art, literature, travel, and Patagonia. Other antiquarian dealers include the Microcentro's **Alberto Casares** (Suipacha 521, tel. 011/4322-6198, www.servisur.com/casares) and **Aquilanti** (Rincón 79, Congreso, tel. 011/4952-4546).

Librerías Turísticas (Paraguay 2457, tel. 011/4963-2866 or 4962-5547, turisticas@sinectis.com.ar) has an outstanding choice of Argentine maps and guidebooks, including its own guides to neighborhood cafés in the capital.

Crafts

Every Argentine province has its own tourist information office in Buenos Aires; the northern provinces with significant indigenous populations carry small but outstanding selections of crafts. The most notable are Balvanera's **Casa del Chaco** (Avenida Callao 322, tel. 011/4372-5209); Retiro's **Casa de Jujuy** (Avenida Santa

---

THE FERIA DE MATADEROS

Gauchesco traditions live in the weekend Feria de Mataderos, where city-bound *paisanos* or would-be *paisanos* immerse themselves in the nostalgia of the campo, or countryside. In addition to a diverse crafts selection, this lively street fair features open-air *parrilladas* and regional delicacies like tamales, live music and dancing in rural styles like *chamamé*, gaucho horseback races, and even, during Carnaval, a neighborhood *murga* (troupe) to kick off the season in the style of Jujuy Province.

Despite occasional exaggeratedly nationalistic overtones, the feria generates genuine enthusiasm. Oddly enough, it was founded in the mid-1980s under the sponsorship of a Jewish *porteña*, Sara Vinocur, who still directs it as the link between city authorities and barrio residents.

In the southwesterly barrio of Mataderos, in the streets surrounding the arcades of the former Mercado de Hacienda at Lisandro de la Torre and Avenida de los Corrales, the feria (info@feriademataderos.com.ar, www.feriademataderos.com.ar) is about an hour from the Microcentro by *colectivo* No. 180, *ramal* (branch) 155 from Tucumán, Talcahuano, or Lavalle. In summer, it takes place 6 P.M.–midnight on Saturday; the rest of the year, it starts at 11 A.M. Sunday.

Fe 967, tel. 011/4393-6096); and the nearby **Casa de Misiones** (Avenida Santa Fe 989, tel. 011/4322-0686).

Monserrat's nonprofit **Arte Indígena** (Balcarce 234, tel. 011/4343-1455) contains a small but representative assortment of indigenous crafts from around the country. In the Galerías Pacífico, **El Boyero** (Florida 760, tel. 011/5555-5307, www.elboyero.com) sells items ranging from leather bags, boots, and belts to gaucho and Mapuche silverwork and *mate* gourds, but also ceramics.

Artesanías Argentinas (Montevideo 1386, Barrio Norte, tel. 011/4812-2650, www.artesaniasargentinas.org) is a well-established artisans' outlet. Nearby **Artesanías Salteñas** (Rodríguez Peña 1775, Recoleta, tel. 011/4814-7562) displays crafts from the northwestern province of Salta.

Leather Goods and Footwear

Retiro has several leather specialists, starting with **Lionel Frenkel** (San Martín 1088, tel. 011/4312-9806), which sells crafts as well. Also try **Casa López** (Marcelo T. de Alvear 640/658, tel. 011/4311-3044), for women's handbags and accessories in particular.

Welcome Marroquinería (Marcelo T. de Alvear 500, tel. 011/4312-8911) is one of BA's best-established leather goods outlets. Others include **Rossi y Carusso** (Avenida Santa Fe 1601, Barrio Norte, tel. 011/4811-1965), and the Microcentro's **Dalla Fontana** (Reconquista 735, tel. 011/4313-4354).

López Taibo (Avenida Alvear 1902, Recoleta) is a men's shoes specialist. Italian immigrant Luciano Bagnasco created one of the capital's most enduring shoe stores in **Guido Mocasines** (Rodríguez Peña 1290, Barrio Norte, tel. 011/4813-4095, guidomocasines@arnet.com.ar).

Music

In addition to their books, the Microcentro's **El Ateneo** (Florida 340, tel. 4325-6801) and Barrio Norte's **El Ateneo Grand Splendid** (Avenida Santa Fe 1880, Barrio Norte, tel. 011/4813-6052) have a wide selection of quality CDs.

Zivals (Avenida Callao 395, tel. 011/4371-7500, www.zivals.com) has a large and varied sale bin in addition to its regular stock. For alternative music, try **Disquería Oid Mortales** (Avenida Corrientes 1145). **Free Blues** (Rodríguez Peña 438, tel. 011/4373-2999) deals in used CDs, cassettes, and even vinyl.

Wine

San Telmo's wine-by-the-glass **Enoteka** (Defensa 891, tel. 011/4363-0011, www.laenoteka.com) is a good place to sample before purchase. Retiro's **Winery** (Avenida Leandro N. Alem 880, tel. 4311-6607) sells Argentine wines by the glass and also carries a stock of imported wines.

The dean of wine outlets, though, is the **Club del Vino** (Cabrera 4737, tel. 011/4833-0048), one of Palermo Soho's top restaurants, bars, and entertainment venues. It also publishes a monthly newsletter, has special events for its members (though it's not necessary to be a member to eat, drink or see a show), and even has a small but beautiful basement wine museum.

SPORTS AND RECREATION

Not just a city for sightseeing, Buenos Aires also offers activities ranging from the calm of a chess match to language study to the energy of a soccer game.

Running

Many *porteños* have taken up running, but the largest open spaces suitable for the activity are in the northern suburbs of Palermo and Belgrano. The major exception is the Reserva Ecológica Costanera Sur, the former rubbish tip near Puerto Madero.

Cycling and Mountain Biking

Buenos Aires's densely built city center, ferocious traffic, and monotonous terrain limit recreational cycling, but a surprising number of *porteños*—even some policemen—get around on bicycles. There is a growing network of paved bicycle trails, and Palermo's parks and the roads of suburban Buenos Aires Province encourage some riders.

Bikes are for rent along Avenida de Infanta Isabel in Palermo's Parque Tres de Febrero, on both sides of the Museo de Artes Plásticas Eduardo Sívori. Speed-riders can test themselves on the track at Parque Tres de Febrero's **Nuevo Circuito KDT** (Jerónimo Salguero 3450, tel. 011/4802-2619, 8 A.M.–9 P.M., daily, one-time admission US$.50 pp, monthly membership US$3.50 pp).

Horseback Riding

In addition to tourist-oriented *estancias,* the city itself offers several riding options: try the **Club Hípico Mediterráneo** (Avenida Figueroa Alcorta 4800, Palermo, tel. 011/4772-3828), or the **Club Alemán de Equitación** (Avenida Dorrego 4045, Palermo, tel. 011/4778-7060).

Golf

The 18-hole **Golf Club Lagos de Palermo** (Avenida Tornquist 1426, tel. 011/4772-7261) is open 7 A.M.–5 P.M. daily except Monday. Greens fees are US$7 weekdays, US$9 weekends (when reservations are advisable).

Soccer

Soccer-mad Buenos Aires has six first-division teams, and it seems like there's a match every night. For participants, there are many pickup games in the parks of Palermo and elsewhere.

For spectators, *entradas populares* (standing-room tickets) are the cheapest, but *plateas* (fixed seats) have better security. The best choices are **Boca Juniors** (Brandsen 805, La Boca, tel. 011/4309-4700, www.bocasistemas.com.ar); **River Plate** (Avenida Presidente Figueroa Alcorta 7597, Núñez, tel. 011/4788-1200); and **San Lorenzo de Almagro** (Avenida Fernández de la Cruz 2403, Nueva Pompeya, tel. 011/4914-2470, www.sanlorenzo.com.ar).

Horse Racing

The country's major track is the **Hipódromo Argentino** (Avenida del Libertador 4101, Palermo, tel. 011/4788-2800, www.palermo .com.ar). Races may take place any day of the week, but mostly Friday–Monday. General admission costs US$1, with minimum bets about the same.

ACCOMMODATIONS

Buenos Aires has abundant accommodations in all categories. Note, though, that since the economic implosion of early 2002, some upscale hotels have enforced differential rates for Argentines and foreigners—sometimes to the point of continuing the former one-to-one exchange rate. If a hotel decides to do this, there's not much you can do except go elsewhere or, if your language skills are good enough, try to argue the point. Note also that advertised rates at upscale hotels often exclude the 21 percent IVA.

Under US$25

Over the past several years, youth hostels have sprung up like tango halls in Gardel's time, and most of them are good to excellent at modest prices. Some but not all are Hostelling International affiliates.

Among nonhostel accommodations, San Telmo's **Hotel Varela** (Estados Unidos 342, tel. 011/4362-1231, hotelvarela@yahoo.com.ar, US$6–7 s or d) is a plain but spotless and reputable backpackers' choice. Some rooms have private bath.

Near Congreso, **Hotel Sportsman** (Rivadavia 1425, tel. 011/4381-8021, fax 011/4383-6263, sportsman@mixmail.com, www.hotelsportsman.com.ar, US$6–11 s/d) is a moldy backpackers' special whose main appeal is low rates; the more-expensive rooms have private bath, but there are few of these. There are discounts for longer stays.

On the edge of Palermo Soho's nightlife zone, the HI affiliate **Tango Backpackers Hostel** (Thames 2212, tel. 011/4776-6871, info@tangobp.com, www.tangobp.com, US$5 pp for dorms, US$14 d) occupies a refurbished house with a rooftop terrace and *parrilla* for barbecues. Because of the location in a party district (though the hostel itself is on a relatively quiet block), they tend to be flexible on the 10 A.M. checkout time.

APARTMENT RENTALS

R ather than just renting a hotel room, visitors spending at least a week in Buenos Aires should consider renting an apartment and living in a neighborhood. Shopping in the same place everyday, buying the morning paper from the corner kiosk, learning the bus lines and Subte system, and making friends with the *portero* (doorman) give one a chance to feel like part of the community.

Daily newspapers like *Clarín, La Nación,* and the *Buenos Aires Herald* all have rental listings. For short-term rentals, though, the best option may be an agency such as **B y T Argentina Travel & Housing** (tel./fax 011/4821-6075 or 011/6057-0129, info@bytargentina.com, www.bytargentina.com); its online inventory of apartments and other housing is a good way to familiarize yourself with the options. **BA House** (tel. 011/4851-0798, www.bahouse.com.ar) has a smaller selection of housing in a more geographically restricted area.

San Telmo's **Sandanzas Cultural Hostel** (Balcarce 1351, tel. 011/4300-7375, info@sandanzas .com.ar, www.sandanzas.com.ar, US$5.50 pp, US$14/17 s/d) is a new independent hostel that's gotten good early reviews. In Monserrat, there's the YMCA-affiliated **Hostel Clan** (Alsina 912, tel./fax 011/4334-3401, www.hostelclan.com.ar, US$6.50 pp).

True budget accommodations are few in the northern barrios, but the **Recoleta Youth Hostel** (Libertad 1216, tel. 011/4812-4419, fax 011/ 4815-6622, reservas@trhostel.com.ar, www .trhostel.com.ar, US$8 pp, US$18 d) boasts the best location in its category (despite the name, it lies within the barrio of Retiro).

In the Microcentro, the independently operated **V&S Hostel Club** (Viamonte 887, tel./fax 011/4322-0994 or 011/4327-5131, hostelclub@hostelclub.com, www.hostelclub.com, US$9 pp, US$20/22 s/d) has both dorms and rooms with private bath. The century-old structure has central heating, a/c, and spacious and attractive common areas including kitchen, dining room, and a *parrilla* for barbecues.

Budget accommodations are scarce in Recoleta and Barrio Norte, but **Hotel del Prado** (Paraguay 2385, tel. 4961-1192, reservas@hoteldelprado-ba .com.ar, www.hoteldelprado-ba.com.ar, US$12/ 15 s/d), near the Facultad de Medicina, is a simply but tastefully remodeled older building with a quiet interior, good beds, and friendly owner-operators. Rooms have private bath, cable TV, telephone, and ceiling fans but no a/c; there are discounts for extended stays.

Also an HI affiliate, Congreso's **St. Nicholas Youth Hostel** (Bartolomé Mitre 1691, tel. 011/4373-5920, US$6 pp with shared bath, US$16 d with private bath) is another rehab with ample common spaces; those common spaces, though, are so close to the dormitories that it can be hard to get to sleep at an early hour.

Near the Plaza de Mayo, in another recycled house, the HI affiliate **Ⅺ Milhouse Youth Hostel**(Hipólito Yrigoyen 959, tel. 011/4345-9604, info@milhousehostel.com, www.milhousehostel.com, US$6 pp, US$20 d) is a well-managed, well-located, immaculate and secure facility with large common areas.

El Hostal de San Telmo (Carlos Calvo 614, tel. 011/4300-6899, fax 011/4300-9028, webs.satlink.com/usuarios/e/elhostal, elhostal @satlink.com, US$10 pp) is an appealingly cozy—perhaps cramped would be closer to the truth—hostel in a prime location. Shared amenities include kitchen facilities, cable TV, and Internet access.

Congreso's **Ⅺ Hotel Chile** (Avenida de Mayo 1297, tel./fax 011/4383-7877, US$14/19 s/d) is an Art Nouveau monument offering modernized rooms with private bath and breakfast. Corner balcony rooms on the upper floors enjoy panoramic views of the Plaza del Congreso and, by craning the neck a bit eastward, the Plaza de Mayo and Casa Rosada; the decibel level rises from the street, though.

US$25–50

Congreso's finest value is the rejuvenated **Ⅺ Hotel de los dos Congresos,** (Rivadavia 1777, tel. 011/4372-0466, fax 011/4372-0317, reservas@hoteldoscongresos.com, www .hoteldoscongresos.com, US$27/31 s/d); its stately exterior is a misleading approach to the refurbished interior, where spacious and comfortable rooms with cable TV, a/c, telephone, and other standard amenities come with a buffet breakfast. Reservations are advisable for one of the stylish loft rooms, which have spiral staircases and hot tub–equipped bathtubs.

Opposite the Luna Park stadium, convenient to Puerto Madero's restaurants and cinemas, **Hotel Plaza Roma** (Lavalle 110, tel. 011/4314-0666, fax 011/4312-0839, info@hotelplazaroma .com.ar, www.hotelplazaroma.com.ar, US$24/ 32 s/d) is an exceptional value with private bath, breakfast, a/c, cable TV, and telephone. Some rooms enjoy views of the Puerto Madero complex.

For large families or groups of friends, one of the capital's best options is **Hotel Lyon** (Riobamba 251, tel. 011/4372-0100, fax 011/4814-4252, info@hotel-lyon.com.ar, www.hotel-lyon .com.ar, US$30/35 s/d), which has spacious apartment-style rooms—the smallest are 40 square meters. For stays longer than three days, paid in cash, there's a 15 percent discount.

The **Ayacucho Palace Hotel** (Ayacucho 1408, tel./fax 011/4806-1815, reservas@ayacuchohotel .com.ar, www.ayacuchohotel.com.ar, US$29/ 36 s/d) offers some of the exterior style of more elegant *porteño* hotels without extravagant prices. Its 70 rooms are plainly but comfortably furnished.

In a charming house dating from 1926, Palermo Viejo's **M Como en Casa** (Gurruchaga 2155, tel. 011/4831-0517, fax 011/4831-2664, info@bandb.com.ar, www.bandb.com.ar, US$15 pp, US$35/45 s/d) has 11 cozy rooms with high ceilings, attractive common areas, and several shady patios on a narrow but deep lot. Rates vary according to whether or not the room has a private bath. It has Internet access and responsive English-speaking personnel, but lacks a/c.

The **M Goya Hotel** (Suipacha 748, tel./fax 011/4322-9311, goyahotel@infovia.com.ar, www.goyahotel.com.ar, US$34–53 s or d) is one of the Microcentro's best small hotels. Rates include private bath, continental breakfast (if the room payment is in cash), cable TV, and a/c; there are some larger, slightly more expensive rooms.

US$50–100

Graham Greene, appropriately enough, once stayed at the British-styled **Hotel Lancaster** (Avenida Córdoba 405, tel. 011/4312-4061, fax 011/4311-3021, lancast@infovia.com.ar, www .lancasterhotel-page.com, US$49/52 s/d), which figures briefly in his novel *The Honorary Consul*. It has an English-style pub on the ground floor; rates include breakfast.

West of San Telmo, the most unique accommodation is the German-run **Pop Hotel Boquitas Pintadas** (Estados Unidos 1393, Constitución, tel. 011/4381-6064, www.boquitas-pintadas.com.ar, US$42 s, US$60–120 d), a flamboyant place that takes its name and inspiration from a work by the even more flamboyant novelist, the late Manuel Puig. Despite the marginal neighborhood, the German owners have given the place a remarkable makeover in a pop-art mode, with a popular bar that pumps thumping techno at night, especially on weekends. Prices vary because each room is different, but the ones at the upper end have hot tubs.

One of the capital's most historic lodgings, dating from 1929, Monserrat's four-star **Castelar Hotel & Spa** (Avenida de Mayo 1152, tel. 011/4383-5000, fax 011/4383-8388, reservas@castelarhotel.com.ar, www.castelarhotel .com.ar, US$50–57 s or d) has hosted the likes of Spanish dramatist Federico García Lorca (who lived six months in room 704), Chilean Nobel Prize–winning poet Pablo Neruda, Nobel Prize–winning scientist Linus Pauling, and many Argentine politicians. Embellished with Carrara marble, it offers comfortable, well-equipped rooms with breakfast and access to its own spa. There are entire nonsmoking floors.

Towering above everything else in its Palermo neighborhood, the **Torre Cristóforo Colombo** (Santa María de Oro 2747, tel. 011/4777-9622, fax 011/4775-9911, reservas@torrecc.com.ar, www.torrecc.com.ar, US$45–63 s or d) contains 160 fully equipped suites with kitchenettes and patios, accommodating two to four persons. Rates include breakfast and IVA; there are also "diplomatic" suites in the US$95 range.

Devaluation has made Monserrat's four-star **Hotel Nogaró** (Diagonal Presidente Julio A. Roca 562, tel. 011/4331-0091, fax 011/4331-6791, reservas@nogarobue.com.ar, www.nogarobue.com.ar, US$60 s or d) a bargain with buffet breakfast included. Dating from 1930 but renovated a few years ago, this French-style, 150-room hotel offers in-room safes and Internet connections.

Recoleta's **Hotel Plaza Francia** (Eduardo Schiaffino 2189, tel./fax 011/4804-9631, contact @hotelplazafrancia.com, www.hotelplazafrancia.com, US$65 s or d) is a boutique-style hotel close to Recoleta cemetery, restaurants and entertainment, and open spaces, but also near downtown. Rates include buffet breakfast, Internet connections, a/c, and many other conveniences—thanks to devaluation.

Congreso's prime upscale option, now part of the Dutch Golden Tulip chain, is the **Savoy Hotel** (Avenida Callao 181, tel. 011/4370-8000, fax 011/4372-7006, info@hotel-savoy.com.ar, www.gtsavoyhotel.com.ar, US$72 s or d). For stays longer than two weeks, there's a 10 percent discount. All windows are double-paned for silence; rates include phones (with voice mail), computer connections and other business amenities, and a buffet breakfast.

In a painstakingly remodeled 19th-century *casa chorizo,* **Malabia House** (Malabia 1555, tel./fax 011/4832-3345 or 011/4833-2410, info@malabiahouse.com.ar, www.malabiahouse.com.ar, US$50–60 s, US$70–90 d) is a more stylish bed-and-breakfast with magnificent natural light, glistening wood floors, handsome furnishings, and small but attractive patio gardens. Standard ground-floor rooms, with breakfast, have external private baths; the slightly more expensive upstairs rooms have a/c and interior baths. There's a 10 percent discount for cash payment.

Just south of the Plaza de Mayo, the **NH City Hotel** Bolívar 160, tel. 011/4121-6464, fax 011/4121-6450, info@nh-city.com.ar, www.nh-hoteles.com, US$97 s or d) is a spectacularly modernized 300-room building (dating from 1931) that had the misfortune to reopen at the nadir of Argentina's economic meltdown of 2001–02. The bad timing, though, has meant good rates for beautifully appointed rooms with all modern conveniences, plus luxuries like a rooftop pool, gym, and sauna, and a first-rate Spanish restaurant.

Barrio Norte's bright, modern **Design Suites** (Marcelo T. de Alvear 1683, tel./fax 011/4814-8700, design@designsuites.com, www.designsuites.com, US$96–144 s or d) is a new boutique-style hotel with a heated pool, gym, restaurant room service, and daily newspaper delivery (of the guest's choice). Each of its 40 suites has cable TV, telephone, Internet and fax connections, kitchenette, minibar, a/c, strongbox, and hot tub.

US$100–150

On the edge of fashionable Recoleta, the 54-room **Hotel Park Plaza Kempinski** (Parera 183, tel. 011/6777-0200, reservas@parkplazahotels.com, www.parkplazahotels.com, US$139 s or d) is a boutique-style hotel.

Part of the highly regarded Spanish luxury business chain, **Hotel NH Jousten** (Avenida Corrientes 240, tel. 011/4321-6750, fax 011/4321-6775, info@nh-jousten.com.ar, www.nh-hoteles.com, US$145 s or d) has 85 rooms in an elegant, tastefully recycled French-style castle. Quiet despite the busy avenue, thanks to double-paned windows, each room has cable TV, stereo, telephone, a/c, and Internet connection. Rates also include a buffet breakfast; its highly regarded basement restaurant serves Spanish cuisine.

In a classic Parisian-styled edifice near Plaza San Martín, Retiro's **Crillón Hotel** (Avenida Santa Fe 796, tel. 011/4310-2000, fax 011/4312-9955, info@hotelcrillon.com.ar, www.hotelcrillon.com.ar, US$90/110–130/150 s/d) enjoys all contemporary comforts including a/c, cable TV, telephone, wireless Internet access, voicemail, and even a cell phone, plus a buffet breakfast. These rates, which are 50 percent higher than Argentines pay, do *not* include the 21 percent IVA.

US$150–200

Retiro's **Meliá Buenos Aires Boutique Hotel**

(Reconquista 945, tel. 011/4891-3800, fax 011/4891-3834, buenosaires@meliaboutique .com.ar, www.solmelia.com, US$190 d) has 125 rooms, including 18 suites, in a modernistic hotel with luminous rooms, a gym and business center, and entire nonsmoking floors. Rates include a sumptuous buffet breakfast but not IVA; there are discounts from mid-December through February.

Near Puerto Madero, across from the Plaza Fuerza Aérea Argentina, the massive 742-room high-rise **Sheraton Buenos Aires Hotel** (San Martín 1225, tel. 011/4318-9000, fax 011/4318-9346, sheraton@sheraton.com.ar, www.starwood.com/redir/sheraton/buenosaires, US$194–224 s or d) gets lots of the international business trade.

Now under international-chain control, the landmark (1909) **⚄ Marriott Plaza Hotel** (Florida 1005, tel. 011/4318-3000, fax 011/4318-3008, marriott.plaza@ba.net, www.marriott .com, US$195–235 s or d) has undergone a significant modernization without losing its German Baroque charm.

Over US$200

Near the Obelisco, the **Hotel Crowne Plaza Panamericano** (Carlos Pellegrini 525, tel. 011/4348-5000, fax 011/4348-5251, hotel @crowneplaza.com.ar, www.crowneplaza.com.ar, US$260–315 d) consists of an older south tower and a newer north tower. Both are comfortable but the more expensive north-tower rooms are technologically superior. Its restaurant *Tomo I* is widely acknowledged as one of the capital's best.

Monserrat's **Hotel Intercontinental** (Moreno 809, tel. 011/4340-7100, fax 011/4340-7199, buenosaires@interconti.com, www.interconti .com.ar, US$303 s or d) consistently makes BA's best-hotels lists in magazines like *Travel & Leisure*. More than half the 305 rooms are nonsmoking. Corporate and other discount rates are possible.

The **Loi Suites Recoleta** (Vicente López 1955, tel. 011/5777-8950, fax 011/5777-8999, recoleta@loisuites.com.ar, www.loisuites.com.ar, US$200–345 s or d plus IVA) is the toniest link of a stylish new four-hotel chain. With some of

BA's most innovative design, it makes magnificent use of natural light.

Popular with international entertainment figures, Retiro's contemporary **Caesar Park Hotel** (Posadas 1232, tel. 011/4819-1100, fax 011/4819-1165, hotel@caesar.com.ar, www.caesarpark.com, US$280 s or d plus IVA) now belongs to a Mexican luxury hotel chain. Rates include an extravagant breakfast buffet.

Since 1928, the **⚄ Alvear Palace Hotel** (Avenida Alvear 1891, tel. 011/4805-2100, fax 011/4804-9246, info@alvearpalace.com, www.alvearpalace .com, US$410 s or d up plus IVA) has symbolized elegance and luxury—not to mention wealth and privilege. This is one place that, despite devaluation, maintains both its standards and its prices—ranging up to US$3,000 for the royal suite—for accommodations with Egyptian-cotton sheets and Hermés toiletries, but even here discounts are possible. Francophobes may find the *ancien régime* decor cloying, but *Travel & Leisure* readers (in 2002) have called it the world's 18th-best hotel and Latin America's second-best, and it also made the Condé Nast Gold List as one of world's finest.

FOOD

Almost everything in BA is affordable at present, at quality ranging from good to world-class, but some places are more affordable than others. The listings below are arranged geographically.

Monserrat/Catedral al Sur and Vicinity

In the barrio of San Cristóbal, near Monserrat's western edge, **Miramar** (Avenida San Juan 1999, tel. 011/4304-4261) is both a reliable *rotisería* and an unfashionable restaurant unsuitable for a formal meal or romantic night out but great for unpretentious lunches or dinners, with quietly professional service. Unlike many recently gentrified—or plasticized—*porteño* cafés, this classic corner bar sports fading posters from classic Argentine movies, thumbtacked to the walls, as a backdrop for tasty entrees like oxtail soup and *gambas al ajillo* (garlic prawns). Prices range US$2.50–5.50 for most items.

Penélope (Avenida Independencia 1702, tel. 011/4381-6715) is a fine Catalán restaurant; for US$16, the diverse fish and seafood *parrillada* easily fills two diners, but also try the lightly breaded *rabas* (large squid) as an appetizer. The staff is professional, the service attentive, and the wine selection ample and reasonably priced.

According to *Buenos Aires Herald* restaurant critic Dereck Foster, BA's best Spanish food comes from the so-new-that-it's-still-nameless restaurant at the **NH City Hotel** (Bolívar 160, tel. 011/4121-6464). Monserrat has several other Spanish/Basque seafood options, though, including my personal favorite **Ñ Laurak Bat** (Avenida Belgrano 1144, tel. 011/4381-0682), a traditional classic.

Microcentro and Vicinity

One of BA's most economical choices is the surprisingly good cafetería at the supermarket **Coto** (Viamonte 1571).

Ñ Pizzería Guerrín (Avenida Corrientes 1372, tel. 011/4371-8141) is a one-of-a-kind that sells by the slice at the standup counter—the *fugazza* (and *fugazzeta*) are exquisitely simple and simply exquisite. There are many more options if you choose table service. **La Americana** (Avenida Callao 83, tel. 011/4371-0202) is a venerable chain pizzería with outstanding empanadas.

Another classic is **Los Inmortales** (Avenida Corrientes 1369, tel. 011/4373-5303), a pizzería seemingly unchanged since the days of Carlos Gardel, whose photographs line the walls.

Open for lunch and dinner, **Broccolino** (Esmeralda 776, tel. 011/4322-9848) is an unfailingly reliable Italian choice, with impeccable service (all the waiters speak at least two languages) and a menu ranging from pizza and pasta to seafood and beef dishes. Entrees range US$3.50–6, but most are in the US$4–5 range. It's open for lunch and dinner.

For a 19th-century experience with contemporary flourishes, try the **Club del Progreso** (Sarmiento 1334, tel. 011/4371-5053, www .clubdelprogreso.com). For about US$5 pp, the fixed-price dinners are a little bland, but the singing waiters alone, with their tangos and boleros, are worth the price. With its high ceilings, classic library, and other features, it served as a location for the film *Imagining Argentina,* with Antonio Banderas and Emma Thompson.

The Microcentro and nearby neighborhoods have several tourist-oriented *parrillas* that make a fetish out of staking their steaks over hot coals in circular barbecue pits, tended by bogus gauchos in full regalia, behind picture windows; while they play for the cliché and serve far too many people for individual attention, their quality is outstanding and their prices reasonable. Among the best choices are **La Estancia** (Lavalle 941, tel. 011/4326-0330) and **La Rural** (Suipacha 453, tel. 011/4322-2654).

For a more characteristic *porteño* experience, though, try one of the cheaper bare-bones *parrillas* like Congreso's **Pippo** (Paraná 356, tel. 4374-0762) or **Chiquilín** (Montevideo 321, tel. 4373-5163). For an antidote, try the vegetarian **La Huerta del Sol** (Lavalle 893, tel. 4327-2862).

Possibly downtown's best restaurant, the banker's favorite **Ñ Sabot** (25 de Mayo 756, tel. 011/4313-6587) serves Italo-Argentine dishes of the highest quality in a very masculine environment—women are few but not unwelcome—with good-humored but extraordinarily professional service. Moderately expensive by current standards, most entrees like *matambre de cerdo* and *chivito,* plus some fish dishes, cost in the US$5–7 range. A pleasant surprise is the *mate de coca* from fresh coca leaves (for digestive purposes only).

Puerto Madero

Over the past few years, redeveloped Puerto Madero has made a big impact on the restaurant scene, but more because of the area's overall tourist appeal than its quality—with a couple of exceptions, the food is unimpressive. Most restaurants, though, have outdoor seating along the yacht harbor, and when the weather's fine it's a great option for people-watching. Because the area is popular with foreigners from nearby luxury hotels, restaurants here are accustomed to dealing with dinnertimes as early as 7 P.M.

Opposite Dique No. 4, the best *parrilla* is 🔟 **Cabaña Las Lilas** (Alicia Moreau de Justo 516, tel. 011/4313-1336). Often packed for lunch despite high prices, it offers complimentary champagne and snacks while you wait; its *bife de chorizo* (US$7) may be the finest in town. Next door, **La Caballeriza** (Alicia Moreau de Justo 580, tel. 011/4314-2648) is also highly regarded for grilled beef. **Puerto Sorrento** (Alicia Moreau de Justo 410, tel. 011/4319-8730) is the area's best seafood choice.

San Telmo and Vicinity

Despite the barrio's tourist allure, San Telmo's gastronomy lags behind that of other barrios. For the most part, restaurants here are better lunchtime bargains than dinnertime indulgences. **Pueblo Indio** (Defensa 702, tel. 011/4361-6365) is a hybrid sandwich shop/furniture store that sells the handmade items that you sit on and eat off.

Medio y Medio (Chile 316, tel. 011/4300-1396) bursts with lunchgoers seeking the Uruguayan caloric overload *chivito,* a steak sandwich piled high with lettuce, cheese, tomato, and bacon; a fried egg crowns the *chivito al plato,* which includes a slab of beef plus potato salad, green salad, and fries.

Sunday visitors to the Plaza Dorrego flea market queue outside **DesNivel** (Defensa 855, tel. 011/4300-9081) for *parrillada* and pasta at bargain prices; it's open for lunch (except Mondays) and dinner daily. Opposite Parque Lezama, 🔟 **1880** (Defensa 1665, tel. 011/4307-2746) is a traditional San Telmo *parrilla* with plenty of barrio atmosphere, including *filete* ornaments by Martiniano Arce. Most entrees fall in the US$3–4 range, including pasta dishes like *ñoquis.*

Abril (Balcarce 722, tel. 011/4342-8000) is an attractive bistro whose US$4 fixed-price dinners are more diverse and lighter than the average Argentine meal. In a late 18th-century house, Plaza Dorrego's **Pappa Deus** (Bethlem 423, tel. 011/4361-2110) is more imaginative than most San Telmo eateries, serving items like arugula and sun-dried tomatoes, plus a tremendous pumpkin-stuffed ravioli, but pricey desserts. Entrees cost around US$3–4.

Hostal del Canigó (Chacabuco 863, tel. 011/4304-5250) specializes in Catalonian seafood, other Spanish dishes, and the occasional standard Argentine item. Best at lunch, it occupies the classic dining room—dark mahogany woodwork and Spanish tiles—of the Casal de Catalunya cultural center.

La Boca

La Boca is not an enclave of haute cuisine, but there's good enough food for lunch—most people visit the barrio during the daytime—and even an occasional dinnertime foray.

With sidewalk seating on the Vuelta de Rocha, adorned with colorful *filete,* **La Barbería** (Pedro de Mendoza 1959, tel. 011/4301-8770) serves empanadas, tapas, pasta, pizza, sandwiches, seafood, and beer and cold hard cider straight from the tap. Prices are moderate, in the US$3–7 range. Next door, **El Corsario** (Pedro de Mendoza 1981, tel. 011/4301-6579) is almost interchangeable.

In an area where taxis are obligatory at night and maybe advisable even in the daytime (though some cabbies have trouble finding it), 🔟 **El Obrero** (Agustín Cafferena 64, tel. 011/4362-9912) is where Argentine and foreign celebrities go slumming for steaks. Its walls plastered with images of soccer icon Diego Maradona and little else, it draws an international clientele on the order of Bono and Robert Duvall, and hasn't even taken down the photo of disgraced ex-president Fernando de la Rúa. There's no printed menu—check the chalkboards scattered around the dining room. No entrée exceeds about US$5.

Retiro

The hippest and most adventurous pizzeria is the garishly decorated **Filo** (San Martín 975, tel. 011/4311-0312). Tourist-oriented *parrillas* include the excellent **Las Nazarenas** (Reconquista 1132, tel. 011/4312-5559) and **La Chacra** (Avenida Córdoba 941, tel. 011/4322-1409).

For contrast, Retiro also has the vegetarian institution 🔟 **La Esquina de las Flores** (Avenida Córdoba 1587, tel. 011/4813-3630), a health-food market and upstairs restaurant that also

COOLING DOWN WITH HELADOS

Buenos Aires has two kinds of *heladerías* (ice creameries). The first are chains that produce large industrial batches; some of these are still very fine, while others are truly awful and most fall in between. The other is the small neighborhood ice creamery that creates *helados artesanales* in smaller quantities.

Gradually overshadowing the fading Freddo, **Chungo** (tel. 0800/888-248646, www.chungo.com.ar) is probably the best industrial-quality ice cream, and is good enough by any standard; the most-convenient branches are in Recoleta (Avenida Las Heras and Rodríguez Peña) and Palermo (Olleros 1660). **Bianca** (Avenida Scalabrini Ortiz 2295, tel. 011/4832-3357) is the Palermo locale of a midsized chain with a wide selection of flavors. Founded by Freddo's former owners, the always-crowded **Persicco** (Salguero 2591, Palermo, tel. 011/4801-5549) is challenging the other chains.

Over the past couple of decades, **Cadore** (Avenida Corrientes 1695, Congreso) has consistently been one of the best ice creameries, but its small storefront (often obscured by construction) gives it a low profile. Across from Parque Lezama, **Florencia** (Brasil and Defensa, tel. 011/4307-6407) is San Telmo's best (and one of the cheapest). Palermo Viejo's **Tempo** (J.L. Borges 2392, tel. 011/4775-2392) features uncommon fruit flavors like mango and *maracuyá* (passion fruit). In Belgrano, try the hole-in-the-wall **Gruta** (Sucre 2356, tel. 011/4784-8417).

works at diversifying the Argentine diet through public workshops and radio and TV programs.

Tancat (Paraguay 645, tel. 011/4312-5442) is a first-rate and wildly popular Spanish *tasca*, with lunches around US$3–5 pp; don't miss the *jamón serrano* (serrano ham) appetizer. Reservations are almost essential for tables, which are few, but plenty of people can jam into the long wooden bar, behind which are shelves of wine covered with business cards, posters, and photos.

Highly regarded **Tres Cuartos** (Florida 947, tel. 011/4314-4045) offers variations on standard Argentine dishes like ravioli (stuffed with hake, for instance), with a midday menu for about US$4. Unfortunately, though they ceremoniously ask whether you prefer smoking or nonsmoking, enforcement is nil and smokers light up wherever they feel like it.

Recoleta and Barrio Norte

For spicy northwestern dishes like *locro*, one of BA's best values is **El Sanjuanino** (Posadas 1515, tel. 011/4804-2909); the empanadas are particularly choice.

José Luis (Avenida Quintana 456, tel. 011/4807-0606) is an Asturian seafood restaurant that stresses fresher and lighter dishes

than most of its counterparts. Entrees are mostly in the US$7 range; it's open daily for lunch and dinner.

The Barrio Norte favorite **Los Pinos** (Azcuénaga 1500, tel. 011/4822-8704) occupies an old-style apothecary, its wooden cases still stocked with antique bottles and rising nearly to the ceiling. Fixed lunch and dinner specials, with substantial choice, fall into the US$3–5 range; the à la carte menu of beef, seafood, and pasta is not much more expensive, as the comparably priced entrees include a side order. Service is well-intentioned but inconsistent.

The **French Bistro** (French 2301, tel. 011/4806-9331) serves a Gallic international menu in European-style surroundings. Charging around US$6 pp, the Middle Eastern buffet at the **Restaurant del Club Sirio** (Pacheco de Melo 1902, tel. 011/4806-5764) is open nightly except Sunday.

Internationally recognized **Oviedo** (Beruti 2602, tel. 011/4822-5415) specializes in seafood but also serves Patagonian lamb and standards like beef, with most entrees in the US$5–8 range. Open for lunch and dinner, it has the unfortunate notion that its air-purification system justifies its being a cigar bar as well.

Palermo

Palermo is, without question, the center of innovation in Argentine dining, mostly in Palermo Soho but also in Palermo Hollywood, the Botánico, and Las Cañitas.

Near the Botánico, **Big Mamma** (Cabello 3760, tel. 011/4806-6822) is a small deli chain with large, good sandwiches.

Down the block, **La Lasagnería** (Cabello 3621, tel. 011/4805-0050) serves exceptional fast-food versions of Italian specialties. Among the Botánico's best, M **Bella Italia Café Bar** (Repúblic Arabe Siria 3330, tel. 011/4807-5120) is the moderately priced café version of the nearby restaurant of the same name. For around US$3.50, it has outstanding squash gnocchi with a subtle cream sauce, along with fine canelloni and salads.

Café Martínez (Scalabrini Ortiz 3195, tel. 011/4804-6804) has a wide selection of gourmet coffees, served indoors and at sidewalk tables, but they're also available fresh-ground in bulk. The croissants, juices, and the like also make it a good breakfast spot.

Mark's Deli & Coffee House (El Salvador 4701, tel. 011/4832-6244) is a United States–style deli, bright and cheerful with indoor and patio seating, and outstanding sandwiches for about US$4; there's a small selection of wines by the glass, and large and tasty glasses of lemonade. Hours are 8:30 A.M.–9:30 P.M. daily except Sunday, when it's open 10 A.M.–7 P.M. only.

For quality-to-price ratio, the hands-down best choice for empanadas and regional dishes is M **La Cupertina** (Cabrera 5300, tel. 011/4777-3711). The service may be inconsistent, but the chicken empanadas and *humitas en chala* (similar to tamales, wrapped in corn stalks) are exquisite and so cheap that price is no object, even with wine; there are also individually sized pizzas. Don't miss the desserts, especially the Spanish custard *natillas* and *arroz con leche*. It keeps limited hours: 11:30 A.M.–3:30 P.M. daily except Monday and 7:30–11 P.M. daily except Sunday and Monday; it's also small, seating only about 20 diners in simple but attractive surroundings.

Near Plaza Serrano, **Spirit** (Serrano 1550, tel. 011/4833-4360) is a tapas-and-oyster bar that serves an ample plate of seafood tapas, sufficient for two persons, for only US$10. Around the corner, with minimalist modern decor, M **Splendid** (Gorriti 5099, tel. 011/4833-4477) prepares perfectly cooked penne with fresh mushrooms, and a fine *maracuyá* (passion fruit) ice cream with raspberry sauce. Open daily for lunch and dinner, it has first-class service and live jazz Thursday and Saturday around 10 P.M.

Across the street, **Rave** (Gorriti 5092, tel. 011/4833-7832) opens at 8:30 P.M. nightly, but it's not unusual to find its split levels packed with 2 A.M. diners. Good choices include *mollejitas* (sweetbreads) for US$4, and chicken/mushroom risotto for US$5. It can get loud, but not deafening.

Social Paraíso (Honduras 5182, tel. 011/4831-4556) is an intimate nouvelle-cuisine place with a US$3.50 lunch special featuring items like bruschetta and risotto; other entrees fall into the US$4.50–6 range. Open for lunch and dinner daily except Sunday and Monday, it also has innovative desserts.

M **El Federal** (Honduras 5254, tel. 011/4832-6500) draws an upper-class clientele to high-priced versions of regional specialties from throughout the country: potatoes and quinoa from Jujuy, *cabrito* (goat) from the western Cuyo provinces, *jabalí* (wild boar) from Bariloche, and Patagonian lamb. Open for lunch and dinner, its entrees fall in the US$6–7 range.

Known for live music in its intimate theater-club, the M **Club del Vino** (Cabrera 4737, tel. 011/4833-8330) is also a fine restaurant with, as its name suggests, an exceptional selection of wines—not to mention an effectively segregated tobacco-free area. The diverse choice of entrees includes the usual beef dishes (US$3–4), but also rabbit stew, conger eel with tomato and basil, chicken breast in orange sauce, and stuffed trout with almonds, all in the US$4–7 range.

Across Avenida Scalabrini Ortiz, the flamboyant **Te Mataré Ramírez** (Paraguay 4062, tel. 011/4831-9156, www.tematareramirez.com) is a self-styled "aphrodisiac restaurant" notorious for suggestive food and decor. Diners are often slow to order as they ogle the salacious menu of entrees (around US$5–7) like *pecado carnal* ("mortal sin," beef in cabernet sauce); *grité tanto de dolor como de placer* ("I screamed as much from pain as from pleasure," flounder in blue cheese sauce); and *paseaba mi rostro por su pecho* ("my mouth brushed your breast," pork loin in sweet-and-sour sauce). Desserts include *anestesiada por el placer* ("anesthetized by pleasure," a cashew semi-freddo), and *un beso ilícito y a oscuras* ("illicit kiss in the dark," a semisweet chocolate dessert). Open only for dinner daily except Monday, its major drawback is poor air quality—go on weeknights or early before the smokers monopolize the relatively small dining room.

Run by a pair of documentary filmmakers, appropriately set in Palermo Hollywood, **Tiempo de Gitanos** (El Salvador 5575, tel. 011/4776-6143) is a bar/restaurant serving an eclectic mix of Spanish and Middle Eastern dishes. Decorated with souvenirs of the owners' extensive travels, it's open from 5 P.M. daily except Monday and Tuesday. There is live music, mostly jazz, on some nights.

Las Cañitas has acquired a reputation for fashionability, but one of its landmark restaurants is the venerable **M El Portugués** (Báez 499, tel. 011/4771-8699), whose half-portion of *bife de chorizo* some might consider a double—consider sharing and then order more if you're still hungry.

M Lotus Neo Thai (Ortega y Gasset 1782, tel. 011/4771-4449) was the pioneer of Thai food in Argentina and one of few places in the country where it's possible to taste truly spicy dishes. Open for dinner only, the quiet upstairs locale with soothing music and imaginative lotus-themed décor is relatively expensive at US$5–9 for entrees, even after the steep devaluation.

Belgrano

Though Belgrano has many decent restaurants—the city's Chinatown is here—it's most notable for BA's best Peruvian restaurant. In a cul-de-sac near the railroad tracks, **M Contigo Perú** (Echeverría 1627, tel. 011/4780-3960) has grown from humble beginnings to become a neighborhood success whose ambience approaches the quality of the food. Prices are moderate, even cheap. Hours are 10 A.M.–midnight daily except Monday. The upside is the attentive service; the downside is

dueling TVs—though one could argue that this is authentically Peruvian.

INFORMATION

The **Secretaría Nacional de Turismo** (Avenida Santa Fe 883, Retiro, tel. 011/4312-2232 or 0800/555-0016, www.turismo.gov.ar) is open 9 A.M.–5 P.M. weekdays only; there's a branch at Aeropuerto Internacional Ezeiza (tel. 011/4480-0292) and another at Aeroparque Jorge Newbery (tel. 011/4771-0104). Both airport branches are open 8 A.M.–8 P.M. daily.

The municipal **Subsecretaría de Turismo** (www.bue.gov.ar) maintains several information kiosks: in the Microcentro (Florida and Diagonal Roque Sáenz Peña, 10 A.M.–6 P.M. daily except Sunday); at Puerto Madero's Dique 4 (tel. 011/4313-0187, noon–6 P.M. weekdays, 10 A.M.–8 P.M. weekends); and at the Retiro bus terminal (tel. 011/4311-0528, daily 7:30 A.M.– 1 P.M. daily except Sunday). All distribute maps and brochures, and usually have English-speaking staff.

SERVICES

Banking

Most visitors find the ubiquitous ATMs most convenient for changing money. In the La City financial district, the numerous *casas de cambio* along San Martín between Corrientes and the Plaza de Mayo usually offer the best exchange rates for U.S. cash, Euros, and travelers checks. For travelers checks, they normally charge a commission or pay a lower rate than for cash, but **American Express** (Arenales 707, Retiro, tel. 011/4310-3000) cashes its own checks for no commission.

Postal Services

The **Correo Central** (Sarmiento 151, 8 A.M.–8 P.M. weekdays, 10 A.M.–1 P.M. Sat.) is a landmark building that's worth a visit in its own right; there are many other branch post offices. International parcels in excess of one kilogram must go from the **Correo Internacional** (Antártida Argentina near the Retiro train station, tel. 011/4316-7777, 11 A.M.–5 P.M. weekdays only).

Federal Express (Maipú 753, tel. 011/4393-6054) offers private courier service.

Communications

Locutorios for long-distance and fax services are so plentiful that it's hardly worthwhile to mention any in particular. Many of these have Internet connections, but there are also locales devoted exclusively to Internet service.

Travel Agencies

North of Plaza San Martín, Retiro's **American Express** (Arenales 707, tel. 011/4310-3535, fax 011/4315-1846, amexbueemp@aexp.com) offers the usual services.

Swan Turismo (Cerrito 822, 9th floor, Retiro, tel./fax 011/4129-7926, swanturismo @teletel.com.ar) is a full-service agency that's earned a reputation for willingness and ability to deal with some of the Argentine travel system's eccentricities.

In the Galería Buenos Aires, affiliated with STA Travel, the nonprofit **Asatej** (Florida 835, 3rd floor, Retiro, tel. 011/4311-6953, fax 011/4311-6840, asatej@asatej.com.ar, www.asatej .com.ar) is transforming its focus to incoming tourism as the Argentine economic crisis has reduced overseas travel by young Argentines. Also an affiliate of Hostelling International, it's good at searching out the best airfares for anyone, not just students.

Libraries

The **Biblioteca Nacional** (National Library, Agüero 2502, Recoleta, tel. 011/4808-6000, www.bibnal.edu.ar) is open 9 A.M.–8 P.M. weekdays, noon–6 P.M. weekends. It holds frequent special exhibitions, lectures and literary events, and free concerts.

The U.S. Information Agency's **Biblioteca Lincoln,** at the Instituto Cultural Argentino-Norteamericano (Maipú 672, Microcentro, tel. 011/4322-3855 or 011/4322-4557) has English-language books, magazines, and newspapers.

Photography

Photo labs are abundant, but for slide film try a specialist like **Kinefot** (Talcahuano 250, tel.

011/4374-7445) or **Color Shot** (Corrientes 1550).

In the basement of Retiro's Galería Buenos Aires, **Gerardo Föhse** (Florida 835, Local 37, tel. 011/4311-1139) can do basic camera repair. Quick, reliable **José Norres** (Lavalle 1569, Oficina 403, tel. 011/4373-0963) can do more-complex jobs except on some of the latest electronic equipment.

Language Study

Buenos Aires has a growing number of language schools at competitive prices, starting with the Universidad de Buenos Aires's **Centro Universitario de Idiomas** (Junín 508, 3rd floor, Balvanera, tel. 011/4372-9674, internacional@cui .com.ar, www.cui.com.ar). Others include the **Centro de Estudio del Español** (Reconquista 715, 11th floor, tel./fax 011/4315-1156, 011/ 4312-1016, spanish@cedic.com.ar, www.cedic .com.ar); **Coined** (Perú 247, 3° E, Monserrat, tel. 011/4342-8556, info@coined.com.ar, www .coined.com.ar); the **Instituto de Lengua Española para Extranjeros** (ILEE, Avenida Callao 339, 3rd floor, tel./fax 011/4782-7173, info@argentinailee.com, www.argentinailee.com); and **Tradfax** (Avenida Callao 194, 2nd floor, Balvanera, tel. 011/4371-0697, fax 011/4373-5581, tradfaxcultural@hotmail.com, www.tradfax.com).

For individual private tutoring, contact English-speaking **Dori Lieberman** (tel./fax 011/ 4361-4843, dori@sinectis.com.ar).

Immigration

Dirección Nacional de Migraciones (Avenida Argentina 1355, Retiro, tel. 011/4317-0237) is open 8 A.M.–1 P.M. weekdays only.

Medical

Public hospitals include Recoleta's **Hospital Rivadavia** (Avenida Las Heras 2670, Recoleta, tel. 011/4809-2002) and Palermo's **Hospital Municipal Juan Fernández** (Cerviño 3356, tel. 011/4808-2600). Public hospitals, however, are under severe personnel and budget constraints in dealing with their Argentine patients; if possible, consider a private hospital or clinic.

The **Hospital Británico** (Perdriel 74, Barracas,

tel. 011/4304-1082) is a highly regarded private hospital. One of the city's best private clinics is Belgrano's **Clínica Fleni** (Montañeses 2325, tel. 011/5777-3200, www.fleni.org.ar), where Argentine presidents have had arthroscopies and soccer star Diego Maradona went for detox, but it does not serve every specialty.

GETTING THERE

Buenos Aires is the main port of entry for overseas visitors, and the hub for domestic travel within the country.

By Air

Most international flights arrive and depart from the suburban airport at Ezeiza, though a handful from neighboring countries use close-in Aeroparque.

Aerolíneas Argentinas has domestic as well as international flights. Their domestic arm, **Austral** (Perú 2, Monserrat, tel. 011/4320-2345), flies to destinations ranging from Puerto Iguazú on the Brazilian border to Ushuaia in Tierra del Fuego.

American Falcon (Avenida Santa Fe 963, Retiro, tel. 011/4328-5541, www.americanfalcon.com.ar) flies from Ezeiza to Montevideo, Uruguay; and from Aeroparque to Paraná, Salta, Tucumán, Puerto Iguazú, Puerto Madryn, and Bariloche. Other foreign capitals, including Santiago de Chile and Asunción, Paraguay, are in the works.

From Aeroparque, **Southern Winds** (Avenida Santa Fe 784, Retiro, tel. 011/4515-8600, www.sw.com.ar) flies to Puerto Iguazú, Tucumán, Salta, Córdoba, Mendoza, Mar del Plata, Neuquén, Bariloche, and Río Gallegos. Ushuaia and Santiago de Chile are on the agenda.

Líneas Aéreas del Estado (LADE, Perú 714, San Telmo, tel. 011/4361-7071, www.lade.com.ar) is the Argentine air force's heavily subsidized commercial aviation branch. Miraculously surviving budget crises and privatizations, it flies to southern Buenos Aires Province and Patagonia on a wing and a prayer.

Aerovip (Cerrito 1318, tel. 011/4813-9686) flies 19-seater air taxis from Aeroparque to Tandil,

Mar del Plata, Rosario, Santa Fe, and Paraná; it also hops the River Plate to the Uruguayan capital of Montevideo and the resort of Punta del Este.

By Bus

Buenos Aires's main bus station is Retiro's **Estación Terminal de Ómnibus** (Avenida Ramos Mejía 1860, tel. 011/4310-0700, www.tebasa.com.ar). The sprawling three-story building is home to nearly 140 separate bus companies that cover the entire country, and international destinations as well. It's walking distance from the northern terminus of Subte Línea C, at the Retiro train station.

The ground floor is primarily for freight; passengers leave from the first-floor *andénes* (platforms). Companies operate out of more than 200 *ventanillas* (ticket windows) on the second floor, roughly arranged according to geographical regions: Zona Sur (South, windows 1–21, 23, 25, 27–30, 32–34, 101); Cuyo (windows 31, 33, 35–43, 45, 47), Zona Noroeste (Northwest, 44, 46–59, 148); Centro (Center, 59–94, 103, 105); Zona Noreste (Northwest, 95–101, 105, 107, 109, 111, 13–153); Costa Atlántica (Atlantic Coast, 152, 154–178); Internacional (International, 179–206).

On the departure level, the Centro de Informes y Reclamos (tel. 011/4310-0700) provides general bus information and also oversees taxis; direct any complaint about drivers to them. There is also a separate tourist office, open 7:30 A.M.–1 P.M. only.

For long-distance and international buses, reservations are a good idea, especially during the summer (Jan.–Feb.) and winter (late July) holiday periods, but also on long weekends like Semana Santa (Holy Week).

Several carriers take the roundabout 600-kilometer overland route to Montevideo, Uruguay, which takes more time (eight hours) than the ferry but costs less (US$23): **Bus de la Carrera** (four nightly, tel. 011/4313-1700); **Cauvi** (once nightly, tel. 011/4314-6999); and **General Belgrano** (once nightly, tel. 011/4315-1226). All leave between 9:30 and 11:30 P.M.

To the Paraguayan capital of Asunción (US$23–43, 17 hours), the main carriers are

Nuestra Señora de la Asunción (tel. 011/4313-2349) and **Chevalier Paraguaya** (tel. 011/4313-2325). For Brazilian destinations such as Foz do Iguaçu (US$40, 18 hours), Porto Alegre (US$59, 20 hours), São Paulo (US$84, 40 hours), and Rio de Janeiro (US$95, 44 hours), try **Pluma** (tel. 011/4313-3893) or **Rápido Iguazú** (tel. 011/4315-6981).

For the trans-Andean crossing to Santiago, Chile (US$36–45, 20 hours), carriers include **Fénix Pullman Norte** (tel. 011/4313-0134) and **Transporte Automotores Cuyo** (TAC, tel. 011/4313-3627). For the Peruvian capital of Lima (via Chile, US$100, a 68-hour marathon), the choices are **El Rápido Internacional** (tel. 011/4315-0804) and **Ormeño Internacional** (tel. 011/4313-2259).

By Train

Railroads were once the pride of the Argentine transportation system, but most people now get around by bus. There is still long-distance train service to the southern beach resorts in and around Mar del Plata, to the northwestern city of Tucumán, and to the Mesopotamian city of Posadas.

From Constitución, **Ferrobaires** (tel. 011/4371-7045, int. 201) goes to Mar del Plata and, in summer, to Pinamar. One-way fares range from US$7 (in stiff-backed *clase única*) to US$10 (reclining Pullman seats). It also goes to Tandil, Bahía Blanca, and Necochea.

From Retiro, **NOA Ferrocarriles** (tel. 011/4312-9506) goes to Rosario (US$4, 5.5 hours) and Tucumán (24 hours) Monday and Friday at 9 P.M. Rates to Tucumán are US$13 *turista*, US$15 *primera*, US$18 Pullman, and US$22 in *camarote* sleepers. Tickets go fast because it's cheap; the office is open 9 A.M.–8 P.M. daily except Sunday.

From Estación Federico Lacroze, on the former Urquiza line, **Trenes Especiales Argentinos** (TEA, info@trenesdellitoral.com.ar) goes two or three times weekly to Posadas. The ticket office is open 9 A.M.–8 P.M. daily; rates to Posadas are US$13 *turista*, US$17 *primera*, US$22 Pullman, and US$35 in *camarote* sleepers.

By Boat

At Puerto Madero's Dársena Norte, **Buquebús**

(Avenida Antártida Argentina 821, tel. 011/4316-6405, www.buquebus.com) coordinates services and schedules with **Ferrylíneas,** whose slow ferry *Eladia Isabel* sails to Colonia (two hours, 45 minutes, US$17 pp tourist, US$23 pp first class) at 12:30 A.M. daily except Sunday, and at 9 A.M. daily; the faster hydrofoil *Atlantic III* (50 minutes, US$27 tourist; US$33 first class) sails at 11:30 A.M. and 7 P.M. daily. Buquebús also has a ticket outlet at Patio Bullrich (Avenida Libertador 750, Retiro).

For direct service to Montevideo (2.5 hours, US$52 tourist class; US$63 first class), the high-speed ferries *Juan Patricio* and *Patricia Oliva III* sail at 8 A.M. daily and 3:30 P.M. weekdays except Monday, and 6 P.M. weekdays only. There are also summer sailings to the port of Piriápolis, midway between Montevideo and the fashionable Atlantic beach resort of Punta del Este.

GETTING AROUND
Airports

Buenos Aires has two airports, both operated by the private concessionaire **Aeropuertos Argentinos 2000** (tel. 011/5480-6111, www.aa2000.com.ar). The main international facility is **Aeropuerto Internacional Ministro Pistarini,** 35 kilometers southwest of downtown, popularly called Ezeiza after its namesake Buenos Aires–Province suburb. The other is Palermo's **Aeroparque Jorge Newbery** (Avenida Costanera Rafael Obligado s/n), which is primarily domestic but handles a few international flights from neighboring countries.

International passengers leaving from Ezeiza pay a US$30.50 departure tax, payable in local currency or U.S. dollars; US$18 of this is normally collected on departure. On flights of less than 300 kilometers to neighboring countries, such as Uruguay, the tax is only US$6; on domestic flights from Aeroparque, it's about US$3. These latter fees are normally included in the price of the ticket.

There is a variety of options for getting to and from the airports, ranging from *colectivos* (city buses) to shuttles, taxis, and *remises* (meterless taxis that quote a fixed price for the trip).

City buses called *colectivos* provide the cheapest transportation to and from the airports, but they are more practical for close-in Aeroparque than distant Ezeiza, as they take circuitous routes on surface streets. To Aeroparque (about US$.35), the alternatives are No. 33 from Plaza de Mayo, the Microcentro, and Retiro; No. 37-C ("Ciudad Universitaria") from Plaza del Congreso, Avenida Callao, Avenida las Heras, and Plaza Italia; No. 45 northbound from Plaza Constitución, Plaza San Martín, or Retiro; and No. 160-C or 160-D from Avenida Las Heras or Plaza Italia. Return buses leave from the Avenida Costanera Rafael Obligado, a short walk outside the terminal.

To Ezeiza (about US$.50), the backpackers' choice is the No. 86-A ("Aeropuerto"), from La Boca to Plaza de Mayo, Plaza del Congreso, and onward, but the roundabout route takes up to two hours. *Servicio Diferencial* buses cost more (US$2) but have more-comfortable reclining seats. At Ezeiza, both leave from just outside the Aerolíneas Argentinas terminal, a short distance from the main international terminal.

Shuttle services are more expensive but more direct, leaving from offices near Plaza San Martín, in Retiro, and using the faster *autopista*. **Transfer Express** (Florida 1045, tel. 011/4314-1999 or 0800/555-0224) operates 20 shuttles daily to Ezeiza (US$4) between 6:30 A.M. and 8:45 P.M.; from Ezeiza, the first leaves at 7:15 A.M. It also has nine trips per day to and from Aeroparque (US$1.50), between 8:50 A.M. and 9:10 P.M.

Manuel Tienda León (Avenida Madero and San Martín, Retiro, tel. 011/4315-5115 or toll-free 0810/888-5366, www.tiendaleon.com.ar) runs 30 buses daily to and from Ezeiza (US$4.50) between 4 A.M. and 9:30 P.M. There are 25 buses daily to Aeroparque (US$1.50); buses from Ezeiza make connections to Aeroparque for domestic flights.

Taxis and *remises* offer door-to-door service and are no more expensive than shuttles for three or more persons. Manuel Tienda León and many other companies, such as **Naon Remises** (tel. 011/4545-6500) have *remises* to Aeroparque (US$3.50) and Ezeiza (US$11). Both *remises* and taxis usually tack on the cost of the toll road to Ezeiza (about US$1).

Colectivos (Buses)

More than 200 separate bus routes serve the Capital Federal and Gran Buenos Aires, but most visitors and even residents need to know relatively few of them. It's helpful, though, to have one of the annually updated city atlases, such as the *Guía Lumi* or *Guía T,* with detailed itineraries; abbreviated pocket versions are also available. Newsstand kiosks and bookstores normally sell these.

Route signs, at fixed stops, do not always indicate the bus's itinerary. In the absence of a written guide, ask someone. *Porteños* often know the system by heart and are generous with information. Fares depend on distance traveled, but within the capital most are US$.35 or less; on telling the driver your destination, he will enter the fare in the automatic ticket machine, which takes only coins but does give small change.

Trains

Buenos Aires has two commuter rail systems: the subway that serves the Capital Federal, and a series of surface commuter trains run by several private companies, connecting downtown with more distant suburbs.

Privatized in 1994 and popularly known as the Subte, the Buenos Aires **subway** opened in 1913 and is still the fastest way to get around the capital. South America's first underground railway, the 13th in the world, has modernized and expanded in recent years, but its antique cars, with their varnished but worn woodwork and elaborately tiled but chipped murals recall the prosperity and optimism of early-20th-century Argentina.

Metrovías, a private concessionaire (www.metrovias.com.ar), operates the five existing underground lines and is building a sixth transverse line from Retiro through Recoleta, Once and the southern part of the city. At present there are 67 stations for 39.5 kilometers of track within the capital; in 2001, the systems carried more than 241 million passengers.

Since taking over the system, Metrovías has also improved the rolling stock, extended existing lines, modernized many stations, and built new

RIDING THE SUBTE

Operated by the private concessionaire Metrovías, the state-owned Subterráneos de Buenos Aires comprises five alphabetically designated lines, four of which (A, B, D, and E) begin in Monserrat or the Microcentro and serve outlying northern and western barrios, with numerous stations in between. Línea C is a north-south connector line between major railway stations at Retiro and Constitución. An additional north-south connector line, Línea H, is under construction between Retiro and outlying southern barrios, beneath Avenida Pueyrredón and Avenida Jujuy.

Subte hours are 5 A.M. to about 11 P.M. except Sundays and holidays, when the system opens later (around 8 A.M.) and closes earlier (about 10:30 P.M.) and services are less frequent. Fares are about US$.35; to save time, purchase magnetic tickets in quantities of two, five, 10, or 30 rides. Two or more people may use the same ticket (legally) by passing it back and forth across the turnstile; you do not need a ticket to exit the system.

Before going through the turnstiles, make sure of the direction; at some stations, trains in both directions use the same platform, but at others the platforms are on opposite sides. A few stations have one-way traffic only, but the next station down the line normally is one-way in the other direction.

For complaints or problems, contact Metrovías's **Centro de Atención al Pasajero** (tel. 0800/555-1616 toll-free).

Subte Routes

Línea A begins at Plaza de Mayo, Monserrat, and runs beneath Avenida Rivadavia to Primera Junta, in the barrio of Chacarita. A westward extension to the edge of Buenos Aires Province is due to open by 2008.

Línea B begins at Avenida Leandro Alem, in the Microcentro, and runs beneath Avenida Corrientes and then northwesterly to Avenida los Incas, in Parque Chas, on an extension that is due to reach Villa Urquiza by 2007. At Federico Lacroze, the former terminus in the barrio of Chacarita, it connects with the suburban Ferrocarril Urquiza.

Línea C connects Retiro, which has commuter surface rail lines to northern suburbs, with Constitución, the transfer point for southern suburban commuter surface lines; Línea C also has transfer stations for all other Subte lines.

Línea D begins at Catedral, on Plaza de Mayo, and runs beneath Avenida Santa Fe and Avenida Cabildo through Palermo and Belgrano to Congreso de Tucumán, in the barrio of Núñez.

Línea E runs from Bolívar, on the Avenida de Mayo, to Plaza de los Virreyes, in the barrio of Flores. From Plaza de los Virreyes there's a light-rail extension known as the Premetro.

Under construction, **Línea H** is due to open in 2006; the economic crisis has slowed but not halted progress. The first stretch will begin at Inclán, in the southern barrio of Parque Patricios, and connect with Plaza Miserere (Once), on Línea A; it should eventually extend north to Recoleta and Retiro, and south to Nueva Pompeya.

ones. Electronic tickets have replaced the traditional Subte *fichas* (tokens) but, while this is perhaps more efficient than in the past, it also means lots of litter. Another negative development is the system of SUBTV monitors with nonstop advertising. Ventilation remains poor in many stations, though some of the newest cars are air-conditioned.

The most useful and best **suburban rail line** is the Ferrocarril Mitre, operated by **Trenes de Buenos Aires** (TBA, tel. 011/4317-4400 or 0800/333-3822, www.tbanet.com.ar), which connects the classic Estación Retiro (Avenida Ramos Mejía 1302) with Belgrano and Zona Norte suburbs including Vicente López, Olivos, Martínez, San Isidro, and Tigre.

TBA also operates the Ferrocarril Sarmiento from Estación Once (Avenida Pueyrredón y Bartolomé Mitre; Subte: Plaza Miserere), which goes to western destinations like Moreno, with connections to Luján. Unlike the immaculate Mitre, this is a run-down line.

Transportes Metropolitano (tel. 0800/666-358736) operates the Ferrocarril Roca from Estación Constitución (Avenida Brasil and Lima) to the Buenos Aires provincial capital of La Plata and intermediate points.

Car Rental

For reasons of safety (ferocious traffic) and practicality (no parking), driving in Buenos Aires makes no sense, but a car can be useful for excursions. Rental agencies include **Ansa Interna-**

Driving in Buenos Aires has its risks.

tional (AI, Paraguay 866, Retiro, tel. 011/4311-0220); **Avis** (Cerrito 1527, Retiro, tel. 011/4378-9640); **Dollar** (Marcelo T. de Alvear 523, Retiro, tel. 011/4315-8800); **Hertz** (Paraguay 1122, Retiro, tel. 011/4816-8001); **Localiza** (Maipú 924, Retiro, tel. 011/4315-8334); and **Thrifty** (Avenida Leandro N. Alem 699, tel. 011/4315-0777).

Buenos Aires and Vicinity

Vicinity of Buenos Aires

When the pressures of city living grow too great, *porteños* escape the capital to the suburbs and countryside of Buenos Aires Province, and across the river to Uruguay. When the capital swelters in summer heat, the Paraná Delta's maze of forested channels is just close enough for an afternoon off, but there's plenty to do for a day trip, a weekend, or even longer. Fewer than 4,000 people, many of whom traditionally bring their produce to Tigre's Mercado de Frutos, live in the 950 square kilometers of "the islands."

TIGRE

After decades of decay, the flood-prone riverside city of Tigre itself seems to be experiencing a renaissance. The train stations are completely renovated, the streets clean, the houses brightly painted and many restored, and it remains the point of departure for delta retreats and historic Isla Martín García. In a decade, the population has zoomed from a little more than 250,000 to 295,561.

From its beginnings as a humble colonial port for Buenos Aires–destined charcoal from the delta, Tigre languished until the railroad connected it to the capital in 1865. From the late 19th century, it became a summer sanctuary for the *porteño* elite, who built imposing mansions, some of which are still standing. Prestigious rowing clubs ran regattas on the river, but after the 1920s it settled into a subtropical torpor until its recent revival.

Tigre is 27 kilometers north of Buenos Aires at the confluence of the north-flowing Río Tigre and the Río Luján, which drains southeast into the Río de la Plata. The delta's main channel, parallel to the Río Luján, is the Río Paraná de las Palmas.

East of the Río Tigre, the town is primarily but not exclusively commercial. West of the river, it is largely residential.

Sights

On the right bank of the Río Tigre, along Avenida General Mitre, two classic rowing clubs are symbols of the town's bygone elegance: dating from 1873: the Anglophile **Buenos Aires Rowing Club** (Mitre 226), and its 1910 Italian counterpart the **Club Canottieri Italiani** (Mitre 74). Though both still function, they're not the exclusive institutions they once were.

Unfortunately, Tigre's revival has also brought fast-food franchises and the dreadful **Parque de la Costa** (Pereyra s/n, tel. 011/4732-6300, Wednesday–Sunday, 11 A.M.–midnight), a cheesy theme park. Open admission, valid for all rides and games, costs US$5 pp for adults, US$3.50 for children ages 9–12.

East of Parque de la Costa is the **Puerto de Frutos** (Sarmiento 160, tel. 011/4512-4493); though the docks of this port no longer buzz with produce transported by launches from the deepest delta islands, it's home to a revitalized crafts fair that's open 11 A.M.–7 P.M. daily, but is most active on weekends. Handcrafted wicker furniture and basketry, as well as flower arrangements, are unique to the area.

In the residential zone across the river, the present-day **Museo de la Reconquista** (Liniers 818, tel. 011/4512-4496, 10 A.M.–6 P.M. Wed.–Sun., free) was the Spanish Viceroy's command post while the British occupied Buenos Aires during the invasions of 1806–07. Not merely a military memorial, it also chronicles the delta, ecclesiastical history, and Tigre's golden age from the 1880s to the 1920s.

Several blocks north, fronting on the Río Luján, the **Museo Naval de la Nación** (Paseo Victorica 602, tel. 011/4749-0608, US$.70) occupies the former **Talleres Nacionales de Marina** (1879), a cavernous naval repair station that closed as military vessels got too large even for its facilities; it now chronicles Argentine naval history from its beginnings under the Irishman Guillermo Brown to the present. Despite sharing the defects of any other Argentine military museum, it houses a remarkable collection of model ships, including civilian riverboats and ocean-going vessels, along with an impressive assort-

TRAVEL IN URUGUAY

The picturesque Uruguayan town of Colonia del Sacramento is an easy day trip or overnight excursion from Buenos Aires. The capital city of Montevideo and the resorts of Carmelo and Punta del Este require a little more investment in time and/or money. For details, see *Moon Handbooks Buenos Aires,* which covers nearly all of the Uruguayan coastline.

Visas and Officialdom
Very few nationalities need advance visas for Uruguay, but requirements can change—if in doubt, check the consulate in Buenos Aires. Ordinarily, border officials give foreign tourists an automatic 90-day entry permit.

Health
Uruguay requires no vaccinations for visitors entering from any country, and public health standards are traditionally among the continent's highest.

Money and Prices
When Argentina sneezes, Uruguay catches cold, and the Argentine political and economic meltdown of 2001–02 has had severe repercussions on the Uruguayan economy. With Argentines unable to travel because of their own weak peso, Uruguayan hotel occupancy has fallen, but the Uruguayan peso slipped more slowly and Uruguayan prices remain somewhat higher than in Argentina.

The U.S. dollar operates as a parallel currency in Uruguay, at least in the tourist sector, where hotel and restaurant prices are often quoted in both currencies. In areas away from the heavily touristed coast this is less common.

Traditionally, Uruguay has the continent's most-liberal banking laws; exchange houses are numerous, and bureaucracy is minimal for U.S. cash and travelers checks. Banks, though, keep limited hours, normally 1–5 P.M. weekdays only. ATMs are common in Montevideo, Colonia, and Punta del Este, but in smaller towns they may not work with foreign plastic.

Communications
Uruguayan communications remain under the state monopoly Antel, despite pressures for privatization, and long-distance phone and Internet offices are fewer than in Argentina. The country code is 598; each city or town has a separate area code, ranging from one to four digits.

Getting Around
Distances in Uruguay are short and roads are good. Rental cars are readily available, but the cost of gasoline is high, approaching US$1 per liter.

Uruguayan buses resemble those in Argentina—modern, spacious, and fast—and service is frequent on most routes. Most, though not all, towns have a main bus terminal, usually on the outskirts of town; some bus lines have separate ticket offices in conveniently central locations.

ment of maps and colonial portraits, including of the Spanish scientist Juan de Ulloa. An outdoor sector includes a sample of naval aircraft and the bridge of a ship destroyed by the British navy during the 1982 Falklands war. Well worth a stop if not quite a special trip to Tigre, it's open 8:30 A.M.–12:30 P.M. Monday–Thursday, 8 A.M.–5.30 P.M. Friday, and 10 A.M.–6:30 P.M. weekends.

At the confluence of the Río del la Reconquista and the Río Luján, dating from 1910, the Belle Epoque **Tigre Club** (Paseo Victorica 972) now serves as the municipal Centro Cultural

(tel. 011/4749-3411). It's all that remains of a complex that included the earlier Tigre Hotel, built in the town's heyday but demolished after upper-class *porteños* abandoned the area for Mar del Plata in the 1930s.

Practicalities
In a recycled mansion on the west side of the Río Tigre, the family-run **B&B Escauriza** (Lavalle 557, tel. 011/4749-2499, fax 011/4749-3150, alebyb@aol.com, excau@aol.com, US$14/20 s/d) has four spacious rooms, attractive gardens and a pool.

The suburb of Tigre is the gateway to the channels of the Paraná Delta.

Standard Argentine eateries are a dime a dozen at locales like the **Mercado de Frutos.** For a more-elaborate menu on a shady riverside terrace with good service, try **María Luján** (Paseo Victorica 611, tel. 011/4731-9613). Homemade pastas cost around US$3.50, more elaborate dishes around US$4.50, and the weekday *menú ejecutivo* around US$5.50. A full dinner, with wine, will cost around US$10 pp.

In the Nueva Estación Fluvial, the **Ente Municipal de Turismo** (Mitre 305, tel. 011/4512-4497, tel. 0800/888-8447, www.puertodetigre .com) is open 9 A.M.–5 P.M. daily. The website is useful but imperfect.

Getting There and Around

Tigre is well-connected to Buenos Aires by bus and train, but heavy traffic on the Panamericana Norte makes the bus slow. Through the delta, there are numerous local launches and even international service to the Uruguayan ports of Carmelo and Nueva Palmira.

The No. 60 *colectivo* from downtown Buenos Aires runs 24 hours a day, but when traffic's heavy it can take two hours to reach Tigre.

Tigre has two **train stations.** From Retiro, Trenes de Buenos Aires (TBA) operates frequent commuter trains on the Ferrocarril Mitre from the capital to **Estación Tigre;** it's also possible to board these trains in Belgrano or suburban stations. The best-run of any suburban provincial rail line, it charges only US$.35 one-way.

Also from Retiro, a separate branch of the Mitre line runs to Estación Bartolomé Mitre, where passengers transfer at Estación Maipú to the Tren de la Costa, a tourist train that runs through several riverside communities and shopping centers to its terminus at Tigre's **Estación Delta,** at the entrance to the Parque de la Costa. This costs about US$1 weekdays, US$1.50 weekends.

To travel by **boat, Catamaranes Interisleña,** at the Tigre's Nueva Estación Fluvial (Mitre 319, tel. 011/4731-0261/0264), operates a number of *lanchas colectivas* to delta destinations. Like a bus on the road, they drop off and pick up passengers at docks along their route. **Líneas Delta Argentino** (tel. 011/4749-0537, www.lineas-delta.com.ar) and **Jilguero** (tel. 011/4749-0987) run similar routes. **Marsili** (tel. 011/4413-4123),

© WAYNE BERNHARDSON

Línea Azul (tel. 011/4401-7641), and **Giacomotti** (tel. 011/4749-1896) use smaller *lanchas taxi*. It's also possible to take short excursions through the delta for about US$3.

Cacciola (Lavalle 520, tel./fax 011/4749-0329, info@cacciolaviajes.com) has daily launches to Carmelo, Uruguay, at 8:30 A.M. and 4:30 P.M. (US$9, three hours), with bus connections to Montevideo. The boat is pretty comfortable at one-third capacity, but when it's full the narrow seats feel cramped.

Líneas Delta Argentino also operates launches to the Uruguayan town of Nueva Palmira (three hours, US$11 plus US$2.50 port taxes), west of Carmelo. Departures are daily except Sunday at 7:30 A.M.; an additional Friday trip leaves at 5 P.M.

THE DELTA

Tigre itself may have been revitalized, but many rusting hulks still line the shore of the Paraná's inner channels. Farther away from Tigre, where colonial smugglers often hid from Spanish officials, summer houses stand on *palafitos* (pilings) to prevent—not always successfully—their being flooded.

Many operators at Tigre's Nueva Estación Fluvial and the Puerto de Frutos offer 40- to 90-minute excursions that are, not quite literally, enough to get your feet wet in the delta. It's also possible to use the *lanchas colectivas* to get where you want to go, including hotels and restaurants. One word of warning: *Porteño* power-boaters, especially those on personal watercraft, can be as reckless as motorists on the capital's roadways—don't jump in the water without looking around first.

A favorite excursion is the **Museo Histórico Sarmiento** (Río Sarmiento and Arroyo Los Reyes, tel. 011/4728-0570). Dating from 1855, built from fruit boxes and now encased by glass, President Domingo F. Sarmiento's onetime summer residence preserves some of his personal effects. Open 10 A.M.–6 P.M. daily except Monday and Tuesday, it charges no admission; there's also a one-kilometer footpath through a gallery forest typical of the delta.

Accommodations and Food

Both accommodations and dining options are increasing in the delta. The following is just a sample of what is now available.

On the Río Carapachay, about 50 minutes from Tigre by Jilguero launch, **La Manuelita** (tel. 011/4728-0248, US$10–12 pp) has differential rates during the week and on weekends. *Parrillada* runs about US$3 pp. On the Río San Antonio, about 50 minutes from Tigre by Interisleña, rates at **Hotel I'Marangatu** (tel. 011/4728-0752, US$15 pp) include breakfast and dinner.

On Canal Honda off the Paraná de las Palmas, about 90 minutes from Tigre by Delta Argentino, **Hotel Laura** (tel. 011/4728-1019, info@riohotellaura.com.ar, www.riohotellaura.com.ar, US$20/26 s/d) has discounts for stays of two nights or longer.

On the Río Tres Bocas, about 25 minutes from Tigre by Interisleña, **La Riviera** (tel. 011/4728-0177) offers outdoor dining in good weather, with a wide selection of beef, fish, and pasta dishes.

M ISLA MARTÍN GARCÍA

Rising out of the Río de la Plata, almost within swimming distance of the Uruguayan town of Carmelo, the island of Martín García boasts a fascinating history, lush forests, and an almost unmatchable tranquility as a retreat from the frenzy of the federal capital and even provincial suburbs.

Only 3.5 kilometers off the Uruguayan coast but 33.5 kilometers from Tigre, 168-hectare Martín García is not part of the sedimentary delta, but rather a pre-Cambrian bedrock island rising 27 meters above sea level. Its native vegetation is a dense gallery forest; part of it is a *zona intangible* provincial forest reserve.

History

Spanish navigator Juan Díaz de Solís was the first European to see the island, naming it for one of his crewmen who died there in 1516. In colonial times, it often changed hands before coming under Spanish control definitively in

1777; in 1814 Guillermo Brown, the Irish founder of the Argentine navy, captured it for the Provincias Unidas del Río de la Plata (United Provinces of the River Plate). For a time, mainlanders quarried its granite bedrock for building materials.

For a century, from 1870 to 1970, the navy controlled the island, and for much of that time it served as a political prison and a regular penal colony; it was also a quarantine base for immigrants from Europe. While serving as Colombian consul in Buenos Aires in the early 1900s, the famous Nicaraguan poet Rubén Darío (1867–1916) lived here briefly.

Political detainees have included presidents Marcelo T. de Alvear (in 1932, after his presidency), Hipólito Yrigoyen (twice in the 1930s), Juan Domingo Perón (1945, before his election), and Arturo Frondizi (1962–63). In the early months of World War II, Argentine authorities briefly incarcerated crewmen from the German battleship *Graf Spee,* scuttled off Montevideo in December 1939.

While the island passed to the United Provinces at independence, it was not explicitly part of Argentina until a 1973 agreement with Uruguay (which was one of the United Provinces). After the navy departed, the Buenos Aires provincial Servicio Penitenciario used it as a halfway house for run-of-the-mill convicts, but it was also a detention and torture site during the 1976–83 military dictatorship.

Sights

Uphill from the island's *muelle pasajero* (passenger pier), opposite the meticulously landscaped **Plaza Guillermo Brown,** the island's **Oficina de Informes** was, until recently, the Servicio Penitenciario's headquarters. It now houses provincial park rangers. Several antique *baterías* (gun emplacements) line the south shore.

At the upper end of the plaza stand the ruins of the onetime **Cuartel** (military barracks, which later became jail cells). Clustered together nearby are the **Cine-Teatro,** the former theater, with its gold-tinted rococo details; the **Museo de la Isla** (Island Museum); and the former **Casa Médicos de Lazareto,** the quarantine center now occupied by the **Centro de Interpretación Ecológica** (Environmental In-

The theater on Isla Martín García, reached from Tigre, is the most distinctive of many historic buildings on the island.

terpretation Center). On the opposite side of the Cuartel, the **Panadería Rocio** (1913) is a bakery that makes celebrated fruitcakes; a bit farther inland, the **faro** (lighthouse, 1881) rises above the trees, but is no longer in use. To the north, the graves of conscripts who died in an early-20th-century epidemic dot the isolated **cementerio** (cemetery).

At the northwest end of the island, trees and vines grow among the crumbling structures of the so-called **Barrio Chino** (Chinatown), marking the approach to the **Puerto Viejo,** the sediment-clogged former port. Across the island, beyond the airstrip, much of the same vegetation grows in the **Zona Intangible,** closed to the public.

Activities

Though the island offers outstanding walking and bird-watching, the river is not suitable for swimming. The restaurant Comedor El Solís, though, has a swimming pool open to the public.

Accommodations and Food

Crowded in summer and on weekends, **Camping Martín García** (tel. 011/4728-1808) charges US$1.50 pp for tent campers, with discounts for two or more nights; it also has hostel bunks with shared bath for US$2.25 pp, with private bath for US$3 pp; again, there are discounts for two or more nights. Cacciola's *Hostería Martín García* charges US$32 pp for overnight packages with full board that include transportation from Tigre. Each additional night costs US$14 pp.

Cacciola's own restaurant **Fragata Hércules** is decent enough, but **Comedor El Solís** is at least as good and a bit cheaper; in winter, however, the Solís may be closed. **Panadería Rocio** is known for its fruitcakes.

Getting There and Around

On the west bank of the Río Tigre, **Cacciola** (Lavalle 520, tel./fax 011/4749-0329, info@cacciolaviajes.com) offers day trips to Martín García on Tuesday, Thursday, Saturday, and Sunday at 8 A.M., but get to the dock by 7:30 A.M. Arriving at the island around 11 A.M., the tour includes an aperitif on arrival, a guided visit, and lunch at Cacciola's restaurant *Fragata Hércules;* there is ample time to roam around before returning to Tigre by 7 P.M.

Cacciola also has a Microcentro office (Florida 520, 1st floor, Oficina 113, tel./fax 011/4393-6100, cacciolacentro@sinectis.com.ar). Fares for a full-day excursion are US$12 for adults, US$4 for children ages 3–10, including port charges.

The Pampas

West of the Capital Federal, Buenos Aires Province is gaucho country, transformed by the herds of cattle that proliferated on the pampas after the Spanish invasion, and by the horsemen who subsisted off those herds. Eventually and ironically, those free-spirited gauchos became the peons of the sprawling *estancias,* or cattle ranches, that occupied almost every square inch of prime agricultural land.

La Plata, an impressively planned city created when Buenos Aires became a separate federal district, is the provincial capital and a worthwhile excursion from BA. San Antonio de Areco is Argentina's unofficial gaucho capital, and the tourist-oriented *estancias* that surround it are some of the country's most historic. Between Buenos Aires and San Antonio, the city of Luján is no less historic, with outstanding architecture and museums, and is also one of South America's major devotional centers.

To the south, the coastal city of Mar del Plata and a string of nearby beach resorts comprise Argentina's—or rather Buenos Aires's—traditional summer vacation destination. This area, though, also boasts the humid pampas' greatest scenic diversity, thanks to the rolling ranges of Tandilia, near the city of Tandil, and the steeper Sierra de la Ventana, north of the city of Bahía Blanca. Scattered around the area are several other *estancias* open to the paying public.

Westerly La Pampa is a thinly populated province that boasts some underrated, off-the-beaten-track attractions like Parque Nacional Lihué Calel. Some of the strongest resistance to Argentina's 19th-century incursions into Mapuche territory took place here.

PLANNING YOUR TIME

Buenos Aires Province is enormous, and La Pampa is large enough that travel in the region can be time-consuming without a base for exploration. Some destinations, like **La Plata, Luján,** and **San Antonio de Areco** make ideal day trips from Buenos Aires, but San Antonio's ambience and accommodations, and the *estancias* in the vicinity, make it an ideal getaway from the capital (San Antonio is calmer and quieter midweek than on weekends). Some overseas visitors make properties like **Estancia La Porteña** destinations in themselves for a week or even more.

For Argentines, **Mar del Plata** is the province's highest-profile destination; foreign beachgoers will probably find a couple of days here enough, though the city has an active cultural scene and a day trip to the **Fangio Automotive Museum** in nearby Balcarce is worthwhile even for non-drivers. The chain of cookie-cutter resorts northeast and southwest of "Mardel" has pockets of peacefulness for those in search of quiet beach holidays, at least outside the January–February peak season, but they're not major destinations for overseas visitors.

Tandilia and Ventania, the modest mountain ranges of southern Buenos Aires Province, fall short of the Andes in both elevation and scenery, but offer many recreational opportunities. Visitors spending months in the country might well enjoy some days in the city of **Tandil** or the town of **Sierra de la Ventana,** but guests at prestigious *estancias* like **La Isolina** and **Cerro de la Cruz** often relish extended stays.

South of Sierra de la Ventana, the tidy port city of **Bahía Blanca** is a pleasant enough place, but its major highlight is the quirky museum at nearby **Puerto Ingeniero White.** This is the best place in the country to appreciate the Argentine immigrant experience—even better than Buenos Aires's recently reopened Hotel de Inmigrantes.

In arid La Pampa, southwest of the provincial capital of Santa Rosa, the rounded granite summits of **Parque Nacional Lihué Calel** are islands of biogeographical diversity surrounded by desert. One of the gateways to Patagonia, isolated Lihué Calel is an ideal destination for anyone seeking serious solitude.

HISTORY

It's tempting to say that the history of the pampas is beef and wheat, but that would omit the presence of the Querandí, the aboriginal hunter-gatherers who stalked guanaco, rhea, and other game animals over the flat grassy horizons before the Spaniards arrived. Though they used bows, arrows and spears, they primarily hunted with *boleadoras,* sinewy thongs weighted with stones. When thrown accurately, these *bolas* (as they are also known) were effective enough to trip and immobilize an animal as large as a horse or bull; in fact, the gauchos of the pampas later used them for this purpose.

Thanks to their mobility, the Querandí were able to harass early Buenos Aires and discourage any inland settlements for more than half a century after the Spaniards first set foot there. Imperial policy also played a role in the area's slow development, as the Crown focused on the wealthy, densely settled Central Andean highlands rather than the poor, sparsely peopled pampas. In fact, for nearly two centuries, all legal trade—not to mention political authority—passed through Lima and overland rather than directly to the Río de la Plata.

Rather than conquering the pampas militarily, the Spaniards did so indirectly—and unconsciously—by abandoning cattle and horses that were free to roam and multiply on grasslands where the only other grazing mammals were deer and guanaco. In contrast to deer and guanaco, cattle had commercial value, and horses were necessary to herd them; in the short term, the new species brought the peoples of the pampas a more abundant and diverse subsistence. In the long term, though, they helped create what

Must-Sees

M **Museo de Ciencias Naturales:** In Buenos Aires Province's capital city of **La Plata,** this is Argentina's premier natural history museum and a great day trip from Buenos Aires (page 126).

M **Complejo Museográfico:** In the pilgrimage city of **Luján,** this exceptional complex of historical museums is among the best in the country (page 131).

M **Fiesta de la Tradición:** In the placid pampas west of Luján, Argentina's "gaucho capital," **San Antonio de Areco,** celebrates its gaucho heritage during this November festival (page 134).

M **Tandil:** The most attractive city in southern Buenos Aires Province's interior is the location of a granite mountain range that's ideal for mountain biking, rock climbing, and other outdoor activities (page 136).

M **Sierra de la Ventana:** In this sleepy town, Buenos Aires Province's most mountainous terrain offers its best hiking. As elsewhere in the province, there are outstanding *estancias,* such as Cerro de la Cruz (page 141).

M **Mar del Plata:** Argentina's top traditional beach resort has also become one of its biggest tourist traps, but it still shows its elegance and sophistication in its historical neighborhoods and cultural offerings—especially outside the summer months of January and February (page 144).

M **Museo del Automovilismo Juan Manuel Fangio:** More than just a tribute to Argentina's legendary Formula One champion, this state-of-the-art automotive museum near Mar del Plata takes an expansive view of transportation technology (page 154).

M **Museo del Puerto:** On Bahía Blanca's outskirts, this whimsical, self-styled "community museum" in **Puerto Ingeniero White** does a lot with a little to illuminate the Argentine immigrant experience (page 160).

M **Parque Nacional Lihué Calel:** Surrounded by the arid pampas that gradually become Patagonian desert toward the southwest, the resistant granite summits and canyons of Lihué Calel are an archipelago of biodiversity (page 166).

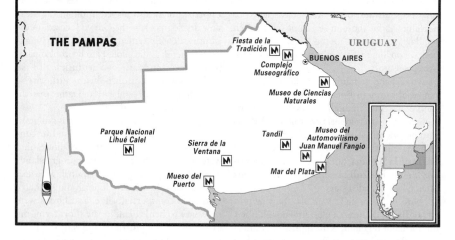

The Pampas

THE PAMPAS

URUGUAY

MONTEVIDEO

ATLANTIC OCEAN

ENTRE RÍOS

BUENOS AIRES

SANTA FE

CÓRDOBA

SAN LUIS

LA PAMPA

MENDOZA

RÍO NEGRO

NEUQUÉN

Fray Bentos
Carmelo
Colonia del Sacramento
La Plata
Río de la Plata
Campana
Zárate
Luján
BUENOS AIRES
San Antonio de Areco
Pergamino
Junín
To Rosario
Gualeguay
Río Uruguay
Río Paraná

M MUSEO DE CIENCIAS NATURALES
M FIESTA DE LA TRADICIÓN
M COMPLEJO MUSEOGRÁFICO
M MUSEO DEL AUTOMOVILISMO JUAN MANUEL FANGIO
M MAR DEL PLATA
M TANDIL
M MUSEO DEL PUERTO
M PARQUE NACIONAL LIHUÉ CALEL

Bahía Samborombón
Chascomús
Dolores
Pinamar
Villa Gesell
Ayacucho
Balcarce
Necochea
Tres Arroyos
Bahía Blanca
Carmen de Patagones
Viedma
San Antonio Oeste
Golfo San Matías

RP 11
RP 2
RP 41
RN 29
RN 226
RN 88
RP 88
RN 228
RN 3
Lobos
Las Flores
Azul
Sierra de Tandil
Benito Juárez
Sierra de la Ventana
Sierra de la Ventana
RN 205
RN 5
RP 51
San Carlos de Bolívar
Olavarría
RP 65
RP 76
Pehuajó
RN 226
Tornquist
Pigüé
RN 188
Trenque Lauquen
RN 33
RN 33
RN 8
RN 7
Rufino
General Villegas
Realicó
General Pico
RN 35
Reserva Provincial Parque Luro
Santa Rosa
General Acha
RP 10
Chacharramendi
RN 188
San Luis
RN 146
San Rafael
Río Salado
Río Atuel
Algarrobo del Aguila
RN 143
RN 151
RP 20
25 de Mayo
RN 152
Puelches
RP 106
Gobernador Duval
Río Negro
RN 22
RN 250
RN 251
RN 154
La Adela
Río Colorado
Neuquén
RN 237
RN 40
RN 143
RN 23

100 mi
100 km
0
0

© AVALON TRAVEL PUBLISHING, INC.

historian Alfred Crosby has called a "neo-Europe" of ecologically exotic animals and plants that helped open the region to immigrants, even as the horse enabled the Querandí and other more westerly peoples to resist the invaders militarily. In areas like La Pampa, they held out nearly into the 20th century.

The numbers of feral cattle, which had no significant natural enemies here, probably reached into the tens of millions; they dramatically impoverished lush grasslands that native peoples had managed skillfully with fire. In the early 19th century, Darwin, witnessing the proliferation of impenetrable European thistles, commented, "I doubt whether any case is on record of an invasion on so grand a scale of one plant over the aborigines."

As wild game gave way to cattle, the hunter became a herdsman on horseback, though this was a gradual process—the rangy cattle were wild enough in the beginning that hunting them was hazardous, and gauchos (as the riders became known) were often gored. Living off the herds, the free-roaming gaucho became an enduring symbol of Argentine nationalism (*argentinidad*) even as his role rapidly diminished with political and economic change.

In Argentina's early independence years, it was customary for gauchos to kill cattle for food as long as they left the hides, which had limited economic value, to the landholder. As Argentina became integrated with the global economy, though, more-intensive land-use practices like sheep- and wheat-farming meant the fencing of the pampas and the end of the autonomous gaucho, who instead became a dependent laborer on the *estancias* that remained.

By the end of the 19th century, sharecroppers and permanent settlers were further displacing the gaucho, Argentina was on its way to becoming the granary of Europe, and the British-built railroads had fanned out from Buenos Aires to transport beef, maize, and wheat to the port. Tensions between the capital and its agricultural hinterland led to a near civil war in the 1880s, when provincial authorities moved the seat of government from BA to the new, planned city of La Plata.

Through much of the 20th century, the richest *estancias* retained a stranglehold on rural social and economic life; their lavish *cascos* (mansions) embodied the pretensions of an oligarchy that aspired to be an aristocracy. Successive crises in the last 30-plus years, though, have weakened their grip, and many traditional landholders have had to open their portals to tourists (often, though not always, the most well-heeled tourists).

Argentina remains a major beef and grain producer, though, its products more competitive since the recent devaluation; like its counterparts in Australia and North America, its mechanized agriculture relies on fossil-fuel fertilizers and pesticides. Smaller farms near Buenos Aires and other cities have benefited from access to urban markets for their fruits, vegetables, and dairy products, but the contemporary gaucho is more symbol than substance.

La Plata

Beyond the southern boundary of the federal district, a new freeway leads to the provincial capital of La Plata, shifted here after indignant provincial authorities, responding to the federalization of the city of Buenos Aires, expropriated six square leagues of land in the former Municipio de la Ensenada to create the new provincial capital of La Plata in 1882.

In a competition to design the city, Governor Dardo Rocha chose Pedro Benoit's standard grid, crisscrossed by diagonals like those of Washington, D.C. Provincial authorities embellished the streets with pretentious neoclassical and Francophile buildings that have, with time, achieved a remarkable harmony.

The province now governs some 14 million people—more than a third of all Argentines and only slightly fewer than the entire population of neighboring Chile, and more than many European countries, including Belgium, Greece, and Portugal. While government may be the motive for La Plata's existence, the city has managed to become one of the country's major cultural foci, with first-rate universities, theaters, concert halls, libraries, and museums.

ORIENTATION

La Plata (population 553,002) is 56 kilometers southeast of Buenos Aires via the Autopista Buenos Aires–La Plata, the recently completed freeway between the two cities. The city itself consists of a rectangular grid, with regularly distributed plazas, but the connecting diagonals (which run north-south and east-west) can make the layout disorienting to pedestrians—a slightly wrong turn can send you far out of your way.

Most public buildings are on or around Plaza Moreno, La Plata's precise geographical center, but its commercial heart is on and around Plaza San Martín, six blocks northeast. Unlike most Argentine cities, its streets and avenues are numbered rather than named; locations are more often described by their intersections and cross streets than by building numeration.

SIGHTS

In 1882, Governor Rocha laid La Plata's **Piedra Fundacional** (Founding Stone) in the center of sprawling **Plaza Mariano Moreno,** a four-block area bounded by Calle 12, Calle 14, Calle 50, and Calle 54. Benoit, along with architects Ernesto Meyer and Emilio Coutaret, designed the French neo-Gothic **Catedral de la Inmaculada Concepción de La Plata** at the southwest corner of Plaza Moreno, but its construction is a story in itself. Begun in 1885, the cathedral did not open officially until 1932, and its three crowning towers went unfinished until 1999. So long, in fact, did the project take that the building underwent its first restoration (1997) even before its completion! Its **Museo de la Catedral** is open 8 A.M.–noon and 2–7 P.M. daily.

Rocha himself resided in what is now the **Museo y Archivo Dardo Rocha,** fronting on Calle 50 on the northwest side of the plaza. Two blocks west, the French-style **Casa de Justicia** fills an entire block bounded by Avenida 13, Calle 47, Calle 48, and Calle 14.

On the northeast side of Plaza Moreno, fronting on Calle 12, Hannoverian architect Hubert Stiers built the elegant German Renaissance **Palacio Municipal** (1886), whose main **Salón Dorado** is adorned with marble staircases, imported oak floors, German stained-glass windows, and bronze chandeliers. Two blocks away, bounded by Calle 9, Calle 10, Avenida 51, and Avenida 53, the architecturally brutalist **Teatro Argentino** is a performing arts center that has finally replaced a far more prestigious building that burned to the ground in 1977.

Two blocks northeast, facing Plaza San Martín on Avenida 7, Hannoverian architects Gustav Heine and Georg Hagemann designed the provincial **Palacio de la Legislatura** in the German Renaissance style of the Palacio Municipal. Across the plaza, fronting on Calle 6, Belgian architect Julio Doral created the Flemish Renaissance **Casa de Gobierno,** home to the provincial executive branch and a remarkable set

The Pampas

LA PLATA

© AVALON TRAVEL PUBLISHING, INC.

Paseo del Bosque

To Museo de Ciencias Naturales

Jardín Zoológico

To República de los Niños

HOTEL SAINT JAMES

HOTEL ROGA

CERVECERIA LA MODELO

HOTEL SAN MARCO

HOTEL CORREGIDOR

PALACIO CAMPODÓNICO

Plaza D. Rocha

Plaza Máximo Paz

TEATRO LA LECHUZA

Plaza Rivadavia

CASA DE GOBIERNO

ASATEJ

Plaza San Martín

CINE SAN MARTÍN

PALACIO DE LA LEGISLATURA

CINE OCHO

TEATRO ARGENTINO

HOTEL LA PLATA

PALACIO MUNICIPAL

TORRE MUNICIPAL

Plaza Mariano Moreno

CATEDRAL DE LA INMACULADA CONCEPCIÓN DE LA PLATA

MUSEO DE BELLAS ARTES BONAERENSE

RECTORADO DE LA UNIVERSIDAD NACIONAL

PASAJE DARDO ROCHA

ING. LUIS MONTEVERDE

CONFITERÍA PARÍS

LOCUTORIO SAN MARTÍN

SUSS UND EIS

LA TRATTORIA

WILKENNY IRISH PUB & RESTAURANT

PREGO

MUSEO Y ARCHIVO DARDO ROCHA

COLEGIO DE ESCRIBANOS

CASA DE JUSTICIA

HOTEL CRISTAL

BANCO DE LA PROVINCIA

LA SORBETIÈRE

TEATRO COLISEO PODESTÁ

HOTEL DEL REY

EL QUIJOTE

Plaza J.J. Paso

Plaza Italia

HOTEL BENEVENTO

CYBERSONIC

ABRUZZESE

ESTACIÓN FERROCARRIL ROCA

TERMINAL DE OMNIBUS

Plaza General Belgrano

CALLE 64
CALLE 63
CALLE 62
CALLE 61
AV. 60
CALLE 59
CALLE 58
CALLE 57
CALLE 56
CALLE 55
CALLE 54
AV. 53
CALLE 50
AV. 51

DIAGONAL 73
DIAGONAL 78
DIAGONAL 79
DIAGONAL 74
DIAGONAL 77
DIAGONAL 80

AV. 1
CALLE 49
CALLE 48
CALLE 47
CALLE 46
CALLE 45
CALLE 4
CALLE 5
CALLE 6
AV. 44
CALLE 8
CALLE 9
CALLE 10
CALLE 11
CALLE 12
AV. 13
CALLE 14
CALLE 43
CALLE 42
AV. 7
CALLE 41
CALLE 40
CALLE 39
CALLE 2
CALLE 3

200 yds
200 m
0
0

of murals by Rodolfo Campodónico. Across Avenida 51, the **Museo de Bellas Artes Bonaerense** (Avenida 51 No. 525, tel. 0221/421-8629, www.lpsat.net/museo) is a contemporary art museum open 10 A.M.–7 P.M. weekdays, 10 A.M.–1 P.M. and 3–7 P.M. weekends.

At the northwest corner of Plaza San Martín, La Plata's first railroad station is now the **Pasaje Dardo Rocha** (1887), home to several museums and other cultural institutions. Two blocks farther on, the **Rectorado de la Universidad Nacional** (1905), on Avenida 7 between Calle 47 and 48, now houses university offices. About three blocks east of the plaza, topped by a view tower, the **Palacio Campodónico** (1892) fills a small triangular lot bounded by Diagonal 70, Calle 5, and Calle 56. Expropriated by the provincial government in 1976, it's now a cultural center with rotating exhibitions.

Several blocks northeast, across Avenida 1, the 60-hectare **Paseo del Bosque** is a forested park that contains recreational and educational facilities including the **Anfiteatro Martín Fierro**, an outdoor theater; the extraordinary **Museo de Ciencias Naturales** (Natural Sciences Museum); the **Observatorio Astronómico** (Astronomical Observatory); the **Jardín de la Paz** (Garden of Peace), with small pavilions for each country with diplomatic representation in Argentina; and the **Jardín Zoológico** (Zoo).

Museo y Archivo Dardo Rocha

Benoit also designed the residence of La Plata's founder (1838–1921), whose varied career included stints as a journalist, soldier, diplomat, provincial legislator, national senator, and then provincial governor. The museum (Calle 50 No. 933, tel. 0221/427-5591, 9 A.M.–6 P.M. weekdays only), though, chooses to focus on Rocha's personal effects, including furniture, art works, clothing, household goods, documents, and photographs, to the virtual exclusion of his role in the controversial shift of the provincial capital from Buenos Aires.

Teatro Argentino

Finally rebuilt after its destruction by fire in 1977, the **Teatro Argentino** reopened in October 2000 with a presentation of *Tosca*. With all the elegance of a multistory parking lot, this 60,000-square-meter concrete structure looks like the product of the military dictatorship that approved it—it's a fortified bunker that (had it been complete) might have bought them a little more time in power after their Falklands debacle of 1982.

Still, the new Teatro Argentino looks and sounds better within than without, and is one of the country's major performing arts venues, with its own orchestra, chorus, ballet, and children's chorus. Its principal theater is the Sala Alberto Ginastera, which seats more than 2,000 spectators; smaller halls seat 300–700 persons. Past performers, prior to the reconstruction, included Arthur Rubenstein, Ana Pavlova, Andrés Segovia, and Richard Strauss.

The Teatro Argentino (Avenida 51 between Calle 9 and Calle 10, tel. 0221/429-1700, ta-relacionespublicas@ed.gba.gov.ar, www.elteatroargentino.com.ar) offers guided tours at 10:30 A.M. and 2 P.M. daily except Monday, by reservation only. These cost about US$1 pp except for bilingual English-Spanish tours, which cost around US$1.70 pp. There are discounts for seniors and students.

Pasaje Dardo Rocha

Formerly the Estación 19 de Noviembre, La Plata's first major railroad station, the French Classic Pasaje Dardo Rocha has undergone an adaptive reuse that has transformed it into a major cultural center with several museums, plus cinemas, auditoriums, conference rooms, cafés, and other venues. The municipal tourist office is also here.

Opened in 1999, the **Museo de Arte Contemporáneo Latinoamericano** (tel. 0221/427-1843,www.macla.laplata.gov.ar) features works by modern Latin American artists. It's open 10 A.M.–8 P.M. Tuesday–Friday all year; weekend hours are 4–10 P.M. in spring and summer, 2–9 P.M. in fall and winter.

The **Museo Municipal de Arte** (tel. 0221/427-1198) is a painting and sculpture museum focusing primarily on local artists. It's open 10 A.M.–8 P.M. weekdays except Monday, and

3–9 P.M. weekends. Dedicated exclusively to photography, the **Museo y Galería Fotográfica** (MUGAFO) keeps the same hours.

Jardín Zoológico

At the west end of the Paseo del Bosque, La Plata's Victorian-style zoo (Paseo del Bosque s/n, tel. 0221/427-3925, daily except Mon. 9 A.M.–6 P.M., US$.70 adult; free for children under 12) billets more than 180 native and exotic species, including giraffes, elephants, lions, monkeys, and rhinoceri, on 14 hectares.

Museo de Ciencias Naturales

Patagonian explorer Francisco Pascasio Moreno donated his personal collections of anthropological, archaeological, and paleontological artifacts to Argentina's premier natural history museum, which opened in 1888 under his own lifetime directorship. Today, more than 400,000 visitors per annum view at least some of the 2.5 million items in its 21 exhibition halls, which also deal with botany geology, zoology, and other fields.

The four-story building is a monument to its era, its exterior a hybrid of Greek regional styles with indigenous American—Aztec and Incaic—flourishes. Home to the university's natural sciences department, its interior also contains classrooms, libraries, offices, workshops, and storage space. That said, the museum's public displays have still not evolved far beyond taxonomy, and the 19th-century Darwinism of their creator.

The Museo de Ciencias Naturales (Paseo del Bosque 1900, tel. 0221/425-7744, www.fcnym .unlp.edu.ar/museo, US$1 pp for those over 12 years of age) is open 10 A.M.–6 P.M. daily except for Mondays and the New Year's, May Day, and Christmas Day holidays. There are guided tours at 2 and 4 P.M. weekdays except Monday, and hourly on weekends from 10:30 A.M.–4:30 P.M.

Observatorio Astronómico

Part of the Universidad Nacional de La Plata, the local observatory has both modern telescopes and historical instruments from the 19th century. Guided tours take place every Friday at 8:30 P.M. in March, 7 and 8 P.M. April–September, 7:30 and 8:30 P.M. October–November, and 8:30 in December. For reservations, contact the Observatorio Astronómico de La Plata (Paseo del Bosque s/n, tel. 0221/423-6953, www .fcaglp.unlp.edu.ar).

ENTERTAINMENT

For event tickets, one option is to visit **Ticketek** (Calle 48 No. 700, corner of Calle 9). **Locutorio San Martín** (Avenida 51 between Avenida 7 and Calle 8) is also a discount ticket outlet.

La Plata is a key theater and live music center, whose major venue is the **Centro de las Artes Teatro Argentino** (Avenida 51 between Calle 9 and Calle 10, tel. 0800/666-5151 toll-free). The box office (tel. 0221/429-1733) is open 10 A.M.–8 P.M. daily except Monday. The Teatro Argentino, by the way, provides free transportation from Buenos Aires for ticket-holders.

Another major performing arts locale is the **Teatro Coliseo Podestá** (Calle 10 between Calle 46 and Calle 47, tel. 0221/424-8457). More-intimate productions take place at spots like the **Teatro La Lechuza** (Calle 58 No. 757, tel. 221/424-6350).

La Plata has two downtown movie theaters: the three-screen **Cine Ocho** (Calle 8 No. 981, between Avenidas 51 and 53, tel. 0221/482-5554) and the two-screen **Cine San Martín** (Calle 7 No. 923 between 50 and 51, tel. 0221/483-9947).

ACCOMMODATIONS

For the truly budget-conscious, the frayed but friendly **Hotel Saint James** (Avenida 60 No. 377, tel. 0221/421-8089, fax 0221/489-4291, hotelsj@lpsat.com, US$7/10 s/d) is a no-frills option with private bath and telephone. At these prices, though, it's often full.

On a quiet block, **Hotel Roga** (Calle 54 No. 334, tel. 0221/421-9553 or 427-4070, US$11/15 s/d) is modern, friendly, and comfortable, with private bath, breakfast, and parking included. There is a five percent surcharge for credit card payments. **Hotel Cristal** (Avenida 1 No. 620, tel. 0221/424-5640, hotelcristal@ciudad.com.ar, US$11/16 s/d) is similar.

With half board included, the central, 70-room **Hotel La Plata** (Avenida 51 No. 783, tel./fax 0221/422-9090, laplatah@cadema.com .ar, US$13/18 s/d) is a phenomenal value for a very good hotel with a/c, cable TV, and similar amenities.

Hotel del Rey (Plaza Paso 180, tel./fax 0221/427-0177 or 425-9181, delrey@infovia .com.ar, US$13/20 s/d) is a 10-story tower at the intersection of 13 and 44; rates for the 40 well-kept midsize rooms, with all modern conveniences, include breakfast.

The star of La Plata's accommodations scene, though, is Ⅻ **Hotel Benevento** (Calle 2 No. 645 at the corner of Diagonal 80, tel./fax 0221/489-1078, info@hotelbenevento.com.ar, www.hotelbenevento.com.ar, US$14/19 s/d). A spectacularly restored 1903 building that once was the provincial labor ministry, it has high ceilings, attractive balconies, and is quiet despite the busy street; the modernized rooms, though, have showers rather than tubs. Rates are negotiable for two nights or more.

The utilitarian exterior at **Hotel San Marco** (Calle 54 No. 523, tel. 0221/422-7202, info @sanmarcohotel.com.ar, US$15/21 s/d) disguises a pretty good hotel. The four-star, 110-room high-rise **Hotel Corregidor** (Calle 6 No. 1026, tel. 0221/425-6800, fax 0221/425-6805, informes@hotelcorregidor.com.ar, US$26/33 s/d) is a good upscale value, but it's by no means twice as good as the Benevento.

FOOD

For breakfast, coffee or pastries, the best option is the tobacco-free **Confitería París** (at the corner of Avenida 7 and Calle 49, tel. 0221/ 482-8840).

The **Colegio de Escribanos,** on Avenida 13 between Calles 47 and 48, is a lunchtime favorite for lawyers and judges from the nearby Tribunales (provincial courts). Plaza Paso's **El Quijote** (Avenida 13 and Avenida 44, tel. 0221/483-3653) specializes in fine, reasonably priced seafood.

There's a pair of fine Italian options with sidewalk seating: **La Trattoría** (Calle 47 and Diagonal 74, tel. 0221/422-6135) and **Prego** (Calle 11 No. 805, tel. 0221/421-0854). For a more formal and elaborate Italian meal, try **Abruzzese** (Calle 42 No. 457, tel. 0221/421-9869).

The line between places to eat and places to drink is not always obvious in La Plata. The best blend of the two is the classic Ⅻ **Cervecería La Modelo** (Calle 5 and Calle 54, tel. 0221/421-1321), which prepares terrific sandwiches, plus draft beer and hard cider, and free unshelled and unsalted peanuts. There is an adequate tobacco-free area.

Another option is the **Wilkenny Irish Pub & Restaurant** (Calle 50 No. 797, tel. 0221/483-1772, www.wilkenny.com.ar), a legitimately Irish-styled pub in the heart of town. The food includes pub grub like lamb stew (though the bulk of the menu is Argentine and there are even a couple of Chinese dishes), plus Irish beers on tap (Guinness, Harp, and Kilkenny) by the pint and half-pint). Lunch or dinner entrees cost around US$2–4; there is a larger selection of bottle brews, plus Irish and specialty coffees. Service is excellent.

For ice cream, try **La Sorbetière** (Calle 47 and Calle 10), or **Süss und Eis** (Calle 47 and Calle 9).

INFORMATION

The improved Información Turística La Plata, the municipal tourist office in the Pasaje Dardo Rocha at the corner of Calles 6 and 50 (tel. 0221/427-1535 or 427-3054) is open 9 A.M.– 6 P.M. weekdays, 9 A.M.–1 P.M. Saturday. It distributes far better city maps, informational brochures, and bus schedules than in the recent past, and the staff has become more accommodating. There's a branch office in the Palacio Campodónico, on Diagonal 79 at Calle 8, open 9 A.M.–6 P.M. daily.

On the 13th floor of the Torre Municipal, the Dirección Provincial de Turismo (Calle 12 and Avenida 53, tel. 0221/429-5553, buenosaires-turismo@hotmail.com, serviciosturisticosbuenosaires @hotmail.com, www.vivalaspampas.com) is open

9 A.M.–3 P.M. weekdays only. Though sometimes bureaucratic, this provincial office can be surprisingly helpful for out-of-town sights.

SERVICES

Banco de la Provincia has an ATM on Avenida 7 between Calle 46 and Calle 47, while Banco Nación has one at the corner of Avenida 7 and Calle 49. There are many others, however.

Correo Argentino is at the corner of Avenida 51 and Calle 4.

Locutorio San Martín, on Avenida 51 between Avenida 7 and Calle 8, provides long-distance services.

Cybersonic, near Plaza Italia (Diagonal 74 and Calle 6, tel. 0221/489-5511) is open 24 hours for Internet access.

Asatej (Avenida 5 No. 990 at the corner of Avenida 53, tel. 0221/483-8673, laplata@asatej .com.ar) is the local branch of Argentina's student- and youth-oriented travel agency.

GETTING THERE AND AROUND

La Plata itself has no airport, but **Manuel Tienda León** (tel. 0221/425-1140) provides door-to-door transportation to Ezeiza and Aeroparque.

La Plata's **Terminal de Ómnibus** is at Calle 42 and Calle 4 (tel. 221/421-2182); there are frequent buses to and from Retiro (US$1.20, one hour) with **Costera Metropolitana** (tel. 0221/489-2284) and **Río de la Plata** (tel. 011/4305-1405). There are also long-distance services along the provincial coastline and to the interior.

La Plata operates the century-old **Estación Ferrocarril General Roca** (Avenida 1 and Avenida 44, tel. 0221/423-2575). **Transportes Metropolitana SA General Roca** (TMR, tel. 011/4304-0021) operates 51 weekday trains from Constitución (Buenos Aires) to La Plata (1.5 hours, US$.50 cents), a number that drops to between 35 and 40 on weekends and holidays. The last train returns to Constitución around 10:30 P.M., but they start up again around 3 A.M.

VICINITY OF LA PLATA

República de los Niños

According to some accounts, Walt Disney took the inspiration for Disneyland from República de los Niños, a 50-hectare children's amusement park on the grounds of what was once a golf course built for the English meat packer Swift, in La Plata's northern suburbs. Disney, though, visited Argentina in 1941—a decade before the Argentine park opened in 1951.

Conceived by Evita Perón, executed by 1,600 laborers under Perón loyalist governor Domingo Mercante, and officially opened by Juan Perón himself, República de los Niños had a strong political subtext that may not be obvious today. In the context of Peronist politics, its origins as an expropriated property and its role as a destination for underprivileged working-class children are significant.

República de los Niños displays a mélange of architectural miniatures from around the world, ranging from the medieval Europe of Grimm's fairy tales to Islamic mosques and the Taj Mahal, but most notably including replicas of the Argentine presidential palace, legislature, and courts—with the obvious implication that its youthful public could aspire to office (and in all likelihood graft, as there's also a jail). A steam train makes the rounds of the park.

República de los Niños (tel. 0221/484-1409, www.republica.laplata.gov.ar, 10 A.M.–10 P.M. daily except Mon., US$.35 adults over 12, parking US$1) is at Camino General Belgrano and 501, in the suburb of Manuel Gonnet.

From Avenida 7 in downtown La Plata, bus No. 518 and 273 go to República de los Niños, but not all No. 273s go all the way—ask before boarding.

Parque Ecológico Cultural

William Henry Hudson, known to Argentines as Guillermo Enrique Hudson, was the Argentine-born son of New Englanders Daniel Hudson and Carolina Kimble, who moved to Argentina in 1836. Born in 1841, Hudson passed his youth on the farm known as Los 25 Ombúes for the

The Pampas

República de los Niños near La Plata

ombú trees that once stood around the humble house in what was, at that time, a very wild and remote area. Today, the 18th-century adobe is a museum and the centerpiece of a compact 54-hectare forest and wetland preserve near the slum suburb of Florencio Varela.

Hudson, who left Argentina for England in 1869, recalled his pampas days in the memoir *Long Ago and Far Away* (1918), but left equally memorable South American stories in *Idle Days in Patagonia* (1893) and *The Purple Land* (1885, republished in 1904). His main interest, though, was natural history, particularly birds.

Along with Hudson's birthplace, which holds his books and family documents, there still stand some of the original 25 trees for which the farm

was named. The best time to see the park is after the spring rains, when the wetlands still teem with bird life—but also with mosquitoes.

The Parque Ecológico Cultural Guillermo E. Hudson (tel. 011/4901-9651) is about midway between Buenos Aires and La Plata. The easiest way there is to take the train from Constitución (Buenos Aires) to Estación Florencio Varela and bus No. 324, Ramal 2 (Terminal) to within a few hundred meters of the entrance, which is up a dirt road.

Nearby, off the Berazategui exit from Buenos Aires, the site where the late cumbia star Rodrigo Bueno rolled his car in 2000 has become an offbeat pilgrimage site for followers convinced he was a saint.

The Pampa Gaucha

Beyond the outskirts of Buenos Aires, the almost endlessly flat pampas are still, symbolically at least, the land of the gaucho. To the west, the city of Luján is one of Argentina's major religious destinations, but it's also home to an exceptional museum complex that brings Argentine history alive. The best place to see the truly living vestiges of gaucho life is the town of San Antonio de Areco, whose historic *estancias* have also acquired an international reputation for get-away-from-it-all holidays.

In the southwestern part of the province, the low mountain ranges of Tandilia and Ventania are the only major exceptions to an almost featureless relief. The city of Tandil and the village of Sierra de la Ventana are the major recreational destinations for Argentines, but they get relatively few foreign visitors despite their attractiveness—Tandil, in particular, is an oasis with a fascinating history. Several more important *estancias* lie in the vicinity of the triangle formed by Tandil, Sierra de la Ventana, and the city of Olavarría.

LUJÁN

History and legend blend in the pampas city of Luján, Argentina's single most important devotional center. Modern Luján, though, is an incongruous potpourri of piety and the profane, where pilgrims purchase shoddy souvenirs and, after making their obligatory visit to the landmark basilica, party until dawn.

Luján may merit a visit for the truly devout or those with an intellectual interest in orthodox Catholicism, but what really shines is its complex of historical museums, in handsome colonial buildings—their recent improvements have turned Luján from a mildly interesting side trip into a nearly obligatory one.

As a sacred symbol, Luján gets four million visitors per year, mostly on weekends and for religious holidays like Easter and May 8 (the Virgin's day). Also important are events like October's Peregrinación de la Juventud (Youth Pilgrimage), a 62-kilometer walk from Once that

acquired a semipolitical character during the Dirty War, but has since returned to its devotional origins.

History

Legend says that in 1630 an oxcart loaded with a terra-cotta image of the Virgin Mary got stuck in the mud, unable to move until gauchos removed the statue. Its devout owner, from the northwestern province of Santiago del Estero, read this as a sign that the Virgin should remain at the spot, and built a chapel for her. Apparently, though, Argentina's patron saint was not totally immovable—she has since shifted to more opulent accommodations in Luján's French Gothic basilica, five kilometers from her original abode.

Orientation

On the right bank of its eponymous river, Luján (population 78,005) is about 65 kilometers west of Buenos Aires via RN7. Most points of interest are on and around Avenida Nuestra Señora de Luján, the broad avenue that enters town from the north, while most services are eastward toward the central Plaza Colón.

Sights

The basilica may be Luján's most imposing site, but its museums have undergone a professional transformation that transcends the standard stuff-in-glass-cases approach of so many provincial institutions.

In the **Basílica Nuestra Señora de Luján,** the "Virgencita" (little virgin) inhabits a separate *camarín* (chamber) behind the main altar; begging her help, pilgrims plod at a snail's pace past plaques left by their grateful predecessors. Glazed in silver to protect her from deterioration and clothed in white-and-blue robes, the ceramic Virgin is a diminutive 38-centimeter image made in Brazil and brought to Argentina in the early 17th century. In the 1880s, on a trip to Europe, the French Lazarist missionary Jorge Salvaire created her elaborate crown; apparently deciding that that was not enough, he worked tirelessly to build the Gothic basilica whose pointed spires now soar 106 meters above the pampas. Not completed until 1937, its facade has recently undergone an extensive restoration. Pope John Paul II said Mass here in 1982, only a few days before the Argentine surrender in the Falklands war.

Immediately west of the basilica, the **Museo Devocional** (1–6 P.M. weekdays except Mon., 10 A.M.–6 P.M. weekends) holds larger *ex-votos* (gifts left in thanks for the Virgin's help).

Complejo Museográfico

On the west side of Avenida Nuestra Señora de Luján, immediately north of the basilica, the former **Cabildo** (colonial town council, 1797) and the **Casa del Virrey** (1803) house one of the country's finest museum complexes—the Complejo Museográfico Enrique Udaondo. No viceroy every lived in Luján, by the way, but the Marqués de Sobremonte once spent a few hours in the house.

Porteño architect Martín S. Noël's 1918 restoration of the Cabildo took some liberties with the building's original unadorned facade and a few other features. Still, the three hectares of buildings and well-kept grounds, bounded by Calles Lezica y Torrezuri, Lavalle, San Martín, and Parque Ameghino, are distinguished for their contents as well.

Within the Cabildo and the Casa del Virrey, the **Museo Histórico** has a vividly thorough display on Argentine history, with a dazzling assortment of maps, portraits, and artifacts (such as caudillo Facundo Quiroga's blood-stained vicuña poncho) that bring history alive. The museum box office, at the corner of Avenida Nuestra Señora de Luján and Lavalle, has a salon for special exhibits such as a remarkable display of crucifixes throughout the ages.

Immediately to the north, the **Museo de Transporte** houses an extraordinary collection of horse carriages in mint condition, including hearses, a carriage that belonged to General Bartolomé Mitre, and the stuffed carcasses of Gato and Mancha, the hardy criollo horses that A. F. Tschiffely rode from Buenos Aires to Washington, D.C. in the 1930s. There is also a Dornier sea-plane cobuilt by Spaniards and Argentines, and the country's first-ever locomotive, from the Ferrocarril Oeste. The upstairs of the main showroom is devoted to an elaborate exhibit on *mate* and its ritual, from colonial times to the present.

The Complejo Museográfico (tel. 02323/420245, Thurs. and Fri. noon–5:30 P.M., weekends 10 A.M.–5:30 P.M.) charges US$.35 admission, paid at the corner of Avenida Nuestra Señora de Luján and Lavalle; admission is good for all its facilities.

Entertainment

For most visitors to Luján, entertainment consists of spontaneous barbecues in Parque Ameghino or, when campgrounds are really crowded, on the median strip of Avenida Nuestra Señora de Luján. Alternatively, there are movies at the **Cine Nuevo Numancia 1** (San Martín 398, tel. 02323/43086), and drinking and dancing at the **Old Swan Pub** (San Martín 546, tel. 02323/433346).

Accommodations

Many if not most pilgrims choose cheap camping; in fact, on major religious holidays, pilgrims camp just about anywhere there's open space, including the median strip of Avenida Nuestra Señora de Luján. More formally, across the Río Luján about 10 blocks north of the basilica, shady **Camping El Triángulo**, (RN7 Km 69.5, tel. 02323/430116, info@lujanet.com.ar, US$4 d) also rents tents for about US$1.50.

Across from the bus terminal, **Hotel Royal** (9 de Julio 696, tel. 02323/421295, US$8/10 s/d) offers smallish but otherwise adequate rooms; it has a restaurant, but breakfast is extra. On the east side of the basilica, the well-managed **Hotel de la Paz** (9 de Julio 1054, tel. 2323/428742, US$10/12 s/d) is a dignified inn that's been around for nearly a century. Rates include breakfast, cable TV, and private bath; weekdays cost about 10 percent less than weekends.

Rooms at **Hotel del Virrey** (San Martín 129, tel. 2323/420797, US$11/13 s/d) include private bath and breakfast. The 45-room **Hotel Hoxón** (9 de Julio 769, tel. 2323/429970, hoxonsa @s6.coopenet.com.ar, US$10–12 s, US$13–16 d) is a step up, the only place in town with its own pool; rates include a buffet breakfast.

Food

Calle 9 de Julio, just north of the basilica, consists of indistinguishable and cheap *parrillas,* lined up wall-to-wall, frequented primarily by pilgrims.

For breakfast and desserts, the best choice is **Berlín** (San Martín 135), half a block east of the basilica. **Don Chiquito** (Colón 964) has a similar menu of higher quality; it's more expensive but considerably more sedate.

Befitting Luján's ecclesiastical importance, the traditional place for a more formal family lunch or dinner is the Carmelite-run **M L'eau Vive**(Constitución 2112, tel. 02323/421774). Fixed-price lunches or dinners, in the US$4–6 range, lean toward French specialties; they sometimes stop to observe a recorded version of *Ave Maria.* Lunch hours are daily except Monday, noon–2:15 P.M., dinner hours daily except Sunday and Monday, 8:30–10 P.M. The main dining room is nonsmoking.

Information and Services

Luján's municipal **Dirección de Turismo** is in Parque Ameghino's Edificio La Cúpula (at the west end of Lavalle, tel. 02323/433500, 9 A.M.–1 P.M. weekdays only). The newly opened **Asociación Lujanina de Turismo,** a block north of the basilica at 9 de Julio 922, keeps irregular hours but is most helpful.

Correo Argentino is at Mitre 575; the postal code is 6700.

Getting There and Around

Luján has good road and rail connections with Buenos Aires. The bus station is walking distance to everything; the train station is across town, but cheap *remises* can carry up to four passengers for only about US$1.

The **Estación Terminal de Ómnibus** (Avenida Nuestra Señora del Rosario between Almirante Brown and Dr. Reat, tel. 02323/420044) is three blocks north of the basilica. Transporte Automotores Luján (Línea 52) runs buses to and from Plaza Miserere (Once) in Buenos Aires, while Transportes Atlántida (Línea 57, tel. 2323/420032, int. 24), connects Luján with Plaza Italia, in Palermo.

For train travel, TBA's Línea Sarmiento (Avenida España and Belgrano, tel. 02323/421312) goes to and from the capital's Estación Once (Subte: Plaza Miserere, Línea A), but it's necessary to change trains in Moreno.

SAN ANTONIO DE ARECO

Bidding for UNESCO World Heritage Site status, the 18th-century town of San Antonio de Areco is Argentina's unofficial gaucho capital, host to its biggest gaucho festivities, and home to a concentration of traditional craftsmen and artists difficult to match in any other place of its size. It's an irony, though, that many of those most closely associated with those gaucho traditions have Italian immigrant surnames.

San Antonio was the home of *gauchesco* novelist Ricardo Güiraldes, who wrote *Don Segundo Sombra* (1927) here. It was also the location for director Manuel Antín's 1969 movie, which featured the author's recently deceased (September 2002) nephew Adolfo Güiraldes in the title role of a dignified rustic whose practical wisdom leaves a lasting imprint on a landowner's son.

Bucking recent economic trends, San Antonio emits an air of tidy prosperity even in the midst of crisis. Its biggest annual event is November's **Día de la Tradición,** celebrating gaucho heritage, but weekends are busy all year round.

Orientation

San Antonio de Areco (population 17,820) is 113 kilometers west of Buenos Aires via RN8, which continues west toward San Luis, Mendoza, and the Chilean border. On the right bank of the Río Areco, it forms a mostly regular grid west of the highway; the commercial street of Alsina, leading south from the main Plaza Ruiz de Arellano, is the liveliest part of town.

Sights

San Antonio is so pedestrian-friendly that, in a country where motorists rarely even slow down for crosswalks, townsfolk often stroll in the middle of the street. That's not really recommended, but San Antonio's leisurely pace and compact core do make it attractive for walkers and cyclists.

Unlike most central plazas, San Antonio's **Plaza Ruiz de Arellano** is not the lively hub of local life, but it's an appealingly shady park surrounded by historic buildings and monuments: the **Casa de los Martínez,** site of the original *estancia* house, at the northwest corner; the **Iglesia Parroquial** (Parish Church, 1869) on the south side; and the **Palacio Municipal** (1885), part of which has become the Draghi family's **Taller y Museo de Platería Criolla y Civil y Salón de Arte,** a combination museum, silversmith's workshop, and art gallery, on the north side. In the center of the plaza, the **Monumento a Vieytes** memorializes San Antonio native Juan Hipólito Vieytes (1762–1815), a participant in the 1810 revolution that eventually brought Argentine independence.

Half a block north of the Plaza, the **Centro Cultural Usina Vieja** (Alsina 66, tel. 02326/452021, 8 A.M.–3 P.M. weekdays, 11 A.M.–4:45 P.M. weekends, free) is an antique power plant (1901) recycled into a fine museum and cultural center. It holds permanent collections of prints by Florencio Molina Campos, massive metal *gauchesco* sculptures by José Perera, and a good sample of work by San Antonio's artisans. It's also managed impressive special exhibits that re-create overlooked everyday institutions like the simple barbershop and *botica* (apothecary), but it hasn't done much in the way of historical and cultural interpretation.

Three blocks northwest, facing the river at the corner of Zerboni and Moreno, is a small zoo, the **Parque de Flora y Fauna Autóctona Carlos Merti** (tel. 02326/453783, 9 A.M.–noon and 2–7 P.M. daily, US$.35).

Across the street, the restored **Puente Viejo** (1857) over the Río Areco may have been the country's first toll bridge; originally designed for cart traffic, it lent its atmosphere to the movie version of *Don Segundo Sombra.* It's now a horse-and-pedestrian shortcut to the **Parque Criollo y Museo Gauchesco Ricardo Güiraldes** (Camino Ricardo Güiraldes s/n, tel. 02326/454780, 11 A.M.–5 P.M. daily except Tues., US$2, US$.35

retired persons, free for children under 12), a museum that's a romantic idealization of the already romantic *gauchesco* literature of Ricardo Güiraldes, whose family lived on the nearby Estancia La Porteña (which is open to visits; see the callout "The Estancias of Areco" for details). Set on 97 hectares of parkland, the museum was created by the provincial government in the 1930s. It lacks the authenticity of the *estancia* itself, but it offers ironic insights into the way Argentines—even *porteños*—have internalized the gaucho heritage.

The main irony, of course, was that the landowning novelist Güiraldes, whatever his sincerity, presumed to speak for the illiterate gaucho—a defiantly independent figure who became a humble dependent laborer on the *estancias* of the oligarchy. Nowhere is this clearer than in the principal Casa del Museo, a 20th-century replica of an 18th century *casco* (big house): it devotes two rooms to Güiraldes himself; another to his wife Adelina del Carril; another to his painter cousin Alberto; a Sala de los Escritores of *gauchesco* literature including Walter Owen's English-language translation of José Hernández's epic poem *Martín Fierro;* a Sala Pieza de Estanciero that includes the bed of tyrant landowner Juan Manuel de Rosas (who exploited gauchos ruthlessly but counted them among his most enthusiastic allies); and, finally, a Sala del Gaucho that stresses horse gear and *gauchesco* art, but not the gaucho's increasingly marginal status.

While the Casa del Museo gives only a partial account of the gaucho, the surrounding park also contains the **Pulpería La Blanqueada,** a real 19th-century roadhouse with a life-size gaucho diorama. Nearby are three other aging structures, the **La Ermita de San Antonio,** an adobe chapel with an image of its patron saint; the **La Tahona** flourmill (1848); and the **Galpón y Cuarto de Sogas,** a carriage house.

It's not the only *gauchesco* institution in town, though: Luis Gasparini, son of the late painter Osvaldo Gasparini, continues to paint and operate the **Museo Gauchesco del Pintor Gasparini** (Alvear 521, tel. 02326/453930, gaspa@areconline.com.ar, 8 A.M.–8 P.M., 365 days a year, free). This *gauchesco* art museum has half a dozen rooms devoted to the gaucho, sculpture, silverwork, and painting (including works by Benito Quinquela Martín and Lino Spilimbergo, among others). There are also a chapel, an atelier with the family's own *gauchesco* works, and a library.

At the intersection of RN 8 and Soldado Argentino, at the south end of San Antonio, the remains of both Ricardo Güiraldes and Segundo Ramírez (the author's model for the fictional Don Segundo Sombra) repose in the **Cementerio Municipal.**

For a day in the country without really leaving town, visit **Estancia la Cinacina** (Mitre 9, tel. 02326/452045, aircampo@areconet .com.ar, www.lacinacina.com.ar), only six blocks west of Plaza Ruiz de Arellano. The fee of about US$12 pp includes snacks, a city tour, lunch, and folkloric music and dance; from Buenos Aires, with transportation, it costs about US$25 pp.

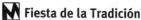 Fiesta de la Tradición

Since 1934, this November festival has feted San Antonio's gaucho heritage with guided visits to historic sites, lectures by top folklorists, crafts fairs, and folkloric music and dance—plus, of course, flamboyant displays of horsemanship. While the principal *Día de la Tradición* is theoretically November 10, the festivities normally stretch over two weekends, climaxing on the final Sunday. Reservations are critical for anyone who wants to stay in San Antonio proper rather than in the surrounding countryside or neighboring towns.

Shopping

San Antonio's silversmiths are the country's finest, so don't expect to find any bargains—a silver *mate* gourd can cost up to US$1,500, though there are, of course, cheaper versions. Other typical silver dress items include the long-bladed *facón* (gaucho knife), *rastra* (studded belt), and *espuelas* (spurs).

THE ESTANCIAS OF ARECO

Just off Ruta Provincial 41, northbound from San Antonio, several historic *estancias* grow soybeans and raise livestock, but tourism pays the bills. All of them take overnight guests, but also offer "day in the country" excursions, including a lunchtime *asado* as well as rural activities like horseback riding. Camping is not out of the question, at least at La Porteña.

Estancia La Porteña

San Antonio's most emblematic *estancia,* La Porteña has belonged to the Güiraldes family since the early 19th century. Of all the area's farms, it has the finest grounds: French landscape architect Charles Thays, who created major public parks like Palermo's Jardín Botánico and Mendoza's Parque General San Martín, designed the plan, including the stately corridor of elmlike hackberries that leads to the *casco* (main house).

La Porteña has only four guest rooms, so reservations are essential. Beef is the standard menu, but the kitchen will accommodate vegetarians with pasta and other meatless dishes, served in a dining room filled with French and British antiques. It eschews television, but there's a large swimming pool and a library, and English is spoken.

Estancia La Porteña (tel. 02326/453770, cell 02325/15-684179, info@estancialaporte-nia.com.ar, www.estancialaportenia.com.ar) charges US$100 d per night with full board. It also has a campground, effectively segregated from the main grounds, which charges US$3.50 pp.

Estancia El Ombú de Areco

El Ombú de Areco, named for Argentina's wide-crowned national tree, was the estate of General Pablo Ricchieri (1859–1936), who first forced military conscription onto Argentina's

Silversmith Juan José Draghi (Alvear 345, tel. 02326/454219, draghi@arecoonline.com) has enlivened the moribund Plaza Ruiz de Arellano with the new **Taller y Museo de Platería Criolla y Civil y Salón de Arte** (Lavalle between Alsina and Ruiz de Arellano, tel. 02326/15-511684). Other silversmiths of note include Raúl Horacio Draghi (Guido 391, tel. 02326/454207), who also works in leather; Gustavo Stagnaro (Arellano 59, tel. 02326/454801); and Miguel and Martín Rigacci (Belgrano 381, tel. 02326/456049).

Sogas Areco (Moreno 280, tel. 02326/453797) specializes in gaucho clothing and horse gear. Cristina Giordano (Sarmiento 112, tel. 02326/452829) is a weaver.

Accommodations

Despite its tourist tradition, San Antonio proper has good but limited accommodations; the level of services has improved in recent years, as even some moderately priced hotels have features like swimming pools, a/c, and the like.

During November's Fiesta de la Tradición, when reservations are imperative, visitors may lodge in communities for miles around. Prices often rise on weekends, when reservations are advisable, but bed-and-breakfast accommodations may also be available—ask at the tourist office.

At the north end of Zapiola, the **Camping Municipal** is cheap (US$2 pp) and shady, but the river floods when it rains heavily. **Hotel San Carlos** (Zapiola and Zerboni, tel. 02326/453106, sancarlos@arecoonline.com.ar, www.hotel-sancarlos.com.ar, US$10 d) is an exceptional value with continental breakfast, cable TV, swimming pool, and other amenities, including free bicycles.

Immediately across the street, the modern **Hotel Los Abuelos** (Zapiola and Zerboni, tel. 02326/456390, US$8/12 s/d) is comfortable,

youth. Set among four hectares of formal gardens, with a pool, on a 300-hectare property, it's the most lavish of all Areco *estancias* in terms of furnishings, facilities, and activities: There's satellite TV and video, telephone, horseback and bicycle riding, and games. There are six impeccable double rooms and three triples; rates for overnight accommodation start at US$100/150 s/d with full board, taxes included. Vegetarians should verify the menu, which leans heavily toward beef.

Estancia El Ombú de Areco (tel. 02326/492080, cell 02325/15-682598, reservas@estancia elombu.com, www.estanciaelombu.com) also offers "day in the country" excursions for US$35 pp and arranges transportation from the capital and its airports for guests. Its Gran Buenos Aires contact is at Cura Allievi 1280, Boulogne, Buenos Aires Province, tel. 011/4710-2795.

Estancia La Bamba

Less elegant than La Porteña and less luxurious than El Ombú, Estancia La Bamba is rougher around the edges, but its unique origins—it began as a *posta*, or way station, on the colonial Camino Real, rather than as an *estancia* per se—define its unique ambience. The least formal of the big three, it's perhaps the most relaxed of them all.

La Bamba, which served as a set for director María Luisa Bemberg's 19th-century drama *Camila,* can accommodate 11 persons in five rooms in the main house, another four in a cottage suitable for a family, and four more in an annex. Amenities include a swimming pool, game and video rooms, and activities such as horseback riding, bird-watching, and fishing. Rates range from about US$70 to US$130 pp with full board, depending on the room.

Estancia La Bamba (tel. 02326/456293, tel. 11/4732-1269 in Buenos Aires, info@la-bamba .com.ar, www.la-bamba.com.ar) also offers a "day in the country" for about US$40 pp.

but what might have been a secluded central garden has instead become a driveway and parking lot. The smallish rooms have private bath, high ceilings with fans, telephone, cable TV, and swimming pool; skip the mediocre breakfast (US$1 extra).

Rates at **La Posada del Ceibo** (Irigoyen between RN 8 and Avenida Dr. Smith, tel. 02326/454614, elceibo@areconet.com.ar, US$8/12 s/d) include breakfast, private bath, cable TV, and pool. Rooms at **Hotel Fuaz** (Avenida Dr. Smith 488, tel. 02326/452487, US$13 d) come with a/c and breakfast, and more-spacious rooms are just a little dearer.

Food

San Antonio has a pair of passable pizzerias: downtown's **Pizzería Dell'Olmo** (Alsina 365, tel. 02326/452506) and **Pizza Morena** (Zerboni and Moreno, tel. 02326/456391), near the river.

La Costa (Belgrano and Zerboni, tel. 02326/452481) serves primarily *parrillada* but also pasta, with friendly service and good prices; most entrees are in the US$3–4 range. Immediately across Belgrano, **Un Alto en la Huella** (tel. 02326/455595) has similar offerings and prices.

Brilliantly recreating a traditional *pulpería* atmosphere, **Puesto La Lechuza** (Alsina 188, tel. 02326/455523) serves home-cooked Argentine food—your basic *bife de chorizo* and a salad, but also appetizers of homemade salami, cheese, bread, and empanadas. There's usually live music on weekends; if not, ask owner Marcelo Salazar to play "Whiter Shade of Pale" on the antique Parisian organ.

The **M Almacén de Ramos Generales** (Bolívar 143, tel. 2326/456376) is a *parrilla* that also sells homemade salami, cheeses, and desserts. **La Olla de Cobre** (Matheu 433, tel. 2326/453105) produces fine artisanal chocolates and other sweets. **Dulces del Pago** (Zerboni 136, tel. 2326/454751) specializes in fruit preserves.

Information and Services

San Antonio's **Dirección de Turismo** (Zerboni and Ruiz de Arellano, tel. 2326/453165) is open 8 A.M.–2 P.M. weekdays, 10 A.M.–8:30 P.M. Saturday, and 10 A.M.–6 P.M. Sunday; on weekends only, for arriving motorists, it maintains a small kiosk on Calle de los Martínez near the intersection with RN8. Their monthly *Don Segundo* is a useful commercial miniguide with a town map; the less-frequently published *Pregón Turismo* provides more detail on things to see and do.

Money is available through ATMs at several banks, including **Banco de la Provincia,** on Mitre immediately west of Plaza Ruiz de Arellano.

There are several *locutorios* for telephone service; **Areco Online** (Arellano 285-A) has reliable Internet access.

The **Hospital Municipal Zerboni** is at Moreno and Lavalle (tel. 02326/452345).

Getting There and Around

San Antonio's main Terminal de Ómnibus is at Avenida Doctor Smith and General Paz, tel. 02326/453904, on the east side of town. **Chevallier** (at Buenos Aires's Retiro bus terminal, tel. 011/4314-5555) charges US$4 to San Antonio (1.5–two hours), with 12 buses daily.

Pullman General Belgrano, next door at the Bar Parador Don Segundo (tel. 02326/15-680368) has three buses daily to Retiro.

There are also westbound long-distance buses on RN 8 toward Córdoba, San Luis, and Mendoza.

M TANDIL

Surrounded by the rounded slopes of its namesake Sierras, Tandil offers literal relief from the relentlessly flat pampas of southern Buenos Aires Province—even though its granitic summits top out at Cerro Albión, only 502 meters above sea level. Still, its irregular terrain has sufficed to make charmingly cobblestoned Tandil one of southern Buenos Aires Province's top recreational destinations.

Tandil is also a major pilgrimage site at Easter, when tens of thousands of the faithful converge at cross-topped Monte Calvario, so called for its supposed resemblance to Golgotha. The city is also known for its gaucho souvenirs and for delectable homemade hams, salamis, and cheeses.

History

Placid Tandil has had a remarkably violent past ever since its origins as Fuerte Independencia, a military outpost established by Martín Rodríguez in 1823, in the course of Argentina's relentless campaign against its indigenous inhabitants. When the dictator Juan Manuel de Rosas assumed power in 1829, the conflict intensified. Between 1820 and 1870, according to one contemporary estimate, the Pampas Indians had rustled 11 million cattle, two million horses, and two million sheep, and had killed 50,000 people and destroyed 3,000 houses.

While the indigenous frontier had largely receded by 1872, violence itself did not vanish. One of the most infamous incidents occurred on New Year's Day of that year, as the messianic healer Gerónimo de Solané, popularly known as Tata Dios (literally, "God the Father") or Médico Dios ("God the Doctor") inspired a brief but bloody reign of throat-slitting terror against foreigners. Some 35 European settlers—British, French, Italian, and Spanish—died at the hands of Solané's gaucho followers; the only Argentine death was an apparent victim of mistaken identity.

In part, the gauchos were motivated by resentment of their own marginal status, but the influence of landowners and corrupt local officials, in an area where Buenos Aires's authority was tenuous, likely played a part as well. Solané, though he himself did not participate in the massacres, died unaccountably of gunshot wounds while detained in the Tandil jail.

The Tandil massacres were not unique in their day, but such extreme and seemingly unprovoked violence had international repercussions. The perception grew, particularly among British observers in Buenos Aires and overseas, that Argentina's federal government could not guarantee the lives and livelihoods of settlers. Immigration declined and foreign investment withdrew, at least temporarily; some historians have argued that this set a pattern of mistrust that continues to the present.

Orientation

Tandil (population 100,869) is 360 kilometers south of Buenos Aires via RN 3 and RN 226, and 160 kilometers northwest of Mar del Plata via RN 226. Plaza Independencia sits precisely in the center of the city's compact original grid, which is bounded by Avenida España to the north, Avenida Rivadavia to the west, Avenida Santamarina to the east, and Avenida Avellaneda to the south.

Sights

Densely wooded, dotted with neoclassical statuary and fountains, **Plaza Independencia** occupies two full blocks; an obelisk in its center marks Tandil's **Piedra Fundamental,** the city's founding stone.

On the former site of Fuerte Independencia (which was demolished in 1864), on the south side of the plaza, the **Municipalidad de Tandil** occupies the former Banco Hipotecario Nacional. Around the corner is the **Museo de Bellas Artes** (Fine Arts Museum, Chacabuco 367, tel. 02293/432067, 5–8 P.M. daily except Monday).

Across the street from the Municipalidad, the neo-Gothic **Templo de la Inmaculada Concepción** (1878) includes stones from Fuerte Independencia, but the triple towers are a late (1969) addition. Its **campanario** (bell tower, 1931) came from Bochum, Germany.

Tandil's **Museo Tradicionalista** (4 de Abril 485, tel. 02293/424025, 4–8 P.M. daily) is a classic kitchen-sink museum that includes just about everything under the sun that has anything to do with Tandil—and it looks like they've tried to make room for every item they possess. It's rather like visiting a thrift shop—hundreds of photographs, works by local artists, a replica of a *pulpería* (rural bar), dozens of horse carriages, and even a 1940s fighter plane, in 17 huge exhibit halls.

Tandil proper is mostly level, but the Sierras start barely six blocks southwest of the plaza in **Parque Independencia,** whose main entrance is at the corner of Avenida Avellaneda and Rondeau.

To the northwest, at the end of Avenida Monseñor de Andrea, **Monte Calvario** is the site of Easter ceremonies.

In 1872, the followers of Tata Dios gathered at **Cerro La Movediza,** about three kilometers

The Pampas

© WAYNE BERNHARDSON

Plaza Independencia, Tandil, Buenos Aires Province

northwest of the plaza, where a 300-ton boulder wobbled in the wind for centuries before finally falling four decades later. According to legend, the so-called **Piedra Movediza** withstood all the efforts of General Rosas's draft animals to pull it down. Bus No. 503 (blue) goes directly there.

Entertainment

The **Teatro Cervantes** (Rodríguez 551, tel. 02293/449607) is Tandil's major performing arts venue and an historical monument—tango legend Carlos Gardel performed five times here, the last time in 1933, only two years before his untimely death.

For movies, try the **Cines Plaza** (Chacabuco 517, tel. 02293/448600) or the **Cinecenter** (Panamá 351, tel. 02293/422332).

Tandil enjoys a lively bar scene at places like the stylishly punning **Bar Tolomé** (Rodríguez and Mitre, tel. 02293/422951), which also has live music; the name derives from its location on the street named for President Bartolomé Mitre. The **Golden Bar** (Pinto 706, tel. 02293/444100)

and the **Scotch Bar** (9 de Julio 760) are also worth checking out.

Shopping

Along with San Antonio de Areco, Tandil is one of the best places on the pampas to shop for gaucho souvenirs such as horse gear, leather, and silver. **Talabartería La Yunta** (Sarmiento 607) has an outstanding selection.

The other local specialty is dairy products and cured meats, such as ham and salami. One of the classic shops is **Época de Quesos** (San Martín and 14 de Julio, tel. 02293/448750).

Sports and Recreation

Tandil is ideal for recreational activities. Swimmers can try the three pools at the **Balneario del Sol** (Avenida Zarini s/n, tel. 02293/435697) on the **Dique del Fuerte,** a sprawling reservoir 12 blocks south of Plaza Independencia.

It's also a major site for mountain biking, with several rental agencies within town, and rock climbing thanks to its steep granite faces (though the summits themselves are walkups). For horseback riding, contact **Gabriel Barletta Cabalgatas** (Avellaneda 673, tel. 02293/427725, cell 15/509609, cabalgatasbarletta@yahoo.com.ar), who also arranges trekking and canoeing.

Accommodations

Reservations are advisable on weekends and especially during Semana Santa, when Tandil is mobbed and many *Tandilenses* rent out their spare rooms.

Tandil has many campgrounds; one of the most convenient is **Camping Pinar de la Sierra** (Avenida San Gabriel s/n, tel. 02993/425370, US$5 for up to four people), the former municipal site south of the Dique del Fuerte. Take the No. 500 (yellow) bus, but verify that it goes all the way to the campground.

For a shoestring sleep, with private bath, **Hotel Kaiku** (Mitre 902, tel. 02293/423114, 440047, luisdelgado2000@yahoo.com, US$5/9 s/d) is even cheaper without TV. The building is rundown, but it's not a desperation choice.

Past its prime, **Hotel Austral** (9 de Julio 725, tel. 02293/425606, US$7/13 s/d) is a worn and slowly declining place that's still a step above the Kaiku. Rates rise slightly on weekends. Under the same management, in a rehabbed older building, friendly **Hotel Torino** (Sarmiento 502, tel. 02293/423454, US$9/13 s/d) is a better value—the rooms have new furniture.

Far superior, though, is the B&B-style **Ⓜ Lo de Olga** (Chacabuco 977, tel. 02293/440258, agandolfi@infovia.com.ar, www.lodeolgagandolfi.com, US$7 pp), which occupies a vintage 1918 house. **Ⓜ Hospedaje Hutton** (Belgrano 39, tel. 02293/426989, myjhutton@ciudad .com.ar, US$14/22/32 s/d/t) is an English-run B&B which, at the time of its construction, was the *casco* of an *estancia* on the outskirts of town. There are only two rooms with private bath, but it's quiet, with spacious grounds, a pool, parking, and everything within easy walking distance. Rates include a self-serve breakfast.

Request a 7th-floor balcony room overlooking Plaza Independencia at **Hotel Dior** (Rodríguez 471, tel. 02293/431901, fax 02293/431903, info@hoteldior.com, www.hoteldior.com.ar, US$19/27 s/d); the view extends to the southern Sierras. The well-kept rooms include a buffet breakfast.

In a 1970s building, the **Plaza Hotel** (General Pinto 438, tel. 02293/427160, plazah@speedy .com.ar, www.plazahoteldetandil.com.ar, US$20/28 s/d) has decent, well-furnished rooms mostly with showers rather than tubs. Rates include breakfast and parking.

The modern **Ⓜ Hotel Libertador** (Mitre 545, tel. 02293/422127, tandil@hotel-libertador.com.ar, www.hotel-libertador.com.ar, US$25/34 s/d) is one of few small-town provincial hotels that truly deserves its four-star rating—by any standard, the rooms are comfortable and spacious, and service is exemplary. With buffet breakfast, this is really a bargain—some places in Buenos Aires charge twice the price for less than half as much.

Ⓜ Hostería Ave María (Avenida Colón 1440 in town, tel. 02293/422843, fax 02293/428737, avemaria@arnet.com.ar, www.avemariatandil .com.ar, US$60/100 s/d) is an elegant Normandy-style farmhouse surrounded by 40 hectares of conifers, magnolias, and oaks at Paraje La Porteña, on Tandil's southern outskirts. Part of what was once a much larger *estancia,* it has eight guest rooms, all with fireplaces and private bath. Activities include horseback riding and carriage excursions, cycling, carriage rides, swimming, and massages; the area beyond the *estancia* offers many more activities. Rates include half board; meals include *asados* and homegrown vegetables.

Food

The **Grill Argentino** (Rodríguez 560, tel. 02293/448666) is an enormously popular *parrilla* and pizzeria that, unfortunately, suffers from a high decibel level. For quieter dining, stroll around the corner to the formal **Club Hípico** (Pinto 636, tel. 02293/435878).

El Estribo (San Martín 750, tel. 02293/425943) is a *parrilla* that specializes in pork. For chicken, there's **El Nuevo Don José** (Monseñor de Andrea 269, tel. 02293/424970). **Taberna Manolo** (Rodríguez 890) specializes in pastas, mostly in the US$3–4 range, with exceptional service.

THE ESTANCIAS OF OLAVARRÍA

Best known as the *Capital del Cemento* (Cement Capital) of Buenos Aires Province, about 400 kilometers southwest of the federal capital, Olavarría is no great destination in its own right, but it's close to two major tourist *estancias*, La Isolina and Sumain.

Estancia La Isolina

In the course of shooting *Imagining Argentina* with Antonio Banderas, British actress Emma Thompson relaxed at Estancia La Isolina, just outside the Olavarría suburb of Hinojo. On the banks of the slow-flowing Arroyo Tapalqué, La Isolina's English-style *casco* (1920) sits on five hectares of manicured grounds on an 1,130-hectare property, and offers horseback and carriages rides, fishing, canoeing, and swimming in a giant-size pool. Owners Jorge and María Louge are descendants of French founder Esteban J. Louge, whose family arrived in 1854.

La Isolina can accommodate up to a dozen guests in rooms furnished, but not cluttered, with antiques in an understated manner. English and French are spoken.

Rates are US$70 pp with full board, with a 50 percent discount for children ages 2–10; dinners are more formal than breakfast or lunch. Their *día de campo* (day in the country) program, which lasts from 11 A.M. to 5 P.M., costs US$30 pp and includes a lunchtime *asado* and late-afternoon tea.

Estancia La Isolina (tel. 02284/491039, 02284/15-652616, or 011/4806-1404, laisolina @hotmail.com, www.laisolina.com.ar) will also pick up passengers at the Olavarría bus terminal (there are no commercial flights to central Buenos Aires Province, but very comfortable buses take five hours from Retiro).

Estancia La Isolina

© WAYNE BERNHARDSON

Estancia Sumain

Closer to the city of Bolívar than to Olavarría, Estancia Sumain has a modern *casco* dating from the 1970s, sheltered by conifers on 17 grassy hectares. Like La Isolina, it offers horseback and carriage rides, walks on the farm, and fishing in a nearby arroyo, as well as bicycle rides. Also like La Isolina, it's a working farm, where the French-Basque Inçaurgarat family employs several gauchos as well as participating actively themselves in farm activities.

There are seven double rooms with private bath, a huge dining room, and an attractive sunken bar. Estancia Sumain (Rivadavia 1378, Olavarría, tel. 02314/493013, info@estanciasumain.com.ar, www.estanciasumain.com.ar) also has a Buenos Aires contact (Libertad 844, 11° B, tel. 011/4816-8634). Rates are US$31 pp weekdays, US$35 pp weekends, including four meals and all activities, but not drinks or IVA. Sumain will pick up or drop off passengers at the Bolívar bus terminal for US$11 pp.

For breakfast, try the **Café y Confitería Renzo** (Rodríguez 792, tel. 02293/443078), which also serves ice cream and desserts. **Helados Pronto** (9 de Julio 629, tel. 02293/441417) is another good ice creamery.

Information

In the summer high season, the **Dirección Municipal de Turismo** (Local 6 in the Galería de los Puentes at 9 de Julio 555, tel. 02293/432073 or 448698, tandilturismo@infovia.com.ar, www.tandil.gov.ar) is open 8 A.M.–8 P.M. weekdays, 8:30 A.M.–8 P.M. Saturday, and 9 A.M.–1:30 P.M. Sunday. The rest of the year, hours are 9 A.M.–7 P.M. weekdays only. It offers a good city map and brochures.

There is also a useful private website, www.gruposierras.com.

For motorists, **ACA** is at Rodríguez 399, tel. 02293/425463.

Services

Jonestur (San Martín 698, tel. 02293/434838) is Tandil's only exchange house. There are numerous ATMs, including **BankBoston** (Pinto 745).

Correo Argentino is at Pinto 623; the postal code is 7000.

Telefónica de la Sierra (Alem 575), two-plus blocks northeast of Plaza Independencia, also has Internet access. **Cyber Plaza,** on Rodríguez on the east side of Plaza Independencia, keeps long hours for Internet access.

The **Hospital Municipal Ramón Santamarina** is at General Paz 1406, tel. 02293/422010. The private **CAMI** (Pinto 851, tel. 02293/425107) comes highly recommended for 24-hour emergency services.

Barbini Turismo (Rodríguez 40, tel. 02293/428912) is a reliable local agency for tours and activities in the area.

Getting There and Around

Tandil's only air service is to Aeroparque (Buenos Aires) with **Aerovip** (Rodríguez 607, tel. 02293/422552), which flies 19-seaters.

The Terminal de Buses (Avenida Buzón 650, tel. 02293/432092) has frequent services to Buenos Aires (US$10, five hours), and several

more to Mar del Plata (US$4, 2.5 hours). There are better connections elsewhere in the country from the city of Azul, 90 kilometers to the northwest.

Localiza (Mitre 585, tel. 02293/447099) has rental cars.

⋈ SIERRA DE LA VENTANA

Rising sharply more than 1,200 meters above sea level, the abrupt topography of the Sierra de la Ventana is a startling contrast to most of the pampas region—even more so than the lower, rounded Sierra de Tandil. Its rugged terrain has made the range, also known as Ventania, a pole for outdoor recreation, centered on its namesake village—a sort of hill station for weekenders from the port city of Bahía Blanca and interior provincial towns like Olavarría.

Even in peak season, Sierra de la Ventana seems a sleepy village, especially during the midday siesta, but the surrounding sierras offer opportunities for camping, hiking, climbing, cycling, horseback riding, and fishing. Cycling is particularly important here, as automobile traffic seems to move slower than elsewhere in the country, but there are also conventional tourist attractions like swimming pools, golf courses, and even a casino.

Orientation

The village of Sierra de la Ventana is 550 kilometers southwest of Buenos Aires via RN 3 to Azul, RN 226 to Olavarría, and RP 76. It is 125 kilometers north of Bahía Blanca via RN 33 to Tornquist, and then RP 76.

Most services are on or near Avenida San Martín in the southerly sector of Villa Tivoli; Villa Arcadia, north of the Río Sauce Grande, is mostly residential.

Accommodations

Most accommodations in Sierra de la Ventana are past their prime, but still good enough for a night or two; in summer, though, it's hard to find a single room. Hotels are about evenly split between Villa Tivoli and Villa Arcadia.

Camping El Paraíso (Diego Meyer s/n, tel.

THE ESTANCIAS OF SIERRA DE LA VENTANA

Estancias in the vicinity of Sierra de la Ventana offer more variety, at least in terms of terrain and activities, than those in the flatter parts of the pampas. Vigorous hiking and fishing are better here than elsewhere.

Estancia Cerro de la Cruz

One of the province's elite *estancias,* only four kilometers north of Sierra de la Ventana, Cerro de la Cruz features a Normandy-style *casco* built by famed architect Alejandro Bustillo, on sprawling formal gardens surrounded by 6,000 hectares of farmland and ranchland. Conspicuous hunting and fishing trophies, displayed between magnificent ceiling beams and burnished *caldén* floors, make the living and dining areas reminders of the lifestyle that oligarchic families like the Bunges, who still own the property, enjoyed before even they felt the brunt of hard times.

Oriented toward the international market, Estancia Cerro de la Cruz (RP 72 Km 9, tel. 0291/15-6486957, cell 0291/15-6449884, www .golfyestancias.com.ar, cerrodelacruz@arnet.com.ar) has five well-furnished rooms with fireplaces for

US$50 pp with full board; reservations are essential. This includes activities such as horseback riding, and there is a large swimming pool, as well as river access for fishing within easy walking distance. The proprietors speak excellent English.

Estancia las Vertientes

Oriented toward a domestic rather than international clientele, Estancia las Vertientes is more conspicuously a working farm than Cerro de la Cruz, but the nine rooms at its two-story 1930s *casco* are ample and well-furnished. Activities include hiking, horseback riding, and farm tasks on its 8,709 hectares, but the swimming pool appears to be cleaned irregularly. Rates are US$22 pp with half board; English is spoken, but not so well as at Cerro de la Cruz.

Estancia las Vertientes (RP 76 Km 221, tel. 0291/491-0064, www.estancialasvertientes.com, info@estancialasvertientes.com) is almost directly opposite the town of Villa Ventana, but is reached by a gated dirt road. There is an inconspicuous sign; again, reservations are essential.

0291/491-5299, US$2 per adult, US$1 per child) has shady riverside facilities.

The rooms at ACA-affiliated **Hostería Maitén** (Iguazú 93, tel. 0291/491-5073, US$6.50 pp) need attention to bring them up to standard—the electric outlets are few and aging, and the paint is peeling in spots, but it offers lush gardens, good parking, a quiet location, and bargain rates with a decent breakfast. Villa Arcadia's **Residencial Carlitos** (Coronel Suárez and Punta Alta, tel. 0291/491-5011, US$7.50 pp) is a better value, though.

Just across the railroad tracks, **Hotel Silver Golf** (Barrio Parque Golf, tel. 0291/491-5079, US$8–12 pp) is not nearly so exclusive as its linkside location might suggest. Standard rooms are acceptable, but a little extra cash gets a much larger and more comfortable but somewhat dark room. There is also a large pool, but not so large as others around town.

Villa Arcadia's **Hotel Pillahuincó** (Avenida Rayces 161, tel. 0291/491-5423, pillahuinco @impsat.com.ar, www.hotelpillahuinco.com.ar, US$15 pp) has expansive wooded grounds, a large pool, and considerable character. It has its share of deferred maintenance too, but even with the wear and tear, rates with half board make it one of the town's best values. The rooms, in four different buildings, vary considerably in size; some are very spacious, with enormous baths, others less so.

Buenos Aires Province has been managing Villa Tivoli's aging **Hotel Provincial Sierra de la Ventana** (Drago s/n, tel. 0291/491-5024, hotel-provincialsierradelaventana@hotmail.com, US$11 pp, US$16 pp with half board) since its private-management contract expired, but they clearly can't afford to invest anything in a slowly declining facility. That said, it has some outstanding features—the town's biggest swimming pool (pushing Olympic-size), extensive grounds, and decent rooms with, on the upper floor at least, balconies with views of the Sierras.

Food

Sol y Luna (Avenida San Martín 393) is a combination restaurant, pizzeria, and teahouse whose specialty is trout, which comes in a delicately spiced sauce of rosemary and shredded almonds. For single diners, they will also make half-pizzas. The service is friendly but a bit distracted.

Rali-Hue (Avenida San Martín between Bahía Blanca and Islas Malvinas) is a conventional *parrilla*. There is a pair of other good pizzerias: **El Establo** (San Martín between Islas Malvinas and Avenida Roca) and **Sher** (Güemes just north of San Martín, tel. 0291/491-5055); Sher also has fine pasta.

Information and Services

Next to the train station, the helpful **Oficina de Turismo y Delegación Municipal** (Avenida Roca 15, tel. 0291/491-5303, info@comarcaturistica.com.ar, www.comarcaturistica.com.ar) distributes maps and brochures, and will phone around to help locate accommodations. Hours are 8 A.M.–2 P.M. and 3–9 P.M. in summer, 8 A.M.–8 P.M. the rest of the year.

Banco de la Provincia (San Martín 260) now has an ATM.

Correo Argentino is at Avenida Roca 195; the postal code is 8168.

Locutorio Televentana (Avenida San Martín 291) has phone and fax services. For Internet, try the **Novabar** (Avenida San Martín 131), but connections are sluggish here.

Laverap (Güemes and San Martín) does laundry.

Getting There and Around

There are daily bus connections to Buenos Aires, but train service is infrequent.

There is **bus service** to Retiro (Buenos Aires) daily except Saturday (US$13, eight hours), from the improvised bus terminal (Avenida San Martín and Güemes). **Geotur Excursiones** (Avenida San Martín 198, tel. 0291/491-5355) goes to Bahía Blanca, as does **Expreso Cabildo,** which leaves from the Video Club at Avenida Roca 100.

Rail services from Buenos Aires to Bahía Blanca pass through Sierra de la Ventana, stopping at the Ferrocarril UPCP station (Avenida Roca and Avenida San Martín, tel. 0291/491-5164). Southbound trains leave Constitución Tuesday and Thursday at 9:10 P.M., arriving here at 7 A.M.; northbound trains leave Sierra de la Ventana at 11 P.M. Wednesday and Friday, arriving at Constitución at 8:30 A.M.

Geotur Excursions (Avenida San Martín 198, tel. 0291/491-5355) links Sierra de la Ventana with surrounding communities including Saldungaray, Villa Ventana, Cerro de la Ventana, and Tornquist. Schedules change with the season, but there are usually four buses daily in each direction, between 7 A.M. and 6 P.M.

VICINITY OF SIERRA DE LA VENTANA

Most sights and activities are not in the village of Sierra de la Ventana, but in the surrounding mountains. **Geotur** (Avenida San Martín 198, tel. 0291/491-5355) and **Excursiones Silver Golf,** immediately to the west, both arrange excursions to local attractions.

Cerro Tres Picos

Some 11 kilometers west of Sierra de la Ventana, 1,239-meter Cerro Tres Picos is the highest point in Buenos Aires Province, and thus a favorite climb for visitors to the area. Unlike the more frequently climbed Cerro de la Ventana, the summit is on private property and requires permission from Estancia Funke (tel. 0291/494-0058). Since the approach is lengthy, this is often done as an overnight backpack trip.

Villa Ventana

With its oval design, sandy streets, and incongruous chalets, 17 kilometers northwest of Sierra de la Ventana via RP 76, Villa Ventana exudes a borderline kitschy charm that's lacking in its more established but now somewhat ragged neighbor. Its **Oficina de Turismo** (tel. 0291/491-0095), at the entrance to town from the highway, is more than helpful.

Immediately opposite the tourist office,

Hostería La Península (tel. 0291/491-0012) is basic but clean for US$10 pp with half board. **Residencial la Colina** (Pillahuincó and Carpintero, tel. 0291/491-0063) is slightly cheaper.

For fine dining, Villa Ventana's **Las Golondrinas** (Cruz del Sur s/n, tel. 0291/491-0047), directly opposite the plaza, outshines anything in Sierra de la Ventana itself. Despite its faux rusticism and Swiss-alpine pretensions, it serves exceptional appetizers like smoked boar (US$2.50), entrees like grilled chicken breast with an Italian sauce (US$3.50), and desserts like raspberries and cream. There's also a long wine list.

Parque Provincial Ernesto Tornquist

Perhaps Argentina's most frequently climbed summit, 1,136-meter **Cerro de la Ventana** is the literal high point of this 6,700-hectare provincial park, with seemingly limitless panoramas of the nearby sierras and the outlying pampas. It's not the highest summit in Buenos Aires Province, though—that honor goes to nearby Cerro Tres Picos.

Cerro de la Ventana is a simple if sometimes steep hike that takes about two hours for anyone in average condition, but rangers (who appear to think every potential trekker is a sedentary *porteño* who smokes) restrict access after around

1 P.M., even though summer sunlight lasts until almost 9 P.M. Truly resolute hikers may persuade them to grant permission, which costs everyone US$1 pp, for an afternoon ascent, but only by signing a waiver. Rangers are on site from 8 A.M.–6 P.M.

The park's main entrance, about midway between Villa Ventana and the Campamento Base trailhead for Cerro de la Ventana, has a helpful, well-equipped **Centro de Visitantes** (tel. 0291/491-0039), open 8 A.M.–6 P.M. daily. Its impressive wrought-iron gates date from the days of the Tornquists, a German immigrant banking family that donated the parkland to Buenos Aires Province.

In summer, rangers lead guided walks to the gorge at **Garganta del Diablo** (Devil's Throat) at 9 A.M. daily except Tuesday and Thursday. Other sights include the gorge at **Garganta Olvidada** and indigenous caves at **Las Cuevas del Toro de Corpus Cristi.**

At the Cerro de la Ventana trailhead, **Campamento Base** (tel. 0291/491-0067, US$2 pp) offers wooded campsites with clean baths and hot showers. Toward the west, **Hotel El Mirador** (RP 76 Km 226, tel. 0291/494-1338) charges US$13/20 s/d with breakfast.

The Atlantic Shore

Buenos Aires Province's Atlantic shore is Argentina's summer playground, whose broad sandy beaches bring families from Buenos Aires and around the country for traditional summer vacations. That said, destinations along the coast vary dramatically in their offerings. Mar del Plata is a large, diverse city with an active cultural life; upper-middle-class to upper-class resorts like Villa Gesell and Pinamar have frenetic night life and are widely perceived as elitist. Those to the south of Mar del Plata, from Chapadmalal to Necochea and beyond, appeal more to working-class vacationers. The port city of Bahía Blanca is a major gateway to Patagonia, and home to one of the country's most interesting museums.

MAR DEL PLATA

In January and February, sun-seekers search for a spot on the sand beyond the colorful canvas tents of the countless *balnearios* that line the beaches of Mar del Plata, Argentina's premier seaside resort. On the southern coast of Buenos Aires Province, far less exclusive than it was when the Argentine counterpart to Britain's Bloomsbury group dominated the social scene, "Mardel" has become *the* affordable destination for working- and middle-class holiday-makers from Buenos Aires and around the country. After Buenos Aires, it's the country's major destination for congresses and conventions, and also a major arts and entertainment center.

The Pampas

Shade umbrellas cover the beach at Mar del Plata, Buenos Aires Province.

Because of its popularity, Mar del Plata can seem suffocatingly crowded in summer. Foreign visitors may enjoy the spring and autumn shoulder seasons, when the weather is often better, prices fall, and lines are shorter for the major attractions, but services may be fewer.

History

In 1581 Juan de Garay, the founder of Buenos Aires, was probably the first European to spot what he called the *costa galana* ("elegant coast," a term still used today), but it took nearly two centuries for Jesuit missionaries to establish a presence inland, in the area known as Laguna de los Padres. It took another century-plus for Portuguese investors to build a *saladero* (meat and hide salting plant) and the port that became Mar de Plata, after they sold out to Patricio Peralta Ramos, in 1874.

Peralta Ramos promoted Mar del Plata as an industrial center and, later, as a beach resort that brought the *porteño* elite to build summer chalets in Barrio los Troncos. The writer Victoria Ocampo, daughter of one of those elite families and founder of the literary magazine *Sur,* put Mardel on the cultural map by bringing famous writers from around Latin America and the world to her own summer house, now a cultural center and museum.

Many families of the Ocampo era have since departed for other provincial beach resorts like Villa Gesell and Pinamar, and even the Uruguayan resort of Punta del Este. Mar del Plata's declining exclusivity is reflected in the number of hotels that belong to labor unions, in the one- and two-star categories, that date from the Perón era. Since then, working- and middle-class families have deluged the city in the summer months, despite the survival of some elite barrios. In others, though, generic highrises have blocked the sun and blighted the neighborhood.

The Pampas

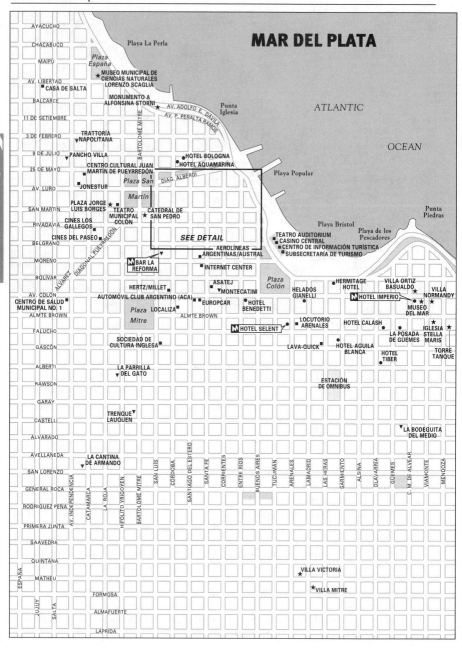

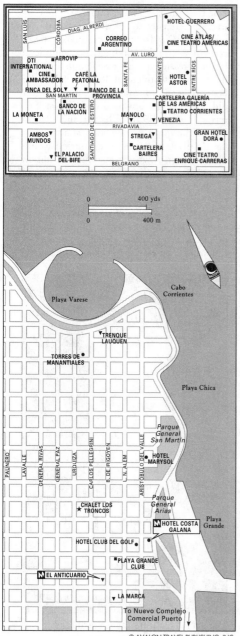

Orientation

Mar del Plata (population 541,857) stretches along eight kilometers of sandy Atlantic beaches, 404 kilometers south of Buenos Aires via RP 2, a four-lane toll road. Most sights lie within the downtown area bounded by the curving coastline, Avenida Independencia (which runs northeast-southwest), and Avenida Juan B. Justo (which leads northwest from the port). The coastal road, popularly known as Blvd. Marítimo, is called Avenida Peralta Ramos in the downtown area but changes names to the north (Avenida Félix U. Camet) and south (Avenida Martínez de Hoz).

For most of the day, the busiest part of town is the parallel pedestrian malls of San Martín and Rivadavia downtown. Other major activity centers are the commercial strip of Güemes, southeast of the bus terminal, and Avenida Leandro N. Alem in the Playa Grande area, to the south, where there are many new restaurants.

Sights

Emtur, Mardel's municipal tourist authority, offers free guided tours known as *Paseos para Gente Inquieta* (Excursions for Restless People), which require advance registration at their office at Blvd. Marítimo 2270. Among the sights visited are Villa Victoria (home of writer Victoria Ocampo and now a major cultural center), the impressive new Museo del Mar (Museum of the Sea), and the Base Naval Mar del Plata (the Argentine navy base).

The densely built downtown has only a handful of sights, such as the century-old, neo-Gothic **Catedral de San Pedro,** on the south side of **Plaza San Martín.** A block to the northwest, at San Martín and La Rioja, the much smaller **Plaza Jorge Luis Borges** features Miguel Repiso's tiled mural of Argentina's great literary figure.

Several blocks east, the **Playa Popular** (People's Beach) is home to the city's most closely packed concentration of summer rental tents. To the north, just beyond Punta Iglesia, the **Monumento a Alfonsina Storni** marks the point where, in 1938, the Argentine poet drowned herself by walking into the South Atlantic.

A few blocks farther north, Plaza España is the site of the **Museo Municipal de Ciencias Naturales Lorenzo Scaglia** (Libertad 3099, tel. 0223/473-8791, 8:30 A.M.–4:30 P.M. weekdays, 3–8 P.M. weekends), Mardel's outstanding natural sciences museum, displaying outstanding paleontological, archaeological, geological, and zoological exhibits. There's also a ground-floor aquarium that highlights ocean-going and freshwater local species. Admission costs US$.65 for adults, half that for children ages 6–11.

Mar del Plata may be a more democratic destination than it once was, but Barrio Stella Maris and Barrio los Troncos, southeast of **Plaza Colón,** still shine with the patina of a patrician past. Rising 88 meters above sea level at Falucho and Mendoza, the terrace of the **Torre Tanque** waterworks (1943) provides a panoramic perspective on the city's most appealing residential neighborhoods. The seemingly endless blocks of tile-roofed chalets to the south show that Mardel retains its upper-middle-class status, at the very least. Designed by architect Cornelio Lange, this unusual tower on the Stella Maris hill was the solution to Mar del Plata's water-distribution problem—Mar del Plata gets all its water from wells—with an elevated tank of 500,000 liters above a two-cistern reservoir of 13 million liters.

The **Torre Tanque** (Falucho 93, tel. 0223/451-4681, 7 A.M.–1:45 P.M. weekdays only, free) has an elevator that carries visitors to the terrace, but there's also a spiral staircase along the walls, for either ascending or descending.

Immediately northwest of the tower, the neo-Gothic **Iglesia Stella Maris** (1910; Brown 1054), is a reminder that Mar del Plata is a major fishing port—its namesake virgin, sculpted by a Rodin disciple, is the fishing fleet's patron saint. If there's a queue outside the **Villa Normandy** (1920), a Francophile residence one block north at Viamonte 2213, it's because economically desperate Argentines are seeking visas at what is now the Italian consulate.

Across the block, the **Museo del Mar** (Avenida Colón 1114, tel. 0223/4513553 or 4519779, fax 0223/4516670, informes @museodelmar.com, www.museodelmar.com,

US$1) is the city's most impressive new attraction. Attached to but well integrated with a house dating from Mar del Plata's aristocratic heyday, this sparklingly new multilevel facility presents collector Benjamín Sisterna's impressive assortment of 30,000 seashells far better than an earlier downtown museum ever did. Following a boyhood enthusiasm, Sisterna (1914–1995) collected shells from around the world over 60 years, and the well-lighted display cases in the cylindrical atrium are only part of what is a stunning addition to the city's attractions.

The new museum features a lower-level tidal pool set within its Confitería Gloria Maris, a perfect choice for coffee or lunch, surrounded by an aquarium. The second level contains the bulk of Cisterna's seashells, a cybercafé, an auditorium, and a museum shop, while the third con-

Mar del Plata's Torre Tanque holds and monitors the city's water supply.

© WAYNE BERNHARDSON

tains more shells, a lecture hall, and an art gallery. The fourth level has an exhibition hall and a rooftop terrace with outstanding views.

The Museo del Mar is open 8 A.M.–2 A.M. (yes, those hours are correct!) daily in summer; the rest of the year, hours are 8 A.M.–8 P.M. daily except Saturday, when it's open 8 A.M.–midnight.

Immediately across the street from the museum, at Avenida Colón and Alvear, the Villa Ortiz Basualdo (1909), former summer home for an elite *porteño* family, now hosts the municipal art museum, **Museo Municipal de Arte Juan Carlos Castagnino** (Avenida Colón 1189, tel. 0223/486-1636, 5–10 P.M. daily, US$.75 adults, US$.35 children and retirees). Mardel's fine arts museum takes its name from the Mardel-born painter who, with the Mexican David Siqueiros and others, was responsible for the awesome ceiling murals at Buenos Aires's Galerías Pacífico. The building itself, in the Francophile style of a Loire Valley castle, still sports its original Belgian furnishings, along with paintings, sculptures, engravings, and photography by Argentine artists.

To the southeast, Avenida Martínez de Hoz leads to the beaches of **Cabo Corrientes** and **Playa Grande,** an area whose Avenida Alem and surrounding streets is now one of the city's most active restaurant and nightlife areas.

To the west is Barrio los Troncos, whose **Chalet los Troncos** (1938; Urquiza 3454) is a distinctive log-style house; all its raw materials, including the *lapacho* and *quebracho* hardwoods and roof tiles, came from Salta Province.

Here you'll also find **Villa Victoria,** the one-time residence of writer-muse Victoria Ocampo and now the **Centro Cultural Villa Victoria** (Matheu 1851, tel. 0223/492-0569, 10 A.M.–1 P.M. and 5–9:30 P.M. daily, US$1). In the 1920s and 1930s, Victoria Ocampo's Mar del Plata residence was the gathering place for a remarkable diversity of artists and intellectuals from around the world, among them her countryman Jorge Luis Borges, Chilean poet Gabriela Mistral, Indian novelist Rabindranath Tagore, and Russian composer Igor Stravinsky—not to mention her sister—poet Silvina—and Silvina's husband, the

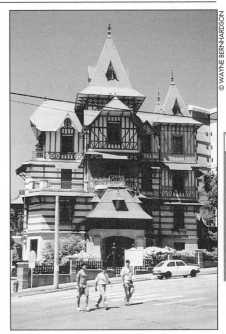

The Pampas

Museo Municipal de Arte Juan Carlos Castagnino

novelist Adolfo Bioy Casares. Founder and editor of the influential literary journal *Sur,* Ocampo donated the building to UNESCO in 1973, but it later reverted to municipal control as a museum and cultural center.

Nearby is **Villa Emilio Mitre** (1930), one of the Argentine oligarchy's classic residences, now the home of the **Museo Archivo Histórico Municipal Roberto T. Barili** (Lamadrid 3870, tel. 0223/495-1200, villamitre@cultura-mgp.com.ar, 9 A.M.–4 P.M. weekdays, 2–6 P.M. weekends).

Mardel's municipal history museum documents the city's history—the good, the bad, and even the ugly high-rises that have come to dominate large parts of the city—through photographs, posters, and a documentary archive.

Admission to the Museo Archivo Histórico costs US$.75 for adults, US$.35 for children. Buses Nos. 523, 524 and 591 go there.

South of downtown, beyond Playa Grande and the Mar del Plata Golf Club, the **Banquina**

de Pescadores is a working fishermen's wharf whose docks double as a magnet for tourists. Thanks to its rainbow fleet, the maned male southern sea lions that gather for scraps at the end of the day, and the cluster of nearby seafood restaurants, it's far more entertaining than a day sunning on the beach.

Male sea lions can be aggressive toward humans but here, at least, a fence safely separates them from their human admirers. They, along with the multicolored fishing boats, are ideal subjects for photography.

Named for a Mardel painter, the maritime-themed **Museo del Hombre del Puerto Cleto Ciocchini** (tel. 0223/480-1228, 4 P.M.–midnight, US$.75 adults, US$.35 kids) occupies new quarters at Centro Comercial del Puerto, at the port entrance.

The Centro Comercial is also home to numerous seafood restaurants where you can order delicacies fresh off the boat. From downtown, local buses Nos. 221, 511, and 581 will drop passengers right at the entrance, only a short walk from the port proper.

From the port, there are also frequent harbor excursions (US$5) on the 30-meter *Crucero Anamora* (tel. 0223/484-0103). **Turimar** (tel. 0223/489-7775) has similar but slightly cheaper outings.

Entertainment

In summer, Mar del Plata is Argentina's entertainment capital, even surpassing Buenos Aires for live theater and musical events. Like the capital, Mardel has *carteleras* that sell discount tickets to movies, live theater, and live music events; try **Cartelera Baires** (Santa Fe 1844) or **Cartelera Galería de las Américas** (Córdoba 1737).

Some venues do not fall easily into a single type. For example, the **Centro Cultural Juan Martín de Pueyrredón** (25 de Mayo 3108, tel. 0223/499-7876, promocion@mgp.com.ar) offers a broad calendar of events including theater, music, film, and lectures.

Befitting a city with a **cinema festival,** Mar del Plata is a big moviegoers' town; some cinemas are *cine teatros* that double as live theater venues. The main locales are the **Cine Ambassador** (Cór-

doba 1673, tel. 0223/495-7271); the **Cine Atlas** (Avenida Luro 2289, tel. 0223/494-3240); the **Cine Teatro América** (also at Avenida Luro 2289, tel. 0223/494-3240); the **Cine Teatro Enrique Carreras** (Entre Ríos 1828, tel. 0223/494-2753); the multiscreen **Cines del Paseo** (Diagonal Pueyrredón 3058, tel. 0223/496-1100); and the two-screen **Cines los Gallegos** (Rivadavia 3050, tel. 0223/499-6977).

The **Teatro Auditorium** (Blvd. Marítimo 2280, tel. 0223/493-7786) is one of the centers of summer musical theater imported from Buenos Aires. Other locales include the **Teatro Municipal Colón** (Yrigoyen 1665, tel. 0223/494-8571) and the **Teatro Corrientes** (Corrientes 1766, tel. 0223/493-7918).

For those with money to burn, Mardel's **Casino Central** (Blvd. Marítimo 2100, tel. 0223/495-7011) is the place to start the fire.

The **Playa Grande Club** (Quintana 238, tel. 0223/486-3727) is a major live music venue. There are many live music and dance clubs along Avenida Constitución, among them **Gap** (Avenida Constitución 5780, tel. 0223/479-6666).

For more-traditional music, try the weekend *peñas* at **Casa del Folklore** (San Juan 2543, tel. 0223/472-3955) and **Casa de Salta** (Libertad 3398).

Events

Argentina's cinematic revival has begun to restore the prestige of Mardel's **Festival Internacional de Cine,** which takes place in March. It's not Cannes, but that's a good thing, and there are plenty of quality offerings from Argentina, the rest of Latin America, and the rest of the world.

Mardel holds a **Festival Celta** of Irish music in January, and celebrates **Fundación de la Ciudad,** the founding of the city in 1874, on February 10.

Shopping

Mardel's open-air crafts market, the Diagonal de los Artesanos, lines Pueyrredón between San Martín and Rivadavia. Plaza Rocha's **Mercado de Pulgas** (flea market), seven blocks northwest on 20 de Septiembre between Avenida Luro and San Martín, is a wide-ranging flea market.

Mar del Plata's signature products are sweaters and jackets from Avenida Juan B. Justo, the so-called "Avenida del Pullover," reached by bus Nos. 561 and 562.

For books, try Librería Galerna (Rivadavia 3050, Local 21, tel. 0223/493-3130).

Sports and Recreation

Most activities in Mar del Plata center on the beach, ranging from sedentary sunbathing to more-active pastimes like swimming, diving, and fishing; even pursuits like parasailing (which seems to go dangerously close to coastal high-rises) take place in the vicinity of the beach. There is also cycling, horseback riding, and even skydiving. For a thorough list of offerings, see Emtur's free quarterly pamphlet *Actividades Recreativas*.

Accommodations

One of Argentina's major domestic destinations, Mar del Plata boasts about 600 hotels with a total of 60,000 beds. Many but by no means all of Mardel's hotels are union-built and -operated, dating from the Peronist heyday of the 1940s and 1950s, and have been unable to modernize in the aftermath of successive economic crises.

Prices below are from the summer high season, when rates can rise considerably and fluctuate dramatically. There are often bargains, though, especially near the bus terminal, and in the current crisis even many upscale places are underpriced. Many *marplatenses* also rent out their apartments and houses in summer.

Under US$25

Cordial **Hotel Tiber** (Olavarría 2580, tel. 0223/451-9958, tiber@mardelcomercial.com.ar, www.mardelcomercial.com.ar/tiber, US$13 d) lacks style—some of the decor is downright tacky—but compensates with modest prices for plain but comfortable rooms.

One of the best of the cheapest, obliging **Hotel Aquamarina** (Córdoba 1432, tel./fax 0223/493-8443, US$9 pp) offers comfortable, medium-sized, no-frills rooms with private bath and breakfast. A few rooms have balconies; the neighborhood, though, seems to have an inordinate number of oversensitive car alarms.

Around the corner, rates are similar at **Hotel Bologna** (9 de Julio 2542, tel. 0223/494-3369, fax 0223/493-8018, hbologna@statics.com.ar). Rooms, though, are slightly smaller, even if some also have balconies.

The family-run **La Posada de Güemes** (Falucho 1285, tel. 0223/451-42878, posadadeguemes@infovia.com.ar, www.mardelcomercial.com.ar/laposada.htm, US$9 pp) attracts plenty of foreign visitors to an appealing chalet-style building whose rooms come with breakfast, cable TV, and similar amenities.

Also family-operated, the nearby **Hotel Calash** (Falucho 1355, tel. 0223/451-6115, calash@copetel.com.ar, US$18/24 s/d) has attractive, comfortable rooms; rates include breakfast.

Hotel Aguila Blanca (Sarmiento 2455, tel. 0223/486-0689, US$18 s or d) is a drab but well-kept older hotel.

Perhaps the best two-star choice, the 30 simple but well-kept rooms at quiet **Ⓜ Hotel Selent** (Arenales 2347, tel. 0223/4940878, fax 0223/492-3920, hotelselent@infovia.com.ar, www.hotelselent.com.ar, US$18 s or d with breakfast) enjoy a substantial setback from the street. This well-maintained older building has ample parking (uncommon in this part of town) for a small extra charge, and the staff can manage English and French.

US$25–50

In its three-star category, the gracefully aging **Ⓜ Hotel Imperio** (Avenida Colón 1186, tel./fax 0223/486-3993, hotelimperio@ciudad.com.ar, US$27 d with breakfast) is a standout for its location, natural light, and spacious rooms, some with balconies.

Clean, quiet and orderly **Hotel Marysol** (Aristóbulo del Valle 3641, tel. 0223/451-7023, US$26/31 s/d) occupies a classic Mardel chalet on attractive grounds; its main drawback is its aging, somewhat fussy owners.

The three-star **Hotel Benedetti** (Colón 2198, tel. 0223/493-0031, hotelbenedetti@hotmail.com, US$32 d) gets high marks for service and only slightly less-than-sumptuous rooms with a buffet breakfast and parking, in addition to standard amenities.

The Pampas

Hotel Club del Golf (Aristóbulo del Valle 3144, tel. 0223/451-3456, fax 0223/451-5878, clubdelgolf@speedy.com.ar, www.hotelclubdelgolf .com.ar, US$32 d) has small but modern and attractive rooms, with fine service.

Reservations are advisable, at least in summer, at popular, efficiently run **Hotel Guerrero** (Diagonal Juan B. Alberdi 2288, tel. 0223/495-8851, info@hotelguerrero.com.ar, www.hotelguerrero.com.ar, US$35 d). Amenities include free Internet access, a gym, a swimming pool, parking, and a strongbox in every room.

Gran Hotel Dorá (Buenos Aires 1841, tel./fax 0223/491-0033, info@hoteldora.com.ar, www .hoteldora.com.ar, US$18 pp with breakfast, US$22 pp with half board) is a 1930s building that's past its prime but still reasonably comfortable, and some rooms have ocean views. It may not match its four-star rating, but prices aren't four-star either; except in the summer months of January and February, half-board guests take their main meal at the sister Hotel Astor.

Hermitage Hotel (Blvd. Pedro Peralta Ramos 2657, tel. 0223/451-9081, fax 0223/451-7255, hermitage@lacapitalnet.com.ar, US$29 d with city views, US$35/42 s/d with sea views) is a classic 1940s hotel undergoing an overdue renovation and modernization, and adding a new wing as well.

US$50–100

Under the same management as the Dorá, **Hotel Astor** (Entre Ríos 1649, tel./fax 0223/492-1616, hotel_astor@yahoo.com.ar, www.hotelastor.com .ar, US$30 pp with buffet breakfast) is more deserving of its four-star status, with more-up-to-date facilities and additional services that include free airport transfers, free beach transfers to the private Club Horizonte del Sol (with a shade tent for guests staying a week or longer), sauna, and similar amenities. Rates fall dramatically in the off-season.

Overlooking Cabo Corrientes, the high-rise **Torres de Manantiales** (Alberti 453, tel. 0223/486-1999, infomdp@manantiales.com.ar, www.manantiales.com.ar, US$90 d) is a luxury apart-hotel where amenities including a sauna, gym, pool and a 28th-floor restaurant that offers the city's most panoramic views. Off-season rates can fall to half.

Overlooking the Playa Grande, **M Hotel Costa Galana** (Blvd. Marítimo 5725, tel. 0223/486-0000, fax 0223/486-2020, reservas @hotelcostagalana.com.ar, www.hotelcosta-galana.com.ar, US$97 d) is a five-star facility that lives up to its luxury billing. Suites are considerably more expensive.

Food

For the first morning coffee, try **Café la Peatonal** (San Martín and Santiago del Estero). **Venezia** (Rivadavia 2301, tel. 0223/495-7205) is also good for coffee and particularly for ice cream. **Helados Gianelli** (Avenida Colón 1802) has fine ice cream as well.

Dating from 1919, the classic **M Bar la Reforma** (San Luis 1958, tel. 0223/494-6331) is an exceptional choice for an afternoon **picada** and a drink. **La Bodeguita del Medio** (Castelli 1252, tel. 0223/486-3096) serves Cuban food in a *cubanísimo* environment of books, photographs—and cigars that despoil the air quality.

Family favorite **Ambos Mundos** (Rivadavia 2644, tel. 0223/495-0450) and the equally popular **Montecatini** (Avenida Colón 2309) offer conventional Argentine menus. There are similar offerings at **La Cantina de Armando** (San Lorenzo 3101, tel. 0223/472-5708).

Italo-Argentine fast food, pizza, and the like, is available at **Manolo** (Rivadavia 2371, tel. 0223/494-5671), which has a credible nonsmoking area, and at **Strega** (Rivadavia 2320, tel. 0223/493-6183). For more elaborate (and expensive) Italian entrees, try **Trattoría Napolitana** (3 de Febrero 3154, tel. 0223/495-3850).

Parrillas of interest include **El Palacio del Bife** (Córdoba 1857, tel. 0223/494-7727) and **La Parrilla del Gato** (Yrigoyen 2699, tel. 0223/495-5309). The comparable **La Marca** (Almafuerte 253, tel. 0223/451-8072) is popular enough that reservations are advisable; figure around US$5 pp. The best in town, despite a higher price tag than the others, is the enormously popular **Trenque Lauquen** (Mitre 2807, tel. 0223/493-7149);

there's also a beachfront branch (Blvd. Marítimo 4099, corner of Bernardo de Irigoyen, tel. 0223/451-4269).

For a beef antidote, try the moderately priced vegetarian buffet at **Finca del Sol** (San Martín 2543, 1st floor, tel. 0223/495-6962). Ethnic food is uncommon in Mardel, but **Pancho Villa** (9 de Julio 3204, tel. 0223/493-2324) does serve Mexican specialties.

Reservations are advisable at one of Mardel's most innovative restaurants, **M El Anticuario** (Bernardo de Irigoyen 3819, tel. 0223/451-6309, www.elanticuarioonline.com.ar). For starters, try the delicate empanadas of mozzarella, tomato, and basil, and the *jamón serrano* (country cured ham, US$3 for two); the exquisite **abadejo al ajo arriero,** a fish cooked in garlic is a bargain for US$6), and the *natillas* (Spanish custard, US$2) make an excellent dessert. There's a good wine list, and excellent service.

On the seaside south of downtown, the Nuevo Complejo Comercial Puerto (Avenida Martínez de Hoz 200) offers a variety of seafood venues. The complex's **Michelangelo** (Local 10, tel. 0223/489-3640) is a good choice for breakfast, coffee, and sandwiches. For more elaborate meals, try locales like the Spanish **La Caracola** (Local 6, tel. 0223/480-9113) and **M El Viejo Pop** (Local 7, tel. 0223/480-0147).

Information

The main source of information is Mardel's municipal **Centro de Información Turística** (Emtur, Blvd. Marítimo 2270, tel. 0223/495-1777, turismo@mardelplata.com.ar, www .mardelplata.gov.ar). Hours are 8 A.M.–9 P.M. daily but, because of high demand for its services, it's often impersonal unless you know exactly what you're looking for, despite its computerized information service, maps, brochures, and activities calendar. In summer only, it operates a branch at the bus terminal.

Nearly alongside the municipal office, the provincial **Subsecretaría de Turismo** (Local 60 in the Rambla del Hotel Provincial, Blvd. Marítimo 2400, tel. 0223/495-5340) is less helpful. It's open 8 A.M.–7 P.M. weekdays most of the year, but stays open until 9 P.M. in summer.

For motorists, **ACA** is at Avenida Colón 1450, tel. 0223/491-2096.

The **library** at the Sociedad de Cultura Inglesa (San Luis 2498, tel. 0223/495-6513) has English-language books, magazines, and newspapers.

Services

Numerous banks have ATMs, including **Banco de la Nación** (San Martín 2594) and **Banco de la Provincia** (San Martín 2563). Exchange houses include **La Moneta** (Rivadavia 2623) and **Jonestur** (San Martín 2574 and Avenida Luro 3191).

Correo Argentino is at Avenida Luro 2460; Mardel's postal code is 7600.

Long-distance phone, fax, and Internet offices are abundant, such as at **Locutorio Arenales** (Arenales 2344). Many *locutorios* have Internet services, but also try the **Internet Center** (Moreno 2840).

Oti International (San Luis 1632, tel. 0223/494-5414) is the AmEx representative. The student- and youth-oriented travel agency **Asatej** is at Santa Fe 2172, tel./fax 0223/495-9000, mardelplata@asatej.com.ar.

Lava-Quick (Las Heras 2471) is one of many laundries.

The **Centro de Salud Municipal** No. 1 (Avenida Colón 3294, tel. 0223/495-0568) is a central clinic. The **Hospital Regional** is less central at J.B. Justo 6700, tel. 0223/477-0030). For emergencies, dial 107.

Getting There

Aerolíneas Argentinas/Austral (Moreno 2442, tel. 0223/496-0101) flies several times daily to Buenos Aires. **Aerovip** (Avenida Córdoba 1621, tel. 0223/494-2376, aerovipmdq@pezzati.com .ar) flies to Buenos Aires, with connections to Rosario, Santa Fe, Montevideo, and Punta del Este.

LADE, Local 5 in the Casino at Blvd Marítimo 2300, tel. 0223/493-8220, flies north to Aeroparque (Buenos Aires) and south to Bahía Blanca, Viedma, San Antonio Oeste, Puerto Madryn, Trelew, Neuquén, Chapelco (San Martín de los Andes), Esquel, and Bariloche.

The Pampas

Northbound flights are normally Tuesday and Friday, southbound flights Monday and Thursday, but all are subject to change.

More than 50 bus companies operate out of Mardel's aging but conveniently central **Estación de Ómnibus** (Alberti 1602, tel. 0223/451-5406) to destinations around the country. In the peak summer season and on holiday weekends such as Semana Santa, fares may rise and reservations are advisable.

Typical destinations, fares, and times include Villa Gesell (US$3.50, 1.5 hours), Necochea (US$5, two hours), Tandil (US$4, 2.5 hours), La Plata (US$12, five hours), Buenos Aires (US$15–18, 5.5 hours), Bahía Blanca (US$16, seven hours), Rosario (US$18, 10 hours), Neuquén (US$23, 14 hours), Córdoba (US$29, 16 hours), Bariloche (US$37, 19 hours), Puerto Madryn (US$28, 16 hours), and Mendoza (US$29, 18 hours).

Ferrobaires, the provincially run rail service, has offices at the bus terminal, (tel. 0223/451-2501), but the **Estación Terminal de Ferrocarril** (Avenida Luro 4500, tel. 0223/475-6076) is some 17 blocks northwest of Plaza San Martín. Ferrobaires operates three or so trains to Buenos Aires daily, but service on the luxury train *El Marplatense* is presently suspended. One-way fares range from US$7 (in stiff-backed vertical *clase única*) to US$10 (in reclining Pullman seats).

Getting Around

Mar del Plata has an extensive bus system; Emtur's quarterly brochure *Actividades Recreativas* (Recreational Activities) lists the appropriate bus lines for sights and activities in the vicinity.

Aeropuerto Félix U. Camet (RN 2 Km 396, tel. 0223/478-3990) is 10 kilometers north of town. City bus No. 542 goes directly there from the corner of Blvd. Marítimo and Belgrano. Taxis and *remises* charge around US$3.50 pp.

For car rentals, try **Hertz/Millet** (Córdoba 2149, tel. 0223/496-2772, hertzmardelplata @sinectis.com.ar); **Localiza** (Córdoba 2270, tel. 0223/493-3461, localizamdp@sinectis.com.ar); or **Europcar** (Avenida Colón 2450, tel. 0223/491-0091).

Museo del Automovilismo Juan Manuel Fangio

Fortunately, the impressive Fangio Automotive Museum (Dardo Rocha and Mitre, tel. 02266/430758, www.museofangio.com, 11 A.M.–6 P.M. daily, US$2 adults, US$1 children), named for Formula One racing legend Juan Manuel Fangio and located in his Balcarce birthplace near Mar del Plata, is not just for fossil-fuel fanatics. While it focuses on the exploits of the five-time world champion, it also gives credit to his competition and, more importantly, places racing in a broader context of the 20th century's evolving transportation technology and related events.

Fangio (1911–1995) won a world title in 1951, and then annually from 1954 through 1957. His life has been the subject of three films: exploitation producer Armando Bó's *Fangio, the Devil of the Racetrack;* the documentary *Fangio* (1976) by Academy Award–winning director Hugh Hudson (*Chariots of Fire*); and director Alberto Lecchi's *Operación: Fangio* (1999), about the racer's kidnapping by Cuban guerrillas in Havana in 1958. Fangio played himself in John Frankenheimer's classic racing film *Grand Prix* (1966), and is also the topic of the biographical tribute *Fangio: A Pirelli Album* (Motorbooks International, 1991), by Fangio's rival Sterling Moss and Doug Nye.

The building that houses the museum is a handsome century-old structure whose recycled interior features a spiral ramp through eight levels of exhibits in 5,000 square meters, dealing with everything from Fangio's childhood through his championships and retirement (though it ignores incidents like his kidnapping). At the same time, it integrates his biography with world events through photographs and a time line. There's an extraordinarily valuable collection of classic automobiles—not just Fangio's racing cars—along with a souvenir shop and a café.

One conspicuously absent topic is highway safety, a critical matter in Argentina, a culture that seemingly idolizes high-speed driving. Fangio himself, for instance, killed his navigator Daniel Urrutia when he rolled his Chevrolet during a road race in Peru in 1948, yet national authorities have named the Buenos Aires–Mar del Plata freeway in his honor. The YPF oil company's highest-octane fuel also bears his name.

On retirement in 1958, Fangio himself spoke of being a role model: "If my efforts have had any value, if racing automobiles has been useful to my homeland, time will tell. I have only one wish, which is that if my conduct in the world can be useful to youth; for that, I will also await the answer of time." Argentina's elevated highway death tolls may be part of that answer.

Balcarce is 60 kilometers northwest of Mar del Plata via RN 226. From the Mar del Plata terminal, frequent El Rápido buses to Balcarce charge about US$1.70.

VILLA GESELL

Turning barren dunes into a botanical garden of ecological exotics traversed by tree-shaded crisscross streets, Carlos Idaho Gesell's transformation of the town that bears his name resembles what William Hammond Hall and John McLaren did in San Francisco's Golden Gate Park. Gesell's vision fashioned one of the province's most appealing coastal resorts, less exclusive than many people believe. Its irregular plan and sandy streets favor pedestrians and cyclists over automobile traffic, except on its cluttered commercial strip—which would likely appall its creator.

Orientation

Villa Gesell (population 21,740) is about 110 kilometers northeast of Mar del Plata via the coastal highway RP 11, and 360 kilometers south of Buenos Aires via RN 2, RP 11 and a couple of shortcuts. Parallel to the beach, the commercial strip of Avenida 3 is the only paved street—bursting with restaurants, souvenir shops, and video game parlors. Most accommodations, though, are on quieter side streets known as *paseos*.

Sights

For a quick orientation to local attractions and activities, a good option is **El Trencito de Villa Gesell,** (Avenida 3 and Paseo 110 bis, tel.

02255/468920). Despite the name, it's in fact a bus whose two-hour outings (US$2 pp, children under five free) visit sights such as Gesell's houses (now a museum and an exhibition hall), the surrounding Parque Cultural Pinar del Norte, early pioneer houses, and the fishing pier.

Farther afield, Turismo Aventura Edy (tel. 02255/463118 or 466797) offers four-hour 4WD excursions to **Faro Querandí,** a landmark lighthouse separated from Gesell by extensive dunefields. Fares are about US$5 pp, with children slightly cheaper.

Parque Cultural Pinar del Norte

Carlos Gesell's vision for the town he created is clearest in these car-free woodlands only a block north of Avenida 3 and Avenida Buenos Aires, the access road from RP 11. Within the reserve, really a large city park, the **Museo Histórico Municipal** (Alameda 201 and Calle 303, tel. 02255/468624, 10 A.M.–1 P.M. and 2–9 P.M. daily, US$.35) was Carlos Gesell's modest original residence (1931). Containing photographs, maps, artifacts, and other items associated with Gesell and his project, it offers guided tours; English-speaking guides are available.

Gesell's later residence, the **Chalet de Don Carlos** (1952), recently opened as an exhibition center; it keeps the same hours and charges the same. There is also a *vivero* (plant nursery) open 7:30 A.M.–12:30 P.M. weekdays only, and an *apícola* that raises honeybees.

Entertainment and Events

In summer, especially, Villa Gesell has many cultural activities and an active nightlife.

Since 1969 the **Anfiteatro del Pinar** (Avenida 10 and Paseo 102) has hosted the annual **Encuentros Corales de Verano,** a national choral competition. The **Sociedad Camping Musical** holds summer chamber music concerts in the auditorium of the Playa Hotel (Alameda 205 and Calle 304).

Gesell's **Casa de la Cultura** (Avenida 3 and Paseo 109, tel. 02255/452839) hosts live theater in summer. Movie theaters include the **Cine Atlantic** (Paseo 105 between Avenida 2 and Avenida 3, tel. 02255/462323) and the **Cine**

Teatro Atlas (Paseo 108 between Avenida 3 and Avenida 4, tel. 02255/462969).

Established dance clubs include **Dixit** (Paseo 106 between Avenida 3 and Avenida 4), **Le Brique** (Avenida 3 between Avenida Buenos Aires and Avenida 1), and **Sabash** (Paseo 103 between the Costanera and Avenida 1). Newer on the scene is **Nyko,** in the Pueblo Límite complex on Avenida Buenos Aires, at the northern approach to town.

Shopping

Gesell's crafts-workers display their wares at the **Feria Artesanal, Regional y Artística** (Avenida 3, between Paseos 112 and 113). From mid-December through mid-March, it's daily, but the rest of the year it takes place only weekends and holidays.

Sports and Recreation

Both rental horses (about US$5 per hour) and guided excursions are available from the **Escuela de Equitación San Jorge** (Circunvalación and Paseo 102, tel. 02255/454464). Local fishing enthusiasts crowd the **Muelle de Pesca,** a pier stretching 15 meters into the South Atlantic at the corner of Playa and Paseo 129. Rental bicycles (about US$1 per hour) are available at **Bicigesell** (Avenida 3 and Paseo 141, tel. 02255/476820).

Accommodations

Gesell has a large selection of accommodations, ranging from campgrounds to simple *hospedajes* to four-star hotels, but many are open only in the peak summer season. Accommodations included here are open all year.

Year-round campgrounds include **Camping Mar Dorado** (Avenida 3 and Paseo 170, tel. 02255/470963, around US$3 pp) and **Camping Monte Bubi** (Avenida 3 and Paseo 168, tel. 02255/470732, around US$3 pp).

For family-run *hospedajes,* charging around US$11 d, try **Hospedaje Villa Gesell** (Avenida 3 No. 812, tel. 02255/466368), **Hospedaje Viya** (Avenida 5 No. 582, tel. 02255/462757), or **Hospedaje Parada 6** (Avenida 6 No. 519, tel. 02255/466256, parada6@gesell.com.ar). One-star hotels, such **Hotel Villa del Sol** (Avenida 3

No. 1469, tel. 02255/467781, grupoce@grupoce .com.ar), are only slightly dearer at around US$14 d.

Two-star hotels, in the US$20 d range, include **Hotel Bellavista** (Paseo 114 between Avenida 1 and Avenida 3, tel. 02255/462293, bellavista@gesell.com.ar), **Hotel La Posada de la Villa** (Paseo 125 No. 182, tel. 02255/464855, la-posadadelavilla@hotmail.com), and **Hotel Romina** (Avenida 1 and Paseo 140, tel. 02255/476074, romina@gesell.com.ar).

The three-star high-rise **Hotel Castilla** (Avenida Buenos Aires 76, tel./fax 02255/ 464100, hotelcastilla@gesell.com.ar) charges US$27 d. The **Hotel Bahía Club** (Avenida 1 No. 855, tel./fax 02255/460838, hotelbahia @gesell.com.ar, US$50 d) is the only prestige hotel that remains open all year.

Food

A Gesell stalwart, **La Jirafa Azul** (Avenida 3 between Paseo 102 and Avenida Buenos Aires, tel. 02255/468968) has been serving vacationers a reasonably priced, conventional Argentine menu for more than 35 years; it has a second branch at Avenida 3 and Paseo 140, tel. 02255/476171.

La Taberna de Don Ramón (Avenida 3 and Paseo 124, tel. 02255/463299) is a good choice for Galician-style seafood, with excellent service and entrees in the US$5–7 range except for pastas, which are cheaper. Try the outstanding chocolate mousse for dessert.

Cantina Arturito (Avenida 3 No. 186, tel. 02255/463037) specializes in pasta and seafood, plus appetizers such as homemade ham.

Information and Services

The exceptionally conscientious **Secretaría de Turismo y Cultura** (tel. 02255/458596 or 457255, turismo@gesell.com.ar) has its main office at Avenida Buenos Aires 1921 and Camino de los Pioneros. Hours are 8 A.M.–8 P.M. daily in summer, 8 A.M.–8 P.M. weekdays and 10 A.M.–6 P.M. weekends the rest of the year. It has an additional Oficina de Información Turística at the bus terminal (Avenida 3 and Paseo 140, tel. 02255/477253), open 5:30–11:30 P.M. daily; and another in the **Municipalidad** (Avenida 3 between Paseo 108 and Paseo 109, tel. 02255/462201).

There is also a useful private website, www .gesell.com.ar.

Gesell also has a Buenos Aires representative (Bartolomé Mitre 1702, Congreso, tel. 011/ 4374-5098).

Correo Argentino is on Avenida 3 between Paseo 108 and Paseo 109; Gesell's postal code is 7165.

Locutorio TPP (Avenida 3 No. 191) has telephone and Internet services.

Hospital Municipal Arturo Illia is at Paseo 123 and Avenida 8, tel. 02255/462618.

Getting There

For the most part, air services to and from Mar del Plata are most convenient. The air-taxi service **Aerovip** (tel. 02255/472828 at the airport) flies up to four times daily to BA in summer only.

The Terminal de Ómnibus is at Avenida 3 and Paseo 140, tel. 02255/476058. As with flights, there are more services to and from Mar del Plata, but there are frequent buses to Buenos Aires (US$20, seven hours) and intermediates, and also south to Mar del Plata (US$3.50, 1.5 hours).

PINAMAR

Exclusive Pinamar bears the stamp of architect Jorge Bunge, one of the biggest names in the Argentine oligarchy. Apparently following Carlos Gesell's precedent, Bunge turned the dunes behind its long, sandy beaches into the most select beach resort in the province.

Orientation

Pinamar (population 20,189) is 127 kilometers north of Mar del Plata via RP 11 and 340 kilometers southeast of Buenos Aires via RN 2, RP 11, and shorter interconnected roads. Avenida Libertador, parallel to the beach, and Avenida Bunge, perpendicular to Avenida Libertador, are the main thoroughfares, but Jorge Bunge's otherwise fan-shaped city plan often confuses first-time visitors. Fortunately, most services are within a few blocks of either avenue.

The tourist office distributes an excellent map of Pinamar.

Sights

Like neighboring Villa Gesell, Pinamar is finally realizing it has a history. The **Museo Histórico Partido de Pinamar,** at De Metz and Niza, Ostende, with lots of historical photos and information, is open 3–6 P.M. weekends in winter, 6–9 P.M. daily in summer. Pinamar is also the site of **La Elenita,** the modest beachfront cabin of former President Arturo Frondizi, on which the dunes are encroaching.

Entertainment and Recreation

Pinamar has three cinemas: the **Cine-Teatro Oasis** (Avenida Shaw and Lenguado, tel. 02254/483334), **Cine Bahía** (Avenida Bunge and De la Sirena, tel. 02254/482747), and **Cine Pinamar** (also at Avenida Bunge and De la Sirena, tel. 02254/481012).

Pinamar is home to the usual beach activities: swimming, sunbathing, surfing, and fishing, as well as cycling and horseback riding.

Accommodations

Like Villa Gesell, Pinamar has abundant accommodations—more than 200 of them—but lacks the cheapest alternatives except for campgrounds such as Ostende's seaside **Camping Saint Tropez** (Quintana 178, tel. 02254/482498) and hostel facilities at Ostende's beachfront **Albergue Bruno Valente** (Nuestras Malvinas and Sarmiento, tel. 02254/482908, US$6 pp), an 85-bed facility. The municipal tourist office does an exemplary job of helping find accommodations when occupancy is high.

One of Pinamar's best bargains is the Italian-run **Hotel Gaviota** (Del Cangrejo 1332, tel. 02254/482079, US$14/20 s/d), a one-star gem with no frills (it's mercifully TV-free, for instance). Rooms are small but impeccable and comfortably furnished, with private bath and breakfast. **Hotel Berlín** (Rivadavia 326, tel. 02254/482320) is comparable but slightly more expensive.

On a woodsy block, the three-star **Hostería Bora Bora** (Del Tuyú 441, tel. 02254/480164 or

482394, bora@telpin.com.ar, www.horqueta
.com/borabora, US$33 d) has good midsize
rooms with private bath and breakfast. The comparable **Hotel Las Araucarias** (Avenida Bunge
1411, tel. 02254/480812 or 480140, fax
02254/495272, araucarias@telpin.com.ar) is a
30-room chalet-style facility.

Ostende's **Hotel Nitra** (Avenida Juan de Garay
299, tel. 02254/486680, fax 02254/496050,
hotelnitra@mixmail.com, www.hotelesnitra
.com.ar, US$35 d) is a new 50-room hotel in a
quiet area near the beach.

Food
Primarily a pizzeria, **Vadinho** (Avenida Bunge
766) also serves decent seafood in the US$4–7
range; in a town where seasonal workers are the
rule, the service is enthusiastic but amateur. Nonsmokers will appreciate the outdoor seating, and
the fact that it's more comfortably spacious than
many Argentine restaurants.

Il Garda (Avenida Shaw 136, tel. 02254/
482582) is a good choice for pastas. **Estilo
Criollo** (Avenida Bunge 768, tel. 02254/495246)
is known for its beef, pork, and especially its
chivito (grilled kid goat).

For breakfast, savor the succulent croissants
and coffee at Confitería La Reina (Avenida Shaw
135, tel. 02254/484727), which also serves snacks
and sweets in the afternoon. **Heladería El Piave**
(Avenida Bunge 449) has excellent ice cream.

Information and Services
Pinamar's tireless **Secretaría de Turismo** (Avenida
Bunge 654, tel. 02254/491680, unestilodev-
ida@telpin.com.ar, www.pinamar.gov.ar) is open
8 A.M.–10 P.M. daily in summer, 8 A.M.–8 P.M.
weekdays and 10 A.M.–6 P.M. weekends the rest of
the year. It's the place to stop for help in seeking
a room, especially in the high season—they will
phone to check on availability in your price range.

For motorists, **ACA** is at Del Cazón 1365, tel.
02254/482744.

Pinamar maintains an information office in
Buenos Aires's Microcentro (Florida 935, 5th
floor, Departamento B, tel. 011/4315-2679).

Correo Argentino is at Jasón 524; the postal
code is 7167. The **Centro Telefónico Pinamar**

(Avenida Shaw 157) has long-distance and Internet services.

For medical emergencies, Pinamar's **Hospital Comunitario** is at Avenida Shaw 250 (tel.
02254/482390).

Getting There and Around
Pinamar itself has only bus and train services,
but it's also convenient to Villa Gesell's airport.

The new Terminal de Ómnibus is at Avenida
Bunge and Intermédanos (tel. 02254/403500).
Several companies go to Mar del Plata (US$3,
two hours) and Buenos Aires (US$10, 5.5 hours).

Pinamar enjoys rail service to and from Constitución (Buenos Aires) several times weekly
(US$8–10). The local stop is Estación Divisadero
(RP 74 Km 4, tel. 02267/497973).

NECOCHEA
From Mar del Plata south, the Atlantic coast
landscape changes from broad sandy beaches
backed by rolling dunes to rugged bluffs with
occasional access points to the shoreline. Beyond
Chapadmalal and Miramar, the terrain levels off
at Necochea, a middle-class resort with a small
but enduring Danish heritage—so much so that
some vehicles proudly bear a European-style
"DK" decal.

Orientation
Straddling the Río Quequén Grande, Necochea
(population 78,566) is 502 kilometers south of
Buenos Aires and 128 kilometers west of Mar
del Plata via RP 88. Most points of interest are
west of the river and south of Avenida 10, also
known as Avenida República del Uruguay, in a
compact grid also bordered by wooded parkland
to the east, the ocean to the south, and Calle 79
to the east. Even-numbered streets run parallel to
the ocean and odd-numbered streets are perpendicular to it. Calle 83 is a pedestrian mall
that runs past Plaza San Martín.

Sights
Like Villa Gesell and Pinamar, Necochea has
its own pine-studded greenbelt in **Parque
Provincial Miguel Lillo;** part of the former

Díaz Vélez *estancia,* it contains the **Museo Histórico Regional** (tel. 02262/425159) and the **Museo Municipal de Ciencias Naturales.** West of the beachfront grid, the park parallels the beach where *balneario* tents line the shore. Sunbathers, swimmers, cyclists, and equestrians share the area.

Across the Río Quequén Grande, itself a popular fishing area, the **Faro de Quequén** (1921) is a 33-meter lighthouse that shines more than 25 nautical miles into the South Atlantic. Farther north, beyond the lighthouse, the surf laps at rusting shipwrecks at **Playa los Ancantilados.**

Entertainment

Necochea has a pair of movie theaters: **Cine París** (Avenida 59 No. 2854, tel. 02262/422273) and **Cine Océan** (Calle 83 No. 450, tel. 02262/435672).

The hottest new nightspot is the beachfront **Sabor Caribe** (Avenida 2 and Calle 87, tel. 02262/432084 or 423791, www.saborcaribe.com). Try also the **El Cairo Bar** (Calle 87 No. 283).

Accommodations

Necochea has plenty of affordable accommodations, starting with Parque Lillo's **Camping Americano** (Avenida 2 and Calle 101, tel. 02262/435832, US$2 pp).

Spacious, friendly **Hostal del Rey** (Calle 81 No. 335, tel. 02262/425170, US$5 pp) is an excellent value with breakfast. Run by responsive management, on a quiet block, recommended **Hotel Suizo** (Calle 22 No 4235, tel. 02262/524008, hotelsuizo@regioneslatinas.zzn.com, US$5/7 s/d) is also a bargain. The 1960s-style **Hotel Perugia** (Calle 81 No. 288, tel. 02262/422020, perugiahot@teletel.com.ar, US$11/15 s/d) is architecturally drab but has comfortable rooms.

Necochea's newest comfort option is the immaculate, four-star **Hotel Nikén** (Calle 87 No. 335, tel./fax 02262/432323, niken@ar.inter.net, www.hotelniken.com.ar, US$22/29 s/d). Four-star **Hotel Presidente** (Calle 4 No. 4040, tel. 02262/423800, US$30 d) offers a 10 percent discount for cash.

Food

La Rueda (Calle 4 No. 4144, tel. 02262/421215) offers a diverse menu of beef, seafood, and pasta at reasonable prices. **La Romana** (Avenida 79 between Calles 4 and 6) specializes in pasta. Recommended **Pizzería Don Peppone** has two branches: on the Peatonal 85 at Avenida 4 (tel. 02262/431364) and at Avenida 59 No. 2828 (tel. 02262/426390).

Open for dinner only, north of Parque Lillo, **La Cabaña** (Avenida República Oriental del Uruguay and Calle 105, tel. 02262/423910) is a welcome new addition to the Necochea scene. Specializing in seafood, with attentive management, it doubles as a pub.

Right on the beach, **El Viejo Contrabandista** (Avenida 2 and Calle 87, tel. 02262/432084) serves very fine pasta, but mediocre starters. Prices tend toward the high end for Necochea.

Keops (Calle 83 No. 251) has pretty good ice cream.

Information and Services

Necochea's main **Oficina de Información Turística** (Avenida 2 and Calle 79, tel. 02262/425983 or 430158, subcom@necochea.mun.gba.gov.ar, www.necocheanatural.com) is open 8 A.M.–10 P.M. daily from December–March; the rest of the year, hours are 9 A.M.–noon and 1–5 P.M. daily. It's a dependency of the municipal **Secretaría de Turismo, Cultura y Deporte** (Calle 56 No. 2945, tel. 02262/422631).

For motorists, the Necochea branch of **ACA** is at Avenida 59 No. 2073 (tel. 02262/422106).

Banco de Galicia (Calle 60 No. 3164) and **Banco de la Provincia** (Calle 60 No. 3000) both have ATMs but are in the downtown area some 20 blocks north of the beach.

Correo Argentino is at Avenida 58 No. 3088 in the downtown area; the postal code is 7630. Most phone offices and Internet locales are in the downtown area, away from the beach, such as **Telefónica y Cibercafé de la Costa** (Calle 57 No. 2798).

Necochea's **Hospital Municipal** is at the northern edge of town (Avenida 59 No. 4081, tel. 02262/422405).

Getting There and Around

Necochea presently has no air services, but there are good bus connections and weekly trains.

The **Terminal de Ómnibus** (tel. 02262/ 422470) is on Avenida 58 (Sarmiento) between Calle 47 (Rondeau) and Avenida 45 (Jesuita Cardiel). In addition to frequent buses to Buenos Aires (US$10, six hours) and up the coast to Mar del Plata, there are interior-provincial services to Córdoba (US$18, 12 hours) and the Cuyo provinces of San Luis and Mendoza. There are also services to the Patagonian lake district resort of Bariloche.

Ferrobaires across the river at Calle 580 and Calle 563 in neighboring Quequén (tel. 02262/ 426028) offers Sunday service to Constitución (Buenos Aires). Trains from the capital leave on Friday.

BAHÍA BLANCA

Home to perhaps Argentina's most unique museum, the Museo del Puerto, which is reason enough for a visit, the southern Buenos Aires Province port of Bahía Blanca is a frequent stopover for Patagonia-bound travelers, especially motorists. It's also a major port for petrochemicals, grains from the pampas, and produce from Patagonia's Río Negro Valley, and it's home to South America's largest naval base.

In addition to its commercial and military importance, Bahía Blanca is the site of Universidad Nacional del Sur. Its suburb of Puerto Ingeniero White, though, deserves a stopover for its extraordinary museum, a self-effacing tribute to immigrants that's a welcome antidote to the pompously nationalistic institutions that pass for historical museums elsewhere in the country.

Bahía Blanca grew around the site of Colonel Ramón Estomba's Fortaleza Protectora Argentina, established in 1828 to enforce an Argentine presence on what, at the time, was an insecure area because of indigenous resistance to the European invaders. Arrival of the railroad from Buenos Aires in 1884 opened the way for it to become the key port in southern Buenos Aires Province. Both the bay and the

city take their name from the dry white salt on the shoreline.

Orientation

Bahía Blanca (population 272,176) is 687 kilometers southwest of Buenos Aires via RN 3, 278 kilometers north of Viedma via RN 3, and 530 kilometers east of Neuquén via RN 22. Most points of interest and services are within a few blocks of Plaza Rivadavia, which occupies four full blocks in the city center. Street names change on either side of the plaza.

Ⓜ Museo del Puerto

On Bahía Blanca's eastern edge, the 19th-century docks of Puerto Ingeniero White were—and still are—Argentina's most important port outside Buenos Aires. Nearly half the country's grain exports leave from here. It was also a thriving multiethnic community with a vigorous street life (though it's now less so), and one of Argentina's most engaging museums still carries the torch for White's immigrant heritage.

The Museo del Puerto occupies the former customs house (1907), which sits inconspicuously atop pilings. Built by Ferrocarriles del Sud, the English-owned southern railway, the rehabbed building houses "a museum of local lifestyles" as reflected in social institutions like barbershops (each immigrant community had its own, represented here by caricature mannequins). Other exhibits include bars, classrooms, and shops.

Named for an Anglo-Argentine engineer by former President Julio A. Roca in 1901, Puerto Ingeniero White actually dates from 1885, when it went by the name "Nueva Liverpool." At the time, the Argentine government actively promoted immigration, with certain restrictions (one official announcement said: "Workers required: if English, French or German, good. No weaklings, sick or anarchists accepted").

Today, though, some of White's inhabitants— who prefer to call themselves *whitenses* rather than *bahienses*—consider the port something of a ghost town, with the decline of its ethnic bars, barbershops, and clubs. Every June, though, they gather to honor San Silverio, the patron saint of fishermen from Ponza, Italy (in Italy, San Silverio puts to sea in June, but here the festival takes place in November because the seasons are reversed).

The Museo del Puerto (Guillermo Torres 4180, tel. 0291/457-3006, mpuerto@bb.mun .gba.gov.ar) is normally open 4–8 P.M. weekends only, but it closes the entire month of January. During the week, it usually hosts school field trips, but private morning visits are possible by phoning ahead. Admission is free of charge, but they request a small donation.

In addition to the permanent exhibits, the museum has an archive with documents, photographs, and recorded oral histories, in both audio and video. A planned expansion will include information on the railroad.

When the museum is open, the kitchen offers meals based on immigrant cookbooks. From downtown Bahía Blanca, colectivo Nos. 500 and 501 take passengers almost to the front door.

Other Sights

Bahía Blanca's neoclassical **Teatro Municipal** (1913) at Alsina and Dorrego, the city's prime performing arts venue, is a notable historical monument. The surrounding neighborhood, especially around the corner of Zeballos and Portugal, boasts a cluster of Deco-style houses and apartments.

In the theater's basement, the **Museo Municipal** (Dorrego 116, tel. 0291/456-3117, 4–9 P.M. daily except Mon.) is more like a quality antique shop—lots of interesting objects from the city's history, in mostly good to excellent condition, all well-arranged, but not particularly enlightening. The focus is on Colonel Estomba and the city's founding, along with the impact of European immigration, but this is covered better, and far more entertainingly, in the museum at Puerto Ingeniero White.

The **Museo de Arte Contemporáneo** (Sarmiento 450, tel. 0291/459-4006, www.macbb.com.ar) is a work-in-progress, but is the first provincial Argentine museum to specialize in contemporary art. Housed in a building dating from the 1920s, it's open 10 A.M.–1 P.M. and 4–8 P.M. weekdays except Monday, 4–8 P.M. only on weekends.

Entertainment

Bahía Blanca's main high-culture performing arts venue is the **Teatro Municipal** (Alsina 425, tel. 0291/456-3973).

Bahía Blanca has several downtown cinemas: the **Cine Plaza** (Alsina 166, tel. 0291/453-3289), **Cine Visión 1** (Belgrano 137), and **Cine Visual** (Chiclana 452, tel. 0291/451-8503).

Try **Ramses** (Alsina 274, tel. 0291/15-405-5979) for live salsa and blues.

Accommodations

Oddly enough for Argentine cities, Bahía Blanca has no hotels near the bus terminal and few near the train station.

Four kilometers southwest of town on RN 3, Parque Marítimo Almirante Brown's **Balneario Maldonado** (tel. 0291/452-9511) is a basic campground (US$1 pp) with saltwater swimming pools, but electricity and hot water in summer only.

Otherwise, the most acceptable shoestring choice is **Residencial Roma,** (Cerri 759, tel. 0291/453-8500, US$4 pp), across from the train station.

In a fairly well-maintained, 75-year-old French-style building, **Hotel Victoria** (General Paz 84, tel. 0291/452-0522, US$10/13 s/d) offers rooms with private bath, high ceilings, and fans; breakfast is also included.

Hotel Chiclana (Chiclana 366, tel. 0291/453-0436, hotel@infovia.com.ar, US$11/18 s/d) is plain but clean, with parking included (uncommon in this part of town). Rooms have showers but not tubs.

Hotel Santa Rosa (Sarmiento 373, tel. 0291/452-0012, hotelsantarosa@bvconline.com.ar, www.bvconline.com.ar/hotelsantarosa, US$14/18 s/d) is a small but friendly spot that, unlike most downtown hotels, has its own parking. There's a five percent discount for cash.

Bahía Blanca's finest value may be **Hotel Italia** (Brown 181, tel./fax 0291/456-2700, hitalia@rcc,com.ar, US$15/19 s/d with breakfast), a handsome French-style building with a mansard roof and completely rehabbed interior. The rooms are compact but well-furnished, the baths glisteningly modern; interior rooms and those facing

The Pampas

the Arribeños alleyway are quieter than those fronting on Brown itself.

Friendly, well-kept **Bahía Hotel** (Chiclana 251, tel. 0291/455-3050, hoteles@bahia-hotel .com.ar, www.bahia-hotel.com.ar, US$17/23 s/d with breakfast) has plain but sizeable rooms, but some of the mattresses are soft. There's a 10 percent discount for cash payments.

Friendly **Hotel Belgrano** (Belgrano 44, tel./fax 0291/456-5446, hbelgrano@impsat1.com.ar, US$13/17 s/d with ceiling fans, US$18/23 s/d with a/c) is well-maintained, though some of the beds are soft. **Hotel Muñiz** (O'Higgins 23, tel. 0291/456-0060, hmuniz@infovia.com.ar, US$16/22 s/d) and **Hotel Austral** (Avenida Colón 159, tel. 0291/561700, haustral@bblanca .com.ar, US$23 s or d) are comparable. Four-star **Hotel Argos** (España 149, tel. 0291/455-0404, pasajeros@hotelargos.com, US$29/36 s/d) is widely considered Bahía Blanca's best.

Food

La Barra (Chiclana 155, tel. 0291/451-7910) is primarily a breakfast spot, with coffee, croissants, juices, and sandwiches. **La Cibeles** (Alsina 301) is another good choice for breakfast and/or coffee.

More like a Spanish *tasca* than the trattoria its name would imply, **Pavarotti** (Belgrano 272, tel. 0291/450-0700) serves a fine *jamón serrano,* ravioli with squash, and a decent pesto by Argentine standards. The diverse menu also includes beef, seafood, and fish, with entrees ranging from US$2–5.

Packed with people relishing Germanic specialties and washing it down with draft beer, **Gambrinus** (Arribeños 164, tel. 0291/452-2380) is a Bahía Blanca institution dating from 1897. Unfortunately, smokers light up with impunity, even in the ostensible nonsmoking section.

El Mundo de la Parrilla (Avenida Colón 379, tel. 0291/451-1588) is the most popular place in town for grilled beef. **Víctor** (Chiclana 83, tel. 0291/452-3814) is a *parrilla* that also offers fine seafood. Other seafood options include the Basque-style **Taberna Baska** (Lavalle 284, tel. 0291/452-1788) and **Bizkaia** (Soler 783, tel. 0291/452-0191).

For pizza, try **Il Pirata** (Lamadrid 360, tel. 0291/454-8829) or **Pizzería Rodelú** (O'Higgins and Saavedra, tel. 0291/455-1332).

El Mago de la Empanada (Undiano near Chiclana, tel. 0291/456-5393) has the best and widest selection of empanadas.

Information

Bahía Blanca's **Oficina de Información Turística** (Alsina 65, tel. 0291/459-4007, www.bahiablanca.gov.ar, 8 A.M.–7 P.M. weekdays and 10 A.M.–1 P.M. Saturday) is directly across from the central Plaza Rivadavia, but in the basement; it has some English-speaking personnel.

Motorists will find **ACA** offices at Chiclana 305 (tel. 0291/455-0076).

Librería Pampa Mar (Alsina 245) is an excellent bookstore.

Services

There are numerous ATMs in the vicinity of Plaza Rivadavia, such as **Banco de la Nación** (Estomba 52) and **Banco Macro Bansud** (San Martín 145). The travel agency **Pullman Tour** (San Martín 171) is also an exchange house.

Correo Argentino is at Moreno 34; the postal code is 8000.

Telefónica is at Arribeños 112, two blocks southwest of Plaza Rivadavia. **CiberPlanet** (Brown 212) has fast Internet connections.

For laundry, **Laverap** is at Avenida Colón 197.

Pullman Tour is at San Martín 171, tel. 0291/455-3344. Student-oriented travel agency **Asatej** is at Zelarrayán 267, tel. 0291/456-0666, bblanca@asatej.com.ar.

Chile has a consulate at Belgrano 503 (tel. 0291/453-1516).

The **Hospital Municipal de Agudos** is at Estomba 968 (tel. 0291/459-8484). The **Hospital Privado del Sur** is at Las Heras 164 (tel. 0291/455-0270).

Getting There

Bahía Blanca has air, bus, and rail services, but the latter are very limited.

Aerolíneas Argentinas and **Austral,** which share offices (San Martín 298, tel. 0291/456-0561), average two flights daily to Aeroparque.

LADE (Darregueira 21, tel. 0291/453-7697) flies shifting schedules north to Mar del Plata and Aeroparque, and south to Viedma, San Antonio Oeste, Puerto Madryn, Trelew, Neuquén, Chapelco (San Martín de los Andes), Esquel, and Bariloche.

The **Argentine Navy** (tel. 0291/486-0595) flies cheaply but irregularly to Buenos Aires.

Bahía Blanca's **Terminal de Ómnibus San Francisco de Asís** (Brown 1700, tel. 0291/481-9615) is about two kilometers east of Plaza Rivadavia. It's a major hub for long overland transportation in southern Buenos Aires Province and long-distance buses north and south, but there are also provincial minibus services elsewhere in the city.

Typical destinations, fares, and times include Mar del Plata (US$16, seven hours) La Plata (US$20, nine hours), Buenos Aires (US$16, eight hours), Viedma (US$7, three hours), Neuquén (US$11, eight hours), Bariloche (US$23, 12 hours), Trelew (US$20, 12 hours), Comodoro Rivadavia (US$25, 15 hours), and Río Gallegos (US$56, 26 hours).

Buses to the hill station of Sierra de la Ventana (US$3.50, two hours) leave from the Terminal de Combis (San Martín 445, tel. 0291/454-0438).

Trains still go from Bahía Blanca to Constitución from the landmark **Estación Ferrocarril Roca,** now operated by Ferrocarril UPCP (Avenida Cerri 750, tel. 0291/452-9196). Departures via Sierra de la Ventana (US$1.50) and Coronel Pringles take place Monday and Wednesday at 8:20 P.M.; departures via Tornquist, Pigüé, and Azul are at 8:20 P.M. Tuesday, Thursday, and Sunday. Fares to Constitución are US$5 *turista,* US$6 *primera,* and US$8 Pullman.

Getting Around

Aeropuerto Comandante Espora (RN 3 Norte, Km 674, tel. 0291/486-1456) is 15 kilometers east of town on the naval base. Aerolíneas/Austral provides its own transfers to and from town (US$1.50 pp).

City buses use magnetic *tarjebús* cards, available from downtown kiosks. Bus Nos. 505, 512, 514, 516, and 517 reach the bus terminal from downtown; No. 504 goes to Ingeniero White, and No. 505 goes to Balneario Maldonado via Avenida Colón.

For car rentals, **AT** is at Avenida Colón 180 (tel. 0291/454-3944); **Localiza** is nearby (Avenida Colón 194, tel. 0291/456-2526).

La Pampa Province

Seemingly, more people travel around thinly populated La Pampa Province rather than through it, which is a pity. Immediately west of Buenos Aires Province, La Pampa has only one substantial city—the capital of Santa Rosa—but a diversity of environments that range from lush grasslands to dense *caldén* forests, broad saline lakes that draw flocks of migratory birds (including flamingos), and rounded pink-granite mountains whose canyons sheltered the indigenous resistance to General Roca's "Conquest of the Desert" in the late 19th century. Its major attraction is Parque Nacional Lihué Calel, a wildlife-rich reserve that's brutally hot in summer but makes a worthwhile stopover for travelers to and from Patagonia.

SANTA ROSA AND VICINITY

One of Argentina's newest cities, Santa Rosa de Toay is the gateway to often-overlooked Parque Nacional Lihué Calel and one of the gateways to Patagonia. Before its founding in 1892, this was a dangerous frontier zone, but today it's a modern provincial capital and agricultural service center.

Orientation

Santa Rosa (population 93,924) is 607 kilometers west of Buenos Aires via RN 5, 641 kilometers south of Córdoba via RN 35, and 327 kilometers northwest of Bahía Blanca via RN 35. Plaza San Martín is the traditional commercial and administrative center of its regular grid, but the

Centro Cívico, seven blocks east, is the seat of provincial government.

Sights

Santa Rosa's **Museo Provincial de Historia Natural** (Pellegrini 190, tel. 02954/422693, 8 A.M.–noon and 2–7 P.M. weekdays, 6–9 P.M. Sun., free) specializes in provincial paleontology, geology, and flora and fauna.

Housed in a handsome building at 9 de Julio and Villegas, the **Museo Provincial de Artes** (tel. 02954/427332, 8 A.M.–1 P.M. daily) deals with provincial and Argentine artists, including works by Antonio Berni, Benito Quinquela Martín, and Juan Carlos Castagnino, but also has special exhibitions.

One of Santa Rosa's most distinguished constructions, the Baroque-style **Teatro Español** (Hilario Lagos 54, tel. 02954/424520) dates from 1908 but took nearly two decades to complete. Other than for scheduled events, it's open to the public 10 A.M.–noon and 4–6:30 P.M. weekdays.

Reserva Provincial Parque Luro

In the early 20th century, Argentines acquired an international reputation for ostentatious excess thanks to figures like Dr. Pedro Luro (1860–1927), a businessman, politician, and sport hunter who created his own private hunting reserve with imported Carpathian deer and European boar, 35 kilometers south of Santa Rosa. Then known as Estancia San Huberto, Luro's property featured an extravagant French-style lodge in the midst of 20,000 hectares of *caldén* forests and grasslands.

Today, reduced to 7,500 hectares and under provincial stewardship, Parque Luro is open to the public and Luro's lodge is a museum—like many other wealthy Argentines whose unrestrained tastes have exceeded even their substantial resources, Luro, his heirs, and even subsequent purchasers were unable to hold onto the deteriorating property. Today, fortunately, it's holding its own, with hiking trails, bicycle paths, and a **Centro de Interpretación** that focuses on the park's environmental and cultural history. There are also a small zoo, places to picnic, and a **Sala de Carruajes** with a collection of classic horse carriages.

Guided tours of the **Castillo Luro** (tel. 02954/499000) and grounds are available on request for US$.75; park admission costs an additional US$.40. Hours are 9 A.M.–5 P.M. daily except in summer, when the park is open until 8 P.M. It is closed Mondays, however.

Meals are available at the park's restaurant **La Frontera** (tel. 02954/454675).

Entertainment

The **Teatro Español** (Hilario Lagos 54, tel. 02954/424520) hosts the biggest performing arts events. The new **Casino Club** (Hilario Lagos 467) has given the city a venue for intermediate acts.

For movies, try **Cine Don Bosco** (Avenida Uruguay 795, tel. 02954/439935).

Shopping

Santa Rosa deserves a stop for souvenir-seekers after gaucho gear. The **Mercado Artesanal,** which shares quarters with the provincial tourist office at Avenida Luro 400, displays quality goods from throughout the province. Other outstanding outlets include **Artesanías Argentinas** (Avenida Luro 430, tel. 02954/427300) down the block, and **El Matrero** (Pellegrini 86).

Accommodations

Camping at the woodsy **Centro Recreativo Municipal Don Tomás** (tel. 02954/455368, US$2–3 pp), about 10 blocks from downtown at the west end of Avenida Uruguay, provides great facilities including picnic tables, barbecue pits, hot showers, and a swimming pool. It can get crowded in summer and on weekends, and the mosquitoes can be abundant and bloodthirsty.

Only a block from the bus terminal, **Hostería Santa Rosa** (Hipólito Yrigoyen 696, tel. 02954/423868, US$7/11 s/d) is likely the best budget choice other than camping. **Hostería Río Atuel** (Avenida Pedro Luro 356, tel. 02954/422597, US$10/12 s/d) is directly across from the bus terminal. **Hotel San Martín** (Alsina 101, tel. 02954/422549, hotelsanmartin@cpenet .com.ar, www.hsanmartin.com.ar, US$10/14 s/d) is more central.

THE OCTOPUS ON LA PAMPA

In pioneer days—which lasted into the 20th century in La Pampa Province—the *pulpería* of Chacharramendi was one of the frontier's most isolated outposts. Built of wood with exterior metal cladding, the only general store in a vast and desolate area, it served as a grocery, hardware store, pharmacy, shoe store, smithery, saddlery, and even justice of the peace—and sold almost anything essential for isolated homesteads.

Though it's now only 200 kilometers southwest of Santa Rosa by a smooth paved highway, this was indigenous territory when Fernando Seijoó established himself here in 1865; long after José Feito acquired the property in 1901 it was still insecure. The architectural details of the restored **Parador Histórico Chacharramendi** show that it could be a dangerous area: There remain several peepholes for pointing pistols or rifles in self-defense, and the main store had a basement hatch leading to an escape tunnel. All the goods were kept behind bars (though this was not an unusual practice on the frontier) and clients pointed out what products interested them.

Also known as the Boliche de Feito and El Viejo Almacén, the *pulpería* served as a hotel, bar, and general gathering place—one of the frontier's few social institutions (according to legend, one of its guests was the famous bandit Juan Bairoletto). It operated until 1975, when the Feito family donated it to the province as a museum; from the surviving account books alone, it would probably be possible to reconstruct the hamlet's history.

For Neuquén-bound motorists on RN 143, Chacharramendi makes an ideal breather and even a stopover for gas, food, and lodging, though its sole hotel and restaurant offer no luxury. To a degree, Chacharramendi still operates on the principle of the *pulpería*—a Spanish-American term that derives from the word for "octopus."

The high-rise **Hotel Calfucurá** (Avenida San Martín 695, tel. 02954/423612, reservas @calfucurahotel.com.ar, www.calfucurah.com.ar, US$16/21 s/d) is more conspicuous than luxurious, thanks to its high-climbing mural of the cacique Calfucurá who led the resistance to Roca's invaders. Still, it's a good value.

Set on eight hectares east of town, Santa Rosa's best is the new **La Campina Club Hotel** (RN 5 Km 604, tel. 02954/426714, lacampina @infovia.com.ar, www.lacampina.com, US$21/30 s/d), In addition to a sauna, a gym, a hot tub, and other recreational facilities, this Spanish-colonial-style hotel has its own restaurant.

Food

Santa Rosa's gastronomic scene is limited but respectable. At the northwest corner of Plaza San Martín, **La Recova** (Hipólito Yrigoyen and Avellaneda) is the best breakfast choice.

Don Pepe (Pellegrini 115) serves *tenedor libre* beef and pasta for around US$4. There are several decent pizzerias, including **Pizza Quattro** (Sarmiento and Pellegrini, tel. 02954/434457); **Pronto Pizza** (Avenida Luro 290, tel. 02954/436993), which also serves *parrillada;* and particularly *La Ochava,* which has sidewalk seating at the corner of Avenida San Martín and Urquiza.

Pimiento (Pellegrini 234, tel. 02954/431068) has a promising but yet-unproven menu of pasta, chicken, and seafood. Entrees range US$4–10.

Heladería Robert (Avenida Luro and Avenida San Martín) has outstanding ice cream.

Information

Directly across from the bus terminal, the **Dirección Provincial de Turismo** (Avenida Pedro Luro 400, tel. 02954/425060, fax 02954/421817, www.turismolapampa.gov.ar) is open 7 A.M.–1:30 P.M. and 5–9 P.M. weekdays, 9 A.M.–noon and 5–9 P.M. weekends. Well-stocked with maps and brochures, it also has English-speaking staff.

At the terminal itself, the municipal **Centro de Informes** (Avenida Pedro Luro 365, tel. 02954/422952, www.santarosa.gov.ar) stays open 24 hours.

For motorists, **ACA** is at Avenida San Martín 102, tel. 02954/422435, at the southeast corner of Plaza San Martín.

Services

Santa Rosa is the only city in the province with a complete range of services.

Several banks in the vicinity of Plaza San Martín have ATMs, including **Banco de la Nación** (Avenida Roca 1) and **Banco de La Pampa** (Pellegrini 255).

Correo Argentino is at Hilario Lagos 258; the postal code is 6300.

Telefónica Centro (Avellaneda 190) has phone and fax services. For Internet connections, try **Cyber Net,** on the north side of Plaza San Martín.

Swiss Travel (Pellegrini 217, tel. 02954/425952) is a full-service agency.

For laundry, **Burbujas** is at Rivadavia 253.

Hospital Lucio Molas is two kilometers north of downtown at Raúl P. Diaz and Pilcomayo (tel. 02954/455000).

Getting There and Around

Santa Rosa has limited air services and extensive bus services, but trains on the Sarmiento line to and from Once (Buenos Aires) are currently suspended.

Aerolíneas Argentinas (Moreno and Hilario Lagos, tel. 02954/422388) flies three times weekly to Aeroparque (Buenos Aires) via Bahía Blanca. The airport, about three kilometers north of town, is easily reached by taxi or *remise* for about US$2.

Santa Rosa is a key crossroads for bus services throughout the republic. The **Estación Terminal de Ómnibus** (Avenida Pedro Luro 365, tel. 02954/422249) is at the Centro Cívico.

Sample destinations and fares include Bahía Blanca (US$8, 4.5 hours), Neuquén (US$9, six hours), Buenos Aires (US$11, 6.5 hours), Córdoba (US$13, nine hours), Mar del Plata (US$15, nine hours), Mendoza (US$22, 12 hours), and Bariloche (US$18, 13 hours).

For Parque Nacional Lihue Calel (US$5), the most convenient choice is Edu Bus (tel. 02954/429101), whose services to Puelches pass the park entrance. Departures are Wednesday and Friday at 6 A.M., Friday and Sunday at

6:30 P.M. Otherwise, Neuquén-bound buses with **TAC** (tel. 02954/437779) and **TUS** (tel. 02954/432140) both pass the park entrance but leave in the very early A.M. hours.

M PARQUE NACIONAL LIHUÉ CALEL

Rising gently but perceptibly above the arid pampas of southern La Pampa Province, Parque Nacional Lihué Calel's landscape stands out not just for its topography, flora, and fauna, but also for its archaeological and historical importance. Its topography has created niches for its surprisingly abundant vegetation and animal life, but it also supported the lifestyle of pre-Columbian hunter-gatherers—still visible in several rock-art sites—and sheltered the indigenous resistance against invasions by Spain and, later, the Argentine state.

After the Mapuche cacique Namuncurá finally surrendered to General Roca's invaders in 1885, Lihué Calel (whose name in Pehuenche means "The Range of Life") fell into private hands as Estancia Santa María. Following decades of exploitation for agriculture, ranching and even copper mining, it was expropriated by the province in 1964. Later donated to the APN for a national park, it's become a regular stop on the itineraries of some international overland expedition companies, but is still a welcome alternative to overcrowded units like Iguazú.

Orientation

Reaching a maximum elevation of 589 meters above sea level, Lihué Calel consists 9,901 hectares of varied terrain, 226 kilometers southwest of Santa Rosa via RN 35 and RN 152. Its northerly slopes are gentle, but the southerly approach is steeper. A further area to the north, comprising the salt flats known Salitral Levalle, is under consideration for inclusion.

Flora and Fauna

Lihué Calel is arid, with only about 400 millimeters of precipitation per annum, but that precipitation supports nearly 350 plant species in a variety of associations and microenvironments. In a sense, the mountains of Lihué Calel are an archipelago surrounded by desert rather than water.

Water, though, contributes to the park's biodiversity. While rain may be infrequent, it collects and remains more easily in some areas than others, and it can support surprisingly lush vegetation. The main plant association is the dry scrub known as *monte,* but more-humid spots support denser groves of *caldén* (*Prosopis caldenia*), a relative of the common mesquite tree. In shadier areas, ferns may even grow within cracks in the rocky terrain, while cacti colonize more exposed areas. Lichens form circular patterns on the more-exposed rocks.

Thanks to both forest cover and wide-open spaces, wildlife is more abundant and conspicuous than in the densely settled areas of Buenos Aires Province. Rare pumas (*Felis concolor*) have been seen in the park, but smaller predators like Geoffroy's cat (*Felis geoffroyi*), the jaguarundi (*Felis yagouaroundi*), and the abundant Patagonian fox also live here. According to a recent census, about 200 guanacos graze the park's open grasslands; other common mammals include the *mara* (Patagonian hare, *Dolichotis patagonicum*) and vizcacha (*Lagostomus maximus*), related to the domestic chinchilla.

Bird life is also plentiful, ranging from the flightless rhea or *ñandú*(Rhea americana) to predators including the common *carancho,* or crested caracara, (*Polyborus plancus*) and the much rarer crowned eagle (*Harpyhaliectus coronatus*). When the *caldén* fruits, there are many *loros barranqueros* (parakeets).

Among reptiles, harmless lizards are common, but beware the rare but highly venomous pit vipers commonly known as *yarará* (*Bothrops* spp.).

Sights and Activities

One of the best areas to view wildlife is the *caldén* forest near the campground and park headquarters—in fact, at dawn and dusk, foxes scurry among the campsites and countless birds call from its shade trees. The campground is also the starting point for the **Sendero El Huitru,** a well-marked nature trail through the *monte* that leads to some sadly vandalized petroglyphs.

Another trail leads to the park's highest point, the melodiously named, 589-meter **Cerro de la**

Sociedad Científica Argentina, but the open granite slopes provide numerous alternative routes. The summit panorama includes the entire Lihué Calel range, the arid pampas, and salt lakes like Salitral Levalle to the north and shallow marshes like Laguna Urre Lauquen to the southwest.

Well west of the visitors center, the ruins of the **Viejo Casco** were the headquarters of the former Estancia Santa María; with a vehicle, it's possible to loop around through the **Valle de las Pinturas,** whose unblemished petroglyphs date from around the time of Christ.

Practicalities

Near the visitors center, the APN operates a free, shady **campground** with firepits, picnic tables, electricity until 11 P.M., and clean bathrooms with flush toilets and cold showers. The solitude and abundant wildlife make it a better choice than the mediocre **ACA Hostería** (tel. 02952/436101, US$7/11 s/d) about one kilometer south of the highway turnoff. ACA has a less-than-mediocre restaurant and limited groceries; the town of Puelches, 35 kilometers to the south, has more and better supplies.

The Administración de Parques Nacionales has a **Centro de Informes** (tel. 02952/436595, apnlc@gralacha.com.ar) only about two kilometers west of the well-marked park entrance on RN 152. Official hours are 8 A.M.–noon and 3–6 P.M. in summer, 9 A.M.–noon and 2–6 P.M. the rest of the year, but in practice the rangers are accessible at almost any reasonable hour.

There is no admission fee for the park.

Edu Bus (tel. 02954/429101 in Santa Rosa) passes the park entrance (US$5) en route to Puelches, departing Wednesday and Friday at 6 A.M., Friday and Sunday at 6:30 P.M. Otherwise, Neuquén-bound buses with **TAC** (tel. 02954/437779) and **TUS** (tel. 02954/432140) both pass the park entrance, but leave in the very early A.M. hours.

Edu Bus's return services from Puelches leave at 12:45 P.M. Wednesday and Friday, and 10:30 P.M. Friday and Sunday. TAC and TUS buses leave Puelches for Santa Rosa between 9:10 and 10:30 P.M.

Mesopotamia and the Paraná

North of Buenos Aires, the Río Paraná is one of the world's great rivers. In all of South America, only the Amazon is longer; at 3,998 kilometers from its source in tropical Brazil to its mouth at the temperate Atlantic, it is the world's 13th longest river, longer than the Mississippi. Draining an area of more than a million square kilometers, it flows south from Brazil, forms much of the border between subtropical Argentina and Paraguay, and

finally meets the Río Uruguay north of Buenos Aires to form the Río de la Plata.

For the northeastern Argentine provinces, the Paraná and the Uruguay are a great part of their visitor appeal. In the area between the rivers, known collectively as Mesopotamia, the provinces of Entre Ríos, Corrientes, and Misiones boast natural attractions like Parque Nacional El Palmar, home to rolling palm savannas;

the matchless Esteros del Iberá, a wildlife-rich wetland comparable to—perhaps even better than—Brazil's better-known Pantanal; and the thunderous falls of Iguazú, by consensus one of the world's greatest sights.

They also have cultural allure: the Entre Ríos city of Gualeguaychú hosts Argentina's liveliest Carnaval celebrations, though the provincial capital of Corrientes comes a close second, and several riverside towns exude colonial charm. Misiones takes its name from the colonial Jesuit outposts (several of which still survive in impressive ruins), which inspired the film *The Mission.*

On the Paraná's western banks, Santa Fe Province is one of the country's economic powerhouses, thanks primarily to its productive agriculture and to the Río Paraná port of Rosario. Rosario, for its part, is a city of monuments and a vigorous cultural life that challenges Córdoba's claim as the republic's second city. North of Santa Fe, Chaco and Formosa Provinces are hot, subtropical lowlands that reward dedicated, environmentally sensitive travelers who seek out their national parks—indeed, the route across the Chaco from Salta to Resistencia, Corrientes (including Iberá) and Misiones (Iguazú) is fast earning a spot on the itineraries of many long-distance travelers.

A word on climate: in summer, northeastern Argentina can be stiflingly hot and humid, and heavy rains can fall in any season. Locals say there are only two seasons—the mild sunny winter (easily the best time to explore the region) and the hot muggy summer. The transition from one to the other, though, can be sudden.

PLANNING YOUR TIME

One of the top attractions on the entire continent, despite recent negative developments, the Iguazú Falls alone demand at least three days from any visitor, preferably during the full moon; if the trip includes the Brazilian side, an additional day or two is desirable, and exploring the more-remote parts of the rain forest in the vicinity could add even more. For the mission at San Ignacio, figure at least one day more.

Add no less than three days to tour the Esteros del Iberá at Colonia Pellegrini, and figure a day to get there and a day to get back via the city of Mercedes (though there's quicker access from the Misiones provincial capital of Posadas in dry weather). Iberá, though, is worth a trip in its own right—even at the cost of bypassing Iguazú. Both Iguazú and Iberá are worthwhile at any time of year—even during the withering summer heat and humidity.

Travelers wishing to explore areas with few foreigners can head northwest to the Chaco provincial capital of Resistencia, with its surprisingly vigorous cultural and artistic life, and use it as a base for visiting the Chaco and Río Pilcomayo national parks. This, though, is best in the cool winter months.

In southernmost Mesopotamia, destinations like Gualeguaychú (for Carnaval), Parque Nacional El Palmar, and the city of Rosario are close enough for weekend excursions from Buenos Aires.

HISTORY

Much of northeastern Argentina's history is inseparable from the two great river systems—the southward-flowing Uruguay and Paraná—that eventually unite to form the Río de la Plata estuary. Between the rivers, the Mesopotamian provinces of Entre Ríos, Corrientes, and Misiones form a virtual island where, in pre-Columbian times, Guaraní-speaking Indians subsisted on beans, maize, and root crops like manioc and sweet potatoes. River fish also played an important role in the diet, though wild game was not so abundant as on the more southerly pampas. On the right bank of the Paraná, and northward into the "green hell" of the Gran Chaco, the aboriginal inhabitants were mostly hunter-gatherers who, like the Guaraní, also relied on fishing for their livelihood.

More numerous than the scattered nomadic inhabitants of the pampas, the semi-sedentary Guaraní attracted the attention of early Spanish explorers. In 1537, Pedro de Mendoza's lieutenant Pedro de Ayolas ascended the Paraná to found the city of Asunción, in present-day

Must-Sees

Look for **N** to find the sights and activities you can't miss and **M** for the best dining and lodging.

N Gualeguaychú: Home to Argentina's liveliest Carnaval for a few late-summer weekends, this is the country's biggest party town. Situated on the Río Uruguay, it's a popular riverside beach resort year-round (page 172).

N Parque Nacional El Palmar: This nearly undeveloped palm savanna on the banks of the Río Uruguay offers a glimpse of Argentine

MESOPOTAMIA AND THE PARANÁ

PARAGUAY

Parque Nacional Río Pilcomayo **M**

Parque Nacional **M** Chaco

Parque Nacional Iguazú **M**

Yacutinga Lodge **M**

San Ignacio **M** Miní

Esteros **M** del Iberá

BRAZIL

Parque Nacional El Palmar **M**

Monumento Nacional a la **M** Bandera

Gualeguaychú **M**

URUGUAY

ATLANTIC OCEAN

Mesopotamia before the arrival of the Spaniards. Its unique environment harbors many kinds of mammals and birds (page 176).

N Esteros del Iberá: The masses throng to thunderous Iguazú, but those in the know prefer the silent, wildlife-rich marshes of central Corrientes Province. This unique environment is at risk, though, from rising water levels caused by Yacyretá dam (page 187).

N San Ignacio Miní: History lives on in the vivid red ruins of Argentina's best-preserved Jesuit mission, among many in the upper Paraná. The missions' details were sculpted by Guaraní artisans under the tutelage of South America's most fascinating missionary order (page 197).

N Parque Nacional Iguazú: One of the continent's greatest natural sights makes Niagara look like a leaky faucet. For a unique perspective, avoiding the crowds, schedule your visit for the full moon—it's more magical under moonlight (page 199).

N Yacutinga Lodge: Only an hour from Iguazú, eco-friendly Yacutinga lacks the thunderous falls but offers everything else in terms of the upper Paraná's subtropical flora and fauna, plus extraordinary accommodations (page 203).

N Monumento Nacional a la Bandera: In **Rosario** (perhaps Argentina's most underrated city), this huge monument is the city's most famous. It pays tribute to the Argentine flag and its designer, Manuel Belgrano (page 213).

N Parque Nacional Chaco: If crossing the Chaco to or from Salta, take a detour to sample the flora and fauna of the humid eastern region in this haven of forest and wetlands (page 225).

N Parque Nacional Río Pilcomayo: In little-visited Formosa Province, this park of shallow shimmering waters along the Paraguayan border is an overlooked gem (page 229).

MESOPOTAMIA AND
THE PARANÁ

PARAGUAY

Río Pilcomayo

Ingeniero
Guillermo Juárez

SALTA

FORMOSA

Río Bermejo

RN
81

RN
86

Parque Nacional
Río Pilcomayo

ASUNCIÓN

Clorinda

Taco Pozo

RN
16

CHACO

RP 3

Formosa

Río Paraguay

Ciudad del Este
Puerto Iguazú

Foz do Iguaçu

Río Iguazú
Andresito

SANTIAGO
DEL
ESTERO

Presidencia Roque
Sáenz Peña

RP 90

Parque
Nacional Chaco

Resistencia

RN
89

RP 90

Parque
Nacional Iguazú

San Ignacio Miní

Yacutinga
Lodge

El Dorado

RN
14

Río Paraná

Corrientes

RN
12

Río Paraná

Posadas

San Ignacio

MISIONES

SANTA FE

P.N.
Mburucuyá

RN
118

Oberá

Ituzaingó

Apóstoles

Esteros
del Iberá

Río Uruguay

RP 40

Colonia
Pellegrini

Santo Tomé

São Borja

BRAZIL

Tostado

RN
98

Reconquista

RN
123

RN
12

Goya

Mercedes

RN
119

Paso de
los Libres

Curuzú Cuatiá

CORRIENTES

Yapeyú

Uruguaiana

RN
34

RP 1

RN
11

RP 1

La Paz

RN
127

Federal

Rafaela

Concordia

RN
19

Santa Fe

ENTRE RÍOS

Salto

CÓRDOBA

Río
Paraná

Paraná

RP 6

RN
18

Parque Nacional El Palmar

Diamante

RP 39

PALACIO
SAN JOSÉ

Colón

Paysandú

RN
9

Monumento
Nacional a la
Bandera

Victoria

Concepción
del Uruguay

RP 11

Gualeguaychú

Rosario

Gualeguay

Fray Bentos

RN
8

RN
33

Pergamino

URUGUAY

Venado Tuerto

Zárate

Campana

Colonia del
Sacramento

RN
7

Junín

San Antonio
de Areco

Luján

Río de la Plata

RN
188

BUENOS
AIRES

RP 3

BUENOS
AIRES

La Plata

MONTEVIDEO

Punta del Este

RN
5

RN
3

RP 2

ATLANTIC

OCEAN

0   100 mi

0   100 km

moon

Mesopotamia & Paraná

© AVALON TRAVEL PUBLISHING, INC.

Paraguay, where the Guaraní provided them food and other essentials. From Asunción, Spanish settlement proceeded south into Corrientes and Santa Fe by the late 16th century.

The most effective colonizers, though, were the Jesuit missionaries who congregated the Guaraní into permanent settlements and taught them the Spanish language, Catholic religion, and even highly skilled trades like violin-making. At the same time, many Guaraní also served as unskilled labor on the Jesuits' *yerba mate* (Paraguayan tea) plantations and cattle ranches in Corrientes and Misiones. The Jesuits' extraordinary success provoked Portuguese slave raids from Brazil and political intrigues in Spain that eventually led to their expulsion from the Amer-

icas in 1767, and lush subtropical forests soon covered their monumental sandstone missions.

In the immediate post-colonial era, Argentine Mesopotamia was an area of caudillos (provincial strongmen)—most notably Justo José Urquiza, who helped topple the dictatorship of Juan Manuel de Rosas—and then the staging point for the War of the Triple Alliance against Paraguay in the 1870s. The west bank of the Paraná, though, surged ahead economically as the river port of Rosario became a major export point for grains from the fabulously productive pampas. Today, Mesopotamia, the Chaco provinces, and even the provincial capital of Santa Fe lag far behind vigorous Rosario in their economic development and cultural life.

Entre Ríos Province

After the unrelentingly level pampas of Buenos Aires Province, the lush rolling hills of Entre Ríos can be a pleasure. As befits its name ("between the rivers"), the province's great natural asset is its access to the enormous southbound rivers, the Paraná and the Uruguay, that converge to form the Río de la Plata (often glossed into English as "River Plate"). Gualeguaychú's summer Carnaval is the province's biggest event, while the palm savannas of Parque Nacional El Palmar preserve one of the country's truly unique environments.

GUALEGUAYCHÚ

Entre Ríos's biggest party town, the riverside city of Gualeguaychú, hosts one of Argentina's top Carnaval celebrations—not quite Rio, but well worth seeing if you're in Buenos Aires instead of Brazil. Dating from 1783, it has a smattering of colonial constructions, but is most popular with Argentines for access to its namesake river. To the east, the Puente Internacional General Libertador San Martín offers the southernmost bridge access into Uruguay, to the city of Fray Bentos.

Orientation

Gualeguaychú (population 73,330) is 220 kilo-

meters north of Buenos Aires via RN 14 and an eastbound lateral that leads directly to the central Plaza San Martín, a square occupying four full blocks. One block south of the plaza, Avenida 25 de Mayo is the main commercial street. Several blocks east, the Río Gualeguaychú, a tributary of the much larger Río Uruguay, meanders southward.

Sights and Activities

The city's only national historical monument is the **Teatro Gualeguaychú** Urquiza 705), dating from 1914. It is still the city's principal high-culture venue, with theater, music, and dance performances.

At the northeast corner of Plaza San Martín, Gualeguaychú's oldest construction (1800) is the **Solar de los Haedo** (San José 105, 9 A.M.–noon Wed.–Sun., and 5–8 P.M. Fri. and Sat. only), which Italian patriot Giuseppe Garibaldi used as his headquarters during the Uruguayan struggle against Rosas. Now the municipal museum. The **Instituto Magnasco** (Camila Nievas 78, tel. 03446/427287, 10 A.M.–noon and 4–8 P.M. weekdays, 10 A.M.–noon Sat.) is a newly renovated private facility focusing on local art, history, and numismatics.

Also dating from late colonial times, the **Casa de Andrade** (Andrade and Borques) was home to versatile Olegario Andrade, a mid-19th-century politician, poet, journalist, and diplomat. José S. Álvarez, better known by his pen name, Fray Mocho, resided at the **Casa de Fray Mocho** (Fray Mocho 135); Álvarez founded the satirical magazine *Caras y Caretas*. Neither the Andrade nor the Fray Mocho house is normally open to the public.

Culture and revelry are not necessarily contradictory in Gualeguaychú, whose enclosed **Corsódromo,** on the grounds of the **Estación Ferrocarril Urquiza,** the old railroad station at the foot of Avenida Rocamora and Avenida Irazusta, is the main site for the midsummer Carnaval parades. The train station is also home to the open-air **Museo Ferroviario,** which displays antique steam locomotives, dining cars, and other railway equipment.

East of the river, reached by bridge, low-lying **Parque Unzué** is Gualeguaychú's favorite recreational resource for campers, picnickers, swimmers, and the like. It is also the site of the city's **Museo Arqueológico Monseñor Manuel Almeida** (archaeological museum, tel. 03446/432643, 9 A.M.–1 P.M. and 6–10 P.M. daily), which offers guided tours during its afternoon hours.

For a roll on the river, the **Expreso Ciudad de Gualeguaychú** (tel. 03446/423248) takes hourlong excursions (US$2) from the Puerto Municipal on the Costanera at the foot of Avenida Irazusta.

Entertainment and Events

The landmark **Teatro Municipal** (Urquiza 705, tel. 03446/431757) remains the principal performing arts locale. **Cinemania** (Camilo Nievas 283, www.cinemania.vaporvos.com.ar) shows recent movies.

Oriented toward visitors from Buenos Aires, Gualeguaychú's **Carnaval del País** celebrations takes place weekends in mid- to late summer, depending on the Lenten calendar. If bad weather intervenes, though, the final weekend may even be pushed back in Lent. Admission to the Corsódromo costs around US$4 pp, with reserved seats for another US$2–3 pp.

The city's other big parade is October's **Fiesta Provincial de Carrozas Estudiantiles,** when secondary students display colorful floats on city streets.

Accommodations

Gualeguaychú is always a popular summer destination, but on Carnaval weekends accommodations are at a premium, reservations almost imperative, and prices can rise. Most choices are very central, but places at the lower end lack a/c.

Residencial Amalfi (25 de Mayo 571, tel. 03446/426818, amalfi@hotmail.com, US$9/12 s/d) is in an attractive older building, but is otherwise plain.

Its Bavarian exterior looks utterly out of place in subtropical Entre Ríos, but the simple **Hotel Alemán** (Bolívar 535, tel. 03446/426153, US$11/17 s/d) is an outstanding value.

Hotel Berlín (Bolívar 733, tel. 03446/425111, hotelberlin@yahoo.com, www.hotelberlin.com.ar) charges US$17/24 s/d with breakfast. **Hotel Viedma** (Bolívar 530, tel. 03446/424262, viedmahotel@ciudad.com.ar) costs US$18/28 s/d.

Rates at three-star **Hotel Embajador** (3 de Febrero 115, tel. 03446/424414, embajador@infovia.com.ar, www.hotel-embajador.com) start around US$14/23 s/d but can rise to US$24/28 s/d, breakfast included. A modern construction, it is also the city casino.

Food

For fish fresh from the river, don't miss **Dacal** (Costanera and Andrade, tel. 03446/4427602), but there are several others along the waterfront. **París** (Pellegrini 162, tel. 03446/422158) is another good seafood/*parrillada* option. **Pizza San Remo** (Alem and Méndez, tel. 03446/426891) serves Italo-Argentine specialties.

For ice cream, the best choice is the riverfront **Bahillo** (Costanera and San Lorenzo, tel. 03446/426240); it also has a downtown branch (25 de Mayo and Italia, tel. 03446/427349).

Information and Services

Gualeguaychú's **Oficina de Información Turística Puerto** is on the riverfront Paseo del Puerto (Tiscornia and Goldaracena, tel. 03446/423668,

Mesopotamia & Paraná

informacion@gualeguaychuturismo.com, www
.gualeguaychuturismo.com). At the bus station,
it also has a convenient **Oficina de Información Turística** terminal (Avenida Artigas and
Blvd. Jurado, tel. 03446/440706). Both have
helpful personnel, thorough information including accommodations details, and many
brochures, but their maps are poor. Hours are
8 A.M.–10 P.M. daily in summer, 8 A.M.–8 P.M.
the rest of the year.

For motorists, **ACA** is at Urquiza 1001, tel.
03446/426088.

Half a dozen banks along Avenida 25 de Mayo
have **ATMs,** but there are no exchange houses.

Correo Argentino is at Urquiza and Angel
Elías; the postal code is 2820. There are **Telecentros** at the bus terminal and at 25 de Mayo
562. **Cibernet** (25 de Mayo 874) has fast Internet access.

For medical services, **Hospital Centenario** is

west of downtown (25 de Mayo and Pasteur, tel.
03447/427831).

Getting There and Around

Gualeguaychú's shiny new **Terminal de Ómnibus** (Avenida Artigas and Blvd. Jurado, tel.
03446/440688) is a long-overdue replacement for
the dilapidated downtown bus station. Its west-
side location, though, is less convenient to all
services.

At noon and 7 P.M. there are international
connections to Fray Bentos, Uruguay, with **Ciudad de Gualeguay** (tel. 03446/440555), which
continues to Mercedes (which has frequent connections to Montevideo). **Cauvi** (tel.
03446/440779) has direct service to Montevideo, but fewer departures. **Encon** (also tel.
03446/440779) stops in Gualeguaychú en route
between Córdoba and Montevideo.

Sample destinations, fares, and times include
Fray Bentos (US$2, one hour); Mercedes,

PALACIO SAN JOSÉ

In a symbolic challenge to his Buenos Aires rival
Juan Manuel de Rosas, Entre Ríos caudillo Justo
José Urquiza (1801–1870) began this improvised
yet imposing palace in 1848, under the supervision
of contractor Jacinto Dellepiane. Italian-born architect Pedro Fossati, though, brought out its full
Italianate grandeur in completing it between 1857
and 1860.

Twin towers mark the location of Urquiza's lavish 38-room residence, still isolated in the middle
of the *entrerriano* countryside, surrounded by an
outer ring of native forest and an inner ring of elegant French-style gardens. The palace itself surrounds two major patios, built of Carrara marble,
while outbuildings include the family's private
chapel, carriage house, bakery, blacksmithery,
aviary, and *pulpería* (store).

Palacio San José

The palace's furnishings include Urquiza's 8.5-meter dining room table, suitable for hosting
prestigious guests like Bartolomé Mitre and Urquiza's onetime critic Domingo F. Sarmiento, who
eventually reconciled with the caudillo. The kitchen includes an equally impressive octagonal
stove, while other sections are decorated with French tiles and distinctive wrought iron.

The chapel contains notable religious images, while marble statuary graces the gardens—
though some of it was stolen in 1991. Declared a national monument in 1935, the complex had
one of the country's first modern plumbing systems, bringing water nearly two kilometers from

Uruguay (US$2.50, 1.5 hours); Buenos Aires (US$8, three hours); Paraná (US$9, four hours); and Córdoba (US$20, 11 hours).

COLÓN

Of all the towns along the Río Uruguay, Colón clearly possesses the most charm. Founded in 1863, it lacks Gualeguaychú's (admittedly limited) colonial character, but its small-town intimacy, 19th-century architecture, and tree-lined streets and riverfront all make it an ideal stopover for north- or southbound travelers along RN 14. It is also a major border crossing, linked to the larger Uruguayan city of Paysandú via the Puente Internacional General Artigas, a bridge over the Río Uruguay.

Orientation

On the west bank of the Río Uruguay, Colón (population 19,194) is 104 kilometers north of Gualeguaychú and 330 kilometers north of Buenos Aires. It is 50 kilometers south of Parque Nacional El Palmar and 101 kilometers south of Concordia, the next major border crossing into Uruguay.

Sights and Activities

The parklike waterfront along **Avenida Costanera Gobernador Quirós** is the city's main attraction, while the **Parque Doctor Herminio Quiros**, at its southerly end, is the site of mid-February's Fiesta Nacional de la Artesanía, an annual crafts fair that also showcases live folkloric music.

General Urquiza himself decreed the construction of the 1860s **Aduana de Colón**, a customs house at the corner of Avenida Costanera and Emilio Gouchón, for the export of farm products from nearby Colonia San José. The distinctive building now serves as the municipal tourist office.

the Río Gualeguaychú by a series of pumps and pipes. In fact, Urquiza even built an artificial lake for recreational sailing.

Urquiza, who earned his fame by defeating Rosas at the battle of Caseros in 1852, did not live to enjoy his retirement here. On April 11, 1870, agents of his political rival Ricardo López Jordán assassinated the caudillo in his own bedroom; Urquiza's wife, 25 years younger than he, made the room into a memorial shrine.

The Palacio San José (tel. 03442/432620, palaciosanjose@infovia.com.ar, www.palaciosanjose.com) is 30 kilometers west of Concepción del Uruguay via RP 39. Hours are 8:15 A.M.–12:45 P.M. and 2–7 P.M. weekdays, 9 A.M.–5:45 P.M. weekends and holidays. Admission costs US$1 adults, US$.50 children. There are occasional nighttime tours, for which visitors should consult the excellent website (in Spanish only).

Accommodations and Food

The nearest accommodations are in Concepción del Uruguay, where the three-star **Hotel Carlos 1°** (Eva Perón 115, tel. 03442/426776, contrataciones@hotelcarlos1.com.ar, www.hotelcarlos1.com.ar, US$17/23 s/d) is a bargain. The Palacio San José's own restaurant serves lunch Thursday–Sunday, and dinner Friday and Saturday only, but there are also many options in Concepción.

Getting There and Away

There's no direct public transportation to Palacio San José, but Basavilbaso- and Paraná-bound buses on RP 39 from Concepción del Uruguay pass within a half-hour's walk of the grounds. There are also tours from Concepción, and the cost of a *remise* is not excessive—about US$8 including a two-hour wait at the site.

Mesopotamia & Paraná

Four kilometers northwest of town, the **Molino Forclaz,** Colón's first flour mill, is a national historical monument. Eight kilometers west, the **Museo Histórico Regional Colonia San José** chronicles the history of the province's second major agricultural colony.

For excursions into the gallery forests and onto the sand banks of the Río Uruguay, contact English-speaking **Itaicorá** (San Martín 97, tel. 03447/423360, www.itaicora.com). Itaicorá also visits nearby overland destinations like Liebig, site of a now-abandoned meat-extract plant.

The **Cine Chaplin** (J.J. Paso 122, tel. 03447/423722) shows recent movies.

Accommodations and Food

The local affiliate of Hostelling International, in a recycled century-old residence, is **M Casamate Hostel** (Laprida 128, tel. 03447/422385, casamate@casamate.com.ar, US$4 pp for dorms, US$9 d for private rooms). Another good budget choice is **Hospedaje Bolívar** (Bolívar 577, tel. 03447/422721, US$9 pp).

In a handsome 1880s building exuding real character, the misleadingly named **M Hostería Restaurant del Puerto** (Alejo Peyret 158, tel. 03447/422698, hosteriadelpuerto@ciudad.com.ar, US$14/21 s/d, a/c US$1.75 extra) is most definitely *not* a restaurant (though it does serve breakfast). Built on a slope, its centerpiece is an attractive sunken patio, while the surrounding rooms all have antique furniture and tile floors.

Its brick walls decorated with photographs of Colón's historic downtown, **M El Viejo Almacén** (Urquiza and J.J. Paso, tel. 03447/422216) serves a surprisingly spicy *boga a la cerveza* (river fish in beer sauce) for US$2.50, with most other entrees slightly more expensive. There are also pastas and *parrillada,* plus fine empanadas and salads.

La Cosquilla del Ángel (Peyret 180) serves three-course meals in the US$3.50 range, including starters like paté, and entrees like fish and ravioli, plus homemade bread.

Information and Services

The exceptionally helpful municipal **Secretaría de Turismo y Ambiente Humano** occupies the historic customs headquarters (Costanera and Gouchón, tel. 03447/421996, 421233, turiscolon@ciudad.com.ar, www.colon.gov.ar, 6:30 A.M.–9 P.M. daily). It distributes decent maps and brochures on Colón and vicinity.

Banco Nación has an ATM at 12 de Abril 151. **Correo Argentino** is at Artigas and 12 de Abril; Colón's postal code is 3280. **Telecentro Shopping Colón** is at 12 de Abril 338. **Barnet,** at Lavalle and San Martín, offers fast Internet access.

Getting There and Around

Colón's **Terminal de Ómnibus** (Rocamora and 9 de Julio, tel. 03447/421716) is a stop for numerous long-distance buses on north-south RN 14; northbound buses pass the entrance to Parque Nacional El Palmar.

Copay buses to Paysandú, Uruguay (US$2, one hour) leave daily at 12:45, 1:45, and 6:50 P.M.

M PARQUE NACIONAL EL PALMAR

Midway between the cities of Colón and Concordia, 8,500-hectare Parque Nacional El Palmar offers a backward glimpse of what Entre Ríos and adjacent areas of Uruguay and Brazil looked like before farming, forestry, and cattle altered the ecology of the native *yatay*-palm savannas in the 19th century. Although *Syagrus yatay* remains in substantial numbers here and its reproduction has improved since the national park's establishment in 1966, its population structure is uneven—some individuals are more than 200 years old, but "middle-aged" trees are few.

Ironically, unnatural clusters of older specimens give real character to the park's surviving savannas, but they are not its only attraction. Along with the gallery forests along the Río Uruguay and its tributary creeks, they provide ample habitat for mammals, birds, and other wildlife.

Orientation

El Palmar is an 8,500-hectare unit 360 kilometers north of Buenos Aires and 50 kilometers north of Colón via RN 14; it is 50 kilometers south of

Concordia via the same highway. Except for a small information center at the highway turnoff, however, all services are 11 kilometers to the east.

Flora and Fauna

The park, of course, takes its name from the *yatay,* which grows up to 18 meters in height with a diameter of 40 centimeters. Its most conspicuous mammals are the innocuous, semi-aquatic *carpincho* (capybara, *Hydrochaerus hydrochaeris,* the world's largest rodent, weighing up to 60 kg), and the chinchilla relative vizcacha *Lagostomus maximus,* abundant here until only recently, but now much reduced in numbers. Wild boar (a European introduction responsible for habitat damage), foxes, and raccoons are also common.

The ostrichlike *ñandú* or rhea (*Rhea Americana*) races across the savannas, but the wetlands and gallery forests are also home to cormorants, egrets, herons, storks, caracaras, kingfishers, parakeets, and woodpeckers. The most conspicuous reptiles are the large but harmless nocturnal toads that invade the campground showers and toilets; the highly venomous yarará (*Bothrops alternata*), a pit viper that reaches upward of two meters, deserves respect in its savanna habitat, though bites are rare.

Sights and Activities

Near the Los Loros campground, the beaches along the **Río Uruguay** are the big draw for swimmers and boaters, but hikers and cyclists can enjoy **Paseo Arroyo los Loros,** a better wildlife-watching area northwest of the campground (rental canoes and bicycles are available at the campground store).

Five kilometers southwest of Los Loros, a gravel road leads across the savanna to **Arroyo El Palmar,** a Río Uruguay tributary that's also one of the best areas to see the *yatay* palms that give the park its name. There's also a fine swimming hole here.

Accommodations and Food

The nearest hotels are in the cities of Colón and Concordia. El Palmar's only accommodations are at shady **Camping Los Loros** (tel. 03447/493031), which has showers, a grocery, and a *confitería* for simple meals. Campers pay a one-time fee of US$2 per tent plus US$1.50 pp per day.

Information

At the park entrance, immediately east of RN 14, there's a small information booth where rangers collect an admission charge (US$1 for residents of Entre Ríos, US$2 for residents of other Argentina provinces, and US$4.50 for foreign residents).

Across from the Los Loros campground, the Administración de Parques Nacionales operates a **Centro de Interpretación** (tel. 03447/493053, pnpalmar@ciudad.com.ar, 8 A.M.–7 P.M. daily). In addition to permanent natural history displays, it offers videos on park attractions and ecology.

© WAYNE BERNHARDSON

yatay palm savanna, Parque Nacional El Palmar

Mesopotamia & Paraná

Getting There and Around

RN 14 goes directly past the park entrance, so any north- or southbound bus between Colón and Concordia will drop passengers there, and even long-distance buses may do so. There is, however, no public transport over the 11 kilometers from the park entrance to the visitors center and camping area. Hitching is feasible, as are *remises* from Colón or Concordia.

CONCORDIA

San Antonio de Padua de la Concordia is a substantial city that, like other Mesopotamian towns, draws visitors to its riverside for water sports. Directly opposite the Uruguayan city of Salto, it's the northernmost border crossing in Entre Ríos Province. A bridge over the Salto Grande dam links the two countries.

With more than its share of handsome buildings, Concordia also holds a place in literary history: the French writer and pilot Antoine St. Exupéry (author of the children's classic *The Little Prince*) made a forced landing here.

Orientation

Concordia (population 137,046) is 425 kilometers north of Buenos Aires and 101 kilometers north of Colón via RN 14. Most sights and services are within a few blocks of the central Plaza 25 de Mayo; the Río Uruguay shoreline is about one kilometer southeast.

Sights

Studded with palms and fountains, the recently rehabbed **Plaza 25 de Mayo** is the center of civic life; overlooking the plaza, the landmark **Catedral San Antonio de Padua** (1899) gave the city its full name. Immediately to the north, the fine arts **Museo de Artes Visuales** (Urquiza 636, tel. 0345/421-5402, 7 A.M.–1 P.M. weekdays, 7–9 P.M. Sat., free) maintains a local focus.

Six blocks north, **Plaza Urquiza** is the site of the Parisian-style **Palacio Arruabarrena** (1919); at the corner of Entre Ríos and Ramírez, it houses the **Museo Regional de Concordia** (tel. 0345/421-1883, 8 A.M.–noon and 4–7 P.M. daily except Mon., free), the regional history museum.

Along the city's northeastern riverfront, **Parque Rivadavia** is the site of the ruined **Castillo San Carlos** (1888), a French industrialist's residence that burned to the ground in 1938. Before his forced landing in the early 1930s, St. Exupéry spotted the building from the air, and during his brief stay here he authored his only Argentine-based short story.

Eighteen kilometers north of town, Argentine and Uruguayan authorities collaborated on the massive **Represa Salto Grande,** a 39-meter dam that created a 78,000-hectare reservoir; its bridge also made Concordia an overland border crossing. Salto Grande's **Oficina de Relaciones Públicas** (tel. 0345/421-6200) offers free guided tours of the project daily except Sunday, 8 A.M.–2 P.M.

Accommodations

Concordia's best budget option is **Hotel Betanía** (Remedios Escalada de San Martín 1120, tel. 0345/431-0456, dantecarmassi@hotmail.com, US$7.50/9 s/d). It's about 2.5 kilometers northeast of the plaza near Playa Nebel, but its quiet garden setting and pool compensate for its relative isolation; a/c costs extra, however.

Two other, more-central hotels are slightly more expensive: **Hotel Concordia** (La Rioja 516, tel. 0345/421-6869, hotel@artcon.com.ar, US$9/12 s/d) and **Hotel Florida** (Hipólito Yrigoyen 715, tel. 0345/421-6536, hotelflorida @concordia.com.ar, US$9/12 s/d).

Concordia's top-of-the-line lodging is four-star **Hotel Salto Grande** (Urquiza 575, tel. 0345/421-0034, hotelsg@concordia.com.ar, US$20/22 s/d).

Food

Despite Concordia's proximity to the river, *parrillada* remains the standard at restaurants like **El Rey del Bife** (Pellegrini 590, tel. 0345/421-2644). On the south side of the plaza, **De La Plaza** (1° de Mayo 59, tel. 0345/421-2899) does serve river-fish specialties; figure about US$5 for fixed-price lunches or dinners.

Yantar (Pellegrini 570, tel. 0345/421-0414) is a pasta specialist that also has a takeaway *rotisería.* **El Reloj** (Pellegrini 580, tel. 0345/422-2822) is a pizzeria with good ambience.

One block east and one block south of the plaza, **Helados Italia,** on Urquiza between Bernardo de Irigoyen and Quintana, has Concordia's finest ice cream.

Information and Services

The municipal **Secretaría de Turismo** (Urquiza 636, tel. 0345/421-2137 or 421-3905, turismo@concordia.gov.ar, www.concordia.gov.ar) is open 7 A.M.–9 P.M. weekdays, 8 A.M.–8 P.M. weekends.

For motorists, **ACA** is at Pellegrini and Corrientes, tel. 0345/421-6544.

Several banks on and around Plaza 25 de Mayo have **ATMs.**

Correo Argentino is on Hipólito Yrigoyen between 1 de Mayo and Buenos Aires; the postal code is 3200. **Telecentro Colón,** (Pellegrini 611 on the east side of Plaza 25 de Mayo) also has long-distance and Internet access. The **Veleta Café** (1° de Mayo 119) is a more appealing Internet outlet. Try **La Mulatona** (Estrada 43, tel. 0345/421-1517) for laundry service.

Uruguay has a consulate at Pellegrini 709, 1° C, tel. 0345/421-0380.

For medical care, try **Hospital Felipe Heras** (Entre Ríos 135, tel. 0345/421-2580).

Getting There and Around

Concordia relies on bus services, but there are also launches across the river to Salto.

Concordia's **Terminal de Ómnibus** is at Blvd San Lorenzo and Hipólito Yrigoyen, 13 blocks north of Plaza 25 de Mayo (tel. 0345/421-7235). Domestic services resemble those to and from other littoral cities, such as Gualeguaychú and Colón. Service to Buenos Aires (six hours) starts about US$10, but costs up to twice as much with fully reclining seats.

International services to Salto (US$3, one hour) operate daily except Sunday. There are four crossings daily between 11:30 A.M. and 6:30 P.M. with **Chadre** (tel. 0345/421-4157) and **Flecha Bus** (tel. 0345/421-4182).

Boats to Salto (US$1.50 one-way, US$2 round-trip) leave from the port at the east end of Carriego at 9:05 A.M., noon, and 2:30 and 6 P.M. daily except Sunday. Return services

from Salto are at 8:45 A.M. and at 12:15, 3 and 6:30 P.M.

PARANÁ

Capital of Entre Ríos Province, across the Río Paraná from Santa Fe, is one of the best access points to the islands and gallery forests of the upper Paraná Delta, including the rarely visited Parque Nacional Pre-Delta to the south. It is in many ways a more livable city that its sweltering neighbor, thanks to shady streets, lush riverside parks and better river access. In the city center, municipal authorities have even widened sidewalks to create "slow streets" in a country where motorists usually consider that might makes right.

Paraná was briefly Argentina's capital, after Entre Ríos native son General Urquiza defeated the Buenos Aires dictator Rosas, but it wasn't even the provincial capital until the late 1880s, when it replaced the previous capital, Concepción del Uruguay. It's maintained a high political profile, even hosting a 1994 convention that revised Argentina's constitution to lift presidential term limits—specifically benefiting the now-disgraced Carlos Menem—and also saw one of the first provincial visits of newly elected President Néstor Kirchner, to settle a teachers' strike in May of 2003.

Orientation

Paraná (population 235,931) is 470 kilometers northwest of Buenos Aires via the Entre Ríos highways of RN 12 and RP 11 through Gualeguay, Victoria, and Diamante; the distance is 500 kilometers via RN 9 to Rosario and A-008 to Santa Fe, which are better and faster highways.

Unlike the low-lying cities along the Río Uruguay, most of Paraná occupies a hilly site above the Río Paraná; constructions are fewer on the floodplain, where Parque Urquiza stretches over a kilometer of mostly open space along the riverfront.

Plaza 1° de Mayo is the center of Paraná's slightly irregular grid; except for the north-south San Martín pedestrian mall and east-west

Avenida Urquiza, street names change on all sides of the plaza.

Sights

Paraná lacks colonial monuments but has no shortage of handsome 19th-century buildings in the vicinity of Plaza 1° de Mayo. On the east side of the plaza, dating from 1885, the neoclassical **Iglesia Catedral** (cathedral) is a national historical monument distinguished by its columnar facade, twin bell towers and a gracefully arched central dome, which reaches a height of 50 meters above street level. Its **Museo Arquidiocesano** (Monte Caseros 51) is open 10 A.M.–noon and 5:30–7 P.M. weekdays, 10 A.M.–noon Saturday, and immediately after weekend Masses.

Adjacent to the cathedral but fronting on Avenida Urquiza, the **Colegio del Huerto** (1858) served as the Argentine Senate when Paraná was briefly capital of the confederation. At the plaza's northeast corner, the **Palacio Municipal** (city hall) dates from 1889; immediately across the street, Domingo F. Sarmiento founded the **Escuela Normal Paraná** (Paraná Normal School, 1926), but the building itself is a later construction on a site once occupied by the confederation's Casa de Gobierno (presidential palace) and Cámara de Diputados (lower house).

Two blocks west of the plaza, the **Museo y Mercado Provincial de Artesanías** (Avenida Urquiza 1239, tel. 0343/422-4540, 8 A.M.–1 P.M. and 4–7 P.M. weekdays and Sat., 9 A.M.–noon Sun.) is a hybrid institution displaying classic crafts from around the province—wood carvings, ceramics, leather goods, and metal work—and selling comparable pieces. One block north of the plaza, dating from 1908, the **Teatro Municipal 3 de Febrero** (25 de Junio 60) is Paraná's prime performing arts venue, distinguished by its horseshoe-shaped auditorium and ceiling frescos.

The San Martín pedestrian mall, a favorite spot for Saturday-morning outings, ends two blocks north at **Plaza Alvear,** the site of three key museums. The **Museo Histórico de Entre Ríos Martín Leguizamón** (provincial history museum, Buenos Aires 286, tel. 0343/420-7869) highlights—and sometimes borders on exaggeration of—Entre Ríos's critical role in mid-19th century Argentine political history. Hours are

Plaza 1° de Mayo and Iglesia Catedral

7:30 A.M.–12:30 P.M. and 3 to 7:30 P.M. weekdays, 9 A.M.–noon weekends and 4–7 P.M. Saturday only. There's a small admission charge.

On the west side of Plaza Alvear, the **Museo de Bellas Artes Pedro E. Martínez** (Buenos Aires 355, tel. 0343/420-7868) showcases provincial painters, sculptors, and illustrators. Hours are 9 A.M.–noon and 4–9 P.M. weekdays except Monday, 10:30 A.M.–12:30 P.M. weekends, and 5:30–8 P.M. Saturday only.

On the north side of the plaza, the recently relocated **Museo de Ciencias Naturales y Antropológicas Doctor Antonio Serrano** (Carlos Gardel 62, tel. 0343/420-8891) specializes in natural history and archaeology. Hours are 7:30 A.M.–12:30 P.M. and 2–7 P.M. weekdays except Monday, 8:30 A.M.–12:30 P.M. and 3–7 P.M. Saturday, and 9 A.M.–noon Sunday.

One block west of Plaza Alvear, Swiss architect Bernardo Rigoli designed the **Casa de Gobierno** (1887), which became the site of the executive, legislative, and judicial branches when the provincial government relocated from Concepción del Uruguay; the courts have since moved to a newer building immediately south. Four blocks north, but also accessible via the diagonal Avenida Rivadavia, **Parque Urquiza** is the city's signature open space, along the Paraná riverfront. The park houses the **Museo de la Ciudad** (tel. 0343/420-1838), detailing Paraná's urban development; hours are 8 A.M.–noon and 3–7 P.M. weekdays except Monday, 10 A.M.–noon and 3–7 P.M. Saturday, and 3–7 P.M. Sunday.

At the Santa Fe approach to town, the **Túnel Subfluvial Uranga Silvestre Begnis** (1969) is a civil engineering monument, a nearly three-kilometer tunnel beneath the Paraná that's the only one of its kind in the country. It's also a political monument, representing cooperation with neighboring Santa Fe at a time when the federal government (exercising a constitutional prerogative) refused to permit the two provinces to build a bridge. Free guided tours (tel. 0343/420-0400) take place 8 A.M.–6 P.M. daily. Passenger vehicles pay a US$1 toll.

Entertainment and Events

The municipal **Teatro 3 de Febrero** (25 de Junio 60, tel. 0343/420-1657) has offerings ranging from live theater and film to art exhibits. For current commercial movies, try the **Cine Rex** (Monte Caseros 266, tel. 0343/423-6004).

The sight of teenagers in little-league uniforms may seem incongruous in soccer-mad Argentina, but for several decades the diamond at Paraná's **Estadio Ingeniero Nafaldo Cargnel,** near the entrance to the Santa Fe tunnel, has hosted slow-pitch and fast-pitch softball tournaments, including the 1995 Panamerican Games. Adult leagues also play here and at the city's other seven fields.

Mid-January's **Fiesta Provincial de Música y Artesanía Entrerriana** invites folk musicians from throughout the region. February's **Maratón Internacional Hernandárias-Paraná** is an 88-kilometer swim drawing competitors from around the world.

Paraná's pre-Lenten **Carnaval del Río,** which takes place along the river, is gaining momentum in a region increasingly known for such celebrations.

Sports and Recreation

Fishing for river species like *boga, sábalo, dorado,* and *surubí* requires a license from the **Dirección de Flora y Fauna** (Avenida Larramendi 3108, tel. 0343/423-0846).

Sponsored by the **Paraná Rowing Club,** hour-long river excursions (US$3.50) leave from the Puerto Nuevo at Costanera and Vélez Sarsfield, tel. 0343/430-6518, at 4:30 and 5:30 P.M. Friday, Saturday, and Sunday.

Accommodations

Seven blocks south of the plaza, **N Hotel City** (Blvd. Racedo 231, tel. 0343/431-0086, info @hotelcityparana.com.ar, www.hotelcityparana .com.ar) merits raves for everything except its slightly inconvenient (though quiet) location across from the old train station. Rates are US$8/12 s/d for expansive rooms with ceiling fans, a/c, and cable TV in a verdant patio setting.

Close to the bus terminal, **Hotel Bristol** (Alsina 221, tel. 0343/431-3961, US$9/13 s/d) is also a good choice.

On the *peatonal*, **Alvear Hotel & Hostel** (San Martín 637, tel. 0343/422-0000, paranacity@yahoo.com, US$9/13 s/d) is now an excellent value at reduced prices. Rates include parking, a/c, and breakfast. The best new choice in town is the charming ⋈ **Hotel San Jorge** (Belgrano 368, tel./fax 0343/422-1685, US$13/20 s/d), a handsome early-20th-century building with a luxuriant patio, stylishly modernized rooms with a/c, and cable TV.

The facade of the **Paraná Hotel** (9 de Julio 60, tel./fax 0343/423-1700, infoph@hotelesparana.com.ar, www.hotelesparana.com.ar) is deceiving, as its interior is more modern and most of its rooms rather smaller—compact, one might generously say—than its exterior would suggest. Several original rooms, surrounding the interior patio, are used only when the hotel is full, as most foot traffic passes through this area. Rates are US$14/21 s/d after bargaining.

Facing Plaza 1° de Mayo, **Gran Hotel Paraná** (Urquiza 976, tel. 0343/422-3900, reservasgranhotel@hotelesparana.com.ar, www.hotelesparana.com.ar) is a mixed bag—rooms on the lower floors, which generally go to tour groups, are utilitarian for US$18/25 s/d, but those on the upper floors live up to its four-star billing for US$29/38 s/d.

Rising high above the river, in the midst of Parque Urquiza, five-star **Hotel Mayorazgo** (Etchevehere and Miranda, tel. 0343/423-0333, www.mayorazgohotel.com) charges US$30/40 s/d with a buffet breakfast. It is also Paraná's casino.

Food

For fresh produce, go to the historic **Nuevo Mercado La Paz** (Pellegrini and Bavio).

Giovani (Avenida Urquiza 1045, tel. 0343/423-0527) is a reliable *parrilla*. The well-established **Luisito** (9 de Julio 140, tel. 0343/431-6912) also deserves consideration.

Overlooking Parque Urquiza, ⋈ **La Urquiza** (Corrientes s/n, tel. 0343/423-5741) is a stylish new *parrilla* that attempts to re-create the atmosphere of mid-19th-century Paraná.

The Gran Hotel Paraná's **La Fourchette** (Urquiza 976, tel. 0343/422-3900) serves good river fish like *pacú and surubí*, but it's expensive by local standards, including high markups on the wine list.

Bahillo (San Martín 724) is one of several excellent ice creameries.

Information

The **Dirección Municipal de Turismo** (Buenos Aires 132, tel. 0343/420-1661, www.turismoenparana.com) is open 8 A.M.–9 P.M. daily. Its riverfront **Oficina Parque** (Avenida Laurencena and Juan de San Martín, tel. 0343/420-1837) keeps similar hours; there is also an **Oficina del Túnel** at the mouth of the tunnel from Santa Fe (tel. 0343/420-1803) and another at the bus terminal (tel. 0343/422-1282).

The **Dirección Provincial de Turismo** (Laprida 5, tel. 0343/420-7989, turismoer@infovia.com.ar) is open 7 A.M.–1 P.M. weekdays only, but has very helpful personnel.

For motorists, **ACA** is at Buenos Aires 333, tel. 0343/431-1319.

Services

Paraná has no exchange houses but numerous ATMs, such as the one at **Banco Francés** (San Martín 763), in the vicinity of Plaza 1° de Mayo.

Correo Argentino is at 25 de Mayo and Monte Caseros; the postal code is 3100. There's a **Telecentro** on San Martín between Uruguay and Pazos that has both long-distance and Internet access.

For medical services, **Hospital San Martín** is at Presidente Perón 450, near Gualeguaychú (tel. 0343/423-4545).

Lavadero Belgrano (Belgrano 306, tel. 0343/431-1556) does the laundry.

Getting There and Around

Represented by **Vikingo Turismo** (Corrientes 563, tel. 0343/423-2425), Aerovip flies 19-seat air taxis from Paraná's small airport to Aeroparque (Buenos Aires). There are more commercial services from neighboring Santa Fe.

Paraná's **Terminal de Ómnibus** (Avenida Ramírez 2300, tel. 0343/422-1282) is opposite

Plaza Martín Fierro, about 10 blocks southeast of Plaza 1° de Mayo. There are frequent buses to Santa Fe (US$1.50, 45 minutes).

Long-distance destinations, fares, and times resemble those from Santa Fe, but there are often more departures from Santa Fe. Among the possibilities here are Rosario (US$6, 2.5 hours), Córdoba (US$12, six hours), Corrientes (US$14, eight hours), Resistencia (US$13, 7.5 hours), Buenos Aires (US$12–16, six hours), Posadas (US$20, 10 hours), Mendoza (US$21, 13 hours), and Puerto Iguazú (US$24, 13 hours). There is also service to Montevideo, Uruguay (US$21, 9.5 hours).

PARQUE NACIONAL PRE-DELTA

Toward the northern end of the Paraná Delta, this little-visited national park protects 2,458 hectares of wetlands and gallery forest just south of the city of Diamante, less than an hour south of the provincial capital. Dating from 1992, it features forested natural levees that become islands when the river rises, and interior depressions that support wildlife-rich marshes and lagoons. It offers a pair of short nature trails, but visitors will see more by hiring a launch to explore its islands and watercourses.

Flora and Fauna

Parque Nacional Pre-Delta's most conspicuous flora are gallery forests of large trees like willows and alders, where the *espinero rojizo* (*Phacellodomus ruffifrons,* common thornbird) builds conspicuous hanging nests of sticks.

Twisted ceibos and the cedarlike *timbó* grow on islands, while mammals like the capybara make their way among floating islands of water hyacinths with violet flowers. Reeds cover lower-lying areas, where there are also nutria and river otters, as well as *yacaré* (caiman). Other birds include ducks, swans, egrets, and the kingfisher (which is the park's symbol).

Practicalities

The ranger station at Paraje La Jaula, at the end of the road from Diamante, has a small **campground,** free of charge, with firepits for barbecues. There's a small **shop** at Paraje La Azotea, immediately before the park entrance, but it's better to bring supplies from Diamante or Paraná.

There is a **ranger station** right at Paraje La Jaula, where the road from Diamante dead-ends; there's a **public telephone** and a small shop at Paraje La Azotea. The park itself has a **Diamante** office (Hipólito Yrigoyen 396, tel. 0343/498-1128 or 0343/498-1496, pnpredelta@infovia.com.ar). Park admission is free.

Parque Nacional Pre-Delta is only six kilometers south of Diamante, where it's easy to hire a *remise* to the park entrance at Paraje La Jaula. There, it's also possible to hire **launches** (tel. 0343/498-1132) to explore the park's intricate waterways.

Mesopotamia & Paraná

Corrientes Province

For travelers continuing up the Río Uruguay littoral through Corrientes Province, there are relatively minor points of interest en route to Misiones Province and its world-famous Iguazú Falls. The capital city of Corrientes, in the northwest corner of the province, has its strong points, including one of the country's best Carnaval celebrations.

What should be Corrientes's biggest attraction is Esteros del Iberá, a wildlife-rich wetland equal (if not superior) to Brazil's better-known Pantanal and even Amazonia—but it remains almost unknown because of its relative isolation and the fact that both provincial and national authorities seem clueless as to its environmental wealth and traveler appeal. Still, anyone pressed for time but eager for a unique experience should consider writing off heavily touristed Iguazú to see Iberá, which is worth a trip to the province—or even to Argentina—in its own right. It is accessible from the western provincial city of Mercedes or, with more difficulty, from the Misiones provincial capital of Posadas.

THE UPPER RÍO URUGUAY

For most foreign travelers, southeastern Corrientes, along the Río Uruguay, is primarily a transit route, with several border crossings into Brazil. For Argentines, though, the village of Yapeyú is a sentimental favorite as the birthplace of José de San Martín, the country's most prominent—and romanticized—national hero.

Paso de los Libres

For most of the year, grubby Paso de los Libres, the first major town along RN 14 for northbound travelers in Corrientes Province, is most significant as a border crossing to the Brazilian city of Uruguaiana, in the state of Rio Grande do Sul. It is also, however, home to a lively summer Carnaval celebration, thanks in part to the Brazilian influence, and its **Cementerio de la Santa Cruz** is the burial place

of the famous French naturalist Aimé Bonpland, who accompanied Alexander von Humboldt on Humboldt's epic 19th-century South American expedition.

Paso de los Libres (population 40,279) is 245 kilometers north of Concordia, 767 kilometers north of Buenos Aires, and 370 kilometers south of Posadas (Misiones) via RN 14. It has key services like exchange houses and a Brazilian consulate (Mitre 892, tel. 03772/425444).

The best budget choice for accommodation is **Hotel Iberá** (Coronel López 1091, tel. 03772/421848, US$7/10.50 s/d); rates include breakfast and a/c. More comfortable is the high-rise **Hotel Alejandro Primo** (Coronel López 502, tel. 03772/424100, US$16/21 s/d).

Paso de los Libres's muddy **Terminal de Ómnibus** is at Avenida San Martín and Santiago del Estero (tel. 03772/425600). There are provincial and long-distance services northbound and southbound on RN 14, and also regular connections to the provincial capital. For connections to Brazilian destinations, cross the border to Uruguaiana.

Yapeyú

To Argentines of all political persuasions, the sleepy village of Yapeyú occupies a special status as the birthplace of José de San Martín (1778–1850), the country's greatest independence hero. Many, indeed, feel a patriotic obligation to visit the remains of his humble house, virtually preserved under glass, though there is little else to see in the area.

Barely a decade earlier, before the Spanish king Carlos III expelled the Jesuits from the Americas in 1767, Yapeyú had been the southernmost of the Jesuit missions in the upper Paraná-Uruguay drainage. After the Jesuits' expulsion, San Martín's father administered what remained of the mission (founded in 1627), which once housed 8,000 Guaraní neophytes with up to 80,000 cattle in the vicinity.

Only the red sandstone foundations remain of the original Jesuit church and school, which burned to the ground in 1800; in 1817, Brazilian troops sacked the town. There is, however, a small but worthwhile Jesuit museum *in situ*.

Yapeyú is 55 kilometers north of Paso de los Libres, 690 kilometers north of Buenos Aires, and 395 kilometers southeast of the provincial capital. It is six kilometers southeast of RN 14 via the Avenida del Libertador turnoff. All sights and services are within easy walking distance of Plaza San Martín, which occupies the high ground above the Río Uruguay, two blocks east of the avenue.

At the east end of Plaza San Martín, its interior adorned with tributary plaques, the **Templete Sanmartiniano** protecting the excavated remains of San Martín's birthplace is a textbook example of chauvinistic hero worship. Interestingly, however, the controversial plaque on which Proceso dictator General Jorge Rafael Videla professed his "most profound faith" in San Martín's ideals of liberty no longer disgraces the Liberator's memory. The official explanation is that all other such plaques are from institutions rather than individuals, but Videla's nonperson status (he remains under house arrest in Buenos Aires for kidnapping of children during the "Dirty War" of 1976–83) is evident.

Two blocks west, at the corner of Sargento Cabral and Obispo Romero, several small contemporary pavilions sit atop Jesuit foundations at the **Museo de Cultura Jesuítica Guillermo Furlong.** Each pavilion has a good photographic display of the missions and their history, while a handful of mission artifacts (most notably a sundial) surround them.

At the south end of Avenida del Libertador, at the army Granaderos regimental headquarters, the **Museo Sanmartiniano** intensifies the hero worship with San Martín family artifacts and documents.

Yapeyú has its charms, but accommodations and food are few and ordinary. The flood-prone **Camping Municipal** (tel. 03772/493013, US$2 per site) has basic installations. On the central Plaza San Martín, **Hotel San Martín** (Sargento Cabral 712, tel. 03772/493120, US$7 pp) has large rooms surrounding a barren courtyard, but some of them lack exterior windows. Rooms

have decent beds and private bath (electric shower), but no breakfast is available.

More visually appealing than the San Martín, **El Parador de Yapeyú** (José de San Martín s/n, tel. 03372/493056, US$9 pp) has motel-style bungalows on sprawling grounds; each free-standing unit has two bedrooms, one with a double bed and the other with four singles, but the rooms themselves are dark and the beds are soft.

There are only two places to eat, both utilitarian with limited menus: Hotel San Martín has its own basic restaurant, **Comedor El Paraíso** (Gregoria Matorras s/n, tel. 03772/493053) is around the corner.

Yapeyú's tiny **bus station,** three blocks northwest of the plaza at Avenida del Libertador and Chacabuco, has services to Buenos Aires, Paso de los Libres, and Posadas.

Santo Tomé

Santo Tomé, another former Jesuit mission, is a much larger city (population 20,063), but its ruins are even less well-preserved than Yapeyú. Here, 140 kilometers north of Yapeyú via RN 14, a bridge over the Río Uruguay leads to the Brazilian city of **São Borja,** which also has nearby Jesuit ruins. There is a Brazilian consulate at Bertrán 842, tel. 03756/420305.

The best place to stay is the **Hotel de Turismo ACA** (Bertrán and Belgrano, tel./fax 03756/420161, US$12/15 s/d with breakfast), which may be aging from ACA's glory days, but is clean and comfortable, with a confitería/restaurant, a large pool, and tennis courts.

Santo Tomé's **Terminal de Ómnibus** is at Avenida Uruguay and Avenida San Martín. There is regular bus service north to Posadas, south to Buenos Aires, and to intermediate points.

MERCEDES

For most foreign visitors, sleepy Mercedes is most significant as the principal gateway to the world-class wetlands of the Esteros del Iberá, an ecological treasure that occupies much of the geographical center of the province.

Because of bus schedules, travelers without their own vehicles almost always have to spend a night in Mercedes. It's worth a stay, though, to appreciate one of Argentina's most popular pilgrimage sites, the spontaneously colorful shrine to the Gaucho Antonio Gil, a 19th-century Robin Hood unjustly executed by provincial authorities, nine kilometers west of town.

Mercedes (population 30,922) is 119 kilometers northwest of Paso de los Libres via RN 123; it is 265 kilometers north of Concordia and 710 kilometers from Buenos Aires via RN 14 and RN 119. Gravel RP 40 leads 120 kilometers northeast to Colonial Pellegrini, the most convenient access point to the Iberá marshes.

Accommodations and Food

Run by a young Bosnian immigrant, **Hospedaje Delicias del Iberá** (Pujol 1556, tel. 03773/ 422508, US$3 pp) is a hostel-style place that's become a backpacker's fixture on the route from Salta across the Chaco to Iberá. It's good value even if maintenance is short of perfect, but its real strength is the outstanding food.

Hotel El Sol (San Martín 519, tel. 03773/ 420283, US$7/11 s/d) has drawn raves for impeccable rooms in an attractive 19th-century building with family-run atmosphere. **Hotel Victoria** (José María Gómez 734, tel. 03773/ 420330, US$9/16 s/d) is also good.

Food here is nothing special, but **La Casa de Chirola,** on Plaza 25 de Mayo at the corner of Pujol and Sarmiento, is a decent *parrilla*. **Delicias del Iberá** (Pujol 1160) is also worth a look.

Other Practicalities

Correo Argentino is at the corner of Rivadavia and Martínez; the postal code is 3470. **Banco de la Nación** has an ATM at Rivadavia 602, and **Banco de Corrientes** has one at San Martín 1099.

Mercedes's **Terminal Hipólito Yrigoyen** is at San Martín and Alfredo Perreyra. Numerous **buses** pass through town en route to the provincial capital of Corrientes (US$5, 3.5 hours) and to Buenos Aires (US$15, nine hours).

Daily except Sunday, **Combi El Rayo** (Pujol 1166, tel. 03773/420184, 15-629598) has minibus service to Colonia Pellegrini (three hours, US$4), in the Esteros del Iberá. Departures are around 11:30 A.M.–noon. **Remis Romero** (tel. 03773/15-627474) provides transfers to Pellegrini in a 4WD vehicle.

THE ROBIN HOOD OF CORRIENTES

Gateway to the Esteros del Iberá, sleepy Mercedes is also the home base of Argentina's fastest-spreading religious cult, the sprawling shrine to the Gaucho Antonio Gil. Second only to San Juan's Difunta Correa as a popular religious phenomenon, the Gauchito (his faithful use the affectionate diminutive) is rapidly gaining adherents (unlike the improbable Difunta, though, Gil really existed).

In the 1850s, as the story goes, Gil was an army deserter who spent years on the run as he took from the rich and gave to the poor. When he was finally apprehended, the police hanged him from an *espinillo* tree; before dying, Gil warned that the sergeant in command would find his own son gravely ill, and the boy would recover only if the sergeant prayed for Gil's soul.

When the boy recovered, the repentant sergeant carved a cross of *espinillo* and placed it at the site of Gil's death. Now every January 8—the anniversary of his death—up to 100,000 pilgrims swarm to a site of chapels, *comedores,* and campgrounds decorated with dozens upon dozens of bright-red flags. Many bring prized possessions to the Gauchito, whom they credit with miracles and life-changing experiences, while they take away souvenirs from a swarm of stands that make a major contribution to the local economy.

Over the past several years, the red flags that mark the Mercedes shrine have spread rapidly to roadside sites from Jujuy to Ushuaia. Just possibly, the perceived injustices of Argentina's economic meltdown require another Robin Hood.

ᴍ ESTEROS DEL IBERÁ

Argentina's biggest unsung attraction, Esteros del Iberá is a breathtaking wetland covering up to 13,000 square kilometers (estimates vary), nearly 15 percent of Corrientes Province. Recharged almost exclusively by rainwater, it's really a broad, shallow river, covered by semisubmerged marsh grasses, reeds, and other water-loving plants; it flows diagonally but almost imperceptibly from the northeast toward the southwest, where the Río Corrientes enters the middle Paraná. There are also, however, open-water stretches like Laguna Iberá, a 24,550-hectare lagoon that's protected under the Ramsar convention on wetlands of international importance.

In terms of wildlife, Iberá is an American Serengeti—while it may lack the total biomass of Africa's famous plain, the variety of species and the sheer numbers of birds, mammals and reptiles is still awesome. For these reasons, it has attracted the attention of international conservationists such as former Esprit clothing magnate Douglas Tompkins, who has purchased several *estancias* in the area in the hopes of preserving their natural wealth.

And Iberá needs defenders, as the marshes have a fragile ecology imperiled by mega-hydro-electric developments of the Yacyretá dam, north of the city of Ituzaingó. As runoff from Yacyretá's rising reservoir seeps into Iberá, deepening waters threaten to break the link between the marsh vegetation and the dissolved sediments from which the plants derive their nutrients.

Orientation

Esteros del Iberá stretches over an enormous area, but the most convenient access point is **Colonia Pellegrini,** a placid hamlet of wide dirt roads on a peninsula jutting into Laguna Iberá, 107 kilometers northeast of Mercedes via RP 40. While Pellegrini has no formal street addresses, it's small and compact enough that orientation is no problem.

Passable under most conditions though sections of it are bumpy, RP 40 can be muddy and difficult for conventional vehicles in very wet weather. It requires caution and moderate speeds at all times.

Flora and Fauna

Iberá's flora and fauna make it a wonderland of biodiversity. Scattered open-water lagoons lie within an endless horizon of marshland grasses, aquatic plants, and *embalsados* ("floating islands"), which some ecologists have compared to tropical peat bogs. Even relatively large trees like the *seibo* (*Erythrina cristagalli*) and laurel (*Nectandra falcifolia*) flourish here and in gallery forests along faster-flowing waters.

Biologists have catalogued over 40 species of mammals, 35 species of amphibians, 80 species of fish, and 250–300 species of birds. The most readily seen mammals are the *carpincho* (capybara, *Hydrochaerus hydrochaeris*), marsh deer (*Blastoceros dichotomus*), and pampas deer (*Ozotocerus bezoarticus;* the *mono carayá* (*Alouatta caraya,* howler monkey) is more easily heard than seen. Less easily seen are the *lobito de río* (Paraná otter, *Lontra longicaudis*) and the largely nocturnal *aguará guazú* (maned wolf, *Chrysocyon brachyurus*).

Among the reptiles, there are two species of caimans, the *yacaré overo* (*Caiman latirostris*) and the *yacaré negro* (*Caiman yacare*). Australians, take note: these skinny, meter-plus creatures are

carpincho (capybara), Esteros del Iberá

not the massive crocodiles of Queensland and the Northern Territory, and will not pounce out of the swamps in search of human nourishment. The endangered water *curiyú* (water boa, *Eunectes notaeus*) is also present.

Birds are far too numerous to mention more than a sample, but the signature species include the *chajá* (horned screamer, *Chauna torquata*), *mbiguá común* (olive cormorant, *Phalacrocorax olivaceus*), several species of storks, herons, and egrets, and many waterfowl, including the endangered *pato crestudo* (comb duck, *Sarkidiornis melanotos*).

Sights and Activities

Iberá is a year-round destination, but the summer months can be brutally hot and humid, and rain can fall at any time of year. Activities include bird-watching and other wildlife watching, hiking on a gallery-forest nature trail, and horseback riding.

Launch tours on Laguna Iberá, which involve poling through floating islands where an outboard motor is useless, are available through all the hotels, and private guides as well. One-hour excursions, on which it's possible to see a lot, begin in the US$15 range for one person, US$7–8 for each additional person. As some animals are nocturnal, nighttime tours are also available, especially under the full moon.

Rental canoes and kayaks are available on Laguna Iberá, but kayaks in particular are unsuitable for exploring the marshes, whose dense vegetation makes visibility poor—there are few landmarks in this nearly featureless terrain and, in any event, you can't stand up in a kayak to get your bearings.

Accommodations and Food

Colonia Pellegrini may be small, but it offers a diversity of quality accommodations and food for all budgets.

The waterside **Camping Municipal** has only basic facilities for less than US$1 pp. For shoestring backpackers, there's a small but growing number of *hospedajes* such as **Posada San Cayetano,** for about US$3 pp for tidy but basic multibedded rooms, with shared bath (electric showers only).

Pellegrini's best value, though, is **Ⅶ Posada Rancho Ypa Sapukai** (tel. 03773/420155, cell 03773/15-629536, info@ypasapukai.com.ar, www.ypasapukai.com.ar, US$12 pp, US$24 pp with full board), where you'll find elegantly simple rooms with private bath, breakfast, and ceiling fans. Set on beautifully maintained grounds on the shores of the lagoon, the *posada* has equally attractive common areas—good enough for just relaxing if bad weather delays excursions. It also has above-average food, though owner Pedro Noailles may dispense with the full-board option if a quality restaurant opens in town.

On a densely wooded property, **Ⅶ Hostería Ñandé Retá** (tel. 03773/499411 or 03773/15629109, tel./fax 03773/420155 in Mercedes, nandereta@nandereta.com, www.nandereta.com) has the atmosphere of a jungle lodge despite its midst-of-the-village location. Run by relatives of the Ypa Sapukai operators, it's also an exceptional value for US$71/107 s/d with full board and excursions included.

Ⅶ Posada de la Laguna (tel. 03773/499413, cell 03773/15-629827, fax 011/4737-7274, posadadelalaguna@ibera.net, www.iberalaguna .8k.com) has six spacious rooms with high ceilings and comfortably stylish furnishings set on sprawling gardens along the lagoon; it also features a swimming pool and a separate bar/restaurant. It's top-of-the-line by local standards, and prices of US$48/80 s/d with full board are by no means excessive. The owner is Elsa Güiraldes, a niece of Ricardo Güiraldes, author of the classic *gauchesco* novel *Don Segundo Sombra.*

The largest of Pellegrini's accommodations is the colonial-style **Ⅶ Posada Aguapé** (tel./fax 03773/499412, aguape@interserver.com.ar, www .iberaesteros.com.ar), which sprawls along the banks of the lagoon in two wings with overhanging galleries for protection from both sun and rain, and a large pool as well. Decorated with high-quality but rustically styled furniture, the 12 suites themselves are substantial and appealing; there is also a bar and a dining room. Rates range from US$48/72 s/d with breakfast only to US$95/160 with full board and several excursions (children under 10 pay half, children under three are free). Its Buenos Aires contact is

María Paz Galmarini (Coronel Obarrio 1038, 1642 San Isidro, Provincia de Buenos Aires, tel./fax 011/4742-3015).

Except for hotel dining rooms, Colonia Pellegrini lacks restaurants, though one may be in the works; if you want to eat where you're not staying, make arrangements in advance, as drop-in customers are uncommon here. Limited groceries are available in Pellegrini, but most locals stock up on shopping trips to Mercedes.

Other Practicalities

At the approach to Colonia Pellegrini, immediately before the military Bayley bridge that crosses Laguna Iberá, former poachers staff the provincial **Centro de Intepretación,** the reserve's visitors center. Hotel staff and guides are also excellent sources of information.

Daily except Sunday, **El Rayo** (tel. 03773/420184) has minibus services from Colonia Pellegrini back to Mercedes (three hours, US$4). The departures are around 3–4 A.M., permitting locals to make shopping trips and return in the same day, but not so great for travelers who want a full night's sleep. They will, however, pick you up at your accommodations in Pellegrini.

From the airport at Posadas, it's possible to arrange direct transfers for up to four persons in a 4WD vehicle for about US$85 with **Guayra Turismo** (tel. 03752/433415, cell 03752/15-690456), **Paul Velázquez** (tel. 03752/457688, 03752/15-684276), or **Honorio Moreno** (tel. 03786/420477).

CORRIENTES

Capital of its namesake province, settled by Spaniards from Asunción in the late 16th century, the city of Vera de las Siete Corrientes took its name from founder Juan Torres de Vera y Aragón and the irregular currents of the Paraná, just below its confluence with the Río Paraguay. Its appeal lies in its colonial core and its riverside location—the views across the Paraná toward the seemingly endless Chaco are soothing, especially at sunset.

Indigenous resistance made the city precarious in its early years. Graham Greene set his semi-satirical novel *The Honorary Consul* in the city's *villas miserias,* its peripheral slums.

Orientation

Corrientes (population 316,486) is 927 kilometers north of Buenos Aires via RN 12 and RN 14. It is 324 kilometers west of Posadas via RN 12, and only 19 kilometers east of Resistencia, the capital of Chaco Province across the Paraná.

Most points of interest fall within a roughly triangular area formed by the riverfront Avenida Costanera General San Martín, north-south Avenida España, and east-west Avenida 3 de Abril. The latter leads west to Puente General Manuel Belgrano, the bridge to Resistencia, and east toward Ituzaingó and Posadas.

Corrientes is a city of plazas; the center of its colonial grid is Plaza 25 de Mayo, but Plaza La Cruz and Plaza J. B. Cabral are also important public spaces. The main commercial street, east-west Calle Junín, is a pedestrian mall between Salta and San Lorenzo.

Sights

Corrientes's compact colonial core makes it a good walker's city, at least in the cool early morning hours or in winter. In practice, the best walk is an evening stroll along the riverfront **Avenida Costanera General San Martín,** which enjoys spectacular sunsets across the glassy surface of the slow-flowing Paraná. On the Costanera at the west end of Junín, the **Jardín Zoológico** (Avenida Costanera 99, tel. 03783/427626, 8 A.M.–1 P.M. and 4–8 P.M. daily) focuses on regional fauna, such as caimans, wild cats like Geoffrey's and the puma, and birds like the toucan; there is also a serpentarium.

One block south of the Costanera, bounded by Quintana, Buenos Aires, Salta, and 25 de Mayo, Corrientes's civic center is **Plaza 25 de Mayo;** it's home to the **Casa de Gobierno** (governor's palace), the legislature, and the **Iglesia de la Merced,** a landmark 19th-century church.

Where the Costanera becomes Plácido Martínez, at Juan Torres de Vera y Aragón, it's a short walk to Calle San Juan's **Paseo Italia,** a monumental tribute to the Italian community, but there's a more impressive feature in the vivid

M

Mesopotamia & Paraná

backdrop of the **Murales Históricos,** a series of murals reaching around the corner of Calle Quintana, which depict the city's history since colonial times.

Immediately to the east, dating from the late 16th century, the **Convento de San Francisco** (Mendoza 450) underwent an impressive restoration in 1939. Its **Museo Francisco** (tel. 03783/422936) is open 8 A.M.–noon and 4–8 P.M. weekdays. Two blocks south of the murals, the **Museo de Bellas Artes Doctor Juan Ramón Vidal** (San Juan 634) is a fine arts facility focusing on sculpture, open 8 A.M.–12:30 P.M. and 4–8:30 P.M. Tuesday–Friday, 9 A.M.–noon and 4–7 P.M. Saturday except in summer, when Saturday afternoon hours are 5–8 P.M.

Two blocks south of here, the **Museo Histórico de Corrientes** (9 de Julio 1044) focuses on colonial art, antique weapons and furniture, and numismatics. Hours are identical to those of the fine arts museum. Four blocks west and a block south, Plaza Cabral is the site of the **catedral,** which contains the mausoleum of local caudillo Colonel Genaro Berón de Astrada.

Three blocks south and two blocks west of the historical museum, bearing the name of Alexander Humboldt's 19th-century travel companion, the **Museo de Ciencias Naturales Amado Bonpland** (San Martín 850) is a sprawling facility focusing on entomology and vertebrates, but also has a good fossil collection. Hours are identical of the art and history museums.

In the 16th century, according to legend, insurrectionary Indians attempted but failed to burn a wooden cross that survives in the **Iglesia de la Cruz,** on the south side of its namesake plaza, bounded by Bolívar, Salta, Buenos Aires, and Belgrano.

Entertainment and Events

Occupying a large tent with long tables, the informal *parrilla* **El Quincho** (Avenida Pujol and Pampir) is less notable for its food than for its live *chamamé,* the accordion-based Mesopotamian music that most closely resembles Tex-Mex *conjunto* in style. The menu is not for single diners or drinkers—beef slabs only, no half bottles of wine,

and beer by the liter. Still, prices are more than reasonable.

Named for the city's founder, the **Teatro Oficial Juan de Vera** (San Juan 637, tel. 03783/427743) is the site for high-culture events such as classical music concerts and live theater. The three-screen **Cine Colón** (9 de Julio between San Juan and Mendoza, tel. 03783/431956) is the main movie theater.

Huge crowds, including performing *comparsas* (troupes) from nearby provinces—and even from Brazil and Paraguay—descend on Corrientes for the **Carnaval Correntino,** whose celebrations take place Friday, Saturday, and Sunday in the summer carnival season. The main parades occur along Avenida Gobernador Ferré, the eastward extension of Avenida 3 de Abril.

Shopping

Something of a hybrid institution, the **Museo de Artesanía Folklórica** (Quintana 905) displays classic crafts from around the province but also sells souvenir versions, some available directly from the artisans themselves. Hours are 8 A.M.–12:30 P.M. and 4–8:30 P.M. Monday and Wednesday–Friday, 9 A.M.–noon Saturday only.

Accommodations

Accommodations are surprisingly scarce for a city of Corrientes's size, but devaluation has brought prices down to realistic levels, in dollar terms at least. True budget accommodations are even fewer, but for summer Carnaval celebrations the provincial tourist office keeps a list of inexpensive *casas de familia,* in which local families rent out their spare rooms.

Overlooking the Costanera, the high-rise **Hotel Hostal del Río** (Plácido Martínez 1098, tel. 03783/436100, hostal_del_rio@infovia.com.ar) charges US$12/16 s/d for rather worn standard rooms with breakfast; so-called superior rooms are better furnished for US$17/21 s/d, but are still fading.

Spacious wooded grounds, a large pool, and proximity to the Costanera are the strengths of the Peronist-vintage **Gran Hotel Turismo** (Entre Ríos 650, tel. 03783/429112, hotelturismo

@arnet.com.ar, US$12/18 s/d), which has pre-served more charm than comfort. Still, its price structure is fair enough.

The business-oriented **Gran Hotel Guaraní** (Mendoza 970, tel. 03783/433800, fax 03783/ 424620, hguarani@espacio.com.ar) has standard rooms at US$17/23 s/d, but superior rooms go for US$22/28 s/d. There's a 10 percent discount for cash payment.

The **Orly Hotel** (San Juan 867, tel. 03783/ 427248, fax 03783/420280, US$17/23 s/d) is impeccably modernized. **Hotel San Martín** (Santa Fe 955, tel. 03783/432326, hsanmartin @impsat1.com.ar) charges US$16/21 s/d.

On the north side of Plaza Cabral, the **Corrientes Plaza Hotel** (Junín 1549, tel./fax 03783/ 466500, reserva@corrienteshotel.com.ar) may not quite live up to its four-star billing, but at US$17/26 s/d for comfortable if cozy standard rooms and US$22/30 s/d for superior rooms, it's at least three-star comfort at one-star prices. There's also a secluded pool, a gym, secure on-site parking, and a 10 percent discount for cash payments.

Food
In general, the Corrientes dining scene is dire. Shockingly enough for a riverside city, no place really specializes in fish.

For breakfast, sandwiches, afternoon tea, and sweets, the best choice in town is **La Perla** (9 de Julio 1198, tel. 03783/423008); it even hosts occasional tango performances.

Pizzería Los Pinos (San Lorenzo 1191, tel. 03783/462025) is a decent pizzeria with varied toppings and reasonable prices. The **Eco Pizza Pub** (Hipólito Yrigoyen 1108, tel. 03783/ 425900) is a slightly more upscale alternative.

Heladería La Terraza (Hipólito Yrigoyen 1135, tel. 03783/423219) sets the standard for ice cream.

Information
The provincial **Subsecretaría de Turismo** (25 de Mayo 1330, tel. 03783/427200, corrientes-turismo@espacio.com.ar, www.planetacorri-entes.com.ar) is open 7 A.M.–1 P.M. and 3–9 P.M. weekdays only. The **Dirección Municipal de**

Turismo maintains an office on the riverfront at Punta Tacura, where 9 de Julio and Junín intersect the Costanera (tel. 03783/423779).

For motorists, **ACA** is at 25 de Mayo and Mendoza (tel. 03783/422844).

Services
Cambio El Dorado (9 de Julio 1341) is the only exchange house. Several downtown banks have ATMs, such as **Banco de Corrientes** (9 de Julio 1092).

Correo Argentino is at the corner of San Juan and Avenida San Martín; the postal code is 3400. There are many *locutorios,* including **Telecentros** at Pellegrini 1239 and at Santa Fe and Junín. **El Paseo Cybercafé** is at San Juan 531.

Quo Vadis, (Pellegrini 1140, tel. 03783/ 423096) is the AmEx representative.

Corrientes's **Hospital Escuela San Martín** is at Avenida 3 de Abril 1251 (tel. 03783/420697 or 421371).

Getting There
Aerolíneas Argentinas/Austral (Junín 1301, tel. 03783/423850) flies most days to Aeroparque (Buenos Aires). Nearby Resistencia also has flights to and from the capital.

From the local **bus terminal** on Avenida Costanera General San Martín at La Rioja, frequent buses link Corrientes to Resistencia (US$1, 30 minutes), across the Paraná, where long-distance connections are better for western and northwestern Argentina.

Corrientes's own long-distance **Estación Terminal de Transporte Gobernador Benjamín S. González** is on Avenida Maipú at the southeast edge of town (tel. 03783/455600). Typical destinations, fares, and times include Posadas (US$7, 4.5 hours), Rosario (US$12, nine hours), Puerto Iguazú (US$13, eight hours), and Buenos Aires (US$13–18, 11 hours). Buses to Mercedes, the transfer point for the Iberá marshes, cost about US$5 (three hours).

Getting Around
From the Estación Terminal de Colectivos Urbanos, on the Costanera at the north end of Salta, local bus No. 8 goes directly to Aeropuerto Doctor

Fernando Piragine Niveyro, about 10 kilometers east of Corrientes on RN 12 (tel. 03783/458332). Aerolíneas provides minibus transfers to Resistencia for flights operating there.

Bus No. 6 goes to the long-distance bus terminal on Avenida Maipú.

Paso de la Patria

At the confluence of the Paraná and Paraguay rivers, 38 kilometers northeast of Corrientes, Paso de la Patria is a favorite weekend getaway for Correntinos and their neighbors from Resistencia as well. It also draws an international sport-fishing crowd to mid-August's **Fiesta Internacional del Dorado,** a contest for capturing the largest individual of the Paraná's favorite fighting fish.

While dorado is the main attraction, other challenging (and appetizing) species include *surubí, boga, and sábalo.* Peak fishing season lasts from July to September; closed season runs from early October to early March. For more detail, contact Paso de la Patria's **Dirección de Turismo** (25 de Mayo 468, tel. 03783/15-604877).

Paso de la Patria enjoys frequent bus service to and from Corrientes.

Parque Nacional Mburucuyá

On the north side of the Esteros del Iberá, 147 kilometers southeast of Corrientes via RN 12 and the paved lateral RP 13, the small town of Mburucuyá is the gateway to its namesake national park, preserving 17,660 hectares of wetlands and palm savannas. Once a Danish-owned *estancia,* the park offers similar habitat and wildlife to those of Esteros del Iberá, and short nature trails among its marshes, gallery forests, and groves of *yatay* palms.

The town of Mburucuyá has a couple of simple accommodations, and there is also a basic campground in the park. There is regular bus service from Corrientes, but the park itself lies 11 kilometers to the east via a dirt road.

For more detail, contact Parque Nacional Mburucuyá (Casilla de Correo 1, 3427 Mburucuyá, Corrientes, tel. 03782/498022 or 498148, mburucuya@impsat1.com.ar, mburucuya@infovia.com.ar).

Misiones Province

Almost surrounded by Brazil and Paraguay, mountainous Misiones has the highest-profile sights of any Mesopotamian province. In the upper Paraná drainage, shared with Brazil, the **Cataratas del Iguazú** (Iguazú Falls) draw visitors from around the world. The Jesuit-mission ruins of San Ignacio and across the border in Paraguay are a strong additional reason to visit the region.

Averaging about 500 meters above sea level, once covered with subtropical forest, the mountains of Misiones are fast giving way to plantations of tea, *yerba mate* and northern-hemisphere pines. In a few areas, coniferous native Araucaria forest still dominates the natural vegetation.

HISTORY

Along with its diverse ecology, Misiones has an epically rich history, thanks to its dense Guaraní

population and the Jesuits who proselytized among them. In the early 17th century, the Jesuits abandoned their efforts among the nomadic hunter-gatherers of the Chaco for the Guaraní, shifting cultivators who were better candidates for missionization. In all, they founded 30 *reducciones,* populated with perhaps 100,000 Guaraní, in a territory that now comprises parts of Argentina, Brazil, and Paraguay.

Hollywood rarely depicts history with any accuracy, but director Roland Joffe got it mostly right in his 1986 film *The Mission,* starring Robert De Niro and Jeremy Irons. Joffe made an admirable effort at portraying the Jesuit experiment in organizing indigenous peoples and educating them not just as farmers but also as skilled craftsmen and even performing artists. He also deftly explained the political and economic intrigues of the time, as Portuguese *malocas* (slavers) and other Spanish settlers coveted the Jesuits' productive *yerba mate* plantations and indigenous labor monopoly.

Eventually, under pressure from these interests, the Spanish king Carlos III expelled the Jesuits from the Americas in 1767. After the Jesuits' expulsion, many of the indigenes fled to the forest and the missions fell into ruins, their walls pried apart by strangler figs and their Guaraní-carved sandstone statuary toppled.

After the South American states gained independence in the early 19th century, Misiones was the object of contention among various countries in an area where it took some time to fix international borders. After the megalomaniacal Paraguayan dictator Francisco Solano López led his country into the hopeless War of the Triple Alliance (1865–1870) against Argentina, Brazil, and Uruguay, his catastrophic loss left Misiones in Argentine hands.

Administratively, Misiones became part of Corrientes Province, but as agricultural colonization proceeded from the west, Misiones broke off as a separate territory with Posadas as its capital. The arrival in 1912 of the Urquiza railway at Posadas provided a way for farmers to get their products to market.

Yerba mate remained the major product of enormous properties acquired under questionable circumstances. By the early 20th century, the federal government expropriated many of these lands and turned them over to agricultural colonists from many countries, including Argentina, Brazil, Denmark, France, Germany, Greece, Italy, Paraguay, Spain, Sweden, Switzerland, the Ukraine, the United States, and countries in Asia and the Middle East. The city of Oberá, in particular, celebrates its immigrant heritage in a major annual festival.

POSADAS

After the war against Paraguay, the growing city of Posadas became the territorial capital when Buenos Aires separated Misiones from Corrientes Province. Today, as the main commercial center for farming communities of the provincial interior, it's also a major border crossing. For travelers, it's important as an access point to the historic Jesuit missions of the upper Paraná, on both the Argentine and Paraguayan sides, and to Parque Nacional Iguazú.

Now capital of its province, Posadas is reclaiming part of its waterfront above the slowly encroaching waters of the downstream Yacyretá hydroelectric project, called "a monument to corruption" by former president Carlos Menem (who should know one when he sees one). In the downtown area, densely planted street trees help offset the summer heat and humidity.

Orientation

On the south bank of the Río Paraná, opposite the smaller Paraguayan city of Encarnación, Posadas (population 280,454) is 1,007 kilometers north of Buenos Aires via RN 14 and RN 105, 324 kilometers east of Corrientes via RN 12, and 302 kilometers southwest of Puerto Iguazú, also via RN 12.

Formerly major avenues mark the limits of Posadas's compact center: Avenida Corrientes to the west, Avenida Guacurarí to the north, Avenida Roque Sáenz Peña to the east, and Avenida Mitre to the south. Most services and points of interest, including the central Plaza 9 de Julio, lie within this area. An attractive new riverfront road, the Avenida Monseñor Kemerer, extends northwest from Avenida Roque Sáenz Peña. Avenida Mitre leads east to the graceful suspension bridge that links Posadas to Encarnación.

Posadas's awkward street numeration continues to confuse nonresidents, as locals continue to prefer the old numbers to the new. Addresses below use the new system but in some cases they indicate the old numbers as well, and occasionally refer to precise locations, as some buildings lack numbers from either system.

Sights and Entertainment

On the east side of Plaza 9 de Julio, the Francophile **Casa de Gobierno** (1883) was actually the work of an Italian, engineer Juan Col. On the north side of the plaza, the famed architect Alejandro Bustillo designed the twin-towered **catedral** (1937).

Mesopotamia & Paraná

Ten blocks north of Plaza 9 de Julio, bounded by the riverfront, **Parque República de Paraguay** is home to the **Museo Regional de Posadas Aníbal Cambas** (Alberdi 600), which focuses on regional history including the Jesuit mission frontier. Hours are 7:30 A.M.– noon and 3–7 P.M. weekdays except Monday, 9 A.M.–noon and 5–8 P.M. Saturday, and 5–8 P.M. only Sunday and holidays.

Posadas's newest attraction is the **Museo Ferrobarcos,** on the waterfront at the east end of Avenida Guacurarí, where trains between Buenos Aires and Asunción once shuttled across the river. Built in Glasgow in 1911, this rail ferry transported up to four passenger cars or eight cargo units at a time across the river from 1913 until 1990, when train service between the two countries ceased. Now staffed by retired railroad workers, it's open 6 P.M.–midnight weekdays, 6 P.M.– 2 A.M. weekends and holidays.

The **Cine Sarmiento,** (Córdoba between San Lorenzo and Ayacucho) shows recent movies. **Teatro El Desván,** (Sarmiento between Colón and San Lorenzo) is a well-established theater company.

Accommodations

For shoestring travelers, the **Residencial Misiones** (Avenida Azara 1960, tel. 03752/430133, US$5.50/9 s/d) is OK for a night. There's much better value, though, at **Hotel Colonial** (Barrufaldi 2419, tel. 03752/436149, US$9/14 s/d).

Its maritime kitsch decor is, well, distinctive, but rooms on the upper floors at the high-rise **Hotel de Turismo Posadas** (Bolívar and Junín, tel. 03752/437104, US$9/14 s/d) enjoy river views from their prominent balconies. Rates are more than reasonable.

The rooms are a little makeshift but the mattresses are firm at friendly **Le Petit Hotel** (Santiago del Estero 1630, tel. 03752/436031, fax 03752/441101, lepetithotel@hotmail.com, www .hotelguia.com/hotels/lepetit/page.htm, US$11/16 s/d). The rates fit the service, though parking is two blocks away.

For US$16/19 s/d, the well-worn **Hotel Libertador** (San Lorenzo 2208, tel. 03752/436901, fax 03752/439448, reservas@libertador-hot.com

.ar) has spacious rooms with a/c, and responsive personnel.

Overlooking Plaza 9 de Julio, the high-rise **Hotel Continental** (Bolívar 1879, tel. 03752/440990, hotel@hoteleramisiones.com.ar, www.hoteleramisiones.com.ar, US$19/27 s/d) is a good alternative. **Posadas Hotel** (Bolívar 1949, tel. 03752/440888, hotelposadas.com.ar, www.hotelposadas.com.ar, US$23/27 s/d) also deserves consideration.

Rates at four-star **Hotel Julio César** (Entre Ríos 1951, tel. 03752/427930, hotel@juliocesarhotel.com.ar, www.juliocesarhotel.com.ar), the city's best, are US$27/34 s/d.

Food

Nouvelle Vitrage, on Plaza 9 de Julio at the corner of Bolívar and Colón, is the place for breakfast, coffee, and snacks, including desserts. **Los Pinos** (San Lorenzo and Buenos Aires, tel. 03752/427252) is the place to go for pizza and cold beer on tap. For river fish, try the simple takeaway **El Doradito** (Avenida Corrientes and La Rioja), which has only a couple of sit-down tables amidst the simplest of decor.

Posadas's finest dining is at **Ⅺ Diletto** (Bolívar 1729, tel. 03752/449784); most entrees, such as their excellent gnocchi, fall into the US$2–5 range. Try the chocolate mousse for dessert. The *parrilla* **La Querencia** (Bolívar between Colón and Avenida Azara, tel. 03752/437117) is an outstanding backup choice.

Information

The provincial **Secretaría de Turismo** (Colón 1985, tel. 03752/441539, turismo@misiones.gov .ar, turismo@misiones.gov.ar) offers a selection of simple maps and brochures for Posadas and the entire province. It's open 7 A.M.–8 P.M. weekdays, 8 A.M.–noon and 4–8 P.M. weekends and holidays.

For motorists, **ACA** is at Córdoba and Colón (tel. 03752/436955).

Services

Cambios Mazza (Bolívar 1932) changes travelers checks. There are several ATMs in the vicinity of Plaza 9 de Julio, including the one at

Banco Nazionale del Lavoro (Bolívar and Félix de Azara).

Correo Argentino is at Bolívar and Ayacucho; the postal code is 3300. **Telecentro Bolívar** is at Bolívar and Colón, at the southwestern corner of Plaza 9 de Julio; Posadas's area code is 0752. **Ciber Soft** (Rivadavia and Santa Fe) has fast Internet connections.

Express Travel (Félix de Azara 2097, tel. 03752/437687) is the AmEx representative.

Hospital General R. Madariaga (Avenida López Torres 1177, tel. 03752/447775) is about one kilometer south of the downtown area.

Getting There

Posadas enjoys pretty good air connections to Buenos Aires, it's a hub for provincial and long-distance buses, and rail service to Bueno Aires has been restored recently. There are also buses and launches across the border to Encarnación.

Between them, **Aerolíneas Argentina** and **Austral** (Ayacucho 1728, tel. 03752/437110) fly once or twice daily to Aeroparque.

Less convenient but far better than the old downtown station, Posadas's new **Terminal de Ómnibus** is at Avenida Quaranta and Avenida Santa Catalina, 44 blocks south and 14 blocks west of Plaza 9 de Julio (tel. 03752/454888). Buses to San Ignacio Miní (US$1.50, one hour) leave roughly hourly starting around 5:30 A.M.

Sample destinations, fares, and times include Corrientes (US$7, 4.5 hours), Resistencia (US$8, five hours), Puerto Iguazú (US$8, four hours) Buenos Aires (US$21–30, 12 hours) and Salta (US$27, 18 hours). There are also international services to Asunción, Paraguay (US$10, 5.5 hours), and to the Brazilian cities of Porto Alegre (US$24, 12 hours) and São Paulo (US$50, 24 hours).

Between 7 A.M. and 10 P.M., international shuttle buses to Encarnación, Paraguay (US$.75), pass along Entre Ríos en route to the international bridge. With border formalities, the crossing can take up to an hour, but is normally faster.

Trenes Especiales Argentinos (TEA, at the east end of Avenida Córdoba) has recently reopened passenger train services on the Urquiza line to Buenos Aires's Estación Federico Lacroze.

Scheduled departures are 9 A.M. Wednesday and Sunday for the 24–25-hour trip, but there have been glitches with provincial authorities in Entre Ríos that may endanger the service.

Local **boats** connect Posadas to Encarnación (US$.50) from the corner of Avenida Guacurarí, but they are mostly for locals—foreigners must still pass through immigration, which means trudging back to the international bridge.

Getting Around

From San Lorenzo between La Rioja and Entre Ríos, city bus No. 8 goes to Aeropuerto Internacional Posadas, 12 kilometers southwest of town via RN 12. A *remise* will cost about US$4.

City bus Nos. 8, 15, 21, and 24 all go to the long-distance bus terminal.

For car rental, try **Express Car** (Colón 1909, tel. 03752/435484, expresscar@arnet.com.ar).

Complejo Hidroeléctrico

Near the town of Ituzaingó, in Corrientes Province, the massive Yacyretá-Apipé hydroelectric project has raised the level of the Río Paraná to form a 1,600-square-kilometer reservoir that reaches 80 kilometers east to Posadas and beyond. Plagued with corruption since its inception under Juan Perón in 1973—the late caudillo's last-gasp contribution to Argentina's unsavory public works history—the biggest dam project on the continent has also helped raise Argentina's foreign-debt burden to unsustainable levels.

It takes two to tango, and it took two countries to create the Argentine-Paraguayan Entidad Binacional Yacyretá (EBY), which in the process has displaced some 40,000 upstream residents, mostly on the Paraguayan side of the border. Despite a reputation for secrecy and authoritarianism, the EBY's **Oficina de Relaciones Públicas** in Ituzaingó (Avenida 3 de Abril and Ingeniero Mermoz, tel. 03786/420050, rrppitu@eby.org.ar, www.eby.org.ar) offers free guided tours at 9 and 11 A.M. and 3:15 and 4:30 P.M. During the second Gulf War, though, they suspended tours for supposed security reasons (go figure!).

A museum at the visitors center shows artifacts discovered during construction, as well as a

Mesopotamia & Paraná

scale model of the project. Bus tours are well-organized, visiting the projects built to house construction workers in what was once a small village, but the guides themselves are on automatic pilot.

Yacyretá has spawned a small cottage industry in academic circles. Those interested in more details can read Gustavo Lins Ribeiro's *Transnational Capitalism and Hydropolitics in Argentina: the Yacyretá High Dam* (Gainesville: University Press of Florida, 1994), and Carmen A. Ferradás's *Power in the Southern Cone Borderlands* (Westbrook, CT: Bergin & Garvey, 1998), which deals primarily with the displacement of local communities.

Hostería Yacyretá (Buenos Aires s/n, tel. 03786/420577, hyacyreta@arnet.com.ar, US$14/ 18 s/d, larger suites US$26) has a restaurant.

There are regular **bus services** to and from Posadas (US$2, one hour).

Trinidad and Jesús (Paraguay)

Immediately across the Paraná via the international bridge, the Paraguayan city of Encarnación barely merits a visit in its own right (though it's morbidly fascinating to see the rising waters of Yacyretá dam slowly submerge its historic downtown). It's well worth crossing the border, though, to see the nearby Paraguayan Jesuit missions of Trinidad and Jesús de Tavarangue. Together, they're an essential complement to the missions on the Argentine side.

Both Trinidad and Jesús were relative latecomers in the Jesuit empire—Jesús, in fact, was still under construction when Carlos III expelled the Jesuits from the Americas in 1767. Trinidad dates from 1706, but took more than five decades to reach its completion in 1760—only seven years prior to the Jesuits' departure.

Trinidad, where more than 4,000 Guaraní once resided, sprawls across a grassy hilltop site, 28 kilometers northeast of Encarnación via Paraguay's paved Ruta 6. Its pride was Jesuit architect Juan Bautista Prímoli's well-preserved red sandstone church, with equally well-preserved details like its intricately sculpted pulpit and statuary (the Guaraní of Trinidad were known for their statuary but also for finely made musical instruments in-

Misión Trinidad, Encarnación, Paraguay

cluding bells, harps, and organs). On a more practical level, the mission supported itself with plantations of *yerba mate* and sugar (which they milled here), and three cattle *estancias*.

Jesús occupies a similar hilltop site, 11 kilometers north of Trinidad via a dirt road off Ruta 6 that can become difficult or impassable with heavy rain. While it lacks the architectural details of Trinidad—after all, Jesús was never finished—together with the older mission it makes an ideal half-day-plus excursion from Posadas. Opening times vary seasonally, but both generally stay open during daylight hours; each collects a token admission charge.

Buses from Encarnación's central terminal, at Avenida Estigarribia and General Cabañas, pass within a kilometer of Trinidad and also go several times daily to Jesús. These are very cheap, but the trip can be done more efficiently (if more expensively) by hiring a taxi at the terminal.

Note that U.S., Canadian, Australian, and Mexican citizens now need visas (US$45 single entry, US$65 multiple entry, three photos required) to enter Paraguay. In Posadas, the Paraguayan consulate (San Lorenzo and Sarmiento, tel. 03752/ 423858, 7 A.M.–2 P.M. weekdays only) provides same-day visa service.

Santa Ana and Loreto

From Posadas, undulating RN 12 climbs and dips northeast over leached red soils past several Jesuit mission ruins, the best-preserved of which is San Ignacio Miní. Santa Ana and Loreto, while less well-preserved, both have their assets; during the 1990s, each was the beneficiary of assistance from the German and Italian governments, but progress in restoration has slowed since the end of European support. Both are national historical monuments.

Founded in 1637, **Santa Ana** once sustained a Guaraní population of more than 4,000, though more than half departed within two decades after the Jesuits' expulsion. Only the mission walls remain, some still covered by strangler figs and other profuse tropical vegetation wedged between the cracks. Immediately alongside it, the disconcertingly open crypts and coffins of an abandoned 20th-century cemetery are a reminder that the Jesuit experiment was only the first failed settlement here.

Santa Ana is 43 kilometers east of Posadas and one kilometer southeast of RN 12 via a dirt road that becomes muddy when it rains; the junction is clearly marked, and buses from Posadas will drop passengers here. There is a small admission charge; hours are 7 A.M.–6 P.M. daily.

Work at **Loreto**, which dates from 1632 but moved here only in 1660, has lagged behind that of Santa Ana, but plaques with descriptive quotations from Jesuit priests help visitors imagine what the site might have been. (The Jesuits brought high culture to the South American wilds— including *Martirologio Romano*, or Roman Martirology, 1700, the first book ever printed within the territory now known as Argentina. It later appeared in Guaraní.)

The turnoff to Loreto is at Km 48, five kilometers beyond that to Santa Ana, but the site itself is three kilometers farther south of RN 12. Both Santa Ana and Loreto have small museums and cafés, and Loreto even offers decent accommodations for US$7 pp in spacious three-bed apartments with kitchen facilities.

SAN IGNACIO

Home to Argentina's best-kept Jesuit-mission ruins, the village of San Ignacio is an essential stopover on the overland route to or from the famous falls at Iguazú. It also enjoys literary celebrity as the home of writer Horacio Quiroga, who produced some of his finest fiction in a residence that still survives here.

San Ignacio (population 6,286) is 56 kilometers northeast of Posadas via RN 12. From the highway junction, Avenida Sarmiento leads to Calle Rivadavia, which leads six blocks north to the ruins.

San Ignacio Miní

In terms of preservation, including the architectural and sculptural details that typify the style known as "Guaraní baroque," San Ignacio Miní may be the most outstanding surviving example of the 30 missions built by the Jesuits in a territory that now comprises parts of Argentina,

Brazil, and Paraguay. It's also a tourist favorite for its accessibility, surrounded as it is by the present-day village of San Ignacio.

San Ignacio's centerpiece was Italian architect Juan Brasanelli's monumental church, 74 meters long and 24 meters wide, with red sandstone walls two meters wide and ceramic-tile floors. Overlooking the settlement's plaza, decorated by Guaraní artisans, it's arguably the finest remaining structure of its kind; the adjacent compound included a kitchen, dining room, classrooms, and workshops. The priests' quarters and the cemetery were also here, while more than 200 Guaraní residences—whose numbers reached 4,000 at the mission's zenith in 1733—surrounded the plaza.

Founded in 1609 in present-day Paraguay, San Ignacio Guazú moved to the Río Yabebiry in 1632 and to its present location in 1697, but declined rapidly with expulsion of the Jesuits in 1767. In 1817, Paraguayan troops under the paranoid dictator Gaspar Rodríguez de Francia razed what remained of the settlement.

Rediscovered in 1897, San Ignacio gained some notoriety after poet Leopoldo Lugones led an expedition to the area in 1903, but restoration work had to wait until the 1940s. Parts of the ruins are still precarious, supported by sore-thumb scaffolding that obscures the essential harmony of the complex but does not affect individual features.

Visitors enter the grounds through the **Centro de Interpretación Regional,** a mission museum (Alberdi between Rivadavia and Bolívar, 6 A.M.–7 P.M. daily, US$1). A nightly light-and-sound show, lasting 50 minutes, costs an additional US$1. Outside the exit, on Rivadavia, there's a growing number of eyesore souvenir stands that detract from the mission's impact.

Casa de Horacio Quiroga

One of the first Latin American writers to reject the city for the frontier, novelist, storyteller, and poet Horacio Quiroga (1878–1937) spent his prime of life in his self-built house overlooking the Paraná, only a short distance southeast of downtown San Ignacio. While he made writing his career, Quiroga also worked as a cotton farmer in the Chaco and as a charcoal maker in San Ignacio, and took notable photographs of San Ignacio's Jesuit ruins, incorporating his outside interests into his literary work.

His life plagued by violence—Quiroga accidentally shot a youthful friend to death, and his stepfather and first wife both committed suicide—the writer lived here from 1910 to 1917, and again from 1931 until his own cyanide-induced death. The home itself is now a museum with furniture from the 1930s, photographs of his life, and personal belongings. This was not Quiroga's first house, a replica of which (built for director Nemesio Juárez's film *Historias de Amor, de Locura y de Muerte* (Stories of Love, Madness and Death, 1996) stands nearby.

The grounds of Quiroga's house (Avenida Quiroga s/n, US$.75) are open 7 A.M.–dusk daily.

© WAYNE BERNHARDSON

San Ignacio Miní

Mesopotamia & Paraná

Accommodations

Just north of the bus terminal, **Hospedaje Los Salpeterer** (Centenario s/n, tel. 03752/470362), is a popular backpackers' choice, charging US$3 pp for basic rooms with shared bath, US$4 pp with private bath. Camping costs only US$1.50 pp.

Hospedaje El Descanso (Pellegrini 270, tel. 03752/470207, US$3 pp with shared bath, US$7 d with private bath) is some distance south of the ruins, but has earned high marks for cleanliness and basic comforts. It also has camping spaces.

There are no luxury choices here, but **Hotel San Ignacio** (Sarmiento 823, tel. 03752/470047, US$8/11 s/d) has the most complete range of services.

Food

Three blocks south of the ruins, **Pizzería la Aldea** (Rivadavia s/n, tel. 03752/470567) serves fine pizza with varied toppings, and has attractive sidewalk seating to boot, but the owner will talk your head off even if you're not keen to chat.

The restaurants near the ruins may be assembly-line operations geared toward large tour groups, but the standard Argentine menus are by no means bad if you can tolerate the crowds and swarms of urchins who want to wash your car and drag you to their restaurant of choice. Opposite the entrance to the ruins, try **Don Valentín** (Alberdi and Bolívar). Opposite the exit, there's **Liana Bert** (Rivadavia 1133, tel. 03752/470151), or **La Carpa Azul** (Rivadavia and Azcuénaga) just to the north.

Other Practicalities

San Ignacio has a new **Oficina de Información Turística** at the junction of RN 12 and Avenida Sarmiento.

Buses arrive and leave from the **Terminal de Ómnibus** at the west end of Avenida Sarmiento, but it's also possible to flag down coaches along RN 12. The main destinations are Posadas (US$1.50, one hour) and Puerto Iguazú (US$7, three hours), but note that milk-run buses are considerably slower than express services.

© WAYNE BERNHARDSON

Iguazú Falls

PARQUE NACIONAL IGUAZÚ

In the Guaraní language of the Tres Fronteras region, Iguazú means "big waters," and the good news is that the thunderous surge of Iguazú Falls—perhaps the planet's greatest chain of cascades—continues to plunge over an ancient lava flow, some 20 kilometers east of the town of Puerto Iguazú. Its overwhelming natural assets, including the surrounding subtropical rainforest, have earned Parque Nacional recognition as a UNESCO World Heritage Site.

The bad news is that Argentina's APN, the state entity charged with preserving and protecting this natural heritage, has buckled to rampant Disneyfication. The falls, its core attraction, have become a mass-tourism destination that might more accurately be called Parque Temático Iguazú—Iguazú Theme Park.

While they've done something right in limiting automobile access—cars must park in a guarded lot and visitors must enter the park on foot—the concessionaire has turned the area surrounding the falls into an area of manicured lawns, fast-food restaurants and souvenir stands, connected by a cheesy narrow-gauge train. Around the falls proper, clean-cut youths with walkie-talkies shunt hikers out by 7 P.M.—the perfect closing hour for a theme park—unless you're fortunate enough to be a privileged guest at the Sheraton, the park's only accommodations. The exception to the rule is the monthly full-moon tour, which is well worthwhile.

That's not to say commercial greed has completely overrun nature—the park still has large extents of subtropical rainforest, with colorfully abundant birdlife along with less conspicuous mammals and reptiles. All of these animals demand respect, but some more so than others—in 1997, a jaguar killed a park ranger's infant son; pumas are even more common, and poisonous snakes are also present.

In 1541 Alvar Núñez Cabeza de Vaca, one of the most intrepid Spaniards in the New World, was the first European to see the falls. But in an area populated by tens of thousands of Guaraní Indians prior to the European invasion, he can hardly have discovered them, despite the assertions of a commemorative plaque.

The Natural Landscape

According to Guaraní legend, a jealous serpent-god created Iguazú Falls by collapsing the riverbed in front of the fleeing lovers Naipi and Caroba; Naipi plunged over the ensuing falls to become a rock at their base, while her lover Caroba became a tree forever condemned to see, but unable to touch, his beloved.

A less fanciful explanation is that the languid Río Iguazú streams over a basalt plateau that ends where an ancient lava flow finally cooled; before reaching the end of the flow, small islands, large rocks and unseen reefs split the river into multiple channels that become the individual waterfalls that, in sum, form the celebrated *cataratas,* some more than 70 meters in height.

At this point, in an area stretching more than two kilometers across the Argentine-Brazilian border, at least 5,000 cubic meters of water per

Garganta del Diablo, Parque Nacional Iguazú

second roar over the edge onto an older sedimentary landscape, but the volume can be far greater in flood. With the water's unstoppable force, the falls are slowly but inexorably receding toward the east.

Some 18 kilometers southeast of the town of Puerto Iguazú, and 1,280 kilometers north of Buenos Aires via RN 12, Parque Nacional Iguazú is a 67,000-hectare unit that includes a roughly 6,000-hectare Reserva Nacional—the presence of which has led to rampant commercial development in the immediate vicinity of the falls.

Flora and Fauna

Misiones's high rainfall (about 2000 mm per annum) and subtropical temperatures create a luxuriant forest flora on relatively poor soils. Unlike the mid-latitudes, where fallen leaves and other plant litter become part of the soil, here they are almost immediately recycled to support a dense, multilevel flora with a variety of faunal habitats. The park's roughly 2,000 identified plant species are home to almost innumerable insects, 448 bird species, 80 mammal species, and many reptiles and fish as well.

The tallest trees, such as the *lapacho* (*Tabebuia ipe*) and *palo rosa* (*Aspidosperma polyneuron*) reach some 30 meters above the forest floor, while the *guapoy* (the appropriately named "strangler fig," *Ficus monckii*) uses the larger trees for support and eventually kills them by asphyxiation. A variety of orchids use the large trees for support only.

Lesser trees and shrubs grow in the shade of the canopy, such as *yerba mate* (*Ilex paraguariensis*), the holly relative that Argentines, Uruguayans, Paraguayans, and Brazilians consume as tea (grown mostly on plantations in Misiones and Corrientes). Ferns are also abundant in the shade thrown by the large trees.

For most visitors, the most conspicuous fauna will be colorful birds such as various species of parakeets and parrots, the piping guan (*Aburria jacutinga*), the red-breasted toucan (*Ramphastos bicolorus*), and the lineated woodpecker (*Dryopus lineaturm*) in the trees, while tinamous (*Crypturellus* spp.) scurry along the forest floor. The tufted capuchin monkey (*Cebus apella nigritus*) is a fruit-eating tree-dweller.

The most commonly seen mammal, though, is the coatimundi (*Nasua nasua*), a raccoon relative that thrives around humans (do not feed it); the largest is the rarely seen tapir (*Tapirus terrestris*), distantly related to the horse. Like the tapir, the puma and *yaguareté* (jaguar) avoid human contact, preferring the denser, more remote parts of the forest, but these wild cats can be dangerous to humans. The most commonly sighted reptile is the innocuous iguana; venomous snakes, while they generally avoid humans, deserve respect in their forest habitat.

Sights

The earliest written record of the falls came from Cabeza de Vaca, who saw them as an obstacle to his downstream progress and reported, with apparent irritation, that "It was necessary . . . to take the canoes out of the water and carry them by hand past the cataract for half a league with great labor." Still, he could not help but be impressed by the noise and mist:

> *The current of the Yguazú was so strong that the canoes were carried furiously down the river, for near this spot there is a considerable fall, and the noise made by the water leaping down some high rocks into a chasm may be heard a great distance off, and the spray rises two spears high and more over the fall.*

Most visitors come to see the falls, and rightly so, but try to arrive early in the morning to avoid the crush of tour buses from Puerto Iguazú and Brazil. The sole exception to Iguazú's Disneyland entry hours are the monthly full-moon hikes, guided by park rangers.

Visitors pay the entrance fee at the Portal Cataratas, the gate to the slickly managed complex of fast food restaurants, souvenir stands, and tour operators. The most worthwhile sight here is the park service's **Centro de Interpretación.**

Traditionally, park visitors walk along three major circuits on mostly paved trails and *pasarelas* (catwalks) that zigzag among the islands and outcrops to make their way to overlooks of the falls. The **Circuito Superior** (Upper Circuit) is a 650-meter route that offers the best panoramas of the Argentine side of the falls, while the 1,700-meter **Circuito Inferior** (Lower Circuit) offers better views of the individual falls, and also provides launch access to **Isla San Martín**, which has exceptional views of the amphitheatrical **Garganta del Diablo** (Devil's Throat), Iguazú's single most breathtaking cataract.

Most visitors take the **Tren de la Selva**, the narrow-gauge railway, to reach the trailhead for the 1,130-meter catwalk to the overlook for the Garganta del Diablo; this means an unavoidable soaking while watching the *vencejo de tormenta* (ashy-tailed swift, *Chaeturo Andrei*) dart through the booming waters to and from nesting sites beneath the falls. The view almost defies description, though the spray can obscure the base of the falls and even on the hottest days can chill sightseers—bring light raingear, plastic bags to protect cameras and other valuables, and perhaps even a small towel.

Far fewer visitors explore forest trails than the *pasarelas,* except for the 20-minute **Sendero Verde,** a short forest walk leading to a small wetland that's home to birds and butterflies. The six-kilometer **Sendero Macuco,** a nature trail that begins near the train station, is the likeliest place to spot or hear the tufted capuchin monkey. Mostly level, it drops to the **Salto Arrechea,** a relatively small waterfall, via a steep, muddy, and slippery segment. Mosquito repellent is desirable.

Sports and Recreation

Above the falls, the Río Iguazú itself is suitable for activities like canoeing, kayaking, and other water sports; it should go without saying that there's serious danger in getting too close to the falls. Below the falls, there are additional opportunities.

The park's principal tour operator is **Iguazú Jungle Explorer** (tel. 03757/421600, int. 582, tel./fax 03757/421696, info@iguazujunglexplorer.com, www.iguazujunglexplorer.com), which has an office in the Sheraton and kiosks at the Portal Cataratas and at the Garganta del Diablo trailhead. Offerings include a 30-minute *Paseo*

Ecológico (US$5.50) through the gallery forests and islands above the falls; a 15-minute *Aventura Naútica* (US$11) that approaches the Garganta del Diablo from below; and the *Gran Aventura* (US$25) that includes and eight-kilometer forest excursion by 4WD vehicle, a motorized descent of the lower Iguazú including two kilometers of rapids; and visits to the various falls.

Explorador Expediciones (tel. 03757/421600, int. 511, tel. 03757/421922, explorador.expediciones@rainforestevt.com.ar) offers two-hour trips through the *selva* (forest) in 4WD vehicles at 10 A.M., noon, and 2 and 4 P.M.

Accommodations and Food

By default, almost everyone will stay in Puerto Iguazú, as the only option within the park itself is the gargantuan **Sheraton Internacional Iguazú Resort** (tel. 03757/421600 or 491800, reservas@iguazu.sheraton.com.ar), an incongruously sited building whose ungainly exterior has a certain Soviet-style presence. That said, it's the only option for those who covet the privilege of roaming the park grounds after hours, with rates starting at US$69 s or d with breakfast; those who demand views of the falls will have to pay rates starting at US$85 s or d.

The hotel itself has several restaurants, but anyone not eating there will have to settle for the tackiest fast-food clones and the odd *parrilla* on the park grounds. Better food is available in Puerto Iguazú itself.

Other Practicalities

Panels at the park's **Centro de Interpretación** (tel. 03757/491444, 8 A.M.–7 P.M. daily in summer, 8 A.M.–6 P.M. daily the rest of the year) give vivid explanations of the park's environment and ecology; there are also helpful personnel on duty.

For foreigners, the admission charge of US$11 is the most expensive to any national park in the country. Provincial residents pay US$2, other Argentines US$4.50, and residents of other Mercosur countries US$6.50. Entry fees include the narrow-gauge Tren de la Selva and launch access to Isla San Martín. The concessionaire Iguazú Argentina has a website (www.iguazuargentina.com) in Spanish, Portuguese, and English.

From the bus terminal at Puerto Iguazú, **El Práctico buses** (US$1) operate frequently between 7:15 A.M. and 8 P.M., taking 45 minutes to or from the park.

⋈ YACUTINGA LODGE

For those can afford it, an even better way of getting to know the Misiones selva is Yacutinga Lodge, set in a 750-hectare private ecological reserve about an hour east of Parque Nacional Iguazú. While the reserve is much smaller than the park, its remaining (and recovering) subtropical rainforest provides a far more up-close-and-personal view of the natural environment, in remarkable accommodations that are far superior to the Sheraton.

For bird-watchers, Yacutinga offers a list of more than 300 species, plus many mammals, reptiles and butterflies; it also, under the sponsorship of the Fundación Vida Silvestre Argentina, operates a small captive breeding program for capybaras. Eight separate nature trails, one of them self-guided and the rest open with local guides, range from 500 meters to eight kilometers (round-trip). There is also a short but fascinating catwalk through the forest canopy, leading to a platform that's an ideal spot for observing birds and other flora (do not, however, encourage the semitame coatimundi, who tries to nibble on your clothes and anything else within reach).

The lodge proper deserves special mention. Using the maximum possible of materials salvaged from the forest, the Argentine owners have created a Gaudiesque combination of tranquility, comfort, and style that amounts to five-star rusticity. The main building is an idiosyncratic architectural masterpiece, with a large living room, dining room, and bar. There are 20 tasteful rooms sleeping up to four people each in five secluded units, but except during major holidays such as Holy Week, the proprietors prefer to have only a small percentage of this capacity occupied to ensure a quality experience. Accommodations are available on a full-board basis only (drinks extra); day excursions are not offered.

Yacutinga also meets many standards for appropriate development as, except for the owners themselves, all 17 employees (including the guides) come from the nearby community of Andresito and from Puerto Iguazú. Insofar as possible, the food is either raised on the reserve or purchased locally; the main exceptions are beverages such as beer, wine, and soft drinks. There is electricity 6–11 P.M. only.

Yacutinga's food is very good, though if you stayed longer than a week it might seem repetitive. Unlike in Argentina's pampas heartland, the beef comes from relatively chewy (though tasty) Zebu cattle. Vegetarian menus are available on request, though sometimes the main dish is vegetarian for everyone. The cinnamon rolls at breakfast deserve special mention.

Yacutinga makes accommodations arrangements and quotes prices through the Internet only (www.yacutinga.com), but it is not cheap. Passengers get picked up at Puesto Tigre, the Gendarmería (Border Guard) post just outside Puerto Iguazú's airport; the transfer vehicle is a high-clearance open-sided truck, which allows views of the *selva* for 45 kilometers en route to Bahía la Blanquita. Here guests board a motorized raft for the last eight kilometers to Yacutinga, seeing the Río Iguazú gallery forest en route. The return to Puesto Tigre is by road on the same vehicle.

PUERTO IGUAZÚ

At the confluence of the Paraná and the Iguazú, Puerto Iguazú is a small riverside town that lives partly from a thriving tourist trade, thanks to its proximity to the famous Iguazú Falls, one of the planet's—not just South America's—most spectacular natural highlights. Visitors from all over the globe pass through or stay in town, though fewer cross the border to the Brazilian side of the falls to Brazil's own national park and the service center of Foz do Iguaçu than in the past because of Brazil's excessive, almost punitive, visa fees.

As part of the Tres Fronteras ("three borders") area that includes the Brazilian city of Foz do Iguaçu and the Paraguayan city of Ciudad del Este, Puerto Iguazú has a dark side as well; on the

Mesopotamia & Paraná

PUERTO IGUAZÚ

BRAZIL
ARGENTINA

Río Iguazú

HITO ARGENTINO

AV. TRES FRONTERAS

HOTEL ESTURIÓN

AV. RÍO IGUAZÚ

RESIDENCIAL
LA CABAÑA

CATAMARCA

SANTA FE

SALTA

25 DE MAYO

CHUBUT

CHACO

RÍO PARANÁ

15 DE NOVIEMBRE

10 DE JUNIO

LA RIOJA

FORMOSA

JANGADERO

CORRIENTES

1° DE MAYO

ENTRE RÍOS

9 DE JULIO

URUGUIZA

TUCUMÁN

LA PAMPA

PETERIBI

CANAFISTOLA

PALO ROSA

INGA

TIMBO

PARAISO

JUAN M. DE ROSAS

BERNABE MENDEZ

A. G. BORTENICH

DTA. C. GRIERSON

FRAY STA. M. DE ORO

SAN L. DE LOYOLA

SARGENTO CABRAL

DIEGO DE BORDA

ANIBAL MORETI

F. VARELA

H. DE CAPRI

ARTURO ILLIA

TAMBOR DE TACUARÍ

DRA. M. SCHWARY

MARMELRO

BASINO BRAÑAS

UMA

ROSETTI

LOCALIZA

TELECOM

AEROLÍNEAS
ARGENTINAS/AUSTRAL

SECRETARÍA DE TURISMO

BANCO DE MISIONES

POST
OFFICE

Plaza
San Martín

PEÑON

ENTE MUNICIPAL
DE TURISMO

AV. MISIONES

BRASIL

BORDLAND

SAN MARTÍN

AV. CÓRDOBA

URUGUAY

FÉLIX DE AZARA

YAPEYÚ

SAN LORENZO

F.L. BELTRAN

HOTEL TIERRA
COLORADA

EL URU

EL MENSU

BRAZILIAN
CONSULATE

HOTEL ALEXANDER

HOSTERÍA SAN
FERNANDO

AV. GUARANI

HOSTERÍA CASA
BLANCA IGUAZÚ

RESIDENCIAL PAQUITA

PIZZA COLOR / TURISMO CUENCA
DEL PLATA

HOSTERÍA
LOS HELECHOS

RESIDENCIAL LILIAN

RESIDENCIAL UNO

RESIDENCIAL
LOS AMIGOS

HIPOLITO HIRIGOYEN

BELGRANO

POMBERO

TAREFEROS

ANDRESITO

AV. PTE. PERÓN

H. QUIROGA

E. LÓPEZ

EL PINDÓ

GÜIRES

AGUAY

LOS CEDROS

LOS YERBALES

REP. ARGENTINA

IND. J. ROMANO

M. MORENO

AV. AGUIRRE

CURUPI

JARDIN DEL
IGUAZÚ

EL TIO
QUERIDO

EL CIELO

P. MORENO

SOUTHERN
WINDS

HOTEL
SAINT GEORGE

LA ESQUINA

CORRECAMINOS IGUAZÚ

CHARO

LA RUEDA

BUS
TERMINAL

J. P. AMARANTE

To Parque Nacional Iguazú
and Foz do Iguaçu (Brazil)

SCALE NOT AVAILABLE

© AVALON TRAVEL PUBLISHING, INC.

entire continent, its only challenger in corruption is the tripartite Amazonian border of Brazil, Colombia, and Peru.

Here, linked by bridges and other less-conspicuous crossings on the two rivers, residents of the three Southern Cone countries pass freely, sustaining plenty of legitimate international trade but also enormous amounts of contraband weapons, drugs, and money. Money is a particularly contentious point, as Brazil- and Paraguay-based merchants of Middle Eastern origins reportedly have financial links to groups like Hamas and Hezbollah, though there have been no terrorist incidents in this area.

This does not mean that the area is unsafe to visit, and most travelers consider Puerto Iguazú positively placid. Devaluation of all three countries' currencies have made the area inexpensive but, while Foz do Iguaçu probably has the best hotels and restaurants, the Brazilian city also has a street-crime problem, particularly at night.

Orientation and Sights

Puerto Iguazú (population 31,371) is about 300 kilometers northeast of Posadas via RN 12, a paved toll road that is gradually being widened; it is 1,287 kilometers north of Buenos Aires. Note that because of widespread smuggling in the Tres Fronteras area, there are thorough Gendarmería (Border Guard) inspections about 30 kilometers south of town.

Unlike the great majority of Argentine cities, Puerto Iguazú lacks a standard grid with a central plaza; instead, it has an irregular plan of triangles, diagonals, and curving streets. The main thoroughfare is the diagonal Avenue Victoria Aguirre, which enters town from the southeast and becomes Avenida Tres Fronteras. Most services are on or north of Aguirre and Tres Fronteras.

At the west end of Avenida Tres Fronteras, the **Hito Argentino** is an obelisk that triangulates the Paraná-Iguazú confluence with similar markers in Brazil and Paraguay, both of which are visible from here.

Accommodations

Puerto Iguazú has abundant accommodations and, while they are even more abundant in Foz

do Iguaçu, many visitors prefer Puerto Iguazú's small-town ambience to the larger Brazilian city's fast-paced and occasionally dangerous lifestyle. Generally, Puerto Iguazú's best places are on the outskirts of town, on the road to the park.

While Puerto Iguazú gets quite a few visitors all year round, demand is highest during Semana Santa and the Argentine patriotic holidays in July, when prices tend to rise.

Under US$10

Two campgrounds on the road to the park offer decent facilities for around US$2–3 pp plus US$2–3 per tent: **Camping El Pindó** (RN 12 Km 3.5, tel. 03757/421795) and **Camping Americano** (RN 12 Km 5, tel. 03757/420190).

Puerto Iguazú has several fine hostel accommodations. **Correcaminos Iguazú** (Paulino Amarante 48, tel. 03757/420967, info@correcaminos.com.ar, www.correcaminos.com.ar) is a bargain at US$3.50 pp for dormitory accommodations with great common spaces, including a high-ceiling bar with a pool table, and spacious grounds. No longer an official HI affiliate, **Residencial Uno** (Fray Luis Beltrán 116, tel. 03757/420529, alberguuno@iguazunet.com, US$3.50 pp with breakfast) is by no means bad and usually has a good crowd, but it lacks the appealing common facilities of the Correcaminos.

Set in sprawling grounds on a quiet block, **Residencial Los Amigos** (Fray Luis Beltrán 82, tel. 03757/420756, infoamigos@vol.com.ar, US$3–5 pp) has both hostel-style accommodations and simple rooms with private bath.

The reception can be indifferent at **Residencial Lilián** (Fray Luis Beltrán 183, tel. 03757/420968, lilian@iguazunet.com), but when improvements on already comfortable place finally end, it will be an even better value than it is now, at US$5.50/9 s/d with shared bath; rooms with private bath are slightly dearer. The rooms themselves, with two or three beds each, surround lushly landscaped patios and the two-story building has wide external corridors that provide shelter from searing sun and subtropical storm alike.

Convenient to the bus terminal, **Residencial Paquita** (Avenida Córdoba 158, tel. 03757/420434, US$7/9 s/d) is a friendlier family hostelry, with personalized attention. Nearby **Hostería San Fernando** (Avenida Córdoba and Guaraní, tel. 03757/421429, US$7/10.50 s/d) deserves consideration if Paquita's full.

US$10–25

Well-worn **Hotel Tierra Colorada** (El Urú 28, tel. 03757/420649, hoteltierra@iguazunet.com, US$9/14 s/d) looks better outside than in, with spartan furnishings including firm beds, but it's quiet, the rooms are sizeable and have a/c, there's secure parking, and it serves a decent breakfast. The hot water supply is spotty, though, because of a firewood-stoked hot water system and erratic water pressure.

Under new management, **Hostería Casa Blanca Iguazú** (Avenida Guaraní 121, tel. 03757/421320, casablancaiguazu@arnet.com.ar, www.casablancaiguazu.com.ar, US$12/16 s/d) is a plain but comfortable alternative.

Like many of its competitors, the motel-style **Residencial La Cabaña** (Av Tres Fronteras 434, tel. 420564, lacabanahotel@hotmail.com, US$11/17 s/d) is also well-worn, but boasts luxuriant grounds and a quiet location.

Reservations are advisable for popular, efficient **M Hostería Los Helechos** (Paulino Amarante 76, tel. 03757/420338, info@hosterialoshelechos.com.ar, www.hosterialoshelechos.com.ar, US$14/16 s/d), an excellent value that's often crowded even off-season. The rooms are in a delightful garden setting, with a large pool and other amenities.

Though a little worn and lacking style, **Hotel Alexander** (Avenida Córdoba 222, tel./fax 03757/420249, alexanderhotel@foznet.com.br, US$17/19 s/d) is still comfortable, with lush gardens, a large swimming pool, and secure parking. Rates are fair enough.

US$25–50

One of Puerto Iguazú's best midrange choices is the tastefully modernized **M Hotel Saint George** (Avenida Córdoba 148, tel. 03757/420633, reservas@hotelsaintgeorge.com, www.hotelsaintgeorge.com, US$26/34 s/d in high season).

At the west end of town, enjoying views of the confluence, **Hotel Esturión** (Avenida Tres Fronteras 650, tel. 03757/420100, hotelesturion@iguazunet.com) charges US$29 s or d with garden vistas or US$29/38 s/d with river views; breakfast is included.

US$50–100

East of Puerto Iguazú, **Hotel Cataratas** (RN 12 Km 4.5, tel. 03757/421100, fax 03757/421090, hotel.cataratas@fnn.net, hotelcataratas@iguazunet.com, www.hotelcataratas.com.ar, US$40/50 s/d) will win no truth-in-labeling awards—it's far closer to town than to the world-famous cascades, and the only falls here are the bogus ones that tumble into its oversize swimming pool. Still, the rooms are large and well-equipped, and the rates are commensurate with its facilities.

Food

Al fresco eating is the norm in Puerto Iguazú, at least in the morning or after the sun sets, and every place has at least some outdoor seating. At lunchtime, when many if not most visitors are in the national park, indoor a/c is more than welcome.

For breakfast, try the **Fechorías** (Eppens 294, tel. 03757/420182), which has sidewalk tables. Its patio particularly packed at dinnertime, **Pizza Color** (Avenida Córdoba 135, tel. 03757/420206) serves a diversity of pizzas.

Puerto Iguazú has several *parrillas,* all of which are pretty good: **Jardín del Iguazú** (Avenida Córdoba and Avenida Misiones, tel. 03757/423200), conveniently alongside the bus terminal; **Charo** (Avenida Córdoba 106, tel. 03757/421529); and **El Tío Querido** (Bonpland s/n, tel. 03757/420750), immediately north of the high-rise Hotel Libertador.

The Hotel St. George's **M La Esquina** (Avenida Córdoba 148, tel. 03757/421597) serves the best food in town, with starters like *jamón crudo* (raw ham) for around US$2.50 and entrees like grilled *surubí* (river fish) in the US$3–5 range. The service, though, can be erratic and even absent-minded. **La Rueda** (Avenida Córdoba 28, tel. 03757/422531) also serves fine grilled fish but is otherwise unimpressive.

Information

There's a helpful provincial **Secretaría de Turismo** (Avenida Victoria Aguirre 311, tel. 03757/420800, 7 A.M.–10 P.M. daily). The local Ente Municipal de Turismo has offices at the bus terminal (tel. 03757/423006, int. 106, 8 A.M.–8 P.M. daily) and downtown (Avenida Tres Fronteras 222, tel. 03757/420113, emturiguazu@yahoo.com.ar, 7 A.M.–1 P.M. weekdays only).

For motorists, **ACA** (tel. 03757/420165) is on the southeastern outskirts of town, just beyond Camping El Pindó.

Services

Banco de Misiones has an ATM at Avenida Victoria Aguirre 330.

Correo Argentino is at Avenida San Martín 780; the postal code is 3370.

Telecom has a large *locutorio* with Internet access at Avenida Victoria Aguirre and Eppens, but connections are very slow here. **El Cielo** is a spacious new Internet café at the corner of Avenida Misiones and Bonpland.

For tours on both the Argentine and Brazilian sides, and into nearby Paraguay as well, try **Turismo Cuenca del Plata** (Paulino Amarante 76, tel. 03757/421062).

Hospital Marta Teodora Shwartz (tel. 03757/420288) is at Avenida Victoria Aguirre and Ushuaia.

Getting There

Air services are in flux since the collapse of LAPA, but bus services are reliable.

Aerolíneas Argentinas/Austral (Avenida Victoria Aguirre 295, tel. 03757/420237) flies several times daily to Aeroparque (Buenos Aires), but Aerolíneas no longer operates international flights from here.

Southern Winds (Perito Moreno 184, Local 2, tel. 03757/420390) also flies to Aeroparque.

Puerto Iguazú's **Terminal de Ómnibus** is on Avenida Córdoba between Avenida Misiones and Belgrano (tel. 03757/420854). In addition to long-distance services throughout Argentina, it is also the terminal for local buses to Foz do Iguaçu (Brazil) and Ciudad del Este (Paraguay), but

note that some nationalities need visas to cross the border.

Sample destinations, fares, and times include Posadas (US$8, 4.5 hours), Corrientes (US$15, nine hours), Resistencia (US$16, 9.5 hours), Buenos Aires (US$24–29, 16.5 hours), and Salta (US$35, 22.5 hours).

Getting Around

Aeropuerto Internacional Iguazú is about 10 kilometers southeast of town. Several local agencies have combined their services to offer airport transfers as Four Tourist Travel, for US$2.50 pp. A *remise* costs about US$7.

El Práctico **buses** to Parque Nacional Iguazú (US$1) operate between 7:15 A.M. and 8 P.M., taking 45 minutes to the park. To Foz do Iguaçu (US$1.10), there are frequent buses with Celeste, Tres Fronteras, Risa, and El Práctico; travelers who must go through border formalities must usually disembark on the Brazilian side and wait for the succeeding bus (of any company) at no additional charge.

Rental **bicycles** are available on Plaza San Martín.

For car rental, try **Localiza** (Avenida Victoria Aguirre 271, tel. 03757/423780 or 422436, localiza_igr@arnet.com.ar).

PARQUE NACIONAL DO IGUAÇU (BRAZIL)

By consensus, the Brazilian side of the border offers the best panoramas of the falls, even if the Argentine side provides better close-ups. Fauna, flora, and services are similar on both sides, but the Brazilian side has fewer easily accessible areas for roaming. The best views are available along the trail leading from Hotel Tropical das Cataratas down to the riverside overlook.

Like the Argentine side, its infrastructure has undergone considerable changes in recent years, with private vehicles consigned to parking lots, and shuttle buses carrying passengers to the falls. One unchanged feature is the noisy 10-minute helicopter overflights (US$60 pp) which, complain Argentine authorities, disrupt nesting birds and other wildlife.

CROSSING TO BRAZIL

Many visitors to Misiones also cross to the Brazilian side of Iguazú Falls, which involves a different set of immigration rules and travel conditions. Here are some basic pointers.

Visas and Officialdom

In the controversial Triple Frontier area, border-crossing regulations can change frequently. Traditionally, visitors entering Brazil for less than 24 hours, simply to visit the Brazilian side of the falls, have crossed freely even when their nationality would require them to obtain an advance visa. According to the Brazilian consulate in San Francisco, the Policía Federal (which enforces the country's immigration laws at the border) can be flexible in this matter, but it falls into a grey area for nationalities that normally must have visas. If in doubt, get the proper visa.

If at all possible, get the Brazilian visa in your home country, where consulates normally issue five-year, multiple-entry visas; if you apply elsewhere, you may get only a 90-day multiple-entry visa. In either case, the first entry to Brazil *must* take place within 90 days of issue, or the visa becomes invalid. Depending on the applicant's nationality, Brazilian consulates require a variable processing fee, which is refunded if the visa is not granted.

Open 7 A.M.–noon weekdays only, Puerto Iguazú's Brazilian Consulate (Avenida Córdoba 264, tel. 03757/421273) is only half a block from the bus terminal. Service is fast, taking only about an hour, and requires two passport-sized photographs. However, it accepts only Argentine pesos and, because of the volatility of exchange rates, builds itself a cushion against devaluation: in March of 2003, for example, the processing fee for U.S. citizens was US$100, but the consulate exchange rate was Ar$4.40 to the dollar, as opposed to Ar$3 at Argentine banks and exchange houses; this meant that the fee was closer to US$150. Other nationalities requiring visas (at the above fixed exchange rate) included Japanese (US$50), Canadians (US$40), Australians (US$35), and Mexicans (US$30), but in practice these fees may be nearly 50 percent higher. Other nationalities needing advance visas pay US$20.

Argentine authorities have been checking the documents of border crossers carefully, the Brazilians less so. While crossing to Brazil for the day without an advance visa *may* be possible, if you have a valid visa, you *must* get a Brazilian stamp in your passport. Buses stop to wait on the Argentine side but not on the Brazilian side; if you need a Brazilian stamp, you may have to wait for the next bus. In this instance, the driver will provide you a chit to continue on the following one.

Health and Safety

Public health conditions are not dramatically different on the Brazilian side of the river, but travelers continuing north into Brazil may want to consider prophylaxis for malaria and other tropical diseases.

Note that auto theft is common in the Triple Frontier area, carjackings have taken place on the Brazilian side, and street crime is more common in Foz do Iguaçu than in Puerto Iguazú. It's better to leave your vehicle in secure parking on the Argentine side and take a bus or hire a taxi or *remise* to the Brazilian side of the falls.

Money and Prices

The Brazilian currency is the *real* (plural *reis*), which is roughly at par with the Argentine peso. In practice, the two currencies circulate almost interchangeably, while the Paraguayan *guaraní* is also acceptable tender. Most businesses, such as hotels and restaurants, also accept U.S. dollars.

Brazilian prices, however, may be slightly higher for comparable services than those in Argentina.

Miscellaneous

Brazilians speak Portuguese rather than Spanish. Travelers with a command of Spanish may be able to read Portuguese, but speaking and understanding it may be more problematic.

At certain times of the year, Argentina is an hour behind Brazil so that, for example, 7 A.M. in Brazil may be 6 A.M. in Argentina.

Brazil's telephone country code is 55; Foz's city code is 045.

The park's only accommodations are at the ℕ **Hotel Tropical das Cataratas** (tel. 45/521-7000, fax 45/574-1688, reservas.iguassu@tropicalhotel.com.br, www.tropicalhotel.com.br, US$146/168 s/d), oozing a tasteful tropicality that the Argentine park's concrete Sheraton bunker can hardly conceive of.

Payable in Brazilian currency only, the park admission charge is equivalent to US$1 for local residents, US$4 for other Brazilians, US$6 for residents of other Mercosur countries, and US$7 for all other foreigners. The park is open 8 A.M.–6 P.M. daily.

From Puerto Iguazú's terminal, take any Celeste, Tres Fronteras, Risa, or El Práctico **bus** over the Puente Internacional Tancredo Neves, the bridge over the Río Iguazú. These buses go to downtown Foz do Iguaçú's local bus terminal, at Avenida Juscelino Kubitschek and Rua Mem de Sá, where Transbalan city buses leave directly for the park. Park-bound passengers from Argentina, however, can disembark at the junction with Avenida das Cataratas, just north of the bridge, and take the Transbalan bus to the park entrance.

FOZ DO IGUAÇU

Compared with pastoral Puerto Iguazú, Foz do Iguaçu is a frantic, fast-moving center of commerce and construction that's grown almost uncontrollably as a result of Itaipú dam, a joint Brazilian-Paraguayan effort that's the Iguazú of hydroelectric projects. Foz has a broader range of services than Puerto Iguazú—with a capacity of 22,000 hotel beds—but lacks the Argentine town's greenery.

Foz's unbridled growth has also focused Brazil's serious social problems here—its downtown streets can be unsafe at night, and its riverside *favelas* (shantytowns) should be avoided at any hour. It's also drawn unfavorable attention for alleged connections to Middle Eastern terrorism: when the Brazilian magazine *Veja* published a report that Osama bin Laden had been seen in Foz some years earlier, local merchants responded with an ironic full-page ad with a photo of the Al Qaeda leader and the caption "if bin Laden visited

Foz, it's because it was worth the trouble." Municipal authorities, though, were livid about the article, which they called unsubstantiated.

Orientation

At the northern confluence of the Rio Iguaçu and the Rio Paraná, Foz do Iguaçu (population 205,000) is immediately north of Puerto Iguazú (Argentina) and immediately east of Ciudad del Este (Paraguay). The Ponte Presidente Tancredo Neves, across the Rio Iguaçú, links the city to Puerto Iguazú, while the Ponte da Amizade crosses the Paraná to Ciudad del Este.

From downtown Foz, the diagonal Avenida das Cataratas leads southeast toward Parque Nacional do Iguaçu and the bridge to Argentina.

Usina Hidrelétrica Itaipú

Other than the Brazilian side of the falls, Foz's biggest attraction—literally—is Itaipú, the world's largest hydroelectric project, 15 kilometers up the Paraná from the city. As a cheap source of hydroelectricity, its legacy is a mixed one; its construction drowned the Sete Quedas, a series of waterfalls that rivaled Iguazú in their dramatic scenery and ecological significance.

Eight kilometers across, with a maximum height of 196 meters, Itaipú is nearly three times the height of Iguazú; with an installed capacity of 12,600 megawatts, it can produce more than one trillion kilowatts of power hourly. Since Paraguay's energy needs are much lower than those of Brazil, Brazil purchases Paraguay's unused portion.

Free guided tours of the Brazilian side take place at 8, 9, and 10 A.M., and at 2 and 3:30 P.M. daily except Sunday; for more information, contact the **Centro de Recepcão de Visitantes** (Avenida Tancredo Neves 6702, tel. 45/520-6398, www.itaipu.gov.br), 10 kilometers north of Foz. From Foz's municipal bus terminal, the Conjunto C bus goes directly to the visitors center via Avenida Juscelino Kubitschek, also stopping at the project's **Ecomuseu** (Avenida Tancredo Neves 6001, tel. 45/520-5813, 9–11:30 A.M. and 2–5:30 P.M. daily except Sunday), an archaeology and natural history museum.

Accommodations

Foz suffers from an overcapacity of accommodations, with 22,000 hotel beds in a city that rarely hosts more than about 5,000 visitors. That means there are some good deals, but many travelers still prefer the Argentine side for its tranquility.

The HI affiliate is the remarkable **M Albergue da Juventude Paudimar** (Avenida das Cataratas, Km 12.5, tel. 45/529-6061, www.paudimar.com .br); see the sidebar "Resort Hostelling in Brazil" for details.

Downtown Foz's best budget option is still the traditional favorite **Pousada da Laura** (Naipi 671, tel. 45/572-3379, US$3.50 pp). **Hotel Tarobá** (Rua Tarobá 1048, tel. 574-3890, US$7/13 s/d) also offers good value; the nearby **Hotel Del Rey** (Rua Tarobá 1020, tel. 45/523-2027, US$11/15 s/d) provides more-spacious rooms and a swimming pool.

Each room at the modern **Hotel Bella Italia** (Avenida República Argentina 1700, tel. 45/523-5300, fax 45/574-4737, bellaitalia@foznet.com .ar, www.hotelbellaitalia.com, US$40/47 s/d) is spacious, spotless, and well-furnished, and comes with a small balcony. It's an exceptional value for a first-rate place.

On almost sprawling, luxuriantly landscaped grounds, the five-star **Bourbon Cataratas Resort & Convention** (Avenida das Cataratas Km 2.5, tel. 45/529-0123, fax 45/529-0000, bourbon .iguassufalls@fnn.net, US$84 s or d) is a legitimate luxury hotel with prices to prove it.

Food

For breakfast, pastries, and short orders, try **Maria's and Maria Confeitaria** (Avenida Brasil 505, tel. 45/574-5472). For vegetarian specialties, there's the inexpensive buffet at **Ver o Verde** (Almirante Barroso 1713, tel. 45/574-5647).

The Brazilian equivalent to Argentina's *parrilla* is the *churascarria,* where grilled beef is the norm. The best choice is **Búfalo Branco** (Rebouças 530, tel. 45/574-5115), but the popular and cheaper **Bier Garten Chopparia** (Avenida Jorge Schimmelpfeng 550, tel. 45/523-3700) also serves pizza and cold draft beer.

Brazil has a large Japanese immigrant community, so specialties like sushi are common here. Two good choices are **Miyako** (Rua Décio Luiz Cardoso 469, tel. 45/523-5724), and the more-expensive **Nissei** (Avenida Juscelino Kubitschek 98, tel. 45/523-3121).

Brazilian ice cream differs from Argentina's in that it features many more tropical-fruit flavors in addition to the standard vanillas and chocolates. For a sample, sold by weight, check out **Ofic-**

RESORT HOSTELLING IN BRAZIL

Sprawling over 16,000 square meters, **Paudimar** is more than just a youth hostel. In fact, it feels more like a destination-in-itself holiday camp, what with its poolside bar, lighted soccer field, buffet breakfast, and nightly buffet dinner, served en masse at 8 P.M. sharp (Brazilians dine earlier than Argentines), for an additional US$2.50 (not including drinks).

Many indolent backpackers spend a week or more here, and those who are *really* on a shoestring can use a separate kitchen to cook for themselves. There are plenty of good hostels in Argentina (and Brazil, for that matter), but Paudimar arguably offers the best value among them.

In addition to its on-site services, Paudimar has managed to persuade the city of Foz do Iguaçu to provide a free shuttle from the main bus line on Avenida das Cataratas to the hostel. It also provides daily transportation to the Argentine side of the falls (US$7 round-trip), leaving the hostel at 8:30 A.M. and returning at 6 P.M.

For HI members, rates with breakfast included are US$3.50 pp for dormitory accommodations, US$5 pp for multibedded rooms with shared bath and ceiling fans, US$7 pp for rooms with private bath and a/c; nonmembers pay slightly more.

ina do Sorvete (Avenida Jorge Schimmelpfeng 244, tel. 45/572-1772).

Information and Services

The downtown office of the **Secretaria Municipal de Turismo** (Praça Getúlio Vargas 260, tel. 45/521-1461, turismo@fozdoiguacu.pr.gov.br, www.fozdoiguacu.pr.gov.br, 7 A.M.–11 P.M. daily) has capable English- and Spanish-speaking staff, plus maps, brochures, and detailed hotel information.

Cambio Leocadio (Avenida Brasil 71) changes both cash and travelers checks (with a three percent commission). **Bamerindus** has an ATM at Almirante Barroso and Xavier da Silva.

Foz's post office is on the east side of Praça Getúlio Vargas, at the corner of Avenida Juscelino Kubitschek and Rio Branco. For international phone calls, try **Telepar** (Marechal Floriano Peixoto 1222).

The Argentine consulate (Travessa Eduardo Bianchi 26, tel. 45/574-2969) is open 10 A.M.– 2:30 P.M. weekdays. Paraguay's consulate (Bartolomeu de Gusmão 738, tel. 45/523-2898) is open 8:30 A.M.–5:30 P.M. weekdays.

Getting There and Around

TAM Mercosur (Rio Branco 640, tel. 45/523-8500) flies out of Ciudad del Este to the Paraguayan capital of Asunción, where there are connections to other South American capitals and to various Brazilian cities; Foz do Iguaçu itself has no air services at present.

Buses to destinations elsewhere in Brazil leave from the Rodoviária (tel. 45/522-2950), six kilometers northeast of downtown on Avenida Costa e Silva.

Local buses use the city bus terminal at Avenida Juscelino Kubitschek and Rua Mem de Sá. Buses to Parque Nacional do Iguaçu, the Rodoviária, Itaipú, and Puerto Iguazú all leave from here, though it's possible to catch them elsewhere along their routes.

Santa Fe Province

Historian Ezequiel Gallo has called wealthy Santa Fe Province the *pampa gringa* for its transformation from humid grasslands into one of the world's great granaries, under the influence of European immigration. Today, its attractions for foreign visitors are primarily urban, in the cities of Rosario and the provincial capital of Santa Fe, but the middle Paraná Delta remains to be explored. There is a new bridge and causeway connection with Entre Ríos Province from Rosario.

ROSARIO

Possibly Argentina's most underrated city, the economic powerhouse of Rosario is an industrial city and a major port for grains from the so-called *pampa gringa,* but it also boasts one of the country's liveliest cultural scenes, with first-rate museums, art, theater, and live music. Among its many creative artists have been comedian Alberto Olmedo, actress Libertad Lamar-

que, actor Darío Grandinetti, and pop musician Fito Páez.

For nationalistic Argentines, Rosario is the "Cuna de la Bandera," (Cradle of the Flag), the city where General Manuel Belgrano designed and first displayed the colors that still wave over the republic today. For Rosarinos themselves, it's the country's "second city," though they may have to argue the point with residents of Córdoba.

History

The first Europeans settled here around 1720, moving southward from the city of Santa Fe. Following the civil wars of the mid-19th century, the railroad to Córdoba made Rosario a major port and spurred agricultural colonization through the Central Argentine Land Company. New European settlers arrived directly from Europe rather than through Buenos Aires, and by the early 20th century Rosario's population of more than 200,000 exceeded that of Santa Fe.

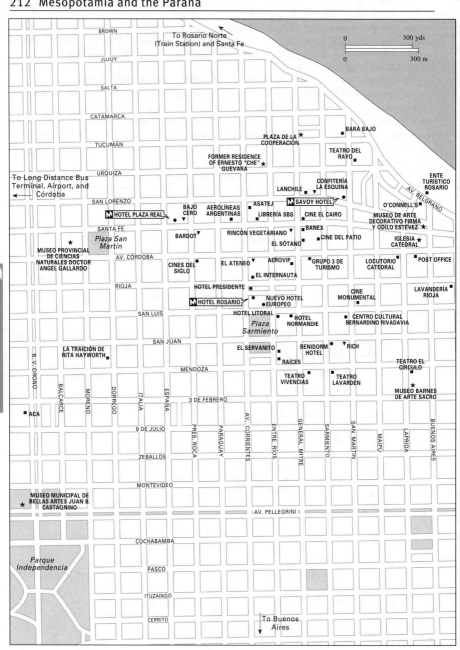

BROWN

To Rosario Norte
(Train Station) and Santa Fe

0   300 yds
0   300 m

JUJUY

SALTA

CATAMARCA

TUCUMÁN

BARA BAJO

PLAZA DE LA ★
COOPERACIÓN

TEATRO DEL
RAYO

FORMER RESIDENCE
OF ERNESTO "CHE" ★
GUEVARA

URQUIZA

ENTE
TURÍSTICO
ROSARIO

To Long Distance Bus
Terminal, Airport, and
Córdoba

CONFITERÍA
LA ESQUINA

LANCHILE

AV. BELGRANO

SAN LORENZO

O'CONNELL'S

BAJO
CERO

AEROLÍNEAS
ARGENTINAS

ASATEJ

SAVOY HOTEL

HOTEL PLAZA REAL

MUSEO DE ARTE
DECORATIVO FIRMA
Y ODILO ESTÉVEZ ★

SANTA FE

LIBRERÍA SBS

CINE EL CAIRO

BANEX

IGLESIA ★
CATEDRAL

Plaza San
Martín

BARDOT

RINCÓN VEGETARIANO

CINE DEL PATIO

EL SÓTANO

MUSEO PROVINCIAL
DE CIENCIAS ★
NATURALES DOCTOR
ANGEL GALLARDO

AV. CÓRDOBA

CINES DEL
SIGLO

EL ATENEO

AEROVIP

GRUPO 3 DE
TURISMO

LOCUTORIO
CATEDRAL

POST OFFICE

RIOJA

EL INTERNAUTA

LAVANDERÍA
RIOJA

HOTEL PRESIDENTE

HOTEL ROSARIO

NUEVO HOTEL
EUROPEO

CINE
MONUMENTAL

SAN LUIS

HOTEL LITORAL

HOTEL
NORMANDIE

CENTRO CULTURAL
BERNARDINO RIVADAVIA

Plaza
Sarmiento

SAN JUAN

LA TRAICIÓN DE
RITA HAYWORTH

EL SERVANITO

BENIDORM
HOTEL

RICH

RAÍCES

TEATRO EL
CÍRCULO

MENDOZA

TEATRO
VIVENCIAS

TEATRO
LAVARDEN

MUSEO BARNES
DE ARTE SACRO ★

3 DE FEBRERO

ACA

9 DE JULIO

B.V. ORONO
BALCARCE
MORENO
DORREGO
ITALIA
ESPAÑA
PRES. ROCA
PARAGUAY
AV. CORRIENTES
ENTRE RÍOS
GENERAL MITRE
SARMIENTO
SAN MARTÍN
MAIPÚ
LAPRIDA
BUENOS AIRES

ZEBALLOS

MONTEVIDEO

MUSEO MUNICIPAL DE
BELLAS ARTES JUAN B. ★
CASTAGNINO

AV. PELLEGRINI

COCHABAMBA

Parque
Independencia

PASCO

ITUZAINGÓ

CERRITO

To Buenos
Aires

Because of its late growth, the best parts of Rosario's cityscape reflect that era's Francophile preferences—or pretensions.

Orientation

On the west bank of the Paraná, Rosario (population 906,004) is 320 kilometers northwest of Buenos Aires via RN 9, a paved four-lane toll road which also leads west to Córdoba (as a two-lane highway). It is 167 kilometers south of Santa Fe via A-008, another four-lane toll road, and now linked to the nearby city of Victoria, Entre Ríos, via a new 57-kilometer series of bridges and causeways across the Paraná Delta.

Sensibly sited Rosario mostly occupies the high ground above the Paraná floodplain; on the floodplain itself, most structures are port facilities or recycled port facilities, set among open green spaces. Shady Plaza 25 de Mayo is not quite typical of the densely built downtown, but it enjoys pleasant pedestrian malls on streets like San Martín and Córdoba. Beyond the downtown core, tree-lined streets and open spaces like the enormous Parque Independencia are the rule.

Monumento Nacional a la Bandera

The most famous—and overwhelming—of Rosario's monuments pays tribute to the Argentine flag and its designer Manuel Belgrano at the colossal Monumento Nacional a la Bandera, bounded by Santa Fe, Rosas, Córdoba, and the Avenida Belgrano (Santa Fe 581, tel. 0341/480-2238, 9 A.M.–7 P.M. daily, except Mon., 2–7 P.M.). It's tempting to call this colossal homage to the Argentine flag a monumental failure or even a shrine to kitsch, as the outline of architect Angel Guido's design represents a ship on whose symbolic mast is a 78-meter tower on its bow. Alfredo Bigatti and José Fioravanti sculpted the patriotic statues that adorn it, while Eduardo Barnes carved the bas-reliefs depicting the country's diverse geography.

The remains of General Manuel Belgrano, who designed the flag and first hoisted it here, lie in a vault at the base of the tower, but the pseudo-grandeur of the monument overshadows

CHE'S FIRST HOME?

Alejandro Bustillo, the architect of Bariloche's landmark Centro Cívico, designed the apartment block at **Entre Ríos 480.** The handsome building, though, is famous not so much for its designer as for the controversy it has engendered as the presumptive birthplace of the famous revolutionary Ernesto "Che" Guevara.

Guevara, of course, is a polemical figure in Argentine (and world) history, with adoring admirers and fierce detractors. Any controversy over whether to honor him here, though, is something of a bogus issue: According to Jon Lee Anderson's exhaustive biography, Che was born in the northern province of Misiones in May 1928, even though his parents registered his birth—officially and falsely—in Rosario on June 14 of that year. Certainly Che slept at this address, though.

Still, Che remains a presence in Rosario—in 2003, the city council presented his Cuban-born daughter Aleida Guevara with a post-mortem "illustrious citizen" award in her father's name. For an idea of how his partisans revere him, visit the watchful mural portrait at **Plaza de la Cooperación,** at the corner of Mitre and Tucumán.

his own unpretentious achievement. Catalina de Vidal actually sewed the original flag, now preserved in the structure's museum. Every June, Rosario observes **La Semana de la Bandera** (Flag Week), which culminates with ceremonies on June 20, the anniversary of Belgrano's death.

For a panoramic view of the Paraná waterfront, it's possible to take the elevator to the top of the tower. Admission to the tower of the Monumento Nacional a la Bandera costs US$.35. A military color guard raises the flag daily at 8:15 A.M. and lowers it at 7 P.M.

Other Sights and Activities

Rosario is a city of monuments and museums, ranging from the subtly unpretentious to the pompously patriotic. Most of these are in and around the city's several attractive parks, both along the waterfront and its bluffs, and farther inland. A handful of sights are scattered elsewhere through the downtown area.

Across Avenida Belgrano, the **Parque Nacional de la Bandera** stretches several blocks along the floodplain in an area that still houses part of Rosario's port facilities.

Continuing its policy of waterfront improvement, Rosario has dramatically upgraded its **Estación Fluvial,** the passenger terminal for the delta islands on Avenida Belgrano. It is home to the **Museo del Paraná y las Islas** (Avenida Belgrano and Rioja, tel. 0341/440-0751, 4–7:30 P.M. daily except Mon. and Tues., US$.35), the site of painter Raúl Domínguez's unassuming murals of delta lifestyles. The heart of its museum, which focuses on life on the river and in the delta, is the series of murals by Rosarino painter Raúl Domínguez.

Like the best muralists, Domínguez (known as "the painter of the river") deals with everyday themes rather than heroic deeds. Among his subjects are the environmental setting in panels such as *Creciente* (In Flood) and *Bajante* (In Drought), travels through the delta in *Recorrido del Paraná* (Exploring the Paraná), folklore in *El Paraná y Sus Leyendas* (The Paraná and Its Legends), and settlers' livelihoods in *Cortador de Paja* (Thatch Cutter) and *El Nutriero* (The Otter Trapper).

The terminal is also the departure point for two-hour river excursions (US$2) on the *Ciudad de Rosario* (tel. 0341/449-8688), which sails at 2:30 and 5 P.M. weekends and holidays.

Several blocks to the southeast, **Parque Urquiza** is the site of the **Complejo Astronómico Municipal** (Municipal Observatory, tel. 0341/480-2533). Although light pollution may make a large city like Rosario less than ideal for viewing the southern skies through the telescopes at its **Observatorio Víctor Capolongo,** visitors can stargaze free of charge from 8:30–10 P.M. weeknights. In the same building, the **Planetario Luis Cándido Carballo** charges US$.70 for its weekly Sunday programs at 8 P.M.

The **Museo Barnes de Arte Sacro** (Laprida 1235, tel. 0341/448-3784) exhibits Bible-themed sculptures from one of the contributors to the Monumento a la Bandera. Actually seeing them, though, can be problematic; museum hours are 4–6 P.M. Thursday only. For a more diverse collection of European art and artifacts (and more-flexible hours), check the **Museo de Arte Decorativo Firma y Odilo Estévez** (Santa Fe 748, tel. 0341/480-2547). Occupying a distinguished Italianate residence, it's open Friday, Saturday, and Sunday, 3–8 P.M.

Occupying the former Tribunales (Law Courts), a national monument dating from 1903) opposite Plaza San Martín, the **Museo Provincial de Ciencias Naturales Doctor Angel Gallardo** (Moreno 758, tel. 0341/472-1449) suffered a devastating fire in July 2003, losing some 70 percent of its natural history collections, and was closed as of writing.

The **Museo Municipal de Bellas Artes Juan B. Castagnino,** (Avenida Pellegrini 2202, tel. 0341/480-2542, museocastagnino@infovia.com .ar, 2–8 P.M. daily except Tues., US$.35) at the corner of Avenida Pellegrini and Blvd. Oroño, is the city's top fine arts museum. Housed in a spacious building dating from 1937, it boasts a diverse collection starting with a small assortment of European masters through 19th-century and later landscapes (both European and South American).

Its strength, though, is modern Argentine art both figurative and abstract, much of it by Rosarinos. Among the prominent artists on display are Prilidiano Pueyrredón, Benito Quinquela Martín, Antonio Berni, and Eduardo Schiavoni.

Immediately across Avenida Pellegrini from Parque Independencia, the museum also holds special rotating exhibits.

Parque Independencia is the city's top recreational area and home to several museums. Throngs of joggers and cyclists lope and pedal along footpaths and trails, while families float on paddle boats in this urban sanctuary that gets heavier recreational use than any other public park in Rosario. Having celebrated its centennial in 2002, the beautifully designed park offers 112 hectares of verdant open space with museums, a small zoo, a rose garden, tennis courts and other athletic fields, a hippodrome, and an important soccer stadium.

Covered with bright-red bougainvillea, a neo-classical pergola follows the shoreline of the lake on Blvd. Oroño where, nightly at 8:30 P.M., colored lights illuminate a fountain of **Aguas Danzantes,** or "dancing waters." Farther south, the **Museo de la Ciudad** (Blvd. Oroño 2350, tel. 0341/480-8665, 9 A.M.–noon weekdays except Mon., 3–6 P.M. weekends, free) focuses on the city's history.

Immediately west of the lake, the **Museo Histórico Provincial Doctor Julio Marc** (tel. 0341/472-1457, 9 A.M.–7 P.M. weekdays except Tuesday, 10 A.M.–1 P.M. weekends and holidays, free) features 30 separate rooms tracing regional development from the earliest cultures through the Spanish invasion and evangelization on the frontier, but its focus is the post-independence period.

Immediately west of the museum, the Newell's Old Boys soccer stadium is colloquially known as **El Coloso** (The Colossus). To its south, the park's largest single construction is the **Hipódromo Independencia,** the racetrack.

Entertainment

Rosario has a diversity of entertainment offerings. The "Cartelera" page of *Rosario/12,* the local edition of the left-of-center *porteño* daily *Página/12,* has the most-complete listings. The bookstore **El Ateneo** (Córdoba 1473) has a Ticketek outlet for purchasing seats.

For the latest updates on live music acts and venues in town, visit the website Rosario Rock (www.rosariorock.com).

The four-screen **Cine Monumental** (San Martín 999, tel. 0341/421-6289) shows recent films. Other cinemas include the multiscreen **Cines del Siglo** (Córdoba and Roca, tel. 0341/425-0761), **Cine del Patio** (Sarmiento 778), **Cine El Cairo** (Santa Fe 1120, tel.

0341/421-9180), and the art-house **Teatro del Rayo** (San Martín 473, tel. 0341/421-3980).

The **Centro Cultural Bernardino Rivadavia** (San Martín 1080, tel. 0341/480-2401) sponsors theater and dance events, along with films, and a large gallery showcases local artists.

Teatro El Círculo (Laprida and Mendoza, tel. 0341/424-5349) is one of the city's main performing arts theaters. **Teatro Lavarden** (Mendoza and Sarmiento, tel. 0341/472-1462) is another prestigious venue.

Teatro Vivencias (Mendoza 1173, tel. 217045) is a small experimental venue. Named for a Manuel Puig novel, **La Traición de Rita Hayworth** (Dorrego 1170, tel. 0341/448-0993) is another intimate local with unconventional offerings.

The bulk of Rosario's pubs and bars lie within a triangle formed by Avenida Belgrano, Avenida Corrientes, and Córdoba.

O'Connell's (Avenida Belgrano 716, tel. 0341/447-3979) is an Irish-style pub serving lunches (US$2), dinners (US$3), and imported beers. There's a 7–9 P.M. happy hour daily, and sidewalk seating as well.

El Sótano (Mitre 785) showcases live local music, normally on weekends. Try also **Bara Bajo** (San Martín 370).

Buy tickets for Newell's Old Boys, the main first-division soccer team, at **Estadio Parque Independencia** (Avenida Las Palmeras s/n, tel. 0341/421-1180). The city's second favorite, Rosario Central, plays at the north end of town at its namesake **Estadio Club Atlético Rosario Central** (Blvd. Avellaneda and Avenida Génova, tel. 0341/438-9595).

Shopping

On weekends and holidays, antiques and bric-a-brac fill the stalls at the **Mercado de Pulgas del Bajo,** a flea market at Avenida Belgrano and Buenos Aires.

For gaucho gear and other souvenirs, try **Raíces** (Mendoza and Entre Ríos) or **El Servanito** (Entre Ríos 1147).

Librería SBS (Santa Fe 1340, tel. 0341/426-1276) sells English-language books.

Accommodations

Amiable **Hotel Normandie** (Mitre 1030, tel./fax 0341/421-2694, hotelnormandie@ciudad.com.ar) has basic but spacious rooms with private bath for US$5.50/8 s/d with breakfast and a/c; rooms with TV cost US$7/11 s/d. In the post-devaluation era, the **M Savoy Hotel** (San Lorenzo 1022, tel. 0341/448-0071, savoy_hotel@arnet.com.ar, US$6.50/11 s/d) has become a budget travelers' favorite. It offers grand hotel nostalgia at a fraction of the cost.

For late arrivals or early departures, there are two decent budget choices almost immediately across from the long-distance bus terminal: **Hotel Esmeralda** (Pasaje Quintanilla 628, tel. 0341/437-3413, US$7/9 s/d) and **Hotel Gran Confort** (Pasaje Quintanilla 657, tel. 0341/438-0486, US$7/11 s/d).

Hotel Litoral (Entre Ríos 1043, tel. 0341/421-1426, hotel_litoral@hotmail.com, US$7/12 s/d) is a friendly, no-frills but clean budget option. Some of its 60 rooms boast balconies, but that's a mixed blessing, given the proximity of busy Plaza Sarmiento.

The **Benidorm Hotel** (San Juan 1049, tel. 0341/421-9368, US$11/18 s/d with private bath) is a good midrange choice. Rosario's best value, though, may be **M Hotel Rosario** (Ricardone 1365, tel. 0341/424-2170, hrosario@infovia.com.ar, www.rosario.com.ar./hotelrosario), on a short block with little traffic. Ample, well-maintained rooms with breakfast, private bath, a/c, cable TV and parking start at US$12 s, but better rooms go for only a little more, about US$16/18 s/d.

Deco-tinged **Nuevo Hotel Europeo** (San Luis 1364, tel. 0341/424-0382, nuevohoteleuropeo @ciudad.com.ar, US$16/22 s/d) has 90 spacious, well-lighted rooms with a/c, phone, TV, breakfast, and hideously garish wallpaper and coverings.

Hotel Presidente (Corrientes 919, tel./fax 0341/424-2545, hotelpresidente@solans.com, www.solans.com) is part of a chain of upscale but not-quite-luxurious business-oriented hotels with excellent service. Rates start at US$23/30 s/d, but try negotiating a lower rate, especially for longer stays.

The sparkling new ⊠ **Hotel Plaza Real** (Santa Fe 1632, tel./fax 0341/440-8800, reservas @plazarealhotel.com.ar, www.plazarealhotel.com, US$35/42 s/d with buffet breakfast) is a legitimate four-star hotel.

Food

Confitería La Esquina (Sarmiento 598) is a good option for breakfast and coffee. The bookstore **El Ateneo** (Córdoba 1473, tel. 0341/425-9306) has an outstanding café for sandwiches and desserts, but closes relatively early, around 9 P.M.

Rincón Vegetariano (Mitre 720, tel. 0341/411-0833) is a longstanding vegetarian favorite. **Rich** (San Juan 1031, tel. 0341/440-8657) is an excellent Italian restaurant, but its adjacent *rotisería* has equally fine (and cheaper) takeaway food.

With a Mediterranean focus, **Bardot** (Roca 749, tel. 0341/411-3363) prepares excellent fixed-price lunches (about US$3) of pasta, beef, chicken, or fish, with gracious service.   For a formal meal in attractive surroundings alongside the Estación Fluvial, try ⊠ **Muelle 1** (Avenida de los Inmigrantes 140, tel. 0341/426-3509). Entrees such as *surubí* start around US$4.50; service is highly professional.

Rosario's ice cream is not Argentina's finest, but **Bajo Cero** (Santa Fe and Roca, tel. 0341/425-1538) is a respectable choice.

Information and Services

The riverfront **Ente Turístico Rosario** (Etur, Avenida Belgrano and Buenos Aires, tel. 0341/480-2230, fax 0341/480-2237, info@rosarioturismo.com, www.rosarioturismo.com) is open 7 A.M.–7 P.M. daily. It has very good maps and obliging English-speaking staff.

For motorists, **ACA** is at Blvd. Oroño and 3 de Febrero, tel. 0341/421-0264.

ATMs are abundant in the downtown area. For cash and travelers checks, try **Banex** at Mitre 701.

Correo Argentino is at Córdoba 721; Rosario's postal code is 2000.

There are numerous phone offices, such as **Locutorio Catedral** (Córdoba 801). **El Inter-**

nauta (Rioja 1378, Local 7) has Internet connections, but again there are many more.

Student- and budget-oriented travel agency **Asatej** is at Corrientes 653, 6th floor (tel. 0341/423-3797, rosario@asatej.com.ar). **Grupo 3 de Turismo** (Córdoba 1147, tel. 0341/449-1783) is the AmEx representative.

Lavandería Rioja is at Rioja 607.

Hospital Clemente Alvarez is (Rueda 1110, tel. 0341/480-2111) is 18 blocks south of the pedestrian junction of Córdoba and San Martín.

Getting There

Rosario has air connections to Buenos Aires, other northern Argentine destinations, and Santiago de Chile, bus connections almost everywhere, and train connections to BA and Tucumán only.

Aerolíneas Argentinas (Santa Fe 1412, tel. 0341/424-9332) flies twice every weekday to Buenos Aires and once on Sunday. **Austral,** at the same address, flies Friday only. **Aerovip** (Mitre 830, Local 32, tel. 0341/449-6800) provides air-taxi service to Aeroparque (Buenos Aires).

LanChile (San Lorenzo 1116, tel. 0341/424-2828 or 0341/426-3232) flies Thursday afternoons to Santiago de Chile.

Rosario is a major hub for **overland transportation** from the **Estación Terminal de Ómnibus Mariano Moreno** (Cafferata 702, tel. 0341/437-2384, www.terminalrosario.com.ar), about 15 blocks west of Plaza San Martin.

Typical domestic destinations, fares, and times include Santa Fe (US$5, two hours), Buenos Aires (US$10, four hours), Córdoba (US$15, six hours), Mendoza (US$13–18, 11–14 hours), Resistencia (US$13, 10 hours), Salta (US$22, 15 hours), Puerto Iguazú (US$23, 18 hours), and Bariloche (US$33, 23 hours).

Rosario has **international bus services** to Asunción, Paraguay (US$16–19, 14 hours) with **Nuestra Señora de la Asunción** (tel. 0341/438-0038); to Curitiba and Rio de Janeiro, Brazil (US$61, 30 hours) with **Pluma** (tel. 0341/437-3152); and to Montevideo, Uruguay (US$22, 10 hours) with **El Rápido Internacional** (tel. 0341/435-3224) or **Encon** (tel. 0341/439-5894). Except for Asunción, these services are few outside the summer peak season.

Trains to Buenos Aires (US$4, 5.5 hours) leave Monday at 5:57 A.M. and Friday at 6:30 P.M. from **Estación Rosario Norte** (Avenida del Valle and Avenida Ovidio Lagos, tel. 0341/430-7272). Tucumán-bound trains (US$13) pass Rosario Norte at 2:40 A.M. Tuesday and Saturday.

Getting Around

Rosario's Aeropuerto Fisherton (tel. 0341/456-7997) is eight kilometers west of town; Aerolíneas Argentinas provides its own transfers, but public buses do not go any closer than about one kilometer from the airport. A taxi or *remise* costs about US$4.

Plaza Sarmiento is the hub of the **city bus** system, which now uses magnetic cards rather than coins. Bus No. 101 goes to the long-distance bus terminal, bus No. 120 to the Rosario Norte train station.

For car rental, **Hertz/Millet** is at Rioja 573 (tel. 0341/424-2408).

SANTA FE

Capital of its namesake province, the city of Santa Fe plays second fiddle to youthful Rosario in economics and culture, but the province's oldest city has a core of colonial monuments that no other nearby place can match. It also enjoys easy recreational access to the islands of the middle Paraná, thanks to a series of bridges that cross the river's tributaries to the city of Paraná, in Entre Ríos Province.

The river, though, is a mixed blessing, as Santa Fe is vulnerable to floods—in May 2003, a major inundation by the Río Salado killed dozens and displaced thousands, causing millions of dollars of economic damage—and even to desiccation, as shallow Laguna Setúbal nearly evaporated in 1964 for lack of rainfall in the upper Paraná drainage. The summer heat and humidity can make Santa Fe a sweatlodge of a city.

History

In 1573, southbound from Asunción in present-day Paraguay, Juan de Garay founded

Santa Fe de la Vera Cruz on the Río San Javier, a Paraná tributary near the site of present-day Cayastá, about 80 kilometers northwest of Santa Fe's present site. The first Santa Fe, though, proved insecure because its isolation exposed it to indigenous raiders, and the location was even more flood-prone than it is now. The ruling *cabildo* (town council) moved and rebuilt the city on the original plan; several significant colonial buildings remain, but others fell to the wrecking ball in a 19th-century Francophile construction boom and 20th-century redevelopment.

Orientation

Sited 10 kilometers east of the main channel of the Paraná, on the Río Santa Fe and shallow Laguna Setúbal, the city of Santa Fe (population 368,369) is 167 kilometers north of Rosario and 475 kilometers north of Buenos Aires via RN 11 and the *autopista* A-008. It is 25 kilometers west of the Entre Ríos provincial capital of Paraná via RN 168 and a subfluvial tunnel, and 544 kilometers south of Resistencia via RN 11.

When the heat permits, all of Santa Fe's historic core is on or within easy walking distance of Plaza 25 de Mayo. Avenida San Martín, the principal shopping street, is a pedestrian mall for seven blocks between Juan de Garay and Eva Perón.

Sights

The river and its tributaries are a palpable presence. One of Santa Fe's most offbeat sights, crossing Laguna Setúbal at the east end of Blvd. Gálvez, is the **Puente Colgante** (1928), the suspension bridge that linked the city to the islands and the city of Paraná until a 1983 flood damaged it beyond usability (pedestrians and bicycles can still cross it, but motor vehicles must use its reinforced-concrete replacement).

Four blocks west of the river, **Plaza 25 de Mayo** is the city's colonial, and contemporary, civic center. On the east side of the plaza, the lavish interior of the Jesuit **Iglesia de la Compañía** (1697, San Martín and Estanislao López) contrasts dramatically with its unadorned exterior. Returned to the Jesuit order in 1862 almost a century after their expulsion from the Americas in 1767, it's a national historical monument.

On the north side of the plaza, the twin-towered **Catedral Metropolitana** (1751, Estanislao López and San Gerónimo) is also a national historical monument. The south side of the civic center, though, underwent a major transformation when the mansard-topped French Renaissance **Casa de Gobierno** (provincial government house) replaced the colonial *cabildo* in the early 20th century.

Immediately southeast of the plaza, the open spaces on the edge of **Parque General Belgrano** contain a cluster of colonial structures that are historical monuments and museums: the Museo Histórico Provincial Brigadier General Estanislao López, the Museo Etnográfico y Colonial Juan de Garay, and most notably the Convento y Museo de San Francisco (1688).

Distinguished by an impressive sample of religious carvings from colonial missions, **Museo Histórico Provincial Brigadier General Estanislao López** (San Martín 1490, tel. 0342/457-3529) contains silverwork, pottery, period furniture, and material on the province's chaotic post-colonial political history, plus paintings from colonial Peru. It occupies a musty but otherwise well-kept early 18th-century residence.

Summer hours are 8:30 A.M.–noon and 4–8:30 P.M. weekdays except Monday, 5:30–8:30 P.M. weekends and holidays. The rest of the year afternoon hours are slightly shorter; it's also closed January 1, May 1, Good Friday, the first Friday of December, and December 25.

The **Museo Etnográfico y Colonial Juan de Garay** (25 de Mayo 1470, tel. 0342/457-3550, etnoc@ceride.gov.ar) focuses on Santa Fe la Vieja, including the area's indigenous heritage and a scale model of the city's original site near present-day Cayastá. Spanish-colonial relics include ceramics and coins; there is also a documentary archive with materials from the 17th, 18th, and 19th centuries.

Summer hours at the Museo Etnográfico are 8:30 A.M.–noon and 5–8 P.M. weekdays except Monday, 5–8 P.M. weekends and holidays. Afternoon hours are shorter and slightly earlier the rest of the year; it's also closed January 1, May 1,

Good Friday, the first Friday of December, and December 25. Admission is free, but donations are welcome.

Begun in 1673 and finished in 1688, Santa Fe's Franciscan church, **Iglesia y Convento de San Francisco** (Amenábar 2257, tel. 0342/459-3303) is its most significant remaining colonial landmark. Damaged by lightning in 1824, it slowly deteriorated, suffered several instances of ill-advised remodeling over more than century, and finally survived thanks to thoughtful restoration between 1938 and the early 1950s.

What survived, thanks to the efforts of architects Angel Guido and Mario Buschiazzo, were the building's original facade, thick adobe walls, and a red-tile ceiling supported by beams of hardwoods and cedar, held together by leather and dowels rather than nails. Its hand-carved exterior doors lead to a nave with a gold-laminated pulpit.

As elsewhere in the city, the church bears witness to the force of the river—in an odd manner in the tomb of Padre Magallanes, who was attacked by a jaguar that entered the church while fleeing the flood of 1825. Provincial caudillo Estanislao López and his wife also repose here.

In one wing of the cloisters, the **Museo Histórico San Francisco** deals with both religious and secular history in colonial and early-independence years. Among the exhibits are ceramics, furniture, silverwork, weapons, religious artifacts from various eras, and sacred and secular art. Its Sala de los Constituyentes displays wax figures of the representatives to the assembly that wrote the Argentine Constitution of 1853.

From October through March, the Convento y Museo is open 8 A.M.–noon and 4–7 P.M. daily except Sunday, when hours are 10 A.M.–noon and 4–7 P.M. The rest of the year, afternoon hours are 3:30–6:30 P.M.

One block west of the plaza, also a national historical monument, the late colonial **Templo de Santo Domingo** (1805, 3 de Febrero and 9 de Julio) is a neoclassical hodgepodge that took a century to complete. Two blocks farther west, **Plaza Italia** is the setting for the **Palacio Legislativo** (provincial legislature); immediately to its east, the outstanding **Museo Provincial de Bellas Artes Rosa Galisteo de Rodríguez** (4 de Enero 1510, tel. 0342/457-3577), the provincial fine arts museum, holds 2,200 paintings, sculptures, and engravings. Hours are 10 A.M.–noon and 4–7 P.M. weekdays except Monday, 4–8 P.M. weekends and holidays except for January 1, May 1, Good Friday, the first Friday of December, and December 25, when it's closed.

One block west of the plaza, dating from 1812, the late colonial **Casa de Estanislao López** (Estanislao López 2792) was home to the caudillo who dominated his province until his death in 1836. One block north and around the corner, bulky walls, overhanging balconies, and red-tile roof make the restored **Casa de los Aldao** (Monseñor Zaspe 2845, tel. 0342/459-3222, 8 A.M.–noon and 4–7 P.M. weekdays) a classic 18th-century residence.

Four blocks north of the plaza, the San Martín pedestrian mall is home to a pair of museums. The **Museo Municipal de Artes Visuales Sor Josefa Díaz y Clucellas** (San Martín 2068, tel. 0342/457-1886, int. 305) showcases contemporary art; it's open 8:30 A.M.–12:30 P.M. and 3:30–8 P.M. weekdays, 9:30 A.M.–12:30 P.M. Saturday and 5–8 P.M. Saturday and Sunday. Immediately adjacent but upstairs, the **Museo de la Ciudad** (San Martín 2076) offers rotating exhibits on *santafesino* customs and tradition. Hours are 8 A.M.–noon and 4–8 P.M. weekdays, 9:30 A.M.–12:30 P.M. and 5–8 P.M. Saturday, and 5–8 P.M. Sunday and holidays.

Popularly known as Granja La Esmeralda, Santa Fe's zoo, **Estación Zoológica Experimental** (Avenida Aristóbulo del Valle 8700, tel. 0342/469-6001, 8 A.M.–7 P.M. daily, US$.75), specializes in regional species, including specimens confiscated from the illegal pet trade, on 13 wooded hectares in suburban surroundings. The enclosures attempt to replicate each species' natural habitat; among the most representative animals are the vizcacha, tapir, coatimundi, puma, jaguar, giant anteater, and caiman. From downtown Santa Fe, bus No. 10 bis goes directly there.

Entertainment

Santa Fe's major performing arts locale is the French Renaissance–style **Teatro Municipal Primero de Mayo** (Avenida San Martín 2020, tel. 0342/457-1883), on the pedestrian mall.

Cine América (25 de Mayo 3073, tel. 0342/452-2246) shows recent movies.

Accommodations

In Santa Fe's sweltering summer, ceiling fans are essential and even budget travelers may wish to splurge a bit for a/c. Every place mentioned here has a/c unless otherwise indicated.

The cheapest options are across from or near the bus terminal: **Hotel Royal** (Irigoyen Freire 2256, tel. 0342/4527359) and **Hotel Alfil** (Belgrano 2859, tel. 0342/4535044) both charge just US$3.50/5 s/d with shared bath, US$5.50/7.50 s/d with private bath. Closer to downtown, **Nuevo Hotel California** (25 de Mayo 2190, tel. 0342/452-3988, US$5.50/9 s/d) compensates for its drab architecture with hospitable service.

It's a little worn around the edges, but the family-run **Emperatriz Hotel** (Irigoyen Freire 2440, tel./fax 0342/4530061, US$8/10 s/d) still evokes the style of a bygone colonial era.

Rates at the aging **Gran Hotel España** (25 de Mayo 2647, tel. 0342/4008834) start at US$13/19 s/d, but its new executive wing is worth consideration at US$19/21 s/d, especially for two people.

A Deco-era classic, the **M Castelar Hotel** (25 de Mayo 2349, tel. 0342/4520141, US$16/19 s/d) has a graceful exterior, an inviting lobby of burnished wood, and friendly staff. The rehabbed rooms are smaller and simpler than one might expect; some have tiny showers but others have tubs.

One of Santa Fe's best values is the comfortable **Meridien Suites Apart Hotel** (25 de Mayo 2620, tel. 0342/456-6111, fax 0342/452-8966, meridiensuites@arnet.com.ar). Rates are US$16/20 s/d with private bath and kitchenette, cable TV, telephone, and Internet modem connections.

At high-rise **Hostal Santa Fe de la Vera Cruz** (Avenida San Martín 2954, tel./fax 0342/455-

1740, hostal_santafe@ciudad.com.ar), the common areas are more impressive than the rooms themselves (which are OK) Rates start at US$15/21 s/d, but more spacious rooms are only a little more expensive.

Under the same management as Gran Hotel España and just across the street, the modern, well-organized **Conquistador Hotel** (25 de Mayo 2676, tel. 0342/400-1195, linverde@gigared.com, US$23/27 s/d) has good rooms with softish beds.

Food

For breakfast, lunch, or coffee, the best choice is the traditional **Confitería las Delicias** (San Martín 2898, tel. 0342/453-2126), alongside the Hostal Santa Fe; the juices deserve special mention. Other good options are **Cafetería La Citi** (La Rioja 2609, tel. 0342/455-4764), and **Clapton** (San Martín 2300, tel. 0342/453-2236).

Italian food is abundant and good. The **Círculo Italiano** (Hipólito Yrigoyen 2457, tel. 0342/452-0628) specializes in pastas, while **Triferto** (San Martín 3301, tel. 0342/453-7070) features a diverse pizza menu.

For inexpensive beef, try **El Brigadier** (San Martín 1607, tel. 0342/458-1607). For Middle Eastern specialties, there's the **Club Social Sirio Libanés** (25 de Mayo 2740, tel. 0342/453-9518).

España (San Martín 2644, tel. 0342/455-2264) serves an outstanding garlic *surubí*, a tasty river fish, for US$3.50, plus an exceptional *arroz con leche* (rice pudding) for dessert. The **Centro Español** (San Martín 2219, tel. 0342/456-9968) may be more elaborate but isn't that much better.

Santa Fe's most promising newcomer is the cheerful tapas bar ⚏ **Tasca Real** (25 de Mayo 3228, tel. 0342/15-631-7592). For only about US$5–6, two people can get their fill of Spanish snacks like *bocados, montaditos* and *pinchos;* there are also beer and hard cider on tap, and wine by the glass.

For fresh river fish, the riverfront ⚏ **El Quincho de Chiquito** (Brown and Obispo Vieytes, tel. 0342/460-2608) is a Santa Fe institution. Beneath a cavernous thatched roof, waiters serve large portions of grilled specialties like *boga,*

sábalo, and *surubí,* for about US$5; take bus No. 16 from Avenida Gálvez, in the northern downtown area.

Via Verona (San Martín 2585, tel. 0342/455-4575) is the place to go for ice cream (a virtual necessity in Santa Fe's steamy summer).

Information

The municipal tourist authority **Safetur** (Belgrano 2910, tel. 0342/457-4123, www.santafeciudad.gov.ar, 7 A.M.–1 P.M. and 3–9 P.M. daily) is downstairs at the bus terminal. It has decent maps and helpful personnel, but technologically it's behind the times. There are additional offices at Boca del Tigre (tel. 0342/457-1812), on the southern approach to the city, and on the north side of town at the Paseo del Restaurador (Blvd. Zavalla and J.J. Paso, tel. 0342/457-1881); both are open 7 A.M.–7 P.M. weekends only.

For motorists, **ACA** is at Avenida Rivadavia 3101 (tel. 0342/455-3862), and at Pellegrini and Avenida San Martín (tel. 0342/455-4142).

Services

Tourfe, San Martín 2500, tel. 0342/455-0157, is a full-service travel agency that also serves as an exchange house. There are numerous ATMs along the Avenida San Martín pedestrian mall.

Correo Argentino is at Avenida 27 de Febrero 2331; the postal code is 3000.

Telecom long-distance telephone services are upstairs at the bus terminal, but there are numerous other *locutorios.* For Internet connections, try the **Cybercafé** at San Jerónimo 2195.

For laundry, **Laverap** is at Rivadavia 2834.

Hospital Provincial José María Cullen is west of downtown at Lisandro de la Torre and Freire (tel. 0342/459-9719 or 455-8770).

Getting There

Santa Fe has air links to Buenos Aires and bus connections around the country, but no rail services.

Aerolíneas Argentinas (Lisandro de la Torre 2633, tel. 0342/459-6313) flies weekday mornings to Aeroparque. **Aerovip** (Lisandro de la Torre 2570, tel. 0342/481-1510) flies smaller planes to the federal capital.

The **Estación Terminal de Ómnibus** (Belgrano 2940) is four blocks west of San Martín. Its Oficina de Informes (tel. 0342/454-7124) conspicuously lists destinations and updated fares.

Typical domestic destinations, fares, and times include Paraná (US$1.50, 45 minutes), Rosario (US$5, two hours), Córdoba (US$10, five hours), Corrientes (US$14, eight hours), Resistencia (US$13, 7.5 hours), Buenos Aires (US$11–15, six hours), Posadas (US$22, 11 hours), San Luis (US$14, nine hours), Santiago del Estero (US$15, eight hours), Mendoza (US$20, 12 hours), Puerto Iguazú (US$25, 14 hours), Tucumán (US$18, 10 hours), Mar del Plata (US$23, 12 hours), Neuquén (US$40, 16 hours), and Bariloche (US$48, 20 hours).

Foreign destinations with service from Santa Fe include Montevideo, Uruguay (US$22, 10 hours); Asunción, Paraguay (US$22, 13 hours); and São Paulo, Brazil (US$50, 30 hours).

Getting Around

Aeropuerto Sauce Viejo is seven kilometers south of town on RN 11, tel. 0342/457-0642. From the corner of Hipólito Yrigoyen and San Luis, Línea Santo Tomé buses go to the airport cheaply.

Hertz/Millet (25 de Mayo 1925, tel. 0342/458-2583) has rental cars.

VICINITY OF SANTA FE

Across the Río Santa Fe, the flood-prone marshlands and islands of the middle Paraná still, to some degree, support a hunter-gatherer sort of lifestyle. Though the new bridge and a paved road now reach the fishing village of **Alto Verde,** for instance, its residents evacuate their homes when the water rises and return when it falls. The area also attracts sportfishing enthusiasts.

An hour to the northeast, RP 1 leads to the location of Santa Fe La Vieja at **Cayastá.** Here, at least where the meandering Río San Javier (formerly called the Quiloazas) has not washed the site away, archaeologists have uncovered part of the original city grid, traced the outlines of some key buildings, and salvaged many artifacts for display in the adjacent **Museo de Sitio Fundacional Argentina** (tel. 03405/493-0556). October–March, hours are 9 A.M.–1 P.M. and 3–7 P.M. weekdays except Monday; weekend and holiday hours are 10 A.M.–1 P.M. and 4–7 P.M. The rest of the year, the afternoon shift opens and closes an hour earlier. Buses from Santa Fe to Cayastá, 78 kilometers northeast of Santa Fe, pass directly by the entrance to the ruins.

Chaco and Formosa Provinces

Together, the provinces of Chaco and Formosa form the Gran Chaco, a hot, humid lowland stretching from the banks of the Paraná and Paraguay to the Andean foothills, and north across international borders into Paraguay and Bolivia. While the Argentine Chaco has a low international profile, the Chaco provincial capital of Resistencia is a magnet for the visual arts and the region's backcountry national parks are treasure troves of wildlife. The trans-Chaco route from Resistencia to Salta has become popular with travelers from the Esteros del Iberá to Salta, and vice-versa.

RESISTENCIA

Named for its defiance of repeated indigenous assaults after its settlement as the Jesuit mission of San Fernando del Río Negro in 1750, Resistencia owes its growth to the tannin industry and westward-advancing agricultural frontier that spurred the construction of a trans-Chaco railroad to Salta. What distinguishes the city, though, is its unexpectedly active cultural life as the "city of sculptures" for its abundant but original public art—not to mention a concentration of educational institutions including a major university and several significant museums, and a smattering of cultural centers.

Orientation

Resistencia (population 274,001, with more than 350,000 in a metropolitan area that includes the nearby port of Barranqueras) is 995 kilometers north of Buenos Aires via RN 11 through Rosario and Santa Fe, 810 kilometers east of Salta via RN 16, and only 19 kilometers west of Corrientes via the Belgrano bridge over the Paraná. RN 16 bypasses the city to the northeast, while RN 11 bypasses it to the northwest, continuing to Formosa and the Paraguayan border.

Filling four entire blocks, palm-studded Plaza 25 de Mayo is the city's geographical center. Street names change on either side of the plaza. Avenida Sarmiento and Avenida 25 de Mayo provide the best access to RN 16 and RN 11, respectively.

Sights

Resistencia prides itself on the literally hundreds of sculptures in its parks, plazas, sidewalks, and boulevards. The highest concentration of them, though, is found in the open-air **Parque de las Esculturas Aldo y Efraín Boglietti,** a 2,500-meter open-air display at Avenida Laprida and Sarmiento, on the grounds of the former **Estación Ferrocarril Santa Fe** (1907), the city's only national historical monument.

Built by French interests, the former railroad station also houses the provincial **Museo de Ciencias Naturales Augusto Schultz** (Pellegrini 802, tel. 03722/423864, free), a natural sciences museum specializing in ornithology and primarily oriented toward school children. Hours are 8:30 A.M.–noon and 2–7 P.M. weekdays only, 4–9 P.M. Saturday; in summer, weekday afternoon hours are 2–8 P.M.

Resistencia's **Museo Provincial de Bellas Artes René Brusan** (Mitre 163, tel. 03722/448000, int. 2511, 8 A.M.–noon and 6–8:30 P.M. weekdays except Mon.) focuses on sculpture but also hosts traveling exhibitions on themes such as graphic design during and after Czechoslovakia's "Prague Spring" of 1968.

Much of the momentum behind Resistencia's reputation as a visual-arts mecca comes from **El Fogón de los Arrieros** (Brown 350, tel. 03722/426418, US$2), a hybrid institution that blends artistic miscellanea from the province, the country, and the globe into a casual, bar-style atmosphere; the exterior is worth a look

even outside the hours of 9 A.M.–noon and 9–11 P.M. weekdays, 9 A.M.–noon Saturday.

Resistencia also has several historical and anthropological museums. Occupying new quarters, the **Museo del Hombre Chaqueño Profesor Ertivio Acosta** (J.B. Justo 280, tel. 03722/453145, cultura@ecomchaco.com.ar, 8 A.M.–noon and 5–8 P.M. weekdays, free) recounts the settlement and transformation of the Chaco from the perspective of its aboriginal Toba, Mocoví, and Wichi peoples, the development of criollo culture, and the European immigration of the early 20th century.

The **Museo Histórico Regional Ichoalay** (Necochea 440, tel. 03722/424200, 9 A.M.–noon Monday, Tuesday, and Wednesday, and 3–7 P.M. Wednesday only, free) adds an institutional focus, dealing with subjects such as the military, churches and missions, and schools and hospitals.

On the grounds of the Universidad Nacional del Noreste, the misleadingly named **Museo Regional de Antropología Juan Alfredo Martinet** (Avenida Las Heras 727, tel. 03722/446958, 9 A.M.–noon weekdays only, free) stresses archaeology rather than anthropology in general, though there are some ethnographic and (outdated) ethnohistorical materials.

Resistencia's most offbeat museum is the **Museo de la Policia del Chaco Carlos Angel Chiesanova** (Roca 233, tel. 03722/421551, 9 A.M.–noon weekdays only, free), if only for its remarkably sympathetic account of the case of two fugitives who, after killing a policeman in the 1960s, spent five years hiding with the assistance of poor people in the countryside. On the other hand, it makes a predictable "reefer madness" attack on drug use, and a fetish of gruesome traffic accidents.

Entertainment and Events

In the last fortnight of July, the **Fundación Urunday** (Avenida San Martín 465, tel. 03722/436694) sponsors the competitive **Concurso Nacional e Internacional de Escultura y Madera,** in the open air on Plaza 25 de Mayo, in which contestants sculpt the reddish trunk of the native *urunday* (*Astronium urundeuva*) into a work of art.

Around the same time or a little later, the Sociedad Rural del Chaco sponsors the **Exposición Nacional de Ganadería,** a longstanding annual livestock show that also includes agriculture and industrial projects. Mid-October's **Muestra de las Colectividades** focuses on the province's immigrant communities and their heritage.

The **Peña Nativa Martín Fierro** (Avenida 9 de Julio 695) showcases folk music such as Mesopotamian *chamamé,* as well as the occasional tango, in the context of a *parrilla* restaurant. The relocated **Nazareno Piano Bar** (Güemes 153) also has weekend tango events.

Resistencia's **Complejo Cultural Provincial Guido Miranda** (Colón 164, tel. 03722/425421) seats more than 500 spectators for current movies, theater productions, and concerts. **Alfonso** (Avenida Sarmiento 408) is a popular new bar.

Shopping

For indigenous crafts from throughout the province, visit the **Centro Cultural y Artesanal Leopoldo Marechal** (Pellegrini 272, tel. 03722/422649). Similar items are available at the **Cooperativa de Artesanos in the Barrio Toba,** a government-built community on the outskirts of town, reached by city bus No. 7 from Plaza 25 de Mayo.

Chac Cueros (Güemes 186) specializes in leather goods.

Accommodations

About 15 blocks north of Plaza 25 de Mayo, the municipal **Camping Parque 2 de Febrero** (Avenida Ávalos 1100, tel. 03722/458366) charges only US$2 per tent plus US$1 pp for shady sites with barbecue grills, and has clean toilets and hot showers. In summer and on weekends, though, it can get crowded and noisy, when the discos on the opposite side of Avenida Ávalos keep late hours.

Better than its drab neighborhood, **Residencial Hernandarias** (Avenida Hernandarias 215, tel. 03722/427088) goes for US$23/35 s/d with a/c and breakfast. Dating from 1927 but recently modernized, **Hotel Marconi** (Perón 352, tel.

03722/421978, marconihotel@ciudad.com.ar, US$10/14 s/d) is one of Resistencia's best values.

The union-run **Hotel Atech Sahara** (Güemes 160, tel. 03722/422970, US$10/17 s/d) is a respectable no-frills choice. Of equivalent vintage to the Marconi, **Hotel Colón** (Santa María de Oro 143, tel. 03722/422863, hotelcolon@lared.com.ar) charges US$14/20 s/d.

Down the block from the Hernandarias, the new **M Atrium Hotel** (Hernandarias 249, tel. 03722/429094, fax 03722/442627, atriumhotel@arnet.com.ar, US$16/21 s/d) adds some much-needed contemporary style to the scene. This business-oriented hotel also has gym facilities and a tennis court. Rates at the institutional-looking **Hotel Lemirson** (Frondizi 167, tel. 03722/421330, lemirson@arnet.com.ar) are US$15/23 s/d for rooms with a/c, telephone, and parking.

Only a block off Plaza 25 de Mayo, **Hotel Covadonga** (Güemes 200, tel. 03722/444444, fax 03722/443444, US$24/26 s/d) is a good traditional hotel but has two drawbacks: the breakfast is poor and, on weekends, the recently developed pub district along Calle Güemes can be noisy; in this case, choose an interior room or turn up the a/c.

A relatively recent addition, the **Gran Hotel Royal** (José M. Paz 297, tel. 03752/443666, fax 03752/424586, hotelroyal@infovia.com.ar, US$21/25 s/d) is a step up.

Food

Perhaps thanks in part to its active cultural scene, Resistencia has a better and more diverse restaurant scene than neighboring Corrientes. The area northeast of Plaza 25 de Mayo, along Güemes and Pellegrini, is the city's "gourmet ghetto."

Café de la Ciudad (Pellegrini 109, tel. 03722/420214), one of the best examples of Resistencia's new wave of *confiterías,* is an exceptional breakfast choice but also keeps late pub hours, especially on weekends. **Barrilito** (Avenida Lavalle 289) is a beer-garden restaurant, while the nearby **Abel Juniors** (Laprida 56, tel. 03722/448449) is a promising pizzeria.

Charly (Güemes 213, tel. 03722/439304) serves a tasty and surprisingly spicy *pacú* (river fish) with cream sauce that, along with most of its other entrees, falls into the US$4–5 range; the service is very professional.

Reservations are advisable for ⚑ **Kebón** (Don Bosco 120, tel. 03722/422385), widely considered Resistencia's best restaurant and certainly its most expensive. If no tables are available or if the prices seem over the top, try its adjacent but far more economical *rotisería* for food to go.

Helados San José (Pellegrini 582, tel. 03722/427008) produces Resistencia's best ice cream.

Information

The **Dirección Provincial de Turismo** (Santa Fe 178, tel. 03722/433880, direccion.turismo @ecomchaco.com.ar, www.chaco.gov.ar) is open 6:30 A.M.–8 P.M. weekdays and 8 A.M.–1 P.M. Saturday only. There's a freestanding tourist kiosk on Plaza 25 de Mayo, at the corner of Avenida Alberdi and Roca (tel. 03722/458289, 8 A.M.–9 P.M. weekdays and 9 A.M.–midnight weekends).

For motorists, **ACA** is at Avenida 9 de Julio and Avenida Italia (tel. 03722/431184).

Services

Cambio El Dorado (Jose María Paz 36) changes travelers checks. There are several ATMs on and around Plaza 25 de Mayo.

Correo Argentino is at Avenida Sarmiento 101, opposite Plaza 25 de Mayo; the postal code is 3500. There are **Telecentros** at J.B. Justo 136, and at Arturo Illia and Colón; **C-Net** (Perón 299) has fast Internet access and large monitors.

Try **Sin Fronteras** (Necochea 70, tel. 03722/431055) if you need a travel agency.

Laverap (Vedia 23, tel. 03722/424223) has laundry service.

For medical aid, **Hospital Julio C. Perrando** is at Avenida 9 de Julio 1101 (tel. 03722/425050).

Getting There

Aerolíneas Argentinas and **Austral** share offices (Frondizi 99, tel. 03722/445550); between them,

they have 12 flights weekly to Aeroparque (Buenos Aires), but there are also flights from nearby Corrientes.

A hub for provincial and long-distance **bus services,** Resistencia's spacious, gleaming **Estación Terminal de Ómnibus** (Avenida MacLean and Islas Malvinas, tel. 03772/461098) is about four kilometers west of Plaza 25 de Mayo. Several long-distance companies share more-central ticket offices at Pellegrini 166/170 (tel. 03722/423738).

La Estrella, which goes four times daily to the village of Capitán Solari (US$3.50, 2.5 hours), the access point for Parque Nacional Chaco, has an office at the corner of Hernandarias and Roca (tel. 03722/446496). There are also direct services to Naick-Neck and Laguna Blanca, near Parque Nacional Pilcomayo on the Paraguayan border.

Other sample destinations, times, and fares include Formosa (US$3, two hours), Posadas (US$7.50, five hours), Puerto Iguazú (US$14, nine hours), Rosario (US$12, nine hours), Buenos Aires (US$14–19, 12 hours), and Salta (US$16–20, 12 hours). There is regular international service to Asunción, Paraguay (US$10, five hours).

Getting Around

Godoy Resistencia buses shuttle regularly between Corrientes and Resistencia.

Aeropuerto San Martín (tel. 03722/436280) is six kilometers south of town on RN 11; from the post office on Plaza 25 de Mayo, take city bus No. 8.

To the bus terminal from the Casa de Gobierno (near the post office) on Plaza 25 de Mayo, take city bus No. 3 or No. 10.

⚑ PARQUE NACIONAL CHACO

West of Resistencia, but not quite to the "Impenetrable" of the mid-Chaco, Parque Nacional Chaco is a serene, little-visited haven of dense forest and scattered, bird-rich wetlands. Most but not all of the park avoided deforestation during the heyday of the tannin trade; some parts are recuperating.

Though not the equal of the magnificent Esteros del Iberá in Corrientes Province, the park's verdant woodland footpaths more than justify a detour for travelers crossing the Chaco in either direction. Because mosquitoes are so abundant here, the dry and relatively cool winter is the best time for a visit.

In the humid eastern Chaco, 15,000-hectare Parque Nacional Chaco is 115 kilometers northwest of Resistencia via the trans-Chaco highway RN 16 and paved RP 9 to the village of Capitán Solari, where it's another five kilometers to the park entrance on a dusty (in dry weather) or muddy (in wet weather) road. After really heavy rains, low-clearance vehicles may not be able to reach the park, but it's possible to hike in or rent horses in Capitán Solari.

Flora and Fauna

At first glance, the Chaco's limited relief—it rises almost imperceptibly from east to west—seems to offer little environmental variety. Relatively minor changes, though, can mean dramatically different habitats.

As part of the Gran Chaco, extending north into Paraguay and Bolivia, the park comprises

part of the "estuarine and gallery forest" subregion, but its marshes and gallery forests are only a fraction of the total area—though they are the richest biologically. Where the winding Río Negro has shifted its course, aquatic plants cover shallow oxbow lakes that are slowly becoming meadows and will eventually be forest.

Away from the watercourse, relatively large trees like the thorny *algarrobo* (*Prosopis chilensis*), *lapacho* (*Tabebuia ipe*), and quebracho ("axebreaker," *Schinopsis lorentzii*) form the forest canopy of the *monte fuerte*. In their shade grow smaller specimens of the same species which, when an older tree dies and topples, take advantage of the ensuing light gap to claim their place in the canopy. There are also many smaller shrubs.

Sparser scrub forests alternate with fan palm savannas of *caranday* (*Copernicia prunifera*) and *pindó*. Human-induced fires and grazing have helped create the savannas, but fire suppression and livestock restrictions are permitting more forest species to invade these areas.

In the park's dense forests, mammals are likelier heard than seen—especially the howler monkey (*Alouatta caraya*). The some 340 bird species

© WAYNE BERNHARDSON

marshland, Parque Nacional Chaco

include the *nandú* (*Rhea Americana,* endangered in this area), jabirú stork (*Jabiru mycteria*), roseate spoonbill, various cormorants, the common caracara, kingfishers, and the like. The Chaco is a wonderland for entomologists—research scientists from the Smithsonian have ongoing projects here—but the common mosquito unavoidably attracts the most attention.

Sights and Recreation

Hiking and bird-watching are the main activities, preferably in the early morning hours or around sunset. There's a 1.5-kilometer nature trail in the vicinity of the campground, but the narrow grassy road that leads northwest from the campground area gets so little automobile traffic that it might as well be a foot path.

A short distance before the road ends, the signed **Sendero Laguna Carpincho** is a three-kilometer forest loop that also leads to **Laguna Yacaré** (both these marshy lakes are prime wildlife areas, with raised and shaded platforms that permit better viewing) before returning to the road. Mosquitoes can be overpowering in the humid summer and for some time thereafter, so bring repellent.

In Capitán Solari, Ñato Mendoza rents horses for about US$1.50 per hour. This is the best alternative for visiting some soggier parts of the park, where slogging through the muck on foot is less appealing.

Practicalities

Camping is the only option at the park, where there are clean toilets, cold showers, fire pits, and collectable firewood; there is no charge, but a tent is necessary to keep out of the rain and insects, particularly the omnipresent mosquitoes. There are simple accommodations only, along with limited supplies, at Capitán Solari; it's better to bring everything from Resistencia.

The **APN** (tel. 03725/496166, chaco@apn.gov.ar) no longer collects an admission charge at the park entrance, but the rangers are happy to provide information on park attractions.

From Resistencia, La Estrella has four buses daily, at 6:30 A.M. and 12:30, 5:30, and 8 P.M., to Capitán Solari (US$4, 2.5 hours); return buses

from Capitán Solari leave at 5:30 and 11:30 A.M. and 5 P.M.

PRESIDENCIA ROQUE SÁENZ PEÑA

Settled by agricultural immigrants of various European nationalities less than a century ago, this barren but hospitable city traditionally draws Argentine visitors to its thermal baths. Until recently, their deplorable state of maintenance had made it a less desirable destination, but recent improvements and a planned US$300,000 upgrade have made it a worthwhile stopover, if not a visit in its own right. Its other attraction is an outstanding zoo focused on species from the Chaco itself.

Presidencia Roque Sáenz Peña owes its awkward official moniker not to the Argentine president who brought about universal male suffrage, but to his term of office (1910–1913); most Argentines, though, simply call it Roque Sáenz Peña. Its thermal baths date from 1937, when drillers seeking potable water struck hot mineral springs instead. Still, it's hard to imagine anyone living here in the summer months until the advent of air-conditioning; during the siesta hour, it's a virtual ghost town.

Orientation

Roque Sáenz Peña (population 76,377) is 165 kilometers northwest of Resistencia and 685 kilometers southeast of Salta via RN 16, the trans-Chaco highway. Willow-shaded Plaza San Martín is the civic center, north-south Avenida San Martín is the main commercial thoroughfare, but it's liveliest in the vicinity of the baths.

Sights and Events

Reopened after a lengthy closure, the **Complejo Termal Municipal** (Brown 545, 6 A.M.–noon and 2:30–10:30 P.M. daily) is a complex of 21 hot mineral baths and a dozen saunas that also offers massages and physical therapy. Thermal baths and saunas cost about US$2 each pp, while a half-hour massage from a professional kinesthesiologist costs only about US$3.

On the eastern outskirts of town, on the south side of the highway, the **Complejo Ecológico**

Municipal (tel. 03732/429660, sunrise to sunset daily, US$.35) features native regional fauna like tapirs and jaguars in spacious enclosures, plus two artificial lakes that attract migratory wildfowl. City bus No. 2 goes from downtown directly to the zoo.

The **Fiesta Nacional del Algodón,** in the second week of October, celebrates the province's role as the country's greatest cotton producer.

Accommodations and Food
At the east end of 9 de Julio, **Camping El Descanso** badly needs an upgrade at what was once a pretty good site. Facilities are free, but not well-maintained, and it's crowded with partying locals on weekends. Take city bus No. 1 from downtown.

The best value for the money is the prosaically named **Hotel Familiar** (Moreno 488, tel. 03732/429906), where medium-sized but immaculate rooms with smallish baths, cable TV, breakfast, and parking cost US$7/11, though a/c (well worth it in summer) is US$2 extra.

Hotel Flamingo (25 de Mayo 442, tel. 03732/426170) may flaunt the decor of a particularly tacky brothel or an *albergue transitorio,* but it's not either. Though barely two years old, it shows signs of shoddy workmanship but is passable for a night at US$9/15 s/d with a/c, TV, and breakfast. Parking costs US$2 more.

Hotel Presidente (San Martín between Palmira and Laprida, tel. 03732/424498) has larger, better, and less lurid rooms, but even here the plaster is already a little moldy. Rates are US$12/16 s/d with a/c, cable TV, parking, and the like.

Though it's stagnated along with the adjacent bath complex, **Hotel Gualok** (San Martín 1198, tel. 03732/420715) has the potential to revive along with them. Rates are US$18/27 s/d, but there are some no-frills third-floor rooms for US$11/17 s/d.

Across from the bath complex, shaded by palms and awnings, **Sky Blue** (Brown and Moreno) is an outdoor beer garden, pizzeria, and sandwich place that draws big evening crowds. In addition to the pizzas, there are welcome appetizers of potato salad, popcorn, and peanuts

(which, of course, tend to increase beer consumption).

Helados Ama Nalec (Moreno 613) serves the city's best ice cream.

Information and Services
In the thermal-bath complex, the **Dirección de Promoción Turística** (Brown 545, tel. 03732/430030, fax 03732/427218, saenzpeniatermal@yahoo.com.ar) generally keeps the same hours as the baths—6 A.M.–noon and 2:30–10:30 P.M. daily.

For motorists, **ACA** is at Rivadavia and 25 de Mayo (tel. 03732/420471).

Banco Credicoop (25 de Mayo 464) and **Banco de la Nación** (Avenida San Martín 301) both have ATMs.

Correo Argentino is at Belgrano 602; the postal code is 3700.

Try **Telecentro Chaco** (San Martín 1016) for telephone services and Internet access.

Hospital 4 de Junio is at Las Malvinas 1350 (tel. 03732/424568).

Getting There and Around
Roque Sáenz Peña's **Terminal de Ómnibus** is east of downtown, on Canteros between Avellaneda and López y Planes (tel. 103—a free local call). City bus No. 1 goes there from downtown Avenida Mitre.

The main destination is Resistencia (US$4, two hours), but there are also direct services to Buenos Aires (US$20, 14 hours). Trans-Chaco services from Resistencia to Salta also stop here.

FORMOSA

Sultry Formosa has little to recommend it as a destination, except for an abundance of public art that falls short of Resistencia's, but visitors en route to Parque Nacional Río Pilcomayo may have to spend a night here.

Orientation
Formosa (population 198,146) is 175 kilometers north of Resistencia and 113 kilometers south of Clorinda, on the border with Paraguay, via RN 11. RN 81 crosses the Chaco to Salta

Province as a highway not yet completely paved, and prone to flooding.

The main thoroughfare, entering town from the west, is Avenida Doctor Luis Gutñiski, which dead-ends at the central Plaza San Martín; on the opposite side of the plaza, Avenida 25 de Mayo continues to the banks of the Río Paraguay.

Museo Histórico Municipal

Formosa's municipal history museum (Avenida 25 de Mayo 84) occupies the **Casa Fotheringham** (1885), built as a private residence by the first territorial governor, a general with the quintessentially Argentine name of Ignacio Hamilton Fotheringham. Enhanced by an attractive veranda but badly in need of restorative maintenance, it's the city's only national historical monument.

On finishing his term, Fotheringham sold the house to the provincial government, under which it housed his successor governors until 1957. Since becoming a museum in 1980, it has chronicled the province's history and political development, particularly after Argentina took this part of the Chaco from Paraguay during the War of the Triple Alliance (1864–1870).

Events

Mid-November's **Fiesta del Río,** in which numerous vessels from Corrientes stage a nocturnal religious procession up the Río Paraguay, is the city's signature event. On the secular side, it includes numerous water-sports competitions.

The **Día de la Fundación de Formosa** takes place on April 8, the date of the city's founding. July 16's **Fiesta de la Virgen de la Catedral** pays homage to Formosa's patron saint, the Virgen del Carmen.

Accommodations and Food

Formosa has several decent but unspectacular accommodations, such as **Hotel Real** (Belgrano 1, tel. 03717/427851, US$9/14 s/d) and **Hotel Plaza** (Uriburu 920, tel. 03717/426767, US$11/19 s/d). **Hotel Colón** (Belgrano 1068, tel. 03717/420719) charges US$14/19 s/d.

Two side-by-side restaurants near the foot of Avenida 25 de Mayo have similar menus stressing freshly caught local fish, but also serves meats and pastas: the tasca-style **El Tano Marino** (Avenida 25 de Mayo 55, tel. 03717) and **Raíces** (Avenida 25 de Mayo 65, tel. 03717/427058). **Pizza Mario** (Rivadavia 792) specializes in pizza and pasta.

Information and Services

The provincial **Dirección de Turismo** (Uriburu 820, tel. 03717/420442) is open 7 A.M.–1 P.M. weekdays only.

Banco de Galicia has an ATM at Avenida 25 de Mayo 160.

Correo Argentino (Avenida 9 de Julio 930) is opposite Plaza San Martín; Formosa's postal code is 3600. The **Telefónica** *locutorio* at Avenida 25 de Mayo 251 also has Internet access.

The **Hospital Central** is at Salta 545 (tel. 03717/426194).

Getting There and Around

Aerolíneas Argentinas (Avenida 25 de Mayo 603, tel. 03717/429314) flies daily except Saturday to Aeroparque, usually stopping in Corrientes. Hire a cab or *remise* to Formosa's Aeropuerto El Pucú, which is only four kilometers south of town along RN 11.

The modern **Estación Terminal de Ómnibus Formosa** (ETOF, Avenida Gutñiski and Antártida Argentina, tel. 03717/451766) is 15 blocks west of Plaza San Martín.

Godoy SRL (tel. 03717/15-613850) goes five times daily to Laguna Naick-Neck (US$3.50), the closest settlement to Parque Nacional Río Pilcomayo, via the border-post city of Clorinda; the first departure is 8:45 A.M., the last 7:30 P.M.

Other sample destinations, fares, and times include Resistencia (US$3, two hours), Rosario (US$15, 11 hours), and Buenos Aires (US$22, 14 hours). There is also international service to Asunción, Paraguay (US$7, three hours).

PARQUE NACIONAL RÍO PILCOMAYO

Nudging the Paraguayan border in the humid eastern Chaco, 47,754-hectare Parque Nacional Río Pilcomayo is an internationally recognized

Ramsar wetland whose centerpiece is the shallow Laguna Blanca, but there are also major marshes, gallery forests, and grasslands.

Parque Nacional Río Pilcomayo is about 45 kilometers west of Clorinda via paved RN 86 and a dirt road that leads to Seccional Laguna Blanca (do not confuse this with the park's administrative headquarters at the town of Laguna Blanca, another 11 kilometers west on the paved highway).

Río Pilcomayo's flora and fauna resemble those of Parque Nacional Chaco, though the distribution of the various environments differs—Pilcomayo has far larger stretches of open water, for instance. Still, visitors will see many of the same birds, mammals, and reptiles that are so abundant to the south.

From the Laguna Blanca campground, the **Sendero Laguna Blanca** is an elevated *pasarela* (boardwalk) leading to the lakeshore over marshy ground to an even higher mirador (overlook) that offers panoramic views across the lake; there are also three shoreline platforms for sunbathing and swimming (the smallish *yacarés,* while they may float ominously on the lake surface, do not attack humans). Capybaras wallow in the marshes along and beneath the boardwalk.

Practicalities

At the park's **Camping Laguna Blanca,** the free facilities include picnic tables, firepits, and toilets with cold showers. Note that the campground is closed to motor vehicles; campers must carry their tents and supplies from the nearby parking lot. Limited supplies are available just outside the park entrance, but it's better to purchase them in the nearby towns of Laguna Blanca, Clorinda, or Formosa.

At the town of Laguna Blanca, **Hotel Guaraní** (San Martín and Sargento Cabral, tel. 03718/ 470024, US$5/8 s/d) is the closest regular accommodations.

Rangers at Seccional Laguna Blanca, near the campground, will provide information and advice. The APN's **Intendencia Parque Nacional Pilcomayo** (Pueyrredón s/n, tel./fax 03718/ 470045, pilcomayo@clorinda-fsa.com.ar) is in the town of Laguna Blanca.

At Laguna Naick-Neck, on RN 86, Godoy and Don Carson buses from Formosa and Clorinda pass a well-marked turnoff to Seccional Laguna Blanca. From the turnoff, though, it's necessary to hike, hitch, or hail a *remise* for the last five kilometers over a dirt road. Minibuses from Clorinda also pass through here.

Cuyo

On the eastern slope of the Andes, comprising the provinces of Mendoza, San Juan, and San Luis, the Cuyo region can claim two world-class attractions in abundance: mountains and wine. The soaring summit of 6,962-meter Cerro Aconcagua is the highest of countless peaks that, in winter, trap the snowfall whose spring thaw irrigates the sandy soils of three-quarters of Argentina's underrated—but rapidly growing—vineyards. Under bright desert sun, the same snowmelt fills the rivers where rafters and kayakers battle white-water waves and rapids, and the reservoirs where windsurfers race across the surface and fishermen troll for trout.

In fact, Cuyo is a year-round destination. As the Western Hemisphere's highest peak,

Aconcagua draws climbers from around the world, but exploring the Andes on foot or horseback is not just for peak-baggers. The provincial capital of Mendoza, for that matter, is one of Argentina's most livable cities, with its numerous wineries and fine food a bonus. In winter, skiers frequent international resorts like Las Leñas and other lesser areas, and others can discover fossil-filled desert parks like San Juan Province's Ischigualasto and San Luis's Las Quijadas, which can be intolerably hot in summer.

To the east, San Luis Province also shares Argentina's lower-central sierras with the province of Córdoba, whose namesake capital city is, arguably, the republic's second city. This area draws far more Argentine than international visitors,

© WAYNE BERNHARDSON

Must-Sees

ᴍ **Cerro Aconcagua:** At 6,962 meters, the "Roof of the Americas" is literally the high point of anyone's trip to the continent. Only a handful of people attempt the summit, but many more make it to base camp, and just about anyone can catch a glimpse of the summit. Other nearby points, like the Cristo Redentor statue on the Chilean border, offer the views without the exertion (page 256).

ᴍ **Bodegas Salentein:** In the Andean foothills southwest of Mendoza, this futuristic winery with a contemporary design is a temple to wine (page 259).

ᴍ **Difunta Correa Shrine:** In the desert 60 kilometers east of San Juan, this sprawling shrine to a popular "saint" will impress skeptics as much as it does the hundreds of thousands of pilgrims who visit every year (page 273).

ᴍ **Parque Provincial Ischigualasto:** In northern San Juan Province, the "Valley of the Moon" badlands are part of a triangle of parks fast becoming stops on the international dinosaur-fossil circuit (page 277). The others are La Rioja's **Parque Nacional Talampaya** and San Luis's **Parque Nacional Sierra de las Quijadas**.

ᴍ **Parque Nacional Sierra de las Quijadas:** In northern San Luis Province, Las Quijadas' sandstone canyons are a scenic maze that recall the canyon country of Utah or New Mexico, and its dinosaur fossils are the source of endless material for Argentina's growing community of paleontologists (page 280).

Pilgrims from all over Argentina and the world visit the Difunta Correa shrine.

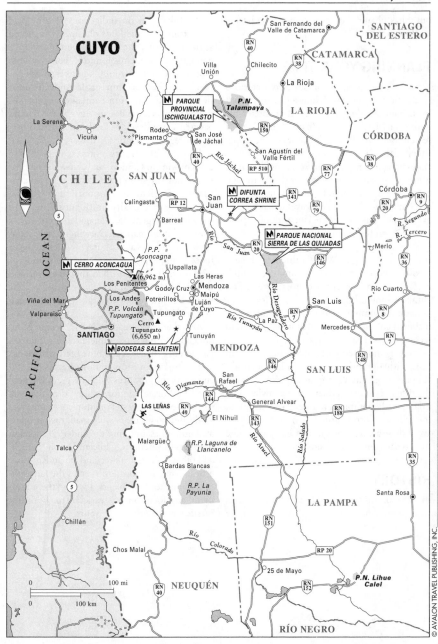

CUYO

San Fernando del
Valle de Catamarca

SANTIAGO
DEL ESTERO

RN
40

CATAMARCA

Villa
Unión

Chilecito

La Rioja

LA RIOJA

CÓRDOBA

RN
38

M **PARQUE
PROVINCIAL
ISCHIGUALASTO**

P.N.
Talampaya

RN
150

La Serena

Vicuña

Rodeo
Pismanta

San José
de Jáchal

San Agustín del
Valle Fértil

Río Jáchal

Córdoba

CHILE

SAN JUAN

RN
40

RP 510

RN
77

RN
38

RN
9

RN
20

Calingasta

RP 12

San
Juan

M **DIFUNTA
CORREA SHRINE**

RN
141

RN
79

Barreal

San Juan

M **PARQUE NACIONAL
SIERRA DE LAS QUIJADAS**

R. Segundo

R. Tercero

Merlo

RN
36

OCEAN

P.P.
Aconcagua

RN
20

RN
146

M **CERRO ACONCAGUA**

Uspallata

(6,962 m)

Las Heras

Río Desaguadero

Río Cuarto

Viña del Mar

Los Penitentes

Los Andes

Godoy Cruz
Potrerillos

Mendoza
Maipú
Luján
de Cuyo

San Luis

RN
8

Valparaíso

P.P. Volcán
Tupungato

Tupungato

La Paz

RN
7

Mercedes

SANTIAGO

Cerro
Tupungato
(6,650 m)

Tunuyán

Río Tunuyán

RN
7

M **BODEGAS SALENTEIN**

MENDOZA

RN
148

PACIFIC

San
Rafael

SAN LUIS

RN
146

Río Diamante

RN
144

General Alvear

RN
188

LAS LEÑAS

RN
40

El Nihuil

RN
143

RN
35

Talca

Malargüe

R.P. Laguna de
Llancanelo

Río Atuel

Río Salado

Bardas Blancas

R.P. La
Payunia

Santa Rosa

LA PAMPA

Chillán

RN
151

Río

Río Colorado

RP 20

Chos Malal

25 de Mayo

P.N. Lihue
Calel

0   100 mi

0   100 km

NEUQUÉN

RN
40

RN
152

RÍO NEGRO

Cuyo

but it has a handful of rewarding off-the-beaten track attractions.

PLANNING YOUR TIME

For wine lovers, Mendoza alone deserves at least a week, and even those with only a passing interest in the vine should spend a few days, preferably during the March *Vendimia* (harvest festival, when reservations are almost obligatory). The upper valley of the Río Mendoza, en route to Chile, is close enough for recreational excursions like whitewater rafting and even for winter skiing, though there are also accommodations on the slopes at Los Penitentes. True wine aficionados may want to extend their stay to visit the vineyards of Tupungato and San Rafael, to the south.

Whether hiking or climbing, Aconcagua is a trip in its own right. While a three-day hike is possible, the long trek to and from base camp is a 10-day commitment for most hikers, and climbers should budget three weeks for an assault on the summit—whether successful or not. It should go without saying that it's important to recognize when to turn back.

Visiting the desert parks of San Juan and San Luis, with a probable side trip to La Rioja's Talampaya, would ideally require a week because of the distances between them, even allowing only a day at each unit (plus a recommended detour to the Difunta Correa shrine). It would be best to avoid these areas in the summer heat, when rare storms can cause flash floods.

HISTORY

In pre-Columbian times, the Cuyo provinces were peripheral to the central Andean empire of the Inkas, but the indigenous Huarpe paid some tribute to the lords of Cuzco. As settled agriculturalists, the Huarpe were numerous enough that Spaniards found it worthwhile to cross the cordillera from Chile to establish *encomiendas*. Because impassable Andean snowfields separated it from Santiago for much of the year and because Buenos Aires was so distant, isolated Cuyo developed a distinctive and persistent regional identity.

By the 17th century, vintners were carting casks of wine to Córdoba and across the pampas to Buenos Aires. Still, it took nearly two centuries to reorient the economy, after the creation of a viceroyalty at Buenos Aires and subsequent Argentine independence effectively closed Chilean markets. Darwin, in 1835, contrasted Mendoza's agricultural productivity with its economic stagnation: "Nothing could appear more flourishing than the vineyards and the orchards of figs, peaches and olives," he wrote, but "the prosperity of the place has much declined of late years."

Arrival of the railroad, in 1884, brought Mendoza into Buenos Aires's orbit and spurred the expansion of grapevines and olive orchards, thanks largely to Italian immigration. Between 1890 and 1910, the province's vineyards grew sevenfold to 45,000 hectares; growth slowed in the next six decades, but they still quintupled. Many vineyards and bodegas are still small, owner-operated businesses, but since the mid-1970s foreign investors—American, Chilean, Dutch, French, and others—have acquired and expanded properties. While Mendoza still serves the large domestic market with blended wines, there is an increasing focus on fine varietals for both domestic consumption and export.

Mendoza Province

At one end of the busiest highway crossing in the Andes, Mendoza gets a constant stream of international travelers but also has a flourishing domestic travel industry. Its biggest attraction, literally, is the formidable Andean range—symbolized by the hemisphere's highest mountain, 6,962-meter Cerro Aconcagua—but it's not the only recreational possibility. Many visitors find the provincial capital of Mendoza and its surrounding wine country so appealing that they stay longer than they expected.

Economically, tourism is a major contributor to the economy, but the province's oil and gas fields supply a quarter of Argentina's fossil fuels. Augmented by hydroelectric power from Andean reservoirs, abundant energy resources have promoted industrial growth.

MENDOZA

In the shadow of the arid central Andes, modern Mendoza lacks the colonial charm of Salta or the scenic immediacy of Bariloche, but the provincial capital delights Argentines and foreigners alike as one of the country's most livable cities. Its dearth of distinctive historic architecture stems from its vulnerability to earthquakes, but *Mendocinos* have compensated by creating a city of sycamore-shaded streets, irrigated by ancient acequias, with broad sidewalks and verdant open spaces. In the words of Mexican novelist Carlos Fuentes, Mendoza "is protected by a roof of leaves woven together like the fingers of a huge circle of inseparable lovers."

On top of that, Mendoza has an active cultural life, thanks to its university, museums, and performing arts venues, and there's a vigorously developing restaurant-and-entertainment district between downtown and the green expanses of Parque General San Martín. Much of Mendoza's present prosperity depends on the provincial petroleum industry, but the area's increasingly fine wines, with dozens of bodegas open for tours and tasting, draw many visitors. It makes an ideal place to organize activities like a white-water de-

scent of the Río Mendoza or an icy ascent of Aconcagua, and to celebrate them afterward.

History

Named for colonial Chilean Governor García Hurtado de Mendoza, the city dates from 1561. Its early history, though, it was one of isolation—for much of the year, it was impossible to cross the Andes to Santiago, and even under the best conditions it was a long, time-consuming trip. In the early 17th century, the Spanish chronicler Vásquez de Espinosa reported only 40 Spaniards and 1,500 Indians under a Mendoza-based *corregidor* (magistrate) and various missionary orders. In the late 18th century, though, it came under the administration of the Buenos Aires–based Virreinato del Río de la Plata (Viceroyalty of the River Plate) through the Intendencia de Córdoba.

Peripheral throughout colonial times, Mendoza became central to the Spanish American wars of independence when General José de San Martín trained his Ejército de los Andes (Army of the Andes) here before crossing the cordillera to Chile. In the aftermath of independence, though, Mendoza struggled (Darwin unfavorably contrasted its "stupid, forlorn aspect" with the Chilean capital of Santiago), but arrival of the railroad linked the burgeoning wine industry to Buenos Aires and the rest of the country.

As the city has grown and earthquakes have forced reconstruction, the city center shifted from the colonial Ciudad Vieja (Old City) at the north end of Parque O'Higgins to contemporary Plaza Independencia in 1861. Earthquakes have been a constant, most recently in 1968, 1985, and 1997, but they've only stalled rather than stopped Mendoza's growth.

Wine has also remained a constant—Mendoza and vicinity account for more than three-quarters of the country's production—but the discovery of major petroleum reserves nearby has also encouraged industrial development. Meanwhile, the tourism industry has taken off because of wine, access to the Andes and, most

Cuyo

MENDOZA

SCALE NOT AVAILABLE

Parque San Martín

Lago del Bosque

HOSTEL NACIONAL ALTAS CUMBRES

CHILEAN CONSULATE

ORVIZ

PRAGA

ZUCKERSÜSS

SOSAHAUS HOSTEL

HOTEL MARCONI

PROMETEUS

CASONA TITTARELLI

DAMAJUANA HOSTEL

HELADO Y CÍA

LA CASA DEL VINO

EXTREM

Streets and features:

CIUDAD SAN FELIPE

GENERAL NICOLAS PLANTAMURA

PASO DE LOS ANDES

PARANA

SUIPACHA

A. DEL VALLE

JUAN DE DIOS VIDELA

ROQUE SAENZ PEÑA

JOAQUIN V. GONZALEZ

URUGUAY

T. BENEGAS

ALFATACAL

AV. JUAN B. JUSTO

MOYANO

J. L. AGUIRRE

NICOLAS AVELLANEDA

URIBURU

AV. DEL LIBERTADOR

CAMINO DEL MEDIO

A. ALVAREZ

AV. EMILIO CIVIT

JULIO A. ROCA

MARTIN ZAPATA

GRANADEROS

MARTINEZ DE ROZAS

OLASCOAGA

CORONEL RODRIGUEZ

RUFINO ORTEGA

VIRGEN

TRABAJO

LOS ROBLES

AV. DE LAS PALMERAS

AV. DEL ROSEDAL

ARISTIDES VILLANUEVA

LAS PICHARDAS

SARGENTO

CABRAL

M. A. SAEZ

CLARK

SOBREMONTE

E. JOFRE

VICENTE GIL

OLASCOAGA

DELGADO

CORONEL RODRIGUEZ

AV. BELGRANO

PERU

LAS TIPAS

BOULOGNE SUR MER

BRAVO

HUARPES

PASO DE LOS ANDES

GRANADEROS

LAMADRID

PUEYRREDON

AV.

LUZURIAGA

E. ALVAREZ

AV. BELGRANO

OLEGARIO V. ANDRADE

M. MORENO

Cuyo

S. RETA

J. A. MAZA

CORONEL PLAZA

EUSEBIO BLANCO

BARCALA

AV. GODOY CRUZ

GENERAL PAZ

MAIPU

CHACABUCO

BELTRAN

CLUB ANDINISTA MENDOZA

ALBERDI

URQUIZA

CORRIENTES

CÓRDOBA

SAN LUIS

ENTRE RÍOS

RIOJA

SALTA

BUENOS AIRES

LAVALLE

CATAMARCA

GARIBALDI

AV. L. N. ALEM

To Airport and San Juan

Plaza Pedro del Castillo ★

MUSEO FUNDACIONAL ★

Parque Bernardo O'Higgins

★ MUSEO HISTÓRICO GENERAL SAN MARTÍN

REZAGOS DE EJÉRCITO

▼ BOCCADORO

N LA MARCHIGIANA

MONTECATINI

■ BANCO DE LA NACIÓN

● CITY HOTEL

MUSEO POPULAR CALLEJERO ★

PIRÉ

ESQUÍ MENDOZA COMPETICIÓN

■ TURISMO MENDOZA

LAS HERAS

LAS VIÑAS

Mercado Central

TEATRO MUNICIPAL MENDOZA ■

PETIT HOTEL

CAFÉ MEDITERRÁNEO ★

MAMBRÚ

HOTEL NECOCHEA ■

GRAND HOTEL BALBI

CENTRO DE INFORMACIÓN TURÍSTICA ■

PALACE ● HOTEL

Plaza Chile

CHILE

BASÍLICA DE ★ SAN FRANCISCO

NECOCHEA

● HOTEL PROVINCIAL

GUTIÉRREZ

Plaza San Martín

HOTEL CAROLLO

TEATRO INDEPENDENCIA

N HOSTEL INDEPENDENCIA

LAS TINAJAS ▼

CINE TEATRO UNIVERSIDAD NACIONAL DE CUYO

HOTEL PRINCESS ●

▼ FACUNDO

M PARK HYATT MENDOZA

LIBRERÍA SBS ■

SARMIENTO

● HOTEL CRILLÓN

Plaza Independencia

LEGISLATURA PROVINCIAL ★

ESPEJO

BETANCOURT RAFTING

MENDOZA VIAJES

EXPRINTER ■

■ CAMBIO SANTIAGO

HUELLAS ANDINAS HOSTEL ●

INSTITUTO CULTURAL ARGENTINO NORTEAMERICANO

ASATEJ

LA CERVECERÍA ▼

AEROLÍNEAS ARGENTINAS ■

RIVADAVIA

FONOBAR ■

SUBSECRETARÍA DE TURISMO, MERCADO ARTESANAL

BOLIVIAN CONSULATE ●

LANCHILE

CITIBANK ■

M HOTEL CADENA DEL SOL ■

MONTEVIDEO

MUSEO DEL PASADO CUYANO

HOSTEL CAMPO BASE ■

SOUTHERN WINDS

AYMARÁ TURISMO

TURISMO SEPEAN ■

Plaza Italia

LA TASCA DE PLAZA ESPAÑA

DA PRAIA ■

ACA ●

● HOTEL HUENTALA

HOSPITAL CENTRAL

SAN LORENZO

EL MESÓN ESPAÑOL ■

Plaza España

GARCÍA SANTOS LIBROS

DOLLAR ■

AVIS ■

LOCALIZA ■

LÍNEA VERDE ▼

LA LAVANDERÍA ■

UVAS MENDOCINAS ■

Plaza Pellegrini

RESIDENCIAL SAVIGLIANO ●

AV. BANDERA DE LOS ANDES

● LAVERAP

AV. COLÓN

25 DE MAYO

LEMOS

AV. MITRE

P. MENDOCINAS

AV. ESPAÑA

9 DE JULIO

DON BOSCO

HOTEL ● MILEN

V. LÓPEZ

AV. PEDRO MOLINA

POST OFFICE ■

PARDO

AV. J. V. ZAPATA

TERMINAL ■ DEL SOL

To Guaymallén, Maipú, San Luis, Córdoba, and Buenos Aires

Barrio Cívico

EL CUERVO ■

RONDEAU

INSTITUTO INTERCULTURAL DE LENGUAS EXTRANJERAS ■

MUNICIPALIDAD ★

AV. GENERAL SAN MARTÍN

SAN JUAN

RIOJA

SALTA

25 DE MAYO

FLORIDA

LAPRIDA

N HOSTEL INTERNACIONAL MENDOZA ■

L. PELTIER

SANTA CRUZ

MOYANO

M. GÜEMES

MORON

ZARATE

ALDOLFO CALLE

R. ESCALADA

J. V. GONZALEZ

To Godoy Cruz, Luján de Cuyo, and Chacras de Coria

BARRAQUERO

To San Rafael, Uspallata and Santiago de Chile

GODOY

AV. GOB. VIDELA

J.N. LENCINAS

ALBERDI

MONTECASEROS

J. F. MORENO

ITUZAINGO

ACUARIO MUNICIPAL ★

ALBANIA

M Cuyo

© AVALON TRAVEL PUBLISHING, INC.

GRAN MENDOZA

Mendoza's relatively small population of just over 100,000 is misleading in that the provincial capital's compact grid borders on several adjacent and nearby municipalities—Guaymallén (to the east), Godoy Cruz (to the south), Las Heras (to the north), Maipú (to the southwest), and Luján de Cuyo (south of Godoy Cruz). Together they form Gran Mendoza (Greater Mendoza), with a population pushing 900,000.

When walking or otherwise traveling around town, it's not always obvious where one municipality ends and the other begins. For the most part, it doesn't matter—the bus station, for instance, is part of Guaymallén, but it's easily accessible from downtown. In some areas, though, there are "villages" within these municipalities, such as Dorrego (Guaymallén), Coquimbito (Maipú), or Chacras de Coria (Luján de Cuyo), that have their own identity (and attractions, such as wineries). Recognizing these will help visitors get oriented.

In a sense, Gran Mendoza's large population is also misleading, in that some municipalities include fairly distant rural communities and sprawling wild areas that are almost unpopulated—Luján de Cuyo, for instance, is an area of 4,847 square kilometers that extends west all the way to the Chilean border.

recently, proximity to Chile, as bargain-seekers from across the Andes have flocked here since the devaluation of late 2001.

Orientation

On the eastern Andean piedmont, 761 meters above sea level, Mendoza (population 110,716, but 846,904 including adjacent municipalities) is 1,073 kilometers west of Buenos Aires via RN 7 and 340 kilometers northwest of Santiago de Chile via RN 7 to the Los Libertadores border complex. It is 168 kilometers south of San Juan via RN 40, 665 kilometers southwest of Córdoba via San Luis, and 825 kilometers north of Neuquén via a series of paved highways that includes RN 40.

Filling four full blocks, Plaza Independencia is the literal city center, around which four satellites—the northwesterly Plaza Chile, northeasterly Plaza San Martín, the southeasterly Plaza España, and the southwesterly Plaza Italia—symbolically revolve. Three blocks east of Plaza Independencia, via the Sarmiento pedestrian mall, the north-south Avenida San Martín (also known as the Alameda) is the main axis of the daily bustle, while three blocks north, Avenida General Las Heras is the downtown shopping area. Five blocks south of Plaza Independencia, the Barrio Cívico is the nucleus of official Mendoza.

Sights

Mendoza makes a great walker's city; to get the lay of the town, take the elevator to the rooftop **Terraza Mirador** at the Municipalidad (9 de Julio 500), two blocks south of Plaza España. Hours are 8:30 A.M.–7:30 P.M. daily except Saturday, when it closes at 7 P.M.

Once you have the aerial layout, consider taking the municipal **Bus Turístico,** which does a twice-daily city tour (US$3.50 adults, US$1.75 children) from January through Semana Santa. Leaving from the information office at the corner of Garibaldi and San Martín, it visits several important locations including Parque San Martín's Cerro de la Gloria; the fee does not include museum admissions, however. Hours are 9:30 A.M.–12:30 P.M. and 2:30–5:30 P.M.

The best place to start a walk, though, is the broad expanse of **Plaza Independencia;** bounded by Espejo, Chile, Rivadavia, and Patricias Mendocinas. Crossed by diagonal and perpendicular pathways and embellished by trees and fountains, it's a major site for civic events, outdoor concerts, and a weekend crafts fair. It also features the subterranean **Teatro Quintanilla** and **Museo Municipal de Arte Moderno** (tel. 0261/425-7279), a mostly contemporary art space open 9 A.M.–1 P.M. and 4–9 P.M. except Sunday, when it's open 4–9 P.M. only.

© WAYNE BERNHARDSON

news kiosk, Avenida San Martín

Immediately east of Plaza Independencia, the pedestrian **Paseo Sarmiento** is home to the **Legislatura Provincial** (provincial legislature), detailed in *celeste* (sky blue) and white according to the Argentine national colors. Sarmiento's shaded sidewalk cafés and benches make it one of the finest spots in town for people-watching.

Two blocks south of Sarmiento, the magnificent tilework of **Plaza España** makes it, arguably, the most attractive in the city; four blocks west, **Plaza Italia** honors the city's Italian community. En route, the Italianate **Casa de Francisco Civit** (1873) was one of the first important residences in the new part of the city after the 1861 earthquake; its **Museo del Pasado Cuyano** (Montevideo 544, tel. 0261/423-6031, 9 A.M.–12:30 P.M. weekdays only) is a regional history museum.

Four blocks north of Plaza Italia, **Plaza Chile** acknowledges Argentina's westerly neighbor. Once part of colonial Chile, Cuyo is probably closer to the adjacent republic than any other part of the country—so close that, since the devaluation of late 2001, Mendoza officials have invited Chilean tourists to celebrate Chile's September patriotic holidays here.

One block north of Plaza Chile, on the southern side of Avenida Las Heras between Avenida Perú and 25 de Mayo, the inventive **Museo Popular Callejero** consists of a series of historical sidewalk dioramas. They depict typical activities on what was once a dry streambed but became one of Mendoza's major shopping streets. Its original designation, in 1830, was Callejón de las Maruleilas, but it's undergone numerous name changes to Calle de la Circunvalación (1863), Calle de las Carretas (1880), Calle Las Heras (1882, after San Martín's ally Gregorio de Las Heras), Calle del Ferrocarril (1885, with arrival of the railroad), Boulevard de las Palmeras (1908, for its newly planted palms), and Calle de los Inmigrantes (1912). The handsome glass cases are now being restored after a shameful vandalization.

Four blocks west of Plaza Chile, **Plaza San Martín** aspires to honor Argentina's icon but oversteps into hero worship. At the northwest corner of the plaza, dating from 1875, the **Basílica de San Francisco** (Necochea and España) is the oldest church in the newer part of the city. It holds the image of Nuestra Señora del Carmen de

N Cuyo

© WAYNE BERNHARDSON

Plaza Independencia

exception is an enormous loggerhead turtle caught off Bahía Blanca in 1985, but not returned to the ocean because of an injury.

At the north end of the park, the so-called **Ruinas de San Francisco** are the remains of a 17th-century Jesuit-built church and school, but the Franciscans claimed the site after the Jesuits' expulsion from the Americas in 1767.

Dating from 1749, the colonial Cabildo stood on Mendoza's Plaza Mayor until 1861, but after that year's devastating earthquake authorities rebuilt the city center to the southwest, at present-day Plaza Independencia. Renamed **Plaza Pedro de Castillo,** the plaza is now the site of Mendoza's **Museo Fundacional** (Alberdi 571, tel. 0261/425-6927, 8 A.M.–8 P.M. weekdays except Mon., 3–8 P.M. Sun. only, US$1 adults, US$.50 children), a spacious modern structure that protects the excavated foundations of the adobe Cabildo (and the subsequent slaughterhouse).

As an archaeological site, there's not a lot left here. As a museum, it's a thorough and thoughtful account of Mendoza's historical development from pre-Columbian times to the present, with ethnographic, historical, and contemporary material. Its strengths are Huarpe Indian artifacts, and historical dioramas and photographs. There's an attractive café and a souvenir shop.

Parque San Martín

At the west end of downtown Mendoza, across Avenida Boulogne Sur Mer, the famed French architect Carlos Thays designed this rolling 420-hectare park on property donated by Governor (later Senator) Emilio Civit. Planted with pines and eucalyptus, its literal high point is the **Cerro de la Gloria,** topped by Uruguayan sculptor Juan Manuel Ferrari's **Monumento al Ejército Libertador,** an equestrian tribute to San Martín's army (interestingly, one of its several mounted soldiers is Afro-Argentine).

At the west end of Avenida Emilio Civit (an extension of Sarmiento), the park's stunning iron-filigree gates are a story—or different stories—in themselves. According to long-standing legend, they were originally forged for the Turkish Sultan Abdul Hamid and crowned by the crescent moon of Islam, but Civit oppor-

Cuyo, the patron of San Martín's army, while its mausoleum is the final resting place of the Liberator's daughter, son-in-law, and granddaughter, repatriated from France in 1951 (the patriarch himself remains in Buenos Aires).

Other points of interest are more scattered toward the north and northeast. To the north, the **Museo Histórico General San Martín** (Remedios Escalada de San Martín 1843, tel. 0261/4257947) focuses specifically on the Liberator but keeps limited hours: 9:30 A.M.–1 P.M. weekdays only.

Seven blocks east of Plaza San Martín, the south end of **Parque Bernardo O'Higgins** is the site of the **Acuario Municipal** (Ituzaingó and Buenos Aires, tel. 0261/425-3824, 9 A.M.–8 P.M. daily, US$.35); the municipal aquarium has small tanks with mostly small to midsized subtropical and tropical species, primarily from the Río Paraná but also elsewhere in the Americas and a few from Asia and Africa. The standout

tunistically purchased them in Paris after Hamid's overthrow. When they were planted at the park's entrance, though, the provincial coat-of-arms and a condor with wings spread replaced the moon of Mohammed. An alternative version of history—far less romantic—says that Civit ordered the gates directly from Glasgow's McFarlane Ironworks.

Parque San Martín is also home to **Estadio Islas Malvinas** (a soccer venue built for the 1978 World Cup), the hillside **Jardín Zoológico** (zoo, tel. 0261/428-1700, 9 A.M.–6 P.M. daily, US$1), and the **Anfiteatro Frank Romero Day** (site of outdoor concerts and festival events). There is also a pair of natural history and archaeology museums: the **Museo de Ciencias Naturales y Antropológicas Juan Cornelio Moyano** (tel. 0261/428-7666, 8 A.M.–1 P.M. and 2–7 P.M. weekdays except Monday and 3–7 P.M. weekends) and the **Museo Arqueológico Salvador Canals Frau** (tel. 0261/423-0915, 9 A.M.–1 P.M. and 3–7 P.M. weekdays only).

The park is an easy 1.5-kilometer walk from Plaza Independencia, but bus No. 110 ("Favorita") also goes directly to the park and onward to the zoo. **Bateas** (open-air buses) also shuttle passengers from the park entrance to Cerro de la Gloria.

Entertainment

For the latest data on what's happening in town, look for the widely distributed *La Guía* (www .culturamendoza.com.ar), a monthly tabloid giveaway.

Most Mendoza **cinemas** are suburban multiplexes, but there are irregular programs downtown at the **Microcine Municipal David Eisenchlas** (9 de Julio 500, tel. 0261/449-5180), in the basement of the Municipalidad. The **Cine Teatro Universidad Nacional de Cuyo** (Lavalle 55, tel. 0261/420-4549) also shows occasional films.

In easterly Guaymallén, try the Mendoza Plaza Shopping's **Village Cinemas** (Avenida Acceso Oeste 3280, tel. 0261/421-0700), reached by the T-Red bus from 9 de Julio. In southerly Godoy Cruz, there's the Palmares Open Mall's **Cinemark** (Panamericana 2650, tel. 0261/439-

5015), reached by bus No. 43 from Plaza Independencia.

The subterranean **Teatro Quintanilla**(tel. 0261/423-2310) is part of Plaza Independencia's Museo de Arte Moderno complex, while the **Teatro Municipal Mendoza** is at San Juan 1427 (tel. 0261/425-3744).

Dating from 1925, Mendoza's major performing arts venue is the remodeled and recently reopened **Teatro Independencia** (Chile 1187, tel. 0261/438-0644).

For live music, downtown **Da Praia** (9 de Julio 976, tel. 0261/423-0190) showcases a variety of musical styles ranging from tango to jazz and bossa nova. **El Cuervo** (San Martín and Pedro Molina) has live music Friday nights and a 1–3 A.M. happy hour.

Prometeus (Arístides Villanueva 480 (tel. 0261/425-0113) is one of the many new and lively bars in the rapidly developing scene on the north side of town.

For live folklore and tango on Thursday, Friday, and Saturday nights, along with regional cuisine, try **El Retortuño** (Dorrego 123, Guaymallén, tel. 0264/431-6300, www.intertour-net.com.ar/elretortuno), only a few blocks south of the bus terminal.

Most **discos** and **dance clubs,** such as **Aloha** and **Runner,** are clustered along the old Panamericana in the suburb of Chacras de Coria, in the southerly department of Luján de Cuyo. It's about a 20-minute cab ride from downtown.

Events

Mendoza's biggest single festival is March's moveable **Fiesta Nacional de la Vendimia** (www .vendimia.mendoza.gov.ar), celebrating the autumn wine harvest for a week. Filled with concerts and parades, it ends with the queen's coronation in Parque San Martín's amphitheater.

Mid-February's **Vuelta Ciclística de Mendoza** is a major road race for bicyclists. Mendoza celebrates the ski season with the **Festival de la Nieve** in August.

Shopping

Plaza Independencia is the site of the **Plaza de las Artes** outdoor crafts fair, which takes place every

Friday, Saturday, and Sunday. The rest of the week, from 8 A.M.–1 P.M., the downtown **Mercado Artesanal** (Avenida San Martín 1143, tel. 0261/420-4239) offers the opportunity to purchase handicrafts from around and beyond the province, including weavings, horse gear, and basketry.

More than its name would suggest, **Las Viñas** (Avenida Las Heras 399, tel. 0261/425-1520, www.lasvinas.com.ar) has plenty of wines but also a bundle of other artisanal items ranging from ceramics and silverwork to leather, hides, ponchos, weavings, and even dried fruits. It's occupied the same site since 1950.

Mendoza also has specialty wine shops such as **Uvas Mendocinas** (Alem 97, tel. 0261/4203924), where knowledgeable sales staff offer a selection of fine wines to premium wines, and **La Casa del Vino** (Arístides Villanueva 160, tel. 0261/423-5862), with a large selection and tasting as well.

García Santos Libros (San Martín 921, tel. 0261/429-2287) has a sophisticated choice of books on Argentina and Spanish-language literature. **Librería SBS** (Gutiérrez 54, tel. 0261/425-2917) has English-language books.

Sports and Recreation

Mendoza Province is one of Argentina's prime outdoor recreation areas, offering climbing and hiking, cycling and mountain biking, skiing, and white-water rafting and kayaking. It's possible to organize many (though not all) activities through the city agencies listed below, but other providers have on-site services in the Andes, along RN 7 (the main route to Chile) and the Río Mendoza. Note that most operators deal in more than one activity.

For specific information on climbing Cerro Aconcagua and on operators who provide support services, see the separate entry on Parque Provincial Aconcagua.

The **Club Andinista Mendoza** (Fray Luis Beltrán 357, tel. 0261/431-9870, Guaymallén) is a good general information source for climbing and hiking. **Orviz** (Avenida J.B. Justo 532, tel. 0261/425-1281) rents and sells climbing and hiking gear.

Mendoza's mountain roads make it one of Argentina's most popular areas for cyclists, though

Upper Río Mendoza

© WAYNE BERNHARDSON

some of the paved highways (such as RN 7) are very narrow and the tunnels (though most of them are short) can be particularly unnerving.

Travesía Mountain Bike (Montecaseros 699, Godoy Cruz, tel. 0261/448-0289) arranges bicycle excursions.

Several places in town rent or sell ski gear, including **Esquí Mendoza Competición** (Avenida Las Heras 583, tel. 0261/429-7544), **Extreme** (Colón 733, Local 1, tel. 0261/429-0733), **Piré** (Avenida Las Heras 615, tel. 0261/425-7699), and **Rezagos de Ejército** (Avenida Mitre 2002, tel. 0261/423-3791).

The only white-water-rafting operator with its own offices in downtown Mendoza is **Betancourt Rafting** (Lavalle 35, Local 8, tel. 0261/429-9665, www.betancourt.com.ar), which does the lower stretches of the Río Mendoza from its Cacheuta base (only 25 km south of town); Cacheuta is, in a sense, a dead-end destination since the rerouting of the Panamericana.

The other main rafting companies, **Ríos Andinos** and **Argentina Rafting,** have their headquarters in Potrerillos, on the upper Río Mendoza, but many of Mendoza's travel agencies and hostels organize groups there and, less frequently, on the Diamante and on the Atuel, both near San Rafael.

Accommodations

Mendoza has plenty of accommodations, including a fast-growing number of quality backpackers' hostels, but the city's popularity occasionally puts pressure on the available resources in all categories. Reservations are essential for March's Fiesta de la Vendimia and highly advisable for Semana Santa and other long weekends—including the Chilean patriotic holidays of mid-September (since the Argentine devaluation of late 2001, Chileans have flocked to Mendoza at every opportunity). Tourist offices at the bus terminal and downtown are more than helpful in locating accommodations.

Under US$10

Campers can stay at Parque San Martín's **Churrasqueras del Parque** (tel. 0261/428-0511, US$1 pp, per tent, and per vehicle). Reached by bus Nos. 50 and 100, it has more than adequate infrastructure but, given the proximity of its namesake *parrilla*, it's not necessarily the place for a sound night's sleep.

Traditionally popular with climbers and trekkers, in an outstanding Plaza Independencia location, the HI-affiliated, 34-bed **Hostel Campo Base** (Avenida Mitre 946, tel./fax 261/429-0707, info@campo-base.com.ar, www.hostelcampobase.com.ar, US$3.50 pp) has become even more popular since devaluation, and reservations are advisable all year. Most rooms are dorm quadruples, but there are a couple doubles; all share the same modernized baths. There's also a bar, and Wednesday- and Saturday-night *asados*.

Also well-located, the new **Huellas Andinas Hostel** (Rivadavia 640, tel. 0261/420-2846) is a small (18-bunk) facility that lacks some of the amenities—restaurants, bars, even swimming pools—of other city hostels. Rates, though, are just US$3.50 pp for a bunk, plus US$.50 for breakfast.

Mendoza's other HI affiliate, the more capacious **Ⓜ Hostel Internacional Mendoza** (Avenida España 343, tel./fax 0261/424-0018 or 0261/424-8432, info@hostelmendoza.net, www.hostelmendoza.net) sleeps up to 80 people and starts at US$4.50 pp in quadruple and sextuple dorms, breakfast included; doubles cost US$6 pp. It also has excellent kitchen facilities, a restaurant, a bar *El Carajo* (where the iconic folk-rock performer León Gieco has been a drop-in performer). It picks up passengers from the bus terminal and arranges excursions in and around the city through its travel agency Choique Turismo Alternativo (www.choique.net).

Occupying a large rehabbed house on Plaza Independencia, congenial **Ⓜ Hostel Independencia** (Mitre 1237, tel. 0261/423-1806, info @hostelindependencia.com.ar, www.hostelindependencia.com.ar) has cramped quarters for sleeping—the dorms average eight beds to a room—but it has great common areas, including a bar, and also offers some unique excursions. Rates are US$5 pp, but there are some slightly dearer doubles.

Opposite Parque San Martín is the **Hostel Nacional Altas Cumbres** (Boulogne Sur Mer 1435, tel. 0261/15-507-2383, hostelnacional @hotmail.com, www.hostelaltascumbres.miarroba.com, US$4 pp for dorm rooms, US$5.50 pp for doubles).

Near Plaza Chile is the tidy, amiable **Petit Hotel** (Perú 1459, tel. 0261/423-2099, US$8/12 s/d with breakfast). For many years **Residencial Savigliano** (Pedro Palacios 944, tel. 0261/423-7746, savigliano@hotmail.com, www.savigliano.com.ar, US$5 pp with breakfast in dorms, US$8/13 s/d with private bath) was one of Mendoza's best budget choices; it's still probably fair to say that it's the best one near the bus terminal, but newer hostels have usurped much of its clientele. It's easily accessible by the pedestrian tunnel beneath Avenida Videla.

US$10–25

Sosahaus Hostel (Juan B. Justo 56, tel. 0261/425-4586, reservas@sosahaus.com, www

.sosahaus.com, US$5.50 pp dorms, US$7 pp doubles) is a modern building in a good neighborhood; rooms have two to six beds.

Austere but otherwise outstanding in its range, the well-kept and well-placed **City Hotel** (General Paz 95, tel. 0261/425-1343, cityhotelmendoza@yahoo.com, US$8/13 s/d with private bath, breakfast, and a/c) is friendly and helpful.

A few doors down from the Sosahaus, **Hotel Marconi** (Juan B. Justo 20, tel./fax 0261/423-3646) is a cheerful and well-kept place where rooms with private bath, cable TV and a/c cost US$10/15 s/d with breakfast. A good value, it's often full.

On a quiet block, **Hotel Necochea** (Necochea 541, tel. 0261/425-3501 or 423-5112, hotelnecochea@supernet.com.ar, www.mendozatour.com.ar/necochea, US$8.50 pp) has small and rather dark rooms that can get stuffy in the summer heat, but good prices.

Don't expect to get to sleep early at **⚑ Damajuana Hostel** (Arístides Villanueva 282, tel./fax 0261/425-5858, info@damajuanahostel.com.ar, www.damajuanahostel.com.ar), since that's not why people stay in the midst of Mendoza's burgeoning restaurant/nightlife district. Though it has only one room suitable for singles or couples, this hostel has extraordinary common areas including spacious gardens, a large swimming pool, and a bar/restaurant that's worth considering even for those who don't care to stay in a hostel. Rates are US$6–7 pp depending on the number of beds; the doubles cost US$20.

The Deco-style **Palace Hotel** (Avenida Las Heras 70, tel. 0261/423-4200, fax 0261/429-5930, hpalace@infovia.com.ar, www.hotelpalace.com.ar, US$13/20 s/d) lacks luxuries but is well-kept and friendly; its Italian restaurant is a local landmark.

On a placid cul-de-sac, the central **Hotel Milena** (Pasaje Babilonia 17, tel. 0261/420-2490, US$16/22 s/d with breakfast) has smallish but well-maintained rooms and parking. There's a 10 percent discount for payments in cash.

Down the block from the Damajuana, **Casona Tittarelli** (Aristides Villanueva 470, tel. 0261/4202486, casonatittarelli@yahoo.com.ar, www.casonatittarelli.com.ar) is a work-in-progress: an enormous family house with energetic youthful management, sprawling gardens, a small pool, and a variety of rooms that range from hostel quadruples (US$8 pp) to more spacious rooms (US$15/24 s/d) with private bath. Slightly cheaper garden rooms with shared bath are also available. Like the Damajuana, it's best for nightlifers, as it's alongside a popular bar.

US$25–50

When its ongoing remodel finally ends, **Hotel Crillón** (Perú 1065, tel. 0261/423-8963, US$25/31 s/d) should be worth the price. The three-star **Hotel Carollo** (25 de Mayo 1184, tel. 0261/423-5666 or 0261/423-5667, reservas@hotelcarollo.com, www.hotelcarollo.com, US$23/26 s/d with breakfast and free airport transfers) is a remodeled business-oriented building.

Despite a misleading modern facade, its adjacent and slightly more expensive sister **Hotel Princess** (25 de Mayo 1168, tel./fax 0261/423-5669, reservas@princess.com.ar, US$27/30 s/d) is not bad but is worn around the edges.

The glisteningly modernized, conveniently central **⚑ Hotel Cadena del Sol** (Garibaldi 82, tel./fax 0261/420-4820, cds-mendoz@arnet.com.ar, US$23/28 s/d) is overtaking some of the more established downtown hotels, with breakfast, cable TV, and similar amenities. Rooms at the immaculate, highly recommended **Hotel Provincial** (Belgrano 1259, tel. 0261/425-8284, fax 0261/425-4022, info@hotelprovincialmza.com, www.hotelprovincialmza.com, US$25/33 s/d) has modern conveniences like card keys, Internet connections, and the like—unusual for the price.

Dating from the 1940s, **Grand Hotel Balbi** (Avenida Las Heras 340, tel. 0261/423-3500, fax 0261/438-0626, balbistarhotel@arnet.com.ar, US$28/37 s/d) may be a four-star anachronism, but it's still good value, with a spacious lobby and other common areas, plus a modest swimming pool.

Arguably the best in town when it opened for the 1978 World Cup, **Gran Hotel Huentala** (Primitivo de la Reta 1007, tel. 0261/420-0766, fax 0261/420-0664, granhotel@huentala.com, www.huentala.com, US$28/48 s/d with buffet breakfast) has maintained its standards, though some newer or rehabbed places may be better values.

US$50–100

Only the facade remains of the landmark Hotel Plaza, which has been gutted, partially demolished, and replaced by a multistory five-star structure that, nevertheless, has managed to blend into a traditional neighborhood as the new **M Park Hyatt Mendoza** (Chile 1124, tel. 0261/441-1234, fax 0261/441-1235, www.mendoza.park .hyatt.com). Once again Mendoza's prestige hotel, it has a restaurant, café, spa, casino, sports bar, and frequent events and entertainment. Rates start at US$58 s or d plus 21 percent IVA, but non-Argentines may have to pay price differentials.

Food

Mendoza's restaurant scene has always been dispersed, but there's a rapidly developing gastronomic axis along the six blocks of Arístides Villanueva, the westward extension of Avenida Colón, toward Parque San Martín. Some places are both food and entertainment venues, so check the Entertainment section above as well.

For lunch on a budget or for picnic fixin's, the best and most diverse option is **Mercado Central** (Avenida Las Heras and Patricias Mendocinas), dating from 1883; a warren of stalls sell groceries and first-rate fast food including empanadas, pizza, and sandwiches.

For a sandwich on downtown's shaded sidewalks, along with cold draft beer, try **La Cervecería** (Sarmiento 63) or any of several others nearby. **Café Mediterráneo** (Avenida Las Heras 596, tel. 0261/420-0322) is similar. **Las Tinajas** (Lavalle 38, tel. 0261/429-1174) is popular for its diverse buffet menu, all-you-can-eat in the US$4–5 range.

La Tasca de Plaza España (Montevideo 117, tel. 0261/423-3466) is a small, informal Spanish-style restaurant with youthful energy, decent lunch specials (entrees in the US$2–3 range), and very fine desserts. **El Mesón Español** (Montevideo 244, tel. 0261/429-6175) is a more traditional Spanish locale. **Praga** (Leonidas Aguirre

413, tel. 0261/425-9585) has earned a reputation for its seafood specialties.

Parrillas, of course, are numerous. Among the good choices for beef-eaters are **Boccadoro** (Mitre 1976, tel. 0261/425-5056); **Arturito** (Chile 1515, tel. 0261/425-1489); the enormously popular and economical **Mambrú** (Avenida Las Heras 510, tel. 0261/425-4482); and **Facundo** (Avenida Sarmiento 641, tel. 0261/420-2866), which has attractive outdoor seating.

Vegetarians have fewer options, but can sample the fare at **Línea Verde** (San Lorenzo 550, tel. 0261/423-9806), which also has takeout food.

The Palace Hotel's **Trevi** (Las Heras 70, tel. 0261/423-3195) is a reliable but run-of-the-mill Italo-Argentine restaurant with moderate prices. **Montecatini** (General Paz 370, tel. 425-2111) is comparable in quality and price.

Relocated after a recent fire, **M La Marchigiana** (España 1615, tel. 0261/423-0751) remains the place to be seen in Mendoza, but its unpretentious Italian kitchen, unexpectedly democratic ambience, and outstanding service combine to keep it one of Mendoza's finest. It's pricier than the standard Italo-Argentine fare, though, with most entrees in the US$5–7 range.

In the atrium of the Escorihuela winery in adjacent Godoy Cruz, celebrity chef Francis Mallman's **M 1884** (Belgrano 1188, tel. 0261/424-2698) is the prestige place to dine in Mendoza, with gourmet versions of what, in Argentina, is standard home cooking; reservations are advisable.

The Damajuana hostel's **Chano** (Arístides Villanueva 282, tel. 0261/425-5858) is remarkably stylish and lively, with variations on standard Argentine dishes.

For fine ice cream, try **Helado y Cía** (Arístides Villanueva 240, tel. 0261/425-7555), which also delivers, or **Zuckersüss** (Martínez de Rozas 1365, tel. 0261/429-2930).

Information

Open 9 A.M.–9 P.M. daily, the municipal **Centro de Información Turística** (CIT, Garibaldi and San Martín, tel. 0261/420-1333) has maps, brochures, and capable personnel that usually includes an English speaker. A second **CIT**

M
Cuyo

(Avenida Las Heras 341, Local 3, tel. 0261/429-6298) is open 9 A.M.–1 P.M. daily except Saturday and 5–9 P.M. weekdays only. Their parent office, the **Dirección Municipal de Turismo** (9 de Julio 500, tel. 0261/449-5185), is open 8 A.M.–1 P.M. weekdays only.

At the bus terminal in Guaymallén, there's a separate and very efficient **Oficina de Informes** (Alberdi and Reconquista, tel. 0261/431-3001, 7 A.M.–11 P.M. daily).

Open 8 A.M.–10 P.M. weekdays, 9 A.M.–10 P.M. on weekends, the improved provincial **Subsec-**

retaría de Turismo (Avenida San Martín 1143, tel. 0261/420-2800, turismo@mendoza.gov.ar, www.turismo.mendoza.gov.ar) has good information on the entire province.

For motorists, **ACA** is at Avenida San Martín 985 (tel. 0261/420-2900).

Services

At one end of one of Argentina's most important border crossings, Mendoza has the most complete services of any provincial city.

Mendoza is one of the easiest places to cash

WINERIES IN MAIPÚ

E ast of downtown Mendoza, the department of Maipú has a huge concentration of wineries, many of them open for tours and tasting. For the most part, weekday tours are the rule, but several are open Saturday morning and a handful on Saturday afternoon and Sunday. The No. 170 *colectivo* reaches several of these from Rioja and Garibaldi in downtown Mendoza; they are arranged according to distance from the capital. Public transportation is the cheapest way, but guided tours or hired *remises* can make logistics simpler—and safer than driving.

Bodegas López

One of Mendoza's largest wineries, dating from 1898, López is an industrial facility that grows 95 percent of its own grapes on 1,060 hectares in the Uco Valley, near Tupungato; 90 percent of its output is for domestic consumption, while 10 percent goes for export. Its diverse line includes Cabernet Sauvignon, Malbec, Merlot, Sangiovese, Pinot Noir, Chardonnay, Chenin Blanc, and Semillón.

One-hour guided tours, with fluent English-speaking guides, begin with a video and then cover the entire production process, from arrival of the grapes to bottling and packaging, and end with a liberal tasting. On request, with reservations, López arranges lunches for a minimum of four people, with unlimited wine, for US$15 pp.

Bodegas López (Ozamis 375, General Gutiérrez, Maipú, tel. 0261/497-2406, lopezmza@bode-gaslopez.com.ar, www.bodegaslopez.com.ar) is 13.5 kilometers from downtown Mendoza. Tours take place at 9 and 11 A.M. and 2 and 6 P.M. weekdays, hourly from 9:30 A.M.–12:30 P.M. Saturday and holidays, Sunday by appointment only.

Antigua Bodega Giol

Seven blocks south of Bodegas López, the former Bodega Giol was once one of Mendoza's major wineries, but it's now a cooperative that operates at only about 10 percent of capacity. Still, its classic historical installations are well worth seeing, even if the operation is a shadow of its past. Note particularly the 75,000-liter French oak barrel, decorated with a bronze sculpture commemorating the centenary of the Revolution of 1810. Bodega Giol (Ozamis 1040, tel. 0261/497-6777) is open 9 A.M.–6:30 P.M. daily except Sunday, when hours are 11 A.M.–2 P.M.

Across the street to the south, the founding Gargantini-Giol family's French Classic mansion is now the **Museo Nacional del Vino y la Vendimia** (Ozamis 914, tel. 0261/497-2448, int. 252), offering a good historical summary of Maipú's winemaking industry (guided tours US$.35). Unfortunately, when the province took over the winery in the 1960s, turning it into offices, it sold off most of the classic furnishings and painted over much of the priceless original woodwork and zinc ceilings. Restoration has barely begun. It's open 9 A.M.–7 P.M. daily except Sunday, when it closes at 2 P.M.

travelers checks in the entire country, thanks to efficient exchange houses like **Exprinter** (Avenida San Martín 1198) and **Cambio Santiago** (Avenida San Martín 1199), which is open late Saturdays; both, however, charge commissions around two percent.

Downtown ATMs are abundant, including the ones at **Citibank** (Sarmiento 20) and **Banco de la Nación** (Necochea and 9 de Julio).

Correo Argentino is at Avenida San Martín and Avenida Colón; central Mendoza's postal code is 5500.

Locutorios such as **Fonobar** (Sarmiento 23) also have Internet access, but there are many others in the downtown area.

Student- and budget-oriented **Asatej** (Sarmiento 223, tel./fax 0261/429-0029, mendoza@asatej.com.ar) will seek out the best deals for airfares. **Isc Viajes** (Avenida España 1016, tel. 0261/425-9259) is the AmEx affiliate.

Other agencies, which offer conventional excursions such as winery tours, include **Turismo Mendoza** (Las Heras 543, tel./fax 0261/429-2013)

Cavas del Conde

Just off RN 7, the main Buenos Aires highway, Cavas del Conde (1919) considers itself a boutique winery with an annual production of about three million liters, 90 percent of which is exported, mostly to the United States. Very well-organized and attentive half-hour tours, with personable guides, include tasting (incorporating a brief but useful lesson in wine appreciation) in the subterranean *cavas* themselves.

Cavas del Conde (Dorrego s/n, Coquimbito, tel. 0261/497-2624, turismo@cavasdelconde.com, www.cavasdelconde.com) is open 9:30 A.M.–7 P.M. from the summer solstice to the fall equinox, 9 A.M.–5:30 P.M. the rest of the year.

Bodega La Rural

One of Mendoza's largest wineries, with a capacity of 10.7 million liters and four vineyards scattered around the province, La Rural produces some of the country's finest premium vintages in its Rutini line. Set on only 10 hectares, its Maipú facility turns out red varietals including Cabernet Sauvignon, Malbec, Merlot, and Syrah, as well as Chardonnay and Gewürztraminer.

Dating from 1885, La Rural is also one of the most popular wineries for guided tours, partly because of its remarkable **Museo del Vino,** a wide-ranging collection of antique wine-making technology. The museum includes vehicles like tractors and trucks, plus horse carriages of many

kinds, and also has a well-integrated, first-rate tasting room and an art gallery.

Despite capable guides, tours can be disappointing—and excruciatingly slow—because La Rural's popularity means groups as large as 50 people. Avoid holidays, in particular, and try to go early in the morning in hopes of joining a smaller group.

Bodega La Rural (Montecaseros 2625, Coquimbito, tel. 0261/497-2013, administracion@bodegalarural.com.ar, www.bodegalarural.com.ar) is open 9:30 A.M.–5:30 P.M. weekdays, 10 A.M.–5 P.M. Saturday and 10 A.M.–1 P.M. Sunday.

Bodega Viña El Cerno

It's tempting to call Viña El Cerno the anti–La Rural, as this tiny artisanal winery's annual production is only about 9,000 bottles each of Malbec, Cabernet Sauvignon, Syrah, Merlot, and Chardonnay, plus some sparkling wines. Genuinely charming, its aged brick *cavas* can accommodate barely a dozen visitors, but the guides are gracious hosts and its ample tasting facility—guides also instruct guests *how* to go about it—is ideal.

Viña El Cerno (Moreno 631, Coquimbito, Maipú, tel. 0261/481-1567, elcerno@lanet.com.ar, www.elcerno.com.ar) is about seven kilometers south of La Rural on the same bus line. It's open 9 A.M.–5 P.M. daily except Sunday, when hours are 10 A.M.–2 P.M. only.

and **Turismo Sepean** (Primitivo de la Reta 1088, tel. 0261/420-4162).

Many agencies offer excursions in the vicinity of Mendoza, ranging from simple city and wine tours to river rafting, climbing, and trekking. Among adventure operators, try **Campo Base Adventures & Expeditions** (Mitre 946, tel. 261/429-0707, www.cerroaconcagua.com.ar), based at downtown Mendoza's Campo Base hostel, specifically for climbing and trekking; **Aymará Turismo** (9 de Julio 1025, tel. 0261/420-2064) for mule trips, trekking, and rafting; and **Choique Turismo Alternativo** (Avenida España 343, tel. 0261/424-0018, info@choique.net, www.choique.net).

Chile's consulate is at Paso de los Andes 1071 (tel. 0261/425-4844), while the Bolivian consulate is at Garibaldi 384, 1st floor (tel. 0261/429-2458).

For visa extensions, **Migraciones** is at Avenida San Martín 1859, Godoy Cruz, tel. 0261/424-3510, but it's probably as cheap to cross the Andes to Chile and come back.

For Spanish-language instruction, try the **Intercultural de Lenguas Extranjeras** (Rondeau 277, tel. 0261/429-0269; info@intercultural.com.ar, www.intercultural.com.ar).

The **Instituto Cultural Argentino Norteamericano** (Chile 987, tel. 0261/423-6367) has an English-language lending library.

For laundry service, try **Laverap** (Colón 502, tel. 0261/435-2035) or **La Lavandería** (San Lorenzo 352, (tel. 0261/429-4782).

The **Hospital Central** is at Salta and Alem (tel. 0261/420-0600). For ambulance service, contact the **Servicio Coordinado de Emergencia** (tel. 107 or 0261/428-0000).

Getting There

Mendoza has both domestic and international connections by air and road. There is talk of reviving rail service across the Andes to Chile, but this is not likely any time soon.

Aerolíneas Argentinas (Sarmiento 82, tel. 0261/420-4100) and close affiliate Austral fly several times daily to Aeroparque, sometimes via Córdoba.

Southern Winds (Avenida España 943, tel. 0261/429-7788) flies to Aeroparque twice each weekday and daily on weekends, with similar schedules to Santiago de Chile. Mendoza's only other international connections are with **Lan-Chile** (Rivadavia 135, tel. 0261/425-7900), which flies twice daily to Santiago de Chile.

Mendoza's gigantic **Terminal del Sol** (Avenida Gobernador Videla and Avenida Acceso Este, Guaymallén, tel. 0261/431-3001 or 0261/431-0500) is just over the departmental line. Provincial, regional, long-distance, and international services (frequently to Chile, less frequently to Perú, and seasonally to Uruguay) are available. There are also restaurants, shops, and even showers.

To the upper Río Mendoza Valley destinations of Uspallata and Los Penitentes (for access to Parque Provincial Aconcagua), there are three or four buses daily with **Expreso Uspallata** (tel. 0261/431-3309). Some agencies offer weekend service, including **Turismo Mendoza** (Avenida Las Heras 543, tel. 0261/429-2013) and **Mendoza Viajes** (Sarmiento 129, tel. 0261/461-0210).

Vallecito (tel. 0261/432-4456) goes daily to San Agustín del Valle Fértil via the provincial capital of San Juan and the Difunta Correa shrine, while several other companies go to San Juan only. There are also services to Barreal and Calingasta, in western San Juan Province, and to Jáchal, north of San Juan.

In ski season, several companies go directly to Las Leñas, including Turismo Mendoza and Expreso Uspallata, but the rest of the year it's necessary to change in San Rafael or Malargüe.

Typical destinations, fares, and times include San Rafael (US$4, three hours), San Juan (US$3.50, two hours), Uspallata (US$3.50, 2.5 hours), Los Penitentes (US$6.50, 3.5 hours), San Agustín del Valle Fértil (US$9, six hours), and Malargüe (US$7, 5.5 hours).

Mendoza is a hub for long-distance bus services, and departures are frequent in almost every direction except perhaps the Mesopotamian littoral (Puerto Iguazú, for instances, usually has only a few departures each week).

Sample destinations, fares, and times include Córdoba (US$16, nine hours), Santa Rosa

(US$22, 12 hours), Neuquén (US$23, 13 hours), Tucumán (US$28, 15 hours), Buenos Aires (US$23–30, 14 hours), Salta (US$35, 19 hours), Bariloche (US$35, 18 hours), Puerto Madryn (US$40, 21 hours), Corrientes (US$39, 20 hours), Puerto Iguazú (US$49, 26 hours), and Río Gallegos (US$71, 37 hours).

Numerous bus companies cross the Andes to the Chilean capital of Santiago (US$8–10, seven hours) and the beach resort of Viña del Mar, but shared *taxis colectivos* like **Coitram** (tel. 0261/431-1999) and **Chiar Autos** (tel. 0261/432-3112) to Santiago are faster and only a little more expensive. **Empresa General Artigas** (EGA, tel. 0261/431-7758) and **El Rápido** (tel. 0261/431-4093) go to Montevideo, Uruguay (US$36, 22 hours), with onward service to Punta del Este and Brazil.

Getting Around

Getting around compact central Mendoza is fairly straightforward on foot, but reaching wineries and other suburban sites requires using taxis (relatively but not extravagantly expensive) or buses. As of writing, the bus system was undergoing a potentially major rerouting effort, so readers should verify any information that appears here. Buses require Mendobús magnetic cards, available at downtown kiosks.

Aeropuerto Internacional Plumerillo (tel. 0261/520-6000) is six kilometers north of downtown along RN 40. From downtown's Calle Salta, bus No. 60 ("Aeropuerto") goes directly to the terminal, or a *remise* costs about US$3.50.

Just across the departmental line in Guaymallén, the Terminal del Sol is easily accessible via a pedestrian underpass from Avenida Alem, or by the "Villa Nueva" trolley bus from Lavalle between Avenida San Martín and San Juan.

Rental agencies include **Avis** (Primitivo de la Reta 914, tel. 0261/420-3178), **Dollar** (Primitivo de la Reta 936, Local 6, tel. 0261/429-9939), and **Localiza** (San Juan 931, tel. 0261/429-0876).

VICINITY OF MENDOZA
Chacras de Coria and Vicinity

Thirty years ago, the Luján de Cuyo suburb of Chacras de Coria was an area of vineyards and orchards on Mendoza's southern outskirts but, while some vintners and farmers hang on, a growing number of trophy houses on giant lots have displaced much of the city's former fruit bowl. The surviving poplar windbreaks and sycamore-lined streets hide many of the worst offenders, though, and Chacras's stylish and diverse restaurants have made it popular for evening outings—or lunch between visits to vineyards.

In and around Chacras, the biggest attractions are the numerous wineries; for details and visiting hours, see the sidebar "Wineries in Luján de Cuyo."

The **Museo Provincial de Bellas Artes Emiliano Guiñazú** (San Martín 3651, Mayor Drummond, Luján de Cuyo, tel. 0261/496-0224, 9 A.M.–6 P.M. daily, free) takes its official name from its owner, but its popular name **Casa de Fader** comes from Fernando Fader, the artist hired to decorate this summer residence. Set among expansive gardens, the building is an attraction in itself, with the artist's own peeling murals and remarkable tiled indoor pools. It also holds collections of Fader's landscapes and portraits, plus exhibitions of contemporary art, some of it very imaginative. From downtown Mendoza, take bus No. 200.

Directly on the plaza, the **Cacano Bar** (Aguinaga 1120, tel. 0261/4962018) has live music with drop-in talents like local guitarist David Lebón and, on occasion, his buddy Charly García. For sampling Mendoza's finest by the glass, try the more sedate **180 Copas & Vinos** (Italia 6076, tel. 0261/496-1731, www.180copasyvinos.com), a quality wine bar.

Chacras has few accommodations, but one option is **Hotel San Francisco** (Pueyrredón 2265, tel. 0261/496-0110, US$10/13 s/d without breakfast), charging a very reasonable rate; it has a pool and spacious wooded grounds, but is otherwise only run-of-the-mill.

A better choice is the new **M Finca Adalgisa** (Pueyrredón 2222, tel./fax 261/496-0713 or 261/15-654-3134, gabriela@fincaadalgisa.com.ar, gabrielafurlotti@hotmail.com), which charges US$50 s or d with breakfast for suites, and US$70 for a full house sleeping up to six persons; for up to eight persons, the rate rises to US$90. Set on two hectares of vineyards and

WINERIES IN LUJÁN DE CUYO

South of Mendoza proper, Luján de Cuyo is one of two key wine-producing areas in the greater metropolitan area. It's possible to get around by public transportation, but the best option would be to contract a tour or to assemble a small group and hire a *remise*—thus reducing the risk of becoming a DUI accident victim. Because several of them are close to Chacras de Coria's gourmet ghetto, a lunch break there is an attractive prospect. It's worth verifying hours before visiting any winery, especially if you need an English-speaking guide, but the facilities listed here are generally accessible on a drop-in basis.

Bodega y Cavas de Weinert

In Chacras de Coria, owned by Brazilians of German descent since 1975, Weinert is a premium industrial winery with a production of three million liters per annum. While the production facilities are state-of-the-art, the historic subterranean *cavas*, with their classic French oak casks, date from the 1890s. A generous tasting can include Cabernet, Chardonnay, Sauvignon Blanc, Rosé, and some blends, from an ample selection in the bodega shop.

Bodega y Cavas de Weinert (Avenida San Martín 5923, Chacras de Coria, tel. 0261/496-4676, bodegaweinert@ciudad.com.ar, www.bodegaweinert.com) is open 9 A.M.–5 P.M. weekdays, 10 A.M.–4:30 P.M. Saturday. Guides speak English, German, and French.

Bodega Nieto Senetiner

In the Vistalba area just south of Chacras de Coria, entered by an alameda of ancient olive trees with a backdrop of the Andean front range, Nieto Senetiner's immaculate grounds are a worthy approach to one of the area's most pleasant wineries. The bodega itself dates from 1904, but the production facilities have undergone modernization; the informative tours conclude with a tasting of Malbec, the main varietal produced here.

Tours at Bodega Nieto Senetiner (Guardia Vieja s/n, tel. 0261/498-0315, www.nietosenetiner.com) take place at 10 and 11 A.M. and 12:30 and 4 P.M. daily, but if guides are available other hours are possible. Some guides speak English. With advance notice, garden lunches are also possible, and a new guesthouse is due to open. From downtown Mendoza, *colectivo* No. 200 goes directly to the portal.

Bodega Fabre-Montmayou

A short distance south of Nieto Senetiner, Fabre-Montmayou is one of two wineries under the French umbrella group Domaine Vistalba (the other one is in Patagonia's Río Negro Valley). Malbec is also the main varietal at this relatively small-scale winery.

Bodega Fabre-Montmayou (Sáenz Peña s/n, tel. 0261/498-2330 or 498-5495) is open 9 A.M.–noon and 3–6:30 P.M. weekdays, 9 A.M.–noon Saturday. Make advance arrangements for English- or French-speaking guides.

Bodega Lagarde

Ideally combined with a visit to the nearby Museo Provincial de Bellas Artes Emiliano Guiñazú, the Lagarde winery comprises 250 hectares of vineyards with an annual production capacity of about

orchards worked by mules, it has only seven rooms, plus a pool and fish and duck ponds, with a small restaurant still in the works. The rooms themselves are spacious and comfortable, with colorful Mexican-style interiors, and fine views across the vineyards to the Andes, at least from the upper floors.

Chacras is becoming Mendoza's gourmet ghetto, but there are both economical and upscale dining choices. Since buses stop running around midnight, consider taking a cab or *remise* back into town.

For Mexican semifast food and very respectable margaritas, try the **Taco Bar** (Viamonte s/n), which has a variety of Mexican dishes beyond its name, including good guacamole. It's also cheap, with the margarita the priciest item on the menu at about US$2. More elaborate is the consulate-sponsored **Casa México** (Carril San Martín 4722, tel. 0261/496-2192), which has a fixed-price dinner or lunch for about US$4.50, and more expensive à la carte items. It's open Friday and Saturday only.

© WAYNE BERNHARDSON

jug wine ready for shipment, Luján de Cuyo

2.5 million liters. Its diverse varietals, for both internal consumption and export, include Chardonnay, Sauvignon Blanc, Cabernet Sauvignon, Malbec, Merlot, and Syrah.

With its original bodega and big house intact, dating from 1897, Bodega Lagarde (San Martín 1745, Mayor Drummond, tel. 0261/498-0011, info@lagarde.com.ar, www.lagarde.com.ar) offers tours at 10 and 11 A.M., noon, and 2:30, 3:30, and 4:30 P.M. weekdays only. There are English- and Portuguese-speaking guides.

Bodega Cabrini

Dating from 1918, under four generations of the same family, Cabrini is a small, unpretentious, Italo-Argentine winery that produces quantities of *vino licoroso,* a blend of Malbec, Tempranillo, Lambrusco, and Bonarda grapes, in demijohns

for Catholic masses. Commercially it produces Malbec, Merlot, Syrah, Bonarda, Cabernet Sauvignon, Chardonnay, and Chenin from its own vineyards in Perdriel and nearby Agrelo, and farther south at Ugarteche and Tupungato. It also makes a rosé—not too good, in all honesty—out of Malbec grapes.

Its tours, which include a generous tasting, are a low-key pleasure. Bodega Cabrini (RP 15 Km 22, Perdriel, tel. 0261/488-0218, ivgcabrini@infovia.com.ar) is open 9 A.M.–noon and 3:30–6:30 P.M. weekdays, 9 A.M.–noon Saturday. Phone ahead for English-language guides.

Bodega Chandon

In Argentina since 1959—its first venture beyond France—Chandon produces blended reds and whites as well as sparkling wines. Directly on the highway to San Rafael, 29 kilometers south of Mendoza, its ultramodern visitors center is becoming a landmark.

In the high-season months of January, February, and July, Bodega Chandon (RN 40 Km 29, Agrelo, Luján de Cuyo, tel. 0261/490-9968, visitorcenter@chandon.com.ar, www.chandon.com.ar) offers weekday tours at 9:30 and 11 A.M., and 12:30, 2:30, and 4 P.M.; the 9:30 A.M. and 12:30 P.M. tours have English-speaking guides. Saturday tours are at 9:30 and 11 A.M., and 12:30 P.M., with the 9:30 and 12:30 P.M. tours in English as well. The rest of the year, tours take place at 10:30 A.M., noon, and 2:30 and 4 P.M. weekdays only; weekend tours are by reservation.

A promising newcomer, the **Almacén Español** (Darragueira 6839, tel. 0261/15-414-2028) has very fine entrees like pepper steak and flounder in the US$2–3 range, and a large wine list, as well as outdoor seating and even a takeaway sector. Service, though, needs improvement—it can be informal to the point of distraction. **La Mitre** (Mitre 1400, tel. 0261/496-1029) is another potentially outstanding new bar/restaurant, with both indoor and outdoor seating.

Occupying a recycled stable leased from the Catena winery, the **Dionisio Wine Bar** (Vi-

amonte 4961, tel. 0261/496-1260) is more than its name would suggest—though the ground floor is indeed a wine bar, which serves a remarkable *tabla* (US$7) of open-faced sandwiches, raw ham, dried figs, olives, and minipizzas to accompany an enormous and well-chosen wine list. The upstairs, though, is a full-fledged restaurant with a creative menu of beef, pork, and seafood specialties in the US$5–7 range, along with delectable desserts like lime mousse and triple chocolate in the US$2–3 range (*tablas* are

M Cuyo

also available as appetizers). There are outside tables in summer, but it bears mentioning that the service in general, if well-intentioned, can't match the kitchen's aspirations.

Cacheuta

Since the realignment of RN 7 (the Panamericana to Chile) for expansion of a hydroelectric and irrigation reservoir on the Río Mendoza, Cacheuta has become an end-of-the-road destination for its hot springs hotel—other places that depended on through traffic to Chile have closed—and the rafting company on the river's lower reaches. At 1,237 meters above sea level, Cacheuta is 36 kilometers southwest of Mendoza.

Mendoza's **Betancourt Rafting** (Lavalle 35, Local 8, tel. 0261/4299665 or 0261/15-650-3616, info@betancourt.com.ar, www.betancourt.com.ar) descends the river below the dam for about US$7 pp, and also does trekking, mountain biking, and riding in Potrerillos. Its Cacheuta address is Ruta Panamericana & Río Cuevas, Godoy Cruz (tel. 0261/439-1949).

Cacheuta's only accommodations, **Hotel Termas Cacheuta** (RP 82 Km 39, tel. 02624/490153, reservas@termascacheuta.com, www.termascacheuta.com, US$58/97 s/d with full board) is an all-inclusive resort offering thermal baths, massage, and various recreational programs including hiking and mountain biking. Nonguests may use the facilities for US$23 pp.

Potrerillos

Since the southerly realignment of RN 7, it's a longer (in distance) but shorter (in time) trip to Potrerillos, the white-water rafting, kayaking, and riverboarding center of the upper Río Mendoza. Now 53 kilometers from the provincial capital—about eight kilometers farther than it used to be—Potrerillos (altitude 1,351 meters, population about 300) is growing because the Embalse de Potrerillos, a hydroelectric project, has relocated displaced people in sharp new houses with fine views and finer conveniences than they've ever had before. Whether once-isolated rural people will prosper in their new village environment on a major international highway is another issue entirely.

Windsurfing is also becoming popular on the newly created reservoir, but water sports are not Potrerillos's only recreational option. Winding RP 89, which leads south to the wine country of Tupungato, is a scenically spectacular and little-traveled mountain bike route—though this stiff climb would be much easier from the other end. It is also close to the modest ski area of Vallecitos; for more details, see the sidebar "Skiing in Mendoza."

Raging with runoff from the snowmelt of the high Andes, the Class III–plus Río Mendoza reaches its spring peak of about 2,000 cubic meters per second in the late spring and summer months of December and January. At this volume, the water is high enough that there aren't many rapids, but the river is fast enough and the waves large enough to provide an enthralling rafting or kayaking experience.

There are two main Potrerillos-based operators. Directly across the highway from the ACA campground, **Argentina Rafting Expediciones** (RN 7 Km 53, tel./fax 02624/482037 or 482006, tel. 0261/15-508-5906 or 0261/508-5909, arg_rafting@hotmail.com, www.argentinarafting.com) and **Ríos Andinos** (RN 7 Km 55, tel. 0261/431-6074 in Mendoza, tel. 0261/15-661-7099 in Potrerillos, info@riosandinos.com.ar, www.riosandinos.com.ar).

Rafting excursions come in various lengths, ranging from one-hour (US$10) and two-hour (US$15) descents to more expensive overnight trips comprising about five hours on the water. Both companies also arrange hiking, horseback riding, and other activities. Transfers to and from Mendoza are available through the many agencies that sell their trips.

Directly on RN 7, the wooded **Camping del ACA** (tel. 02624/482013) charges US$3.50 per site for members, US$4 for nonmembers.

Languishing in neglect under provincial administration, the Spanish-colonial-style **Gran Hotel Potrerillos** (RN 7 Km 53, tel. 02624/482130, US$27 d with breakfast and dinner) isn't bad, but there's nobody with the will to reverse the indifference toward guests.

Ríos Andinos founder Sergio Brunetti is planning to add an *hostería* to the company's new riverside headquarters east of town, which should be worth watching for. Argentina Rafting has its own pub/restaurant, **El Futre,** along the river.

Uspallata

From the west, the long lines of Lombardy poplars flanking RN 7 offer a dramatic approach to Uspallata, a crossroads village in an area that, thanks to its resemblance to the central-Asian highlands, enjoyed 131 minutes of cinematic fame as the base for French director Jean-Jacques

Annaud's movie (and Brad Pitt vehicle) of Heinrich Harrer's memoir **Seven Years in Tibet.** Yaks were flown in from a herd in Montana for the filming, and journalist Orville Schell recounted the experience in his book *Virtual Tibet* (New York: Metropolitan Books, 2000).

Since losing out to Luján de Cuyo as a *zona franca* (duty-free zone) for exports to Valparaíso, Chile, Uspallata (population 3,284) has returned to its pre-Hollywood tranquility. In a broad valley surrounded by colorful Andean peaks, 1,751 meters above sea level, it is 52 kilometers northwest of Potrerillos.

SKIING IN MENDOZA

In winter, Pacific storms drop enormous amounts of snow on the western slopes of the Andes, where Chilean resorts like Valle Nevado and Portillo draw skiers from around the continent and the world. Some of this snow makes it over the Andean crest—southerly Las Leñas is Mendoza Province's biggest and best winter resort—but Vallecitos and Los Penitentes are more convenient to the provincial capital.

Area ski resorts generally open in July and close by early October, but in poor snow years they may shut down in early September. Several Mendoza shops have rental equipment, including **Piré Ski & Montaña** (Avenida Las Heras 615, tel./fax 0261/425-7699, piremont@slatinos.com.ar), which also has camping gear and mountaineering equipment.

Vallecitos

About 80 kilometers from Mendoza and 15 kilometers west of Potrerillos in the Cordón del Plata, Vallecitos is a modest 100-hectare ski area at a base of 2,900 meters, ranging up to 3,350 meters. Many if not most visitors are day-trippers from Mendoza, who pay about US$14 per day for lift access; the resort provides its own transport from the capital for US$6 round-trip.

Shoestring travelers can share dorm space at the resort's **Refugio Ski y Montaña Hostel Inn** for US$9 pp with breakfast; at the **Refugio Hostería Valle Nevado,** quadruples cost US$60 (US$15 pp), also with breakfast. Half board and full board are also available.

The season runs from July to early October, but accommodations remain open the entire year; for more details, contact **Valles del Plata** (Perú 1523, Mendoza, tel. 0261/423-6569, informes@skivallecitos.com, www.skivallecitos.com).

Los Penitentes

The summer gateway to Aconcagua, 165 kilometers from the provincial capital, Los Penitentes is an accessible winter resort at a base altitude of 2,580 meters. It has better infrastructure and snow cover than Vallecitos, but in dry years the season can still be short.

Covering 300 hectares, Los Penitentes has 28 separate runs totaling 25.5 kilometers; lift tickets range US$17–25 per day, depending on the time of the season. Many people, however, buy multiday tickets and contract full packages at the resort or other hotels in town. For more details, contact Los Penitentes (Paso de los Andes 1615, Departamento C, Godoy Cruz, Mendoza, tel. 0261/4271641, info@lospenitentes.com).

Cuyo

While westbound RN 7 continues to Parque Provincial Aconcagua and the Chilean border, RP 39 leads north into remote parts of San Luis Province; RP 52 makes a 102-kilometer loop back to Mendoza via the hot springs of **Villavicencio,** on a route followed by San Martín's army in crossing the Andes to liberate Chile, and later by Darwin in crossing the Andes from Santiago. The latter is probably a safer route for cyclists than RN 7, which has several tunnels and heavy truck traffic.

There's not much to see in Uspallata proper, which is primarily a service center along RN 7, but there are several worthwhile sights in the vicinity. About two kilometers north of the highway junction, the **Bóvedas Históricas Uspallata** contains a series of conical kilns used for metallurgy during the 17th century, but even before the Spanish invasion the local Huarpe population processed local ores here. The kilns themselves comprise a museum (10 A.M.–8 P.M. daily, US$.35) that contains a series of dioramas on General Gregorio de Las Heras's trans-Andean campaign in support of San Martín (several key battles took place nearby), but also includes exhibits on mineralogy and the indigenous Huarpe. Descriptions are in Spanish and fractured English.

On RP 39, the road to Calingasta, at Km 12 in San Alberto, the **Comunidad Huarpe Guaytamari** (10 A.M.–8 P.M. daily in summer, US$.35) is a small llama farm and crafts center run by a handful of Huarpe Indians.

About seven kilometers northeast of town, on RP 52 to Villavicencio, volcanic **Cerro Tunduqueral** (10 A.M.–8 P.M. daily in summer, US$.35) offers a fading series of pre-Columbian petroglyphs. Nearby is a monument to Ceferino Namuncurá, a Mapuche Indian who succumbed to pulmonary disease while studying and tending to patients in Italy; promoted as a saint in Argentina, he has not yet cracked the Catholic hierarchy for lack of any miracles attributed to him.

Beyond Cerro Tunduqueral, the **Caracoles de Villavicencio** is a zigzag gravel road that leads to the now-closed hot springs hotel of the same name, where it becomes a straight-as-an-arrow paved highway into Mendoza. En route, the road passes a plaque to Darwin, who found fossil Araucaria trees (now extinct in this area) here, and reaches the scenic heights of the 3,800-meter **Cruz del Paramillo.** A warning sign at the northern outskirts of Uspallata indicates regulated hours for ascending and descending the Caracoles, but its presence owes more to bureaucratic inertia than current reality.

Half a kilometer north of the highway junction, the wooded **Camping Municipal** costs US$3 per site with picnic tables and barbecue pits; the bathrooms have wood-fired showers, so the availability of hot water can vary.

East of the junction, **Hotel Viena** (Avenida Las Heras 240, tel. 02624/420046) charges only US$5 pp for utilitarian rooms with private bath and cable TV. Directly at the junction, the more spacious **Hostería Los Cóndores** (tel./fax 02624/420002, US$17/23 s/d) has a restaurant.

Built for a labor union during the 1940s Peronist heyday, on RN 7 about one kilometer west of the highway junction, **Hotel Uspallata** (tel./fax 02624/420066, cds-uspa@elsitio.net, US$15/22 s/d with breakfast) has improved considerably since coming under management of the Cadena del Sol chain. It's particularly notable for its spacious and manicured grounds, which include a large swimming pool, but the rooms are comfortable enough and it's clearly the best value in town.

On the highway at the south end of town, appealing **Hotel Valle Andino** (tel. 02624/420033) charges US$20/28 s/d with breakfast; amenities include tennis courts and an indoor pool.

In a strip mall at the highway junction, **Café Tibet** (tel. 0261/15-512-0971) opened during the brief cinema boom, but has managed to outlast the Brad Pitt blip with a menu of inexpensive but good-quality pizza and sandwiches.

Other offerings are almost exclusively *parrillas,* including **San Cayetano** (tel. 02624/420049), behind the YPF station; **La Estancia de Elías** (tel. 02624/420165) at the southern approach to town; and **La Bodega del Gato** (tel. 02624/420381).

At last visit, Uspallata was building a new tourist office at the junction of RN 7 and RP 39, across from the YPF gas station. It has a post office (postal code 5545) but no bank or ATM, so bring money from Mendoza. **Comunicación Alta Montaña,** just north of the highway junction, provides phone services, but there is no Internet access as yet.

In the same strip mall as Café Tibet, just north of the highway junction, Expreso Uspallata operates three or four **buses** daily to and from Mendoza (US$3.50, 2.5 hours); westbound services continue to Puente del Inca. If continuing to Chile, it's best to buy a ticket in Mendoza and pick up your bus here or at Penitentes; through buses are often full.

Los Penitentes

Westbound RN 7 splits the settlement of Penitentes, the main base for Aconcagua-bound trekkers and climbers in summer, and for skiers in winter. For details on sights and activities, see the separate Parque Provincial Aconcagua entry and the sidebar "Skiing in Mendoza."

Affiliated with Mendoza's Campo Base Hostel, the **Hostel Refugio Penitentes** (tel. 0261/429-0707), just west of the YPF gas station, is open all year; ski season rates range from US$6–8 pp, but are lower in summer. Across the highway, **Refugio Cruz de Caña** (tel. 0261/15-511-4447) charges US$3 pp for dark bunkrooms without windows, but it's friendly and has a pub/restaurant, satellite TV, hot water, and central heating.

Now open in summer, the ski area's hospitably staffed **Hostería Penitentes** (RN 7 Km 166, tel. 02624/420110) charges US$13 pp with private bath and breakfast included (ski-season prices, though, are parts of packages). Its restaurant serves lunch and dinner as well.

Penitentes's best accommodations, the 50-room **Hotel Ayelén** (RN 7 Km 165, tel. 02624/420229 or 420230, hotelayelen@speedy.com.ar, www.ayelen.net) has become a major base for summer trekkers and climbers visiting Aconcagua, as most of the companies that arrange excursions to the park occupy offices in their next-door apartments. Accommodations include shuttle service to and from the park entrance, and they also offer other excursions in the vicinity. Summer rates are US$42/58 s/d for spacious rooms with, however, limited views. There is also a restaurant.

Nearby, under the same management, **Hostería Ayelén** (Juan B. Justo 1490, Godoy Cruz, tel. 0261/427-1123 or 427-1283, US$7 pp) is a cheaper but still very good alternative with accommodations in doubles, quadruples, and sextuples with private bath; it also has an inexpensive pizzeria.

Puente del Inca

Seven kilometers west of Penitentes, also split by RN 7, Puente del Inca takes its name from the natural bridge over the Río Mendoza. It's also notable for the **Cementerio de los Andinistas,** the climbers' cemetery that reminds visitors that nearby Cerro Aconcagua demands the respect—and sometimes the lives—of those who try to climb it (not all those buried here died on

climbers' cemetery, Puente del Inca

© WAYNE BERNHARDSON

Cuyo

the mountain, though—some chose this as their final resting place). At 2,720 meters above sea level and 177 kilometers west of Mendoza, it's the closest settlement to the Horcones entrance to Parque Provincial Aconcagua, but Penitentes has more-abundant and better accommodations and food.

Puente del Inca enjoys spectacular panoramas of the mountains surrounding Aconcagua and south to the 6,650-meter massif of **Cerro Tupungato,** also part of a Mendoza provincial park; most easily accessible from Tunuyán, its summit route is a technical climb suitable for accomplished snow-and-ice mountaineers only.

Chile-bound travelers, especially those in private vehicles, should note that all border formalities—immigration and customs—take place on the Chilean side; those coming from Chile complete formalities at Los Horcones, immediately west of Penitentes on the Argentine side. Penitentes has the last gas station before the border; the next one is some 50 kilometers west at Río Blanco, Chile.

Shoestring travelers can pitch their tents at **Camping Los Puquios,** on the north side of the highway, but it's a barren, exposed site.

Built for the climate, with smallish bedroom windows that minimize heat loss in winter but also reduce the natural light, **Hostería Puente del Inca** (RN 7 Km 175, tel. 02624/420266, US$17/21 s/d with breakfast) is a mountain lodge with multibedded rooms. Its so-so restaurant serves lunch and dinner.

Cristo Redentor

From Las Cuevas, the last outpost of Argentine territory before the tunnel into Chile, a zigzag dirt road, barely wide enough for a single vehicle in some spots, climbs eight kilometers to a blustery border ridge where Uruguayan sculptor Mateo Alonso's eight-meter, six-ton statue **Cristo Redentor** marks the limit between Chile and Argentina. Taken by train to Uspallata in 1904, it went the rest of the way by mule; it commemorates the peaceful conclusion, in 1902, of a territorial dispute between the two countries.

Reaching 4,200 meters above sea level, this forbidding road was the main route between the two countries until the three-kilometer Cristo Redentor tunnel opened in 1980; today it is the province of tourists and tour buses. Upward-bound vehicles have preference, but not every Argentine driver appears to appreciate this, so be on guard. It's still possible to continue to the Chilean border post at Los Libertadores by foot or bicycle, but the road is not open to motor vehicles beyond the ridge.

At the pass, there are two *refugios,* one Argentine and one Chilean; the former sells cheap sandwiches and coffee; the latter gives away hot chocolate (tips appreciated). Befitting a monument devoted to peace between peoples, Cristo Redentor has its own binational website (www.cristoredentorchiar.galeon.com).

PARQUE PROVINCIAL ACONCAGUA

Approaching the Chilean border, Parque Provincial Aconcagua is the site of the province's most prominent attraction—literally so, as the bulky, 6,962-meter Cerro Aconcagua is the "the roof of the Americas," the highest peak on two continents.

Parque Provincial Aconcagua, encompassing 71,000 hectares, lies entirely north of RN 7. The main point of entry is Laguna Horcones, immediately east of Puente del Inca, but there's also access from Punta de Vacas, 20 kilometers to the east.

Cerro Aconcagua

An irresistible magnet for climbers (and aspiring climbers) from around the world, Aconcagua also draws casual visitors in private motor vehicles and tour buses, as well as day-hikers and long-distance trekkers, to enjoy the big-sky views of the Andean high country.

Of the world's highest summits, Aconcagua probably draws the most climbers because the main route requires no technical expertise—simply good conditioning (and willingness to acknowledge physical limitations), suitable equipment, and the readiness to recognize when conditions become dangerous. The extreme and changeable weather, in particular, has claimed

ACONCAGUA TOUR OPERATORS

Seasoned mountaineers can and have climbed Aconcagua with only their backpacks and boots for support, but less-experienced travelers with the yen (or dollars or pesos) to stand atop the Roof of the Americas usually contract overseas package tours or make logistical support arrangements with local guides and muleteers. Most local operators are based at Penitentes in summer, but also have offices in Mendoza proper or nearby suburbs like Godoy Cruz or Guaymallén. Aconcagua Express has its main office in Santiago, Chile, however.

All of the following operators have substantial experience on the mountain and either have or can arrange pack mules. For suggestions on overseas operators, who usually subcontract with one of those listed here, see Organized Tours in the Know Argentina section.

Aconcagua Express
Avenida Las Condes 12265, Oficina 1,
Las Condes
Santiago, Chile
tel. 56/2-217-9101, fax 215-1243
tel. 0261/510-7822 in Mendoza
info@aconcagua-express.com
www.aconcagua-express.com

Aconcagua Trek
Güiraldes 246
Dorrego, Mendoza
tel./fax 0261/431-7003
aconcagua@rudyparra.com
www.rudyparra.com

Andesport
RN 7 Km 164
Los Penitentes
andes@andesport.com
www.andesport.com

Campo Base
Avenida Mitre 946
Mendoza
tel. 0261/429-0707
info@campo-base.com.ar
www.campo-base.com.ar
www.cerroaconcagua.com

Expediciones Aconcagua Atmir
Vicente Gil 471
Mendoza
tel./fax 0261/420-2536, cell 0261/15-658-5011
antoniomir@aconcaguatmir.com.ar
www.aconcaguatmir.com.ar

Fernando Grajales Expediciones
25 de Mayo 2985, Villa Nueva
Guaymallén, Mendoza
tel./fax 0261/428-3157, cell 0261/15-500-7718
expediciones@grajales.net
www.grajales.net

Gabriel Cabrera Expediciones y Aventura
tel. 0261/452-0641
info@aconcagua2002.com.ar
www.aconcagua2002.com.ar

Inka Expediciones
Juan B. Justo 343
Mendoza
tel./fax 0261/425-0871
inka@aconcagua.org.ar
www.inka.com.ar

Mallku Expediciones
Roque Sáenz Peña 873
Mendoza
tel. 0261/4232582, cell 0261/15-512-4163
info@mallkuexpediciones.com
www.mallkuexpediciones.com

Cuyo

the lives of even experienced mountaineers: in total, 108 have died on the mountain, and there are fatalities almost every year, including four in 2003.

In 1897, Swiss climber Mathias Zurbriggen made Aconcagua's first confirmed ascent, but the 1985 discovery of an Inka mummy on the southwest face, at an altitude of 5,300 meters, demonstrated that pre-Columbian civilizations explored the wild high country of the central Andes. There is disagreement over the etymology of "Aconcagua"—some claim the word comes from the Quechua language and others from the Mapuche—but everyone recognizes its indigenous genesis. Geologically, the mountain consists of uplifted marine sediments covered by volcanic andesite.

Flora and Fauna

Discussions of Aconcagua rarely mention flora and fauna, partly because the mountain's sheer size and altitude overwhelm most other considerations, and partly because of the focus on climbing. Another reason is that, in the rain shadow of the Andean crest, the park is one of the most barren parts of the Andes, with only a discontinuous cover of prostrate shrubs and grasses. At the highest altitudes, it is almost pure scree and snow.

That does not mean it lacks wildlife, as the Andean condor soars above the ridges and summits, and lesser birds are also present along the watercourses that descend from its glaciers and snowfields. Mammals like guanacos and red foxes may be conspicuous, along with smaller rodents.

Hiking and Climbing

The main sight is Aconcagua itself, which is visible from RN 7, but there are better views from **Laguna Horcones,** about two kilometers north of the highway and about 20 minutes from the ranger station (though probably a bit farther than the 400 meters the trail sign suggests).

For day-hikers, the best outing is **Confluencia,** about eight kilometers from the ranger station, at an elevation of 3,368 meters. For a three-day camping trip, the best option is to **Plaza Francia,**

another 13 kilometers to the north, at an elevation of 4,500 meters. This is the base camp for Aconcagua's highly difficult and technical **Pared Sur** (South Face), first ascended by a French group in 1954.

Most climbers take the longer but technically simpler **Ruta Noroeste** (Northwest Route) to Plaza de Mulas, 4230 meters above sea level, where there is camping and even a hotel, and then try for the summit. Hikers can go as far as Plaza de Mulas, for which it makes sense to have a seven-day permit.

An alternative approach, longer than the Ruta Noroeste but less technical than the Pared Sur, is the **Ruta Glaciar de los Polacos** (Polish Glacier route), pioneered by Polish nationals in 1934. Starting at Punta de Vacas, 15 kilometers southeast of Puente del Inca, this route is less crowded than the others but more time-consuming and expensive.

Note that there are variations on all these routes. By whatever route, Aconcagua is a serious mountain that requires excellent physical conditioning, time to adapt to the great altitude, and proper gear for snow, ice, wet, and cold. People have done the summit in as little as seven days from Puente del Inca, but at least an additional week is desirable.

Accommodations and Food

Independent camping is possible at the base camps and along the trails, but tour operators and climbing guides monopolize the best sites during the season. It's also possible to stay and eat at the provincial **Hotel Plaza de Mulas** (tel. 02624/490440 or 02624/490442); this is a radio-telephone connection), which also features electricity, hot showers, telephone, and luggage deposit.

Rates for dorm rooms are US$17 pp with breakfast, US$38 pp with half board, and US$50 pp with full board. More comfortable "B" rooms cost US$27 pp with breakfast, US$48 pp with half board, and US$60 pp with full board; for "A" rooms, the corresponding rates are US$40 pp, US$60 pp, and US$72 pp. Argentine residents get a 20 percent discount in high season, a 40 percent discount the rest of the year.

Other Practicalities

The main information post is at **Los Horcones,** where the rangers have good information and suggestions, and supply trash bags for climbers and trekkers; it's open 8 A.M.–9 P.M. weekdays, 8 A.M.–8 P.M. Saturdays. There are also rangers at Confluencia, Plaza de Mulas, Las Leñas on the Polish route up the Río de las Vacas, and at Plaza Argentina, the last major base camp along the Polish route.

Both hikers and climbers must have permits; those with hiking permits may not continue beyond the base camps. In Mendoza, for most of the year, get permits from the provincial **Dirección de Recursos Naturales Renovables** (Avenida de los Plátanos s/n, tel. 0261/425-2090, aconcagua@mendoza.gov.com.ar, www.recursosnaturales.mendoza.gov.ar), just inside the gates of Parque San Martín. It's open 8 A.M.–6 P.M. weekdays, 9 A.M.–1 P.M. weekends. In summer only, though, permits are available from the nearby Edificio Cuba, and in winter hiking permits are available at Los Horcones itself (though climbing permits are not).

In past years, though, they have been available through the provincial Subsecretaría de Turismo in Mendoza, and this could change again. For the most up-to-date information, check the park's website (www.aconcagua.mendoza.gov.ar), in Spanish and very readable English as well. Climbers must present proof of their experience and show their equipment.

Permit prices depend on season and nationality (there is now a differential pricing system for Argentines and resident foreigners, and for non-Argentines). Low season runs from November 15–30 and February 21–March 15, mid-season December 1–14 and February 1–20, and high season December 15–January 31. Outside these seasons, fees are reduced.

There is no charge for the short hike to Laguna Horcones, but rangers collect a US$1.50 fee for the day hike to Confluencia. For non-Argentines, three-day hiking permits cost US$20 except in high season, when they cost US$30. Seven-day permits (more desirable for their greater flexibility) cost US$30 in low season, US$40 in mid-season, US$50 in high season; climbers pay US$100 in low season, US$200 in mid-season, and US$300 in high season. Argentines and resident foreigners pay around half the above numbers, but in Argentine pesos, so in practice they pay about one-sixth the U.S.-dollar price.

For more detail on hiking in the park and climbing Aconcagua, look for the improved fifth edition of Tim Burford's *Chile and Argentina: the Bradt Trekking Guide* (Bradt Travel Guides, 2001), and for the second edition of R.J. Secor's climbing guide **Aconcagua** (Seattle: The Mountaineers, 1999).

Buses from Mendoza to Uspallata continue to Penitentes, where most hikers and climbers stay. From Penitentes, it's necessary to walk or hire a car to the trailhead at Horcones.

ⓜ BODEGAS SALENTEIN

Built by Dutch capital near Tunuyán, in the Andean foothills southwest of Mendoza, Bodegas Salentein (RP 89 and Videla, Los Arboles, Tunuyán, tel. 02622/423550, info@bodegasalentein.com, www.bodegasalentein.com) is a futuristic—one might even say New Age—winery built with a contemporary aesthetic sensibility. At ground level, stainless-steel tanks hold the wine in four separate wings, each of which operates autonomously; eight meters below ground level, forming the shape of a cross, the four wings meet in a subterranean central amphitheater where the subdued light on circular rows of oak barrels creates a cathedral atmosphere. It is, in fact, a temple of wine.

At 33° S latitude, Salentein vineyards enjoy sunny days and cool nights (the annual average temperature is 14°C), on rocky alluvial soils at a mean elevation of 1,250 meters. Ranging from 1,050 to 1,500 meters above sea level, the vineyards are up to 30 years old, but new plantings are also underway.

While open to tours, Salentein is a work-in-progress; its wines have barely begun to appear on the market and tasting facilities are improvised. In the long run, they will offer *picadas* of cheese and other snacks along with wine-tasting.

Bodegas Salentein can be most easily reached by private car or by *remise* from the town of Tunuyán,

82 kilometers south of Mendoza by RN 40. Hours are 10 A.M.–4 P.M. daily except Sunday. Tunuyán is 17 kilometers east of Salentein.

There are four double rooms available at **Posada Salentein** (Humboldt 2355, 1° Piso, Buenos Aires, tel. 011/4776-6262, fax 4778-0294, www.salenteintourism.com), in an isolated part of the vineyard with a trout-stocked reservoir. Rates are US$80/140 s/d with half board, US$120/200 s/d with full board; this includes wine as well as activities like hiking and horseback riding, along with tours of the bodega.

SAN RAFAEL

Irrigated by the Atuel and Diamante rivers, vineyards and orchards still survive within the limits of San Rafael, heart of a prosperous wine-and-fruit-producing area southeast of the provincial capital. Recreationally, the city is also a base for rafting on the Atuel and Diamante, and for other activities in the nearby Andean foothills.

Dormant during the afternoon siesta, when there is little or no traffic on its sycamore-shaded avenues, San Rafael comes alive in the evening, when locals fill the café tables that occupy its broad clean sidewalks. Most of the local wine route, a good enough reason to visit in its own right, is negotiable on foot.

Orientation

San Rafael (population 104,782) is 236 kilometers southeast of the provincial capital via paved RN 40 and RN 143, and 186 kilometers northeast of Malargüe via RN 144 and RN 40. It is 996 kilometers west of Buenos Aires via RN 7 to Junín (Buenos Aires Province), RN 188 to General Alvear, and RN 143.

Trending northwest to southeast, RN 143 is the main thoroughfare. On the Andean side of the perpendicular Avenida El Libertador/Avenida San Martín axis, its western segment is called Avenida Hipólito Yrigoyen; on the pampas side, its eastern segment is Avenida Bartolomé Mitre. Most sights and services are within a few blocks on either side of the highway.

Wineries

San Rafael grew around its wineries and, while some of them have moved to the outskirts of town, others are very central. On foot and/or by public transportation, it's possible to visit four or five in a single day.

Dating from 1928, **Bodegas Valentín Bianchi** (Ortiz de Rosas and Comandante Torres, tel. 02627/422046, informes@vbianchi.com, www.vbianchi.com), offers guided tours (Spanish, English, and Italian) with tasting at 9:15, 10:15, and 11:15 A.M., and at 2:15 and 4:15 P.M. When it began, this five-story bodega (three levels of which are underground) was far less central than it is now, in what has become a residential neighborhood only five blocks south of Avenida Mitre. Eventually, Bianchi will move nearly all of its operations to its champagne-processing plant, about five kilometers west of town on RN 143, but it will continue to store wines here and may turn the structure into a museum (San Rafael, in general, lacks museums).

About two kilometers west of downtown, founded by a Franco-Swiss family in 1956, **Bodega Juan Rivier e Hijos** (Avenida Hipólito Yrigoyen 2385, tel. 02627/432676, fax 02627/432675, bodega@jeanrivier.com, www.jeanrivier.com) is open 8–11 A.M. daily except Sunday, and 3–7 P.M. weekdays only. Still a small-scale family affair, its spontaneous tours (one-on-one if necessary, Spanish, or French on request) and generous tasting that includes its specialty *tocai friulano,* a varietal of Italo-Hungarian origin.

Recently shifted from family ownership to a partnership, the Swiss-founded **Bodega Suter** (Avenida Hipólito Yrigoyen 2850, tel. 02627/430135, suter@satlink.com) is a more industrial winery, presently replacing its huge epoxy-lined concrete vats with even larger stainless-steel tanks. While its guided tour is informative and there's a shop on site, this well-known winery inexplicably fails to offer tasting. In addition to reds and whites, they are also producing champagne (note the eye protection employees wear to avoid accidental damage by high-speed corks). Monday–Thursday, and Saturdays and holidays, tours (English-speaking guides available) take place hourly 9–4 P.M.; on Friday, hours are 9 A.M.–3 P.M. only.

On the western outskirts of town, the **Bodega de Champaña Valentín Bianchi** (RN 143 and Valentín Bianchi, Las Paredes, tel. 02627/435600, informes@vbianchi.com, www .vbianchi.com) is a state-of-the-art operation—even the rack on which the bottles are turned to concentrate their sediments is automated—that contrasts dramatically with its original downtown bodega. While the focus is sparkling wines, it also has processing capacity for regular reds and whites. The tours (English-speaking guides available), which include tasting in a magnificent new facility, are highly professional; hours are 9 A.M.–12:30 P.M. and 3–6:30 P.M. daily except Sundays. It closes at 6 P.M. in winter, however.

Entertainment
Cines Altos del Sol (San Martín 153, tel. 02627/420850) shows recent movies.

Accommodations
Six kilometers west of downtown via RN 143 is Isla Río Diamante's **Camping El Parador** (tel. 02627/420492, complejoelparador@infovia .com.ar, US$2/3 s/d).

On two hectares of palm-studded grounds, about 1.5 kilometers west of downtown, is the HI affliate **Puesta del Sol Hostel** (Deán Funes 998, tel. 02627/434881, puestadelsol@infovia.com.ar, US$4 pp for dorm accommodations, US$11 d for private rooms).

Easily San Rafael's best budget option, better than some places charging twice as much, amiable **La Esperanza Housing** (Nicolás Avellaneda 263, tel. 02627/427978, wet73@hotmail.com, www .laesperanza-sr.com.ar) has spacious, well-lighted rooms for US$5/8.50 s/d with shared bath, US$6/10 s/d with private bath, breakfast included. It still needs a little work, but new management seems determined to do the job.

At friendly **Hotel España** (Avenida San Martín 292, tel. 02627/421192, tel./fax 02627/424055) the older colonial-style sector around the back patio has more personality than the newer parts, though the rooms themselves are a bit smaller.

Not all the beds are equally firm, though, the hot water takes time to get to the showers, and the owner's son is a rock 'n' roll drummer (who, fortunately, doesn't play when most people are trying to sleep). Rates are US$9/14 s/d with private bath, cable TV, phone (which works off an antiquated PBX), and a decent breakfast. Rates at the newer sector are US$12/20 s/d.

Opposite the cathedral, only half a block off Plaza San Martín, **Hotel Tonín** (Pellegrini 330, tel. 02627/422499, 425802, toninhotel@san-rafael.com, www.sanrafael-tour.com/tonin, US$9 pp) is good value with cable TV, a/c, parking, and breakfast. **Hotel Dalí** (Belgrano 44, tel. 02627/430059, US$9 pp) offers smallish multibedded rooms with breakfast.

On a quiet, tree-lined street, three-star **Hotel Millalén** (Ortiz de Rosas 198, tel./fax 02627/422776, US$15/21 s/d) is modern and comfortable, with a/c, TV, phone, parking, and breakfast.

Rising 10 stories above low-rise San Rafael, the sparkling new 97-room **Tower Inn & Suites** (Avenida Hipólito Yrigoyen 774, tel. 02627/427190, gerenciatower@infovia.com.ar, www .towersanrafael.com) is, ironically, a hotel with a history. The province's tallest hotel, it occupies a building whose white-elephant skeleton stood empty for 35 years until it opened in 2001, and its spa still awaits completion. Maybe the results weren't worth the wait, but they're good enough to make it the best in town. Rates are US$31/37 s/d for standard rooms, US$37/41 s/d for slightly more capacious executive rooms, and US$55 s or d for suites.

Food
Best for breakfast or afternoon tea, **Gath & Chávez** (San Martín 98, tel. 02627/434960) is an upscale-looking café-bar with a sandwich and drinks menu, but no wines by the glass. The service is perfunctory, and the kitchen can be slow.

At first glance **El Gran Pollo** (Avenida Hipólito Yrigoyen and Pueyrredón, tel. 02627/428754) has a fast-food feel, but the kitchen and conscientious service are far better than its deceptively simple menu of chicken, pasta, empanadas, and the like would suggest. Meals start around US$3, with excellent empanadas only about US$.25; it also has takeout service.

El Pancho (Avenida Hipólito Yrigoyen 1110, tel. 02767/425085) is an open-flame *parrilla* whose specialty is *chivito* (grilled goat). **Grill Las Vegas** (San Martín 226, tel. 02627/421390) is a decent second choice. **El Romancero** (Belgrano 338, tel. 02627/422336), the Jockey Club restaurant, has a standard Argentine menu in agreeable surroundings.

Information

The **Dirección Municipal de Turismo** (Avenida Hipólito Yrigoyen 745, tel. 02627/437870, www.sanrafael-tour.com) has good maps but printed matter is otherwise limited. Hours are 7 A.M.–10 P.M. daily in summer, 8 A.M.–9 P.M. the rest of the year.

In the provincial capital, the Casa de San Rafael is at Avenida Alem 308 (tel. 0261/420-1475).

Services

Banco Regional de Cuyo (Hipólito Yrigoyen 124) has one of several ATMs in the downtown area.

Correo Argentino is at San Lorenzo 35; the postal code is 5600. Across the street, **Telefónica** (San Lorenzo 68) has long-distance services. **Punto.com** (J.A. Maza 2) and **Miyagi Cybercafé** (Avenida Hipólito Yrigoyen 650) offer Internet connections.

For medical services, contact **Hospital Teodor J. Schestakow** (Comandante Torres 150, tel. 02627/424290).

Getting There and Around

In the winter ski season, **Aerolíneas Argentinas** flies here three or four times per week for connections to Las Leñas, but it has no permanent representative. Travel agencies like **Buttini Hermanos** (Corrientes 495, tel. 02627/421413) can make reservations and sell tickets.

San Rafael's **Terminal de Ómnibus** is on Coronel Suárez between Avellaneda and Almafuerte, one block south of Avenida Hipólito Yrigoyen. Sample destinations, fares and times include Malargüe (US$3, 2.5 hours), Mendoza

(US$4, three hours), San Juan (US$7, five hours), Buenos Aires (US$21, 13 hours), Tucumán (US$25, 15 hours), Mar del Plata (US$25, 15 hours), Neuquén (US$14, eight hours), and Bariloche (US$22, 13 hours).

Localiza (Avenida Balloffet 2840, tel. 02627/420995, 0800/999-2999 toll-free, cell 15/401679, localizasanrafael@infovia.com.ar) has rental cars.

VICINITY OF SAN RAFAEL

Most things to see and do are in the vicinity of San Rafael, rather than in the town itself. Six kilometers west of town, the **Museo de Historia Natural** (tel. 02627/422121, int. 290, 8 A.M.–1 P.M. and 3–8 P.M. weekdays, 8 A.M.–8 P.M. weekends) occupies a site at Isla Diamante's Parque Mariano Moreno. Regionally focused, it has sectors on anthropology and archaeology, botany and zoology, paleontology and geology, and astronomy.

En route to Malargüe, southwestbound RP 144 zigzags for 32 kilometers up the **Cuesta de los Terneros,** where the **Parque Sierra Pintada,** a 5,000-hectare private reserve, contains pre-Columbian rock-art sites and indigenous fauna like the guanaco. It has also, inexplicably, introduced nonnative fauna like the Indian water buffalo.

South of San Rafael, despite the presence of three hydroelectric dams, the **Cañón del Atuel** retains enough water for Class II–III descents of its namesake river. **Turismo Aventura Raffeish** (RP 173 Km 35, tel./fax 02627/436996, raffeish @infovia.com.ar, www.raffeish.com.ar) is the most popular rafting and kayaking operator on the Río Atuel, and will also organize descents of the Class IV Río Diamante, in rugged country west of San Rafael.

Covering 9,600 hectares, **Dique El Nihuil,** 79 kilometers south of San Rafael, is the main reservoir for the hydroelectric project and a popular site for sailing windsurfing. There are several cabañas, campgrounds and restaurants here; there is no scheduled public transportation, but Exploring TA (Coronel Suárez 255, tel. 02627/436439) offers frequent excursions to and from the Dique.

MALARGÜE

West of San Rafael, the isolated massifs of 5,189-meter El Sosneado, 4,589-meter Cerro Paraguay, and other peaks soar above the plains west of RN 40. At the foot of the Andes, the town of Malargüe is primarily a winter sports destination that relies on tourism, especially to the upscale ski resort of Las Leñas. Otherwise, it's a truly out-of-the-way place despite the presence of nearby wildlife reserves at Payunia and Laguna Llancanelo, caves at Caverna de las Brujas and Pozo de las Ánimas, archaeological and paleontological sites, and access to an adventurous summer route across the Andes to Talca, Chile.

In colonial times, Malargüe and its surroundings were Pehuenche territory, and it takes its name from a Mapudungun (Mapuche language) word meaning "Place of Rocky Mesas." Today the Pehuenche are largely a memory, and the regional economy lives by ranching and mining, in addition to tourism.

Orientation

Malargüe (population 17,710) is 186 kilometers southwest of San Rafael via RN 144 and RN 40. At 1,402 meters above sea level, it's 151 kilometers from the Chilean border at the 2,553-meter Paso Pehuenche via paved RN 40 and gravel RP 224; on the Chilean side, the excitingly narrow Ruta 115 (passable in summer only) continues another 180 kilometers to Talca.

Malargüe is eminently walkable, with most of its services on or near the central strip of RN 40, known as Avenida San Martín through town. Many residents, though, get around on bicycles.

Sights

Immediately south of the tourist office, antique farming implements embellish the landscaped spaces of the 10-hectare **Parque del Ayer,** a handsome city park. At the north end of the park, the **Museo Regional Malargüe** (tel. 02627/470154, 8 A.M.–1 P.M. and 5–9 P.M. Tues.–Fri., free) protects a selection of mostly mismatched artifacts from local history.

At the south end of the park, Malargüe's founder built the **Molino de Rufino Ortega,** an historic flour mill dating from 1876.

Events

Every town needs a festival, and Malargüe's is

Andean goatherd near Malargüe

© WAYNE BERNHARDSON

N Cuyo

the **Fiesta Nacional del Chivo** (National Goat Festival), a fixture on the fiesta scene since 1986. For a week in early January, hotels fill and major folkloric figures like Antonio Tarragó Ros and Suna Rocha perform before substantial crowds.

Accommodations and Food

Malargüe's accommodations are nothing to write home about, as their primary goal is to cram the maximum number of shoestring skiers (who can't afford to stay at ritzy Las Leñas) into each room (the average is about three beds each). Peak rates are in winter, summer is substantially cheaper, and the shoulder seasons are almost giveaways.

Unquestionably cheapest is the **Camping Municipal Malargüe** (Alfonso Capdevila s/n, tel. 02627/470691, US$2.25), at the north end of town. Perhaps the best value is the simple but spotless and friendly **Hotel Andysol** (Rufino Ortega 158, tel. 02627/471151, fax 02627/427072, hotelandysol@yahoo.com.ar), where beds go for just US$5.50 pp in summer, in rooms with private bath. It lacks luxuries, but for this price there's nothing better.

About four kilometers south of town, the new HI affiliate **Hostel Internacional Malargüe** (tel. 02627/15-402439, info@hostelmalargue.net, www.hostelmalargue.net) has four quadruples for US$7 pp, and doubles for US$20, with a country-style breakfast included. It also has its own travel agency and transportation for excursions in the vicinity, and arranges activities like horseback riding and mountain biking.

Hotel Rioma (Fray Inalicán 68, tel. 02627/471065, hotelrioma@infovia.com.ar, about US$11 pp) has more amenities, but for the price, it's not twice as good as the Andysol. A step up is the newish **El Cisne Hotel** (General Villegas and Emilio Civit, tel. 02627/471350, about US$12.50 pp), where the rooms have TV and telephone, but it fills up quickly.

On the northern outskirts of town, the **Río Grande Hotel** (RN 40 s/n, tel. 02627/471589, hotelriogrande@slatinos.com.ar, US$20/23 s/d in summer) has ample rooms with comfortable beds, but the dreary wallpaper needs replacement or, even better, a coat of cheerful white

paint; the hot water takes a while to reach the showers at the back of the building. Breakfast and cable TV are available.

La Posta (Avenida Roca 374, tel. 02627/471306) has an extensive Argentine menu; its specialties are trout and *chivito* (roast kid), but the latter is not always available. Entrees run about US$3–4; try the Salafia house wines, especially the white blend of Chenin Blanc and Torrontés.

Information

At the northern approach to town is the well-organized **Dirección de Turismo y Medio Ambiente** (RN 40 s/n, tel./fax 02627/471659, turismun@slatinos.com.ar, www.malargue.gov.ar, 8 A.M.–midnight daily). Its personnel are friendly, thorough, and knowledgeable, and it has an excellent selection of printed material.

In the provincial capital, the **Casa de Malargüe** is at Avenida España 1075 (tel. 0261/425-9564).

Services

Banco de la Nación has an ATM at Avenida San Martín and Fray Inalicán.

Correo Argentino is at Adolfo Puebla and Saturnino Torres; the postal code is 5613. There are several *locutorios* along Avenida San Martín, but their Internet connections are slow.

Karen Travel (Avenida San Martín 1056, tel. 02627/470342, www.karentravel.com.ar), which has English-speaking personnel, can arrange excursions in the vicinity of Malargüe.

For medical attention, **Hospital Malargüe** is at Avenida Roca and Esquivel Aldao (tel. 02627/471048).

Getting There and Around

In ski season, Aerolíneas Argentina sometimes flies between Aeroparque and nearby **Aeródromo Malargüe** (tel. 02627/471600). The Aerolíneas representative is **Karen Travel** (Avenida San Martín 1056, tel. 02627/470342, www.karentravel.com.ar).

Malargüe's **Terminal de Ómnibus** (Avenida General Roca and Aldao) has frequent service to San Rafael (US$4, two hours), where it's usually but not always necessary to transfer for Mendoza (US$9, six hours). **Transporte Viento Sur** (San Martín 891, tel. 02727/470455) has direct services to Mendoza.

In summer only, there is service over the 2520-meter Paso Pehuenche and down the Río Maule canyon to Talca, Chile.

In ski season, there is service to Las Leñas with several different carriers including **Transportes Payún** (Avenida Roca 416, tel. 02627/471426), **Autotransportes Malargüe** (tel. 02627/470317), and **Karen Travel.**

VICINITY OF MALARGÜE

Estancia Coihueco

About 10 kilometers north of the RP 222 turnoff to Las Leñas, Estancia Coihueco belongs to that upscale ski resort, but this 1880s farmhouse, rehabbed with modern conveniences and a bar/restaurant, is a comfortable (but not extravagant) tourist *estancia*. It does enjoy friendly management, with rustically decorated rooms, offers mountain biking and horseback excursions, and produces organic produce and preserves for sale. It also, in season, offers transportation to Las Leñas and half-price lift tickets.

Rates for accommodations are US$13 pp with half board, a phenomenal bargain. For more information, contact Estancia Coihueco (tel. 02627/15-580803) directly or through Las Leñas (informes@laslenas.com, www.laslenas.com).

Los Molles

For those who can't afford to stay or ski at high-powered and high-altitude Las Leñas, Los Molles is a budget alternative that's closer to the slopes than Malargüe. Here, 55 kilometers northwest of Malargüe and 1,900 meters above level, 1,100-meter lifts serve 90 hectares of snowy slopes, but because it's 340 meters lower than Las Leñas the season is shorter. It is only 15 kilometers east of the more elaborate and prestigious resort, though.

Los Molles's cheapest accommodations is the basic **Club Andino Pehuenche** (tel. 02627/499700, US$5 pp), on the north side of the Río Salado. On the south side of the river, the tunnel-like **Hostería Termas Lahuen-co** (tel. 02627/499700 in Los Molles, tel. 02627/427171 in San Rafael) is suffering from deferred maintenance and the south-facing rooms have small windows, but at summer prices of US$16 pp with full board, it's hard to complain. Its thermal

---

THE POWER OF EL ZONDA

Everybody gripes about the weather, but nobody suffers it like the Cuyanos when "El Zonda" is blowing. In many of the world's regions, similar hot, dry winds descend the easterly slopes of longitudinal mountain ranges, but El Zonda easily tops the Föhn of the Alps, the Chinook of the Rockies, and other similarly strong air currents.

El Zonda is a katabatic wind, a sinking mass of air that gusts up to 40 knots or more, raises temperatures 10 to 15°C in just a few minutes, stirs up clouds of dust and pollen, blows over signs, breaks branches, strips off roofing, and shrivels crops. Starting around midday and lasting up to 10 hours, Zonda episodes usually take place between May and October, but they can happen at any time of year.

But it's the impact on humans that's really striking. When the Zonda hits, atmospheric pressure drops, humidity plummets to near zero, and the few folks on the streets all act hypoglycemic or hung over, rubbing their eyes red against their better judgment. The rest stay at home with low blood pressure or migraines.

Some might say that this is no different than similar occurrences in the Alps or Rockies, but that isn't necessarily so because of the Andes' sheer altitude. Recent research has suggested that if the Andes were lower Zonda events would be more frequent but less intense.

winter at Las Leñas ski area

baths are open to hotel guests for no additional charge; nonguests pay US$2 pp.

The nearby **Los Molles Hotel** (RP 222 Km 30, tel. 02627/499712, losmolleshotel@hotmail.com, US$18 pp with half board in summer) is a pretty comfortable alternative; even though the carpets could use replacement, the rooms have good views and the price is right. It has a bar with satellite TV, a restaurant, and other spacious common areas.

Las Leñas

Near the end of a winding mountain highway, 2,240 meters above sea level, self-contained Las Leñas is Argentina's most exclusive ski resort and, because of its isolation, most visitors come on week-long package tours. That said, it's close enough to Malargüe and Los Molles that even some shoestring skiers can afford to spend the day here—especially when the resort offers half-price lift tickets to those who lodge in nearby towns.

Open mid-June to early October, Las Leñas claims 40 separate runs, the longest of which exceeds four kilometers, with a maximum eleva-tion of 3,430 meters; there are seven chairlifts, the steepest of which gains 786 meters, and four other lifts. Slopes range from easy to very difficult, and there is even one sector with restricted access where helmets are obligatory. Some of the runs are lighted for night skiing, and there is a ski school with instruction in Spanish, English, French, German, Italian, and Portuguese.

In addition, Las Leñas enjoys an active nightlife, with pubs, discos, cinemas, and casinos, and it even has its own radio station (which specializes in truly bland Anglo-pop). It is trying to make itself into a year-round destination as well, offering non-winter activities like rafting, hiking, climbing, mountain biking, tennis, paddle-ball, volleyball, and basketball.

Las Leñas is 445 kilometers south of Mendoza via RN 40, RN 143, RN 144 and RP 222 (note that the rough unpaved segment of RP 40 south of Pareditas makes the longer paved detour via RN 143 and RN 144 more desirable, especially in winter. It is 204 kilometers southwest of San Rafael via RN 144, RN 40, and RP 222, and also 70 kilometers northwest of Malargüe, also via RN 40 and RP 222.

© WAYNE BERNHARDSON

summer at Las Leñas ski area

Prices for **lift tickets** vary throughout the ski season, which runs from mid-June to early October. Half-day tickets range from US$16 in low season to US$26 in peak season; there are corresponding rates for one day (US$23–34), three days (US$62–92), four days (US$82–119), one week (US$124–184), 15 days (US$222–340), one month (US$340–414), and the entire season (US$467).

Children and seniors get a roughly 30 percent discount, while skiers lodged in Malargüe get a 50 percent discount.

Lifts operate 9 A.M.–5 P.M. daily, and sometimes at night when lighting is available. Rental equipment, including snowboards, is readily available.

Las Leñas has five four-star **luxury hotels** (tel. 02627/471100 for all) with capacity for 740 skiers, plus apart-hotel accommodations for another 2,219. Since it's oriented toward package tours in ski season, this is obviously not a drop-in situation, but when things are slow in summer it's possible to stay at places like **Hotel Géminis** and **Aparthotel Delphos** (info@maxisol.com.ar, www.maxisol.com.ar) for as little as US$15 pp.

Las Leñas' five hotels all have restaurants, but there is also **Johnny's Restaurant** and **Innsbruck** (tel. 02627/471100, int. 1205), which also delivers from a menu that's primarily pasta and sandwiches.

Las Leñas' on-site **Oficina de Informes** (tel. 02627/471100, int. 1241, 1243) is open 9 A.M.–8 P.M. daily. Its Buenos Aires contact is **Ski Leñas** (Cerrito 1186, 8th floor, tel. 011/4816-6999, ventas@laslenas.com, www.laslenas.com).

In season, **Aerolíneas Argentinas** operates charters from Buenos Aires to Malargüe, including transfers to and from Las Leñas. There is seasonal **bus** service from Mendoza and San Rafael, and year-round service from Malargüe.

Provincial Reserves

Thinly populated southern Mendoza Province can pride itself on several important and diverse reserves of various sizes and accessibility. For the most complete information, visit the website for the provincial **Dirección de Recursos Naturales Renovables** (www.recursosnaturales.mendoza.gov.ar).

Cuyo

Immediately west of Malargüe, a 28-kilometer gravel road leads toward the Andes and the 650-hectare **Reserva Natural Castillos de Pincheira,** a series of volcanic sedimentary landforms resembling castles, that were a hideout for caudillo and bandit José Antonio Pincheira.

On the southwestern slopes of Cerro Moncol, 80 kilometers from Malargüe via paved southbound RN 40 and an eight-kilometer dirt lateral, the 450-hectare **Reserva Natural Caverna de las Brujas** (8 A.M.–5 P.M. daily, US$3.50 adults, US$1.75 children) is a limestone cave previously open only for guided visits, but now open to the public in general.

About 65 kilometers southeast of Malargüe via RN 40 and RP 186, the most significant feature of the 40,000-hectare **Reserva Natural Laguna de Llancanelo** is a shallow wetland that's home to 220 bird species, many of them migratory, including three species of flamingos. While it's ostensibly open for guided visits only, in practice things are much more flexible.

Immediately south of Laguna de Llancanelo, Mendoza Province's largest reserve is the 442,996-hectare **Reserva Natural La Payunia,** a volcano-studded landscape whose high point is 3,680-meter Cerro Payún (it is only one of 800 volcanoes within the reserve, however). It has abundant wildlife, including more than 10,000 guanacos as well as pumas, condors, and rheas. Accommodations are available through Malargüe's **Kiñe Turismo Rural Ecológico** (tel. 02627/471344, tel. 011/4299-2577 in Buenos Aires, kine-turismo-rural@sinectis.com.ar).

San Juan Province

Immediately north of Mendoza, San Juan Province stands in the shadow of its more populous and prosperous southern neighbor, but its tidy namesake capital city has a progressive wine district, the offbeat Difunta Correa shrine is a popular religious phenomenon, and its desert and mountain back country—including the fossil-rich Parque Provincial Ischigualasto—offers almost unlimited possibilities for adventure travel. To the west, the 4,750-meter Agua Negra pass, the highest between Argentina and Chile, is an exhilarating alternative to the usual Libertadores route from Mendoza to Santiago.

SAN JUAN

San Juan de la Frontera dates from 1562, but its predominantly modern aspect is the result of repeated earthquakes. The event with the most impact—and not just seismically—was the 1944 temblor that brought Juan Domingo Perón, then a minor political figure, to prominence for his disaster-relief efforts. Perón used this role as a springboard to found the controversial political movement known formally as Justicialism, but more commonly as Peronism.

Though smaller, poorer, drier, and hotter than Mendoza, San Juan has much in common with the larger city: wide tree-shaded avenues, sidewalk cafés, a wine industry that's lifting the local economy, and a work schedule that starts early but shuts down for several hours at midday in the smothering summer heat. It has not, however, been as successful in diversifying its economy, which is largely administrative and agricultural.

San Juan was the birthplace and home of statesman, educator, and author Domingo F. Sarmiento, who wrote the famous polemic *Civilization and Barbarism* about the excesses of provincial caudillos.

Orientation

San Juan (population 115,556, elevation 650 meters) is 168 kilometers north of Mendoza via RN 40, and 1,138 kilometers northwest of Buenos Aires; a ring road, the Avenida Circunvalación, keeps most through traffic out of the city center. Its relatively small population is misleading as, like Mendoza, it's the center of a larger metropolitan area (which exceeds 400,000).

© WAYNE BERNHARDSON

roadside fruit stand

Occupying a full block, Plaza 25 de Mayo is the civic center; north-south Calle Mendoza and east-west Avenida San Martín divide the standard grid into quadrants. Street addresses all have cardinal points to simplify orientation, but beyond the central grid the layout is more irregular.

Sights

Lushly landscaped **Plaza 25 de Mayo** is a handsome central plaza, with its palms, fountains, and statuary, but buildings like its brutalist **Iglesia Catedral** (Mendoza and Rivadavia) seem to have been designed primarily to withstand earthquakes, despite some appealing details.

One block west and one block north, **Celda Histórica de San Martín** (Laprida 57 Oeste), where the general stayed while raising funds and shoring up support for his daring Chilean campaign, is the only part of the colonial **Convento de Santo Domingo** (9 A.M.–1 P.M. daily except Sun., US$.35) to survive the 1944 earthquake.

Barely a block farther west, the **Casa Natal de Sarmiento** (Sarmiento 21 Sur, tel. 0264/422-4603, US$.35), Domingo F. Sarmiento's boyhood home, is now a museum and national historical

monument. Despite provincial origins that might have made him a caudillo, Domingo Faustino Sarmiento (1811–1888) became a renaissance man with a distinguished public career that included stints as an educator, journalist, diplomat, and the first president from Argentina's interior provinces. While exiled in Chile during the Rosas dictatorship, he wrote the famous anti-caudillo polemic *Civilization and Barbarism,* often subtitled *Life in the Argentine Republic in the Days of the Tyrants* and still in print in many languages.

Dating from 1801, built by Sarmiento's mother Paula Albarracín, Sarmiento's birthplace grew in time from the original one-room adobe to a 12-room brick house with two patios and a surviving fig tree that appears prominently in his memoir *Recuerdos de Provincia.* The first building ever to be declared an Argentine national monument, it suffered damage in the 1944 earthquake, but underwent a successful restoration.

The Casa Natal de Sarmiento is open 9 A.M.–7 P.M. daily in winter, 9 A.M.–1 P.M. and 3–8 P.M. in summer except Monday and Saturday, when it's open mornings only.

Cuyo

Where Laprida meets Avenida España, Plaza Julieta Sarmiento is the site of the reinforced concrete skeleton of the proposed **Casa de Gobierno,** a corruption-plagued project that, nearly two decades on, shows no signs of progress.

Four blocks north, beyond Plaza España, the former **Estación Belgrano** (railway station) is now home to the **Centro Cultural María Eva Duarte de Perón** (Avenida España and San Luis) and the anthropological **Museo El Hombre y La Naturaleza** (Avenida España and 25 de Mayo); hours are 9 A.M.–1 P.M. and 4–7 P.M. daily. Admission is US$.35.

One block farther north, the most worthwhile item at the **Museo de Ciencias Naturales** (Avenida España 400 Norte, tel. 0264/421-6774, 9 A.M.–1 P.M. weekdays only, US$.65) is the reconstructed **Herrerasaurus** skeleton from Parque Provincial Ischigualasto. One block east and two blocks north, the **Antigua Bodega Chirino** (Salta 782 Norte, tel. 0264/421-4327, 8:30 A.M.–12:30 P.M. daily, and 4:30–8:30 P.M. daily except Sun.) is no longer a working winery—that moved out of town—but parts of the old facilities are a museum and there is a tasting room.

About one kilometer southeast of Plaza 25 de Mayo, two museums share a building at Avenida Rawson and General Paz. The **Museo de Bellas Artes Franklin Rawson** (Avenida Rawson 621 Sur, tel. 0264/422-9638, 8 A.M.–1 P.M. weekdays only, free) boasts an impressive roster of works by 19th-century Argentine artists, including Rawson himself and Prilidiano Pueyrredón, plus more contemporary figures like Antonio Berni, Raquel Forner, Lino Spilimbergo, and others.

The same building holds the **Museo Histórico Provincial Agustín Gnecco,** which traces San Juan's history from prehistory through the 19th century via archaeological artifacts and items like silverwork, furniture, wine technology, and numismatics. Hours and contact numbers are identical to those of the fine arts museum.

Entertainment and Events

On the south side of Plaza 25 de Mayo, the two-screen **Cine San Juan** (Mitre 41 Este, tel. 0264/423-3503) shows recent films. For live theater and music, there's the **Teatro Sarmiento** (Avenida Alem Norte 34, tel. 0264/421-7363).

Shopping

Raíz Sanjuanina (Avenida Córdoba 617 Oeste, tel. 0264/4216128) has diverse offerings that range from food products like jams, dried fruits, olive oil, vinegar, and herbs to art works and crafts. Immediately south of the tourist office, **El Carrascal** (Sarmiento 40 Sur, tel. 0264/422-6733) has many of the same items, with a focus on items like weavings and basketry.

Accommodations

At **Hostal Suizo** (Salta 272 Sur, tel. 0264/422-4293, US$6 pp), the beds are firm, the interior is quiet, and the price is right, but disagreeably greasy odors sometimes emanate from the kitchen. Another good basic choice is friendly **Hotel Bristol** (Entre Ríos 368 Sur, tel. 0264/421-4629, fax 0264/421-4778, bristol-sanjuan@yahoo.com.ar, US$8/12 s/d with breakfast), which has 45 decent rooms with repellent wallpaper.

Though it stands in dreary surroundings five blocks north of the bus terminal, **Petit Hotel Dibú** (Avenida San Martín and Patricias Sanjuaninas, tel. 0264/420-1034, US$8/13 s/d with breakfast) has clean, sizeable rooms. The best budget option, though, is well-kept **Ⅺ Hotel Nuevo San Francisco** (Avenida España 284 Sur, tel. 0264/427-2821, fax 0264/422-3760, nhsf @sinectis.com.ar, US$11/14 s/d with private bath and breakfast), with firm beds, plus bright and spacious common areas; it also arranges excursions in the area.

The tiny reception at **Hotel Selby** (Avenida Rioja 183 Sur, tel. 0264/422-4766, hotelselby @sinectis.com.ar, www.hotel-selby.com.ar, US$12/16 s/d with breakfast) is a misleading approach to an aging but well-maintained hotel with smallish but otherwise good rooms with private bath.

On the south side of Plaza 25 de Mayo is business-oriented **Hotel Capayán** (Mitre 31 Este, tel. 0264/421-4222, fax 0264/422-5442, hca-payan@infovia.com.ar, US$13/15 s/d).

In a quiet neighborhood near Plaza J.M. Paz, the amiable **Jardín Petit Hotel** (25 de Mayo 345 Este, tel. 0264/421-1825, fax 0264/421-1464, jardinpetithotel@hotmail.com, US$13/17 s/d with breakfast) is a little worn and some baths are small, but the beds are good and it has a verdant back garden. It sometimes offers discounted rates.

Near the bus terminal, popular **Hotel América** (9 de Julio 1062 Este, tel. 0264/421-4514, fax 0264/427-2692, hotelam@impsat1.com.ar, US$13/18 s/d) is an outstanding value with breakfast and amenities like a/c, phone, and cable TV.

Central **Hotel Nogaró** (Ignacio de la Roza 132 Este, tel./fax 0264/422-7501, hotel@nogarosanjuan.com.ar, for US$23/27 s/d) is aging but tidy and efficient. San Juan's top hotel is the five-star **Hotel Alkazar** (Laprida 82 Este, tel. 0264/421-4965, reservas@alkazarhotel.com.ar, US$33/40 s/d with breakfast).

Food

There are several good places to eat downtown, but the classiest concentration of restaurants is on Avenida San Martín Oeste, about two kilometers to the west.

San Juan's greatest simple pleasure is the fresh-squeezed orange juice from the mobile carts at the northeast corner of Plaza 25 de Mayo and other nearby locations—only about US$.20 for a paper cup of sweet chilled refreshment.

For breakfast, sandwiches, or afternoon tea, try **Freud** (General Acha 282 Sur). For specialty sandwiches—large enough to be a meal in their own right—the best choice is **Pirandello** (San Martín 3105 Oeste, tel. 0264/426-0260), which has indoor and outdoor seating.

For pastas, pizzas, and draft beer, **Un Rincón de Napoli** (Rivadavia 175 Oeste) has zero atmosphere but prices that aren't much higher than that. The historic Club Español's once-grand **El Quijote** (Rivadavia 32 Este, tel. 0264/422-3389) serves decent food at moderate prices with adequate service, but needs to upgrade or it will just fade away.

It could take a lesson from the equally classic ◤ **Club Sirio Libanés** (Entre Ríos 33 Sur, tel. 0264/422-3841), where there's genuine Middle Eastern ambience and hospitality, and the diverse US$7 buffet includes items like kebbe, tabouleh, and stuffed grape leaves. À la carte items like beef with an almond sauce cost around US$4.

Remolacha (Avenida Jose I de la Roza 199 Oeste, tel. 0264/422-7070) is a popular downtown *parrilla,* almost impossibly full on Sunday afternoons. **Soychú** (Ignacio de la Roza 223 Oeste, tel. 0264/422-1939) is a San Juan tradition in vegetarian *tenedor libre.*

◤ **Il Duomo** (Avenida Libertador San Martín 1802 Oeste, tel. 0264/423-9819) is a *parrilla* that also has a superb Italian menu—or an Italian restaurant with superb *parrillada*—that serves upscale versions of beef, stuffed gnocchi, and Spanish desserts like *natillas,* with both indoor and outdoor seating.

Estancia Los Toneles (Avenida Libertador San Martín 1931 Oeste, tel. 0264/423-4979) is a popular *parrilla* that serves goat Friday and roast pork Sunday. The comparable **Las Leñas** (Avenida San Martín 1674 Oeste, tel. 0264/423-5040) serves hordes of carnivores in its thatched premises.

West of the Circunvalación, **Maloca** (Del Bono 321, Barrio del Bono, tel. 0264/15-566-6344) is a pan-Latino restaurant with Mexican tacos, Venezuelan *arepas* and the like; the kitchen isn't quite there yet, but it's cheap and promising.

The outstanding ice creamery **Soppelsa** has two outlets (Mendoza 163 Sur; Avenida Ignacio de la Roza 639 Oeste).

Information

The **Dirección Provincial de Turismo** (Sarmiento 24 Sur, tel. 0264/422-7219, dirturismo @ischigualasto.com, www.ischigualasto.com) is open 7:30 A.M.–8 P.M. weekdays, 9 A.M.–8 P.M. weekends. It has up-to-date hotel information, and distributes a good city map plus brochures on destinations elsewhere in the province. An airport office is open for arriving flights only.

For motorists, **ACA** is at 9 de Julio 802 Este (tel. 0264/421-4245).

Services

Cambio Santiago is at General Acha 52 Sur, but there are several downtown ATMs, including the one at **Banco de San Juan** (José Ignacio de la Roza 85 Oeste).

Correo Argentino is at José Ignacio de la Roza 259 Este; the postal code is 5400.

Telefónica has a *locutorio* on Avenida San Martín between Sarmiento and Entre Ríos. **Cyber Planeta** (Entre Ríos 355 Sur) has 24-hour Internet access.

Several agencies arrange excursions to destinations like Ischigualasto and Talampaya (La Rioja), including **Patricio Viajes** (25 de Mayo 1208 Oeste, tel. 0264/422-7786) and **Mario Agüero Turismo** (General Acha 17 Norte, tel. 0264/422-3652).

Laverap is at Rivadavia 498 Oeste.

Hospital Rawson is at General Paz and Estados Unidos (tel. 0264/422-2272).

Getting There and Around

Austral (Avenida San Martín 215 Oeste, tel. 0264/422-5049) flies daily to Aeroparque except Friday (no flights).

San Juan's **Terminal de Ómnibus** (Estados Unidos 492 Sur, tel. 0264/422-1604) has provincial, long-distance, and international services (though it's usually necessary to change in Mendoza for Santiago or Viña del Mar/Valparaíso).

Sample destinations, fares, and times include the Difunta Correa shrine (US$1.50, one hour), Mendoza (US$3.50, two hours), San Agustín del Valle Fértil (US$5, 3.5 hours), Córdoba (US$9, eight hours), San Luis (US$5.50, four hours), La Rioja (US$5.50, six hours), Catamarca (US$10, eight hours), Santiago de Chile or Valparaíso/Viña (US$11, nine hours), Tucumán (US$16, 13 hours), Buenos Aires (US$15–20, 16 hours), Neuquén (US$18, 15 hours), Salta (US$20, 17 hours), Mar del Plata (US$25, 19 hours), and Bariloche (US$27, 19 hours).

A cab or *remise* to **Aeropuerto Las Chacritas** (tel. 0264/425-0487), about 13 kilometers southeast of town via RN 20, costs about US$3.50.

For rental cars, contact **Avis** (tel. 0264/425-3962 at the airport, cell 0264/15-504-3333).

VICINITY OF SAN JUAN

Local operators arrange excursions to some of the province's better but less easily accessible sights, including the Jáchal/Pismanta area and

Parque Provincial Ischigualasto (sometimes combined, in a long day trip, with la Rioja's Parque Nacional Talampaya). In addition to those listed above, try Money Tur (Santa Fe and Sarmiento, tel. 0264/420-1010), and Raphael Joliat at Swiss-run **Fascinatur** (tel. 0264/15-504-3933, fascinatur_dahu@arnet.com.ar), where English and French are spoken.

Ruta del Vino San Juan (Pocito)

On San Juan's southern outskirts, the locality of Pocito is home to a cluster of wineries which, even if they can't quite match Mendoza's size and diversity, are well worth sampling. All are on or near RN 40, the paved highway to Mendoza.

Closest to San Juan is **Champañera Miguel Más** (Calle 11 s/n, tel. 0264/422-5807, miguelmas@infovia.com.ar), 300 meters east of RN 40. It's a tiny family-run bodega with only 2.5 hectares of organic grapes, producing 6,000 bottles of sparkling wine per annum. Hoping to increase production, it also makes some Cabernet Sauvignon and Malbec, a small amount of muscatel, and quantities of jam and honey. At this mom-and-pop operation, tours and tasting are about as personal as can be.

About two kilometers farther south, fronting on the west side of the highway, **Fabril Alto Verde** (RN 40 between Calle 13 and Calle 14, tel. 0264/492-1905, altoverde@arnet.com.ar) is another organic winery with a more high-tech and diverse production that includes varietals like Chablis, Chardonnay, Malbec, and Syrah, plus some sparkling wines. Its spacious, contemporary tasting room may add a *tapas* menu to complement the wine. Hours are 9 A.M.–6 P.M. weekdays, 9 A.M.–1 P.M. Saturdays.

Another kilometer south but well west of the highway, the structures at **Bodega Viñas de Navas** (Mendoza and Calle 15, tel. 0264/427-3100, mnavas@infovia.com.ar) date from 1876, but the installations within are modern. Its espaliered vines yield relatively limited quantities of Cabernet Sauvignon, Malbec, Merlot, and Syrah, along with Chardonnay and Sauvignon Blanc.

In sheer tourist appeal, the best choice is **Viñas de Segisa** (Aberastain y Calle 15, tel. 0264/492-2000, segisa@saxsegisa.com.ar, www.saxsegisa

.com.ar, 10:30 A.M.–8 P.M. daily), a boutique winery that's made a special effort to conserve its century-old facilities and adapt them to individualized guided tours—which include tastings directly from their cellar casks. It is, nevertheless, a contemporary bodega producing Cabernet Sauvignon, Syrah, Malbec, Chardonnay, and a Torrontés/Chardonnay blend.

Dique Ullum

In San Juan's hot, arid climate, the vineyards thrive on water from 3,200-hectare Dique Ullum, 18 kilometers west of town via RP 60, but it's also the place where *sanjuaninos* go to beat the heat by swimming, sailing, windsurfing, and fishing. From the bus terminal, take bus No. 29; for schedules, contact **Empresa Ullum** (tel. 0264/422-1910).

If the heat relents, hike from the dam outlet to the top of 1,800-meter **Cerro Tres Marías,** a waterless two-hour walk that traces the crest of the southwest-trending Serranía de Marquesado. The conspicuous zigzag trail begins at the Stations-of-the-Cross; carry plenty of liquids and high-energy snacks.

Museo Arqueológico La Laja

Under the auspices of the Universidad Nacional de San Juan, this first-rate archaeological museum chronicles 8,000 years of pre-Columbian peoples in what is now San Juan Province. Arranged sequentially in a Moorish-style structure that was once a hotel, the exhibits explore the region's cultural evolution in considerable depth through artifacts that include tools, ceramics, basketry, and mummies—extraordinarily well-preserved in San Juan's hot, dry climate. Once a hot springs resort, the building still offers hot mineral baths.

In the village of La Laja, the Museo Arqueológico (9 A.M.–1 P.M. daily, US$.65)is 25 kilometers north of San Juan via RN 40 and a paved lateral. From the terminal, bus No. 20 runs five times daily; verify schedules with **Empresa Albardón** (tel. 0264/423-4396).

 Difunta Correa Shrine

Until very recently, Roman Catholicism was Argentina's official faith, and it still permeates daily

Pilgrims from all over Argentina and the world visit the Difunta Correa shrine.

life. When the shepherd fails the flock, though, the people seek help from popular saints like the Difunta Correa—whose shrine draws upward of 100,000 Semana Santa pilgrims to the desert hamlet of **Vallecito,** about 60 kilometers east of San Juan. More than just a religious experience, it's an economic force, and even nonbelievers will find plenty to contemplate in the mixture of the sacred and the profane.

According to legend, María Antonia Deolinda Correa died of thirst in the desert while following her conscript husband—a small landowner—during the mid-19th-century civil wars. When passing muleteers found her body, though, her baby son was still alive, feeding at her breast. While it seems far-fetched that any infant could survive on milk from a lifeless body, the legend had such resonance among local folk that the waterless site became a spontaneous shrine. The Difunta ("Defunct," as dead

© WAYNE BERNHARDSON

Pilgrims leave models of houses, thanking the Difunta Correa for granting their wishes.

people are known in the countryside) became a popular "saint," despite limited proof that she even existed.

In the 150-plus years since the Difunta first colonized the consciousness of poor *sanjuaninos* and other Argentines, millions have come to regard her as a miracle worker. She is *not* a saint, though, and at best the official church regards belief in her as superstition; at worst, it has denounced her as contrary to its dogma, and has even installed its own priest and built its own church to combat the heresy.

Their efforts have been futile. From its negligible origins as a solitary cross atop a knoll, the shrine has grown into a complex that includes hotels and a campground, restaurants, a police station, a post office, a school, souvenir shops, and even its own tourist office. There is also the bureaucracy of the Fundación Vallecito, the nonprofit entity that administers the site.

For queues of pilgrims, though, the goal is the chamber in which lies a prostrate image of the Difunta, her baby at her breast. To fulfill promises they have made, and to thank her for favors granted, some crawl the concrete steps on their backs. They leave an astonishing assortment of license plates, model cars and houses, photographs, and other personal items that signify their gratitude; the foundation, for its part, "recycles" many items to finance its activities (which include delivery of 2,000 liters of water daily from the town of Caucete).

Pilgrims visit the shrine all year. It's most impressive on holidays like Easter, May Day, and Christmas, but events like mid-April's *gauchesco* **Cabalgata de la Fe** (Ride of Faith) from San Juan and December's **Festival del Camionero** (Trucker's Festival) are increasingly important.

Writing in the 19th century, Domingo F. Sarmiento—himself a *sanjuanino*—expressed what the official church still privately believes about rural religious practices like the Difunta Correa:

Christianity exists . . . as a tradition which is perpetuated, but corrupted; colored by gross superstitions and unaided by instruction, rites, or convictions.

Believers, for their part, see no contradiction between their formal faith and their devotion to the Difunta. That devotion has spread throughout the republic, as shown in roadside shrines—some of them astonishingly elaborate—from the Bolivian border at La Quiaca to the tip of Tierra del Fuego. Their marker is the water-filled bottles left to slake her thirst, but there are also banknotes (from the hyper-inflationary past), low-value coins, and miscellaneous auto parts (truckers are among her most committed adherents).

It also bears mention that, while the Difunta remains the most widespread of popular religious figures, as measured by numbers of roadside shrines, she's not the only one. Sites devoted to the Gaucho Antonio Gil, an unjustly executed "Robin Hood" figure from the Corrientes provincial town of Mercedes, are proliferating alongside the Difunta in the wake of Argentina's economic and political implosion of late 2001.

The shrine has its own branch of the provincial tourist office; there is also an ostensibly official website (www.visitedifuntacorrea.com.ar).

Informally, pilgrims camp just about anywhere they like, but the shrine's own **Hotel Difunta Correa** (tel. 0264/496-1018) has spartan rooms with private bath (electric showers) for US$5.50/8.50 s/d with breakfast. There's plenty of *parrillada,* plus empanadas and similar snacks at any of several streetside *comedores.*

From San Juan, **Empresa Vallecito** has direct service to the shrine (US$1.50, one hour), but any other eastbound bus, toward cities like La Rioja or Córdoba, will stop at the shrine's entrance.

Jáchal and Vicinity

From San Juan, paved RN 40 leads 156 kilometers north to the vineyards and olive orchards of San José de Jáchal (population 10,901), a town renowned for its gaucho customs and its handmade blankets and ponchos. November's **Fiesta de la Tradición** highlights this reputation, while its most notable sight is the **Iglesia San José** (1878), a national historical monument. Also notable is the church's **Cristo Negro** (Black Christ) or **Señor de la Agonía** (Lord of Agony),

a gruesome 18th-century image imported from Bolivia.

East of Jáchal, the scenic graveled RP 491 links up with the discontinuous RN 40 (presently under construction) to the village of **Huaco,** the birthplace of poet Buenaventura Luna and the site of the late-colonial **Viejo Molino** (flour mill). To the west, RN 150 leads over the pass known as the **Cuesta del Viento** to the town of **Rodeo,** where **Rafting San Juan** (Paoli s/n, tel. 0264/427-6143 or 40264/33-2352, cell 0264/15-505-1150) descends the Class III Río Jáchal, a good beginners' river.

Jáchal has numerous **campgrounds.** A block-plus north of the plaza, **Hotel San Martín** (Echegaray 367, tel. 02647-420431) charges US$2 pp with shared bath, but has more commodious rooms with private bath for US$8/13 s/d. Half a block east of the plaza, **Hotel Plaza** (San Juan 545, tel. 02647/420431) charges US$6/10 s/d with shared bath, US$8/13 s/d with private bath. For dining, try **Chatito Flores** (San Juan and Echegaray), half a block west of the plaza.

Jáchal's **Terminal de Ómnibus** is at San Juan and Obispo Zapata, four blocks east of the plaza. From San Juan, the main carriers are **Empresa 20 de Junio** (tel. 0264/421-4108) and **TAC** (also tel. 0264/421-4108).

Pismanta and Vicinity

West of Rodeo, paved RN 150 leads southwest to the foothill hot springs of Pismanta, where the comfortable **Hotel Termas de Pismanta** (tel. 02647/497002, reinaldo_echavarravia@hotmail.com, US$17/30 s/d to US$22/36 s/d) has enormous hot baths and very good restaurant that are open to nonguests. Shoestring travelers can stay at **Hospedaje La Olla** (tel. 02647/497003, US$5 pp with breakfast, US$8 with half board, US$12 pp with full board).

From Pismanta, RN 150 climbs 92 kilometers through the upper Río Jáchal drainage to the Chilean border at 4,722-meter **Paso de Agua Negra,** the highest pass between the two countries. Open at least December–March, it features an impressive glacier and the snowmelt pinnacles known as *penitentes* along the narrow highway,

Cuyo

penitentes (snow formations) at Paso de Agua Negra on the Chilean border

© WAYNE BERNHARDSON

which continues to the scenic Elqui Valley and the beach resort of La Serena.

SAN AGUSTÍN DEL VALLE FÉRTIL

The mountainous microclimate around San Agustín del Valle Fértil (population 3,889), on the eastern edge of the province, helps create a well-watered enclave of lush hills and valleys that's seemingly a mirror image of the rest of this desert province. San Agustín itself is a refreshingly tranquil and hospitable "hill station" that draws weekend visitors from the searingly hot provincial capital, but it's also a base for visiting Parque Provincial Ischigualasto. Founded in 1788, the town commemorates its anniversary on April 4.

On the eastern slopes of the sedimentary Sierras Pampeanas, San Agustín is 247 kilo-meters northeast of San Juan via paved RN 141 and RP 510, which continues unpaved to Baldecitos (the turnoff to Ischigualasto), beyond which it meets paved RP 26 to Parque Nacional Talampaya and RN 150 toward La Rioja. While locals generally ignore street names, it's small and regular enough to make orientation easy.

Sights

San Agustín's main points of interest are archaeological: the petroglyphs of **Piedra Pintada,** about 300 meters over the Río Seco; the **Morteros Indígenas** (Indian mortars) another 500 meters on; and the **Meseta Ritual** (Ritual Mesa), on the grounds of the Escuela Agrotécnica. Known for its fresh dairy products, the nearby farming village of **La Majadita,** a seven-kilometer hike or ride in the dry winter, is even calmer than San Agustín.

Accommodations and Food

Many visitors stay at campgrounds, such as the riverside **Camping Municipal** (Rivadavia s/n, tel. 02646/420104, US$1 pp). The woodsy and popular **Camping Valle Fértil** (Rivadavia s/n, tel. 02646/420115, US$3.50 per tent plus US$1 pp) has better infrastructure.

There's a cluster of family-run accommodations in the US$3–4 pp range with private bath, slightly less with shared bath: **Pensión Doña Zoila** (Mendoza s/n, tel. 02646/420147), **Pensión Villalón** (Tucumán s/n, tel. 02646/420148), **Hospedaje San Agustín** (Rivadavia s/n, tel. 02624/420004), **Hospedaje Los Olivos** (Santa Fe s/n, tel. 02646/420115), and **Hospedaje Santa Fe** (Santa Fe s/n, tel. 02646/420012).

San Agustín's best, though, is the hilltop **Hostería Valle Fértil** (Rivadavia 1510, tel. 02646/420015, vallefertil@alkazarhotel.com.ar, US$16/21 s/d with breakfast, US$19/27 s/d with half board). Under the same management as San Juan's Hotel Alkazar, it also has a restaurant/confitería.

Except for the *hostería* and **Rancho Criollo** (Tucumán s/n), an established *parrilla,* places to eat are few.

Other Practicalities

Open 7 A.M.–11 P.M. weekdays and 8 A.M.–1 P.M. weekends, the **Dirección de Turismo** (General Acha s/n, tel. 02646/420104) is directly across from the plaza; it's quick to offer suggestions and help organize excursions. The private **Cámara de Turismo** keeps an office at the bus terminal, but its hours are very irregular.

The post office is at Laprida and Mendoza. **Telefónica** has a *locutorio* on Tucumán between Mitre and Santa Fe, but Internet access has been slow to arrive at isolated San Agustín.

Patricio Viajes (Mitre s/n, tel. 02646/420143) organizes excursions to Ischigualasto and Talampaya.

San Agustín's **Terminal de Ómnibus** is at Entre Ríos and Mitre. **Empresa Vallecito** (tel. 02646/420427) links the town with San Juan (US$4.50, four hours) daily, and with La Rioja (US$2.50) Thursday and Sunday, passing the Ischigualasto turnoff.

⚑ PARQUE PROVINCIAL ISCHIGUALASTO

Nicknamed *Valle de la Luna* for the lunar landscapes formed from its colorless clay, reddish sandstone, and black volcanic ash, Parque Provincial Ischigualasto also deserves to be called "Triassic Park" for fossil-rich sediments that have yielded dinosaur skeletons from 228 million years ago. Finds like the early predator *Eoraptor lunensis,* the *Tyrannosaurus*-like *Herrerasaurus,* and the herbivorous *Riojasaurus,* have made Ischigualasto, together with neighboring Parque Nacional Talampaya, a UNESCO World Heritage Site. Of the roughly 35,000 visitors every year, only about 1,000 are foreigners.

About 80 kilometers northwest of San Agustín via bumpy RP 510 and smoothly paved RN 150, Ischigualasto encompasses 63,000 hectares of eroded sedimentary badlands between the easterly Cerros Colorados and the westerly Quebrada de los Jachalleros. RP 150 dead-ends about 15 kilometers to the west, and it's likely to be some time before it reaches the last 35 kilometers or so to the junction with RN 40 and Jáchal.

Flora and Fauna

Rather than plants and animals, most visitors come to see whatever the sparse vegetation of hillside cacti and streambed shrubs and algarrobos doesn't cover. In Ischigualasto's withering summer heat, most wildlife is nocturnal, but there are guanacos, foxes, hares, rheas, and pumas, as well as rodents, snakes, and other reptiles.

Sights and Activities

From the visitors center, rangers accompany both private vehicles and guided tours on the **Circuito Vehicular,** an unpaved 40-kilometer loop past distinctive landforms like the **Cancha de Bochas** (The Ball Court), **El Esfinge** (The Sphinx), **El Gusano** (The Worm), **El Hongo** (The Mushroom), and **El Submarino** (The Submarine)—all of which bear some resemblance to the objects from which they take their names. Normally, the circuit takes about two hours but, after summer storms, some park roads may be impassable.

Local guides (contracted at the visitors center for about US$2.50) are obligatory, and plenty of water and snacks are essential, for the three- to four-hour climb of the 1,748-meter **Cerro Morado,** which gains about 800 meters en route to the solitary summit.

Practicalities

Camping is permitted at the visitors center, but there is no shade whatsoever and, while the **Comedor Dante Herrera** has toilets and showers, that doesn't necessarily mean there's water to wash and flush—that comes in on trucks. The *comedor* serves decent meals, cold beer and sodas, and regional products like olives and dried fruit, along with a selection of crafts.

Visitors pay a US$2 entrance fee at the park's **Centro de Visitantes,** whose museum contains dioramas of the park in Triassic times, and also includes fossils of some of its dinosaurs. Spanish-speakers should purchase Raúl Romarión's informative booklet *Valle de la Luna: Tierra de Dinosaurios,* which is on sale here.

The Thursday and Sunday Empresa Vallecito **buses** from San Juan to La Rioja stop at the Los Baldecitos checkpoint on RP 510, but that still leaves several kilometers' walk to the visitors center and raises the question of getting around the circuit (which could be dangerous for hikers and even cyclists in the unrelenting summer heat).

Visiting Ischigualasto without a vehicle may be possible, but a rental car or a tour certainly simplifies things. San Juan's **Grupo Zonda** (Mendoza 122 Sur, tel. 0264/421-4200, leo@leonardo-galvez.com) offers daily excursions for US$25 pp; this normally requires a four-person minimum, but the Saturday trip goes with or without the minimum. Other operators in both San Juan and San Agustín arrange trips to the park. It's also possible to hire a private vehicle with driver in San Agustín.

San Luis Province

San Luis is a contradiction, a tiny province with a small population that's maintained a high national profile through the notorious dynasty of the Rodríguez Saá family. Its most prominent figure, the erratic authoritarian populist Adolfo Rodríguez Saá ("El Adolfo"), proudly declared Argentina's debt default while serving as a caretaker president during the crisis of late 2001; still, the province itself is solvent despite widespread corruption in what opponents of El Adolfo and his brother Alberto punningly call a *dictadura Saátanica*.

San Luis prefers to be called *La Puerta de Cuyo* (The Door to Cuyo); its roads are among the country's best, and its namesake city is a clean, attractive provincial capital. For foreign visitors, though, its most worthwhile sight is the dinosaur-rich sandstone canyon country of Parque Nacional Sierra de las Quijadas; for *puntanos* (natives of the province) and other Argentines, it's the underrated Sierras on the border of Córdoba Province.

SAN LUIS

Capital of its province, San Luis itself has no internationally significant attractions, but it's the best place to arrange excursions to Parque Nacional Las Quijadas and overland travelers to Mendoza often stop over here. It's also a backdoor approach to Córdoba Province and its Sierras.

Orientation

San Luis (population 152,918) is 820 kilometers west of Buenos Aires via RN 7, 257 kilometers east of Mendoza via RN 7, and 405 kilometers southwest of Córdoba via RN 148. Most points of interest lie between Plaza Pringles, at the north end of the commercial axis formed by the parallel streets Rivadavia and San Martín, and Plaza Independencia four blocks south.

Sights

Most of San Luis's sights lie on or between the city's two principal plazas. The neoclassic **Iglesia Catedral** (1883, but not finished until 1944) faces lushly landscaped **Plaza Pringles** from Rivadavia, while the **Colegio Nacional Juan Crisóstomo Lafinur** (1869), facing the opposite side of the plaza from San Martín, is the province's most prestigious school.

The provincial **Casa de Gobierno** (1913) overlooks the equally well-landscaped **Plaza Independencia** from Calle 9 de Julio. On the opposite side of the plaza, the city's oldest building is the Moorish-style, 17th-century **Iglesia de Santo Domingo** (25 de Mayo s/n), but most of it is a 1930s reconstruction; its outstanding original feature is the carved *algarrobo* doors.

Entertainment and Events

Bar-hoppers will find a flourishing pub scene on Avenida Illia, running northwest from Plaza Pringles; several of these double as restaurants. Among them are the **Liberato Pub** (Avenida Illia 378, tel. 02652/445041); **Baco's Bar** (Avenida Illia 180), which also has live music; and **The Movie** (Avenida Illia 187, tel. 02652/441470), immediately across the street. **Taboo** (San Martín 488, tel. 02652/426014) is also worth a look, while **Morrison** (Pringles 830, tel. 02652/440818), as in Jim, is a lively rock 'n' roll theme bar with above-average food.

Accommodations

San Luis has good to excellent accommodations in all price ranges. The best budget option is **Residencial María Eugenia** (25 de Mayo 741, tel. 02652/430361, US$6/10 s/d with private bath), in a quiet area near Plaza Independencia. The nearby, family-run **Hotel Buenos Aires** (Buenos Aires 834, tel. 02652/424062) is a comparably priced alternative.

Rates at the more central **Hotel Castelmonte** (Chacabuco 769, tel. 02652/424963) are US$9/11 s/d, without breakfast but with friendly management, for well-kept midsize rooms whose opaque windows open onto interior patios.

Inca Hotel (Bolívar 943, tel. 02652/424923, yannice@arnet.com.ar) charges US$9 pp for decent medium-size rooms, but mattresses are on the soft side.

Well but simply furnished, **Gran Hotel España** (Avenida Illia 300, tel. 02652/437700, granhotelespana@tuhotel.net.ar) is an aging, deco-style hotel whose original woodwork makes the room deceptively dark when the blinds are closed. Rates are US$10/14 s/d without TV, US$13/17 s/d with TV and other amenities.

Rates seem a little steep at **Hotel Regidor** (San Martín 848, tel. 02652/423303, fax 02652/424756, US$14/21 s/d) for smallish rooms with showers only, but it's friendly, features a pleasant garden with a pool, and there's even a good bookstore within.

It's past its peak of about 20 years ago, but the midsize rooms at **Hotel Dos Venados** (Perón and República del Líbano, tel. 02652/422312, fax 02652/422503, hoteldosvenados@infovia .com.ar, US$17/21 s/d) are still respectable. It also has a pool, the largest gardens of any hotel in town, and restaurant.

One of the highlights at **Hotel Aiello** (Avenida Illía 431, tel. 02652/425609, fax 02652/425694, US$17/23 s/d with buffet breakfast) is the good-humored staff, but the ample rooms are impeccable even if relatively small windows limit the natural light.

The four-star **Hotel Quintana** (Avenida Illia 546, tel. 02652/438400, quintanahotel@infovia.com.ar, www.quintanahotel.com.ar) charges US$23/26 s/d.

Food

La Gran Avenida (Avenida Illia 168, tel. 02652/422942) provides large servings—the "small" pizza consists of four huge portions—from a diverse menu. A San Luis institution since 1945, **La Porteña** (Junín 696, tel. 02652/431722, 423807) has plain decor but an excellent menu with unusual (for Argentina) items such as pineapple chicken. **Los Robles** (Avenida Colón 684, tel. 02652/436767) is the top *parrilla.*

For breakfast, the bus terminal's **Confitería La Terminal** (Avenida España s/n) is better than most of its kind, with fresh croissants and espresso drinks. **Il Gelato** (Pringles 925) is the best bet for ice cream.

Information

The staff at the provincial **Secretaría de Estado de Turismo y Deporte** (Avenida Illia and Junín, tel. 02652/423957, turismo@sanluis.gov .ar, www.turismoensanluis.com, 8 A.M.– 9 P.M. daily) can be indifferent, and its glossy flyers are more notable for their photography than their utility.

For motorists, **ACA** is at Avenida Illia 401 (tel. 02652/423188).

Services

Banco de la Nación has an ATM at San Martín 695, at the southwest corner of Plaza Pringles, but there are several others in the vicinity.

Correo Argentino is at Arturo Illia and San Martín; the postal code is 5700.

Locutorio San Luis (Avenida Illia 305) has both phone and Internet access. **Ego** (Avenida Illia 352) is an Internet bar/café.

Dasso Viajes (Rivadavia 540, tel. 02652/ 421017) does excursions to provincial destinations like Las Quijadas and Merlo.

The **Hospital Regional** is at Avenida República Oriental del Uruguay 150 (tel. 02652/ 422627).

Getting There and Around

Aerolíneas Argentinas (Avenida Illia 468, tel. 02652/425671) flies four or five times weekly to Aeroparque via San Rafael.

San Luis's **Terminal de Ómnibus** (Avenida España between Francia and Estado de Israel, tel. 02652/424021), six blocks north of Plaza Pringles, has frequent provincial and long-distance services, and direct connections to Chile.

Typical destinations, fares, and times include San Juan (US$5.50, four hours), Mendoza (US$5, three hours), Merlo (US$4, 2.5 hours), and Buenos Aires (US$20–26, 12 hours). Tur-Bus goes directly to Santiago de Chile at 2:30 A.M. Wednesday and Sunday (US$13, 10 hours).

Aeropuerto Brigadier Mayor César R. Ojeda (tel. 02652/422457) is only about three kilometers north of town, on RN 146, so a cab or *remise* is inexpensive.

For rental cars, try **Hertz** (Avenida Illia 300, tel. 02652/422820) or **Avis** (Avenida Illia 470, tel. 02652/440288).

⋈ PARQUE NACIONAL SIERRA DE LAS QUIJADAS

Evoking the red sandstone ravines of Utah's Bryce Canyon, Parque Nacional Sierra de las Quijadas is rich in scenery, fossils, and pre-Columbian archaeological sites. In Lower Cretaceous times, about 120 million years ago, pterosaurs and their contemporaries left tracks in a lush subtropical wetland that has since become a jumble of barren cliffs, cornices, terraces, and dried-up lakebeds. Far later, the Huarpe and their predecessors left evidence of their camps and settlements.

Comprising 150,000 hectares in northwestern San Luis Province, the park is the site of ongoing paleontological research by Universidad Nacional de San Luis and New York's Museum of Natural History, as well as excavations of early Huarpe sites. It's open all year, but the mild spring and autumn months are the best times to visit; in the suffocatingly hot summer, thunderstorms can cause dangerous flash floods.

Las Quijadas is about 120 kilometers northwest of San Luis via paved RN 147 and a signed six-kilometer westbound gravel lateral. Most of the enormous park, though, is accessible only on foot or horseback.

Flora and Fauna

When the pterosaurs roamed here, Las Quijadas was a most-level marshland, but climate changes over the last hundred million years have left it a desert where summer temperatures often exceed 40° C, and plants and animals have adapted to this regime. Typical of the flora is the endemic *chica* (*Ramarinoa girolae*), a small, slow-growing tree whose hard, dense wood forms a twisted trunk. Truncated shrubs like the *jarilla* and several species of cacti are also typical.

The most notable mammals are the collared peccary, guanaco, puma, and red fox, while the endangered Argentine land turtle is also present here. Peregrine falcons and other raptors dive for small prey.

The canyons of Parque Nacional Sierra de las Quijadas are dinosaur country.

Sights and Activities

Las Quijadas's most unforgettable sight is the natural amphitheater of **Potrero de la Aguada,** where the last 25 million years of runoff—from precipitation that now averages only about 300 millimeters per annum—has eroded ancient sediments to expose the bright sandstone beds and conglomerates to the west. An easy trail follows the Aguada's rim toward the south for about half an hour, but hikers should refrain from descending into the intricate canyons without orienteering skills, plenty of water, high-energy snacks and, ideally, a local guide.

Along the gravel road to Potrero de la Aguada, stop to look at the recently excavated **Hornillos Huarpes,** the ovens where the park's pre-Columbian inhabitants prepared their food and fired their ceramics.

Practicalities

About one kilometer east of the Potrero de la Aguada overlook, there's a free APN campground, where there's also a small grocery with cold drinks. Near the park entrance, there's a new *comedor* that serves full meals and cold drinks.

There's no formal visitors center as yet, but rangers at the park entrance—where they collect a US$4 admission for foreigners, US$2 for Argentine residents—can answer questions. For guides, contact English-speaking geologist **David Rivarola** (tel. 02652/15-543629, rivarola@unsl .edu.ar, www.lasquijadas.com) in San Luis. Spanish-speaking visitors should look for Rivarola's self-published guidebook *El Parque Nacional Sierra de las Quijadas y Sus Recursos Naturales.*

Buses between San Luis and San Juan can drop passengers on the access road just north of the hamlet of Hualtarán. Travel agencies in the provincial capital sometimes organize day tours.

MERLO

Rapidly modernizing Merlo, a traditional *puntano* hill station on the western slope of the Sierras de Comenchingones, is increasingly popular with Argentines from elsewhere in the country. Foreign travelers are few, though, despite its refreshing climate and recreational opportunities. Like towns in the nearby Sierras de Córdoba, it's busiest in summer, during holiday periods like Semana Santa, and on weekends.

Orientation

Merlo (population 11,165), 900 meters above sea level, is 194 kilometers northeast of San Luis via RP 20 to La Toma, an eight-kilometer detour via RP 10 and RN 148 to Santa Rosa del Conlara, where eastbound RP 5 goes to Merlo. Plaza Sobremonte is the traditional town center, but most services are on or near Avenida del Sol, two blocks south, which climbs steeply east to the barrio of El Rincón.

Sports and Recreation

Adventure sports such as hiking, climbing, rappelling, and even parasailing are possible at **Mirador de los Cóndores** (tel. 02656/476329), at 2,100 meters in the Comenchingones immediately east of town. It also operates a bar and teahouse on the site.

Accommodations

Space prohibits mention of more than a handful of Merlo's abundant accommodations. It's worth emphasizing that prices are highest in summer, and during Semana Santa and winter holidays; the prices here are for the high season, and may be as much as 30 percent lower at other times.

Hotel Mirasierras (Avenida del Sol and Pedernera, tel. 02656/475045, consultas@hotelmirasierras.com.ar, www.hotelmirasierras.com.ar) charges US$18 s or d with breakfast for good but plain and decent-sized rooms; it also has a pool.

Posada del Valle (Poeta Lugones and Neptuno, tel./fax 02656/476103, posadadelvalle @merlo-sl.com.ar, US$20 s or d) is a very fine place with six double rooms in a recycled older house; rates include a large homemade breakfast. It accepts no children younger than 14.

The rooms are good but the management a little touchy at **Hostería Argentina** (Los Almendros 102, tel. 02656/475825, hosteriargentina@ merlo-sl.com.ar, www.hosteriargentina.8m.com, US$13/21 s/d).

M
Cuyo

Hotel Parque y Sol (Avenida del Sol 715, tel. 02656/475150, US$14–24 s or d) has motel-style units on spacious grounds. **Apart Hotel Piscú Yaco** (Pasaje los Teros 235, tel. 02656/475419, hotelpiscuyaco@merlo-sl.com.ar, www.aparthotelpiscuyaco.com.ar) enjoys a great location on a quiet alleyway, with ample grounds and a pool. Rates are US$13 pp for simply furnished, medium-sized rooms with breakfast.

Food

The **Montana Café** (Avenida del Sol 25) is a good breakfast spot, with exceptionally succulent croissants. **Heladería Michelangelo** (Avenida del Sol 100, tel. 02656/477418) has exceptional ice cream.

Unlike the other Cuyo provinces, San Luis is not wine country, but the restored **La Vieja Bodega** (Poeta Conti and Cerro Champaquí, tel. 02656/476564) was once a winery and, dating from 1870, is the oldest building in town. Recently restored, it has a diverse menu of pasta, fish, and meat—try the *chivito* (kid goat)—and the best atmosphere of any restaurant in town. Its former cellar is now a stylish pub, with occasional live entertainment.

Information and Services

At the entrance to town, at the traffic circle where RP 1 and RP 5 intersect, the **Dirección Provincial de Turismo** (tel. 02656/476079) is open 8 A.M.–8 P.M. daily except in summer, when it stays open until 10 P.M. It has an excellent city map and brochures, and will help find suitable accommodations in your price range.

The municipal **Oficina de Informes** (Coronel Mercau 605, tel. 02656/476078, sectur@merlo-sl.com.ar, 8 A.M.–9 P.M. daily) is helpful but less encyclopedic in its information.

There are ATMs in the vicinity of Plaza Mercau. **Correo Argentino** is at Coronel Mercau 579; the postal code is 5881. The **Cooperativa Telefónica** is at Juan de Videla 112; **Merlo Digital** (Presbítero Becerra 624), facing Plaza Mercau, has Internet access.

Lavandería Marva (Avenida del Sol 202, tel. 92656/476173) does the washing.

Getting There and Around

The new **Aeropuerto Internacional Valle del Conlara** (tel. 02656/492852) is about 18 kilometers west of Merlo on RN 148, about three kilometers south of the town of Santa Rosa del Conlara. **Cata Líneas Aéreas** (tel. 02656/478460), in the same building as the provincial tourist office at the Rotonda, flies Monday, Thursday, Friday, and Sunday to and from Aeroparque.

Merlo's new **Terminal de Ómnibus** is at RP 1 and Independencia, about 500 meters south of the Rotonda junction. Typical destinations, fares, and times include Buenos Aires (US$18, 12 hours), San Luis (US$4, 2.5 hours), and Mendoza (US$10, six hours). There are also services northeast across the Sierras to the capital city of Córdoba.

The Andean Northwest

Worth a trip to Argentina in its own right, the traditionally underrated northwest, comprising the Andean provinces of Jujuy, Salta, Santiago del Estero, Tucumán, Catamarca, and La Rioja, is fast becoming a popular destination for foreign visitors. Argentina's most indigenous region, part of the Inka empire in immediate pre-Columbian times, still shares much of the heritage of the highland civilizations of the central Andes. It also reveals a palpable colonial legacy, visible in adobe churches and other monuments of the city of Salta, and the Humahuaca and Calchaquí Valleys.

The northwest also boasts a cornucopia of diverse natural landscapes and ecosystems, many of them protected by national parks and other reserves. One unusual ecological feature is the *yungas,* a discontinuous longitudinal strip of subtropical cloud forest along the eastern edge of the Andes; there are also vividly colorful deserts and desolately beautiful high-altitude steppes, punctuated by volcanoes soaring above vast dry salt pans and shallow lakes crowded with migratory birds.

PLANNING YOUR TIME

In terms of logistics and services, Salta is the best base for visiting the region. Strategically central, it is almost equidistant from sights such as the

Quebrada de Humahuaca, the national parks of the *yungas,* the altiplano altitudes toward the Chilean border, and the circuits of the Valles Calchaquíes. Many of these may be done as day trips or multiday loops; about the only major sight too distant for an easy excursion is Parque Nacional Talampaya, in La Rioja Province.

To see the region's key attractions, at least a week is essential, two weeks or more desirable, and a month or more would be worthwhile. In these subtropical latitudes, the climate is agreeable most of the year, though the highest altitudes above 4,000 meters can be very cold in the winter months of June, July and August, especially at night. Many visitors, though, prefer these months, as most of the region has a dry-winter, wet-summer climate. Summer rains can cause flash floods in desert areas and make roads into the humid *yungas* impassable; ironically enough, summer snowstorms can make the highest elevations harder to reach than in the dry winter.

Because Argentines often head north during winter school holidays, which take place the last two weeks of July, demands on services can be high and reservations desirable for the best-value accommodations, rental cars, and attractions like the Tren a las Nubes (which does not operate in the summer months).

HISTORY

For travelers who see Europeanized Buenos Aires before visiting the mountainous Andean provinces, the northwest sometimes seems a historical relic that's failed to match the advances of the megalopolis of the pampas. What has happened, in fact, is a reversal of fortune—in immediate pre-Columbian times, the pampas were a peripheral backwater peopled with hunter-gatherers, while the highland valleys of what is now northernmost Argentina were an integral part of one of the world's most sophisticated civilizations. It may seem marginal now, but when the Spaniards first saw South America, this region held a good two-thirds of the population of what is now Argentine territory.

Until the mid-15th century A.D., indigenous groups like the Diaguita, Omaguaca, and Lules lived in more or less autonomous communities in the well-watered canyons, where they could grow corn, beans, and squash; and on the eastern Andean slopes. At higher altitudes, they grew potatoes and *quinoa* (a native grain); military fortifications, agricultural terraces, and complex irrigation systems were a measure of their political and technological sophistication.

Around A.D. 1480, the expanding Inka state brought more and more distant regions, including what is now northwestern Argentina, under the control of Cuzco. While the Inkas were a military juggernaut when necessary, they only required that the new subject peoples acknowledge the Inka Viracocha as their deity and pay tribute to the Inka state.

In the early 16th century, the Spanish invasion and exploration proceeded from Peru and Alto Perú (as present-day Bolivia was known during colonial times). In 1535, Diego de Almagro became the first Spaniard to set foot in the region—a year before Pedro de Mendoza's initial landing in Buenos Aires. Almagro's massive expedition, consisting of 500 Spaniards and thousands of Indians, traveled south through what is now Jujuy and Salta but endured tremendous hardship crossing to Chile via high and brutally cold Puna de Atacama; consequently, he returned to Peru by a different route.

In the 1550s, after subjecting the populations of the central Andean highlands to labor and tribute obligations under the *encomienda*, the Spaniards moved into what is now northwestern Argentina, but the sparser population of this area never rewarded its *encomenderos* with the same riches. Over the next century-plus, introduced European diseases devastated the indigenous populations and made those *encomiendas* worthless.

Still, the Spaniards founded a string of cities along the Andean front range and beyond, starting with Santiago del Estero (1553) and followed by San Miguel de Tucumán (1565), Córdoba (1573), Salta (1582), La Rioja (1591), and San Salvador de Jujuy (1592). Catamarca's first settlement was Belén (1555), but Diaguita resistance destroyed it and delayed permanent

Must-Sees

M **Iglesia San Francisco:** This 18th-century church with a four-story tower and reddish hue is the most unusual in **Salta,** northwestern Argentina's best-kept colonial city (page 292).

M **Valles Calchaquíes and the Altiplano:** West and south of Salta, explore the polychrome Quebrada de Cafayate and its nearby wine country, the vertiginous mountain road to remote Cachi, and the scenic "Train to the Clouds" (page 297).

M **Quebrada de Humahuaca and Vicinity:** The deep canyon's stunning landscapes, archaeological monuments, and settlements have preserved so much indigenous integrity that the valley received UNESCO World Heritage Site designation in 2003 (page 310).

M **National Parks of the Yungas:** In this strip of eastern Andean cloud forest, several national parks display some of Argentina's greatest biodiversity.

Calilegua and El Rey are easier to visit, while access to Baritú is difficult (page 320).

M **San Miguel de Tucumán:** This capital of a poverty-stricken province takes pride in its role as the cradle of Argentine independence. Its historical legacy, represented by several colonial monuments, makes it an interesting stop for history buffs (page 323).

M **Quilmes:** At the south end of the Valles Calchaquíes in Tucumán Province, but also easily reached from Cafayate, these hillside ruins of a pre-Columbian fortress make up what is arguably the country's most impressive archaeological site (page 331).

M **Parque Nacional Talampaya:** Reminiscent of Utah and Arizona, the thinly settled western desert of La Rioja Province is rich in scenery, fossils, and pre-Columbian rock-art sites (page 347).

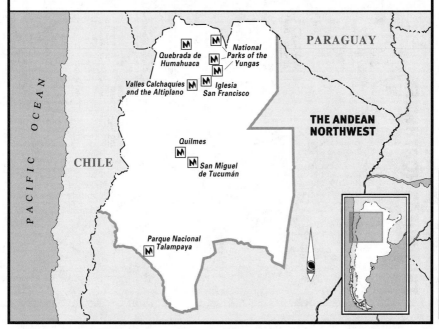

THE ANDEAN NORTHWEST

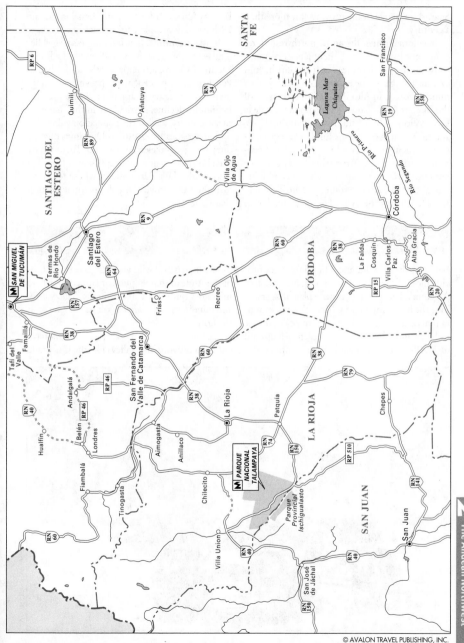

Spanish presence in the province for more than a century.

In colonial times, the entire northwestern region went by the name "Tucumán." Economically, it supplied mules, cotton, cloth, and eventually sugar to the enormously wealthy silver mine at Potosí, in Alto Perú. With formation of the Buenos Aires–based Virreinato del Río de la Plata (Viceroyalty of the River Plate) in 1776, and the opening of Buenos Aires to foreign commerce, Tucumán reversed its political and economic orientation. Argentine independence reinforced this trend but also left Salta and Jujuy out of the loop, as the routes to Alto Perú and Lima fell into disuse. Arrival of the railroad from Buenos Aires-Córdoba to San Miguel in the late 19th century completed the process.

In the meantime, political progress lagged behind economic growth, as caudillos like La Rioja's Facundo Quiroga, Felipe Varela, and Chacho Peñaloza set a precedent for provincial strongmen whose legacy is apparent to the present. Economic decline, particularly in the Tucumán sugar industry, has left the population vulnerable to demagogues like Antonio Domingo Bussi, a dirty war general elected mayor of Tucumán by the slimmest majority in 2003, and La Rioja labor leader Luis Barrionuevo, whose followers disrupted the provincial gubernatorial election that same year.

Salta and Jujuy Provinces

Between them, Salta and Jujuy Provinces provide most of the reasons for visiting northwestern Argentina. Except for an easterly plain that grades into the low-lying Gran Chaco, this is a mountainous area whose highest western peaks, on the Bolivian and Chilean borders, reach well upward of 5,000 meters. Beneath those summits, domestic llamas and wild vicuñas graze the grasses of the Andean steppe (puna or altiplano), where migratory birds frequent enormous shallow lakes and blindingly white *salares* (salt pans) open onto the horizon.

East and south of the altiplano, rivers have cut deep canyons and valleys like the Quebrada

© WAYNE BERNHARDSON

salt pan of Salinas Grandes

de Humahuaca, the Quebrada del Toro, and the Valles Calchaquíes, where most of the pre-Columbian population lived; there are still many archaeological sites but also colonial villages and modern vineyards. Where the rivers leave their canyons, the provincial capitals of Salta and San Salvador de Jujuy are contemporary urban centers that still show their colonial origins. Where the Andes meet the Chaco, east of Salta and San Salvador, the *yungas* comprise a longitudinal strip of cloud forest that has given the region several national parks.

While Salta and Jujuy Provinces are legitimate destinations in their own right, they are also becoming popular with trans-Chaco travelers en route to or from Mesopotamian attractions like Parque Nacional Iguazú, the Jesuit missions, and the biologically wealthy wetlands of the Esteros del Iberá.

SALTA

Experiencing a tourist boom from within and beyond Argentina's borders, the colonial city of Salta is the urban gateway to Argentina's Andean northwest, thanks to its picturesque plazas, impressive architecture, cultural life, and the region's best and widest offerings of accommodations, food, tours, and other services. Nearly surrounded by mountains, it also enjoys one of the most scenic settings of any Argentine city, making it an ideal base for excursions to the nearby Andes in any of several directions. Appropriately enough, it is nicknamed *Salta la Linda* (Salta the Beautiful).

Salta dates from 1582, when Tucumán's tyrannical governor Hernando de Lerma led colonists to the fertile alluvial valley that now bears his name. Ecologically, thanks to its mild climate and rich soils, it was an ideal location where the Spaniards could raise crops and pasture animals for the high-altitude silver-mining industry of Potosí, in Alto Perú (present-day Bolivia). After Argentine independence, Salta briefly declined but soon reoriented itself toward Buenos Aires and other Pampas cities that, thanks to the arrival of the railroad, became the primary destinations for sugar and other subtropical crops.

Orientation

In the sheltered Lerma Valley, 1,200 meters above sea level, Salta (population 462,668) is 1,495 kilometers northwest of Buenos Aires via RN 9, which turns abruptly west at General Güemes before dropping into town. It is 92 kilometers south of San Salvador de Jujuy via RN 9, a stretch of which is a paved but narrow mountain road not suitable for buses or similar large vehicles; it is 120 kilometers from San Salvador via RN 34 and RN 66, the safer but more roundabout route taken by buses. It is 813 kilometers northwest of Resistencia via the trans-Chaco RN 16 and RN 9.

Plaza 9 de Julio is the centerpiece of Salta's colonial grid, from which most points of interest are within a few blocks. North-south streets change names on either side of Caseros, but east-west streets are continuous. Toward the east, across Avenida Virrey Toledo, the grid gives way to streets that follow the contours of Cerro 20 de Febrero and Cerro San Bernardo.

Sights

For an overview of the city, take the *teleférico* (gondola, tel. 0387/431-0641, 10 A.M.–7:30 P.M. daily, US$2 pp) from Parque San Martín to the top of 1,454-meter **Cerro San Bernardo.** From the summit, a zigzag footpath descends to the **Monumento a Güemes,** the memorial to Salta's favorite caudillo.

Salta's compact center is ideal for walkers, and palm-studded **Plaza 9 de Julio** is the best starting point for exploring it. Nearly all the surrounding buildings feature *recovas* (porticos), beneath which hotels, cafés, and small businesses have their entrances.

On the west side of the plaza, the Francophile eclectic Centro Cultural América (Mitre 23) served as an elite private club from its completion in 1913 until 1950, when it became the provincial **Casa de Gobierno;** in 1987, when executive offices moved to the western suburbs, it became a cultural center. Immediately to its north, currently occupying a former girls school dating from 1860, the new **Museo de Antropología y Arqueología de Alta Montaña** (Mitre 71) will replace the former anthropology museum on

The Andean Northwest

SALTA

RÍO BERMEJO

B. FIGUEROA

ESTACIÓN
FERROCARRIL
BELGRANO

EL ANDÉN DE ▼
LOS ANDES

EL RANCHO DE
■ LOS ALEGRES

M LA VIEJA ESTACIÓN

● EL ESTAR
■ EN SALTA

ADOLFO ALSINA

LA TORRE

LAVANDERÍA
SOL DE MAYO ■

BAR 22 ■

AV. ENTRE RÍOS

RIVADAVIA

ACA ■

Plaza
Güemes

M FIAMBRERÍA LA
CORDOBESA

▼

J. TODD

LEGUIZAMON

25 DE MAYO

20 DE FEBRERO

BALCARCE

F. ACUNDO DE ZUVIRIA

M HOTEL SOLAR
DE LA PLAZA

HOTEL RESIDENCIAL
BALCARCE

SANTIAGO DEL ESTERO

M. ALVEAR

A. GÜEMES

AV. SARMIENTO

M HOTEL DEL
VIRREY

M. CASTRO

B. MITRE

SOCIEDAD ▼
ITALIANA

CHILEAN
CONSULATE ●

GENERAL GÜEMES

CIBERCITY ■

MAIPÚ

IBAZETA

MARTÍN CORNEJO

GUILLERMO BROWN

GENERAL SIMON BOLIVAR

HELADERÍA ▼
FILI

ARTEAGA

ESPAÑA

BANCO DE
LA NACIÓN ■

■ MIGRACIONES

FALCON CALCHAQUI

HOTEL PROVINCIAL ●

JULIO CASEROS

Plaza
9 de Julio

MUSEO DE ★
BELLAS ARTES

SEE DETAIL

GENERAL ALVARADO

SANTA ROSA

● HOTEL CRISTIÁN

JUSTO J. DE URQUIZA

PJE. RUIZ DE LOS LLANOS

ESTECO

CARLOS PELLEGRINI

MERCADO
CENTRAL
▼

PLURAL LIBROS ■
RESIDENCIAL ELENA ●

DIRECCIÓN MUNICIPAL
DE TURISMO ■

AV. SAN MARTÍN

HELADOS GIANNI ▼

LAPRIDA

10 DE OCTUBRE

GENERAL LAMADRID

GENERAL J. M. PAZ

GENERAL J. J. GORRITI

MENDOZA

ALVAREZ ▼

IL CAVALLINO ▼

JUJUY

EL BOLICHE DE
BALDERRAMA ■

ITUZAINGO

CASA MARÍA
DE TOFFOLI ●

LA FLORIDA

JUAN BAUTISTA ALBERDI

BUENOS AIRES

SAN JUAN

CUMBRE HOTEL ●

To
Hostal
Patras

▼

CLUB AMIGOS DE
LA MONTAÑA ■

SAN LUIS

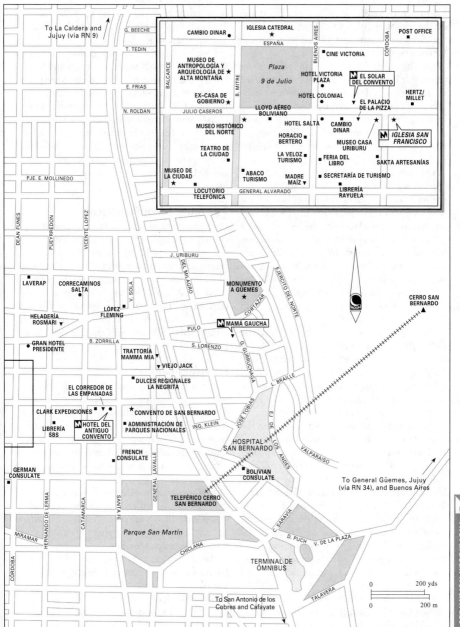

To La Caldera and Jujuy (via RN 9)

G. BEECHE

T. TEDIN

E. FRIAS

N. ROLDAN

CAMBIO DINAR

IGLESIA CATEDRAL

ESPAÑA

BUENOS AIRES

CORDOBA

POST OFFICE

CINE VICTORIA

MUSEO DE ANTROPOLOGÍA Y ARQUEOLOGÍA DE ★ ALTA MONTAÑA

Plaza 9 de Julio

HOTEL VICTORIA PLAZA

EL SOLAR DEL CONVENTO

HERTZ/ MILLET

EX-CASA DE GOBIERNO ★

HOTEL COLONIAL

EL PALACIO DE LA PIZZA

JULIO CASEROS

LLOYD AÉREO BOLIVIANO

MUSEO HISTÓRICO DEL NORTE

HOTEL SALTA

CAMBIO DINAR

IGLESIA SAN FRANCISCO

TEATRO DE LA CIUDAD

HORACIO BERTERO

MUSEO CASA URIBURU

MUSEO DE LA CIUDAD

LA VELOZ TURISMO

FERIA DEL LIBRO

SAKTA ARTESANÍAS

ABACO TURISMO

MADRE MAÍZ

SECRETARÍA DE TURISMO

LOCUTORIO TELEFÓNICA

GENERAL ALVARADO

LIBRERÍA RAYUELA

PJE. E. MOLLINEDO

DEAN FUNES

PUEYRREDON

VICENTE LOPEZ

J. URIBURU

DEL MILAGRO

V. SOLA

CORTAZAR

MONUMENTO A GÜEMES ★

EJERCITO DEL NORTE

CERRO SAN BERNARDO ▲

LAVERAP

CORRECAMINOS SALTA

LÓPEZ FLEMING

PULO

MAMÁ GAUCHA

HELADERÍA ROSMARI ▾

B. ZORRILLA

S. LORENZO

G. GURRUCHAGA

L. BRAILLE

GRAN HOTEL PRESIDENTE

TRATTORÍA MAMMA MIA

VIEJO JACK

DULCES REGIONALES LA NEGRITA

JOSE TOBIAS

EL CORREDOR DE LAS EMPANADAS

CLARK EXPEDICIONES

CONVENTO DE SAN BERNARDO ★

ADMINISTRACIÓN DE PARQUES NACIONALES

ING. KLEIN

EJ. DE LOS ANDES

VALPARAISO

LIBRERÍA SBS

HOTEL DEL ANTIGUO CONVENTO

HOSPITAL SAN BERNARDO

FRENCH CONSULATE

GENERAL LAVALLE

GERMAN CONSULATE

BOLIVIAN CONSULATE

To General Güemes, Jujuy (via RN 34), and Buenos Aires

HERNANDO DE LERMA

CATAMARCA

SANTA FE

TELEFÉRICO CERRO SAN BERNARDO

MIRAMAR

Parque San Martín

CHICLANA

C. SARAVIA

D. PUCH

V. DE LA PLAZA

CÓRDOBA

TERMINAL DE ÓMNIBUS

TALAVERA

0   200 yds
0   200 m

To San Antonio de los Cobres and Cafayate

The Andean Northwest

© AVALON TRAVEL PUBLISHING, INC.

Cerro San Bernardo; its signature exhibit will be the mummies of Inka children found atop the Andean summit of Llullaillaco, on the Chilean border.

On the north side of the plaza, Salta's 19th-century *Iglesia Catedral* (España 596) replaced an earlier cathedral destroyed by an earthquake; it contains several significant religious images, along with the remains of independence hero and provincial caudillo General Martín Miguel de Güemes, a native *salteño* and independence hero.

On the south side of the plaza, distinguished by its asymmetrical style, the colonial **Cabildo** (1780) replaced a series of precarious earlier buildings; it underwent a major restoration in 1945. It now serves as the **Museo Histórico del Norte** (Caseros 549, tel. 0387/421-5340, US$.70), whose collections include antique furniture, ecclesiastical and contemporary art, and animal-powered transportation technology. Hours are 9:30 A.M.–1:30 P.M. and 3:30–8:30 P.M. weekdays, 9:30 A.M.–1:30 P.M. and 4:30–8 P.M. Saturday, and 9:30 A.M.–1 P.M. Sunday.

One block west of the plaza, Salta's **Museo de Bellas Artes** (Florida 20, tel. 0387/421-4714, 9 A.M.–1 P.M. and 4–8 P.M. daily except Sun., US$.35) occupies the colonial **Casa Arias Rengel** (1752), a two-story mansion with thick adobe walls and a hanging balcony. Its collections focus on contemporary painting and sculpture.

At the south end of the same block, on the opposite side of the pedestrian street, the **Casa de Hernández** (1780) is another handsome colonial residence with a second-story corner balcony and an attractive interior patio. It houses the **Museo de la Ciudad** (Florida 97, tel. 0387/437-3352, www.museociudadsalta.gov.ar, US$.30), which deals with municipal government history and objects of daily usage in the evolution of the city. The most imposing item, though, is Lorenzo Gigli's historical oil. Hours are 9 A.M.–1 P.M. daily except Sunday, and 4–8:30 P.M. weekdays only.

One block east of the plaza, the 18th-century **Museo Casa Uriburu** (Caseros 417, tel. 0387/421-5340, US$.30) was the residence of José Evaristo Uriburu (1831–1914), who twice served

as president of Argentina. It's open 9:30 A.M.–1:30 P.M. daily except Monday, and 4:30–8 P.M. Tuesday–Saturday.

One block farther east, dating from 1582, the **Convento de San Bernardo** (Caseros and Santa Fe) is a Carmelite convent not open to the public, though its cobblestone patio, dazzling adobe walls and intricately carved algarrobo doors (1762) impart a colonial dignity to the city's oldest surviving religious landmark. In practice, it has served other functions—it was once a hospital, for example—and has undergone several modifications because of earthquake damage and changing uses.

Iglesia San Francisco

Immediately to the east, Salta's most outlandish church is the Iglesia San Francisco (Caseros and Córdoba, 9 A.M.–12:30 P.M. and 5–8 P.M. daily except Sunday), dating from 1796 but embellished by Franciscan architect Luis Giorgi from 1868 to 1872; the soaring four-story tower—terraced like a ziggurat—also dates from this period. It's the reddish color, gilt trim, and ornamental details that really grab the viewer's attention, though.

Entertainment

The line between entertainment and dining is not always clear in Salta, especially when it comes to the well-established folkloric venues scattered around town, and the newer, more fashionable locales along Balcarce. In some instances, especially along Balcarce, the same performers may work at several different places on the same night.

El Rancho de los Alegres (Balcarce 926, tel. 0387/15-404-6906) offers a fine regional-food menu including goat, pizza, *humitas,* tamales, and the usual *parrillada,* plus *peña* entertainment daily except Monday.

Bar 22 (Balcarce 717, tel. 0387/431-3930) holds a folkloric peña every Thursday, with food as well.

Some 20 blocks west of Plaza 9 de Julio, the participatory **La Casona del Molino** (Luis Burela 1, tel. 0387/434-2835) has adapted itself to the traditional layout of a sprawling residence to offer live folkloric music in intimate surroundings. There's also a prime regional menu of *locro, humitas,* empanadas, and wines.

On the lower slopes of Cerro San Bernardo, east of downtown, the **Peña Gauchos de Güemes** (Avenida Uruguay 750, tel. 0387/492-1621) has regular dinner-and-show packages for around US$7.50. Reservations are essential at **El Boliche de Balderrama** (San Martín 1126, tel. 0387/421-1542), in the same location for more than 40 years. Its dinner-and-show package is comparably priced to the one at Peña Gauchos de Güemes.

The **Cine Victoria** (Zuviría 70) shows recent films.

Occupying the former Gran Cine Alberdi, the **Teatro de la Ciudad** (Alberdi 56, tel. 0387/431-3330) offers live theater and concerts.

Shopping
Sakta Artesanías (Córdoba 32, tel. 0387/15-683-3720) sells woodcarvings, pottery, silverwork, handmade clothing, regional sweets, and the like. **Dulces Regionales La Negrita** (España 79, tel. 0387/421-1833) also sells homemade sweets.

Silversmith Horacio Bertero (Buenos Aires 16, tel. 0387/431-3585) produces *gauchesco* items like those of his mentor Raúl Horacio Draghi, of San Antonio de Areco.

Salta has an outstanding selection of bookstores, including **Librería Rayuela** (Alvarado 570, tel. 0387/431-2066 or 0387/431-8886, rayuela@arnet.com.ar), **Feria del Libro** (Buenos Aires 83), and **Plural Libros** (Buenos Aires 220). **Librería SBS** (Lerma 45, tel. 0381/431-8868) carries English-language books.

Accommodations
Thanks to its increasing tourist appeal and traditional commercial importance, Salta has a wide variety of accommodations in many categories, ranging from backpackers' favorites to business-oriented hostelries.

Under US$10
Salta's cheapest choice is the sprawling 500-site **Camping Municipal Carlos Xamena** (Avenida

República de Líbano s/n, tel. 0387/423-1341, US$2 pp, US$1 per car and US$2 per tent), which features a gigantic swimming pool that makes it uncomfortably crowded and noisy during daylight hours, at least in summer. From downtown Salta, take city bus No. 1A.

In recent years, Salta has seen an eruption of hostel facilities where backpackers can sleep cheaply and comfortably, find traveling companions, and arrange excursions into the Andes. The cheapest is **Correcaminos Salta** (Vicente López 353, tel. 0387/422-0731, salta@correcaminos.com.ar, www.correcaminos.com.ar, US$3 pp).

The oldest of these is Salta's HI affiliate **Backpacker's Hostel** (Buenos Aires 930, tel./fax 0387/423-5910, hostelsalta@backpackerssalta .com, www.backpackerssalta.com, US$3.50 pp), 10 blocks south of Plaza 9 de Julio. So popular that some shoestring travelers stay for weeks or even months on end, the hostel organizes tours, has weekly Wednesday barbecues, and arranges outings to local restaurants and clubs. The non-smoking rules, though, are only pro forma. The same management runs the nearby **Hostel Patras** (Rioja 573, tel. 0387/423-4401), which offers a bit more comfort, quiet, and privacy.

Lodged in an older house north of Plaza Güemes, **El Estar en Salta** (Mitre 833, tel. 0387/422-2380, elestarensalta@yahoo.com.ar, US$3.50 pp dorms, US$4.50 pp d) is a casual facility with amenities like a climbing wall, hammocks, minigym, and rental bikes; there are even occasional live music performances.

Until the recent devaluation, private *casas de familia* were the best values in town, and they're still worth consideration. The traditional favorite has been the **Casa María de Toffoli** (Mendoza 915, tel. 0387/431-8948, US$4 pp); María de Toffoli's two sisters can usually accommodate any overflow at their adjacent houses.

US$10–25
Rooms at the simple but clean and friendly **Hotel Residencial Balcarce** (Balcarce 460, tel. 0387/431-8135, hotelbalcarce@hotmail.com, www.hotelbalcarce.8m.com, US$5/7 s/d with shared bath, US$7/11 s/d with private bath and

breakfast) surround a shady grape arbor. Rates at this well-located place, close (but not too close) to the city's main restaurant and nightlife district, are a bargain.

Two-plus blocks south of Plaza 9 de Julio, recommended **Residencial Elena** (Buenos Aires 256, tel. 0387/421-1529, US$7/11 s/d) offers cozy neocolonial style; it's one of the best choices in its price range.

The **M Hotel del Antiguo Convento** (Caseros 113, tel. 0387/422-7267, arancibiasara @arnet.com.ar, US$11/17 s/d with breakfast) is the best new value in Salta's hotel scene. All the smartly furnished rooms enjoy a quiet setback from the streetside snack bar, and there's also a small pool.

The spacious rooms at the modern **Cumbre Hotel** (Ituzaingó 585, tel. 0387/421-4747, cumber@salnet.com.ar, US$9 pp) are an excellent value, but the dull semi-industrial neighborhood is a drawback. **Hotel Cristián** (Islas Malvinas 160, tel. 0387/431-9600, hotelcristian@uolsinectis.com.ar, US$14/23 s/d) enjoys a quiet, secure location on pleasant grounds.

On the east side of Plaza 9 de Julio, **Hotel Colonial** (Zuviría 6, tel. 0387/4310760, hotelcolonial@salnet.com.ar), charges US$16/23 s/d. The adjacent multistory **Hotel Victoria Plaza** (Zuviría 16, tel./fax 0387/431-8500, vplaza @arnet.com.ar, US$19/25 s/d with a decent breakfast) is a three-star hotel that hasn't quite managed to keep up with the times—it remains comfortable but commonplace, though the rates are reasonable.

US$25–50

One of Salta's traditional favorites is its namesake **Hotel Salta** (Buenos Aires 1, tel. 0387/431-0740, US$31/41 s/d); though it hasn't kept pace with recent improvements elsewhere in the city, it's fairly priced. In the same category is **Hotel Provincial** (Caseros 786, tel. 0387/432-2000, reservas@provincialplaza.com.ar, US$41/43 s/d).

US$50–100

Gran Hotel Presidente (Avenida Belgrano 353, tel./fax 0387/431-2022, granhotelpresidente @salnet.com.ar, $38/55 s/d) is a four-star facility

with average- to plus-sized rooms that lack tubs but otherwise have everything.

Furnished with style, the boutiquish **M Hotel del Virrey** (20 de Febrero 420, tel./fax 0387/422-8000, hoteldelvirrey@arnet.com.ar, US$41/55 s/d) is an eight-room colonial-style accommodation that's an excellent value. Its pool is for wading or soaking only, but it has all other amenities.

Facing Plaza Güemes, the most stylish new hotel in town is business-oriented **M Hotel Solar de la Plaza** (J.M. Leguizamón 669, tel./fax 0387/431-5111, reservassolar@salnet.com.ar, www.newage-hotels.com), a magnificently retrofitted family house. Rates are US$65 d with breakfast, parking, taxes, pool, gym, sauna, a/c, safe deposit boxes, and the like; superior rooms are only slightly dearer at US$70 d. Suites cost US$98.

Food

There are plenty of good places to eat scattered around downtown and other areas, but the focus of Salta's gastronomic scene has shifted north to Calle Balcarce, between Plaza Güemes and the old railroad station. In style, if not in scale, the area resembles Buenos Aires's Palermo Soho, with inventive restaurants occupying recycled premises.

For fresh groceries at the stalls and cheap snacks like empanadas and pizzas at the stands, try the **Mercado Central,** which occupies most of the block bounded by Avenida San Martín, Ituzaingó, Urquiza, and Florida.

Among sit-down restaurants, **Alvarez** (Buenos Aires 302, tel. 0387/421-4523) is one of the most economical Argentine choices, and it offers live tango on Saturday nights. Other traditional inexpensive choices include **El Palacio de la Pizza** (Caseros 437) and the **Sociedad Italiana** (Santiago del Estero 497). **Madre Maíz** (Alvarado 508, tel. 0387/432-9425) is a vegetarian alternative.

Parrillada is available at **El Corredor de las Empanadas** (Caseros 117, tel. 0387/422-0345), but instead try *norteño* specialties like tamales (US$.50), *empanadas salteñas* (spicier and even cheaper), and *locro* (US$1). With wines stacked from the floor to the ceiling and hanging hams twirling on strings, out-of-the-way ⚑ **Fiambrería La Cordobesa** (J.M. Leguizamón 1502, tel. 0387/422-2794) is a delightful deli that also serves early-evening tapas at a handful of tables. It may get crowded, but it's well worth any wait.

Quiet with fine service, downtown's best *parrilla* is ⚑ **El Solar del Convento** (Caseros 444, tel. 0387/421-5124), with an outstanding *bife de chorizo* for US$3 and regional specialties like empanadas and *humitas*. Five blocks east of Plaza 9 de Julio, **Viejo Jack** (Avenida Virrey Toledo 145, tel. 0387/421-7568) is another good option for beef-eaters.

Immediately to the north, **Trattoría Mamma Mia** (Pasaje Zorrilla 1, tel. 0387/422-5061) is a more upscale but still reasonable choice for pastas. On the lower slopes of Cerro San Bernardo, ⚑ **Mamá Gaucha** (Gurruchaga 225, tel. 0387/431-7307) affects a *pulpería* style of faux rusticism, but regional specialties like *pastel de choclo* (a maize casserole) and the standard *parrillada* are all excellent. In warm weather, it offers comfortable sidewalk seating, and the service is outstanding; most entrees are in the US$2–3.50 range.

Just walking the length of Balcarce between Plaza Güemes and the train station can offer any number of choices, but one of the most popular is ⚑ **La Vieja Estación** (Balcarce 885, tel. 0387/421-7727, www.laviejaestacionsalta.com .ar). With *locro* and kid goat on the menu, and live folkloric entertainment on the stage, it's open until 5 A.M. Down the block, **El Andén de los Andes** (Balcarce 999, tel. 0387/431-4021) is another fine folk music venue, with good meals and an outstanding bar.

Salta boasts an abundance of quality ice creameries, among them **Il Cavallino** (Buenos Aires 303, tel. 0387/421-3356), **Heladería Fili** (General Güemes 1009), **Helados Gianni** (San Martín 595), and **Heladería Rosmari** (Pueyrredón 202).

Information

The well-organized provincial **Secretaría de Turismo** (Buenos Aires 93, tel. 0387/431-0950, info@turismosalta.gov.ar, www.turismosalta .gov.ar) is open 8 A.M.–9 P.M. weekdays, 9 A.M.– 8 P.M. weekends and holidays; it distributes brochures and maps, and has English-speaking personnel.

The **Dirección Municipal de Turismo** (Avenida San Martín and Buenos Aires, tel. 0387/437-3341) is open 8 A.M.–9 P.M. daily; in high season, at the bus terminal, it maintains a smaller office that closes 1–4 P.M.

For motorists, **ACA** is at Rivadavia and Mitre, tel. 0387/431-0229.

For information on national parks in Salta and Jujuy Provinces, visit the **Administración de Parques Nacionales** (APN, Santa Fe 23, tel. 0387/422-7093, drnoa@apn.gov.ar). Hours are 10 A.M.–noon and 3–5 P.M. daily.

For information on mountaineering in the northern Argentine Andes, visit the **Club Amigos de la Montaña** (San Luis 510, cam1956@hotmail.com), which meets Tuesday, Wednesday, and Thursday at 8 P.M.

Services

Cambio Dinar (Mitre 101), at the northwest corner of Plaza 9 de Julio, changes cash and travelers checks (with commission). Numerous banks in the vicinity have ATMs, such as **Banco de la Nación** (Mitre 151).

Correo Argentino is at Deán Funes 170; the postal code is 4400.

For visa renewals, **Migraciones** is at Maipú 35 (tel. 0387/422-0438), 11 blocks west of Plaza 9 de Julio.

Argentina's immediate neighbors have Salta consulates: Chile at Santiago del Estero 965 (tel. 0387/431-1857), Bolivia at Mariano Boedo 34 (tel. 0387/421-1040). Several European countries also have consulates, including France (Santa Fe 156, tel. 431-4726), Germany (Urquiza 409, tel. 0387/421-6525), and Italy (Santiago del Estero 497, tel. 0387/432-1532).

There are numerous telephone offices such as **Locutorio Telefónica,** Alvarado 686. Internet outlets are also abundant, such as **CiberCity** (Zuviría 255, Local 1).

Abaco Turismo (Alberdi 53, Local 33, tel. 0387/431-3116, abaco@ciudad.com.ar) is the AmEx representative.

Lavandería Sol de Mayo is at 25 de Mayo 755 (tel. 0387/431-9718); hotel pickup and delivery are free. **Laverap** is at Santiago del Estero 363 (tel. 0387/15-605-3839).

Hospital San Bernardo is at Boedo 69 (tel. 0387/432-0300).

Getting There and Around

Salta has the most complete transportation options in northwestern Argentina.

Aerolíneas Argentinas (Caseros 475, tel. 0387/431-1331) flies once or twice daily to Aeroparque (Buenos Aires), sometimes via Córdoba; some flights from Aeroparque continue to Jujuy. **Austral,** at the same office, flies daily to Aeroparque.

Lloyd Aéreo Boliviano (Caseros 529, tel. 0387/431-0320 or 431-1389) flies Wednesday and Saturday to Santa Cruz de la Sierra (US$166 one-way, US$201 round-trip, plus US$18 airport taxes).

Aeropuerto Internacional Martín Miguel de Güemes (tel. 0387/424-7356) is nine kilometers southwest of town on RP 51; for transfers, contact Airbus (tel. 0387/15-683-2897).

At the east end of Parque San Martín, Salta's **Terminal de Ómnibus** (Avenida Hipólito Yrigoyen s/n, tel. 0387/401-1143) has provincial, long-distance, and even international services (to Chile only).

Once or twice weekly, either **Pullman Bus** (tel. 0387/431-9719) or **Géminis** crosses the Andes to San Pedro de Atacama (US$55, 11 hours) and Calama, Chile (US$60, 13 hours). At Calama, there are connections to Antofagasta (US$65, 15.5 hours), Iquique (US$70, 23 hours), and the border city of Arica (US$70, 24 hours).

Nearly a score of bus companies offer long-distance service throughout the country. Typical long-distance destinations, fares, and times include Jujuy (US$5, two hours), Tucumán (US$9, four hours), Catamarca (US$10, seven hours), Resistencia (US$20, 13 hours), La Rioja (US$12, eight hours), Córdoba (US$17–20, 10 hours), San Juan (US$16–20, 15 hours), Mendoza (US$23–30, 18 hours), Rosario (US$24–29, 17 hours), and Buenos Aires (US$25–32, 22 hours).

El Indio (tel. 0387/431-4389) goes three times daily to Cafayate (US$5, three hours). **El**

An international bus crosses the Andes from Salta Province.

Quebradeño (tel. 0387/427-1127) climbs daily to San Antonio de los Cobres (US$4, five hours).

Empresa Marcos Rueda (tel. 0387/421-4447) goes to Cachi (4.5 hours, US$6) daily at 7 A.M., Tuesday and Saturday at 1:30 P.M., Thursday at 3:30 P.M., and Sunday at 6 P.M.; Molinos (6.5 hours, US$9), Monday, Wednesday, Friday, and Sunday at 7 A.M., Saturday at 1:30 P.M. (with change in Cachi); and La Poma (6.5 hours, US$8) Tuesday and Saturday at 1:30 P.M., Wednesday at 7 A.M. (with change in Cachi). The Wednesday and Sunday Molinos buses continue to Angastaco, where it's possible to make connections to Cafayate.

While the **Ferrocarril Belgrano** (Ameghino 690, tel. 0387/431-0809) has no regular passenger services, it is still the departure point for the legendary **Tren a las Nubes** (Train to the Clouds), now a tourist train that, from April to November, goes beyond San Antonio de los Cobres to a spectacular viaduct before returning to Salta (in January and February, it operates a shorter itinerary).

For more details, see the sidebar "A Train to the Clouds," and the entry for San Antonio de los Cobres, or contact the local representative **La Veloz Turismo** (Buenos Aires 44, tel. 0387/401-2000, info@lavelo.turismo.com.ar). Really determined travelers can explore the possibilities of crossing the Andes to Chile via the freight train to the border post of Socompa, but this is more difficult than in the past.

Car rental agencies include **Hertz/Millet** (Caseros 374, tel. 0387/421-6785) and **López Fleming** (Avenida Güemes 92, tel. 0387/421-4143).

◩ VALLES CALCHAQUÍES AND THE ALTIPLANO

West and south of Salta, the Andean canyonlands bear the collective name of the Valles Calchaquíes, after the indigenous Calchaquí or Diaguita peoples who inhabited the area before the Spanish invasion, while the altiplano uplands are a high, thinly populated steppe. Rich in scenery and archaeological heritage, its highlights are the Quebrada del Toro, through which the fa-

mous Tren a las Nubes chugs northwest to the Chilean border, the polychrome Quebrada de Cafayate and its wine country, and the picturesque towns of the Río Calchaquí proper.

Several Salta operators offer excursions in the area. **MoviTrack** (Buenos Aires 28, tel. 0387/431-6749, fax 0387/431-5301, movitrack@movitrack.com.ar, www.movitrack.com.ar) does a one-day Safari a las Nubes (US$68) including San Antonio de los Cobres, Salinas Grandes, and Purmamarca; a two-day excursion that also includes the Quebrada de Humahuaca (US$100); a one-day trip to Los Cardones and Cachi (US$45); and a two-day version that also includes Quilmes and Cafayate (US$80). There are also one-day trips to Cafayate and Quilmes (US$35), to Humahuaca (US$40), and to Dique Cabra Corral (US$27).

Another reliable operator, specializing in natural history and bird-watching in particular, is **Clark Expediciones** (Caseros 121, Local 2, tel./fax 0387/421-5390, clark@clarkexpediciones.com, www.clarkexpediciones.com), which focuses on the *yungas* but also travels to the altiplano and other remote areas of the northwest. English-speaking operator Ricardo Clark has written several bird-watching guides, which are for sale along with other books on the region.

Quebrada del Toro

West of Salta, graveled RP 51 parallels the railroad as it climbs the narrow canyon of the Quebrada del Toro en route to the mining town of San Antonio de los Cobres, the largest settlement in the provincial altiplano, and the stunning viaduct at La Polvorilla. While many people enjoy the Tren a las Nubes, the famous "Train to the Clouds," the highway has its own appeal and is usually open in the summer months, when the train does not run.

Before the train, which dates from the 1940s, and even before the road, the Quebrada del Toro was the route by which stockmen drove cattle and mules across the Andes to the nitrate mines of Chile's food-deficient Atacama desert. By the time the animals got to Chile after crossing the altiplano, they were usually far scrawnier than when they left Salta (on Diego de Almagro's initial

A TRAIN TO THE CLOUDS

One of South America's most impressive engineering achievements has been, from an economic standpoint, one of its most useless. From its base at Salta, 1,187 meters above sea level, a 571-kilometer westbound rail line climbs the vividly colorful Quebrada del Toro and traverses the monochrome puna beneath intense blue Andean skies to Socompa, at 3,858 meters on the Chilean border. At Abras Chorrillos, its highest point, it scrapes 4,575 meters.

freight train on the Tren a las Nubes line

Its greatest feature is the **Viaducto La Polvorilla,** the turnaround point for excursions on the popular Tren a las Nubes (Train to the Clouds) excursion. Sixty-four meters above the desert floor, at an altitude of 4,220 meters, the 224-meter viaduct straddles a scenic desert canyon. En route to La Polvorilla, the line passes through more than 20 tunnels and 19 stations, zigzagging up hillsides at El Alisal (1,806 meters) and Chorrillos (2,111 meters), and literally spiraling twice between Tacuara (3,036 meters) and Diego de Almagro (3,503 meters).

In conception, this was an international railway that linked Salta to the Chilean port of Antofagasta; in practice it still is, but not in the way its founders envisaged. In the first instance, it took 60 years to complete a line first proposed in 1888 to supply Chile's nitrate mines with fresh produce, by which time the nitrate boom had fizzled.

After opening in 1948, it failed as a passenger line because demand was too small and the 38-hour trip, which required changing trains at Socompa, was simply too exhausting. In 1973, when

Spanish expedition, in the 16th century, both men and horses froze to death with the cold, and subsequent expeditions scavenged meat from the preserved animal carcasses).

About 55 kilometers from Salta, the train and the highway intersect at **Estación Chorrillos,** 2,111 meters above sea level, where there's a small campground suitable for cyclists and other travelers. **Santa Rosa de Tastil,** 3,110 meters above sea level and 110 kilometers from Salta, is the site of pre-Inka archaeological ruins; while tour buses cannot easily approach the ruins, smaller operators do. In any event, there's a modest archaeological museum here, open 10 A.M.–6 P.M. Tuesday–Saturday and 10 A.M.–2 P.M. Sunday only, along with an indigenous crafts market.

Befitting its name, **San Antonio de los Cobres** (population 4,281) relies on a nearby copper mine for its economy, but for most visitors it is

the last station on the Tren a las Nubes before the La Polvorilla viaduct, where the train turns around and returns to Salta. At 3,775 meters above sea level, 168 kilometers from Salta, it's also a stop for loop tours to the Salinas Grandes salt flats along RN 40, to the north, which return to Salta via Purmamarca and the Quebrada de Humahuaca. In dry weather, this route is passable for any vehicle, but in rainy weather it can be treacherous.

Note that even when the train is not running, volunteer guides from the Municipalidad's Instituto Terciario del Turismo will take visitors to the viaduct for the cost of gasoline (a tip, though, would be appropriate).

San Antonio has several basic accommodations, such as **Hospedaje Belgrano** (Belgrano s/n, tel. 0387/490-9025), and **Hotel El Milagro** (Zavaleta and Avellaneda, tel. 0387/15-402-

Chile used the link to freight a trial load of copper to the Brazilian port of Santos, it took more than two weeks to reach the Atlantic; only recently has the shipment of motor vehicles across the Andes to Paraguay justified keeping the line open. According to British rail historian Ian Thomson, "It's a superlative railroad both in terms of its technical achievements and of the expenses to keep it in service."

For those who want to appreciate these superlatives, the Salta representatives for Tren a las Nubes (www.trenalasnubes.com.ar) include **La Veloz Turismo** (Buenos Aires 44, tel. 0387/401-2000, info@lavelozturismo.com.ar) and **Dinar** (Mitre 101, tel./fax 0387/432-2600, lfarias @dinarsa.com). Check-in time at the station (Balcarce and Ameghino) is 6:30 A.M.; the train itself departs from the station at 7:05 A.M. and returns by 10:05 P.M. This is a winter dry-season-only trip, with approximately four departures in April, five in May, four in June, 15 in July, seven in August, four each in September and October, and two in November.

The fare for the 438-kilometer round-trip to La Polvorilla is US$68 pp; meals, ranging from snack-bar sandwiches and hamburgers (US$3–4) to four-course dining-car lunches (US$8), are extra. On-board services include guides, translators, live music, video, medical staff, and telephones.

For those who want to live the entire experience, it's been possible to reach the border on the infrequent freights; though the service has been suspended recently, it's worthwhile to investigate the current status. According to a reliable source, though, the last foreigner to wrangle a spot, in 2002, needed nearly three weeks to convince the engineer.

Anyone lucky enough to reach Socompa can try to switch to the run-down Chilean freight, which continues to the town of Baquedano on Ruta 5, Chile's main north-south highway. Through wild, high scenery that's about as far off the beaten track as you can get in Argentina and Chile, this uncertain trip requires language skills, patience, and lots of time. Carry Chilean pesos from Salta to meet expenses until you can get to a city.

4720) for about US$3 pp with private bath, slightly less with shared bath. The best in town, though, is the well-heated **Hostería de las Nubes** (RN 51 s/n, tel. 0387/490-9059, US$12/17 s/d), which offers large but simply furnished rooms with private bath, breakfast, and TV. It also has a large crafts shop, and its restaurant has a decent but limited lunch and dinner menu for US$3 pp.

El Quebradeño operates daily buses to and from Salta (US$4, five hours).

Quebrada de Escoipe

South of Salta, RN 68 rises slowly out of the Lerma Valley pass the westbound RP 33 turnoff through the Quebrada de Escoipe, a mostly gravel road that's one of Argentina's most spectacular mountain highways, to Parque Nacional Los Cardones and the picturesque town of Cachi.

Where the paved road ends and the gravel section begins, RP 33 snakes through a gorge so narrow that there's barely room for a single lane of traffic, and washouts are a serious hazard in wet weather. That said, it does not require 4WD. Cyclists interested in making the strenuous 520-kilometer loop trip from Salta, though, are advised to take the more gradual climb via Cafayate and Cachi, rather than the very steep ascent from here to the 3,600-meter **Cuesta del Obispo.** Looking back east toward Salta, the views—and the descent—are vertiginous.

Located mostly on the high plateau west of the Cuesta del Obispo, the 65,000-hectare **Parque Nacional los Cardones** also occupies arid canyons and summits ranging from 2,700 to 5,000 meters above sea level. About 100 kilometers from Salta, its emblematic species is the columnar *cardón* or candelabra cactus (*Trichocereus pasacana*), which

The Andean Northwest

© WAYNE BERNHARDSON

Estación Chorrillos, Quebrada del Toro

forms imposing stands at altitudes up to 3,400 meters. In the otherwise-treeless aridity of the puna, the *cardón* was the only source of construction wood for the pre-Columbian population, and colonial Spaniards adapted it to their own houses and churches. Now paved, the straight-as-an-arrow **Recta de Tin Tin** parallels an Inka road to the village of Payogasta.

The park itself lacks infrastructure, though many Salta travel agencies offer excursions here. There is a ranger at Piedra del Molino, near the Cuesta del Obispo, while the park headquarters is at Payogasta (San Martín s/n, tel. 03868/491066), 11 kilometers north of Cachi.

Quebrada de Cafayate and Vicinity

About 50 kilometers south of Salta, paved RP 47 leads east to **Embalse Cabra Corral,** a hydroelectric reservoir whose carefully timed releases permit white-water rafting through the scenic canyon of the Río Juramento.

Another 50 kilometers to the south, beyond the hamlet of Alemanía, the landscape undergoes an abrupt transition from lush upper Lerma Valley to the arid canyon of the north-flowing Río de las Conchas, popularly known as the Quebrada de Cafayate. At the foot of the Sierra de Carahuasi, the river has eroded the range's sedimentary strata into uniquely shaped and colorful landforms reminiscent of the canyon country of the southwestern United States.

Dams, in general, aren't worth a visit, but the regular releases from **Embalse Cabra Corral,** the reservoir formed by the General Manuel Belgrano hydroelectric dam, ensure a reliable flow that permits white-water rafting all year through the canyon of the Río Juramento.

Based at Cabra Corral, **Salta Rafting** (RP 47 Km 34, tel. 0387/15-685-6085, info@saltarafting.com, www.saltarafting.com) offers two-hour, 12-kilometer, Class III descents of the river for US$16 pp plus US$7 pp for round-trip transport from Salta, where their office is at Buenos Aires 88, Local 13 (tel. 0387/401-0301); they also organize other activities such as kayaking, rappelling, and mountain biking. Try also **Norte**

Rafting (RP 47 Km 18, consultasweb@norte rafting.com, www.norterafting.com).

On the southbound bus from Salta to Cafayate, grab a left-side window seat for the best views of landforms like the **Garganta del Diablo** (Devil's Throat), **El Anfiteatro** (The Amphitheatre), **El Sapo** (The Toad), **El Fraile** (The Friar, **El Obelisco** (The Obelisk), **Los Castillos** (The Castles), and the dunefield of **Los Médanos,** on the outskirts of the town. From Cafayate to Salta, sit on the right side of the bus.

For more in-depth explorations of these landmarks and box canyons, which are mostly concentrated in the last 58 kilometers before Cafayate, it's possible to disembark and continue on a subsequent bus, while hiking between the closer sights. It's also possible to hire a bicycle in Cafayate and ride through the canyon, returning on the bus if you don't care to ride back. Whether walking or riding, carry high-energy snacks and plenty of water.

Cafayate

Thanks to its mild dry climate and high altitude, the town of Cafayate is the hub of one of Argentina's major wine regions, with producers ranging from tiny artisanal bodegas and boutique wineries to full-scale industrial operations. Its specialty is the dry white Torrontés, a varietal long since disappeared from its Spanish origins, that one French grower considers akin to "eating the grape."

With the additional attraction of its scenic surroundings, Cafayate is southwestern Salta Province's top tourist destination, but underappreciated by non-Argentines. It tends to become crowded with visitors from the provincial capital on weekends, when hotel reservations are advisable.

At 1,660 meters above sea level, Cafayate (population 10,729) is 236 kilometers south of Salta via paved RN 68; RN 40 leads northwest toward Molinos and Cachi, and south toward the ruins of Quilmes, in Tucumán Province. The town itself has a compact regular grid, whose main drag is north-south Avenida Güemes (RN 40). Addresses on Avenida Güemes are known directionally, depending

whether they are north (Norte) or south (Sur) on the central Plaza San Martín.

Sights

For most visitors, Cafayate's wineries will be the main attraction; for details, see the sidebar "Wines and Wineries of Cafayate."

The other attraction is the private **Museo de Arqueología e Historia Calchaquí** (Colón and Calchaquí, tel. 03868/421054, 11 A.M.–8 P.M. daily, US$.50), founded by the late historian/archaeologist Rodolfo Bravo. Bravo, an autodidact who undertook research in the archives of Salta and Tucumán Provinces, as well as those of local farms and ranches, collected an enormous and impressive assortment of pre-Columbian arrow and spear points, ceramics, textiles, and funerary urns, plus colonial and post-colonial weapons, horse gear, musical instruments, and leather goods.

Entertainment and Events

Late February's misleadingly named **Semana de Cafayate** is in fact a three-day folklore celebration. The annual **Fiesta de la Virgen** takes place October 7.

At the Quebrada de Cafayate's appropriately named canyon El Anfiteatro, there is an annual musical event known as the **Concierto en la Montaña,** the last Sunday in July.

Cafayate's **Mercado Artesanal,** on Güemes across from Plaza San Martín, is the main handicrafts outlet.

Accommodations

At the south end of town, the municipal **Camping Lorohuasi** (RN 40 s/n, tel. 03868/421051) costs US$1 pp plus US$.30 for access to the swimming pool. There are also tiny *cabañas* with four single bunks for US$6 (US$1.50 pp). The next cheapest choice is the **Road Runner's Den** (Avenida Güemes Norte 441, tel. 03868/421440, US$3.50 pp), a simple hostel facility.

The comparably priced **Hospedaje Familiar Daruich Plaza** (Nuestra Señora del Rosario 165, tel. 03868/421098) has tidy rooms with private bath and breakfast. The pick in this price range, occupying a period house, is **El Hospedaje**

WINES AND WINERIES OF CAFAYATE

Cafayate is one of South America's most elevated wine regions, whose signature varietal is the fruity white Torrontés. Five wineries are within staggering distance of the plaza, another couple within weaving distance on a bicycle, and more are likely to open in the future.

© WAYNE BERNHARDSON

It's theoretically possible to visit all seven in a single day; those who need intellectual justification can start at the **Museo de Vitivinicultura** (Güemes Sur and Colón, tel. 03868/421125), Cafayate's wine museum, which is open 10 A.M.–1 P.M. and 5–8 P.M. weekdays. Admission costs US$.30.

East of the plaza, the organically certified **Bodega Nanni** (Chavarría 151, tel. 03868/421527) is an informal family business with only 10 hectares of vineyards and a handful of employees. In addition to Torrontés, it produces Cabernet Sauvignon, Malbec, and Tannat, and is open on a drop-in basis.

South of the plaza, **Domingo Hermanos** (Nuestra Señora del Rosario and 25 de Mayo, tel. 03868/421225) offers the most-professional tours, where a

unloading the grapes, Yacochuya

generous tasting in appealing surroundings includes Malbec, Torrontés, and their own goat cheese (which can be purchased separately). Guided visits take place in Spanish only, 8:30 A.M.–noon and 4–6:30 P.M. weekdays, 8:30 A.M.–noon Saturday, and 11–12:30 P.M. Sunday and holidays. The vineyards stand above 2,000 meters in nearby Yacochuya.

Just south of town, dating from 1850, **Bodega Etchart** (RN 40 Km 1047, tel. 03868/421310) devotes half of its 300 hectares on Finca La Florida to whites, including Tor-

(Quintana del Niño and Salta, tel. 03868/421680, elhospedaje@nortevirtual.com, www.nortevirtual.com).

Hotel Confort (Güemes Norte 232, tel. 03868/421091) charges US$5.50 pp for rooms with private bath but no exterior windows; consequently, it can feel claustrophobic. Though it's fairly drab, **Hotel Tinkunaku** (Diego de Almagro 12, tel. 03868/421148, US$8/14 s/d) does have sizeable rooms and a pool.

Hotel Asturias (Güemes Sur 154, tel. 03868/421328, asturias@infonoa.com.ar, US$11/17 s/d) boasts a large swimming pool and ample secure parking, but the building itself is a little worn and the beds, the singles at least, are a bit narrow. Rates are fair enough, though, and with 70 rooms there's usually something available.

At the north end of town, ACA's **Hostería de Cafayate** (RN 40 s/n, tel. 03868/421296) has the best gardens and quietest location, but the original large rooms have been subdivided into smaller quarters that are not quite cells. Rates are US$11/16 s/d for members of ACA and affiliates, but about 20 percent more for nonmembers.

New in 2003, on a quiet block west of the plaza, comfortable **Hotel los Sauces** (Calchaquí 62, tel. 03868/421158, lossauces @arnet.com.ar, US$13/21 s/d with breakfast) is an exceptional value; the grounds are a bit barren as yet, but as the landscaping matures it should be even more appealing.

Food

For a town that gets that so much tourist traffic,

rontés and Chardonnay, and the rest to reds including Cabernet Franc, Cabernet Sauvignon, Malbec, Merlot, Pinot Noir, Syrah, and Tannat. Free 45-minute tours include tasting; for English-languages guides, it's necessary to make advance arrangements. In January, February, July, and August, hours are 9 A.M.–5 P.M. daily except Sunday, when hours are 9 A.M.–1 P.M. only; the rest of the year, it's open 9 A.M.–5 P.M. weekdays, 9 A.M.–noon Saturday .

Occupying a mid-19th-century structure at the north edge of town, the 800-hectare **Bodega la Banda** (Avenida Güemes Norte s/n, tel. 03868/421850, www.vasijasecreta.com) conducts individualized tours and tasting 8:30 A.M.–12 P.M. and 2:30–6:30 P.M. daily. Varietals include the usual Cabernet, Merlot, and Torrontés, but there's also Burgundy and a Cabernet/Merlot blend.

Now owned by U.S. investors, at the north-end highway junction, Michel Torino's **Bodega la Rosa** (RP 68 and RN 40, tel. 03868/421201, www.micheltorino.com.ar) has gracious guides and fine tasting facilities. Hours are 8 A.M.–5 P.M. Monday–Thursday, 8 A.M.–4 P.M. Friday, and 9 A.M.–1 P.M. weekends. At the highway junction, its historic **Casa de Alto,** an Italian-style villa, is not part of the property, but the winery's separate 19th-century mansion has five huge, comfortable rooms, furnished with antiques, starting at US$36/54 s/d. Its restaurant is open to nonguests by reservation only.

Co-owned and operated by Etchart and French interests, **Bodega San Pedro de Yacochuya** (tel. 03868/421233) lies eight kilometers northeast of town at an elevation of 2,035 meters. On only 14 hectares of grounds, it produces especially outstanding Torrontés and Malbec, and has recently opened a new visitors center.

For a different sort of experience, there's **Finca Animaná** (RN 40 Km 1064, tel. 03868/492019, finca_animana@arnet.com.ar), a more industrial facility that produces for the regional market only, on 200 hectares of its own vineyards 15 kilometers north of Cafayate. As a commercial winery, it dates from the early 20th century; it's the only one in the province to produce commercialized, cheap, boxed table wines. Dating from 1797–1806, the handsome *casco* alongside the offices features a colonnade with Moorish arches.

Cafayate's restaurant scene is unexceptional. **El Criollo** (Güemes Norte 254, tel. 03868/421140) is a run-of-the-mill eatery better known for quantity than quality, though it's passable and cheap.

Ruperta (Avenida Güemes Sur 2, tel. 03868/421838) serves regional dishes and presents occasional live entertainment. Immediately to the south, **La Carreta de Don Olegario** (Güemes Sur 2, tel. 03868/421004) is comparable.

The best choice, for both food and appealing decor, is probably **El Rancho** (Toscano 10, tel. 03868/421256), on the south side of Plaza San Martín; the beef is surprisingly so-so but the rest of the diverse menu is more appealing and the service is outstanding.

Heladería Miranda (Güemes Norte near Córdoba) has earned a reputation for its inventive wine-flavored ice cream—the fruity white Torrontés is a better choice than the Cabernet.

Information and Services
Plaza San Martín's **Oficina de Información Turística** (Güemes and San Martín, municafayate@hotmail.com) is open 8 A.M.–10 P.M. daily.

Banco de la Nación and **Banco Macro,** both facing Plaza San Martín, have ATMs.

Correo Argentino is at Güemes Norte 197; the postal code is 4427. **Telecentro Cafayate** is at Güemes Norte and Belgrano, while **Telecabinas** is at Güemes Sur and Rivadavia. Internet connections here are agonizingly slow, but try **Salamanca.com** (Güemes Sur 155), half a block south of Plaza San Martín.

La Lavandería (Toscano and Nuestra Señora

del Rosario), opposite Plaza San Martín, does the laundry.

Getting There and Around
El Indio (Belgrano 34, tel. 03868/421002) operates three buses daily to Salta (US$5, four hours). It also has two or three daily to San Carlos (US$.50, 30 minutes) and two daily to Angastaco (US$2.50, two hours), where there are onward connections to Molinos, Cachi, and back to Salta.

El Aconquija (Mitre 77, tel. 421052) goes twice daily to San Miguel de Tucumán (US$7.50, 6.5 hours) via Tafí del Valle (US$5) and Santa María (US$2.50). These buses are the best option to visit the pre-Columbian ruins at Quilmes, just over the provincial border.

Rudi Ramos Generales (Güemes Norte 175) rents mountain bikes for visiting nearby wineries or riding the Quebrada de Cafayate (it's easiest to take the El Indio bus to El Anfiteatro and ride back downhill to town.

Valle Calchaquí

The Valle Calchaquí proper begins at the headwaters of its namesake river, just south of the 4,895-meter Andean pass known as the Abra del Acay, about 30 kilometers south of San Antonio de los Cobres. Dusty RN 40 parallels the river south through picturesque hamlets and villages including La Poma, Payogasta, Cachi, Seclantás, Molinos, Angastaco, and San Carlos, and south beyond Cafayate to the pre-Columbian fortress of Quilmes.

Until the mid-17th century, the Quilmes Indians of the region held off the Spanish invasion before finally suffering deportation to the Buenos Aires suburb that now bears their name. Their irrigated lands fell under control of Spanish landowners, while the Quilmes themselves either scattered or died out in the century-plus before Argentina became an independent country. In colonial times, the valley was one of the main routes across the Andes to Chile and Peru.

Set among the vividly colored sedimentary canyons and high summits of the Andes, ruins like Quilmes and other archaeological sites are the legacy of the native peoples of the valley. In the autumn months, red peppers drying on the hillsides add another intense hue to a distinctive cultural landscape, many of whose rural adobe houses display neoclassical flourishes like Doric columns and Moorish arches.

Fifty kilometers south of Cafayate via paved RN 40, the restored fortress of **Quilmes** is the area's most important archaeological site and a national historical monument. Though frequently visited from Cafayate, it lies within Tucumán Province. It is described in more detail later in this chapter.

North of San Carlos, 22 kilometers from Cafayate, paved RN 40 soon becomes a rugged dusty route that parallels the Río Calchaquí as it passes through a geological wonderland of folded Tertiary sediments that strongly resemble the Quebrada de Cafayate but for their more subdued colors.

At the 70-kilometers point, a short turnoff leads west to the village of **Angastaco,** home to pepper fields, vineyards, a modest archaeological museum, and nearby pre-Columbian ruins. There is also an increasing number of weekend and summer homes, with some very offbeat architecture.

For accommodations, there's the simple but decent **Pensión Cardón** (Juan Martín s/n, tel. 03868/491123, US$3 pp) and the more elaborate **Hostería Angastaco** (Avenida Libertador s/n, tel. 03868/15-639016, US$9/13 s/d with breakfast); the latter has a swimming pool, a restaurant, and arranges excursions on horseback.

El Indio has two buses daily to Cafayate; there are Marcos Rueda connections from here to Cachi and Salta Thursday and Monday at 5:30 A.M.

Founded in the 17th century as the administrative base for Diego Díaz Gómez's *encomiendas* (labor and tribute grants) on the upper Río Calchaquí, **Molinos** preserves the setting of a slow-moving colonial village with its namesake flourmill, landmark church, and a magnificent historical residence converted into a stunning hotel. At 2,020 meters above sea level, it's 39 kilometers north of Angastaco and 39 kilometers south of Cachi via RN 40.

Molinos's **Iglesia de San Pedro de Nolasco** has its origins in Díaz Gómez's original chapel, enlarged by his son-in-law Domingo de Isasmendi, but the current structure is a late-18th-century construction that's also the burial site of Nicolás Severo de Isasmendi, an *encomendero* and Salta's last royalist governor. Its twin bell towers, linked by a semicircular arch that shades the main entrance, rise above the thick adobe wall and traditional red-tiled roof; the interior has one central nave with a pair of lateral chapels.

Nicolás Isasmendi (1753–1837) also built and occupied the **Casa de Isasmendi,** immediately across from the church. It's now the provincial tourist hotel and reason enough in its own right to consider a stay at Molinos. About 1.5 kilometers west of town via a good dirt road, the **Criadero Coquera** is a captive breeding site for the endangered vicuña, at a relatively low elevation (around 1,900 meters) for this high puna camelid. Part of the former Estancia Luracatao, now belonging to the state agricultural extension service INTA, the **Casa de Entre Ríos** contains a little-visited but excellent artisans' market, including the province's characteristic red-striped *ponchos de Güemes,* woven from alpaca wool.

The cheapest accommodations option is **Camping Municipal** (tel. 03868/494037, US$1.25 per tent), with access to hot showers and use of the nearby swimming pool, though the shade trees have been slow to grow. The adjacent, spotless **Albergue Municipal** has a dozen rooms charging US$3.50 pp in single beds. Set around a pepper-shaded patio, the **Ｍ Hostal Provincial de Molinos** (tel. 03868/494004, hostaldemolinos@salnet.com.ar, US$35/41 s/d with breakfast) features colonially stylish rooms; it also offers a small archaeological museum and an artisans' shop that's open to the general public.

Marcos Rueda buses via Cachi to Salta (US$8, 6.5 hours) leave at 7 A.M. Monday, Tuesday, Thursday, and Saturday, and 1 P.M. Sunday. At 1:45 P.M. Wednesday and Sunday, it goes to Angastaco, where it's possible to connect with El Indio buses to Cafayate.

Nineteen kilometers north of Molinos, an eastbound bridge crosses the Río Calchaquí to **Seclantás,** a hillside hamlet with a shady plaza, the early 19th-century **Iglesia de Nuestra Señora del Carmen,** and an atmospheric cemetery with a ruined chapel. There are decent accommodations at **Hostería La Rueda** (Cornejo s/n, tel. 03868/498041, US$14 d).

Eleven kilometers north of Cachi, **Payogasta** is a quiet village that's the headquarters of **Parque Nacional Los Cardones** (San Martín s/n, tel. 03868/491066), 11 kilometers north of Cachi. There's a fine crafts shop here, and surprisingly good accommodations at **Hostería Payogasta** (Los Incas s/n, tel. 03868/496034, US$5.50/9 s/d).

Cachi

Scenic Cachi dates from an 18th century *encomienda* which, as the indigenous population declined, turned into the Aramburu family's private hacienda and then the picturesque village it is today. Reachable from either Salta or Cafayate and blessed with some of the region's finest scenery, Cachi (population 2,235) makes an ideal stopover on the scenic 520-kilometer loop that connects the three localities. At 2,280 meters above sea level, with narrow cobbled streets, it enjoys a spectacular setting at the base of the imposing 6,380-meter Nevado de Cachi.

Sights

Cachi's architecture and museums are a large part of its charm. Immediately east of shady **Plaza 9 de Julio,** the colonial **Iglesia San José** (1796) has an elegantly simple facade with three bells facing south, in a line, over the entrance. Craftsmen fashioned many of its interior features, including the ceiling and confessional, from cardón-cactus wood.

Immediately south of the church, Cachi's **Museo Arqueológico Pío Pablo Díaz** (Juan Calchaquí s/n, tel. 03868/491080), always a good museum, has improved thanks to a sophisticated account of the area's cultural development from its hunter-gatherer origins to the Inka conquest and the Spanish invasion. Well-arranged and illustrated, the exhibits have good explanatory text (in Spanish only). Hours are 8 A.M.–6:30 P.M. weekdays, 10 A.M.–2 P.M.

Saturday and 10 A.M.–1 P.M. Sunday. The admission charge of US$.30 is voluntary.

Events and Shopping

The **Festival de la Tradición,** taking place the third weekend of January, is a folkloric happening. March 29's **Día de San José** celebrates Cachi's patron saint.

On the west side of Plaza 9 de Julio, Cachi's **Centro de Artesanías** (Güemes s/n) sells regional crafts.

Accommodations and Food

Sites at Cachi's hilltop **Camping Municipal** (Avenida Tavella s/n, tel. 03868/491053), about one kilometer southwest of Plaza 9 de Julio, cost US$2 or a bit less in the more open areas. Dorm beds at the **Albergue Municipal,** on the same property, costs US$2–3 pp depending on whether you provide your own sheets. Otherwise, the more central **Hospedaje Nevado de Cachi** (Ruiz de los Llanos and Federico Suárez, tel. 03868/491063, about US$3.50 pp) is the cheapest option.

On a quiet block full of adobes, about 100 meters south of Plaza 9 de Julio, **Hospedaje Don Arturo** (Bustamante s/n, tel. 03868/491087, hospedajedonarturo@infonoa.com.ar, US$9 d with shared bath, US$11 d with private bath) is simple but comfy and friendly; it offers terraces for sunbathing, guided excursions, and even a little free wine-tasting.

Having undergone a stunning transformation that's turned it into one of the country's best hotel values while conserving local style, ACA's **M Hostería de Cachi** (Automóvil Club Argentino s/n, tel. 03868/491105, reservas@hosteriacachi .com.ar, www.hosteriacachi.com.ar) sits on immaculate grounds, with a pool; its rooms surround an expansive courtyard, in one corner of which rises and spreads a gigantic pepper tree. Rates start at US$13/17 s/d for members, US$16/20 s/d for nonmembers, with superior rooms slightly more expensive. It also has Cachi's most sophisticated restaurant.

Immediately across the street, an equal if not even better value, the 15-room **M Hostal el Cortijo** (Automóvil Club Argentino s/n, tel.

03868/491034, elcortijo@hostalelcortijo.com.ar, www.hostalelcortijo.com.ar, US$17 pp with private bath) is an elegantly transformed colonial farmhouse, its central patio sculpted with a fountain and running water to mimic the sounds of acequias (canals) that irrigate local vineyards. The rooms are furnished in an appropriate antique style and offer friendly family attention. Rates include an exceptional breakfast.

There are also two country inns in the vicinity. Six kilometers west of town, furnished partly with antiques and enjoying spectacular views of the Nevado de Cachi, **Samay Huasi** (tel. 0387/425-0625 in Salta, tel. 03868/15-684-4541 in Cachi, samayhuasi@ciudad.com.ar) was once the *casco* of an *estancia*. With simpatico staff, rates start at US$14/21 s/d with breakfast; other meals are also available.

Eight kilometers south of town, en route to Molinos, the **Hostería La Paya** (tel. 03868/ 491139) is a country inn dating from 1878. Rooms with fireplaces start at US$21 d; there is also a pool.

In addition to the ACA restaurant, there are several good but less elaborate and less expensive eateries focusing on regional food. Among them are **Confitería del Sol** (Ruiz de los Llanos s/n, tel. 03868/491103), on the north side of Plaza 9 de Julio; the **Oliver Café** (Ruiz de los Llanos s/n, tel. 03868/491052), immediately to the west; **El Aujero** (Ruiz de los Llanos s/n), alongside Hospedaje Nevado de Cachi; and especially **El Jagüel** (Güemes s/n, tel. 03868/ 491135), two blocks south of the plaza.

Information and Services

On the west side of Plaza 9 de Julio, **Cachi's Oficina de Turismo** (Güemes s/n, tel. 03868/ 491053, www.salnet.com.ar/cachi) is open 8:30 A.M.–9 P.M. weekdays, 10 A.M.–6 P.M. Saturday, and 11 A.M.–5 P.M. Sunday.

On the west side of the plaza, **Banco Macro** (Güemes s/n) also has an ATM around the corner on Ruiz de los Llanos.

For postal services, **Correo Argentino** (Güemes s/n) is one block south of the plaza. One block east of the plaza, **Telecabinas del**

Valle (Ruiz de los Llanos s/n) has phone and fax services, but no Internet.

Try the **Hospital Regional** (Benjamín Zorrilla s/n, tel. 03868/491085) for medical services.

Getting There

Marcos Rueda buses to Molinos go at 11:30 A.M. Monday, Wednesday, Friday, and Sunday, and at 6 P.M. Saturday. There is service to Seclantás at 11:30 A.M. daily; to Luracatao at 11:30 A.M. Tuesday, Thursday, and Saturday; to La Poma at 6 P.M. Tuesday and Saturday, and 12:45 P.M. Wednesday. Buses back to Salta (US$6, 4.5 hours) leave at 9:05 P.M. daily except Sunday, 3 P.M. Monday, Thursday, Friday, and Sunday, and Sunday at 4:15 P.M.

For about the same price, given a full complement of four passengers, **Remises Interurbanos San José** (tel. 03868/491907, tel. 0387/424-3077 in Salta) and **Remises Interurbanos Los Calchaquíes** (tel. 03868/491071, tel. 0387/424-7877 in Salta) can also take passengers to and from Salta. This would more easily permit photo ops along the spectacular Cuesta del Obispo and the Quebrada de Escoipe.

SAN SALVADOR DE JUJUY

Settled from Perú in 1592, San Salvador de Jujuy (commonly called "Jujuy") was then the northernmost Spanish settlement in the territory that is now Argentina. While it has some worthwhile colonial monuments, for most travelers it's the gateway to the Quebrada de Humahuaca, the scenic and culturally rich Río Grande canyon that slopes southward from the altiplano, the high Andean plateau that extends into Chile, Bolivia, and Peru.

At 1,200 meters above sea level, Jujuy enjoys a consistently springlike climate and rich alluvial soils that made it agriculturally productive from its earliest days: according to the Spanish chronicler Vásquez de Espinosa, early-17th-century Jujuy had about "100 Spanish residents, mostly muleteers, who freight flour, corn, cheese, and other foodstuffs to the Chichas and Lipes mines; they have mule and cattle ranches, and drive their stock to Potosí."

Jujuy played a major role in the independence wars of the early 19th century, when General Manuel Belgrano ordered the city's evacuation to prevent the population's falling into Spanish hands. In post-independence times, sugar has dominated the local economy.

Orientation

Jujuy (population 230,999) is 1,523 kilometers northwest of Buenos Aires via RN 9, RN 34 and RN 66; RN 9 continues north through the Quebrada de Humahuaca to the Bolivian border at La Quiaca/Villazón. Salta is only 88 kilometers to the south via RN 9, a narrow road not suitable for bus traffic, which must take a longer, more roundabout route of 115 kilometers.

Jujuy's historic core occupies an elevated site between the Río Grande and the smaller Río Xibi Xibi, just above the confluence of the two rivers. Its civic center is Plaza Belgrano, bounded by Belgrano, Gorriti, Sarmiento, and San Martín. Most services are on or near east-west Belgrano.

Sights

Most of Jujuy's sights are on or within a few blocks of **Plaza Belgrano,** whose outstanding feature is the west-side **Iglesia Catedral** (1763, but with an Italianate facade dating from the early 20th century); its exquisitely Baroque, gold-laminated pulpit is one of the country's finest. On the north side of the plaza, the colonnaded **Cabildo** (1864) replaced an earlier building destroyed by an earthquake; it now houses the lackluster **Museo Histórico Policial** (Belgrano 493), open 8 A.M.–1 P.M. and 4–9 P.M. weekdays, 9 A.M.–noon and 6–8 P.M. weekends. Across the plaza, fronting on San Martín, the **Casa de Gobierno** (1920) reflects the Francophile fashionability of the early 20th century.

Two blocks west of the plaza, the **Iglesia y Convento San Francisco** (1912), at Belgrano and Lavalle, is another relatively recent addition on the cityscape. Its even newer **Museo Histórico Franciscano Jujuy** (tel. 0388/423-3434, 10 A.M.–1 P.M. and 5–8 P.M. daily, free) is a small but outstanding two-room facility that illuminates the Franciscan order's early colonial presence and boasts an impressive assortment of sacred art from the Cuzco school.

Half a block south, the **Museo Histórico Provincial** (Lavalle 256, tel. 0388/422-1345, US$.35) occupies the 19th-century Casa Alvarado, named for its owner Ramón Alvarado. The house witnessed history before it chronicled it—during the extended civil wars of the post-independence era, Unitarist General Juan Lavalle died here from a gunshot that, according to an aide, pierced the building's bulky wooden door. The museum details this incident, but also the Alvarado family, colonial art, the wars of independence and Belgrano's evacuation, and provincial political history. Hours are 8 A.M.–8 P.M. weekdays, 9 A.M.–1 P.M. and 3–9 P.M. Saturday.

Half a block north of the Franciscan church, the **Museo Arqueológico Provincial** (Lavalle 434, tel. 0388/422-1343, 8 A.M.–1 P.M. and 3–8 P.M. weekdays, free) impressively chronicles pre-Columbian cultural sequences from the Quebrada de Humahuaca, the altiplano, and other parts of the province.

Three blocks west, the elegant **Teatro Mitre** (1901; Alvear 1009) is the city's finest performing arts venue. Two blocks south of the Mitre, Jujuy's oldest surviving church is the **Iglesia Santa Bárbara** (1777), at Lamadrid and San Martín, a national historical monument adorned with paintings from the Cuzco school.

Jujuy is the most indigenous of Argentina's major cities, and the best place to appreciate that fact is the **Mercado del Sur** (Avenida Dorrego and Leandro Alem), opposite the long-distance bus terminal. Here Quechua merchants market products from the countryside and neighboring countries (some of these items, like fresh coca leaves, are semi-illicit) to their city-bound clients.

Entertainment

The **Teatro Mitre** (Alvear 1009, tel. 0388/422-1342), an architectural and cultural landmark dating from 1901, hosts live theater and concerts.

For recent movies, try the two-screen **Cine Opera** (Alvear 1125, tel. 0388/422-2234) or the **Cine Teatro Alfa** (Patricias Argentinas 360, tel. 0388/423-0426).

Events

Jujeños take a week to celebrate August's **Éxodo Jujeño,** Belgrano's evacuation of the city. There are several other major events, though, including March's **Festival de la Humita y El Folclor,** the harvest festival; and October 7's **Peregrinaje a la Virgen del Río Blanco & Paypaya,** a religious pilgrimage. One of the most colorful, though, is September's **Fiesta Nacional de los Estudiantes,** a student festival known for its spontaneity and colorful floats.

Shopping

For provincial crafts, visit the various booths at the Paseo de los Artesanos (Sarmiento 240), immediately south of the cathedral.

Rayuela Libros (Belgrano 638, tel. 0388/423-0658) is Jujuy's best bookstore.

Accommodations

For shoestring travelers, the best bets are **Residencial Río de Janeiro** (José de la Iglesia 1356, tel. 0388/422-3700, US$3 pp with shared bath, US$6/7 s/d with private bath), three blocks west of the bus station; and the more central **Residencial Chungking** (Alvear 627, tel. 0388/422-8142, US$3/5 s/d with shared bath, US$6/8 s/d with private bath). The utilitarian **Hotel Avenida** (Avenida 19 de Abril 469, tel. 0388/423-6136, info@quintar.com.ar, www .quintar.com.ar, US$5 pp with private bath) is also good value.

Far better value than any of these, though, is the six-room **Hostería Munay** (Alvear 1222, tel. 0388/422-8435, munayhotel@hotmail.com, www.munayhotel.jujuy.com, US$9/13 s/d), an inviting B&B-style place. **Hotel Alvear** (Senador Pérez 398, tel. 0388/424-4580, hotelalvear @jujuy.com, www.hotelalvear.jujuy.com, US$11/ 17 s/d) is a comfortable midsize hotel that offers an almost equally good bargain.

Rates at the centrally located **Hotel Sumay** (Otero 232, tel. 0388/423-5065, sumayhotel @imagine.com.ar), are US$13/17 s/d with breakfast. At nearby **Hotel Augustus** (Belgrano 715, tel. 0388/423-0203, hotelaugustus@arnet .com.ar), they start at US$18/26 s/d, but better rooms cost only a little more.

Under the same management as the budget Hotel Avenida, the more commodious **Hotel Fenicia** (Avenida 19 de Abril 427, tel. 0388/423-1800, info@quintar.com.ar, www.quintar.com.ar, US$18/28 s/d) has rooms with river-view balconies. The four-star **Hotel Jujuy Palace** (Belgrano 1060, tel. 0388/423-0433, jpalace @imagine.com.ar) charges US$33/41 s/d.

Food

For inexpensive regional dishes, try any of several locales within the **Mercado Municipal** (Alvear and Balcarce), which is also the place to purchase groceries. Part of its namesake hotel, nearby **Chung King** (Alvear 627, tel. 0388/422-8142) is not a Chinese *tenedor libre,* but rather a combination of *parrilla* and pizzeria that's a local fixture, with moderate prices.

Krysys (Balcarce 272, tel. 0388/423-1126) is an appealing *parrilla* with entrees in the US$2–4.50 range. **Ruta 9** (Lavalle 287, tel. 0388/423-7043) is a classic for spicy specialties like *locro,* while the **Sociedad Española** (Belgrano 1102, tel. 0388/423-5065) is the best choice for fish. The well-established **Madre Tierra** (Belgrano 619, tel. 0388/422-9578) is a reliable vegetarian alternative to the standard Argentine menu. **Ｍ Manos Jujeñas** (Avenida Senador Pérez 222, tel. 0388/15-682-2087) has become a Jujuy institution for its exceptional regional cuisine—and this is one place where you can get legitimately spicy food like *picante de pollo,* (US$3.50) along with outstanding empanadas. Other items on the menu include *locro,* tamales, and *humitas.*

Helados Pingüino (Belgrano near Lavalle) has better-than-average ice cream.

Information

The genial but disorganized **Secretaría de Turismo y Cultura de la Provincia** (Gorriti 295, tel. 0388/422-1326, turismo@jujuy.gov.ar) is open 7 A.M.–9 P.M. weekdays and 8 A.M.–9 P.M. weekends. In summer and in the July winter holidays, the city maintains an office on Avenida El Éxodo, at the southeastern approach to town.

For motorists, **ACA** is at Senador Pérez and Alvear (tel. 0388/422-3865).

Services

Graffiti Turismo (Belgrano 601, tel. 0388/423-4033) changes U.S. cash dollars and travelers checks. **Banco de la Nación** (Alvear 801) has an ATM, but there are several others along both Belgrano and Lamadrid.

Correo Argentino has moved to Belgrano 877; the postal code is 4600.

The Bolivian consulate (Independencia 1098, tel. 0388/424-0501) is open 8 A.M.–1 P.M. weekdays.

There's a convenient **Telecentro** at Belgrano and Lavalle. For Internet, **Chat.ar** (Belgrano 574) is open 24 hours.

Tea Turismo (San Martín 128, tel. 0388/423-6270, fax 0388/422-2357) is a well-established travel agency.

For laundry, **Laverap** is at Belgrano 1214.

Hospital Pablo Soria is at Güemes and General Paz (tel. 0388/422-2025, or tel. 107 for emergencies).

Getting There and Around

Aerolíneas Argentinas (Belgrano 1053, tel. 0388/422-7198) flies daily to Aeroparque (Buenos Aires), usually nonstop but some days via Córdoba. It is also possible to make connections to Mendoza via Córdoba, rather than backtracking from Aeroparque.

Aeropuerto Internacional Dr. Horacio Guzmán (tel. 0388/491-1106) is 32 kilometers southeast of town via RN 66. **Tea Turismo** (San Martín 128, tel. 0388/423-6270) arranges minibus transfers.

Jujuy's **Terminal de Ómnibus** (Avenida Dorrego and Iguazú, tel. 0388/422-1373) has provincial, long-distance, and international services (to Chile), which begin in Salta. There are frequent services up the Quebrada de Humahuaca to La Quiaca, on the Bolivian border, via Purmamarca, Maimará, Tilcara, Humahuaca, and Abra Pampa, and additional services to western-altiplano destinations like Susques. Buses also go to Libertador General San Martín (for Parque Nacional Calilegua) and to Aguas Blancas and Pocitos, both of which are close to Bolivian border crossings.

Typical destinations, fares, and times include Purmamarca (US$2.50, one hour), Salta (US$5, two hours), Tucumán (US$10, five hours), La Quiaca (US$9, four hours), Susques (US$9, 6.5 hours), Córdoba (US$20, 11 hours), Catamarca (US$15, nine hours), La Rioja (US$17, 10 hours), San Juan (US$27, 16 hours), Mendoza (US$33, 19 hours), Resistencia (US$32, 15 hours), and Buenos Aires (US$26–33, 22 hours).

Chile-bound buses from Salta stop here before crossing the Paso de Jama to San Pedro de Atacama and Calama (US$50), with onward connections to Antofagasta (US$55), Iquique (US$70), and Arica (US$70); make reservations as far in advance as possible at **Géminis** (tel. 0388/15-682-1213) or **Pullman** (at the same number). Frequencies vary, depending on the time of year.

QUEBRADA DE HUMAHUACA AND VICINITY

Recently declared a UNESCO World Heritage Site for its cultural and historical riches—not to mention its stunning scenery—the Quebrada de Humahuaca may finally become the attraction for foreign visitors that it long has been for Argen-

tines. Linked to the Andean highland civilizations of pre-Columbian times, the route includes some 200 archaeological sites, plus major colonial monuments and ecological treasures. There is also the intangible legacy of its indigenous musical, linguistic, and religious heritage.

West of San Salvador, RN 9 climbs slowly northwest past the turnoff to the Termas de Reyes hot springs, and then steadily north toward and up the Quebrada to the Bolivian border at La Quiaca. Past Humahuaca, the highway rises higher yet to the barren altiplano at Abra Pampa, on a greatly improved surface that has cut travel times significantly. If driving, watch for livestock on the road, including cattle, sheep, goats and, at higher elevations, llamas.

Termas de Reyes

Spanish conquistadors named the Termas de Reyes, 1,800 meters above sea level in the mountains west of Jujuy, for the Inka royalty that enjoyed the thermal baths above the precipitous canyon of the Río Reyes. In the past century, the baths and their historic hotel have been kicked around like a soccer ball, changing hands

Quebrada de Humahuaca

from private ownership to the Fundación Eva Perón in the 1940s to the military in the 1950s and again in the 1970s, and to the provincial government. Privatization in 1999 has granted it some of the grandeur to which it has always aspired but never quite reached.

In the vicinity of the hotel, there is free but very rustic camping, along with baths, and excellent hiking. Guests at the **Hotel Termas de Reyes** (RP 4 Km 19, tel. 0388/492-2522, info @termasdereyes.com, www.termasdereyes.com) pay US$54 s or d with breakfast for interior rooms, US$63 s or d for rooms with exterior views; there are also a few suites with private hot tubs (Evita, by the way, slept in room No. 100). Nonguests can use the hotel's public baths, and its outdoor swimming pool, for a fee; there is also a restaurant.

From Calle Dorrego, near the bus terminal in San Salvador, *colectivo* No. 14 goes to the Termas hourly between about 6:30 A.M. and 8:30 P.M.

© WAYNE BERNHARDSON

street crafts market, Purmamarca

Purmamarca

At the base of the vivid Cerro de los Siete Colores, peaceful Purmamarca's adobe ambience is, ironically, making it one of the Quebrada de Humahuaca's fastest-growing settlements. While the arrival of town-dwellers to these Andean foothills could undermine the colonial character of a village with only a few hundred inhabitants, to this point the newcomers have respected Purmamarca's captivating style, despite a growing abundance of tourist-oriented services.

In the long run, a likelier villain is heavy truck traffic along the international highway that stretches from Pacific Chile to Atlantic Brazil and, when paving is finally complete, may see ever more movement along the so-called *Corredor Bi-Oceánico* (Bi-Coastal Corridor). For the present, though, Purmamarca remains one of the most pleasing points in the entire Quebrada.

Purmamarca (altitude 2,190 meters) is 65 kilometers northwest of San Salvador de Jujuy via RN 9 and RN 52, which continues west through the altiplano to the Chilean border, for access to San Pedro de Atacama, Calama, and Antofagasta.

Purmamarca is a sight in itself, what with its pepper-shaded plaza and, at its south end, the colonial **Iglesia Santa Rosa de Lima**. The church itself dates from 1778 or 1779; a lintel dated 1648 probably came from an earlier construction.

Starting from and returning to the plaza, the **Paseo de los Colores** is a cactus-studded three-kilometer loop that winds around its namesake hill behind town. While it's plenty wide for automobiles, it makes an equally good or even better hike, but take water and snacks.

Purmamarca's **Mercado Artesanal,** on the east side of the plaza, has grown with increasing numbers of tourist buses from Salta and Jujuy.

Accommodations and Food

Both accommodations and food are remarkably good for a village of Purmamarca's size, and prices are reasonable. Immediately behind the church, **Alojamiento y Camping Bebo Vilte** (Salta s/n, tel. 0388/490-8038) provides camping for US$1.50 pp and simple accommodations for US$11 d.

La Falda (Salta and Sarmiento, tel. 0388/490-8028, US$9 pp) is a two-room bungalow-style accommodation on a dead-end street, with views of the town and plaza below. It has comfortable double beds and private bath, but there is no breakfast.

Also immediately behind the church, **El Viejo Algarrobo** (Salta s/n, tel. 0388/490-8286, elviejoalgarrobo@hotmail.com) exudes all the style of the striking wood from which it takes its name, but the downstairs rooms are rather dark for US$12/16 s/d with shared bath; if available, the upstairs rooms with private bath are a better option at US$16 s or d. Breakfast is included.

M **Hostal La Posta de Purmamarca** (Santa Rosa de Lima s/n, tel./fax 0388/490-8040) is a lovely but simple hotel, in local style, with friendly staff and rates of US$16 s with breakfast. It has a separate eponymous restaurant on Rivadavia, on the east side of the plaza.

Across the highway to Susques and Chile, set among orchards, Purmamarca's finest accommodations are at **M** **Hotel El Manantial del Silencio** (RN 52 Km 3.5, tel. 0388/490-8080, elsilencio@cootepal.com.ar, US$42/50 s/d), a colonial-style country inn featuring large rooms with tiled floors, modern baths, and a large pool.

Relocated *porteños* run **La Sombra del Sauce** (Pantaleón Cruz and Santa Rosa), offering a diverse menu focusing on regional dishes like tamales and *humitas* but also including *parrillada,* pizza, house wines served in distinctive carafes, and fresh coca-leaf tea. Entrees cost around US$3; the rustically styled building includes surprisingly solid eucalyptus furniture, but the service can be a little too casual. The operators speak English and French.

Other Practicalities

On the west side of the plaza, Purmamarca's helpful **Oficina de Información Turística** (Belgrano s/n, tel. 0388/490-8077, 8 A.M.–8 P.M. or so daily) has a rudimentary but useful town map.

There are many buses to San Salvador de Jujuy, and four daily up the Quebrada to Maimará, Tilcara, and Humahuaca (US$2): at 7 A.M. and 11:20 A.M., and 1 and 5 P.M. Many more pass by on RN 9, which is three kilometers east of town.

La Posta de Hornillos

In late colonial times, when the Quebrada de Humahuaca was the main route between Buenos Aires and Perú, the restored Posta de Hornillos was one of a chain of way stations that connected the two viceregal capitals, though the original building was much earlier than this. During the wars of independence, General Manuel Belgrano slept at the now-restored facility, on RN 9, 11 kilometers north of the Purmamarca junction. More recently, in mid-2003, President Néstor Kirchner presided over the Quebrada's dedication as a UNESCO World Heritage Site here.

As a museum, the Posta holds pre-Columbian artifacts such as mortars and mummies, and more recent millstones and weapons. Hours are 9 A.M.–6 P.M. daily except Tuesday; buses up and down the Quebrada will deposit visitors at the gate.

Maimará

Maimará's most memorable view, only a few kilometers north of Hornillos, may be the dazzling hillside cemetery seen from RN 9 as the highway passes through the Quebrada. Then again, it may simply be its scintillating setting beneath the polychrome La Paleta del Pintor (the Painter's Palette), comparable to Purmamarca's Cerro de los Siete Colores. In either event, this small, dusty farming village (elevation 2,320 meters) is something to look at.

The attractive **Hostería Posta del Sol** (Martín Rodríguez and San Martín, tel. 0388/499-7156, posta_del_sol@hotmail.com, from US$17/21 s/d) offers spacious view rooms with stylish *algarrobo* furniture. There is also a pool and a restaurant.

Buses up the Quebrada pass through town en route to Tilcara and Humahuaca.

Tilcara

Thanks to its Andean archaeological heritage, living indigenous presence, artist-colony atmosphere, and scenery equal to the rest of the Quebrada de Humahuaca, many visitors enjoy Tilcara more than any other settlement along the route. In the sheltered valley of the Río

© WAYNE BERNHARDSON

cemetery at Maimará

six of its eight rooms host permanent displays, while the other two usually have special exhibitions. Hours are 9 A.M.–6 P.M. daily except Tuesday, when it's closed; in January, it may stay open until 7 P.M. Admission (US$1) is also valid for the Pucará de Tilcara.

Immediately west of the archaeological museum, the **Museo Ernesto Soto Avendaño** (Belgrano s/n, tel. 0388/495-5354, US$1, free Thurs.) displays some of the more modest efforts of the sculptor of Humahuaca's hubris-laden *indigenista* monument to the heroes of Argentine independence, of which there is a scale model here; the colonial building itself belonged to gaucho colonel Manuel Alvarez Prado, to whom one room is dedicated. Hours are 9 A.M.–1 P.M. and 3–6 P.M. daily except Monday and Tuesday.

Half a block west of Plaza Prado, the five-room **Museo Irureta de Bellas Artes** (Belgrano and Bolívar, tel. 0388/495-5124, 10 A.M.–1 P.M. and 3–6 P.M. daily except Mon., free) presents some 150 paintings, illustrations, engravings and sculptures by modern Argentine artists including its founder, the sculptor Hugo Irureta.

On the east side of Plaza Prado, the **Museo José Antonio Terry** (Rivadavia 459, tel. 0388/495-5005, US$.35) honors a *porteño* painter who, living in Tilcara 1910–1953, chronicled local and regional traditions and landscapes through his oils. Hours are 9 A.M.–6 P.M. daily except Monday, when it's closed, and Sundays and holidays, when hours are 9 A.M.–noon and 2–6 P.M.

Before the Spaniards arrived, the Quebrada de Humahuaca was an outlier of the Inka empire, but more than five centuries earlier the peoples of the region had built hilltop fortifications like the **Pucará de Tilcara** to detect invaders—such as the Inka latecomers—and defend their settlements. About one kilometer south of Tilcara's Plaza Prado, this reconstructed archaeological site (tel. 0388/495-5073) appears to have some Incaic features. Admission (valid also for the archaeological museum on Plaza Prado) costs about US$1, well worth it for the panoramas that the site's defenders were probably unable to appreciate; there is also a native-plant botanical garden.

Grande, it's warmer than Humahuaca, with far better services.

Tilcara (population 4,364) is 86 kilometers north of San Salvador de Jujuy and 2,461 meters above sea level via RN 9, which passes west of the Río Grande; a bridge connects the town to the highway. Plaza Prado is its civic center, but a few blocks from the plaza the streets are highly irregular. It is small enough, though, that orientation is no major problem despite the uneven terrain and frequent lack of street signs.

Sights
On the south side of Plaza Prado, specializing in regional archaeology in general and the Quebrada de Humahuaca in particular, the **Museo Arqueológico Doctor Eduardo Casanova** (Belgrano 445, tel. 0388/495-5006) showcases many of its 5,000 pieces in this colonial-style house;

The Andean Northwest

About 10 kilometers north of Tilcara, just before the hamlet of Huacalera, a monolith on the west side of RN 9 marks the **Tropic of Capricorn.**

Events and Shopping

Tilcara holds a number of special events, of which the most specifically local is January's **Enero Tilcareño,** a month-long celebration that encompasses many individual cultural activities, including music and sports. Both February's **Carnaval Norteño** and April's **Semana Santa** are observed throughout the Quebrada. The indigenous **Festival de Pachamama** (Mother Earth Festival) takes place in August.

Plaza Prado is sinking beneath the weight of its souvenir stands. For distinctively decorated calabashes, cross the river to the **Taller Artesanal,** in Quebrada Sarahuaico.

Accommodations and Food

Near the river, **Autocamping El Jardín** (Belgrano s/n, tel. 0388/495-5128, autocampingtilcara@yahoo.com.ar, US$1 pp) is a spacious garden campground.

Reports suggest falling standards at **Hospedaje El Pucará** (Patillo s/n, tel. 0388/495-5050, camarquez@cootepal.com.ar, US$7 d with shared bath, US$10 d with private bath), though it still enjoys a delightful garden setting (its namesake restaurant, by the way, is a completely separate entity).

Half a block south of **Residencial El Antigal** (Rivadavia s/n, tel. 0388/495-5020, elantigal@yahoo.com.ar, US$7/9 s/d with shared bath, US$9/12 s/d with private bath) is one of Tilcara's longest-operating hostelries, but its restaurant gets higher marks than its accommodations, which lag behind some newer alternatives.

Perched on the hillside several blocks north of Plaza Prado (follow the signs), steadily improving **N Hostel Malka** (San Martín s/n, tel. 0388/495-5197, malka_tilcara@cootepal.com.ar, www.tilcarajujuy.com.ar/malka, US$5.50 pp; US$7–9 s, US$11–14 d) has dorm accommodations but also a few private rooms for individuals or couples.

Also on the hillside is the secluded **Posada La Hoyada de los Molles** (tel. 0388/495-5359,

US$14 d with breakfast), where a relocated couple from Córdoba offers rustically stylish accommodations; it also functions as a teahouse. To get there, follow Lavalle east from Plaza Prado up the hill and then ask.

Set among orchards and poplars on a quiet block two blocks north of the plaza, **Casa Hostal de los Alamos** (Alberro s/n, 0388/495-5172, jujuylosalamos@hotmail.com, US$7 pp) is well worth consideration. The owner, however, is more often in Jujuy than Tilcara, so the service can be less than personalized despite its B&B feeling.

One of Tilcara's real gems is **N Quinta La Paceña** (Padilla s/n, tel. 0388/495-5098, quintalapacena@argentina.com, US$14/24 s/d), where small but private and romantic garden rooms come with personalized service; the breakfast takes place in the main house, which has inviting common spaces in a contemporary southwestern style.

The **Hotel de Turismo** (Belgrano 590, tel. 0388/495-5002, tilcahot@imagine.com.ar, US$11/18 s/d with private bath and breakfast) exudes an institutional atmosphere that contrasts with Tilcara's indigenous ambience, though it's by no means bad.

Built in the 1930s, **Hostal Villar del Ala** (Padilla 100, tel. 0388/495-5100, adriantilcara@hotmail.com, US$26/31 s/d with private bath and breakfast) is, by contrast, a unique castle-like residence on sprawling grounds, with striking views across the Quebrada from its breakfast nook. The basement room, while not unattractive, is rather dark, but the rest of the house is more appealing.

Adjacent to the archaeological museum, the **Café del Museo** (Belgrano 445, tel. 0388/495-5006) is an ideal place for coffee, cakes, and croissants, or snacks like sandwiches. It's also an architecturally appealing adobe, with cardón ceilings.

With a *porteño*-trained chef incorporating native Andean crops and other regional touches, the **N Pucará Restó** (Padilla s/n) serves the Quebrada's most creative cuisine—and probably the best as well. Savor the extraordinarily creative quinoa/spinach pasta, and the rich chocolate desserts, in stylish surroundings. Also oriented toward regional dishes, Tilcara's next most worthwhile dining option is **Pachamama** (Belgrano 590, tel. 0388/495-5293). Offerings include *salteñas* (spicier than mainstream empanadas), the spicy stew *locro,* and *parrillada.*

Other Practicalities

Tilcara has a new **Centro de Informes** on Belgrano, on the village side of the bridge, but it keeps inconsistent hours. There is a useful website, www.tilcarajujuy.com.ar.

Correo Argentino is at Belgrano and Rivadavia, directly on Plaza Prado. **Telecentro Tilcara** (Lavalle 448) has phone services but Tilcara lacks Internet connections as yet.

The **Terminal de Ómnibus** has, fortunately, relocated from overcrowded Plaza Prado to a new location at the west end of Belgrano. At least two dozen buses daily go to Jujuy, some of them continuing to Salta, while an equivalent number head north to Humahuaca. There are also several daily to Purmamarca.

Uquía

Only a few kilometers south of Humahuaca, straddling RN 9, the hamlet of Uquía is notable for its **Capilla de San Francisco de Paula,** a colonial chapel dating from 1691. It's also notable for the chapel's series of restored Cuzco-school paintings featuring the *ángeles arcabuceros,* nine angels armed with 15th-century European matchlock guns, and for its Baroque altarpiece, possibly the work of a craftsman from Potosí. The church is open 10 A.M.–noon and 2–4 P.M. daily.

Alongside the church, the shiny new **Hostal de Uquía** (tel. 03887/490523, elportillo@cootepal .com.ar, US$11/14 s/d) has comfortable rooms with private bath and breakfast, and has a bar/restaurant.

Humahuaca and Vicinity

North of Tilcara, the higher, colder climate of Humahuaca has discouraged the influx of lowlanders that have built weekend houses in Purmamarca and Tilcara, so that the village has remained more visibly indigenous and its narrow, cobbled, adobe-lined streets more typically Andean. Though services are not so good as those in Tilcara, it's cheaper and, therefore, a popular stop for budget travelers.

Beyond Uquía, RN 9 climbs steeply toward and then bypasses Humahuaca (population 8,010), which straddles the Río Grande to the east; in a more exposed location than Tilcara, the town sits 2,939 meters above sea level. Most but not all sights and services are west of the river; some, though, are across the bridge in the neighborhood known as La Banda. The key archaeological site of Coctaca is 10 kilometers to the northeast via the La Banda bridge.

Sights

Humahuaca's colonial core is a sight in itself, with narrow cobbled streets that can barely accommodate automobiles, and some alleyways through which motorcycles would have problems passing. Facing the central Plaza Sargento Gómez from the west, the 17th-century **Iglesia de la Candelaria y San Antonio** is a national historical monument that's needed frequent repairs because of earthquake damage, and underwent an almost total rehab between 1926 and 1938. The twin bell towers are an 1880 addition, but the rococo altarpiece dates from around 1680. The Cuzco school's Marcos Sapaca created *Los Doce Profetas* (The Twelve Prophets), an 18th-century series of paintings that decorates the church's walls.

Immediately north of the church, a broad flight of stone steps rises to Tilcara sculptor Ernesto Soto Avendaño's pompous **Monumento a la Independencia** (Monument to Independence, 1950), which took 10 years to complete. Out of place in a town whose populace is largely indigenous, it's also out of proportion to its surroundings.

On the south side of the plaza, a full-size replica of San Francisco Solano emerges from the clock tower at the **Cabildo de Humahuaca,** occupied by municipal offices; in theory, this happens daily at noon, but in practice it's often earlier.

The privately run **Museo Folklórico Regional** (Buenos Aires 447, tel. 03887/421064) is the work of author and activist Sixto Vázquez Zuleta, also known by his Quechua name of Toqo. Hours are 8 A.M.–8 P.M. daily for guided tours only, which cost US$2 pp. Toqo himself is at the museum only irregularly because of family commitments in San Salvador de Jujuy. The museum is alongside the local youth hostel.

Across the bridge and about 10 kilometers to the north, the bench terraces of **Coctaca** cover about 40 acres of what once were intensively cultivated lands, irrigated by canals and sluices, on an alluvial fan. Now almost uncultivated, they suggest that the area once supported a much larger population.

Events and Shopping

Humahuaca celebrates February 2 as the **Fiesta de la Virgen de Candelaria,** in honor of its patron saint. February is also the month of the **Carnaval Norteño,** which takes place in many communities along the Quebrada.

The old train station, just west of the river, is the site of Humahuaca's **Mercado Artesanal;** woolens are the pick of the crafts.

Accommodations and Food

Immediately across the bridge, **Camping Municipal** is a free site that lacks services. No longer affiliated with Hostelling International, the 70-bed **Albergue Juvenil Humahuaca** (Buenos Aires 447, tel. 03887/421064, toqohumahuaca @yahoo.com, US$2 pp with shared bath, US$3.50 pp with private bath) has kitchen facilities and some rooms with private bath. The increasingly popular **Hostel El Portillo** (Tucumán 69, tel. 03887/421288, elportillo@cootepal .com.ar, US$3 pp) has a good economical restaurant.

Also across the bridge, in Barrio Medalla Milagrosa about one kilometer east of the center, the best of the cheapest is **Posada El Sol** (03887/ 421466, elsolposada@imagine.com.ar, US$4.50 pp; private rooms US$11 d), an improving hostel-style place on spacious grounds.

Convenient to the bus terminal is **Residencial Humahuaca** (Córdoba 401, tel. 03887/ 421141, US$3.50/6.50 s/d with shared bath, US$7/9 s/d with private bath). **Residencial Colonial** (Entre Ríos 110, tel. 03887/ 421007, US$4.50/6.50 s/d with shared bath,

US$11/14 s/d with private bath) is slightly more expensive.

M Hostal Azul (tel. 03887/421107 or 421596, hostalazul@cootepal.com.ar, www.hostal azulhumahuaca.com.ar, US$11 pp), across the bridge, may have Humahuaca's finest facilities— a cozy living room with fireplace, central heating, a breakfast nook with homemade bread in the morning, and eight attractive rooms surrounding a delightful interior patio. Rates are more than fair, though it has imperfections: the single beds are narrow even if the mattresses are firm, the service is a little erratic, and the garish exterior paint job (it is, after all, the "blue house") is not really appropriate to its desert setting. Suitable only in an emergency, the rapidly deteriorating **Hotel de Turismo** (Buenos Aires 650, tel. 03887/421154, US$7/12 s/d low season, US$14/18 s/d in the peak winter holidays) has spacious rooms with balconies and parking, but the state of the facilities is deplorable. Look instead for the new hotel that at last visit was due to open immediately behind it.

Just across the bridge, opposite the municipal campground, the new **Hostería Camino del Inca** (Ejército del Norte s/n, 03887/421136, hosteriainca@imagine.com.ar, US$21 d) has attractive common areas and friendly management, but the rooms are unexpectedly small and the beds softer than some may like.

Part of its popular namesake hostel, **El Portillo** (Tucumán 69, tel. 03887/421288) has a limited regional menu that does, however, include llama dishes.

La Cacharpaya (Jujuy 295, tel. 03887/ 421016) seats large numbers of diners for regional specialties like *locro, salteñas,* and tamales. **El Fortín** (Buenos Aires 200, tel. 03887/421178) has similar fare and ambience.

Other Practicalities

Humahuaca's **tourist office,** in the Cabildo at Tucumán and Jujuy, is supposedly open 7 A.M.–noon weekdays only.

Correo Argentino is on Buenos Aires, across from the plaza; the postal code is 4630. There's a **Telecentro** at Jujuy 399, behind the Municipalidad.

road to Iruya

For medical services, **Hospital Belgrano** (Santa Fe 34) is open 8 A.M.–1 P.M. and 2–6 P.M. daily, but there's always someone on duty for emergencies.

All northbound and southbound buses, between Jujuy and La Quiaca, stop at the **Terminal de Ómnibus** (Belgrano and Entre Ríos). Transportes Mendoza (tel. 03887/421016) provides daily connections to the remote Andean village of Iruya (US$5, 2.5 hours), which is in Salta Province but is easily accessible only via a lateral highway that leads northeast from RN 9. Buses leave Humahuaca at 10:15 A.M. and return from Iruya at 3 P.M.

Iruya

Perched on a hillside above its namesake river, Iruya is a settlement of steep cobbled streets where a handful of automobiles can go no faster than the far more numerous burros. Its colonial **Iglesia de Nuestra Señora del Rosario y San Roque** rises above the squat adobe houses that conserve their heat at 2,780 meters above sea level.

Iruya is also the terminus of RP 13, a stunningly scenic gravel road that passes through several hamlets to an altitude of 4,000 meters at the Abra del Cóndor. At this point, entering Salta Province, it begins a vertiginous descent through terrain that evokes the most remote Peruvian highlands, with pre-Columbian agriculture clinging to nearly sheer hillsides fast being undercut by the river.

Iruya (population 1,200) is about 100 kilometers northeast of Humahuaca via RN 9 and RP 13, which is open all year, but a couple of stream crossings can be tricky for passenger cars in the wet summer months. This would be an exhilarating mountain bike ride on arrival, as the climb from Humahuaca makes a strenuous but relatively gradual workout, but the return trip from Iruya would be exhausting, as the climb is much steeper.

Iruya has a couple of simple accommodations in the US$2–3 pp range: **Hospedaje Tacacho** is Spartan but clean and friendly, while the improvised **Café del Hostal** (tel. 03887/15-629152, which is also a restaurant) has a certain ramshackle charm.

The Andean Northwest

Were it not beyond and above the village proper, the sore-thumb **Hostería de Iruya** (tel. 03887/15-630019) would stick out even more, as it's larger than any other building in town. In its own right, the spacious provincial hotel boasts bright, cheerful, well-furnished rooms, a well-decorated, airy lobby and restaurant, and attentive service. Rates are US$14/21 s/d for hillside rooms (which lack views) and US$21/31 s/d for rooms with valley views. Entrees on the restaurant menu, which includes locally grown Andean tubers, run from US$3.50–6.

From Humahuaca, Transporte Mendoza has daily buses to Iruya, returning the same day.

Abra Pampa

Ninety kilometers north of Humahuaca, paved RN 9 emerges onto the altiplano at windswept Abra Pampa, a low-slung treeless town nearly 3,500 meters above sea level. Though it's often cold and cloudy, when the sky clears and the wind drops, the vastness of the landscape can be enthralling.

Most of Abra Pampa's 7,495 inhabitants are Quechua Indians who live off the wealth of their herds of goats, sheep, llamas (look for llama-crossing signs on the highway!) and a handful of cattle. Otherwise, there's little to see or do here, but southbound travelers from Bolivia, especially those descending the Quebrada de Humahuaca on bicycles, may have to stay here. The best accommodations option is probably **Residencial La Coyita** (Gobernador Fascio 123, tel. 0388/749-1052, US$4.50/7 s/d); breakfast is US$1 extra.

La Quiaca

Where RN 9 ends at the international border, the altiplano town of La Quiaca is often an obligatory stopover for international travelers to or from Bolivia. While neither La Quiaca nor the Bolivian border town of Villazón has much to see in its own right, the nearby village of Yavi is worth at least a detour and preferably an overnight stay. During the convertibility decade, commerce nearly died in La Quiaca, but since the devaluation of the Argentine peso, Bolivians

have begun to cross the border to make their purchases here, while Argentines cannot afford Bolivian products.

La Quiaca (population 13,736) is 280 kilometers north of San Salvador de Jujuy. Most of its services are west of the tracks of the inoperative Belgrano railroad, but the border crossing itself is east of the tracks via a bridge over the Río Villazón. The border is open 24 hours.

Hotel Frontera (Belgrano and Árabe Siria, tel. 03885/422269), charges US$3.50/6 s/d for shared accommodations. A better choice is **Hotel Cristal** (Sarmiento 539, tel. 03885/422255, US$7/11 s/d). The best, though, is the comfortable, spic-and-span **Hotel de Turismo** (San Martín and Arabe Siria, tel. 03885/422243, hotelmun@laquiaca.com.ar, US$11/18 s/d with private bath); rates include breakfast and access to a heated swimming pool.

La Quiaca's few eateries are below average by Argentine standards, but try the *parrilla* **La Taberna** (Avenida España and Belgrano) or the **Club Atlético Argentino** (Balcarce and 25 de Mayo).

The **ACA** service station, east of the tracks on Sánchez de Bustamante, has provincial maps for sale, but there is no tourist office.

Correo Argentino is at San Juan and Sarmiento; the postal code is 4650. The **Cooperativa Telefónica** is at Avenida España and 25 de Mayo, but phone calls are more expensive here than elsewhere in the country.

The ATM at **Banco de Jujuy** (Árabe Siria 445) facilitates money exchange, especially for those crossing the border at odd hours.

The **Bolivian Consulate** (Sarmiento 529, tel. 03885/422283) charges US$20 pp for visas; hours are 9:30 A.M.–1 P.M. weekdays. Argentina has a consulate in Villazón (Avenida Cornelio Saavedra, tel. 591/2597-2011), but most foreigners do not need a visa to enter Argentina. Note that the Argentine Gendarmería (border guards) may search your person or belongings on demand, but they are usually polite and professional.

Buses south to Jujuy (US$9, four hours), Salta, and intermediate points leave from the **Terminal de Ómnibus** at 25 de Mayo and Avenida España.

Yavi

Only a short drive east of La Quiaca, where the Río Yavi has cut into the altiplano to create a sheltered valley, out-of-the-way Yavi has a colonial charisma that's utterly lacking in its dowdy, neighboring border town. Southbound travelers should spend at least an afternoon here, and increasing numbers of visitors are choosing to stay a night or more.

Yavi dates from the late 17th century, when Juan Fernández Campero y Herrera married into the family of the area's original *encomendero;* the settlement became the *encomienda*'s administrative base and, later, the base of the family's extensive landholdings.

Sights and Events

When Juan Fernández Campero y Herrera laid the cornerstone of Yavi's **Iglesia de San Francisco** in 1682, it was only a modest chapel. Today's austere but handsome church is the result of various exterior improvements during colonial times; it's the ornate interior, though, that makes the trip to Yavi worthwhile. From the forged ironwork of its doors to the wooden choir and the laminated gold altarpiece and pulpit, this is a colonial treasure. Ostensibly, hours are 9 A.M.–noon and 3–6 P.M. weekdays except Monday, 9 A.M.–noon Saturday, but it's sometimes necessary to track down the custodian elsewhere in the village.

Immediately across from the church, the slowly crumbling **Casa del Marqués Campero** was the *encomendero*'s residence and is now a hybrid museum/library, though its eclectic exhibits include none of the family's personal effects. It has no fixed hours; ask around for the custodian (who may or may not be the same as the church's). Two blocks south of the house is a ruined **molino,** a water-powered flourmill.

Immediately north of town, the reddish hills known as the **Cerros Colorados** contain pre-Columbian rock-art sites at **Las Cuevas.** About five kilometers northeast via an undulating gravel road, the terrain near the village of **Yavi Chico** resembles a scale model cutaway of the Grand Canyon.

Toward the end of March, the **Encuentro de la Comida Regional y la Música Popular** offers regional cooking and live folkloric music in the campground at the riverside park. Dishes include tamales, *humitas,* and the like.

Practicalities

There is free camping in the shady riverside park, which has picnic tables but no other services.

Otherwise, **Hospedaje Aborígen** (Senador Pérez s/n, tel. 03387/491138, lapachos@jujuy-tel.com.ar, US$5.50 pp) is stylistically simple but remarkably inviting. For the same price, the casual **Hostal la Casona** (Senador Pérez and San Martín, tel. 03885/422316 in La Quiaca, mccalizaya@laquiaca.com.ar) is a hostel-style adobe with rooms surrounding a sheltered courtyard; it also has a small restaurant.

The **Hostal de Yavi** (tel. 03887/490523, tel./fax 03887/490508, elportillo@cootepal.com.ar, US$11/14 s/d) enjoys an attractive view and fine common areas, but the rooms themselves are fairly drab. There is also a restaurant.

From La Quiaca, Flota La Quinqueña offers public transport to Yavi, but there's also a frequent pickup truck from the Mercado Municipal on Avenida Hipólito Yrigoyen, east of the railroad tracks.

Monumento Natural Laguna de los Pozuelos

In the altiplano's azure clarity, northwest of Abra Pampa and southwest of La Quiaca, Laguna de los Pozuelos is a shallow but biologically bountiful wetland that's a breeding site for coots, ducks, geese, and three species of flamingos, along with many other migratory and resident species like plovers and avocets. Because of this rich but sensitive habitat, it's a designated critical wetland under the international Ramsar convention; in all, there are 44 breeding bird species.

The biggest attention-getters, though, are the 25,000 flamingos, which build conical mud nests on the shoreline. The lake itself is seven level kilometers north of the Río Cincel ranger station on RP 7.

Laguna de los Pozuelos (elevation about 3,600 meters) covers some 15,000 hectares, about 50 kilometers northwest of Abra Pampa via RP 7 or 85 kilometers southwest of La Quiaca via RP 5 and RP 69. All of these are unpaved routes that can be impassable in wet summer weather.

There is basic camping at the Río Cincel ranger station, on RP 7 at the south end of the reserve, but no other services or supplies. The village of Rinconada, 11 kilometers west, has basic accommodations and food.

Locally, ask at the Río Cincel ranger station; in Abra Pampa, try the offices of the **Monumental Natural Laguna de los Pozuelos** (Rivadavia and Alberdi, Barrio 31 de Agosto, tel. 03887/491315).

From Abra Pampa, midmorning buses to Rinconada pass the Río Cincel ranger station, at the south end of the reserve. A car provides more flexibility, but carry extra fuel—none is available beyond Abra Pampa.

ⓜ NATIONAL PARKS OF THE YUNGAS

In subtropical northwestern Argentina, most storms come out of the east and, as they lose their power, drop most of their moisture on the eastern Andean slopes. The fragmented terrain creates a number of microclimates, one of which is the narrow longitudinal strip of cloud forest known as the *yungas,* stretching from the Bolivian border through Jujuy and Salta south into Tucumán and even a spot of northernmost Catamarca.

Within Jujuy and Salta, three major national parks preserve remnants of the rare ecosystem: Calilegua, Baritú, and Finca El Rey. As public transportation is limited and access is especially difficult in the wet summer months, rental cars or guided tours are the best options for visiting them. Salta travel agencies organize tours, but for more information also check the website www.yungasandinas.com.

Parque Nacional Calilegua

Much if not most of Jujuy Province is high-altitude desert. The major exception is the area along the province's eastern limits, where the verdant subtropical *yungas* cover the slopes of the Serranía de Calilegua, home to the most accessible of several national parks that preserve

this ecosystem in Jujuy and Salta. Its dense woodlands and deeply incised canyons provide one of the last Argentine refuges of the endangered *yaguareté* (jaguar).

In recent years, the area between Calilegua and Parque Nacional Baritú, to the north, was the subject of a contentious dispute between environmental organizations and indigenous communities of the altiplano on the one hand, and commercial interests on the other, over construction of a gas pipeline from the Chaco to Chile. According to the Fundación Vida Silvestre Argentina, perhaps the country's leading environmental organization, the controversy has reached a satisfactory conclusion, with significant environmental mitigation on the part of gas and construction interests, plus the provision of natural gas to the indigenous communities of the altiplano.

Encompassing 76,306 hectares of rugged terrain, Parque Nacional Calilegua is about 110 kilometers northeast of San Salvador via a roundabout route via eastbound RP 56 and northbound RN 34 to Libertador General San Martín, and westbound RP 8. It is 170 kilometers from Salta via RN 34.

Flora and Fauna

One of Argentina's greatest centers of biodiversity, Calilegua boasts a variety of ecological zones that depend partly on altitude and partly on the microclimates created by its rugged topography, as the annual rainfall varies between 800 and 1,800 millimeters. There are also seasonal differences, as the winter months are almost invariably dry.

At the lower elevations, between 350 and 500 meters, the *selva de transición* (transitional forest) most closely resembles the arid Chaco, with deciduous trees like *lapacho* (*Tabebuia* spp.) and *palo amarillo* (*Phyllostilon rhamnoides*). Between 500 and 1,800 meters, though, the *selva montana* consists of dense cloud forest that also supports clusters of epiphytes, verdant ferns, and climbing lianas. Above 1,800 meters, the *bosque montano* consists of various conifers and *queñoa* (*Polylepis* spp) until the roughly 2,600-meter tree line, where drier puna grasslands take over.

Rare mammals like the jaguar, tapir, and otter inhabit the densest forest at lower elevations, where there are also fruit-eating bats. The grayish deerlike *taruca,* or northern huemul (*Hippocamelus antisensis*), grazes the higher elevations. There are hundreds of bird species, among them the toucan, torrent duck, brown eagle, and condor (the latter at the highest elevations).

Sights and Activities

There are several trails in the vicinity of the Aguas Negras and Mesada de la Colmena, all of which offer opportunities for wildlife sightings, though birds are easier to spot than mammals in this densely wooded country. At Aguas Negras, the **Sendero Burgo** is a 600-meter nature trail through the transitional forest, while the **Sendero Mirador** leads to an overlook of the Río San Lorenzo. The **Sendero a la Lagunita** is a two-kilometer walk to a bird-rich wetland.

Also near Aguas Negras, the **Sendero Tataupá** is a steep and longer hike through the forest that returns by the streambed of the Arroyo Negrito. The **Sendero a la Junta** passes through similar terrain to the confluence of the Arroyo Negro and Arroyo Toldos. **Sendero La Herradura** is an easy nature trail.

At Mesada de la Colmena, the **Sendero a la Cascada** is a steep descent to a waterfall in Arroyo Tres Cruces, where there are plenty of animal tracks. It's also possible to climb 3,600-meter **Cerro Hermoso** for spectacular panoramas toward the east, but this is cross-country walking.

From Valle Grande, west of the park, it's possible to hike through the Sierra de Zenta to Humahuaca. For details, see the fifth edition of Tim Burford's *Chile and Argentina: the Bradt Trekking Guide* (Bradt Travel Guides, 2001).

Practicalities

Near the park entrance, **Camping Aguas Negras** (tel. 03886/425388) has picnic tables, barbecue pits, and latrines, but also mosquitoes—don't forget repellent. Basic camping is permitted at **Mesada de las Colmenas** near the ranger station.

Libertador General San Martín's **Hotel Los Lapachos** (Entre Ríos 400, tel. 03886/423790) charges US$12/16 s/d. The leisurely **Hotel Posada del Sol** (Los Ceibos and Pucará, Barrio La Loma, tel. 03886/424900, posadadelsol @cooperlib.com.ar, US$21/27 s/d) has a swimming pool, restaurant, and Internet access, and also offers excursions to the park and other areas of interest.

Next door to the Intendencia (park headquarters) in Calilegua, the **Club Social San Lorenzo** has excellent inexpensive meals.

Bequeathed by the Ledesma sugar mill, the park's Intendencia at the town of Calilegua, immediately north of Libertador General San Martín, includes a **Centro de Visitantes** (San Lorenzo s/n, tel. 03886/422046, pncalilegua@cooperlib .com.ar), open 8 A.M.–noon weekdays only. The visitors center provides information on all the area's national parks, including those in neighboring Salta Province such as Baritú and Finca El Rey, and current road conditions. Information is also available at ranger stations at Aguas Negras and Mesada de las Colmenas.

Libertador General San Martín's Hotel Posada del Sol arranges guided trips to the park.

From Libertador General San Martín, daily except Wednesday, 8 A.M. buses to the village of Valle Grande travel through the park on RP 83, passing the Aguas Negras ranger station and campground, and the Mesada de las Colmenas ranger station. Schedules are subject to change, however, so travelers should confirm services at the park visitors center.

Parque Nacional Baritú

Along with Calilegua, Parque Nacional Baritú is one of Argentina's only two truly tropical national parks, lying north of the Tropic of Capricorn on the border with Bolivia (Calilegua is just south of the line). Like Calilegua, it preserves a substantial sector of *yungas* cloud forest; like the isolated village of Iruya, the 72,000-hectare unit belongs to Salta Province, but access is even more difficult because the only road passes through Bolivian territory via the border post of Aguas Blancas, at the northern terminus of RN 50.

There is, however, access to the park via westbound RP 19 from Aguas Blancas and a northbound footpath that follows the course of the

Río Lipeo—in winter only, as the rising and fast-moving river can be dangerous in the wet summer months. Thanks to its inaccessibility, the park is a refuge for rare mammals like the Brazilian tapir, jaguar, capuchin, and howler monkeys, and the southern river otter. It also offers habitat for the harpy eagle, the world's largest eagle.

While the park proper has no tourist infrastructure, the nearby **Portal del Baritú** (tel. 0388/422-6998 or 0338/15-685-4357, portaldelbaritu@hotmail.com, www.portaldelbaritu.com.ar) offers half a dozen forest *cabañas* with full board for US$190 for up to four people. For more information on the park, contact the national parks office in Salta or the visitors center at Parque Nacional Calilegua (tel. 03886/422046) in the village of Calilegua, Jujuy Province.

Parque Nacional El Rey

Created in 1948 by expropriation from private land, Parque Nacional El Rey protects 44,162 hectares of *yungas* forest and similarly diverse environments on the eastern edge of Salta Province. Because of its proximity to Salta, it's probably the most visited of several similar parks in the region.

Directly east of Salta, Parque Nacional El Rey is 200 kilometers from the provincial capital by paved RN 9 and RP 5, and dusty (in winter) or muddy (in summer) RP 20.

Flora and Fauna

El Rey's flora and fauna closely resemble those of Calilegua and Baritú, the other national parks of the *yungas,* though it does not reach the same high altitudes. El Rey is a particularly good bird-watching destination, however, as evidenced by its emblematic giant toucan. In the wet summer, though, mosquitoes are the most abundant fauna.

Sights and Activities

From the visitors center, there are several short footpaths and one main vehicular trail, the 10-kilometer **Senda Río Popayán** on the drier Chaco side of the park. Of the footpaths, the best is the 12-kilometer **Senda Pozo Verde,** a bird-rich trail that climbs through dense forest to a small lake; the first part of the trail follows an abandoned road. Another worth consideration is the 10-kilometer **Sendero Chorro de los Loros,** which climbs the watershed of its namesake creek.

Practicalities

Except for basic, free campgrounds with running water and pit toilets near park headquarters, Parque Nacional El Rey lacks infrastructure; a handsome hostería nearby has been closed for more than a decade. Bring food and other supplies from Salta.

On private land, on the north side of the park via RP 23, **Finca Aquisto** (San Juan 444, Salta, tel. 0387/424-3607 or 421-0981, info@fincaquisto.com.ar, www.fincaquisto.com.ar, US$40 pp with full board) offers accommodations and will arrange transportation from Salta as well.

Prior to going, consult with the national parks office in Salta; at the park itself, rangers staff the **Centro de Visitas,** which has a small museum.

Except for tours from Salta, there is public transportation only as far as the intersection of RN 9 and RP 5. Hitching is difficult because there is almost no traffic along the 46 kilometers of RP 20 to park headquarters. For motorists, RP 20 involves fording several streams that may require high clearance; 4WD is advisable in wet weather, but it's not foolproof.

Tucumán and Santiago del Estero Provinces

Traditionally known as the *Jardín de la República* (Garden of the Republic), Tucumán is rich in history as the cradle of Argentine independence, declared in the provincial capital of San Miguel in 1816. Its garden reputation stems from the subtropical fertility that turned it into the Southern Cone's sugar bowl in the post-independence period.

Tucumán still stands on a platform of sugar but, as that industry declines due to falling prices, so does the province that even some Argentines have begun to call "the Ethiopia of Argentina" for its rural poverty and high child mortality. Only during the winter *zafra* (harvest) do the industrial *ingenios* (sugar mills) need laborers, who spend most of the rest of the year jobless.

The province of Santiago del Estero, even more historic in the sense that its namesake capital is the country's oldest city, is more popular with Argentine than foreign travelers. Its main attraction is the hot springs resort of Termas de Río Hondo, a popular winter destination in a subtropical lowland province that suffers bru-tally hot summers. Like Tucumán, it is poverty-stricken, due largely to the dynasty of a provincial caudillo, ex-Governor Carlos Juárez.

SAN MIGUEL DE TUCUMÁN

For patriotic Argentines, the provincial capital of San Miguel de Tucumán is a pilgrimage site, the place where delegates declared the country's independence on July 9, 1816. Its historical legacy, which also includes several colonial monuments plus its access to the nearby Sierra de Aconquija, makes it a worthwhile visit, though it really owes whatever prosperity it conserves to the province's struggling sugar industry.

During the current crisis, though, Tucumán has become a politically divided city where former dirty warrior General Antonio Domingo Bussi won a closely contested mayoral election in early 2003 before being jailed for 1970s human-rights violations on the request of Spanish judge Baltasar Garzón. Capital of a nearly bankrupt province, the city retains a certain vigor, but it's a vigor of

© WAYNE BERNHARDSON

Plaza Independencia, Tucumán

The Andean Northwest

© WAYNE BERNHARDSON

forests of the Sierra de Aconquija

and Santa Fe and Rosario to the southeast. By the early 17th century, wrote the Spanish chronicler Vásquez de Espinosa, the region had begun to acquire a reputation for its fertile soils, plentiful irrigation water and abundant livestock, making it the region's wealthiest city.

Following independence, declared by a largely Unitarist congress of clergy, lawyers, merchants, and military (Federalist forces boycotted the gathering), Tucumán quickly adapted to the changed economic and political circumstances. With its frost-free subtropical climate, the province was well positioned to supply the burgeoning Buenos Aires market with sugar, and arrival of the railroad from Córdoba reduced transportation costs, further fueling the boom.

In recent decades, though, falling world sugar prices, obsolete equipment and low levels of reinvestment have caused many sugar mills to close, and more capital-intensive farming for crops like cotton, grains and soybeans have superseded labor-intensive cane. This, in turn, has increased rural unemployment and fomented immigration to the capital.

Orientation

Between the steep, densely wooded Sierra de Aconquija to the west and the banks of the Río Salí to the east, San Miguel de Tucumán (population 525,853) is 1,191 kilometers northwest of Buenos Aires via RN 9, and 303 kilometers south of Salta via the same highway.

Bounded by San Martín, 25 de Mayo, Laprida and east-west Avenida 24 de Septiembre, Plaza Independencia is the pivot of Tucumán's standard grid; street names change on either side of 24 de Septiembre, and outside the boundaries of Avenida Alem and Avenida Mitre to the west, Avenida Sarmiento to the north, Avenida Avellaneda and Avenida Sáenz Peña to the east, and Avenida Roca to the south. The largest open space is the wooded 100-hectare Parque 9 de Julio, only six blocks east of Plaza Independencia.

Sights

Tucumán's civic center is **Plaza Independencia,** whose provincial **Casa de Gobierno** (1912) is the site of frequent demonstrations, thanks to the

protest from the strikers at the tourist office to the demonstrating teachers in the central Plaza Independencia, opposite the provincial government house. Tucumán is also one of Argentina's noisiest cities, and that's saying something.

In the aftermath of the sugar collapse, unemployment is epidemic, and it may be a symptom of Tucumán's plight that even relatively upscale businesses find it hard to make change (provincial *bonos* (bonds or funny money) have been more common here than elsewhere in the country—there's just not been enough money in circulation). One index of its misery may be the numbers of bucket-bearing car washers lining both sides of the highway on the eastern approach to the city.

History

San Miguel de Tucumán dates from 1565, when it was a highway hub connecting the highlands of Alto Perú (present-day Bolivia) and the city of Salta, to the north, with Córdoba to the south

THE POLITICS OF TUCUMÁN

In a country renowned for bizarre politics and politicians, Tucumán has some of the most outlandish. Crooner Ramon "Palito" Ortega, a onetime provincial governor, once tried to get the federal government to bail him out when he lost big money bringing Frank Sinatra to Buenos Aires.

Tucumán's champion of corruption, though, must be former General Antonio Domingo Bussi, who wiped out the Ejército Revolucionario del Pueblo (ERP), a hapless leftist guerrilla group that operated in the Sierras de Aconquija in the 1970s. Bussi later ran for and won the provincial governorship before running into legal problems due to a hidden Swiss bank account.

In 2003, with his son inheriting the governorship, Bussi won the mayoralty of the provincial capital in a razor-thin election victory against the brother of one of his human-rights victims from the 1976–83 dictatorship. His victory was brief, though, as he soon found himself arrested under a warrant issued by Spanish judge and human-rights crusader Baltasar Garzón, the nemesis of Chilean general Augusto Pinochet.

province's perpetual financial plight and contentious history. Across the street to the north, the **Templo y Convento de San Francisco** (1879) is a rebuilt version of a colonial church that passed into Franciscan hands after the Jesuit expulsion from the Americas in 1767; the convent sits atop Jesuit foundations.

Immediately to the south of the government house, the mid-19th century **Casa Padilla** (25 de Mayo 36, 9:30 A.M.–12:30 P.M., US$.30), built by provincial governor José Frías and furnished in the fashion of its time, is now a museum of European art (it takes its name from Frías's son-in-law, a city mayor).

On the south side of the plaza, its twin bell towers topped by cupolas, the neoclassical **Iglesia Catedral** (1847–1856) is a national historical monument. Half a block south, dating from 1836, the **Museo Histórico de la Provincia** (Congreso 56, tel. 0381/431-1039, 9:30 A.M.–12:30 P.M. weekdays only, US$1) was President Nicolás Avellaneda's birthplace; it holds some 10,000 items including maps, documents, paintings, coins, and the like.

One block farther south, Tucumán's most important historical landmark is the colonial **Casa de la Independencia** (Congreso 151). Two blocks east of the historical museum, the **Museo Iramaín** (Entre Ríos 27, tel. 0381/421-1874, 8 A.M.–noon and 2–7 P.M., Saturdays 8 A.M. noon only) showcases Argentine painting and sculpture.

Half a block south of the plaza, the **Museo de Bellas Artes Timoteo Navarro** (9 de Julio 44, tel. 0381/422-7300, 8 A.M.–noon and 4–8 P.M. weekdays, 5:30–8:30 P.M. weekends) offers rotating art exhibitions. One block farther south, the **Basílica Santo Domingo** (on 9 de Julio between Crisóstomo Alvarez and San Lorenzo) dates from 1860.

Half a block west of the plaza, the **Museo Folklórico Manuel Belgrano** (24 de Setiembre 565) is a hybrid museum and crafts shop in a house that once belonged to the influential bishop José Eusebio Colombres. One block north of the plaza, part of the Universidad Nacional de Tucumán, the **Museo Arqueológico** (25 de Mayo 265, tel. 0381/423-3962, 8 A.M.–noon and 4–8 P.M. weekdays only) specializes in northwestern Argentine prehistory, with some 6,000 archaeological and ethnographic items.

Beyond the city center there is a pair of other notable museums. To the north, beyond Avenida Sarmiento, the Instituto Miguel Lillo operates the **Museo Pedagógico de Ciencias Naturales** (Miguel Lillo 251, tel. 0381/423-3026, 9 A.M.–noon and 5:30–9 P.M. weekdays), a natural sciences facility that specializes in geology and paleontology. On the west side of Parque 9 de Julio, the early 19th-century **Casa del Obispo Colombres** (Avenida Capitán Casares s/n) was the bishop's residence and site of the local sugar industry's first oxen-driven *trapiche,* a mill that's

The Andean Northwest

still in working condition. Hours are 8:30 A.M.–6 P.M. daily, with informative guided tours available in Spanish only.

In the handsome late-colonial **Casa de la Independencia,** arguably Argentina's single most important historical site, the signatories to the country's definitive declaration of independence met at the invitation of then-owner Francisca Bazán y Esteves de Laguna. They signed the declaration on July 9, 1816, and though the congress itself moved to Buenos Aires the following year, the heirs sold the building to the federal government in 1872, when it became the site of judicial and postal offices.

Much of the building was demolished in 1903, but for the renovated facade and the restored salon in which the declaration was signed; in 1943, however, architect Mario Buschiazzo rebuilt the structure based on documents and photographs antedating the demolition. From the walls, portraits of the signatories face the table at which the declaration was signed.

The **Museo de la Independencia** (Congreso 151, tel. 0381/431-0826, US$.65, half that for retirees and students) is open 9 A.M.–12:40 P.M. and 3–7 P.M. weekdays except Monday, 10 A.M.–12:40 P.M. and 4–7 P.M. weekends and holidays; there's a light-and-sound show at 8:30 P.M. nightly except Tuesday.

Housed in a colonial construction that belonged to the family of independence figure Bishop José Eusebio Colombres, also a pioneer in the sugar industry, the misnamed **Museo Folklórico Manuel Belgrano** has nothing to do with General Belgrano, but rather is a hybrid institution that displays and sells museum-quality versions of indigenous carvings, weavings and ceramics, leather goods and horse gear, and the intricately woven lace known as *randa,* from the provincial village of Monteros.

The Museo Folklórico Manuel Belgrano (24 de Setiembre 565, tel. 0381/421-8250, free) is open 7 A.M.–1 P.M. and 3–9 P.M. weekdays, 9 A.M.–1 P.M. and 4–9 P.M. weekends.

Entertainment and Events

July 9's **Día de la Independencia** (Independence Day) is Tucumán's single biggest celebration, but September 24's anniversary of the **Batalla de Tucumán** (Battle of Tucumán) is also important.

Plaza de Almas (Maipú 791, tel. 0381/430-6067, www.plazadealmas.com.ar), is a cultural café/bar (open from 8:30 P.M.), exhibition center, and native-art shop (open 10 A.M.–1 P.M. only).

At the northeast corner of Plaza Independencia, the **Victoria Plaza** (San Martín and Laprida, tel. 0381/430-4349) provides live music, theater and/or comedy, Friday and Saturday nights only.

The **Teatro Orestes Caviglia** (San Martín 251) also has live theater.

The Universidad Nacional de Tucumán's **Centro Cultural Eugenio Flavio Virela** (25 de Mayo 265, tel. 0381/422-1692) holds theater and music events, along with art exhibits, and also has a crafts shop.

The **Centro Cultural Doctor Alberto Rougués** (Laprida 31, tel. 0381/427-7976) is a fine arts facility, open 8:30 A.M.–12:30 P.M. and 5–9 P.M. weekdays, 10:30 A.M.–12:30 P.M. and 6:30–8:30 P.M. Saturday.

Downtown movie theaters survive in Tucumán: the two-screen **Cine Candilejas** (Mendoza 826, tel. 0381/430-1901), the **Cine Atlas** (Monteagudo 250, tel. 0381/422-0825), and the **Cine Majestic** (24 de Setiembre 666, tel. 0381/421-7515).

Shopping

For regional crafts, try the Museo Folklórico Manuel Belgrano (24 de Septiembre 565, tel. 0381/421-8250). Another possibility is the Plaza de Almas (Maipú 791, tel. 0381/430-6067).

Accommodations

Except for its up-and-coming hostels and the upscale categories, Tucumán's hotel scene is pretty drab, with only a handful of exceptions.

Under US$10

The **Ⅿ Tucumán Hostel** (Buenos Aires 669, tel. 0381/420-1584, info@tucumanhostel.com, www.tucumanhostel.com) charges US$3.50 pp in dorm rooms, US$9 d. The **Albergue Jóven Argentina Norte** (Laprida 456, tel. 0381/430-2716), hostel@argentinanorte.com), is comparably priced.

Ask for the larger, more luminous upstairs rooms at the central **Hotel Florida** (24 de Setiembre 610, tel. 0381/422-6674, US$5.50/9 s/d). Another passable, comparably priced place is **Hotel Petit** (Cristóstomo Alvarez 765, tel. 0381/421-3902, US$6.50/11 s/d).

US$10–25

A little dark but otherwise OK, **Hotel Astoria** (Congreso 88, tel. 0381/421-3101) charges US$8/11 s/d with shared bath, US$10/13 s/d with private bath and a/c; the noisy block is a drawback. Modern **Hotel Impala** (Crisóstomo Alvarez 274, tel. 0381/431-0371) costs US9 12 s/d with private bath.

Hotel América (Santiago del Estero 1064, tel. 0381/430-0810) is not a bad choice in its category. It starts at US$10/14 s/d, with more spacious and better-furnished rooms for US$13/17 s/d. **Hotel Francia** (Crisóstomo Alvarez 467, tel. 0381/431-0781, hotelfrancia @arnet.com.ar, www.franciahotel.com, US$11/ 14 s/d) is a decent choice with breakfast, a/c, and a good range of other services.

With its awkward effort to incorporate colonial elements into a contemporary building, **Hotel Colonial** (San Martín 35, tel. 0381/431-1523) might more accurately be called "Hotel Pseudo-Colonial." It benefits, though, from friendly, helpful management and rates of US$12/15 s/d with private bath, comfortable beds, cable TV and breakfast. That said, this well-worn hotel, with chipped mirrors and warped doors, has clearly seen better days.

Amiable **Hotel Versailles** (Crisóstomo Alvarez 481, tel. 0381/422-9760, hotelversailles@ciu-dad.com.ar, US$13/16 s/d) has smallish rooms with narrow beds, but is adequate in this price range. Friendly but tacky **Hotel París** (Francia 2, tel. 0381/421-1104, US$14/16 s/d) draws a borderline recommendation. **Gran Hotel Premier** (Crisóstomo Alvarez 502, tel. 0381/431-0381, US$16/19 s/d) is an acceptable but worn and dreary deco-style hotel.

US$25–50

Opposite Plaza Independencia, the best value in this range is business-oriented ⚑ **Hotel Mediter-** **ráneo** (24 de Setiembre 364, tel. 0381/431-0025, info@hotelmediterraneo.com.ar, www .hotelmediterraneo.com.ar, US$20/28 s/d).

Hotel del Sol (Laprida 35, tel. 0381/431-0393, US$31/41 s/d) is a downtown high-rise. One of Tucumán's finest, the **Swiss Hotel Metropol** (24 de Setiembre 524, tel. 0381/431-1180, fax 0381/431-0379, info@swisshotelmetropol.com.ar, www.swisshotelmetropol.com.ar) charges US$32/ 41 s/d, but 20 percent discounts are there for the asking, at times at least.

Opposite Parque 9 de Julio, the **Hotel Garden Park Suites** (Avenida Soldati 330, tel. 0381/431-0700, gardenpark@infovia.com.ar, US$41/48 s/d) is a legitimately four-star facility.

Food

Il Postino (Córdoba 501) is good for croissants, coffee, and breakfast, but also has pizza. **Café 25** (Mendoza 502, tel. 0381/422-8688) serves a mostly standard Argentine menu with a few surprises, most notably decent fajitas and other Tex-Mex dishes, and has good service.

More a snack bar than a restaurant, **El Portal** (24 de Septiembre between Laprida and Rivadavia) is a worthwhile stop for regional delicacies like *humitas,* empanadas, and *locro.*

The **Jockey Club** (San Martín 451, tel. 0381/421-3946) is a traditional favorite for *parrillada* and other Argentine specialties. **Mi Nueva Estancia** (Córdoba and Laprida, tel. 0381/430-7049) is a newer upscale *parrilla.*

For Middle Eastern dining, try **Doña Sara Figueroa** (24 de Septiembre 358, tel. 0381/422-6533) or **La Sirio Libanesa** (Maipú 575). **Kló & Kló** (Junín 663, tel. 0381/422-3340) provides a diverse menu of pasta and seafood.

When they finish their lunches, local businessmen chew fresh coca leaves at the traditional favorite ⚑ **La Corzuela** (Laprida 866, tel. 0381/421-6402), which boasts a large, diverse menu that includes the usual *parrillada* and pasta, but also regional dishes, fish (fresh trout), seafood, poultry and salads. Its high brick walls are covered with weavings, paintings, and gaucho gear; it also offers great service, a small but fine wine list, an exquisitely refreshing lemonade (more than welcome in this climate), and entrees in the US$3–6 range.

Pigalle (25 de Mayo 22) is the best bet for ice cream.

Information

On the south side of Plaza Independencia, Tucumán's provincial **Secretaría de Estado de Turismo** (24 de Setiembre 484, tel. 0381/430-3644, turismo@tucuman.gov.ar, www.tucumanturismo.gov.ar) is perpetually short of printed matter and vulnerable to work stoppages. When it's working, hours are 8 A.M.–10 P.M. daily. There is also an office at the bus terminal, open 8 A.M.–1 P.M. and 5–10 P.M. daily.

For motorists, **ACA** is at Crisóstomo Alvarez 901, tel. 0381/430-3384.

Services

As a provincial capital, San Miguel has a full complement of services.

Maxicambio (San Martín 779) is a convenient exchange house. Several downtown banks have ATMs, including **Citibank** (San Martín 859).

Correo Argentino is at 25 de Mayo and Córdoba; the postal code is 4000.

Bolivia has a consulate at Avenida Aconquija 1117-B, tel. 0381/425-2224, while the Chilean consulate is at Laprida 714, tel. 0381/424-5668.

Telecentro Margarita (Córdoba 402) also has Internet access.

The student- and discount-oriented **Asatej** travel agency is at Mendoza 916, tel. 0381/430-3034, fax 0381/422-3432, tucuman@asatej.com.ar. **Patsa Turismo** (Chacabuco 38, tel. 0381/421-6806) is the AmEx affiliate. **Duport Turismo** (Mendoza 720, Local 3, tel. 0381/422-0000) organizes half-day city tours (US$8) and full-day excursions to Tafí del Valle (US$17; US$25 with an extension to the ruins at Quilmes).

Lavadero Laprida (Laprida 325, tel. 0381/421-6573) does the laundry inexpensively.

Hospital Angel C. Padilla is at Alberdi 550, tel. 0381/424-8008.

Getting There

Tucumán enjoys air, road and even rail connections to Buenos Aires and much of the rest of the republic.

Aerolíneas Argentinas (9 de Julio 112, tel. 0381/431-1030) flies 12 times weekly to Aeroparque; one flight daily stops in Córdoba, except on Saturday. Austral, at the same address, flies twice each weekday to Aeroparque.

Six blocks east of Plaza Independencia, Tucumán's shiny **Estación de Ómnibus** (Avenida Brígido Terán 350, tel. 0381/430-4696) also contains a post office, supermarket, restaurants and a major shopping center, the **Shopping del Jardín** (tel. 0381/430-6400), which also provides information on buses. There is now a tourist information booth, open 8 A.M.–1 P.M. and 5–10 P.M. daily. Within the province, Aconquija (tel. 0381/227620) goes to Tafí del Valle at 10 A.M., 12:30 P.M., and 4 P.M., to America del Valle four times daily, and to Cafayate at 6 A.M. and 2 P.M. daily, with a transfer at Santa María.

Sample destinations, fares, and times include Termas de Río Hondo (US$2.50, 1.5 hours), Santiago del Estero (US$3.50, two hours), Tafí del Valle (US$5, three hours), Catamarca (US$9, 4.5 hours), Salta (US$$9, four hours), Jujuy (US$11, 5.5 hours), La Rioja (US$12, six hours), Cafayate (US$12, seven hours) Córdoba (US$15, eight hours), Corrientes (US$23, 13 hours), San Juan (US$25, 13 hours), Mendoza (US$28, 15 hours), Santa Fe/Paraná (US$23, 12 hours), Rosario (US$21, 11 hours), Posadas (US$35, 18.5 hours), Buenos Aires (US$25–40, 15 hours), Neuquén (US$40, 21 hours), Bariloche (US$50, 26 hours), Puerto Madryn (US$51, 25 hours), Comodoro Rivadavia (US$55, 30 hours), and Río Gallegos (US$70, 40 hours). International service to Santiago de Chile (22 hours) costs US$38.

NOA Ferrocarriles, at the Estación Mitre (Corrientes 1023, tel. 0381/422-0861) operates **trains** to Retiro at 8 A.M. Wednesday and Sunday. Rates are US$12 *turista,* US$14 *primera,* US$17 Pullman and US$21 in *camarote* sleepers. The ticket office is open 9 A.M.–8 P.M. daily except Sunday.

Getting Around

Aeropuerto Internacional Benjamín Matienzo (tel. 0381/426-4906) is eight kilometers east of downtown via Avenida Gobernador del Campo, which runs along the northern edge of Parque 9 de Julio. **Transfer Express** (tel. 0381/426-7945) provides door-to-door transfers.

City buses use *cospeles* (tokens), available from downtown kiosks, but also accept coins.

Car rental agencies include **Móvil Renta** (San Lorenzo 370, tel. 0381/431-0550, info@movil-renta.com.ar) and **Dollar** (Mendoza 1020, tel. 0381/430-6154).

TAFÍ DEL VALLE AND VICINITY

When San Miguel de Tucumán becomes a subtropical summer sauna, the residents of the capital flee to the cooler heights in and around Tafí del Valle, 107 kilometers to the west via a scenic highway that's a highlight in itself. At an elevation of 1,976 meters, Tafí's permanent population is only 3,290, but when every bed in its hotels and weekend houses is occupied, those numbers can double or triple.

Unlike steamy San Miguel, Tafí's microclimate is subject to fogs and drizzle that can require sweaters, jackets, and mufflers even in midsummer, but when the weather clears the scenery is magnificent. There's a certain tension between rural residents and weekenders, as locals generally ignore the numerous street signs that prohibit the presence of horses in the center, where road apples often cover the pavement. In addition to tourism, the local economy depends on cool-weather crops like potatoes and temperature fruits like apples and pears, which grow in the immediate vicinity. Farther afield, farmers pasture cattle, sheep and even llamas at the highest elevations.

History

In pre-Columbian times, Calchaquí farmers and llama herders lived in scattered settlements in and around Tafí, but the Spanish invasion brought them under the labor and tribute obligations of the *encomienda*. As the population declined and the *encomienda* lost its value, Jesuit missionaries gained control and, under their relative benevolence and philosophy of self-sufficiency, the economy rebounded. After the Jesuits' expulsion from the Americas in 1767 and Argentine independence half a century later, the valley faltered in isolation. Completion of a new highway, however, brought improved access to the markets of San Miguel, and brought the tourist trade to the hill station of Tafí.

Orientation

From Acheral, 42 kilometers southwest of the provincial capital via RN 38, paved RP 307 meanders up the narrow canyon of the Río de los Sosas until, at roughly the 100-kilometer mark, the landscape widens into Tafí's open valley where, when the fog clears, the 4000-meter-plus summits of the Nevados de Aconquija tower toward the north. The highway continues over the 3,050-meter Abra del Infiernillo to Amaicha del Valle (55 km), Quilmes (77 km), and Cafayate (123 km, in Salta Province).

Tafí has a very irregular street plan, but most tourist services are on or around a triangle formed by east-west Avenida Gobernador Critto, north-south Avenida Presidente Perón (ex-Diego de Rojas), and the roughly diagonal Avenida Belgrano that links the two. At the northwest corner of the triangle is the distinctively semicircular Plaza Angel Miguel Estéves; immediately south, the Centro Cívico is home to public services.

Sights

Most points of interest are not in Tafí proper, but nearby and en route from Tucumán, and beyond toward Quilmes and Cafayate.

Built in the early 18th century, across the bridge over the Río Tafí at the south end of Perón, the **Capilla La Banda** was part of the Jesuit *estancia* that dates from the order's takeover of the 17th-century *encomienda*. Restored in 1970s after multiple modifications in the post-independence era, it is now Tafí's **Museo Histórico y Arqueológico** (Avenida Gobernador Silva s/n, tel. 0387/421685, 10 A.M.–4 P.M. daily except Sun. 9 A.M.–noon, small admission charge for guided tours), with collections of pre-Columbian funerary urns, colonial religious art and ecclesiastical items, along with typical 19th-century furnishings and an escape tunnel.

The Andean Northwest

About 10 kilometers south of Tafí, a paved lateral leads to the village of El Mollar, where authorities recently moved the **Parque de los Menhires,** a collection of some 80 pre-Columbian granite monuments gathered in the vicinity. While the monuments themselves, carved with representations of humans and animals, are intriguing, it's worth repeating that they've been wrenched out of their geographical context more than once.

Events

Tafí's major annual event is February's **Festival del Queso,** celebrating the local cheese industry.

Shopping

Try Los Artesanos (Avenida Perón 252, tel. 03867/421758) for souvenirs.

Sports and Recreation

Local guide Juan Carlos Yapura leads hikes to nearby summits including 2,650-meter Cerro El Pelao (US$13 pp, four hours), 4,437-meter Cerro Muñoz (US$13, four hours) and 4,660-meter Cerro Negrito (US$17, full day), with discounts for groups of up to five persons. For details, ask at the Casa del Turista.

Accommodations

At the east end of town, Tafí's **Autocamping del Sauce** (Avenida Palenques s/n) charges US$.60 pp, per tent and per vehicle for passable facilities with minimal shade. There are also bunks in claustrophobic prefab *cabañas* for US$1.50 pp, and marginal toilets and showers.

Other than camping, the next cheapest accommodations are at **Hospedaje La Cumbre** (Perón 311, tel. 03867/421016, US$4–5 pp) and **Hospedaje Celia Correa** (Avenida Belgrano 443, tel. 03867/421170, US$4–5 pp).

The rooms are large and the beds comfortable at **Hostería Huayra Puca** (Los Menhires s/n, tel. 03867/421190, info@huayrapuca.com .ar, www.huayrapuca.com.ar, US$14/19 s/d with a buffet breakfast), but the plaster is peeling in Tafí's damp climate and there are other cosmetic shortcomings like cracked mirrors and light fix-

tures. New in 1998, it still has attractive common areas and rates are not unfair.

The stylishly modern and spacious **Hostería La Rosada** (Avenida Belgrano 322, tel. 03867/421323, miguel_torres@sinectis.com.ar, US$17/24 s/d) is enormously appealing for the price and has buffet breakfast, but the mattresses are on the soft side.

Down the block, the placid **Hotel Tafí** (Avenida Belgrano 177, tel. 03867/421007, fax 03867/ 421452, info@hoteltafiweb.com.ar, hoteltafi@imp-sat1.com.ar, www.hoteltafiweb.com.ar) offers simply furnished, midsize rooms, some of which have views; it also enjoys sprawling gardens and large common areas with high ceilings. On the other hand, the rates of US$19/23 s/d with buffet breakfast are higher than some comparable places.

Immediately north of Plaza Estéves, the recommended **Hostería del ACA** (Gobernador Campero and Avenida San Martín, tel. 03867/ 421027) charges US$21/27 s/d for members, US$24/33 s/d for nonmembers.

Clearly the best of the standard accommodations, **ⵎ Hostería Lunahuaná** (Avenida Gobernador Critto 540, tel./fax 03867/421360, info@lunahuana.com.ar, www.lunahuana.com.ar, US$25/33 s/d) offers a mix of contemporary comforts and traditional design; some rooms even have lofts. It's well worth consideration.

For colonial style in a rehabbed *estancia* house, try any of the half-dozen rooms at the intimate **ⵎ Posada las Tacanas** (Perón 372, tel. 03867/421821, fax 03867/421222, lastacanas @hotmail.com, US$42 s or d). It's an outstanding value.

Food

Tafí's restaurant scene is by no means bad, but it does lack variety. Most eateries are on Avenida Perón, within a block or two of each other. The **Tequila Pub Bar** (Avenida Perón s/n) has sidewalk seating, good breakfasts, and excellent empanadas and pizzas. **Pub El Ciervo** (Perón s/n, tel. 03867/421518) and **Bar El Paraíso** (Perón s/n) are both inexpensive dining options.

TO (LITTLE) HELL AND BEYOND

From Tafí del Valle, RP 307 climbs steeply northwest over the curiously named **Abra del Infiernillo** (literally "Little Hell"), a fog-shrouded 3,050-meter pass that marks the transition to the western desert. As the highway descends into the drainage of the Valles Calchaquíes, at an elevation of 2,560 meters, it passes the **Observatorio Astronómico Ampimpa** (RP 307 Km 107, tel. 03867/15-609-2286, ampimpa@turismoentucuman.com), a small teaching-oriented observatory that offers both day and night astronomical programs, along with simple accommodations and a restaurant.

Another 10 kilometers west, in the village of Amaicha, Héctor Cruz's **Centro Cultural Pachamama** or **Casa de Piedra** (RP 307 Km 118, tel. 03892/421004) is a stunning, sprawling juxtaposition of sculptures (by Cruz and other regional artists) on indigenous themes, set among cactus gardens and fountains. It's also a museum that includes informative thematic exhibits on geology, mining, natural history, and art, and is well worth a detour from either Tafí del Valle or Cafayate. Informative guided tours, in Spanish only, cost US$4 pp (this is a private, not a state-run, facility), but the price, like the trip, is well worth it.

Regional specialties like *humitas* and *locro,* along with pizza, are the items at **El Rancho de Félix** (Perón and Belgrano, tel. 03867/421022); **La Posta del Tafí** (Perón 464, tel. 0381/15-588-1632) has a comparable menu.

Having shed its hideous great-white-hunter decor, the greatly improved **Ⲙ El Portal de la Villa** (Avenida Perón s/n, tel. 03867/421834) serves great *cabrito* (kid goat) for US$2 per half portion; it also offers good empanadas and *humitas.*

Information and Services

On the south side of Plaza Estéves is Tafí's **Casa del Turista** (Los Faroles s/n, tel. 03867/421519, int. 23, 8 A.M.–8 P.M. daily except in summer, when it stays open to 11 P.M.).

Banco de Tucumán, in the Centro Cívico at Gobernador Critto 311, has an ATM. **Telecom** is at Gobernador Critto s/n; Tafí's area code is 03867. For postal services, **Correo Argentino** is at San Martín s/n, half a block north of Plaza Estéves; the postal code is 4137.

Getting There and Around

From Tafí's handsome new bus terminal, **Empresa Aconquija** (Avenida Gobernador Critto s/n, tel. 03867/421035) has five to nine buses daily to the provincial capital of San Miguel

(US$3.50, two hours). Several buses from San Miguel continue to Amaicha del Valle, Santa María (Catamarca) and Cafayate (Salta), passing the major ruins at Quilmes.

Ⲙ QUILMES

Arguably northwestern Argentina's single most impressive pre-Columbian ruins, the fortified settlement of Quilmes ascends the arid eastern slope of the Cerro Alto del Rey, 77 kilometers northwest of Tafí del Valle and 55 kilometers south of Cafayate. Covering about 30 hectares, the city supported a population upwards of 5,000 in terraced structures with thick walls, overlooking irrigated farmlands.

Dating from about A.D. 1000, Quilmes developed autonomously as part of the regional Diaguita/Calchaquí culture, but came under Inka influence in the late 15th century. The Quilmes Indians fiercely resisted the Spaniards who, when they defeated them in 1667, deported the last 2,000 survivors to Buenos Aires, where an industrial southern suburb, known for its beer factory, is their sad legacy.

Climbing and exploring the ruins of Quilmes is a rewarding experience that justifies at least half a day in its own right, and the ideal would be to spend the night camping at the site or staying

ruins of Quilmes

at its low-impact hotel. Admission to the museum (US$1), where there's also an excellent crafts selection at the museum shop, includes access to the ruins.

Accommodations and Food

Camping is free but shade is minimal and there are no showers, though there are toilets at the museum. Fortunately, since devaluation, rates at the magnificently sited and designed, virtually camouflaged **M Hotel Ruinas de Quilmes** (tel. 03892/421075) have fallen to US$21/28 s/d with breakfast; other meals are also available. Since it has only a handful of rooms, reservations are a good idea. The museum at the ruins also has a *confitería* serving basic meals.

Getting There and Around

Empresa Aconquija buses from San Miguel de Tucumán and Tafí del Valle to Cafayate will drop passengers at the junction, as will return services from Cafayate to Santa María or Tafí. From the junction, though, it's a five-kilometer hike or hitch (vehicles are few) to the ruins, which are five kilometers west of the highway.

TERMAS DE RÍO HONDO

Roughly midway between the provincial capitals of San Miguel de Tucumán and Santiago del Estero via RN 9, Termas de Río Hondo draws crowds of visitors to its thermal springs in the cool months from May to September. The rest of the year, it belongs to its 27,696 permanent inhabitants, and most of its 150-plus hotels and other services shut down. The whole year, though, it's a cheerful place that welcomes travelers of any sort.

In addition to its thermal waters—virtually every accommodation has huge tubs for hot soaks—Río Hondo's main attraction is the nearby **Dique Frontal,** a 33,000-hectare reservoir used for water sports such as swimming, boating, fishing for *dorado,* and windsurfing. Avenida Alberdi (RN 9) is the main thoroughfare, and most services are on or near it.

Accommodations

Many visitors to Río Hondo stay in campgrounds rather than hotels. Rates are around US$1.40 pp at nearby riverside sites like **Camping Mi-**

rador (tel. 03858/421392), **Camping La Olla** (tel. 03858/421857), and the more secluded and wooded **Camping del ACA** (tel. 03858/421648), on the road to the Dique Frontal.

Many hotels close in the summer months, when prices for those that remain open are real bargains; remember that even the most modest have hot mineral baths, though the quality of the infrastructure obviously varies. The prices that follow, however, are from peak season, with breakfast included.

Shoestring travelers can try the simple **Hotel Mon Petit** (Alberdi 602, tel. 03858/421822, US$4 pp). A step up is **Hotel Termal Los Felipe** (San Francisco Solano 230, tel. 03858/421484, US$11 pp).

Recently renovated and substantially upgraded, the **Casino Center Hotel** (Caseros 126, tel. 03858/ 421346, hoteltermalcasinocenter@yahoo .com.ar, www.hotelcasinocenter.com.ar, US$17 pp with breakfast); the expectation, of course, is that losses at the slots and tables will offset relatively low room rates.

For an all-inclusive experience, there's the self-contained **Hotel Los Pinos** (Maipú 201, tel. 03858/421043, infor@lospinoshotel.com.ar, www.lospinoshotel.com.ar, US$57/81 s/d), set on lush extensive grounds with an enormous pool and other luxuries.

Food
Recently relocated to new and more elaborate quarters, **La Casa de Rubén** (Sarmiento 35) is a traditionally outstanding *parrilla.*

San Cayetano (Caseros 204, tel. 421878) grills a tasty *chivito* (kid goat), with first-rate service. **Chorizo Loco** (Avenida Alberdi and Sarmiento) also specializes in beef.

Game fish, particularly the feisty *dorado,* are the forte at **La Cabaña de los Changos** (Avenida Alberdi and Libertad).

Information and Services
Hours at the **Ente Municipal de Turismo** (Caseros 132 tel. 03858/421721, www.lastermasderiohondo.com) are 7 A.M.– 1 P.M. and 3–9 P.M. in the peak winter months, 6:30 A.M.– 12:30 P.M. and 4–10 P.M. the rest of the year. It's

worth adding that its website is useful for the entire province.

Banco de la Nación (Caseros 56) has an ATM.

Correo Argentino is on Avenida Alberdi between 9 de Julio and Maipú; the postal code is 4220. There are numerous *locutorios,* but the best Internet outlet is **Cybertermas** (25 de Mayo and San Lorenzo, 9 A.M.–midnight daily except Sunday, when it opens at 4 P.M.).

Laverap (Avenida San Martín 465) does the washing.

The **Hospital Zonal** (Antonino Taboada s/n, tel. 03858/421578) provides medical services.

Getting There and Around
Termas de Río Hondo has no commercial airport, but Tucumán is only a little more than an hour away (Santiago del Estero is even closer, but has very few flights).

Buses to and from Buenos Aires (US$22, 15 hours) along RN 9 stop at Río Hondo's Terminal de Ómnibus, on Las Heras between España and 12 de Octubre, six blocks west of the triangular Plaza San Martín and two blocks north of Avenida Alberdi. Long-distance services closely resemble those to and from Santiago del Estero and Tucumán.

SANTIAGO DEL ESTERO
Capital of a province that sometimes seems a semifeudal fiefdom, the city of Santiago del Estero has failed to sustain its birthright as the colonial "Madre de Ciudades" (Mother of Cities) and has become more a stopover than a destination in its own right. That said, a night spent here need not be a wasted one.

In 1553, Francisco de Aguirre founded the first city in what is now Argentine territory on the south bank of the meandering, flood-prone Río Dulce. Since independence, though, this city that occupies a transitional site between the arid Chaco and the Andes has suffered some of the worst politicians ever in a country notorious for misgovernment.

In the 1990s, political discontent resulted in arson attacks on government offices, partly in

The Andean Northwest

response to official impunity, but for many years the dynasty of 86-year-old former Governor Carlos Juárez and his wife (and present Governor) Mercedes Aragonés survived any efforts to reduce their influence. A recent high-profile murder case, involving several lower-level provincial politicians, proved their undoing.

Orientation

Santiago del Estero (population 230,424) is 1,045 kilometers northwest of Buenos Aires and 440 kilometers north of Córdoba by RN 9; it's 170 kilometers southeast of Tucumán by the same route. The main thoroughfare is southeast-to-northwest-trending Avenida Belgrano, as RN 9 is known until it turns southwest at Avenida Sáenz Peña; most services and points of interest are northeast of Belgrano, on and around Plaza Libertad, though the bus terminal is several blocks to the southwest. Street names change on each side of Avenida Belgrano and Avenida Libertad, which runs southwest-northeast along the plaza.

Sights

As Argentina's oldest city, Santiago has managed to retain a handful of colonial construction and a representative sample of museums, along with some more-contemporary landmarks. Most but not all of these are northwest of Plaza Libertad.

Fronting on Plaza Libertad, the neoclassical **Iglesia Catedral** (1868–1877) is the fifth of a series of successors to the country's first cathedral, which dated from 1578. Striking bas-reliefs decorate the triangular facade above its Corinthian columns, flanked by twin bell towers.

Santiago's best museum is the **Museo Wagner de Ciencias Antropológicas y Naturales** (Avellaneda 355, tel. 0385/421-1380, 7 A.M.– 1 P.M. and 4–8 P.M. weekdays, 10 A.M.–noon weekends, free), one of the country's most orderly in its presentation of natural history, archaeology, and ethnography, specializing in the Chaco. The museum offers free informative guided tours (Spanish-only).

Two blocks to the southeast, the **Museo Histórico Provincial Dr. Oreste di Lullo** (Urquiza 354, tel. 0385/421-2893) occupies a colonial architectural landmark, but stresses post-colonial history as viewed through sacred and secular art, the first families of the province, and numismatics. Hours are identical to those of the Museo Wagner, and admission is also free.

Just beyond the Museo Wagner, the **Palacio Legislativo** is home to the provincial legislature and also the performing arts **Teatro 25 de Mayo;** in the early 1990s, an "energetic social protest" set the building afire, but it has since been restored. Two blocks beyond the Museo Wagner, the Spanish missionary San Francisco Solano occupied a 16th-century cell in the **Convento de San Francisco** (Avellaneda between Avenida Roca and Olaechea), an 18th-century reconstruction; it namesake neo-Gothic church dates from 1895. Both are national historical monuments; their **Museo de Arte Sacro** (Museum of Sacred Art, tel. 0385/421-1548) is open 9 A.M.–noon and 6–9 P.M. daily.

Beyond Olaechea, offering relief from Santiago's torrid summers, sprawling and densely wooded **Parque Aguirre** features a small zoo, a swimming pool (though the water supply is unpredictable), a municipal campground, and other simple attractions.

Two blocks southeast of Plaza Libertad, the **Iglesia de la Merced** (1836) superseded an earlier building that suffered damage from floods and other natural disasters; the cubical bell tower rises to a cupola. One block beyond, the **Casa Museo de Andrés Chazarreta** (Mitre 127, tel. 0385/421-1905) was the residence of the well-known Santiago teacher, musician, and composer, and reflects his folkloric interests.

Entertainment and Events

The **Teatro 25 de Mayo** (Avellaneda and 25 de Mayo, tel. 0385/ 214141), in the same building as the provincial legislature, is Santiago's main performing arts facility.

Santiago celebrates a raucous **Carnaval** in February. Late July's weeklong **Fundación de Santiago** commemorates the city's founding.

Accommodations

About a kilometer northeast of Plaza Libertad via Avenida Libertad, Parque Aguirre's municipal

Campamento Las Casuarinas is securely fenced and has clean toilets and showers, but sleep is almost impossible when locals overrun the park for their weekend *asados*. For US$2 per site, it's a good deal off-season or during the working week.

Near the bus terminal, the five-room **Residencial Emaus** (Moreno Sur 673, tel. 0385/421-5893, US$6.50/11 s/d) is a tidy and friendly shoestring choice. More central, precariously hanging onto its historical charm, the 80-year-old **Hotel Savoy** (Tucumán 39, tel. 0385/421-1234, fax 0385/421-1235, savoysantiago@savoysantiago.com.ar, www.savoysantiago.com.ar, US$7/10 s/d) is an excellent deal; sweeping marble staircases climb to rather worn but otherwise well-kept rooms. Almost next door is the aging deco landmark **Hotel Palace** (Tucumán 19, tel. 0385/421-2700, US$7/11 s/d).

The large rooms—some very large—at **Nuevo Hotel Santiago** (Buenos Aires 60, tel. 0385/421-4949, nuevosantiago@radar.com.ar, US$9/12 s/d) are excellent values; though luxuries are few, it does have a snack bar and room service. Alongside the Emaus, rates at **Hotel Bristol** (Moreno Sur 677, tel. 0385/421-8387) start at US$10/14 s/d.

Business-oriented **Hotel del Centro** (9 de Julio 131, tel./fax 0385/421-9502, ly@ocanet.com.ar, US$14/21 s/d) is modern and well-maintained, though the single beds are soft and narrow; the double beds are firmer.

In a quiet neighborhood opposite a triangular plaza, the inconspicuous **Libertador Hotel** (Catamarca 47, tel./fax 0385/421-9252, administracion@hotellibertadorsrl.com.ar, US$17/22 s/d with a buffet breakfast) offers a 20 percent discount for cash payment. The staff is friendly and there's ample parking among the extensive gardens, but the single beds are soft and narrow, and the pool sometimes lacks water. The doubles, though, are firm and the rooms spacious.

The multistory **M Hotel Carlos V** (Independencia 110, tel. 0385/424-0303, hotelcarlosv@arnet.com.ar, www.carlosvsantiago.com.ar, US$24/31 s/d), a legitimate four-star facility, serves a sumptuous buffet breakfast and has amenities that include a pool, sauna, and gym.

Food

Santiago's restaurant scene is only adequate. For fresh produce and the cheapest *comedores,* try the **Mercado Armonía,** fronting on Pellegrini between the Tucumán and Rojas pedestrian malls.

Tequila (Independencia 46, tel. 0385/422-0745) is a typical confitería suitable for breakfast and short orders. With a comfortable outdoor patio but even better indoor seating, **Puerto Coyote** (24 de Septiembre and Mendoza, tel. 0385/424-1172) makes decent pizza but, oddly for an Argentine restaurant, serves no wine.

One of Santiago's standbys is the Italo-Argentine **Mía Mamma** (24 de Setiembre 15, tel. 0385/421-9715), which serves a wide assortment of pastas, *parrillada,* and salads. The **Jockey Club** (Independencia 68, tel. 0385/421-4722) is a standard Argentine eatery in what has been an elite Argentine institution.

Parque Aguirre's **La Casa del Folclorista** (Pozo de Vargas s/n) is a *parrilla* that also, as its name suggests, offers folkloric entertainment.

Geleé Helados (Independencia 171) has fine ice cream, especially the fresh peach.

Information

Facing Plaza Libertad, the **Dirección Provincial de Turismo** (Avenida Libertad 417, tel. 0385/421-4243) is open 7 A.M.–1 P.M. and 3–9 P.M. weekdays, 9 A.M.–noon weekends except in the winter peak season, when it's also open 3–6 P.M. weekends.

For motorists, **ACA** is at Avenida Sáenz Peña and Avenida Belgrano Norte, tel. 0385/421-8899.

Services

Several downtown banks have ATMs, including **Citibank** (Avellaneda 41). **Correo Argentino** is at Buenos Aires 250; the postal code is 4200.

Telefónica (24 de Septiembre 220) has long distance and fax services. **El Escondite** (24 de Septiembre 369) has Internet access.

Laverap (Independencia 265) does the washing.

Getting There and Around

Santiago has limited air and rail services, but frequent buses almost everywhere.

Aerolíneas Argentinas (24 de Septiembre 547, tel. 0385/422-4335) flies daily except Friday and Sunday to Aeroparque via Tucumán.

City bus No. 19 goes to **Aeropuerto Mal Paso** (Avenida Madre de Ciudades s/n, tel. 0385/422-2386), six kilometers northwest of downtown via Avenida Belgrano Norte.

Santiago's run-down **Estación Terminal de Ómnibus** (Pedro León Gallo and Saavedra, tel. 0385/421-3746) is eight blocks southwest of Plaza Libertad.

Sample destinations, fares, and times include Termas de Río Hondo (US$1, one hour), Tucumán (US$3.50, two hours), Córdoba (US$10, 5.5 hours), Rosario (US$17, nine hours), and Buenos Aires (US$15–25, 13 hours).

It's not really worth taking the twice-weekly **train** from Buenos Aires to Tucumán, which uses the Mitre station in the northern suburb of La Banda, since bus services are so frequent. The longer southbound train to Buenos Aires, which stops here Wednesday and Sunday mornings, is significantly cheaper than the bus, but much slower.

Several buses from Avenida Libertad go to the Ferrocarril Mitre station in La Banda, including Nos. 10, 14, 18, and 21.

Catamarca and La Rioja Provinces

West and south of Tucumán, Catamarca and La Rioja are Andean desert provinces that remind some visitors of the Middle East, and many immigrant settlers came from that part of the world—the most prominent of which is the Syrian family of former President Carlos Menem, an ex-governor of La Rioja. Both provincial capitals, nevertheless, are major pilgrimage sites for Argentine Catholics.

Both provinces boast wild, high, and rarely visited country near the Chilean border that will reward adventurous travelers. The highest-profile destination, though, is La Rioja's Parque Nacional Talampaya, a series of fossil-rich desert canyons near the limit with San Juan Province.

In post-independence times, La Rioja has come under the control or influence of 19th-century strongmen like Felipe Varela and, most recently, labor leader Luis Barrionuevo, whose forces physically disrupted a mid-2003 gubernatorial election after provincial courts declared their hero ineligible as a nonresident of the province (Barrionuevo, who lives in Buenos Aires, once remarked that "nobody in Argentina ever got rich by working" and that Argentina's foreign-debt problems could be resolved "if we just stop stealing for a couple years"). Barrionuevo later attempted an end-run around the courts by running his sister Liliana for the governorship, but she lost to the (conceivably) less corrupt Eduardo Brizuela del Moral.

SAN FERNANDO DEL VALLE DE CATAMARCA

Home to the revered image of the Virgen del Valle, one of the most important pilgrimage sites in the entire country, San Fernando del Valle de Catamarca—more simply known as Catamarca—lives by faith and faith-based tourism. Images of the virgin are ubiquitous, and religious holidays like December 8 bring masses to the city.

Catamarca's founding date of 1683 is relatively late for a capital in the colonial northwest—because indigenous resistance to the Spaniards prevented any permanent presence until then. As capital of a province with perhaps the most dysfunctional politics of any in Argentina, it's tempting to say that Catamarca needs that faith to survive the poverty and political backwardness to which its caudillos have condemned it.

Orientation

In the valley of the Río del Valle, between the western Sierra del Colorado and the eastern Sierra Graciana, Catamarca (population 140,556) is 1,131 kilometers northwest of

Buenos Aires via RN 9 to Córdoba, northbound RN 60, and RP 33. It is 154 kilometers northeast of La Rioja and 230 kilometers from Tucumán via RN 38, and 209 kilometers from Santiago del Estero via RN 64.

For residents and pilgrims alike, Plaza 25 de Mayo is the center of Catamarca's universe and a *microcentro* bounded by Avenida Belgrano to the north, Avenida Alem to the east, Avenida Güemes to the south, and Avenida Virgen del Valle to the west. South of the plaza, five blocks of Rivadavia are a permanent pedestrian mall that connects to Avenida Güemes and Plaza 25 de Agosto.

Sights

Famed French landscape architect Carlos Thays designed shady **Plaza 25 de Mayo** but, unfortunately, city authorities haven't been willing or able to maintain it in the manner it deserves. Fortunately, at least, it blends almost seamlessly with the pedestrian mall that provides access to Italian architect Luis Caravati's landmark **Catedral Basílica de Nuestra Señora del Valle** (Sarmiento 653), immediately to the west. Most visitors to Catamarca are pilgrims who come to visit the basilica and see its 17th-century image of the **Virgen del Valle,** the city's patron saint (who, appropriately enough, is also the Patrona Nacional de Turismo, the national patron saint of tourism). Most pilgrims time their visits for and following Semana Santa and December 8, her patronal day, which are the only times her diamond-studded crown is on display.

The Italianate building, which dates from 1859 to 1869, rises impressively above Thays's landmark plaza design, but like the plaza it has suffered deferred maintenance and looks better at night. The interior boasts a decorative Baroque pulpit and an equally impressive carved altar. Immediately north of the basilica, Caravati also created the provincial **Casa de Gobierno** (1859).

In a province where the governor is traditionally a caudillo with scant regard for the political process, it's fitting that the **Palacio Legislativo** (República and Ayacucho), four blocks west, has all the charm of an unusually unsightly 1950s apartment block. Two blocks farther west, under-

© WAYNE BERNHARDSON

Iglesia y Convento de San Francisco, Catamarca

going a major renovation, the **Paseo General Navarro** is a city park with a quirky subterranean **Museo Folklórico Juan Alfonso Carrizo** (tel. 03833/437564, 9 A.M.–noon daily, 3–8 P.M. weekdays, and 5–8 P.M. weekends), whose collections look more like those at a country flea market.

In new quarters half a block north of the plaza, the **Museo de Bellas Artes Laureano Brizuela** (Sarmiento 347, tel. 03833/437563, 7 A.M.–1 P.M. and 3–9 P.M. weekdays) is a fine arts facility named for a local painter but also including works by internationally known Argentine artists including Antonio Berni, Raúl Soldi, and Benito Quinquela Martín.

One block farther north, the **Museo Arqueológico Adán Quiroga** (Sarmiento 450, tel. 03833/437413, 8 A.M.–noon and 3–7 P.M. weekdays only, US$.35) is both more and less than it suggests: in addition to extensive artifacts from

The Andean Northwest

regional prehistory, it also showcases materials from colonial and religious history (including the belongings of Franciscan priest and constitutionalist politician Fray Mamerto Esquiú), but the presentation is pedestrian and ill-organized.

One block immediately east, architect Luis Giorgi's Italianate **Iglesia y Convento de San Francisco** (Esquiú 550; 1882–1905) is the third in a series of Franciscan churches to occupy the site; it still contains remnants of the original colonial cloisters and the cell of Padre Esquiú (whose heart, in a bizarre incident resembling the theft of Juan Perón's hands, once ended up in a crystal urn on the church's roof but now lies locked away safely).

Dating from 1895, the former **Seminario Lourdista** (San Martín 954, tel. 03833/434299) now includes a museum with collections of archaeology and colonial religious art. The highlight of the municipal **Museo Histórico** (Chacabuco 425, tel. 03833/437562, 8 A.M.–noon and 3–7 P.M. weekdays only) is a rogues' gallery of provincial governors.

At the north end of town, Avenida Virgen del Valle becomes RP 108, a paved road that leads seven kilometers to the **Gruta de la Virgen del Valle,** where the virgin herself supposedly appeared in the early 17th century—decades before the founding of the city. City bus No. 104 goes directly to the grotto, whose present image is a replica of the original in the basilica.

For the finest views in the area, take a tour or a *remise* up the narrow, zigzag **Cuesta de El Portezuelo,** a paved 17-kilometer portion of RP 2 that climbs the steep western face of the Sierras de Ancasti, where it connects with gravel RP 42 toward Santiago del Estero. The panoramas of the valley and the high westerly Sierra del Ambato, which separates the provincial capital from its western deserts and altiplano, are stupendous.

Entertainment and Events

Catamarca's multiscreen **Cinemacenter** is at the bus terminal (Avenida Güemes 850, tel. 03833/423040). The **Cine Teatro Catamarca** (San Martín 555, tel. 03833/437565) is a mixed film and performing arts venue.

Following Semana Santa, for two weeks pilgrims from Catamarca and other Andean provinces celebrate the **Fiesta de Nuestra Señora del Valle,** which includes a *novena* (nine days of prayer) after which they parade the Virgen del Valle out of her chamber in the cathedral and around Plaza 25 de Mayo.

July 5's **Fundación de Catamarca** recalls the founding of the city in 1683. During winter holidays, the last two weeks of July, the **Fiesta Nacional del Poncho** honors traditional weavers with folkloric music and dance—including performances from high-profile performers from around the country—and traditional cuisine.

Throngs of pilgrims from around the entire country occupy all available accommodations, campgrounds, and all other services for December 8's **Día de la Virgen,** honoring the city's patron saint.

Shopping

Catamarca's biggest crafts outlet is the **Mercado Artesanal Permanente y Fábrica de Alfombras** (Avenida Virgen del Valle 945, tel. 03833/437862), which showcases the province's traditional handmade rugs, blankets, and ponchos, as well as jewelry and similar items. There's a evenings crafts market on **Plazoleta 5 de Julio,** a miniplaza on the Rivadavia pedestrian mall just south of Mota Botello.

La Yunta (Sarmiento 489, tel. 03833/428101) sells regional products such as leather goods and woolens, *mate* paraphernalia, and sweets like sugared walnuts.

Accommodations

Four kilometers west of Catamarca via RP 4, in a verdant canyon on the banks of the Río El Tala reached by city bus No. 101, the **Autocamping Balneario Municipal** charges reasonable rates of US$2.50 per tent, plus US$.50 per vehicle, and US$.50 pp for sites with clean toilets, hot showers, electricity and a *confitería* for food. Its swimming pools, though, make it a major recreation site for *catamarqueños,* so that sleep is difficult except out of season and during the week. Mosquitoes are also abundant.

Improbably claiming five-star status, **Hotel Comodoro** (República 855, tel. 03833/423490, US$5.50/7 s/d with shared bath, US$7/11 s/d for private rooms with a/c) isn't a desperation choice either, at least for shoestring travelers. The modest **Residencial Esquiú** (Esquiú 365, tel. 03833/422284, US$5.50/9 s/d), though, is a better value.

Hotel Colonial (República 802, tel. 03833/423502, US$7/11 s/d with private bath) is decent and congenial. Increasingly worn, the boxy, undistinguished **Sol Hotel** (Salta 1142, tel. 03833/430803, US$10/13 s/d with breakfast) redeems itself, in part, with large rooms and secure parking.

Also worn, but with bright rooms in a contemporary style, the respectable **Hotel Suma Huasi** (Sarmiento 541, tel. 03833/435699, US$11/14 s/d), has a/c, cable TV, and the like, but the beds are a little soft.

One of the best in its range is quiet **Hotel Pucará** (Caseros 501, tel./fax 03833/430688, US$14/18 s/d with plain but comfortable furnishings, breakfast and cable TV); there's a surcharge for credit card payments, though.

The rooms at **Hotel Arenales** (Sarmiento 542, tel. 03833/430307, catamarca@hotel-arenales .com.ar, US$14/19 s/d) are larger and a third cheaper than the more prestigious Hotel Ancasti, though the beds are a little softer. It also has a gym and pool. The slightly more expensive **Hotel Inti Huasi** (República 299, tel. 03833/435705, intihuasihotel@hotmail.com, US$15/19 s/d) has most of the same amenities but indifferent service.

The business-oriented **Hotel Ancasti** (Sarmiento 520, tel. 03833/435951, hotelancasti @cedeconet.com.ar, US$21/28 s/d) offers good, decent-sized rooms with desks, but the bathrooms lack tubs.

Amerian Catamarca Park Hotel (República 347, tel. 03833/425444, reservascat@amerian .com, www.amerian.com) is a marble-and-travertine tower that seems vaguely out of place in Catamarca, but it is impressive. Rack rates are US$47/83 s/d with buffet breakfast, but there are some substantial discounts.

Food

Nobody comes to Catamarca for its cuisine, but it's possible to find passable food. Penurious pilgrims eat cheaply at **Comedor El Peregrino** (San Martín s/n), in the gallery immediately behind the cathedral, where basic pasta and *parrillada* are the rule.

The **Bar Richmond** (República 534, tel. 03833/423123) has a larger, more diverse menu, but it's hit-and-miss as to what they've got and whether it's good or not—though it's worth a look. **Trattoría Montecarlo** (República 548, tel. 03833/423171) is a pasta specialist, as is **Las Tinajas** (Sarmiento 533, tel. 03833/435853). **Los Maestros** (Rivadavia 973, tel. 03833/432357) is for pizza.

For relatively upscale dining, try the Spanish specialties at the **Sociedad Española** (Avenida Virgen del Valle 725, tel. 03833/431896). **Plaza Bonita** (Sarmiento 683) is a new bistro-style place that's worth a look.

Coppo di Sabore (Rivadavia 620) has Catamarca's finest ice cream, but **Heladería Venecia** (Avenida Virgen del Valle 730) ain't bad.

Information

The **Dirección Municipal de Turismo** (Sarmiento 450, tel. 03833/437413, 7 A.M.–8 P.M. weekdays, 8 A.M.–8 P.M. weekends) occupies offices in the same building as the anthropological museum. Reasonably helpful and friendly, it has maps and brochures.

The provincial **Secretaría de Turismo y Cultura** (General Roca, 1° Cuadra, tel. 03833/437594, turismocatamarca@cedeconet.com.ar, 9 A.M.–9 P.M. daily) occupies offices in the Manzana del Turismo (Tourism Block) at the corner of Avenida Virgen del Valle and General Roca; the entrance is on General Roca.

There is a very thorough private website (www.guiacatamarca.com.ar) in Spanish only.

For motorists, **ACA** is at República 102 (tel. 03833/424513).

Services

Several downtown banks have ATMs, including **Banco de Galicia** (Rivadavia 554) and **Banco de la Nación** (San Martín 632). There is also one at the bus terminal.

Correo Argentino is at San Martín 753; the postal code is 4700. There's a **Telecentro** at

Rivadavia 758; for Internet access, try **La PCra** (Esquiú and Maipú).

Yokavil Turismo (Rivadavia 916, tel. 03833/430066) arranges tours in the vicinity of Catamarca.

Espumitas (Mota Botello 343, tel. 03833/424504) does the laundry.

For medical emergencies, try the **Hospital San Juan Bautista** (Avenida Illia 200, tel. 03833/437654).

Getting There and Around

Aerolíneas Argentinas (Sarmiento 589, tel. 03833/424460) flies daily to La Rioja and Aeroparque except Saturday, when the flight does not continue to Aeroparque.

Aeropuerto Felipe Varela (tel. 03833/430080) is 22 kilometers east of Catamarca on RP 33; Aerolíneas's Servicios Diferenciales minibus charges US$3 pp to or from.

Nearly a decade in the completion, Catamarca's state-of-the-art **Terminal de Ómnibus** (Avenida Güemes 850, tel. 03833/437578) offers services throughout the province and the country.

Sample destinations, fares, and times include La Rioja (US$3.50, 2.5 hours), Tucumán (US$4.50, 3.5 hours), Fiambalá (US$5, four hours), Andalgalá (US$5.50, 4.5 hours), Córdoba (US$7, 5.5 hours), Salta (US$10, seven hours), Mendoza (US$13, 10 hours), Resistencia/Corrientes (US$18, 14 hours), and Buenos Aires (US$18–22, 15 hours).

ANDALGALÁ

Across the Sierra de Ambato, northwest of the provincial capital, enormous extents of new planted, irrigated olive groves are rapidly transforming the landscape in and around Andalgalá, a gateway to Catamarca's scenic but little-visited highlands.

At the north end of the Sierra de Manchao, Andalgalá (population 11,360) is 245 kilometers from the provincial capital via the roundabout southwesterly route of paved RN 38, RN 60, and RP 46; a shorter route via RP 1 and RP 48 is only partially paved. Graveled RP 46 continues west to the early colonial town of Belén.

Sights

Shaded by sycamores and studded with orange trees, Andalgalá's **Plaza 9 de Julio** is the center of street life. The south side of the plaza features two adjacent museums; the **Museo Arqueológico Provincial** (Pérez de Zurita 345, 8 A.M.–7 P.M. weekdays except Saturday, and 8–10:30 P.M. Sunday), which features artifacts like ceramics and mummies, and the **Museo Folklórico** (Pérez de Zurita 345, 7 A.M.–noon and 3–10 P.M. weekdays only), which specializes in locally crafted tools, horse gear, and medicinal herbs.

Practicalities

Andalgalá's best accommodations option is **Hotel Aquasol** (Avenida Carranza Norte s/n, tel. 03835/422615, US$9/14 s/d for rooms with private bath, a/c, and breakfast); there is also a pool. **El Búfalo** (Núñez de Prado 350) serves pizza and the usual *minutas.*

From the provincial capital, **Empresa Lazo** (tel. 03833/432478) provides daily service to Andalgalá. Westbound Gutiérrez buses link Andalgalá to Belén.

BELÉN

Convenient to a number of worthwhile but underappreciated sights including Inka ruins, and popular for its woolen ponchos, the western highlands town of Belén is one of Catamarca's oldest settlements. The Inkas themselves had a tenuous presence in the area, which was inhabited by native Calchaquí peoples, until the Spaniards established an almost equally tenuous presence in the mid-16th century. It was ultimately settled from La Rioja, to the south.

Where RN 40 meets the westbound road from Andalgalá, 89 kilometers to the east, Belén (population 11,281) is the best place to stay between Chilecito (221 km to the south, in La Rioja Province) and Santa María (180 km to the north).

Sights

Belén's main gathering place is the pine- and pepper-studded **Plaza Olmos y Aguilera,** the site of its **Iglesia Nuestra Señora de Belén** (1907), a brick construction that's unusual in this part of Argentina. At the southeast corner of the plaza, the provincial **Museo Arqueológico Cóndor Huasi** (San Martín 310, 1st floor, 8 A.M.–1 P.M. and 3–7 P.M. daily except Monday) is a small but well-organized facility specializing in regional cultural evolution.

Three blocks west of the plaza, a 1,900-meter footpath climbs steeply to far-larger-than-life-size statues of the Virgin Mary and Jesus on the **Cerro de la Virgen.** The base of the mountain is the site of preparatory activities for December 20's **Día de la Fundación,** which start up to a week earlier.

Accommodations and Food

The cheapest choice, by no means bad for the price, is **Hotel Gómez** (Calchaquí 213, tel. 03835/461388, US$5/7 s/d), one block west of the plaza.

The former provincial hotel **Complejo Turístico Belén** (Belgrano and Cubas, tel. 03835/461501, hotelbelen@hotmail.com, www.belencat.com.ar, US$9/12 s/d) is undergoing a badly needed renovation that may take several years to complete. The rooms themselves are still aesthetically unappealing but comfortable enough and, if the eventual results resemble the model on display in the lobby, it's hard to imagine that prices won't rise.

One block west, **Hotel Samay** (Urquiza 349, tel. 03835/461320, US$12/15 s/d) has adequate but smaller and darker rooms with softer beds.

Parrillada is the dining standard, best sampled at **El Único** (General Roca and Sarmiento), which serves a fine *lomo a la pimienta* (pepper steak) for around US$2.50. **Fénix** (Sarmiento and Rivadavia) serves both *parrillada* and some Middle Eastern dishes.

Other Practicalities

For woolens, especially ponchos, try **Regionales Los Antonitos** (Lavalle 418, tel. 03835/461940) or **El Collita** (Belgrano 267, tel. 03835/461712).

Belén's **Oficina Municipal de Turismo** is at the foot of Cerro de la Virgen, three blocks west of the plaza.

Inka ruins of El Shinkal, Londres

Southwest of the plaza, Belén's **Terminal de Ómnibus** (Sarmiento and Rivadavia) has eastbound provincial services to and from Andalgalá (US$2.50, 1.5 hours) and to Catamarca (US$5.50, 4.5 hours), northbound to Hualfín and Santa María (US$4, 2.5 hours), and southbound to La Rioja and Córdoba.

Vicinity of Belén

From Belén, paved RN 40 leads south 15 kilometers through **Londres** (population 2,128), named by founder Juan Pérez de Zurita in 1558 for the marriage of Mary Tudor to the Spanish King Felipe II. The oldest Spanish settlement in the area, repeatedly abandoned and resettled for political and military reasons, it holds the **Festival Provincial de la Nuez** (Provincial Walnut Festival) the first two weeks of February.

About six kilometers west of Londres, at the base of the Sierra de Quimivil, the Inka fortress of

© WAYNE BERNHARDSON

The Andean Northwest

El Shinkal is a 21-hectare site where the lords of Cuzco maintained a presence from around A.D. 1470–1536. While it's no Macchu Picchu, Shinkal contains more than a hundred constructions including ceremonial platforms, depositories, staircases, and roads.

From Belén, there are seven buses daily to Londres where, from Plaza Eusebio Colombres, a westbound dirt road leads to the ruins; at the sign that says "La Toma," turn right. Admission to the site costs US$.65.

SANTA MARÍA

About 60 kilometers north of Belén, following the old Inka route, RN 40 enters the village of **Hualfín,** whose simple **Capilla de Nuestra Señora del Rosario** is a national historical monument dating from 1770. Another 120 kilometers to the northeast, the paved highway arrives at Santa María de Yokavil, a Valles Calchaquíes settlement more often visited from Cafayate (Salta) or Tafí del Valle (Tucumán).

Santa María (population 10,794) is known for its **Museo Arqueológico Provincial Eric Boman** (Belgrano and Sarmiento, tel. 03838/421282, 9 A.M.–1 P.M. and 5–9 P.M. daily). Named for an early-20th-century French archaeologist who did substantial field research in the vicinity, it focuses on early hunter-gatherers, but also contains a substantial collection of Diaguita/Calchaquí ceramics.

Practicalities

Residencial Inti Huayco (Belgrano 146, tel. 03838/420476, US$5 pp) provides good value. The unusual adobe **Complejo Arquitectónico Artesanal Santa María** (Avenida 9 de Julio s/n, tel. 03838/421627, www.caasama.8m.net, US$8/10 s/d) has 24 rooms with private bath and breakfast, and also has a pool. The **Hotel Cielos del Oeste** (San Martín 450, tel. 0838/420240, US$10/13 s/d) is another good choice.

Santa María has several *parrillas;* for regional cuisine, try **Rancho El Cardón** (Abel Acosta 158, tel. 03838/420172).

Some but not all **buses** to and from Cafayate and Tucumán via Tafí del Valle pass through

Santa María. There are also southbound buses to Hualfín and Belén.

LA RIOJA

Dating from 1591, Todos los Santos de la Nueva Rioja has managed to maintain a genuine colonial ambience in a city that has somehow survived repeated political conflicts and natural disasters since its founding by *encomendero* Juan Ramírez de Velasco. Missionaries of several Catholic orders defused the earliest conflicts, between the Spanish invaders and the indigenous Diaguita, while caudillos like Facundo Quiroga and his present-day counterparts have kept the city under their thumbs. In the meantime, earthquakes have leveled much of the city's historical heritage, but the rebuilding effort has largely succeeded in preserving the feeling, if not every feature, of the Andean past.

Orientation

At the foot of the eastern face of the Sierra de Velasco, 498 meters above sea level, La Rioja (population 143,921) is 1,151 kilometers northwest of Buenos Aires via RN 9 and RN 38. It is 456 kilometers northwest of Córdoba and 154 kilometers southwest of Catamarca via RN 38, and 452 kilometers northeast of San Juan via a series of national and provincial highways.

La Rioja's compact city center features two main squares, with most sights and businesses on and around Plaza 25 de Mayo; some major public buildings surround Plaza 9 de Julio. Most north-south streets change names on either side of Rivadavia, but east-west streets do not change names.

Sights

Earthquake-prone La Rioja has few buildings of any real antiquity, but most of those are on or around Plaza 25 de Mayo.

On the south side of the Plaza, the Byzantine **Iglesia Catedral** (1899) holds the venerated image of the city's patron San Nicolás de Bari, a colonial Franciscan missionary known for defending the indigenous population. The provincial **Casa de Gobierno** (25 de Mayo 10) faces the west side of the plaza.

Franciscans were the first order to establish themselves in La Rioja, in the **Convento de San Francisco** (25 de Mayo 218) one block north of the plaza. It was here that San Nicolás de Bari lived in a now-reconstructed cell with the current church and convent, which are also later constructions. An image of the Niño Alcalde, a Christ Child figure acknowledged as the city's symbolic mayor, resides here.

Another block north is the underachieving **Museo Inca Huasi** (Alberdi 650, tel. 03822/427310, 9 A.M.–noon daily except Monday). Poor organization and presentation detracts from an otherwise impressive assortment of artifacts ranging from early hunter-gatherers to Diaguita ceramics and cloth, plus a selection of colonial religious art.

One block west of the plaza, the **Convento de Santo Domingo** (Pelagio Luna and Lamadrid) is Argentina's oldest convent, built by Diaguita labor from the *encomienda* of Juan Ramírez de Velasco. The carved *algarrobo* door frame bears the original date of 1623, though only the stone exterior church walls survived the earthquake of 1894. One block south of the plaza, the **Iglesia de la Merced** (Rivadavia and 9 de Julio) superseded an earlier Mercedarian church that fell in the 1894 temblor. The **Museo Histórico de La Rioja** (Dávila 79), one block west, is the province's historical museum, but it's closed for the foreseeable future. One-plus block west of the plaza, the neoclassical **Escuela Normal de Maestros** (teachers' school, Pelagio Luna 749) dates from 1884.

Another block west, the **Museo Folklórico** (Pelagio Luna 811, 9 A.M.–noon daily except Mon., 4–8 P.M. weekdays except Mon., US$.35), in excellent quarters, is thematically outstanding. Unlike many similar institutions, this misleadingly named folklore museum is more and better than its prosaic name suggests. Though it stresses local customs, beliefs, and artifacts, it places them in a historic household context rather than in glass-case isolation; it also offers many of these same items for sale (appropriately enough, given their economic significance in everyday life). Among the items on display are ponchos, wood carvings, silver and leather work, and the like. The museum occupies a handsome 19th-century house with a shady central patio that's suitable for a break.

Despite its Spanish colonial style, the **Palacio Legislativo** (Vélez Sarsfield 874) on the south side of Plaza 9 de Julio, two blocks to the south, dates only from 1937. Half a block west of the plaza, the **Casa de Joaquín V. González** (Rivadavia 952) was the residence of a true renaissance man who founded the Universidad de La Plata, whose written works totaled 25 volumes, and who also served as a legislator and diplomat.

Entertainment and Events

The **Cinema Show** (Avenida Perón and Pelagio B. Luna, tel. 03822/429987) shows recent movies.

La Chaya, an indigenous version of Carnaval, takes place in February or March and can get raucously wet with water balloons—the Diaguita-derived deity known as Pujllay appears, according to popular belief, as a rain cloud in the Andes before dying on the final Sunday of the celebration.

December 31's **El Tinkunako** also has indigenous origins in San Francisco Solano's 1593 mediation between the Spanish invaders and the Diaguitas, who insisted on replacing the Spanish *alcalde* (mayor) with the Niño Alcalde, a Christ Child image that still resides in the Franciscan church. In a procession that ends in front of Plaza 25 de Mayo's government house, the indigenous patron saint San Nicolás de Bari bows three times to acknowledge the authority of the image.

Shopping

The modestly priced **Mercado Artesanal de La Rioja** (Pelagio Luna 792) displays and sells provincial crafts such as weavings, ceramics, silver and leather work, and the like. A virtual crafts museum, its hours are 8 A.M.–noon and 4–8 P.M. weekdays except Monday, 9 A.M.–1 P.M. weekends only.

For wines, try the wide selection at the **Paseo del Aljibe** (San Martín 211, tel. 03822/435074), a wine bar that also stocks regional sweets like dried fruit and jams, and crafts like basketry, ceramics, and weavings.

Accommodations

There's no suitable camping within city limits, but there are several options in the lush Quebrada de los Sauces west of town, such as **Country Las Vegas** (RN 75, Km 8) and the **Sociedad Siriolibanesa** (RN 75, Km 11). Rates are around US$2 per tent plus US$1.50 pp; city bus No. 1 from Avenida Perón goes as far as the Las Vegas before returning to town.

Cozy family-run **Residencial Anita** (Lagos 476, tel. 03822/427008, US$5.50 pp) is one of La Rioja's best bargains. Once a classic but now a budget option, **Residencial Petit** (Lagos 427, tel. 03822/427577) is comparable. Though it fronts on a busy thoroughfare and the interior rooms can be dark, tidy **Hospedaje Don José** (Avenida Perón 409, US$6.50 pp) is also a good shoestring choice.

As Parque Yacampis, northwest of downtown, recovers some of its former luster, ACA's rehabbed **Motel Yacampis** (Avenida Ramírez de Velasco s/n, tel. 03822/425216, US$7 pp for members, US$11 pp for nonmembers) is a better value.

Facing a narrow alleyway on downtown's western edge, **Hotel Savoy** (Avenida Roque A. Luna 14, tel. 03822/426894, hotelsavoy@infovia.com.ar) has slightly claustrophobic downstairs rooms (US$9/12 s/d), but those on the upper floors are bright and cheerful, reached through spacious and well-kept common areas, for only a little more (US$11/15 s/d). All rooms have cable TV and a/c, and come with breakfast.

Gran Hotel Embajador (San Martín 250, tel. 03822/438580, US$12/15 s/d) is a typically passable but past-its-prime hotel with narrow single beds. Toward the south end of town, the provincial **Hotel de Turismo** (Avenida Perón and Avenida Quiroga, tel. 03822/422005, US$17/21 s/d) may boast a pool and a solarium, but the residential floors look like cellblocks with balconies.

Its boxy interior limits its curb appeal, but **Hotel Plaza** (9 de Julio and San Nicolás de Bari, tel. 03822/425215, fax 03822/422127, plaza-hotel@plazahotel-larioja.com.ar, www.plazahotel-larioja.com.ar, US$28/33 s/d) has comfortable midsized rooms with balconies. It also has a swimming pool and bar.

King's Hotel (Avenida Quiroga 1070, tel. 03822/422122, US$27/38 s/d) is one of the better values in its price range. It has a pool.

Food

Café del Paseo (Pelagio Luna and 25 de Mayo, tel. 03822/422069) is good for breakfast, coffee, and sandwiches. **El Gran Comedor** (Bazán y Bustos 978, tel. 03822/422020) is a basic Argentine eatery, as is **El Milagro** (Avenida Perón 1200, tel. 03822/430939).

La Vieja Casona (Rivadavia 427, tel. 03822/425996) serves the usual *parrillada* but also regional specialties like *locro* and tangy empanadas. **Cavadini** (Avenida Quiroga 1131, tel. 03822/422183) is Italo-Argentine.

Though ex-President Carlos Menem may be *persona non grata* outside his home province, **El Ancla Dorado** (Vélez Sarsfield 742, tel. 03822/464455) is proud to have hosted him and his beauty-queen wife, Cecilia Bolocco, for fish, seafood, and pasta. On warm nights, the colonial-style patio is ideal for outdoor dining.

A new gastronomic quarter is developing in the vicinity of the old railroad station on Avenida Gordillo, at the east end of Rivadavia. One good choice is the smartly stylish **Open Piazza** (Avenida Gordillo and Rivadavia, tel. 03822/425390).

Golfo Azul (Avenida Perón 936) has excellent ice cream.

Information

Heavily hit by budget crises, the **Dirección Municipal de Turismo** (Dimutur, Avenida Perón 715, turismo@larioja.gov.ar, 7 A.M.–1 P.M. and 3–9 P.M. daily) has fewer maps and brochures than in the past, but the personnel do their best.

The improving provincial **Dirección General de Turismo** (Pelagio B. Luna 345, tel. 03822/453978, 8 A.M.–10 P.M. daily) has a slightly better supply of printed material.

For motorists, **ACA** is at Vélez Sarsfield and Copiapó (tel. 03822/425381).

Services

Several banks have ATMs, including **Nuevo Banco de la Rioja** (Rivadavia 702).

Correo Argentino is at Av Perón 764; the postal code is 5300. **Telecentro Avenida** is at Avenida Perón 1066, but there are several others. For Internet access, try **CyberStation** (Avenida Rivadavia 684).

There are two convenient laundries: **Mamá Espuma** (Avenida Perón 324) and **Lavadero Rocío** (Avenida Perón 946).

For medical attention, try **Hospital Presidente Plaza** (San Nicolás de Bari Este 97, tel. 03822/427814).

Getting There and Around

Aerolíneas Argentinas (Belgrano 63, tel. 03822/426307) flies daily except Saturday to Aeroparque.

From Plaza 9 de Julio, city bus No. 3 goes to **Aeropuerto Vicente Almonacid** (tel. 03822/439211), seven kilometers east of town on RP 5. A *remise* costs around US$2.50.

La Rioja's **Estación Terminal de Ómnibus** (Arias and España, tel. 03822/427991) is seven blocks south of Plaza 25 de Mayo. Sample destinations, fares, and times include Catamarca (US$3, two hours), Chilecito (US$3, 2.5 hours), Tucumán (US$8, five hours), Córdoba (US$9, 5.5 hours), San Juan (US$12, 6.5 hours), Mendoza (US$15.50, 8.5 hours), Salta (US$20, 11 hours), and Buenos Aires (US$23–30, 16 hours).

A few minibus companies, serving regional destinations, have separate offices elsewhere. **Maxi Bus** (Rivadavia and Dávila) operates minibuses to Chilecito, as does **La Riojana** (Rivadavia 578, tel. 03822/435279). **Carhuva** (Dorrego 96, tel. 03822/436380) goes to Villa Unión, Vinchina, and Villa Castelli, in the province's western cordillera, for connections to Parque Nacional Talampaya.

King's Rent A Car is in the King's Hotel (Avenida Quiroga and Copiapó, tel. 03822/422122).

VICINITY OF LA RIOJA

From La Rioja, westbound Avenida Roque A. Luna becomes RN 75 to **Las Padercitas,** where a 20th-century structure encloses ruins once inhabited, says popular belief, by San Francisco Solano as he proselytized among the Diaguita. The second Sunday of August, pilgrims walk to the site, seven kilometers from town, but the less devout can take city bus Nos. 1 or 3.

RN 75 continues west to **Dique Los Sauces,** a reservoir 15 kilometers from La Rioja that's a popular recreational resource for townies, before turning north up the canyon of the Río de los Sauces to **Villa Sanagasta,** a summer-house village (permanent population 2,072) that's home to the private folkloric **Museo Rumy May,** open 9 A.M.–6 P.M. Sundays only. There's lodging at the **Hostería Achay Sacat** (Carlos Alvarez s/n, tel. 03822/492022) for US$7 pp with breakfast.

Nobody at **Anillaco,** at an elevation of 1,800 meters some 100 kilometers farther north, apologizes for the widely despised ex-President Carlos Menem—it's his home town and his late father's winery **Bodega Saúl Menem** (open for tours) is one of its main employers (it over-optimistically produced wines to be opened on Menem's anticipated third inauguration after the presidential elections of 2003, but the candidate withdrew in the face of a certain crushing defeat by now-President Néstor Kirchner).

Thanks to Menem, this village of fewer than 1,000 residents also has an airport built to international standards (which acquired the sarcastic nickname *la pista de las aceitunas* after the former president suggested it was built to export olives) and an 18-hole golf course that raised more than a few eyebrows during and since his tenure. He has been investigated for illegal enrichment, though no charges have yet been brought.

Visitors to Anillaco can stay at a pair of pretty good accommodations. Try ACA's **Hostería Anillaco** (Coronel Barros s/n, tel. 03827494064, US$7/11 s/d for members, US$11/14 s/d for nonmembers) or **Hostería Los Amigos** (Castro Barros s/n, tel. 03827/494107, US$11/17 s/d).

CHILECITO

In the longitudinal valley between the eastern Sierra de Velasco and the western Sierra de Famatina, Chilecito is a onetime mining town that's now the base for a key wine-producing area that also grows olives and walnuts. Founded in 1715 as Santa Rita de Casia, it grew to fame, and acquired its present name, from the Chilean miners who worked the gold deposits of Famatina for most of the 19th century. When caudillo Facundo Quiroga occupied La Rioja in the 1820s, it briefly served as the de facto provincial capital.

With its refreshing climate, at an altitude of 1,100 meters, Chilecito (population 29,321) is the province's most appealing town and the gateway to Parque Nacional Talampaya, the province's number-one attraction. At the base of the massive 6,250-meter Nevado de Famatina, the town is directly west of the provincial capital, but reaching it requires a detour around the southern end of the Sierra de Velasco via RN 38 and RN 74, a distance of 192 kilometers.

Sights

In the late 19th century, the mines of Famatina were so important that Chilecito became the site of the second branch of **Banco de la Nación** (Joaquín V. González and 19 de Febrero), at the northwest corner of **Plaza Sarmiento;** the current building, though impressive, is not the original.

One block west, the **Centro Cultural Gonzaliano** (Joaquín V. González and Santiago Bazán) is a period house recycled as an art space. Three blocks farther west, Chilecito founder Domingo de Castro y Bazán built and owned the **Molino de San Francisco** (Ocampo 63), an exceptionally well-restored colonial flour mill that now operates as a museum displaying local minerals, pre-Columbian tools, colonial documents, and historic weapons, leather work and wood carvings, and weavings and paintings. Hours are 8 A.M.–noon and 3–7 P.M. daily except Monday.

One block farther west, the **Bodega La Riojana** (La Plata 646, tel. 03825/423150, lariojana@lariojana.com.ar, www.lariojana.com.ar) is an area cooperative specializing in Torrontés *riojano* but also producing Malbec, Cabernet, and others, as well as dried fruit. Free guided tours, with tasting, take place at 8 and 10 A.M. and at noon, weekdays only.

At the southern approach to town, the **Cablecarril La Mejicana** is a Leipzig-built aerial tramway that, from 1904 until 1929, connected the railway station with the smelter at Santa Florentina and the mine at La Mejicana. Replacing an obsolete mule-back system, it carried labor and materials 34 kilometers to and from the mine, with an elevation gain of some 3,500 meters. The longest of its kind in the Americas and the second-longest in the world, it consisted of nine stations, each of which had dormitories for the laborers, linked by 262 towers; the 450 ore-carts and passenger carts traveled at speeds up to 28 kilometers per hour.

Now a museum, the Cablecarril's base station is open 8 A.M.–noon and 4–7 P.M. daily, with free tours led by municipal guides. In addition to the tower platform and carts, the former mine offices at ground level hold a variety of tools, minerals, and other items. The entire system is a national historical monument.

About three kilometers east of town via RP 12, **Samay Huasi** (tel. 03825/422629, 8 A.M.–noon and 2–6 P.M. daily, US$.65) was educator Joaquín V. González's country house and the Universidad Nacional de La Plata, which he founded, administers the building as a natural sciences museum and research base; there is also a collection of Argentine art. When space is available, people unaffiliated with the university may stay here.

Accommodations

Hospedaje Nuevo Bellia (Maestro 198, tel. 03825/422525, US$3 pp with shared bath, US$5 pp with private bath) is the cheapest in town. An excellent shoestring choice, **Residencial Americano** (Libertad 68, tel. 03825/422804, US$3.50 pp with shared bath, US$7 pp with private bath) has plain but immaculately clean rooms with firm beds.

Chilecito's best value may be family-run **Hostal Mary Pérez** (Florencio Dávila 280, tel./fax 03825/423156, hostal_mp@hotmail .com, US$8.50 pp), which offers large comfy rooms with good beds, cable TV, and a decent breakfast. It is normally quiet, but the walls are a little thin.

On ample shaded grounds, ACA's **Hotel Chilecito** (Timoteo Gordillo 101, tel. 03825/422201, US$7/11 s/d for members and affiliates, US$10/16 s/d for nonmembers) is architecturally unremarkable but has no major flaws. Breakfast is included in room rates. The location of **Hotel Bel-Sa-Vac** (9 de Julio and Dávila, tel. 03825/422977, US$9/14 s/d) is a little noisy.

Food

Plaza Sarmiento's **Bar Capri** (25 de Mayo and Joaquín V. González) is an upgraded bar/confitería that's fine for breakfast and sandwiches, as well as drinks.

Having changed hands recently, the **Club Arabe** (25 de Mayo 250) is a no-frills venue that produces tasty versions of Middle Eastern specialties like *niños envueltos* (stuffed grape leaves) at low prices.

The best new place in town is **La Rosa** (Alberto G. Ocampo 149, tel. 03825/424693), which serves good pizza in attractive surroundings, with attentive service. **Helados Vanessa** (Joaquín V. González 50) has the best ice cream.

Information and Services

The competent, helpful **Dirección Provincial de Turismo** (Castro y Bazán 52, tel. 03825/422688, www.chilecitotour.com) is open 8 A.M.–1 P.M. and 4–9 P.M. weekdays, and on long weekends. The municipal **Dirección General de Turismo** operates a small branch at the bus terminal.

Several banks with ATMs have branches facing the central Plaza Sarmiento.

Correo Argentino is at Joaquín V. González and Pelagio B. Luna; the postal code is 5360. **Cabinas Telefónicas** (Córdoba and Dávila) has long-distance phone services, but the Internet access is excruciatingly slow in Chilecito.

Getting There and Around

Chilecito's **Estación Terminal de Ómnibus** (La Plata and 19 de Febrero) has frequent regional and some long-distance services. Sample destinations, fares, and times include La Rioja (US$3.50, 2.5 hours), Córdoba (US$11, seven hours), and Buenos Aires (US$45).

Several minibus carriers provide service to La Rioja from separate offices: **Inter Rioja** (Castro Barros s/n, tel. 03825/425949), **Maxi Bus** (Santiago Bazán 138, tel. 03825/423134), and **La Riojana** (El Maestro 61, tel. 03825/435279).

Opposite the main bus terminal, local carriers serve outlying settlements like Famatina and Tinogasta.

ⓜ PARQUE NACIONAL TALAMPAYA

On the waterless western slopes of the Sierra de Sañogasta, the colorful canyon country of Parque Nacional Talampaya is a jumble of wildly eroded landscapes that draws more overseas visitors than any other part of La Rioja. Many combine it with a trip to neighboring San Juan Province's Parque Provincial Ischigualasto, colloquially known as the Valle de la Luna (Valley of the Moon).

Talampaya takes its name from a Quechua term, with sacred allusions, meaning "Dry Riverbed of the Tala," a place where the *tala* tree once grew. While the riverbed may be dry, running water has played the key role in creating its steep-walled sandstone canyons and distinctive silhouette landforms from an enormous lakebed that covered the Talampaya basin during Permian and Triassic times.

One of ex-President Carlos Menem's least controversial decisions in office was to grant this deserving area, which along with San Juan Parque Provincial Ischigualasto is a UNESCO World Heritage Site, its national park status in 1997 (prior to then, it was a provincial park). In addition to its natural attractions, it boasts archaeological and rock-art sites (both figurative and abstract) that date from around A.D. 100–1200.

From a junction 15 kilometers south of Chilecito, westbound RN 40 becomes a gravel road as it climbs the hairpin turns of the scenic Río Miranda gorge to the 2,020-meter **Cuesta de Miranda**, before descending to La Unión or

© WAYNE BERNHARDSON

Parque Nacional Talampaya

alternatively, via RP 18, to the village of Pagancillo. From Pagancillo, RN 76 leads south to Parque Nacional Talampaya, for a total distance of about 140 kilometers.

Sprawling over 215,000 hectares of desert, the park is 217 kilometers from La Rioja on a roundabout route via southbound RN 38, westbound RN 150, and northbound RN 76. Midway between La Unión and Los Baldecitos, a paved 14-kilometer road leads east to Puerta de Talampaya, the staging point for park visits.

Flora and Fauna

Talampaya's sparse vegetation consists largely of shrubs, including the nearly leafless *retamo* (*Diostea juncea*) and the resinous **jarrilla** (*Larrea tridentate*), as well as cacti including the *cardón*. In some areas, subterranean water supports larger trees like the *algarrobo* and pepper (*Schinus molle*).

The most conspicuous mammal is the common grey fox, but the *chinchillón,* or vizcacha (*Lagidium vizcacia*), is also present. Armadillos are also seen. Birds include scavengers like the Andean condor and turkey vulture, and raptors including the peregrine falcon.

Talampaya's most distinctive fauna, such as

the dinosaur *Lagosuchus talampayensis* and the turtle *Palaeocheris talampayensis,* have been extinct since the early Triassic, some 250 million years ago.

Sights and Activities

Park access is by guided tour only, which may be on foot or bicycle, or by 4WD vehicle. Visitors using their own 4WD must still hire a licensed guide. The park is open 9 A.M.–5 P.M. in the winter months, 10 A.M.–6 P.M. in the summer months, but the relatively cool mornings are better than the hot afternoons. All tours start at the **Puerta de Talampaya** (Gate of Talampaya) entrance to the canyon.

For hikers, there is the three-hour **Sendero Jardín Botánico,** which also visits rock-art and mortar sites, for US$3 pp; the slightly longer **Sendero Quebrada Don Eduardo** (US$4 pp) covers much of the same ground but visits some additional areas. The same circuits can be done faster, and slightly more expensively, on rental bicycles.

Visitors with vehicles, or those hiring vehicles on site, have access to more remote parts of the park. They see some of the same sites as

© MARÍA MASSOLO

Chimenea del Eco, Parque Nacional Talampaya

foot and bicycle visitors, but during a two- to three-hour excursions they also spend time at the **Chimenea del Eco,** a natural echo chamber also known as **La Catedral** because of it towering vertical recesses. Condors are a common sight at **El Cañón de los Farallones** (Canyon of Cliffs). The five-hour excursion to the **Ciudad Perdida** (Lost City, so called because its landforms resemble ruined buildings) includes a 2.5-hour hike.

Note that guides' vehicles carry up to eight persons, who may divide the cost among them. Two-hour tours cost US$20, four-hour excursions US$40–50 depending on the itinerary. For visitors with their own vehicles, guides charge US$10 for the shorter tours, US$20–25 for the longer ones.

Practicalities

While there's no campground proper, self-contained **campers** can crash at the Puerta de Talampaya *confitería* for about US$1 pp; there are toilets but no showers. Otherwise, the nearest accommodations are at Pagancillo.

At the RN 76 junction for Puerta de Talampaya, a new toll booth collects park-entrance fees (US$4 pp for foreigners, US$2 pp for Argentine residents) at the beginning of the paved 14-kilometer eastbound road to the Puerta de Talampaya entrance, where a *confitería* prepares basic meals and sells cold drinks. Bids are out for a new visitors center to be built here.

From La Rioja, **Ivanlor buses** leave daily at 1:15 P.M. for Pagancillo (US$3, three hours), which means they arrive too late for same-day tours. Since many park personnel live in Pagancillo, though, they can help arrange transportation to the park the next morning. One reputable individual is **Adolfo Páez** (tel. 03825/470115; this is the village's general message number).

Córdoba Province

Geographically, historically, politically, and culturally, Córdoba's key feature is its centrality. Bordering every major region except Patagonia, it shares the pampas with Santa Fe and Buenos Aires Provinces and the Gran Chaco with Santiago del Estero, and borders the northwestern Andean provinces of La Rioja and Catamarca. Most significantly for travelers, it shares its central sierras—a major vacation land for Argentines—with the Cuyo province of San Luis, so it's easy to travel back and forth between the two on the dense road network. The main gateway to the Sierras, however, is the capital city of Córdoba.

Ironically, the centrally located province has traditionally held less appeal to foreign visitors

© WAYNE BERNHARDSON

Must-Sees

M Iglesia Catedral: In Argentina's historic second city, **Córdoba,** this 17th-century church features a richly decorated interior and is the resting place of several notable locals (page 356).

M Manzana de las Luces: This site in Córdoba, featuring the Iglesia de La Compañía, is just one of

CÓRDOBA PROVINCE

Manzana de las Luces — Iglesia Catedral

M

M **M** Estación Astrofísica de Bosque Alegre

Senda a la Quebrada del Condorito **M** Alta Gracia

many examples of Jesuit heritage and architecture scattered around the province. The urban legacy and rural *estancias* of the Jesuit order became a UNESCO World Heritage site in 2000 (page 357).

M Alta Gracia: This gracious colonial town features notable Jesuit monuments, well worth a day trip from the capital. Alta Gracia was the boyhood home of Ernesto "Che" Guevara; one of his family's one-time rental homes is now a museum dedicated to the charismatic hero of the Cuban revolution (page 363).

M Estación Astrofísica de Bosque Alegre: On a winding mountain road between Villa Carlos Paz and Alta Gracia, the focus of Argentine astronomy has modernized its antique equipment, but its site and installations still impart the sense of interstellar pioneers (page 365).

M Senda a la Quebrada del Condorito: In Parque Nacional Quebrada del Condorito, this trail is the best way to experience the area's open skies and peek in on the Andean condor's nesting sites, perched on rocky outcroppings over the Río Condorito Canyon (page 370).

Villa Nydia, Che Guevara's boyhood home, Alta Gracia

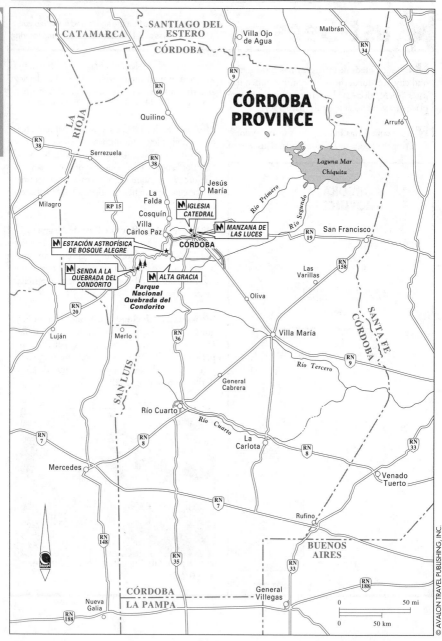

CÓRDOBA
PROVINCE

© AVALON TRAVEL PUBLISHING, INC.

than peripheral regions like Patagonia, but its capital is one of the country's most vibrant cities, and its countryside is full of recreational opportunities.

PLANNING YOUR TIME

Córdoba's urban attractions are independent of the seasons, and its Sierras are popular getaways throughout the year (but very crowded in summer). Travelers coming great distances to spend only a few weeks in the country may not spend much time in the province—it's more popular with Argentines—but overland explorers will enjoy the province's numerous Jesuit ruins, as well as off-the-beaten-path places like Quebrada del Condorito, recently designated a national park.

HISTORY

Córdoba's aboriginal inhabitants were the Comechingones, settled agriculturalists who also herded llamas, collected wild fruit—and opposed the Spanish invasion with guerrilla tactics which, however, ultimately failed. After Jerónimo Luis de Cabrera founded the city of Córdoba in 1573, Dominican, Franciscan, and Jesuit missionaries streamed into the province, but they and other Spaniards also introduced

diseases that wiped out the remaining indigenes within a century.

For more than two centuries, Córdoba was, arguably, the most important city in what is now Argentina, linked overland to the viceregal capital of Lima, Peru. From the late 18th century, though, it suffered a literal reversal of fortune—Buenos Aires's enhanced status as capital of the new Viceroyalty of the River Plate made Córdoba second fiddle to the up-and-coming port city. This, in turn, aroused resentment among Córdoba's traditionalist political and ecclesiastical elites—provincial royalists opposed independence and, in the aftermath of the wars of independence, fanatical Federalists shouting the slogan "Religion or Death" opposed the secular Unitarists of Buenos Aires.

From the late 19th century, though, European immigration, agricultural colonization, expansion of the railroads and industrialization reinforced Buenos Aires's primacy and eclipsed Córdoba's conservatism. Ironically enough, the province's political revival came through radicalism, when student rebels and labor activists helped bring down the 1960s military dictatorship of General Juan Carlos Onganía in the so-called *cordobazo*, an event that had repercussions throughout the country.

Córdoba

Córdoba preserves the most impressive colonial remains of any large Argentine city, and that architectural heritage embodies its tradition as an educational and cultural center. Though much of the mid-1950s downtown construction is insipidly utilitarian, and the area is nearly treeless, the creation of several pedestrian malls, the broadening of sidewalks, and the restriction of automobile traffic in the *microcentro* are hopeful signs. Another encouraging development is the renascent Nueva Córdoba neighborhood, full of popular restaurants and bars, fronting on the open spaces of Parque Sarmiento.

ORIENTATION

Sprawling Córdoba (population 1,267,774), 400 meters above sea level on the eastern piedmont of its namesake Sierras, is 701 kilometers northwest of Buenos Aires via RN 9, and about 400 kilometers northeast of San Luis via paved routes either over or around the Sierras de Córdoba. There are another 100,000 people in the metropolitan area.

The eastward-flowing Río Primero (also known as the Suquía) meanders around the north end of downtown Córdoba, whose Plaza San Martín is the heart of a compact area bounded by

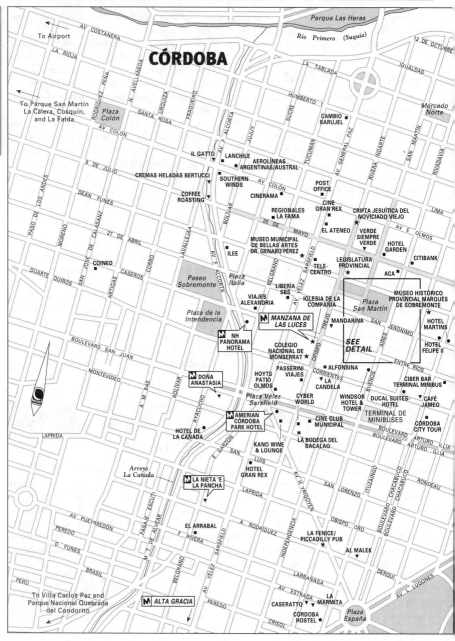

CÓRDOBA

To Airport

AV. COSTANERA

Parque Las Heras

Río Primero (Suquía)

12 DE OCTUBRE

LA RIOJA

IGUALDAD

To Parque San Martín
La Calera, Cosquín,
and La Falda

Plaza
Colón

Mercado
Norte

IL GATTO LANCHILE

AERLÍNEAS
ARGENTINAS/AUSTRAL

CREMAS HELADAS BERTUCCI

SOUTHERN
WINDS

COFFEE
ROASTING

CINERAMA

POST
OFFICE

CINE
GRAN REX

CRIPTA JESUÍTICA DEL
NOVICIADO VIEJO

REGIONALES
LA FAMA

EL ATENEO

MUSEO MUNICIPAL
DE BELLAS ARTES
DR. GENARO PÉREZ

VERDE
SIEMPRE
VERDE

HOTEL
GARDEN

CITIBANK

ILEE

LEGISLATURA
PROVINCIAL

ACA

COINED

Paseo
Sobremonte

Plaza
Italia

TELE-
CENTRO

LIBRERÍA
SBS

MUSEO HISTÓRICO
PROVINCIAL MARQUÉS
DE SOBREMONTE

VIAJES
ALEXANDRIA

Plaza de la
Intendencia

IGLESIA DE LA
COMPAÑÍA

Plaza
San Martín

MANZANA DE
LAS LUCES

MANDARINA

HOTEL
MARTINS

NH
PANORAMA
HOTEL

COLEGIO
NACIONAL DE
MONSERRAT

SEE
DETAIL

HOTEL
FELIPE II

DOÑA
ANASTASIA

PASSERINI
VIAJES

ALFONSINA

CIBER BAR
TERMINAL MINIBUS

HOYTS
PATIO
OLMOS

LA
CANDELA

Plaza Vélez
Sarsfield

CYBER
WORLD

WINDSOR
HOTEL &
TOWER

DUCAL SUITES
HOTEL

CAFÉ
JAMEO

AMERIAN
CÓRDOBA
PARK HOTEL

TERMINAL DE
MINIBUSES

CÓRDOBA
CITY TOUR

HOTEL DE
LA CAÑADA

CINE CLUB
MUNICIPAL

KANO WINE
& LOUNGE

LA BODEGA DEL
BACALAO

Arroyo
La Cañada

HOTEL
GRAN REX

LA NIETA 'E
LA PANCHA

EL ARRABAL

LA FENICE/
PICCADILLY PUB

AL MALEK

To Villa Carlos Paz and
Parque Nacional Quebrada
del Condorito

ALTA GRACIA

CASERATTO

LA
MARMITA

CÓRDOBA
HOSTEL

Plaza
España

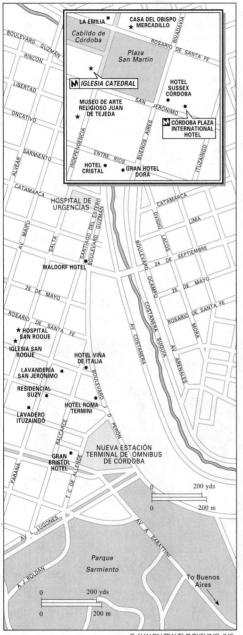

Avenida Olmos to the north, Avenida Chacabuco to the east, Blvd. Illia to the south, and Avenida General Paz to the west. Many businesses line the perpendicular pedestrian malls 25 de Mayo and Rivera Indarte, northwest of the Plaza.

All these avenues have extensions that, together, form Córdoba's *microcentro;* south of Blvd. Illia, fashionable Nueva Córdoba is less densely built, with many upgraded houses, restaurants and pubs, and Parque Sarmiento.

SIGHTS

Córdoba's compact center, on and around **Plaza San Martín,** lends itself to walking. For US$1.50 pp, the Centro de Información Turística Cabildo (Deán Funes 15, tel. 0351/428-5856) conducts theme-oriented city tours, including the city's Jesuit heritage, at 9:30 and 10:30 A.M., and 3 and 4 P.M. There are double-decker bus tours (US$4.50) two or three times daily from Plaza San Martín, opposite the cathedral, with **Córdoba City Tour** (Chacabuco 325, tel. 0351/424-6605); another option is bicycle-based tours with **Viajes Alexandria** (Belgrano 194, tel. 0351/428-1995, bicitour@alexandria.com.ar, www.alexandria .com.ar), which also operates out of the municipal tourist office behind the Casa del Obispo Mercadillo on the plaza.

On the west side of the plaza, the colonial **Cabildo de Córdoba** (Independencia 30) dates from 1775, though it took more than a decade to finish. Immediately to the south, the **Iglesia Catedral** (1758) required well over a century, as well as several architects. On the north side of the plaza, dating from 1700, the **Casa del Obispo Mercadillo** (Rosario de Santa Fe 39) was the home of the bishop who transferred the episcopate from Tucumán to Córdoba, reinforcing Córdoba's religious primacy; note the baroque facade and forged-iron balcony.

Two blocks east, the **Museo Histórico Provincial Marqués de Sobremonte** (Provincial History Museum, Rosario de Santa Fe 218) occupies an 18th-century house distinguished by its balcony and corner pillar. One block farther east, at Rosario de Santa Fe and Salguero, the **Hospital**

© AVALON TRAVEL PUBLISHING, INC.

San Roque (1763) stands alongside the better preserved **Iglesia San Roque** (1764).

Half a block south of the plaza, the 18th-century **Iglesia de Santa Teresa y Convento de Carmelitas Descalzas de San José** houses the **Museo de Arte Religioso Juan de Tejeda** (Independencia 122, tel. 0351/423-0175, 9:30 A.M.–12:30 P.M. Wed.–Sat., US$.35). One block west of the plaza, at the corner of the Rivera Indarte and Rosario de Santa Fe pedestrian malls, there are guided tours of the **Legislatura Provincial** (Provincial Legislature) weekdays at 11 A.M.

Two blocks north, beneath Avenida Colón, neophyte priests studied at the **Cripta Jesuítica del Noviciado Viejo.** To the south, the pedestrian mall of Obispo Trejo was Córdoba's **Manzana de las Luces** (Block of Enlightenment) in Jesuit times and, together with remains of Jesuit establishments throughout the province, is now a UNESCO World Heritage Site; its standout landmark is the 17th-century **Iglesia de La Compañía.**

Cabildo de Córdoba

Replacing an earlier building that had deteriorated over a century and a half, the colonial Cabildo dates from 1775, though it took more than a decade to finish. Its outstanding feature is the ground-floor gallery, with 15 graceful arches; the clock tower (1885) is a post-independence addition. A plaque on the Pasaje Santa Catalina side acknowledges an unsavory part of its history—during the 1976–83 dictatorship, the police station here was a torture center. Today, the ground floor is an exhibition center.

Iglesia Catedral

Dominating the prospect from Plaza San Martín, one of Argentina's few notable 17th-century buildings, Córdoba's cathedral was the work of a succession of architects, most notably the Jesuit Andrés Blanqui (who designed the neoclassical facade) and the Franciscan Vicente Muñoz (responsible for the Romanesque dome). Begun in 1677, this long-term project sometimes resulted in contradictory styles—the towers were the work of an anonymous architect, and postdated the building's inauguration in 1758. The richly decorated interior is the work

Iglesia Catedral, Plaza San Martín

of Catamarca-born painter Emilio Caraffa (1863–1939).

The cathedral is also the final resting place of several distinguished *cordobeses,* including the priest-politician Gregorio Funes (1749–1829), who played a key role in the independence movement, and General José María Paz (1791–1854), whose military career spanned the wars of independence and the civil wars against Rosas. The most offbeat presence, though, is the literally heartless Fray Mamerto Esquiú (1826–1883)—following his sudden death and an autopsy, the onetime Franciscan bishop of Córdoba left his heart in his birthplace of Catamarca. There, preserved in alcohol in a glass urn, the organ once appeared mysteriously on the roof of the order's landmark church; it now remains locked in the convent.

Museo Histórico Provincial

With its corner pillar, flanked by separate entrances on perpendicular streets and a balcony that looks onto both, the residence of colonial governor (and later viceroy) Rafael Núñez adds more than a touch of architectural distinction to downtown Córdoba. The ecclesiastical artwork, musical instruments, gaucho gear, and elaborate furniture that fill its 26 rooms and five courtyards are worthy complements to the building itself.

The Museo Histórico Provincial Marqués de Sobremonte (Rosario de Santa Fe 218, tel. 0351/4331661, US$.35) is open 10 A.M.–4 P.M. Tuesday–Saturday.

Manzana de las Luces

Córdoba owes much of its intellectual heritage to the Jesuit order, whose Belgian architect Philippe Lemaire solved the problem of roofing the **Iglesia de La Compañía** (Obispo Trejos and Caseros) by adapting the shipbuilding techniques of French architect Philibert Delorme. Beams of Paraguayan cedar, imported from the Paraguayan missions, sit atop the austere stone walls—more than 1.5 meters thick—while solid wooden doors provide access to the interior's carved Baroque altarpiece.

Immediately south of the church, the **Rectorado de la Universidad Nacional de Cór-**

Iglesia de La Compañía, Manzana de las Luces

doba (Obispo Trejo 242) is a direct descendent of the Seminario Convictorio de San Javier, the continent's second university (the first was in Lima, Peru). The building's walls and vaults date from Jesuit times, but the rest of the building has undergone substantial, if tasteful, modification over the centuries. Immediately south of it, dating from 1782, the Spanish Renaissance **Colegio Nacional de Monserrat** (Obispo Trejo 294) is a prestigious high school whose alumni include three Argentine presidents, as well as educator Joaquín V. González and poet Leopoldo Lugones.

Cripta Jesuítica del Noviciado Viejo

Uncovered in 1989, this subterranean Jesuit chapel dates from the early 18th century, when it was part of a more extravagant project terminated on orders from Rome. With the expulsion of the Jesuits in 1767, the Bethlemite order used it as a hospital, but soon abandoned it for the Hospital San Roque. It was later used for burials, but the creation of Avenida Colón in the 1920s filled it with rubble.

Thick but unfinished walls of stone separate its three naves. In its restored state, it now hosts exhibits, small theater presentations, and concerts. Hours are 9 A.M.–6 P.M. weekdays, 10 A.M.–1 P.M. Saturday. Admission costs US$.20.

Museo Municipal de Bellas Artes

Focusing on Argentine art, with paintings by 20th century figures like Antonio Berni, Juan Carlos Castagnino, Benito Quinquela Martín, Lino Spilimbergo and Raúl Soldi, Córdoba's municipal fine arts museum also includes illustrations, engravings, and sculptures among its 800-plus works. Built in 1905 for then vice-governor (later governor) Félix Garzón, the building itself displays European influence, with its Louis XVI facade and sweeping ceremonial staircase; details by Córdoba artist Emilio Caraffa adorn the rooms themselves.

The Museo de Bellas Artes Dr. Genaro Pérez (Avenida General Paz 33, tel. 0351/428-5906, museogenaroperez@cordoba.gov.ar, free) is open 9 A.M.–9 P.M. daily except Monday.

ENTERTAINMENT AND EVENTS

July 6 is **Fundación de la Ciudad,** the anniversary of Córdoba's founding in 1572. From early to mid-September, the **Feria del Libro** reinforces the city's intellectual history and its status as a regional publishing center.

The bookstore **El Ateneo** (General Paz 156, tel. 0351/423-4718) has a Ticketek outlet for performing arts events.

Cinema

Córdoba's commercial cinemas include the multiscreen **Hoyts Patio Olmos** (Avenida Vélez Sarsfield 361, tel. 0351/420-4237), **Cine Gran Rex** (Avenida General Paz 174, tel. 0351/424-8709), and the three-screen **Cinerama** (Avenida Colón 345, tel. 0351/422-0866). The **Cine Club Municipal** (Blvd. San Juan 49), which reprises older films, occupies the former headquarters of the Sociedad Italiana.

Bars

Most but not all of Córdoba's bar scene is in and around the Nueva Córdoba area. There are exceptions, though, like El Ateneo's literary wine bar **La Imprenta** (Avenida General Paz 156, tel. 0351/428-4371, www.cafeyletras.com.ar), and the less pretentious, highly popular **Alfonsina** (Duarte Quirós 66), which is also a good spot for simple regional cuisine.

Nueva Córdoba's stylish **Kano Wine & Lounge** (Avenida Hipólito Yrigoyen 81, tel. 0351/422-5135) is a very fashionable wine bar, with a late-twenties to early-thirties crowd. Not too noisy, it offers both bar and table seating, along with benches against the walls; it serves abundant Spanish tapas (a US$5 order suffices for two), wines by the glass as well as the bottle, and also features live music.

El Arrabal (Belgrano 899, tel. 0351/460-2990, www.elarrabal.com.ar) showcases tango but also *milonga* and salsa music in a nightclub-style ambience. The popular **La Bodega del Bacalao** (Montevideo 86, tel. 0351/15-528-4149) is another wine bar, with Spanish cuisine and tapas. The **Piccadilly Pub** (Avenida Hipólito Yrigoyen 464, tel. 0351/468-4628) is precisely what its name suggests, an English-style pub.

Spectator Sports

Córdoba's only remaining first-division soccer team is **Talleres de Córdoba** (Rosario de Santa Fe 15, tel. 0351/423-3576); it plays in the western suburbs at the **Estadio Olímpico** (General Ricchieri 3100, tel. 0351/481-2829), which seats nearly 50,000 spectators.

SHOPPING

For leather goods and other souvenirs, try La Emilia (Deán Funes 18, tel. 0351/423-8402) or Regionales La Fama (9 de Julio 336, 0351/422-8354), whose specialty is woolens.

El Ateneo (General Paz 156, tel. 0351/423-4718) is the local branch of Buenos Aires's outstanding bookstore. **Librería SBS** (27 de Abril 227, tel. 0351/423-6448) sells English-language books.

SPORTS AND RECREATION

Hiking and climbing in the nearby Sierras is a popular activity for locals. The **Club Andino de Córdoba** (7 de Abril 2050, tel. 0351/476-4795 or 480-5126, info@clubandinocordoba.com.ar, www.clubandinocordoba.com.ar) is the best source of information.

ACCOMMODATIONS

Córdoba has abundant accommodations ranging from campgrounds to simple *hospedajes* to five-star hotels, with good values in all categories. At peak seasons, like Semana Santa and winter holidays, reservations are a good idea.

Under US$10

Facilities at Parque General San Martín's **Camping Municipal** (tel. 0351/433-8011, about US$1.50 pp), 13 kilometers west of downtown, are only so-so, it lacks shade, and public transportation (city bus No. E-1 from Plaza San Martín) stops about one kilometer short of the site. Still, the price is right.

In a sprawling rehabbed Nueva Córdoba house with a secluded shady garden, the HI-affiliate **Córdoba Hostel** (Ituzaingó 1070, tel. 0351/468-7359 or 0351/15-657-4103, www.cordobahostel.com.ar, info@cordobahostel.com.ar, US$3 pp dorms, US$7 d, plus US$1 for breakfast) has amenities including kitchen and laundry facilities, lockers, Internet access, and a barbecue. Guests must, however, rent sheets or bring their own.

The best nonhostel shoestring selection is frills-free **Residencial Suzy** (Entre Ríos 528, US$5/8 s/d with shared bath). Immediately west of the bus terminal, the lackluster **Gran Bristol Hotel** (Pasaje Oliver 64, tel. 0351/423-9950, US$7/10 s/d) has little else to offer but that very convenience, friendly personnel, and good rates. Though it's a little farther from the terminal, the ordinary **Hotel Roma Termini** (Entre Ríos 687, tel. 0351/421-8721, dedesimone@arnet.com.ar, US$7/10 s/d with private bath but without breakfast) is a better choice.

US$10–25

On the pedestrian mall a block north of Plaza San Martín, **Hotel Garden** (25 de Mayo 35, tel. 0351/421-4729) charges US$8.50/14 s/d without breakfast for plain but passable rooms. Under new management, **Hotel Martins** (San Jerónimo 339, tel. 0351/421-1819, martins@cordoba.com.ar) charges US$9/13 s/d.

The best feature of the otherwise unexceptional **Hotel Gran Rex** (Avenida Vélez Sarsfield 601, tel. 0351/423-8659, granrexhotel@hotmail.com, US$10/15 s/d with breakfast) is its Nueva Córdoba location. In an aging deco-style building near the old railroad station, the friendly **Hotel Viña de Italia** (San Jerónimo 611, tel. 0351/422-6589, vitalia@arnet.com.ar, www.hotelnet.com.ar/hotel/vitalia.asp, US$11/18 s/d) has decent but smallish rooms that could use contemporary upgrades.

Well-worn but also well-kept—some of the original wallpaper survives in surprisingly good shape—the deco-style **Waldorf Hotel** (Avenida Olmos 513, tel./fax 0351/422-8051, reservas@hotelwaldorfcba.com.ar, www.hotelwaldorfcba.com.ar, US$14/18 s/d) has some rooms with balconies. There is live tango Wednesday and Saturday nights.

Half a block from Plaza San Martín, west-facing upper floors at **Hotel Sussex Córdoba** (San Jerónimo 125, tel. 0351/422-9070, fax 0351/421-8563, hotelsussex@arnet.com.ar, US$18/25 s/d) have the best views of any hotel in town. Its shadowy lobby is a misleading approach to a generally well-maintained, if aging, 1950s building.

A block south of Plaza San Martín, **Hotel Cristal** (Entre Ríos 56, tel. 0351/424-5000, hoteles@arnet.com.ar, www.hotelcristal.com.ar) charges US$21/25 s/d for relatively small but otherwise acceptable rooms. The single beds, however, are very narrow.

US$25–50

Hotel Felipe II (San Jerónimo 279, tel. 0351/425-5500, info@hotelfelipe.com.ar, www.hotelfelipe.com.ar, US$21/28 s/d) is a popular three-star choice. Though past its prime, **Gran Hotel Dorá** (Entre Ríos 70, tel. 0351/421-2031, reservas@hoteldora.com, www.hoteldora.com, US$24/28 s/d) is still a decent option.

West of downtown, **Hotel de la Cañada** (Marcelo T. de Alvear 580, tel. 0351/421-4649, fax 0351/423-1227, info@hoteldelacaniada.com .ar, US$28/37 s/d with breakfast) projects a progressive stylishness in materials—wood and brick—that's lacking in most other Córdoba hotels. There's a pool, sauna, and other amenities.

Rooms at the professionally run **Ducal Suites-Hotel** (Corrientes 207, tel. 0351/570-8888, fax 0351/570-8840, ventas@hotelducal.com.ar, www.hotelducal.com.ar, US$24/38 s/d with breakfast) are spacious and good, but even the new beds are surprisingly soft.

The Spanish-chain affiliate **M NH Panorama Hotel** (Marcelo T de Alvear 251, tel. 0351/420-4000, info@nh_panorama.com.ar, US$37/47 s/d) has contemporary rooms with buffet breakfast, and access to amenities like the pool, gym, and sauna.

US$50–100

The **M Amerian Córdoba Park Hotel** (Blvd. San Juan 165, tel. 0351/420-7000, fax 0351/420-7021, reservascor@amerian.com, www.amerian .com, US$40/47 s/d) is a new full-service hotel with pool, sauna, gym, and buffet breakfast.

The **Windsor Hotel & Tower** (Buenos Aires 214, tel./fax 0351/422-4012, informe@windsor tower.com, www.windsortower.com) has adequate standard rooms in its older hotel sector for US$42/50 s/d. The king-size beds in the more ample and comfortable 1998 addition, though, are worth the difference at US$54/62 s/d. Guests in both sections, though, get the buffet breakfast and use of the pool, sauna, and gym.

Rates at the **M Córdoba Plaza International Hotel** (San Jerónimo 137, tel. 0351/426-9800, reservas@corplaza.com, www.corplaza.com, US$45/52 s/d) are an outstanding value for a five-star facility, but multinight discounts are an even better deal. Included are breakfast buffet, pool, gym, and similar amenities.

FOOD

For cheap eats, especially at lunchtime, try the empanadas and pizza at the municipal **Mercado Norte** (La Tablada and San Martín), a 1927 landmark that's also a lively wholesale and retail grocery market. For coffee and snacks, try **Café Jameo** (Avenida Chacabuco 294) or **Coffee Roasting** (Avenida Figueroa Alcorta and 9 de Julio).

In the university district, **Mandarina** (Obispo Trejo 171, tel. 0351/426-4909) is a student hangout for fixed-price lunches. Nueva Córdoba's **La Fenice** (Buenos Aires 779, tel. 0351/460-1311) serves savory sandwiches and other pub food, as well as crepes, pasta, and some beef, plus draft beer; there is also sidewalk seating.

For regional versions of empanadas and *locro,* there's no better choice than **La Candela** (Duarte Quirós 69, tel. 0351/428-1517). It can get loud and crowded, though, and its informality has an opportunity cost (embodied in its motto "he who knows how to eat knows how to wait"); either that reflects its philosophy of service, or the staff's inability to walk and wait tables at the same time.

Verde Siempre Verde (9 de Julio 36, tel. 0351/421-8820) has a decade's credibility in vegetarian cuisine. **Il Gatto** (Avenida Colón 628, tel. 0351/426-1270) is an Italian chain restaurant that's economical and good.

M Doña Anastasia (Blvd. San Juan 325, tel. 0351/424-1716) serves excellent specialties like *cabrito* (kid goat) in the US$3–4 range, appetizers like *rabas* (squid rings) for about US$1, and an effectively isolated tobacco-free sector. The desserts, though, are a bit below par.

Nueva Córdoba's **M La Nieta 'e la Pancha** (Belgrano 783, tel. 0351/468-1920) produces regional versions of empanadas (sweetish but slightly spicy), lamb stew, pork chops, and pastas, with most entrees in the US$3.50 range. The service can be erratic, though, and folkloric music would be more appropriate than symphonic versions of Queen's greatest hits.

Open for lunch Tuesday–Sunday, dinner Monday–Saturday, Nueva Córdoba's **Al Malek** (Derqui 255, tel. 0351/468-1279) serves Lebanese food. Nearby **La Marmita** (Estrada 130, tel. 0351/460-0100) is the place for empanadas.

Also in Nueva Córdoba, **Caseratto** (Buenos Aires and Estrada, tel. 0351/468-2060) has the best ice cream, but downtown's **Cremas Heladas Bertucci** (Avenida Figueroa Alcorta 181) is worth a stop.

INFORMATION

The quantity and quality of information available here varies considerably, but on balance it's below average. The best of the bunch is the municipal **Dirección de Turismo** (Rosario de Santa Fe 39, tel. 0351/428-5600, int. 9159, munturis@cordoba.gov.ar, visitecordobaciudad@cordoba.gov.ar), downstairs in the Casa del Obispo Mercadillo on the north side of Plaza San Martín. It keeps weekday business hours only, however.

In the colonial Cabildo, staff at the privatized **Agencia Córdoba de Turismo** (Deán Funes 15, tel. 0351/428-5856, agencia.turismo@cba.gov.ar) do the minimum necessary from 8 A.M.–8 P.M. weekdays, 9 A.M.–8 P.M. weekends. The office at the bus terminal (Blvd. Perón 380, tel. 0351/433-1980, 7:30 A.M.–8:30 P.M. weekdays, 8 A.M.–8 P.M. weekends) is most useful for hotel information. The office at **Aeropuerto Internacional Ingeniero A.L. Taravella** (Camino Pajas Blanca Km 11, tel. 0351/434-8390) is open 8 A.M.–8 P.M. weekdays.

For motorists, the **Automóvil Club Argentino (ACA)** is at Avenida General Paz 499 (tel. 0351/421-4636).

SERVICES

Downtown has many ATMs, including the one at **Citibank** (Rivadavia 104). Nearby **Cambio Barujel** (Rivadavia 97) changes travelers checks.

Correo Argentino is at Avenida General Paz 201; central Córdoba's postal code is 5000.

Locutorios are numerous, including **Telecentros** at General Paz 36 and at the bus terminal. **Ciber Bar Terminal Minibus** (Entre Ríos 358) keeps long hours for Internet access. **Cyber World** (Obispo Trejos 443) is tobacco-free.

Student- and budget-oriented travel agency **Asatej** is in Shopping Patio Olmos (Avenida Vélez Sarsfield 361, Local 318, tel./fax 0351/444-

4444, cordoba@asatej.com.ar). The AmEx representative is **Passerini Viajes** (Obispo Trejo 324, tel. 0351/422-6269).

Córdoba has a pair of good language schools: **Coined** (Caseros 873, tel. 0351/422-6260, fax 0351/429-9402, info@coinedcom.ar, www.coined.com.ar) and **ILEE** (Bolívar 12, 7th floor, tel. 0351/425-4715, jagold@datafull.com, www.ilee.com.ar).

For clean clothes, try **Lavandería San Jerónimo** (San Jerónimo 556, tel. 0351/425-5093) or **Lavadero Ituzaingó** (Paraná 290).

The **Hospital de Urgencias** is at Blvd. Guzmán and Catamarca (tel. 0351/421-0243).

GETTING THERE

Córdoba has better air connections than any other Argentine city but Buenos Aires, and also has extensive bus services.

Aerolíneas Argentinas and **Austral** (Avenida Colón 520, tel. 0351/410-7676) fly frequently to Aeroparque, twice daily to Mendoza, and less frequently to Tucumán, Salta, Jujuy, Puerto Iguazú, and Bariloche.

Southern Winds (Avenida Figueroa Alcorta 192, tel. 0810/777-7500) averages three flights daily to Aeroparque, flies weekdays to Neuquén and Bariloche, daily except Saturday to Neuquén only, and weekends to Bariloche only.

LanChile (Avenida Figueroa Alcorta 206, tel. 0351/425-3447) flies daily to Santiago de Chile.

Facilities at the **Nueva Estación Terminal de Ómnibus de Córdoba** (NETOC, Blvd. Perón 300, tel. 0351/4234199, 4230532) include a tourist information office, ATMs, postal, telephone, and Internet services, restaurants, newsstands, toilets, and hot showers. Since Córdoba is a hub for overland travel throughout the country, it has dozens of bus companies traveling just about everywhere, and even some international connections.

Sample destinations, fares, and times include Mina Clavero (US$5, three hours); Catamarca (US$9, 5.5 hours); Santiago del Estero (US$8, five hours); Santa Fe (US$9, five hours); Tucumán (US$13, eight hours); Buenos Aires (US$14–17, nine hours); Mendoza (US$16, nine hours); Posadas (US$28, 16 hours); Salta (US$18, 11 hours); Montevideo, Uruguay (US$23, 15 hours); and Bariloche (US$35, 21 hours).

For provincial destinations like Alta Gracia, Jesús María, Cosquín, La Falda, and Mina Clavero, there are frequent services from the Terminal de Minibuses at the Mercado Sud, on Blvd. Illia between Buenos Aires and Ituzaingó; note that the buses park in a passageway on the north side of the market.

GETTING AROUND

Aeropuerto Internacional Ingeniero A.L. Taravella (tel. 0351/475-0392), popularly known as "Pajas Blancas," is 11 kilometers north of town via Avenida Monseñor Pablo Cabrera. Empresa Ciudad de Córdoba's "Salsipuedes" buses go directly to the airport from the NETOC terminal, but **Diferencial Ecuador** (tel. 0351/ 475-9111) offers door-to-door service for US$1.50 pp. A *remise* costs about US$3.50.

City buses require *cospeles* (tokens), available for US$.25 from kiosks, or rechargeable magnetic cards.

Europcar (Entre Ríos 70, tel. 0351/422-4867 or 0351/15-650-2288, rentacar@powernet.net .ar) occupies an office alongside the Gran Hotel Dorá. **Localiza** (tel. 0351/15-403-2936) has an office alongside the ACA station (Avenida General Paz 499), but fronting on Humberto Primo.

VICINITY OF CÓRDOBA

From downtown Córdoba, Avenida Colón leads northwest to **La Calera,** one of the city's closest getaways. It's most notable for its restored early-18th-century **Capilla Jesuítica** (Jesuit chapel); rubble from other Jesuit constructions surrounds the site. It's also noteworthy for the roadside stands selling the local specialty *salame casero* (homemade salami) and fresh bread. The road continues west to Lago San Roque, an alternative route to Villa Carlos Paz.

In a secluded wooded canyon at the foot of the Sierra Chica, about 40 kilometers northwest of Córdoba via the hamlet of El Manzano, the **Capilla del Rosario de Candonga** is a landmark Jesuit chapel dating from 1730. With its rounded archway entrance and red-tiled roof, it remains a vision of the 18th century, surrounded by ruined walls and foundations of the Jesuit Estancia Santa Gertrudis.

Some 48 kilometers north of the capital via RN 9, the former *estancia*—now a small city—of Jesús María is the site of the **Museo Jesuítico Nacional de Jesús María** (Pedro de Oñate s/n, tel. 03525/420126, www.coop5.com.ar/museo, US$.65), the church and convent of an enterprise whose vineyards, orchards, and pastures helped the Jesuits finance their other activities in the province. On nine hectares of beautifully landscaped grounds, the museum holds collections of Comechingones archaeology and colonial art; it's open 8 A.M.–6 P.M. weekdays, 10 A.M.–noon and 2–6 P.M. weekends.

Five kilometers north of Jesús María, independence figures such as Manuel Belgrano and Juan Lavalle slept at the **Museo de la Posta Rural de Sinsacate,** a post house on the colonial road between Alto Perú and Córdoba. Its most famous visitor, though, may have been the caudillo Facundo Quiroga, whose wake took place here after his assassination in 1835. Open 3–7 P.M. daily from mid-November to mid-March, 2–6 P.M. daily the rest of the year, it charges US$.35 admission.

Sierras de Córdoba

Between the Andes and the pampas, the Sierras de Córdoba comprise several parallel mountain ranges, including the Sierras Chicas immediately west of the capital and the higher Sierra de Comechingones toward San Luis, separated by longitudinal valleys. Most Argentine visitors flock to the foothills town of Villa Carlos Paz, a middle-class casinos-and-discos resort, but the region's real pleasures are historic hill towns like Alta Gracia (boyhood home of revolutionary icon Ernesto "Che" Guevara) and La Falda, and the backcountry of Parque Nacional Quebrada del Condorito.

January, February, Semana Santa, and July are the peak season here, but weekends can be busy at any time. Because the Sierras do not exceed 2,800 meters, the high country is normally accessible even in mid-winter, and the area's dense road system makes it a favorite with cyclists. The roads, however, are narrow, and the many unpaved surfaces make a mountain bike desirable.

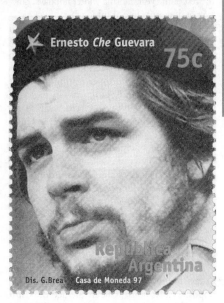

Che Guevara

ALTA GRACIA

On the gentle western slopes of the Sierra Chica, Alta Gracia was a major Jesuit *estancia* that became a town, and the place where Che Guevara's parents relocated in hopes of relieving their son's chronic asthma. Jesuit monuments in excellent repair grace the main plaza, and a German group is bidding to restore the historic Hotel Sierras, once *the* destination of choice for the socially prominent from around the country, as a casino.

Alta Gracia was also the residence of Viceroy Santiago Liniers, a resistance hero during the British invasions of Buenos Aires whose royalist convictions brought about his execution during the wars of independence, and Spanish composer Manuel de Falla, who fled the Franco dictatorship after the Spanish Civil War. It's an easy day trip from the capital, but worth considering for an overnight.

Orientation

Some 35 kilometers southwest of Córdoba via paved RP 5, Alta Gracia (population 42,600) has a compact center based on Plaza Manuel Solares. The northwestern road over the Sierra Chica offers an interesting alternative route to Villa Carlos Paz and the high country to the west.

Sights

Overlooking Plaza Solares, Alta Gracia's Jesuit monuments are the main reason to come here. The **Iglesia Parroquial Nuestra Señora de la Merced,** finished only five years before the Jesuits' expulsion from the Americas, stands alongside the **Museo Histórico Nacional del Virrey Liniers** (tel. 03547/421303, www.museoliniers.org .ar, US$.65), where the viceroy resided for just a few months in 1810. With 17 permanent exhibit rooms on topics ranging from Comechingones ethnology to daily life and customs in the province, it's open 9 A.M.–8 P.M. weekdays except Monday, 9:30 A.M.–8 P.M. weekends and holidays in summer; the rest of the year hours are

9 A.M.–1 P.M. and 3–7 P.M. weekdays except Monday, 9:30 A.M.–12:30 P.M. and 3:30–6:30 P.M. the rest of the year. During winter holidays, however, it does not close at midday.

Other Jesuit constructions flank the church and museum: to the south, the workshops known as **El Obraje** (1643) survive as a public school; to the north, the **Tajamar** (1659) diked a field to create a reservoir used for irrigating the Jesuit vineyards and orchards. It's now a city park.

Several blocks northwest, Che Guevara's family frequented the deteriorating **Sierras Hotel** (Avenida Vélez Sarsfield s/n), though their diminished economic standing undercut their social position. Manuel de Falla lived seven years in the house known as **Chalet Los Espinillos,** now home to **Museo Manuel de Falla** (Avenida Pellegrini 1011, tel. 03547/421592, US$.35). It still contains the composer's Eavestaff minipiano and other personal items. Hours are 3–8 P.M. daily except Monday and Saturday; in February only, there are weekday morning hours (9:30 A.M.–12:30 P.M. except Monday) and Saturday afternoon hours (3–8 P.M.). Immediately opposite Falla's house, Che frequented the **Club de Golf,** acquiring a taste for the game that lasted into his Cuban years.

Che and his family moved from house to rented house, but their principal residence was **Villa Nydia** (known until recently as Villa Beatriz), a solid, spacious, middle-class residence—despite frequent financial setbacks, the Guevaras were not poor people. It is now home to the **Museo Ernesto Che Guevara** (Avellaneda 501, tel. 03547/428579, museocheguevara@latinmail.com.ar, 9 A.M.–7 P.M. daily).

While the museum does a good job of reconstructing Che's boyhood—through a photographic history of Ernesto and his family in Alta Gracia society, his school report cards, and memories by his classmates, cook Rosario González and others—it doesn't really place it in any larger historical context. Admittedly this may not be the place for a complete summary of his life, but from its contents one would hardly know that Che was a controversial figure, or have any idea why it was converted into a museum, and why so many neighbors opposed the conversion.

Entertainment

Cinecenter Alta Gracia (Avenida Belgrano 466, tel. 03547/422459) is a comfortable, modern movie theater.

© WAYNE BERNHARDSON

Villa Nydia, Che Guevara's boyhood home

Accommodations and Food

In a handsome building dating from Argentina's railroad heyday, **Hostería Asturias** (Vélez Sarsfield 127, tel. 03547/423668) costs US$7/10 s/d with private bath. More utilitarian in style, but comfortable enough, **Hotel Cavadonga** (Presidente Quintana 285, tel. 03547/423456) charges US$7/11 s/d, breakfast not included. Immediately west of the plaza, **Apart Hotel La Posada** (Avenida del Tajamar 95, tel. 03547/422809, laposadaaparthotel@onenet.com.ar, US$18 s or d) has huge comfortable rooms.

For specialties like pasta, paella, and goat in the US$2–4 range, **El Casco** (Avenida Sarmiento 399, tel. 03547/426787) is an excellent dining choice. On the south side of Plaza Solares, **Trattoria Oro** (España 18, tel. 03547/425619) has an equally diverse menu focused on regional dishes.

Information and Services

The municipal **Dirección de Turismo** (Avenida del Tajamar 1, tel. 03547/428128, www.altagracia.gov.ar, turismoycultura@altagracia.gov.ar) is on the ground floor of the Reloj Público, the clocktower at the northwest corner of Plaza Manuel Solares. It's open 8 A.M.–8 P.M. daily.

Banco de Córdoba has an ATM at Belgrano and Lozada.

Correo Argentino is at Avenida Libertador 577; the postal code is 5186. There's a **Telecentro** at Avenida del Libertador 1909.

Getting There and Around

The long-distance **Terminal de Ómnibus,** which has direct service to Buenos Aires, is at Avenida Sarmiento and Vélez Sarsfield. Opposite Plaza Solares, **Sarmiento Diferencial de Pasajeros** (Belgrano 71, tel. 03547/426001) operates about 20 buses daily to and from Córdoba; it also has half a dozen daily to Villa Carlos Paz.

ⓜ ESTACIÓN ASTROFÍSICA DE BOSQUE ALEGRE

Midway between Alta Gracia and Villa Carlos Paz via a winding mountain road, protruding above the pines on a 1,250-meter hilltop, the Estación Astrofísica de Bosque Alegre is one of the main resources for Argentina's small community of about a hundred astronomers. Begun in 1928 but not opened until 1942, the observatory measures 20 meters in diameter and 25 meters in height.

Within, it rotates a Pittsburgh-built 60-inch, 28-ton Warner & Swasey reflector telescope that dates from 1922; the instrument itself has undergone continual upgrades to the latest electronic instrumentation. Part of the provincial capital's **Observatorio Astronómico de Córdoba** (Laprida 854, tel. 0351/433-1064, www.oac.uncor.edu), the Bosque Alegre facility is open for grad-student-guided tours Friday, Saturday, and Sunday 10 A.M.–1 P.M. and 3–6 P.M. all year. During summer and Semana Santa, it's open daily except Monday. There's technically no admission charge, but parking costs US$1.50 per automobile, US$.35 per motorcycle.

VILLA CARLOS PAZ

Only half a century ago, densely built Villa Carlos Paz was a bucolic hill town in the Sierra Chica at the outlet of the Río Suquía. Development around sailboat-studded Lago San Roque—the result of a dam project originally built to store drinking water for the capital in the 1890s—turned it into a summer madhouse for tourists from all over Argentina, as well as a popular weekend destination for *cordobeses*.

More recently, a four-lane toll road has turned it into a bedroom community for capital commuters. Packed with upwards of 10,000 hotel beds, receiving 850,000 visitors per year, it's become a small-scale Mar del Plata, with fresher water but without the cultural appeal of Argentina's premier beach resort.

Orientation

Crawling up and down the south arm of Lago San Roque, 640 meters above sea level, fast-growing Villa Carlos Paz (population 56,246) is 36 kilometers west of Córdoba via four-lane RN 20. Two-lane RN 38 continues north to the resorts of Cosquín and La Falda, while RN 20 continues southwest past Parque Nacional Quebrada del Condorito to Mina Clavero and San

Luis Province. Through town, RN 20 is known as Avenida San Martín.

Sights

Villa Carlos Paz looks better at a distance, from the 953-meter summit of **Cerro de la Cruz,** reached by foot or by chairlift from the **Complejo Turístico Aerosilla** (Florencio Sánchez s/n, tel. 03541/422254). Since opening in 1955, it's been a traditional activity for Argentine families—nearly all of whom seem to have purchased photos from its lurking photographers. The chairlift charges US$3 pp round trip, but many mountain bikers now use it just to get up the hill.

At the summit, a passenger monorail *aerotrén* loops past grazing goats on other parts of the hillside for US$.65 pp more. Soft drinks, beer, and sandwiches at the hilltop *confitería,* which offers good panoramas of the higher Sierras to the west, are reasonably priced.

Accommodations and Food

Many visitors stay at campgrounds like ACA's waterfront **Centro Turístico Villa Carlos Paz** (Av San Martín and Nahuel Huapi, tel. 03541/422132, about US$2 pp).

Typical of two-star accommodations is the very decent **Hotel Alpre** (Avenida San Martín 1035, tel. 03541/426012, informes@hotelalpre .com.ar, www.hotelalpre.com.ar, US$20 d with breakfast). It also has a pool.

The four-star resort **Hotel Portal del Lago** (Avenida Gobernador Alvarez and Gobernador Carrera, tel. 03541/424931, hotel@portal-del-lago.com, www.portal-del-lago.com) charges US$45/65 s/d for first-rate accommodations.

The cinema-themed **Villapaz** (General Paz 152, tel. 03541/433230) is primarily but not exclusively a *parrilla,* with excellent *bife de chorizo,* outstanding provoleta for a starter, and superb desserts. Most entrees are in the US$3–6 range.

In an area where outside-the-box cuisine is *really* the exception, the Mexican-ish **Guacamole** (9 de Julio 50, tel. 03541/432613) serves enchiladas, fajitas, and tacos to the accompaniment of—on weekends at least—live mariachis.

Information and Services

On a traffic island at the north end of town, the well-stocked and helpful Secretaría de Turismo (San Martín 1100, tel. 0810/888-2729, www.carlospaz.gov.ar) is open 7 A.M.–11 P.M. in summer, 7 A.M.–9 P.M. the rest of the year. Its office at the **Estación Terminal de Ómnibus** (Avenida San Martín 400) is also helpful.

ATMs, Telecentros, and Internet outlets are abundant along Avenida San Martín.

Correo Argentino is at Avenida San Martín 190; the postal code is 5152.

Getting There and Around

Buses to Córdoba leave at least every 15 minutes from the **Estación Terminal de Ómnibus** (San Martín 400); **Sarmiento Diferencial de Pasajeros** (tel. 03541/421571) has half a dozen buses daily to Alta Gracia.

Some long-distance companies from Buenos Aires start and end their Córdoba routes here, and there are also westward routes toward San Luis and Mendoza. Fares and times are similar to those from the provincial capital.

COSQUÍN

Nearly as cluttered as Carlos Paz with hotels and *parrillas,* Cosquín is the events center of the Valle de Punilla, which rises gradually north toward and beyond La Falda. It has few sights in its own right, but major folk and rock festivals take place here in summer.

Orientation

At 700 meters above sea level, Cosquín (population 18,795) is 52 kilometers from Córdoba via La Calera, and 63 kilometers from the provincial capital via Villa Carlos Paz. RN 38 goes directly through the middle of town as Avenida San Martín, passing the central Plaza San Martín and, four blocks farther north, the Plaza Próspero Molino, site of Cosquín's biggest musical events.

Sights

After straggling out of bed around midday, Argentine tourists head for the 1,260-meter summit of **Cerro Pan de Azúcar,** about seven kilometers east of town, for views of the Sierras to the west and the city of Córdoba to the east. A gravel road takes you most of the way, but there is no scheduled public transport; from the parking area, the peak is a half-hour climb or a US$3.50 chairlift ticket away. At the foot of the chairlift, souvenirs and simple meals are available from a pair of *confiterías;* at one of these, owner Luis de Giacomo has built a museum/shrine to Carlos Gardel, including a larger-than-life monument to the great *tanguero.*

Events
Traditionally, Cosquín's biggest draw is the **Festival Nacional del Folklore** (national folklore festival); held the last week of January for more than 30 years, it lasts around 10 days and brings in artists like Horacio Guarany, Mercedes Sosa, and Soledad (who normally omits her surname Pastorutti). In early February, the four-day **Cosquín Rock** draws performers of the stature of Divididos, Las Pelotas, Los Piojos, Charly García, and Fito Páez.

Both the folklore and rock festivals normally fill the 8,100-seat open-air theater on Plaza Próspero Molino, where hanging advertisement on the chain-link fence block the views of non-ticketholders (who can nevertheless hear the proceedings). Events at both start around 10 P.M. and finish about 3–4 A.M.

Accommodations and Food
Cosquín has an enormous roster of hotels and other accommodations, but many of them are open in summer only or, perhaps, as late as Semana Santa; off-season, rates can drop dramatically. Visitors in search of peace and quiet, but still wishing to attend the folk or rock festivals, should consider staying nearby in La Falda.

The inviting **Petit Hotel** (Sabattini 730, tel. 03541/451311, US$10/13 s/d) has kept high standards for simple, economical accommodations for many years. The impeccable, modern **Hotel del Valle** (San Martín 330, tel. 03541/452802, hoteldelvalle@cosquinturismo .com.ar, US$14/18 s/d) has the drawback of being on the main drag.

Upgraded **Hotel Paraíso de las Sierras** (San Martín 733, tel. 03541/452190, US$23/26 s/d) has a dozen nonsmoking rooms and spa facilities.

Parrillada is the standard at places like **San Marino** (Avenida San Martín 707), whose specialty is *chivito* (grilled goat). Pizza and pasta are also popular, as at **Pizzería Riviera** (Avenida San Martín and Sabattini, tel. 03541/451152).

Information
The helpful Dirección Municipal de Turismo (San Martín 560, tel. 03541/450921) is open 8 A.M.–9 P.M. weekdays, 9 A.M.–8 P.M. weekends.

Getting There and Around
Cosquín's Terminal de Ómnibus is at Perón and Salta, one block west of Plaza San Martín. There are frequent buses to Córdoba, and up and down the Valle de Punilla.

LA FALDA

Forested La Falda owes its origins to the railroad to Cruz del Eje, which arrived here in 1892, and the grand Hotel Edén—now in ruins—that opened six years later. For much of the first half of the 20th century, it was *the* place for the socialite set to summer in the Sierras—though its later history had a dark side. Though La Falda has become a more democratic destination, its quiet tree-lined streets are still a contrast to raucously populist Carlos Paz and Cosquín.

Orientation
At the foot of the steeper western slope of the Sierra Chica, 934 meters above sea level, La Falda (population 15,114) is 19 kilometers north of Cosquín and 45 kilometers north of Villa Carlos Paz via RN 38. Most businesses are on or near Avenida El Edén, which runs eastward off the highway. For travelers with their own vehicles, the eastbound gravel road that switchbacks to 1,500 meters at Cerro El Cuadrado before descending to Salsipuedes and Río Ceballos is a scenic and much less traveled alternative.

Sights
In its heyday, 1898 to about 1945, the **Hotel**

Edén hosted figures of the stature of President Julio A. Roca, Nicaraguan poet Rubén Darío, Albert Einstein, and the Prince of Wales. Its second set of German owners, though, were open Nazi sympathizers and the Argentine government, after belatedly declaring war on Germany in the closing days of WWII, expropriated the property.

After closing in 1965 and being ransacked by locals—including its supposed custodians—in the 1970s and 1980s, today it's a ghostly grand hotel offering only hints of what it once was. Some locals, though, take pride in at least part of its history and dream of the day that it might reopen—many years and millions of dollars in the future, if ever. Meanwhile, the municipality offers guided tours 9:30 A.M.–12:30 P.M. all year and 4–7 P.M. in summer; winter afternoon hours are 3–5:30 P.M. Admission costs US$1.

The **Trenshow** (Las Murallas 200, tel. 03548/423041, US$2) is a miniature-train museum, open 9:30 A.M.–8:30 P.M. daily in summer; the rest of the year, hours are 10 A.M.– 12:30 P.M. and 3–7 P.M., weekends and holidays only.

The **Museo del Deporte Pierre de Coubertin** (Meincke 32, 1st floor, tel. 03548/15-631835) is a private sports museum whose trophies including Olympic materials. Hours are 10 A.M.–1 P.M. and 6–9 P.M. daily in summer; 11 A.M.–1 P.M. and 7–9 P.M. the rest of the year.

Entertainment and Events

The only functioning part of the old hotel, the **Bar Edén Hotel** has live music Friday, Saturday, and Sunday. At other times, it still offers sandwiches, desserts, drinks, and coffee.

The **Cine Teatro Rex** (9 de Julio 186, tel. 03548/424784) shows commercial films.

Events at late July's **Semana del Tango** take place at various locales around town.

Shopping

The **Feria Artesanal del Andén,** alongside the tourist office at the old rail station, is a summer crafts fair, also open on holiday weekends like Semana Santa; hours are 6 P.M.–1 A.M.

former Hotel Edén

© WAYNE BERNHARDSON

Accommodations and Food

La Falda has abundant accommodations that offer, in general, more spacious grounds and more quiet than those in Cosquín or Carlos Paz. Good shoestring choices, for around US$6 pp, include **Hostería Marina** (Güemes 134, tel. 03548/422640) and **Hotel San Remo** (Avenida Argentina 105, tel. 03548/424875). Well-landscaped **Hotel Old Garden** (Capital Federal 28, tel. 03548/422842, US$16 d) has greater amenities, including a pool.

East of the commercial center, with spacious gardens and a pool, the castle-like **Hotel La Asturiana** (Avenida Edén 835, tel./fax 03548/422923, hotelasturiana@yahoo.com.ar, US$11 pp) has decent-size rooms with firm beds, private bath, and breakfast. The standard for excellence, though, is **Hotel Tomaso di Savoia** (Avenida Edén 732, tel. 03548/423013, hotel @tomasodisavoia.com.ar, US$31/38 s/d) which has an outstanding restaurant.

La Parrilla de Raúl (Avenida El Edén 1002, tel. 03548/15-635674) is cavernous *parrilla* that's cool in winter even when the grills are smoking, but the huge buffet for US$4 is an exceptional value. **Restaurant de las Cabañas El Edén** (Avenida El Edén 1233) has excellent desserts and coffee.

Information and Services

Occupying the former train station, La Falda's Ente de Turismo (Avenida España 50, tel. 0351/423007, turismolafalda@punilla.net.com. ar) is open 8 A.M. to 8:30 P.M. daily except in summer, when it stays open until 9 P.M.

Banco de Córdoba (Avenida El Edén 402) has an ATM.

Correo Argentino is at Avenida Argentina 199; La Falda's postal code is 5172. There's a *locutorio* at Diagonal San Martín 23.

Nuevo Estilo Internet (Avenida El Edén 629) has cheap Internet access.

Getting There and Around

La Falda's Estación Terminal de Ómnibus is at RN 38 and Avenida Güemes. There are frequent buses up and down the Valle de Punilla and to Córdoba, and long-distance services to the Cuyo cities of San Juan and Mendoza, as well as Buenos Aires and intermediates.

Parque Nacional Quebrada del Condorito

The world's most famous carrion carnivore, the majestic Andean condor, reaches its easternmost range in the Altas Cumbres (High Summits) of the Sierras de Córdoba, where it lends its name to the area's only national park. Because of its year-round accessibility, it makes an ideal excursion from Villa Carlos Paz or even the capital city of Córdoba, or a stopover en route to or from San Luis Province.

Quebrada del Condorito is 55 kilometers southwest of Villa Carlos Paz and 90 kilometers southwest of Córdoba via RP 20, the Camino Altas Cumbres, which continues west to Mina Clavero and San Luis Province. Comprising some 37,000 kilometers of rolling high terrain cut by eastward-draining streams on the Pampa de Achala, up to 2,300 meters above sea level, the park lies mostly south of the highway. Another 145,000 hectares of provincial watershed reserve nearly surround the park.

The average annual temperature is about 8°C, but at these altitudes winter temperatures can fall to -25°C. Since most precipitation falls in the spring and summer months (Nov.–Mar.), it snows only three to five times per year.

FLORA AND FAUNA

Most of the park's vegetation consists of high-altitude grasslands where high evaporation discourages trees and even shrubs. The slopes of its sheltered, well-watered canyons, though, support dwarf forests of *tabaquillo* (*Polylepis australis*) and *maitén* (*Maytenus boaria*), along with ferns and a host of endemics.

Its signature animal, of course, is the condor (*Vultur gryphus*), which soars overhead and breeds

high steppe of Parque Nacional Quebrada del Condorito

© WAYNE BERNHARDSON

on rocky outcrops in the canyon that bears its name. It is also, however, home to mammals like the puma and red fox (*Dusicyon culpaeus*), and a host of other birds including the red-and-black-headed turkey vultures. If hiking, watch carefully for the highly venomous pit viper *yarará ñata* (*Bothrops ammodytoides*); fortunately, most park reptiles are harmless lizards.

⛰ SENDA A LA QUEBRADA DEL CONDORITO

The most accessible sight and activity is the nine-kilometer hike, a signed trail from Paraje La Pampilla, on the highway, to Balcón Norte, the northern overlook of the Río Condorito canyon. Unlike many, if not most, mountain trails, this one starts high and descends gradually, over undulating terrain, to the edge of the Quebrada.

The Quebrada itself is a V-shaped canyon, 800 meters deep, 1.5 kilometers wide, and about 12 kilometers long; a short lateral descends through scrub forest and ferns to an overlook for the condor nesting site—colloquially known

as the **Escuela de Vuelo** (Flight School)—on the nearly vertical walls on the south side.

Hiking the trail—really an abandoned road for most of its length—takes about 2–2.5 hours one-way; carry water and snacks. While the trail is well-signed and the weather is normally clear, occasional fog banks can disrupt visibility. Note that bicycles are permitted on the trail in dry weather only.

ACCOMMODATIONS AND FOOD

The nearest hotels are in Villa Carlos Paz and in Mina Clavero, both some distance from the park. Park rangers, though, will grant permission to camp at Cañada del Hospital, near the new visitors center; Pampa Pajosa, near Balcón Norte; and at Puesto Condorito, about 20 minutes across the Río Condorito. The latter involves a steep descent and river ford.

About nine kilometers before Paraje La Pampilla, the **Fundación Cóndor** has a very respectable restaurant with standard Argentine food and regional specialties like *locro*. Campers must bring campstoves—no fires are allowed within the park.

INFORMATION

Until the new visitors center about two kilometers south of Paraje La Pampilla comes online, the main source of information is the **Fundación Cóndor,** nine kilometers east of La Pampilla. The foundation also has a Córdoba office (José J. Díaz 1036, tel. 0351/464-6537, ramallotr@arnet .com.ar or mldepi@yahoo.com.ar).

Park rangers, currently stationed at Seccional Achala about three kilometers south of La Pampilla, are exceptionally helpful. The **APN** has its Intendencia in Villa Carlos Paz (Sabat-

tini 33, tel. 03541/433371, pncondor@villacarlospaz.com.ar). There is no entry fee as yet, but this could change.

GETTING THERE

Contact travel agencies in Córdoba or the Fundación Cóndor for guided excursions to the park. Otherwise, it's possible to take the **Ciudad de Córdoba buses** (tel. 0351/428-2811) from Córdoba to La Pampilla (about 1.5 hours) at 10:30 A.M., and 1:15, 4:45, 7:30, and 11:20 P.M.; return buses pass La Pampilla at 12:30, 2:40, 4, 6:30, and 8:30 P.M. Schedules can change, however, so visitors should verify times. These buses can also be caught in Villa Carlos Paz.

Northern Patagonia

On a bridge over the Río Colorado in southern Buenos Aires Province, midway between Bahía Blanca and the Río Negro, a roadside sign reading "Patagonia Starts Here" marks the boundary of southernmost South America's vast, legendary region. No other part on the continent—not even Amazonia—excites the imagination like it. Ever since Magellan's chronicler Antonio Pigafetta reported encounters with a giant "so tall that the tallest among us reached only to his waist," the unknown southern latitudes have projected a mystique that's been a mixture of anticipation and apprehension.

Geographically, Patagonia is more diverse than simple statistics would suggest, with its long Atlantic coastline, boundless steppes, and Andean lakes, forests, and peaks. Many of the country's finest wildlife sites and national parks

Must-Sees

M **Volcán Lanín:** In the northernmost sector of Argentina's fabled lake district, this snow-capped peak is one of the region's most recognizable summits and the centerpiece of **Parque Nacional Lanín** (page 399).

M **Parque Nacional Los Arrayanes:** *Arrayán* forests are the highlight of this park on the shore of Lago Nahuel Huapi. The upscale town of **Villa la Angostura** provides easy access (page 402).

M **Centro Cívico:** The buildings around this square in **San Carlos de Bariloche** represent the best of Argentine Patagonia's architecture, setting a standard for the entire lake district with their steep roofs and arched *recovas* (page 407).

M **Lago Nahuel Huapi:** This glacial lake is the centerpiece of **Parque Nacional Nahuel Huapi,** one of Argentina's most-visited national parks.

From the alluring lakeshore, the parkland rises to the forests, pinnacles, and icefields of some of the Andes' most accessible scenery (page 417).

M **Feria Artesanal:** This thrice-weekly market surrounding Plaza Pagano in **El Bolsón** is the perfect place to find local crafts and sample regional food and drink (page 421).

M **Cerro Piltriquitrón:** This 2,284-meter granite summit rises east of Bolsón, where a clear day reveals snow-covered peaks along the Chilean border. There's a parking area at 1,200 meters, with a forest of 25 stump sculptures nearby (page 424).

M **Circuito Lacustre:** The most popular excursion in **Parque Nacional Los Alerces** is this lake circuit, by boat and by foot, starting at Puerto Limonao, on the south end of Lago Futalaufquen, and ending at Puerto Sagrario (page 434).

Northern Patagonia

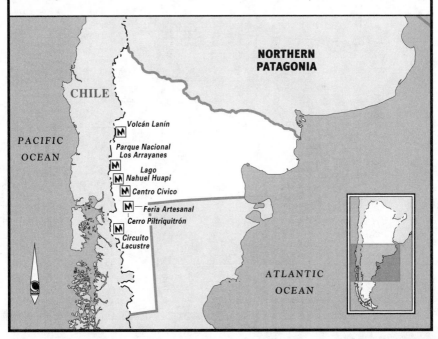

NORTHERN PATAGONIA

CHILE

PACIFIC OCEAN

M Volcán Lanín

M Parque Nacional Los Arrayanes

M Lago Nahuel Huapi

M Centro Cívico

M Feria Artesanal
Cerro Piltriquitrón

M Circuito Lacustre

ATLANTIC OCEAN

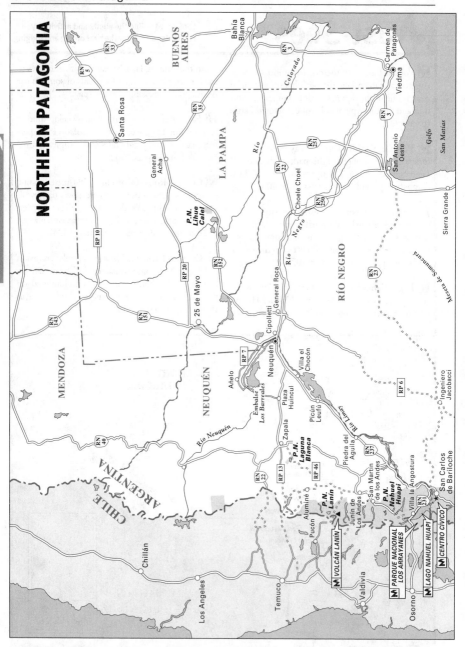

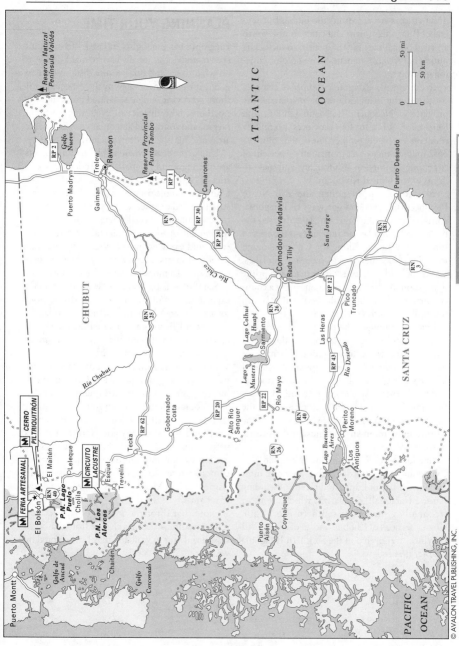

draw visitors from around the globe, but several of Patagonia's towns and cities are also worth a visit. Though they vary in quality, an increasing number of *estancias* (ranches) have become enticing getaways.

In Argentina, Patagonia comprises the area south of the Río Colorado, primarily the provinces of Neuquén, Río Negro, Chubut, and Santa Cruz. While the four provinces' 1.6 million residents are barely 4.5 percent of the country's 36.2 million, they cover more than 27 percent of Argentine territory, an area roughly equivalent to Texas or the United Kingdom.

Between them, Neuquén and Río Negro Provinces, the overland gateways to Patagonia, contain most of the Argentine lake district, the traditionally popular vacation area on the eastern slope of the Andes. Along the Chilean border, its alpine peaks and glaciers, indigo finger lakes, and thick Valdivian forests have made it a prime destination for decades; if Patagonia were a country, its logical capital might be the Río Negro resort of San Carlos de Bariloche.

Together, though, the two provinces extend from the Andes to the Atlantic, and the coastal zone features the colonial city of Carmen de Patagones and the Río Negro provincial capital of Viedma, as well as a scattering of wildlife reserves and beach resorts. An energy storehouse for its petroleum reserves and hydroelectric resources, the intervening steppe is also the site of some of the world's most momentous dinosaur discoveries of recent decades.

In addition to Río Negro and Neuquén, this chapter includes parts of Chubut Province, most notably the city of Esquel and vicinity, including Parque Nacional Los Alerces, which are most frequently visited from southern Río Negro. Coastal sections of Chubut, and all of Santa Cruz Province, are covered in the Southern Patagonia chapter that follows.

PLANNING YOUR TIME

Patagonia has highlights to last a lifetime, but even repeat visitors usually have to make decisions on what to see and do. Because distances are so great, it's often necessary to fly, especially for those who visit widely separated areas like the northerly lake district of Neuquén and Río Negro, and southern Patagonia's coastal wildlife areas and massive Andean glaciers.

Unlike the coast, where sights and settlements are often few and far apart, the Andean lake district of Neuquén, Río Negro, and northwestern Chubut is a more compact area with dense infrastructure and easy accessibility. A week here can be rewarding for special-interest visitors like fly-fishing aficionados, but general-interest travelers would easily enjoy two weeks or more, and dedicated sports-oriented travelers like climbers could spend a month or an entire summer.

San Carlos de Bariloche makes an ideal hub for excursions in and around the lake district, but towns like San Martín de los Andes, Villa la Angostura, El Bolsón and Esquel are also good choices—not to mention the lodges and *estancias* in the surrounding countryside.

In Patagonia's southerly latitudes, January and February are the most popular vacation months, but they are also the most expensive months. The shoulder months of November–December and March–April have lesser crowding, lower prices and almost equally good (and sometimes better) weather. By April, though, the days are getting significantly shorter, but the region becomes a winter destination, thanks to skiing in Bariloche, San Martín de los Andes, and a few lesser areas.

Note that throughout Patagonia, overland transportation schedules change from season to season and year to year, and may be disrupted by weather.

PATAGONIA, THEN AND NOW

For such a thinly populated territory, Patagonia has a complex, even epic history. At least 11,000 years ago, probably several thousand years earlier, the first inhabitants arrived as aboriginal hunter-gatherers who subsisted on guanaco, rhea, and other wild game, and may even have contributed to the extinction of megafauna like the ground sloth mylodon and the American horse *Onohippidium saldiasi.*

In cave sites ranging from present-day Neuquén to the tip of Tierra del Fuego, they left clues as to the peopling of Patagonia. Their successors painted vivid evidence of their way of life in rocky overhangs like Cueva de las Manos, in Santa Cruz Province. These were essentially self-sufficient bands; only much later, around A.D. 1000, does ceramic evidence indicate contact between northernmost Patagonia and the central Andean civilizations.

The first encounter between Europeans and Patagonia took place in 1520, when Magellan's crew wintered at what is now Puerto San Julián, before rounding Cape Horn on the first circumnavigation of the globe. This was a cordial meeting, but many succeeding encounters were not.

The word Patagonia itself is a matter of confusion. One explanation is that it derived from the Tehuelches's supposedly oversized feet, but the Spanish word *pata* more correctly means "paw." More probably, it came from the Spanish romance *Primaleón,* in which a giant named Patagón inhabits an island of fur-wearing hunter-gatherers.

Though little-explored, the northern Patagonian interior was also a source of tall tales like the kingdom of Trapalanda or Trapananda, a southern city of gold (ironically enough, real marvels like the Moreno Glacier remained unseen by Europeans until the 19th century). If Patagonia was a source of tall tales, though, it also saw scientifically serious expeditions, like those of Englishman John Narborough, Frenchman Louis de Bougainville, Spaniard Alejandro Malaspina, and of course, Darwin on the *Beagle.* It was Darwin, in fact, who credibly debunked the lingering legends of "Patagonian giants":

> *We had an interview at Cape Gregory with the famous so-called gigantic Patagonians, who gave us cordial reception. Their height appears greater than it really is, from their large guanaco mantles, their long flowing hair, and general figure; on an average their height is about six feet, with some men taller and only a few shorter; and the women are also tall; altogether they are certainly the tallest race which we anywhere saw.*

The Conquest of Patagonia

In immediate pre-Columbian times, the semi-sedentary Mapuche and their allies crossed the northern Patagonian Andes freely, occupying Tehuelche territory and mixing with them, and they continued to do so after the Spanish invasion. Acquisition of the Old World horse, which the Mapuche soon mastered, allowed them to keep their autonomy even as the Spaniards and then the Argentines advanced southward from the pampas. After Darwin met the dictator Rosas, he sorrowfully foretold the demise of the aborigines:

> *Every one here is fully convinced that this is the justest war, because it is against barbarians. Who would believe that in this age in a Christian civilised country that such atrocities were committed? . . . Great as it is, in another half century I think there will not be a wild Indian in the Pampas north of Río Negro.*

continued on next page

PATAGONIA, THEN AND NOW (cont'd)

The Argentines and their European immigrant allies advanced on several fronts, by differing means. In the 1860s foreign minister Guillermo Rawson struck a deal to grant Welsh dissidents farms in coastal Chubut, from where they moved westward up the river to the Andes. Not long after, with land grants from the Argentine government, Scottish settlers from the Falkland Islands began to conquer Santa Cruz with sheep.

In 1879—proving Darwin's prescience—General Julio Argentino Roca began his so-called *Conquista del Desierto* (Conquest of the Desert) to displace the Mapuche of Neuquén and Río Negro in favor of settlers' cattle and sheep. The subsequent arrival of the railway from the coast accelerated the process and opened the fertile Río Negro Valley to agricultural development.

Patagonia Today

Today, thanks to fishing, industrial preferences, and tourism, Patagonia (including Tierra del Fuego) is Argentina's fastest-growing region, with the most positive demographic indicators. Since 1980, Tierra del Fuego's population has nearly quadrupled, while Neuquén has nearly doubled. Santa Cruz has grown 70 percent, Chubut 57 percent.

Patagonia now has the highest employment rates outside of Buenos Aires, the highest mean monthly income at US$245, the lowest poverty rates at 18.5 percent, lowest mortality rate at 4.7 per thousand (the nationwide figure is 7.4), the lowest rate of death by heart disease and infection, and the lowest infant mortality. It has the highest percentage rate of potable water and sewer service, and the highest literacy rates.

Ironically, the Argentine economic implosion of 2001–02 revived the wool industry, as the new exchange rate made Argentine wool more competitive internationally; at the former one-to-one rate with the U.S. dollar, production costs were impossibly high. At the same time, Australia's depleted wool stocks raised demand elsewhere, and oil-price increases made wool more competitive with petroleum-based fibers: Prices that were US$3 per kilogram rose to US$9 per kilogram and, in pesos terms, earnings quadrupled. In 2002, mutton exports in Santa Cruz doubled to about US$500 million, thanks partly to worries about mad cow disease in Europe. A delegation of rabbis even visited Río Gallegos to explore the idea of setting up a kosher slaughterhouse for exports to Israel.

Before World War II, Santa Cruz Province had had 1,500 *estancias* with 7.5 million sheep, a figure which fell in the 1990s from four million on 1,200 to two million on 600. After a series of bad winters and an unforeseen natural disaster in the ash-laden 1992 eruption of Chile's Volcán Hudson, some farms were abandoned. Some economically desperate *estancieros* may have even set fires to collect on insurance, and even burned down outbuildings to avoid their designation as historic structures they would have been obliged to maintain without economic assistance.

Many of the beneficiaries of the new boom have been foreign companies who bought the best properties at bargain prices. In Santa Cruz, sheep still outnumber humans by ten to one, and Patagonia's largest wool producer, the Italian conglomerate Benetton, owns flagship ranches like Estancia El Cóndor near Río Gallegos. In total, Benetton runs about 280,000 sheep on 900,000 hectares.

Devaluation also made tourism competitive. For much of the 1990s, Argentines took their vacations in Chile or other "inexpensive" countries like the United States, but the exchange rate trend has totally reversed, so that Chileans and other foreigners are flocking to Patagonia. The summers of 2003 and 2004 were a bonanza for Patagonian tourism, and increased demand may result in rising prices.

Coastal Río Negro Province

CARMEN DE PATAGONES

On the north bank of the Río Negro, founded in 1779, Carmen de Patagones was once the farthest outpost of the Spanish empire in what is now Argentina, and it's the only Patagonian city that can legitimately claim a colonial heritage. Modern "Patagones" is also the most southerly city in Buenos Aires Province, but the Río Negro capital of Viedma on the south bank, with which it forms a significantly larger metropolitan area, has a wider variety of hotels, restaurants, and other services.

Befitting its dual heritage, the city's name is a blend of the indigenous (Patagones, after the region's aborigines) and the European (after its patron, the Virgen del Carmen). The original Spanish colonists came from Maragatería, in the province of León; in 1827, in the conflict over the buffer state of Uruguay, their descendents fended off Brazilian invaders. Locals still go by the nickname of *maragatos.*

Orientation

Carmen de Patagones (population 18,095) is 279 kilometers south of Bahía Blanca and 915 kilometers south of Buenos Aires via RN 3, the coastal highway that continues west and then south to Chubut, Santa Cruz, and Tierra del Fuego. Two bridges connect it to Viedma, but most locals commute via the frequent launches that shuttle across the river. Most points of interest are between the river and the Centro Cívico on Plaza 7 de Marzo, two blocks inland.

Sights

Patagones's most conspicuous landmark, the twin towers of the Salesian-built **Iglesia Parroquial Nuestra Señora del Carmen** (1883) rise above the west side of **Plaza 7 de Marzo,** which commemorates the date of victory over Brazil in 1827. Immediately to the west, engineer José Pérez Brito's **Torre del Fuerte** (1780) is the sole remnant of Patagones's frontier fortifications.

Iglesia Parroquial Nuestra Señora del Carmen, Carmen de Patagones

Immediately south of the tower, between a set of antique cannons, the broad staircase of **Pasaje San José de Mayo** descends to the adobe **Rancho de Rial** (1820), home of the town's first elected mayor. One block east, dating from 1823, the restored **Casa de la Cultura** (Mitre 27) was once a flourmill. Immediately across the street, fitted with period furniture, the 19th-century **Casona La Carlota** (Bynon and Mitre) is open for guided tours; contact the museum for details.

To the south, on the flood-prone waterfront, the restored **Mazzini & Giraudini** was a thriving merchant house in the early 20th century. The adjacent open space of **Parque Piedra Buena** was once the home of naval hero and Patagonian/South Atlantic explorer Luis Piedra Buena; a

Northern Patagonia

block west, the **Casa Histórica del Banco de la Provincia de Buenos Aires** (J.J. Biedma 64), the former provincial bank, is now the regional history museum.

At Patagones's historical museum, **Museo Histórico Regional Emma Nozzi,** a stereotypically chauvinistic attitude—the unspoken but unmistakable notion that General Roca's 19th-century "Conquest of the Desert" was a greater good that justified a genocidal war against the native peoples of Patagonia—undercuts the quality of its pre-Columbian artifacts. In context, its most interesting exhibit is the so-called **Cueva Maragata,** one of several riverbank excavations that sheltered the first Spanish colonists. There are other examples of these caves five blocks west of Plaza 7 de Marzo.

The building itself has served a variety of roles, ranging from a naval-stores depot to a girls' school to branches of Banco de la Provincia and Banco de la Nación to commercial locales. Banco de la Provincia restored the structure, which suffered serious flood damage in 1899, for use as a museum in 1984; a series of historical photographs displays the flood's devastation, which caused the evacuation of lower-lying Viedma.

Immediately opposite the dock for launches to and from Viedma, the Museo Histórico (J.J. Biedma 64, tel. 02920/462729, US$.35) is open 9 A.M.–noon weekdays only and 7–9 P.M. daily except Sunday December–February. The rest of the year, hours are 10 A.M.–noon and 2:30–4:30 P.M. weekdays, 7–9 P.M. Saturday only.

Entertainment and Events

The **Cine Garibaldi** (España 206) shows recent films.

Carmen holds its annual **Fiesta del 7 de Marzo,** commemorating the date of the victory over Brazilian forces, the entire first week of March. Most festivities take place on Plaza Villarino, four blocks north of Plaza 7 de Marzo.

Accommodations and Food

Viedma has a bigger and better selection of hotels and restaurants, but there are adequate shoe-string accommodations at **Residencial Reggiani** (Bynon 422, tel. 02920/464137, US$6/10 s/d

with private bath), a basic older home opposite Plaza Villarino. The Francophile-style **Hotel Percaz** (Comodoro Rivadavia 384, tel. 02920/ 464104, US$8/12 s/d) is drab but tidy.

Confitería Sabbatella (Rivadavia 218) is ideal for breakfast, coffee, or sandwiches. **Pizzería Neptuno** (Rivadavia 310) sells the obvious, while the riverfront **Rigoletto** (J.J. Biedma 10) serves seafood.

Information and Services

The **Dirección Municipal de Turismo** (Bynon 186, tel. 02920/461777, int. 253, subcom @patagones.mun.gba.gov.ar) is helpful and well-stocked with maps and brochures. Summer hours are 7 A.M.–9 P.M. weekdays, 10 A.M.–1 P.M. and 6–9 P.M. weekends; the rest of the year hours are 7 A.M.–7 P.M. weekdays only.

Banco de la Nación (Paraguay 2) has an ATM at the southeast corner of Plaza 7 de Marzo. **Correo Argentino** (Paraguay 38) is immediately to the east; the postal code is 8504. **Locutorio Patagones** (Olivera 9) is on the south side of Plaza 7 de Mayo.

Getting There and Around

Services to and from Patagones's **Terminal de Ómnibus** (Barbieri and Méjico, tel. 02920/ 462666), two blocks north and three blocks east of Plaza 7 de Marzo, are less frequent than those to and from Viedma; many long-distance buses stop at both, however.

Balsas (passenger launches) travel to and from Viedma cross the river every few minutes.

VIEDMA

While it lacks Patagones's colonial character, fast-growing Viedma long ago surpassed the older city in services and significance, as it's the capital of the Río Negro despite its distance from other population centers in this Atlantic-to-the-Andes province. Locals swim and kayak along its upgraded, willow-shaded riverfront, with its new riverside *parrilla* restaurants and sailing school.

Founded simultaneously with Patagones, in 1779, Viedma became the de facto capital of

Patagonia exactly a century later and then, following the "Conquest of the Desert," capital of Río Negro territory, though the capital was relocated briefly to Choele Choel after the flood of 1899. In 1955, it became capital of the new province of Río Negro and, in the 1980s, President Raúl Alfonsín tried to transfer the federal capital here from Buenos Aires—a foolishly visionary boondoggle that, fortunately, never came to be.

Orientation

Viedma (population 46,767) is 280 kilometers south of Bahía Blanca and 439 kilometers north of Puerto Madryn via the coastal highway RN 3. It is 982 kilometers east of Bariloche, Río Negro's largest city, via Neuquén on a series of paved highways through the Río Negro Valley.

Like most Argentine cities, Viedma has a regular grid, but there are at least separate activity zones: the waterfront Costanera Avenida Villarino and its Centro Cívico; the provincial government center around Plaza San Martín, four blocks southwest; and the traditional Plaza Alsina, several blocks south of the Centro Cívico. Street names change on either side of Colón, which runs roughly northeast-southwest, except for the diagonal Buenos Aires, which is continuous between 25 de Mayo and Yrigoyen.

Sights

On the southwest side of **Plaza Alsina,** the entire block bounded by Yrigoyen, Colón, Rivadavia, and Alvaro Barros is a national historical monument dating from the 1880s, when the Salesian order first installed itself here. Among its works were the Italian-built **Vicariato Apostólico de la Patagonia Septentrional** (Vicarage of Southern Patagonia, 1883–1897); Padre Juan Aceto envisioned its neo-Renaissance brick facade and tower.

For many years, the structure served as the **Colegio San Francisco de Sales,** a boys' school, and an orphanage. Since 1975, it has been the **Centro Histórico Cultural Salesiano,** comprising two separate museums: the **Museo Salesiano Cardenal Cagliero** (Rivadavia 34, 8 A.M.–1 P.M. daily), which presents the Salesian viewpoint on

evangelizing the Patagonian frontier, and the **Museo Tecnológico del Agua y del Suelo** (Colón 498, 1st floor, tel. 02920/431569, 4–6:30 P.M. daily), which focuses on the role of irrigation in the province.

Part of the same complex but facing Plaza Alsina, the **Catedral de la Merced** (1912) replaced an earlier church that came down after the flood of 1899; alongside it, the neoclassical **Obispado de Viedma** (Bishopric of Viedma, 1945) replaced the **Hospital de San José.**

Key provincial public buildings cluster around Plaza San Martín, including the **Casa de Gobierno** (Government House), the dignified **Residencia del Gobernador** (Governor's Residence), and the **Legislatura Provincial,** a hideous deco high-rise. On the north side of the plaza, the **Museo Gobernador Eugenio Tello** (San Martín 263, tel. 0290/425900, 9 A.M.–12:30 P.M. and 5–9:30 P.M.) is an archaeological and secular historical museum.

Daily except Monday at 5 P.M., the catamaran *Curru Leuvu II* (the aboriginal name for the Río Negro) offers 1.5-hour excursions (US$2 adults, US$1 children to age 12) on the river from the **Muelle de Lanchas,** at the foot of 25 de Mayo.

Entertainment and Events

Viedma's craftsworkers operate an informal **Mercado Artesanal** on Plaza Alsina. For wines, try the large selection at **La Bodega de Marzio** (San Martín 319, tel. 02920/422087).

Viedma's biggest annual event is January's **Regata del Río Negro** (www.regatadelrionegro .com.ar), whose highlight is a 500-kilometer kayak race beginning in Neuquén. It bills itself as "the longest regatta in the world."

Accommodations

Across RN 3 on the west side of town, the well-kept waterside **Camping Municipal** (tel. 02920/421341, US$1.50 pp, plus US$1.50 per tent) offers some shade, hot showers, clean toilets, and mosquitoes.

Residencial Luis Eduardo (Sarmiento 366, tel. 02920/420669, US$7/11 s/d with breakfast) offers good shoestring value.

Viedma's biggest surprise is the former Hotel Nuevo Roma, a dreary place literally rejuvenated as the **Hotel Spa Inside Patagónico** (25 de Mayo 174, tel. 02920/430459, US$11 pp), a work in progress that includes a pool, sauna, and gym; it also offers personal trainers, dance classes, massage, and even cellulitis treatment.

Overlooking Plaza Alsina, the utilitarian **Hotel Peumayén** (Buenos Aires 334, tel. 02920/425222, fax 02920/425243, US$10/16 s/d with cash or US$12/17 s/d with credit card) is a decent choice with carpeted rooms, a/c, parking, TV, and the usual.

Friendly **Hotel Nijar** (Mitre 490, tel. 02920/422833, nijarh@arnet.com.ar, US$14/19 s/d; 10 percent discount for cash) is a comfortable, immaculate modern hotel with good service, parking, breakfast, and other amenities. Overlooking the river is the four-star **Hotel Austral** (Avenida Villarino 292, tel. 02920/422615, paradoresviedma@infovia.com.ar, www.hoteles-austral.com.ar, US$24/28 s/d).

Food

El Nuevo Munich (Buenos Aires 161, tel. 02920/421108) has pizza, substantial sandwiches, and draft beer. **Camila's Café** (Buenos Aires and Saavedra) is a good choice for coffee and desserts.

Sahara Pizza & Pasta (Saavedra 326, tel. 02920/15-607790) is Viedma's most popular pizzeria, but **Los Tíos** (Belgrano 265, tel. 02920/422790) runs a close second. For *parrillada*, try **El Tío** (Avenida Zatti and Colón).

Best along the riverside, ideal for lunch beneath the willows, **La Balsa** (Avenida Villarino 55, tel. 02920/431974) specializes in fish and seafood at moderate prices. **El Náutico** (Avenida Villarino 207, tel. 0290/430086) is a waterside pizzeria.

The most promising development in Viedma's culinary scene is the ambitious **Ⓝ Capriasca** (Alvaro Barros 685, tel. 02920/426754), with diverse entrees (US$4–5) that include pastas, Patagonian lamb, beef, and seafood; the bittersweet chocolate mousse is a good dessert choice. The kitchen is prompt and the rehabbed period house, its walls partly opened to reveal its struc-

ture and the rest painted in pastels, is a plus, but it suffers from an out-of-the-way location.

Fiore Helados (Buenos Aires and Aguiar) serves fine ice cream.

Information

The riverfront **Oficina de Informes Turísticos** (Villarino s/n between Colón and Alvaro Barros), though it's open 8 A.M.–8 P.M. daily in summer, seems to operate on automatic pilot. Winter hours are 9 A.M.–1 P.M. and 4–8 P.M. daily. There's also an office at the bus terminal.

The provincial **Secretaría de Turismo** (Avenida Caseros 1425, tel. 02920/422150, www.rionegrotur.com.ar) provides information and printed matter for the entire province.

For motorists, **ACA** is at RN 3 Km 692 (tel. 02920/422441).

Services

Banco Patagonia (Buenos Aires 184) and several others have ATMs. **Tritón Turismo** (Namuncurá 78, tel. 02920/430129) changes money, rents cars, and arranges excursions.

Correo Argentino is at Rivadavia 151; the postal code is 8500. **Telefónica** has a *locutorio* at Mitre 531, while **Inter.com Servicios** (Saavedra 213) provides Internet access.

Lavandería Automática Siglo XXI (Mitre 343) does the laundry.

For medical emergencies, try **Hospital Artémides Zatti** (Avenida Rivadavia 351, tel. 02920/422333).

Getting There

Austral (Guido 398, tel. 02920/423033) flies Thursday to Bahía Blanca and Aeroparque. **LADE** (Saavedra 403, tel. 02920/424420) flies Wednesday and Thursday to Puerto Madryn, Trelew, and Comodoro Rivadavia, and Friday to Bahía Blanca, Mar del Plata, and Aeroparque. **Sapsa** (San Martín 57, tel. 02920/421330) flies occasionally to Bariloche.

Sefepa (Cagliero s/n, tel. 02920/422130, www.trenpatagonico.com.ar) connects Estación Viedma, on the southeast edge of town, with Bariloche via **train** Monday and Friday at 6 P.M. The 15-hour trip costs US$7 in hard-backed *turista,* US$18 in reclining Pullman, or US$28 in *camarote* sleepers; children 5 to 12 pay half.

Viedma's **Terminal de Ómnibus** (Guido 1580, tel. 02920/426850) is 13 blocks south of downtown, at the corner of Avenida General Perón.

Sample destinations, fares, and times include Las Grutas (US$3.50, 2.5 hours), Bahía Blanca (US$5.50, 3.5 hours), Puerto Madryn (US$9, five hours), Trelew (US$9.50, 5.5 hours), Neuquén (US$16, nine hours), Esquel (US$16, 10 hours), La Plata (US$20, 12 hours), Comodoro Rivadavia (US$18, 11 hours), Buenos Aires (US$21–25, 12 hours), Bariloche (US$19, 14 hours), and Río Gallegos (US$29, 20 hours).

Getting Around

There is no bus service to **Aeropuerto Gobernador Castello** (tel. 02920/425311), which is five kilometers south of town on RP 51, but a cab or *remise* costs only about US$2.50.

On-demand *balsas* leave the Muelle de Lanchas for Carmen de Patagones from the Muelle de Lanchas at the foot of 25 de Mayo, from 7 A.M.–8 P.M. weekdays.

Tritón Turismo (Namuncurá 78, tel. 02920/430129) is the only car rental option.

GOLFO SAN MATÍAS AND VICINITY

From Viedma, RN 3 turns west and slightly inland toward the port of San Antonio Oeste, paralleling the shoreline of the Golfo San Matías, but day-trippers and visitors with their own vehicles should consider a detour along coastal RP 1. Here, about 30 kilometers east of Viedma at the mouth of the Río Negro, **Balneario El Cóndor** draws beachgoers from the provincial capital; there are decent accommodations at **Hospedaje Río de los Sauces** (tel. 02920/497193, US$11/14 s/d) and several seafood restaurants. From Viedma's Plaza Alsina, Empresa Ceferino (tel. 02920/424542) has five buses daily (US$.65).

Buses and RP 1 continue another 30 kilometers to **La Lobería,** where the **Reserva Faunística Provincial Punta Bermeja** protects a colony of some 4,000 southern sea lions (*Otaria flavescens*), present all year; the scenic coastline is also a prime bird-watching area. There is a visitors center, a *confitería* for light meals, and exposed tent sites at **Camping La Lobería** (tel. 02920/428883, US$1 pp and per tent).

West of La Lobería, the pavement ends but the RP 1 scenery improves to include massive dunes at **Bahía Creek** (for secluded camping) and another sea lion colony at **Reserva Provincial Caleta de los Loros;** fishing is also popular. Here, at Punta Mejillón, the highway swerves inland, where it's possible to return to RN 3 via unpaved RP 52, or else continue west toward San Antonio Este, where paved RN 251 also turns north to RN 3.

Some 187 kilometers west of Viedma but east of RN 3, hordes of summer and weekend visitors converge on the beach resort of **Las Grutas** (permanent population 2,708), so called because of the wave-eroded grottoes that have penetrated the sedimentary headlands. Because of Las Grutas' phenomenal tidal range, the available beachfront can recede to just tens of meters, making it suitable for only the most gregarious beachgoers. There are nearly a hundred hotels, *hospedajes* and campgrounds; for suggestions, visit the **Secretaría Municipal de Turismo** in the Galería Antares (Primera Bajada s/n, tel. 02934/497470). Las Grutas has frequent bus links to San Antonio Oeste, 12 kilometers northeast.

About 125 kilometers south of San Antonio Oeste and 140 kilometers north of Puerto Madryn, RN 3 passes through **Sierra Grande** (population 6,768), a onetime iron-mining town that is the northernmost point to purchase gasoline at Patagonian discount prices—at least a third cheaper than in Las Grutas or San Antonio Oeste. Southbound drivers should nurse their fuel to get here, while the northbound should top off the tank.

While the mine has closed, the highway helps keep Sierra Grande alive, filling its modest hotels and simple roadside restaurants. In an attempt to encourage stopovers, the municipality has promoted descents into the inoperative iron mine once run by **Hierro Patagónico Rionegrino** (Hiparsa). These cost around US$5 pp, with discounts for children; for details, contact **Hotel Jarillal** (RN 3 Km 1270, tel. 02934/481095, hoteljarillal@infovia.com.ar). The **Subsecretaría de Turismo** (Calle 2 No 300, tel. 02934/15-447776) can also provide information.

NEUQUÉN

Capital of its namesake province, Neuquén is primarily a gateway city to the northern Patagonian lake district, but it's also an ideal base for visiting a triangle of dinosaur sites to the northwest, west, and southwest. At the confluence of two major rivers, once a major railroad junction, it's a clean contemporary city that benefits from its proximity to the agricultural plenty of the upper Río Negro Valley, its abundant energy resources, and its productive financial sector.

Orientation

At the confluence of the Río Neuquén and the Río Limay, Neuquén (population 201,729) is 537 kilometers east of Bahía Blanca via RN 22, 559 kilometers southwest of Santa Rosa via a series of paved highways, and 429 kilometers northeast of San Carlos de Bariloche via RN 237. It is also the main access point to destinations like Aluminé, in the little-visited northernmost part of the lake district. Note that RN 22 through the upper Río Negro Valley and west toward Zapala is a narrow highway with heavy truck traffic and many dangerously impatient drivers.

Most points of interest and services lie north of Félix San Martín, the main east-west thoroughfare (also known as RN 22); the main north-south street is Avenida Argentina/Avenida Olascoaga; street names change on either side of Avenida Argentina and either side of the old railroad station, which is now the Parque Central. North of the Parque Central, several diagonals complicate the otherwise regular grid.

Sights

Pretty much all of Neuquén's sights are in the **Parque Central,** the recycled railyard bounded by Avenida San Martín/Avenida Independencia on the north, Salta/Manuel Láinez to the west, Tu-

cumán/Tierra del Fuego on the east, and Sarmiento/Mitre on the south.

Occupying the 1902 repair shed for the Ferrocarril del Sud, **Museo Nacional de Bellas Artes** (Avenida San Martín and Brown, 9 A.M.–9 P.M. weekdays, 6–10 P.M. weekends, US$.35) is now a branch of the national fine arts museum, with rotating exhibits of painting, sculpture, and other plastic arts. It is due, however, to be replaced by a nearby and more contemporary facility.

Just north of the bus terminal, the **Sala de Arte Emilio Saraco** (Avenida Olascoaga s/n, tel. 0299/449-1200, int. 4490) occupies the railroad station's former cargo terminal, with exhibits of contemporary art. Hours are 9 A.M.–8 P.M. weekdays, 4–8 P.M. weekends; admission is free. Just across the tracks to the north, **Juntarte en el Andén** is an outdoor art space at the former passenger terminal.

Two blocks east, the **Museo de la Ciudad Paraje Confluencia** (Avenida Independencia and Córdoba, 8 A.M.–9 P.M. weekdays, 6–10 P.M. weekends and holidays, free) traces Neuquén's cultural evolution and history from its earliest archaeological sites through the first European contact, the development of the Mapuche nation, and their resistance to General Roca's euphemistically named "Conquest of the Desert."

Entertainment and Events

La Casona (Alvear 59) is a bar with live music some nights. For current films, there's the **Cine Teatro Español** (Avenida Argentina 271, tel. 0299/442-2048).

January's annual **Regata del Río Negro** is a 500-kilometer kayak marathon that starts here and ends a week later in Viedma.

Shopping

Near Avenida Independencia and Avenida Argentina, the Parque Central's **Paseo de los Artesanos** (Vuelta de Obligado s/n) is open 10 A.M.–9 P.M. daily except Monday and Tuesday.

The province of Neuquén sponsors **Artesanías Neuquinas** (San Martín 57, tel. 0299/442-3806, www.artesaniasneuquen.com.ar), which has an excellent, diverse crafts selection at reasonable prices. **Cardón** (Avenida Argentina 392, tel.

0299/448-0155) sells leather goods, *mates,* and silverwork. **Artesanías Mapuches** (Roca 62, tel. 0299/443-2155) focuses on indigenous crafts, primarily silverwork.

Accommodations

Oddly enough, nearly all of Neuquén's accommodations lie in the somewhat scruffy but not unsafe retail area between RN 22 and the bus terminal.

Under US$10

On the banks of the Río Limay on the south side of town lies Neuquén's **Camping Municipal** (Obreros Argentinos and Copahue, tel. 0299/448-5228, US$1 pp plus US$1.50 per tent). Closed in the winter months, it's easily reached by *colectivo* No. 103.

US$10–25

Residencial Inglés (Félix San Martín 534, tel. 0299/442-2252, US$5.50/9 s/d) is quiet, clean, and family-run, but rates do not include breakfast. Rooms at friendly, centrally located **Residencial Belgrano** (Rivadavia 283, tel. 0299/4480612, US$6.50/11 s/d) are small—some claustrophobically so—but also immaculate.

Modernized **Hotel Alcorta** (Ministro Alcorta 84, tel. 0299/442-2652, hostaldos@infovia.com.ar, US$7.50/11 s/d) has the most-contemporary conveniences, but lacks the intangibles. **Hotel Ideal** (Avenida Olascoaga 243, tel. 0299/442-2431, hotelidealneuquen@yahoo.com.ar, US$10/17 s/d) has clean, comfortable rooms with breakfast, parking and modern amenities.

Rooms at family-run **Residencial del Neuquén** (Roca 109, tel. 0299/442-2403, macaflo@infovia.com.ar, US$12/16 s/d) are also very small, but it's spotless with breakfast, cable TV, and private bath. Rooms at **Hotel Charbel** (San Luis 268, tel. 0299/442-4143, hotelcharbel@hotmail.com, US$12/16 s/d) are clean and substantially larger, with most conveniences, and a bar/restaurant.

The classic **Hotel Iberia** (Avenida Olascoaga 294, tel. 0299/442-2372, luislo@neunet.com.ar, US$12/22 s/d) has tidy, ample rooms with basic conveniences.

US$25–50

Remodeled three-star **Hotel Royal** (Avenida Argentina 145, tel. 0299/442-2408, hotelroyal@arnet.com.ar, US$23/32 s/d) has large rooms and baths, with cable TV and breakfast included; there's also a 10 percent cash discount.

Neuquén's best value may be the nearly new **M Hotel El Prado** (Perito Moreno 484, tel. 0299/448-6000, hotelelprado@hotmail.com, US$21/33 s/d), which has large, well-furnished rooms with private bath, a/c, cable TV, telephone, key cards, and Internet-access jacks. In addition, there's an abundant buffet breakfast and superb service.

Over US$50

Downtown, four-star **Hotel del Comahue** (Avenida Argentina 387, tel. 0299/442-2439, reservas@hotelcomahue.com.ar, US$48/54 s/d) is the pick of the litter, and also offers 10 percent cash discounts.

Food

Neuquén is strong on pizza and pasta, at places like the traditional **La Mamma** (9 de Julio 56, tel. 0299/442-5291), **El Sótano** (Brown 162, tel. 0299/443-1122), **La Tartaruga** (Roca 193, tel. 0299/443-6880), and the more fashionable **Vuestra Pizzería** (Yrigoyen 90, tel. 442-8888). **Franz y Peppone** (9 de Julio and Belgrano, tel. 0299/448-3399) is a blend of the Teutonic and the Mediterranean.

La Obra (9 de Julio 70, tel. 0299/447-3137) is a leading *parrilla,* while **La Tejuela** (Alberdi 59, tel. 0299/443-7114) has a beef and seafood menu. **Pasty** (Félix San Martín 246, tel. 0299/4435860) serves fine, fairly priced pasta and chicken dishes, with well-intentioned but inconsistent service; the sidewalk seating is a mixed blessing, as the highway runs almost alongside it.

Decorated in soothing pastels, **M Mediterráneo** (Avenida Argentina 584, tel. 0299/442-9325) lives up to its name in both food and decor, with an exceptional Middle Eastern and Mediterranean buffet of appetizers; the seafood and succulent meat entrees run about US$6–9. This is Neuquén's one real can't-miss dining choice.

NEUQUÉN'S DINOSAUR TRIANGLE

Where there's oil, there are dinosaurs, and Neuquén's sedimentary steppe is one of Argentina's late-Cretaceous hot spots. By rental car, a triangle of sites northwest, west, and southwest of the provincial capital makes an ideal (if long) full-day excursion, though one of these, Lago Barreales, is more difficult to reach and open only in the fall and winter months. The other two, Plaza Huincul and Villa El Chocón, are easily accessible by public transportation.

Centro Paleontológico Lago Barreales

The best place to see an on-site excavation is this reservoir northwest of Neuquén, where paleontologists demonstrate the separation and rescue of fossils deposits, as well as the cleaning and extraction of the fossils themselves. Beasts in the sediments here include the sauropod *Futalognkosaurus* (a long-tailed quadruped with a long neck and small head), teropods (bipedal carnivores with huge claws such as *Megaraptor*), and ornithopods (small bipedal herbivores), as well as bivalves, crocodiles, turtles, and pterosaurs.

Only when the water level falls in autumn, usually in early April, can the Museo de Geología y Paleontología de la Universidad Nacional del Comahue, under the direction of Jorge Calvo, resume its work, so this is the ideal time to go. The long-term plan is to create an open-air dinosaur park in the vicinity.

On the north shore of Barreales, the Centro Paleontológico Lago Barreales (RP 51 Km 65, tel. 0299/15-404-8614, info@proyectodino.com.ar, www.proyectodino.com.ar) is open 9 A.M.–

12:30 P.M. and 3–7 P.M. daily. Admission costs US$.65 for adults, US$.35 for kids under 12. Foreign university students can hire on to participate in the digs (US$420 for a week, US$700 for two weeks, tent accommodations, full board, and transportation from Neuquén included).

Actually reaching the site can complicated, but the simplest route is to take RP 7 from Cipolletti almost to Añelo, about 100 kilometers northwest of Neuquén, and then turn south on a gravel road to the north shore of Barreales. It's signed, but still not easy.

Museo Municipal Carmen Funes (Plaza Huincul)

At the oil town of Plaza Huincul, about midway between Neuquén and Zapala, the municipal museum's prize exhibit is a replica skeleton of *Argentinosaurus huinculensis*, the world's largest dinosaur at 45 meters long and 18 meters high. So large is the herbivore *A. huinculensis* that an adult male human barely reaches its knee, and one of the dorsal vertebrae measures 1.6 meters.

Former oil worker Guillermo Heredia found the fossil only three kilometers away, along the highway, in 1987. In addition to the imposing skeleton, there's a clutch of dinosaur eggs some 80 million years old, and remains of crocodiles found in Picún Leufú, about 75 kilometers to the south.

Directly on the highway, the expanding Museo Municipal Carmen Funes (Avenida Córdoba 55, tel. 0299/496-5486) is open 8:30 A.M.–8 P.M. weekdays; weekend hours are 3–7 P.M. in winter, 4–8 P.M. in summer. Admission costs US$.35. In consultation with museum director Rodolfo Coria,

---

Neuquén may not have Argentina's finest ice cream, but **Helados Las Malvinas** (Avenida Argentina 12) and **Heladería Pire** (Diagonal Alvear 29) are both above average.

Information

Directly on RN 22, the **Subsecretaría de Turismo** (Félix San Martín 182, (tel. 0299/442-4089, turismo@neuquen.gov.ar, www.neuquentur.gov.ar) is open 7 A.M.–8 P.M. weekdays, 8 A.M.–8 P.M. weekends. In terms of content, accuracy,

and usefulness, their brochures and maps are among the country's best. There is sometimes an office at the bus terminal.

For motorists, **ACA** is at Rivadavia and the diagonal 25 de Mayo (tel. 0299/442-4860).

Services

As a provincial capital, Neuquén has a full complement of services.

There are ATMs at **Banco de la Provincia de Neuquén** (Avenida Argentina 13) and several

metallurgist Omar Vejar (tel. 0299/496-0522, cell 0299/15-5884076) produces skilful scale models of Patagonian dinosaur skeletons; prices start around US$70 for the smallest items, around 30 centimeters in length.

Plaza Huincul (population 12,047), 110 kilometers west of Neuquén via RN 237 and RN 22, has an **Oficina de Información Turística** (RN 22 s/n, tel. 0299/496-7637) directly on the highway. Bus services from Neuquén are frequent and comfortable.

Museo Paleontológico Municipal Ernesto Bachmann (Villa El Chocón)

Plaza Huincul boasts the world's largest herbivore, but Villa El Chocón can claim its carnivorous counterpart in *Giganotosaurus carolinii*. On the

Pianitzskysaurus floresi, Museo Paleontológico Municipal Ernesto Bachmann

© WAYNE BERNHARDSON

shores of the Embalse Exequiel Ramos Mexía, an enormous hydroelectric reservoir southwest of Neuquén, the municipal museum also features models of *Carnotaurus* and the smaller *Pianitzkysaurus*. There are also dinosaur tracks in the vicinity.

G. carolinii takes its name from amateur paleontologist Rubén Carolini, who discovered the fossil, while Rodolfo Coria, Leonardo Salgado, and Jorge Calvo first identified it. Measuring 14 meters in length and 4.65 meters high at the hip, it weighed up to 10,000 kilograms.

Unfortunately, because the hydroelectric dam generating 3.35 million kwh per annum drowned the sedimentary canyon of the Río Limay here, many probable paleontological sites have disappeared beneath the water. The Museo Paleontológico Municipal Ernesto Bachmann (8 A.M.–9 P.M. daily, US$.35) also offers exhibits on the area's archaeology and a whitewashed history of the dam and former *estancia*-owner Manuel Bustigorry.

Villa El Chocón, 136 kilometers southwest of Neuquén via RN 237, originated as a company town during the dam's construction. The **Dirección Municipal de Turismo** (tel. 0299/490-1230), at the northern approach to town off RN 22, is open 8 A.M.–7 P.M. daily; there's a paleontological excavation site within easy walking distance.

On the shoreline, **La Posada del Dinosaurio** (tel. 0299/490-1200, fax 490-1201, posadadino @infovia.com.ar, www.posadadeldinosaurio.com, US$40 d) offers excellent accommodations, with a good, reasonably priced restaurant and outstanding service. Camping also exists nearby.

others along the same street. Neuquén has two exchange houses, **Cambio Olano** (J.B. Justo 97) and **Cambio Pullman** (Ministro Alcorta 144).

Correo Argentino is at Rivadavia and Santa Fe; the postal code is 8300.

Arlequín I (Avenida Olascoaga 222) has both telephone and Internet access, but there are many other *locutorios*.

Neighboring Chile has a consulate at La Rioja 241 (tel. 0299/442-2727). **Migraciones** is at Santiago del Estero 466 (tel. 0299/442-2061).

The travel agency **Zanellato** (Avenida Independencia 366, tel. 0299/443-0105) is the AmEx representative, but there are many others downtown.

Lava Ya (Avenida Independencia 326, tel. 0299/443-4318) does the washing.

Try the **Hospital Regional** (Buenos Aires 421, tel. 0299/449-0800) for emergencies or routine care.

Getting There

Aerolíneas Argentinas and **Austral** (Santa Fe

Northern Patagonia

52, tel. 0299/442-2409) average three or four flights daily to Aeroparque.

Southern Winds (San Martín 107, tel. 0299/442-0124) flies every morning except Sunday to Aeroparque, weekday afternoons to Aeroparque and Córdoba, and weekdays to Bariloche.

LADE (Brown 163, tel. 0299/443-1153) flies Thursday only to Comodoro Rivadavia, which has next-day milk-run connections to Aeroparque.

On the south side of the Parque Central, Neuquén's **Terminal de Ómnibus** (Mitre 147, tel. 0299/442-4903) is a hub for provincial, national, and some international bus services (to the Chilean cities of Temuco and Osorno/Puerto Montt). Reservations are advisable for international buses.

Sample provincial and long-distance destinations, fares, and times include Zapala (US$4, 2.5 hours), Aluminé (US$10, 5.5 hours), Bariloche (US$9–11, five hours), San Martín de los Andes (US$12, 6.5 hours), Santa Rosa (US$13, seven hours), Villa La Angostura (US$11, 6.5 hours), Bahía Blanca (US$13, seven hours), Puerto Madryn (US$15, 9.5 hours), Trelew (US$19, 10.5 hours), El Bolsón (US$13, 7.5 hours), Mendoza (US$19, 11 hours), Esquel (US$17, 10 hours), Buenos Aires (US$25–30, 13 hours), Comodoro Rivadavia (US$25, 14 hours), Córdoba (US$25, 16 hours), and Río Gallegos (US$47, 25 hours).

Services to Chile normally leave around 11 P.M. or midnight. Carriers include **Narbus/Igi Llaima** (tel. 0299/442-3661) to Temuco, Chile (US$18, 11–12 hours) via Zapala and the Pino Hachado pass; **Igi Llaima** (tel. 0299/442-3661) to Temuco (US$18, 122 hours) over Paso Tromen via Junín de los Andes; and **Andesmar** (tel. 0299/442-2216), which goes Tuesday, Thursday, and Saturday to Osorno and Puerto Montt via Paso Cardenal Samoré (US$21, 12 hours). These services can vary seasonally.

Getting Around

Aeropuerto Internacional J.D. Perón (tel. 0299/444-0244) is seven kilometers west of town on the north side of RN 22 (despite its name,

there are no international services at present). A taxi or *remise* costs US$3–4.

Neuquén has several car rental agencies, including **AI** (Perticone 735, tel. 0299/443-8714), **Avis** (Lastra 1196, tel. 0299/443-0216), and **Dollar** (Belgrano 14, tel. 0299/442-0872).

ZAPALA

Argentine backpackers once used forlorn Zapala, the erstwhile end of the line for the northern spur of the Ferrocarril Roca, as a jumping-off point to the least-visited parts of the Patagonian lake district. Since the railroad shut down, and there's little immediate prospect of connecting the dots across the Andes to Chile in a binational transit corridor from Bahía Blanca, this bleak steppe area draws far fewer visitors than it once did. It's a convenient stopover en route to San Martín de los Andes, though, and has good access to bird-rich Parque Nacional Laguna Blanca and an outrageously scenic route to the trout-fishing mecca of Aluminé.

Orientation

Zapala (population 31,265) is 189 kilometers west of Neuquén via RP 22, which continues northwest toward Las Lajas and the Chilean border at Pino Hachado, and 244 kilometers northeast of San Martín de los Andes via RN 40 and RN 234. RP 13 leads west to the ski resort of Primeros Pinos, while paved RP 46 leads southwest to Parque Nacional Laguna and down the spectacular Bajada de Rahue into the Río Aluminé Valley.

Zapala's main drag is Avenida San Martín, which leads south from the traffic-circle intersection of RN 22 and RN 40.

Museo Olsacher

Zapala's most worthwhile sight is its mineralogical museum, filling a recycled warehouse with minerals from around the world and paleontological exhibits from Neuquén. Its prize exhibit is the remains of the herbivorous dinosaur **Zapalasaurus antipani,** but there are also displays on marine reptiles, paleobotany, systematic mineralogy (with 2,035 minerals from 84 countries), economic minerals from Argentina, and invertebrate and vertebrate paleontology. A specialized library holds more than 11,500 items.

Alongside the bus terminal, the Museo Olsacher (Etcheluz and Ejército Argentino, tel. 02942/431959, free) is open 8 A.M.–2 P.M. and 6–9 P.M. weekdays except Monday, and 5–9 P.M. weekends and holidays.

Shopping

Zapala's Escuela de Cerámica (Luis Monti 240) has a long tradition in artisanal pottery.

Accommodations and Food

While Zapala's accommodations and food options are limited, their quality is more than acceptable.

South of the old railroad line, the **Camping Municipal** (Sapag s/n, free of charge) has poplar windbreaks, hot showers, and marginal toilets. Otherwise, Zapala's cheapest is **Residencial Coliqueo** (Etcheluz 165, tel. 02942/421308, US$6.50/10 s/d). **Hotel Huincul** (Avenida Roca 311, tel. 431442, US$7.50/11 s/d) has a restaurant.

Near the bus terminal, the immaculate **Pehuén Hotel** (Etcheluz and Elena de la Vega, tel. 02942/423135, US$7.50/12.50 s/d) stays cool even in summer. **Hotel Hue Melén** (Almirante Brown 929, tel. 02942/422391, US$14/22 s/d) also has a restaurant.

For breakfast, coffee, and snacks, there's **El Chancho Rengo** (Avenida San Martín and Etcheluz, tel. 02942/422795). Directly on RN 22 near the roundabout, **La Zingarella** (Houssay 654, tel. 02924/422234) is the choice for pasta and *parrillada*.

Capriccio (Etcheluz 151, tel. 02942/423156) prepares very good homemade pasta, such as fresh ravioli and pizza, in utilitarian surroundings. **Helados Don Héctor** (Etcheluz 527) is only so-so compared with ice creameries elsewhere, but it's not a desperation choice.

Information

The **Dirección Municipal de Turismo** (Avenida San Martín and Almirante Brown, tel. 02942/421132, turismozapala@argentina.com) occupies an A-frame on the median strip of the main av-

enue. Summer hours are 7 A.M.–8 P.M. weekdays, 8 A.M.–noon and 4–7 P.M. weekends; the rest of the year, it's open 8 A.M.–8 P.M. weekdays only.

The local **APN** office (Ejército Argentino 260, tel. 02942/431982, lagunablanca@zapala.com.ar) provides information on Parque Nacional Laguna Blanca.

Services

Banco de la Provincia del Neuquén (Cháneton 460) has an ATM.

Correo Argentino is at Avenida San Martín and Cháneton; the postal code is 8340. **Telefónica** (Etcheluz 527) has long-distance telephone service and slow Internet connections.

For medical needs, try the **Hospital Regional** (Luis Monti 155, tel. 02924/431555).

Getting There and Around

LADE (Uriburu 397, tel. 02942/430134) flies Wednesdays to Bariloche and to Neuquén.

Taxis or *remises* to Aeropuerto Zapala (tel. 02924/431496), at the junction of RN 40 and RP 46 southwest of town, cost about US$3.

Zapala's **Terminal de Ómnibus** (Etcheluz and Uriburu, tel. 02924/423191) has provincial and long-distance services, and some Chile-bound carriers will pick up passengers here. Ruta Sur goes to Temuco (US$15) at 3 A.M. Monday, Thursday, and Sunday.

Typical destinations, fares, and times include Neuquén (US$4, 2.5 hours), San Martín de los Andes (US$6, 3.5 hours), Bariloche (US$9, five hours), Mendoza (US$26 13.5 hours), and Buenos Aires (US$29, 18 hours). Most often, though, it's easiest to transfer in Neuquén.

Albus goes to Laguna Blanca (US$2, one hour) and Aluminé (US$4, 2.5 hours) Monday, Wednesday, and Friday at 9:20 P.M., while Aluminé Viajes goes to Laguna Blanca and Aluminé at 7:15 P.M. Monday, Wednesday, and Friday, and at 6 P.M. Tuesday, Thursday, and Saturday.

PARQUE NACIONAL LAGUNA BLANCA

In the stark volcanic steppe southwest of Zapala, alkaline Laguna Blanca is a shallow but plankton-rich interior drainage lake that supports large breeding populations of the black-necked swan (*Cygnus melancoryphus*). Protected as an internationally significant wetland under the Ramsar convention, it's also the spot to spot coots, ducks, grebes, gulls, upland geese, and occasional flamingos; even the flightless *choike* (rhea) sometimes scurries along the barren shoreline for a drink.

From a junction 10 kilometers south of Zapala via RN 40, paved RP 46 leads 20 kilometers southwest to the park, which covers 11,250 hectares of undulating terrain, 1,276 meters above sea level; the lake itself covers 1,700 hectares to a depth of 10 meters. RP 46 continues southwest to Rahue and Aluminé, a recommended scenic detour to San Martín de los Andes.

Sights

From the visitors center on RP 46, a short-signed nature trail winds through the steppe to the shoreline, the best place to sight the lake's abundant bird life. A roofed shelter, open on the leeward side, holds a classic 1915 Zeiss telescope that awaits repair; even if the money comes through, it's still worth carrying a pair of lightweight binoculars. Swans are present all year, but the bird life is best November–March.

Practicalities

On the north side of RP 46, about one kilometer east of the visitors center, a free APN campground offers both shade and shelter from the strong, steady westerlies that gust across the steppe. There is no food available here, though—bring everything from Zapala or elsewhere. In reality, Laguna Blanca makes a better day trip than an overnight stay.

Directly on RP 46, Laguna Blanca's steadily improving **Centro de Visitantes** has helpful rangers, informative exhibits, clean toilets, and a crafts outlet. It's open 9 A.M.–6 P.M. daily mid-December to March; the rest of the year, it's open weekends and holidays only.

Public transportation is limited; for details, see the Zapala section. If these schedules are inconvenient, considering hiring a cab or *remise.*

The Lake District

ALUMINÉ AND VICINITY

West of Laguna Blanca, RP 46 passes 2,839-meter Cerro Chachil, with more distant views of Volcán Lanín and fuming Volcán Villarrica, across the border in Chile. From the **Cuesta del Rahue,** where the first Araucaria, or monkey-puzzle trees, make their appearance, the zigzag road descends into the valley of the Río Aluminé, a prime trout-fishing and white-water-rafting river whose very name, appropriately enough, derives from a Mapuche compound that means "glittering jewel."

Aluminé proper is nothing special but, for those who have their own vehicles, it offers the best traveler services in an area with almost unlimited recreational opportunities in the northernmost parts of Parque Nacional Lanín. The drive south through the scenic Aluminé Valley, to Junín de los Andes and San Martín de los Andes, is far more appealing than RN 40.

Aluminé (population 3,384) is 138 kilometers southwest of Zapala via RP 46, which is gradually being paved, and a paved stretch of RP 23; it is 102 kilometers north of Junín de los Andes via RP 23, a good but mostly gravel road. It is 900 meters above sea level.

White-Water Rafting

In November and December, the spring runoff makes the Class II–IV Río Aluminé an excellent white-water experience, but low water the rest of the year makes the rock-strewn riverbed hazardous. For river excursions, which cost about US$10–15 pp, contact **Aluminé Rafting** (tel. 02942/496322), **Mali Viajes** (Joubert and Julio Ayoso, tel. 02942/496310, malialumine@alumine.com.ar), or **Amuyén Servicios Turísticos** (Villegas 348, tel. 02942/496368).

© WAYNE BERNHARDSON

Northern Patagonia

Cuesta del Rahue, the easternmost habitat of the Araucaria (monkey-puzzle) tree

Events

Mid-March's **Fiesta del Pehuén** pays tribute to the distinctive monkey-puzzle tree whose nuts provided sustenance to the aboriginal inhabitants of the region; there are still several Mapuche communities in the area.

Accommodations and Food

Hostería Nid-Car (Cristián Joubert 559, tel. 02942/496131, cagonzalez@hotmail.com, US$9/16 s/d with breakfast) is the shoestring choice. Across from Plaza San Martín, looking better without than within, **Hostería Aluminé** (Cristián Joubert 336, tel. 02942/496347, hosteriaalumine@hotmail.com, US$11/16 s/d with breakfast) offers rooms that are spartan but spacious. Rooms with shared bath are about 20 percent cheaper.

Aluminé's best hotel, **Pehuenia Hotel & Resort** (Capitán Crouzelles and RN 23, tel. 02942/496340, hotelpehuenia@uol.com.ar, US$16/23 s/d) is a multistory European-style chalet with comfortable rooms, some of them with river views, though the beds are little soft;

some of the common areas are worn, their walls scuffed, and their carpets frayed. Rates include an abundant but mediocre breakfast; the dinner is better, however.

At Rahue, 16 kilometers south of Aluminé, **Hostería Rahue-Quillén** (RP 46, tel./fax 02942/496129, panchoyaliciaquillen@alumine.com.ar, US$31/38 s/d) is a comfortable lodge catering primarily to hunters and fishermen. Rates include an abundant, diverse breakfast; lunch and dinner cost an additional US$9 each. It's open January to mid-April only.

Information and Services

For information, consult the diligent **Subsecretaría de Turismo** (Cristián Joubert 321, tel. 02942/496001, subsecretariadeturismo@alumine.com.ar, www.alumine.net), directly on the central Plaza San Martín. In summer, it also operates a Centro de Informes in the hamlet of Rahue, at the junction of RP 46 and RP 23.

Banco de la Provincia del Neuquén (Villegas 392) has an ATM.

Correo Argentino is at Villegas 560; the postal code is 8345. There's a *locutorio* at Benigar 334.

Getting There and Around

The **Terminal de Ómnibus** (4 de Caballería 139, tel. 02942/496048) occupies a triangular block immediately south of Plaza San Martín. Albús goes daily to Neuquén via Zapala. Aluminé Viajes make the same trip Monday, Wednesday, Friday, and Saturday. Transporte Tillería goes to Junín de los Andes and San Martín de los Andes (US$6, three hours) Tuesday and Friday at 7 A.M.

JUNÍN DE LOS ANDES

Where the steppe meets the sierra, the Río Chimehuin gushes from the foot of 3,776-meter Volcán Lanín to become one of Argentina's top trout streams in the vicinity of Junín de los Andes. Styling itself Neuquén Province's "trout capital," economical Junín also provides the best access to the central sector of Parque Nacional Lanín, which takes its name from the symmetrical cone along the Chilean border.

In addition to its natural attractions, Junín is promoting itself as a pilgrimage site for links to the recently beatified Chilean Laura Vicuña, a young girl who willed her own death to protest her widowed mother's affair with an Argentine landowner, and for the ostensible blend of Catholic and Mapuche traditions here. Founded in 1883 as a military camp, during General Roca's euphemistically named "Conquista del Desierto," it's Neuquén's oldest city.

Orientation

At the confluence of the Río Chimehuin and its tributary Río Curruhué, Junín (population 10,243) is 402 kilometers southwest of Neuquén via RN 22, RN 40, and RN 234, and 41 kilometers northeast of San Martín de los Andes via RN 234. It is 218 kilometers north of San Carlos de Bariloche, the hub of the lake district, via RN 234, RN 40, and RN 237. RP 23 leads north to Aluminé, while nearby RP 60 and RP 62 are unpaved roads that lead west to the Chilean border.

Junín's main thoroughfare is north-south RN 234, known as Blvd. Juan Manuel de Rosas within the city limits. The compact city center, a regular grid around Plaza San Martín, lies east of the highway and west of the Chimehuin. Avoid confusing the Avenida San Martín, which runs north-south along its namesake plaza, and the parallel Félix San Martín, two blocks west.

Sights

The focus of the Salesian-organized **Museo Mapuche** (Ginés Ponte 540, 9 A.M.–noon daily except Sun., and 2–7 P.M. weekdays only) is its indigenous artifacts and historical exhibits, but it also displays a sample of fossils.

In what was once a Lebanese-run general store, the private **Museo Moisés Roca Jalil** (Coronel Suárez 311) houses an ample selection of Mapuche artifacts, including very elaborate weavings. It was closed at last visit, but may reopen.

Recent developments reflect Junín's ambition to become a religious-tourism destination. Just modernized, the **Santuario Nuestra Señora de las Nieves y Beata Laura Vicuña** (Ginés Ponte and Don Bosco) is now an airy, luminous structure that incorporates Mapuche elements into its design; it also shelters an urn that contains one of Laura Vicuña's vertebrae. East of town, the **Vía Crucis** is an ambitious stations-of-the-cross project that stretches two kilometers to the cross-topped summit of **Cerro de la Cruz.**

Entertainment and Events

Junín's **Paseo Artesanal,** on Padre Milanesio immediately north of the tourist office, accommodates a cluster of artisans who work in ceramics, leather, wood, and wool.

January's **Feria y Exposición Ganadera** is the landowner's extravaganza of blue-ribbon cattle, horses, and sheep, as well as rabbits and poultry. Gauchos get to show off their skills here as well, but they hold center stage at mid-February's **Festival del Puestero.**

Junín's pre-Lenten **Carnaval del Pehuén** fills the streets with parades, costumed celebrants, and water balloons and confetti. The **Semana de Artesanía Aborígen** at the end of August gives the Mapuche a chance to showcase their finest crafts.

Sports and Recreation

Both Argentines and foreigners flock to Junín for fishing on the Chimehuin, the Aluminé, their tributaries, and the lakes of Parque Nacional Lanín. Catch-and-release is the norm; for licenses and a list of fishing guides, visit the tourist office on Plaza San Martín. For nonresidents of the province, licenses cost US$11 per day, US$50 per week, or US$70 for the season; note that the national parks have their own separate fishing licenses.

The Club Andino Junín de los Andes in the Paseo Artesanal (Padre Milanesio 568) will provide information on hiking and climbing Volcán Lanín and other excursions in the park, as can the Parques Nacionales office.

Accommodations and Food

The riverside municipal **Camping La Isla** (Ginés Ponte s/n, tel. 02972/491461, US$2 pp) has good facilities but collects a small additional charge for showers, which have limited hours: 8–10 A.M. and 8–10 P.M. Across the way, **Camping y Albergue Beata Laura Vicuña** (Ginés Ponte 861, tel. 02972/491149, campingl@jandes.com.ar, US$1.50 pp) is comparable but also has four-person hostel accommodations (US$4 pp).

Directly on the highway is **Residencial Marisa** (Blvd. Juan Manuel de Rosas 360, tel. 02972/491175, rmarisa@jandes.com.ar, US$7/9 s/d); breakfast is an inexpensive extra. Plaza San Martín's basic **Hostería del Montañés** (San Martín 555, tel. 02972/491155) costs US$7/12 s/d, while **Residencial El Cedro** (Lamadrid 409, tel. 02972/492044) costs US$8/14 s/d; its main amenity is cable TV. Rates at **Hostería Posada Pehuén** (Coronel Suárez 560, tel. 02972/491569, posadapehuen@hotmail.com) are US$9/14 s/d.

On Junín's northern outskirts, **Hotel Alejandro Primero** (Blvd. Juan Manuel de Rosas and Chubut, tel. 02972/491182, alejandro1@jandes .com.ar, US$12/19 s/d) has a restaurant.

Aging but agreeable, the riverside **Hostería Chimehuin** (Coronel Suárez and 25 de Mayo, tel. 02972/491132, fax 02972/492503, hosteria chimehuin@jandes.com.ar, www.hosteria chimehuin.com.ar) has 23 comfortable rooms and a restaurant. Rates with private bath are US$14/21 s/d but rooms with shared bath go for just US$8.50 pp; the breakfast includes home-made scones and other specialties.

For pizza and pasta, plus sandwiches and empanadas, try the traditional favorite **Roble Bar** (Ginés Ponte 331, tel. 02972/491111). For greater diversity, there's **Ruca Hueney** (Padre Milanesio 641, tel. 02972/491113).

In an attractive new building styled after Bariloche's landmark civic center, the awkwardly named **Casa de Turismo** (Padre Milanesio 586, tel. 02972/492555) has a good but mostly standard Argentine menu; the standout item is the butter-grilled trout (US$5.50).

Information

Facing Plaza San Martín, the **Subsecretaría de Turismo** (Padre Milanesio 596, tel. 02972/491160, turismo@jdeandes.co.ar) is open 8 A.M.–11 P.M. daily in summer, 8 A.M.–9 P.M. the rest of the year. Fishing permits are also available here.

For information on Parque Nacional Lanín, the **APN** is on the Paseo Artesanal, immediately north of the tourist office. Here you can buy entry tickets to Parque Nacional Lanín, valid for one week, for US$4.50. It's open 9 A.M.–8:30 P.M. weekdays, 2:30–8:30 P.M. weekends.

Services

Banco de la Provincia del Neuquén (Avenida San Martín and Lamadrid) has an ATM.

Correo Argentino is at Suárez and Don Bosco; the postal code is 8371. For telephone services, use the *locutorio* at Padre Milanesio 540, half a block north of the tourist office.

Laverap Pehuén (Ginés Ponte 340) washes clothes.

A new hospital is under construction, but meanwhile use the **Hospital de Area** (Ginés Ponte and Padre Milanesio, tel. 02972/491162).

Getting There and Around

Aeropuerto Aviador Carlos Campos–Chapelco

(RN 234 Km 24, tel. 02972/428388) lies midway between Junín and San Martín de los Andes. For flight details, see the Getting There section for San Martín de los Andes later in this chapter.

Services to and from Junín's **Terminal de Ómnibus** (Olavarría and Félix San Martín, tel. 02972/491110) resemble those to and from San Martín, including services across the Andes to Pucón and Temuco, Chile.

Estancia Huechahue

On the banks of the Río Aluminé, about 30 kilometers east of Junín via RN 234, the 15,000-hectare Anglo-Argentine Estancia Huechahue is a forested cattle ranch that doubles as a recreational getaway for riding, hiking, bird-watching, fishing, and even tennis. From November through April, owner Jane Williams also leads hard-riding pack trips into Parque Nacional Lanín for a maximum of 12 riders. Most visitors arrange packages from overseas. Drop-ins are not possible, but with at least a few days' notice it may be possible to arrange a stay.

The basic rate of $211 pp, in twin-bedded rooms in two separate guest houses, includes full board, drinks (beer, wine, and spirits), and activities (though fishing guides are extra). It also includes transportation between Huechahue and San Martín de los Andes's Aeropuerto Chapelco; transportation from Bariloche is available for an additional charge. For more information, email Jane Williams at huechahue @fronteradigital.net.ar.

SAN MARTÍN DE LOS ANDES

In little more than a century since its founding as a frontier military outpost, San Martín de los Andes has become one of the Patagonian lake district's most fashionable—and expensive—resorts. Nestled in the hills near Lago Lácar, it owes its tourist appeal to its surrounding scenery, the trout that thrash in the lakes and streams of Parque Nacional Lanín, and the ski boom that began in the 1940s at nearby Chapelco.

San Martín is picturesque in its own right, thanks to the legacy of architect Alejandro Bustillo, whose rustically stylish Centro Cívico builds on his

designs at Bariloche. San Martín, though, has shunned the high-rise horrors that have degraded his legacy in Bariloche; its biggest blight is the growing number of timeshares and the increasingly aggressive marketing of them. The height limit has its own downside, though, in promoting its perceived exclusivity—in that sense, San Martín de los Andes is Argentina's Jackson Hole, where fashion sometimes trumps nature.

Orientation

At the east end of Lago Lácar, 642 meters above sea level, San Martín de los Andes (population 22,269) is 189 kilometers north of San Carlos de Bariloche via RN 237, RN 231, and RN 234; it is 109 kilometers north of Villa la Angostura via RN 234, part of which is a narrow and unpleasantly dusty but scenic road through the southern sector of Parque Nacional Lanín. It is 259 kilometers from Bariloche via the roundabout but faster alternative of RN 237, RN 40, and RN 234 via Junín.

San Martín's main thoroughfare is RN 234, which divides into the one-way avenues of Avenida Roca and Avenida San Martín (the main commercial drag) as it runs northeast-southwest through town. Most points of interest and services lie within a few blocks of the Centro Cívico surrounding Plaza San Martín, bounded by the two avenues and the block-long streets of Rosas and Frey.

Centro Cívico

The masterpiece of lavishly landscaped **Plaza San Martín** is Alejandro Bustillo's **Intendencia Parque Nacional Lanín** (Emilio Frey 749), which matches the style of its Bariloche counterpart for Parque Nacional Nahuel Huapi and has influenced constructions throughout the region. The exterior consists of roughly hewn stone blocks, rustically carved wooden beams, attic windows that jut out from the main structure, and wooden roof shingles. Other buildings in the vicinity resemble, but cannot quite match, Bustillo's model.

On the opposite side of the plaza, the **Museo Primeros Pobladores** (Rosas 758, tel. 02792/427315, museoprimerospobladores@yahoo.com

.ar, US$.35) is a modest but worthy effort at acknowledging all the area's cultural influences, from pre-Columbian hunter-gatherers to settled Mapuche farmers and their struggles with the Spanish and Argentine invaders, and the European colonists who helped create the contemporary city. The material exhibits include items such as arrowheads, spear points, and ceramics, but there is also an account of the creation of Parque Nacional Lanín and its significance to the area. Hours are 10 A.M.–7 P.M. weekdays, 4–7 P.M. weekends.

Entertainment and Events

San Martín's main performing arts outlet is the **Centro Cultural Amancay** (Roca 1154, tel. 02972/428399), which offers recent movies at its **Cine Amankay** (tel. 02972/427274).

This is also a bar-goer's town, at places like the theme-oriented **Austria Ski-Bar** (San Martín and Moreno, tel. 02972/427071) and **Downtown Matías** (Coronel Díaz and Calderón, tel. 02972/421699).

El Almacén (Capitán Drury 857, tel. 02972/425663) is a wine bar worth watching.

At February 4's **Día de la Fundación,** the anniversary of San Martín's creation as a frontier fortress in 1898, the military still marches down the avenues, followed by firemen and an offbeat equestrian array of foxhunters, gauchos, and riders on polo ponies.

Shopping

San Martín has a significant concentration of souvenir outlets, starting with the Mapuche weavings, silverwork, and carvings at **Artesanías Neuquinas** (Rosas 790, tel. 02972/428396), the provincially sponsored crafts cooperative.

El Establo (San Martín 1141, tel. 02972/429257) specializes in rural clothing like boots, leather, and ponchos, plus *mate* gourds and paraphernalia. For textiles, try **La Oveja Negra** (Avenida San Martín 1025, tel. 02972/428039) or **Kosem** (Capitán Drury 838, tel. 02972/427269).

Fenoglio (Avenida San Martín 836, tel. 02972/427515) is a popular choice for homemade-style chocolates.

Sports and Recreation

Like Jackson Hole, and thanks to the proximity of Parque Nacional Lanín, San Martín de los Andes is a mecca for outdoor recreationists for everything from hiking and climbing to mountain biking, white-water rafting, trout fishing, and skiing (for details on Cerro Chapelco, see the sidebar "The Slopes of Chapelco").

Climbing snow-topped Volcán Lanín requires some technical skill, but it's possible for enthusiastic amateurs with a guide such as **Horacio Peloso,** at Cerro Torre (San Martín 950, tel. 02972/429162), which also rents equipment.

Secondary roads around Lago Lácar and the park are ideal for mountain biking. Rental bikes are available from **HG Rodados** (Avenida San Martín 1061, tel. 02972/427345).

Rivers on the Argentine side generally have lower flows and fewer challenging rapids than their Chilean counterparts, but the Class III-plus Río Aluminé goes through spectacular scenery a couple of hours north of San Martín. It's best with the spring runoff in November and December; contact **Pucará Viajes** (Avenida San Martín 941, tel. 02972/427862, pucara@smandes.com.ar).

Closer to San Martín, the Class II Río Hua Hum provides a gentler experience; contact **ICI Viajes** (Villegas 459, tel. 02972/427800, iciviajes@smandes.com.ar, www.interpatagonia .com/iciviajes), **El Claro Turismo** (Villegas 977, tel. 02972/428876, elclaro@smandes.com .ar, www.elclaroturismo.com.ar), or **Tiempo Patagónico** (San Martín 950, tel. 02972/ 427113, info@tiempopatagonico.com.ar, www .tiempopatagonico.com).

For fishing gear and advice, visit the **San Martín Orvis Shop** (Villegas 835, tel. 02972/ 425892), or **Jorge Cardillo Fly Shop** (Villegas 1061, tel. 02972/428372).

Accommodations

San Martín has abundant accommodations, but prices are higher than almost anywhere else in the region, and reservations are advisable in the summer months, at Semana Santa, and throughout ski season. At these peak times, single occupants may have to pay double rates, but the devaluation of 2002 has made and kept things relatively affordable.

Under US$10

On the highway to Junín, the wooded **Camping ACA** (Avenida Koessler 2176, tel. 02972/429430, US$2.50 pp off season, US$9 per site in summer) is spacious enough even in peak season, but the best sites go early. There are other campgrounds north and south of town, in Parque Nacional Lanín.

US$10–25

Albergue Rukalhue (Juez del Valle 682, tel. 02972/427431, US$5.50 pp) offers hostel accommodations in very respectable facilities. Peak-season reservations are essential at the HI-affiliated **Puma Hostel** (Fosbery 535, tel. 02972/422443, fax 02972/428545, puma@smandes .com.ar, www.pumahostel.com.ar, US$5–7 pp dorms, US$19 d), an attractive and well-run facility on the north side of the arroyo.

There are several simple and economical *residenciales:* **Residencial Laura** (Mascardi 632, tel. 02972/427271, US$18 d), **Residencial Los Pinos** (Almirante Brown 420, tel. 02972/427207, US$18 d), **Residencial Casa Alta** (Obeid 659, tel. 02972/427456, casaalta @smandes.com.ar, US$21 d), and **Residencial Italia** (Coronel Pérez 977, tel. 02972/427590, US$21 d).

Hostería Las Lucarnas (Coronel Pérez 632, tel. 02972/427085, US$18 d) is also a decent budget choice. Slightly larger and only slightly more expensive, with greater privacy, is **Hostería Cumelén** (Elordi 931, tel. 02972/427304, cumelen@smandes.com.ar, US$21 d).

Hotel Crismalú (Rudecindo Roca 975, tel. 02972/427283, crismalu@smandes.com.ar, US$23 d) may be the best choice in this range. Just far enough off the main drags to ensure some quiet, **Hotel Colonos del Sur** (Rivadavia 686, tel. 02972/427224, colonoshotel@smandes .com.ar, US$24 d) has midsize rooms with bathtubs in a category where showers are the rule.

US$25–50

Hotel Rosa de los Viajes (Avenida San Martín 821, tel. 02972/427484, rosahotel@smandes .com.ar, US$27 d) is a small (only 20 rooms) and homey place, but both foot and auto traffic are heavy in this part of town. Set among attractive gardens, **Hostería Anay** (Capitán Drury 841, tel. 02972/427514, anay@smandes .com.ar, US$27 d) has 10 cozy rooms and enjoys a welcome setback from the street in a bustling area.

Sedate **Hotel Intermonti** (Villegas 717, tel./fax 02972/427454, info@hotelintermonti.com.ar, www.hotelintermonti.com.ar, US$21/31 s/d) has 24 well-furnished midsize rooms, plus attractive common areas.

Central **Hotel Chapelco Ski** (Belgrano 869, tel. 02972/427480, hotelchapelcoski@smandes .com.ar, US$31 d) is a little worn and has limited parking, but is otherwise OK. Near the lake, **Hostería del Chapelco** (Brown 297, tel. 02972/427610, hcchapelco@smandes.com.ar, US$31 d) has the best location of any hotel in its price range, and some second-story rooms have balconies with lake or mountain views.

Upstairs rooms are better than those downstairs at **Hostería La Posta del Cazador** (Avenida San Martín 175, tel. 02972/427501, laposta @satlink.com, US$42 d), a Middle European-style place on a quiet block near the lake. The credit card surcharge is high—pay cash.

Also try nearby **Hostal del Esquiador** (Coronel Rohde 975, tel. 02972/427674, hostaldelesquiador@smandes.com.ar, UD$44 d), only a block from the bus terminal. The alpine-styled **Hotel Caupolicán** (Avenida San Martín 969, tel. 02972/427900, hotelcaupolican@smandes .com.ar, US$48 d) offers ample rooms with contemporary furnishings on the busiest part of the avenue.

Hostería Las Lengas (Coronel Pérez 1175, tel. 02972/427659, navarroclaudia@speedy .com.ar, US$47 d) is an intimate B&B with a French-Swiss style and ample natural light. On sprawling wooded grounds, with rustic style and contemporary comforts, **Hostería La Masía** (Obeid 811, tel. 02972/427688, info@hosterialamasia.com.ar, www.hosterialamasia.com.ar, US$45 d) is exceptional for the price.

US$50–100

Hostería La Cheminee (Avenida Roca and Mariano Moreno, tel. 02972/427617, lacheminee @smandes.com.ar, US$94 d) is one of San Martín's best.

US$100–200

Four-star **⋈ Hotel Patagonia Plaza** (San Martín and Rivadavia, tel./fax 02972/422280, patagoniaplaza@smandes.com.ar, US$110–270 d) has become one of the city's premier accommodations, with 90 rooms ranging from relatively simple doubles to sprawling suites.

Food

Try **Café de la Plaza** (Avenida San Martín and Coronel Pérez, tel. 02972/428488) for coffee, croissants, sandwiches, and desserts. **Abolengo** (Avenida San Martín 806, tel. 02972/427732) is a cozy, comfortable place for relaxing with rich hot chocolate on a cool night. **Alihuen** (Rivadavia 759) is a teahouse with outstanding desserts.

Pizzería La Nonna (Capitán Drury 857, tel. 02972/422223) serves about 30 varieties of pizzas, including wild boar, trout, and venison, in the US$3–7 range; there are also calzones and empanadas. **Trattoria Mi Viejo Pepe** (Villegas 725, tel. 02972/427415) is a more elaborate Italian option.

Though not strictly vegetarian, tobacco-free **⋈ Pura Vida** (Villegas 745, tel. 02972/429302) has plenty of excellent vegetarian dishes; its tasty ñoquis and other pastas make it one of San Martín's best values.

Reflecting San Martín's Lebanese roots, **Salsabil** (Obeid 832, tel. 02972/427556) prepares Middle Eastern dishes like hummus, tabouleh, falafel, and kebabs. For smoked meats, as well as cheeses and mushrooms, go to **Ahumadero El Ciervo** (Villegas 724, tel. 02972/427361).

⋈ La Chacha (San Martín and Rivadavia, tel. 02972/422564) is primarily a *parrilla* that serves out-of-the-routine items like kid goat, roast pig, and a flavorful chicken in plum sauce, along with fresh raspberries in season. Dinner lines form early outside popular *parrilla* **Piscis**

Patagonia (Villegas 598, tel. 02972/427601), and the more fashionable **Mendieta** (San Martín 713, tel. 02972/429301).

For ice cream, there are two locations of **Charlot** (Avenida San Martín 467 or Avenida San Martín 1017, tel. 02972/428561), with dozens of imaginative flavors. **Abuela Goye** (Capitán Drury 812, tel. 02972/429409) is another outstanding choice, with superb chocolate confections as well.

Information

At the east end of Plaza San Martín, the **Secretaría Municipal de Turismo** (Avenida San Martín and Rosas, tel. 02972/427347, munitur @smandes.com.ar, www.smandes.gov.ar, 8 A.M.– 9 P.M. daily.) does an outstanding job of providing advice, maps, and brochures, plus an up-to-the-minute database of accommodations and rates; in peak season, though, its resources can be stretched to the breaking point. National park entry permits are available here.

On the opposite side of the plaza, the APN's **Intendencia de Parque Nacional Lanín** (Emilio Frey 749, tel. 02972/427233 or 429004, 8 A.M.–1 P.M. weekdays only) provides information on the park, with a selection of maps and brochures.

Services

Banco de la Nación (Avenida San Martín 687) and several others have ATMs. **Andina Internacional** (Capitán Drury 876) is the only exchange house.

Codesma (Capitán Drury 761) has telephone, fax, and Internet services.

Chapelco Turismo (Avenida San Martín 876, tel. 02972/427611) offers conventional overland excursions to Parque Nacional Lanín (including Lago Huechulafquen), Villa Traful, Villa la Angostura, and even San Martín's Chilean counterpart of Pucón.

For laundry, **Laverap** has two locations (Capitán Drury 880 and Villegas 972, tel. 02972/428820).

Hospital Zonal Ramón Carrillo (Avenida San Martín and Coronel Rohde, tel. 02972/ 427211) is very central.

Getting There

Note that air schedules, in particular, are subject to changes, especially in the winter ski season.

Aerolíneas Argentinas (Capitán Drury 876, tel. 02972/427004) flies occasionally to Buenos Aires, sometimes to Aeroparque and others to Ezeiza; its partner Austral flies daily and twice on weekends to Aeroparque.

LADE (Villegas 231, tel. 02972/427672) occupies an office in the bus terminal; it flies Sundays to Buenos Aires, Bariloche, and Esquel, and alternate Sundays to Neuquén.

San Martín's **Terminal de Ómnibus** (Villegas 231, tel. 02972/427044) has regional, long-distance, and international connections (to Chile).

Transportes Ko Ko (tel. 02972/427422) goes to Villa la Angostura (US$6, three hours) via the scenic Siete Lagos route, sometimes continuing to Bariloche, but most of their services to Bariloche (US$8, 4.5 hours) go via Rinconada. **Albus** (tel. 02972/428100) also goes to Villa la Angostura, three times daily by the Siete Lagos route, twice to Bariloche. Transporte Tillería goes to Aluminé (US$6, three hours) Tuesday and Friday at 4 P.M.

Internationally, **Igi-Llaima** (tel. 02972/425325) and **Empresa San Martín** (tel.

02972/427294) alternate service to Temuco, Chile (US$15, eight hours), continuing to Valdivia, daily except Sunday. In summer, Buses Lafit goes once or even twice daily to the Chilean border post of Pirehueico (US$4.50, two hours) and on to Panguipulli (US$9, 4.5 hours).

Other typical destinations, fares, and times include Junín de los Andes (US$2, one hour), Neuquén (US$10, 5.5 hours), Mendoza (US$33, 18 hours), and Buenos Aires (US$40–45, 21 hours).

From the pier at the foot of Obeid, **Naviera Lácar y Nonthue** (Avenida Costanera s/n, tel. 02972/427380) goes seven times daily to Quila Quina (US$5.50 round-trip), on the south shore of the lake, and daily to Hua Hum (US$18).

Getting Around

Aeropuerto Aviador Carlos Campos-Chapelco (RN 234 Km 24, tel. 02972/428388) lies midway between San Martín and Junín de los Andes. For airport transfers, contact **Traslados Chapelco** (tel. 02944/425808) or **Caleuche** (tel. 02972/422115).

In summer only, **Transportes Ko Ko** (tel. 02972/427422) runs several buses daily (US$1) to Lago Lolog.

THE SLOPES OF CHAPELCO

O verlooking San Martín de los Andes, at a maximum elevation of 1,920 meters, Cerro Chapelco draws enthusiastic winter crowds to 29 different runs, the longest combination of which is about 5.3 kilometers. The diversity of conditions means it's suitable for both experienced skiers and novices. The **Fiesta Nacional del Montañés,** the annual ski festival, takes place in August, when there are also provincial skiing championships.

Chapelco Aventura (Avenida San Martín and Elordi, tel. 02972/427460, nieves_cerro@smandes.com.ar, www.chapelco.com.ar) is the resort office in San Martín. Rental equipment is available on-site, but also in town at **Bumps** (Villegas 465, tel. 02972/428491) and **La Colina** (San Martín 532, tel. 02972/427414).

Lift-ticket prices depend on timing; the season runs from mid-June to mid-October, but is subdivided into low, mid-, and peak season. One-day rates range US$16–28 for adults, US$13–22 for children ages 5 to 11 and seniors age 60 and above. The corresponding prices for three-day passes are US$47–82 for adults, US$38–66 for children and seniors. Week-long passes cost US$90–157 for adults, US$72–127 for children and seniors, while the rates for 15-day passes are US$176–307 and US$142–247 respectively. Season passes cost US$750 for adults, US$600 for children and seniors. Those over age 70 ski free.

For rental cars, try **Avis** (Avenida San Martín 998, tel. 02972/427704) or **Localiza** (Villegas 977, tel. 02972/428876).

PARQUE NACIONAL LANÍN

In westernmost Neuquén, stretching from Lago Ñorquinco in the north to a southeasterly diagonal that runs between Lago Nonthué on the Chilean border and Confluencia on RN 237, Parque Nacional Lanín comprises 412,000 hectares of arid steppe, verdant mid-altitude forests ringing glacial finger lakes, alpine highlands, and volcanic summits. From Aluminé in the north to Junín de los Andes and San Martín de los Andes in the south, several longitudinal highways intersect westbound access roads, all of them graveled.

Where the park's eastward-flowing Pleistocene glaciers receded, they have left a series of deep finger lakes that drain into the upper and lower tributaries of the Río Limay. Unlike Parque Nacional Nahuel Huapi, to the south, these lakes and the dense Valdivian forests that surround them have suffered much less commercial development, but they are recovering from timber exploitation in the early 20th century and livestock grazing that, in some areas, still persists.

Flora and Fauna

Precipitation that reaches up to 3,000 millimeters per annum encourages the growth of dense humid Valdivian woodlands. Lanín's signature species is the coniferous *pehuén* or monkey-puzzle tree (*Araucaria araucana*), for centuries a subsistence resource for the Mapuches and Pehuenches (a subgroup whose own name stresses their dependence on the tree's edible nuts). Along with the broadleaf deciduous southern beech *raulí* (*Nothofagus nervosa*), the *pehuén* forms part of a transitional forest that overlaps southern beech species that dominate the more southerly Patagonian forests, such as the *coihue, lenga,* and *ñire.* In places, the solid bamboo *colihue* forms almost impenetrable thickets within the forest.

At higher elevations, above 1,600 meters, extreme cold and wind reduce the vegetative cover to shrubs and grasses. At lower elevations, to the east, the drier climate results in a gradation to Patagonian steppe grasses.

Except for its trout, Lanín is less celebrated for its wildlife than for its landscapes. Fortunate visitors, though, may see the secretive spaniel-size deer known as the *pudú* (*Pudu pudu*) or the larger Andean *huemul* (*Hippocamelus bisulcus*). The major predator is the puma, present on the steppes and in the forest, while the torrent duck frequents the faster streams and the Andean condor glides on the heights. The lakes and rivers attract many other birds.

From north to south, Aluminé, Junín de los Andes, and San Martín de los Andes are the main access points to the park. This section begins at Aluminé and works southward, though most park visitors use either Junín or San Martín as their base.

Except in nearby towns, accommodations and food are in short supply, as the park is far less developed than Nahuel Huapi to the south.

Sector Aluminé

Immediately east of Aluminé, RP 18 follows the south bank of the Río Rucachoroi for 23 kilometers to Lago Rucachoroi, site of a Mapuche reserve. From Rahué, 17 kilometers south of Aluminé, RP 46 leads west to **Lago Quillén,** an area of dense monkey-puzzle forests that's also home to Mapuche families.

Volcán Lanín

Looming above the landscape, 3,776 meters above sea level on the Chilean border, lop-sided Volcán Lanín is the literal and metaphorical center of its namesake national park. Covered by permanent snow, rising 1,500 meters above any other peak in the vicinity, its slightly irregular cone is an elevated beacon visible for hundreds of kilometers to the east and, where the rugged terrain permits, to the north and south.

Sector Lago Tromen

From a junction 11 kilometers north of Junín, northwesterly RP 60 leads to the Chilean border at Paso Mamuil Malal, where Lago Tromen marks the most convenient approach to the summit of **Volcán Lanín.** Because of the northeasterly exposure, both hiking and climbing routes open earlier here than on the southern side of the peak, which lies partly in Chile.

Before climbing Lanín, obtain permission from the APN in San Martín, who will ask to inspect your gear, which should contain crampons, an ice axe, plastic tools, and appropriate clothing and peripherals (gloves, hats, insulated jackets, sunglasses, and sunscreen).

From the trailhead at the Argentine border, the **Camino de Mulas** route takes five to seven hours to the **Refugio Club Andino Junín de los Andes** (altitude 2,600 meters; capacity 10 persons); beyond here, snow gear is essential. The shorter but steeper **Espina del Pescado** route starts at the Argentine army's **Refugio Regimiento Infantería de Montaña** (elevation 2,350 meters; capacity 15 persons); it's possible to approach either route from the Lago Huechulafquen side as well. A new *refugio*, with a capacity of 60 persons at an elevation of 2,600 meters, is under consideration.

Alongside the Gendarmería post, **Camping Lanín** (tel. 02972/491355, US$1 pp, open Jan.–Mar. only) has facilities that include picnic tables, firepits and bathrooms with showers.

Appealing chiefly to fly-fishing fanatics, **Hostería San Huberto** (RP 60 Km 28, tel. 02972/491238) charges from US$150/200 s/d with full board. Reservations are essential as it has only six twin rooms.

Sector Lago Huechulafquen

About four kilometers north of Junín, RP 61 leads northwest along the Río Chimehuin and the north shore of Lago Huechulafquen for 52 kilometers to Puerto Canoas (the end of the road) and **Lago Paimún.** En route, several trailheads lead north, the most interesting of which is the **Cara Sur** (Southern Face) approach to Volcán Lanín along the wooded Arroyo Rucu Leufú, which meets the trail coming south from Lago Tromen. Hikers not wishing to continue to the base of Lanín, about a four-hour walk, or the seven hours to the RIM *refugio,* can still enjoy the stroll through the Araucaria forest; climbers should get permission from the APN ranger here.

From the Piedra Mala campground at Lago Paimún, a 30-minute hike goes to **Cascada El Saltillo,** a 20-meter waterfall. It's no longer possible to walk around Lago Paimún, most of whose north shore is closed for environmental reasons, but summer hikers can cross the narrows, known as La Unión, that separates Huechulafquen and Paimún on a *balsa* (cable platform) for about US$1. The rest of the year, it's possible to hire a rowboat to get across.

From La Unión, the trail continues for about five hours to **Aila,** where there's a Mapuche-run campground, and another eight hours to the rustic **Termas de Epulafquen.** From Epulafquen, RP 62 returns to Junín de los Andes.

THE SIETE LAGOS ROUTE

Between Villa la Angostura and San Martín de los Andes, northbound RN 234 traverses the forests and skirts the lakes of two national parks, Nahuel Huapi and Lanín, on the popular **Ruta de los Siete Lagos.** It takes its name from the seven scenic alpine lakes that it passes along or near, but only the northern half through Lanín is paved. This is notable because the southern Nahuel Huapi section may well be Argentina's dustiest road or, when it rains heavily, one of the muddiest.

Because of these clouds of dust, tours that take this otherwise enjoyable route don't necessarily see the landscape; the ideal time is immediately after a light rain. The Nahuel Huapi section is also narrow, requiring defensive driving to avoid head-on collisions; vehicles are also a serious hazard for cyclists, but many international adventure-travel companies include the route as part of their mountain bike itineraries.

In addition to tours, the Siete Lagos route offers scheduled bus service; see the Getting There and Getting Around sections for Villa la Angostura and San Martín de los Andes for details.

Free **campgrounds** along the shores of Lago Huechulafquen and Lago Paimún are very rustic, while the pay sites are better maintained, with better services, and are community-oriented.

Camping Bahía Cañicul (RP 61 Km 48) has sites without electricity for US$2 pp, with electricity for US$3 pp; it also has a small store, but supplies are cheaper and more diverse in Junín. **Camping Raquithué** (RP 61 Km 54) costs US$1 pp, while the attractive **Camping Piedra Mala** (RP 61 Km 60) charges US$1.50 pp.

A few kilometers before Lago Paimún, **Hostería Huechulafquen** (RP 61 Km 55, tel. 02972/426075, lafquen@smandes.com.ar) charges US$90 d with full board. For US$70/90 s/d with full board, the three-star **Hostería Paimún** (RP 61 Km 58, tel. 02972/491211, fax 02972/491201, adelvalle@jandes.com.ar) is primarily a fishing lodge.

Lago Lolog

Only about 15 kilometers north of San Martín, little-developed Lago Lolog has several campgrounds and regular transportation; the basic **Camping Puerto Arturo** is free. See Getting Around in the San Martín de los Andes section for details.

Lago Lácar

San Martín's own lake, Lago Lácar, is wilder toward the Chilean border, where there is camping, hiking, and white-water rafting at the outlet of the Río Hua Hum. For transportation details, both overland and by water, see the San Martín de los Andes section of this chapter.

Other Practicalities

In addition to the APN Intendencia at San Martín, there are **ranger stations** at all the major lakes and some other points of interest. While the personnel are helpful they do not, in general, have maps or other printed matter. The park entry fee, valid for one week, is US$4.50 pp for foreigners, and also covers neighboring parks like Nahuel Huapi.

San Martín de los Andes, Junín de los Andes, and Aluminé are the main gateways to the park. Public transportation is limited, but consult the entries on those areas for further information. While international buses to Chile, via the southerly Hua Hum and the northerly Tromen passes, may carry passengers, they are often full.

VILLA LA ANGOSTURA AND VICINITY

On the north shore of Lago Nahuel Huapi, Villa la Angostura traditionally lies within Bariloche's economic orbit. Thanks to its proximity to less-developed parts of the lake, to Parque Nacional Los Arrayanes, and the winter sports center of Cerro Bayo, though, it's quickly establishing its own identity as a destination for both Argentines and foreign visitors. It has excellent accommodations and restaurants, but there's an air of exclusivity and prices are on the high side.

Snow falls on a *Nothofagus* forest, Villa la Angostura.

Orientation

Villa la Angostura (population 7,311) is 80 kilometers northwest of Bariloche via RN 237 and RN 231 (the international highway to Osorno, Chile) and 109 kilometers south of San Martín de los Andes via RN 234, the scenic but narrow and dusty Siete Lagos (Seven Lakes) route. It is 870 meters above sea level, but the surrounding mountains rise sharply from the Nahuel Huapi shoreline.

RN 231 passes directly through the part of town known as El Cruce, where many services line both sides of the highway (which is known as Avenida Los Arrayanes and its westward extension as Avenida Los Lagos). Three kilometers south, the largely residential La Villa also has a cluster of hotels and restaurants; Parque Nacional Los Arrayanes occupies the entirety of Península Quetrihué, the southward-jutting peninsula linked to La Villa by the 91-meter isthmus that gives Villa la Angostura its name (The Narrows). There are other sectors of interest as well, including Las Balsas and Puerto Manzano to the southeast, and Barrio Norte and Río Correntoso to the northwest.

Sights

Foot and bicycle are the best means of seeing Villa la Angostura's attractions. For hiking in the nearby mountains, where the trails are too steep and narrow for bicycles, consider hiring a taxi or *remise* to the trailhead.

Villa la Angostura's relocated **Museo Histórico Regional** (11 A.M.–5 P.M. weekdays, 2:30–5 P.M. Sat. and holidays, free) occupies a new facility at Boulevard Nahuel Huapi and El Calafate, in El Cruce. Its contents deal primarily with the pioneering timber industry, the agriculture that followed it, and the families who established themselves here. It does, however, acknowledge the enduring presence of the Mapuche who constituted a separate nation overlapping the Argentine and Chilean borders, and their displacement by the Argentine state.

From June to September at nearby Cerro Bayo, **Centro de Ski Cerro Bayo** (tel. 02944/ 494189, informes@cerrobayoweb.com, www .cerrobayoweb.com) operates 26 kilometers of

runs ranging from 1,050 to 1,782 meters above sea level, with five chairlifts and five towbars. Lift passes depend on the time of the season, but range from US$11–17 for a half-day, US$13–21 for a full day, US$33–55 for three days, and US$75–125 for a week. Season passes costs US$440; there are discounts for children and seniors.

Only nine kilometers southeast of El Cruce, Cerro Bayo also has accommodations, restaurants, and rental equipment on site. Empresa 15 de Mayo operates four buses daily US$1) from town, starting at 11 A.M.; the last one returns at 7 P.M.

From El Cruce, a narrow four-kilometer road zigzags to **Mirador Belvedere,** a wide parking area and overlook with views along Lago Correntoso to the north, the almost absurdly short Río Correntoso that connects it with Lago Nahuel Huapi, and the snowy peaks that mark the Chilean border to the west.

About midway up the route, an eastbound forest trail leads to **Cascada Inayacal,** a 50-meter waterfall. From the parking area, a three-kilometer trail to 1,992-meter **Cerro Belvedere** climbs through *coihue* forest before dipping into a saddle and then ascending steeply over Cerro Falso Belvedere before continuing to the summit. Note that the road can be difficult in wet weather, and has several blind curves.

Parque Nacional Los Arrayanes

According to local folklore, Walt Disney took the idea for the forest in his cartoon feature *Bambi* from the *arrayán* forest at the tip of Península Quetrihué, a former *estancia* that became a national park in 1971. The eye-catching red-barked forests of *Myrceugenella apiculata,* with their bright-white flowers, do indeed bear a resemblance, but a Disney archivist has pointed out that Walt never visited the area. In fact, *Bambi* was in production prior to his 1941 trip to Argentina.

So close to La Villa that it feels more like a sprawling city park—though it's larger than the city itself—the park occupies the entire 1,753 hectares of Península Quetrihué, which stretches south into Lago Nahuel Huapi. Its namesake

© WAYNE BERNHARDSON

cyclists in Parque Nacional Los Arrayanes, near Villa la Angostura

forest comprises only about 20 hectares, but the rest of the peninsula bristles with trees like the *maitén* and the southern beeches *coihue, lenga,* and *ñire,* colorful shrubs like the *notro* and *chilco,* and dense thickets of the bamboo *colihue.*

The park's environmental standout may be the *arrayán,* individuals of which reach 25 meters and 650 years of age, but it's also an ideal place for hiking and mountain biking—the undulating 12-kilometer trail to or from the tip of the peninsula makes an ideal half-day excursion (on a bicycle or doing one-way by boat) or a full-day by hiking in both directions. Frequently, in Argentina, rangers exaggerate the time needed on certain trails, but the three hours they suggest is about right for this highly pleasurable walk in the woods, which passes a pair of lakes; only at the park entrance, near La Villa, are there any truly steep segments.

At the entrance, rangers collect a US$4.50 admission charge (US$2.25 for Argentine resi-

dents). Unfortunately, even those who only intend to make the 20-minute hike to the panoramic **Mirador Arrayán** must also pay the fee. Near the dock at the southern tip of the peninsula, a *confitería* with a cozy fireplace serves sandwiches, coffee, and hot chocolate.

Nonhikers can reach the *arrayán* forest in about half an hour on the *Catamarán Futaleufú,* run by El Cruce's **Angostura Turismo** (Avenida Arrayanes 208, Local 1, tel. 02944/494405); the cost is US$7 one-way, plus a US$1 boarding tax. Cyclists can rent bikes in El Cruce, but note that hikers and bikers must leave the park by 4 P.M. Horses are prohibited, as is camping.

Shopping and Events

On weekends only, locals and parachutists peddle their own wares at **Feria de Artesanos,** El Cruce's artisan's fair, on Belvedere between Avenida Los Arrayanes and Las Fucsias.

For four days in early February, the provincial **Fiesta de los Jardines** (Garden Festival) occupies center stage.

Sports and Recreation

English-speaking Anthony Hawes operates Patagonian Adventures (Avenida Arrayanes 21, Local 5, tel. 02944/15-550318, info@patagonianadventures.com, www.patagonianadventures.com), which arranges activities ranging from fishing to horseback riding, mountain biking, and whitewater rafting.

Accommodations

Some 500 meters west of the tourist office, the improved **Camping Unquehue** (Avenida Los Lagos s/n, tel. 02944/494922, unquehue@ciudad.com.ar, US$2 pp for wooded sites) has hot showers available in the communal baths.

The next cheapest choices are the **Bajo Cero Hostel** (Río Caleufú 88, tel. 02944/495454, US$6.50 pp dorms, US$15 d) and the **Hostel la Angostura** (Barbagelata 157, tel. 02944/494384, hostellaangostura.com.ar, www.hostellaangostura.com.ar, US$6.50 pp in dorms, US$9 pp), an attractive place on spacious grounds.

About one kilometer from El Cruce, **Hostería Las Cumbres** (Avenida Siete Lagos s/n, tel.

02944/494945, info@hosterialascumbres.com, www.hosterialascumbres.com, US$25 d) is an eight-room, owner-operated hotel that's a fine budget choice. Home-cooked dinners are also available.

In a secluded location near Lago Correntoso, skier-friendly **M Hostel lo del Francés** (Lolog 2057, tel. 02944/15-564063, lodelfrances@hotmail.com, www.interpatagonia.com/lodelfrances, US$9 pp for hostel bunks, US$27 d) has only three rooms but offers home-cooked dinners, great gardens, a bar and other common areas, including a walk-in fireplace for recharging the batteries in ski season. It is an HI affiliate; because capacity is so limited, reservations are essential.

Two blocks north of the bus terminal, **Residencial Río Bonito** (Topa Topa 260, tel. 02944/494110, riobonito@ciudad.com.ar, US$18 d), the private rooms enjoy a quiet garden setting; breakfast is included. El Cruce's **Residencial Don Pedro** (Belvedere and Los Maquis, tel. 02944/494269, US$18 d) is comparable.

Dating from 1938, originally built for the APN, La Villa's lakeside classic **M Hotel Angostura** (Nahuel Huapi 1911, tel. 02944/494224, info@hotelangostura.com, US$32 d) has 20 rooms, some with lake views, and three separate bungalows sleeping up to six people. Its restaurant is also worth consideration.

Just off Avenida Arrayanes, **Hostería Posta de los Colonos** (Los Notros 19, tel. 02944/494386, postadeloscolonos@arnet.com.ar, US$28/42 s/d) has nearly pristine, well-heated rooms with comfy beds, cable TV, and breakfast, but also thin walls and creaky floors. While it's not a noisy locale per se, small noises carry well and the planned addition of sound insulation will be welcome.

In Puerto Manzano, about six kilometers southeast of El Cruce, **Hostería Naranjo en Flor** (Chucao 62, tel. 02944/494863, naranjoenflor@infovia.com.ar, US$58 d) is an eight-room hotel on a forested lot that has views of Lago Nahuel Huapi and the Andes. It also has a pool, and offers simple but tasty dinners.

Across the Río Correntoso, three kilometers northwest of El Cruce, the historic **M Hotel Correntoso** (tel. 02944/15-556903, info@correntoso.com, www.correntoso.com, US$95 d) started as a fishing lodge in 1917 and became a major attraction before burning nearly to the ground. Almost abandoned, it underwent a recent rehab that's restored its former glory plus—there's a lakeside fishing bar, a wine bar, and an outstanding restaurant as well. It also has a Buenos Aires contact (Avenida Figueroa Alcorta 3351, tel. 011/4803-0030).

The area's standout is the sophisticated Relais & Chateaux affiliate **M Hostería Las Balsas** (tel. 02944/494308, balsas@satlink.com, US$200 d, US$300 suite), a 12-room, three-suite Bustillo classic on Bahía las Balsas south of El Cruce. All rooms have lake views; rates include unlimited spa access and breakfast, and there's a highly regarded hybrid restaurant with French and traditional Argentine dishes.

Food

In addition to its hotel restaurants, Villa la Angostura offers a diversity of dining options at moderate to upscale prices. There's a cluster on and around Avenida Arrayanes in El Cruce, but several other worthwhile options in the vicinity.

For breakfast, sandwiches, coffee, and desserts, try the **Rincón Suizo** (Avenida Arrayanes 44, tel. 02944/494248). **Las Varas** (Avenida Arrayanes 235, tel. 02944/494405) is a standard *parrilla*. **Tante Frida** (Avenida Arrayanes 209) is a teahouse with exceptional ice cream.

The spacious but still crowded **Nativa Café** (Avenida Arrayanes 198, tel. 02944/495093) is a very fine pizzeria whose toppings include *jabalí* (wild boar) and *ciervo* (venison, which is farmed in the region). **La Buena Vida** (Avenida Arrayanes 167, Local 4, tel. 02944/495200) is a smaller, homier place, with excellent service, that serves a fine risotto.

Reservations are essential at the current star of the cuisine scene, the **M Tinto Bistro** (Blvd. Nahuel Huapi 34, tel. 02944/494924). Run by brother-to-royalty Martín Zorreguieta (whose sister Máxima married the Dutch Crown Prince William in 2002), it offers an Asian/Patagonian fusion food, with what is probably the area's finest wine selection.

North of Puente Correntoso, **El Mirador de los Cerros** (Avenida Siete Lagos 5018) enjoys a spectacular panorama from its hillside deck, though the kitchen and the service can be slow, and the menu is limited to pizza, sandwiches, and regional appetizers. Also enjoying fine views, especially at sunset, **Raíces** (Avenida Siete Lagos 3314, tel. 02944/15-556903) is another fine choice for appetizers and drinks.

Set on wooded grounds, Puerto Manzano's comfy **Ⅺ Waldhaus** (Avenida Arrayanes 6431, tel. 02944/495123) serves continental-style dishes like fondue, goulash, and raclette, with a Patagonian touch. It's also known for its wine list.

Information and Services

At El Cruce, the **Secretaría Municipal de Turismo** (Avenida Siete Lagos 93, tel. 02944/494124, www.villalaangostura.gov.ar) is open 8 A.M.–9 P.M. daily except in winter, when it closes at 8 P.M.

The APN's **Seccional Villa la Angostura** (Nahuel Huapi s/n, tel. 02944/494152) is in La Villa.

Virtually all services are in El Cruce, where Banco Patagonia (Avenida Arrayanes 275) has an **ATM.**

Correo Argentino is at Avenida Arrayanes 282, Local 4; the postal code is 8407. **VLA Comunicaciones** (Avenida Arrayanes 90, Local 2) has phone and Internet connections, but those connections are significantly slower than in Bariloche.

Getting There

El Cruce's **Terminal de Ómnibus** (tel. 02944/494961) sits at the intersection of Avenida Siete Lagos and Avenida Arrayanes. There are frequent connections to Bariloche, several buses daily to San Martín de los Andes via the dustily scenic Siete Lagos route, and long-distance services to Neuquén. Chile-bound buses from Bariloche stop here, but reservations are advisable because these often run full.

Typical destinations, times, and fares include Bariloche (US$2.50, 1.5 hours), San Martín de los Andes (US$5.50, three hours), and Neuquén (US$11, six hours).

SAN CARLOS DE BARILOCHE AND VICINITY

If Patagonia ever became independent, its logical capital might be San Carlos de Bariloche—"Bariloche" to most visitors—the highest-profile destination in an area explorer Francisco P. Moreno once called "this beautiful piece of Argentine Switzerland." It's not just that Bariloche, with its incomparable setting on the shores of Lago Nahuel Huapi, is the lake district's largest city, transportation hub, and gateway to Argentina's first national park; in the 1930s, the carved granite blocks and rough-hewn polished timbers of its landmark Centro Cívico made a promising precedent for harmonizing urban expansion with the wild surroundings.

Dating from 1902, Bariloche was slow to grow—when former U.S. President Theodore Roosevelt visited in 1913, he observed:

Bariloche is a real frontier village. . . . It was like one of our frontier towns in the old-time West as regards the diversity in ethnic type and nationality among the citizens. The little houses stood well away from one another on the broad, rough, faintly marked streets.

When Roosevelt crossed the Andes from Chile, Bariloche was more than 700 kilometers from the nearest railroad, but it began to boom after completion of the southern branch of the Ferrocarril Roca in 1934. Its rustic style has spread throughout the region—even to structures as commonplace as phone booths—but unrelenting growth, promoted by unscrupulous politicians and developers, has cost the city much of its hybrid Euro-Andean charm. For much of the day, for instance, the Bariloche Center, a multistory monstrosity authorized by the brief and irregular repeal of height-limit legislation, literally overshadows the Centro Cívico.

As the city's population has grown from about 60,000 in 1980 to almost 90,000 today, its downtown *microcentro* has become a congested clutter of chocolate shops, hotels, and time-shares, and is notorious for high school

Northern Patagonia

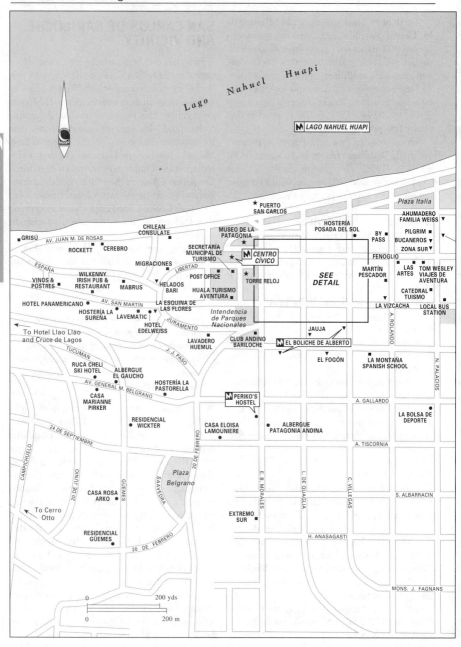

GRISÚ
AV. JUAN M. DE ROSAS
ROCKETT   CEREBRO
ESPAÑA
VINOS &   WILKENNY
POSTRES   IRISH PUB &
           RESTAURANT   MABRUS
HOTEL PANAMERICANO
HOSTERÍA LA   LAVEMATIC
SUREÑA
To Hotel Llao Llao
and Cruce de Lagos
TUCUMAN
RUCA CHELI
SKI HOTEL   ALBERGUE
             EL GAUCHO
AV. GENERAL M. BELGRANO
CASA
MARIANNE
PIRKER
             RESIDENCIAL
             WICKTER
24 DE SEPTIEMBRE
CAMPICHUELO
To Cerro
Otto
CASA ROSA
ARKO
             RESIDENCIAL
             GÜEMES
20 DE JUNIO
GÜEMES
SAAVEDRA
Plaza
Belgrano
20 DE FEBRERO

Lago Nahuel Huapi

LAGO NAHUEL HUAPI

Plaza Italia

★ PUERTO
   SAN CARLOS
CHILEAN
CONSULATE
MUSEO DE LA
PATAGONIA
SECRETARÍA
MUNICIPAL DE
TURISMO
MIGRACIONES
LIBERTAD
POST OFFICE
HELADOS
BARI
HUALA TURISMO
AVENTURA
LA ESQUINA DE
LAS FLORES
JURAMENTO
HOTEL
EDELWEISS
LAVADERO
HUEMUL
J. J. PASO
HOSTERÍA LA
PASTORELLA
20 DE FEBRERO
PERIKO'S
HOSTEL
CASA ELOISA
LAMOUNIERE
ALBERGUE
PATAGONIA ANDINA
EXTREMO
SUR
E. B. MORALES
L. DE QUAGLIA
H. ANASAGASTI

HOSTERÍA
POSADA DEL SOL
CENTRO
CÍVICO
TORRE RELOJ
SEE
DETAIL
Intendencia
de Parques
Nacionales
CLUB ANDINO
BARILOCHE
JAUJA
EL BOLICHE DE ALBERTO
EL FOGÓN
A. GALLARDO
A. TISCORNIA
C. VILLEGAS

BY
PASS
FENOGLIO
MARTÍN
PESCADOR
LA VIZCACHA
A. ROLANDO
LA MONTAÑA
SPANISH SCHOOL

AHUMADERO
FAMILIA WEISS
PILGRIM
BUCANEROS
ZONA SUR
LAS
ARTES   TOM WESLEY
         VIAJES DE
         AVENTURA
CATEDRAL
TUISMO
LOCAL BUS
STATION
N. PALACIOS
LA BOLSA DE
DEPORTE
S. ALBARRACIN
MONS. J. FAGNANS

0   200 yds
0   200 m

SAN CARLOS DE BARILOCHE

CLUB DE CAZA Y PESCA ■

IGLESIA CATEDRAL ★

SECRETARÍA TURISMO DE RÍO NEGRO

AV. 12 DE OCTUBRE

ACA ■

To Terminal de Ómnibus, Train Station, Airport, Villa la Angostura, and Neuquén

E. O'CONNOR

HOSTERÍA SUR ●

● HOSTERÍA PIUKÉ

PIZZERÍA VOGUE

DIRTY BIKES

HOSPEDAJE TITO

B. MITRE

LADE

EL MUNDO DE LA PIZZA ▼

BARILOCHE BIKE'S ■

HOTEL LOS ANDES ■

ÓMNIBUS 3 DE MAYO ■

P. MORENO

HOSPITAL ZONAL

C. ONELLI

AV. ELFLEIN

F. BESCHTEDT

E. FREY

J. O'CONNOR

O. GOEDECKE

HOSTERÍA IVALÚ ●

EL CÍVICO

BARILOCHE RAFTING

L. DE QUAGLIA

EL VIEJO MUNICH

BANCO DE LA NACIÓN

CAMBIO SUDAMÉRICA

B. MITRE

TELEFÓNICA TEMPO

COCODRILOS

AMERICAN FALCON ■

ABUELA GOYE ▼

LOCUTORIO QUAGLIA

AEROLÍNEAS ARGENTINAS/ AUSTRAL

■ DE LA GRANJA

E. B. MORALES

BARUZZI ■ FLY SHOP

■ SOUTHERN WINDS

C. VILLEGAS

HELADOS JAUJA

PASEO DE LOS ARTESANOS

LANCHILE ■

LA ALPINA ▼

P. MORENO

CINE ARRAYANES

BANCO GALICIA ■

■ HAYLAND TRAVEL

DEL LAGO TURISMO ■

To El Bolsón and Esquel

© AVALON TRAVEL PUBLISHING, INC.

Northern Patagonia

graduation bashes that leave some hotel rooms in ruins. Student tourism may be declining, in relative terms at least, but Bariloche still lags behind aspirations that were once higher than the ski areas of nearby Cerro Catedral.

Bariloche holds a peculiar place in Argentine cinema as the location for director Emilio Vieyra's *Sangre de Vírgenes* (Blood of the Virgins), a Hammer-style vampire flick that was well ahead of its time when shot in 1967 (it's now available on DVD). Perhaps Vieyra envisaged the unsavory side of things to come, but Bariloche's bloodsuckers are only part of the story—the city and its surroundings still have much to offer, at reasonable cost. Many of the best accommodations, restaurants, and other services lie along Avenida Bustillo between Bariloche proper and Llao Llao, about 25 kilometers to the west.

Orientation

On Lago Nahuel Huapi's southeastern shore, 764 meters above sea level, Bariloche (population 89,475) is 1,596 kilometers from Buenos Aires and 429 kilometers southwest of Neuquén via RN 237, but 982 kilometers west of the Río Negro provincial capital of Viedma, on the Atlantic coast. It is 123 kilometers north of El Bolsón via RN 258.

As RN 237 enters Bariloche from the east, it becomes Costanera Avenida 12 de Octubre, Avenida Juan Manuel de Rosas, and then Avenida Bustillo, as it continues west to the resort of Llao Llao. En route, it skirts the landmark Centro Cívico; one block south, the parallel Avenida Bartolomé Mitre is the main commercial street, but the entire area within a few blocks of the lake is densely built. North-south streets—some of them staircases—climb steeply from the lakeshore.

◼ Centro Cívico

Despite the kitsch merchants who pervade the plaza with Siberian huskies and St. Bernards for photographic poses, and the graffiti that often deface sculptor Emilio Sarneguet's equestrian statue of the controversial General Roca, the handsome array of buildings that border it would be

© WAYNE BERNHARDSON

Torre Reloj (Clock Tower) in Bariloche's Centro Cívico, which set a precedent for architecture in the Argentine lake district

the pride of many cities around the world. The view north to Lago Nahuel Huapi is a bonus, even when the boxy Bariloche Center blocks the afternoon sun.

The Centro Cívico was a team effort, originally envisioned by architect Ernesto de Estrada in 1936 and executed under the stewardship of APN director Exequiel Bustillo until its inauguration in 1940. On its south side, when the Municipalidad's **Torre Reloj** (Clock Tower) sounds at noon, figures from Patagonian history appear to mark the hour. Other buildings of interest, with steep-pitched roofs and gracefully arched *recovas* that offer shelter from inclement winter weather, include the **Correo** (post office) and the **Museo de la Patagonia.**

Exequiel Bustillo's brother, the famous architect Alejandro Bustillo, designed the **Intendencia de Parques Nacionales** (National Park Headquarters, San Martín 24), one block to the north, to harmonize with the Centro Cívico. Together, the structures form a national historical monument and represent the best of Argentine Patagonia.

Museo de la Patagonia

At the northeast corner of the Centro Cívico, Bariloche's Patagonian museum is an admirably comprehensive effort at placing the region (and more) in ecological, cultural, and historical context. Its multiple exhibition halls touch on natural history through taxidermy (far better than most of its kind); insects (inexplicably including subtropical areas like Iguazú); the population of Patagonia from antiquity to the present; the region's aboriginal Mapuche, Tehuelche, and Fuegian peoples; caudillo Juan Manuel de Rosas; the Conquista del Desierto that displaced the region's first peoples; and Bariloche's own urban development. There is even material on Stanford University geologist Bailey Willis, a visionary consultant who did the first systematic surveys in the region in the early 20th century.

The Museo de la Patagonia Francisco P. Moreno (Centro Cívico s/n, tel. 02944/422309, US$1) is open 10 A.M.–12:30 P.M. and 2–7 P.M. weekdays except Monday, and 10 A.M. to 1 P.M. Monday and Saturday only.

Entertainment

The densely built *microcentro* has an active nightlife, with pubs, theaters, cinema and discos open until all hours.

Cine Arrayanes (Perito Moreno 39, tel. 02944/422860) shows recent movies.

Bariloche's cluster of downtown bars offers menus of palatable pub grub. Choices include the **Wilkenny Irish Pub & Restaurant** (San Martín 435, tel. 02944/424444), which has a 6–9 P.M. happy hour; **Pilgrim** (Palacios 167, tel. 02944/421686), also an Irish-style venue; and the traditional German-style **El Viejo Munich** (Mitre 102, tel. 02944/422336), a customary stop for sandwiches, snacks, and cold draft beer.

Like their Buenos Aires counterparts, Bariloche nightspots open late—around 1 A.M.—

and close around daybreak. The most central of the bunch is **By Pass** (Rolando 155, tel. 02944/420549), while several others lie a few blocks west of the Centro Cívico: **Cerebro** (Juan Manuel de Rosas 406, tel. 02944/424965), **Rockett** (Juan Manuel de Rosas 424, tel. 02944/431940), and **Grisú** (Rosas 574, tel. 02944/422269).

Events

More than just a pretty landscape, the Nahuel Huapi area has an active cultural life as well. Llao Llao's Camping Musical Bariloche (cmbariloche @infovia.com.ar) sponsors the summertime **Festival de Música de Verano,** which includes chamber music and brass concerts in January and February.

March's **Muestra Floral de Otoño** is an end-of-the-summer flower show, while May 3 marks the **Fiesta Nacional de la Rosa Mosqueta,** in which local bakers and confectioners make the most of the wild rosehips, a European introduction that's become a weed in the lake district. July's **Fiesta Nacional de la Nieve** (National Snow Festival) marks the beginning of the ski season.

Gardeners get their turn again at October's **Fiesta del Tulipán** (Tulip Festival) and the **Muestra Floral de Primavera** (Spring Flower Show). Late December is the time for **Navidad Coral** (Christmas Chorus).

Shopping

Bariloche artisans live off souvenir shoppers, who frequent the outdoor **Paseo de los Artesanos** (Villegas and Perito Moreno), open 10 A.M.–9 P.M. daily. For leather goods and gaucho gear, try **Mabrus** (España 268, tel. 02944/522313).

Vinos & Postres (Avenida San Martín 597, tel. 02944/436300) is the Bariloche outpost of Buenos Aires's Club del Vino, with a wide selection of wines from around the country.

Traditionally, chocoholics flock to places like **Fenoglio** (Mitre 301, tel. 02944/423119), **Las Artes** (Mitre 369, tel. 02944/424434), and **Abuela Goye** (Quaglia 221, tel. 02944/423311), which is also a standout ice creamery.

RISING COSTS

Shortly after completion of this book's manuscript, tourism sector prices in parts of Argentina (and in Chile) underwent notable increases in dollar terms, primarily in accommodations and, to a lesser degree, food and transportation.

Argentina's peso gained against the dollar, but even more significant was the rejuvenated tourist economy in the capital city of Buenos Aires and popular Patagonian destinations like San Carlos de Bariloche, San Martín de los Andes, Puerto Madryn, El Calafate, and Ushuaia.

Prices began rising because of increased domestic demand—for the most part, Argentines can still not afford to travel beyond their own borders, and thus spend their pesos at home. At the same time, foreigners were flocking to Argentina as their dollars and Euros bought far more than in the days of dollar-peso parity. Travelers should be prepared for steadily rising prices for food, accommodations, and transportation.

Sports and Recreation

Thanks to the proximity of Parque Nacional Nahuel Huapi, Bariloche is the base for organizing outdoor activities ranging from fishing, to hiking and climbing, mountain biking, horseback riding, white-water rafting and kayaking, and skiing. For details on skiing, see the sidebar "The Slopes of Bariloche."

From mid-November to mid-April, the entire lake district is an angler's paradise for its lakes (where trolling is the rule) and streams (for fly-fishing). Bariloche's **Club de Caza y Pesca** (Costanera 12 de Octubre and Onelli, tel. 02944/422785) is a good source of information. For rental equipment, try **Baruzzi Fly Shop** (Urquiza 250, tel. 02944/424922) or **Martín Pescador** (Rolando 257, tel. 02944/422275).

Non-Argentines can purchase licenses at the APN's Intendencia on the Centro Cívico at a cost of cost US$11 per day, US$50 per week, or US$70 per month; note that the national parks have fishing regulations which may differ from those of the province.

The APN can provide some information on hiking and climbing in the park, but the best source is the **Club Andino Bariloche** (20 de Febrero 30, tel. 02944/422260, cab@bariloche .com.ar, www.clubandino.com.ar), which also organizes excursions to the park, and sells trail maps.

Bariloche's generally high-quality roads, both paved and gravel, and the many wide trails in the vicinity make cycling an attractive option for seeing the area. Mountain bike rental, with gloves and helmet, costs about US$15 per day.

Dirty Bikes (Eduardo O'Connor 681, tel. 02944/425616, dirtyb@bariloche.com.ar, www .dirtybikes.com.ar) rents bikes and also offers half-day to multiday excursions that include other activities as well. **Bariloche Bike's** (Moreno 520, tel. 02944/424657) also rents bikes.

Local horseback trips can last anywhere from two hours (about US$10) to a full day, with multiday excursions also possible. The main operators are **Cabalgatas Carol Jones** (Modesta Victoria 5600, tel. 02944/426508, caroljones@infovia .com.ar, www.caroljones.com.ar) and **Tom Wesley Viajes de Aventura** (Mitre 385, tel. 02944/ 435040, viajesyaven@infovia.com.ar).

For rafters and kayakers, the Río Limay, at the outlet of Lago Nahuel Huapi, is a half-day, Class II float through agreeable scenery east of Bariloche. The more challenging Río Manso, midway between Bariloche and El Bolsón to the south, is a full-day, mostly Class III descent (around US$40 pp) with some taxing Class IV rapids on multiday trips.

Operators offering river trips include **Aguas Blancas** (Morales 564, tel. 02944/432799, aguasblancas@infovia.com.ar), **Bariloche Rafting** (Mitre 86, Local 5, tel./fax 02944/422997, rafting@bariloche.com.ar), **Extremo Sur** (Morales 765, tel. 02944/427301, info@extremosur.com, www.extremosur.com), and **Huala Turismo Aventura** (San Martín 66, tel. 02944/522438, info@patagoniarafting.com, www.patagoniarafting.com).

Accommodations

Bariloche has plentiful accommodations options in all categories, from camping to hostels, B&Bs, hotels, and luxury lodges. Quality hostel accommodations, in particular, have proliferated; for B&Bs, the best area is Barrio Belgrano, southwest of the Centro Cívico. The

Hotel Llao Llao, near Bariloche, is one of the most famous accommodations on the continent.

finest hotels are west of the city, on and along the Llao Llao road.

Bariloche's municipal tourist office keeps a thorough database of accommodations and, when demand is high in summer, they're an excellent resource. Remember that many low- to mid-range hotels cater to high school graduation trips, so may it be better to avoid them toward the end of the academic year.

Under US$10

There are numerous campgrounds west of town on and around Avenida Bustillo, such as the lake-front **Camping Petunia** (Avenida Bustillo 13500, tel. 02944/461969, campingpetunia@bariloche .com, www.campingpetunia.com, US$2.50 per adult, US$1.25 per child).

Bariloche's cheapest hostel—still very decent— is **La Bolsa del Deporte** (Palacios 405, tel. 02944/423529, viaene@bariloche.com.ar, www .labolsadeldeporte.com.ar, US$4 pp for dorms, US$10 d). It is tobacco-free. For a shoestring hotel, try **Hotel Los Andes** (Perito Moreno 594, tel. 02944/422222, US$6.50/7.50 s/d).

US$10–25

The HI affiliate **Ⓝ Periko's Youth Hostel** (Morales 555, tel. 02944/522326, US$5.50 pp) has mostly dorm rooms, but also some new stylish doubles (US$19 d) on the upper floors and a secluded garden (uncommon in this part of town); it's a nonsmoking facility. On forested grounds in a quiet neighborhood, its more cramped sister **Alaska Hostel** (Lilinquén 326, tel. 02944/461564, info@alaska-hostel.com, US$5.50 pp) is walking distance from Avenida Bustillo Km 7.5. Several buses, including Nos. 10, 20, and 21 will drop passengers here.

Across the street from Periko's, **Albergue Patagonia Andina** (Morales 564, tel. 02944/ 422783, info@elpatagoniaandina.com.ar, US$5–6 pp) is a little less spacious but equally welcoming, with ample common areas. Also good is the newly popular **Albergue El Gaucho** (Belgrano 209, tel. 02944/522464, albergueelgaucho@hotmail.com, www.hostelelgaucho.com.ar, US$4–5.50 pp), which has mostly dorms but also a handful of doubles (US$13); all rooms have private bath. It also rents bicycles, and the staff manage English, German, and Italian.

Other shoestring choices include **Hospedaje Tito** (Eduardo O'Connor 745, tel. 02944/ 523563, US$11 d), and Barrio Belgrano's **Residencial Wickter** (Güemes 566, tel. 02944/ 423248, wikter@hotmail.com, US$14 d) and **Residencial Güemes** (Güemes 715, tel. 02944/ 424785, US$9/15 s/d). Downtown's **Hostería Posada del Sol** (Villegas 148, tel. 02944/423011, posadadelsolbariloche@hotmail.com, US$17 d) is comparable.

West of Barrio Belgrano, **Hostería Quime Quipán** (Avenida de los Pioneros Km 1, tel. 02944/425423, quimequipan@bariloche.com.ar, www.hosteriaquimequipan.com.ar, US$15/17 s/d) is adequate but a steep walking distance away from downtown. The hillside **Hostería Ivalú** (Frey 535, tel. 02944/423237, US$17 d) is a decent out-of-the-center choice to the south.

Near the cathedral, try **Hostería Piuké** (Beschtedt 136, tel. 02944/423044, US$12/17 s/d), or the rather cluttered **Hostería Sur** (Beschtedt 101, tel. 02944/422677, hosteriasur@ciudad.com.ar, US$14/21 s/d).

Hostería La Sureña (San Martín 432, tel. 02944/422013, hosteria@infovia.com.ar, US$17/24 s/d) is an attractive chalet-style place whose main drawback is its busy avenue setting.

Barrio Belgrano is home to several family-run B&Bs that, in the US$6–7 pp range, are good alternatives to the city's otherwise impersonal budget-hotel scene. Among them are **Casa Rosa Arko** (Güemes 691, tel. 02944/423109), **Casa Eloisa Lamouniere** (24 de Septiembre 55, tel. 02944/422514), and **Casa Marianne Pirker** (24 de Septiembre 230, tel. 02944/429689, franzpirker@bariloche.com.ar).

US$25–50

Though it's not kept pace with the times—the first shower of the morning is slow to arrive via the aging plumbing and the breakfast is utterly forgettable—**La Posada del Angel** (Avenida Bustillo Km 12.5, tel. 02944/461263, posadadelangel @infovia.com.ar, www.hosteriasargentinas.com, US$27/32 s/d) does enjoy friendly family service, a large pool, and five wooded hectares screened by pines from the busy avenue. The rooms themselves are ample and comfortable, but their windows are too small to appreciate the alpine views.

Barrio Belgrano's obliging **Ruca Cheli Village Ski Hotel** (24 de Setiembre 275, tel./fax 02944/424528, rucacheli@ciudad.com.ar, www .rucacheli.com.ar, US$17/28 s/d) has reasonably large rooms that are good enough if you can endure the lurid wallpaper; rates include a buffet breakfast.

On the Llao Llao road, the woodsy  **Hostería Pájaro Azul** (Avenida Bustillo 10800, tel. 02944/461025, hostpajaroazul@bariloche .com.ar, www.hosteriapajaroazul.com.ar, US$24/ 28 s/d) has cozy pine-sided rooms with mountain views through relatively small windows.

Some of the 13 rooms at the attractive **Hostería La Pastorella** (Avenida Belgrano 127, tel. 02944/424656, lapastorella@bariloche.com .ar, www.lodgebariloche.com/pastorella, US$33/ 41 s/d) are a little too cozy for comfort, but it does offer a diverse breakfast and amenities including a sauna.

Past its prime, the **Hotel Aconcagua** (San Martín 286, tel. 02944/424718, aconcagua @invofia.com.ar, www.aconcaguahotel.com.ar, US$45 s or d) was once one of the city's best, but it's now only average in its price range.

US$50–100

Hotel Edelweiss (San Martín 202, tel. 02944/426165, reservas@edelweiss.com.ar, www .edelweiss.com.ar, US$90–105 s or d) has 100 spacious standard to superior rooms, plus more elaborate suites.

Over US$100

Llao Llao's  **Hotel Tunquelén** (Avenida Bustillo Km 24, tel. 02944/448600, recepciontunquelen@infovia.com.ar, US$160 s or d) might be the area's top choice were it not for the nearby Hotel Llao Llao.

Not just a hotel but an attraction in its own right,  **Hotel Llao Llao** (Avenida Bustillo Km 25, tel. 02944/448530, fax 02944/445781, llaollao @datamarkets.com.ar, www.llaollao.com) is an Alejandro Bustillo classic dating from 1940, its interior completely renovated in the 1990s. High-season rates run from US$184–283 s or d, depending on the size, view, and amenities of the room; there are also more-elaborate suites.

Fresh-made chocolates are one of the most popular items in Bariloche.

Downtown's top hotel is the five-star **Hotel Panamericano** (San Martín 536, tel. 02944/ 425846, hotel@panameri.com.ar, www.panamericanobariloche.com, US$350 s or d), a sprawling complex on both sides of the avenue, linked by a glassed-in, elevated walkway. It also holds a casino and a spa, but it's just not up to the standards—not to mention the style or location—of the Llao Llao.

Food

For breakfast, coffee, sandwiches, and sweets, try confiterías like **La Alpina** (Perito Moreno 98, tel. 02944/425693) or **Zona Sur** (Mitre 396, tel. 02944/434258).

Primarily a takeaway place, **La Esquina de las Flores** (20 de Febrero 313) is the Bariloche outpost of Buenos Aires's famous natural foods market and restaurant. For smoked *ciervo* (venison), *jabalí* (wild boar), and *trucha* (trout), pay a visit to **Ahumadero Familia Weiss** (Palacios and V.A. O'Connor, tel. 02944/435789), a *parrilla* and beer garden that packages these items for takeaway as well.

Downtown's **De la Granja** (Villegas 216, tel. 02944/435939) isn't the best of Bariloche's offerings, but its crepes (particularly the smoked trout) and fried empanadas are above average at moderate prices; the desserts, though, are below average.

Unrelated to its namesake ice creamery, **Jauja** (Quaglia 366, tel. 02944/422952) is a long-time fixture for its derivative European-style menu at higher-than-average prices.

Bariloche abounds in pizzerias, starting with the inexpensive, unpretentious, but nevertheless excellent **Cocodrilos** (Mitre 5, tel. 02944/ 426640), though **El Mundo de la Pizza** (Mitre 759, tel. 02944/423461) has greater variety. **Pizzería Vogue** (Palacios 156, tel. 02944/ 431343) is arguably hipper—or smugger—than either. Across the street, **Bucanero** (Palacios 187, tel. 02944/423674) is more engaging if less inventive.

The full-portion *bife de chorizo* at **El Boliche de Alberto,** Avenida Bustillo Km 8.8, tel. 02944/462285) is too big for all but the most ravenous adolescents, even the fatty half-portion (US$3.50) and the side dishes are far

too large for a single diner and even for some couples. Given its popularity, it's best to go a little early, around 8–8:30 P.M.; it also has downtown branches specializing in *parrillada* (Villegas 347, tel. 02944/431433) and pasta (Elflein 49, tel. 02944/431084).

Other worthwhile downtown *parrillas* include **La Vizcacha** (Rolando 279, tel. 02944/422109), which offers exceptional value for the money, and **El Fogón** (Elflein 163, tel. 02944/524603).

For *picadas*, pizzas, and draft beer, don't miss **Cervecería Blest** (Avenida Bustillo 11600, tel. 02944/461026); it closes relatively early, at midnight. The kitchen at **Paraje Bairoleto** (Avenida Bustillo 7966, tel. 02944/525251) prepares a brilliant *lomo a la pimienta* (pepper steak) in its airy but rather impersonal dining room; the service, however, is exemplary, and it also has a pub on site.

Possibly Bariloche's best—perhaps even one of the country's top 10— **Chachao** (Avenida Bustillo 3800, tel. 02944/520574, chachaobistro@terra.com) offers what can only be called nouvelle Patagonian cuisine; offerings include an assortment of cheeses and smoked game, crepes, guanaco, *lomo a la frambuesa* (steak with a raspberry sauce), Patagonian lamb with elaborate vegetable garnishes, teriyaki trout, and beer from El Bolsón. It's on the high side, with entrees about US$10 and up, but worth every centavo.

Bariloche has several exceptional ice creameries, starting with **Helados Bari** (España 7, tel. 02944/422305), near the Centro Cívico, and **Abuela Goye** (Quaglia 221, tel. 02944/ 422311). The real standout, though, is **Helados Jauja** (Perito Moreno 18, tel. 02944/437888), whose dizzying diversity includes unconventional wild fruit flavors, half a dozen or more chocolates, and the remarkable *mate cocido* (there's even greater variety at their home base in El Bolsón).

Information

Bariloche's **Secretaría Municipal de Turismo** (Centro Cívico s/n, tel. 02944/429850 or 429896, securismo@bariloche.com.ar) is open 8 A.M.– 9 P.M. daily, but in peak season it's overwhelmed with visitors in search of accommodations and other information. There's a satellite office in a kiosk at the Paseo de los Artesanos (Perito Moreno and Villegas, 9:30 A.M.–1 P.M. and 5–8:30 P.M. daily).

The APN's **Intendencia del Parque Nacional Nahuel Huapi** (San Martín 24, tel. 02944/423111) is one block south of the Centro Cívico. One block farther south, the **Club Andino Bariloche** (20 de Febrero 30, tel. 02944/424531, 9:30 A.M.–1 P.M. and 4:30–8:30 P.M. daily except Sunday) provides details and permits for hiking in the park.

The **Secretaría de Turismo de Río Negro** (Avenida 12 de Octubre and Emilio Frey, tel. 02944/425973, secturrn@rnonline.com.ar) distributes information on the entire province.

For motorists, **ACA** is at 12 de Octubre 785 (tel. 02944/422611).

Services

Bariloche has the most complete traveler services of any city in the lake district.

Cambio Sudamérica (Mitre 63) changes foreign cash and travelers checks. **Banco de la Nación** (Mitre 180) and **Banco Galicia** (Moreno and Quaglia) are two of many downtown banks with ATMs.

Correo Argentino (Centro Cívico s/n) is alongside the municipal tourist office; the postal code is 8400.

Banco Galicia (Quaglia 220) and **Telefónica Tempo** (Mitre 201) have phone and fax only; **El Cívico** (Urquiza 187), just off the Centro Cívico, has Internet service until 1 A.M.

Hayland Travel (Moreno 126, 6th floor, tel. 02944/426377) is the AmEx representative. **Del Lago Turismo** (Villegas 222, tel. 02944/430056, cordille@bariloche.com.ar) is a full-service agency that will arrange a variety of excursions around the city and the area.

For trips throughout the region and beyond, including Patagonian excursions via the still-rugged RN 40 to El Calafate, contact **Overland Patagonia** through either of Bariloche's Hostelling International affiliates: **Periko's Youth Hostel** (Morales 555, tel. 02944/522326, www.perikos.com) or **Alaska Youth Hostel** (Lilinquén 326, tel.

02944/461564, www.alaska-hostel.com). They also offer four-day tours on the Siete Lagos route, four days to Los Alerces, an 11-day combination of the two that adds three days' hiking, and an 18-day adventure to Ushuaia, Tierra del Fuego.

Spanish-language instruction is available at **La Montaña Spanish School** (Elflein 251, tel. 02944/524212, info@lamontana.com, www.lamontana.com), US$4 per hour.

Neighboring Chile has a consulate at Avenida Juan Manuel de Rosas 180, tel. 02944/422842.

For visa matters, visit **Migraciones** (Libertad 191, tel. 02944/423043).

Launderettes include **Lavadero Huemul** (Juramento 37, tel. 02944/522067) and **Lavematic** (San Martín 325, tel. 02944/426319).

The **Hospital Zonal** is at Perito Moreno 601 (tel. 02944/426119).

Getting There

Bariloche is the transportation hub for the Patagonian lake district.

LanChile (Moreno 234, 2nd floor, tel. 02944/431043) has recently begun flights from Santiago to Bariloche Thursday, returning to the Chilean capital via Puerto Montt; a Sunday flight goes from Santiago to Bariloche via Puerto Montt.

Domestically, **Aerolíneas Argentinas/Austral** (Mitre 185, tel. 02944/422425) normally flies to Aeroparque but a handful of flights make international connections at Ezeiza; a few flights go to El Calafate, and there's the occasional connection to Esquel and Trelew.

Bariloche is something of a hub for **LADE** (Mitre 531, 1st floor, tel. 02944/423562), with low-priced flights to Buenos Aires and to Patagonian destinations including Comodoro Rivadavia, Trelew, Neuquén, Zapala, El Bolsón, El Maitén, Esquel, and Río Mayo, but most of these are only weekly and schedules change frequently.

American Falcon (Mitre 159, tel. 02944/425200) flies daily to and from Aeroparque. **Southern Winds** (Quaglia 262, Local 13, tel. 02944/423704) flies to Aeroparque and to El Calafate.

On the eastern outskirts of town, across the Río Ñireco, Bariloche's new but relatively small **Terminal de Ómnibus** (Avenida 12 de Octubre s/n, tel. 02944/432860) is immediately east of the train station, with which it shares taxis and parking facilities. There are international services (to Osorno and Puerto Montt, Chile), long-distance services throughout the republic, and provincial and regional routes.

Sample destinations, fares, and times include Villa La Angostura (US$3, 1.5 hours), El Bolsón (US$4.50, two hours), San Martín de los Andes (US$8, 4.5 hours), Esquel (US$7.50, four hours), Neuquén (US$8–12, five hours), Viedma (US$19, 14 hours), Trelew (US$22, 13 hours), Bahía Blanca (US$23, 12 hours), Puerto Madryn (US$25, 14 hours), Santa Rosa (US$18, 13 hours), Mendoza (US$35, 18 hours), Comodoro Rivadavia (US$23, 12 hours), Mar del Plata (US$37, 19 hours), Buenos Aires (US$45–50, 22–23 hours), and Río Gallegos (US$47, 24 hours).

Sefepa (Avenida 12 de Octubre s/n, tel. 02944/431777, trenpatagonico@bariloche.com.ar, www.trenpatagonico.com.ar) connects Bariloche with Viedma via train Thursday and Sunday at 5 P.M. The 15-hour trip costs US$7 in hard-backed *turista*, US$18 in reclining Pullman, or US$28 in *camarote* sleepers; children 5 to 12 pay half.

Cruce de Lagos (www.crucedelagos.com) operates the long-running bus-boat shuttle over the Andes to Puerto Montt (US$178 with lunch) via Puerto Pañuelo, Puerto Blest, Puerto Frías, Peulla (Chile), Petrohué, and Puerto Varas. With an overnight at Peulla, the trip costs US$220 pp. For bookings, contact the local representative **Catedral Turismo** (Palacios 263, tel. 02944/425444). Foreigners pay an additional US$4.50 in national park entry fees; it is possible to do this trip in segments or as a round trip, say Puerto Pañuelo to Puerto Blest and back.

Getting Around

Aeropuerto Teniente Candelaria (tel. 02944/422767) is 15 kilometers east of Bariloche via RN 237 and RP 80. Micro Ómnibus 3 de Mayo's No. 72 bus goes directly to the airport (US$.50), while cabs and *remises* cost about US$2.50.

Ómnibus 3 de Mayo (Perito Moreno 840, tel. 02944/425648) goes to Cerro Catedral (US$1) every 30 minutes, sometimes via Avenida de los Pioneros and others via Avenida Bustillo. In summer, 3 de Mayo goes four times daily to Lago Mascardi.

Ómnibus 3 de Mayo's bus No. 20 goes every 20 minutes to Llao Llao and Puerto Pañuelo, which is also the final destination of some of its seven No. 10 and No. 11 buses via Colonia Suiza, on the Circuito Chico route through Parque Nacional Nahuel Huapi, at 8:05 A.M., noon, and 5:20 P.M. Return times from Puerto Pañuelo via Colonia Suiza are 9:40 A.M. and 1:40 and 6:40 P.M.

Ómnibus 3 de Mayo's No. 50 and No. 51 buses go to Lago Gutiérrez (US$1.10) every 30 minutes, while in summer the company's Línea Mascardi goes to Villa Mascardi (US$2) and Puente Los Rápidos (US$3) three times daily. Their Línea El Manso goes twice Friday and once Sunday to Río Villegas and El Manso (US$2), on the southwestern edge of Parque Nacional Nahuel Huapi.

Bariloche has several car rental agencies, including **Baricoche** (Moreno 115, 1st floor, tel. 02944/427638), **Budget** (Mitre 106, 1st floor, tel. 02944/422482), **Correcaminos** (Libertad 114, tel. 02944/426076), **Dollar** (Villegas 282, tel. 02944/430333), **Europcar** (Rolando 258, tel. 02944/426420), and **Localiza** (Avenida San Martín 531, tel. 02944/424767).

PARQUE NACIONAL NAHUEL HUAPI

In 1903, Patagonian explorer Francisco Pascasio Moreno donated three square leagues of "the most beautiful scenery [his] eyes had ever seen," at the west end of Lago Nahuel Huapi near the Chilean border, to "be conserved as a natural public park." Explicitly acknowledging the example of the United States in creating large public reserves, Moreno's burst of idealism actually returned part of a personal land grant to the Argentine state. This property, first known as Parque Nacional del Sur, was the forerunner of today's Parque Nacional Nahuel Huapi.

Since then, countless Argentine and foreign visitors have enjoyed the benefits of Moreno's charity and foresight in a reserve that now encompasses a far larger area of glacial lakes and limpid rivers, densely forested moraines and mountains, and snow-topped Andean peaks that mark the international border, connecting two countries via a series of scenic roads and waterways. So many, in fact, have experienced the park that it's questionable whether authorities have fulfilled Moreno's wish that "the current features of their perimeter not be altered, and that there be no additional constructions other that those that facilitate the comforts of the cultured visitor."

Prior to the "Conquest of the Desert," the Araucanians freely crossed the Andes between Chile and Argentina, via the Paso de los Vuriloches south of ice-covered, 3,554-meter Cerro Tronador, the park's highest peak. The pass lent its name to Bariloche which, a century after its founding in 1903, has morphed from a lakeside hamlet to a sprawling city whose wastes threaten the pure air, water, and woodlands that surround it.

For all that, Nahuel Huapi remains a beauty spot with almost unlimited options for excursions, some traditional and others less so. In 1979, unfortunately, Argentine and Chilean military dictatorships fortified the borders and mined the approaches because of a territorial dispute

HONORING THE EXPERT: THE LEGACY OF PERITO MORENO

The career of Francisco Pascasio Moreno (1852–1919) began improbably at his father's Buenos Aires insurance agency, but by age 20, the young, inquisitive Moreno had founded the Sociedad Científica Argentina (Argentine Scientific Society). From 1875, a time when much of Patagonia was hostile and unknown territory, he explored the Río Negro and Limay Valleys up to Lago Nahuel Huapi (twice), and the Río Santa Cruz to its source at Lago San Martín. On his 1879–80 Nahuel Huapi expedition, he fell prisoner to previously friendly Manzanero Indians—for whom he evinced a sympathy that was unfashionable in the era of General Roca's Conquista del Desierto—and escaped down the Limay on a precarious log raft.

In 1884, Moreno, dedicated to the public good, donated his extensive natural history collections to the Museo Antropológico y Etnológico de Buenos Aires, an institution that became the Museo de Historia Natural de La Plata—which U.S. Patagonian surveyor Bailey Willis compared with the Smithsonian Institution. In 1897, recognizing Moreno's intimate knowledge of the region, the government named the *perito* (expert) its delegate to a commission settling border differences with Chile; five years later, he oversaw the placement of permanent boundary markers.

The following year, in honor of his services, the government granted him a substantial Nahuel Huapi property near the Chilean border, which the altruistic Moreno gave back on the stipulation that it become the cornerstone of a national park system. Five years later, in 1908, he founded the Argentine Boy Scouts; in 1913, he hosted former U.S. President Theodore Roosevelt at Bariloche.

Only a few years later, dismayed by changes in a country that ignored his ideas, and betrayed and bitter like San Martín a century earlier, Moreno died in near-poverty in Buenos Aires. In Patagonia, his public legacy is a few frequently confused place-names—a street in Bariloche, his namesake lake to the west, the dusty provincial town of Perito Moreno, Parque Nacional Perito Moreno, and the famous Glaciar Perito Moreno.

Yet according to Bailey Willis (whose own name graces a peak near Bariloche), Moreno was the first to grasp Patagonia's potential as a "national asset" that needed impartial research to be properly unlocked: "Among men of Moreno's nationality personal ambition is more often than not the ruling motive. But he was selfless where knowledge of the truth was his objective."

in Tierra del Fuego, but a papal intervention cleared the air and perhaps reflected Moreno's aspirations:

This land of beauty in the Andes is home to a colossal peak shared by two nations: Monte Tronador unites both of them. . . . Together, they could rest and share ideas there; they could find solutions to problems unsolved by diplomacy. Visitors from around the world would mingle and share with one another at this international crossroads.

Orientation

From Moreno's original gift of 8,100 hectares along the Chilean border, the park has grown dramatically. Stretching from the northerly Lago Queñi, west of San Martín de los Andes, to the southerly Río Manso, midway between Bariloche and El Bolsón, it now covers 750,000 hectares in southwestern Neuquén and western Río Negro Provinces. Together with the contiguous Parque Nacional Lanín to the north, it forms an uninterrupted stretch of well over a million hectares, but part of the area is a *reserva nacional* that permits commercial development. At the park's western edge, the imposing Tronador is the highest of a phalanx of snow-covered peaks that signifies the border.

Flora and Fauna

Nahuel Huapi's flora and fauna resemble those of Parque Nacional Lanín to the north and Parque Nacional Los Alerces to the south, but differ in some important respects. There are three principal ecosystems: the easterly Patagonian steppe; the Andean-Patagonian forest; and the high Andes above 1,600 meters, which consists of low shrubs and sparse grasses adapted to cold, wind, and snow.

Guanacos graze the semiarid grasslands of the eastern steppe, stalked by foxes and even pumas, while raptors like the cinereous harrier (*Circus cinereus*) and American kestrel (*Falco sparverius*) patrol the skies. Toward the west, open woodlands of coniferous cypress, the southern false beech *ñire* and *maitén* cover the rocky soils.

Farther to the west, at slightly higher altitudes, dense false-beech forests of *coihue, lenga,* and *ñire* cover the slopes, while the lakeshores and stream banks burst with a flowering understory of *notro* and climbing vines like *mutisia,* with scattered clusters of the cinnamon-barked *arrayán* (*Myrceugenella apiculata*).

In the vicinity of Puerto Blest, rainfall up to 4,000 millimeters per annum supports a humid Valdivian forest of Guaiteca cypress (*Pilgerodendron uviferum*), *mañío macho* (*Podocarpus nubigena*), *mañío hembra* (Prince Albert's yew, *Saxegothaea conspicua*), and the tree fern *fuinque* (*Lomatia ferruginea*). Nahuel Huapi, though, lacks Lanín's Araucaria forests and the more southerly *alerce* tree is less abundant here than in Chubut Province.

The *huemul* (Andean deer, *Hippocamelus bisulcus*) and the miniature deer *pudú* (*Pudu pudu*) both exist here, but sightings are rare. Other mammals include the carnivorous *huillín* (otter, *Lontra provocax*) and the gopherlike *tuco-tuco* (*Ctenomys sociabilis*), an endemic rodent.

Normally ocean-going, the king cormorant has a colony along Lago Nahuel Huapi, where the kelp gull (*Larinus dominicanus*) often trails the boats that sail the lake. Nahuel Huapi, its tributary streams, and other lakes teem with trout and other fish as well.

Lago Nahuel Huapi

Nahuel Huapi's focal point is its namesake lake, whose several fingerlike fjords converge near the Llao Llao peninsula to form the main part of its 560-square-kilometer surface. With a maximum depth of 454 meters, it drains into the Río Limay, a major tributary of the Río Negro, east of Bariloche.

In the middle of Nahuel Huapi's northern arm, **Isla Victoria** is the former site of the APN's park ranger's school (since relocated to the Universidad Nacional de Tucumán) that trained rangers from throughout the Americas. From Puerto Pañuelo, the *Modesta Victoria* sails to the island (US$13 plus US$4.50 national park entry fee) at 10:30 A.M. and 2 P.M., continuing to Parque Nacional Los Arrayanes, on Península Quetrihué. To Isla Victoria only (US$6.50),

THE SLOPES OF BARILOCHE

After decades of decline and eclipse by resorts like Las Leñas (Mendoza), Bariloche is reestablishing itself as a ski destination with new investment and technological improvements at **Catedral Alta Patagonia** (Base Cerro Catedral, Casilla de Correo 1630, tel. 02944/423776, info@catedralaltapatagonia.com, www.catedralaltapatagonia.com), only a short hop west of town. It's still more popular with Argentines and Brazilians than long-distance travelers, but new snow-making and grooming equipment have complemented the blend of 15 beginner-to-advanced runs, and lift capacities have also improved. From a base of 950 meters, the skiable slopes rise another 1,000.

As elsewhere, ticket prices depend on timing; the season runs from mid-June to mid-October, but is subdivided into low, mid-, and peak season. One-day rates range US$16–28 for adults, US$13–23 for children ages 5 to 11 and seniors age 65–74. The corresponding prices for three-day passes are US$43–75 for adults, US$34–61 for children and seniors. Week-long passes cost US$90–157 for adults, US$72–127 for children and seniors, while the rates for 15-day passes are US$164–285 and US$132–232 respectively. Season passes cost US$714 for adults, US$580 for children and seniors. Those over age 74 are free.

Basic rental equipment is cheap, but quality gear is more expensive. In addition to the on-site facilities, try downtown's **Baruzzi Fly Shop** (Urquiza 250, tel. 02944/424922) or **Martín Pescador** (Rolando 257, tel. 02944/422275).

In addition to downhill skiing, there are also cross-country opportunities at close-in Cerro Otto.

Bioceánica has departures at 10 A.M., noon, and 2 P.M. Note that Los Arrayanes is more accessible from Villa la Angostura, on the north shore of the lake.

Circuito Chico

Bariloche's single most popular excursion leads west out Avenida Bustillo to Península Llao Llao and returns via the hamlet of Colonia Suiza, at the foot of Cerro López. En route, it passes or touches several points of interest worthwhile in their own right; buses along the route will pick up and drop off passengers almost anywhere.

For a panoramic view of Nahuel Huapi and its surroundings, take the **Aerosilla Campanario** (Avenida Bustillo Km 17.5, tel. 02944/427274) to the 1,050-meter summit of **Cerro Campanario,** where there's an expensive *confitería.* Operating 9 A.M.–6 P.M. daily, the chairlift charges US$4.50 pp.

The bus-boat "Cruce de Lagos" to Chile starts at **Puerto Pañuelo,** but excursions to Isla Victoria and Parque Nacional Los Arrayanes (across the lake) also leave from here. The area's outstanding

cultural landmark is the **Hotel Llao Llao,** a Bustillo creation opened to nonguests for guided tours (free of charge, except for parking); for details on accommodations here, see the Bariloche entry earlier in this chapter.

From Puerto Pañuelo the paved road continues west and then south before looping northeast toward Bariloche; a gravel alternative leads east to **Colonia Suiza,** known for its Sunday crafts fair (Wednesday also in summer). There is also a regular Sunday *curanto* (a mixture of beef, lamb, pork, chicken, sausage, potatoes, sweet potatoes, and vegetables, baked on heated earth-covered stones) and a spectacular assortment of sweets and desserts.

From Colonia Suiza, a zigzag dirt road suitable for mountain bikes climbs toward the Club Andino's **Refugio López,** 1,620 meters above sea level; near the junction of the paved and gravel roads, a steep footpath climbs 2.5 hours to the *refugio,* which is open mid-December to mid-April.

For most of the way, the route is obvious, but where it seems to disappear into a grove of *lengas,* it actually climbs steeply to the left, brushing the dirt road, before continuing toward the *refugio.* In fact, it's much simpler if a little longer to walk the upper sections along the road (in any event, the last kilometers are on the road itself, which deteriorates into something not even suitable for 4WD).

From Refugio López, a good place to take a break and a beer, the route climbs to **Cerro Turista,** a strenuous scramble over rugged volcanic terrain. With an early start, it's possible to reach the summit of 2,076-meter **Cerro López.**

Many Bariloche agencies offer the Circuito Chico as a half-day tour (about US$7 pp), but it's also possible on cheaper public transportation; for details, see Getting Around in the Bariloche section of this chapter.

Cerro Otto

From Bariloche's Barrio Belgrano, westbound Avenida de los Pioneros intersects a gravel road that climbs first gently and then steeply to the 1,405-meter summit of Cerro Otto. While it's a feasible eight-kilometer hike or mountain bike ride, it's also possible to reach the peak via the gondolas of **Teleférico Cerro Otto** (Avenida de los Pioneros Km 5, tel. 02944/441035) for US$9 pp; city buses No. 50 and No. 51 go directly to the base station.

On the summit road, at 1,240 meters, the Club Andino's **Refugio Berghof** has 40 bunks, serves meals and drinks, and also houses the **Museo de Montaña Otto Meiling** (guided tours US$.50), honoring an influential early mountaineer who built his residence here. There is a nearby area suitable for cross-country skiing and rock climbing.

Cerro Catedral

About 20 kilometers southwest of Bariloche, the 2,388-meter summit of Cerro Catedral overlooks **Villa Catedral,** the base of the area's major winter-sports complex (see the sidebar "The Slopes of Bariloche" for ski details). From Villa Catedral, the **Cablecarril y Silla Lynch** (US$6.50 pp, operating 10 A.M.–5 P.M. daily) carries visitors to **Confitería Punta Nevada** at 1,900 meters, and the **Refugio Lynch,** which also has a *confitería.* Hikers can continue along

© WAYNE BERNHARDSON

hikers on the trail to Refugio Cerro López, Parque Nacional Nahuel Huapi

the ridgetop route to the Club Andino's 40-bed **Refugio Emilio Frey,** 1,700-meters above sea level; it's open all year in an area whose spirelike summits are a magnet for rock climbers.

Monte Tronador

Though its inner fire died long ago, the ice-clad volcanic summit of Tronador still lives up to its name ("Thunderer") when frozen blocks plunge and crash off its face into the valley below. The peak that surveyor Bailey Willis called "majestic in savage ruggedness" has impressed everyone from early Jesuit explorer Miguel de Olivares to Perito Moreno, Theodore Roosevelt, and the hordes of tourists that view it every summer. Its ascent, though, is for skilled snow-and-ice climbers only.

Source of the Río Manso, Tronador's icy eastern face gives birth to the **Ventisquero Negro** (Black Glacier), a mixture of ice, sand, and rocky detritus, and countless waterfalls. Passing Pampa Linda, at the end of the road from Lago Mascardi, whistle-blowing rangers prevent novice (and other) hikers from approaching the **Garganta del Diablo,** the area's largest accessible waterfall, too closely.

From Pampa Linda, hikers can visit the Club Andino's basic **Refugio Viejo Tronador,** a kiln-shaped structure that can sleep a maximum of 10 climbers in bivouac conditions, via a trail on the south side of the road. On the north side, another trail leads to its more comfortable 60-bed **Refugio Meiling,** 2,000 meters above sea level. Well-equipped backpackers can continue north to Laguna Frías via the 1,335-meter Paso de las Nubes and return to Bariloche on the bus-boat shuttle via Puerto Blest and Puerto Pañuelo; it's also possible to do this route from Bariloche.

Reaching the Tronador area requires a roundabout drive via southbound RN 258 to the south end of Lago Mascardi, where westbound RP 81 follows the south bank of the Río Manso; at Km 9, a northbound lateral crosses the river and becomes a single-lane dirt road to Pampa Linda and the base of Tronador. Because of its narrowness, traffic is one-way inbound in the morning (until 2 P.M.) and outbound in the afternoon (after 4 P.M.). At other hours, it's open to cautious two-way traffic. Starting in mid-November, the Club Andino provides transportation from its Bariloche headquarters to Pampa Linda at 9 A.M. daily, returning at 5 P.M., for US$4.50 pp (two hours).

Hostería Pampa Linda organizes horseback rides in the vicinity.

Accommodations and Food

Park campgrounds are numerous, especially in those areas accessible by road. The Club Andino's *refugios* charge around US$3 pp for overnight stays, US$$.50 for day use, US$.75 for breakfast, and US$1 more for kitchen use. Since bunks are limited, it's a good idea to make reservations through the Club Andino, but day hikers can buy simple meals and cold drinks at them.

Hotels and other accommodations are scattered around various sectors of the park. At the Villa Catedral ski area, the cheapest option is the Club Andino's **Hostería Knapp** (tel./fax 02944/460021, hosteria@hosteria-knapp.com.ar, www.hosteria-knapp.com.ar, US$23 pp with breakfast), which has a restaurant, bar, and ski-equipment rentals (though it's open all year). Half board is also available, and triples and quadruples are available for slightly less pp; rates fall considerably in spring and summer.

At the northwest end of Lago Mascardi, on the Pampa Linda road, **Hotel Tronador** (tel. 02944/441062) is a lake district classic in the Bustillo tradition; rates of US$50/56 s/d with full board are more than reasonable. Near the end of the road, the rustically contemporary **Hostería Pampa Linda** (tel. 02944/490517, pampalinda @bariloche.com.ar, US$30/45 s/d with breakfast, US$38/58 s/d with half board, US$45/73 s/d with full board) charges reasonable rates.

Information

For detailed information on the park, contact the APN office or the Club Andino in Bariloche. The *refugios* in the highlands are good sources of information within the park.

The Club Andino's improved trail map *Refugios, Sendas y Picadas,* at a scale of 1:100,000 with more-detailed versions covering smaller areas at a scale of 1:50,000, is a worthwhile acquisition. The fifth edition of Tim Burford's *Chile and Argentina: The Bradt Trekking Guide* (Bradt Travel Guides, 2001) covers several park trails in considerable detail, but its maps are for orientation only. The third edition of Clem Lindenmayer's *Trekking in the Patagonian Andes* (Lonely Planet, 2003) has more-useful maps.

EL BOLSÓN

El Bolsón, the counterculture capital of Argentine Patagonia, may be the place to replace your worn-out tie-dyes, but it's also a beauty spot in a fertile valley between stunning longitudinal mountain ranges that provide some of the region's finest hiking. So far, despite completion of the paved highway from Bariloche, this self-styled "ecological municipality" and declared nonnuclear zone has managed to stymie the incursion of five-star hotels and stylish ski areas in favor of simpler—earthier, even—services and activities.

El Bolsón's alternative lifestyle dates from the 1960s, and grew in the 1970s as an island of tolerance and tranquility even during the nastiest military dictatorship Argentina ever endured. More affordable than Bariloche, it embraces visitors, turns the valley's agricultural bounty—apples, cherries, pears, raspberries, strawberries—into delectable edibles, and makes local hops into a distinctive beer. This is the northernmost place to buy gasoline at Patagonian discount prices.

Orientation

Río Negro's southernmost city, on the border of Chubut Province, El Bolsón (population 13,845, elevation 300 meters) is 123 kilometers south of Bariloche via RN 258 and 167 kilometers north of Esquel via RN 258 and RN 40. West of the Río Quemquemtreu, which flows south through the valley, the snowy ridge of Cordón Nevado marks the Chilean border, while the north-south ridge of Cerro Piltriquitrón rises steeply to the east.

Most services are on or around north-south Avenida San Martín, the main thoroughfare, which leads south to Lago Puelo; the diagonal Avenida Belgrano becomes the main southbound highway to Chubut. The center of civic life is the elliptical Plaza Pagano, which surrounds an artificial lake and is the site of the popular street fair.

Feria Artesanal

Nearly encircling Plaza Pagano, the buskers, bakers, candle-makers, flower arrangers, and countless other crafts workers of Bolsón's popular Feria Artesanal (street fair) have transformed it from a once-a-week gathering to a Tuesday, Thursday, and Saturday event. Instead of eating a restaurant lunch, snack to the max on the homemade empanadas, sandwiches, sausages, and sweets, and wash them all down with fresh-brewed draft beer. It all starts around 10 A.M. and winds down around 3 P.M.

Other Shopping

In addition to the crafts at the Feria Artesanal, the Mapuche-oriented **Centro Artesanal**

Cumey Antú (Avenida San Martín 2020, sells indigenous textiles. On the east side of town, **Cabaña Micó** (Islas Malvinas 2753, tel. 02944/492691) is the place to find fresh fruit from its own vines in season, and homemade preserves the rest of the year.

Entertainment and Events

Founded in 1926, the city celebrates its **Aniversario** every January 28. Bolsón's brewers take center stage in mid-February's four-day **Festival Nacional del Lúpulo** (National Hops Festival).

In summer, the **Morena Café** (San Martín and Pablo Hube, tel. 02944/492725) offers live music. **La Bandurria** (Perito Moreno and Dorrego, tel. 02944/491929) and **La Posada del Alquimista** (Avenida Belgrano and Beruti, tel. 02944/492908) also have live music.

Sports and Recreation

Several El Bolsón travel agencies arrange excursions such as boating on Lago Puelo, hiking and climbing, horseback riding, mountain biking, rafting on the nearby Río Azul and the more distant Río Manso, parasailing, and the like. Where logistics are complex, as in reaching some trailheads, they can be a good option.

Among the operators are **Grado 42** (Avenida Belgrano 406, Local 2, tel. 02944/493124, grado42@elbolson.org), **Patagonia Adventure** (Pablo Hube 418, tel. 02944/492513, patago @red42.com.ar), and **Viva Patagonia** (Avenida San Martín 2526, tel. 02944/455555, vivamaspatagonia@elbolson.com).

Accommodations

El Bolsón has quality accommodations for every budget except the four- and five-star luxury category. Some of the best values are not in town, but scattered around its northern and southern outskirts.

At the north end of town, directly on the highway, a truly unique option is **Camping El Bolsón** (RN 258 s/n, tel. 02944/492595, info@cerveza-elbolson.com, US$2.50 pp), perhaps the only campground in the country with its own brewery and beer garden. At the southeast edge of town, grassy **Camping La Chacra** (Avenida Belgrano s/n, tel. 02944/492111, US$3 pp) is a good alternative.

Albergue Sol del Valle (25 de Mayo 2329, tel. 02944/492087, US$3.50 pp) is a good downtown hostel. About four kilometers north of town, the HI affiliate **El Pueblito Hostel** (Barrio Luján s/n, tel. 02944/493560, reservas@hostels .org.ar, US$3 pp dorms, US$9 d) is a comfortable, sociable place on a large property, with bunks for 40 people. From downtown Bolsón, there are hourly buses between 7:45 A.M. and 8:45 P.M., except at 9:45 A.M. and 7:45 P.M.

Residencial Edelweiss (Angel del Agua 360, tel. 02944/492594, US$3.50 pp) is basic, with shared bath and kitchen privileges. **Residencial Salinas** (Roca 641, tel. 02944/492396, US$4.50 pp) may be cozy in summer but cold in winter; rates include kitchen privileges. Somewhat better choices include **Residencial Valle Nuevo** (25 de Mayo 2329, tel. 02944/492087, US$13 d) and **Hospedaje Unelén** (Azcuénaga 350, tel. 02944/492729, US$14 d).

About three kilometers southeast of Plaza Pagano, Alejandro Canale raises brilliantly colorful flowers for dried arrangements on the lower slopes of Piltriquitrón at **Hostería Sukal** (Subida los Maitenes s/n, tel. 02944/492438, sukal@elbolson.com, www.sukalelbolson.com, US$15 d). A miracle for the price, it also enjoys spectacular views of the Andean crest across the valley.

Casablanca Hostería (José Hernández and Onelli, tel. 02944/492464, US$18 s or d) offers smallish but well-furnished rooms with private bath and breakfast, which varies daily (a strong point, as Argentine hotel breakfasts are often uniformly mediocre). It's open from January to Semana Santa, and again in the July winter holidays. **La Posada de Hamelin** (Granollers 2179, tel. 02944/492030, US$12/18 s/d) is comparably priced.

On the west side of the highway on the northern outskirts of town, the **Hostería del Campo** (RN 258 s/n, tel. 02944/492297, US$16/20 s/d) has quiet motel-style rooms with covered parking, set among spacious gardens, but breakfast is extra and there's a credit card surcharge.

Amancay Hotel (Avenida San Martín 3217, tel. 02944/492222, htlamancay@yahoo.com.ar, US$13/21 s/d) is an aging but still serviceable hotel that shows wear but not tear; rates include breakfast. Across the street, the **Cordillera Hotel** (Avenida San Martín 3210, tel. 02944/492235, cordillerahotel@elbolson.com, US$26/37 s/d) has large rooms whose east-facing balconies have fine views of Cerro Piltriquitrón; it's the best in its category in town, but there are more distinctive options surrounding town. Rates include buffet breakfast.

Six kilometers north of town, by a well-signed dirt road that diverges from the main highway to Bariloche, the French-run riverside **La Casona de Odile** (Barrio Luján s/n, tel. 02944/ 492753, odile@red42.com.ar, www.interpatagonia.com/odile, US$16 pp) is a bargain with breakfast; a home-cooked French dinner with wine doubles the price, though, and Odile herself is a heavy smoker (nonguests may also partake of dinner with reservations).

Food

Given the ready accessibility of fresh fruit and vegetables, food in El Bolsón exceeds expectations, even though it may lack Buenos Aires's (or even Bariloche's) sophistication. Forego at least one restaurant lunch to snack at Plaza Pagano's **Feria Artesanal. Verde Menta** (San Martín 2137) is a natural foods grocery.

There are several good breakfast-and-coffee spots, including **La Calabaza** (San Martín 2524, tel. 02944/492910) and **La Tosca** (San Martín and Roca, tel. 02944/493669), immediately behind the tourist office; the latter has occasional live music. Relocated **La Salteñita** (Avenida Belgrano 515, tel. 02944/493749) still serves the best spicy northern empanadas for takeaway.

Economical **Arcimboldo** (Avenida San Martín, tel. 02944/492137) specializes in pastas. **Las Brasas** (Sarmiento and Hube, tel. 02944/492923) is one of Bolsón's best *parrillas*.

Martín Sheffield (Avenida San Martín 2500, tel. 02944/491920) is a welcome new presence on the dining scene, with cooked-to-order chicken, Patagonian trout, and lamb, plus local beer on tap. Service is excellent and attentive. **Il**

Rizzo (Avenida San Martín 2500, tel. 02944/491380) is for pizza and pasta.

Cerro Lindo (Avenida San Martín 2524, tel. 02944/492899) has evolved from a good but simple pizzeria (try the smoked boar) to a full-fledged restaurant with regional specialties that include half a dozen versions of trout, plus venison, stuffed leg of lamb, and the like, in the US$4–5.50 range. It badly needs a tobacco-free section, though—the air is fresher on the sidewalk.

Still, Bolsón's best is ⚑ **Jauja** (San Martín 2867, tel. 02944/492448), where Alejandro Canale's vivid flower arrangements set the stage for succulent pastas such as gnocchi with a garlic cream sauce, vegetarian dishes such as *milanesa de soja* (soybean steak), a diversity of fish and pizza, outstanding homemade bread, and local brews.

Ignore the in-house desserts, though, and step out the door to their **Helados Jauja,** one of the country's top two or three ice creameries, with an almost paralyzing choice of inventive flavors. One longstanding favorite is *mate cocido con tres de azúcar* (boiled and slightly sweetened *mate*), though some Argentines blanch at the idea of consuming their favorite bitter infusion in frozen form.

Information

At the north end of Plaza Pagano, El Bolsón's improved **Dirección Municipal de Turismo** (Avenida San Martín and Roca, tel./fax 02944/492604, sec_turismo@elbolson.com, www.bolsonturistico.com.ar) provides decent maps of accommodations and other services, and even employs a helpful accommodations specialist who will make suggestions and book hotels. Summer hours are 9 A.M.–11 P.M. Monday–Saturday and 10 A.M.–10 P.M. Sunday; the rest of the year, hours are 9 A.M.–10 P.M. daily.

For details on hiking and climbing in the vicinity, visit the **Club Andino Piltriquitrón,** on Sarmiento between Roca and Feliciano (tel. 02944/492600).

For motorists, **ACA** is at Avenida Belgrano and San Martín (tel. O2944/492260).

Services

Banco de la Nación (Avenida San Martín 2598) and **Banco Patagonia** (Avenida San Martín 2831) have ATMs.

Correo Argentino is at Avenida San Martín 2806; the postal code is 8430. At the south end of Plaza Pagano, **La Barra** (Juez Fernández 429) has long-distance phone service. **Rancho Internet** (Avenida San Martín and Pablo Hube) has the best Internet connections.

Laverap (José Hernández 223, tel. 02944/493243) does the washing.

The **Hospital de Area** (Perito Moreno s/n, tel. 02944/492240) is behind Plaza Pagano.

Radio Alas (FM 89.1 Mhz) provides an eclectic blend of music and community service programs 8 A.M.–2 P.M. weekdays and 8 A.M.–midnight weekends.

Getting There

El Bolsón has regional air and bus connections, but Bariloche has more-complete services.

LADE (Roca 446, tel. 02944/492206) flies Tuesdays to El Maitén and Bariloche, and Thursday to Río Mayo and Comodoro Rivadavia. Flights leave from the **Aero Club El Bolsón** (tel. 02944/491125), at the north end of Avenida San Martín.

Although El Bolsón currently lacks a single central **bus** terminal, most companies are within a few blocks of each other. A new bus terminal is under discussion. It would be located at the north end of San Martín at the aerodrome and could open before the next edition of this book is completed.

Andesmar (Belgrano and Perito Moreno, tel. 02944/492178) goes to Bariloche and Buenos Aires (usually with a change in Neuquén), and south to Esquel. **Vía Bariloche** (Roca 359, tel. 02944/455554) goes to Esquel, Bariloche, and Buenos Aires; **Transportes Esquel,** at the same address, also goes to Esquel, via Parque Nacional Los Alerces.

Grado 42 (Belgrano 406, tel. 02944/493124) represents TAC, which goes to Esquel and to Bariloche, and makes connections in Neuquén for Mendoza, Córdoba, and other northern destinations. **Don Otto** (Belgrano and Berutti, Local 3, tel. 02944/493910) goes to Bariloche and Comodoro Rivadavia, with connections in Esquel for Trelew and Puerto Madryn.

The usual destinations from El Bolsón are Bariloche (US$4.50, two hours) and Esquel (US$5, 2.5 hours). Fares to other northbound destinations are slightly more expensive than those from Bariloche; fares to southbound destinations are slightly cheaper than those from Bariloche.

Getting Around

For a small town, El Bolsón has excellent public transportation for excursions like Cerro Piltriquitrón, Mallín Ahogado, and Lago Puelo. There are also abundant radio taxis and *remises*.

For rental bikes, try **La Rueda** (Avenida Sarmiento 2972, tel. 02944/492465).

VICINITY OF EL BOLSÓN

One of El Bolsón's greatest virtues is its convenience to trailheads for hiking and secondary roads for mountain biking. Most are just far enough away, though, to require an early start for those without their own vehicle.

Two blocks north of Plaza Pagano, westbound Azcuénaga crosses the Quemquemtreu and continues six kilometers to a footpath overlooking its southerly confluence with the Río Azul and, in the distance, Lago Puelo; the precipitous northbound trail leads to the natural metamorphic silhouette colloquially known as the **Cabeza del Indio** ("Indian's Head"). The local Mapuche themselves sometimes hold ceremonies here.

About 10 kilometers north of town, but west of the highway via a gravel road, the **Cascada Mallín Ahogado** is a 20-meter waterfall on the Quemquemtreu tributary of the Arroyo del Medio. Another gravel road continues 15 kilometers northwest to the Club Andino's 80-bunk

Refugio Perito Moreno (tel. 02944/493912, US$3.50 pp); a small ski area, at a base elevation of 1,000 meters, has a T-bar lift to 1,450 meters. Meals are also available here. From the *refugio,* the 2,206-meter summit of **Cerro Perito Moreno** is about a 2.5- to three-hour hike.

Cerro Piltriquitrón

East of Bolsón, the piedmont rises steadily and then sharply to the granite summit of 2,284-meter Piltriquitrón, where a clear day reveals the snow-covered phalanx of peaks along the Chilean border, from Tronador and beyond in the north to Lago Puelo and beyond the Cordón Esperanza in the south. Over the border, the Fuji-perfect cone of Volcán Osorno lies almost immediately west of Tronador.

From Bolsón, a winding dirt road climbs 13 kilometers to an overlook and parking area at the 1,200-meter level, where a steep footpath leads to the **Bosque Tallado** (www.elbosquetallado.com, US$1), where chainsaw sculptors from around the country have transformed trunks from a scorched *lenga* forest into 25 memorable sculptures.

Beyond the Bosque Tallado, the trail climbs to the Club Andino's **Refugio Piltriquitrón** (tel. 02944/492024, bunks US$2.50 pp), at 1,400-meters, where you need your own sleeping bag; meals are also available here. This was once a ski area, and the path climbs even more steeply along the rusty T-bar cable before leveling off and rounding Piltriquitrón; marked by paint blazes, it then climbs steeply again, over loose rock debris, to the summit. From the *refugio,* it takes about two hours; carry water and high-energy snacks.

In summer, Bolsón's **Grado 42** (Avenida Belgrano 406, Local 2, tel. 02944/493124) goes to the parking area at 9 A.M. daily, returning at 5 P.M. The fare is US$3.50 one-way, US$5 round-trip.

Interior Chubut Province

PARQUE NACIONAL LAGO PUELO

Fed by four rivers and numerous arroyos, nearly surrounded by forested peaks, the turquoise body of Lago Puelo is the showpiece of its namesake national park. In addition to its scenery, it's popular for camping, swimming, boating, and hiking, and offers a little-used option for crossing into Chile (unlike most Argentine lakes and streams, Lago Puelo drains toward the Pacific).

Just 15 kilometers south of El Bolsón, Lago Puelo lies across the Chubut provincial line. The park itself encompasses 27,675 hectares of mostly mountainous forested land, except for the lakeshore deltas of the Río Azul in the north, and the Río Turbio, across the lake to the south. Though the lake is only 200 meters above sea level, the summits rise above 1,500 meters.

Flora and Fauna

Lago Puelo's flora and fauna closely resemble those of Nahuel Huapi to the north and Los Alerces to the south. Its relatively low elevations and exposure to Pacific storms, however, create a milder microclimate around the lakeshore that permits the growth of tree species like the *ulmo* (*Eucryphia cordifolia*), with its showy-white flowers, and the *lingue* (*Persea lingue*). The *huemul* (Andean deer) and *pudú* (miniature deer) are both present but rarely seen.

Sports and Recreation

There are several trailheads near the park's scantily outfitted Centro de Informes, where a couple of bilingual guides hang out to offer inexpensive guided hikes. The most popular is the **Sendero al Mirador del Lago,** to the east, which climbs 130 meters to an overlook.

To the west, the **Senda Los Hitos** fords the Río Azul and leads five kilometers east to Arroyo Las Lágrimas, where through-hikers to Chile can complete Argentine border formalities with the Gendarmería. Five kilometers farther west, just beyond Los Hitos, the Chilean Cara-

bineros handle their part of the paperwork; from there, it's possible to continue to the Chilean town of Puelo, with onward connections to Puerto Montt.

For most visitors, though, the chance to sail the lake is the main attraction. The *Juana de Arco* (tel. 02944/493415) and *Popeye 2000* carry passengers on half-hour excursions (US$3.50 pp) after 2 P.M.; they also offer midmorning departures to the Chilean border (US$11 pp).

The *Catamarán Lago Puelo* (tel. 02944/492663, lagopuelo@elbolson.com) sails daily all year to Río Turbio (US$11), on the south shore of the lake.

Practicalities

Immediately east of the visitors center, **Camping Lago Puelo** (tel. 02944/499186) charges US$2 pp. There's a free site at Arroyo Las Lágrimas, about five kilometers west of the visitors center, on the footpath to the Chilean border; there are other free sites at Río Turbio, at the south end of the lake. There's a small *confitería* here, and limited supplies are available.

Near the park entrance, the APN's understaffed **Oficina de Informes** (tel. 02944/499232, pnpuelo@red42.com.ar) lags behind the area's other park offices, with scanty exhibits on its natural attractions. At the entrance, they collect fees of US$2.25 pp for Argentine residents, US$4.50 pp for foreigners; that admission is valid for 48 hours at nearby parks, including Nahuel Huapi and Los Alerces.

From El Bolsón, Vía Bariloche **buses** shuttle down Avenida San Martín to the park entrance and back 11 times every weekday between 7 A.M. and 9 P.M., but only nine Saturday between 9:15 A.M. and 9:15 P.M. The only Sunday buses leave at 10:45 A.M. and 1:45, 4:45, and 7:45 P.M. Return times are 45 minutes later.

EL MAITÉN

In 1979, Paul Theroux's overrated opus *The Old Patagonian Express* made the dying

locomotive plaque at El Maitén

narrow-gauge railway that ran south from Ingeniero Jacobacci to Esquel known in households worldwide. Its antique steam locomotives no longer traverse the entire 402-kilometer route from Río Negro to Chubut, but the dusty township of El Maitén, with its rusting rails, weathered workshops, and twirling turntables, is the best place to savor a picturesque line that was an economic folly. Like Esquel, it retains enough rolling stock to let committed trainspotters board this anachronism and fill their photo albums in the process.

El Maitén (population 3,399) is 70 kilometers southeast of El Bolsón via gravel RP 6 or paved RN 258 and gravel RP 70. It is 130 kilometers north of Esquel via RP 40, the last 32 kilometers of which is unpaved.

La Trochita

Gringos may cite the Gospel according to Theroux, but Argentines know the train as *La Trochita* (a diminutive for "gauge") or *El Trencito* ("Little Train"). The yards are still open, though only a couple of locomotives (an American Baldwin and a 1922 German Henschel) are in running order; the mostly Belgian cars date from 1922 to about 1960.

February's combined **Fiesta Provincial del Trencito** and **Fiesta Nacional del Tren a Vapor** (National Steam Train Festival) fill El Maitén's handful of hotels and campgrounds. Celebrating the railroad, it also features live music, horseback races and bronco-busting, and regional delicacies.

In summer, the train does a 2.5-hour excursion to Bruno Thomae and back (US$5.50 pp) Tuesday, Thursday, Friday, and Saturday at 3 P.M.; the rest of the year, frequencies fall to weekly. For current schedules, contact El Maitén's **Secretaría de Turismo** (tel. 02945/495150, turismai@ar.inter.net).

Practicalities

On the Río Chubut on the east side of town, **Camping Municipal** (tel. 02945/495189) charges about US$1 pp. **Hostería Refugio Andino** (Avenida San Martín 1317, tel. 02945/15-681121, US$4.50 pp) has both accommodations and a restaurant.

LADE (Avenida San Martín s/n, tel. 02945/495159) flies once or twice per week to destinations like El Bolsón, Bariloche, Esquel, Río Mayo, and Comodoro Rivadavia.

Transportes El Maitén (tel. 02944/493124) goes from El Bolsón to El Maitén Wednesday and Saturday at 1 P.M., returning at 3 P.M. **Transportes Jacobsen** (Avenida San Martín 1317, tel. 02945/15-681121) goes to Esquel (US$4.50, two hours) Tuesday, Thursday, and Saturday at 1 P.M.

ESQUEL

Across the Chubut border, the gateway to Parque Nacional Los Alerces and the end of the line for the famous narrow-gauge train internationally known as The Old Patagonian Express, Esquel is a deceptively tranquil town of wide avenues divided by densely wooded medians. It is also, though, a city divided by a dispute and a plebiscite that rejected a nearby gold mine, promoted by Canadian interests and local politicians, which would have used highly toxic cyanide to leach the gold. What's more, it's a place where Mapuche militancy is palpable, in graffiti that says "neither Argentine nor Chilean, but Mapuche."

© WAYNE BERNHARDSON

La Trochita, the famous narrow-gauge railroad, arriving at Esquel

Orientation

Esquel (population 28,117) is 167 kilometers south of El Bolsón via RN 258, RN 40, and RN 259, all of which are smoothly paved. Alternatively, many visitors take the gravel highway RP 71, south of the town of Epuyén, to go directly to Parque Nacional Los Alerces. Esquel is also 608 kilometers west of Trelew via a series of paved highway across the Patagonian steppe, and 581 kilometers northwest of Comodoro Rivadavia via equally good roads.

The city itself is a compact grid on the north bank of the Arroyo Esquel. Southbound RN 259 leads to a junction to Parque Nacional Los Alerces, the Welsh-settled town of Trevelin, and the Chilean border at Futaleufú.

Sights

Esquel's most notable sight, not to mention one of its most popular excursions, is the narrow-gauge steam train **La Trochita,** which arrives and departs from the **Estación Ferrocarril Roca** (Roggero and Urquiza).

Esquel has a pair of modest museums. The **Museo de Culturas Originarias Patagónicas** (Belgrano 330, tel. 02945/451929, US$.35) is an archaeological and ethnographic institution focusing on Patagonia's first peoples; it's open 7 A.M.–12:30 P.M. and 4–9 P.M. weekdays, 9 A.M.–1 P.M. weekends.

The **Museo de Arte Naif** (Avenida Alvear and Avenida Fontana, US$.35) occupies new quarters on the first floor of the old bus terminal; it's open 9:30 A.M.–noon and 5–8 P.M. weekdays, 10 A.M.–12:30 P.M. and 6–8 P.M. weekends.

La Trochita

From the old Roca railway station, now a museum, La Trochita still makes daily excursions in summer to the nearby station of Nahuel Pan, and operates less frequently the rest of the year; its wooden passenger wagons, equipped with salamander stoves, are classics of their era, and the entire line is national historical monument. The theoretical top speed of the antique steam engines is 60 km/h, but these rarely exceed 45 km/h and average only about 30 km/h.

Normally, the train to Nahuel Pan and back leaves at 10 A.M. and returns to Esquel at 1 P.M. The fare is US$9 pp; for more detail, contact **La Trochita** (Roggero and Urquiza, tel. 02945/451403).

Events and Shopping

The **Semana de Esquel** marks the city's founding in 1906. The **Fiesta Nacional de Esqui** (national ski festival) takes place in September.

The Asociación de Artesanos de Esquel sponsors the **Feria Artesanal Permanente** in Plaza San Martín; hours are 7–10:30 P.M. Thursday and Friday, 6–11:30 P.M. weekends.

For wood carvings, try **Artesanías Manolo** (Alsina 483). **Casa de Esquel** (25 de Mayo 415, tel. 02945/452544) is a bookstore and crafts outlet. **La Casona de Olgbrun** (San Martín 1137, tel. 02945/453841) sells crafts but also edibles such as chocolates and smoked salmon.

Sports and Recreation

Hiking, climbing, horseback riding, white-water rafting and kayaking, fishing, and skiing are all on the docket; for information on skiing, see the separate entry for La Hoya later in this chapter. Rafters and kayakers should note that the Río Futaleufú, across the border in Chile, is one of the world's top white-water rivers; Argentina's Corcovado is an easier Class II–IV outing.

Patagonia Verde (9 de Julio 926, tel. 02945/454396) arranges activities like hiking, climbing, and horseback riding. **Frontera Sur** (Sarmiento 784, tel. 02945/450505, fronterasur@fronterasur.net, www.fronterasur.net) organizes water sports like rafting (US$30 for a full day) and kayaking on the Class II–III Río Corcovado, as well as hiking, riding, and mountain biking. Rincón Andino (Miguens 40, tel. 02945/451891) has similar offerings.

For fishing licenses, contact the **Dirección de Pesca** (9 de Julio 1643, tel. 0297/451226); the season runs from November through mid-April.

Accommodations

Esquel has abundant budget accommodations but not much in the upper categories. Standards in general, though, are good.

There are several campgrounds around and just outside of town: **Autocamping La Colina** (Humphreys 554, tel. 02945/454962, US$3 pp), **Camping Millalén** (Ameghino 2063, tel. 02945/456164, US$9 d), and **Autocamping La Rural** (RN 259 Km 1, tel. 02945/15-681429, US$2 pp, plus a one-time charge of US$2 per car, tent, and family group).

Shoestring backpackers can try the basic **Hotel Argentino** (25 de Mayo 862, tel. 02945/452237, US$3.50–6 pp), which has rooms with shared or private bath. There are also, however, simple B&Bs like the **Casa Familiar Rowlands** (Rivadavia 330, tel. 02945/452578, US$3.50 pp) with shared bath.

Other inexpensive options include **Hostería El Cisne** (Chacabuco 778, tel. 02945/452256, US$5.50.9 s/d) and **Hotel Huemul** (Alvear 1015, tel. 02945/450817, US$5.50/9 s/d). No longer a Hostelling International affiliate, **Parador Lago Verde** (Volta 1081, tel. 02945/

452251, fax 02945/453901, patagoniaverde@ciudad.com.ar, US$10 d) is still a good value.

Hostería Lihuén (San Martín 822, tel. 02945/452589, ejarque@ar.inter.net, US$11/15 s/d) is a friendly, decent place. **Residencial Ski** (San Martín 961, tel. 02945/451646, elcalafate@ciudad.com.ar, US$13/17 s/d) is a bit worn.

Comfortable **Hostería los Tulipanes** (Avenida Fontana 365, tel. 02945/452748, US$12/16 s/d) is a real find—the decor is tacky, but the beds are firm, the baths spacious, and the breakfast abundant and diverse. There's also a genuine warmth that shows up in small details, like chocolates by the bedside.

Improved **Hotel Esquel** (San Martín 1044, tel. 02945/452534, hotelesquel@hotmail.com, US$23 d) and **Hostería La Tour D'Argent** (San Martín 1063, tel. 02945/454612, latourdargent@ciudad.com.ar, US$18/25 s/d) are also good choices.

Despite its unimpressive facade, the spacious, well-furnished rooms at the exceptionally friendly **M Hostería Angelina** (Avenida Alvear 758, tel./fax 02945/452763, hosteriangelina@argentina.com, US$20/26 s/d) make it the best value in its category. Rates include a buffet breakfast, telephone, TV, parking, and central heating.

Esquel has a pair of solid three-star hotels: **Hotel Sol del Sur** (9 de Julio 1086, tel. 02945/452189, soldelsur@ar.inter.net, US$18/28 s/d) and spacious **Hotel Tehuelche** (9 de Julio 825, tel. 02945/452420, tehuelche@ar.inter.net, US$34/42 s/d).

Food

Esquel is no place for haute cuisine, but local restaurants do what they do well. **María Castaña** (25 de Mayo 605, tel. 02945/451752) serves breakfast, coffee, and good sandwiches. **La Luna** (Rivadavia 1080) offers palatable lunches for about US$5, with limited sidewalk seating. **La Empanadería** (Molinari 633) bakes a variety of empanadas.

Fitzroya Pizza (Rivadavia 1048, tel. 02945/450512) is a first-rate pizzeria, with an enormous variety of toppings, in the US$3.50–7 range; solo diners can order half portions. Other good pizzerias include **Don Pipo** (Fontana 649, tel. 02945/453458) and **Pizzería Dos-22** (Ameghino and Sarmiento, tel. 02945/454995).

La Española (Rivadavia 940, tel. 02945/ 451509) is a *parrilla* that also serves Middle Eastern dishes. **Vascongada** (9 de Julio and Mitre, tel. 02945/452229) serves large portions of regional specialties.

Serenata (Rivadavia 975, tel. 02945/455999) has Esquel's best ice cream.

Information

Keeping long hours, the **Secretaría de Turismo y Medio Ambiente** (Avenida Alvear 1120, tel. 02945/451927, turismo@esquel.gov.ar, www.esquel.gov.ar) maintains a thorough database on accommodations and other services here and in Parque Nacional Los Alerces, and has a representative at the bus terminal as well. The private **Ente Mixto de Turismo** (tel. 02945/451566) has a desk at the bus terminal, but its information is skeletal.

For motorists, **ACA** is at 25 de Mayo and Ameghino (tel. 02965/452382).

Services

Banco del Chubut (Alvear 1131) and **Banco Macro Bansud** (25 de Mayo 737) have ATMs.

Correo Argentino is at Alvear 1192; the postal code is 9200. **Su Central** (25 de Mayo 415) has both phone and Internet access, but the best Internet connections are at **Locutorio El Alerce** (25 de Mayo and 9 de Julio). **Cyber Planet** (San Martín 978) also has good connections.

Chile's honorary consulate (Molinari 754, tel. 02945/451189) is open 8:30 A.M.–1:30 P.M. weekdays only.

Lavandería Marva (Avenida San Martín 941) does the laundry for about US$3 per load.

For medical services, contact the **Hospital Zonal** (25 de Mayo 150, tel. 02945/450222).

Getting There and Around

Austral (Avenida Fontana 406, tel. 0297/ 453614) flies twice or three times weekly to Buenos Aires via Bariloche.

LADE (Alvear 1085, tel. 02945/452124) usually flies twice weekly to Bariloche and Chapelco

(San Martín de los Andes), weekly to Comodoro Rivadavia and Puerto Madryn, weekly to Río Mayo, El Maitén, and El Bolsón, and weekly to Aeroparque.

Aeropuerto Esquel is 20 kilometers east of town on RN 40; a taxi or *remise* is the only option.

Esquel's **Terminal de Ómnibus** (Avenida Alvear 1871, tel. 02945/451566) has finally moved from its congested downtown location to a more contemporary facility four blocks to the northeast. It has good local and regional connections, but long-distance services are better in Bariloche.

Transportes Jacobsen (tel. 02945/453528) connects Esquel with El Maitén at 12:30 P.M. Tuesday, Thursday, and Saturday, returning at 3 P.M.

Jacobsen also serves the nearby provincial destinations of Trevelin (frequently); La Balsa/Futaleufú (Monday and Friday at 8 A.M. and 5:30 P.M., with Wednesday service in summer); and Corcovado/Carrenleufú (Sunday and Monday at 4 P.M., Wednesday and Friday at 10 A.M.).

In summer, **Transportes Esquel** (tel. 02945/ 453529) goes to Parque Nacional Los Alerces and Lago Puelo at 8 A.M. (connecting with lake excursions) and 2 P.M. daily; a 7.30 P.M. bus goes only as far as Lago Verde. Fares are US$2.50 to La Villa, US$3.50 to Bahía Rosales, US$4 to Lago Verde, US$5 to Lago Rivadavia, US$6 to Cholila, and US$7 to Puelo, where there are easy connections to El Bolsón. Winter schedules may differ.

Other typical destinations, fares, and times include Trevelin (US$1.40, 30 minutes), La Balsa/Futaleufú (US$3.50, 1.5 hours), El Maitén (US$4.50, two hours), El Bolsón (US$5, 2.5 hours), Corcovado/Carrenleufú (US$4, three hours), Bariloche (US$9.50, five hours), Neuquén (US$16, nine hours), Trelew (US$14, eight hours), Puerto Madryn (US$16, nine hours), and Comodoro Rivadavia (US$14, nine hours). For Buenos Aires, it's necessary to change in Bariloche.

For the moment, La Trochita (tel. 02945/ 541403) is a **tourist train** only, but there's talk of reopening the line to Ingeniero Jacobacci.

Northern Patagonia

La Hoya

Only 13 kilometers north of Esquel, run by the provincial government, La Hoya is a modest ski area with improving infrastructure. Thanks to its location on the drier eastern side of the Andes, it gets a fine powder that compensates for its relatively small size, and it's also substantially cheaper than Bariloche.

Ranging from 1,200 to 2,500 meters above sea level, La Hoya has 25 runs totaling about 22 kilometers on 60 hectares. Its modern lifts include the 1,100-meter Telesilla del Bosque, which also carries hikers to high-country trailheads in summer (US$2); and the 1,018-meter Telesilla del Cañadón. In season, which runs from June to October, it also has a ski school; the **Fiesta Nacional del Esquí** (National Ski Festival) takes place the second week of September.

Full-day lift passes run from US$7 (low season) to US$9 (high season), with small children's discounts. Six-day passes cost US$35–45 for adults, US$25–35 for children, while season passes cost US$70 for adults, US$50 for children.

Equipment can be rented on site or in Esquel at **Bolsa de Ski** (Rivadavia and 25 de Mayo, tel. 02945/452379). In town, contact the **Centro de Montaña La Hoya** (25 de Mayo 646, tel. 02945/453018, www.camlahoya.com.ar).

Museo Leleque

Midway between Esquel and El Bolsón, on what was one of Argentina's largest *estancias,* the Museo Leleque covers Patagonia from prehistory to the present. Funded by Italian fashion icon Carlo Benetton, who purchased the Argentine Southern Land Company and several other Patagonian properties, it houses and organizes the collections of Ukrainian immigrant Pablo S. Korschenewski, who left Buenos Aires half a century ago to live in Patagonia, exploring the countryside on foot and by horseback.

In the process, Korschenewski collected over 14,000 artifacts including arrowheads, thin stone blades, bone drills, ceremonial stone axes, grinding stones, and pottery shards; making contact with Benetton, he struck a chord and persuaded him to turn the historic buildings at Leleque, once a general store, hotel, and school, into a contemporary museum that now gets 8,500 visitors, mostly Argentines, per annum. Not just archaeological, the exhibits stress contact and post-contact history of the region's first peoples, regional and oral histories, photographs and documents. One prize is a receipt signed by Butch Cassidy, who lived in nearby Cholila from 1901 to 1905 under the alias Santiago Ryan.

Administered by the Fundación Ameghino, the Museo Leleque (RN 40 Km 1440, museoleleque@ciudad.com.ar, US$1) is 90 kilometers north of Esquel. It's open 11 A.M.–7 P.M. daily except Wednesday in January and February; the rest of the year, hours are 11 A.M.–5 P.M. except Wednesday and in May and June, when it shuts down entirely. The museum also has a souvenir shop and a *confitería.*

Cholila

Though it's barely a wide spot in the road, the community of Cholila has become an offbeat pilgrimage site ever since U.S. author Anne Meadows pinpointed the house of North American outlaws Robert Leroy Parker and Harry Longabaugh in her historical travelogue *Digging Up Butch and Sundance* (third edition, University of Nebraska Press, 2003). Bruce Chatwin also told the tale of the Cholila cabin—perhaps taking literary license—in his classic *In Patagonia.*

Butch and Sundance apparently tried to go straight here, but fled to Chile in 1905 when accused of a robbery in Río Gallegos and the Pinkertons got on their scent. Since the death of its elderly occupant Aladín Sepúlveda in 1999, the unoccupied and now-crumbling cabin has become a target for souvenir hunters. It is also in legal limbo, unsaleable since one of the Daher family owners died intestate; the Sepúlveda family also claims a right of occupancy. The provincial government hopes to lease the cabin from the Daher survivors, restore it, and hire the Sepúlvedas as caretakers.

Near the northeastern entrance of Parque Nacional Los Alerces, just north of Cholila at Km 21 of RP 71 near the signed junction to the Casa de Piedra teahouse, the house is visible on the west side of the highway; there are informal direc-

© WAYNE BERNHARDSON

Northern Patagonia

Butch Cassidy and the Sundance Kid's cabin at Cholila

tional signs. Transportes Esquel buses between El Bolsón and Esquel via Los Alerces pass within sight of the cabin.

Beyond the cabin entrance, a westbound lateral leads to the **Casa de Piedra** (tel. 02945/498056, US$25 d with breakfast), a hybrid B&B/teahouse that's open from December through Semana Santa. It makes an ideal detour even for day-trippers.

TREVELIN AND VICINITY

Unlike coastal Chubut, the Andean interior has few settlements where the Welsh imprint remains, but tranquil Trevelin, with historic houses and teahouses to rival Gaiman, is the exception. Only half an hour south of Esquel, it owes its very name to a Welsh compound meaning "mill town" after its first flour mill, since preserved as a history museum.

Trevelin (population 4,849), 24 kilometers south of Esquel via RN 259, is also unique for its disorientingly octagonal Plaza Coronel Fontana, from which RN 259 continues southward as Avenida San Martín; it is the main commercial street and thoroughfare to Corcovado and the

Chilean border post of Futaleufú. Other streets fan out from the plaza.

Sights

In 1922, Welsh immigrants founded the Molino Harinero de la Compañía Andes, the flour mill that is now the **Museo Molino Viejo** (Molino Viejo 488, tel. 02945/480189, US$1 adults, US$.50 children under age 12). Closed in 1953, it was then used to store wool; a fire gutted its interior in 1972, but the solid brick walls survived to become the city's historical museum. Its contents include everyday artifacts of early Trevelin, such as clothing, furniture, carriages, and agricultural machinery, but also photographs, maps, and documents. From November to March, hours are 10 A.M.–9 P.M. daily; the rest of the year hours are 9 A.M.–noon and 2–8 P.M. daily.

Two blocks northeast of the plaza, the offbeat historical monument known as the **Tumba de Malacara** (Malacara s/n, tel. 02945/80108, 9 A.M.-12:30 P.M. and 2 P.M.–dusk, US$.65) holds the stuffed remains of the horse that helped its rider, John Evans, flee an Araucanian raid during the Argentine army's 1880s war against the indigenes.

At the south end of town, built of brick, the **Capilla Bethel** (Aplwan and Laprida) is a Welsh chapel that dates from 1897; it has also served as a school.

About 19 kilometers south of Trevelin via RN 259 and a short southbound lateral, **Reserva Provincial Nant-y-Fall** is a provincial park with a 400-meter footpath to a string of waterfalls, the highest of which is 67 meters. The source for Nant-y-Fall is **Lago Rosario,** a subalpine lake on a Mapuche reservation, 24 kilometers southwest of Trevelin via RP 17 and a short eastbound lateral.

Six kilometers west of Nant-y-Fall, the provincial **Estación de Salmonicultura** (salmon hatchery) offers guided tours 8 A.M.–1 P.M. weekdays. There are several campgrounds and *cabañas* along RN 259, which leads to the Chilean border.

For information on the Chilean settlement of **Futaleufú,** which offers some of the world's most thrilling white-water rafting and kayaking, see *Moon Handbooks Chile.*

In summer, there's a Sunday **crafts market** on Plaza Coronel Fontana; the rest of the year, it takes place alternate Sundays.

Accommodations

Except for *cabañas,* which are primarily for large family groups, accommodations are scarce. On the high ground east of the plaza, the HI affiliate **M Casaverde Hostel** (Los Alerces s/n, tel. 02945/480091, casaverdehostel@ciudad .com.ar, US$5 pp dorms, US$10 d) is a true prize: comfortable rooms, a bar, and extensive grounds, with views of the Andes in the distance. It's small, though, so reservations—or good timing—are essential.

Other good options include **Residencial Pezzi** (Sarmiento 353, tel. 02945/480146, US$6 pp) and **Residencial Estefania** (Perito Moreno and Sarmiento, tel. 02945/480148, US$6/9 s/d).

Food

Like Gaiman, Trevelin is the place to go for Welsh tea; though teahouses are not so numerous here, the quality is still outstanding. The traditional favorite, though its quarters are contemporary, is **M Nain Maggie** (Perito Moreno 179, tel.

02945/480232), but there's nothing wrong with **Las Mutisias** (Avenida San Martín 170, tel. 02945/480165). Late-afternoon teas, which are very filling, cost about US$5 pp.

Four blocks south of the plaza, **Ruca Laufquén** (Avenida San Martín 419, tel. 02945/480400) is a reliable *parrilla.* **Kuimey Ruca** (Avenida Fortín Refugio s/n, tel. 02945/480088), a block northwest of the plaza, is a fine pizzeria.

Reservations are advisable at **M Patagonia Celta** (25 de Mayo s/n, tel. 02945/15-687243), which has a more diverse menu of Argentine regional specialties. Despite the name, it has no direct Welsh connections.

Information

From December to March, the **Secretaría de Producción, Turismo, y Medio Ambiente** (Plaza Coronel Fontana s/n, tel. 02945/480120, turismotrevelin@ciudad.com.ar, www.trevelin .org) is open 8 A.M.–10 P.M. weekdays, 9 A.M.– 10 P.M. weekends; the rest of the year, hours are 9 A.M.–6 or 7 P.M. daily. Unfortunately, the level of service has fallen off in recent years.

Services

Banco del Chubut (Avenida San Martín and Brown) has an ATM.

Correo Argentino (Avenida San Martín and Brown) is across the street from the bank; the postal code is 9203. **Locutorio Central San Martín** (San Martín 559) is five blocks south of Plaza Coronel Fontana.

Gales al Sur (Avenida Patagonia 185, tel. 02965/480427) organizes excursions and activities in Trevelin and vicinity.

Lavitrev (Avenida San Martín 559, tel. 02945/480393) does the washing.

Hospital Trevelin (Avenida San Martín and John Evans, tel. 02945/480132) is three blocks south of Plaza Coronel Fontana.

Getting There and Around

Transportes Jacobsen shuttles between Esquel and Trevelin frequently during the daylight hours; some of its buses continue to the main Chilean border crossing at La Balsa/Futaleufú (Mon.,

Wed., and Fri. at 8:30 A.M. and 5:30 P.M.), while others use the alternate Chilean border post at Carrenleufú (weekdays at 5:30 P.M.). Long-distance travelers have to return to Esquel.

PARQUE NACIONAL LOS ALERCES

Parque Nacional Los Alerces owes its existence and its name to the coniferous *Fitzroya cupressoides,* the monarch of the humid Valdivian forests, also known as false larch or Patagonian cypress. Easily western Chubut's most popular attraction, the park draws campers and fishing aficionados to its lush forests and deep-blue finger lakes. Despite the magnificent setting, with the snowy summits of the Andean range to the west, hikers may find it frustrating because it has relatively few trails, forcing them to walk along dusty roads with heavy automobile traffic.

Geography and Climate
About 45 kilometers west of Esquel via RN 259 and RP 71, Los Alerces is a 263,000-hectare unit on the eastern Andean slope. The highest summit is 2,253-meter Cerro Torrecillas, but most of the cordillera here is low enough to permit the penetration of Pacific storms while areas to the north or south might lie completely in the rain shadow.

Past glaciations have left a series of navigable finger lakes that provide access to some of the park's greatest attractions. Summers are mild, temperatures reaching 24°C with cool nights, but winters average barely 2°C, with considerable snowfall.

Most destinations within the park are described with reference to "La Villa," the village-like cluster of services at the south end of Lago Futalaufquen.

Flora and Fauna
In addition to its signature *alerce,* the park's other conifers include the Chilean incense cedar (*Austrocedrus chilensis*) and the Guaiteca cypress (*Pilgerodendron uviferum*), both of which have very limited geographical distribution. Most of the rest of the forest consists of the broadleaf south-

THE REDWOOD OF THE SOUTH

Like the redwoods of California, the coniferous *alerce* (*Fitzroya cupressoides*) is long-lived (up to 4,000 years), tall (up to 70 meters, though most mature specimens top out around 40), and an attractive, easily worked, and water- and insect-resistant timber. Native to Chile and Argentina, it is much more abundant on the Chilean side, where its native habitat ranges from coastal Valdivia south to archipelagic and continental Chiloé. In Argentina, it's found from Lago Nahuel Huapi south to Parque Nacional Los Alerces.

Although it grows mostly between 400 and 700 meters above sea level, the *alerce* also occurs in poorly drained marshlands at lower altitudes. The branches of younger specimens touch the ground, but the reddish-barked lower trunks of mature trees are barren. The Mapuche know it as the *lawen,* but Darwin gave the tree its botanical name, after the famous commanding officer of his equally famous vessel. Still, the great scientist offers only a few descriptive remarks in his *The Voyage of the Beagle.*

ern beeches *coihue* (*Nothofagus dombeyi*), *lenga* (*Nothofagus pumilio*), and *ñire* (*Nothofagus Antarctica*). The *arrayán* is near the southern limit of its range here.

For hikers, one of the worst plagues is the *colihue* (*Chusquea coleou*), a solid bamboo that forms impassable thickets at ground level. The exotic *Rosa mosqueta,* a European introduction, is an aggressive species that is displacing native plants in many parts of the park.

In the dense forest, the fauna is less conspicuous, but the Andean deer or *huemul* is present, along with its distant miniature relative the *pudú.* Birds include the chucao (a common songbird), the austral parakeet and the Patagonian woodpecker.

Sights and Activities
Travel agencies in Esquel sell tickets for the **Circuito Lacustre,** the park's most popular traditional excursion to the old-growth *alerce* forests.

On the Río Desaguadero, east of RP 71 at the south end of Lago Futalaufquen, the **Sendero del Poblamiento Prehistórico** is an easy 500-meter nature trail that passes a natural overhang with fading pre-Columbian rock art, some of it clearly geometrical; it then climbs through forest to an overlook with expansive panoramas to the north.

Hikers need to register with rangers to hike the steep route to the 1,916-meter summit of **Cerro Alto El Dedal,** reached by a trailhead from Puerto Bustillo, two kilometers north of La Villa; figure about five hours round-trip. From the same trailhead, **Cinco Saltos** is a shorter and easier hike to a series of waterfalls.

From Puerto Limonao, four kilometers north of La Villa, the 25-kilometer **Sendero Lago Krüger** follows the southern shore of Lago Futalaufquen to the smaller Lago Krüger, where there are a campground and a *refugio,* which is due to reopen after repairs; register with rangers before beginning the hike. Daily boat service to Lago Krüger costs about US$17 pp.

In the park's southernmost sector, reached via Trevelin, the 448-megawatt **Central Hidroeléctrica Futaleufú** is a massive dam project that drowned several natural lakes to create a 9,200-hectare reservoir that powers the Aluar aluminum plant at Puerto Madryn, 550 kilometers to the east. Guided tours (US$1 pp) take place 8 A.M.–8 P.M. daily.

Circuito Lacustre

Los Alerces' traditional excursion is the "lake circuit" starting at Puerto Limonao, at the south end of Lago Futalaufquen, to the Río Arrayanes outlet of Lago Verde; at **Puerto Mermoud,** a catwalk crosses to **Puerto Chucao,** on **Lago Menéndez,** where another boat continues to **Puerto Sagrario.**

From Puerto Sagrario, passing blue-green **Lago Cisne,** a looping nature trail goes to the *alerce* grove of **El Alerzal** and the landmark **El Abuelo,** the oldest and most impressive single specimen. While there are guides on the hike to and from El Abuelo, it's possible to separate from the group; it is not, however, possible to hike elsewhere in an area that's mostly limited-access *zona intangible.*

It's possible to start the excursion at either Puerto Limonao (US$24 pp) or Puerto Chucao (US$15 pp. Scheduled departures are at 10 A.M. from Limonao, returning by 6:30 P.M.; and noon from Chucao, returning by 4:45 P.M. Esquel travel agencies can make reservations, which are highly advisable, but it's possible to purchase tickets here on a space available basis. The Esquel representative is **Empresa Cleona** (Avenida Alvear 442, tel. 02945/450795).

Accommodations and Food

Los Alerces has numerous campgrounds and a handful of other accommodations, mostly in the vicinity of Lago Futalaufquen. In addition to organized campgrounds, which are reasonably priced, there are free sites but maintenance is poor at most of these.

Accessible by road, organized campgrounds all have picnic tables, firepits, toilets with hot showers, and easy access to groceries and restaurants. Among them are **Camping Los Maitenes** (tel. 02945/451003, US$2 pp), only 200 meters from the Intendencia at the south end of Lago Futalaufquen; **Camping Bahía Rosales** (tel. 02945/471004, US$2.50 pp), 14 kilometers from La Villa on the eastern lakeshore; **Camping Lago Verde** (tel. 02945/454421, US$2 pp), 36 kilometers north of La Villa, on its eponymous lake; and **Camping Lago Rivadavia** (tel. 02945/454381, US$2.50 pp), 42 kilometers north of La Villa at the south end of its namesake lake.

Reached only by a 25-kilometer footpath or launch from Puerto Limonao, **Camping & Refugio Lago Krüger** (tel. 02945/454690) is the only backcountry campsite and hostel in the park. Having undergone a major renovation, it now charges US$5 pp for camping, and US$70 pp with full board in the *refugio.*

About 25 kilometers north of La Villa, on Futalaufquén's north arm, **Hostería Cume Hue** (RP 71 s/n, tel. 02945/453639, US$33/38 s/d with breakfast) has clean, comfortable rooms in an attractive setting, but seems to make little effort to promote itself. The restaurant is mediocre. About 10 kilometers north of La Villa, there's **Motel Pucón Pai** (RP 71 s/n, tel.

Hotel Futalafquen, Parque Nacional Los Alerces, was the work of the famous architect Alejandro Bustillo.

02945/452828, puconpai@ciudad.com.ar, US$32/52 s/d).

For groups of any size, the cheapest noncamping options are places like **Cabañas Los Tepues** (RP 71 s/n, tel. 02945/452129, los tepues@hotmail.com, US$45 for up to eight persons), eight kilometers north of La Villa; and **Cabañas Tejas Negras** (RP 71, tel. 02945/471046, US$60–70 for five to six persons), about 12 kilometers north of La Villa.

About six kilometers north of La Villa, **Hostería Quimé-Quipán** (RP 71 s/n, tel./fax 02945/471021, cell 0291/15-501537, 691658, US$60 d with half board) has simple but comfortable rooms, some with lake views; its restaurant is adequate, but hardly haute cuisine.

Four kilometers north of La Villa, the park's prestige accommodations is the Bustillo-built  **Hostería Futalaufquen,** (tel. 02945/471008, fax 02945/471009, www.newage-hotels.com, hosteria@ar.inter.net, www.brazosur.com, US$80–110 to US$110–164 s or d, depending on view). With only nine rooms, it enjoys a privileged end-of-the-road location on Lago Futalaufquen's western shore; distinctive features

include beamed Tudor-style ceilings, a walk-in granite fireplace, copper chandeliers, and a long wooden bar. Rates vary from low season (mid-October to mid-December and March to the end of April; high season is mid-December to late February and Semana Santa.

Other Practicalities

Colloquially known as "La Villa," **Villa Futalaufquen,** at the south end of Lago Futalaufquen on the eastern approach from Esquel, is the park headquarters. The APN's **Museo y Centro de Informes** (tel. 02945/471015, int. 23, losalerces@apn.gov.ar or infoalerces@apn.gov.ar) is both a museum, with exhibits on the park's history and natural history, and a notably helpful ranger information center. Hours are 7 A.M.–9 P.M. daily from mid-December to April, and 9 A.M.–5 P.M. daily the rest of the year.

At both the northern Lago Rivadavia and eastern La Portada entrances, rangers collect an admission fee of US$4.50, valid for one week here and at Nahuel Huapi, Lago Puelo, and Lanín. After 9 P.M., when the toll booths close, there is no one to collect the charge.

In addition to the APN headquarters, La Villa also has a gas station, grocery, post office, public telephones, and a first-aid station.

Transportes Esquel **buses** between Esquel and El Bolsón pick up and drop off passengers along RP 71 within the park; some northbound buses go only as far as Lago Rivadavia before returning to Esquel.

GOBERNADOR COSTA

Some 153 kilometers south of Esquel, the tiny cowtown of Gobernador Costa has little to see, but offers the best motorist services on the long haul between Esquel and Río Mayo on RN 40 (south of here, the paved route becomes RP 20, while graveled RN 40 detours west through Alto Río Senguer). **Lago General Vintter,** on the Chilean border via graveled westbound RP 19, is popular with fishermen.

Accommodations and Food

On the north side of the highway, the **Camping Municipal** (US$2 pp) has hot water and electricity. **Residencial Jair** (San Martín and Sarmiento, tel. 02945/15-680414, US$5.50) has decent rooms with private bath.

Hostería y Parrilla Mi Refugio (Avenida Roca s/n, tel. 02945/491097, US$9 pp) provides newish rooms with firm, comfortable beds, but the cheap bathroom fixtures could use an upgrade. Breakfast is included, and its restaurant serves pretty good versions of Argentine standards like beef, pasta, and *milanesa.*

Other Practicalities

Banco del Chubut (Sarmiento and San Martín) has an ATM.

Gobernador Costa's **bus terminal** has northbound services to Esquel, eastbound services to Trelew, and southbound services to Río Mayo, Sarmiento, and Comodoro Rivadavia.

RÍO MAYO

For southbound travelers on RN 40, the crossroads of Río Mayo is the end of the line for pub-

lic transportation; in fact, few vehicles of any kind use the spine-jarring gravel section that intersects RP 43, the paved route between Comodoro Rivadavia and the Chilean border, 124 kilometers to the south. Though it has little to see in its own right, it's a common stopover for cyclists, bikers, and others with their own mobility, as well as the odd southbound safari from Bariloche.

Depending primarily on wool for its livelihood, Río Mayo (population 2,940) is 224 kilometers south of Gobernador Costa, and 274 kilometers west of Comodoro Rivadavia via paved RN 26 and RP 20. There is public transportation on the 189 kilometers of westbound RN 26 to Coyhaique, Chile; some buses take the slightly longer route via RP 55. For information on the southern reaches of RN 40, between Perito Moreno and the Chilean border, see the Southern Patagonia chapter.

Sights and Events

Río Mayo's modest **Museo Regional Federico Escalada** (Avenida Ejército Argentino s/n) shares quarters with the tourist office and keeps the same hours, 9 A.M.–noon and 4–6 P.M. weekdays only.

Featuring sheep-shearing contests and horseback races, early January's **Festival Nacional de la Esquila,** in the Predio Olegario Paillaguala (fairgrounds) is the principal festival.

Accommodations and Food

At the fairgrounds, **Camping Municipal** (tel. 02903/420121) charges US$3 per vehicle. Modernized **Hotel Akatá** (San Martín 640, tel. 02903/420054, US$7 pp) has rooms with private bath and a restaurant as well.

Reservations are a good idea for **Hotel El Viejo Covadonga** (San Martín 573, tel. 02903/420020, elviejocovadonga@hotmail.com, US$7/13 s/d), which is popular with tour operators who do the circuit between Bariloche and El Calafate along RN 40. Though it no longer sports its classic Old West–style bar, which the previous owners absconded with, this spruced-up hotel has gracious management and it's also the best place to eat.

Information and Services

For tourist information, visit the Casa de la Cultura (Avenida Ejército Argentino s/n, tel. 02903/420400, turismoriomayo@yahoo.com.ar or riomayoturistico@yahoo.com.ar, 9 A.M.–noon and 4–6 P.M. weekdays only).

Banco del Chubut (Yrigoyen and Antártida Argentina) has an ATM. Río Mayo's postal code is 9030. **Hospital Río Mayo** (Sarmiento and Belgrano, tel. 02903/420022) provides medical services.

Getting There and Around

LADE (San Martín 520, tel. 02903/420060) flies semiregularly to Comodoro Rivadavia and to Esquel, El Maitén, El Bolsón, and Bariloche.

Schedules are subject to change from Río Mayo's **Terminal de Ómnibus** (Fontana and Irigoyen). **Etap** (tel. 02903/420167) has northbound services to Esquel (US$9, seven hours) twice weekly, usually Monday and Thursday, and eastbound services daily to Comodoro Rivadavia (US$6, four hours). Westbound international services to Coyhaique, Chile (US$8, four hours) leave Monday and Friday at 5:30 P.M., but often fill up in Comodoro, so reservations are essential.

Northern Patagonia

Southern Patagonia

Argentina's second and third largest provinces, extending from the ocean to the Andes, Santa Cruz and Chubut might be considered Argentina's "Deep South," whose vast open spaces and small population lend themselves to Patagonia's "wild and remote" stereotype. That said, there are several substantial cities and towns with hotels and other services, many good roads (and others not so good), and a decent public-transportation infrastructure.

Note that details on the northern stretches of RN 40, from the Río Negro provincial border to the town of Río Mayo in southern Chubut, appear in the Northern Patagonia chapter. Those sections of RN 40 southbound to the Chilean border and north to the town of Perito Moreno appear in this section.

PLANNING YOUR TIME

Like northern Patagonia, southern Patagonia has virtually limitless highlights, but distances are even greater and flying is almost essential for short-term visitors—overland transportation is

Must-Sees

M Ecocentro Puerto Madryn: This environmental center is home to living tidepools, gardens, a research library, and more. It is a testament to the ecological commitment of **Puerto Madryn,** coastal Patagonia's largest beach resort (page 444).

M Reserva Provincial Península Valdés: It's hard to choose among coastal Patagonia's countless wildlife reserves, but Península Valdés has everything: guanacos, rheas, penguins, elephant seals, sea lions, orcas, and the great right whales. It doesn't have everything at the same time, though, which makes every season a different experience (page 449).

M Reserva Provincial Punta Tombo: Every austral spring, nearly 250,000 pairs of Magellanic penguins come ashore to nest in this remote spot, but you'll also see plenty of other seabirds here (page 461).

M Parque Nacional Monte León: This newly created, less-visited coastal park features plenty of opportunities for wildlife-viewing. But the landscape is also unique—where the sea meets the headlands, the tides formed deep caverns (page 474).

M Estancia Monte Dinero: On the coastal steppe southeast of Río Gallegos, Monte Dinero is a model working ranch that also provides homey accommodations and access to the giant penguin colony and other sites at **Cabo Vírgenes** (page 478).

M Hostería Alta Vista: Southwest of El Calafate, this country lodge on the historic Estancia Anita is the place to vacation like the Braun-Menéndez dynasty (page 486).

M Parque Nacional Los Glaciares: The constantly calving 60-meter face of groaning **Glaciar Moreno,** west of El Calafate, is one of the continent's most awesome sights (and sounds). **Sector Fitz Roy,** near the hamlet of El Chaltén, offers some of the Andes' most exhilarating scenery, hiking and climbing (page 487).

M Parque Nacional Perito Moreno: In what is perhaps Patagonia's wildest park, you'll find varied terrain—from sub-Antarctic forest to high Andean pastures—that makes braving RN 40 worthwhile (page 499).

M Cueva de las Manos: Some of this area's rock paintings (of hundreds of human hands and other more abstract forms) are nearly 10,000 years old. It's one of the finest detours off RN 40 (page 501).

SOUTHERN PATAGONIA

Reserva Provincial Península Valdés

Ecocentro **M** Puerto Madryn

Reserva **M** Provincial Punta Tombo

ATLANTIC OCEAN

Cueva de las Manos **M**

M Parque Nacional Perito Moreno

Parque Nacional Los Glaciares **M**

M Hostería Alta Vista

Parque Nacional Monte León

Estancia Monte Dinero **M**

CHILE

Southern Patagonia

RESERVA PROVINCIAL
PENINSULA VALDÉS

RP 2

Golfo
Nuevo

Puerto
Pirámides

Reserva
Provincial Punta
Loma

RESERVA PROVINCIAL
PUNTA TOMBO

ECOCENTRO
PUERTO MADRYN

Puerto Madryn

Trelew

Gaiman

Rawson

RP 1

Reserva Provincial
Cabo dos Bahías

Camarones

RP 30

RP 28

RN
3

RN
25

SOUTHERN
PATAGONIA

RÍO NEGRO

CHUBUT

Río Chico

Comodoro Rivadavia

Rada Tilly

Golfo

San Jorge

RN
281

Caleta Olivia

RP 12

Pico
Truncado

Lago Colhué
Huapi

Sarmiento

RN
26

Río Desado

Las Heras

RP 43

Lago
Musters

RP 20

RP 22

Río Mayo

RN
40

CUEVA DE LAS MANOS

RP 57

Perito
Moreno

Río Chubut

Gobernador
Costa

Tecka

ARGENTINA

Alto Río
Senguer

RN
26

Lago
Buenos Aires

Los
Antiguos

Andes

RP 41

El Maitén

Leleque

RN
40

Cholila

Esquel

Trevelin

RP 62

Cordillera   de   los

Coyhaique

P.N.
Nahuel
Huapi

RN
258

El Bolsón

P.N. Lago
Puelo

P.N. Los
Alerces

Chaitén

RN
7

Puerto
Aisén

Puerto
Montt

Golfo de
Ancud

Golfo
Corcovado

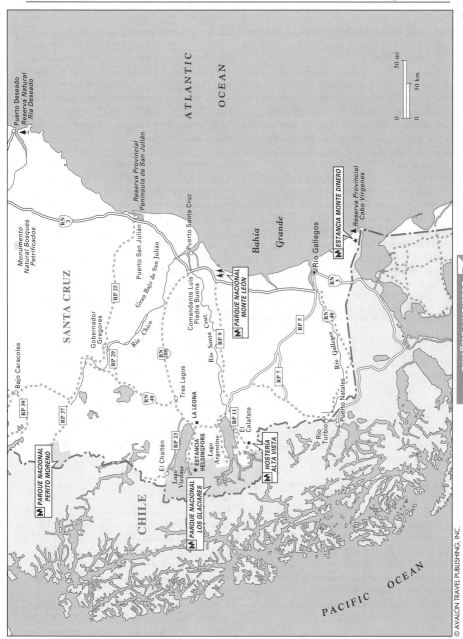

too time-consuming to see widely separated sights like the world-class wildlife of Península Valdés and the stunning Glaciar Moreno (Moreno Glacier).

Glaciar Moreno visitors should make additional time—perhaps at least a week—to hike the Fitz Roy Sector of Parque Nacional Los Glaciares and even Chile's Parque Nacional Torres del Paine (dedicated climbers can wait the entire summer for the weather to clear at these latitudes). Many choose an extension to Tierra del Fuego as well.

For visitors with time, money, and a vehicle, one of the best ways to see the region is to drive south on RN 3—all the way to the Glaciar Moreno or even Tierra del Fuego— and return via RN 40 to Bariloche or beyond. In addition to a sturdy vehicle, this would require at least a month, preferably two, and ideally three.

Coastal Patagonia's best base is Puerto Madryn, which has the largest and most diverse selection of accommodations and other services, and the best access to secondary attractions like the Welsh settlements of Trelew and Gaiman. For the national parks of the far south, El Calafate and El Chaltén are best options, along with full-service *estancias*.

As in northern Patagonia, January and February are the most popular vacation months, but they are also the most expensive. The shoulder months of November–December and March–April have lesser crowding, lower prices and almost equally good (and sometimes better) weather. By April, the days are getting significantly shorter, but winter whale-watching has become big business at Puerto Madryn.

As in northern Patagonia, overland transportation schedules change from season to season and year to year, and may be disrupted by weather.

Coastal Chubut Province

PUERTO MADRYN

For foreigners and many Argentines, Puerto Madryn is the gateway to coastal Patagonia's wealth of wildlife; the sheltered waters and sandy shoreline of the Golfo Nuevo have also made it, for better or worse, the region's premier beach resort. In January and February, sunbathers, cyclists, inline skaters, joggers, and windsurfers irrupt onto the *balnearios* along the Costanera Avenida Brown, while divers seek out reefs and wrecks as the shallow waters warm with the season.

In winter, the great right whales of nearby Península Valdés help fill the hotels, and the city, conscious of its ecological birthright, has promoted itself as an environmentally friendly destination. Its new Ecocentro complex, with its focus on maritime conservation, is a positive development, but mushrooming souvenir stores and chocolate shops have turned parts of the waterfront into tourist traps.

At the same time, the bright-green lawns of Madryn's suburban-style homes have worsened the city's water deficit, while the burning dunes along the barren Costanera could use a visionary like Carlos Gesell to plant more shade trees. Stimulated by the Muelle Storni (commercial pier), the Aluar aluminum plant, and the fishing fleet, three decades of rapid growth have almost obliterated the city's Welsh heritage (though it still has a sister city in Nefyn, Gwynedd). On the positive side, Madryn's cultural life has blossomed with a university campus, theater, and cinema.

Orientation

Puerto Madryn (population 57,571) is 1,308 kilometers south of Buenos Aires and 1,219 kilometers north of Río Gallegos via RN 3. It is 673 kilometers east of Esquel via RN 3, RN 25, and RN 40, 719 kilometers southeast of Neuquén, and 896 kilometers from Bariloche. It is only 65 kilometers north of Trelew.

Most services are within a few blocks of the waterfront Avenida Roca and Avenida Brown, with their sandy beaches and *balnearios,* which are the main points of interest in the city itself.

PUERTO MADRYN

To Playa El Doradillo and
RESERVA PROVINCIAL PENÍNSULA VALDÉS

0   200 yds
0   200 m

MUELLE PIEDRABUENA

Golfo Nuevo

MUELLE PIEDRABUENA

AQUATOURS ■

TEATRO DEL MUELLE ■

AV. RAWSON

MUSEO OCEANOGRÁFICO Y DE CIENCIAS NATURALES ■

HOSPITAL SUBZONAL

TERMINAL 12 DE JULIO

DOMECQ GARCÍA
A. PUJOL
GÓMEZ
C. ALT
J. A. COSTA
ROBERTO GÓMEZ
MOSCONI TOSCHKE
NECOCHEA
FONTANA
G. GENERAL

MONUMENTO A LA GESTA GALESA ★

MUSEO DE ARTE MODERNO ★

SEE DETAIL

BELGRANO

28 DE JULIO

R.S. PEÑA

ANTIGUA PATAGONIA ■

H. YRIGOYEN

HOTEL TOLOSA ■

ESTACIÓN DEL FERROCARRIL PATAGÓNICO ★

MANOS DEL SUR ■

KEBOM ■

★ MARY Y MESETA
GAMBO
VÍA ROCA ▼ THALER
TENTEMPIE ▼

TELEFÓNICA PATAGÓNICA ■

HOTEL GRAN PALACE ■

POST OFFICE ■

Plaza San Martín

9 DE JULIO

■ EL GUALICHO HOSTEL

LA VACA Y EL POLLITO
HOSTAL DEL REY
PRESTO-LAV
CAFÉ MARES
LIZARD CAFÉ

XT MOUNTAIN BIKE
COSTANERA HOTEL
BALNEARIO NA PRAIA
LA BARRA

BALNEARIO KRILL
BALNEARIO YOAQUINA
BALNEARIO PLAYA MIMOSA

SCUBA DUBA ■
HOTEL GRAN MADRYN ■
CANTINA EL NÁUTICO ■
HOTEL EL CID ■

RESIDENCIAL MANOLO'S ■
LAVERAP ■
FUNDACIÓN PATAGONIA NATURAL ■

YOUTH HOSTEL HUEFUR ■
HOTEL CARRERA ■

HOTEL AGUAS MANSAS ■
ALQUILER DE MOUNTAIN BIKE

PETIT RESIDENCIAL ■

HOTEL MORA ■

HOSTEL VIAJEROS ■

RESIDENCIAL JO'S ■

To RN 3, Trelew, and Viedma

To Parque Histórico Punta Cuevas, Punta Loma, Camping ACA, and **ECOCENTRO PUERTO MADRYN**

BALNEARIO NATIVO SUR

INACAYAL
VESTA
VIAMONTE
LAVALLE
MAIPU
MIMOSA

BOULEVARD ALTE. GUILLERMO BROWN

LOVE PERRY
FOURNIER
J.M. THOMAS
VILLARINO
ALEM
RIVADAVIA
MORENO
ESTIVARIZ
ALBARRACÍN
ESPAÑA
AV. GALES
SARMIENTO

LEWIS JONES
JULIO A. ROCA
25 DE MAYO
MITRE
MARCOS A. ZAR
SAN MARTÍN
GOBERNADOR

SAN MARTÍN
FRAY LUIS BELTRÁN
PERITO MORENO
MAIZ
M.T. DE ALVEAR
J.B. JUSTO

RECONQUISTA
VILLEGAS
ROSALES
COLÓN
BOUCHARD
H. YRIGOYEN
LAPRIDA
BOLÍVAR
OHIGGINS
ESPORA
INDEPENDENCIA

Detail

HOTEL PENÍNSULA VALDÉS ■

HOTEL BAHÍA NUEVA ■
RESIDENCIAL LA POSTA ■
LA CABILDO ■
HOTEL VASKONIA ■
ESTELA ■
HOTEL PLAYA ■
LADE ■
AMBIGÚ ■
MARGARITA BAR ■
RECREO ■
LOBO LARSEN ■
LA OVEJA NEGRA ■
R.S. PEÑA
H. YRIGOYEN

TELEFÓNICA PATAGÓNICA ■
SECRETARÍA DE TURISMO Y DEPORTES ■
TURISMO PUMA ■
CINE AUDITORIUM ■
CAFÉ PARÍS 43 ■
BANCO DEL CHUBUT ■
ACA ■
HOTEL DEL CENTRO ■
AIKE TOUR ■
BANCO DE LA NACIÓN ■
BANCO DEL CHUBUT ■

9 DE JULIO
25 DE MAYO
MITRE
JULIO A. ROCA
BELGRANO
28 DE JULIO

© AVALON TRAVEL PUBLISHING, INC.

Southern Patagonia

Sights

At the north end of downtown, the **Museo Oceanográfico y de Ciencias Naturales** (Domecq García and Menéndez, tel. 02965/451139, free, but donations are appropriate) stresses the regional environment, wildlife, and history, including geology and paleontology, botany and oceanography, invertebrates, marine mammals, fish, birds, and the Welsh colonization of Chubut. It occupies the **Chalet Pujol** (1915), a neoclassical building with a domed hexagonal tower, that was the residence of Agustín Pujol, a businessman and, later, mayor of Madryn. Hours are 9 A.M.–noon and 2:30–8:30 P.M. weekdays, 4:30–8:30 P.M. weekends.

One of Madryn's oldest structures, the former **Estación del Ferrocarril Patagónico** (Hipólito Yrigoyen and Marcos A. Zar) dates from 1889; after serving briefly as the city bus terminal, it's due to become the Museo y Archivo Histórico de la Ciudad (City Historical Museum and Archive). The **Museo Municipal de Arte** (Municipal Art Museum, Avenida Roca 444, tel. 02965/453204, US$.35) is open 2–8 P.M. weekdays, 4–10 P.M. weekends.

At the point where the first Welsh colonists came ashore in 1865, about three kilometers southeast of town via Blvd. Brown, the **Parque Histórico Punta Cuevas** preserves the remnants of the humble shelters whose foundations they dug into the bluff above the high-tide mark. A visitors center, open 3–7 P.M. daily and 5–9 P.M. daily December–March, provides more details; admission costs US$.35.

For Puerto Madryn's 1965 centennial, *porteño* artist Luis Perlotti created two monumental sculptures: the downtown **Monumento a La Gesta Galesa** (on the waterfront at Avenida Roca and Belgrano) to honor the role of Welsh in the area's settlement, and the **Monumento al Indio Tehuelche** at Punta Cuevas, a well-deserved tribute to the province's aboriginal inhabitants.

Ecocentro Puerto Madryn

In season, southern right whales approach the promontory of this emblem of Madryn's ecological commitment, a striking building that draws on Patagonia's "Magellanic" architec-

Ecocentro Puerto Madryn

tural tradition and permits the maximum penetration of natural light. Crowned by a tower that yields distant views of Península Valdés across the Golfo Nuevo, it's the work of a nonprofit institution striving to bring environmental education, research, and the arts under the same roof.

As a maritime-life educational center, the Ecocentro has superb displays of South Atlantic fauna, including birds, seals, and especially whales; one of the most interesting, though, is a living tidal pool. Even the surrounding gardens, though, serve an educational purpose—rather than planting water-hungry lawns, the directors have chosen to preserve the coastal desert flora native to the region.

Reached by a spiral staircase, the three-level tower holds a library, an exhibition room for local artists and authors, and a reading room. Painting, photography, and sculpture are all on display; the spacious ground-floor atrium accommodates the larger works. There is also a theater, seating about

150 persons for concerts and other events, a crafts and souvenir shop, and a café.

Reached by Boulevard Almirante Brown, about five minutes from downtown by taxi, 15 minutes by bicycle, and 40 minutes on foot, the **Ecocentro** (Julio Verne 3784, tel. 02965/457470, mar@ecocentro.org.ar, www.ecocentro.org.ar, 10 A.M.–7 P.M. daily except Tuesday) charges admission of US$3 adults, US$2 retired individuals, and US$1 kids. English-speaking personnel can answer specific questions.

Entertainment and Events

The **Teatro del Muelle** (Rawson 60, tel. 02965/457966) hosts theater programs, usually on weekends. The **Cine Auditorium** (28 de Julio 129, tel. 02965/455653) shows current movies and hosts theater productions as well.

For occasional live music, try the **Margarita Bar** (Roque Sáenz Peña 15, www.margarita-pub .com.ar), which has good pub food and drinks, but the drinks are considerably costlier than the food (which is rock-bottom cheap). **La Oveja Negra** Hipólito Yrigoyen 144) is another popular bar.

July 28's **Fundación de la Ciudad** celebrates the anniversary of the initial Welsh landing at Punta Cuevas. Festivities continue for several days.

Shopping

The waterfront avenues are full of souvenir shops now, but the best choice for souvenirs and crafts remains **Manos del Sur** (Avenida Roca 546, tel. 02965/472539).

Recreo (25 de Mayo and Roque Sáenz Peña, tel. 02965/472971) carries an outstanding selection of books on Patagonia.

Sports and Recreation

Water sports are the primary attraction, on the crescent of sandy beaches that stretches from Aluar's Muelle Storni in the north almost to Punta Cuevas in the south. In these sheltered waters, hazards like rip currents are nonexistent, but at low tide the water retreats hundreds of meters on the gradually sloping beach.

At the beaches along Boulevard Almirante Brown, several *balnearios* rent water-sports equip-

ment and have snack bars and restaurants. From north to south, they are **Balneario Na Praia** (Blvd. Brown between Lugones and Perlotti); **Balneario Krill** (Blvd. Brown and Luis Perlotti); **Balneario Yoaquina** (Blvd. Brown and José Hernández); **Balneario Playa Mimosa** (Blvd. Brown and Fragata Sarmiento); and **Balneario Nativo Sur** (Blvd. Brown and Inacayal).

Several *balnearios* also rent items like inline skates and mountain bikes, and some of the operators who arrange diving excursions and other activities have space at them; other operators are scattered around town.

Divers favor Madryn because of its clear waters, natural and artificial reefs, and shipwrecks; most operators do initial dives for novices, PADI certification courses, and underwater photography. Operators working out of the *balnearios* include **Ocean Divers** (Balneario Yoaquina, tel. 02965/472569,oceandivers@oceandivers.com.ar, www.oceandivers .com.ar); **Tito Botazzi** (Balneario Krill, tel. 02965/474110, teresa@titobottazzi.com.ar, www.titobottazzi.com.ar); and **Madryn Buceo** (Balneario Nativo Sur, 3ra Rotonda, tel. 02965/15-513997, madrynbuceo@mixmail .com, www.madrynbuceo.com). Operators elsewhere include **Aquatours** (Rawson 6, tel. 02965/451954, patagonia9@hotmail.com, www.aquatours.com.ar); **Lobo Larsen** (Avenida Hipólito Yrigoyen 144, tel. 02965/451954, lobolarsenbuceo@infovia .com.ar); and **Scuba Duba** (Blvd. Brown 893, tel. 02965/452699, info@scubaduba.com .ar, www.scubaduba.com.ar).

Accommodations

In addition to up-to-date hotel prices, the Secretaría de Turismo keeps a register of rental apartments on a daily, weekly, or monthly basis. Note that in peak season, hotels may double rates even for a single person.

Under US$10

On the Punta Cuevas road, the wooded 800-site **Camping ACA** (tel. 02965/452952) charges US$6.50 per site for up to four persons, with discounts for members and affiliates. A short

Southern Patagonia

distance beyond, sites at the Club Náutico Atlántico Sud's more spacious **Camping El Golfito** (tel. 02965/454544, US$1.60 pp) are more exposed; rates are comparable to the ACA campground.

US$10–25

The Hostelling International affiliate is the excellent ⓜ **El Gualicho Hostel** (Marcos A. Zar 480, tel. 02965/454163, info@elgualichohostel.com.ar, www.elgualichohostel.com.ar, US$4 pp dorms, US$13 d). Freshly modernized, the amiable **Hostel Viajeros** (Gobernador Maíz 545, tel. 02965/456457, info@hostelviajeros.com, US$5.50) has double and triple rooms in a motel-style place with pleasing garden spaces. A step down is the **Youth Hostel Huefur** (Estivariz 245, tel. 02965/453926, huefur245@hotmail.com, US$5–6 pp).

Hotel del Centro (28 de Julio 149, tel. 02965/473742, US$5.50/10 s/d) and **Residencial Jo's** (Bolívar 75, tel. 02965/471433, residencialjos@infovia.com.ar, US$7 pp) are the cheapest nonhostel options.

The spartan **Petit Residencial** (Marcelo T. de Alvear 845, tel. 02965/451460, fax 02965/456428, hotelpetit@arnet.com.ar, US$9/14 s/d) is a friendly place with small motel-style rooms and ample parking; rates include breakfast. **Hotel Vaskonia** (25 de Mayo 43, tel. 02965/472581, buce23@infovia.com.ar, US$9/14 s/d) is also a good shoestring option.

Simple but tidy, the 40-room **Hotel Gran Palace** (28 de Julio 390, tel. 02965/471009, US$13/16 s/d) is a decent choice in its price range. Set back from the busy avenue, **Residencial Manolo's** (Avenida Roca 763, tel. 02965/472390, US$14/18 s/d) has firm beds but slightly cramped rooms.

Attractive **Residencial La Posta** (Avenida Roca 33, tel. 02965/472422, fax 02965/454573, residenciallaposta@infovia.com.ar, US$14/18 s/d) fills up fast. Others in this category include **Hotel Gran Madryn** (Lugones 40, tel. 02965/472205, granmadryn1@hotmail.com, US$14/18 s/d) and **Hotel Mora** (Juan B. Justo 654, tel. 02965/471424, nelyomarmora@hotmail.com, US$15/17 s/d).

Though its smallish rooms don't get many style points, the homey, well-kept **Hotel Carrera** (Marcos A. Zar 844, tel. 02965/450759, carrerah@infovia.com.ar, US$17/21 s/d) offers personalized service in a quiet neighborhood, with a very decent breakfast to boot.

On a quiet residential block, one of the best values in its range, tranquil **Hotel Aguas Mansas** (José Hernández 51, tel. 02965/473103, aguasmansas@aguasmansas.com, www.aguasmansas.com, US$16/23 s/d) is a contemporary place that doesn't raise rates in summer.

Adequate but clearly showing its age, the **Costanera Hotel** (Almirante Brown 759, tel. 02965/453000, hotelcostanera@infovia.com.ar, US$18/25 s/d) lives mostly off its convenient beachfront location.

US$25–50

Hostal del Rey (Blvd. Brown 681, tel. 02965/471093, US$21/28 s/d) has a central beachfront location. Nicely furnished, in a quiet area, **Hotel El Cid** (25 de Mayo 850, tel./fax 02965/471416, hotelcid@infovia.com.ar, US$23/28 s/d) is a good choice.

Re-creating the style of Madryn's early Welsh houses but with contemporary comforts, ⓜ **Hotel Bahía Nueva** (Avenida Roca 67, tel./fax 02965/451677, hotel@bahianueva.com.ar, www.bahianueva.com.ar, US$28/35 s/d) also has spacious gardens and ample parking in a central beachfront location. **Hotel Playa** (Avenida Roca 181, tel. 02965/451446, playahotel@playahotel.com.ar, US$28–36 s or d) draws its character from its age.

Hotel Tolosa (Roque Sáenz Peña 253, tel. 02965/471850, tolosa@hoteltolosa.com.ar, US$27–34 s, US$29–47 d) lacks that retro touch, but is still a fine downtown choice.

US$50–100

Top-of-the line **Hotel Península Valdés** (Avenida Roca 155, tel. 02965/471292, fax 02965/452584, info@hotel-peninsula-valdes.com) has fine standard rooms for US$45 s or d, but spectacular ocean views makes the larger panoramic rooms worth consideration for only a little more, US$55 s or d.

Food

Good choices for breakfast, snacks, and coffee include **Café París 43** (Roque Sáenz Peña 112) and the **Lizard Café** (Avenida Roca and Gales, tel. 02965/455306).

Madryn's only Welsh teahouse, **Del Chubut** (Avenida Roca 369, tel. 02965/451311) also sells takeaway *alfajores* (cookies sandwiched around sweet fillings) and *torta galesa* (a dense black cake).

La Barra (Blvd. Brown and Lugones, tel. 02965/455550) is one of Madryn's better pizzerias, with moderate prices, but **Tentempié** (Avenida Gales 191, tel. 02965/455384) has lighter versions. Reinvented as a sports bar, **Ambigú** (Avenida Roca 97, tel. 02965/472541) has eight TVs, but pizza is still the best bet here (though the scallops aren't bad). **La Cabildo** (Hipólito Yrigoyen 36, tel. 02965/471284) serves pizza and especially good empanadas.

Though the service can seem surly, **La Vaca y El Pollito** (Avenida Roca and Alfonsina Storni, tel. 02965/458486) serves a thick, juicy *bife de chorizo* (US$5) that's arguably the best-value steak in town; truly fresh bread accompanies every meal. **Estela** (Roque Sáenz Peña 27, tel. 02965/451573) is another worthwhile *parrilla*.

Made in the metal-clad Magellanic style, with Georgian flourishes and a brick interior adorned with artifacts from the early days of settlement, **Antigua Patagonia** (Mitre and Sáenz Peña, tel. 02965/458738) has a varied menu of meat, excellent seafood (try the *abadejo*), and pasta, with most entrees in the US$3.50 range. For warm nights, there's outdoor seating and a play area for kids, as well.

The large menu at ⚑ **Mar y Meseta** (Avenida Roca 485, tel. 02965/458740) boasts intriguing dishes like gnocchi with lamb, prawn ravioli, and rabbit in chocolate sauce, but not everything is available every night; consider the king-crab salad (SU$4.50) or the seafood *parrillada* (US$6), which includes fresh fish, king crab, and scallops. Service is attentive and cheerful, but the kitchen seems a little *too* quick at times for a leisurely meal.

Cantina El Náutico (Avenida Roca 790, tel. 02965/471404) and **Puerto Marisko** (Avenida Rawson 7, tel. 02965/450752) are traditional seafood favorites.

Madryn has several excellent ice creameries, including the 40-plus flavors at **Vía Roca** (Avenida Roca 517, tel. 02965/450704), **Kebom** (Avenida Roca 540), and **Café Mares** (Avenida Roca 600).

Madryn's most ambitious menu is at ⚑ **Nativo Sur** (Blvd. Brown 1900 at Humphreys, tel. 02965/457403), with delicious appetizers like bruschetta (US$2.50) and gazpacho with chicken chunks, and entrees like grilled pork (US$5.50) and an abundant mixed-seafood plate (US$6) of fish, king crab, octopus, scallops, and shrimp. Be prepared to wait, though—the service is haphazard at best, and the kitchen can be so slow you may think they've left to hunt the Patagonian hare (US$5.50). Fortunately, there's a good wine list; in summer, the shady interior *quincho* stays cooler than the exposed beachside tables.

Information

The **Secretaría de Turismo** (Avenida Roca 223, tel. 02965/453504, informes@madryn.gov.ar, www.madryn.gov.ar) does an exemplary job of providing information (in Spanish, English, French, and German), and will help find accommodations when beds are scarce. Hours are 7 A.M.–9 P.M. January–March; the rest of the year, weekday hours are 7 A.M.–1 P.M. and 3–9 P.M. weekdays, 8:30 A.M.–1:30 P.M. and 3:30–8:30 P.M. weekends and holidays.

For motorists, **ACA** is at Belgrano 19 (tel. 02965/456684).

The **Fundación Patagonia Natural** (Marcos A. Zar 760, tel. 02965/474363, patagonianatural@speedy.com.ar, www.patagonianatural.org) is an NGO that works to preserve Patagonia's environmental heritage.

Services

There are numerous ATMs, including those of **Banco de la Nación** (9 de Julio 117) and **Banco del Chubut** (25 de Mayo 154). The only exchange house is **Cambio Thaler** (Avenida Roca 497).

Correo Argentino is at Belgrano and Gobernador Maíz; the postal code is 9120.

Telefónica Patagónica (Marcos A. Zar 289; Avenida Roca and 9 de Julio) has phone, fax, and Internet services, and there are several others. Nievemar (Avenida Roca 493, tel. 02965/455544) is the AmEx affiliate. Laverap (Avenida Gales 112) or Presto-Lav (Avenida Brown 605, tel. 02965/451526) can do the washing.

Puerto Madryn's Hospital Subzonal is at Pujol 247 (tel. 02965/451240).

Getting There

Commercial flights land at Trelew, 65 kilometers to the south. LADE (Avenida Roca 119, tel. 02965/451256) uses nearby Aeródromo El Tehuelche (tel. 02965/451909) for sporadic southbound flights to Trelew and Comodoro Rivadavia, and northbound flights to San Antonio Oeste, Viedma, Bahía Blanca, Mar del Plata, and Aeroparque.

Madryn's new Terminal 12 de Julio (Italia s/n, tel. 02965/451789) stands directly behind the old terminal (and former railroad station). It has frequent connections to nearby Trelew with Línea 28 de Julio (tel. 02965/472056), plus extensive regional and long-distance connections. Mar y Valle (tel. 02965/472056) goes to Puerto Pirámides at 9:55 A.M. daily; in summer and during the whale-watching season, it adds a 5 P.M. departure.

Sample destinations, fares, and times include Trelew (US$2, one hour), Puerto Pirámides (US$3, 1.5 hours), Comodoro Rivadavia (US$10, six hours), Bahía Blanca (US$13, eight hours), Esquel (US$14, nine hours), Neuquén (US$16, nine hours), Bariloche (US$20, 12 hours), Córdoba (US$21–30, 18 hours), Río Gallegos (US$20–24, 17 hours), and Buenos Aires (US$22–30, 18 hours).

Getting Around

For LADE flights from Aeródromo El Tehuelche, use a taxi or *remise*. For commercial flights to and from Trelew, Transportes Eben-Ezer (tel. 02965/472474, 02965/15-660463) charges US$4.50 pp for door-to-door service.

Bicycle rental outlets include XT Mountain Bike (Avenida Roca 742, tel. 02965/472232), which also leads guided tours, and Alquiler de

Mountain Bike (25 de Mayo 1136, tel. 02965/474426).

Because its attractions are so spread out but roads are relatively good, renting a car is a good option here. Agencies include Avis (Avenida Roca 27, tel. 02965/451491); Localiza (Avenida Roca 536, tel. 02965/456300); Puerto Madryn Turismo (Avenida Roca 624, tel. 02965/452355); and Rent A Car Patagonia (Avenida Roca 293, tel. 02965/452095).

VICINITY OF PUERTO MADRYN

Tour agencies in Madryn go farther afield as well, to Trelew, Gaiman, Punta Tombo, and, of course, Península Valdés. Operators include Aike Tour (Avenida Roca 353, tel. 02965/450720); Cuyun-Co (Avenida Roca 165, tel. 02965/451845); Puerto Madryn Turismo (Avenida Roca 41, tel. 02965/456453 and Avenida Roca 624, tel. 02965/452355); and Turismo Puma (28 de Julio 46, tel. 02965/451063). Full-day excursions run in the US$25–30 range, not including meals; whale-watching is additional, even on full-day tours to Península Valdés.

Reserva Provincial Punta Loma

Close enough to Madryn to make it an ideal mountain bike excursion, Punta Loma lacks the large numbers and diversity of wildlife of the more famous Península Valdés, but its ample sea lion colonies, along with cormorants, giant petrels, gulls, terns, and snowy sheathbills are reason to visit. Though only 15 kilometers southwest of Madryn via an undulating gravel road, it still gets many fewer visitors than Valdés.

Near the sea lion colony, there's a visitors center and an overlook that permits good views of the animals. Hours are 8 A.M.–8 P.M. daily; admission costs US$3.50 for foreigners, US$1.50 for Argentine residents, and US$.75 for Chubut residents. There is no regular public transportation, but Madryn operators will arrange excursions, or a small group can go cheaply by hiring a *remise*.

Playa El Doradillo

From the headlands at Playa El Doradillo, 17

kilometers northeast of Madryn via RP 42, deep water lets whales approach the shore—the next best choice to an in-the-water view at Península Valdés. Like Punta Loma, this is close enough for a bicycle trip or a shared taxi.

⋈ RESERVA PROVINCIAL PENÍNSULA VALDÉS

Coastal Patagonia's top destination, the UN-ESCO World Biosphere Reserve of Península Valdés is the place where the great southern right whale arrives to breed and birth in the winter months. Protected since 1935, the *ballena franca* occupies an almost unique position as a "natural monument"—a designation normally reserved for territorial ecosystems—within the Argentine national park system.

Península Valdés itself, a provincial reserve rather than a national park, has much more to offer than just the whales. Some species of marine mammals—ranging from sea lions to elephant seals and orcas—cover the beaches or gather in the waters of the Golfo San José, Golfo Nuevo, or the open South Atlantic all year. There are also concentrations of burrowing Magellanic pen-guins and flocks of other seabirds, plus herds of grazing guanacos and groups of sprinting rheas in the arid interior grasslands.

The peninsula's main activity center is the hamlet of Puerto Pirámides, which like Puerto Madryn enjoys a longer tourist season because of the whale- and orca-watching periods. Once the export point for salt from the Salina Grande depression, it has grown haphazardly, and water continues to be a problem in this desert environment.

Sometimes called Puerto Pirámide, the village has recently reasserted its plurality. According to local accounts, when the Argentine navy used the area as a firing range, they destroyed two of the three pyramidal promontories that gave the settlement its original moniker.

Geography and Climate

Connected to the mainland by the narrow Istmo de Ameghino, Península Valdés is 56 kilometers northeast of Puerto Madryn via RP 2, but a visit to the major wildlife sites involve a circuit of roughly 400 kilometers to Puerto Pirámides and Punta Delgada via RP 2, Caleta Valdés and Punta Norte via RP 47, and RP 3 back to Puerto

© WAYNE BERNHARDSON

cliffs near Puerto Pirámides, Península Valdés

Pirámides. Beyond Puerto Pirámides, all these are gravel and dirt roads that can be hazardous to inexperienced drivers, especially with low-clearance vehicles.

Broad sandy beaches line much of the coast, but the steep headlands that rise above many of them are dangerous to descend because of unconsolidated sediments. Sheep *estancias* take up most of the interior, whose Salina Grande depression lies 42 meters below sea level, one of the lowest points on the globe. The climate is extremely dry, with high evaporation due to long hours of sunlight and almost perpetual winds.

Fauna

Most of Peninsula Valdés consists of rolling *monte* (scrubland) with patches of pasture that can expand considerably in wet years. The stocking rate for the sheep *estancias* is relatively low, permitting the guanacos and rheas to thrive alongside domestic stock.

Marine mammals—whales, orcas, elephant seals, and sea lions—are the big draw here, but there are also Magellanic penguin colonies. In addition to penguins, there are breeding populations of the Dominican gull (*Larus domincanus*),

white heron (*Casmerodius albus*), black-crowned night heron (*Nycticorax nycticorax*), olivaceous cormorant (*Phalacrocorax olivaceus*), black cormorant (*Phalocrocorax magellanicus,*) steamer duck (*Tachyeres leucocephalus*), Patagonian crested duck (*Lophonetta specularoides*), Magellanic oystercatcher (*Haematopus ostralegus*), and black oystercatcher (*Haematopus ater*). Several species of gulls, terns, and plovers are visitors, along with the Chilean flamingo and the snowy sheathbill.

From June to December, the breeding, breaching, blowing, and birthing of *Eubalaena australis* brings whale-watchers from around the world to the warm, shallow waters of the Golfo Nuevo and Golfo San Jorge. Since 1971, when the first census was taken, the Península Valdés population has grown from 580 to about 3,000.

Inhabiting the South Atlantic from about 20° S to 55° S, the southern right whale is a giant that reaches 17 meters in length and weighs up to 100 tons, though most individuals are smaller; females are larger than males. They are baleen whales, filtering krill and plankton as seawater passes through sieves in their jaws.

Right whales acquired their English name from whalers who sought them out because

© WAYNE BERNHARDSON

A right whale swims along the surface near Puerto Pirámides, Península Valdés.

dead specimens, instead of sinking, floated to the surface; hence, they were the "right whales" for hunting. Identifiable by calluses of keratin on their heads, about 1,300 of Valdés's population have names; this has given researchers the ability to follow their movements and even trace their kinship.

After the cows give birth, whale calves get closest to the catamarans and rafts that do commercial whale-watching at Puerto Pirámides. Over the course of the season, though, it is possible to witness all stages of the species' mating and breeding cycle.

For much of the year, *Orcinus orca* swims the South Atlantic waters in search of squid, fish, penguins, and dolphins, but from October to April, pods of "killer whales" patrol the Punta Norte shoreline in search of sea lion pups—a nine-meter specimen can kill and consume up to eight pups per day. The largest of the dolphin family, the 950-kilogram animal is a conspicuous sight thanks to its sleek black body, white underbelly, and menacing dorsal fin, which can rise two meters above the water's surface.

The peninsula's sandy beaches are the only continental breeding site for *Mirounga leonina* (elephant seals) though there are also breeding colonies on sub-Antarctic islands in Chile and the Falklands (Malvinas), as well as South Georgia and other circumpolar islands. Largest of the pinnipeds, it is a true seal with no external ear (as opposed to the southern sea lion, for example), but its distinguishing characteristic is the male's inflatable proboscis, which resembles an elephant's trunk.

Ungainly on land, the 2,500–4,000-kilogram "beachmaster" males come ashore in the spring to take charge of harems that number up to 100 females; the much smaller females weigh only about 500 kilograms. Reaching seven meters in length, the beachmasters have to fend off challenges from younger bachelors in bloody fights that leave all parties scarred and even disfigured.

Females spend most of their pregnancy at sea, giving birth when they return to land in the spring. Pups spend only a few weeks nursing, gaining weight quickly, before the mother abandons them (some die crushed beneath battling

males). At sea, the elephant seal is an extraordinary diver, plunging up to 600 vertical meters in search of squid before surfacing for air half an hour later.

Present all year on the beaches and reefs beneath the peninsula's headlands, *Otaria flavescens* (sea lion) is common from southern Brazil and Uruguay all the way around the tip of South America and north to Peru. With its thick mane, the 300-kilogram, 2.3-meter male reminds many observers of the African lion, though Spanish-speakers know it as the *lobo marino* (sea wolf). The female is only about 1.8 meters long and weighs only about 100 kilograms.

Unlike the larger elephant seal, the sea lion has external ears. Also unlike the elephant seal, it propels itself with both front and rear flippers on land, and the male is quick enough to attack and drag away elephant seal pups. More often, though, it feeds on krill and the odd penguin.

For Spanish-speakers, by the way, this is the *lobo marino de un pelo;* the *lobo marino de dos pelos* is *Arctocephalos australis,* the southern fur seal, whose pelt was far more valuable to commercial sealers.

Spheniscus magellanicus, the braying and burrowing jackass penguin, is the only species present on the peninsula. From September to March or April, it breeds and raises its young in remote areas like Caleta Valdés and Punta Norte, but summer swimmers in the shallow waters at Puerto Pirámides have had close encounters.

Sights and Activities

Many visitors book excursions in Puerto Madryn, but these day trips are often too brief for more than a glimpse of what the peninsula has to offer, especially if the operators spend too much time at lunch. Staying in Puerto Pirámides and contracting tours there can be a good alternative, especially for whale-watching, as you have the flexibility to pick the best time to go out.

Five operators, some of whom also have offices in Puerto Madryn, offer whale-watching in semirigid rafts (which get low down and closer to the animals) and in larger catamarans: **Tito Botazzi** (Primera Bajada, tel. 02965/495050, www.titobottazzi.com); **Hydrosport** (Primera Bajada, tel. 02965/495065, www.hydrosport .com.ar); **Pinino Aquatours** (Primera Bajada, tel. 02965/495015, capitanpinino@infovia .com.ar, www.whalesargentina.com.ar); **Jorge Schmid** (Segunda Bajada, tel./fax 02965/495012, puntaballena@puntaballena.com.ar, www.punt-aballena.com.ar); and **Peke Sosa** (Segunda Bajada, tel. 02965/471291, www.pekesosa.com.ar). Prices range around US$17–35, depending on the vessel and the length of the tour.

In the waters of Golfo San José, 800 meters north of the isthmus, penguins, gulls, cormorants, and herons all nest on the offshore bird sanctuary of **Isla de los Pájaros.** The island itself is off-limits to visitors, but a stationary telescope on the shoreline permits views of the breeding birds. Near the telescope is a replica of a chapel from Fuerte San José, the area's first Spanish settlement (1779, but destroyed by the Tehuelche in 1810).

Argentina's primary whale-watching center, **Puerto Pirámides,** has the peninsula's major concentration of tourist services, including its most affordable accommodations and food. From June to December, whales are the main attraction, but traditional beachgoers take over in January and February. Visitors without their own vehicle can hike or bike to the southern sea lion colony at Punto Pirámide, four kilometers to the west, which offers outstanding panoramas and sunsets over the Golfo Nuevo.

Beneath the headlands at the southeastern tip of the peninsula, **Punta Delgada** is the site of substantial elephant seal and sea lion colonies, reached by a trail from the lighthouse at the former naval station (now a hotel). The hotel concessionaires provide well-prepared English-speaking guides to lead tour groups and individuals free of charge; they have also turned the lighthouse into a small but well-presented museum. Their restaurant is open to the public, and they also offer horseback tours of the area.

Another large colony of elephant seals and sea lions is visible from the cliffs a short distance north of Punta Delgada, but there is no safe access.

On the peninsula's eastern shore, about midway between Punta Delgada and Punta Norte,

© WAYNE BERNHARDSON

lighthouse at Punta Delgada, Península Valdés

Caleta Valdés is a sheltered bay that is fast becoming a lagoon as its ocean outlet fills with sediments. In the meantime, though, Magellanic penguins swim north to a breeding colony and elephant seals haul up onto the shore in the mating season. Even guanacos may be seen along the beach.

Where RP 47 and RP 3 meet at the northern tip of the peninsula, **Punta Norte's** big attraction is the mixed colony of southern elephant seals and sea lions, but from October to April this is also the best place to see the orcas that lunge onto the beach to grab unwary pups. Punta Norte also has a small but outstanding museum that puts marine mammals in both natural and cultural perspective—thanks to exhibits on the aboriginal Tehuelche, and a historical account of the sealing industry.

In the vicinity of Punta Norte, reached by a northwesterly road off RP 3, **Estancia San Lorenzo** conducts tours of its own Magellanic penguin colony, but is not open as accommodations.

Accommodations and Food

Puerto Pirámides has sprouted many more places to stay, eat, and partake of activities than ever before. Demand is high, though; in summer and in the whale-watching season reservations are advisable. There are *estancia* accommodations scattered around Punta Delgada, Caleta Valdés, and Punta Norte, but no camping is permitted beyond Puerto Pirámides.

Immediately behind the dunes, Puerto Pirámides's shoreline **Camping Municipal** (tel. 02965/495084) charges US$1.50 pp plus US$.40 per shower (water is limited and the showers timed). The bathrooms are clean, and there's a store with basic supplies, but only a few sites have shade.

The next cheapest option is **Hospedaje El Español** (Avenida de las Ballenas s/n, tel. 02965/495025, US$3 pp), which can accommodate up to 36 people in Spartan accommodations with shared baths and hot showers. **Hostería La Estancia del Sol** (Avenida de las Ballenas s/n, tel. 02965/495007, estancia@arnet .com.ar, US$17 d) is a significant step up, but by no means luxurious. At the entrance to town, the **Hostería ACA** (tel. 02965/495004, US$14/ 19 s/d for members, US$18/23 s/d for nonmembers) was once Piramides's top choice, but several others have overtaken it.

Right on the beach, the **Posada Austral Patagonia Franca** (Primera Bajada, tel. 02965/495006, info@patagoniafranca.com, www.patagonia franca.com) is a sparkling new construction with views across the Golfo Nuevo. Rates are US$35/42 s/d Monday–Thursday, US$42/48 s/d weekends.

Its handsome brick superstructure reflecting the region's Welsh heritage, **Ⓜ Hostería Paradise** (Avenida de las Ballenas s/n, tel./fax 02965/495003, 495030, paradise@satlink.com, www.hosteriaparadise.com.ar) is a substantial improvement on the traditional choices. Rates are US$110 s or d with breakfast, and there's a spacious suite for US$170. Fixed-price lunches or dinners cost US$15 for foreigners, US$9 for

Argentines; there's a sandwich and pizza menu as well.

In a casual ambience that blends traditional artifacts and artwork with pop music, **La Estación** (Avenida de la Ballenas s/n, tel. 02965/495047) serves excellent fresh fish and salads, but the kitchen is slow and the service amateurish.

On the bluffs overlooking Punta Delgada, alongside the lighthouse at the east end of RP 2, **Ⓜ Hotel Punta Delgada** (tel. 02965/15-406304; Avenida Roca 536, Puerto Madryn, tel. 02965/458444, faro@puntadelgada.com, www .puntadelgada.com) is an upgraded property on lease from the navy, with 30 comfortable double rooms with private baths. High-season rates, September 1–January 1, are US$79/96 s/d with breakfast, US$96/132 with half board, and US$107/154 with full board; low season rates, from January 1 to April 15, are about 10 percent cheaper. Tour buses often stop at its restaurant, which is open to nonguests.

Near Punta Delgada, run by a young Madryn couple, the best of the new tourist-oriented *estancias* is **Ⓜ Estancia Rincón Chico** (tel. 02965/15-688302, Blvd. Almirante Brown 1783, tel. 02965/471733, rinconchico@infovia.com.ar, www.rinconchico.com.ar). Five kilometers south of RP 2, its purpose-built hotel has eight comfortable, well-furnished doubles, with a sheltered *quincho* for barbecues. For three months a year, they host elephant seal researchers from the University of California at Santa Cruz, as the seals frequent their long coastal frontage. High-season rates, September 1–January 31, are US$80/110 s/d with breakfast, US$100/150 with half board, and US$115/185 with full board; low-season rates, February 1–April 15 and June 15–August 30, are about 10–15 percent less.

Set in a sheltered depression west of Caleta Valdés, along RP 47, **Estancia La Elvira** (tel. 02965/15-698709, 02965/15-406183, laelvira @laelvira.com.ar, www.laelvira.com.ar) lacks the mature landscaping of Rincón Chico, but the rooms and common areas are attractive enough. Rates are US$65/80 s/d with breakfast, US$80/98 s/d with half board, and US$100/ 145 s/d with full board. For nonguests, they operate the roadside **Parador Punta Cantor,** which gets tour buses at lunchtime, near the elephant seal colony.

Toward Punta Norte, along the west side of RP 47, the seven-room **Estancia la Ernestina** (tel. 02965/15-661079; Avenida Gales 54, Puerto Madryn, tel. 02965/471143, info@laernestina .com.ar, www.laernestina.com.ar, US$115/180 s/d with full board and excursions) is an amiable place with access to the large Magellanic-penguin colony at Estancia San Lorenzo. Three of the rooms have only two baths among them.

Information

At El Desempeño, at the west end of the Istmo de Ameghino, provincial authorities have erected a toll booth to collect an admission fee of US$9 for foreigners, US$5 for Argentine residents, and US$2 for Chubut residents. A short distance to the east, the reserve's **Centro de Interpretación** (open 8 A.M.–8 P.M. daily) includes a complete right-whale skeleton and other natural history items, but also historical material ranging from the Tehuelche presence to Spanish colonization and Argentine settlement for salt-mining and sheep-ranching. An adjacent observation tower offers panoramas across the Golfo San José to the north to the Golfo Nuevo in the south, and east across the interior of the peninsula.

Sarah Mansfield Taber's *Dusk on the Campo: a Journey in Patagonia* (New York: Henry Holt and Company, 1991) tells the tale of pioneer life on the peninsula, in both historical and ethnographic perspective.

Getting There and Around

In summer, from Puerto Madryn, **Mar y Valle** (tel. 02965/472056) has daily bus departures for Puerto Pirámides (US$6.50, 1.5 hours) at 8:55 A.M. and 5 P.M.; return buses leave at 11 A.M. and 7 P.M. In the winter months, there are morning departures only, Thursday and Saturday only.

Tour buses may permit passengers to disembark at Puerto Pirámides and return another day on a space-available basis, but make arrangements in advance.

Distances from Puerto Pirámides to other destinations on the peninsula are too great for any transport except motor vehicles, so it's worth considering a **rental car** in Puerto Madryn. Many consider day trips from Madryn too rushed.

TRELEW

Though less conspicuously tourist-oriented than Puerto Madryn, the Río Chubut city of Trelew retains more visible remnants of its Welsh birthright than its oceanside sister city. It also offers excellent access to the lower Chubut Welsh communities of Gaiman and Dolavon, to the dolphin-watching beach resort of Playa Unión, and the massive penguin colonies at Punta Tombo. Its own main attraction, though, is the state-of-the-art paleontological museum that documents the great Argentine dinosaur discoveries of recent decades.

Dating from 1886, when the railroad united Puerto Madryn with the farms of the lower Río Chubut, Trelew takes its name from Welsh colonist and railroad promoter Lewis Jones (in Welsh, *tre* means "town" while *lew* was an abbreviation of "Lewis." It has since experienced several waves of immigration—Italians and Spaniards, as well as Argentines from elsewhere in the country—and boom-and-bust cycles thanks to the wool industry, customs preferences, and industrial promotion.

Through all this, Trelew has retained its immigrant identity by way of events like the Eisteddfod (a Welsh poetry and music festival) and other cultural activities.

Orientation

On the north bank of the Río Chubut, Trelew (population 88,397) is 65 kilometers south of Puerto Madryn and 377 kilometers northeast of Comodoro Rivadavia via RN 3. It is 608 kilometers west of Esquel via paved RN 25, RP 62, and RN 40.

Most points of interest and services lie on or within a few blocks northeast of the central Plaza Independencia.

Sights

From its office opposite **Plaza Independencia,** Entretur distributes an informative brochure (Spanish only) that describes most of the city's

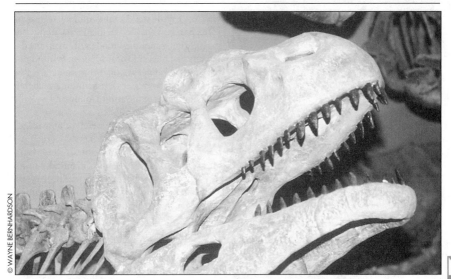

dinosaur, Museo Egidio Feruglio, Trelew

landmarks. On the pleasingly landscaped plaza itself, the Victorian-style **Kiosco del Centenario** (1910) marked the centennial of Argentine independence.

Several other landmarks surround the plaza. First serving as police headquarters and then as municipal offices, the former **Distrito Militar** (army headquarters, Mitre 350) was for decades isolated from the rest of the plaza by walls and gates; it now houses the **Museo de Artes Visuales,** with exhibits of historical photography, as well as contemporary photography, painting, and sculpture. Dating from 1900, it's overdue for maintenance; Entretur's own offices occupy the complex's **Anexo** (Annex, Mitre 387). Museum hours are 9 A.M.–noon and 6–9 P.M. weekdays only.

In 1920, Trelew's Spanish community built the **Teatro Español** (25 de Mayo 237) on the north side of the plaza to replace an earlier construction destroyed by fire. Half a block east of the plaza, at San Martín between Belgrano and Rivadavia, the **Teatro Verdi** (1914) served the Italian community; at the corner of San Martín and Belgrano, the Welsh community's **Salón San David** (1913) frequently hosts the musical festivities of the Eisteddfod. Half a block north, the Welsh **Capilla Tabernacl** (1889) is Trelew's oldest surviving building.

Two blocks northeast of the plaza, early Patagonian tourists stayed at the **Hotel Touring Club** (1906), the former Hotel Martino, which underwent a major upgrade in the 1920s with materials imported from Europe (the Touring Club Argentino, which still exists, is a moribund organization that once rivaled the Automóvil Club Argentino). It is still, however, a popular meeting place for *trelewenses.*

Half a block north, the **Antigua Estación del Ferrocarril** (Fontana and Lewis Jones) was the city's second railway station, dating from 1889, and is now the regional history museum. Immediately to its north, the Museo Egidio Feruglio is a state-of-the-art paleontological museum.

From 1889 to 1961, the Ferrocarril Central Chubut from Puerto Madryn to Trelew stopped at the English-style railway station, a national historical monument, that now houses the **Museo Regional Pueblo de Luis.** An antique

© WAYNE BERNHARDSON

The Victorian-style Kiosco del Centenario marked the centennial of Argentine independence on Plaza Independencia, Trelew.

steam locomotive and other equipment still stand outside the building. The interior, while it's packed with memorabilia of the Welsh immigration, including historical photographs, furnishings, and clothing, is short on interpretation; this, however, is due to be remedied as the museum expands its mission to become an "Ecomuseo" to document the transformation of landscape by aboriginal peoples and European settlers.

The Museo Regional (Avenida Fontana and Lewis Jones, tel. 02965/424062, US$.75 adults, half that for children) is open 8 A.M.–8 P.M. weekdays and 5–8 P.M. Sunday only.

The central Patagonian steppe west of Trelew is one of the prime dinosaur digs in the entire country, and the constantly improving paleontological museum **Museo Egidio Feruglio** (Avenida Fontana 140, tel. 02965/420012, info@mef.org.ar, www.mef.org.ar, US$3 adults,

US$1.50 children 12 and under) is reason enough to visit the city. Its main attraction is the magnificently mounted models of Argentine dinosaurs like the carnivorous *Pianitzskysaurus floresi* and *Carnotaurus sastrei,* but there are also items like dinosaur eggs, a genuine touchable dinosaur femur in the atrium lobby, and a working lab visible to the public.

At the same time, the museum acknowledges the achievements of pioneering Patagonian researchers like Florentino Ameghino, George Gaylord Simpson, and Alejandro Pianitzsky in its own hall of fame. The museum owes its name to an Italian paleontologist who came to Argentina in 1925 as a petroleum geologist for the state petroleum company YPF.

The museum is open 10 A.M.–6 P.M. daily except from mid-March to September 1, when it's closed on weekends. There is also a small café and a souvenir shop. The museum also arranges excursions to Geoparque Paleontológico Bryn Gwyn, near Gaiman.

Entertainment and Events

The **Cine Coliseo** (Belgrano 371, tel. 02965/425300) shows recent films.

Mid-September's **Certamen Internacional de Coros,** which takes place in odd-numbered years, draws on the Welsh tradition of choral music. Later that same month, the **Fiesta Provincial del Pingüino** coincides with the spring arrival of penguins at the Punta Tombo reserve.

October 20's **Aniversario de la Ciudad** celebrates Trelew's founding in 1886. Late October's **Eisteddfod de Chubut** focuses on the Welsh traditions, particularly folk music and poetry, of the lower Chubut Valley.

Accommodations

The best shoestring choices are **Hotel Avenida** (Lewis Jones 49, tel. 02965/434172, US$3.50/6.50 s/d), which has rooms with shared bath and a cheap breakfast; and **Hotel Argentino** (Mathews 186, tel. 02965/436134, US$5.50/9 s/d).

For a taste of old Patagonia—perhaps because it's well past its prime—try the landmark **Hotel Touring Club** (Avenida Fontana 240, tel.

02965/433998, htouring@internet.siscotel.com, US$9/13 s/d).

The fast-aging, 1970s-era **City Hotel** (Rivadavia 254, tel./fax 02965/433951, cityhotelsrl@infovia.com.ar, US$11/14 s/d) is central and remains tidy; the rooms are smallish but bright and cheerful.

Upstairs rooms at **Hotel Rivadavia** (Rivadavia 55, tel. 02965/434472, fax 02965/423491, hotelriv@infovia.com.ar, www.cpatagonia.com/rivadavia, US$11–13 s, US$13–16 d) have better beds and bathrooms, in addition to cable TV, than the more economical downstairs rooms. Breakfast costs about US$1.25 extra. **Hotel Centenario** (San Martín 150, tel. 02965/420542, hotelcentenario@infovia.com.ar, www.hotelcentenario.com.ar, US$15/18 s/d) is comparable.

Recently rehabbed **⚑ Hotel Galicia** (9 de Julio 214, tel. 02965/433802, hotelgalicia@arnet.com.ar, www.sipatagonia.com/hotelgalicia, US$13/16 s/d) has impressive common areas—note the curving marble staircase—along with rooms that are slightly less impressive; still, with cable TV and breakfast, this is one of Trelew's best values.

Four-star **Hotel Rayentray** (San Martín 101, tel. 02965/434702, rcvcentral@ar.inter.net, www.cadenarayentray.com.ar, US$22/25 s/d) has amenities including a restaurant, gym, sauna, and swimming pool. Four-star in designation but not quite in reality, the 90-room **Hotel Libertador** (Rivadavia 31, tel./fax 02965/420220, hlibertador@infovia.com.ar, www.hotellibertadortw.com, US$21/26 s/d) is a decent but by no means exceptional hostelry with friendly personnel and a buffet breakfast, but rather dull rooms.

Food

Even those who don't stay at the hotel should take breakfast or coffee at the **Confitería Touring Club** (Avenida Fontana 240, tel. 02965/433998), to partake of its timeless ambience. **Sugar** (25 de Mayo 247, tel. 02965/435978) is a sandwich and short-order option.

The misleadingly named **Los Tres Chinos** (San Martín 188, tel. 02965/437280) is primarily a *parrillada* rather than the Chinese

tenedor libre it once was. **Quijote** (Rivadavia 457, tel. 02965/15-402937) serves a US$3.50 *parrillada*.

La Bodeguita (Belgrano 374, tel. 436276) serves good pasta (particularly cannelloni) and pizza, with decent service. **Lo de Juan** (Moreno 360, tel. 02965/421534) is a pizzeria with a diversity of other dishes as well. **Delikatesse** (Belgrano 409, tel. 02965/430716) serves mainly pasta and pizza, but also wild-game dishes.

About three blocks north of Plaza Independencia, in a former flour mill dating from 1910, **⚑ El Viejo Molino** (Avenida Gales 250, tel. 02965/428019) is the most ambitious new restaurant in town.

For ice cream, try **Heladería Venecia** (Belgrano 321), **Mares** (25 de Mayo 195), and **Vía Roca** (Belgrano and Roca).

Roger Shop (Moreno 463, tel. 02965/430690) is Trelew's only Welsh teahouse, and the place to purchase traditional black cake.

Information

Occupying recycled quarters at the southeast corner of Plaza Independencia, the municipal **Entretur** (Mitre 387, tel. 02965/420139, turismo@trelew.gov.ar, www.trelewpatagonia.gov.ar) is open 8 A.M.–9 P.M. weekdays and 9 A.M.–1 P.M. and 3–8 P.M. weekends. There are also offices at the bus terminal (open daily except Sunday, 10 A.M.–noon and 6–9 P.M.) and airport (for arriving flights only).

For motorists, **ACA** is at Avenida Fontana and San Martín (tel. 02965/435197).

Services

Several banks have ATMs, including **Banco de la Nación** (Avenida Fontana and 25 de Mayo) and **Banco Macro Bansud** (9 de Julio 320). **Patagonia Grandes Espacios** (Belgrano 330, tel. 02965/434550) changes cash and travelers checks.

Correo Argentino is at Calle 25 de Mayo and Mitre; the postal code is 9100. **Locutorio del Centro** (25 de Mayo 219) has telephone, fax, and Internet connections.

Many visitors stay in Puerto Madryn, but Trelew agencies also operate excursions to destinations like Rawson and Playa Unión, the Welsh villages of the lower Río Chubut Valley, as well as Punta Tombo and even Península Valdés. **Nievemar** (Italia 98, tel. 02965/434114), the AmEx representative, arranges excursions to the Welsh settlements and Punta Tombo.

Lavadero Sarmiento (Sarmiento 363, tel. 02965/434233) washes clothes.

For souvenirs and clothing, including horse gear, leather, and woolens, visit **Los Jagüeles** (25 de Mayo 144, tel. 02965/422949).

For medical services, contact the **Hospital Zonal Adolfo Margara** (28 de Julio 160, tel. 02965/427542).

Getting There

Aerolíneas Argentinas/Austral (25 de Mayo 33, tel. 02965/420210) flies once or twice daily to Aeroparque, and occasionally to destinations such as Bariloche, El Calafate, and Ushuaia.

LADE (Urquiza 150, tel. 02965/435749) occupies offices in the bus terminal; it flies sporadically to Puerto Madryn, Viedma, Bahía Blanca, Mar del Plata, and Aeroparque northbound; Esquel, Bariloche, and Neuquén westbound; and Comodoro Rivadavia southbound.

The **Terminal de Ómnibus** (Urquiza 150, tel. 02965/420121) is six blocks northeast of Plaza Independencia.

Empresa Mar y Valle (tel. 02965/432429) has regular service to Puerto Pirámides, leaving Trelew at 7:45 A.M., with additional summer service; for more detail, see the Puerto Madryn section. **El Ñandú** (tel. 02965/427499) goes to the coastal town of Camarones Monday and Friday at 8 A.M. and Wednesday at 6 P.M., but departures may be daily in summer.

Typical destinations, fares, and times include Camarones (US$5.50, three hours), Puerto Pirámides (US$4.50, three hours), Comodoro Rivadavia (US$7.50, five hours), Viedma/Carmen de Patagones (US$11, seven hours), Esquel (US$14, nine hours), Neuquén (US$16, 10 hours), Bahía Blanca (US$18, 12 hours), Río Gallegos (US$25, 17 hours), Bariloche (US$18, 13 hours), Mar del Plata (US$28, 17 hours), Córdoba (US$22–29, 19 hours), Buenos Aires (US$22–30, 21 hours), and Mendoza (US$28–35, 24 hours).

Getting Around

Aeropuerto Internacional Marcos A. Zar (RN 3 s/n, tel. 02965/433443) is five kilometers north of town on the east side of the Puerto Madryn highway. Cabs or *remises* cost about US$3.

Línea 28 de Julio (tel. 02965/432429) has hourly **buses** to Puerto Madryn (US$1.50), and 18 daily to Gaiman (US$.65) and Dolavon (US$1.20) between 7:10 A.M. and 11 P.M. weekdays; on Saturday there are 14 between 7:20 A.M. and 9:40 P.M., and 11 on Sundays and holidays between 7:30 A.M. and 9:30 P.M.

Empresa Rawson goes to Rawson (US$.50) every 15 minutes, starting at 5:30 A.M.

Car rental agencies include **Avis** (Paraguay 105, tel. 02965/434634) and **Localiza** (Urquiza 310, tel. 02965/435344), both of which also have airport desks. For camper and motor-home rentals, contact the local agent for **Gaibu Motorhome Time** (Salvador Allende 1064, tel. 02965/15-407412, claudiofrasch@hotmail.com, infovaldes@gaibu.com).

RAWSON AND PLAYA UNIÓN

Rawson (population 22,355) is Chubut's low-profile capital and, in truth, there's not a lot to see in this nondescript bureaucratic outpost. Its suburb of Playa Unión, though, is a minor ecotourism destination for the glossy black-and-white Commerson's dolphins that dart around and under the launches that motor along the waters fronting its long sandy beach.

To see the dolphins (which are also common in other coastal destinations like Puerto Deseado), contact Toninas Adventure (tel. 02965/15-666542, toninas_adventure@yahoo.com), which charges about US$8 pp. While waiting, or afterward, consider a seafood lunch at dockside cantinas like **El Marinero** or **Cantina Marcelino** (tel. 02965/496960) at the south end of town.

Playa Unión also has decent accommodations at **Hotel Atlansur** (Costanera Avenida Rawson 339, tel. 02965/15-698735, US$10/13 s/d, breakfast extra) and **Hostería Le Bon** (Rifleros 68, tel. 02965/496638, US$13/17 s/d).

In Rawson, the Secretaría de Turismo y Areas Protegidas de la Provincia del Chubut (Avenida 9 de Julio 280, tel. 02965/481113, chubutur @arnet.com.ar, info@chubutur.gov.ar, www .chubutur.gov.ar) has information on the entire province. Playa Unión has its own Centro de Atención al Turista (Avenida Rawson and Centenario, tel. 02965/4496887), open 7:30 A.M.– 7:30 P.M. daily except Sunday, when hours are 9 A.M.–noon and 4–9 P.M.

Buses from Trelew to Rawson run every 15 minutes; from the Rawson terminal, it's necessary to catch another local bus or taxi to Playa Unión.

GAIMAN AND VICINITY

More than any other settlement in the lower Chubut Valley, Gaiman has sustained and capitalized on its Welsh heritage. Traditionally famous for its tourist teahouses, sturdy stone buildings, and community events like the Eisteddfod, it's recently become more of a destination, thanks to the addition of several B&B accommodations, rather than a simple excursion.

© WAYNE BERNHARDSON

Welsh teahouses line the streets of Gaiman.

Gaiman (population 4,300), 17 kilometers east of Trelew via RN 25, dates from 1874, when Welsh immigrants first harnessed the river to irrigate their fields and orchards. The aboriginal Tehuelche gave it the name Gaiman, meaning "Stony Point."

Sights

The best starting point for a visit to Gaiman is the **Amgueddfa Hanesyddol** (Sarmiento and 28 de Julio, tel. 02965/491007, US$.35), the regional historical museum that occupies the former train station. Staffed by Welsh and English-speaking volunteers, it holds documents, photographs, and possessions of early immigrants. Hours are 10 A.M.–11:30 P.M. and 3–7 P.M. weekdays except Monday, when it's closed, and 3–7 P.M. weekends.

Two blocks to the northwest, Dolavon-bound trains no longer pass through the **Twnnel yr Hen Reilfford,** a 300-meter brick tunnel that's now open to pedestrians and slow-moving vehicle traffic (westbound only). One block west of the tunnel exit, dating from 1899, the **Coleg Camwy** (Bouchard and M.D. Jones) may have been Patagonia's first secondary school. At the east end of 28 de Julio, the **Mynwent** (cemetery) is full of historic headstones, many of them in Welsh.

Parque El Desafío

Though it has nothing to do with Gaiman's Welsh heritage, founder Joaquín Alonso's magnum opus is a whimsical labor of love by a man who seems incapable of throwing anything away, turning everyone else's trash into lighthearted *objets d'arts.* In the process, he's created credible mural replicas of works by Florencio Molina Campos, Benito Quinquela Martín, and even Pablo Picasso's *Guernica.* Perhaps the most amusing single item is the *palo borracho* (a pun on the spiny Mesopotamian tree *Chorisia speciosa,* colloquially known as "drunken stick" because of its water-swollen trunk); the leaves of this drunken stick, though, are beer and wine bottles.

According to the Guinness Book of Records, Alonso's one-hectare property contains 50,000

"palo borracho," Parque El Desafío, Gaiman

wine and beer bottles, 30,000 aluminum cans, 25,000 spools of thread, 12,000 bottle caps, and 5,000 plastic bottles, along with automobiles, TVs, refrigerators, washing machines, and 200-liter water tanks. It's easy to amuse yourself for an hour or so just looking at the odds and ends, and even more if your Spanish is good enough to appreciate the aphorisms on small plaques scattered around the park.

Parque El Desafío (Avenida Almirante Brown s/n, tel. 02965/491340, US$2 adults, US$.80 children) is open from dawn to 6 P.M. With every admission, Alonso hands out a small souvenir.

Shopping

For crafts, visit the Paseo Artesanal Crefft Werin (Avenida Eugenio Tello and Miguel Jones, tel. 02965/491134), opposite Plaza Roca. Try El Arbol (Belgrano 259, tel. 02965/15-685582) for chocolates, cheeses, and the like.

Accommodations

The quality of accommodations here is pretty high, especially as some of the top teahouses have begun to offer B&B-style lodging. Options are still limited, though, so reservations are a good idea.

Alongside the fire station, the flood-prone **Camping Bomberos Voluntarios** (Hipólito Yrigoyen between Libertad and Independencia, US$1 pp) has picnic tables, clean toilets, and hot showers.

Hostería Dyffryn Gwirdd (Avenida Eugenio Tello 103, tel. 02965/491777, infodw @dwhosteria.com.ar, US$8 pp) is not a teahouse, but it's a very respectable place with private bath and breakfast, though definitely a work-in-progress. Run by Italo-Argentines, its Welsh name is a little misleading.

Gaiman's only proper hotel, **Hotel Unelem** (Avenida Eugenio Tello and 9 de Julio, tel. 02965/491663, unelem@arnet.com.ar, US$11 d) has rooms with private bath, some with fireplaces, and breakfast. **Plas y Coed** (M.D. Jones 123, tel. 02965/491133, US$15 d) is an annex of Gaiman's landmark teahouse.

At **Hostería Gwesty Tywi** (Michael D. Jones 342, tel. 02965/491292, gwestywi@infovia.com .ar, www.advance.com.ar/usuarios/gwestywi, US$13/20 s/d), the rooms vary considerably and some have shared rather than private baths. There are discounts for stays longer than a few days.

M Te Gwyn (9 de Julio 147, tel. 02965/ 491009, tygwyn@cpsarg.com, US$14 pp) is a quality teahouse that has built several stylishly furnished rooms—the beds are new and handsome, and antique sewing machines have been adapted into desks. Some rooms have balconies facing the river—a mixed blessing, as they also face a playground where families with children play until midnight or even later, and the mosquitoes are ferocious. Still, it's a remarkable bargain with breakfast (a satisfying reprise of the previous afternoon's tea), and would still be a good value at the old 1:1 exchange rate.

Food

Gaiman may be picturesque, but it's pointless

to come here without indulging yourself on cakes, jams, scones, pies, and a bottomless teapot. Since tea starts around 3 P.M., either skip lunch or go later and then skip dinner; for about US$5.50–6 pp, it's a de facto all-you-can-eat. Watch for the arrival of tour buses—when one is parked outside, slow service is almost certain.

Gaiman's oldest teahouse is ⚑ **Plas y Coed** (M.D. Jones 123, tel. 02965/491133), which wins points for exceptional sweets and personalized service. Ivy-covered **Ty Nain** (Hipólito Yrigoyen 283, tel. 02965/491126) is the most stylish of the bunch, but **Ty Gwyn** (9 de Julio 147, tel. 02965/491009) is also appealing. The newest teahouse, **Ty Cymraeg** (Mathews 74, tel. 02965/491010) blends a traditional style with all modern conveniences; its scones, grape jam, and lemon pie are all outstanding.

Across the river, reached by a roundabout route over the bridge at the south end of J.C. Evans, **Ty Caerdydd** (tel. 02965/491053) is an enormous teahouse that sits among its own irrigated fields, which produce fresh fruits and berries used in its own products, and elaborate flower gardens. Lady Di, as Princess of Wales, was once a celebrity guest.

Overnighters can't gorge themselves on Welsh teas every day. New restaurants include **Pizzería Gustos** (Avenida Eugenio Tello 156, tel. 02965/491453) and **La Vieja Cuadra** (M.D. Jones 418). Gaiman's most ambitious and atmospheric restaurant, **El Ángel** (M.D. Jones 257, tel. 02965/491460) is open for dinner Saturdays only; reservations are essential.

Other Practicalities

In the Casa de Cultura (Belgrano 235), the **Oficina de Informes Turísticos** (tel. 02965/491571) is open 8 A.M.–3 P.M. weekdays only.

Correo Argentino is at Juan Evans and Hipólito Yrigoyen, just north of the bridge over the river; the postal code is 9105. There's a *locutorio* on Avenida Tello between 25 de Mayo and 9 de Julio.

Empresa 28 de Julio's frequent **buses** between Trelew and Dolavon stop on the south side of Plaza Roca.

GEOPARQUE PALEONTOLÓGICO BRYN GWYN

Exposed by early meanderings of the Río Chubut after an earlier subtropical sea evaporated, the sedimentary badlands of Bryn Gwyn are an open book of ancient fossils. While the oldest Tertiary beds are too young to yield dinosaur bones, there is evidence of giant anteaters and ungulates from the time when this was savanna, and marine mammals like seals, dolphins, and whales, as well as penguins.

Visitors to the park, eight kilometers south of Gaiman via RP 5, can hike the well-organized trail, which climbs gradually and then steeply up the cliffs, from the confitería at the south end. There are at least a dozen excavation sites, with some fossils in the open and others preserved in glass cases.

Affiliated with Trelew's Museo Feruglio, the park charges US$1.50 admission for adults, US$1 for children, with discounts for provincial residents; groups of more than 20 can arrange guided visits. Hours are 10 A.M.–7 P.M. daily. There is no regular public transportation, but *remises* from Gaiman are not unreasonable.

DOLAVON

Unlike Gaiman, sleepy Dolavon (population 2,481) has never become a tourist town, but the brick buildings along its silent streets display a greater architectural harmony than its larger neighbor—even though, founded in 1919, it's much newer. Its major landmark, dating from 1930, is the **Molino Harinero** (Maipú 61), a grain mill that's now a hybrid museum and teahouse. *Norias* (waterwheels) in the nearby canals still distribute Río Chubut water to the fields and orchards.

From the Trelew terminal, Empresa 28 de Julio runs 10 buses daily to and from Dolavon via Gaiman.

⬛ RESERVA PROVINCIAL PUNTA TOMBO

On the barren shores of the South Atlantic, 110 southeast of Trelew, nearly a quarter million pairs

THE WILDLIFE ROUTES OF COASTAL CHUBUT

For Patagonia travelers, arrow-straight RN 3 is the quickest ticket south, but visitors with their own wheels—whether two or four—should explore coastal Chubut's dusty backroads. It's common enough to rent a car for Península Valdés, where a bicycle is less useful because camping is prohibited, but the loop from Rawson south to Punta Tombo and Camarones, returning via RN 3, is an intriguing alternative for automobiles, motorbikes, and bicycles.

Along southbound RP 1, the big attraction is Punta Tombo's **penguins**, but most visitors see them on a tour. Rather than returning to Puerto Madryn or Trelew, the self-propelled can get an *estanciero's* view of the thinly settled area by following the dusty, narrow, but smooth gravel road south past desolate Cabo Raso, with its steep gravel beach, and on to picturesque Camarones.

From Camarones, the **provincial wildlife reserve** at Cabo Dos Bahías makes an ideal excursion before returning to RN 3 via a smooth paved lateral and heading back north—perhaps for tea in Gaiman—or continuing south toward Comodoro Rivadavia. With an early start, this could be a day trip, but an overnight in Camarones is a better option.

of Magellanic penguins come ashore every austral spring to nest on only 210 hectares at remote Punta Tombo. Despite its isolation, 50,000 visitors a year find their way down graveled RP 1 and a dusty southeasterly lateral to the continent's largest single penguin colony. In addition to penguins, though, there are impressive numbers of other seabirds, including giant petrels, kelp and dolphin gulls, king and rock cormorants, and shorebirds including oystercatchers and flightless steamer ducks.

Tours from Trelew (around US$27 pp) arrive at the site around 11 A.M., but the birds are dispersed enough that it rarely seems crowded. Provincial authorities have fenced off most of the nesting grounds and human visitors must stay on marked trails and boardwalks; still, since the penguins themselves do not respect the fences, it's possible to get up-close-and-personal photographs while respecting the birds' distance. Note, though, that penguin beaks can inflict a nasty gash.

Punta Tombo's infrastructure is still very limited—a visitors center is in the works, but local *estancieros* are disinclined to part with any more property than they already have. Still, the simple *confitería,* while nothing special, has fresh-baked lamb empanadas and clean, modernized toilets.

At the entrance, provincial authorities collect US$5.50 pp for adult foreigners, US$2.50 for Argentine residents, and US$1 for Chubut residents. No camping is permitted; if you're driving, penguins have right-of-way.

While it's also possible for a group to hire a taxi for a day trip to the reserve, renting a car in Trelew or Puerto Madryn would make it possible to follow the scenic desert coastline south past the ghost town of Cabo Raso to the picturesque fishing port of Camarones and the wildlife reserve of Cabo Dos Bahías, which has both penguins and sea lions. From Camarones it's possible to return to Trelew or Puerto Madryn via paved RN 3.

CAMARONES AND VICINITY

Toward the south end of its namesake bay, the sleepy fishing port of Camarones has only two paved streets, but so many wide gravel ones that it seems as if the town is waiting for something big to happen. Its citizens may wait for quite a while, but Camarones is just picturesque enough, close to enough to the wildlife reserve at Cabo Dos Bahías, and getting here from Punta Tombo via the desolate Cabo Raso route is interesting enough, that it's a worthwhile off-the-beaten-road loop for anyone with a vehicle.

Alternatively, there's public transportation via southbound RN 3 from Trelew and eastbound RP 30, a distance of about 250 kilometers. The town holds a **Fiesta Nacional del Salmón** (National Salmon Festival) the second weekend of February.

Reserva Provincial Cabo Dos Bahías

Only 30 kilometers southeast of Camarones, Dos Bahías is one of several similar but by no means identical reserves in coastal Chubut. Like Punta Tombo, it has a substantial Magellanic penguin colony, which at 12,000 breeding pairs is much smaller than Punta Tombo. In some ways, though, it's a better place to see penguins, as Dos Bahías' more open terrain makes it easier to appreciate the extent of the colony.

In addition to penguins, Dos Bahías has a substantial colony of southern sea lions on offshore **Isla Moreno,** though they're hard to see from the mainland without binoculars. It also has abundant terrestrial wildlife, including ar-

© WAYNE BERNHARDSON

Magellanic penguin, Cabo Dos Bahías

madillos, foxes, guanacos, and rheas, not to mention many of the same seabirds that characterize Punta Tombo.

Unlike Punta Tombo, it's possible to camp at the beaches en route to Dos Bahías and at the reserve itself, though there are no other services. There is also no regular transportation, though it's possible to hire a car with driver in Camarones (try Hotel Viejo Torino). At the entrance to the reserve, provincial authorities collect at US$2 admission fee per adult foreigner.

Accommodations and Food

Open all year, the sheltered sites at the waterfront **Camping Camarones** (US$2 per site) have electricity, and the clean bathrooms have hot showers.

Residencial Bahía del Ensueño (Belgrano and 9 de Julio, tel. 0297/496-3077, US$4.50 pp) is the shoestring choice. **Hotel Kau-i-keukenk** (Sarmiento and Roca, tel. 0297/496-3004, US$4.50 pp) is better and only slightly dearer with breakfast, and its restaurant is reliable if no longer exceptional.

Though it's a work-in-progress, the new and cheerful **Hotel Viejo Torino** (Brown 100, tel. 0297/496-3003, US$7/13 s/d) represents an effort to create a decent hotel with an attractive seafood-and-pasta restaurant, which is doing good business—though the food is not quite up to its aspirations and the service is well-intentioned but inexperienced. Rooms are simply but comfortably furnished, with firm beds and up-to-date baths with plenty of hot water.

Getting There

There are still only three or four buses weekly with El Ñandú to Trelew (US$5, 3.5 hours), which arrive and leave the same afternoon.

COMODORO RIVADAVIA AND VICINITY

Comodoro Rivadavia's motto is "a city with energy," and in that sense Chubut's most southerly city is Houston-by-the-Sea. For almost a century, ever since drillers looking for water hit an oil gusher instead, it's been the locus of Argentina's

Southern Patagonia

petroleum industry; thanks to the former state oil company Yacimientos Petrolíferos Fiscales (YPF), now a private enterprise, it has an outstanding petroleum museum.

On the hills north and south of town, the landscape is a jumble of drilling rigs, petroleum pipelines, storage tanks, and seismic-survey lines. Ironically enough, though, Comodoro appears to be leading the way in alternative energy—the high-tech windmills overlooking downtown from the north are a conspicuous symbol of change.

As the only large coastal city between Trelew and Río Gallegos, Comodoro Rivadavia's services make it a frequent stopover for southbound motorists. Other destinations, though, have more to see and do.

Orientation

Comodoro Rivadavia (population 135,813) is 377 kilometers south of Trelew and 780 kilometers north of Río Gallegos via RN 3. It is 581 kilometers southeast of Esquel via paved RN 26, RP 20, and RN 40.

Hilly Comodoro lacks a central plaza, and most activity takes place within a triangular area formed by the Atlantic shoreline, east-west Avenida San Martín (the main commercial street), and north-south Avenida Alsina and Avenida Chiclana.

Sights

For a panoramic view of the city and the curving shoreline of Golfo San Jorge, climb the footpath to the summit of **Cerro Chenque,** immediately north of downtown.

On the Avenida Rivadavia median strip, a stiff climb from downtown, the **Museo Patagónico Antonio Gárces** (Rivadavia and Chacabuco, tel. 0297/447-7101, 8 A.M.–7 P.M. weekdays, 3–7 P.M. weekends, free) is an orderly but uninspiring facility that offers vignettes of Comodoro's development through fossils, aboriginal artifacts, and photographs.

Railroads were never the factor in Patagonia, especially southern Patagonia, that they were in the pampas. In Comodoro's old railway station, though, the developing **Museo Ferroportuario** (Avenida Rivadavia and 9 de Julio, tel. 0297/

447-3330, int. 345, 8 A.M.–7 P.M. weekdays, 3–7 P.M. weekends, free) tells the tale of the train that hauled wool and other agricultural produce from the city of Sarmiento, 149 kilometers to the west; intended to reach Lago Buenos Aires, the line never penetrated any farther west, though it also carried crude from nearby oilfields to the port.

About three kilometers north of downtown, the Universidad Nacional de Patagonia's first-rate **Museo Nacional del Petróleo** (Lavalle and Tehuelches, tel. 0297/455-9558, US$1.25, senior discounts available) is a YPF legacy. Occupying the grounds of Comodoro's initial gusher, it presents a professional account of Argentina's oil industry, from the natural and cultural environment to the evolution of petroleum technology and its social and historical consequences. Summer hours are 8 A.M.–1 P.M. and 3–8 P.M. weekdays except Monday, and 3–8 P.M. weekends only; the rest of the year, it's open 8 A.M.–5 P.M. weekdays except Monday and 3–8 P.M. weekends and holidays. From the Comodoro bus terminal, take the No. 7 Laprida or No. 8 Palazzo bus.

About 15 kilometers north of town, on the west side of RN 3, the **Museo Paleontológico Astra** has two elements: a roadside display of antique drilling equipment, and an elaborate exhibit of Patagonian fossils and minerals that keeps erratic hours but is well worth a visit if it's open.

Rada Tilly

About 17 kilometers south of Comodoro via RN 3, Rada Tilly is Comodoro's main beach resort and the access point for a sea lion colony at **Punta del Marqués,** where the animals are visible from an overlook. The **Museo Regional** (Combate de Martín García 175, tel. 0297/445-1598, US$.35) has exhibits on natural history but also ethnography and rock art; it's open 9:30 A.M.–8 P.M. Tuesday–Friday, 4–8 P.M. Saturday, Sunday, and holidays.

For further information, Rada Tilly's **Dirección de Turismo** (Avenida Brown 117, tel. 0297/445-2423, turismoradatilly@infovia.com.ar, www.radatilly.com) is open 7:30 A.M.–2:30 P.M.

weekdays and 1–7 P.M. weekends and holidays. There are frequent buses from Comodoro's downtown terminal.

Entertainment

A classic of its era, the **Cine Teatro Español** (Avenida San Martín 664, tel. 0297/447-7700) offers recent movies and theater productions. There's also the **Cine Coliseo** (San Martín 570, tel. 0297/444-5500).

Accommodations

Because Comodoro is the largest city in almost a 1,000 kilometers of highway, hotels can fill up fast and reservations are a good idea in summer.

Comodoro proper has no campgrounds, but Rada Tilly's **Camping Municipal** (Avenida Capitán Moyano s/n, tel. 0297/445-2918, US$1 pp, plus US$1 per tent) has sheltered sites with firepits and electricity, plus clean toilets and hot showers.

Downtown Comodoro has several run-of-the-mill shoestring choices: **Hospedaje Belgrano** (Belgrano 546, tel. 0297/447-8349, US$5–7 s, US$8–11 d); **Hospedaje Cari-Hue** (Belgrano 563, tel. 0297/447-2946, US$6.50/11 s/d) with shared bath; and the drab but well-located **Hotel Español** (9 de Julio 850, tel. 0297/446-0116, US$6-US$8 pp).

Hostería Rua Marina (Belgrano 738, tel. 0297/446-8777, US$7.50–11 s, US$10–14 d) is suitable in a pinch. **Residencial Comodoro** (España 919, tel. 0297/446-2582, fax 0297/444-0718, US$13/20 s/d) is deservedly the city's most popular budget choice. The aging public areas at **Hotel Azul** (Sarmiento 724, tel./fax 0297/447-4628, US$15/20 s/d) are a misleading introduction to what are, in reality, pretty decent rooms.

Hotel Comodoro (9 de Julio 770, tel. 0297/447-2300, info@comodorohotel.com.ar, US$25–28 s, US$32–35 d) is a traditional upscale choice, but it's fallen behind some newer options.

Really two hotels in one, the **Austral Hotel** (Rivadavia 190, US$27/34 s/d) and the recent addition ℕ **Hotel Austral Plaza** (Moreno 725, tel. 0297/447-2200, fax 0297/447-2444, info@australhotel.com.ar, www.australhotel.com.ar, US$49/57 s/d) share a reception, telephones, bar, *confitería,* and restaurant. While the Austral Hotel's rooms are comfy enough, if a little small, they are less extravagant than the Plaza's, which cost almost twice as much. Guests at both eat the same buffet breakfast.

The new **Hotel Lucania Palazzo** (Moreno 676, tel. 0297/449-9300, reserva@lucania-palazzo.com, www.lucania-palazzo.com, US$55/62 s/d) is a new four-star high-rise with all the amenities.

Food

For breakfast and sandwiches, try the **Café del Sol** (Avenida San Martín and 25 de Mayo).

Comodoro has several quality *parrillas,* including **Bom Bife** (España 789, tel. 0297/446-8412 and **La Rastra** (Rivadavia 348, tel. 0297/446-2140).

Pizzería Giuletta (Belgrano 851, tel. 02965/446-1201) serves fine pasta as well; in the same vein, there's **La Cantina** (Belgrano 845).

Peperoni (Rivadavia 481, tel. 0297/446-9683) serves fish and seafood, pastas, and short orders like *milanesa.* **La Barca** (Belgrano 935, tel. 0297/447-3710) is a fish and seafood specialist.

Under the direction of a disciple of *porteño* celebrity chef Joan Coll, the Hotel Austral Plaza's ℕ **Tunet** (Rivadavia 190, tel. 0297/447-2200) has become Comodoro's top restaurant, and even if they bring you the wrong dish—the service isn't quite up to snuff—it's likely to be so good you won't care. Good choices are the seafood risotto and the Ensalada Williams, a mixed salad of smoked salmon, mozzarella, carrots, and mushrooms; most entrees, especially seafood, are in the US$6–8 range.

Chocolate's (San Martín 231) serves Comodoro's best ice cream.

Information

Comodoro's **Dirección de Turismo** (Rivadavia 430, tel. 0297/446-2376, turismocomodoro@comodoro.gov.ar, www.comodoro.gov.ar), is open 8 A.M.–7 P.M. weekdays, 2–7 P.M. weekends in summer; the rest of the year, hours are

8 A.M.–3 P.M. weekdays only. It also has quarters at the bus terminal, open 8 A.M.–10 P.M. weekdays and 9 A.M.–9 P.M. weekends.

For motorists, **ACA** is at Dorrego and Alvear (tel. 0297/446-4036).

Services

Banco de la Nación (San Martín 102) is one of several ATMs along the main commercial drag. **Cambio Thaler** (San Martín 272) is the only specialized exchange house.

Correo Argentino is at Avenida San Martín and Moreno; the postal code is 9000. **Locutorio Pellegrini** (Pellegrini 930) has phone, fax, and Internet services, but there are several others.

Turismo Ceferino (9 de Julio 880, 1st floor, tel. 0297/447-3805) is the AmEx representative.

The Chilean consulate is at Almirante Brown 456, Oficina 3 (tel. 0297/446-2414).

Laverap (Rivadavia 287) does the laundry.

For medical assistance, try the **Hospital Regional** (Hipólito Yrigoyen 950, tel. 0297/444-2287).

Getting There and Around

Aerolíneas Argentinas/Austral (9 de Julio 870, tel. 0297/444-0050) flies twice or three times daily to Aeroparque.

Comodoro is the best place to catch a flight on **LADE** (Rivadavia 360, tel. 0297/447-0585), which flies irregularly northbound to Trelew, Puerto Madryn, Viedma, Bahía Blanca, Mar del Plata, and Aeroparque; westbound to Neuquén; and southbound to Perito Moreno, Gobernador Gregores, El Calafate, Río Gallegos, Río Grande, and Ushuaia.

From the downtown bus terminal, the No. 8 Patagonia Argentina (Directo Palazzo) bus goes directly to **Aeropuerto General Mosconi** (RN 3, tel. 0297/454-8093), which is nine kilometers north of town.

Comodoro's **Terminal de Ómnibus Teniente General Angel Solari** (Pellegrini 730, tel. 0297/446-7305) has regional, long-distance, and limited international bus service (to Coyhaique, Chile).

Buses to Coyhaique (US$25, 11 hours) often run full, so reservations are essential. **ETAP** (tel. 0297/447-4841) departs at 1 A.M. Mondays and Fridays for Coyhaique, while **Turibús** (tel. 0297/446-0058) goes there Tuesday and Saturday at 8 A.M.

Other typical destinations, fares, and times include Caleta Olivia (US$2.50, one hour), San Julián (US$7, 5.5 hours), Trelew (US$7.50, six hours), Puerto Deseado (US$7, four hours), Puerto Madryn (US$9, seven hours), Los Antiguos (US$11, six hours), Esquel (US$13, eight hours), Río Gallegos (US$12, 10 hours), Bariloche (US$20, 14 hours), and Buenos Aires (US$32, 24 hours).

Car rental agencies include **Localiza** (9 de Julio 770, tel. 0297/446-0334) and **Dubrovnik** (Moreno 941, tel./fax 0297/444-1844).

Coastal Santa Cruz Province

CALETA OLIVIA

South of Comodoro Rivadavia, entering Santa Cruz Province, there's heavy truck traffic and plenty of reckless driving on winding RN 3, before arriving at the forlorn oil port of Caleta Olivia. Caleta (population 36,323), 79 kilometers south of Comodoro, is a hub for westbound traffic to Lago Buenos Aires, Los Antiguos, and the Chilean border. It is 346 kilometers north of Puerto San Julián, the next major stop on RN 3, but only 216 kilometers northwest of Puerto Deseado, a uniquely underrated wildlife destination.

The city's only conspicuous attraction, dominating a downtown traffic circle that marks the center of town, is the **Monumento al Obrero Petrolero** (1969), popularly known as "El Gorosito," Facing north, Sculptor Pablo Daniel Sánchez's 10-meter sculpture of a shirtless oil worker turning an oil valve symbolizes thinly populated Patagonia's contribution to (or exploitation by) the populous Argentine heartland.

Accommodations and Food
The seaside **Balneario Municipal** (Brown and Guttero, tel. 0297/485-0976, US$1 pp, US$2 for a family) has clean toilets and hot showers.

Hotel Capri (José Hernández 1145, tel. 0297/485-1132, US$5.50/9 s/d) has some cheaper rooms with shared bath; breakfast is US$1 extra. **Posada Don David** (Hipólito Yrigoyen 2385, tel. 0297/485-7661, US$6–11 s/d) has rooms with shared or private bath.

Hospedaje Rodas (Matheu 12, tel. 0297/485-1880, US$5.50 pp) offers good value with private bath. **Hotel Robert** (Avenida San Martín 2151, tel. 0297/485-1452, hrobert@mcolivia.com.ar, US$14–18 s, US$21–25 d) passes for a top hotel here, and its restaurant **La Rosa** comes recommended.

Pizzería Variedades (Independencia and Fagnano, tel. 0297/485-2653) also has a wide variety of takeaway empanadas. Down the block, **El Puerto** (Avenida Independencia 1060, tel. 0297/485-1313) is a good option.

Heladería Centro (Independencia and Namuncurá) has fine ice cream.

Information and Services
The municipal **Centro de Informes** (Avenida San Martín and Güemes, tel. 0297/485-0988) is open 8 A.M.–9 P.M. in summer, 8 A.M.–5 P.M. the rest of the year.

There are several ATMs along Avenida San Martín. **Correo Argentino** is at Hipólito Yrigoyen 2194. **Telefonía Caleta** (Avenida Independencia 1147) has long-distance services.

Getting There
Caleta's **Terminal de Ómnibus** (Avenida Tierra del Fuego and Humberto Beguín) is some 15 blocks northwest of the monument. There are north- and southbound services along RN 3, but also westbound connections to Los Antiguos and Chile Chico via paved RP 43.

Typical fares include Comodoro Rivadavia (US$2.50, one hour), Puerto Deseado (US$6, 3.5 hours), Río Gallegos (US$10, eight hours), Los Antiguos (US$10, five hours), and Buenos Aires (US$35, 25 hours).

PUERTO DESEADO AND VICINITY

Bypassed by rerouted RN 3—but not by nature or history—Puerto Deseado is one of Patagonia's hidden pleasures. Visited by Magellan, originally settled by Spanish whalers, explored by Darwin in 1833 and resettled half a century later, it hasn't lost its 19th-century pioneer ambience. In recent years, it's become a home port for the booming South Atlantic shrimp fishery—some businesses have signs in Spanish, English, and Russian. In an area that Francisco P. Moreno called "the most picturesque place on the eastern Patagonian coast," though, the star attraction is the Ría Deseado, where strong tides rush dozens of kilometers up the estuary to create a wildlife-rich zone that's the focus of a growing ecotourism sector.

© WAYNE BERNHARDSON

abandoned railroad station at Puerto Deseado

Orientation

On the north shore of the Ría Deseado, Puerto Deseado (population 10,252) is 216 kilometers southeast of Caleta Olivia and 295 kilometers from Comodoro Rivadavia via RN 3 and paved RN 281. It is, however, 125 kilometers from the RN 3 junction.

Compact Deseado is a walker's town, with most sights and services on and around the waterfront and Avenida San Martín.

Sights

For a small town, Deseado has plenty to see; the big draw is the **Reserva Provincial Ría Deseado.** The town's various historical monuments, though, all have good stories behind them.

By the late 19th century, Deseado seemed destined to become a railroad town, as authorities planned a northwesterly line for freight and passengers to Bariloche. Service never progressed beyond Las Heras, 283 kilometers to the northwest; it closed in 1977, leaving the stately **Estación del Ferrocarril Patagónico** (Avenida Oneto s/n) as an empty shell that's slowly undergoing restoration for municipal offices.

Several historic monuments date from this era, most notably the railroad's **Vagón Histórico** (1898), a historical railcar placed in a small plaza at San Martín and Almirante Brown. To the west, immediately across the street, **Banco de la Nación** has preserved its classic lava-block style; unfortunately, the supermarket that occupies the former **Compañía Argentina del Sud** (1919), immediately to the north, has covered up its vintage features with hideous painted signs on all sides of the building—for no reason whatsoever, as they have no competition in town (perhaps the people who stood up for the Vagón Histórico will make this their next cause). One block west, dating from 1915, stands the **Sociedad Española.**

Along the waterfront, the **Museo Regional Mario Brozoski** (Brown and Colón, tel. 0297/487-0673, 8 A.M.–5 P.M. weekdays) holds artifacts from the English corvette *Swift,* sunk nearby in 1770 and located only in 1982. Several kilometers northeast of town, **Balneario Las**

REMEMBERING A BRUTAL PAST

The handsome wooden railcar that now stands at the corner of San Martín and Almirante Brown is more than an object of trainspotter nostalgia. During the Santa Cruz Anarchist rebellion of 1921 (a struggle dramatized in Osvaldo Bayer's film *La Patagonia Rebelde*), it was the mobile command center for Colonel Héctor Benigno Varela, who led government forces against striking farm workers throughout the province. At Jaramillo station, near the present-day junction of RN 281 and RN 3, Varela himself executed gaucho insurgent José Font (popularly known as "Facón Grande" or "Big Knife") under false pretenses (appropriately enough, Varela died from a bomb and bullets by German Anarchist Kurt Gustav Wilckens in Buenos Aires in 1923).

As a symbol of military brutality in the province—in total, some 1,500 people died at the hands of Varela's forces—the car is an enduring monument. Nearly six decades later, in a December 1980 demonstration of defiance against Argentina's fiercest dictatorship ever, Deseado residents encircled the historic railcar with 40 private automobiles to prevent its removal by a truck. Not only did they challenge armed authority—in a town with a tank regiment—but the demonstrators bravely signed their names and ID card numbers in a petition to Santa Cruz Province's military governor. Astonishingly, under pressure, the de facto government backed down.

Piletas is a volcanic beach area where retreating tides leave shallow pools warm enough for swimming, at least in summer.

At the north end of Almirante Zar, after passing beneath a railroad bridge, the road leads five kilometers into the isolated **Cañadon Quitapeña,** where there are excellent wild camping sites with no services. Ten kilometers west of town, a southbound lateral off RN 281 leads to the **Gruta de Lourdes,** a secluded pilgrimage site where the faithful have left devotional plaques (it might be sacrilegious to say this would be a good rock-climbing area, but it would be no more so than spray-painting the rocks themselves already is). A rare rainstorm produces an ephemeral waterfall in the grotto.

Reserva Natural Ría Deseado

One of coastal Patagonia's primo wildlife sites, the Ría Deseado differs from a typical estuary in that it submerges a long, narrow valley that, in the past, probably carried a much greater volume of fresh water. As the fresh water flow diminishes, seawater penetrates farther and farther inland, creating new islands and other fauna-rich habitats. Offshore islands also form part of the reserve.

Several local operators organize wildlife-watching excursions in and around the Ría, to locations including the Magellanic penguin colony at **Isla Chaffers** and cliffside colonies of rock cormorants (*Phalacrocorax magellanicus*) and grey or red-legged cormorants (*Phalacrocorax gaimardi*) at **Banca Cormorán,** where the deep water permits easy approaches to the nests. On any excursion, swiftly swimming *toninas overas* (*Cephalorhynchus commersonii,* Commerson's dolphin) are constant companions, breaching and diving around and under the outboard launches; in mating season, they leap completely out of the water.

At **Isla de los Pingüinos,** 30 kilometers offshore, there are breeding elephant seals and colonies of the tireless rockhopper penguin (*Eudyptes crestatus*), which braves crashing waves to bound up steep stone faces to get to its nesting sites. Some operators also follow Darwin's route up the ría where, wrote the great naturalist, "I do not think I ever saw a spot which appeared more secluded from the rest of the world, than this rocky crevice in the wild plain."

Three Deseado operators organize excursions in the vicinity for the increasing number of Argentine and foreign visitors. Ricardo Pérez of **Darwin Expediciones** (Avenida España s/n, tel.

elephant seal pups, coastal Patagonia

0297/15-624-7554, info@darwin-expeditions .com, www.darwin-expeditions.com) has extensive experience here, and also does sea kayaking. Half-day trips to Isla Chaffers cost only about US$20 pp; full-day trips, following Darwin's route up the Deseado estuary, cost US$80 pp. A full-day excursion to offshore Isla de los Pingüinos, where there are rockhopper penguins, runs about US$90 pp, with a minimum of four passengers.

Turismo Aventura Los Vikingos (Estrada 1275, tel. 0297/487-0020, tel. 0297/15-624-4283) also organizes a diversity of itineraries, and goes farther afield to destinations like the petrified Araucaria forest at Monumento Natural Bosques Petrificado. A new entrant is **Kren Excursiones Náuticas** (Pueyrredón 238, tel. 0297/15-621-0875, krenturismo@hotmail.com, www.krenturismo.com).

Entertainment

Deseado is a quiet place, but for drinks there's the **Hotel Los Acantilados** (España and Pueyrredón). The **Jackaroe Boliche** (Moreno 633) is a dance club.

Accommodations and Food

Open all year, but windy and exposed, **Camping Refugio de la Ría** (Avenida Marcelo Lotufo s/n, tel. 0297/15-625-2980) charges US$2.50 per site, and also has claustrophobic trailers US$2.50 pp. At the western approach to town, **Camping Cañadón Giménez** (US$2 per tent) is more protected.

There are several shoestring options: **Hotel Colón** (Brown and Ameghino, tel. 0297/487-0522, US$7/13 s/d); **Residencial Sur** (Ameghino 1640, tel. 0297/487-0522, US$8/11 s/d); and **Hotel Oneto** (Doctor Fernández and Oneto, tel. 0297/487-0455, US$5.50 pp with shared bath, US$11/15 s/d with private bath).

Hotel Chaffers (San Martín and Moreno, tel. 0297/487-2246 or 0297/487-2168, US$16/24 s/d) is a substantial upgrade. At **Hotel los Acantilados** (España and Pueyrredón, tel. 0297/487-2167, acantour@puertodeseado.com, US$13–20 s, US$18–26 d), downstairs budget rooms come with small but serviceable baths; the upstairs rooms are better furnished and have sea views, but the baths are small and lack tubs. Its bar/*confitería*, with high ceilings and sea vistas, is the best place in town for a drink.

Dining options are limited, but good enough at places like **Pizzería La Balsa** (12 de Octubre 641, tel. 0297/487-1275), the pizzeria **Kokomos** (San Martín and Sarmiento, tel. 0297/487-2134), and the *parrilla* **El Pingüino** (Piedrabuena 958, tel. 0297/487-0373). Both

Viejo Marino (Pueyrredón 224, tel. 0297/487-0509) and **Puerto Cristal** (España 1698, tel. 0297/487-0387) have decent seafood, but the intangibles are lacking.

Information and Services

Deseado's **Dirección Municipal de Turismo** (Avenida San Martín 1525, tel. 0297/487-0220, turismo@pdeseado.com.ar) is open 8 A.M.–9 P.M. daily in summer, 9 A.M.–4 P.M. daily the rest of the year.

From December through Semana Santa, there is also an information table within the Vagón Histórico (San Martín and Almirante Brown), the city's historic rail car; hours are 10 A.M.–9 P.M. daily.

Banco de la Nación (San Martín 1001) and **Banco de Santa Cruz** (San Martín 1056) have ATMs.

Correo Argentino is at San Martín 1075; the postal code is 9050. **Telefonía Deseado** is at Almirante Brown 544. **TPP** (San Martín 1259) has slow Internet connections.

For medical services, try the **Hospital Distrital** (Brown and Colón, tel. 0297/487-0200).

Getting There and Around

Deseado has limited public transportation options, both by air and land. The government air service **LADE** (tel. 0297/487-1204) has its offices at the **Terminal de Ómnibus** (Sargento Cabral 1302), which is about 10 blocks northeast of the downtown area. The only flights are to and from Comodoro Rivadavia, usually on Mondays; cabs and *remises* are the only options to the airport, which is about six kilometers from town.

There are five buses daily to Caleta Olivia (US$6, 3.5 hours) and Comodoro Rivadavia (US$8, 4.5 hours), three with Transporte La Unión (tel. 0297/15-592-8598) and two with Sportman (tel. 0297/487-0013).

MONUMENTO NATURAL BOSQUES PETRIFICADOS

One of RN 3's most desolate stretches is the 350 kilometers between Caleta Olivia and Puerto San Julián, but just north of the midway point there's an incomparable detour to this 13,700-hectare desert badland, scattered with fossil tree trunks. In Jurassic times, long before the Andes rose in the west, this was a humid region of coniferous *Proaraucaria* woodlands before catastrophic volcanic eruptions flattened the forests and covered them with ash. In the 130 million years since, water and wind have eroded the ash layers and left the petrified trunks strewn on the surface.

Measuring up to three meters in diameter and 35 meters in length, *Proaraucaria* was a forerunner of the contemporary Araucaria of the Andes. Until 1954, when the area became a natural monument (meriting the highest possible level of protection under Argentine law), the best and biggest specimens were regularly looted. Proposed additions would increase the protected area to 60,000 hectares.

Solitary Bosques Petrificados, 50 kilometers west of RN 3 via graveled RP 49, gets about 3,500 visitors per annum, mostly in summer. In addition to its petrified forests, it has typical desert-steppe vegetation and wildlife like guanacos and rheas. It has no water, and there is no public transportation, but tour operators in Río Deseado will organize excursions to the site. For camping, try Estancia La Paloma, midway between RN 3 and the forest; in the past, authorities have permitted camping near the ranger station.

PUERTO SAN JULIÁN AND VICINITY

Arguably coastal Patagonia's single most historical settlement, windswept Puerto San Julián was the place where Magellan's crew wintered in 1520, en route to the first circumnavigation of the globe. Both Magellan and Sir Francis Drake, half a century later, faced mutinies that they put down ruthlessly. Antonio de Viedma founded a short-lived Spanish colony at nearby Floridablanca in 1780. Darwin, who found the countryside here "more sterile" than Deseado, uncovered a fossil specimen of *Macrauchenia patachonica*, a llamalike animal with an elephantlike trunk.

Southern Patagonia

From the late 19th century, British settlers from the Falklands and Scotland finally established a permanent presence in the area, thanks to the powerful San Julián Sheep Farming Company. Even in the late 1930s, according to John Locke Blake, "English was spoken freely round town," and the Company's extensive holdings—175,000 hectares of pastureland—dominated economic life into the 1960s. Today the town is a minor ecotourism destination, thanks to the presence of dolphins and penguins, and a common stopover as the largest town between Caleta Olivia and Río Gallegos.

San Julián (population 6,152) is 351 kilometers south of Caleta Olivia and 355 kilometers north of the provincial capital of Río Gallegos via RN 3. Avenida San Martín, the main thoroughfare, is an extension of the eastward lateral that connects the town with the highway.

Sights and Entertainment

In the bay just north of town, **Isla Cormorán** has a substantial Magellanic penguin colony; nearby **Isla Justicia,** with a king-cormorant colony, is also the site where Magellan decapitated one mutineer, quartered another, and left two others to starve. Excursiones Pinocho (Brown 739, tel. 02962/452856) takes visitors on harbor tours (US$6 pp) that include dolphin-watching, but when the winds are too strong it may not be able to sail.

Occupying an archetypal Patagonian house, San Julián's **Museo Regional y de Arte Marino** (Vieytes and Rivadavia) is so bursting with archaeological and historical artifacts that it may have to move to new quarters. Fortunately enough, it has knowledgeable staff, since the clutter means it's poorly organized; hours are 9 A.M.–noon and 4–9 P.M. weekdays, 10 A.M.–1 P.M. and 4–9 P.M. weekends.

Immediately across from the museum entrance, the memorial **Plazoleta Albino Argüelles** commemorates one of the victims of the army in the Anarchist rebellion of 1921. From here, the coastal Avenida Hernán de Magallanes leads north along the coast, past the marked grave of *Beagle* crewman Robert Sholl, who died on the voyage prior to Darwin's. The road continues to the abandoned **Frigorífico Swift,** a mutton freezer that operated from 1912 to 1967; its crumbling shell and pier are suitable subjects for post-industrial photographers.

In a century-old building, atmospheric **Casa Lara** (Avenida San Martín and Ameghino) is the only bar worthy of the name.

Accommodations and Food

The waterfront **Autocamping Municipal** (Avenida Hernán de Magallanes 560, tel. 02962/452806, US$1 pp plus US$1.50 per vehicle) has well-sheltered sites with picnic tables and firepits, clean bathrooms with hot showers, laundry facilities, and even a playground.

M Hospedaje La Casona (Avenida Hernando de Magallanes s/n, tel. 02962/452940, US$5.50 pp) is a B&B that occupies a recycled waterfront house—the most distinctively Patagonian lodgings in town. **Hotel Alamo** (RN 3 s/n, tel. 02962/454092, US$9/13 s/d) is a utilitarian motel-style facility at the highway junction.

Government-run hotels have a reputation for shoddy service and maintenance, but the **Hostería Municipal de Turismo** (25 de Mayo 917, tel. 02962/452300, US$11/17 s/d) is an exception. It's not luxurious, but the staff take pride in the place, and the rooms are comfortable and spotless, even though the breakfast is forgettable.

Under new management, **Hotel Sada** (Avenida San Martín 1112, tel. 02962/452013, US$12/17 s/d) has 18 rooms with private bath. **Hotel Bahía** (Avenida San Martín 1075, tel. 02962/454028, US$14–18 s, US$23–28 d) is an attractive new hotel that fills up fast.

Right on the waterfront, the popular **M Cantina El Muelle Viejo** (9 de Julio 1106, tel. 02962/453009) has a quick kitchen and attentive service, with fish and seafood at the top of the menu. Try the fresh and tasty *robalo a la maitre'd* (US$3.50), garnished with garlic, butter, and parsley, and the diverse house salad of lettuce, tomato, green beans, palm hearts, and hard-boiled egg.

La Rural (Ameghino 811, tel. 02962/454066) is primarily a *parrilla* serving beef and lamb, but they've expanded their fish and seafood offerings. **La Juliana** (Zeballos 1130, tel. 02962/452074) has made good early impressions with relatively expensive home-style cooking.

M&M (Avenida San Martín 387) has superb ice cream; there's another branch in El Calafate.

Information and Services

From mid-December to March, there's a municipal information office, open 10 A.M.–10 P.M. daily, in a trailer at the highway junction. The **Centro de Informes** is on the median strip on Avenida San Martín between Moreno and Rivadavia (tel. 02962/452871, int. 116, 7 A.M.–midnight in summer, 7 A.M.–2 P.M. weekdays the rest of the year).

Banco de Santa Cruz (Avenida San Martín and Moreno) and **Banco de la Nación** (Mitre 101) have ATMs.

Correo Argentino is at Avenida San Martín 155; the postal code is 9310. For telecommunications, try **Cabinas Telefónicas Noé** (Avenida San Martín 1375). CTK.com provides much-improved Internet access, but can be noisy with video gamers.

Lavandería Arco Iris (Roca 1077) does the washing.

For medical services, try the **Hospital Distrital** (9 de Julio s/n, tel. 02962/452020).

Getting There and Around

LADE (tel. 02962/452137) maintains an office in the **Terminal de Ómnibus** (Avenida San Martín 1552), but had no flights as of writing; flights normally leave from the airfield near the highway junction. On a highway as long as RN 3, somebody has to draw the short straw, and nearly all San Julián buses arrive and leave between midnight and 6 A.M., most of these between 1:30 and 4 A.M. There are several services to Buenos Aires and intermediates, and south to Río Gallegos.

Cerro San Lorenzo (Berutti 970, tel. 02962/452403) goes to Gobernador Gregores (US$9) at 7:30 A.M. Tuesday, Thursday, and Saturday, and 11 A.M. Sunday, returning at 6 P.M. on the same days.

COMANDANTE LUIS PIEDRA BUENA

When Darwin and the *Beagle*'s crew ascended the Río Santa Cruz in 1834, the swift current beyond Isla Pavón obliged them to walk the shore and drag their boats on lines—a slow process that limited their progress to about 10 miles per day. Twenty-five years later, naval explorer Luis Piedra Buena first raised the Argentine flag in the area where the mostly forgettable town that bears his name now stands.

The surprising quality of Piedra Buena's limited services, though, makes it worth a lunch break or even an overnight stay before visiting Parque Nacional Monte León.

On the north bank of the Río Santa Cruz, Piedra Buena (population 4,175) is 127 kilometers south of San Julián and 235 kilometers north of Río Gallegos via RN 3. About 45 kilometers south of town, westbound RP 9 provides a motorist's or cyclist's shortcut along the Río Santa Cruz Valley to El Calafate.

While Piedra Buena itself is nondescript, **Isla Pavón,** reached by a turnoff from the bridge over the Río Santa Cruz about three kilometers south of the highway junction, is a wooded beauty spot that's popular for fishing; a small museum honors Comandante Piedra Buena's efforts.

Accommodations and Food

On the island, the **Camping Vial Isla Pavón** (tel. 02962/497303, US$2.50 per site) has electricity, clean toilets, and hot showers (which cost US$.50 extra).

Its name lacks attraction and imagination, but the **Hotel Sur Atlantic Oil** (RN 3 Km 2404, tel. 02962/497008, suratlantic@alantecpsc.com .ar, US$15 s or d) has spacious and comfortable motel-style rooms along its gas station. Popular with southbound travelers, it also has a tremendous restaurant with a diverse menu, and particularly choice pastas (be sure to lunch in the restaurant proper, rather than the utilitarian *confitería*.

On Isla Pavón itself, **M Confitería y Hostería Isla Pavón** (tel. 02966/15-638380, US$14/23 s/d) offers 10 attractive rooms, a sauna, and one hot tub–equipped suite. While parts of the grounds can flood at high tide, the hotel itself would be a good value even at the old 1:1 exchange rate, and the restaurant is equally inviting.

Getting There and Around

The **Terminal de Ómnibus** is at Ibáñez Norte 130, in the town proper. There are north- and southbound services along RN 3, but it's also possible to catch buses on the highway.

M PARQUE NACIONAL MONTE LEÓN

Recently donated to the APN by the Fundación Vida Silvestre and the Patagonia Land Trust, 60,000-hectare Monte León's 25-kilometer shoreline and headlands are an ecological wonderland of copious wildlife and uncommon landscapes. Little known and even less visited, this former *estancia* is only Argentina's second coastal national park, after Parque Nacional Tierra del Fuego (other reserves in Río Negro, Chubut, and Santa Cruz are provincial domains).

Flora and Fauna

Monte León's coastline is home to populations of Magellanic penguins, king cormorants, Dominican gulls, and sea lions, while its interior grazes guanacos and rheas and shelters armadillos, among other species. The vegetation is primarily grasses and prostrate shrubs associated with the Patagonian steppe.

Sights and Activities

Wildlife-watching is, of course, the principal activity. The landscape itself, though, is something special: where the tides meet the headlands, the sea has eroded deep caverns. One of these, **La Olla** ("the kettle"), is so called because, seen from the steppe above, it has an almost perfectly circular opening (for safety's sake, do not approach too closely).

The coastline itself differs from the rest of Patagonia in that it abounds with prominent offshore rocks and stacks. Guano collectors worked one of these, **Isla Monte León,** by

stringing a still-existing cable tram from the mainland. Exploring both La Olla and Isla Monte León is possible at low tide, but hikers need to be aware of the tide tables to avoid being stranded—at best.

Practicalities

At Monte León proper, **camping** is possible, but there are better accommodations at **M Hostería Monte León** (RN 3 Km 2385, tel. 011/4621-4780 in Buenos Aires, consultas@monteleon-patagonia.com, US$90/150 s/d with full board), the former *estancia's casco,* which also arranges excursions to the shoreline.

For information (especially on the state of the road, which is subject to washouts) ask at **Estancia Monte León** on the highway (tel. 02962/498184, pnmonteleon@yahoo.com.ar), where there is an APN office.

There is no public transport to Monte León, which is 58 kilometers south of Piedrabuena via paved RN 3 and graveled RP 63, but heavy rains can cause washouts on this route; if this happens, the gate will be locked.

RÍO GALLEGOS

Travelers often dismiss windy Río Gallegos as merely a port and service center for Anglo-Argentine wool *estancias* and, more recently, the petroleum industry. Dating from 1885, near continental Argentina's southern tip, it has a handful of worthwhile museums, historical landmarks and other distinctive Magellanic buildings; it's also the gateway to one of the continent's largest penguin colonies and several historic *estancias* that are open to visitors. It is no longer the main gateway to El Calafate, since construction of the new international airport there, but many overland travelers to or from Punta Arenas (Chile) and Tierra del Fuego still have to spend a night here.

Orientation

Río Gallegos (population 79,072) is 696 kilometers south of Comodoro Rivadavia and 351 kilometers south of Puerto San Julián via RN 3, and 67 kilometers north of the Chilean border post of Monte Aymond; from Monte Aymond, it's another 196 kilometers to Punta Arenas or, alternatively, 571 kilometers to Ushuaia, Tierra del Fuego (including a ferry crossing at Primera Angostura). It is 305 kilometers southeast of El Calafate via paved RP 5.

Most points of interest and services are on and around Avenida Roca, which runs northwest-southeast, and the perpendicular Avenida San Martín. The redeveloped open space along the waterfront to the northeast has added a touch of class, but it can't stop the almost incessant winds.

Sights

Opposite Plaza San Martín, dating from 1899, the **Catedral Nuestra Señora de Luján** (Avenida San Martín 755) was the work of the Salesian priest Juan Bernabé, also responsible for the cathedrals of Punta Arenas and Ushuaia. Like other pioneer buildings, it reflects the typically Magellanic wood-framed, metal-clad style. Guided tours are available 10 A.M.– 3 P.M. daily except Sunday, when hours are 2–6 P.M.

On the south side of the plaza, named for an influential local sculptor, the **Museo de Arte Eduardo Minnicelli** (Maipú 13, tel. 02966/436323, museominnicelli@aike.zzn.com) showcases provincial artists. Hours are 8 A.M.–7 P.M. weekdays except Monday, 3–7 P.M. weekends.

Three blocks south, the **Museo Provincial Padre Jesús Molina** (Ramón y Cajal 51, tel. 02966/423290, cultura@spse.com.ar) is a comprehensive museum in the Complejo Cultural Santa Cruz, a larger cultural center; its holdings include material on geology and natural history, ethnology, and local history, including a good photographic collection. Hours are 10 A.M.–6 P.M. weekdays, 11 A.M.–7 P.M. weekends and holidays.

Appropriately located in a pioneer house that was the residence of Arthur and Victor Fenton, the city's first physicians, the **Museo de los Pioneros** (Elcano and Alberdi, tel. 02966/437763) does an outstanding job of documenting southern Patagonia's early settlers. English-speaking Scots-Argentine volunteers greet visitors and explain the details. Hours are 10 A.M.–8 P.M. daily.

Entertainment and Shopping

The **Cine Carrera** (Avenida Roca 1012, tel. 02966/420204) shows recent movies.

Artesanías Santacruceñas Yatén (Sarmiento 80, tel. 02966/420026) contains handmade items from throughout the province, some of which are made on the premises. **Rincón Gaucho** (Avenida Roca 619, tel. 02966/420669) specializes in horse gear and the like.

Originally sponsored by *estancieros,* **Artesanías Keokén** (Avenida San Martín 336, tel. 02966/420335) specializes in woolens, but also sells leather goods and food items including preserves and candies.

Accommodations

Traditionally, prices are high and quality mediocre in the accommodations sector, but things are improving.

Not quite so good as its fresh exterior paint job would suggest, **Residencial Laguna Azul** (Estrada 298, tel. 422165, US$4.50 pp) is a no-frills choice with multibedded rooms; for a little more, you can have a room to yourself. Homey **Hotel Colonial** (Rivadavia and Urquiza, tel. 02966/422329, US$5.50 pp) is probably the best in this range.

Amiable **Hostería La Posada,** Ameghino 331, tel. 02966/436445, hosterialaposada@infovia.com.ar, US$13 s or d) is a major step up for comfortable rooms with private bath (including a tub) and cable TV, but breakfast costs US$1 extra. Lunch or dinner is available for US$3.50. In the same range, try **Hotel Nevada** (Zapiola 480, tel. 02966/425990, US$7/13 s/d).

Ill-advised remodeling has cost **Hotel París** (Avenida Roca 1040, tel. 02966/422432, US$10/15 s/d) most of its original charm, but it's still a respectable place though rough around the edges. Modern motel-style rooms at the back have high ceilings and firm single beds; breakfast is extra. **Hotel Oviedo** (Libertad 746, tel. 02966/420118, US$10/15 s/d) is comparable, **Hotel Croacia** (Urquiza 431, tel. 02966/422997, US$12/16 s/d) a bit better.

Aging but reliable **Hotel Covadonga** (Avenida Roca 1244, tel. 02966/420190, US$7.50–13 s, US$13–18 d) has rooms with both shared and private bath. The spacious, friendly, and well-kept **Ⓜ Hotel Sehuen** (Rawson 160, tel. 02966/425683, hotelsehuen@hotmail.com, www.hotelsehuen.unlugar.com, US$13–17 s, US$17–22 d) is a new and welcome presence on the scene.

Once one of the city's best, still better than its unimpressive exterior might suggest, **Hotel Comercio** (Avenida Roca 1302, tel. 02966/420209, fax 02966/422172, hotelcom@internet.siscotel.com, US$21/27 s/d) has large and spotless rooms that are a bit worn around the edges; the lighting is dim and electrical outlets are few and antiquated. The private baths do have tubs, there is phone service and cable TV, and the public areas, including the bar, are excellent. The breakfast is only so-so, but there's a 10 percent discount for payment in cash.

Hotel Santa Cruz (Avenida Roca 701, tel. 02966/420601, fax 02966/420603, htlscruz@infovia.com.ar, www.advance.com.ar/usuarios/htlscruz, US$23/31 s/d) is starting to show its age, and the management can be a little brusque, but it still offers good value for money.

The **Costa Río Apart Hotel** (Avenida San Martín 673, tel./fax 02966/423412, costario @infovia.com.ar, www.advance.com.ar/usuarios/fjmontes, US$35/45 s/d) offers huge suites with twin-sized beds that can sleep three or four people comfortably, making it a good choice for a family or a group.

Food

As with accommodations, Río Gallegos' restaurant scene is also improving. For takeaway breads, croissants, and other baked goods, try **Panadería Zapiola** (Zapiola and Estrada).

Misleadingly named **Confitería Díaz** (Avenida Roca 1143, tel. 02966/420203) is a *parrilla* as well as a breakfast and sandwich spot. **18 Horas** (Avenida Roca 1315, tel. 02966/434541) is comparable.

Pizzería Bartolo (Avenida Roca 854, tel. 02966/427297) has a particularly fine fugazzeta (US$2). **La Vieja Esquina** (Vélez Sarsfield 96, tel. 02966/426991) is a backup choice for pizza. **Café Bohemia** (Chacabuco 104) has an interesting tapas menu.

Anyone who has ever been, or aspired to be, an Anglo-Argentine wool baron will dine at classic **Club Británico** (Avenida Roca 935, tel. 02966/425223), though the atmosphere still trumps the food.

The classiest choice in town remains **Ⓜ El Horreo** (Roca 862, tel. 02966/426462), whose upgraded facilities replace older ones that burned down a couple of years back. Local lamb (about US$4) is the specialty, but the *empanada gallega* makes an ideal appetizer.

Acuarela (Avenida Roca 1084, tel. 02966/420249) produces exceptional ice cream, perhaps even better than the traditional favorite **Heladería Tito** (Zapiola and Corrientes, tel. 02966/422008).

Information

One of the country's most efficient tourist offices, the **Subsecretaría de Turismo** (Avenida Roca 863, tel. 02966/422702, fax 02966/438725, turismosantacruz@speedy.com.ar, www.scruz.gov.ar/turismo) is open 9 A.M.–9 P.M. weekdays, 10 A.M.–10 P.M. weekends in the peak summer season; the rest of the year, hours are 9 A.M.–8 P.M. weekdays, 10 A.M.–3 P.M. weekends. It has maps and extensive details on accommodations, excursions, and transportation.

At the bus terminal, the Dirección Municipal de Turismo maintains a **Centro de Informes** (tel. 02966/442159, 10 A.M.–3 P.M. daily).

For motorists, **ACA** is at Orkeke 10 (tel. 02966/420477), on the riverfront end of Avenida San Martín.

Services

Cambio Luis Lopetegui (Zapiola 469) and **Cambio Thaler** (Avenida San Martín 484) exchange U.S. dollars, Chilean pesos, and travelers checks. There are numerous ATMs, such as those of **Banco Santa Cruz** (Avenida Roca 809) and **Banco de la Nación** (Avenida Roca 799).

Correo Argentino occupies a historic building at Avenida Julio Roca 893; the postal code is 9400. **Telefax** (Avenida Roca 1328), one of many *locutorios,* also has Internet services. **J@va Cybercafé** (Avenida Roca 923, tel. 02966/422775) is the comfiest Internet outlet.

Tur Aike (Zapiola 63, tel. 02966/422436) is one of the city's best established travel agencies.

For visa matters, **Migraciones** (Urquiza 144, tel. 02966/420205) is open 8 A.M.–8 P.M. weekdays only. The Chilean consulate (Mariano Moreno 148, tel. 02966/422364) is open 9 A.M.–2 P.M. weekdays only.

Lavadero El Tumbaito (Alberdi 397) can do the laundry.

For medical attention, try the **Hospital Regional** (José Ingenieros 98, tel. 02966/420025).

Getting There

Río Gallegos is still a hub for travel in southern Patagonia, though air services are less important since the opening of El Calafate's airport. Overland, there are connections west to El Calafate and Parque Nacional Los Glaciares, as well as the coal town of Río Turbio, with connections to Chile's Puerto Natales and Parque Nacional Torres del Paine; south to Punta Arenas, Chile; and to the Argentine side of Tierra del Fuego.

Aerolíneas Argentinas/Austral (Avenida San Martín 545, tel. 02966/422020) flies daily to Aeroparque and to Ushuaia. **Southern Winds** (Mitre 943, tel. 0297/446-7200) flies from Buenos Aires to Comodoro and on to Río Gallegos.

LADE (Fagnano 53, tel. 02966/422316) flies northbound to Buenos Aires and Comodoro Rivadavia, westbound to El Calafate, Gobernador Gregores, and Perito Moreno, and southbound to Río Grande and Ushuaia.

Once a month, **LanChile** flights between Punta Arenas and the Falkland Islands pick up and drop off passengers in Río Gallegos; for details, contact a travel agency.

About two kilometers west of downtown, Río Gallegos's **Terminal de Ómnibus** (Charlotte Fairchild s/n, tel. 02966/442159) fronts directly on RN 3 near Avenida Eva Perón. There are provincial, long-distance, and international services (to Chile).

A new and welcome development is direct service to Río Grande (US$20, eight hours) and Ushuaia (US$29, 12 hours), in Argentine Tierra del Fuego, avoiding the former necessity of traveling to Punta Arenas, Chile (which is still possible but considerably longer and slower).

Tecni-Austral (tel. 02966/442447) has departures daily except Sunday in high season.

Between them, **El Pulgarcito** (Avenida Roca 1074, Local 2, tel. 02966/15-623780) and **El Pegaso** (Comodoro Rivadavia 35, Local 3, tel. 02966/426758) alternate almost-daily service to Gobernador Gregores (US$13, 6.5 hours), the almost-gateway to Parque Nacional Perito Moreno (*not* the famous Moreno Glacier). Departures are 7–8 A.M.

Other typical destinations, fares, and times include San Julián (US$6.50, 4.5 hours), Río Turbio (US$11, five hours), El Calafate (US$10, 4.5 hours), Caleta Olivia (US$10, eight hours), Comodoro Rivadavia (US$12, nine hours), Trelew (US$23, 13 hours), Puerto Madryn (US$25, 14 hours), Buenos Aires (US$40–55, 36 hours), and Mendoza (US$50, 38 hours).

Several carriers go to Punta Arenas, Chile (US$8, 5.5 hours), including **El Pingüino** (tel. 02966/442169), **Buses Ghisoni** (tel. 02966/442687) **Magallanes Tour** (tel. 02966/442765), and **Pacheco** (also tel. 02966/442765). El Pingüino and **Bus Sur** (tel. 02966/442687) both go to Puerto Natales, the gateway to Torres del Paine, but it's also possible to bus to the Argentine border town of Río Turbio, where there are frequent services over the line.

Getting Around

Aeropuerto Internacional Brigadier General D.A. Parodi is about five kilometers west of town on RN 3. Taxis and *remises* (about US$3.50) are the only public transport to and from the airport.

From downtown Avenida Roca, city bus Nos. 1 and 12 ("Terminal") go directly to the Terminal de Ómnibus, on the southwestern outskirts of town, but cabs are also a reasonable option.

Car rental agencies include **Localiza** (Rivadavia 535, tel. 0297/446-3526), **Riestra** (Avenida San Martín 1504, tel. 02966/421321), and **Servicar** (España 311, tel. 02966/427293).

VICINITY OF RÍO GALLEGOS

Thanks to its proximity to historic *estancias* and wildlife sites, most notably the Cabo Vírgenes penguin colony, Río Gallegos is earning

Southern Patagonia

a newfound respect even though it's not a major destination in its own right. Río Gallegos travel agencies, such as Tur Aike, can arrange excursions to outlying attractions.

Returning from Cabo Vírgenes, Chile-bound travelers with their own transportation can take the RP 51 shortcut to the border at Monte Aymond, but should ask directions before doing so, as it is not always clearly marked.

Hill Station (Estancia Los Pozos)

One of Santa Cruz's most historic *estancias,* Hill Station embodies the experience of the Scots and Irish families who, after immigrating to the Falkland Islands in the 1870s, found their advancement blocked by large farms that already owned all pastoral lands. Unwilling to remain simple shepherds, many left for "the coast" of Patagonia, where large blocks of nearly free land were still available.

Dating from the winter of 1885, Hill Station began inauspiciously when, disembarking, William Halliday and his family lost most of their supplies to a sudden storm and a high tide on the north side of the Río Gallegos estuary. Despite the setbacks, Halliday and his descendents persevered; today, Estancia Los Pozos remains a family farm—running some 9,000 Corriedale and Merino sheep on 30,000 hectares—and a getaway destination for visitors from around Argentina and the world.

Visitors to Hill Station are welcome to participate in farm activities, which include horseback riding, and to stay at the sizable Magellanic-style farmhouse, which has two large comfortable rooms, accommodating a maximum of four persons, with period furnishings; there is one shared bath, plus a large sitting room. Dating from 1929, this is not the *estancia's* original *casco,* which was near the shoreline immediately across from the city of Río Gallegos. For more on Hill Station's history, look for Michael Mainwaring's *From the Falklands to Patagonia* (London: Allison & Busby, 1983).

Reservations are obligatory at Hill Station (Libertad 1057, Río Gallegos, tel. 02966/423970; 02966/15-621783, hillstation@arnet.com.ar), which is only a short distance north of the city as

the crow flies, but it's 64 kilometers by road via paved RN 3 and gravel RP 55. Rates are US$100 pp with full board, US$140 pp with horseback excursions included; nonguests can order breakfast or afternoon tea (US$15 pp, including a guided tour), an executive lunch (US$35 pp), or dinner (US$25 pp, also including a guided tour).

ⓜ Estancia Monte Dinero

At a junction about 15 kilometers south of Río Gallegos, RP 1 turns southeast through an area of rolling pasturelands and, increasingly, gas-and-oil derricks reminding you that Santa Cruz is an energy storehouse. The gravel road is smooth as far as **Estancia Cóndor,** an immaculate settlement that belongs on picture postcards (though neighboring farmers consider that the Benetton empire, which now owns Cóndor, is at best an indifferent neighbor in what was once a close-knit community).

Beyond Cóndor, the road deteriorates toward **Estancia Monte Dinero,** a pioneering sheep farm that has also opened its doors to tourists. Some 120 kilometers from Río Gallegos, 26,000-hectare Monte Dinero benefits from its proximity to the penguin colony at Cabo Vírgenes, but it's also interesting as a ranch that, unlike most others in the area, is subdivided into relatively small paddocks to manage its 19,500 sheep and fragile pastures more intensively. Also unlike other *estancias,* it trains its own contract shearers to use manual rather than electric shears, pays them a premium to do so, and shears the ewes prior to lambing to ensure a higher lambing rate.

Founded by the Fentons, another pioneer Patagonian family, **Hostería Monte Dinero** has four downstairs bedrooms, three with private bath and two with shared bath upstairs, while the *casco's* former sun porch has been expanded into an attractive and spacious, but not extravagant, bar and dining room. A small museum holds family keepsakes (including a perfect puma skull), and there's also a billiard table (*not* a pool table).

Estancia Monte Dinero (tel./fax 02966/ 428922, tel./fax 02966/426900, int. 23, turismo@montedinero.com.ar, www.montedinero .com.ar) is open October to April. Rates are

US$40/60 s/d with breakfast; lunch or dinner costs US$10 additional. Excursions to Cabo Vírgenes cost US$30 pp, and horseback riding is available for US$10 per hour.

Reserva Provincial Cabo Vírgenes

Beyond Monte Dinero, the road improves as it approaches Cabo Vírgenes, second only to Punta Tombo among Argentina's Magellanic penguin colonies with about 120,000 breeding pairs. It is also growing rapidly, having increased by a third since 1998.

The abundance of brush here, though, means the birds are less visible than at Dos Bahías, and there is no direct access to the beach. There is, however, a 1,500-meter nature trail that permits close approach to the birds, and an interpretive brochure in good English; at the entrance to reserve, there's an admission fee of US$2.50 for foreigners, US$1.60 for Argentines, and US$.80 for Santa Cruz residents.

At the northeast corner of the reserve, the Universidad Nacional de la Patagonia is rehabbing the hilltop **Faro Cabo Vírgenes,** the historic Argentine lighthouse, as a museum. In front of the lighthouse, facing the ocean, there remain foxholes dug to repel British commandos who might have landed here during the 1982 Falklands war (the Brits did conduct operations on Argentine territory in Patagonia and Tierra del Fuego, escaping into Chile with collusion from the Pinochet dictatorship, which feared an Argentine attack).

At the so-called **Cementerio Histórico,** the only truly legitimate tomb may be that of Conrado Assinbom, a hermit who lived in the shack beneath the lighthouse. There is one older cross, but it's almost illegible and there's no certainty anyone's buried there.

At the southern end of the reserve, visitors can cross the border—technically illegally—for a guided tour of **Faro Punta Dungeness** (1897), the Chilean lighthouse at the end of Chile's narrow strip of land along the Strait of Magellan. When their duties permit, Chilean navy personnel there offer guided tours of the facility.

The nearest accommodations are at Estancia Monte Dinero, but Monte Dinero's sparkling new *confitería* **Al Fin y al Cabo** has become the place to stop for lunch and sweets—try the rhubarb cake with calafate sauce. While it's fairly expensive, the quality is excellent and the building has a magnificent view of the shoreline south to Cabo Dungeness.

© WAYNE BERNHARDSON

The coastline at Cabo Vírgenes is one of Argentina's largest penguin reserves.

Interior Santa Cruz Province

EL CALAFATE

On the south shore of Lago Argentino, a giant glacial trough fed by meltwater from the icefields of the Campo de Hielo Sur, fast-growing El Calafate is the gateway to Argentina's Parque Nacional Los Glaciares and its spectacular Glaciar Moreno. While the town has few points of interests, its population has more than doubled in a decade, it has good and improving services, including hotels and restaurants, and it's the main transport hub for southwestern Santa Cruz Province. A sparkling new international airport provides direct connections to Buenos Aires and even, in season, to Puerto Natales, Chile.

Orientation

El Calafate (population 6,439) is 320 kilometers northwest of the Santa Cruz provincial capital of Río Gallegos, and 32 kilometers west of northbound RP 40, which leads to the wilder El Chaltén Sector of Parque Nacional Los Glaciares and a rugged, little-used overland route back to Chile. While it's only about 50 or 60 kilometers from Torres del Paine as the crow flies, El Calafate is 215 kilometers from the Cerro Castillo border crossing and about 305 kilometers from Puerto Natales via RN 40, RP 5, and RP 11, including a small additional distance on the Chilean side.

A former stage stop, El Calafate has an elongated city plan that has spread only a few blocks north and south of its main east-west thoroughfare, the pompously named Avenida del Libertador General José de San Martín. Nearly all services and points of interest are close to what is colloquially known as "Avenida Libertador" or simply "San Martín."

Sights

After years of apparent abandonment, the **Museo Regional El Calafate** (Avenida Libertador 575, tel. 02902/491924, 10 A.M.–5 P.M. weekdays only) has finally reopened, but it's hard to say it was worth the wait for the sparse and poorly presented exhibits on paleontology, natural history, geology, and ethnology. The photographic histories of pioneer families show promise, but it would be nice to have some explanation of the labor unrest that led to several shooting deaths on the *estancias* in the 1920s.

Just north of town, municipal authorities have transformed a onetime sewage pond into **Reserva Municipal Laguna Nimez,** a fresh water body frequented by more than 100 bird species. It's open 8 A.M.–9 P.M. daily; Cecilia Scarafoni, an English-speaking biologist, leads two-hour birdwatching excursions (US$4 pp) here through her **Ecowalks** (tel. 02902/493196, ecowalks @cotecal.com.ar). Scheduled walks take place at 9 A.M. and 6 P.M. daily except Sunday, unless there is rain.

Entertainment and Shopping

El Calafate is surprisingly light on nightlife, which consists mostly of dining out and drinking at venues like the brew pub **Whirra** (Almirante Brown 1391, tel. 02902/492515), on the road to Laguna Nimez. It also offers *picadas* (bar snacks). On the western outskirts of town, the best new place for drinks is the **Shackleton Lounge** (Avenida Libertador 3287, tel. 02902/493516), which has views over the lake.

Downtown Avenida Libertador is lined with souvenir shops such as Open Calafate (Avenida Libertador 996, tel. 491254), which also sells books and maps. For premium homemade chocolates, try Casa Guerrero (Avenida Libertador 1246, tel. 491042), or any of several similar locales.

Accommodations

El Calafate has a wide variety of accommodations at generally high standards in each category, ranging from camping to five-star comfort. Unless otherwise indicated, prices below are for high season, usually October to April, but specific dates can vary and, if business is slow, rates can be negotiable. Breakfast is usually (though not always) extra.

Under US$10

On the grounds of its namesake *hospedaje*, **Camping Los Dos Pinos** (9 de Julio 218, tel. 02902/491271, US$2 pp) has basic tent sites. At the eastern approach to town, flanking the Arroyo Calafate, the fenced and forested **Camping Municipal** (José Pantín s/n, tel. 492622, campingmunicipal@cotecal.com.ar, US$2 pp) has good common toilets and hot showers, and each site has its own firepit. Areas on the east side of the creek are for walk-in campers only.

Adolescent boys—not necessarily bad kids, but still adolescents—hang around friendly **Hospedaje Jorgito** (Moyano 943, tel. 02902/491323, US$4.50 pp), which has good multibedded rooms with shared bath.

US$10–25

A block south of the bus terminal, **Albergue Lago Argentino** (Campaña del Desierto 1050, tel. 02902/491423, fax 02902/491139, hostel-lagoargentino@cotecal.com.ar, US$5.50 pp) offers so-so hostel-style accommodations. Other places in the same range include Chilean-run **Hospedaje Alejandra** (Espora 60, tel. 02902/491328), which is old and a bit dark but otherwise OK, and **Hospedaje Lago Azul** (Perito Moreno 83, tel. 02902/491419).

"Think big" seems to be the motto at the **Calafate Hostel** (Gobernador Moyano 1296, tel. 02902/492450, calafatehostel@cotecal.com.ar, www.hostelspatagonia.com, US$7 pp), openly challenging the more established Hostal del Glaciar Pioneros. In a stylish new building with vast common areas, it has hostel accommodations with shared bath and balconies, plus rooms with private bath (US$20/25 s/d).

East of the arroyo, open October to mid-April, the HI-affliate **Ⓜ Hostal del Glaciar Pioneros** (Los Pioneros 251, tel./fax 02902/491243, info@glaciar.com, www.glaciar.com, US$7.50 pp, US$30/35 s/d) has extensive common spaces, including a large lounge, kitchen space and laundry facilities, provides information, and offers its own excursions to Glaciar Moreno. There is also floor space above the restaurant for US$2 pp, as well as large comfortable but no-frills hotel-style rooms.

Under the same management, the brand-new **Ⓜ Hostal del Glaciar Libertador** (Avenida Libertador 587, tel./fax 02902/491792, info@glaciar.com, www.glaciar.com, US$7.50 pp, US$30/35 s/d) has 22 rooms with private bath; some are four-bed dorms, while others are twins or doubles. Both the Pioneros and Libertador hostels offer roughly 15 percent discounts for HI members, and 30 percent low-season discounts in October and April (except for Semana Santa).

Immediately east of the municipal campground, **Ⓜ Albergue América del Sur** (Puerto Deseado s/n, tel. 02902/493525, info@america hostel.com.ar, www.americahostel.com.ar, US$9 pp, US$36 d) has made good first impressions.

Just south of the bus terminal is the basic **Hospedaje Buenos Aires** (Ciudad de Buenos Aires 296, tel. 02902/491147, buenosaires@cotecal.com.ar, US$17 d). **Hospedaje los dos Pinos** (9 de Julio 358, tel./fax 02902/491271, losdospinos@cotecal.com.ar, US$18 d) has plain but spacious and immaculate accommodations with in-room heating.

At **Hospedaje del Norte** (Los Gauchos 813, tel. 02902/491117, caltur@cotecal.com.ar, US$10–18 s, US$17–25 d), rates vary for rooms with shared or private bath; breakfast costs US$2 extra. Breakfast is also additional at the new and appealing **Hospedaje Sir Thomas** (Espora 257, tel. 02902/492220, fax 02902/491300, hospedajesirthomas@cotecal.com.ar, US$22/25 s/d).

Hospedaje Familiar Las Cabañitas (Valentín Feilberg 218, tel. 02902/491118, lascabanitas@cotecal.com.ar, US$18/25 s/d) offers chalet-style accommodations and perhaps the most *simpático* management in town. This is a popular choice, and reservations are advisable; despite the suggestive name, it lacks kitchen facilities for guests.

US$25–50

Tidy, well-regarded **Residencial Los Lagos** (25 de Mayo 220, tel. 02920/491170, fax 02920/491347, loslagos@cotecal.com.ar, US$27 d) also charges extra for breakfast. Toward the west end of town, just beyond the EG3 gas station on Avenida Libertador, **Home Garden** (Guillermo

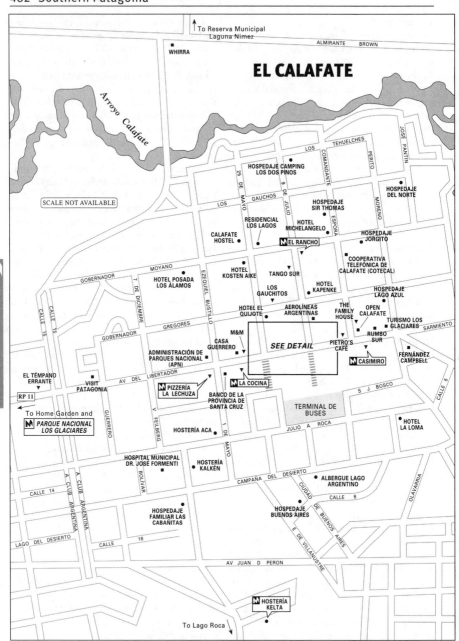

To Reserva Municipal
Laguna Nímez

ALMIRANTE   BROWN

WHIRRA

EL CALAFATE

Arroyo Calafate

SCALE NOT AVAILABLE

LOS   TEHUELCHES

JOSÉ PANTIN

PERITO

COMANDANTE

9 DE JULIO

25 DE MAYO

MORENO

ESPORA

HOSPEDAJE CAMPING
LOS DOS PINOS

HOSPEDAJE
DEL NORTE

LOS   GAUCHOS

HOSPEDAJE
SIR THOMAS

RESIDENCIAL
LOS LAGOS

HOTEL
MICHELANGELO

HOSPEDAJE
JORGITO

CALAFATE
HOSTEL

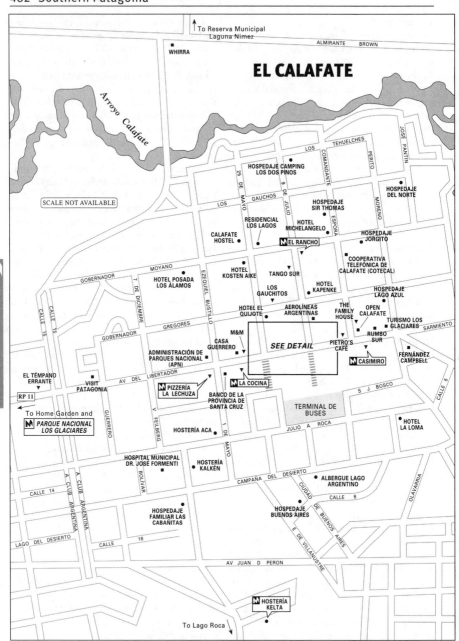EL RANCHO

COOPERATIVA
TELEFÓNICA DE
CALAFATE (COTECAL)

MOYANO

HOTEL
KOSTEN AIKE

TANGO SUR

GOBERNADOR

HOTEL POSADA
LOS ÁLAMOS

LOS
GAUCHITOS

HOTEL
KAPENKE

HOSPEDAJE
LAGO AZUL

7 DE DICIEMBRE

EZEQUIEL BUSTILLO

HOTEL EL
QUIJOTE

AEROLÍNEAS
ARGENTINAS

THE
FAMILY
HOUSE

OPEN
CALAFATE

TURISMO LOS
GLACIARES

SARMIENTO

GREGORES

M&M

SEE DETAIL

RUMBO
SUR

GOBERNADOR

CASA
GUERRERO

PIETRO'S
CAFÉ

FERNÁNDEZ
CAMPBELL

ADMINISTRACIÓN DE
PARQUES NACIONAL
(APN)

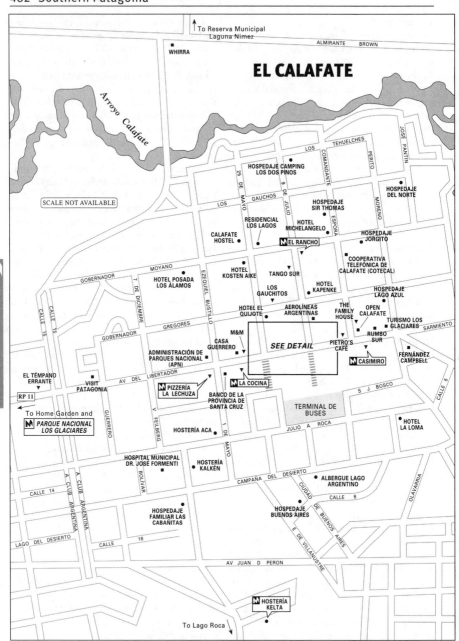CASIMIRO

CALLE 15

CALLE 5

EL TÉMPANO
ERRANTE

VISIT
PATAGONIA

AV DEL LIBERTADOR

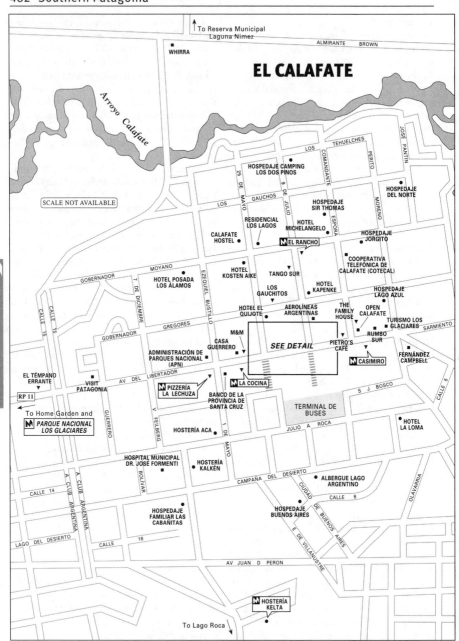PIZZERÍA
LA LECHUZA

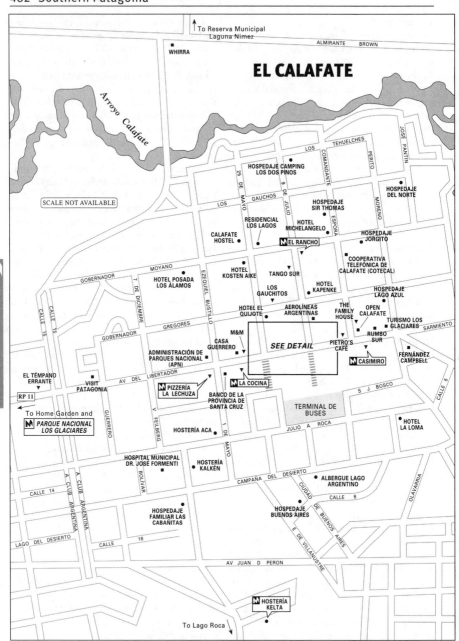LA COCINA

S J BOSCO

CALLE 5

RP 11

To Home Garden and

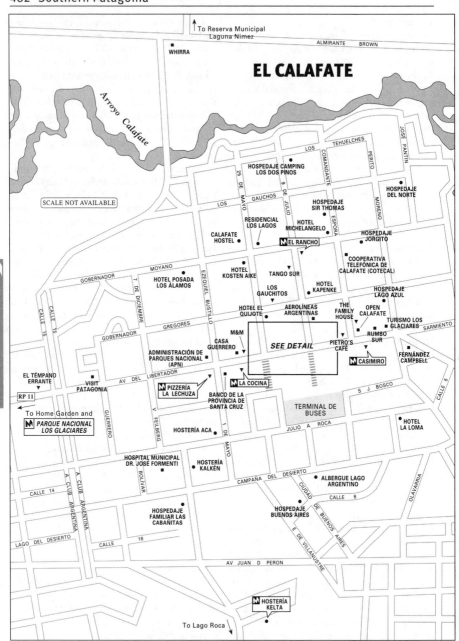PARQUE NACIONAL
LOS GLACIARES

GUERRERO

FEILBERG

BANCO DE LA
PROVINCIA DE
SANTA CRUZ

TERMINAL DE
BUSES

HOTEL
LA LOMA

HOSTERÍA ACA

1 DE MAYO

JULIO A ROCA

BOLÍVAR

HOSPITAL MUNICIPAL
DR. JOSÉ FORMENTI

HOSTERÍA
KALKÉN

CAMPAÑA DEL DESIERTO

ALBERGUE LAGO
ARGENTINO

CIUDAD DE BUENOS AIRES

OLAVARRÍA

CALLE 14

A CLUB ARGENTINA

CALLE 8

HOSPEDAJE
FAMILIAR LAS
CABAÑITAS

HOSPEDAJE
BUENOS AIRES

E DE VILLANUSTRE

LAGO DEL DESIERTO

CALLE   18

AV JUAN D PERON

HOSTERÍA
KELTA

To Lago Roca

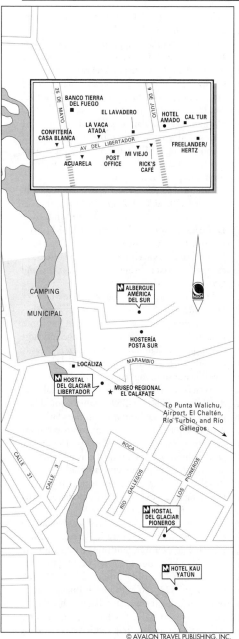

Eike 14, tel./fax 02902/493396, homegarden@yahoo.com.ar, US$20/30 s/d) has smallish rooms with private bath and breakfast, and an exceptionally friendly family atmosphere.

At the **Hostería ACA** (Primero de Mayo 50, tel. 02902/491004, fax 02902/491027, robertolugo@cotecal.com.ar, US$19–23 s, US$25–31 d), rates differ for members (including those of overseas affiliates) and nonmembers. **Hotel Amado** (Avenida Libertador 1072, tel. 02902/491134, familiagomez@cotecal.com.ar, US$22/32 s/d) is central but mediocre; breakfast costs extra.

Recommended **Hostería Kalkén** (Valentín Feilberg 119, tel. 02902/491073, fax 02902/491036, hotelkalken@cotecal.com.ar, US$39/44 s/d) includes an outstanding breakfast in its rates. **Hostería Kelta** (F.M. Portoriero 109, tel. 02902/491966, kelta@kelta.com.ar, www.kelta.com.ar, US$40/50 s/d) is a handsome, homey new B&B with 11 rooms.

US$50–100

Attractive **Hotel Kapenke** (9 de Julio 112, tel. 02902/491093, kapenke@cotecal.com.ar, www.kapenke.com.ar, US$35/54 s/d) is a conveniently central choice.

Hotel Michelangelo (Gobernador Moyano 1020, tel. 02902/491045, fax 02902/491058, michelangelohotel@cotecal.com.ar, US$46/61 s/d) includes breakfast, but its restaurant gets raves for other meals as well. Set back from the street, **Hotel La Loma** (Avenida Roca 849, tel. 02902/491016, lalomahotel@cotecal.com.ar, www.lalomahotel.com, US$29–36 s, US$40–57 d) is an unpretentious place where rates can vary dramatically from off-season to high season.

Near the old airfield, **Hostería Posta Sur** (Puerto San Julián 490, tel./fax 02902/492406, US$57/62 s/d, hosteriapostasur@cotecal.com.ar) has made good first impressions. The 60-room **Hotel Kosten Aike,** Gobernador Moyano 1243, tel. 02902/492424, fax 02902/491538, kosten aike@cotecal.com.ar, US$88 s or d) is a new and impressive four-star, facility with every modern convenience, including gym and spa, modem access, and even handicapped facilities.

Southern Patagonia

US$100–200

Its exterior handsomely rehabbed in wood and glass, **Hotel El Quijote** (Gregores 1191, tel. 02902/491017, fax 02902/491103, elquijote@cotecal.com.ar, US$93/107 s/d) is one of El Calafate's most stylish hotels. Rates include breakfast.

When El Calafate was smaller, four-star ⋈ **Hotel Kau Yatún** (tel. 02902/491259, fax 02902/491260, kauyatun@cotecal.com.ar, www.kauyatun.com, US$100/110 s/d) was part of the Estancia 25 de Mayo; the older part was the *casco,* which has suites with hot tub, fireplace, and other amenities, including a full buffet breakfast. In January only, it offers a nightly string quartet. Note that its business address of Avenida Libertador 1190 is not the same as the property itself, which is east of the arroyo and up the hill from the Albergue del Glaciar.

In the same economic range is **Hotel Posada Los Álamos** (Gobernador Moyano 1355, tel. 491144, posadalosalamos@cotecal.com.ar, www.posadalosalamos.com.ar, US$126/137 s/d).

Food

El Calafate has several decent *confiterías* for *minutas* (short orders), sandwiches, coffee, and the like. Among them are **Pietro's Café** (Avenida Libertador 1000); **Confitería Casa Blanca** (Avenida Libertador 1202, tel. 02902/491402); and **Rick's Café** (Avenida Libertador 1105, tel. 02902/492148). **Los Gauchitos** (Gregores 1170, tel. 02902/492298) has the best takeaway empanadas.

Decorated in a Buenos Aires motif, **Tango Sur** (9 de Julio 265, tel. 02902/491550) has pizzas in the US$4–7 range, with more-complex entrees around US$10.

Another fine choice is ⋈ **El Rancho** (Gobernador Moyano and 9 de Julio, tel. 02902/491644, back in action after an unfortunate absence). A breakaway from El Rancho, ⋈ **Pizzería La Lechuza** (Avenida Libertador and 1° de Mayo, tel. 02902/491610) deserves special mention for its *super cebolla y jamón crudo* (onion and raw ham). The most imaginative Italian option, though, is ⋈ **La Cocina** (Avenida Libertador 1245, tel. 02902/491758, where entrees start around US$5.

Simply decorated, appropriately named **The Family House** (Comandante Espora 18, tel. 02902/492156) is a respectable *parrilla* that also serves trout and pasta dishes in the US$3–4 range and up, with good service as well. **La Vaca Atada** (Avenida Libertador 1176, tel. 02902/491227) is a popular *parrilla* that also has fine soups and pasta, with most entrees in the US$4–7 range. **Mi Viejo** (Avenida Libertador 1111, tel. 02902/491691) is comparable but a bit more expensive.

Relocated **El Témpano Errante** (Avenida Libertador 1630, tel. 02902/493723) is worth a detour for its diverse menu and cheerful ambience. **La Posta** (Bustillo and Moyano, tel. 491144) is the outstanding upscale restaurant at Hotel Posada Los Álamos; entrees are upward of US$10 except for pasta dishes, which start around US$5–6.

Hotel El Quijote's ⋈ **Sancho** (25 de Mayo 80, tel. 02902/492442) has become one of the town's top dining options, with entrees ranging from pasta to lamb in the US$4.50–7 range and large portions—the half *picada* of appetizers is easily enough for four hungry mouths. It also has a credible nonsmoking section.

Even better is ⋈ **Casimiro** (Avenida Libertador 963, tel. 02902/492590), which would be a good choice almost anywhere in the world; the plate of smoked Patagonian appetizers is exquisite. Other entrees, in the US$4.50–11 range, are close behind but less unique, though portions are large in pastas, trout, and lamb. It's also a by-the-glass wine bar, with an enormous list of vintages ranging up to US$100 (truly extravagant by current Argentine standards).

Astonishingly, El Calafate went nearly a decade without a quality ice creamery, but now it has two outstanding ones. **Acuarela** (Avenida Libertador 1177, tel. 02902/491315) and **M&M** (Avenida Libertador 1222, tel. 02902/492422) can both match Buenos Aires's best; for a local treat, try the fresh calafate berry flavor at M&M, which is slightly better than that at Acuarela (which nevertheless has many very fine flavors).

Information

At the bus terminal, the **Secretaría de Turismo de la Municipalidad de El Calafate** (Avenida Roca 1004, tel. 02902/491466, fax 02902/491090, info@elcalafate.gov.ar, www.elcalafate.gov.ar) maintains a database of hotels and other services, and has English-speaking personnel, maps, brochures, and a message board. Hours are 8 A.M.–10 P.M. from November to March, 8 A.M.–8 P.M. the rest of the year.

The **Administración de Parques Nacionales** (APN, Avenida Libertador 1302, tel. 02902/491755, 491545, apnglaciares@cotecal.com.ar, www.losglaciares.com) is open 7 A.M.–2 P.M. weekdays only.

Services

As the gateway to the glaciers, El Calafate has a full complement of services.

Both **Banco de la Provincia de Santa Cruz** (Avenida Libertador 1285) and **Banco de Tierra del Fuego** (25 de Mayo 40) have ATMs; the latter is more reliable.

Correo Argentino is at Avenida Libertador 1133; the postal code is 9405.

The **Cooperativa Telefónica de Calafate** (Cotecal, Espora 194) also has the best and cheapest Internet access in town; there are no collect phone calls, however. **Open Calafate** (Avenida Libertador 996, tel. 02902/491254) provides some competition in both telephone and Internet services, but its connections are notably slower than Cotecal's.

El Lavadero (Avenida Libertador 1118, tel. 02902/492182) charges around US$3.50 per load of laundry.

The **Hospital Municipal Dr. José Formenti** is at Avenida Roca 1487 (tel. 02902/491001, 02902/491173).

Getting There

El Calafate is the transport hub for western Santa Cruz, thanks to its new airport, road connections to Río Gallegos, and improving links north and south along RN 40.

Aerolíneas Argentinas (9 de Julio 57, tel. 02902/492815) normally flies north to Trelew and Aeroparque, and south to Ushuaia, but sometimes has service to or from Bariloche as well. **Southern Winds** (9 de Julio 69, tel. 02902/491349) flies north to Bariloche and Buenos Aires, and south to Río Gallegos and Ushuaia.

LADE (tel. 02902/491262, ladecalafate@cotecal.com.ar) keeps an office at the bus terminal (Avenida Roca 1004). It flies northbound to Gobernador Gregores, Perito Moreno, and Comodoro Rivadavia, and southbound to Río Gallegos, Río Grande, and Ushuaia.

From November to March, Chilean carrier **Aerovías DAP** flies to Puerto Natales (US$50) twice each weekday. Its local representative is **Rumbo Sur** (Avenida Libertador 960, tel. 02902/492155, 02902/491854).

El Calafate's **Terminal de Ómnibus** overlooks the town from its perch at Avenida Roca 1004; for pedestrians, the easiest approach is a staircase from the corner of Avenida Libertador and 9 de Julio. For long-distance connections to most of the rest of the country, it's necessary to backtrack to Río Gallegos.

Interlagos (tel. 02902/491179) and **Taqsa** (tel. 02902/491843) shuttle between El Calafate and the Santa Cruz provincial capital of Río Gallegos (US$10, four hours), where there are northbound connections to Buenos Aires and intermediates, and southbound connections to Punta Arenas (Chile). These buses will also drop passengers at the Río Gallegos airport.

In summer, three carriers connect El Calafate with El Chaltén (US$14, five hours), in the Fitz Roy Sector of Parque Nacional Los Glaciares: **Cal Tur** (tel. 02902/491842); **Chaltén Travel** (tel. 02902/491833); and **Los Glaciares** (tel. 02902/491158). Services generally leave 7:30–8 A.M., though there are sometimes afternoon buses around 5–6 P.M. Winter services may be only once or twice weekly.

From December until April or so, Chaltén Travel provides alternate-day bus service from El Calafate to Perito Moreno and Los Antiguos (the border crossing for Chile Chico), in Chubut Province, along desolate RN 40 (US$80, 13 hours); while this is expensive on the face of it, it's much more direct, quicker, and cheaper than alternative routes via coastal

RN 3, especially if you factor in accommodations. Passengers from El Chaltén can board the northbound bus from El Calafate at the junction of RN 40 and RP 23 without having to return to El Calafate. Buses depart Calafate on odd-numbered days and return from Los Antiguos on even-numbered days.

In summer, **Turismo Zaahj/Bus Sur** (tel. 02902/491631) and **Cootra** (tel. 02902/491444) alternate daily services to Puerto Natales, Chile (US$17, 5.5 hours); occasionally there are direct services to Parque Nacional Torres del Paine. In winter, these services may be as infrequently as once a week.

Getting Around

The glossy new **Aeropuerto Internacional El Calafate** (tel. 02902/491220, aerocal@cotecal.com.ar) is 23 kilometers east of town, just north of RP 11. For US$3 pp, **Aerobús** (tel. 02902/492492) provides door-to-door service.

For car rental, the local Hertz representative is **Freelander** (Avenida Libertador 1029, tel. 02902/491437). **Localiza** is at Avenida Libertador 687, tel. 02902/491398.

VICINITY OF EL CALAFATE

Tours and transport to the Glaciar Moreno and other nearby attractions are possible with a variety of operators. Among them are **Turismo Los Glaciares** (Avenida Libertador 924, tel. 02902/491159, losglaciares@cotecal.com.ar); **Solo Patagonia** (Avenida Libertador 867, tel. 02902/491298, fax 02902/491790, www.solopatagonia.com.ar); **Cal Tur** (Avenida Libertador 1080, tel. 02902/491368, caltur@cotecal.com.ar); **Mundo Austral** (Avenida Libertador 1114, tel. 02902/492365, fax 02902/492116, mundoaustral@cotecal.com.ar); **Aventura Andina** (Avenida Libertador 761, Local 4, tel. 02902/491726, aventuraandinafte@cotecal.com.ar); **Visit Patagonia** (Avenida Libertador 1532, visitpatagonia@cotecal.com.ar); and **Interlagos Turismo** (Avenida Libertador 1175, tel. 491175, interlagos@cotecal.com.ar), which some locals suggest has been living on its reputation.

Private guides such as **Mariano Besio** (tel. 02902/493196, marianobesio@cotecal.com.ar) can also provide services.

Punta Walichu

Seven kilometers west of El Calafate, a northbound dirt road leads three kilometers to Punta Walichu, a commercialized pre-Columbian rock-art grotto on the south shore of Lago Argentino. A small visitors center displays a few fossils and some stone tools, and shows a 25-minute video, not to mention spurious replicas of similar sites elsewhere in the province. On the plus side, devaluation has dropped the admission price to about US$2.50 pp.

Punta Walichu (tel. 02902/491059) also has a small library, a souvenir stand, a *confitería*, and bathroom facilities.

Estancia Alice

One of El Calafate's most convenient *estancias*, open for day excursions that may include breakfast and outdoor activities like bird-watching and horseback riding, as well as exhibitions of sheep-herding and -shearing, afternoon tea, and a barbecued lamb dinner, is Estancia Alice, west of El Calafate en route to Glaciar Moreno. Morning excursions cost around US$22 pp, afternoon excursions with dinner around US$28, horseback rides around US$8 per hour.

Estancia Alice also offers accommodations (US$113/122 s/d with breakfast and limited activities included); there are also multiday packages with more-comprehensive services. For details, contact **Agroturismo El Galpón** (Avenida Libertador 761, El Calafate, tel. 02902/491793, elgalpon@estanciaalice.com.ar, www.estanciaalice.com.ar); the *estancia* itself is at RP 11 Km 22. Their Buenos Aires office is at Avenida Leandro Alem 822, 3rd floor (tel./fax 011/4313-0679).

⋈ Hostería Alta Vista

Once a separate *estancia*, recently absorbed by the adjacent **Estancia Anita,** Hostería Alta Vista (RP 15 Km 33, tel./fax 02902/491247, altavista@cotecal.com.ar, US$220 s or d all-inclusive) is an outpost of the Braun dynasty that dominated the wool industry of Chilean and Argentine Patagonia. As such, its seven-room *casco,* which includes one luxury suite, is the place to be spoiled; surrounded by luxuriant gardens in a sheltered location at the foot of 1,294-meter Cerro Freile, it has a first-rate bar/restaurant open to guests only, a separate *quincho* for lamb *asados,* and flawless service from its English-speaking staff. The all-inclusive package does not include incidentals like telephone charges and laundry.

In addition to accommodations, Alta Vista offers excursions that include horseback riding in the hills immediately behind the *estancia,* offering a small lagoon full of wildfowl, condors soaring above, and distant views of Glaciar Moreno. Nonguest may take tours of the *estancia.* It is arguably the most upscale *estancia* in the vicinity of El Calafate—unlike Nibepo Aike, it has been gentrified beyond rusticism.

Near the entrance to Estancia Anita stands a memorial to the "Patagonia Rebelde" strikers of 1921–22; erected by the provincial Chamber of Deputies, it reads "If the winners write history, that means there's another history: the Santa Cruz strikers, their histories present in our memory."

ⓜ PARQUE NACIONAL LOS GLACIARES

On the eastern slope of the Andes, Parque Nacional Los Glaciares comprises more than 759,000 hectares of slowly flowing ice, interspersed with Magellanic forests that gives birth to clear, frigid rivers, and vast lakes along the Chilean border east and north of El Calafate. A UNESCO World Heritage Site, it's most famous for the Glaciar Moreno, which draws thousands of relatively sedentary visitors on day trips from El Calafate but also pulls in international scientists absorbed in glaciology and climate studies. The northerly sector—a five-hour bus trip from El Calafate—attracts those seeking to spend several days in vigorous exercise, either trekking or the far more demanding and dangerous technical climbing for which the area is well-known. The park's wildlife includes the endangered Andean huemul.

Geography and Climate

When the Campo de Hielo Sur receded at the end of the Pleistocene, it left behind the two huge glacial troughs that are now Lago Argentino and, to the north, the roughly parallel Lago Viedma. While these lakes are only about 250 meters above sea level, the Andean summits along the Chilean border rise to 3,375 meters on Cerro Fitz Roy and nearly as high on pinnacles like 3,102-meter Cerro Torre, which matches the Torres del Paine for sheer majesty.

Most of these bodies of water lie outside the park boundaries, but the eastern Andean slopes still contain their remnants, some of the world's most impressive and accessible glaciers. Thirteen major glaciers flow toward the Argentine side, including the benchmark Glaciar Moreno; ice covers 30 percent of the park's surface.

Despite the abundance of snow and ice, the Argentine side of the cordillera is substantially drier than the Chilean, receiving only about 400 millimeters of precipitation on the eastern steppe,

Cerro Torre, Parque Nacional Los Glaciares

© WAYNE BERNHARDSON

Southern Patagonia

rising to about 900 millimeters at higher elevations to the west, where the terrain is forested. The warmest month is February, with an average maximum temperature of 22°C and a minimum of 9°C, while the coolest month is August, when the maximum averages only 5°C and the minimum -1°C. Like the rest of Patagonia, it often receives ferocious winds, which are strongest in spring and summer.

Flora and Fauna

Where rainfall is insufficient to support anything other than coirón grasses and thorny shrubs like the calafate (*Berberis buxifolia*) that gave the nearby town its name, the guanaco grazes the Patagonian steppe. Foxes and Patagonian skunks are also conspicuous, the flightless rhea, or *ñandú*, scampers across the open country, the *bandurria*, or buff-necked ibis (*Theristicus caudatus*), hunts invertebrates, and flocks of upland geese (*Chloephaga picta*)

browse the wetter areas along the lakeshores. The Andean condor soars above the plains and even the highest peaks, but occasionally lands to feast on carrion.

In the forests, the predominant tree species are the *lenga* (*Nothofagus pumilio*) and the *coigüe* (*Nothofagus betuloides,* also known here as *guindo.* The puma still prowls the forest, while the *huemul* and perhaps the *pudú* survive in the vicinity of Lago Viedma. Squawking flocks of austral parakeets (*Enicognathus ferruginaeus*) flit between trees, and the Patagonian woodpecker (*Campephilus magellanicus*) pounds on their trunks. Perching calmly, awaiting nightfall, the austral pygmy owl (*Glaucidium nanum*) is a common sight in the late afternoon.

Along the lakeshores and riverbanks, aquatic birds like coots and ducks are abundant. The most picturesque is the Patagonian torrent duck (*Merganetta armata*), which dives for prey in the rushing creeks.

Glaciar Perito Moreno

Where a low pass in the Andes lets Pacific storms cross the cordillera, countless storms have deposited hundreds of meters of snow that, over the millennia, have compressed into the Moreno Glacier, the flowing river of ice that's one of the continent's greatest sights. Fifteen times during the late 20th century, the advancing glacier blocked the **Brazo Rico** (Rico Arm) of Lago Argentino to form a rising body of water that eventually, when the water's weight became too much for the natural dam, triggered an eruption of ice and water toward the lake's main glacial trough.

In March 2004, before more than 2,000 eager spectators who had camped with their cameras at the ready, the dammed glacier erupted for the first time since 1988—though the event was smaller than previous instances. It will be several years more before any reoccurence, but in the interim, massive icebergs will continue to calve off the glacier's 60-meter face and crash into the **Canal de los Témpanos** (Iceberg Channel) with astonishing frequency. Perched on catwalks and overlooks, many visitors spend entire days either gazing at, or, eyes closed, simply lis-

© WAYNE BERNHARDSON

pygmy owl, Parque Nacional Los Glaciares

Moreno Glacier, Parque Nacional Los Glaciares

tening to, this awesome river of ice as it rumbles forward. Descending to lake level is prohibited because of the danger of backwash and flying chunks of ice; it's possible, though, to contract a full-day "minitrekking" excursion onto the ice for about US$64 pp with **Hielo y Aventura** (Avenida Libertador 935, El Calafate, tel. 02902/492205 or 492094, fax 02902/491053, www.losglaciares.com/hieloyaventura). Hielo y Aventura also does one-hour boat excursions on the lake, approaching the glacier's face, for US$9 pp.

Only seven kilometers east of the glacier, **Camping Bahía Escondida** (tel. 02902/491005) charges US$3.50 pp for 30 sites with running water and firepits; there are hot showers 7–10 P.M. only and electricity 8 P.M.–midnight only. Backpackers can camp free at the Seccional de Guardaparques, the ranger station at the glacier itself, for a maximum of two nights.

The only accommodation close to the glacier itself, **⋈ Hostería Los Notros** (tel. 02902/499510, fax 02902/499511 in El Calafate, US$189–274 s or d) rivals Torres del Paine's Hotel Explora in the "room-with-a-view" category; its 32 rooms all face the ice. Reservations are essential here, and multiday packages with full board and excursions included are the rule rather than the exception. For more details contact Hostería Los Notros in Buenos Aires (Arenales 1457, 7th floor, Buenos Aires, tel. 011/4814-3934, fax 011/4815-7645, info@losnotros.com, www.losnotros.com).

Near the glacier, the **Unidad Turística Ventisquero Moreno** operates both a snack bar (sandwiches for US$2–3.50, plus coffee and desserts) and a separate restaurant with set meals for US$7–12 pp; there is also an à la carte menu.

The Moreno Glacier is 80 kilometers southwest of El Calafate via RP 11; the trip takes somewhat more than an hour. Both Interlagos and Taqsa, at the El Calafate bus terminal, have scheduled bus services at 9 A.M. daily (US$17 round-trip), returning in the afternoon.

In addition to these regularly scheduled services, guided bus tours are frequent, but both are less frequent in winter; for suggested operators, see the Vicinity of El Calafate section. El Calafate's Albergue del Glaciar runs its own minivan excursions, leaving about 8:30 A.M. and returning about 5 P.M., for US$25 pp, including the navigation in front of the glacier.

Glaciar Upsala

Even larger than Glaciar Perito Moreno, 50 kilometers long and 10 kilometers wide at its foot, Glaciar Upsala is accessible only by crowded catamaran excursions from Puerto Bandera via Lago Argentino's Brazo Norte (North Arm). Impressive for its sheer extent, the size of the bergs that have calved off it, and their shapes and colors, it's the trip's outstanding sight.

At midday, the boat anchors at Bahía Onelli, but bring a bag lunch (skipping the restaurant) to walk to ice-clogged **Lago Onelli.** The land portion of this excursion is highly regimented, and the pace the guides suggest—30 minutes from the dock to the shores of Onelli—are appropriate for those on crutches. Smoking is prohibited on the forest trail.

Travelers should realize that this is a mass tourism excursion that may frustrate hikers accustomed to the freedom of the hills. If you take it, choose the biggest available ship, which offers the greatest deck space to see the

Spegazzini and Upsala Glaciers. On board, the freshest air is within the cabin of the *ALM,* whose seats are cramped but where smoking is prohibited. Reasonably priced cakes, sandwiches, coffee, tea, and hot chocolate are available on board.

Puerto Bandera is 45 kilometers west of Calafate via RP 11 and RP 8. For information and reservations, contact concessionaire **René Fernández Campbell** (Avenida Libertador 867, El Calafate, tel. 2902/491155, 491428, fax 491154, rfcino@cotecal.com.ar). The full-day trip costs about US$53 pp; the fare does not include transportation from El Calafate (about US$4 pp round-trip) to Puerto Bandera or the obligatory US$7 park admission fee for nonresidents of Argentina.

Lago Roca

Less visited than other parts of the park, the southwesterly sector also known as La Jerónima, along the Brazo Sur (South Arm) of Lago Roca, offers camping and cross-country hiking—there are no formal trails, only routes like the one up the summit of **Cerro Cristal** from the campground, 55 kilometers from El Calafate. The most striking characteristic of the landscape, though, is the conspicuously high, but now dry, shoreline from the days when the lake backed up behind the advancing Moreno Glacier. Unlike other sectors of the park, this one charges no admission fee.

At La Jerónima, **Camping Lago Roca** (tel. 2902/499500) charges US$3 pp for adults, US1.50 pp for children, and also has four-bed *cabañas* for US$18. Hot showers are available, and its restaurant/*confitería* serves decent meals.

At the terminus of RP 15, 56 kilometers southwest of El Calafate, **Estancia Nibepo Aike** (Perito Moreno 229, Río Gallegos, tel./fax 02966/436010, nibepo@ciudad.com.ar, www .nibepoaike.com.ar, US$75/84 s/d with breakfast, US$98/138 s/d with full board) is a Croatian-founded ranch whose former *casco* preserves its original rustic style but is now a five-room guesthouse with contemporary conveniences— all rooms have private bath, for instance. Open October 1 to April 30, it also has a newer **Quin-**

cho **Don Juan** for day-trippers to lunch or dine, though overnight guests may eat in the restaurant rather than the main house's dining room if they wish.

Sector Fitz Roy

In the park's most northerly sector, the Fitz Roy Range has sheer vertical spires to match Torres del Paine, but even if you're not one of the world's top 10 technical climbers, the several trails from the village of El Chaltén to the base of summits like Fitz Roy and Cerro Torre make some of the Southern Hemisphere's most enthralling hiking. There are even opportunities for crossing the southern Patagonian icefields, but visitors looking for a more sedate outdoor experience will find a handful of former sheep *estancias,* onetime Patagonian wool producers that have reinvented themselves as tourist accommodations.

From a signposted trailhead at the north end of El Chaltén, just south of the basic Camping Madsen, the **Sendero Laguna Torre** is an 11-kilometer track that gains only about 200 meters in elevation as it winds through southern beech forests to the climbers' base camp for Cerro Torre; figure about three to 3.5 hours. At the lake itself, in clear weather, there are extraordinary views of the 3,102-meter summit of Cerro Torre, crowned by the so-called "mushroom" of snow and ice that technical climbers must surmount. While the Italian Cesare Maestri claimed that he and the Austrian Toni Egger reached the summit in 1959 (Egger died in an avalanche and took the expedition's camera with him), the first undisputed ascent was by the Italian Casimiro Ferrari in 1974.

From the Madsen pack station, the more demanding **Sendero Río Blanco** rises steeply at the outset before leveling out through boggy beech forest and continuing to the Cerro Fitz Roy base camp, a total climb of about 350 meters in 10 kilometers. About midway to Río Blanco, a signed lateral leads south to **Laguna Capri,** where there are backcountry campsites but campfires are not permitted.

From Río Blanco, the vertiginous zigzag trail ascends 400 meters in only 2.5 kilometers to **La-**

guna de los Tres, a glacial tarn whose name commemorates three members of the French expedition, René Ferlet, Lionel Terray, and Guido Magnone, who reached Fitz Roy's summit in 1952. Truly a top-of-the-world experience, Laguna de los Tres offers some of Patagonia's finest Andean panoramas.

From the Río Blanco campground (reserved for climbers only), a northbound trail follows the river's west bank north to **Laguna Piedras Blancas,** whose namesake glacier continually calves icebergs into the lake. The trail continues north to the Río Eléctrico, beyond the park boundaries, where a westbound trail climbs the river to Piedra del Fraile and a possible circuit of the Campo de Hielo Sur, suitable only for experienced snow-and-ice trekkers. At the Río Eléctrico, it's also possible to rejoin the road from El Chaltén to Laguna del Desierto.

Accommodations, services, and other practicalities in the northern sector of the park are covered in the following El Chaltén section.

Glaciar Viedma

From Puerto Bahía Túnel on Lago Viedma's north shore but south of El Chaltén, the park's best lake excursion is the catamaran *Viedma Discovery*'s voyage to the face of the Viedma glacier, a full-day trip that includes an ice-climbing exploration of the glacier itself.

Sailing from Bahía Túnel, the ship rounds the ironically named **Cabo de Hornos** ("Cape Horn") and enters an iceberg-cluttered section of the lake (though Viedma's lakeside face is small, it's Argentina's largest glacier) before anchoring in a rocky cove. After disembarking, visitors hike to an overlook of the glacier and 2,677-meter Cerro Huemul; those who wish can strap on crampons and continue with the guides onto the glacier for about 1.5 hours (even some pretty sedentary *porteños* do so).

The guides themselves are well-versed in glaciology, speak both Spanish and English, and provide much more personalized service than the Fernández Campbell excursion from Puerto Bandera. While the excursion price here does not include lunch, it does include an aperitif on the glacial rocks.

ice hiking on Glaciar Viedma, Parque Nacional Los Glaciares

© WAYNE BERNHARDSON

On Lago Viedma's secluded south shore, open mid-October to mid-April, **Ⓜ Hostería Helsingfors** (San Martín 516, Río Gallegos, tel. 02966/420719; Avenida Córdoba 827, 11° A, C1054AAH Buenos Aires, tel. 011/4315-1222, info@helsingfors.com.ar, www.helsingfors.com.ar) was one of the area's first *estancias,* and also one of the first to open its door to tourists. Room rates are US$195/350 s/d with full board, excursions, and transportation from El Calafate (including the airport). Children under age eight pay half.

Restaurante Bahía Túnel is a good breakfast choice, with exceptional picture-window views across the lake, and also serves lunch, afternoon tea, and an especially good sunset dinner.

Departure time from El Chaltén is 8:30 A.M., while the boat sails from Bahía Túnel at 9 A.M.; the cost is US$45 pp plus US$6.50 pp for transportation from El Chaltén for those who need it. For more information, contact **Patagonia Aventura,** (Güemes s/n, tel. 02962/493110, fax 02962/493017, El Chaltén).

Lago del Desierto

Elongated Lago del Desierto, 37 kilometers north of El Chaltén, is a scenic end-of-the-road destination with several worthwhile hiking trails, boat excursions, and even a challenging border crossing to the remote Chilean settlement of Villa O'Higgins.

From the south end of the lake, a short trail winds west through dense southern beech forest to a vista point and the hanging glacier at **Laguna Huemul,** while a longer route follows the eastern shore to the border, a 20-kilometer trek over relatively easy terrain. In 2002, more than 200 people crossed the Argentine-Chilean border in a place that was once such a bone of contention between Chile and Argentina that, decades ago, a Chilean Carabinero even lost his life in a firefight with Argentine soldiers.

Despite objections by a handful of extreme Chilean nationalists, the matter is resolved, the border is peaceable, and determined hikers or mountain bikers can readily cross to Villa O'Higgins. Before attempting the route, though, clear it with the Argentine Gendarmería (Border Patrol) in El Chaltén, and make arrangements to be picked up at Lago O'Higgins on the Chilean side by contacting the Carabineros (tel. 0056-67/215167) and Antonio Vidal (tel. 0056-67/234813), operator of the Chilean ferry *El Pirincho.*

North of El Chaltén, in an out-of-the-way location on the road to Lago del Desierto, **◪ Hostería El Pilar** (tel./fax 02962/493002, hosteriaelpilar@infovia.com.ar, www.hosteriaelpilar.com.ar, US$91/111 s/d) has the classic style of a Patagonian *casco,* but it's really a recent construction (1996). Room reservations are a must for this cozy, popular place (it's open October to April), but it's possible to eat in the restaurant without.

From El Chaltén, **Mermoz** (San Martín s/n, tel. 02962/493098) minibuses go to Lago del Desierto (US$9 round-trip pp) at 9:30 A.M. daily, returning at 4:30 P.M. Hitching is feasible but vehicles are few and often full. At the lake itself, the launches *Viedma 1* and *La Mariana* take passengers to the north end for US$12.50 pp.

Accommodations

There are limited accommodations in the southern sector of the park since most people stay at El Calafate; see the previous sections for various park attractions and accommodations in those areas. El Chaltén has, if not exactly an abundance, at least a reasonable selection of places to stay. See the following El Chaltén section for accommodations there.

Food

Backpackers should note that no campfires are permitted within the park—carrying a campstove is obligatory for cooking. According to rangers, water is potable throughout the park.

Hikers and climbers can stock up on groceries in El Chaltén. Otherwise, for its size, El Chaltén offers a pretty good selection of places to eat as well. See following section for listings.

Tour Operators

At El Chaltén, it's possible to arrange a one-day trek and ice climb on Glaciar Torre (US$35 pp) with **Fitzroy Expediciones** (Lionel Terray 212, tel./fax 02962/493017, fitzroy@infovia.com.ar), which also offers lengthier guided hikes—nine-day expeditions, really—on the Campo de Hielo Sur, the Southern Continental Ice Field. **Camino Abierto** (tel. 02962/493043), **Alta Montaña** (Lionel Terray s/n, tel. 02962/493018), and **Viviendo Montañas** (Güemes 68, tel. 02962/493068, info @vivmont.com.ar) also conduct expeditions onto the great icefields.

NYCA Adventure (San Martín 591, tel. 02962/493093, www.nyca.com.ar) offers half-day excursions including activities like climbing, hiking, mountain biking, rafting, and rappelling. **Lago San Martín** (Riquelme and Rojo, tel. 02962/493045, lagosanmartin@videodata.com.ar) arranges excursions to and from Lago San Martín, across the mountains to the northeast.

Equipment

Just north of Albergue Rancho Grande, **Viento Oeste** (San Martín s/n tel. 02962/493021, vientooeste@infovia.com.ar) rents and sells climbing, camping, and wet-weather gear.

Information

At the Río Mitre entrance to the park, the main approach for the Moreno Glacier, the Administración de Parques Nacionales (APN) collects a US$7 park admission fee for nonresidents of Argentina. At present, there is no fee collected at either the Lago Roca or at El Chaltén Sectors.

At El Chaltén, just before the Río Fitz Roy bridge at the approach to town, the APN (tel. 02962/493004, 8 A.M.–8 P.M. daily) offers information in both Spanish and English, and issues climbing permits (free of charge).

Hikers may want to consult Tim Burford's *Chile and Argentina: The Bradt Trekking Guide* (Bradt Travel Guides, 2001), and Clem Lindenmayer and Nick Tapp's *Trekking in the Patagonian Andes* (Lonely Planet, 2003); the latter has better maps. There is also the new edition of Miguel A. Alonso's locally available, bilingual *Trekking en Chaltén y Lago del Desierto* (Los Glaciares Publishers, 2003), which covers numerous hikes in the vicinity. Alonso has also written *Lago Argentino & Glaciar Perito Moreno Handbook* (Buenos Aires: Zagier & Urruty, 1997), a more general guide to the park that's available in English, Italian, German, and French.

EL CHALTÉN

While exposed to fierce westerly winds and to potential floods from the Río de las Vueltas, El Chaltén has achieved a feeling of permanence in what, only a few years ago, seemed only a bleak assortment of government offices intended to uphold Argentina's presence in a then-disputed border zone (the last of many Chilean-Argentine territorial quarrels, over Lago del Desierto to the north, was settled only a few years ago).

One reason for El Chaltén's popularity is its easy access to Fitz Roy–range trailheads—so much so that the village bills itself as "Capital Nacional del Trekking," the national trekking capital. Although many of the trails are suitable for overnight backpacks, access is so good that day-hikers can cover nearly as much ground.

Note that while El Chaltén now has street names and addresses, they don't really mean very much in a town this size, and people pay little attention to them.

Events

El Chaltén celebrates several events, including October 12's **Aniversario de El Chaltén,** marking the town's formal founding in 1985; November 10's **Día de la Tradición,** celebrating the gaucho heritage; and early February's **Fiesta Nacional del Trekking,** which lasts a week.

Accommodations

Many places close in winter, but there's always something available.

At the north edge of town, the APN's woodsy **Camping Madsen** has running water and is free of charge but lacks toilets—dig a latrine—and fires are prohibited. Directly across from the APN office there's another free site, on the banks of the Río Fitz Roy, but it's more exposed.

Commercial campgrounds, with services like hot showers, generally cost around US$3 pp, plus an additional peso or two for hot showers. Among these are **Camping El Relincho** (San Martín s/n, tel. 02962/493010, elrelincho@cotecal.com.ar) and **Camping El Refugio** (San Martín s/n).

El Chaltén has several hostel-style accommodations, starting with the smallish **Albergue Los Ñires** (Lago del Desierto s/n, tel. 02962/493009, losnires@videodata.com.ar, US$7 pp), **Cóndor de los Andes** (Avenida Río de las Vueltas and Halvorsen, tel. 02962/493101, www.condordelosandes.com), and **Albergue del Lago,** (Lago del Desierto 135, tel. 02962/493010, US$7 pp).

Open all year, the HI-affiliate **Ⓜ Albergue Patagonia** (San Martín 493, tel. 02962/493019, alpatagonia@infovia.com.ar, US$7–8 pp) has cozy dorm accommodations—four to six beds per room—and also provides cooking facilities, laundry service, meals, a book exchange, and bike rentals, and organizes excursions. English and Dutch are spoken; its main drawback is that the bathroom facilities, while good enough, are arguably too small.

The 44-bed **🕅 Albergue Rancho Grande** (San Martín 635, tel./fax 02962/493005, rancho@cotecal.com.ar, US$7 pp) also offers B&B packages with transportation from El Calafate. For reservations in El Calafate, contact **Chaltén Travel** (Avenida Libertador 1177, tel. 2902/491833, chaltentravel@cotecal.com.ar).

Nothofagus Bed & Breakfast (Hensen s/n, tel. 02962/493087, nothofagus@infovia.com.ar, US$16–18 s, US$20–24 d) is a small but friendly place that's also tobacco-free. Like many other places, family-run **Hospedaje La Base** (Lago del Desierto 97, tel./fax 02962/493031, US$24 s or d) closes June–November.

Casa de Piedra (Lago del Desierto s/n, tel./fax 02962/493015, US$27/30 s/d) provides large and comfy but tackily decorated rooms with private bath but without breakfast. It has well-kept grounds and is quiet, but the new power plant going up nearby could change things. Recently opened **Posada Altas Cumbres** (Lionel Terray 342, tel. 02962/493060, altas_cumbres@hotmail.com, US$40 s or d) has five spacious rooms and a restaurant.

Hotel Lago del Desierto (Lago del Desierto s/n, tel. 02962/493010, hotelldd@infovia.com.ar, US$50 s or d) closes May–October; it also rents six-bed *cabañas* with kitchen facilities for US$110, and has camping facilities for US$2.50 pp.

It's a work in progress—the landscaping still needs attention—but **Hostería Posada Lunajuim** (Trevisan s/n, tel. 02962/493047, posadalunajuim@yahoo.com, US$80/90 s/d) has made good first impressions with its attractive common areas (including a bar/restaurant) and private bath, central heating, and breakfast.

Rates at the **Fitzroy Inn** (San Martín 520, tel. 493062, US$50–65 s, US$53–68 d, caltur @cotecal.com.ar) vary from low season (Sept.–Oct. and Apr.) to high season (Nov.–Mar.); it also has multiday packages with half board or full board, but the full-board option would preclude eating at other good places in town.

Food

For groceries, try **El Chaltén** (Lago del Desierto s/n), **Kiosko Charito** (Güemes s/n), and **El Gringuito** (San Martín s/n).

Chocolatería Josh Aike (Lago del Desierto s/n, tel. 02962/493008) is more than it sounds—while the desserts are good enough, the breakfasts and pizzas are also excellent. **Domo Blanco** (Costanera Sur 90, tel. 02962/493036) serves exceptional ice cream but closes in winter.

Open in summer only, **🕅 Ruca Mahuida**, (Lionel Terray 501, tel. 02962/493018) is one of the most imaginative eateries in town and also ships smokers outside to indulge their habit, but the service can be forgetful. Lamb is the specialty at **La Casita** (San Martín 535, tel. 02962/493042), which otherwise serves a standard Argentine menu—beef, pizza, pasta and the like—its major downside is the cramped and smoke-heavy ambience. In midsummer, it can be hard to get a table at popular **Pizzería Patagonicus** (Güemes s/n, tel. 02962/493025), perhaps the only Argentine eatery to have lamb on the pizza menu; the decor, with natural wood and mountaineering photos, fits El Chaltén perfectly.

Chaltén's best new place is the Albergue Patagonia's bistro-style **🕅 Fuegia** (San Martín s/n, tel. 02962/493019), which is small and popular enough that reservations are a good idea, especially in summer.

Information and Services

The town of El Chaltén has a very useful website (www.elchalten.com).

There's an increasing diversity of services in town. **Chaltén Travel** (corner of Güemes and Lago del Desierto) now has Internet access, but it is slow and expensive compared to other localities.

Locutorio de la Morsa (Güemes s/n) has long-distance phone and fax service.

Getting There

El Chaltén is 220 kilometers from El Calafate via a roundabout route that follows paved RP 11 east to the Río Bote junction, northbound RN 40 (presently being paved to the east end of Lago Viedma), and inconsistently maintained but always passable RP 23, westbound along the north shore of Lago Viedma. The latter road is also being paved.

Several companies connect El Chaltén with El Calafate (US$15, five hours): **Cal Tur** (San Martín s/n, tel. 02962/493062; **Chaltén Travel** (San Martín s/n, tel. 02962/493005); and **Los Glaciares** (Güemes s/n, tel. 02962/493084). Departures are usually in late afternoon, between 5 and 6 P.M. There are several buses daily in summer, but only one or two weekly in winter.

With Chaltén Travel, it's possible to travel north on gravel RN 40 to the towns of Perito Moreno and Los Antiguos (the border crossing for Chile Chico), in Chubut Province (US$80, 13 hours). These services leave El Calafate on alternate days in summer; passengers from El Chaltén can board the bus at La Leona, on RN 40, without having to return to El Calafate. The rest of the year, there may be only one bus weekly.

An alternative is Daniel Bagnera's **Itinerarios y Travesías** (Perito Moreno 152, tel. 02962/ 493088) a minivan that sometimes makes a side excursion to the pre-Columbian rock-art site of Cueva de las Manos en route to Perito Moreno and Los Antiguos. At US$77 pp, this is competitive with the bus in an area little-served by public transportation. Departures are almost daily in summer, but only weekly in the winter months.

RN 40 SOUTH

Southeast of El Calafate, RN 40 and RP 5 are contiguous as far as El Cerrito, where RN 40 forks southwest toward the Chilean border. At the junction of RN 40 and east-west RP 7, about halfway to Puerto Natales, Tapi Aike is a wide spot in the road where there's a gas station, a convenience store, and accommodations at nearby Estancia Tapi Aike.

From here, the road continues southwest to the border crossing at **Cancha Carrera**, the easiest access to Torres del Paine, but there is no regular public transportation here. Most travelers cross into Chile at Río Turbio, an otherwise bleak coal

town that features a remarkably modern ski resort and a historic narrow-gauge railway.

Estancia Tapi Aike

Historically part of the Braun empire, the sheep farm of Tapi Aike sprawls over 60,000 hectares of the steppes of southern Santa Cruz Province, but the settlement itself is a compact one near the junction of RN 40 and RP 7. Open November to April, the *estancia's* comfortable *casco*, reinvented as **Posada Tapi Aike** (tel. 02966/420092 in Río Gallegos, bvdesign@fibertel.com.ar, US$40 pp), offers the only B&B accommodations between Calafate and the border; some visitors stay here and make Torres del Paine a day trip.

In addition to accommodations, Tapi Aike prepares simple but well-made lunches and dinners for US$10 pp, including a main dish, salad, soda, wine, and dessert. The resident Viel family, descendents of the Brauns, speaks English as well as Spanish. Estancia Tapi Aike also has a Buenos Aires contact (tel./fax 011/4784-4360).

Río Turbio

In one of Argentina's most remote corners, the gritty coal town of Río Turbio has been slowly declining as its underground seams reach exhaustion, but it got an ironic shot in the arm with the 2001 peso meltdown—as locals could no longer afford to do their shopping in Chile, supermarkets and other businesses here actually opened and expanded during the country's worst economic crisis ever.

Though it's no beauty spot, Río Turbio holds some interest for its aging locomotives and railcars—the narrow-gauge railway still carries coal to Punta Loyola, near Río Gallegos—and its modest winter-sports center.

Río Turbio (population 6,652) is 270 kilometers west of Río Gallegos via RN 40, and 30 kilometers north of Puerto Natales, Chile. It's 242 kilometers south of El Calafate via RN 40 and RP 11.

Near the Villa Dorotea border post, about four kilometers south of town, the **Centro de Deportes de Invierno Valdelén** (tel. 02902/ 421900, angeli@oyikil.com.ar) is a modest but lighted ski area, with elevations ranging from

Southern Patagonia

GET YOUR FLATS ON LA CUARENTA

From the Bolivian border near La Quiaca to its terminus near Río Gallegos, RN 40 is Argentina's great unfinished interior highway. Some segments of "La Cuarenta," in the Cuyo provinces, are smoothly paved, while others in the Andean northwest are rough and rugged. None of those, though, has quite the notoriety of the segment between the El Calafate junction and the town of Perito Moreno, on the cusp between the Patagonian steppe and the icy southern Andes.

It may not be Argentina's loneliest road—some of the dead-end routes that spin off it seem simply abandoned—but for Argentines and foreigners alike it's become the standard for adventurous driving and cycling, thanks to its secluded Andean lakes, isolated *estancias*, plentiful wildlife, and rare sights like the pre-Columbian rock art of Cueva de las Manos. Even the advent of (infrequent) public transportation has not diminished its mystique.

When I first drove the 594 kilometers in early 1991, I saw only three other vehicles in four days, and services were almost nil. Since then, traffic has not exactly burgeoned, but the peak summer season now sees a small but steady procession of motorists, motorcyclists, and bicyclists. It's as if a selective bunch has

© WAYNE BERNHARDSON

Settlements are few and far apart on "La Cuarenta," Santa Cruz Province.

180 to 690 meters; there are about 12 hectares of downhill slopes and 160 suitable for cross-country. Hours are 10 A.M.–10 P.M. daily when snow is sufficient.

Whatever its shortcomings as a place to live, Río Turbio has decent accommodations, starting with **Hotel Nazo** (Gobernador Moyano 464, tel. 02902/421800, nazo@oyikil.com.ar, US$14/ 22 s/d). At the Valdelén ski area, **Hostería de la Frontera** (tel. 02902/421979, US$14/23 s/d) is an exceptional value.

Don Pablo I (Pellegrini and Roque Saenz Peña, tel. 02902/421220) is a pizzería that also serves *minutas*.

Río Turbio's **Centro de Información Turística** (Plazoleta Agustín del Castillo s/n, tel. 02902/ 421950, www.rioturbioturismo.com.ar) is pre-

sumably open 8 A.M.–10 P.M. weekdays and 9 A.M.–9 P.M. weekends.

LADE (Avenida Mineros 375, tel. 02902/ 421224) had suspended flights as of press time.

Unlike other cities, Río Turbio has no central terminal, but all the bus companies are fairly close to each other. **Cootra** (Teniente del Castillo 01, tel. 02902/421448) operates five to seven buses daily to Puerto Natales (US$1.50, one hour) except on weekends, when there are only two or three. **Bus Sur** (Avenida Mineros 262) goes once or twice daily. Cootra also goes to El Calafate at 7 A.M. daily (US$7, 4.5 hours).

Taqsa (Teniente del Castillo 130, tel. 02902/421422) goes to Río Gallegos (US$11, five hours) at 1 A.M. daily.

absorbed Darwin's insight that the appeal of the bleak Patagonian plains was "the free scope given to the imagination."

It's clearly not for everyone, though, and a trip up or down La Cuarenta requires planning and preparation. With accommodations and supplies few and far between, bicyclists and motorcyclists *must* carry tents and cold-weather gear, even in midsummer, and plenty of food. Detailed maps, like ACA's Chubut and Santa Cruz provincial sheets, are essential. Automobiles should carry at least two spare tires.

Also carry extra fuel—between El Calafate and Perito Moreno, the only dependable supplies are at El Chaltén (a 90-kilometer detour), Tres Lagos, Gobernador Gregores (a 70-kilometer detour), and Bajo Caracoles. Some tourist *estancias* will sell gasoline to their clients or in an emergency, but don't count on it.

Road hazards are numerous. Bicyclists and motorcyclists have to contend with powerful Patagonian winds that can knock them down in an instant, and deep gravel adds to the danger. Even high-clearance vehicles are vulnerable to flipping on loose gravel, especially on sudden braking, and 50-knot gusts only make things worse. Though 4WD is not essential, some drivers prefer it to avoid fishtailing on gravel.

Chipped, cracked, and even shattered windshields are par for the course on RN 40 and other graveled Patagonian roads. Normally, rental-car insurance policies do *not* cover such damage, and replacements are expensive in Argentina (though fairly cheap in Punta Arenas, Chile). Approaching vehicles usually brake to minimize the possibility of such damage, but some drivers find they need to play chicken to slow down an onrushing SUV.

If none of these methods appeals to you, but you still want to see the loneliest road, summer bus and minivan services now connect El Calafate and El Chaltén, at the south end, with Perito Moreno and Los Antiguos at the north end of the province.

For a longer, slower experience, Bariloche's **Overland Patagonia** (tel. 02944/461564, www.overlandpatagonia.com) offers a four-day excursion from Bariloche to El Calafate that overnights in Río Mayo (Chubut), Estancia Los Toldos (for Cueva de las Manos), and Estancia Menelik (for Parque Nacional Perito Moreno).

RN 40 NORTH

About 30 kilometers east of El Calafate, northbound RN 40 covers 596 kilometers of rugged gravel road in the arid eastern Andean foothills, before finally arriving at the cowtown of Perito Moreno near Lago Buenos Aires, the oasis of Los Antiguos, and the Chilean border town of Chile Chico. In recent years, this desolate highway has seen increasing numbers of overland travelers but it gets mixed reviews: the unrelenting westerly winds bowl over cyclists and bikers alike, sharp rocks blow tires and shatter windshields, and vehicles can break down in the middle of nowhere.

Still, this particular section of "La Cuarenta"— running from Río Gallegos almost to La Quiaca, it's Argentina's longest interior highway—has a mystique all its own. Some love it, some dislike it, and some are ambivalent, but no one forgets it.

La Leona

Little more than a wide spot alongside the road, at the Helsingfors junction of RN 40 and westbound RP 21, **Hotel La Leona** is a local landmark where travelers brake for chocolate and lemon pie, banana bread, and tea and coffee. At the same site since 1916, it has only two simple rooms with a total of four beds, but makes an excellent stop for cyclists, either north or southbound, who can't be bothered to set up the tent. Water shortage warning in the toilet: "If it's yellow, let it mellow; if it's brown, flush it down."

Nearby, the newly discovered **Bosque Petrificado La Leona** is a badlands reserve of petrified forests and dinosaur fossils on nearby Estancia Santa Teresita, accessible by guided tour only. For details on this full-day excursion (US$45), contact any travel agency in El Calafate.

Tres Lagos

Beyond La Leona, after passing the westbound turnoff to El Chaltén, RN 40 turns east to climb over the volcanic Meseta Escorial before it drops into the enigmatically named hamlet of Tres Lagos (the only water in the vicinity is the humble Río Shehuen). Northbound motorists *must* fill up at the YPF station, which has the only gasoline this side of Bajo Caracoles, 338 kilometers to the north.

Tres Lagos has few other services, though there is a pretty good municipal **Camping Comunal** (tel. 02962/495031, US$1 pp) with hot showers (US$.65). Fresh-baked empanadas and other snacks are available at the YPF station.

To the northwest, gravel RP 31 and RP 33 leads 100 kilometers to **Lago San Martín** and 19 kilometers farther to **Estancia La Maipú,** which has upscale facilities with breakfast (US$60/80 s/d) but also a cozy backpackers' *refugio* (US$10 pp). For details, contact Estancia La Maipú (Chaco 167 2° B, Buenos Aires, tel. 011/4901-5591, fax 011/4311-6689, lamaipu@fibertel .com.ar); there is also a contact in Puerto Santa Cruz (9 de Julio 570, 02962/498233).

Estancia La Siberia

North of Tres Lagos, RN 40 winds north over the Meseta Cascajosa before coming within sight of **Lago Cardiel,** a deep interior drainage lake that's a bellwether for ongoing climate-change studies. On the west side of the highway, 22 kilometers south of the RP 29 junction to Gobernador Gregores, English-speaking Alejandro Luiz runs **Estancia Siberia,** the casual doppelganger of the stereotypical tourist *estancia.*

La Siberia's only livestock have been two exceptionally tame guanacos, who are even more affectionate than dogs, but they're also rapidly defoliating an orchard of its apricot, cherry, pear, and plum trees. Open from September to March

or April, after which Luiz winters in Brazil, he operates a one-of-a-kind *confitería*/bar with light meals and desserts, a large CD collection, and a *fogón* for *parrilladas*. He also rents rooms for US$17 pp with shared bath and hot showers; camping is free, so it's a popular stop for cyclists.

Estancia La Angostura and Vicinity

About 60 kilometers northwest of La Siberia on RN 40, midway between RP 29 and RP 25, an eastbound dirt road drops into the Río Chico marshlands, dotted with birds including upland geese, coots and lapwings. In a sheltered location among densely planted trees, La Angostura has seven comfortable guest rooms (US$30 pp with breakfast), but also has a decent campground (US$3.50 pp) on a farm that's closer to the rustic end of the tourist *estancia* continuum. The food is heavy on Argentine standards like *milanesa.* For more details, contact Estancia La Angostura (tel. 02902/491208, jck@intervia.com .ar); it's open September to May.

North of La Angostura, the 200 or so kilometers of northbound RN 40 to Bajo Caracoles is one of Patagonia's most service-free areas, especially since the owner's death forced closure of the landmark **Hotel Las Horquetas,** an out-of-the-wind dive near the junction with westbound RP 37. Some campers like the sites along the Río Chico near the junction of RN 40 and RP 25, but the best spots go early.

Gobernador Gregores

Though it's 60–70 kilometers east of RN 40 via either RP 29 or RP 25, Gobernador Gregores (population 2,513) can be an essential detour for bikers or motorists running short of gasoline. It's also the easiest place to obtain other supplies, and to hire a car and driver to otherwise-inaccessible Parque Nacional Perito Moreno, some 200-plus kilometers to the northwest.

The free **Camping Municipal Nuestra Señora del Valle** (Roca and Chile) has hot showers. There's a pair of decent hotels: **Hotel San Francisco** (San Martín 463, tel. 02962/491039, US$5.50 pp) and **Hotel Cañadón León** (Roca 397, tel. 02962/491082, US$713 s/d), which also has the best restaurant.

The **APN** (San Martín 882, tel./fax 02962/ 491477, pnmoreno@uvc.com.ar, pnmoreno @servisur.com.ar,) can provide information on Parque Nacional Perito Moreno.

LADE (Colón 544, tel. 02962/491008) flies northbound to Perito Moreno and Comodoro Rivadavia, and southbound to El Calafate, Río Gallegos, and Río Grande.

Cerro San Lorenzo (San Martín and Alberdi, tel. 02966/15-631768) has bus service to San Julián at 6 P.M. Wednesday, Friday, Saturday, and Sunday, returning from San Julián at 7 A.M. Tuesday and Saturday, and 1 P.M. Thursday and Sunday.

El Pulgarcito (San Martín 704, tel. 02962/491102) goes to Río Gallegos (US$13, 6.5 hours) Tuesday, Thursday, and Saturday at 6 A.M., returning Wednesday, Friday, and Sunday at 7 A.M. **El Pegazo** (Mariano Peikovic 520, tel. 02962/491274) goes to Gallegos Monday, Wednesday, and Friday at 6 A.M., returning at 8 A.M. Tuesday, Thursday, and Saturday.

Parque Nacional Perito Moreno

The intensely colored sedimentary summits of the Sierra Colorada are the backdrop for the lake-laden, wind-whipped, and wildlife-rich high country of Parque Nacional Perito Francisco P. Moreno, named for the founder of Argentina's national park system. Possibly the wildest of Patagonian parks, where Paleo-Indians covered cave walls with images of guanacos and human hands, it's one major reason travelers are braving the rigors of La Cuarenta.

Besides the park itself, the Patagonia Land Trust has acquired 14,000 hectares in the adjacent area of El Rincón, which may be incorporated into the park.

Comprising 115,000 hectares of Patagonian steppe, sub-Antarctic forest, glacial lakes and fjords, and high Andean pastures, the park is 220 kilometers northwest of Gobernador Gregores via RP 25, RN 40, and RP 37. It is 310 kilometers southwest of the town of Perito Moreno via RN 40 and RP 37.

At 900 meters above sea level, the park's base altitude is significantly higher than Los Glaciares, and its climate colder, wetter, and more unpre-

dictable. Its highest summit is 2,254-meter Cerro Mié, but snow-capped 3,700-meter Cerro San Lorenzo, north of the park boundary, is the area's highest peak.

In the drier eastern steppes, the dominant vegetation consists of bunch grasses known collectively as *coirón;* to the west, there's a transitional wind-flagged, sub-Antarctic forest of *lenga* and *ñire,* the ubiquitous southern beeches (*Nothofagus* spp.) In more sheltered areas, there are dense and nearly pure *lenga* forests along the shores of Lago Azara and Lago Nansen.

Troops of guanacos patrol the steppes and even some of the high country where there is summer pasture; the *huemul* (Andean deer) also grazes the uplands in summer but spends the winter at lower altitudes. The puma is the alpha predator, but there are also smaller killers: red and grey foxes. The *pilquín* or *chinchillón anaranjado* (*Lagidium wolffsohni*) is a species of vizcacha unique to Santa Cruz Province and southernmost Chile.

The largest birds are the Andean condor and the flightless rhea, but other impressive species include the *águila mora* (*Geranoaetus melanoleucus,* black-chested buzzard eagle), the large owl *ñacurutú* (*Bubo virginianus*), Patagonian woodpeckers, and the *carancho* (crested caracara). Perito Moreno's many lakes and streams support abundant wildfowl, including, flamingos, black-necked swans, grebes, wild geese, and steamer ducks. Unlike other Patagonian lakes, those within the park have remained free of introduced fish species.

Sights and Recreation

While **Lago Burmeister** is still worth a visit, the cave paintings have been closed to public access. There are large troops of guanacos on **Península Belgrano,** reached by an isthmus immediately west of Estancia Belgrano (which is not a tourist *estancia*).

One of the best day hikes is 1,434-meter **Cerro León,** a 2.5-hour climb immediately north of Estancia La Oriental, which offers the best easily accessible panoramas in the vicinity (though hikers must be prepared for the changeable weather). The nearby volcanic overhang known as the

Southern Patagonia

Cerro de los Cóndores is the flight school for condor chicks.

Accommodations and Food

There are free but barren campsites with pit toilets at the Centro de Informes, at the park entrance, but the more appealing campground at Lago Burmeister consists of Tehuelche-style lean-tos in dense *lenga* forest. The water here is potable, but no supplies are available within the park; campers must bring everything they need.

Open November to March, within the park boundary on the north shore of Lago Belgrano, **Estancia La Oriental** (Rivadavia 936, San Julián, tel. 02962/452196, fax 02962/452445, elada @uvc.com.ar, US$50 s/d) has both conventional accommodations (seven rooms sleeping up to 22 guests) and protected campsites (US$6, with hot showers) near the lodge. The US$5 homemade breakfasts (homemade scones, bread and jam, plus ham and cheese) deserve a detour, but the dinners (US$14 pp) can't quite match them.

Just outside the park boundary,  **Estancia Menelik** occupies a windy, oddly exposed site—most *estancieros* chose protected valley-bottom locations for their settlements—but the popular explanation is that its original German homesteader wanted to advertise his presence, and spot the approach of any strangers. Despite the barren landscape, the welcome is warm at both the comfortably furnished farmhouse, which has ample bedrooms (US$40–70 d with breakfast) plus a large sitting room (with library) and dining areas, and at the simpler hostel (a rehabbed bunkhouse, US$10–15 pp). Though well off the beaten path, it does get tour groups, so reservations are advisable; for details, contact **Cielos Patagónicos** (Corrientes 531, 7th floor, tel. 011/5371-5580, fax 011/5371-5581, www.cielospatagonicos.com). Given Menelik's isolation, the quality of the food (US$15 for lunch or dinner) is very good. It's open November to April.

Other Practicalities

Rangers at Perito Moreno's Centro de Informes, at the park entrance, provide maps and brochures, and offer a variety of guided hikes and visits; they can also be reached through the **APN** in Gobernador Gregores (tel./fax 02962/491477, pnmoreno@uvc.com.ar or pnmoreno@servisur

Hotel Bajo Caracoles is one of few accommodations along isolated RN 40, Santa Cruz Province.

© WAYNE BERNHARDSON

.com.ar,); the postal address is Casilla de Correo 103, (9311) Gobernador Gregores.

Rental cars offer the greatest flexibility to get around, though it's possible to hire a car and driver in Gobernador Gregores or the town of Perito Moreno. Hitching from the highway junction is feasible but by no means certain.

In season, Overland Patagonia's four-day "safari" from Bariloche to El Calafate visits the park during the day and spends the night at Menelik; for details, see the sidebar "Get Your Flats on La Cuarenta."

Bajo Caracoles

Midway between Las Horquetas and the town of Perito Moreno, barren Bajo Caracoles is an oasis for automobiles and motorcycles, as it has the only gas station in nearly 500 kilometers of RN 40. Southbound travelers should fill the tank here, but northbound travelers should buy only enough to reach Perito Moreno, 128 kilometers to the north.

Bajo Caracoles is also the southern gateway to the major rock-art site of Cueva de las Manos, 41 kilometers to the northeast via RP 57, but there are alternative access points to the north. RP 39 leads east to the hamlet of Hipólito Yrigoyen and **Lago Posadas,** near the Chilean border, while RP 41, a short distance north of Bajo Caracoles, goes directly to the border crossing at **Paso Roballos.**

The legendary **Hotel Bajo Caracoles** (tel. 02963/490100, US$10 pp) is far better than anyone might expect in this remote outpost, and it fills up early despite its cantankerous owner—after all, it's the only option. It also has groceries and surprisingly good meals.

Lago Posadas and Vicinity

Bajo Caracoles is no beauty spot, but it's hard to improve on aquamarine Lago Posadas, 90 kilometers to the east, and nearby Lago Pueyrredón, nudging the Chilean border. While the main route from Bajo Caracoles to the border passes Lago Ghío, along RP 41 to the north, southerly RP 39 via Lago Posadas is a more scenic alternative.

It also permits a stay at ◼ **Estancia Turística Lagos del Furioso,** an unpretentious but more than comfortable getaway occupying a privileged site on the isthmus between Lago Pueyrredón and Lago Posadas. *Porteño* owners Ana Bas and Jorge Cramer oversee attentive service, a first-rate restaurant, and excursions to the wild surrounding countryside with rates starting at US$98/110 s/d. Lunches cost US$10, dinners US$20.

Lagos del Furioso (Paraná 1255 6° D, Buenos Aires, tel. 011/4812-0959) can also be reached via **Estancias Turísticas de Santa Cruz** (Suipacha 1120, Buenos Aires, tel. 011/4325-3098, estancias @interlink.com.ar). It's open November to April.

◼ Cueva de las Manos

Beyond Baja Caracoles, rugged RN 40 traverses the northern steppe until the point where, over millions of years, the Río Pinturas has cut a deep, scenic canyon. In the process, it has left countless

The canyon of the Río Pinturas is the site of Cueva de las Manos, a pre-Columbian rock-art site recognized by UNESCO.

aleros, stony overhangs often mistakenly called *cuevas* or caves. One of these is the famous **Cueva de las Manos,** a UNESCO World Heritage Site where stencils of hundreds of human hands, guanacos, and abstract forms cover the rock walls in orange, red, and yellow ochres.

Dating from around 7370 B.C. the oldest paintings at Cueva de las Manos represent hunter-gatherers from immediate post-glacial times, but the more-abstract designs, which are fewer, are far more recent. Oddly enough, nearly all the hands from which the site takes its name are left hands.

Along with Parque Nacional Perito Moreno, this is one of the finest detours off RN 40, with two main access points. From Bajo Caracoles in the south, gravel RP 41 goes directly to the site, where the municipality of Perito Moreno operates a small *confitería* and a rocky campground (US$1 per tent), and charges US$1.50 pp admission to the caves. Bars now block access to the paintings to discourage vandalism (even touching the paintings repeatedly could damage them), but they do not obscure the view.

The other main access point is from the Río Pinturas drainage itself, with two separate alternatives (both of which also offer accommodations). From **Estancia Casa de Piedra,** 45 kilometers north of Bajo Caracoles, there's a 12-kilometer access road, at the end of which it's a three-kilometer hike to the paintings; from **Estancia los Toldos,** another 23 kilometers north and seven kilometers east, another 15-kilometer access road permits a close approach. Note that, by either the northern or southern route, mountain bikers can avoid backtracking to RN 40 by hauling their bikes over the river (there is a pedestrian bridge) and out the other direction.

On the east side of RN 40 (ideal for cyclists), the bucolic **Estancia Casa de Piedra** (tel. 02963/432199) allows camping for $1.25 per tent, plus US$1 for showers; it also rents basic but passable rooms for US$5.50/9 s/d with shared bath. At Estancia Los Toldos, **Hostería Cueva de las Manos** (tel. 011/4901-0436, fax 011/4903-7161, cuevadelasmanos@hotmail.com) has four modern carpeted rooms with private bath

(US$30 d) with breakfast, plus very fine hostel accommodations (US$9 pp) without breakfast. Good restaurant lunches cost about US$3.50. It's open November–March, and for Semana Santa.

Estancia Telken

Only 30 kilometers south of Perito Moreno, a short drive west of the highway, Estancia Telken is a 21,000-hectare working ranch that doubles as a restful guest house and campground. It also offers excursions in the vicinity, most notably to the rock-art site of Cañadón del Arroyo Feo, as well as Cueva de las Manos, Los Antiguos, Lago Posadas, and other provincial destinations.

Dating from 1915, Telken has a main house comprising two rooms with private bath and one with shared bath, while a separate guest house has a triple with private bath and an apartment that can sleep up to five persons. Guests dine with gracious Dutch-Argentine proprietors Coco and Petty Nauta, who speak Spanish, English, and Dutch. The grassy campground has a covered *quincho* with a full kitchen for cooking and a full bath with hot showers.

Open October to the end of April, Estancia Telken (tel. 0293/432079, tel./fax 02963/432303, jarinauta@yahoo.com.ar, telkenpatagonia @argentina.com) charges US$40/50 s/d with shared bath, US$45/60 s/d with private bath, both with breakfast. With half board, rates are US$55/80 s/d with shared bath, US$60/90 s/d with private bath. Camping costs US$5 per tent or vehicle, plus US$5 pp. In addition to more-distant excursions, visitors can rent horses (US$10 for the first hour, US$5 per additional hour).

In the off-season, contact Coco and Petty Nauta at Roque Sáenz Peña 2480, (1636) Olivos, Provincia de Buenos Aires, tel. 011/4797-7216.

Perito Moreno

Where RN 40 meets the smoothly paved international highway from Comodoro Rivadavia to Chile Chico, the nondescript cowtown of Perito Moreno marks the return to civilization for northbound travelers and the start of the adventure for the Calafate-bound. Often confused with its namesake national park, as well as the eponymous glacier in Parque Nacional Los Glaciares, it has reasonably good services, but most visitors prefer the lakeside town of Los Antiguos to the west.

Perito Moreno (population 3,598) is 398 kilometers southwest of Comodoro Rivadavia via Caleta Olivia, and 58 kilometers east of Los Antiguos via smoothly paved RP 43. It is 124 kilometers south of Río Mayo, Chubut Province, via one of the more rugged stretches of RN 40, which continues toward Esquel and the Andean lake district; for more details on this route, see the Northern Patagonia chapter. Note that there is no regularly scheduled public transportation between Perito Moreno and Río Mayo.

Early February's **Festival Folklórico Cueva de las Manos** is a musical event that capitalizes on the proximity of Santa Cruz's World Heritage Site.

Practicalities

Opposite Laguna de los Cisnes, the city park at the south end of town, the **Camping Municipal** (Roca and Moreno, US$1.25 plus US$1.25 per vehicle or tent) is small but sheltered from the wind, and has flawless bathrooms with hot showers (US$1 extra).

Otherwise, the pickings are slim. **Hotel Santa Cruz** (Belgrano 1565, tel. 02963/432133, US$4.50 pp) is a no-frills shoestring option, while **Hotel Americano** (San Martín 1327, tel. 02963/432074, US$6.50/11 s/d) is a hair better. The respectable **Hotel Belgrano** (Avenida San Martín 1001, tel. 02963/432019, US$9/13 s/d) also has a restaurant, but the best option is the homey B&B **Posada del Caminante** (Rivadavia 937, tel. 02963/432204, matejedor@interlap .com.ar, US$11/17 s/d); since it has only three rooms, call ahead.

The **Oficina Municipal de Turismo** (Avenida San Martín 1059, tel. 02963/432732, turis-mompm@interlap.com.ar) is open 7 A.M.–11 P.M. and 8 A.M.–10 P.M. daily the rest of the year, but closes noon–2 P.M. on weekends.

Banco de la Nación (Avenida San Martín 1385) has an ATM.

Correo Argentino is at Avenida Juan D. Perón 1331; the postal code is 9040. The **Call Center**

(Rivadavia 1055) has long-distance services, while **Crazy.net** (Perito Moreno 1070) provides Internet access.

Perito Moreno Travel (Avenida San Martín 1779, tel./fax 02963/432730) rents cars and organizes excursions. Run by family of the Estancia Telken operators, bilingual **Guanacondor Tours & Expeditions** (Perito Moreno 1087, tel. 02963/432303, jarinauta@yahoo.com.ar or jarin-auta@santacruz.com.ar) arranges excursions including Cañadón del Arroyo Feo.

For medical services, the **Hospital Distrital** is at Colón 1237 (tel. 02963/432045).

LADE (Avenida San Martín 1065, tel. 02963/432055) maintains an office here, but has no flights to the area at present. The airstrip is at the north end of town.

The sharp new **Terminal de Ómnibus** is also at the north end of town, at the traffic circle where RN 40 (Avenida San Martín) meets RP 43. Note, however, that there is are is no regular overland transport on that stretch of RN 40 between Perito Moreno and Río Mayo, 124 kilometers to the north.

La Unión (tel. 02963/432638) and **Sportman** (tel. 02963/432177) have westbound service to Los Antiguos (US$1.50, one hour) and eastbound service to Comodoro Rivadavia (US$8, five hours). Sportman also has a daily service to Río Gallegos (US$18, 12 hours).

Transporte Lago Posadas (Saavedra 1357, tel. 02963/432431) has irregular minibus service to Lago Posadas.

Chaltén Travel buses from Los Antiguos to El Calafate will pick up passengers here; for details, see the El Calafate entry. For southbound travel to El Chaltén, contact **Itinerarios y Travesías** (tel. 0297/15-400-0335 or 011/15-5325-9302); for more details, see the Parque Nacional Los Glaciares entry earlier in this chapter.

Los Antiguos

Rows of upright poplars announce the approach to laid-back Los Antiguos, the garden spot of Santa Cruz Province, where riotously colorful flowers fill the median strip of Avenida 11 de Julio, flats of soft fruits like raspberries, cherries, and strawberries go for a song, and baskets of

Southern Patagonia

apples, apricots, pears, peaches, plums, and prunes fill the stores.

Thanks to its mild microclimate, Los Antiguos has been a getaway since Tehuelche times, its Spanish name ("the ancient ones") derived from an indigenous term meaning "Place of the Elders." For a few years, after the eruption of Chile's nearby Volcán Hudson in August 1991 buried the area in ash, both the fruit harvest and the tourist trade suffered, but there's been a recent recovery. Fishing and hiking are the main attractions.

On the south shore of Lago Buenos Aires, Los Antiguos (population 2,047) is 58 kilometers west of Perito Moreno via RP 43. As it enters town, the highway becomes the divided Avenida 11 de Julio, which continues to the Chilean border; the Argentine border post is on the western edge of town, while the Chilean Carabineros are across the Río Jeinemeni, about five kilometers farther.

Early January's three-day **Fiesta de la Cereza** (cherry festival) can put a strain on accommodations and other facilities. February 5's **Día de los Antiguos** marks the town's anniversary, while **Día del Lago Buenos Aires** is October 29.

For fresh fruit, as well as preserves, try any of several farms such as **Chacra El Porvenir** (walking distance from Avenida 11 de Julio) and the lakeshore **Chacra El Paraíso.**

Practicalities

Protected by poplars and cypresses, the lakeshore **Camping Municipal** (Avenida 11 de Julio s/n, tel. 02963/491265, US$1 pp plus US$1 per tent) has picnic tables and firepits at every site. Hot showers are available 5:30–10 P.M. only.

Hotel Argentino (Avenida 11 de Julio 850, tel. 02963/491132, US$9/16 s/d) is a utilitarian hotel with a decent restaurant. On the eastern outskirts of town, **Hostería Antigua Patagonia** (RP 43 s/n, tel. 02963/491055, US$36/50 s/d) is a modern three-story hotel.

The **Subsecretaría de Turismo** (Avenida 11 de Julio 432, tel. 02963/491261, fax 02963/491261) is open 7 A.M.–8 P.M. daily from October to March, 9 A.M.–4 P.M. weekdays only the rest of the year.

Banco de la Provincia (Avenida 11 de Julio 531) now has an ATM.

Correo Argentino is at Gobernador Gregores 19; the postal code is 9041. **Locutorio Los Antiguos** (Alameda 436) has long-distance telephone services, but has been slow to enter the digital age.

La Unión (Alameda 428, tel. 02963/491078) and **Sportman** (Patagonia Argentina 170, tel. 02963/15-621-6082) both go to Caleta Olivia (US$7, five hours) and Comodoro Rivadavia (US$8, six hours). Sportman also has daily service to Río Gallegos.

Acotrans (Patagonia Argentina 170, tel. 02963/15-621-6082) crosses the border to Chile Chico (US$2 return) three times every weekday and twice Saturday, but never on Sunday.

For up-to-date information on Chaltén Travel buses and Itinerarios y Travesías trips to El Chaltén via southbound RN 40, contact the **Subsecretaría de Turismo** (Avenida 11 de Julio 432, tel. 02963/491261).

Tierra del Fuego and Chilean Patagonia

If Patagonia is exciting, Tierra del Fuego—with its reputation as the "uttermost part of the earth"—is electrifying. In the days of sail, the reputation of its sub-Antarctic weather and ferocious westerlies obsessed navigators, whether or not they had ever had experienced the thrill—or terror—of "rounding the Horn." After Richard Henry Dana survived the southern seas en route to California in November 1834, he vividly recalled conditions that could change from calm to chaos in an instant:

"Here comes Cape Horn!" said the chief mate; and we had hardly time to haul down and clew up, before it was upon us. In a few moments, a heavier sea was raised than I had ever seen before, and . . . the little brig . . . plunged into it, and all the forward part of her was under water; the sea pouring in through the bow ports and hawse-hole, and over the knight-heads, threatening to wash everything overboard . . . At the same time sleet and hail were driving with all fury against us.

Must-Sees

Look for **M** to find the sights and activities you can't miss and **N** for the best dining and lodging.

Ushuaia: With one of the world's most spectacular settings, its southernmost city is the base for excursions along the famed Beagle Channel, including wildlife-rich islands and historic Estancia Harberton, not to mention winter skiing only half an hour outside town. It's also the gateway to Antarctica (page 510).

Estancia Harberton: Head out from Ushuaia to this historic *estancia*, where you can take a guided tour of the 19th-century grounds and outbuildings or stay overnight in the former cookhouse or shepherds' house (page 522).

Parque Nacional Tierra del Fuego: Argentina's first coastal national park stretches east of Ushuaia along the north shore of the Beagle Channel to the Chilean border. It rises from the seashore to high wild country of southern beech forests and glacial peaks and is *the* destination for visitors who make it to the end of the road (page 523).

Puerto Williams (Chile): On Isla Navarino, across the Beagle Channel from Ushuaia, little Puerto Williams retains much of the "uttermost part of the earth" ambience that Ushuaia once had. It also provides access to the rugged hiking trails of the Dientes de Navarino, a series of summits that rise like inverted vampire's fangs (page 525).

Punta Arenas (Chile): Parisian-style mansions and numerous museums provide glimpses of the city's Gold-Rush past. Punta Arenas is the base for excursions to nearby penguin colonies and historic sites, and the gateway to Torres del Paine for airborne arrivals (page 537).

The Fjords of Fuegia: It's expensive to cruise the ice-clogged inlets of the archipelago of Tierra del Fuego, from Punta Arenas to Ushuaia, Cape Horn, and back, but it's still cheaper than buying and sailing your own yacht. Even backpackers occasionally splurge for a leg of this unforgettable itinerary (page 549).

Parque Nacional Torres del Paine (Chile): The world's most intensely beautiful mountain range compresses the splendor of Alaska into only 180,000 hectares (page 566).

TIERRA DEL FUEGO AND CHILEAN PATAGONIA

ARGENTINA

CHILE

Parque Nacional Torres del Paine

ATLANTIC OCEAN

Punta Arenas

Parque Nacional Tierra del Fuego

Ushuaia

Estancia Harberton

The Fjords of Fuegia

Puerto Williams

PACIFIC OCEAN

Tierra del Fuego

TIERRA DEL FUEGO AND CHILEAN PATAGONIA

ATLANTIC OCEAN

ARGENTINA

CHILE

PACIFIC OCEAN

Isla de los Estados

Estrecho de Le Maire

Isla Grande de Tierra del Fuego

ESTANCIA POLICARPO

ESTANCIA HARBERTON

Cabo de Hornos

Parque Nacional Cabo de Hornos

Isla Nueva

PUERTO WILLIAMS

Isla Navarino

Isla Hoste

Canal de Beagle

Peninsula Mitre

Tolhuin

Lago Fagnano (Kami)

USHUAIA

THE FJORDS OF FUEGIA

PARQUE NACIONAL TIERRA DEL FUEGO

Puerto Navarino

Cordillera Darwin

P.N. Alberto de Agostini

Paso Radman

RN 3

Bahía San Sebastián

MUSEO SALESIANO

ESTANCIA VIAMONTE

Río Grande

Cabo Vírgenes

Punta Delgada

RN 3

255

P.N. Pali Aike

ESTANCIA SAN GREGORIO

Cerro Sombrero

Onaisín

Cameron

Lago Blanco

Isla Dawson

Porvenir

Bahía Inútil

Estrecho de Magallanes

Río Gallegos

Bahía Grande

To Puerto San Julián and Comodoro Rivadavia

Comandante Luis Piedra Buena

Puerto Santa Cruz

RN 40

RP 9

RP 2

RP 7

RP 5

RN 40

Laguna Blanca

Villa Tehuelches

Río Verde

Seno Skyring

L. Pinguino

Seno Otway

Pen. Muñoz Gamero

Pen. Brunswick

Isla Riesco

R.N. Magallanes

R.N. Laguna Parrillar

PUNTA ARENAS

FUERTE BULNES

El Calafate

To El Chaltén and Perito Moreno

GLACIAR MORENO

GLACIAR BALMACEDA

MONUMENTO NATURAL CUEVA DEL MILODÓN

PARQUE NACIONAL TORRES DEL PAINE

Cerro Paine Grande

Villa Cerro Castillo

Lago del Toro

Puerto Natales

Río Turbio

9

Ferry To Puerto Montt

Isla Hanover

Isla Jorge Montt

Isla Diego de Almagro

Reserva Nacional Alacalufes

Isla Santa Inés

Isla Desolación

0   60 mi

0   60 km

© AVALON TRAVEL PUBLISHING, INC.

In Dana's time, such voyages were the price of admission to one of the most spectacular combinations of sea, land, ice, and sky on the face of the earth. In a landscape whose granite pinnacles rise nearly 2,000 meters straight out of the sea, only a handful of hunter-gatherers living among the fjords and forests could know the area with any intimacy. Today, fortunately, there are ways to reach the archipelago of Tierra del Fuego that involve less hardship—not to mention motion sickness—than Dana and his contemporaries suffered.

Though it has much in common with Santa Cruz, Chubut, and Argentina's other Patagonian provinces, Tierra del Fuego retains its own distinctive identity. This chapter also includes adjacent parts of Chilean Patagonia (which shares Tierra del Fuego with Argentina, as part of its own Patagonian province of Magallanes); Magallanes' greatest attraction is the world-famous spires of Parque Nacional Torres del Paine.

PLANNING YOUR TIME

Like the rest of southern South America, Tierra del Fuego and Chilean Patagonia deserve all the time you can give it, but most visitors have to make choices. Ushuaia is the best base for sightseeing in Tierra del Fuego proper, given its access for excursions to the nearby national park, the Beagle Channel, and Estancia Harberton, with a minimum of three days. Hikers may wish to spend several days more, and fly-fishing aficionados—who often prefer the vicinity of Río Grande—can easily stay a week or two.

Exploring the thinly populated Chilean part of Tierra del Fuego requires a vehicle, or even an airplane—connections to Puerto Williams, though it's not far from Ushuaia as the crow flies, are haphazard except by commercial flights from Punta Arenas. Once you're there, it takes at least a week to hike the Dientes circuit.

Like Ushuaia, Punta Arenas can be a base for sightseeing, but usually only for a day or two; for those who haven't seen Magellanic penguins elsewhere, it's worth scheduling or waiting for the boat to Isla Magdalena. Punta Arenas is also the homeport for the spectacular cruise to Tierra del Fuego's remotest fjords and Cape Horn, a trip that deserves its full week but is worth doing even in a three- or four-day segment.

Puerto Natales, the urban gateway to Torres del Paine, is primarily a place to prepare for the trek, but its seaside setting, the youthful vitality of its visitors, and nearby hiking excursions often extend the stay. The park itself deserves no less than a week, for day-hikers and backpackers alike, but even an abbreviated day trip—some people do it, despite the time and difficulty of getting here—is worth the trouble.

Tierra del Fuego

In his autobiography, pioneer settler Lucas Bridges labeled Tierra del Fuego the "Uttermost Part of the Earth" for its splendid isolation at the southern tip of the southern American continent. Shared between Chile and Argentina, it's a place where fur seals, sea lions, and penguins cavort in the choppy seas of the strait named for the celebrated navigator Ferdinand Magellan, where Darwin sailed on the *Beagle* and the first 49ers found their route to California. From the seashore, behind the city of Ushuaia, glacial horns rise like sacred steeples nearly 2,000 meters above sea level. The beaches and southern beech forests of Parque Nacional Tierra del Fuego, west of the city, are the terminus of the world's southernmost highway.

Tierra del Fuego is not just one island, but an archipelago, though the Isla Grande de Tierra del Fuego is South America's largest island. While parts of the Argentine side of the Isla Grande are urbanized, the Chilean part of the archipelago has only a few small towns and isolated *estancias*. Roads are relatively few but improving, and some of them are now paved, especially on the Argentine side; the unpaved roads, though, are hazardous to windshields, which are mostly cheaply replaced in Punta Arenas.

© WAYNE BERNHARDSON

Chilean ferry crossing from Tierra del Fuego to the South American mainland at Primera Angostura

There are two ferry routes from the Chilean mainland to Tierra del Fuego: a shuttle from Punta Delgada, only 45 kilometers south of the Argentine border, across the Primera Angostura narrows to Puerto Espora, and a daily service from Punta Arenas to Porvenir, one of the widest parts of the strait.

History

Prior to their European "discovery" by Magellan in 1520, southern South America's insular extremes were inhabited by dispersed bands of hunter-gatherers like the Selknam (Ona), Kawasqar (Alacaluf), and Yámana (Yahgan) who lived off maritime and terrestrial resources that they considered abundant—only in the European view was this a land of privation. The archipelago acquired its name from the fires set by the region's so-called "Canoe Indians," the Kawasqar and Yámana, for heating and cooking; in this soggy region, though, it might have been more accurate to call it Tierra del Humo (Land of Smoke).

Early navigators dreaded rounding Cape Horn's wild seas, and their reports gave their countrymen little reason in settle in or even ex-

plore the area. In the early 1830s, Captain Robert Fitzroy of the *Beagle* abducted several Yámana, including the famous Jemmy Button, to England and subjected them to missionary indoctrination before returning them to their home on a later voyage. On that voyage, a perplexed Charles Darwin commented on the simplicity of their society: "The perfect equality among the individuals composing the Fuegian tribes, must for a long time retard their civilization."

The first to try to bring "civilization" to the Yámana were Anglican missionaries from the Falkland Islands, some of whose descendents still live in Tierra del Fuego. After abortive attempts that included both Fuegian assaults and the starvation death of British evangelist Allen Gardiner, the Anglican Thomas Bridges settled at present-day Ushuaia, on the Argentine side of the Isla Grande, where he compiled an English-Yahgan dictionary. His son Lucas, who grew up with Yámana playmates, wrote the extraordinary memoir *The Uttermost Part of the Earth,* published a few years before his death in 1950.

In the meantime, both the Chilean and Argentine governments established a presence in the region, and gigantic sheep *estancias* occupied

Tierra del Fuego

the sprawling grasslands at the expense of native peoples who once hunted guanaco and other game on them. When, as the guanaco slowly disappeared, the desperate Fuegians began to hunt domestic sheep, they often found themselves facing the wrong end of a rifle—though introduced European diseases like typhoid and measles killed more native people than did bullets.

Borders in the archipelago were never clearly defined and the two countries nearly went to war over three small islands in the Beagle Channel in 1979. Positions were uncompromising—one Argentine poster boldly declared "We will never surrender what is ours!"—but papal mediation successfully avoided warfare and brought a settlement within a few years. There are lingering issues, though, like transportation across the channel from Ushuaia to Puerto Williams.

Since then, travel to the uttermost part of the earth has boomed, especially on the Argentine side in the summer months. Other important economic sectors are sheep-farming and petroleum, on both the Chilean and Argentine sides.

 USHUAIA (ARGENTINA)

Beneath the serrated spires of the Martial range, on the north shore of the Beagle Channel, the city of Ushuaia is both an end—virtually the terminus of the world's most southerly highway—and a beginning—the gateway to Antarctica. The surrounding countryside is increasingly popular with activities-oriented visitors who enjoy hiking, mountain biking, fishing, and skiing.

After two decades–plus of economic growth and physical sprawl, the provincial capital is both declining and improving. On the one hand, the duty-free manufacturing, fishing, and tourist boom that transformed a onetime penal colony and naval base into a bustling city has weakened, but on the other, it's begun to clean up the waterfront and restore some of the historic buildings that gave the town its personality. The streets are cleaner, and there are parks and plazas and green spaces, but it still has one of the worst particulate pollution problems of any Argentine city because high winds kick up clouds of dust in the unpaved streets of its newer neighborhoods.

Ushuaia

USHUAIA

To RN 3; Ski Areas, Lago Kami/
Fagnano, Río Grande, and
ESTANCIA HARBERTON

MUSEO
MARITIMO

YAGANES

VOLVER

MUSEO DEL FIN
DEL MUNDO

ANTARTIDA

ARGENTINA

RIVADAVIA

GODOY

ROCA

KAUPÉ

MUELLE
TURISTICO

SECRETARIA
DE TURISMO

SEE DETAIL

MARTIN

SAN

MAIPU

**HOTEL
POSADA
FUEGUINA**

EL REFUGIO DEL
MOCHILERO

LASSERRE

AVENIDA

OFICINA
ANTARTICA
INFUETUR

MAGALLANES

25 DE MAYO

**HOTEL
CAP
POLONIO**

TRANSPORTE
PUKY/BODY/
BELLAVISTA

MUELLE
COMERCIAL

**HOSTAL DEL
BOSQUE**

JUANA

CAMPOS

FADUL

HOTEL
CESAR

HOTEL CAP
POLONIO

TRANSPORTES
PASARELA/BUSS
EBEN-EZER/ALVAREZ

9 DE JULIO

**MARTIN
FIERRO B&B**

LOS TRES
ANGELES

THALER

CAMBIOS
THALER

BANISUD

Bahía Ushuaia

J.M. DE ROSAS

LIDER

MANUEL
TIENDA LEON

CARDOS

CAPILLA
ANTIGUA

EUROPCAR

SOLIS

MONSEÑOR FAGNANO

DON BOSCO

HOSTERÍA
MUSTAPIC

DELOQUI

GOBERNADOR

BOUTIQUE
DEL LIBRO

LOCALIZA

CLUB
NAUTICO

PIEDRABUENA

OPIPARO

BELGRANO

PAZ

Plaza Islas
Malvinas

MAGALLANES

GOBERNADOR

SARMIENTO

DTT
CYCLES
SPORT

PATAGONIA

Plazoleta
Perito Moreno

Plaza
Gendarmería
Nacional

PASARELA LUIS FIQUE

ONAS

HOSPEDAJE
TORRE AL SUR

GOBERNADOR

PIZZERIA
EL TURCO

200 yds

200 m

GOMEZ

ADMINISTRACIÓN
DE PARQUES
NACIONALES

TÉ PARA DOS

0

0

Parque
Paseo del
Centenario

CEMENTERIO
MUNICIPAL

CASA BEBAN

To Glaciar Martial and
Camping la Pista del Andino

AVENIDA SAN MARTIN

ARGENTINAS

To Camping Municipal, Airport, and
PARQUE NACIONAL TIERRA DEL FUEGO

DARWIN

HOSTAL
AMÉRICA

AVENIDA

MALVINAS

HOSPITAL
REGIONAL

AUTOMÓVIL
CLUB ARGENTINO

LUIS VERNET

12 DE OCTUBRE

HOTEL MAITEN

CHILEAN
CONSULATE

O.V. ANDRADE

ONACHAGA

JAINEN

SANCHEZ DE CABALLERO

PAZ

FLORENCIA

LUGONES

25 DE AGOSTO

Detail

LA
RUEDA

**TANTE
SARA**

CANAL FUN
& NATURE

RIVADAVIA

TOLKEYÉN

RANCHO
ARGENTINO

LA CASA
DE LOS
MARISCOS

MUSEO DE
MAQUETAS MUNDO
YAMANA

GODOY

LA GRAN
ESTANCIA

MOUSTACCHIO

POST
OFFICE

RUMBO
SUR

TANTE
NINA

TRANSPORTE KAUPÉN/GONZALO

TECNI-AUSTRAL/
TOLKAR

BARCITO
DEAL

YISHKA TURISMO
Y AVENTURA

TIA ELVIRA

ROCA

AEROLÍNEAS
ARGENTINAS

BANCO DE LA
PROVINCIA

AVENIDA

RUMBO SUR/TRES MARIAS
EXCURSIONES/TOLKEYÉN

MARTIN

SAN

PODER
LEGISLATIVO

LASSERRE

DELOQUI

FIN DEL
MUNDO

AVENIDA

HOTEL
ALBATROS

25 DE MAYO

LOCUTORIO

CABO DE HORNOS

CAFÉ DE LA
ESQUINA

LADE

AEROVIAS
DAP

HOSTAL
MALVINAS

GOBERNADOR

**ALBERGUE
CRUZ DEL SUR**

BARCLEIT 1912

CAFÉ-BAR
TANTE SARA

HELADOS
GADGET

SECRETARIA DE
TURISMO

ALL PATAGONIA

MAYO

JUANA

FADUL

© AVALON TRAVEL PUBLISHING, INC.

N Tierra del Fuego

History

Ushuaia dates from 1870, when the Anglican South American Missionary Society decided to place the archipelago's first permanent European settlement here. Pioneer missionary Thomas Bridges and his descendants have left an enduring legacy in Bridges's Yahgan (Yámana) dictionary, the memoir of his son Lucas, and the family *estancia* at nearby Harberton (sadly, the Yahgans whom Thomas Bridges hoped to save succumbed to introduced diseases and conflict with other settlers).

Not long after Ushuaia's settlement, Argentina, alarmed by the British presence, moved to establish its own authority at Ushuaia and did so with a penal settlement for its most infamous criminals and political undesirables. It remained a penal settlement until almost 1950, when Juan Domingo Perón's government created a major naval base to help support Argentina's claim to a share of Antarctica. Only since the end of the military dictatorship of 1976–83 has it become a tourist destination, visited by many cruise ships as well as overland travelers and air passengers who come to see the world's southernmost city.

Orientation

Ushuaia (population 45,205) is 240 kilometers southwest of Río Grande, the island's only other city, and 3,220 kilometers south of Buenos Aires. It stretches east and west along the north shore of the Beagle Channel. Now bedecked with flowerbeds, the main thoroughfare is Avenida Maipú, part of RN3 which continues west to Bahía Lapataia in Parque Nacional Tierra del Fuego. The parallel Avenida San Martín, one block north, is the main commercial street; the focus of Ushuaia's night life, it gets gridlocked on summer nights as surely as any avenue in Buenos Aires. From the shoreline, the perpendicular northbound streets rise steeply—some so steeply that they become staircases.

Museo Marítimo de Ushuaia

Misleadingly named, this museum most effec-

RISING COSTS

Shortly after completion of this book's manuscript, tourism sector prices in parts of Argentina and in Chile underwent notable increases in dollar terms, primarily in accommodations and, to a lesser degree, food. The reasons and degree of increases were different in each country, however.

Argentina's peso gained against the dollar, but even more significant was the rejuvenated tourist economy in the capital city of Buenos Aires and, especially, in popular Patagonian destinations like San Carlos de Bariloche, San Martín de los Andes, Puerto Madryn, El Calafate, and Ushuaia.

The reason for price pressures in Argentina, though, was not so much the peso's strength and the economy at large as increased domestic demand—for the most part, Argentines could still not afford to travel beyond their own borders, and thus spent their pesos at home. At the same time, foreigners flocked to Argentina as their dollars and Euros bought far more than in the days of dollar-peso parity. Fortunately, there has been no return to the hyperinflation of the 1970s and 1980s, and prices have not skyrocketed anywhere close to their pre-devaluation levels. Still, travelers should be prepared for steadily rising prices for food, accommodations, and transportation.

In Chile, thanks to booming copper prices, the local peso strengthened nearly 20 percent against the U.S. dollar before subsiding slightly. Visitors should probably count on dollar prices some 15 to 20 percent above those listed in this book, except in transportation, which has remained fairly stable. Domestic inflation remains near zero, but prices in South America's most stable economy are, on the whole, higher than in Argentina.

tively tells the story of Ushuaia's inauspicious beginnings as a penal settlement for both civilian and military prisoners. Alarmed over the South American Missionary Society's incursions among the indigenous peoples of the Beagle Channel, Argentina reinforced its claims to the territory by building, in 1884, a military prison on Isla de los Estados (Staten Island), across the Strait of Lemaire at the southeastern tip of the Isla Grande.

Barely a decade later, in 1896, it established Ushuaia's civilian Cárcel de Reincidentes for repeat offenders; after finally deciding, in 1902, that Isla de los Estados was a hardship post even for prisoners, the military moved their own facility to Ushuaia. Then, in 1911, the two institutions fused in this building that, over the first half of the 20th century, held some of the country's most famous political prisoners, celebrated rogues, and notorious psychopaths.

Divided into five two-story pavilions, with 380 cells intended for one prisoner each, the prison held as many as 600 prisoners at a time before closing in 1947. Its most famous inmates were political detainees like immigrant Russian anarchist Simón Radowitzsky, who killed Buenos Aires police chief Ramón Falcón with a bomb in 1909; Radical politicians Ricardo Rojas, Honorio Pueyrredón, and Mario Guido (the deceptively named Radicals are in fact a bland middle-class party); and Peronist politician Héctor Cámpora, who was president briefly in the 1970s.

Many if not most of the prisoners, though, were long-termers or lifers like the diminutive strangler Cayetano Santos Godino, a serial killer dubbed "El Orejudo" for his oversized ears (the nickname also describes a large-eared bat that is native to the archipelago). Julio Ordano has written a play, performed in Buenos Aires, about Santos Godino, "El Petiso Orejudo."

Life-size figures of the most infamous inmates, modified department-store dummies clad in prison stripes, occupy many of the cells. A particularly interesting exhibit is a wide-ranging comparison with other prisons that have become museums, such as San Francisco's Alcatraz and South Africa's Robben Island.

The museum does justify its name with an exceptional exhibit of scale models of ships that have played a role in local history, such as Magellan's galleon *Trinidad*, the legendary *Beagle*, the South American Missionary Society's three successive sailboats known as the *Allen Gardiner*, and Antarctic explorer and conqueror Roald Amundsen's *Fram*. In addition, there are materials on Argentina's Antarctic presence since the early 20th century, when the corvette *Uruguay* rescued Otto Nordenskjöld's Norwegian expedition, whose crew included the Argentine José María Sobral. On the grounds outdoors is a full-size model of the Faro San Juan de Salvamento, the Isla de los Estados (Staten Island) lighthouse that figures in Jules Verne's story "The Lighthouse at the End of the World."

In addition, this exceptional museum contains a philatelic room, natural history exhibits, and admirable accounts of the region's aboriginal peoples. In fact, it has only two drawbacks: there's too much to see in a single day, and the English translations could use some polishing—to say the least.

The Museo Marítimo (Yaganes and Gobernador Paz, tel. 02901/437481, museomar @satlink.com, 9 A.M.–8 P.M. daily) offers guided tours at 11 A.M. and 2, 4:30, and 5:45 P.M. Admission costs US$4.50 pp but, on request, the staff will validate your ticket for another day; since there's so much here, splitting up sightseeing sessions is not a bad idea. There are discounts for children (US$1), students and senior citizens (US$1.75), and families (US$9 including up to four children). It has an excellent book and souvenir shop, and a fine *confitería* for snacks and coffee.

Other Sights

Even if it's leveled off, Ushuaia's economic boom provided the wherewithal to preserve and even restore some of the city's historic buildings. Two of them are now museums: the **Casa Fernández Valdés** (1903), on the waterfront at Avenida Maipú 175, houses the historical Museo del Fin de Mundo, while the **Presidio de Ushuaia** (1896), at Yaganes and Gobernador Paz, is now the Museo Marítimo.

Three blocks west of the Casa Fernández Valdés, at Maipú 465, the classically Magellanic

mural of Yámana Indians on post office building

Poder Legislativo (1894) houses the provincial legislature. Five blocks farther west, at the corner of Avenida Maipú and Rosas, prisoners built the recently restored **Capilla Antigua,** a chapel dating from 1898. Ushuaia's municipal tourist office now occupies the **Biblioteca Sarmiento** (1926), San Martín 674, the city's first public library. At the corner of Avenida Malvinas Argentinas and 12 de Octubre, the waterfront **Casa Beban,** is an elaborate reassembled pioneer residence dating from 1913; it now houses the municipal Casa de la Cultura, a cultural center.

Benefiting greatly from its exterior restoration of its block-style construction, Ushuaia's impressively evolving **Museo del Fin del Mundo** (Avenida Maipú 175, tel. 02901/421863, museo@tierradelfuego.org.ar, US$3.50 adults, US$2 students and retirees, free for children 14 and under) contains improved exhibits on the Yámana, Selknam, and other Fuegian Indians, and on early European voyages to the area. There remain permanent exhibits on the presidio; the Fique family's El Primer Argentino general store; the original branch of the state-run bank, Banco de la Nación (which occupied the building for more than 60 years); and run-of-the-mill taxidermy. Its celebrity artifact is one of few existing copies of Thomas Bridges's Yámana-English dictionary.

On the grounds outside, an open-air sector includes representations of a Yámana encampment and dwellings, plus machinery used in early agriculture and forestry projects. The museum also contains a bookstore/souvenir shop and a specialized library on southernmost Argentina, the surrounding oceans, and Antarctica. Hours are 9 A.M.–8 P.M. daily in summer. The rest of the year, hours are 3–8 P.M. daily except Monday. There are guided tours at 11 A.M. and 5 P.M. daily.

While both the Museo del Fin del Mundo and the Museo Marítimo do a creditable job of covering Tierra del Fuego's indigenous heritage, the small, private **Museo de Maquetas Mundo Yámana** (Rivadavia 56, tel. 02901/422874, mundoyamana@infovia.com.ar, 10 A.M.–8 P.M. daily) consists of skillfully assembled dioramas of life along the Beagle Channel prior to the European presence, at a scale of 1:15. It also includes cartographic representations of the Yámana and their neighbors, interpretations of the European impact, and panels of historical photographs.

SOUTH TO THE ICE

Since the demise of the Soviet Union, Ushuaia has become the main jumping-off point for Antarctic excursions on Russian icebreakers that, despite being chartered under American officers, sometimes still carry the shield of the hammer and sickle on their bows. For travelers with flexible schedules, it's sometimes possible to make last-minute arrangements at huge discounts—no ship wants to sail with empty berths—for as little as US$1,100. Normal rates, though, are around US$3,000 for nine to 14 days, including several days' transit across the stormy Drake Passage—seasickness medication is advisable.

former Soviet research icebreaker, now an Antarctic cruise ship, in Ushuaia

© WAYNE BERNHARDSON

If your timing is bad and budget cruises are not available, many Ushuaia travel agencies can make alternative arrangements. The season runs from mid-November to mid-March.

On the waterfront Muelle Comercial, Ushuaia's **Oficina Antarctica Infuetur** (tel. 02901/424431, antartida@tierradelfuego.org.ar) has the latest information on Antarctic cruises. Guidebooks to the white continent include Jeff Rubin's *Antarctica* (Lonely Planet, 2000), Ron Naveen's *Oceanites Site Guide to the Antarctic Peninsula* (Chevy Chase, MD: Oceanites, 1997), and the third edition of Tony Soper and Dafila Scott's *Antarctica: A Guide to the Wildlife* (Bradt Publications, 2001).

The museum charges US$1.75 pp for adults, US$1 for students and retirees, and is free for children under 13. The staff speak fluent English.

Shopping

Boutique del Libro (San Martín 1129, tel. 02901/424750) offers an excellent selection of Spanish-language books and a smaller choice of English-language materials. **Fin del Mundo** (San Martín 505) has a wide selection of kitschy souvenirs but also maps and books.

Accommodations

Ushuaia has abundant accommodations, but it's long been one of the most expensive destinations in what was, until recently, an expensive country. Demand is also high, though, in the summer months of January and February, when prices rise and reservations are advisable. One heartening development on the accommodations scene is the arrival of several bed-and-breakfasts—known by the semi-English acronym ByB—several of which are excellent alternatives.

Under US$10

Eight kilometers west of Ushuaia on the road to Parque Nacional Tierra del Fuego, the **Camping Municipal** is free of charge but has limited facilities (firepits and pit toilets only). Four kilometers west of town, **Camping del Rugby Club Ushuaia** (tel. 02901/435796, camping-pipo@tierradelfuego.org.ar, US$2 pp) has sites with running water, bathrooms with hot showers, and firepits with grills for barbecuing.

A stiff climb to the northwest of downtown Ushuaia, **La Pista del Andino** (Alem 2873, tel. 02901/435890 or 02901/15-568626, pistadelandino@hotmail.com, US$3 pp) has slightly sloping campsites at the Club Andino's ski area; the first transfer from downtown or the airport is free. It also allows guests with sleeping bags to crash in the *refugio* above its bar/restaurant, but

Tierra del Fuego

this is less than ideal for anyone who wants to get to bed early.

US$10–25

On the edge of downtown, high enough to offer spectacular views of the Beagle Channel, expanding **Albergue Torre al Sur** (Gobernador Paz 1437, tel. 02901/437291, fax 02901/430745, torrealsur@impsat1.com.ar, www.torrealsur.com.ar, US$5.50–6 pp) has been one of Argentina's finest backpacker facilities, but it's gotten mixed reviews recently because of overcrowding and noise. Rooms have two or four beds, with lockers; there's hot water, Internet access, and free luggage storage.

Central but quiet, Ⅺ **Albergue Cruz del Sur** (Deloqui 636, tel. 02901/430062, ibar72@yahoo .com or xdelsur@yahoo.com, US$6.50 pp) is an independent hostel facility whose rooms have four, six, or eight beds; there is also cable TV, Internet access, two kitchens, and a free initial pickup. Guests also get a series of discounts and specials at various services around town.

El Refugio del Mochilero (25 de Mayo 241, tel. 02901/436129, refmoch@infovia.com.ar, US$7 pp) has almost equally good facilities but perhaps a little less ambience than it once had.

US$25–50

Hotel Maitén (12 de Octubre 140, tel. 02901/ 422745, maiten@tierradelfuego.org.ar, US$18/26 s/d) is a reasonable budget choice. Improvements at rehabbed **Hotel César** (Avenida San Martín 753, tel. 02901/421460, fax 02901/ 432721, cesarhostal@infovia.com.ar, US$27/36 s/d) have turned it into one of the central area's better values.

The same is not true of **Hostería Mustapic** (Piedrabuena 230, tel. 02901/421718, mustapic @sinectis.com.ar, US$33/41 s/d), whose management seems to have turned grumpy, but it's still adequate. **Hostal Malvinas** (Gobernador Deloqui 615, tel./fax 02901/422626, hostalmalvinas@arnet.com.ar, US$27–36 s, US$32–43 d) provides simple but quiet and immaculate rooms with large baths but no frills—not even TV.

Ⅺ **Martín Fierro B&B** (9 de Julio 175, tel. 02901/430525, javiersplace@hotmail.com, US$34

d) is a stylish new hillside place with bunks— two people each in small but well-designed rooms with shared baths. The common areas are simultaneously spacious and cozy, and the breakfast is varied and filling; its main drawback is the tiny stalls that make showering with a friend impossible without being *really* intimate. There are also two downstairs "aparthotel" rooms (US$55) sleeping up to four people.

US$50–100

Hostería América (Gobernador Paz 1665, tel. 02901/423358, fax 02901/431362, hosteria america@arnet.com.ar, US$37/54 s/d) is a good choice that enjoys a fine location above the Parque Paseo del Centenario.

Hostal del Bosque (Magallanes 709, tel./fax 02901/430777, 02901/421723, info@hostaldelbosque.com.ar, www.hostaldelbosque.com.ar, US$50–77 s or d) is an aparthotel whose two-room suites, with kitchenette, can sleep up to four people. There are large baths, with shower and tub, and cable TV; it also has its own restaurant.

Only its location on a busy street detracts from the bright and cheerful **Hotel Cap Polonio** (San Martín 746, tel. 02901/422140, 02901/422131, cappolonio@tierradelfuego.org.ar, www.cappolonio.com.ar, US$90 s or d). All rooms are carpeted, with cable TV; the private baths have tubs as well as showers, and there's a good restaurant/*confitería* with breakfast included. Tango shows take place at 10 P.M. Saturday.

Three-star **Hotel Albatros** (Avenida Maipú 505, tel. 02901/433446, albatros@tierradelfuego.org.ar, www.albatroshotel.com.ar, US$82/ 96 s/d) is the pick of the waterfront accommodations, but it hasn't kept up with places like the Cap Polonio.

US$100–200

Hillside, four-star **Hotel Ushuaia** (Lasserre 933, tel. 02901/430671, hushuaia@tierradelfuego .org.ar, US$80/110 s/d) is a good value in its price range.

Offering awesome views from its cul-de-sac hillside perch, Ⅺ **Hotel Posada Fueguina** (Lasserre 438, tel. 02901/423467, pfueguina

@tierradelfuego.org.ar, US$89/128 s/d) also provides breakfast, cable TV, and similar amenities.

The interior is more impressive than the surprisingly plain exterior at the luxury **Hotel del Glaciar** (Luis Martial 2355, tel. 02901/430640, fax 02901/430636, delglaciar@speedy.com.ar, www.hoteldelglaciar.com, US$172 s or d). At Km 3.5 on the road to the Martial glacier, each room has either a mountain or sea view.

At Km 3 on the glacier road, the nearby **Ⓜ Hotel y Resort Las Hayas** (Luis Martial 1650, tel. 02901/430710, fax 02901/430719, lashayas @overnet.com.ar, www.lashayas.com.ar, US$186 s or d) enjoys nearly all conceivable luxuries, including an elaborate buffet breakfast, gym, sauna, hot tubs and a heated indoor pool; it picks up guests with reservations at the airport, and offers a regular shuttle to and from downtown Ushuaia. Despite its surprisingly utilitarian exterior, some of its 102 rooms suffer from hideous decor—the wallpaper is to cringe at—but all are comfortable and the staff are highly professional.

Food

Ushuaia has always been one of Argentina's more expensive places to eat, but the peso collapse of 2001 has reined in prices. That said, there are still some truly expensive choices; the financially challenged should look for *tenedor libre* specials, or be particularly cautious with extras like dessert and coffee.

The Hotel Cap Polonio's **Marcopolo** (San Martín 730, tel. 02901/430001) is a café-restaurant that serves excellent coffee, chocolate, and croissants for breakfast—try the *submarino* for a cold morning's pickup. **Café de la Esquina** (Avenida San Martín 602, tel. 02901/421446) is a popular meeting place with similar offerings, as well as sandwiches for late-afternoon tea.

Open for lunch only weekdays, but with Saturday-evening hours, **Pizzería El Turco** (San Martín 1440, tel. 02901/424711) is good and moderately priced, but it lacks the variety of the slightly more expensive **Opíparo** (Avenida Maipú 1255, tel. 02901/434022), a pizzería that also serves pasta dishes. Well-established **Barcleit 1912** (Fadul 148, tel. 02901/433422) seems to

have fallen a step behind some of the other pizzerias, but also has a variety of moderately priced short orders.

One of Ushuaia's finest, **Ⓜ Tante Sara** (San Martín 137, tel./fax 02901/435005) serves outstanding pasta with a broad selection of imaginative sauces, as well as pizza, with good service in pleasant surroundings. Most entrees are in the US$4–6 range, such as ravioli with king crab. For sandwiches and desserts, try their **Café-Bar Tante Sara** (San Martín 701, tel. O2901/423912).

Tante Nina (Gobernador Godoy 15, tel. 02901/432444) focuses on Fuegian fish and seafood, Patagonian lamb, and "homely pasta."

Barcito Ideal (San Martín 393, tel. 02901/437860) seems always to draw crowds to its US$6 *tenedor libre* buffet. **La Rueda** (San Martín 193, tel. 02901/436540) charges only slightly more for its own buffet *parrillada*. Nearby **La Estancia** (San Martín 253, tel. 02901/421241) has similar fare.

For US$6, **Rancho Argentino** (San Martín 237, tel. 02901/430100) serves a fixed-price four-course meal including grilled Fuegian lamb, but it also has a more diverse à la carte menu including beef and baked empanadas. The well-established **Moustacchio** (Avenida San Martín 298, tel. 02901/423308) has similar fare but also emphasizes seafood.

Ushuaia has a wider choice of seafood restaurants than almost any other Argentine provincial city. **La Casa de los Mariscos** (San Martín 232, tel. 02901/421928) specializes in *centolla* (king crab), but also has many other fish and shellfish options in the US$3–7 range. Looking like a *porteño* antique shop housed in a classic Magellanic residence, tango-themed **Volver** (Avenida Maipú 37, tel. 02901/423977) doesn't quite live up to its potential—the fish and seafood dishes, like *abadejo al ajillo* (US$5) and king-crab soup (US$3) are disappointingly bland.

Other possibilities include **El Náutico** (Avenida Maipú and Belgrano, tel. 02901/424028), where entrees start around US$4; **Tía Elvira** (Avenida Maipú 349, tel. 02901/424725), where four-course dinners cost around US$10–12;

and Ⓜ **Kaupé** (Roca 470, tel. 02901/422704), which serves an exclusively (and exclusive) à la carte menu. The latter has specialties like king crab (US$11), exquisite lemon ice cream, carpaccio, and wine by the glass. Even with devaluation, a full meal here runs about US$25, but it's worth the splurge.

Top of the line—both literally and geographically—is the dining-with-a-panoramic-view at Ⓜ **Chez Manu,** (Luis Martial 2135, tel. 02901/423253), immediately below the Hotel del Glaciar. Using local ingredients like king crab and lamb, the French-run restaurant is *the* place for a truly elaborate meal at equally elaborate prices: US$25 and up even in times of devaluation. Along with Kaupé, this is one Ushuaia restaurant with food to match its views.

Té Para Dos (San Martín 1463, tel. 435535) is a promising teahouse. **Helados Gadget** (Avenida San Martín 621) has all the conventional Argentine ice cream flavors—good enough in their own right—but also incorporates regional specialties like calafate and rhubarb.

Information

Ushuaia's well-organized municipal **Secretaría de Turismo** (San Martín 674, tel. 02901/424550, muniush@speedy.com.ar, www.e-ushuaia.com) is open 8 A.M.–10 P.M. weekdays and 9 A.M.–8 P.M. weekends and holidays. English-speaking staff are normally present.

In addition, there is a subsidiary office at the **Muelle Turístico** (tel. 02901/437666, 8 A.M.–6 P.M. daily), and another at the airport (tel. 02901/423970) that's open for arriving flights only.

The provincial **Instituto Fueguino de Turismo (Infuetur)** has ground-floor offices at Hotel Albatros (Avenida Maipú 505, tel. 02901/423340).

For motorists, the **Automóvil Club Argentino** (ACA) is at Malvinas Argentinas and Onachaga (tel. 02901/421121).

The **APN** (Avenida San Martín 1395, tel. 02901/421315) is open 9 A.M.–noon weekdays.

From October to March, at the waterfront Muelle Comercial, the **Oficina Antártica Infuetur** (tel. 02901/423340 or 421423, antar-

tida@tierradelfuego.org.ar) has information on Antarctic tours.

Services

Several banks have ATMs, including **Banca Nazionale del Lavoro** (Avenida Maipú 297), **Banco Macro Bansud** (Avenida Maipú 781), and **Banco de la Provincia** (San Martín 396); the latter accepts travelers checks at a three percent commission. **Cambios Thaler** (Avenida San Martín 788, tel. 02901/421911) also takes three percent on travelers checks but keeps longer hours: 9:30 A.M.–1:30 P.M. and 4–8 P.M. weekdays, 10 A.M.–1:30 P.M. and 5:30–8 P.M. Saturday, and 5:30–8 P.M. Sunday.

Correo Argentino is at San Martín 309; Ushuaia's postal code is 9410.

Locutorio Cabo de Hornos (25 de Mayo 112) provides telephone, fax, and Internet access, as do many other businesses.

The **Chilean consulate** (Jainén 50, tel. 02901/430970) is open 9 A.M.–1 P.M. weekdays only.

The **Dirección Nacional de Migraciones** is at Beauvoir 1536 (tel. 02901/422334).

Los Tres Angeles (Juan Manuel de Rosas 139, tel. 02901/422687) has quick and reliable laundry service.

The **Hospital Regional** is at Maipú and 12 de Octubre (tel. 02901/422950, tel. 107 for emergencies).

Getting There

Aerolíneas Argentinas/Austral (Roca 116, tel. 02901/421218) normally flies twice or thrice daily to Aeroparque, sometimes via El Calafate or Trelew. On occasion, Buenos Aires–bound flights land at Ezeiza instead of Aeroparque.

In the Galería Albatros, **LADE** (Avenida San Martín 564, Local 5, tel. 02901/421123) flies weekly to Río Gallegos, El Calafate, and Comodoro Rivadavia.

From November to March, the Chilean carrier **Aerovías DAP** (25 de Mayo 64, tel. 02901/431110, 02901/431111) flies 20-passenger Twin Otters Monday, Wednesday, and Friday to Punta Arenas, Chile (US$100), Ushuaia's only scheduled international service.

For Puerto Williams, across the channel in Chile, it may be possible to arrange a private-charter flight through the **Aeroclub Ushuaia** (tel. 02901/421717 or 421892) for about US$100 pp.

Lider (Gobernador Paz 921, tel. 02901/436421) runs buses to Tolhuín (US$4) and Ushuaia (US$7.50) eight times daily except Sunday and holidays, when it goes only five times. Transportes Montiel (Marcos Zar 330, tel. 02901/421366) goes to Río Grande seven times daily except Sunday and holidays, when it goes six times only.

Tecni-Austral (Roca 157, tel. 02901/431612) goes daily at 6 A.M. to Río Grande (US$7.50, 3.5 hours); the Monday, Wednesday, and Friday buses continue to Río Gallegos (US$29, 12 hours) and connect with Pacheco buses to Punta Arenas, Chile (US$25, 12 hours).

Tolkeyén (Maipú 237, tel. 02901/437073) goes to Río Grande 5:30 A.M. Monday, 6:30 A.M., Tuesday, Thursday and Saturday, 8 A.M. Wednesday and Friday, and 7 P.M. Friday and Sunday. The Tuesday, Thursday, and Saturday services hook up with the 11:30 A.M. Pacheco bus from Río Grande to Punta Arenas.

Political complications between Chile and Argentina have held up regular transportation across the Beagle Channel to Puerto Williams, but in December 2001 the two countries agreed to open Puerto Navarino, at the east end of Isla Navarino, as a port of entry to Chile. What that means for regular public transportation is not yet clear. In the meantime, ask around the Club Náutico, at Avenida Maipú and Belgrano, for private yachts that may be willing to take passengers (a large enough group should be able to charter a boat for around US$70–100 pp). One possibility is **Claudio Don Vito** (claudio_don_vito@hotmail.com).

Getting Around

A causeway links the city with **Aeropuerto Internacional Malvinas Argentinas,** which has the country's highest airport taxes: US$5 to elsewhere in Argentina, and US$20 for international flights. Taxis and *remises* cost only about US$3

with **Manuel Tienda León** (San Martín 995, tel. 02901/422222).

Several bus companies charge around US$7.50 round-trip to Parque Nacional Tierra del Fuego; it's normally possible to stay in the park and return on a later day. Note that the companies listed here, as indicated, use several different stops along the waterfront but do not have offices there; some have telephones and others do not. The schedules listed are summer hours that may change; during other seasons, schedules are reduced.

From Avenida Maipú and 25 de Mayo, **Transporte Pasarela** (tel. 02901/433712), **Buses Eben-Ezer** (tel. 02901/431133), and **Transportes Alvarez** have 21 buses daily to the park between 7:30 A.M. and 8 P.M., returning between 9 A.M. and 8 P.M.

From Maipú and Fadul, **Transporte Puky** (tel. 02901/435418 or 02901/15-618547), Body, and Bellavista go a dozen times daily between 8:30 A.M. and 7:45 P.M., returning between 9:30 A.M. and 8:30 P.M.

From Maipú and Roca, **Transportes Kaupén** and **Gonzalo** operate seven buses daily between 9 A.M. and 7 P.M., returning between 10 A.M. and 8 P.M.

Most of the same companies have slightly less frequent services to the chairlift at the Glaciar Martial (US$2.50 pp), normally with a minimum two passengers. Trips to Estancia Harberton (US$14 pp) need a minimum three passengers.

Car rentals start around US$30 per day and range up to US$60 per day for a 4WD vehicle. Some agencies offer unlimited mileage within the province of Tierra del Fuego, but others limit this to 150 kilometers per day or even less, so verify before signing the contact.

Ushuaia rental agencies include **Cardos** (San Martín 845, tel. 02901/436388, cardosr@hotmail.com), **Europcar** (Maipú 857, tel. 02901/430786, europcar@carletti.com.ar), **Hertz** (at the airport, tel. 02901/432429, hertzushuaia @infovia.com.ar), and **Localiza** (San Martín 1222, tel. 02901/430739, ultimoconfin@tierradelfuego.com.ar).

DTT Cycles Sport (Avenida San Martín 903) rents mountain bikes.

The Chilean M/V *Mare Australis* operates luxurious sightseeing **cruises** to Puerto Williams and through the fjords of Chilean Tierra del Fuego to Punta Arenas; while not intended as simple transportation, they can serve the same purpose for those who can afford them. It's possible to either disembark in Punta Arenas (three days) or return to Ushuaia (in a week). These cruises are usually booked far in advance, but on rare occasion—normally just before Christmas—it may be possible to board more spontaneously.

VICINITY OF USHUAIA

Ushuaia has more than a dozen travel agencies offering varied excursions in and around Ushuaia, ranging from conventional city tours (US$7, 1.5 hours) to Parque Nacional Tierra del Fuego (US$14, four to five hours) and historic Estancia Harberton (US$50–65, eight hours). They also organize activities such as hiking, climbing, horseback riding, fishing, and mountain biking.

Local operators include **All Patagonia** (Juana Fadul 54, tel. 02901/433622, fax 02901/430707, allpat@satlink.com), which is the AmEx representative; **Canal Fun & Nature** (Rivadavia 82, tel. 02901/437610, tel./fax 02901/435777, info@canalfun.com; **Rumbo Sur** (San Martín 342, tel. 422441, fax 02901/430699, informes@rumbosur.com.ar; **Tolkar** (Roca 157, Local 1, tel. 02901/431408, tolkarturismo@infovia.com.ar); **Tolkeyén** (Maipú 237, tel. 02901/437073); and **Yishka Turismo** (Gobernador Godoy 62, tel./fax 02901/437606, yishka@tierradelfuego.org.ar).

CROSSING THE BEAGLE CHANNEL

In 1978, the military dictatorships of Chile and Argentina barely avoided war over three small islands in the Beagle Channel and, though successive civilian governments have resolved the territorial dispute, freedom of movement across the channel is not yet what it could be.

According to the Chilean viewpoint, the Argentines have failed to live up to their part of the 1978 agreement, which implied reciprocal border openings at Agua Negra (between the Argentine city of San Juan and the Chilean city of La Serena) for Argentina and Puerto Almanza (opposite Puerto Williams) for Chile. For the Chileans, it's also a matter of principle that, since they provide overland access to Argentine Tierra del Fuego through Chilean territory, the Argentines should supply access to Isla Navarino for the Chileans.

This sounds reasonable enough, but Argentina's federal government (unlike Chile, which is a unitary state) has to deal with elected provincial authorities still obsessed with territoriality, as well as Ushuaia business interests who astonishingly fear a loss of commerce to flyspeck Puerto Williams. In practice, improved communications would probably encourage more tourists to stay longer in the area, and Puerto Williams shoppers to cross to Ushuaia, where prices are lower.

In early 2001, at the invitation of the Chilean navy, President Ricardo Lagos paid a visit to Puerto Williams in the company of Sernatur head Oscar Santelices and Argentine ambassador Daniel Olmos, but so far there have been no concrete transportation developments between Puerto Williams and Puerto Almanza. In December of 2001, though, Chile declared Puerto Navarino a port of entry for Chilean-flagged vessels, permitting day excursions from Ushuaia to the southern Beagle Channel fjords.

Because excursionists would have to stay in Argentina, there were hopes that this step would begin to satisfy Ushuaia interests who, apparently, worry that Puerto Williams might undermine Ushuaia's claim to be the world's southernmost city. Reportedly, a Chilean businessman purchased a catamaran for this purpose, but no further movement has taken place. Still, the situation bears watching.

Beagle Channel Boat Excursions

From the Muelle Turístico, at the foot of Lasserre, there are boat trips to Beagle Channel wildlife sites like **Isla de los Lobos,** home to the southern sea lion (*Otaria flavescens*) and the rarer southern fur seal (*Arctocephalus australis*), and **Isla de Pájaros,** a nesting site for seabirds, mostly cormorants. These excursions cost around US$18–25 for a 2.5-hour trip on oversized catamarans like the *Ana B, Ezequiel B,* and *Luciano Beta.* With extensions to the penguin colony at Estancia Harberton and a visit to the *estancia* itself, the cost is about US$50.

Rumbo Sur and Tolkeyén sell tickets for these excursions from offices at the foot of the Muelle Turístico, where Héctor Monsalve's **Tres Marías Excursiones** (tel./fax 02901/421897, marias3@satlink.com) operates four-hour trips on a smaller vessel (eight passengers maximum) that can get closer to Isla de Lobos than the large catamarans. They can also land on Isla Bridges, a small but diverse island with cormorant colonies, shellmounds, and even the odd penguin.

Ferrocarril Austral Fueguino

During Ushuaia's early days, prison labor built a short-line, narrow-gauge steam-driven railroad west into what is now Parque Nacional Tierra del Fuego to haul the timber that built the city. Only a few years ago, commercial interests rehabilitated part of the roadbed to create a gentrified, antiseptic tourist version of the earlier line that pretty much ignores the unsavory aspects of its history to focus on the admittedly appealing forest scenery of the Cañadon del Toro.

The train leaves from the **Estación del Fin del Mundo** (tel. 02901/431600, fax 02901/437696, ush@trendelfindelmundo.com.ar) eight kilometers west of Ushuaia at the municipal campground. From October to mid-April, there are four departures daily, while the rest of the year there are only two. The two-hour-plus excursion costs US$22 pp in tourist class, US$25 pp in first class, and US$75–100 pp with a buffet lunch or dinner.

Round-trip transportation from Ushuaia to the station costs US$5 pp with **Manuel Tienda León** (San Martín 995, tel. 02901/422222). Passengers can also use the buses from Ushuaia to Parque Nacional Tierra del Fuego.

Ski Areas

Ushuaia gets most of its visitors in summer, but it's becoming a winter-sports center as well, thanks to its proximity to the mountains. Downhill skiing, snowboarding, and cross-country skiing are all possible. There is also dog sledding.

The major annual ski event is the **Marcha Blanca,** which symbolically repeats Argentine liberator José de San Martín's heroic winter crossing of the Andes from Mendoza to assist his Chilean counterpart Bernardo O'Higgins against the Spaniards. Luring upward of 400 skiers, it starts from the Las Cotorras cross-country area and climbs to Paso Garibaldi, the 430-meter pass between the Sierra Alvear and the Sierra Lucas Bridges. It takes place in the second half of August, presumably on the 17th, the anniversary of San Martín's death (Argentine novelist Tomás

© WAYNE BERNHARDSON

view of the Beagle Channel from Glaciar Martial, Parque Nacional Tierra del Fuego

Eloy Martínez has called his countrymen "cadaver cultists" for their apparent obsession with celebrating death rather than birth dates of their national icons).

The nearest area, only three kilometers west of downtown, is the Club Andino's modest **Pista Andina Wolfgang Wallner,** which has a single lift, capable of carrying 300 skiers, and one 859-meter run on a 30° slope. For more information, contact the **Club Andino Ushuaia** (Juana Fadul 50, tel. 02901/422335). The principal downhill area, though, is the **Centro de Deportes Invernales Luis Martial** (tel. 02901/421423, 02901/423340, seven kilometers northwest of town at the end of the road, which has a single 1,130-meter run on a 23° slope, with a double-seat chairlift capable of carrying 224 skiers per hour.

Most of the areas east of Ushuaia, along RN 3, are for cross-country skiers: **Valle de los Huskies** (Km 17, tel. 02901/431902; **Tierra Mayor** (Km 21, tel. 02901/437454); **Las Cotorras** (Km 26, tel. 02901/499300); and **Haruwen** (Km 35, tel./fax 02901/424058). All of them rent equipment and offer transportation from Ushuaia.

The only downhill resort east of Ushuaia is the modern **Cerro Castor** (Km 27, castor@infovia.com.ar, www.cerrocastor.com), which has up-to-the-minute facilities, including four lifts and 15 different runs. Lift tickets cost US$18–25 per day, with discounts for multiday packages.

Estancia Harberton

Historic Harberton dates from 1886, when missionary pioneer Thomas Bridges resigned from the Anglican mission at Ushuaia to settle at his new *estancia* at Downeast, later renamed for the Devonshire home town of his wife Mary Ann Varder. Thomas Bridges, of course, was the author of the famous English-Yámana dictionary, and their son Lucas continued the family literary tradition with *The Uttermost Part of the Earth,* an extraordinary memoir of a boyhood and life among the Yámana.

Harberton continues to be a family enterprise—its present manager and part-owner, Tommy Goodall, is Thomas Bridges's great-grandson. While the livestock industry that spawned it has declined in recent years, the *estancia* has opened its doors to organized English- and Spanish-language tours of its grounds

© WAYNE BERNHARDSON

Estancia Harberton

Tierra del Fuego

and outbuildings; these include the family cemetery, flower gardens, the wool shed, woodshop, boathouse, and a native botanical garden whose Yámana-style lean-tos are far more realistic than their Disneyfied counterparts along the Ferrocarril Austral Fueguino tourist train.

In addition, Tommy Goodall's wife, American biologist Rae Natalie Prosser, has also created the **Museo Acatushún de Aves y Mamíferos Marinos Australes** (www.acatushun.com), a bone museum stressing the region's marine mammals but also seabirds and a few shorebirds; it's open 10 A.M.–7 P.M. daily, with guided tours for US$2 pp. It is also possible to visit Magellanic penguin rookeries at Isla Martillo (Yecapasela) with Piratur for US$18 pp; a small colony of gentoo penguins has recently established itself on the island, making this a more intriguing trip for those who've seen Magellanic penguins elsewhere.

Estancia Harberton (tel. 02901/422742, fax 029091/422743 in Ushuaia, estanciaharberton@tierradelfuego.org.ar) is 85 kilometers east of Ushuaia via paved RN 3 and gravel RC-j, but a new coastal road from Ushuaia is likely to shorten the distance soon. From mid-October to mid-April, the *estancia* is open for guided tours (US$3.50 pp) 10 A.M.–7 P.M. daily except Christmas, New Year's, and Easter.

With written permission, **camping** is permitted at unimproved sites; the *estancia* has also remodeled the former cookhouse (two rooms with four or five beds each and shared bath) and shepherds' house (two rooms of three beds with private bath), for US$60–80 pp, depending on the room.

Harberton's **Casa de Té Mánacatush** serves a tasty afternoon tea for US$4.50 pp, and serves lunch and dinner as well (US$11, reservations advised).

In summer, Transportes Pasarela and others provides round-trip transportation from Ushuaia (US$20–30 pp), but these services change frequently. Piratur offers a US$50 package that includes transportation, the farm and museum tour, and the penguin colony.

Catamaran tours from Ushuaia are more expensive and spend less time at Harberton, but do include the farm and museum tour fee.

PARQUE NACIONAL TIERRA DEL FUEGO

For pilgrims to the uttermost part of the earth, Parque Nacional Tierra del Fuego, where RN 3 ends at Bahía Lapataia, on the north shore of the Beagle Channel, is mecca. Despite its size, over 63,000 hectares, only relatively small parts of its mountainous interior, with its lakes, rivers, glaciers, and summits, are open to public access. Most visitors see only the area in and around the highway.

Geography and Climate

About 18 kilometers west of Ushuaia, Parque Nacional Tierra del Fuego hugs the Chilean border as its 63,000-hectare stretch from the shores of the Beagle Channel north across Lago Fagnano (Kami). Elevations range from sea level on the channel to 1,450 meters on the summit of Monte Vinciguerra.

hikers at Glaciar Martial

Tierra del Fuego

Most of the park has a maritime climate, with frequent high winds. While rainfall is moderate at about 750 millimeters per annum, humidity is fairly high, as relatively low temperatures also inhibit evapotranspiration—the summer average is only about 10°C. The record maximum temperature is 31°C, while the record minimum is a fairly mild -12°C. At sea level, snow rarely sticks for any length of time, but at higher elevations there are permanent snowfields and glaciers.

Flora and Fauna

As in southernmost Chile, thick southern beech forests cover the Argentine sector of Tierra del Fuego. Along the coast, the deciduous lenga (*Nothofagus pumilio*) and the Magellanic evergreen coigue (*Nothofagus betuloides*) are the main tree species, while the stunted, deciduous ñire (*Nothofagus antarctica*) forms nearly pure stands at higher elevations. In some low-lying areas, where cool annual temperatures do not permit complete decomposition, dead plant material compresses into *Sphagnum* peat bogs with a cover of ferns and other moisture-loving plants; the insectivorous *Drosera uniflora* swallows unsuspecting bugs.

Until recently Argentina's only protected coastal area, Parque Nacional Tierra del Fuego has a seashore protected by thick beds of kelp that serve as incubators for fish fry. Especially around Bahía Ensenada and Bahía Lapataia, the shoreline and inshore waters swarm with cormorants, grebes, gulls, kelp geese, oystercatchers, flightless and flying steamer ducks, snowy sheathbills, and terns. The maritime black-browed albatross skims the channel waters, while the Andean condor sometimes soars overhead. Marine mammals, mostly sea lions but also fur seals and elephant seals, cavort in the ocean. The rare southern sea otter (*Lutra felina*) may exist here.

Inland parts of the park are fauna-poor, though foxes and guanacos are present in small numbers. The most conspicuous mammals are the European rabbit (*Oryctolagus cunniculus*) and the Canadian beaver (*Castor canadiensis*), both of which were introduced for their pelts but have proved to be pests.

Sights and Activities

Within the park boundaries, but also within walking distance of Ushuaia, the **Glaciar Martial** is the area's best single hike, offering expansive views of the Beagle Channel and across to the jagged peaks of Chile's Isla Navarino. Reached not by RN 3 but rather by the zigzag Camino al Glaciar (also known as Luis Martial) that climbs northwest out of Ushuaia, the trailhead begins at the Aerosilla del Glaciar, the ski area's chairlift, that operates 10 A.M.–4:30 P.M. daily except Monday. The 1.2-kilometer chairlift, which charges US$2.50 pp, reduces the two-hour climb to the foot of the glacier by half; in summer are frequent buses to the lift (US$2.50–3 round-trip) with Pasarela, Eben Ezer, and Bellavista from the corner of Avenida Maipú and 25 de Mayo, between 9 A.M.–9 P.M. Though the straightforward trail itself is steep, especially the middle segment and the descent require particular caution because of loose rocks and soil. There is no admission charge to this sector of the park.

Where freshwater Lago Roca drains into the sea at Bahía Lapataia, the main sector of the park has several short nature trails and a handful of longer ones; most of the backcountry is off-limits to casual hikers. Slightly less than one kilometer long, the **Senda Laguna Negra** uses a boardwalk to negotiate boggy terrain, studded with ferns, wildflowers, and other water-tolerant species. The 400-meter **Senda de los Castores** (Beaver Trail) winds among southern beeches gnawed to death to form dams and ponds where the beavers themselves occasionally peek out of their dens.

From Lago Roca, the five-kilometer **Senda Hito XXIV** follows the lake's northeastern shore to a small obelisk that marks the Chilean border. If someday Argentine and Chilean authorities can get it together, this would be an ideal entry point to the wild backcountry of Estancia Yendegaia, but at present it's illegal to continue beyond the marker. From a junction about one kilometer up the Hito XXIV trail, **Senda Cerro Guanaco** climbs four kilometers northeast up the Arroyo Guanaco to the 970-meter summit of its namesake peak.

From Bahía Ensenada, near the southeastern edge of the park, there are boat excursions to **Isla Redonda** (US$14 pp) from 10 A.M.–5:30 P.M.

Accommodations and Food

Camping is the only option in the park itself, where there are free sites with little or no infrastructure at **Camping Ensenada, Camping Río Pipo, Camping Las Bandurrias, Camping Laguna Verde,** and **Camping Los Cauquenes.** The only paying site, which has hot showers, a grocery, and a *confitería,* is **Camping Lago Roca** (tel. 2901/445714, US$1.75 pp). The latter tends to be substantially cleaner than the free campgrounds, though the latter are improving.

Information

At the park entrance on RN 3, the APN has a Centro de Información where it collects an US$4.50 pp entry fee.

Several books have useful information on Parque Nacional Tierra del Fuego, including William Leitch's *South America's National Parks* (Seattle: The Mountaineers, 1990), which is now out of print; the fifth edition of Tim Burford's *Backpacking in Chile & Argentina* (Bradt Publications, 2001); and the third edition of Clem Lindenmayer's *Trekking in the Patagonian Andes* (Lonely Planet, 2003). The latter two are hiking guides.

Bird-watchers may want to acquire Claudio Venegas Canelo's *Aves de Patagonia y Tierra del Fuego Chileno-Argentina,* Ricardo Clark's *Aves de Tierra del Fuego y Cabo de Hornos* (Buenos Aires: Literature of Latin America, 1986), or Enrique Couve's and Claudio Vidal Ojeda's bilingual *Birds of the Beagle Channel* (Punta Arenas: Fantástico Sur Birding & Nature, 2000).

Getting There and Around

For details on transportation to and from the park, see Getting Around under Ushuaia earlier in this chapter.

⬛ PUERTO WILLIAMS (CHILE)

On the north shore of Isla Navarino, across the Beagle Channel from Argentine Tierra del Fuego, Puerto Williams is the so-called "Capital of Antarctica" and gateway to the rugged Los Dientes backcountry circuit, a difficult five-day hike through rugged soggy terrain. Local residents look forward to establishment of a permanent ferry link to nearby Argentina, but there is much political opposition across the channel because myopic Ushuaia impresarios fear losing business to tiny Williams—however unlikely that possibility.

Founded in the 1950s, formerly known as Puerto Luisa, the town (population 1,952) has paved sidewalks but gravel streets. Most of its residents are Chilean naval personnel living in relatively stylish prefabs, but there are also some 60 remaining descendants of the Yámana, of whom only about five speak the language—now a hybrid including many Spanish and English words—among themselves.

Sights

Overlooking the harbor is the **Proa del Escampavía Yelcho,** the prow of the famous cutter

directional signs in Puerto Williams, Isla Navarino, Chilean Tierra del Fuego

© WAYNE BERNHARDSON

Tierra del Fuego

which, at the command of Luis Pardo Villalón, rescued British Antarctic explorer Edward Shackleton's crew from Elephant Island, on the Antarctic Peninsula, in 1916. A national monument, the bow survived collisions with icebergs to get to its destination; returning to Punta Arenas, the entire ship makes a cameo appearance in original newsreel footage in British director George Butler's *Endurance,* an extraordinary documentary of the Shackleton expedition.

Very professional for a small-town museum, the **Museo Martin Gusinde** has small exhibits on geology, economic plants, and taxidermy, a marker for the former post office, and a sign for the coal mine at Caleta Banner, on nearby Isla Picton, which provisioned the *Yelcho* on its mission to rescue Shackleton's crew. Admission costs US$1.75 pp; nearby is the **Parque Botánico Omora,** an organized selection of native plants.

Built in Germany for operations on the Rhine, the **MV Micalvi** shipped supplies between remote *estancias* and other settlements before sinking in Puerto Williams's inner harbor in 1962; the upper deck and bridge remain as the yacht club's bar/restaurant.

Practicalities

The **Pingüino Pub** is at the Centro Comercial.

Pensión Temuco (Piloto Pardo 224, tel. 061/621113) charges US$12.50 pp with shared bath, US$17 pp with private bath, and also serves meals. Try also the nearby **Residencial Pusaky** (Piloto Pardo 242, tel. 061/621116).

Refugio Coirón (Ricardo Maragaño 168, tel. 061/621227, coiron@simltd.com, US$13 pp) has very good accommodations with kitchen privileges and shared bath. It's a better choice than the friendly but basic **Hostería Onashaga** (Uspachún 290, tel. 061/621081), which costs US$15 pp for multibedded rooms with shared bath; those with private bath go for US$33 d. Lunch or dinner costs US$3.

South America's southernmost bar/restaurant, the **Club de Yates Micalvi,** occupies the main deck and the bridge of the historic vessel that lies grounded in Puerto Williams's inner harbor.

Nearly all of Puerto Williams's services are concentrated around the Centro Comercial, a cluster of storefronts just uphill from the Muelle Guardián Brito, the main passenger pier. These include the post office, several telephone offices, **Banco de Chile,** the Cema-Chile crafts shop, and **Manualidades,** which rents mountain bikes.

DAP (tel. 061/621051), at the Centro Comercial, flies 20-seat Twin Otters to Punta Arenas (US$64) Tuesday, Thursday, and Saturday from April to October. The rest of the year, flights leave daily except Sunday. DAP flights are often heavily booked, so make reservations as far in advance as possible.

Regular boat connections between Puerto Williams and Ushuaia, on Argentine Tierra del Fuego, continue to be problematical, but hitching a lift across the channel with a yacht is feasible—for a price. For up-to-date information, contact the **Gobernación Marítima** (tel. 061/621090), the **Club de Yates** (tel. 061/621041, int. 4250), or **Turismo Sim** (tel. 061/621150).

In summer, the ferry *Patagonia* sails to Punta Arenas (38 hours) Friday at 7 P.M. Fares are US$150 in a bunk, US$120 for a seat.

VICINITY OF PUERTO WILLIAMS

The German-Venezuelan **Sea, Ice & Mountains Adventures Unlimited** (Austral 74, tel. 061/621150, fax 061/621227, coiron@simltd.com, www.simtld.com) organizes trekking, climbing, and riding expeditions on Isla Navarino and the Cordillera Darwin, week-long yacht excursions around the Beagle Channel and to Cape Horn, and even Antarctica. Advance booking is advisable.

The Coastal Road

From Puerto Williams, a coastal road runs 54 kilometers west to the village of Puerto Navarino, now a legal port of entry, and 28 kilometers east to Caleta Eugenia; only two kilometers east of Williams, **Villa Ukika** is the last refuge of the Yámana. From Caleta Eugenia, the road is gradually advancing southeast to **Puerto Toro,** where some 60 boats employ about four persons each in search of *centolla* (king crab).

Cordón de los Dientes

Immediately south of Puerto Williams, Cordón de los Dientes is a range of jagged peaks rising more than 1,000 meters above sea level that offers the world's southernmost trekking opportunities. There are, however, few trails through this rugged countryside—anyone undertaking the four- to five-day "circuit" should be experienced in route-finding.

RÍO GRANDE (ARGENTINA)

Most visitors who stay in and around Río Grande, on the Isla Grande's barren, blustery Atlantic shoreline, do so for the fishing. For the rest, the once-desolate city is more a point of transit than a destination in itself, but thanks to smoothly paved streets, the huge dust clouds that once blew through this wool and oil town have subsided. There are limits to beautification, though, as all the trees planted in Plaza Almirante Brown are stiffly wind-flagged.

Bus schedules used to dictate that travelers pass the night here, but recent improvements mean quicker connections to Ushuaia for overland travelers. Still, services have improved, and there's enough to do that an afternoon spent here need not be a wasted one.

Orientation

On the north bank of its namesake river, Río Grande (population 52,786) is 79 kilometers southeast of the Chilean border post at San Sebastián and 190 kilometers northeast of Ushuaia via RN 3, which is still unpaved between Tolhuin and Rancho Hambre. As of writing, the mountainous section between Tolhuin and the Hostería Petrel turnoff was still a loose gravel surface on which cracked windshields were a daily event, and the blinding dust kicked up by every vehicle makes this one of the country's most hazardous roads.

RN 3 bypasses the compact city center, which is reached by southeasterly Avenida San Martín, the main commercial street. Most services are within a few blocks of the axis formed by San Martín and the perpendicular Avenida Manuel Belgrano, which leads east toward the waterfront.

Sights

Río Grande's **Museo de La Ciudad Virginia Choquintel** does a lot with a little, with good materials on natural history, surprisingly sophisticated exhibits on ethnology and aboriginal subsistence, and historic displays on maps and mapmaking, the evolution of communications on the island, and astronomical science. Now occupying the former storehouses of the Asociación Rural de Tierra del Fuego, the **Museo de la Ciudad** (Alberdi 553, tel. 02962/430647) is open 10 A.M.–5 P.M. weekdays and 3–7 P.M. Saturday.

Río Grande has few architectural landmarks—or few buildings of any antiquity, for that matter—but the **Obras Sanitarias** (1954) waterworks tower (Lasserre 386) at the northeast corner of the plaza, dates from the Juan Perón era.

Entertainment

El Cine 1 & 2 (Perito Moreno 211, tel. 02962/433260) shows current films in modern facilities, but sometimes turns up the volume to excruciating levels—bring or improvise ear plugs, just in case.

La Guanaca (Lasserre 592) is an informal, low-key bar with live music.

Accommodations

Accommodations are fairly scarce, but there are good values, particularly at the budget end. Nearly every mid- to upscale place offers a 10 percent discount for payment in cash.

Río Grande's first backpackers' hostel, at the south end of town, is the promising **Hotel Argentino** (San Martín 64, tel. 02964/422546, hotelargentino@yahoo.com, US$6 pp). It gets especially high marks from cyclists; standards are good for B&B with shared bath, there are kitchen facilities and other usable common spaces, and they'll fetch guests from the bus terminal for free.

Perhaps the next best value in town, cozy **Hotel Rawson** (J.M. Estrada 750, tel. 02954/430352, US$7.50/12 s/d) has smallish rooms with private bath. The simple but spotless, family-run **Hospedaje Noal,** (Obligado 557, tel. 02954/427515, US$13 d) has spacious rooms with shared bath but plenty of closet space and good beds.

Close to the bus terminal, the seaside **Hotel Isla del Mar** (Güemes 936, tel. 02964/422883, fax 02964/427283, isladelmar@arnet.com.ar, US$20/24 s/d) is frayed, rather than just worn around the edges, what with loose doorknobs, scuffed walls, and slowly eroding wooden built-ins. Still, it exudes a certain funky charm, even if "seaview" is a relative term here—with Río Grande's enormous tidal range, the ocean sometimes seems to be on the distant horizon. Rates include breakfast, and there's a cash discount.

A glass palace that looks out of place in Río Grande, **Hotel Atlántida** (Avenida Belgrano 582, tel./fax 02964/431914, atlantida@netcombbs.com.ar, US$25/30 s/d) has decent rooms, but it's also well worn. Beds are softer than some might prefer in the aging but tidy rooms at **Hotel Federico Ibarra** (Rosales 357, tel. 02964/430071, US$31/38 s/d), but it's worth consideration with breakfast and a 10 percent cash discount.

Río Grande's most professional operation, **M** **Posada de los Sauces** (Elcano 839, tel. 02964/432895, info@posadadelossauces.com, US$35/43 s/d) is easily the top of the line. One of the suite bathrooms is large enough for a hot-tub party, and the restaurant is far and away the city's most elegant.

Food
La Nueva Piamontesa (Belgrano and Mackinlay, tel. 02964/424366) is a longstanding favorite for varied and delicate baked empanadas and the pizzas in its deli; it has an inexpensive sit-down restaurant as well, open 24/7.

Two other places specialize in pizza and pasta: **Café Sonora** (Perito Moreno 705) and **La Nueva Colonial** (Fagnano 669).

Leymi (25 de Mayo 1335, tel. 02964/421683) serves fixed-price lunches for about US$3, and has a broad menu of *parrillada*, pasta, and other short orders. **El Rincón de Julio** (Elcano 805, tel. 02964/15-604261) is a hole-in-the-wall *parrilla*, highly regarded by locals, with lunch-counter-style service.

Mamá Flora (Avenida Belgrano and Rafael Obligado) is a good breakfast choice that also has coffee and exquisite chocolates. There are two outstanding ice creameries on the plaza: **Limoncello** (Rosal and Fagnano, tel. 02964/420134) and **Lusso** (Fagnano and Lasserre).

Several upscale hotels have their own restaurants, most notably the **Posada de los Sauces** (Elcano 839, tel. 02964/430868), which deserves special mention for superb service, the cooked-to-order *lomo a la pimienta* (pepper steak, US$6), and a complementary glass of wine. There's also a 10 percent cash discount.

Information
Río Grande's municipal **Oficina de Información Turística** (Rosales 350, tel. 02964/431324, rg-turismo@netcombbs.com.ar) is a kiosk on Plaza Almirante Brown; open 9 A.M.–9 P.M. daily in summer, 9 A.M.–8 P.M. weekdays, and 10 A.M.–5 P.M. Saturday the rest of the years, it's exceptionally helpful.

The provincial **Instituto Fueguino de Turismo** (Infuetur, Belgrano 319, tel. 02962/422887, infuerg@satlink.com) is open 10 A.M.–4 P.M. weekdays only.

Services
Cambio Thaler (Rosales 259) is the only exchange house. Banks with ATMs include **Banco de Tierra del Fuego** (San Martín 193), **Banco Macro Bansud** (Rosales 241), and **Banca Nazionale del Lavoro** (San Martín 194).

Correo Argentino (Rivadavia 968) is two blocks west of San Martín; the postal code is 9420. **Locutorio Cabo Domingo** (Avenida San Martín 458) has long-distance services, while **Telefónica** (San Martín and 9 de Julio) has Internet access.

El Lavadero (Perito Moreno 221) does the washing.

For medical services, the **Hospital Regional** is at Ameghino s/n (tel. 02954/422088).

Getting There
Aerolíneas Argentinas/Austral (San Martín 607, tel. 02964/422748) flies daily to Río Gallegos. **LADE** (Lasserre 447, tel. 02964/421651)

flies with some frequency to Río Gallegos, less frequently to El Calafate, Gobernador Gregores, Perito Moreno, and Comodoro Rivadavia.

Río Grande's **Terminal de Buses** (Avenida Belgrano 16, tel. 421339) is near the waterfront, but some companies have offices elsewhere in town.

At the main terminal, **Lider** (tel. 02964/420003), **Transportes Montiel** (tel. 02964/420997), and **Tolkeyén** (tel. 02964/427354) have multiple departures to Tolhuín (US$3.50) and Ushuaia (US$7.50). **Buses Pacheco** (tel. 02964/425611) goes to Punta Arenas, Chile (US$18, eight hours) Monday, Wednesday, and Friday at 10:30 A.M.

Tecni-Austral (Moyano 516, tel. 02964/430610) goes to Punta Arenas Monday, Wednesday, and Friday at 10:30 A.M., to Río Gallegos (US$20, eight hours) via Chile the same days at 9:30 A.M., and to Ushuaia (US$9, four hours) Tuesday, Thursday, and Saturday at 10 A.M.

Getting Around

City bus Línea C goes directly to **Aeropuerto Internacional Río Grande** (tel. 02964/420600), a short distance west of downtown on RN 3, for US$.50. It's also a reasonable cab ride.

Ansa International (AI, Ameghino 612, tel. 02964/422657) rents cars and pickup trucks.

VICINITY OF RÍO GRANDE

As the area surrounding Río Grande does not have a well-developed transport infrastructure, hiring a vehicle is worth consideration.

Reserva Provincial Costa Atlántica

From Cabo Nombre, at the north end of Bahía San Sebastián, to the mouth of the Río Ewan southeast of Río Grande, the Isla Grande's entire shoreline is a major bird sanctuary because of the abundance of plovers and sandpipers, some of which migrate yearly between the Arctic and South America (the sanctuary's full name is Reserva Provincial Costa Atlántica de Tierra del Fuego). Near the San Sebastián border post is the privately owned **Refugio de Vida Silvestre Dicky,** a prime wetland habitat of 1,900 hectares.

FISHING IN FUEGIA

Fishing for Atlantic salmon, brown trout, and rainbow trout is a popular pastime throughout Argentine Tierra del Fuego, but the rules are a little intricate. In the first instance, there are separate licenses for Parque Nacional Tierra del Fuego and for the rest of the island, and fees differ for residents of the province, nonresidents of the province, and foreigners.

For fishing within the park, licenses are available only from the APN in Ushuaia; rates are US$5 per day or US$20 per season (November to mid-April) for residents. For nonresidents or foreigners, rates are US$11 per day, US$53 per week, or US$71 per season. Children under age 18 pay US$3.50 and retired Argentine citizens pay nothing.

For fishing outside the park boundaries, daily rates vary depending on the river, but range from US$18–35 for foreigners; there's a 15-day license for US$35–70, and monthly rates are US$71–140. Fuegian residents and Argentines pay a fraction of these rates.

In Ushuaia, licenses are available at the **Asociación Caza y Pesca** (Maipú 822, tel. 02901/423168, cazpescush@infoviar.com.ar), or **Óptica Eduardo's** (San Martín 830, tel. 02901/433252). In Río Grande, contact the **Club de Pesca John Goodall** (Ricardo Rojas 606, tel. 02964/424324).

Museo Salesiano

One exception to the area's lack of historic sites is the Salesian museum, on the grounds of a mission founded by the order to catechize the Selknam; after the aboriginals died out from unintentionally introduced diseases and intentional outright slaughter, the fathers turned their attention to educating rural youth in their boarding school. The well-preserved **Capilla** (chapel) is a national historical monument, but the rest of the Magellanic-style structures need renovation, and the museum collections, dealing with natural history and ethnography, need organization and preservation.

About 11 kilometers north of Río Grande the Museo Salesiano (RN 3 Km 2980, tel. 02964/

421642, US$1 adults, US$.50 children) is open 10 A.M.–12:30 P.M. and 3–7 P.M. daily except Sunday, when it keeps afternoon hours only. From Río Grande, Línea B goes hourly to the mission from 7:30 A.M.–8:30 P.M.

Historic Estancias

Several of the region's largest and most important *estancias* are in the vicinity of Río Grande. Founded by the Menéndez dynasty's Sociedad Explotadora de Tierra del Fuego, **Estancia María Behety,** 17 kilometers west via gravel RC-c, is the site of the world's largest shearing shed.

Also Sociedad Explotadora property, **Estancia José Menéndez,** 25 kilometers southwest of town via RN 3 and RC-b, is one of the island's most historic ranches; RC-b continues west to an obscure summer border crossing at **Radman,** where few visitors of any kind cross the line to Lago Blanco on the Chilean side.

For potential overnighters, though, the gem is the Simon Goodall family's **M Estancia Viamonte** (tel. 02964/430861, info@estanciaviamonte .com, www.estanciaviamonte.com), its Sea View Guest House is the only place on the island that can offer the opportunity to sleep in Lucas Bridges's bedroom. Directly on RN 3, about 42 kilometers southeast of Río Grande, it fronts on a bird-rich beach; the house itself can sleep up to six people with two shared baths, plus living and dining rooms. There are extensive gardens, and chances for fishing, riding, and farm activities.

Lago Fagnano (Kami)

Named for the Salesian priest who headed the Salesian evangelical effort among the Selknam,

THE FALKLAND ISLANDS

In 1982, Britain and Argentina fought a 10-week war over the isolated Falkland Islands (which Argentines claim as the Malvinas) that ended in a decisive British victory and the end of a brutal military dictatorship. The territorial dispute has not disappeared, but in the interim the islands have become an important destination for a select group of international travelers interested primarily in sub-Antarctic wildlife.

What the Falklands can offer, 500 kilometers east of the continent in the open South Atlantic, is six species of penguins, including easy access to the uncommon king and gentoo, marine mammals including elephant seals, sea lions, and fur seals; there are many more birds, with enormous nesting colonies of black-browed albatrosses and several species of cormorants. Most of these are not easily seen on the continent, and many of them would normally require a trip to Antarctica.

For several years after the war, the only way to reach the islands was an expensive Royal Air Force flight from England, but for the last several years LanChile has offered Saturday flights to and from Punta Arenas; one flight per month picks up and drops off passengers in the Argentine city of Río Gallegos. Cruise ships pay frequent visits in the southern summer as well.

Despite their small population, only about 2,000, the islands have good tourist infrastructure in the capital city of Stanley and at wildlife sites in offshore island farms that are the local equivalent of Argentine and Chilean *estancias*. The big drawback is that most, though not all, of these sites are accessible by relatively expensive internal flights on small planes.

Because of complicated logistics, visitors heading from the continent to the islands should consider arranging an itinerary in advance to take maximum advantage of their time—accommodations are relatively few and internal flights have limited capacity. Contact **International Tours and Travel** (P.O. Box 408, Stanley, Falkland Islands, tel. 500/22041, fax 500/22042, se.itt@horizon.co.fk).

For further information, consult the Falkland Islands Tourist Board's thorough, well-organized website, www.tourism.org.fk.

this elongated body of water fills a structural depression that stretches across the Chilean border to the west. Also known by its Selknam name, Kami, its shoreline is nearly 200 kilometers long and its surface covers nearly 600 square kilometers.

The most westerly part of the lake, along the Chilean border, belongs to Parque Nacional Tierra del Fuego, but is virtually inaccessible except by boat. As might be expected, the lake is popular with fishing enthusiasts.

At the moment, since the closure of Hostería Kaikén at the east end of the lake, the main accommodations this side of Ushuaia are Lago Escondido's **Hostería Petrel** (RN 3 Km 3186, tel. 02901/433569, hpetrel@infovia.com.ar, US$43 d), which has lakeview rooms with hot tubs and a restaurant that's a popular stopover for tour groups.

At the east end of the lake, about midway between Río Grande and Ushuaia, pilgrims stop at Tolhuin to taste the goods at **Panadería la Unión,** a bakery whose celebrity visitors have ranged from ex-President Carlos Menem to folk-rocker León Gieco, hard-rockers Los Caballeros de la Quema, and actress China Zorrilla. It has the usual bread but loads of *facturas* (pastries), *alfajores,* and sandwiches; what it

lacks, astonishingly, is coffee other than machine-dispensed instant.

PORVENIR (CHILE)

Chilean Tierra del Fuego's main town, Porvenir sits on a sheltered harbor on the east side of the Strait of Magellan. Local settlement dates from the 1880s, when the area experienced a brief gold rush, but stabilized with the establishment of wool *estancias* around the turn of the century. After the wool boom fizzled in the 1920s, it settled into an economic torpor that, ironically enough, has left it a remarkable assortment of corroding metal-clad Magellanic buildings.

Porvenir's inner harbor is a great place for spotting kelp geese, gulls, cormorants, steamer ducks, and other seabirds, but its main tourist role has been as a gateway to the Argentine sector of the Isla Grande. This may change as small local enterprises begin to provide access to parts of the archipelago that, up to now, have been accessible only through expensive cruises.

Only 30 nautical miles east of Punta Arenas, Porvenir (population 4,734) occupies a protected site at the east end of Bahía Porvenir, an inlet of the Strait of Magellan. Its port, though, is three

wool truck at Porvenir ferry dock, Chilean Tierra del Fuego

© WAYNE BERNHARDSON

kilometers west of the town proper, whose mostly regular grid occupies a sloping south-facing site centered on the Plaza de Armas.

From Porvenir Ruta 215, a smooth gravel road, leads south and then east along the shore of Bahía Inútil to the Argentine border at San Sebastián, 150 kilometers away; an alternate route leads directly east through the Cordón Baquedano before rejoining Ruta 215 about 55 kilometers to the east. If it's too late to catch the ferry back to Punta Arenas, another gravel road follows the coast to Puerto Espora, 141 kilometers to the northeast.

Sights

Directly on the water, **Parque Yugoslavo** is a memorial to the earliest gold-seeking immigrants, most of whom were Croatians; it's also one of the best spots in town for bird-watching. The tourist office provides a small map/brochure, in English, of the city's distinctive architectural heritage; many of its houses and other buildings were Croatian-built.

Most public buildings surround the neatly landscaped **Plaza de Armas,** two blocks north of Parque Yugoslavo. Among them is the ex-

panded and improved **Museo de Tierra del Fuego Fernando Rusque Cordero** (Zavattaro 402, tel. 061/580098, US$.80), a regional museum that deals with the island's natural history, indigenous heritage, the early gold rush, the later but longer-lasting wool rush, and even cinematography—German-born local filmmaker José Bohr actually went to Hollywood in 1929, and enjoyed a long if inconsistent career. It has added a skillfully done replica of an early rural store, and a good photographic display on local architecture.

The museum takes its name from a Carabineros officer who helped found it—and was no doubt responsible for the permanent exhibit on police uniforms. Hours are 9 A.M.–5 P.M. weekdays; in January and February only, weekend hours are 10:30 A.M.–1:30 P.M. and 3–5 P.M.

Accommodations and Food

Rates at **Hotel España** (Croacia 698, tel. 061/ 580160, US$8.50–10 pp) depend on whether the room has shared or private bath. It also has a restaurant, but breakfast costs extra. **Residencial Colón** (Damián Riobó 198, tel. 061/ 581157, US$8.50 pp) and **Hostal los Canelos**

Plaza de Armas, Porvenir

© WAYNE BERNHARDSON

(Croacia 356, tel. 061/580247, US$8.50 pp) are comparable.

Hotel Central (Philippi 295, tel. 061/580077, US$15–18 s, US$28–32 d) also varies according to shared or private bath, but rates include breakfast. All rooms at **Hotel Rosas** (Philippi 296, tel. 02901/580088, US$22/30 s/d) have private bath and include breakfast; its restaurant is one of the best values in a town with, admittedly, only a few options.

Hostería Los Flamencos (Teniente Merino s/n, tel. 061/580049, US$35–42 s, US$44–54 d, ventas@hosterialosflamencos.com) has undergone a recent rehab, including much-needed interior and exterior paint, but it kept prices reasonable for what it offers. The higher rates are from peak season, October to April.

Other than hotel restaurants, the main dining options are the basic **Puerto Montt** (Croacia 1199, tel. 061/580207), the very decent waterfront **Club Social Croata** (Señoret 542, tel. 580053), and the **Club Social Catef** (Zavattaro 94, tel. 061/581399). **El Chispa** (Señoret 202, tel. 061/580054) is a *picada*, a Chilean term that denotes good home cooking at moderate prices.

Information

Porvenir's steadily improving **Oficina Municipal de Turismo,** in the museum building at Padre Mario Zavattaro 434 (tel. 061/580098, int. 324, muniporvenir@terra.cl) is open 8:30 A.M.–5 P.M. weekdays except Friday, when it closes at 4 P.M. Weekend hours are 11 A.M.–2 P.M. and 3–5 P.M. If emailing them, include *asunto turismo* in the header.

Information is also available at the kiosk on the Costanera between Mardones and Muñoz Gamero.

Services

Banco del Estado (Philippi 263) is the only option for changing money.

Correos de Chile is at Phillipi 176, at the southwest corner of the Plaza de Armas. The **Compañía Chilena de Teléfonos** is at Philippi 277.

For medical services, the **Hospital Porvenir** is at Carlos Wood s/n, between Señoret and Guerrero (tel. 061/580034).

Getting There and Around

Porvenir has regular but infrequent connections to the mainland and to Argentina.

Aerovías DAP (Manuel Señoret s/n and Muñoz Gamero, tel. 061/580089) operates air-taxi service to Punta Arenas (US$23) at least daily, often more frequently.

Unfortunately, there are no longer regular buses between Porvenir and Río Grande, on the Argentine side, so hitching is the only option. Tuesday and Friday at 4 P.M., there's a free municipal bus from the DAP offices on Señoret to Camerón and Timaukel (2.5 hours), in the southwestern corner of the island; another goes to Cerro Sombrero (1.5 hours) at 5 P.M. Monday, Wednesday, and Friday from Santos Mardones 330.

There are also buses to Camerón and Timaukel (US$6, 2.5 hours) Monday, Wednesday, and Friday at 5 P.M.; these leave from the DAP offices on Señoret.

In the same office as DAP, **Transbordadora Broom** (Manuel Señoret s/n, tel. 061/580089) sails the car-passenger ferry *Melinka* to Punta Arenas (2.5 hours) Tuesday, Thursday, and Saturday at 1 P.M., Wednesday and Friday at 2 P.M., and Sunday and holidays at 5 P.M. The ferry leaves from Bahía Chilote, about three kilometers west of town. For fares, see the Punta Arenas section.

VICINITY OF PORVENIR

Vicinity is a relative term on Tierra del Fuego, as some fascinating locales are exceptionally difficult—or expensive—to reach. **Cordillera Darwin, Ltda.** (Croacia 675, tel. 061/580296, cell 09/6407204, info@explorepatagonia.cl, www.explorepatagonia.cl) does brief launch tours around Bahía Chilote, three-day horseback excursions to the Río Cóndor, and a six-day trip to the Cordillera Darwin that's substantially cheaper than the only other option, the week-long luxury cruise on the *Mare Australis* (see The Fjords of Fuegia section for details).

Monumento Natural Laguna de los Cisnes

Bird-watching groups often make a detour to this 25-hectare saline lake reserve, which sometimes dries out, just north of Porvenir. While it takes its name from the elegant black-necked swan, it's also home to many other species.

Cordón Baquedano

After Chilean naval officer Ramón Serrano Montaner found gold in the rolling hills east of Porvenir in 1879, goldpanners from Chile and Croatia flocked to the valley of the Río del Oro, between the Cordón Baquedano and the Sierra Boquerón. Living in sod huts that insulated them from the wind and cold, in hopes of eking out a kilogram per year—though yields were usually smaller—more than 200 worked the placers until they gave out and, by the turn of the century, dredges and steam shovels replaced them. Decreasing yields ended the rush by 1908–09, though a few individuals hang on even today.

Estancia Yendegaia and Cordillera Darwin, Chilean Tierra del Fuego

From Porvenir, the eastbound road through the Cordón Baquedano passes several of these gold-rush sites, some of them with interpretive panels; the literal high point is the **Mirador de la Isla,** an overlook 500 meters above sea level. In many places guanacos, which seem to outnumber sheep, gracefully vault meter-high fences that stop the sheep cold.

Onaisín

About 100 kilometers east of Porvenir, a major north-south road crosses Ruta 215 at Onaisín, a former Sociedad Explotadora *estancia* whose **Cementerio Inglés** is a national historical monument. Northbound, the road goes to the petroleum company town of Cerro Sombrero, while southbound it goes to Camerón and Lago Blanco.

Lago Blanco

Some 50 kilometers southwest of Onaisín, the road passes through **Camerón,** a well-preserved former *estancia* that is now a municipality, then angles southeast to Lago Blanco, an area known for its fishing and, until recently, a speculative and controversial project for native forest exploitation by the US-based Trillium Corporation. In summer, there's a bumpy border crossing to Río Grande, Argentina, via a dirt road with many livestock gates and a ford of the Río Rasmussen. The Argentine border post is called Radman.

On Isla Victoria, in the middle of Lago Blanco, **Lodge de Pesca Isla Victoria** (tel. 061/241197, US$144/174 s/d) caters to fly-fishermen.

Estancia Yendegaia

Visited primarily by Chilean cruise ships and private yachts, Estancia Yendegaia conserves 44,000 hectares of native Fuegian forest in the Cordillera Darwin between the Argentine border and Parque Nacional Alberto de Agostini. While the owners hope to establish a private national park and create an unbroken preservation corridor along the Beagle Channel (Yendegaia borders Argentina's Parque Nacional Tierra del Fuego), there is government pressure to pave the *estancia's* airstrip at Caleta María, at the northern end of the property, and a road south from Lago Blanco is already under construction. The owners, for their part, would rather see the border opened to foot traffic from Argentina, but they have consulted with public works officials to minimize the road's environmental impact.

In the meantime, the *estancia* is open to visitors—though access is difficult without chartering a plane or boat or taking an expensive tour like the *Mare Australis* cruise through the Fuegian fjords; even this stops only on occasion. While naval boats between Punta Arenas and Puerto Williams may drop passengers here, these are infrequent enough that getting back could be a problem. In the near future, there should be accommodations available.

CERRO SOMBRERO (CHILE)

About 70 kilometers north of Onaisín and 43 kilometers south of the Puerto Espora ferry landing, Cerro Sombrero is a company town where employees of Chile's Empresa Nacional de Petróleo (ENAP, National Petroleum Company) reside in orderly surroundings with remarkable amenities for a town with only about 150 houses. Dating from the early 1960s, it has an astronomical observatory, a bank, a botanical garden, a cinema, a hospital, recreational facilities including a heated swimming pool, and restaurants. Buses between Río Grande and Punta Arenas take a meal break at **Restaurant El Conti,** just outside town.

Magallanes Region (Chile)

Chilean Patagonia's exact boundaries are imprecise because, in a sense, the region exists only in the imagination. In Chile, Patagonia has no juridical reality, though nearly everybody would agree that both Region XI (Aisén) and Region XII (Magallanes) are at least part of it. Other more northerly areas would like to be included, if only to partake of the Patagonian mystique; this section, though, covers only Magallanes, a popular destination in an area where travelers cross borders frequently.

Chile's most southerly region has acquired international fame thanks to the Torres del Paine, the magnificent granite needles that rise above the Patagonian plains. Pacific storms drench the nearly uninhabited western Andean cordillera, feeding alpine and continental glaciers and rushing rivers, but rolling grasslands and seemingly unstoppable winds typify the eastern areas in the Andean rain shadow. Along the Strait of Magellan, the city of Punta Arenas is the center for excursions to a variety of attractions, including easily accessible penguin colonies and Tierra del Fuego's remote fjords. The region has no direct road connections to the rest of Chile—travelers must arrive by air, sea, and through Argentine Patagonia.

Administratively, Region XII (Magallanes) includes all Chilean territory beyond 49° S—

theoretically all the way to the South Pole, as Chile claims a slice of Antarctica between 53° and 90° W longitude. It also takes in the Chilean half of the Isla Grande de Tierra del Fuego, west of about 68° 35', and most of archipelagic Tierra del Fuego.

Over the past decade, improved cross-border communications have meant that many visitors to the Argentine side also visit Chile to see Puerto Natales, Torres del Paine, and other Chilean attractions. While prices are presently higher in Chile than in Argentina, they are also stable and, after the initial surprise, most visitors adapt accordingly.

As in Argentina, January and February are the peak months, and prices drop considerably in the off-season—though many places also close. Like El Calafate, the area enjoys a lengthening tourist season.

History

Some of the oldest archaeological evidence for human habitation on the entire continent comes from Magallanes, from volcanic rock shelters in and near Parque Nacional Pali Aike on the Argentine border. Pleistocene hunter-gatherers once stalked now-extinct species like giant ground sloths and native American horses, but later adopted more broad spectrum forms of subsistence that included marine and coastal resources. These peoples were the predecessors of today's few surviving Tehuelche and Kawasqar (Alacaluf) peoples, and the nearly extinct Selknam (Ona) and Yámana (Yahgan) who gathered shellfish on the coast and hunted guanaco and rhea with bows and arrows and *boleadoras.*

European familiarity with southernmost South America dates from 1520, when the Portuguese navigator Fernando Magalhaes, in the service of Spain, sailed through the strait that now bears his name (Magallanes in Spanish, Magellan in English). Ranging from three to 25 kilometers in width, the Strait of Magellan became a major maritime thoroughfare en route to the Pacific.

Spain's 16th-century colonization attempts failed miserably, as did the initial Chilean and Argentine efforts, but the city of Punta Arenas finally took hold after 1848—thanks largely to the fortuitous discovery of gold in California only a year later. While gold fever soon subsided, the introduction of sheep brought a wool and mutton boom that benefited from the Franco-Prussian War of the 1870s, and led to the creation of enormous *estancias* that dominated the region's political, social, and economic life for nearly a century.

While the livestock industry hangs on, commercial fisheries, the state-run oil industry and the tourist trade have superseded it in the regional economy. Even these industries, though, have proved vulnerable to fluctuations, declining reserves, and international developments beyond their control, so that Magallanes cannot count on the prosperity that once seemed assured. The Zona Franca free-trade zone that once fueled the regional economy, even drawing immigrants from central Chile, has largely stagnated.

TRAVEL IN CHILE

Many visitors to Argentine Patagonia also cross the border into Chilean Patagonia and Tierra del Fuego. In fact, anyone traveling overland to Argentine Tierra del Fuego *must* pass through Chile, though air passengers can avoid Argentina's smaller neighbor. Not that they would necessarily want to, as there's plenty to see and do there.

Because so many travelers to Patagonia visit bordering Magallanes and the Chilean side of Tierra del Fuego, key destinations like Punta Arenas, Parque Nacional Torres del Paine, and Puerto Williams are covered in detail in this book. For details on the rest of the country, see *Moon Handbooks Chile.*

Visas and Officialdom

Very few nationalities need advance visas, but requirements can change—if in doubt, check Chilean consulates in Río Gallegos, Río Grande, or Ushuaia. Ordinarily, border officials grant foreign tourists an automatic 90-day entry permit, but if arriving by air some nationalities must pay a so-called reciprocity fee, equivalent to what their own countries charge Chileans for a visa application.

In the case of U.S. citizens, for instance, it's a hefty US$100.

The paramilitary Carabineros (Border Guards) serve as both immigration and customs officials at some Patagonian crossings; at the larger ones, most notably San Sebastián (Tierra del Fuego) and Monte Aymond (south of Río Gallegos), the Policía Internacional (International Police), the Servicio Nacional de Aduanas (National Customs Service), and the Servicio Agrícola y Ganadero (SAG, Agriculture and Livestock Service) have separate presences. Fresh fruit is the biggest taboo, but electronic items like video cameras sometimes attract their attention.

Health

Chile requires no vaccinations for visitors entering from any country, and public health standards are high. As in Argentina, both Chagas' disease and hantavirus are present, but health risks in Patagonia and Tierra del Fuego are small indeed.

Money and Prices

Until the Argentine economic meltdown of early

ⓜ PUNTA ARENAS

Patagonia's largest city, Punta Arenas is also the regional capital and the traditional port of entry, whether by sea, land, or air. Stretching north-south along the Strait of Magellan, the city boasts an architectural heritage that ranges from the Magellanic vernacular of metal-clad houses with steeply pitched roofs to elaborate Francophile mansions erected by 19th-century wool barons. It is home to several museums and is a good base for excursions to historical sites and nearby penguin colonies.

Punta Arenas has a diverse economy that depends on fishing, shipping, petroleum, duty-free retail and tourism. Historically, it's one of the main gateways to Antarctica for both research and tourism, but in recent years the Argentine port of Ushuaia has taken away much of this traffic. Ironically, in a region where there are millions of sheep, it's hard to find woolens here because of the influx of artificial fabrics through the duty-free Zona Franca.

History

After the collapse of Chile's initial Patagonian settlement at Fuerte Bulnes, Governor José Santos Mardones relocated northward to a site on the western shore of the Strait of Magellan, long known to British seamen as "Sandy Point." Soon expanded to include a penal colony, the town adopted that name in Spanish translation.

The Chileans' timing was propitious, as the California Gold Rush of 1849 brought a shipping surge through the strait; it helped keep the new city afloat, even if supplying seal skins, coal, firewood, and lumber did not exactly portend prosperity. A mutiny that resulted in the death of Governor Benjamín Muñoz Gamero did little

2002, Chile had been a relatively inexpensive destination compared with its larger neighbor, but Argentina's dramatic devaluation reversed this relationship. It was not that Chilean prices increased significantly, but rather that Argentine prices dropped so precipitously that Chile became relatively more expensive. In late 2003, a steady revaluation of the Chilean peso against the U.S. dollar did raise prices somewhat.

Nevertheless, Chile has maintained economic stability and a low-inflation economy for at least a decade and a half. Travelers should keep a close eye on exchange rates, however.

Travelers checks are relatively easy to cash, but ATM cards are far more convenient. A small reserve of cash in dollars is also a good idea.

One economic advantage of travel in Chile is that midrange to upscale hotels deduct IVA (value added tax) for foreign tourists who pay in U.S. dollars or by credit card. This means, for instance, that a US$100 hotel becomes a US$80 hotel, but it's not automatic—you must ask for it. The very cheapest accommodations, which are usually IVA-exempt, generally do not follow this practice.

Schedules and Hours

Chileans, in general, rise later than Argentines, many businesses do not open until 10 A.M., and it's often difficult to get breakfast in a Chilean hotel before 8 A.M. Lunch tends to be a bit later than in Argentina, around 2 P.M., but dinner maybe as early as 8 P.M.

Communications

Telephone, Internet, and postal services are all moderately priced. Chile's country code is 56; the area code for Magallanes and Chilean Tierra del Fuego is 061. The prefix for cell phones in the entire country is 09.

Getting Around

Distances in Chilean Patagonia are shorter than in Argentina, and the main highways are excellent. On the Chilean side of Tierra del Fuego, some roads are paved but most are gravel or dirt.

Chilean buses mostly resemble those in Argentina—modern, spacious, and fast. Neither Punta Arenas nor Puerto Natales, the two main cities in Magallanes, has a central terminal. Prices are similar to those in Argentina.

to improve matters, and traffic fell off in the following years.

What did bring prosperity was Governor Diego Dublé Almeyda's introduction of breeding sheep from the Falkland Islands, their proliferation on the Patagonian plains, and a vigorous immigration policy that brought entrepreneurs like the Portuguese José Nogueira, the Spaniard José Menéndez, and the Irishman Thomas Fenton—not to mention the polyglot laborers who made their fortunes possible. Together, they transformed the city from a dreary presidio to the booming port of a pastoral empire, with mansions to match those of Buenos Aires, though the maldistribution of wealth and political power remained an intractable issue well into the 20th century.

As the wool economy declined around the end of World War II, petroleum discoveries on Tierra del Fuego and commercial fishing have sustained the city economically. Creation of Zona Franca duty-free zones gave commercial advantages to both Punta Arenas and the northern city of Iquique in the 1970s, and the tourist trade has flourished since the end of military dictatorship in 1989.

Orientation

Punta Arenas (population about 116,105) is 210 kilometers southwest of Río Gallegos via the Argentine RN 3 and the Chilean Ruta 255 and Ruta 9; it is 241 kilometers southeast of Puerto Natales via Ruta 9. A daily vehicle ferry connects Punta with Porvenir, while a gravel road, the most southerly on the South American continent, leads to Fuerte Bulnes and Cabo San Isidro.

On the western shore of the Strait of Magellan, it occupies a narrow north-south wave-cut terrace, but the ground rises steeply farther west. Only in recent years has the city begun to spread eastward rather than north to south.

Most landmarks and services are within a few blocks of the central Plaza Muñoz Gamero; street names change on each side of the plaza, but the numbering system is continuous.

Sights

For a panoramic overview of the city's layout,

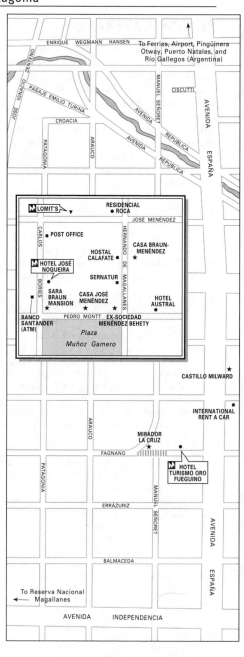

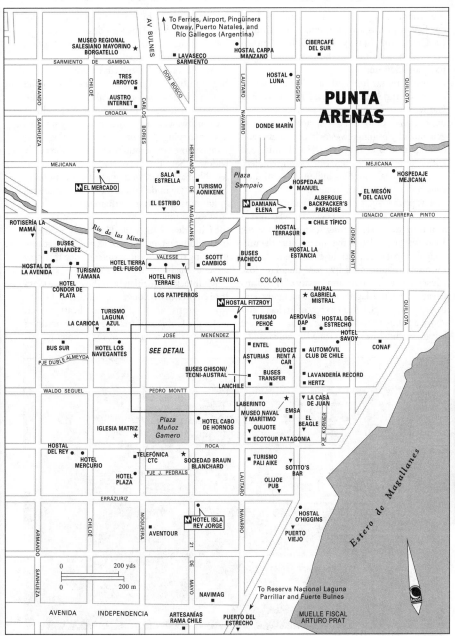

© AVALON TRAVEL PUBLISHING, INC.

the Strait of Magellan and the island of Tierra del Fuego in the distance, climb to **Mirador La Cruz,** four blocks west of Plaza Muñoz Gamero via a staircase at the corner of the Fagnano and Señoret.

Unlike plazas founded in colonial Chilean cities, Punta Arenas's central **Plaza Muñoz Gamero** was not initially the focus of civic life, but thanks to European immigration and wealth generated by mining, livestock, commerce, and fishing, it became so by the 1880s. Landscaped with Monterey cypress and other exotic conifers, the plaza and surrounding buildings constitute a *zona típica* national monument.

The plaza takes its name from early provincial governor Benjamín Muñoz Gamero, who died in a mutiny in 1851. Among its features are the Victorian kiosk (1910) that now houses the municipal tourist office and the elaborate sculptural monument sponsored by wool magnate José Menéndez on the 400th anniversary of Magellan's voyage of 1520. Magellan's imposing figure, embellished with a globe and a copy of his log, stand above a Selknam Indian representing Tierra del Fuego, a Tehuelche symbolizing Patagonia, and a

mermaid with Chilean and regional coats-of-arms. According to local legend, anyone touching the Tehuelche's now well-worn toe will return to Punta Arenas.

After about 1880, the city's burgeoning elite began to build monuments to their own good fortune, such as the ornate **Palacio Sara Braun** (1895), a national monument in its own right, at the northwest corner of the plaza. Only six years after marrying the Portuguese José Nogueira, Punta's most prosperous businessman, the newly widowed Sara Braun contracted French architect Numa Mayer, who applied contemporary Parisian style in designing a two-story mansard building that contrasted dramatically with the city's earlier utilitarian architecture. Now home to the Club de la Unión and Hotel José Nogueira, the building retains most of its original features, including the west-facing winter garden that now serves as the hotel's bar/restaurant.

Midblock, immediately to the east, the **Casa José Menéndez** belonged to another of Punta's wool barons, at the plaza's northeast corner, while the Comapa travel agency now occupies the former headquarters of the influential **So-**

former Sara Braun mansion, Punta Arenas, Chile

© WAYNE BERNHARDSON

Tierra del Fuego

ciedad **Menéndez Behety** (Magallanes 990). Half a block north, dating from 1904, the **Casa Braun-Menéndez** (Magallanes 949) houses the regional museum.

At the southwest corner of the Plaza, Punta Arenas's **Iglesia Matriz** (1901) has since earned cathedral status. Immediately to its north, both the **Residencia del Gobernador** (Governors' Residence) and the **Gobernación** date from the same period, filling the rest of the block with offices of the Intendencia Regional, the regional government. On the south side, directly opposite the Victorian tourist kiosk, the former **Palacio Montés** now holds municipal government offices, while the building at the southeast corner, the **Sociedad Braun Blanchard,** belonged to another powerful commercial group (as should be obvious from the names, Punta Arenas's first families were, commercially at least, an incestuous bunch).

Like European royalty, Punta's first families formed alliances sealed by matrimony, and the **Casa Braun-Menéndez** (Museo Regional de Magallanes, 1904) is a classic example: the product of a marriage between Mauricio Braun (Sara's brother) and Josefina Menéndez Behety (daughter of José Menéndez and María Behety, daughter of a major wool-growing family in Argentina— though international borders meant little to wool merchants). Still furnished with the family's belongings, it now serves as the regional museum, replete with pioneer settlers' artifacts and historical photographs.

From November to April, the Casa Braun-Menéndez (Magallanes 949, tel. 061/244216, musemag@entelchile.net, US$1.50 adults, US$1 children, free on holidays) is open 10:30 A.M.–2 P.M. daily.

The **Museo Regional Salesiano Mayorino Borgatello** holds the collection of Italian mountaineer priest Alberto de Agostini (1883–1960). Agostini, along with many others in the Salesian order, made major contributions to both physical geography and ethnographic understanding of the region from the 19th century, when the order played a key role in evangelizing southern Patagonia and Tierra del

© WAYNE BERNHARDSON

headstone of the wool baron José Menéndez, Cementerio Municipal, Punta Arenas, Chile

Fuego, in both Chile and Argentina. Punta Arenas was their base, but their rosy view of Christianity's impact on the region's native people may be debatable.

Agostini left a sizeable collection of photographs, both ethnographic and geographical, preserved in the museum, which also has a library and a small regionally oriented art gallery. Permanent exhibits deal with regional flora and fauna, a handful of early colonial artifacts, regional ethnography, the Salesian missionization of Isla Dawson and other nearby areas, regional cartography, and the petroleum industry. For Darwinists, there's a scale model of the *Beagle* and, for Chilean patriots, one of the *Ancud,* which sailed from Chiloé to claim the region in 1843.

The museum (Avenida Bulnes 336, tel. 061/221001, musbora@tnet.cl, US$1.60 adults, US$.80 children) is open daily except Monday 10 A.M.–12:30 P.M. and 3–6 P.M.

Tierra del Fuego

© WAYNE BERNHARDSON

Castillo Milward, Punta Arenas, Chile

Pleasantly surprising, Punta Arenas's naval and military museum, the **Museo Naval y Marítimo,** provides perspectives on subjects like ethnography—in the context of the Strait of Magellan's seagoing indigenous peoples—even while stressing its military mission. It features interactive exhibits, such as a credible warship's bridge, a selection of model ships, and material on the naval history of the southern American oceans.

The most riveting material, though, concerns Chilean pilot Luis Pardo Villalón's 1916 rescue of British explorer Ernest Shackleton's crew at Elephant Island, on the Antarctic peninsula. On board the cutter *Yelcho,* with neither heat, electricity, nor radio in foggy and stormy winter weather, Pardo brought the crew back to Punta Arenas in short order; he later served as Chilean consul in Liverpool.

The Museo Naval (Pedro Montt 981, tel. 061/205479, US$1.20 adults, US$.50 children) is open daily except Sunday and Monday, 9:30 A.M.–12:30 P.M. and 2–5 P.M.

Run by the Instituto de la Patagonia, itself part of the Universidad de Magallanes, the **Museo del Recuerdo** is a mostly open-air facility displaying pioneer agricultural implements and industrial machinery, reconstructions of a traditional house and shearing shed, and a restored shepherd's trailer house (hauled across the Patagonian plains on wooden wheels). In addition to a modest botanical garden, the Instituto itself has a library/bookshop with impressive cartographic exhibits.

Admission to the Museo del Recuerdo (Avenida Bulnes 01890, tel. 061/207056, 8:30 A.M.–11:30 P.M. and 2:30–6 P.M. weekdays) costs US$1.50 for adults, free for children. From downtown Punta Arenas, taxi *colectivos* to the Zona Franca (duty-free zone) stop directly opposite the entrance.

Four blocks south of Plaza Muñoz Gamero, at the foot of Avenida Independencia, naval vessels, freighters, cruise ships, Antarctic icebreakers, and yachts from many countries dock at the **Muelle Fiscal Arturo Prat,** the city's major port facility until recently. Open to the public 10 A.M.–6 P.M. only, it's also a departure point for cruises to the fjords of Tierra del Fuego and to Antarctica.

The late, gifted travel writer Bruce Chatwin found the inspiration for his legendary stories *In Patagonia* through tales of his distant relative

THE SOUTHERNMOST GRAPES

When the wool barons of Patagonia built their mansions and *cascos* in the 19th century, one amenity they all demanded was a glassed-in greenhouse or conservatory. In a region where high winds and snowstorms were not all that unusual in any season, they could enjoy balmy indoor sunshine and grow vegetables like eggplants and tomatoes that could never survive the climate outdoors.

Both Argentina and Chile are famous for their grapes (thanks to their wine industries), but the two countries can also boast the world's southernmost grape arbors. The most readily seen is the conservatory restaurant at Punta Arenas's Hotel José Nogueira, the former Sara Braun mansion, at 53° 9' S. According to Sara Braun's descendent Julia Braun, though, the vines at the *casco* of Estancia Sara, on the Argentine side of Tierra del Fuego, push the grape line to 53° 25' S. The original *casco* at Estancia María Behety (53° 48' S), west of the city of Río Grande, may have had a conservatory, but the house burned to the ground several years back.

© WAYNE BERNHARDSON

Some of the world's southernmost grapes grow in the conservatory restaurant of the former Sara Braun mansion, Punta Arenas, Chile.

Charley Milward, who built and resided at the **Castillo Milward** (Milward's Castle, Avenida España 959), described by Chatwin as "a Victorian parsonage translated to the Strait of Magellan." With "high-pitched gables and gothic windows," the building features a square tower streetside and an octagonal one at the back.

At the corner of Avenida Colón and O'Higgins, gracing the walls of the former **Liceo de Niñas Sara Braun** (Sara Braun Girls' School), rises the seven-meter **Mural Gabriela Mistral,** honoring the Nobel Prize poetess.

Ten blocks north of Plaza Muñoz Gamero, the **Cementerio Municipal** (Avenida Bulnes 029) is home to the extravagant crypts of José Menéndez, José Nogueira, and Sara Braun, but the multinational immigrants who worked for them—English, Scot, Welsh, Croat, German, and Scandinavian—repose in more modest circumstances. A separate monument honors the vanished Selknam (Ona) Indians who once

flourished in the strait, and another memorializes German fatalities of the Battle of the Falklands (1914).

Entertainment

Except on Sunday, when the whole city seems as dead as the cemetery, there's usually something to do at night.

Punta Arenas has one movie theater, the **Sala Estrella** (Mejicana 777, tel. 061/241262).

Laberinto (Pedro Montt 951, tel. 061/223667) is primarily a dance club. The stylish **Olijoe Pub** (Errázuriz 970) has the feel of an upscale English pub, with paneled walls, ceiling, and bar, and reasonably priced drinks; the music, though, can get a little loud for conversation.

At the north end of town, **Makanudo** (El Ovejero 474, tel. 09/6492031) has 7–10 P.M. happy hours weekdays except Friday, and live music Friday and Saturday nights from around 1:30 A.M.

Tierra del Fuego

The **Club Hípico** (municipal racetrack) fronts on Avenida Bulnes between Coronel Mardones and Manantiales, north of downtown. Professional soccer matches take place at the **Estadio Fiscal,** a few blocks north at Avenida Bulnes and José González.

Shopping

Though it's faltered in recent years, Punta Arenas's major shopping destination is the duty-free **Zona Franca,** four kilometers north of downtown but easily reached by taxi colectivo from Calle Magallanes. Traditionally, consumer electronics were the big attraction, so much so that Santiaguinos flew here for the bargains, but price differentials are not so great as they used to be. If you're traveling by automobile, you should know that prices for replacement tires and similar items are much lower here than in Argentina or mainland Chile.

Puerto del Estrecho (O'Higgins 1401, tel. 061/241022) serves as the waiting room for *Mare Australis* cruises to the Chilean fjords but is also a good if fairly pricey souvenir shop; in addition, it has an upstairs café, Internet access and long-distance telephone service.

For crafts, well-stocked **Artesanías Rama Chile** (Independencia 799, tel. 061/244244) contains items like wool socks and sweaters and wood carvings of penguins. For media like metal (copper and bronze) and semiprecious stones (lapiz lazuli), visit **Chile Típico** (Ignacio Carrera Pinto 1015, tel. 061/225827). **Tres Arroyos** (Bories 448, tel. 061/241522) specializes in custom chocolates.

For books (including some local guidebooks and travel literature in English), maps, and keepsakes, try **Southern Patagonia Souvenirs & Books;** since its central Bories location burned down, it has outlets at the airport (tel. 061/211591) and at the Zona Franca (tel. 061/216759).

Accommodations

Sernatur maintains a complete list of accommodations with up-to-date prices. Note that what in many parts of Chile would be called *residenciales* are *hostales* in Punta Arenas. Some relatively expensive places have cheaper rooms with private bath that can be excellent values.

US$10–25

Open November to March only, the **Albergue Backpacker's Paradise** (Ignacio Carrera Pinto 1022, tel. 061/222554, backpackersparadise_chile @hotmail.com, US$5 pp) is a hostel-style facility that jams 30 bunks into only four dorm rooms, but for the price it has its public. On the plus side, it has adequate common spaces with cable TV, a kitchen for cooking, and Internet access.

Israeli favorite **Hospedaje Manuel** (O'Higgins 648, tel. 061/220567, fax 061/221295, turmanmi@entelchile.net, US$4 pp for dorms) has more spacious quarters for US$7/10 s/d. Open January and February only, six blocks south of Plaza Muñoz Gamero, the **Colegio Pierre Fauré** (Bellavista 697, tel. 061/226256, US$5 pp) also offers the option of camping (US$2.50 pp) in the adjacent garden (or pitching a tent indoors in the gymnasium); a simple breakfast costs US$1 more.

Often full despite mixed reviews, **Hostal Dinka's House** (Caupolicán 169, tel. 061/226056, tel./fax 061/244292, fueguino@entelchile.net, US$6–8 pp) has rooms with private and shared bath, with breakfast included; the nearby annex is definitely substandard.

Only a block from the plaza, **Residencial Roca** (Magallanes 888, 2nd floor, tel./fax 061/243903, US$10/17 s/d) has cable TV, laundry service, and a book exchange. **Hostal del Rey,** Fagnano 589, Departamento B, tel./fax 061/223924, US$10/17 s/d) is a friendly family place with only three doubles and two singles, so it's often full—call ahead. Rates include an ample breakfast, but the toxic smoke-laden atmosphere may tip the balance against it.

Hospedaje Mejicana (Mejicana 1174, tel. 061/227678, cell 09/4246903, yoya_h@hotmail.com, US$10 pp) has made favorable first impressions. **Hostal La Estancia** (O'Higgins 765, tel./fax 061/249130, reservas_laestancia@hotmail.com, US$13/20 s/d) has spacious rooms with telephone and shared bath only, with breakfast included.

About 10 blocks northwest of the plaza, **Hostal Sonia** (Pasaje Darwin 175, tel./fax 061/248543, hostalsk@entelchile.net, www .hostalsk.50megs.com, US$12 pp) has hostel accommodations for HI members only at an otherwise midrange place. Near the old port, improved **Hostal O'Higgins** (O'Higgins 1205, tel. 061/227999, US$10 pp, US$25 d) has rooms with shared and private bath.

US$25–50

Near the cemetery, **Hostal Parediso** (Angamos 1073, tel./fax 061/224212, US$13–25 s, US$20–33 d) compensates for kitsch décor—note the stalactite ceilings—with genuine hospitality and reasonable comfort. Each room has comfy beds, telephone, and cable TV, though they tend to be overheated and the building can squeak when someone walks to the shared baths. Rates include a simple but abundant breakfast, and kitchen privileges are available; the more-expensive rooms have private bath.

Well-regarded **Hostal Sonia** (Pasaje Darwin 175, tel. 061/248543, hostalsk@entelchile.net, US$23/34 s/d) has rooms with private bath, breakfast included, in addition to its hostel accommodations.

Hostal Luna (O'Higgins 424, tel. 061/221764, fax 061/224637, hostalluna@hotmail .com, US$18 pp) has plain but well-furnished and even homey rooms—every bed has a cozy duvet—with a simple breakfast included. The spacious dining room has cable TV, but the rooms do not.

M Hostal Turismo Oro Fueguino (Fagnano 356, tel./fax 061/249401 or 061/246677, tel. 09/2183690, fueguino@ctcinternet.cl, US$20–30 s, US$30–38 d) occupies a deco-style house with an outlandish interior paint job that somehow holds the place together. Rates include cable TV, telephone, central heating, breakfast, and private bath; some rooms are windowless but have skylights. A few cheaper rooms have shared bath.

Low-key, family-run **Hostal Terrasur** (O'Higgins 723, tel. 061/225618, hostalterrasur@entelchile.net, US$40 s or d) is one of the more appealing B&B-style places in its range.

M Hostal Fitzroy (Lautaro Navarro 850, tel./fax 061/248415, calafate@entelchile.net, US$19–33 s, US$28–41 d) is an old-fashioned B&B offering some modern comforts—notably cable TV and phones in each room—along with peace and quiet. It falls short in some details, though, and the breakfasts are mediocre. The cheaper rooms have shared bath, and there's free parking.

Despite its misleadingly small streetside facade, its sister **M Hostal Calafate** (Magallanes 922, tel./fax 061/241281, hostal@calafate.cl, www.calafate.cl, US$19–33 s, US$28–41 d) is a rambling building with spacious rooms that once held the former Hotel Oviedo; recently remodeled, it charges the same prices as its more traditional counterpart but also keeps a couple of so-called *celdas de castigo* ("prison cells") for backpacker clients for just US$10 pp–a pretty good deal in a well-kept, central facility.

Hostal de la Avenida (Avenida Colón 534, tel./fax 061/247532 or 061/249486, US$36/43 s/d) is a respectable choice for the price The so-so **Hostal del Estrecho** (José Menéndez 1048, tel./fax 061/241011, estrecho@chileanpatagonia.com, US$17/27 s/d with shared bath, US$40/45 s/d with private bath) is suitable in a pinch, but **Hotel Cóndor de Plata** (Avenida Colón 556, tel. 061/247987, fax 061/241149, US$40/50 s/d) is a better choice with private bath and breakfast.

US$50–100

Hotel Savoy (José Menéndez 1073, tel./fax 061/247979, hotelsavoy@terra.cl, US$30–42 s, US$45–52 d) lacks style—some of the walls have cheap plywood paneling—but the rooms are large and comfortable, and the staff is responsive.

Occupying a tastefully modernized building, **Hotel Mercurio** (Fagnano 595, tel./fax 061/242300, mercurio@chileaustral.com, US$42/53 s/d) offers both convenience and charm, with gracious staff to boot. Rates include private bath and breakfast.

Hostal Carpa Manzano (Lautaro Navarro 336, tel. 061/242296, fax 061/248864, US$42/54 s/d) gets good marks in its category. Half a block south of Plaza Muñoz Gamero, **Hotel**

Plaza (Nogueira 1116, tel. 061/241300, fax 061/248613, hplaza@chileaustral.com, US$72/87 s/d) is a classic of its era, but the **Hotel Tierra del Fuego** (Avenida Colón 716, tel./fax 061/|226200, tierradelfuego@entelchile.net, US$89/98 s/d) has better contemporary fixtures.

US$100–200

Punta Arenas has a good selection of upscale, mostly modern hotels, such as **Hotel Los Navegantes** (José Menéndez 647, tel. 061/244677, fax 061/247545, hotelnav@chilesat.net, www.hotellosnavegantes.com, US$110/139 s/d), which has standard conveniences in midsized rooms. **Ⱅ** **Hotel Isla Rey Jorge** (21 de Mayo 1243, tel. 061/222681, fax 061/248220, reyjorge@ctcinternet.cl, www.islareyjorge.com, US$119/146 s/d) is a favorite with foreign tour groups.

Hotel Finis Terrae (Avenida Colón 766, tel. 061/228200, fax 061/248124, finister@ctcreuna.cl, www.hotelfinisterrae.com, US$140/160 s/d) is a fine newer hotel.

Traditionally one of the city's best, built by the Sociedad Ganadera Tierra del Fuego, the 1960s high-rise **Hotel Cabo de Hornos** (Plaza Muñoz Gamero 1025, tel./fax 061/242134, rescabo @entelchile.net, US$126–140 s, US$149–166 d) is gradually recovering from years of neglect.

Punta Arenas's most distinctively historic accommodations, the **Ⱅ** **Hotel José Nogueira** (Bories 959, tel. 061/248840, fax 061/248832, rvanogueira@entelchile.net, www.hotelnogueira .com, US$149/179 s/d) occupies part of the Sara Braun mansion. Its greenhouse bar/restaurant deserves a visit even if you can't afford to stay here.

Food

Los Patiperros (Avenida Colón 782, tel. 061/245298) is a modest but popular café serving full meals in the US$5 range. **Quijote** (Lautaro Navarro 1087, tel. 061/241225) also serves inexpensive lunches, as does the outstanding **Rotisería La Mamá** (Sanhueza 720, tel. 061/225812).

Upstairs in the Casa del Turista, at the entrance to Muelle Prat, **Café Puerto del Estrecho** (O'Higgins 1401, tel. 061/241022) has a

variety of espresso-based specialty coffees, such as mocha and amaretto, plus snacks and desserts to accompany them.

Ⱅ **Lomit's** (José Menéndez 722, tel. 061/243399) is a dependable sandwich chain that's almost always packed. By contrast, **La Carioca** (José Menéndez 600, tel. 061/224809) is a one-of-a-kind sandwich outlet that also serves passable pizza, pasta, and draft beer.

Donde Marín (O'Higgins 504, tel. 061/245291) delivers on its modest pretensions, serving fine if simply prepared fish entrees, including a side order, in the US$5–7 range. The decor is only utilitarian, but the service is professional.

Stick with the meat at **El Estribo** (Ignacio Carrera Pinto 762, tel. 061/244714); their fish dishes are only so-so, but the beef and lamb choices, in the US$4–10 range, are consistently better. The English menu translation is occasionally hilarious, but the service is attentive.

One of Punta's best new restaurants is **Ⱅ** **Damiana Elena** (O'Higgins 694, tel. 061/222818), where reservations are essential on weekends and advisable even on weeknights. Decorated with antiques, this restored period house serves beef and seafood specialties in the US$4–8 range—very modest prices for the quality it offers—with unobtrusive service. There is limited tobacco-free seating, for which reservations are particularly advisable.

A good seafood choice is the nautically themed **Ⱅ** **Puerto Viejo** (O'Higgins 1205, tel. 061/ 225103), doing bang-up business in its first months with an almost exclusively seafood menu. Open for lunch and dinner daily, with knowledgeable waiters and terrific service, it serves specialties like *centolla* (king crab) and *merluza* (hake); for US$12, the *centolla al Puerto* appetizer is sufficient for two hungry diners. On the other hand, the pisco/calafate sours are mixed in advance, though they're still pretty fresh.

Under the same management, a couple of kilometers north of the plaza, **Ⱅ** **Los Ganaderos** (Avenida Bulnes 0977, tel. 061/214597) is a classy *parrilla* specializing in succulent Patagonian lamb grilled on a vertical spit—for US$10 *tenedor libre* (all-you-can-eat). There is also a more diverse *parrillada* for two (US$23), and pasta dishes in the US$7 range. Other treats include the regional Patagonian desserts, such as *mousse de calafate* and *mousse de ruibarbo* (rhubarb).

Four blocks south of the plaza, the most creative new place is **☒ La Leyenda del Remezón** (21 de Mayo 1469, tel. 061/241029), which serves game dishes (beaver and guanaco are now being farmed in the region) in the US$17 range—not cheap, obviously, but unique. Seafood specialties include krill, king crab, and spider crab.

Punta Arenas's classic seafood locale, open 24/7, is **☒ El Mercado** (Mejicana 617, 2nd floor, tel. 061/247415); serving a diverse fish and shellfish menu at midrange prices, it affixes a 10 percent surcharge from 1–8 A.M. Another seafood classic, upstairs from the Teatro Cervantes, is the **Centro Español** (Plaza Muñoz Gamero 771, tel. 061/242807); though it never seems to have many clients, it still manages to turn out good food at slightly higher prices than El Mercado.

Other seafood choices, more upscale but not dramatically better, include **Asturias** (Lautaro Navarro 967, tel. 061/243763), **La Casa de Juan,** (O'Higgins 1021, tel. 061/223463), **El Beagle** (O'Higgins 1077, tel. 061/243057), and highly regarded **Sotito's Bar** (O'Higgins 1138, tel. 061/245365).

Information

A couple of doors north of Plaza Muñoz Gamero, **Sernatur** (Magallanes 960, tel. 061/225385, infomagallanes@sernatur.cl) is open 8:15 A.M.–6 P.M. weekdays only. One of Chile's better regional tourist offices, it has English-speaking personnel, up-to-date accommodations and transportation information, and a message board.

In summer, Plaza Muñoz Gamero's municipal **Kiosko de Informaciones** (tel. 061/200610) is open 8 A.M.–8 P.M. weekdays, 9 A.M.–6 P.M. Saturday, and 9:30 A.M.–2:30 P.M. Sunday. It also has free Internet access for brief periods (longer if no one is waiting).

For motorists, the local branch of the **Automóvil Club de Chile** (Acchi, O'Higgins 931, tel. 061/243675) also rents cars.

Conaf (José Menéndez 1147, tel. 061/223841) is Chile's national parks agency.

Services

Punta Arenas is one of the easier Chilean cities in which to change both cash and travelers checks, especially at travel agencies along Lautaro Navarro. Most of these close by midday Saturday, but **Scott Cambios** (Avenida Colón and Magallanes) will cash travelers checks then.

There are many ATMs, such as the one at **Banco Santander** (Bories 970), half a block north of Plaza Muñoz Gamero.

Correos de Chile is at Bories 911, just north of Plaza Muñoz Gamero.

Long-distance call centers include **Telefónica CTC** (Nogueira 1116), at the southwest corner of Plaza Muñoz Gamero, and **Entel** (Lautaro Navarro 931). Try also **Hostal Calafate** (Magallanes 922), which has expanded its hotel business with an Internet café and phone center.

Austro Internet (Croacia 690, tel. 061/229297) is open 9 A.M.–8 P.M. weekdays, 10 A.M.–8 P.M. Saturday, and 4–8 P.M. Sunday, but also keeps Sunday morning hours (9 A.M.–1 P.M.) when cruise ships are in port. **Cibercafé del Sur** (Croacia 1028, tel. 061/235117) stays open 24 hours. Both charge around US$1.50 per hour.

The **Argentine consulate** (21 de Mayo 1878, tel. 061/261912) is open weekdays 10 A.M.–3:30 P.M. Several other countries have honorary consulates, including Brazil (Arauco 769, tel. 061/241093), Spain (José Menéndez 910, tel. 061/243566), and the United Kingdom (tel. 061/211535).

Lavandería Record is at O'Higgins 969 (tel. 061/243607). Also try **Lavaseco Sarmiento** (Sarmiento de Gamboa 726, tel. 061/241516).

Punta Arenas's **Hospital Regional** (Arauco and Angamos, tel. 061/244040) is north of downtown.

Getting There

Punta Arenas has good air connections to mainland Chile, frequent air service to Chilean Tierra del Fuego, infrequent air service to Argentine Tierra del Fuego, and regular weekly service to the

Tierra del Fuego

Falkland Islands. There are roundabout overland routes to mainland Chile via Argentina, regular bus service to Argentine Tierra del Fuego via a ferry link, direct ferry service to Chilean Tierra del Fuego, and expensive (but extraordinarily scenic) cruise-ship service to Ushuaia, in Argentine Tierra del Fuego.

LanChile/LanExpress (Lautaro Navarro 999, tel. 061/241232) flies four times daily to the capital city of Santiago, normally via Puerto Montt, but some flights stop at Balmaceda, in northern Chilean Patagonia. It also flies Saturday to the Falkland Islands; one Falklands flight monthly stops in the Argentine city of Río Gallegos.

Aerovías DAP (O'Higgins 891, tel. 061/223340, fax 061/221693, ventas@aeroviasdap.cl) flies seven-seater Cessnas to and from Porvenir (US$23), in Chilean Tierra del Fuego, at least daily except Sunday, more often in summer. Daily except Sunday and Monday, it flies 20-seater Twin Otters to and from Puerto Williams on Isla Navarino (US$64 one way). In summer, it flies Twin Otters to Ushuaia Monday, Wednesday, and Friday only (US$100). It also has extensive charter services.

Punta Arenas has no central **bus terminal,** though some companies share facilities. Most are within a few blocks of each other, north of Plaza Muñoz Gamero.

Regional Buses: Several carriers go to Puerto Natales (US$5, three hours), including **Bus Sur** (José Menéndez 565, tel. 2061/27145), with four buses daily; **Buses Fernández** (Armando Sanhueza 745, tel. 061/242313), which has older but still serviceable vehicles (seven daily); **Buses Pacheco** (Avenida Colón 900, tel. 061/242174, two daily); and **Buses Transfer** (Pedro Montt 966, tel. 061/229613, one daily).

Long-Distance Buses: In addition to its Puerto Natales services, Buses Pacheco goes to the Chilean cities of Osorno, Puerto Montt, and Castro (US$58, 30–32 hours) Wednesday at 8 A.M., via Argentina.

Queilén Bus (Armando Sanhueza 745, tel. 061/221812) and **Cruz del Sur** (Armando Sanhueza 745, tel. 061/227970) alternate services to Puerto Montt and Castro most mornings at 9:30 A.M.

Besides Puerto Natales, Bus Sur goes to Coyhaique (US$50, 20 hours) Monday at 10:30 A.M. and to Osorno, Puerto Montt, and Castro Tuesday at 8:30 A.M.

International Buses: Several carriers go to Río Gallegos (US$12, four hours): **Buses Pingüino** (Armando Sanhueza 745, tel. 061/221812, 061242313), daily at 12:45 P.M.; **Buses Ghisoni** (Lautaro Navarro 975, tel. 061/222078), Monday at 12:45 P.M., Wednesday and Saturday at noon, and Thursday at 3 P.M.; and **Buses Pacheco** at 11:30 A.M. Tuesday, Friday, and Sunday.

Tecni-Austral (Lautaro Navarro 975, tel. 061/222078) goes directly to Río Grande (US$22–25, eight hours), in Argentine Tierra del Fuego, daily except Monday at 8:30 A.M.; the Tuesday, Thursday, Saturday, and Sunday buses continue to Ushuaia (US$33, 12 hours). Buses Pacheco goes Monday, Wednesday, Friday, and Sunday at 7:30 A.M. to Río Grande, with connections to Ushuaia.

If you'd like to travel by boat, **Transbordadora Austral Broom** (Avenida Bulnes 05075, tel. 061/218100, tabsa@entelchile.net) sails from Punta Arenas to Porvenir (2.5 hours) at 9 A.M. daily except Sunday, when sailing time is 9:30 A.M. Adult passengers pay US$6 pp except for drivers, whose own fare is included in the US$37 charge per vehicle (motorcycles pay US$11). Children pay US$2.50 pp. Since the ferry has limited vehicle capacity, reservations are a good idea on the *Melinka,* which leaves from Terminal Tres Puentes, at the north end of town but is easily accessible by taxi colectivo from the Casa Braun-Menéndez, on Magallanes half a block north of Plaza Muñoz Gamero.

Broom also sails the ferry *Patagonia* to Puerto Williams (36 hours) every Wednesday at 6 P.M., returning Friday at 10 P.M. The fare is US$150 for a bunk, US$120 for a reclining seat.

Getting Around

Punta Arenas's **Aeropuerto Presidente Carlos Ibáñez del Campo** is 20 kilometers north of town on Ruta 9, the Puerto Natales highway. **Buses Pacheco** (Avenida Colón 900, tel. 061/229613) goes to the airport at 11 A.M. and

2:30 P.M. daily (US$4 pp); buses returning from Puerto Natales will usually drop their passengers at the airport to meet outgoing flights, but make arrangements before boarding. Otherwise, from Punta, it's necessary to hire a taxi (US$8).

Punta Arenas has numerous car rental options, including **Adel Rent a Car** (Pedro Montt 962, tel. 061/235471 or 061/235472, gdreyes@entelchile.net); the **Automóvil Club de Chile** (O'Higgins 931, tel. 061/243675, fax 061/243097; **Budget** (O'Higgins 964, tel./fax 061/241696, budget@ctcinternet.cl); **Emsa** (Roca 1044, tel./fax 061/229049, rentacar@chilesat.net); **Hertz** (O'Higgins 987, tel. 061/248742, fax 061/244729); **International** (Waldo Seguel 443, tel. 061/228323, fax 061/226334, internationalrac@entelchile.net); and **Lubag** (Magallanes 970, tel./fax 061/242023, luis_barra @entelchile.net).

For rental **bikes**, contact **Claudio Botten** (Sarmiento 1132, tel. 061/242107 or 09/6913475).

It's neither a cheap nor conventional way of getting to Argentina, but passengers on the luxury M/V *Mare Australis,* which sails from Punta Arenas every Saturday for a week-long cruise of the fjords of Chilean Tierra del Fuego, can disembark in Ushuaia (or board there, for that matter). Normally the *Mare Australis* requires reservations well in advance. For more details, see The Fjords of Fuegia section.

VICINITY OF PUNTA ARENAS

Punta Arenas's many travel agencies operate a variety of excursions in the vicinity, to nearby destinations like Reserva Nacional Magallanes, Fuerte Bulnes, the Seno Otway penguin colony, Río Verde, Estancia San Gregorio, and even Parque Nacional Torres del Paine. The most popular half-day excursions, like Fuerte Bulnes and Otway, cost US$10–15 pp, while full-day trips like Pali Aike can cost up to US$70 pp.

Among the established operators are **Aventour** (José Nogueira 1255, tel. 061/244197, fax 061/243354, aventour@entelchile.net); **Ecotour Patagonia** (Lautaro Navarro 1091, tel. 061/221339, fax 061/223670, ecopatagonia @entelchile.net); **Turismo Aonikenk** (Magallanes 619, tel. 061/228332); **Turismo Laguna Azul** (José Menéndez 631, tel. 061/225200, fax 061/240278, lagunaazul@chileaustral.com); **Turismo Pali Aike** (Lautaro Navarro 1129, tel. 061/229388, fax 061/223301, paliaike @entelchile.net); **Turismo Viento Sur** (Fagnano 585, tel. 061/226530, fax 061/225167, agencia@vientosur.com); and **Turismo Yámana** (Avenida Colón 568, tel. 061/221130, yamana @chileaustral.com).

The Fjords of Fuegia

Short of Antarctica itself, some of the Southern Hemisphere's most awesome scenery occurs in the Beagle Channel, southern Tierra del Fuego, and the legendary Cape Horn. And as usual, Charles Darwin left one of the most vivid descriptions of the channel named for the vessel on which he sailed:

> *The scenery here becomes even grander than before. The lofty mountains on the north side compose the granitic axis, or backbone of the country, and boldly rise to a height of between three and four thousand feet, with one peak above six thousand feet. They are covered by a wide mantle of perpetual snow, and numerous cascades pour their waters, through the woods, into the narrow channel below. In many parts, magnificent glaciers extend from the mountain side to the water's edge. It is scarcely possible to imagine anything more beautiful than the beryl-like blue of these glaciers, and especially as contrasted with the dead white of the upper expanse of the snow. The fragments which had fallen from the glacier into the water, were floating away, and the channel with the icebergs presented, for the space of a mile, a miniature likeness of the Polar Sea.*

Even today, fairly few visitors see Tierra del Fuego's splendid fjords, barely changed since Darwin described them in 1833. Many who do venture out do so onboard the week-long excursion from Punta Arenas to Ushuaia and back on

Tierra del Fuego

the Chilean vessel M/V *Mare Australis*. Unlike the Navimag ferry from Puerto Montt to Puerto Natales, this is a cruise in the traditional sense—the passengers are waited on hand and foot, and it's not cheap. Yet for the foreseeable future, it remains the only way to see the area short of sailing or hiring your own private yacht, and for that reason it's worth consideration even for those with limited finances.

Routes can vary depending on weather conditions in this notoriously changeable climate. After an evening departure from Punta Arenas's Muelle Prat, the *Mare Australis* crosses the Strait of Magellan to enter the **Seno del Almirantazgo** (Admiralty Sound), a westward maritime extension of the freshwater Lago Fagnano trough. Passengers usually go ashore at the sound's lesser inlet **Bahía Parry,** on the north side of the Cordillera Darwin; here, hikers can approach the groaning **Ventisquero Parry** (Parry Glacier), named by Philip Parker King, captain of HMS *Adventure* and hydrographer on the *Beagle* expedition, in honor of Sir William Edward Parry (1790–1855), who made four unsuccessful attempts at the Northwest Passage to the Pacific. With its numerous icebergs and low salinity, Bahía Parry has little wildlife.

From Bahía Parry, the ship sails back west, pausing at a small elephant seal colony at **Bahía Ainsworth,** near the **Ventisquero Marinelli,** where there's a short hiking trail through what was once forest until escaped beavers dammed the area into a series of ponds. Farther west, at **Isla Tucker,** there's a small Magellanic-penguin colony and it's also possible to see the rare striated caracara, *Phalcoboenus australis.*

After a night's sailing, the ship enters the **Fiordo D'Agostini,** a glacial inlet named for the Italian priest and mountaineer who explored the farthest recesses of the Cordillera Darwin in the early 20th century. When high winds make it impossible to approach the **Glaciar Serrano** (named for Chilean naval Lieutenant Ramón Serrano Montaner, who charted the strait in 1879), an option is the more sheltered **Glaciar D'Agostini.** Even here, though, seracs fall off the face of the glacier, touching off a rapid surge of water and ice that runs parallel to a broad

gravel beach and, when it subsides, leaves the beach littered with boulders of ice.

Darwin, again, described the dangers of travel in an area that sea kayakers are beginning to explore:

> *The boats being hauled on shore at our dinner hour, we were admiring from the distance of half a mile a perpendicular cliff of ice, and were wishing that some more fragments would fall. At last, down came a mass with a roaring noise, and immediately we saw the smooth outline of a wave traveling toward us. The men ran down as quickly as they could to the boats; for the chance of their being dashed to pieces was evident. One of the seamen just caught hold of the bows, as the curling breaker reached it: he was knocked over and over, but not hurt; and the boats, though thrice lifted on high and let fall again, received no damage . . . I had previously noted that some large fragments of rock on the beach had been lately displaced; but until seeing this wave, I did not understand the cause.*

Prior to navigating Canal Cockburn, the ship anchors at **Ventisquero Cóndor** where condors glide low and cormorants nest on the bluffs. Briefly exposed to swells from the open ocean, the vessel turns into the calmer **Canal Ocasión** and eventually enters the Beagle Channel's north arm, sailing past the so-called **Avenida de los Glaciares,** a series of glaciers named for various European countries.

Traditionally, the *Mare Australis* proceeds to **Puerto Williams,** where it spends a few hours before sailing for the Argentine port of **Ushuaia,** but a new Chilean port of entry at Puerto Navarino, directly south of Ushuaia, may expedite immigration formalities and the itineraries, as it will allow Chilean-flagged vessels to avoid doubling back to Puerto Williams, to reenter Chile after leaving Ushuaia.

After reentering Chile at Puerto Williams, the ship sails south to **Cabo de Hornos** (Cape Horn) and then back north to **Bahía Wulaia** where passengers go ashore at the site of a one-time Yámana mission. Returning to the Beagle Channel, it turns westward through the north arm of the channel, again passing the Avenida de los Glaciares and entering **Fiordo Pía** (Pía Fjord), where dozens of waterfalls cascade down sheer metamorphic slopes from the **Glaciar Pía**. A bit farther west, it enters **Fiordo Garibaldi,** at least to the point where thick ice prohibits any further progress—even on a comfortable cruise ship, sailing through Tierra del Fuego has the feeling of passing through uncharted waters. After a short backtrack, the most vigorous passengers disembark for a short but strenuous and slippery hike through sopping Magellanic rain forest.

On the last full day, the boat passes through the Angostura Gabriel, a narrows only about 250 meters wide, before entering **Bahía Brooke,** where a nameless river of ice is slowly but inexorably transporting granite boulders down to the sea, and fresh snow avalanches off hanging glaciers. On the final morning, it sails north to **Isla Magdalena** (see the separate entry for Monumento Natural Los Pingüinos) before returning to its home port of Punta Arenas.

Well-organized without being regimented, the cruise is informal in terms of dress and behavior. As it begins, passengers sign up for meal tables; places are fixed for the duration except at the buffet breakfast, when people tend to straggle in at different times. In general, passengers are grouped according to language, though they often place together people who speak English as a second language. The staff themselves can handle Spanish, English, German, French, and occasionally other languages.

After a welcome drink accompanied by snacks in the bar, there's an introduction of the captain, crew, and staff, a brief folkloric show, and an obligatory safety drill. Smoking is prohibited everywhere except on the topmost deck and outdoors; bar consumption is now included in the package.

The cabins themselves are simple but spacious, with either a double or two single beds, built-in reading lights, a writing desk, and a private bath with good hot showers (though it takes a while for the hot water to arrive if you're the first shower of the morning). Each room has a closet with hangers and a small lock box for valuables. Note that cabins on the *Mare Australis,* which was built in 2002, have 110-volt outlets, with United States–style plugs. The food is ample and occasionally excellent, though breakfasts are a little monotonous; the wine is superb, and the service exceptional. Vegetarian menus are available on request.

For those who tire of the landscape or when the weather is bad, onboard activities include line-dancing(!), PowerPoint slide lectures on flora and fauna, engine-room tours, and demonstrations of culinary artistry with carved cucumbers, peppers, zucchinis, and other vegetables in the shapes of birds and flowers. The farewell dinner is a gala affair, followed by champagne on the topmost deck. As on the *Puerto Edén* ferry from Puerto Montt to Puerto Natales, the crew hands out diplomas on the final night.

At several locations, there are optional shore-based activities as well. At Puerto Williams, supplementary excursions include a US$30 anthropological bus trip, led by the local museum director, and a US$180 Twin Otter overflight of Cabo de Hornos—South America's most remote outlier—for a maximum of 20 passengers. Many passengers leave and others board at Ushuaia, the only major stopover on the trip, where the possibilities for full-day excursions are numerous, Many, though, opt for independent sightseeing.

Punta Arenas is *Mare Australis*'s home port; check-in takes place at the Casa del Turista (O'Higgins 1401), at the entrance to Muelle Prat, and boarding begins in late afternoon. Some passengers, especially those on the shorter three- or four-day options, begin or end the trip in Ushuaia.

Usually this very popular cruise runs full for the whole season from October to April, except for the last trip before Christmas, which is often only half full; in this case, it may be possible to negotiate a deal in Punta Arenas, getting a private cabin without paying a single supplement, for instance. In addition, at this time of year, days are so long that it's possible to enjoy the landscape until after 11 P.M., and there's sufficient light to read by 4 A.M.

Tierra del Fuego

Reservations are made through **Cruceros Australis** (Avenida Bosque Norte 0440, 11th floor, Las Condes, Santiago, tel. 02/4423110, fax 02/2035173, www.australis.com), which also has offices in Buenos Aires (Carlos Pellegrini 989, Retiro, tel. 011/4325-8400, fax 011/4325-6600) and in Miami (4014 Chase Ave. Suite 202, Miami Beach, FL 33140, 305/695-9618 or 877/678-3772, fax 305/534-9276). Per person rates on the Punta Arenas–Ushuaia leg start at US$785–1,393 in low season up to US$1,244–2,229 in high season. On the Ushuaia–Punta Arenas leg, the comparable rates are US$681–1,207 in low season to US$1,078–1,931 in high season.

Reserva Nacional Magallanes

Only eight kilometers west of downtown Punta Arenas, 13,500-hectare Reserva Nacional Magallanes is a combination of Patagonian steppe and southern beech forest which, in good winters, accumulates enough snow for skiing. Despite its proximity to Punta Arenas, official statistics say it gets only about 2,800 visitors per year.

From westbound Avenida Independencia, a good gravel road that may require chains in winter climbs gradually to a fork whose southern branch leads to the reserve's **Sector Andino,** where the local Club Andino's **Centro de Esquí Cerro Mirador** includes a *refugio* that serves meals, a ski school, and a single well-maintained chairlift. In summer, the **Sendero Mirador,** a two-hour loop hike, winds through the forest and crosses the ski area; there's also a mountain bike circuit.

The northwesterly **Sector Las Minas,** which includes a gated picnic area, charges US$1.50 pp for adult admission, but nothing for kids. A longer footpath links up with the trail to the El Mirador summit, which offers panoramas east toward Punta Arenas, the strait, and Tierra del Fuego, and west toward Seno Otway.

Though some Punta Arenas travel agencies offer tours to the reserve, it would also be a good mountain bike excursion.

Pingüinera Seno Otway

Burrowing Magellanic penguins abound along the Atlantic coast of Argentine Patagonia, but they are fewer in Chile. Barely an hour from Punta Arenas, though, the *Spheniscus magellanicus* colony at Seno Otway (Otway Sound) is the closest to any major city on the continent. Under the administration of the nonprofit Fundación Otway, it grew in a decade from no more than 400 penguins to about 8,000 breeding pairs at present. From October, when the first birds arrive, to April, when the last stragglers head out to sea, it attracts up to 40,000 visitors. The peak season, though, is December–February.

While the site is fenced to keep human visitors out of critical habitat, the birds are relatively tame and easy to photograph; on the down side, this did not prevent stray dogs from killing more than a hundred birds in 2001. The land-owning Kusanovic family has recently taken over management from the Fundación Otway.

During the season, any number of Punta Arenas operators shuttle visitors to and from the Otway site for about US$10–12 pp, not including the US$3.50 pp admission charge. Half-day tours take place either in morning (which photographers may prefer) or afternoon.

Otway is only about 70 kilometers northwest of Punta Arenas via Ruta 9 and a gravel road that leads west from a signed junction at the Carabineros Kon Aikén checkpoint; the gravel road passes the **Mina Pecket** coal mine before arriving at the *pingüinera.*

During the season, the **Pinguin Adventure Line** (Gabriela Mistral 679, Puerto Natales, tel. 061/411113, pinguin_adventure@yahoo.com) connects Puerto Natales with Punta Arenas (US$19 pp) via the scenic Río Verde alternative and the Otway colony, which makes it easy to visit to combine the penguin colony with door-to-door transportation. It departs from Puerto Natales at 8 A.M., arriving at Punta Arenas at 1 P.M.; the return trip leaves Punta Arenas at 3 P.M., arriving 8 P.M. at Natales.

While the Otway colony is a worthwhile excursion, visitors with flexible schedules and a little more money should consider the larger Isla Magdalena colony in Monumento Natural Los Pingüinos, in the Strait of Magellan.

PINGÜINOS AND PINGÜINERAS AT PUNTA ARENAS

Chilean Patagonia's largest city is close to two breeding colonies of the burrowing Magellanic penguin, *Spheniscus magellanicus*. The Otway Sound colony is about a 45-minute drive from Punta Arenas, and is interesting enough, but the larger colony on Isla Magdalena, an island in the Strait of Magellan, is two hours away by ferry.

Also known to English speakers as the jackass penguin because its call resembles that of a braying burro, the Magellanic is present from October to April. It's most numerous in January and February, when the chicks hatch in the sandy burrows that the birds have dug beneath the coastal turf. After the chicks have hatched, the parents alternate fishing trips in search of food that they later regurgitate to their young (combined with the scent of bird droppings, this makes any visit to a penguin colony an olfactory as well as a visual and auditory experience).

While the birds appear tame, they are wild animals, and their sharp beaks can draw blood—maintain a respectful distance for photography. Even though both the Otway and Magdalena colonies have fenced walking routes to restrain tourists, the birds themselves cross them constantly.

Besides the countless seabirds and dolphins en route, the Magdalena trip has the added bonus of a historic lighthouse that now serves as a visitors center on an island that's one big warren of penguin burrows. While neither trip is strenuous, any walk in the roaring Patagonian winds can be a workout.

Otway trips leave every day, but Magdalena trips no more than two or three times a week, in January and February, with fewer or no trips outside those months.

Monumento Natural Los Pingüinos

From early October, more than 60,000 breeding pairs of Magellanic penguins paddle ashore and waddle to burrows that cover nearly all of 97-hectare Isla Magdalena, 20 nautical miles northeast of Punta Arenas, before returning to sea in April. Also the site of a landmark century-old lighthouse, Isla Magdalena is the focal point of Monumento Natural Los Pingüinos, one of Conaf's smallest but most interesting reserves.

While the mainland Otway penguin colony gets upwards of 40,000 visitors per year, Isla Magdalena gets only about 4,600 because of its limited accessibility. In the summer months, though, the ferry *Melinka* visits the island three times weekly from Punta Arenas. Though more expensive than Otway tours, these excursions also offer the chance to see penguins and dolphins in the water, as well as black-browed albatrosses, cormorants, kelp gulls, skuas, South American terns, and other seabirds in the surrounding skies.

From a floating dock on the east side of the island, a short trail leads along the beach and up the hill to Scottish engineer George Slight's **Faro Magdalena** (1901), a lighthouse whose iron tower rises 13.5 meters above the island's highest point; still functioning, the light has a range of 10 nautical miles. A narrow spiral staircase ascends the tower.

In the building's first five decades, a resident caretaker maintained the acetylene light, but after its automation in 1955 the building was abandoned and vandalized. In 1981, though, the Chilean navy entrusted the building to Conaf; declared a national monument, it has since become a visitors center. It boasts remarkably good exhibits on the island's history (discovery and early navigation, cartography, and construction of the lighthouse) and natural history in both Spanish and English (though the English text is less complete). The U.S. archaeologist Junius Bird, best known for his 1930s work at the mainland site of Pali Aike, also undertook excavations here.

For excursions to Isla Magdalena, contact **Turismo Comapa** (Magallanes 990, tel. 061/200200, fax 061/225804, tcomapa@entelchile.net). In

M
Tierra del Fuego

December, January, and February, after its regular Tuesday/Thursday/Saturday ferry run to Porvenir, the *Melinka* makes a passengers-only trip to Isla Magdalena (US$30) from Terminal Tres Puentes; sailing time is 3 P.M. (bring food—the *Melinka*'s snack bar is pretty dire). Visitors spend about 1.5 hours on the island, returning to Punta Arenas around 9 P.M.

Passengers on the *Terra Australis* cruise through the Tierra del Fuego fjords stop here on the return leg of the trip.

Fuerte Bulnes

In 1584, Spanish explorer Pedro Sarmiento de Gamboa organized an expedition of 15 ships and 4,000 men to control the Strait of Magellan, but after a series of disasters only three ships with 300 colonists arrived to found **Ciudad del Rey don Felipe,** at Punta Santa Ana south of present-day Punta Arenas. Even worse for the Spaniards, the inhospitable climate and unsuitable soils made agriculture impossible; when the British privateer Thomas Cavendish landed here three years later, in 1587, he found only a handful of survivors and gave it the name Port Famine, which has survived as the Spanish **Puerto del Hambre.**

For many years, the consensus was that starvation alone determined the fate of Puerto del Hambre, but Punta Arenas historian Mateo Martinic has suggested that disease, mutual acts of violence, Tehuelche attacks, and a simple sense of anguish or abandonment contributed to its demise. Unfortunately, the Chilean military controls much of the area, making archaeological excavations that might resolve the question difficult.

The area remained unsettled until 1843, when President Manuel Bulnes ordered the cutter *Ancud* south from Chiloé with tools, construction materials, food, and livestock to take possession for the expansionist Chilean state. The result was Fuerte Bulnes, a military outpost that survived only a little longer than the original Spanish settlement before being relocated to Punta Arenas in 1848.

Modern Fuerte Bulnes, on the site of the first Chilean settlement, is a national monument

more for its site than for its reconstructions of 19th-century buildings and the defensive walls of sharpened stakes that surround them. Among the structures were residences, stables, a blockhouse, a chapel, a jail, and warehouse.

Archaeologists located nearby remnants of Ciudad del Rey don Felipe in 1955, and later excavations turned up human remains, bullets, tombs, and ruins of Puerto del Hambre's church. A relatively recent plaque (1965) celebrates the 125th anniversary of the Pacific Steam Navigation Company's ships *Chile* and *Peru* and their routes around the Horn.

Puerto del Hambre and Fuerte Bulnes are 58 kilometers south of Punta Arenas via Ruta 9, which is paved about halfway; the rest is bumpy but always passable. There is no regular public transportation, but most Punta Arenas tour operators offer half-day excursions to the area. Admission is free.

Reserva Nacional Laguna Parrillar

About 45 kilometers southwest of Punta Arenas via paved Ruta 9 and a gravel westbound lateral, Laguna Parrillar attracts only about 3,200 visitors per year to its 18,000 hectares of forest and wetland. While it's open to day use only, it has picnic areas and hiking trails to commend it, and makes a worthwhile excursion from the city.

Río Verde

Some 43 kilometers north of Punta Arenas on Ruta 9, a gravel road loops northwest along the shore of Seno Otway to Seno Skyring and the former Estancia Río Verde, which has seemingly made the transition from a shipshape sheep farm to a model municipality of exquisitely maintained public buildings in the Magellanic style. Note particularly the manicured gardens surrounding the **Escuela Básica** the local boarding school, which has a small natural history museum.

Ninety kilometers from Punta Arenas and six kilometers south of Río Verde village, **Hostería Río Verde** (tel. 061/311122, tel./fax 061/241008, rioverde@chileaustral.com, US$30 pp) draws big crowds to its Sunday Patagonian lamb barbecues, though it also serves seafood. Accommodations come with private bath and breakfast.

The loop road rejoins Ruta 9 at Villa Tehuelches, a wide spot in the road about 90 kilometers from Punta Arenas. This would make a good alternative route north or south for both motorists and mountain bikers, and is now part of an alternative tour between Puerto Natales and Punta Arenas that takes in the Otway penguin colony.

Río Rubens

About halfway between Villa Tehuelches and Puerto Natales, Río Rubens is a prime trout stream that flows northeast into Argentina. At Km 183 on Ruta 9, the nearby **Hotel Río Rubens** has resisted the temptation to upgrade itself from a modest rural inn, with a decent restaurant at modest prices, though it has added cabañas and camping. Hotel rates are US$12 pp with private bath and breakfast.

Estancia San Gregorio

From a highway junction about 45 kilometers north of Punta Arenas, paved Ruta 225 leads east-northeast to the Argentine border at Monte Aymond, passing the former Estancia San Gregorio, once one of Chilean Patagonia's largest landholdings. Part of the Menéndez wool empire, San Gregorio dates from the 1890s, though it reached its peak between 1910 and 1930. Besides wool, it produced frozen mutton, hides, and tallow.

Now run as a cooperative, 120 kilometers from Punta Arenas, San Gregorio is a *zona típica* national historical monument. It exemplified the Anglo-Scottish model of the Patagonian sheep *estancia,* in which each unit was a self-sufficient hierarchy with a nearly omnipotent administrator at the top. Geographically, it consisted of discrete residential and production sectors: the former included the administrator's house, employee residences, shearers' dormitories, chapel, and the like, while the latter consisted of the shearing shed, warehouses, a smithery, company store, and similarly functional buildings. It had its own railroad and a pier to move the wool clip directly to freighters.

Most of San Gregorio's construction dates from the 1890s, but French architect Antoine Beaulier's **Casa Patronal,** still occupied by a descendent of the Menéndez dynasty, dates from 1925. The farm featured an extensive system of windbreaks ranging upward of five meters in height, later planted with Monterey cypress for beautification.

While San Gregorio is technically not open to the public, many of its buildings line both sides of the highway to Monte Aymond. Beached on shore are the corroded hulks of the *Ambassador* (a national monument) and the company steamer *Amadeo,* which gave up the ghost in the 1940s.

Kimiri Aike

About 30 kilometers east of San Gregorio, paved Ruta 257 leads southeast to **Punta Delgada,** the port for the ferry crossing to Tierra del Fuego via the Primera Angostura narrows. Depending sometimes on tidal conditions, the ferries *Bahía Azul* and *Patagonia* shuttle across the channel every 1.5 hours between 8:30 A.M. and 11 P.M. Fares are US$2 pp for passengers, US$1 for kids ages 10–14, US$16 for automobiles, and US$5 for motorcycles. Most buses to Argentine Tierra del Fuego use this route because the longer ferry to Porvenir goes only once daily.

Directly at the highway junction, **Hostería Tehuelche** (tel. 061/1983002) was once the *casco* (big house) for the formerly British-run Estancia Kimiri Aike; now, from November to May, it offers satisfactory accommodations for US$28/38 s/d with shared bath. Buses between Punta Arenas and Río Gallegos usually stop here for lunch; breakfast, dinner,and snacks are also available. The Barros Luco sandwich can be good, but ask them to hold the mayonnaise.

Parque Nacional Pali Aike

Hugging the Argentine border north of Kimiri Aike and west of the Monte Aymond border crossing, little-visited Pali Aike is an area of volcanic steppe and rugged lava beds that once supported megafauna like the ground sloth known as the *milodón* and the native American horse, both of which disappeared soon after humans first inhabited the area some 11,000 years ago.

While Paleo-Indian hunters may have contributed to their extinction, environmental changes after the last major glaciation may also have played a role. In the 1930s, self-taught archaeologist Junius Bird, of New York's American Museum of Natural History, conducted the earliest systematic excavations of Paleo-Indian sites like Cueva Pali Aike, within the park boundaries, and Cueva Fell, a short distance to the west. These archaeologically rich volcanic shelters (not caves in the strictest sense of the word) are the prime reason Chilean authorities have nominated the area as a UNESCO World Heritage Site.

Findings at Cueva Pali Aike include human remains that have yielded insights on Paleo-Indian funerary customs, while materials from Cueva Fell have helped reveal the transition from relatively simple Paleo-Indian hunting to more complex forms of subsistence. These include sophisticated hunting tools like the bow and arrow and *boleadoras,* and a greater reliance on coastal and marine resources. There are also indicators of ceremonial artifacts.

Part of arid eastern Magallanes, 5,030-hectare Pali Aike consists of rolling steppe grasslands whose porous volcanic soils and slag absorb water

quickly. Almost constant high winds and cool temperatures make it a better summer or autumn excursion.

While the *milodón* and native horse may have disappeared, the park's grasslands swarm with herds of wild guanaco, and flocks of rheas, upland geese, *bandurria* (ibis), and other birds. Pumas and foxes are the major predators.

Accessible by road, **Cueva Pali Aike** is a volcanic tube seven meters wide and five meters high at its mouth; it is 17 meters deep but tapers as it advances. In the 1930s, Bird discovered both human and megafauna remains, at least 8,600 years old and probably much older, in the cave.

Tours from Punta Arenas visit Cueva Pali Aike and usually hike the 1.7-kilometer trail through the **Escorial del Diablo** (the appropriately named Devil's Slag Heap, which is hell on hiking boots). The trail ends at the volcanic **Crater Morada del Diablo.**

From Cueva Pali Aike, a nine-kilometer footpath leads to **Laguna Ana,** where waterfowl are abundant, and the main road, five kilometers from the park entrance. Mountain bikes should be ideal for this sort of rolling terrain, but it could be even tougher on tires than it is on boots.

guanacos, Parque Nacional Pali Aike, Chile

A campground is under construction, but there are no tourist services as yet. At the main park entrance, Conaf has a ranger station; there is no admission charge. A great destination for seekers of solitude, Pali Aike officially gets only about 600 visitors per annum.

Parque Nacional Pali Aike is 196 kilometers northeast of Punta Arenas via Ruta 9, Ruta 255, and a graveled secondary road from the hamlet of Cooperativa Villa O'Higgins, 11 kilometers beyond Kimiri Aike. Just south of the Chilean border post at Monte Aymond, a hard-to-follow dirt road also leads to the park.

There is no public transportation, but Punta Arenas travel agencies can arrange visits. Hiring a car, though, is probably the best alternative, especially if shared among several people.

PUERTO NATALES

In the past 20 years, Puerto Natales has changed from a sleepy wool and fishing port on what seemed the aptly named Seno Última Esperanza—"Last-Hope Sound"—to a bustling tourist town whose season has lengthened well beyond the traditional summer months of January and February. Its proximity to the now-famous Parque Nacional Torres del Paine, coupled with its status as the southern terminus for the scenic and increasingly popular ferry route from Puerto Montt, has placed it on the international travel map, utterly transforming the local economy.

Although Puerto Natales has no knockout attractions in its own right, the town enjoys a magnificent seaside setting, with the snow-capped Cordillera Sarmiento and Campo de Hielo Sur, the southern Patagonian ice cap, visible over the water to the west. For visitors to Paine and other regional sights, it has abundant services, including tour operators and rental-equipment providers; there are also convenient connections to the Argentine town of El Calafate and Parque Nacional Los Glaciares.

In the aftermath of the Argentine economic meltdown of 2001–02, though, Natales has taken a triple hit: retired Chilean coal workers from Río Turbio saw their incomes trapped in Argentine banking restrictions and their pensions cut by two-thirds because of the Argentine devaluation, even as their cost of living remains high, and active workers have seen their wages decline. At the same time, local merchants have seen their Argentine business dry up as things are no longer cheaper on the Chilean side. Only tourism remains reliable.

One possible strong point is the pending construction of a 150-meter cruise-ship pier, which would simplify transfers from both the ferry and visiting cruisers to land.

History

Última Esperanza acquired its name because expeditions led by the 16th-century Spaniards Juan Ladrilleros and Pedro Sarmiento de Gamboa failed to find a westbound route to the Pacific here. Puerto Natales proper dates from the early 20th century, a few years after German explorer Hermann Eberhard founded the area's first sheep *estancia* at Puerto Prat. Within a few years, the Sociedad Explotadora de Tierra del Fuego had built a slaughterhouse at nearby Bories to process and pack mutton for the export market. While the livestock economy declined in the second half of the 20th century, the tourist boom has reactivated and diversified the economy.

Orientation

On the eastern shores of Seno Última Esperanza, Puerto Natales (population 16,978) is 250 kilometers northwest off Punta Arenas via paved Ruta 9. It is 150 kilometers south of Parque Nacional Torres del Paine, also by Ruta 9, which is paved for 13 kilometers north of the city.

Entering town from the north, Ruta 9 becomes the roughly north-south Costanera Pedro Montt; most services and points of interest are within easy walking distance to the east. The principal commercial streets are east-west Manuel Bulnes and north-south Avenida Baquedano.

Sights

The **Municipalidad,** a gingerbread-style construction dating from 1929 on the east side of the Plaza Arturo Prat, had its construction financed by the Sociedad Explotadora de Tierra del Fuego, which owned large amounts of land

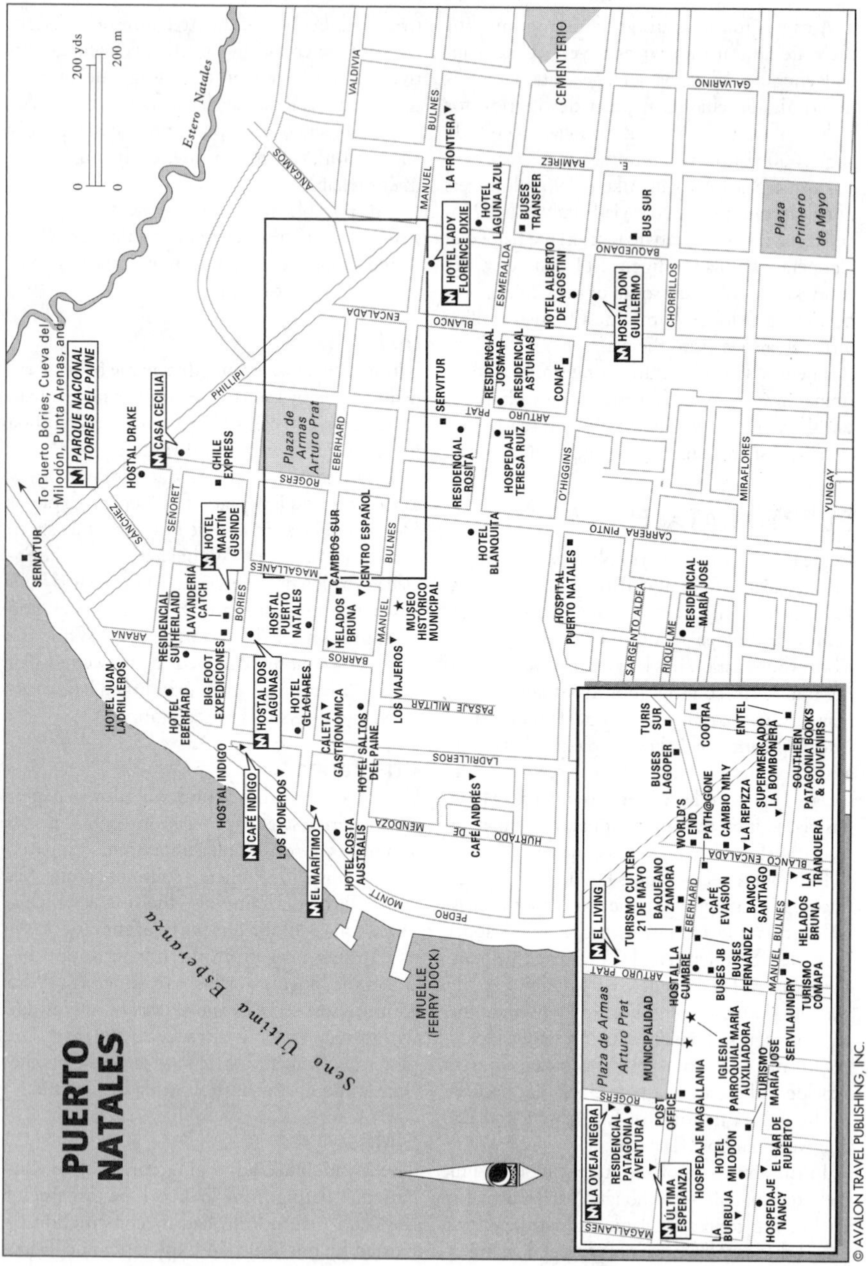

PUERTO NATALES

Seno Última Esperanza

MUELLE (FERRY DOCK)

Estero Natales

To Puerto Bories, Cueva del Milodón, Punta Arenas, and PARQUE NACIONAL TORRES DEL PAINE

0   200 yds
0   200 m

© AVALON TRAVEL PUBLISHING, INC.

Tierra del Fuego

Streets:
VALDIVIA, BULNES, MANUEL, ANGAMOS, PHILLIPI, SEÑORET, SÁNCHEZ, ARANA, BORIES, MAGALLANES, ROGERS, EBERHARD, ENCALADA, BLANCO, PRAT, ARTURO, ESMERALDA, O'HIGGINS, BAQUEDANO, CHORRILLOS, RAMÍREZ, GALVARINO, MIRAFLORES, YUNGAY, CARRERA PINTO, SARGENTO ALDEA, RIQUELME, LADRILLEROS, HURTADO DE MENDOZA, CAFÉ ANDRÉS, PEDRO MONTT, BARROS, LOS VIAJEROS, MANUEL, PASAJE MILITAR

Map labels:
SERNATUR
HOTEL JUAN LADRILLEROS
RESIDENCIAL SUTHERLAND
LAVANDERÍA CATCH
HOTEL EBERHARD
BIG FOOT EXPEDICIONES
HOSTAL DOS LAGUNAS
HOTEL GLACIARES
HOSTAL INDIGO
CAFÉ INDIGO
LOS PIONEROS
CALETA GASTRONOMICA
HOTEL SALTOS DEL PAINE
HOTEL COSTA AUSTRALIS
EL MARITIMO
HOSTAL DRAKE
CASA CECILIA
CHILE EXPRESS
HOTEL MARTIN GUSINDE
HOSTAL PUERTO NATALES
HELADOS BRUNA
CENTRO ESPAÑOL
CAMBIOS SUR
MUSEO HISTÓRICO MUNICIPAL
HOTEL BLANQUITA
SERVITUR
RESIDENCIAL ROSITA
HOSPEDAJE TERESA RUIZ
RESIDENCIAL JOSMAR
RESIDENCIAL ASTURIAS
CONAF
HOTEL LADY FLORENCE DIXIE
LA FRONTERA
HOTEL LAGUNA AZUL
BUSES TRANSFER
BUS SUR
HOTEL ALBERTO DE AGOSTINI
HOSTAL DON GUILLERMO
HOSPITAL PUERTO NATALES
RESIDENCIAL MARÍA JOSÉ
CEMENTERIO
Plaza Primero de Mayo
Plaza de Armas Arturo Prat

Inset map labels:
Plaza de Armas Arturo Prat
POST OFFICE
MUNICIPALIDAD
IGLESIA PARROQUIAL MARÍA AUXILIADORA
TURISMO MARÍA JOSÉ
RESIDENCIAL PATAGONIA AVENTURA
LA OVEJA NEGRA
ÚLTIMA ESPERANZA
LA BURBUJA
HOTEL MILODON
HOSPEDAJE MAGALLANIA
HOSPEDAJE NANCY
EL BAR DE RUPERTO
EL LIVING
TURISMO CUTTER 21 DE MAYO
BAQUEANO ZAMORA
HOSTAL LA CUMBRE
WORLD'S END
CAFÉ EVASIÓN
BUSES JB
BUSES FERNANDEZ
SERVILAUNDRY
BANCO SANTIAGO
TURISMO COMAPA
HELADOS BRUNA
LA TRANQUERA
PATH@GONE
CAMBIO MILY
LA REPIZA
TURIS SUR
BUSES LAGOPER
COOTRA
ENTEL
SUPERMERCADO LA BOMBONERA
SOUTHERN PATAGONIA BOOKS & SOUVENIRS

Municipalidad de Puerto Natales, Chile

in both Chile and Argentina. Immediately to its east, the **Iglesia Parroquial María Auxiliadora** dates from the same era and shares its Magellanic style.

In the same exterior fashion but with a roomier interior that displays its holdings to advantage, the **Museo Histórico Municipal** (Bulnes 285, tel. 061/411263, muninata@ctcinternet.cl, US$1 adults, US$.35 children) offers displays on natural history, archaeology and the region's aboriginal peoples, European settlement and the rural economy (including the powerful Sociedad Explotadora), Puerto Natales's own urban evolution, and the Carabineros police, who played a role in the museum's creation. Noteworthy individual artifacts include a Yámana (Yahgan) dugout canoe and Aonikenk (Tehuelche) *boleadoras,* plus historical photographs of Captain Eberhard and the town's development. Summer hours are 8:30 A.M.–12:30 P.M. and 2:30–8 P.M. weekdays, 3–8 P.M. weekends; the rest of the year, hours are 8:30 A.M.–12:30 P.M. and 2:30–6 P.M. weekdays, 3–6 P.M. weekends.

Entertainment

Puerto Natales's nightlife is limited mostly to low-key bars like **Café Indigo** (Ladrilleros 105), a Chilean-run but gringo-oriented gathering place with nightly slide shows about Natales and Torres del Paine.

El Bar de Ruperto (Bulnes 371) takes its name from the pisco-swilling burro so popular on Chilean TV ads.

Shopping

For books, travel literature (some of it in English), maps, and the like, there's a branch of **Southern Patagonia Souvenirs & Books** (Bulnes 688, tel. 061/413017).

Ñandú Artesanía (Eberhard 586) sells maps and books in addition to a selection of quality crafts. **World's End** (Blanco Encalada 226, tel. 061/414725) is a Chilean-map specialist.

Accommodations

Over the past two decades, Puerto Natales has developed one of the densest offerings of

Tierra del Fuego

accommodations in all Chile. This is especially true in the budget category, where competition keeps prices low. There are good values in all categories, but plenty of mediocre and ordinary places as well. Off-season rates can drop dramatically.

Under US$10
Residencial Josmar (Prat and Esmeralda, tel. 061/414417, US$3 pp) has built a spacious campground with clearly delineated sites, privacy from the street, electricity, and hot showers. Among the regular accommodations, Israeli favorite **Residencial María José** (Magallanes 646, tel. 061/412218, US$5 pp) is one of Natales's best bargains.

US$10–25
Hospedaje Magallania (Tomás Rogers 255, tel. 061/414950, US$5.50 pp) is an informal hostel-style facility with spacious but multibedded rooms, kitchen privileges, a TV room, and *buena onda* (good vibes).

    Residencial Rosita (Prat 367, tel. 061/412259, US$6 pp) occupies the upstairs of a crowded family house; the rooms, all with shared bath, are smallish but fairly priced.

    Residencial Asturias (Prat 426, tel. 061/412105, US$6 pp) is a little cramped but otherwise fine. Other respectable choices are **Hospedaje Teresa Ruiz** (Esmeralda 463, tel. 410472, US$5–6 pp); and **Residencial Sutherland** (Barros Arana 155, tel. 061/410359, US$6 pp).

    The local HI affiliate is **Albergue Path@gone** (Eberhard 595, tel. 061/413291, US$8 pp), which has very good facilities. Friendly **Residencial Patagonia Aventura** (Tomás Rogers 179, tel. 411028, US$8–10 pp) provides a bit more privacy than others in its range, and the knowledgeable operators also rent equipment.

    Rates at friendly, responsive **Hospedaje Nancy** (Bulnes 343, tel. 061/415644, nancy@patagoniadiscovery.cl, US$8 pp) include breakfast. In an older house with considerable character, steadily upgrading **Ⅶ Hostal Dos Lagunas** (Barros Arana 104, tel. 061/415733, doslagunas

@hotmail.com, US$9 pp) is fast becoming a travelers' favorite; rates include an ample and varied breakfast.

US$25–50
Stuck in an off-the-beaten-sidewalk location, **Ⅶ Hostal Don Guillermo** (O'Higgins 657, tel./fax 061/414506, US$12–20 s, US$20–25 d) gets less business than it deserves, perhaps because it looks more expensive than it is. Though it lacks private baths and some rooms are small, this immaculate hostelry is seriously underpriced compared to competitors; rates vary according to whether the room has cable TV. In all likelihood, it will either go out of business or jack up prices as demand increases.

    Its decor is tacky—the interior looks more like a house trailer than a house—but cheerful **Hotel Blanquita** (Ignacio Carrera Pinto 409, tel. 061/411674, US$9 pp, US$23/30 s/d) is spotlessly maintained and often full. Rates include breakfast, but vary according to shared or private bath.

    Setting local standards since its inception many years ago, **Ⅶ Casa Cecilia** (Tomás Rogers 60, tel. 061/411797, redcecilia@entelchile.net, US$13–25 s, US$21–32 d, US$27 t) has become a Natales institution—on occasion, nonguests even ask for tours of the hospitable Swiss-Chilean B&B. The rooms are simple and some are small, but all enjoy central heating. There there are kitchen facilities, and the cheerful atrium is a popular gathering place. Rates, which vary according to shared or private bath, include the usual sumptuous breakfast.

    Hostal La Cumbre (Eberhard 533, tel. 061/412422, US$18 pp) has one of the better-preserved landmark houses in town. Hip **Hostal Indigo** (Ladrilleros 105, tel. 061/413609, fax 061/410169, indigo@entelchile.net, US$17 pp, US$40 d with breakfast) has carved itself a niche as much for its ground-floor pub/restaurant as for its comfortable upstairs accommodations; most but not all rooms have private bath. Climbers can work out on the wall outside.

US$50–100
Some of the city's best values are in this cate-

gory, starting with **Hotel Laguna Azul** (Baquedano 380, tel./fax 061/411207, laguna.azul@entelchile.net, US$42/51 s/d) and **Hotel Milodón** (Bulnes 356, tel. 061/411727, fax 061/411286, US$45/60 s/d).

Recently rehabbed **Hostal Drake** (Philippi 383, tel./fax 061/411553, francisdrake@chileaustral.com, US$52/69 s/d) is a comfortable hostelry that tour operators often choose for their clients. Rates include breakfast, but you may have to be persistent to get IVA discounts.

The striking **Hotel Lady Florence Dixie** (Manuel Bulnes 659, tel. 061/411158, fax 061/411943, florence@chileanpatagonia.com, US$66–76 s, US$82–92 d) has expanded and upgraded what was already a good hotel without becoming a budget-breaker. It's getting competition, though, from the newish **Hotel Glaciares** (Eberhard 104, tel./fax 061/411452, glaciares@entelchile.net, www.hotelglaciares.co.cl, US$74/86).

US$100–150

Hotel Internacional Alberto de Agostini (O'Higgins 632, tel. 061/410060, fax 061/410070, hotelagostini@entelchile.net, US$68/102) has spacious rooms with good natural light, but the hotel seems moribund despite its relative newness. While it's dropped its rack rates, it's still worth bargaining here.

Hotel Eberhard (Costanera Pedro Montt 25, tel. 061/411208, fax 061/411209, hoteleberhard@busesfernandez.com, US$95/104 s/d) used to be one of the best in its range; it's still OK, but there are better values. **Hotel Juan Ladrilleros** (Pedro Montt 161, tel. 061/411652, fax 061/412109, aventour@entelchile.net, US$93/105) is about average; try instead the handsome **Hotel Saltos del Paine** (Bulnes 156, tel. 061/413607, fax 061/410261, informacion@netline.cl, www.saltosdelpaine.cl, US$85/108 s/d).

The best value in this category is the **Hotel Martín Gusinde** (Bories 278, tel. 061/412770, fax 061/412401, mgusinde@uoie.com, US$116/140 s/d)—especially when off-season rates drop by 50 percent.

Rates at the waterfront classic **Hotel Costa Australis** (Costanera Pedro Montt 262, tel. 061/412000, fax 061/411881, costaus@ctcreuna.cl, US$130–164 s, US$147–181 d) depend on whether the room has a city or sea view. Off-season rates also fall substantially.

Food

To stock up on supplies for hiking at Puerto Natales, visit **Supermercado La Bombonera** (Bulnes 646). For breakfast, sandwiches, and desserts (especially the Sachertorte), try the British-run **El Living** (Arturo Prat 156), on the north side of the Plaza de Armas. The owner arrived here by way of Explora's extravagant Hotel Salto Chico, in Torres del Paine, but his food is more upscale than his prices.

Known for its seafood, Puerto Natales has plenty of moderately priced eateries and a handful of upscale choices, if nothing truly exceptional. Relying on their waterfront locations to draw crowds, **El Marítimo** (Pedro Montt 214, tel. 061/410819) and **Los Pioneros** (Pedro Montt 166, tel. 061/410783) offer good value. For better atmosphere, though, try the casual **La Tranquera** (Bulnes 579, tel. 061/411039).

La Caleta Gastronómica (Eberhard 169, tel. 061/413969) is a moderately priced (US$4–7) locale that offers excellent value—try the salmon with king-crab sauce. Another well-established option is **Café Andrés** (Ladrilleros 381, tel. 061/412380), for cooked-to-order seafood.

La Burbuja (Bulnes 300, tel. 061/414204) specializes in seafood and meats, but also has vegetarian offerings; try the *ostiones al pil pil* (US$5), a spicy scallop appetizer, and *congrio* (conger eel). **La Oveja Negra** (Tomás Rogers 169, tel. 061/415711) has made good early impressions for seafood and beef.

Underrated **Última Esperanza** (Eberhard 354, tel. 061/411391) deserves more attention than it gets for exceptional seafood at reasonable prices with outstanding service. **Los Viajeros** (Bulnes 291, tel. 061/411156) is a recent entry in the seafood category. The **Centro Español** (Magallanes 247, tel. 061/411181) promises Spanish cuisine, but it's work-in-progress.

Evasión (Eberhard 595-B, tel. 061/414605) is a moderately priced café-restaurant with daily lunch specials. **La Frontera** (Bulnes 819), open for lunch only, is comparable.

Basic Chilean dishes outshine the Italian at **La Repizza** (Blanco Encalada 294, tel. 061/441036). The most diverse food in town may be at ▨ **Café Indigo,** (Ladrilleros 105, tel. 061/413609), part of its namesake accommodations.

Natales's best ice creamery, **Helados Bruna,** has two locales: Bulnes 585 and Eberhard 217. Rhubarb is the regional specialty.

Information

In a freestanding chalet-style structure on the waterfront, **Sernatur's** local delegation (Pedro Montt 19, tel./fax 061/412125) is open 8:30 A.M.–1 P.M. and 2:30–6:30 P.M. weekdays throughout the year; from December to March it's also open 9 A.M.–1 P.M. weekends. It has helpful personnel, occasionally English-speaking, and fairly thorough information on accommodations, restaurants, and transportation.

For national park information, contact **Conaf** (O'Higgins 584, tel. 061/411438).

Services

Puerto Natales has several exchange houses: **Cambio Mily** (Blanco Encalada 266); **Cambios Sur** (Eberhard 285); and **Stop Cambios** (Baquedano 380). **Banco Santiago** (Bulnes 598) has an ATM.

Correos de Chile (Eberhard 429) is at the southwest corner of Plaza Arturo Prat.

Long-distance operators include **Telefónica CTC** (Blanco Encalada and Bulnes), **Chile Express** (Tomás Rogers 143), and **Entel** (Baquedano 270).

Internet connections are water-torture slow here, but there are several outlets for about US$3 per hour, including **Turismo María José** (Bulnes 386) and **Café Indigo** (Ladrilleros 105).

Servilaundry (Bulnes 513, tel. 061/412869) or **Lavandería Catch** (Bories 218) can do the washing.

Hospital Puerto Natales is at Ignacio Carrera Pinto 537 (tel. 061/411582).

Getting There

LanChile/LanExpress no longer has a separate office here, but **Turismo Comapa** (Bulnes 533, tel. 061/414300, fax 061/414361) can handle reservations and tickets. Punta Arenas–bound buses will drop passengers at that city's Aeropuerto Presidente Carlos Ibáñez del Campo.

Path@gone (Eberhard 599, tel./fax 061/413290, pathgone@chileaustral.com, www.pathagone.com) is the representative for Aerovías DAP, which flies weekdays to El Calafate (Argentina) from November to March. Puerto Natales has a small but modern airfield just north of town.

There is frequent bus service to and from Punta Arenas and Torres del Paine, and regular but less frequent service to the Argentine destinations of Río Turbio, Río Gallegos, and El Calafate.

Carriers serving **Punta Arenas** (US$5.50, three hours) include **Bus Sur** (Baquedano 558, tel. 061/411325); **Buses Fernández** (Eberhard 555, tel. 061/411111); **Buses Pacheco** (Baquedano and O'Higgins, tel. 061/414513); and **Buses Transfer** (Baquedano 414, tel. 061/412616).

Services to **Torres del Paine** (US$9, two hours) vary seasonally, and there is often frequent turnover among the agencies; there are small discounts for round-trip tickets. **Buses JB** (Prat 258, tel. 061/412824) goes three times daily to Torres del Paine (US$9, two hours), while **Buses Gómez** (Prat 234, tel. 061/410595) goes at 7:30 A.M., returning at 2:30 P.M. **Turismo María José** (Bulnes 386, tel. 061/414312) goes at 7 A.M. daily, returning at 1:30 P.M.

For the Argentine border town of **Río Turbio** (US$1.50, one hour), where there are connections to El Calafate and Río Gallegos, try **Buses Lagoper** (Angamos 640, tel. 061/411831), which has one or two daily; or **Buses Cootra** (Baquedano 244, tel. 061/412785), which has five to seven daily except on weekends, when there are only two or three. **Turismo Zaahj** (Prat 236, tel. 061/412260), Bus Sur, and Cootra alternate daily service to El Calafate (US$17, 5.5 hours). In winter, services are less frequent, perhaps only weekly.

To **Río Gallegos, Buses El Pingüino,** (Eberhard 555, tel. 061/411111) at the Fernández terminal, goes Wednesday and Sunday at 11 A.M.

(US$10–13, 4.5 hours). Bus Sur goes Tuesday and Thursday at 9 A.M.

Turismo Comapa/Navimag (Bulnes 533, tel. 061/414300, www.navimag.cl), operates the car/passenger ferry M/V *Magallanes* to the mainland Chilean city of Puerto Montt. Northbound sailing day is usually Friday at 4 A.M., but weather and tides can change schedules.

Passengers often spend the night on board before early morning departures, but Navimag also has a Sala de Espera (waiting room) improvised from two shipping containers at the corner of Pedro Montt and O'Higgins.

Getting Around

Emsa/Avis (Bulnes 632, tel. 061/410775) rents cars, but there's a better selection in Punta Arenas. **World's End** (Blanco Encalada 226, tel. 061/414725) rents bicycles (US$20 per day) and motorcycles (US$65 per day). **Path@gone** (Eberhard 599, tel./fax 061/413290) also rents bicycles.

VICINITY OF PUERTO NATALES

Increasing numbers of operators arrange excursions to nearby sites of interest and, of course, to Parque Nacional Torres del Paine and even Argentina's Parque Nacional Los Glaciares.

Several operators have organized complementary, one-stop arrangements for Torres del Paine under the umbrella of **Path@gone** (Eberhard 599, tel./fax 061/413290, pathgone @chileaustral.com, www.pathagone.com). These include **Andescape** (tel./fax 061/412592, andescape@terra.cl, www.andescape.cl); **Fantástico Sur** (Magallanes 960, Punta Arenas, tel. 061/710050, info@lastorres.com, www.lastorres.com); **Onas Aventura Patagonia** (tel./fax 061/412707, onas@chileaustral.com), which also does sea kayaking, trekking, and full-day excursions to Paine; and **Turismo Stipe** (tel./fax 061/411125, turismostipe@entelchile.net).

Other tour operators include **Big Foot Adventure Patagonia** (Bories 206, tel. 061/414611, fax 061/414276, explore@bigfootpatagonia.com, www.bigfootpatagonia.com) for sea kayaking, trekking, ice hiking, climbing, mountaineering, and more-general excursions as well; **Chile Na-**tivo (Barros Arana 176, tel. 061/411385, fax 061/415474, info@chilenativo.com, www.chile-nativo.com) for riding, trekking, and bird-watching; and **Servitur** (Prat 353, tel./fax 061/411858). **Baqueano Zamora** (Eberhard 566, tel. 061/413953, baqueano@chileaustral.com) specializes in horseback trips in the park and is also the concessionaire for Posada Río Serrano.

Frigorífico Bories

Only four kilometers north of Puerto Natales, the Sociedad Explotadora de Tierra del Fuego built this state-of-the-art (for its time) meat freezer to prepare excess livestock, primarily sheep, for shipment to Europe. Built of brick masonry between 1912 and 1914 in the Magellanic style, it's the only plant of its kind in a reasonable state of preservation. After expropriation by the Allende government in 1971, the plant was partially dismantled and finally shut down a few years back.

Among the remaining structures are the rendering plant, which converted animal fat into tallow, the tannery that prepared hides for shipment, and the main offices, smithery, locomotive-repair shop (Bories had its own short line), freight jetty, power plant, and boilers. The power plant still works.

Accommodations and food are available here at **Hotel Cisne Cuello Negro;** make reservations through **Turismo Pehoé** (José Menéndez 918, Punta Arenas, tel. 061/244506, fax 061/248052, pehoe1@ctcreuna.cl). Rack rates are US$90/100 s/d with private bath and breakfast; there is also a restaurant.

Puerto Prat

About 15 kilometers northwest of Puerto Natales via a gravel road, sheltered Puerto Prat is the nearest thing to a beach getaway that *Natalinos* have—on rare hot days, its shallow waters warm up enough to let the truly intrepid dip their toes into the sea. It is also the starting point for one-day sea-kayak trips to **Fiordo Eberhard** (US$90 pp); for details, contact Big Foot Adventure Patagonia in Puerto Natales.

A short distance north, settled by Captain Hermann Eberhard, **Estancia Puerto Consuelo** was the area's first sheep farm. Now open to the public for day visits (US$10 pp), it also has a small museum. It's open 9 A.M.–7 P.M. daily; for details, contact Turismo Comapa in Natales.

Difunta Correa Shrine

About six kilometers east of Puerto Natales, on the south side of Ruta 9, the mounting number of water-filled plastic bottles at this spontaneous roadside shrine suggests one of two things: either many Argentines are traveling here, or Chileans are becoming devoted to the folk saint of the Argentina's San Juan Province. Or it may be a changing combination of the two, as the recent Argentine economic crisis has reversed the traditional flow of Argentine tourists into Chile.

Cerro Dorotea

About seven kilometers east of Puerto Natales on Ruta 9, along the Argentine border, the hike

The Argentine folk saint Difunta Correa has a large roadside shrine near Puerto Natales, Chile.

to the ridgetop of the Sierra Dorotea makes an ideal half-day excursion, with some of the area's finest panoramas. Well-marked with red blazes and signs, the route to the summit of 549-meter Cerro Dorotea is, after the initial approach, unrelentingly uphill but never exhaustingly steep. This is not pristine nature—much of the lower slopes are cutover *lenga* forest, some of which has regenerated itself into an even-aged woodland. The ridge itself is barren, with a telephone-relay antenna on the top.

Access to the trailhead is over private property, where farmer Juan de Dios Saavedra Ortiz charges US$4 pp. The fee, though, includes a simple but welcome Chilean *onces* (afternoon tea with homemade bread, butter, ham, and cheese) on your return from the hike.

Monumento Natural Cueva del Milodón

Northwest of present-day Puerto Natales, on the shores of a small inlet known as Fiordo Eberhard, the giant Pleistocene ground sloth known as the mylodon (*Mylodon darwini*) took shelter in this wave-cut grotto some 30 meters high and 80 meters wide at its mouth, and 200 meters deep. While the mylodon has been extinct for nearly as long as humans have inhabited the area—some 11,000 years ago—the discovery of its remains caused a sensation in Europe, as their state of preservation induced some scientists to believe the animal might still be alive.

German pioneer sheep farmer Hermann Eberhard gets credit for discovering the cave in 1895, but Erland Nordenskjöld (1900) was the first scientist to study the cave, taking sample bones and skin back to Sweden. Its manure has been carbon-dated at roughly 10,400 years before the present, meaning the large herbivore coexisted with humans, but it was most definitely *not* a domesticate. In all probability, though, hunting pressure contributed to its demise (and that of many other Pleistocene megafauna). Oddly enough, no complete skeleton has been found.

The mylodon has gained a spot in the Western imagination, both among scientists and the lay public. U.S. archaeologist Junius Bird described the animal in his journals, published as *Travel* and *Archaeology in South Chile* (University of Iowa Press, 1988), edited by John Hyslop of the American Museum of Natural History. Family tales inspired Bruce Chatwin to write his masterpiece *In Patagonia,* which relates far-fetched legends that Paleo-Indians penned the mylodon in the cave and that some animals survived into the 19th century.

Conaf's **Museo de Sitio,** open 8 A.M.–8 P.M. daily, has excellent information on the 192-hectare park, which attracts some 41,000 visitors per annum, more than half of them Chilean, but there are no other facilities except for a picnic area. A tacky full-size statue of the mylodon stands in the cave itself.

Many tours from Puerto Natales take in the sight, but there is no regular public transportation except for Paine-bound buses that pass on Ruta 9, five kilometers to the east. Mountain bike rental could be a good option.

Parque Nacional Bernardo O'Higgins

Chile's largest national park, covering 3,525,901 hectares of islands and icecaps from near Tortel in Region XI (Aisén) to Última Esperanza in Region XII (Magallanes), has few easy access points, but the **Glaciar Balmaceda,** at the outlet of the Río Serrano, is one of them. From Puerto Natales, it's now a four-hour sail northwest—where Juan Ladrilleros and Pedro de Sarmiento de Gamboa ended their futile quests for a sheltered route to the Pacific—past Puerto Bories, several wool *estancias* reachable only by sea, and nesting colonies of seabirds and breeding colonies of southern sea lions, among U-shaped valleys with glaciers and waterfalls. Andean condors have been sighted in the area.

At the end of the cruise, passengers disembark for an hour or so at **Puerto Toro,** where a half-hour's walk through southern beech forest leads to the receding Glaciar Balmaceda. Visitors remain about an hour before returning to Natales, unless they take advantage of the option to travel upriver to Torres del Paine, which may be visible in the distance.

Accommodations and Food

There are no formal accommodations in the park

proper. However, across the sound from Puerto Toro, in virtually the most peaceful imaginable location—but for the wind—the nearly new **Hostería Monte Balmaceda** (José Nogueira 1255, Punta Arenas, tel. 061/220174, fax 061/243354, aventour@entelchile.net) charges US$110/145 s/d with breakfast.

As it's mostly accessible by sea, a stay here is usually part of a package including a visit to the park and/or Torres del Paine. There is, however, a footpath suitable for a two-day trek from the park to the hotel.

Practicalities

Two Puerto Natales operators sail up the sound to Glaciar Balmaceda, usually daily in summer, less frequently the rest of the year. Bad weather and high winds may cause cancellations at any time of year.

Turismo Cutter 21 de Mayo (Eberhard 554, tel. 061/411978 or Ladrilleros 171, tel./fax 061/411176, 21demayo@chileaustral.com) operates its eponymous vessel or the yacht *Alberto de Agostini* to the park. Fares are US$60 pp; on the return the boat stops at Estancia Los Perales, where there's an optional *asado* for US$12 pp. The 18-meter yacht *Nueva Galicia* (Eberhard 169, tel. 061/412352, nuevagalicia@terra.cl, www.nuevagalicia.com) does the same circuit.

Instead of returning to Puerto Natales, it's possible to continue upriver to Torres del Paine with either 21 de Mayo or **Onas Patagonia** (Eberhard 599, tel. 061/414349, tel./fax 061/412707, onas@chileaustral.com). In open Zodiac rafts, supplying all passengers with warm wet-weather gear, Onas passes scenic areas not normally seen by visitors to Paine, makes a lunch stop along the Río Serrano, and requires a brief portage around the Serrano rapids before arriving at the Río Serrano campground. The total cost is US$90; the excursion can also be done in the opposite direction.

Cerro Castillo

One of Chile's most thinly populated municipalities, the *comuna* of Torres del Paine has only 739 inhabitants according the 2002 census; more than half of them live in Cerro Castillo, 60

Tierra del Fuego

kilometers north of Puerto Natales on Ruta 9, alongside the Río Don Guillermo border crossing. Called Cancha Carrera on the Argentine side, this is the most direct route from Parque Nacional Torres del Paine to El Calafate (Argentina) and Parque Nacional Los Glaciares. Once seasonal, it is now open all year.

Formerly an *estancia* belonging to the powerful Sociedad Explotadora de Tierra del Fuego, Cerro Castillo has an assortment of services, including a dismal museum at the municipal **Departamento de Turismo** (Avenida Bernardo O'Higgins s/n, tel. 061/691932), and the only gas station north of Puerto Natales.

It also has accommodations at the basic **Residencial Loreto Belén** and more-elaborate lodgings at **Hostería El Pionero** (tel. 061/413953, fax 061/412911, baqueanoz@terra.cl, US$45–95 s, US$55–115 d); the cheaper rooms belong to an annex. Open September to April only, it serves meals to nonguests as well as guests, and also rents horses.

PARQUE NACIONAL TORRES DEL PAINE

Several years ago, when a major Pacific Coast shipping company placed a two-page ad in Alaska Airlines' in-flight magazine, the landscape chosen to represent Alaska's grandeur was . . . Parque Nacional Torres del Paine! While an opportunistic or uninformed photo editor may have been the culprit—appropriately enough for a Southern-Hemisphere destination, the image was reversed—the soaring granite spires of Chile's premiere national park have become an international emblem of alpine majesty.

But there's more—unlike many of South American's national parks, Torres del Paine has an integrated network of hiking trails suitable for day trips and backpack treks, endangered species like the wild guanaco in a UNESCO-recognized World Biosphere Reserve, and accommodations options ranging from rustic campgrounds to cozy trail huts and five-star luxury hotels. Popular enough that some visitors prefer the shoulder seasons of spring (Nov.–Dec.) or fall (Mar.–Apr.)—the park re-

ceives upwards of 70,000 visitors yearly—Torres del Paine has become a major international destination, but it's still wild country.

Nearly everybody visits the park to behold extraordinary natural features like the **Torres del Paine** themselves, the sheer granite towers that have defied erosion even as the weaker sedimentary strata around them have weathered, and the jagged **Cuernos del Paine,** with their striking interface between igneous and metamorphic rocks. Most hike its trails uneventfully, but for all its popularity, this is still hazardous terrain. Hikers have disappeared, the rivers run fast and cold, the weather is unpredictable, and there is one documented case of a tourist being attacked and killed by a puma.

Orientation

Parque Nacional Torres del Paine is 112 kilometers northwest of Puerto Natales via Ruta 9 through Cerro Castillo; 38 kilometers beyond Castillo, a westbound lateral traces the southern shore of Lago Sarmiento de Gamboa to the park's isolated Laguna Verde Sector. Three kilometers beyond the Laguna Verde junction, another westbound lateral leaves Ruta 9 to follow Lago Sarmiento's north shore to Portería Sarmiento, the park's main gate; it continues southwest for 37 kilometers to the Administración, the park headquarters at the west end of Lago del Toro.

Twelve kilometers east of Portería Sarmiento, another lateral branches northwest and, three kilometers farther on, splits again; the latter leads to Guardería Laguna Azul, in the park's little-visited northern sector, while the latter enters the park at Guardería Laguna Amarga, the most common starting point for the popular Paine Circuit, and follows the south shore of Lago Nordenskjöld and Lago Pehoé en route to the Administración. Most public transportation takes this route.

Geography and Climate

Parque Nacional Torres del Paine comprises 181,414 hectares of Patagonian steppe, lowland, and alpine glacial lakes, glacier-fed torrents and waterfalls, forested uplands and nearly vertical granite needles. Altitudes range from only about 50 meters above sea level along the lower Río

Serrano to 3,050 meters on the summit of Paine Grande, the central massif's tallest peak.

Paine has a cool temperate climate characterized by frequent high winds, especially in spring and summer. The average summer temperature is about 10.8°C, with the maximum reaching around 23°C; the average minimum in winter is around freezing. Average figures are misleading, though, as the weather is highly changeable. The park lies in the rain shadow of the Campo de Hielo Sur, where westerly storms drop most of their load as snow, so it receives only about 600 millimeters of rainfall per annum. Still, snow and hail can fall even in midsummer. Spring is probably the windiest time; in autumn, March and April, the winds tend to moderate, but days are shorter.

It should go without saying that at higher elevations temperatures are somewhat cooler and snow is likelier to fall. In some areas it's possible to hut-hop between *refugios,* eliminating the need for a tent and sleeping bag but not for warm clothing and impermeable rain gear.

Flora and Fauna

Less diverse than in areas farther north, Paine's vegetation still varies with altitude and distance from the Andes. Bunch grasses of the genera *Festuca* and *Stipa,* known collectively as *coirón,* cover the park's arid southeastern steppes, often interspersed with thorny shrubs like the calafate (*Berberis buxifolia*), which produces edible fruit, and neneo (*Anathrophillum desideratum*). There are also miniature ground-hugging orchids like the zapatito (*Calceolaria uniflora*) and capachito (*Calceolaria biflora*).

Approaching the Andes, forests of the deciduous lenga (*Nothofagus pumilio*) blanket the hillsides, along with the evergreen *coigue de Magallanes* (*Nothofagus betuloides*) and the deciduous ñire (*Nothofagus antarctica*). At the highest elevations, there is little vegetation of any kind among the alpine fell fields.

Among Paine's mammals, the most conspicuous is the guanaco (*Lama guanicoe*), whose numbers—and tameness—have increased dramatically over the past two decades. Many of its young, known as *chulengos,* fall prey to the puma (*Felis*

concolor). A more common predator, or at least a more visible one, is the gray fox (*Dusicyon griseus*), which lives off the introduced European hare and, outside the park boundaries, off sheep). The endangered *huemul* or Andean deer (*Hippocamelus bisulcus*) is a rare sight.

The monarch of South American birds, of course, is the Andean condor (*Vultur gryphus*), not a rare sight here. Filtering the lake shallows for plankton, the Chilean flamingo (*Phoenicopterus chilensis*) summers here after breeding in the northern altiplano. The *caiquén,* or upland goose (*Chloephaga picta*), grazes the moist grasslands around the lakes, while the black-necked swan (*Cygnus melancoryphus*) paddles peacefully on the surface. The fleet but flightless rhea, or ñandú (*Pterocnemia pennata*), races across the steppes.

Paine Circuit

More than two decades ago, under a military dictatorship, Chile attracted few foreign visitors, and hiking in Torres del Paine was a solitary experience—on a 10-day trek over the now-famous Paine Circuit, I met only three other hikers, two Americans and a Chilean. Some parts of the route were easy-to-follow stock trails (the park was once an *estancia*), while others, on the east shore of Lago Grey and into the valley of the Río de los Perros in particular, were barely boot-width tracks on steep slopes, or involved scrambling over granite boulders and fording waist-deep glacial meltwater. In the interim, as raging rivers have destroyed bridges at the outlets of Lago Nordenskjöld and Lago Paine, the original trailhead on the north shore on Lago Pehoé no longer exists, and the Laguna Azul exit in the park's northeastern corner is no longer feasible.

At the same time, completion of a trail along the north shore of Lago Nordenskjöld several years back created a new loop and simultaneously provided access to the south side of the Torres, offering easier access up the Río Ascencio and Valle del Francés in what is often done as the shorter "W" route (see The "W" Variant section) to Lago Pehoé. Where the former circuit crossed the Río Paine and continued along its north bank to the Laguna Azul campground,

Tierra del Fuego

the new circuit now follows the river's west bank south to Laguna Amarga.

In the interim, trail maintenance and development have improved dramatically, rudimentary and not-so-rudimentary bridges have replaced fallen logs and traversed stream fords, and comfortable concessionaire *refugios* and organized campgrounds have supplanted the lean-tos and *puestos* (outside houses) that once sheltered shepherds on their rounds. Though it's theoretically possible to complete most of the circuit without a tent or even a sleeping bag, showering and eating at the *refugios,* hikers should remember that this is still rugged country with unpredictable weather.

Most hikers now tackle the circuit counter-clockwise from Guardería Laguna Amarga, where buses from Puerto Natales stop for passengers to pay the park admission fee. An alternative is to continue to Pudeto and take a passenger launch to Refugio Pehoé, or to the park's Administración (which involves a much longer and rather less interesting approach); both of these involve doing the trek clockwise.

At least a week is desirable for the circuit; before beginning, registration with park rangers is obligatory. Camping is permitted only at designated sites, a few of which are free. Purchase supplies in Puerto Natales, as only limited goods are available with the park, at premium prices.

For counterclockwise hikers beginning at Laguna Amarga, there is no *refugio* until Lago Dickson (roughly 11 hours), though there is a pay campground at **Campamento Serón** (five hours) and a free one at **Campamento Coirón** (three hours farther).

Under Conaf concession are Puerto Natales's **Andescape** (Eberhard 599, tel. 061/412877, fax 061/412592, andescape@terra.cl); **Refugio Lago Grey;** and **Refugio Lago Dickson,** where there are also campgrounds; plus the **Campamento Río de los Perros.** All these *refugios* resemble each other closely, with 32 bunks charging US$16 pp, and providing kitchen privileges and hot showers but not sheets or sleeping bags, which are available for rental but are sometimes scarce. Breakfast costs US$6–7, lunch US$8, dinner US$11; a bunk with full board costs

US$38 pp. Campers pay US$5 pp, plus US$1.50 for showers (*refugio* guests, however, have priority on the hot showers). Tents, sleeping bags, mats, and campstoves are also for rent.

Puerto Natales's **Vértice** (tel. 061/412742) is the new concessionaire for cramped and traditionally overcrowded **Refugio Lago Pehoé** (but make reservations, which are strongly recommended, at Turismo Comapa, Bulnes 533, tel. 061/414300); a new *refugio* has been under construction here and should be operating in the summer of 2005. Rates are US$20 pp without breakfast.

The "W" Variant

From Guardería Laguna Amarga, a narrow undulating road crosses the Río Paine on a narrow bridge to the grounds of **Estancia Cerro Paine,** beneath the 2,640-meter summit of Monte Almirante Nieto. The *estancia* operates a hotel, *refugios,* and campgrounds on its property, and also shuttles hikers back and forth from Laguna Amarga for US$4 pp.

From Estancia Cerro Paine, a northbound trail parallels the route from Guardería Laguna Amarga, eventually meeting it just south of Campamento Serón. The *estancia* is more notable, though, as the starting point for the "W" route to Lago Pehoé, a scenic and popular option for hikers lacking time for the full circuit. On the western edge of the *estancia* grounds, the trail crosses the Río Ascencio on a footbridge to a junction where a northbound lateral climbs the river canyon to Campamento Torres, where a short but very steep trail ascends to a nameless glacial tarn at the foot of the Torres proper. This is an easy day hike from the *estancia,* though many people prefer to camp or spend the night at the *refugio.*

From the junction, the main trail follows Lago Nordenskjöld's north shore, past another *refugio* and campground, to the free Campamento Italiano at the base of the **Río del Francés** Valley. While the main trail continues west toward Lago Pehoé, another northbound lateral climbs steeply up the valley, between the striking metamorphic Cuernos del Paine to the east and the 3,050-meter granite summit of Paine Grande to the west, to the free Campamento Británico.

Technically outside the park boundaries, most of the "W" route along the north shore of Lago Nordenskjöld is under the private control of **Fantástico Sur** (Magallanes 960, Punta Arenas, tel. 061/226054, fax 061/222641, lastorres@chileaustral.com), which runs the 36-bunk **Refugio Las Torres** on the *estancia*'s main grounds, the 36-bunk **Refugio Chileno** in the upper Río Ascencio Valley, and the 28-bunk ◪ **Refugio Los Cuernos,** all of which also have campgrounds. Fantástico Sur's *refugios* are more spacious, diverse and attractive in design than the Conaf *refugios,* and the food is better as well.

Bunks at any of the Fantástico Sur *refugios* cost US$20 pp (US$42 pp with full board), while camping costs US$4 pp with hot showers. Separately, a continental breakfast costs US$5, a U.S.-style breakfast US$6, lunch US$8 or dinner US$10; a full meal package costs US$22. Rental tents, sleeping bags, mats, and stoves are also available.

Other Trails

After heavy runoff destroyed the once-sturdy bridge at the outlet of Lago Paine in the early 1980s, the north shore of the Río Paine became, and has remained, isolated from the rest of the park. A good road, however, still goes from Guardería Laguna Amarga to the east end of Laguna Azul, where there are a campground and *cabañas,* and the **Sendero Lago Paine,** a four-hour walk to the lake and a simple *refugio.* A trekkers' alternative is the **Sendero Desembocadura,** which leads north from Guardería Laguna Amarga through open country to the west end of Laguna Azul and continues to Lago Paine, but this takes about eight hours. From the north shore of Lago Paine, the **Sendero Lago Dickson** (5.5 hours) leads to the Dickson glacier.

Several easy day hikes are possible in the vicinity of Guardería Lago Pehoé, directly on the road from Laguna Amarga to the Administración. The short **Sendero Salto Grande** leads to the thunderous waterfall, at the outlet of Lago Sarmiento, that was the starting point of the Paine Circuit until unprecedented runoff swept away the iron bridge that crossed to Península Pehoé. From Salto Grande, the **Sendero Mi-** rador Nordenskjöld is a slightly longer but still easy hike to a vista point on the lakeshore, directly opposite the stunning Cuernos del Paine.

From the Guardería Lago Grey, 18 kilometers northwest of the Administración by road, a short footpath leads to a sandy beach on the south shore of Lago Grey, where icebergs from Glaciar Grey often beach themselves. The longer and less visited **Sendero Lago Pingo** ascends the valley of the Río Pingo to its namesake lake (5.5–six hours); there are two basic *refugios* along the route.

Further Recreation

Despite the similarity of terrain, Paine attracts fewer climbers than Argentina's neighboring Parque Nacional Los Glaciares, perhaps because fees for climbing permits have been very high here. At present, permits are free of charge; before being granted permission, though, climbers must present Conaf with current climbing résumés, emergency contact numbers, and authorization from their consulate.

When climbing in sensitive border areas (meaning most of Andean Chile), climbers must also have permission from the Dirección de Fronteras y Límites (Difrol) in Santiago. It's possible to obtain permission through a Chilean consulate overseas or at Difrol's Santiago offices; if you arrive in Puerto Natales without permission, request it through the **Gobernación Provincial** (tel. 061/411423, fax 061/411992), the regional government offices on the south side of Plaza Arturo Prat. The turnaround time is at 48 hours. Ask Conaf for more time than you'll need, as each separate trip could require a separate fee.

While climbing and mountaineering activities may be undertaken independently, local concessionaires can provide training and lead groups or individuals with less experience on snow and ice. Puerto Natales's Big Foot Adventure Patagonia, for instance, has a base camp at Refugio Grey where it leads full-day traverses of the west side of Glaciar Grey (US$75 pp) daily at 9 A.M. and 3 P.M., returning at 2 and 8 P.M. Except for warm, weather-proof clothing, they provide all equipment. For more detail, contact **Big Foot Adventure Patagonia** (Bories 206,

◪ Tierra del Fuego

tel. 061/414611, fax 061/414276, explore@big-footpatagonia.com, www.bigfootpatagonia.com). Big Foot also arranges guided three-day, two-night descents of the Río Serrano for US$380 pp.

The only concessionaire offering horseback trips in Parque Nacional Torres del Paine is Río Serrano–based **Baqueano Zamora** (Eberhard 566, Puerto Natales, tel. 061/413953, baque-anoz@terra.cl). Rates are about US$15 for two hours or US$50 per day (including lunch).

Accommodations and Food

Park accommodations range from free trailside campgrounds to first-rate luxury hotels with just about everything in between; in summer, reservations are almost obligatory at hotels and are advisable at campgrounds and *refugios*. For options along the Paine Circuit and other trails, see the separate entries earlier in this chapter.

River water and pit toilets are the only amenities at Conaf's free **Refugio y Camping Laguna Amarga,** where people wait for the bus to Puerto Natales. At Estancia Cerro Paine, **Camping Las Torres** (US$5 pp) gets hikers heading up the Río Ascencio Valley to the Paine overlook and/or west on the "W" route to Lago Pehoé, or finishing up the circuit here. Formerly insufficient shower and toilet facilities have improved here.

Also at Las Torres, the ◪ **Cascada Eco-Camp** is a dome-tent facility designed for minimum impact; on raised platforms, heated by gas stoves, each tent is five meters wide, with wooden floors and two single beds, with towels and bedding including down comforters. Another large tent includes a common living area, dining room, and kitchen; the separate bathrooms have hot showers and composting toilets. It is open, however, only to Cascada clients; for more detail consult their listing under Organized Tours in the Know Argentina section, or visit their website, www.cascada-expediciones.com.

On the small peninsula on the eastern shore of its namesake lake, just west of the road to the Administración, sites at the concessionaire-run **Camping Lago Pehoé** (tel. 061/226910 in Punta Arenas, US$20) hold up to six people; fees include firewood and hot showers. A few kilometers farther south, **Camping Río Ser-**rano has recently been closed but should reopen in the near future.

In the park's isolated northeastern sector is **Camping Laguna Azul** (tel. 061/411157 in Puerto Natales, US$17 per site).

Near the Administración, Conaf's **Refugio Lago Toro** charges US$5 pp for bunks (bring your own sleeping bag) plus US$2 for hot showers. The extremely basic **Refugio Pudeto,** on the north shore of Lago Pehoé, has been long overdue for a makeover to put it on a par with other park *refugios,* but for the moment it remains a backpackers' crash pad.

Posada Río Serrano (tel. 061/413953, US$79–107 d, baqueanoz@tie.cl) is a former *estancia* house retrofitted as a B&B. Rates, which include breakfast, depend on whether the room has shared or private bath; there a restaurant/bar for additional meals and for drinks.

Reachable by road along Lago Sarmiento's south shore or by foot or horseback from the Río Paine, well-regarded **Hostería Mirador del Payne** (tel. 061/410498, US$112/138 s/d) lies in the park's isolated southeastern Laguna Verde Sector. Its Punta Arenas representative is **Turismo Viento Sur** (Fagnano 585, tel./fax 061/228712).

Where Lago Grey becomes the Río Grey, you'll find **Hostería Lago Grey** (US$173/199 s/d with breakfast); lunch or dinner costs US$25 pp. For reservations, contact **Austro Hoteles** (Lautaro Navarro 1061, Punta Arenas, tel./fax 061/225986, hgrey@terra.cl). Off-season rates are about half; it also arranges excursions.

On a five-hectare island linked to the mainland by a footbridge, the 25-room **Hostería Pehoé** US$145–180 s, US$160–195 d) has improved substantially since the operator won a lawsuit against Conaf and began to reinvest in what had been a run-down facility with substandard service in an undeniably spectacular setting. For reservations, contact **Turismo Pehoé** (José Menéndez 918, Punta Arenas, tel. 061/244506, fax 061/248052, pehoe1@ctcreuna.cl).

At Estancia Cerro Paine, ◪ **Hostería Las Torres** (US$131–179 s, US$149–197 d) is one of the park's gems due to its setting, seven kilometers west of Guardería Laguna Amarga beneath Monte Almirante Nieto, its professionalism, and the recent addition of a spa. The restaurant is open to both guests and nonguests. For reservations, contact Hostería Las Torres (Magallanes 960, Punta Arenas, tel. 061/226054, fax 061/222641, info@lastorres.com); off-season rates are about half.

Open for packages only, **N Hotel Salto Chico** is a megaluxury resort that, somehow, manages to blend inconspicuously into the landscape while offering some of the grandest views of any hotel on the globe. Rates start at US$1,974/2,876 s/d for three nights in the least expensive room, ranging up to US$6,808/8,544 for seven nights in the costliest suite, including transfer to and from Punta Arenas and unlimited excursions within the park. For details and/or reservations, contact **Explora Hotels** (Américo Vespucio Sur 80, 5th floor, Las Condes, Santiago, tel. 02/3952533, fax 02/2284655, reservexplora@explora.com, www.explora.com).

Just beyond park boundaries, reached by launch over the Río Serrano, the stylish **Hostería Lago Tyndall** (Croacia 731, Punta Arenas, tel./fax 061/2354457, www.hosteriatyndall.com, US$130/150 s/d) enjoys peace, quiet and magnificent views. Nearby is the less stylish **Hostería Cabañas del Paine** (tel. 061/220174, fax 061/243354 in Punta Arenas, US$110/140 s/d).

Information

Conaf's principal facility is its **Centro de Informaciones Ecológicas** (tel. 061/691931, 8:30 A.M.–8 P.M. daily in summer), at the Administración building on the shores of Lago del Toro, which features good natural history exhibits. Ranger stations at Guardería Laguna Amarga, Portería Lago Sarmiento, Guardería Laguna Azul, Guardería Laguna Verde, and Guardería Lago Grey can also provide information.

For foreigners, Torres del Paine is Chile's most expensive national park—US$13 pp except from May 1 to September 30, when it's only US$7 pp. Rangers at Portería Lago Sarmiento, Guardería Laguna Amarga (where most inbound buses now stop), Guardería Laguna Verde, or Guardería Laguna Azul collect the fee and issue receipts.

The text and coverage of the fifth edition of Tim Burford's *Chile & Argentina: The Bradt Trekking Guide* (Bradt Publications, 2001) are greatly improved over previous editions, though the maps are only so-so. Clem Lindenmayer and Nick Tapp's new third edition of *Trekking in the Patagonian Andes* (Lonely Planet, 2003) has significantly better maps than Bradt and expanded coverage compared to its own previous editions. Only a few of those maps, though, are as large as the 1:100,000 scale that's desirable for hiking, though the rest are suitable for planning hikes.

Climbers should look for Alan Kearney's *Mountaineering in Patagonia* (Seattle: The Mountaineers, 1998), which includes both historical and practical information on climbing in Torres del Paine and Argentina's Parque Nacional Los Glaciares. Gladys Garay N. and Oscar Guineo N. have collaborated in **The Fauna of Torres del Paine** (1993), a locally produced guide to the park's animal life.

Conaf sells a very inexpensive map, at a scale of 1:160,000 with erratic contour intervals, that's suitable for orientation but not for trekking. The trekking map of choice, for about US$5.50, is Daniel Bruhin's *Torres del Paine,* at a scale of 1:100,000. At the same scale and about the same price, JLM Mapas's *Torres del Paine Trekking Map* is widely available in Punta Arenas and Puerto Natales, and less dependably at Portería Lago Sarmiento and the park's Centro de Informaciones Ecológicas.

Getting There

Most people choose the bus as the cheapest and quickest way to and from the park, but the more expensive trip up Seno Última Esperanza and the Río Serrano by cutter and Zodiac is a viable and more interesting alternative.

For overland transportation details, see the Puerto Natales section. All bus companies enter the park at Guardería Laguna Amarga, where many people begin the Paine Circuit, before continuing to the Administración at Río Serrano. Round trips from Natales are slightly cheaper, but companies do not accept each others' tickets.

In summer only, there may be direct bus service from Torres del Paine to El Calafate, Argentina, the closest town to that country's Parque Nacional Los Glaciares. Inquire in Puerto Natales or at the park Administración.

Transportation up and down the Río Serrano, between the park and Puerto Natales, has become a popular if considerably more expensive alternative than the bus; for details, see Parque Nacional Bernardo O'Higgins. Visitors who want to see only this sector of the river, without continuing to Puerto Natales, can do so as a day trip to Puerto Toro and back.

Getting Around

Buses to and from Puerto Natales will also carry passengers along the main park road, but as their schedules are very similar, there are substantial blocks of time with no public transportation. Hitching is common, but competition is heavy and most Chilean vehicles are full with families. There is a regular shuttle between Guardería Laguna Amarga and Estancia Cerro Paine (Hostería Las Torres).

From October to April, reliable transportation is now available from Refugio Pudeto to Refugio Pehoé (US$17, 30 minutes) with the catamaran *Hielos Patagónicos* (tel. 061/411380 in Puerto Natales). In October and April, there is one departure daily, at noon, from Pudeto, returning at 1 P.M. In November and from mid-March to April, there are departures at noon and 6 P.M., returning at 1 and 7 P.M. From December through mid-March, there is another departure at 9 A.M., returning at 10 A.M. Schedules are subject to change.

Also in season, the catamaran *Grey II* goes daily from Hotel Lago Grey to Glaciar Grey (US$60 pp) at 9 A.M. and 3 P.M. daily. A US$3.50 shuttle between the Administración and Hotel Lago Grey connects with the cruise.

Tierra del Fuego

Know
Argentina

The Land

Argentina's diverse geography, stretching from the northern desert tropics through the temperate pampas grasslands to the sub-Antarctic and rising from sea level to puna zones well above 4,000 meters, alpine fell fields, and continental glaciers, contains almost every possible South American environment.

GEOGRAPHY

With an area of about 2.8 million square kilometers (apart from its South Atlantic and Antarctic claims), Argentina is the world's eighth-largest country, only slightly smaller than India. From the tropical latitudes of the Bolivian border, at about 22° S, it stretches more than 3,700 kilometers as the crow flies, to almost exactly 55° S at the city of Ushuaia, on the Argentine side of Tierra del Fuego. It's more than 1,300 kilometers across at its widest, in the north, but narrows to barely 400 kilometers at the tip of the continent.

Most of Argentina is temperate lowlands, but its natural landscapes run the gamut from the subtropical wetlands of the northeast to the endless grasslands of the pampas, the uplands of the Andes, and the steppes of Patagonia.

Pampas

On the right bank of the Río de la Plata, the capital city of Buenos Aires sits atop the coastal margin of the flat, fertile, sedimentary pampas whose beef and grain exports made Argentina a wealthy country throughout much of the 19th and 20th centuries. Receiving up to 1,200 millimeters of rainfall per annum, Buenos Aires Province's easterly pampas are lush, green, and vulnerable to flooding; rainfall diminishes as the landscape stretches westward into Córdoba and La Pampa Provinces, where it is nearly desert.

Mountains

Argentina's most imposing physiographic feature is the longitudinal Andean range that extends from its northern borders with Chile and Bolivia to southernmost Patagonia, where it gradually disappears beneath the Pacific Ocean. The highest point in the Americas is the 6,962-meter summit of Cerro Aconcagua, west of the city of Mendoza, but much of the northern Andes and altiplano (high steppe) or puna exceeds 4,000 meters. The southern Patagonian Andes are not so high, but have many heavily glaciated peaks because of their higher latitude.

In addition to the Andes, there are several lesser mountain ranges. The interior of northern Misiones Province is mostly undulating hill country that rarely exceeds 600 meters. Near the country's geographical center, most of the rolling Sierras de Córdoba top out around 1,500 meters, though the highest peaks fall just short of the

Pucará de Tilcara, Quebrada de Humahuaca, Jujuy Province

© WAYNE BERNHARDSON

Misiones rainforest, Misiones Province

3,000-meter mark; the range extends into neighboring San Luis Province. In southern Buenos Aires Province, the Tandil and Ventania ranges lie mostly beneath 1,000 meters, but still offer relief from the otherwise numbingly flat pampas.

Steppes

In Jujuy, Salta, and other northwestern provinces, sparse pasture grasses and prostrate shrubs cover the broad level areas of the high-altitude puna, between the soaring volcanoes along the Chilean and Bolivian borders. In the high latitudes of Patagonia, similar grasses and shrubs punctuate the *meseta* between the Atlantic coast and the Andean foothills to the west.

Rivers

The Río de la Plata, misleadingly glossed into English as the River Plate, is one of the world's great river systems, in a class with the Amazon, the Nile, and the Mississippi in terms of length, width, and flow. Originating in the heights of the Bolivian altiplano, draining an area of more than 3.1 million square kilometers, it is in reality an estuary at the confluence of the Río Paraná (length 3,945 km) and the Río Uruguay (length 1,650 km).

Its delta, northwest of Buenos Aires proper, is a series of islands in a maze of muddy channels whose sedimentary surface is largely covered by dense gallery forest. The combined waters of the Paraná and Uruguay carry sediments far out into the southern Atlantic Ocean.

In the west, descending from the Andes, rushing rivers create recreational rafting runs and water to irrigate the vineyards of Mendoza Province and other wine-growing areas. Some of these reverse direction to flow through gaps into the Pacific on the Chilean side, while others traverse the Patagonian steppe to reach the Atlantic.

Wetlands

Between the Río Paraná and the Río Uruguay, the Mesopotamian lowland provinces of Entre Ríos, Corrientes, and Misiones are home to lush gallery forests along the rivers and shallow, biologically rich wetlands between them. The most notable, one of the country's most spectacular attractions, is Corrientes's Esteros del Iberá.

Lakes

Argentina is famous for its southern lake district, where the melting ice of Pleistocene glaciers has left a legacy of indigo-filled troughs. Even in the desert north, though, there are surprises like Laguna Pozuelos, which is home to a wealth of bird life including flamingos and giant coots.

CLIMATE

Located in the Southern Hemisphere, Argentina's seasons are reversed from the Northern Hemisphere: the summer solstice falls on December 21, the autumn equinox on March 21, the winter solstice on June 21 and the spring equinox on September 21. For most Argentines, the summer months are January and February, when schools are out of session and families take their holidays.

Because Argentina stretches from the desert tropics, where solar insolation and daylight hours vary little over the year, to far southern latitudes where blustery maritime conditions are the rule and seasonal variations can be dramatic, it's difficult to generalize about climate. Moreover, altitude plays a major role in all regions of the country.

Thanks to their midlatitude setting and proximity to the ocean, Buenos Aires and the surrounding pampas have a humid temperate climate, with annual precipitation of about 1,200 millimeters distributed evenly throughout the year. Summer can be hot, wet, and sticky, as temperatures frequently exceed 30° C and thunderstorms are common. Pamperos (southwesterly cold fronts) and *sudestadas* (cool high winds from the southeast) are the most problematic climatic phenomena; winter temperatures are mild, frosts are rare, and snow is unheard of.

Between the Río Paraná and the Río Uruguay, the Mesopotamian provinces of Entre Ríos, Corrientes, and Misiones can be hot, humid, and prone to flooding, but nighttime winter temperatures occasionally approach freezing even in the northernmost subtropical parts near the Brazilian and Paraguayan borders. West of the Paraná, the arid Argentine Chaco encompasses parts of northern Santa Fe and Córdoba Provinces, plus Santiago del Estero, Chaco, and Formosa; rainfall diminishes toward the west in this summertime furnace, whose dry winter is the best time to visit. Santiago del Estero gets less than half of Corrientes's 1,200-millimeter annual rainfall.

In the desert canyons and high puna of the northernmost Andes, warm or even hot daytime temperatures often fall to or near freezing at night. Summer thunderstorms can bring heavy rains and even floods or, at higher elevations, snow; the winter months of July and August are nearly rain-free, and a fine time to travel here. In some favored microclimates, such as Tucumán, rainfall is sufficient for unirrigated agriculture. South of Tucumán, summer can be brutally hot (especially in La Rioja and Catamarca) and rainfall is inadequate for agriculture, but irrigation has turned the Cuyo region (Mendoza and San Juan Provinces, primarily) into the country's vineyard. The dry katabic wind known as *El Zonda* brings stifling heat and even physical distress.

Its receding glaciers particularly sensitive to warming, Patagonia is a living laboratory for climate-change studies. While it's the coolest part of the country, its inclemency is often overstated—despite its geographical position at the southern tip of the continent, it is not Antarctica. Eastern portions of the Patagonian provinces are even arid steppe, with low rainfall but frequent high winds, especially in summer. Climatically, Tierra del Fuego is an extension of mainland Patagonia.

Flora

With latitudinal limits comparable to those between Havana and Hudson Bay, and elevations ranging from oceanic to alpine, Argentina possesses a diversity of flora, much of which will be novel to foreign visitors, especially those from the Northern Hemisphere.

VEGETATION ZONES

Floral associations are strongly, but not perfectly, correlated with latitude and altitude. The environments below appear in more detail in the listings for individual national parks and other locations in the destination chapters.

Temperate Grasslands

As European sheep, cattle, and horses consumed the succulent native grasses of the pampas, they so impoverished the native vegetation that opportunistic colonizers like thistles turned much of the region into a botanical desert. As the land grew too valuable for grazing, grain farms supplanted the livestock industry in many areas.

Gallery Forests

Dense, nearly impenetrable forests still cover large extents along the banks and on the islands of the Paraná, the Uruguay, and other northern rivers. Twisted trunks of the *ceibo* (*Erythrina cristagalli*, whose blossom is Argentina's national flower) mix with *sauces* (willows), *canelones* (*Rapanea* spp.), and lesser species.

Subtropical Forests and Savannas

Argentina has no strictly tropical rainforests, but much of Misiones Province is a panhandle of verdant subtropical forest jutting northeast between Paraguay and Brazil; Araucaria pines punctuate its interior uplands. On the most easterly slopes of the Andes, in Salta, Jujuy, and Tucumán Provinces, the *yungas* are a narrow longitudinal fringe of cloud forest with a unique microclimate.

Between these two geographical extremes, the Gran Chaco of Formosa, Chaco, and Santiago del Estero Provinces is a mix of broad savannas and dense thorn forests. Away from the rivers, *yatay*

© WAYNE BERNHARDSON

Patagonian steppe, Santa Cruz Province

palm savannas survive on the higher ground of Entre Ríos.

Puna

In the canyons of the northwest, the dry hillsides sprout stands of the *cardón* cactus, which eventually yield to broad level areas of the perennial bunch grasses *ichu,* interspersed with shrubs known collectively as *tola.* Their sparse vegetation provides year-round pasture for wild guanacos and vicuñas, and domestic llamas and sheep.

Broadleaf and Coniferous Forest

In the Patagonian lake district, various species of broad-leafed southern beech (*Nothofagus* spp), both evergreen and deciduous, are the most abundant trees. There are, however, several notable conifers, particularly the *paraguas* (umbrella) or monkey-puzzle tree *Araucaria araucaria,* so called because its crown resembles an umbrella and its limbs seem to take the shape of a monkey's curled tail. The long-lived *alerce* or *lawen* (*Fitzroya cupressoides*) is an endangered species because of its high timber value, though most stands of the tree are now protected.

Note that Argentines other than specialists may refer indiscriminately to conifers as *pinos* (pines), even though the Southern Hemisphere has no true pines (of the genus *Pinus*) other than ornamentals in gardens or timber species in forest plantations.

Patagonian Steppe

In the rain shadow of the Andes, on the eastern Patagonia plains, Chilean Magallanes, and even parts of Tierra del Fuego, decreased rainfall supports extensive grasslands where the wind blows almost ceaselessly. In some areas, thorn scrub such as the fruit-bearing *calafate* (*Berberis buxifolia*), a barberry, is abundant. From the late 19th century, sheep grazing for wool had a tremendous detrimental impact on these natural pastures.

Magellanic Forest

From southern Patagonia to the tip of Tierra del Fuego, Argentine woodlands consist primarily of dense *Nothofagus* forests that, because of winds and climatic extremes, are nearly prostrate except where high mountains shelter them.

Fauna

As with the flora, Argentina's fauna is largely correlated with latitude and altitude. In the warm northeastern lowlands, for instance, the range of many species overlaps into the South American tropics, while the high altitudes of the Andean northwest have much in common with the high latitudes of the Patagonian steppe.

MARINE, COASTAL, AND AQUATIC FAUNA

Argentina's lengthy Atlantic coastline and many estuaries are a storehouse of biological wealth, though that wealth is more abundant in terms of individuals than diverse in terms of species.

Fish and Shellfish

In the murky, sediment-saturated waters of the La Plata estuary, it can be difficult to spot any aquatic fauna, but it's there in ocean-going **fish** species like the **yellow corvina** (*Micropogonias furnieri*) and the **black corvina** (*Pogonias cromis*), as well as crustaceans like **crabs** and shellfish like **mussels.** *Congrio* (conger eel, *Genypterus* spp) and the overexploited *merluza* (hake, *Merluccius hubbsi*) are among the top pelagic fish.

Shellfish and crustaceans include the relatively commonplace *ostión* (scallop, *Argopecten purpuratus* or *Chlamys patagonica*) and *calamares* (squid, *Loligo gahi* or *Ilex argentinus*).

Marine Mammals

The most important aquatic mammal in the estuaries is the endangered La Plata **river dolphin** (*Pontoporia blainvillei*). The nutria or La Plata **river otter** (*Lutra platensis*) is also present here and farther up the delta.

© WAYNE BERNHARDSON

Male sea lion, coastal Patagonia

The **southern sea lion** (*Otaria flavescens*) inhabits the coastline from the River Plate all the way south to Tierra del Fuego. From Chubut south, the **southern elephant seal** (*Mirounga leonina*) and **southern fur seal** (*Arctocephalus australis*) are both on Appendix II of the Endangered Species List (CITES), classified as threatened or regionally endangered.

The most famous of Argentine whales is the **southern right whale** (*Eubalaena australis*), which breeds in growing numbers in the waters around Península Valdés. Other cetaceans found in south-Atlantic waters include the **blue whale** (*Balaenoptera musculus*), the **humpback whale** (*Megaptera novaeangliae*), the **fin whale** (*Balaenoptera physalus*), and the **sei whale** (*Balaenoptera borealis*). The **orca** or killer whale (*Orcinus orca*) is also present, along with smaller marine mammals such as **Commerson's dolphin** (*Cephalorhynchus commersonii*).

TERRESTRIAL FAUNA

Argentina's land fauna, especially large mammals, are often nocturnal or otherwise inconspicuous, but they are a diverse lot.

Mammals

The largest, most widely distributed carnivore is the secretive **puma** or mountain lion (*Felis concolor*). The most spectacular wild cat, though, is the *yaguareté* (jaguar, *Panthera orca palustris*), limited to Misiones Province, the *yungas* of Jujuy and Salta, and possibly parts of the Gran Chaco. Other wild felines include the smaller **Andean cat** (*Felis jacobita*) and the **jaguarundi** (*Felis yagouarundi*), both endangered species.

Two species of otters are also endangered: the **long-tailed otter** (*Lutra platensis*) and the **southern river otter** (*Lutra provocax*). The only **wolf** is the nocturnal *aguará guazú* (maned wolf, *Chrysocyon brachyurus*) of the northern wetlands; there are several species of foxes, including the threatened **Argentine gray fox** (*Dusicyon griseus*).

The northern subtropical forests are also home to the rarely sighted **tapir** (*Tapirus terrestris*), related to the horse, and to the **tufted capuchin monkey** (*Cebus apella nigritus*) and **howler monkey** (*Alouatta caraya*). A much more common sight is the **coatimundi** (*Nasua nasua*), related to the raccoon. The world's largest rodent, the *carpincho* (capybara, *Hydrochaerus hydrochaeris*), has a wide distribution from the Paraná Delta north into Corrientes and the Gran Chaco.

Wild grazing mammals include the **vicuña** (*Vicugna vicugna*), an endangered relative of the domestic **llama** (*Lama glama*) and **alpaca** (*Lama pacos*) that occurs only in the northern puna. Their more widely distributed cousin the wild **guanaco** (*Lama guanicoe*) is most abundant on the Patagonian steppe but inhabits parts of the high Andes. **Domestic livestock** like cattle, horses, burros, and goats are of course very common.

The **South Andean huemul** (*Hippocamelus bisulcus*), a cervid that appears on Chile's coat-of-arms, is the subject of a joint conservation effort between the two countries. In the mid-19th century, there were some 22,000 in both countries, but at present only about 1,000 survive in each country south of Chile's Río Biobío because of habitat destruction, contagious livestock diseases, and unregulated hunting.

The **North Andean huemul** (*Hippocamelus antisensis*) is closely related but found only in the Andean northwest. The **pudú** (*Pudu pudu*) is a miniature deer found in densely wooded areas on both sides of the Patagonian Andes. Farther north, the main cervids are the subtropical **marsh deer** (*Blastoceros dichotomus* and the declining **pampas deer** (*Ozotocerus bezoarticus*).

The northern puna is home to two noteworthy rodent species, the Andean **vizcacha** (*Lagidium vizcacia*) and its smaller nocturnal cousin the short-tailed **chinchilla** (*Chinchilla brevicaudata*). Inhabiting large rookeries, the former is fairly easy to spot.

Reptiles and Amphibians

The northeastern wetlands have two small species of *yacaré* (caimans), which ignore humans unless provoked. The same is not true of the several species of the highly venomous pit vipers known collectively as *yarará* (*Bothrops* spp.), which can be aggressive and range from the northernmost lowlands well into the pampas and beyond. The mostly widely distributed is the *yarará ñata* (*Bothrops ammodytoides*), which reaches altitudes upward of 2,000 meters in the Sierras de Córdoba, and latitudes south of

Península Valdés. They are less common in the southern part of their range than in the subtropical north, however.

The amphibian **rana criolla** (Creole frog, *Leptodactylus ocellatus*) is large (up to 130 mm in length) and meaty enough that it's occasionally eaten.

Freshwater Fish

In the upper reaches of the Plata estuary, as far as the confluence of the Paraná and the Uruguay, freshwater game fish like the **boga** (*Leporinus obtusidens*), the **dorado** (*Salminus maxillosus*, a 30-kg fighter), **sábalo** (*Prochilodus platensis*), the 80-kilogram **surubí** (*Pseudoplatystoma coruscans*, a giant catfish), and **tararira** (*Hoplias malabaricus*) mix with some of the oceanic species. These freshwater species, though, are abundant throughout the Mesopotamian provinces.

In the Andean region, introduced species include **brook trout** (*Salvenilus fontinalis*), **European brown trout** (*Salmo trutta*), **rainbow trout,** and landlocked **Atlantic salmon** (*Salmo selar sebago*). Native species (catch-and-release only) include *perca bocona* (big-mouthed perch, *Percichtys colhuapiensis*), *perca boca chica* (*Percichtys trucha*, small-mouthed perch), *puyén* (*Galaxis* spp.), Patagonian *pejerrey* (*Basilichtys microlepidotus*), and *peladilla* (*Aplochiton taeniatus*).

BIRDS

Argentina can be a wonderland for bird-watchers, especially in the northeastern marshes and gallery forests along the great river systems, the humid pampas, and the steppe and oceans of southern Patagonia. For visitors and especially dedicated bird-watchers from the Northern Hemisphere, the great majority are new additions to their life lists. For recommended bird-watching guides, see Suggested Reading later in this section.

In the gallery forests along the Plata estuary, common birds include the *boyero negro* or black cacique, an oriole-like species that breeds in hanging nests; the rufous-capped **antshrike** (*Thamnophilus ruficapillus*), and *pava de monte* (*Penelope obscura*, black guan). Common aquatic species include **coots, ducks,** and **swans.**

© WAYNE BERNHARDSON

Rock cormorants, Beagle Channel near Ushuaia

Marshland species include the *junquero* or marsh wren (*Phleocryptes melanops*), the polychromatic *sietecolores* (literally, "seven colors," *Thraupis bonariensis*), and the striking *federal,* with black plumage crowned by a scarlet hood. There are also several species of **rails** and **crakes**.

Many of these same species extend across the pampas, especially in inundated low-lying areas, which also attract large numbers of migratory birds. The pampas' signature species may be the southern **lapwing** or *tero* (*Vanellus chilensis*), whose local name derives from its call, but it and other similar species have a wide distribution. With its curved beak, the widely distributed **buff-necked ibis** or *bandurria* is a striking presence.

In the Mesopotamian marshlands, the diversity is astounding—Iberá has more than 250 species, including large conspicuous ones like the *chajá* (horned screamer, *Chauna torquata*), **cormorants,** several species of **storks, herons,** and **egrets,** and many waterfowl. Subtropical Misiones is habitat for overlapping tropical species like the red-breasted **toucan** (*Ramphastos bicolorus*).

The Andean condor soars above the deserts and puna of the north, while migratory birds like **flamingos,** along with **coots, ducks,** and

geese, frequent its shallow lakes. Common throughout the Andes, the **condor** reaches its most easterly point in the Sierras de Córdoba.

In northern Patagonia's dense forests, some birds are heard as often as they're seen, especially the reticent songbird *chucao*. Others, like the flocks of squawking **Patagonian parakeets** that flit through the woods, are more visibly conspicuous.

Some 240 bird species inhabit the south-Atlantic coastline and Tierra del Fuego, including the wandering **albatross** (*Diomedea exulans*), with its awesome four-meter wingspan, the **black-necked swan** (*Cygnus melanocoryphus*), **Coscoroba swan** (*Coscoroba coscoroba*), **flightless steamer duck** (*Tachyeres pteneres*), **kelp gull** (*Larus dominicanus*), and several species of **penguins,** most commonly the Magellanic or jackass penguin (*Spheniscus magellanicus*).

Its numbers reduced on the pampas, where it roamed before cattle, horses, and humans turned native grasslands into ranches and granaries, the ostrich-like *choike* or *ñandú* (greater rhea, *Rhea americana*) still strides across some less-densely settled parts of the country. The smaller *ñandú petiso* (lesser rhea, *Pterocnemia pennata*) is fairly common in the Patagonian provinces of Neuquén, Río Negro, Chubut, and Santa Cruz; a rare subspecies (*Pretocnemia pennata garleppi*) survives on the heights of the northwestern puna.

INVERTEBRATES

For purely practical purposes, visitors should pay attention to pests and dangers like mosquitoes, flies, and ticks, which can be serious disease vectors, even though maladies like malaria and dengue are almost unheard of (the mosquito vector for dengue has been spreading southward from the tropics, but the disease itself has not yet been detected). In well-watered rural areas like the Paraná Delta, mosquitoes can be a real plague, so a good repellent is imperative.

The vinchuca (Reduvid or assassin bug), which bears trypanosomiasis (Chagas' disease), is present in Argentina, though it is hardly cause for hysteria. For more information, see Health and Safety later in this section.

The Cultural Landscape

While Argentina's natural landscapes, flora, and fauna are fascinating and enchanting, the country also has a cultural landscape, one transformed by human agency over the millennia. Few parts of the country are truly pristine, but their landscapes are no less interesting for all that.

As an outlier of the great Andean civilizations, northwestern Argentina shows tangible testimony of those times. While their monuments are not so grand as those of Peru and Bolivia, many pukarás (fortresses), pircas (walls), agricultural terraces, and pre-Columbian roads survive in places like the Quebrada de Humahuaca and Quilmes.

Except for the shifting cultivators of the upper Mesopotamian provinces, most of the rest of pre-Columbian Argentina was a thinly populated place of hunter-gatherers who left few conspicuous landmarks—notwithstanding aboriginal rock-art sites like the Cueva de las Manos in Santa Cruz Province. Some of the continent's most important early-man archaeological sites are just over the border from Santa Cruz, in the Chilean region of Magallanes.

In immediate pre-Columbian times, bands of nomadic Querandí hunter-gatherers peopled what is now Buenos Aires and its surrounding pampas. Living in smallish bands with no permanent settlements, they relied on wild game like the guanaco (a relative of the domestic llama) and the flightless ostrichlike ñandú or rhea, as well as fish, for subsistence. What remains of their material culture is primarily lithic (arrow-heads, spearpoints, and the rounded stone balls known as *boleadoras*) and ceramic.

AGRICULTURE AND THE LANDSCAPE

In some areas, such as the more remote parts of Quebrada de Humahuaca, local communities have retained control of their better lands and constructed durable terrace systems that have conserved soil and maintained productivity. Native crops such as quinoa (*Chenopodium quinoa*) are still grown in some areas, while indigenous llama-herders persist in the northwestern puna well upward of 3,000 meters. Cultivation along the eastern Andean slopes extended south into what is now Mendoza Province.

The pre-Columbian peoples of northern Mesopotamia were shifting cultivators and, as such, their impact on the landscape is less obvious. Because they cut the forest and used fire to clear the fields before planting, their impact was significant, but long fallow periods allowed the woodlands to recover. Much of what seems to be virgin forest may in fact be secondary growth.

The arrival of the Spaniards, of course, led to major transformations. At first content to collect tribute from the indigenous population, they became landholders as that population declined from various causes, most importantly introduced diseases. Their large rural estates, known as haciendas, consisted of relatively small areas of in-

Sorting sheep at Estancia Monte Dinero, Santa Cruz Province

tensively cultivated land surrounded by large areas on which grazed cattle, horses, and other European livestock.

From the pampas south, the European invasion utterly transformed the landscape into first an open-range cattle zone and then, successively, large fenced sheep and cattle ranches known as *estancias* that dominated the rural economy for more than a century. Parts of the pampas, in turn, became large-scale grain ranches. In Patagonia, the sheep *estancia,* an extensive unit producing wool for export to Europe and North America, was the dominant agricultural institution.

SETTLEMENT LANDSCAPES

After the Spaniards took control of Argentina, as in the rest of their American dominions, they tried to institute a policy of *congregación* or *reducción*. This meant concentrating native populations in villages or towns for the purpose of political control, tribute, or taxation, and religious evangelization.

The only area in which this really worked was the Andean northwest, which had much in common with the highland civilizations of Peru and Bolivia; still, descendents of the same natives who had resisted the Inka invasions of the 15th century made things difficult for the Spaniards. For indigenous peoples, who lived in dispersed settlements near their fields or their animals, this was an inconvenience at best, and contributed to land disputes both within indigenous communities and between indigenous communities and Spaniards.

Still, in many areas, the need to be close to one's fields or animals has reinforced a dispersed rural settlement pattern—in the puna, for instance, some villages have become primarily ceremonial sites where people gather for the festival of their patron saint. The standard house is often an adobe, usually with a thatched or tiled roof, and small windows to conserve heat; the frequency of earthquakes, though, has encouraged reinforced-concrete-block construction, and galvanized roofing has become more common.

A different model prevailed in the northeast, where Jesuits organized Guaraní-speaking peoples into self-sufficient missions against the raids of Brazilian slavers. While the Jesuits may have been paternalistic, they also taught their wards useful skills, such as carpentry and masonry, which helped them create the monumental mission architecture that survives in ruins along the upper Paraná drainage in Argentina, Paraguay, and Brazil.

In the Mapuche country of the northern Patagonian lake district, traditional *rucas,* plank houses with thatched roofs traditionally erected with community labor rather than by individual families, have nearly disappeared; they are more common on the Chilean side, where the indigenous population is larger and more cohesive. In southern Patagonia, dating from the 19th century, so-called "Magellanic" houses often affect a Victorian style, with wooden framing covered by metal cladding and topped by corrugated zinc roofs.

Cities, of course, differ greatly from the countryside. By royal decree, Spanish cities in the Americas were organized according to a rectangular grid surrounding a central plaza where all the major public institutions—*cabildo* (town council), cathedral, and market—were located. Buenos Aires and other Argentine cities were no exception to the rule; though the transformation from colonial city to modern metropolis obliterated some landmarks, the essential grid pattern remains.

Traditionally, as in Buenos Aires, colonial houses fronted directly on the street or sidewalk, with an interior patio or garden for family use; any setback was almost unheard of. This general pattern has persisted, though building materials have mostly changed from adobe to concrete, and high-rise apartment blocks have replaced single-family houses in many city neighborhoods.

It is also true, though, that many wealthier Argentines have built houses with large gardens, on the North American suburban model, in a frenzy of conspicuous consumption—but still surrounded by high fences and state-of-the-art security.

Environmental Issues

Like other countries, Argentina suffers from environmental degradation, though not all indicators are negative.

AIR, WATER, AND NOISE POLLUTION

Aging diesel buses may be the primary culprit in deteriorating urban air quality, but private vehicles (some of which still run on leaded gasoline) and taxis contribute more than their share (some taxis and private vehicles, though, run on natural gas). Superannuated factories, with their subsidized smokestacks, are another source.

A different sort of air pollution is the deterioration of the Antarctic ozone layer, which has exposed both humans and livestock in far southern Argentina to ultraviolet radiation in summer. Though ozone depletion from aerosols is a global problem over which Argentines have rel-

atively little control, they suffer the consequences of the growing ozone hole.

Just as motor vehicles cause urban air pollution, so they produce most of its noise pollution, due partly to inadequate mufflers. According to one study, vehicular noise accounts for 80 percent of levels that, at corners like Rivadavia and Callao in Buenos Aires, reach upward of 80 decibels. Buses and motorcycles are the worst offenders.

Drinking water is normally potable, but a historical legacy of polluted waterways derives from, first, the proliferation of European livestock on the pampas, followed by the processing of hides and livestock, and then by heavy industry. The textbook case is Buenos Aires's Riachuelo, in the working-class barrio of La Boca, which more closely resembles sludge than water; its bottom sediments, thanks to chemical runoff from factories here and in nearby Avellaneda, are an even greater toxic hazard. In the provinces, mining is also a factor; near the town of Esquel, Chubut, there has been concern and vociferous opposition to a Canadian project that would use cyanide, which might find its way into streams and aquifers, to extract gold from local ores.

SOLID WASTE

Buenos Aires and other cities produce prodigious amounts of garbage—in 2001, for example, the Gran Buenos Aires conurbation generated more than 400,000 tons of solid waste per month. Sidewalk pickups take place daily, but in the aftermath of the 2002 economic crisis, garbage-strewn streets became more common because of spontaneous recycling by *cartoneros* who ripped open plastic bags in search of reusable materials like cardboard. Recently, the city government has sought to create a landfill near the city of Olavarría, 400 kilometers to the southwest.

There's another dark side to this recycling, as some *cartoneros*—apparently in league with criminal elements—have also absconded with valuable metals covering utility boxes and other similar objects accessible from the street. Sold and melted into ingots of bronze and other metals, these are almost untraceable.

Another sort of solid waste is even more problematic. Greenpeace Argentina has protested an agreement with Australia to import that country's nuclear waste for reprocessing near the Buenos Aires suburb of Ezeiza. Argentina's constitution prohibits storage of nuclear waste, though Argentina has its own 357-megawatt Atucha I reactor near the town of Lima, northwest of the capital.

ENERGY

Argentina is self-sufficient in fossil fuels and has substantial hydroelectric resources in the subtropical north and along the Andean foothills, but Argentine governments have promoted nuclear power since the 1950s. While the country has renounced any intention to build nuclear weapons, the 357-megawatt Atucha I reactor has powered the capital's electrical grid since 1974. For much of the time since then it has operated at reduced capacity thanks partly to the availability of cheaper hydroelectricity, but also due to inadequate maintenance; the controlling Comisión Nacional de Energía Atómica (CNEA, National Atomic Energy Commission) is not known for its transparency. Atucha I is due to close in 2014.

Even hydroelectricity is no panacea, as the creation of the massive Yacyretá dam along the Paraguayan border in Corrientes Province may be raising water levels in the Iberá marshlands; this could sever the "floating islands," on which their wildlife depends, from their anchoring soils. Similarly, upstream water diversions on the Río Iguazú could affect the flow over the spectacular falls that are one of the continent's greatest natural features.

SOIL CONSERVATION AND DEFORESTATION

Centuries of livestock activities, both grazing and trampling, have caused serious erosion even in areas where there were never native forests, such as the pampas and the Patagonian steppes. Even today, some forested national parks—most notably Lanín and Los Glaciares—have been unable to eliminate grazing within their boundaries. There has been pressure to create presumably sustainable forest-exploitation projects in the Magellanic woodlands of Tierra del Fuego.

The hot-button forest issues, though, are in the northern subtropical forests. In Misiones Province, agricultural colonists and commercial tea and *yerba mate* plantations have cut over much of the *selva misionera,* a diverse, wildlife-rich rainforest that cannot easily reestablish itself when its natural recycling mechanisms are disturbed. In Jujuy and Salta Provinces, the *yungas* cloud forest on the edge of the Andes is in double trouble, from a natural gas pipeline over the Andes to Chile, and from sugar-cane expansion by the giant Ledesma mill.

CONSERVATION ORGANIZATIONS

For information on protected areas, contact the **Administración de Parques Nacionales** (Avenida Santa Fe 680, Retiro, tel. 011/4312-0820, informes@parquesnacionales.gov.ar, www.parquesnacionales.gov.ar).

Argentina's preeminent wildlife advocacy organization is the **Fundación Vida Silvestre Argentina** (Defensa 251, tel. 011/4331-4864, Monserrat, Buenos Aires, socios@vidasilvestre.org.ar, www.vidasilvestre.org.ar). Foreign member-

ship rates are US$60 per annum; it publishes the monthly newsletter *Otioso* and the magazine *Revista Vida Silvestre*.

For bird-watchers, it's the **Asociación Ornitológica del Plata** (25 de Mayo 749, 2nd floor, Buenos Aires, tel. 011/4312-8958, info@avesargentinas.org.ar, www.avesargentinas.org.ar); hours are 3–9 P.M. weekdays.

The international conservation organization **Greenpeace** also has a Buenos Aires representative (Mansilla 3046, Barrio Norte, tel. 011/4962-0404, www.greenpeace.org.ar).

History

From inauspicious beginnings, Argentina has fashioned an epic but contentious, even divisive, history. Both Argentine and foreign historians who write about Argentina find it hard to separate scholarship from politics—even when they have no overt political agenda, almost everyone interprets their work in an ideological context.

PREHISTORY

Human occupation of the Americas, unlike that of Africa, Europe, and Asia, is relatively recent. The earliest immigrants reached North America from East Asia more than 12,500 years ago, when sea levels fell during the last major period of continental glaciation and united the two continents via a land bridge across the Bering Strait. Some researchers believe this migration, interrupted by various interglacials during which rising sea levels submerged the crossing, began tens of thousands of years earlier. Nevertheless, by the time the bridge last closed about 10,000 years ago, the entire Western Hemisphere was populated, at least thinly, with bands of hunter-gatherers in environments ranging from barren, torrid deserts to sopping rainforests to frigid uplands.

Evidence of Paleo-Indian hunter-gatherers is relatively scarce in Argentina, but one of the continent's oldest confirmed archaeological sites is at Monte Verde, Chile, just across the Andes from present-day Bariloche. Radiocarbon dating here has given a figure of 13,000 years at a site at which, according to University of Kentucky archaeologist Tom Dillehay, has some of the continent's earliest evidence of architecture, as well as use of wild potatoes and other native tubers. The most geographically proximate early-man sites—later than Monte Verde—are 900 kilometers or more to the north.

As important as hunting was to the first Americans, gathering wild foods probably contributed more to the diet. As population gradually reached the saturation point under hunter-gatherer technology, they began to rely on so-called incipient agriculture, one of whose hearths was the Peruvian highlands. In the process of gathering, incipient agriculturalists had acquired knowledge of the annual cycles of seed plants, and selected, scattered, and harvested them in a lengthy domestication process. In fact, the earliest domesticated plants could have been root crops like manioc in the Amazon lowlands, but as these are perishable tubers rather than durable seeds, there is little archaeological evidence to support this supposition.

In any event, starting about 6000 B.C., beans (*Phaseolus* spp.), squash (*Cucurbita* spp.), and potatoes (*Solanum* spp.) became the staples of an agricultural complex that, as population grew, supported a settled village life and, eventually, the great Andean civilizations. Maize was a later addition, acquired from Mexico. In Argentina, the outliers of these civilizations appeared on the eastern Andean slopes as far south as present-day San Juan Province, and in the highlands of Córdoba; across the Gran Chaco, in Mesopotamia, semisedentary shifting cultivators raised maize, manioc (cassava), and sweet potatoes.

When the Spaniards finally arrived, according to one scholar, they found "the richest assemblage of food plants in the Western Hemisphere." Domestic animals were few, however—only the dog (sometimes raised for food), the guinea pig (definitely raised for food), and the llama and alpaca (both raised for food and fiber, with the llama also serving as a pack animal).

Slower to develop than the Andean region, due at least partly to late demographic saturation, most indigenous societies in what is now Argentina remained nomadic or semisedentary until shortly before the Spanish invasion. In Patagonia, some indigenous peoples sustained a hunter-gatherer way of life even into the 20th century.

PRE-COLUMBIAN CIVILIZATION AND CULTURES

In pre-Columbian times, what is now Argentina comprised a diversity of native peoples who ranged from small isolated bands of hunter-gatherers to semiurbanized outliers of Inka Cuzco (in present-day Peru). The Inka were never quite able to impose their will on the agricultural Diaguita peoples, who maintained considerable autonomy in what are now Salta, Tucumán, La Rioja Catamarca, and San Juan Provinces.

Likewise, the Inka had little control over the southerly Araucanians—the semisedentary Mapuche and the closely related Pehuenche and Puelche—who withstood both the Inka expansion and, for more than three centuries, the Spanish invasion. More numerous on the Chilean side of the Andes, they survived because of distance from Cuzco, their mobility as shifting cultivators, and their decentralized political structure—not easily conquered or co-opted by the bureaucratic Inka. Likewise, the decentralized Guaraní of Mesopotamia were a more or less independent people.

In Patagonia, groups like the Chonos, Tehuelche (Aónikenk), Kawasqar (Alacaluf), Yámana (Yahgan), and Selkn'am (Ona) subsisted by hunting, fishing, and gathering, but introduced European diseases and outright extermination devastated their already small numbers, and sheep displaced the guanaco and rhea on which many of them relied.

The Inka Empire and Its Collapse

At the time of the Spanish invasion, the Inka ruled an administratively centralized but geographically unwieldy empire; their hold was especially tenuous on the southern Araucanian (Mapuche) frontier, just as it would be for the Spaniards in only a few years. Though Inka political achievements were impressive, their realm having stretched into present-day Colombia in the north, it's important to recognize that they were relative latecomers in the pre-Columbian Andes, only consolidating their power around A.D. 1438. Building on earlier Andean advances in mathematics, astronomy, and other sciences, they were a literate and administratively sophisticated society, but their hierarchical organization, like that of the modern Soviet Union, was ultimately unsustainable.

Toward the end of the 15th century, just prior to the Spanish invasion of the New World, the Inka empire was no monolith, but rather a diverse empire ruling a mosaic of peoples who resisted domination, especially on its most remote frontiers. Because of internal divisions after the premature deaths of the Inka ruler Huayna Capac and his immediate heir, there developed a struggle between potential successors Atahualpa and Huáscar. The fact that the Inka state was a house divided against itself helps explain why a relatively small contingent of Spanish invaders could overcome vastly superior numbers, but it's only part of the story.

EARLY HISTORY

Early Argentine history is complex because of multiple currents of European exploration and settlement. The Florentine Amerigo Vespucci's expedition of 1501, in the service of Portugal, brought what were probably the first Europeans to enter the Río de la Plata estuary, followed by Cristóbal de Haro (1514); Juan Díaz de Solís (1516), who died at the hands of the indigenous Charrúa on the Uruguayan side of the river; and Sebastian Cabot (1527), who went some distance up the river and returned to Spain with small amounts of Peruvian silver—giving the river the name that has survived to the present.

Solís's crew, who landed on Isla Martín García, was probably the first European group to actually set foot in what is now Argentina. Ferdinand Magellan's legendary expedition of 1519, though, spent the winter of 1520 in San Julián, Santa Cruz Province; Magellan himself died before returning to Spain on the first circumnavigation of the globe, but his Italian chronicler Antonio Pigafetta aroused European imaginations with exaggerated tales of Patagonian "giants."

Cabot's expedition, combined with the first news from of wealthy Cajamarca and Cuzco, spurred Pedro de Mendoza's massive expedition (1535), which founded Buenos Aires on the right bank of the river. Mendoza's effort failed within five years due to poor planning, lack of supplies, and stiff resistance from the native Querandí, whom the Spaniards treated with disdain. A contingent of Mendoza's forces had headed north to Asunción, Paraguay, where the Guaraní were more receptive to the Spaniards; in 1580, moving south from Asunción, Juan de Garay reestablished Buenos Aires. In the meantime, more-momentous events in the central Peruvian Andes were to have a greater impact on Argentina.

From the North

Christopher Columbus's so-called "discovery" of the "New World" was, of course, one of the signal events of human history. While he may have bungled his way into fame—according to geographer Carl Sauer, "the geography in the mind of Columbus was a mixture of fact, fancy and credulity"—the incompetently audacious Genovese sailor excited the interest and imagination of Spaniards and others who, within barely half a century, brought virtually all of what is now known as Latin America under at least nominal control.

Europeans had roamed the Caribbean for more than three decades after Columbus's initial voyage, but the impulse toward conquest in South America came from Mexico and especially Panama, which Francisco Pizarro and his brothers used as a base to take Peru. From there, in 1535, Pizarro's partner/rival Diego de Almagro made the first attempt to take Chile by traveling south through Jujuy, Salta, and Catamarca. Crossing the 4,748-meter Paso de San Francisco from the east, Almagro's poorly organized expedition ended in grisly failure as most of his personnel, retainers, and even livestock died, but this marked the start of Spain's presence in Argentina.

The Spanish Imposition

The Spanish presence in the Americas had contradictory goals. Most Spaniards came in hopes of getting rich, but there were also Christian idealists who sought to save the souls of the millions of Indians they found in highland Mexico, Peru, and elsewhere (ignoring for the moment the fact that these millions already had their own elaborate religious beliefs).

Consequently, the Spanish Crown obliged its forces to offer their opposition the option to accept Papal and Spanish authority in lieu of military subjugation. Whether or not they accepted, the result was the same—they became subject to a Spanish colonial system that was overwhelmingly stacked against them.

Many prisoners of war became Spanish slaves and were shipped elsewhere in the Americas. Others who remained were obliged to provide labor for individual Spaniards through forced-labor systems like *repartimiento* and geographically based tribute systems like the *encomienda*. In principle, the Spanish *encomendero* (holder of an *encomienda*) was to provide Spanish-language and Catholic religious instruction, but this was almost unenforceable. The *encomienda*, it should be emphasized, was *not* a land grant, though many *encomenderos* became large landholders.

Spanish institutions were most easily imposed in areas that had been under Inka influence, as a long history of hierarchical government made it possible for the Spaniards to place themselves at the top of the pyramid. Subjects accustomed to paying tribute to the Inka's delegate now paid it to the *encomendero,* the Spanish Crown's representative. This was different, though, with the unsubjugated Araucanians of the south.

The Demographic Collapse and Its Consequences

One of the invasion's perpetual mysteries, at least on its face, was how so few Spaniards could dominate such large indigenous populations in so little time. Spanish weapons were not markedly superior to their indigenous equivalents—it took longer to reload a harquebus than a bow, for example, and the bow and arrow were probably more accurate. Mounted cavalry gave the Spaniards a tactical edge in open terrain, but this was only occasionally decisive. Certainly the Spaniards took advantage of factionalism within South American societies, but that was not the entire story either. The Spaniards' greatest allies may have been microbes.

From the time the Bering Strait land bridge closed, the Americas had been geographically isolated from Europe and Asia. Diseases that had evolved and spread in the Old World, such as smallpox, measles, plague and typhus, no longer took a catastrophic toll there, but in the New World they encountered immunologically defenseless human populations and spread like the plague did in 14th-century Europe. In some lowland tropical areas, fatal infections reduced the population by nearly 95 percent in less than a century.

In the cooler, drier highlands, disease did not spread so quickly nor so thoroughly, but was still overwhelming. In some parts, it even preceded direct contact with the Spaniards—the death of the Inka Huayna Capac may have been the result of European smallpox spread indirectly. For this reason, historian Murdo Macleod has called introduced diseases "the shock troops of the conquest."

While the population was numerous, *encomiendas* were a valuable source of wealth for those who held them (including the Catholic church). As the population plummeted, however, *encomiendas* lost their value—dead Indians paid no tribute. In the absence of large Indian

populations to exploit, Spaniards took economic refuge in large rural estates, or haciendas, though they struggled to find labor to work them.

European settlement, then, proceeded south from Lima (capital of the Viceroyalty of Peru) and the silver-rich highland town of Potosí (in present-day Bolivia). Before Juan de Garay reestablished Buenos Aires in 1580, southbound Spaniards had founded Santiago del Estero (1553); San Miguel de Tucumán (1571), which supplied cloth, food, and mules to high, cold, barren Potosí; and Córdoba (1573). Salta (1582), La Rioja (1591), and Jujuy (1593) soon followed. Spaniards from Chile settled the Cuyo cities of Mendoza (1561), San Juan (1562), and San Luis (1596), which produced wine and grain. Buenos Aires, legally barred from trade with the mother country except overland through Lima, suffered in remote isolation from the viceregal capital.

In the lake district, on both sides of the Andes, the mobile Araucanians staved off the Spaniards and then the Argentines and Chileans for more than three centuries. In far-off Patagonia, the situation was even more tenuous, as tentative Spanish colonization efforts failed disastrously because of poor planning and extreme environmental conditions.

COLONIALISM

Barred from direct contact with Europe by Spain's mercantile bureaucracy, early colonial Buenos Aires had to survive on the resources of the sprawling pampas grasslands. The Querandí and other indigenous groups had subsisted on guanacos, rheas, and other game, in addition to edible fruits and plants they gathered, but these resources were inadequate and culturally inconceivable for the Spaniards.

The Mendoza expedition, though, had left behind horses that proliferated on the lush but thinly populated pastures of the pampas, and the multiplication of escaped cattle from the Garay expedition soon transformed the Buenos Aires backcountry into a fenceless feral-cattle ranch. The presence of horses and cattle, nearly free for the taking, resulted in the gaucho culture for which Argentina became famous. Hides were the primary product because they were durable; beef had little value because it was perishable.

Buenos Aires had no easily accessible markets, though, because hides were too low-value a product to ship to Spain via Lima and Panama; consequently, there developed a vigorous contraband trade with British and Portuguese vessels in the secluded channels of the Paraná Delta. As this trade grew, Spain acknowledged Buenos Aires's growing significance by making it capital, in 1776, of the newly created Virreinato del Río de la Plata (Viceroyalty of the River Plate). Reflecting its significance and the need to curb a growing Portuguese influence in the region, the viceroyalty even included the silver district of Potosí.

Buenos Aires's population grew slowly at first, but by the time of the new viceroyalty it exceeded 24,000, and nearly doubled by the early 19th century. Open to European commerce, as Madrid loosened its control, the livestock economy expanded with the development of *saladeros,* or meat-salting plants, giving value to a product that was almost worthless before.

Unlike the densely populated central-Andean area, Buenos Aires lacked an abundant labor force. The improving economy and growing population, which previously consisted of peninsular Spaniards, criollos (creoles, or American-born Spaniards), *indígenas* (Indians), and mestizos (the offspring of Spaniards and *indígenas*), soon included African slaves. Increasing political autonomy and economic success paved the way for the end of Spanish rule.

The Dissolution of Colonial Argentina

Appointed by the Spanish Crown, all major officials of the viceroyalty governed from Buenos Aires, and economic power was also concentrated there. Outside the capital, isolated by geographical barriers, provincial bosses created their own power bases. When Napoleon invaded Spain in the early 19th century, the glue that held Spain's colonial possessions together began to dissolve, leading to Argentine independence in several steps.

Contributing to this tendency was a changing sense of identity. In the early generations, of course, people identified themselves as Spaniards, but over time criollos began to differentiate themselves from *peninsulares* (European-born Spaniards). It bears mention that while the mestizos and even the remaining indigenous population may have identified more closely with Argentina than with Spain, it was the criollo intelligentsia to whom the notion of independence had the greatest appeal.

The South American independence movements commenced on the periphery, led by figures like Argentina's José de San Martín, Venezuela's Simón Bolívar, and Chile's Bernardo O'Higgins, but their heroism rested on a broader base of support. In Buenos Aires, this base developed as opportunistic and unauthorized British forces, taking advantage of Spain's perceived weakness, occupied the city in 1806 and 1807.

As the shocked Viceroy Rafael de Sobremonte fled to Córdoba, city residents organized a covert resistance that, under the leadership of the Frenchman Santiago de Liniers, dislodged the invaders. On the rationale that Spain's legitimate government had fallen, the *porteños* of the capital chose Liniers as viceroy in an open *cabildo* (town meeting). The royalist Liniers, ironically enough, died at the hands of independence fighters during the Revolution of 1810.

Returning from Spain, San Martín led independence forces against royalist forces, deployed from Peru, in what is now northwestern Argentina, and over the Andes into Chile. In 1816, in the city of Tucumán, delegates of the Provincias Unidas del Río de la Plata (United Provinces of the River Plate) issued a formal declaration of independence but this was only a loose confederation that papered over differences between "Federalist" caudillos—provincial landholders and warlords intent on preserving their fiefdoms—and the cosmopolitan "Unitarists" of Buenos Aires.

The struggle between Federalists and Unitarists was slow to resolve itself; in the words of historian James Scobie, "It took seventy years for Argentina to coalesce as a political unit." Even today, tensions between the provinces and the central government have not disappeared, but it took a Federalist to ensure Buenos Aires's supremacy.

REPUBLICAN ARGENTINA

Having achieved independence but united in name only, the Provincias Unidas became an assortment of quarrelsome ministates. After they failed to agree upon a constitution, Federalist caudillo Juan Manuel de Rosas took command of Buenos Aires, the largest and most populous province, and ruled it ruthlessly from 1829 until his overthrow in 1852. Ironically enough, the opportunistic Rosas did more than anyone else to ensure the city's primacy, though it did not become the country's capital until 1880.

In the early independence years, Unitarist visionaries like Mariano Moreno and Bernardino Rivadavia had advocated an aggressive immigration policy to Europeanize the new republic, but Rosas's dictatorial rule, obstinate isolationism, and continual military adventures discouraged immigration. His defeat at the battle of Caseros, followed by his departure for England, opened the country to immigration. It also helped diversify the economy from extensive *estancias* and *saladeros* to the more intensive production of wool and grains for export.

War, Expansion, and Consolidation

The exile of Rosas did not mean the end of conflict, as it took nearly a decade of civil war for General Bartolomé Mitre's Buenos Aires army to defeat the other provinces, led by Justo José Urquiza of Entre Ríos, and unite the country. Even then, Federalist resistance lingered in northwestern provinces such as La Rioja, and only a few years later Argentina became embroiled in the bloody War of the Triple Alliance (1864–70) against Paraguay. Allied with Brazil and Uruguay, Argentina gained the provinces of Misiones and Formosa, but the real challenge was the Patagonian frontier to the south and west of Buenos Aires Province.

With encouragement from foreign minister Guillermo Rawson, Welsh colonists had given Argentina a beachhead in the southern territory of Chubut in 1865. General Julio Argentino Roca, though, wanted to complete the job begun by Rosas, who had driven the Araucanian Indians westward toward the Andean lake district in the 1830s. The Araucanians, for their part, continued to raid the frontier for cattle and horses.

In 1879, the politically ambitious Roca initiated the *Conquista del Desierto* (Conquest of the Desert), a euphemistically titled military campaign that rode ruthlessly across La Pampa, Neuquén, and Río Negro to dispossess the Mapuche and Tehuelche east of the Andes; at the same time, it was a preemptive strike against Chilean ambitions in the region. On the strength of his military victory, Roca became president in 1880 and made prosperous Buenos Aires a separate federal district (the Capital Federal). Economically and politically, the provinces beyond the pampas lagged far behind.

Around the same time, the government began to encourage settlers, primarily British sheep farmers from the Falkland Islands, into the southern territories of Chubut, Santa Cruz, and Tierra del Fuego. With the definitive settlement of southern Patagonia, Argentina reached its maximum territorial expansion, though precise boundaries with Chile remained to be settled.

The Transformation of Argentina

Rosas's expulsion reversed Argentina's inward-looking isolationism, opening the country to "liberalism" in the form of foreign immigration, investment, and export opportunities. The first beneficiary was the wool industry, as sprawling sheep *estancias* in Buenos Aires Province provided countless bales of wool for the mills of England, while traditional cattle *estancias* floundered except on the frontier. Close to the capital, intensively farmed *chacras* produced food for the burgeoning urban market.

After 1880, the humid pampa of Buenos Aires, along with Santa Fe and parts of Córdoba and Mesopotamia, became one of the world's great granaries, as it still is today. This also, however, resulted in the proliferation of latifundios, large landholdings that precluded the rise of any independent class of freehold farmers.

Meanwhile, the influx of British capital modernized the transportation system. Supplanting cart roads, rail lines fanned out from Buenos Aires like the spokes of a wire wheel. The export economy, though, was susceptible to negative developments like the 1879 depression that followed the Franco-Prussian War, and to land speculation by *latifundistas* (large landholders) that resulted in financial collapse as the century drew to a close.

In the new century, the economy recovered thanks to grain and meat exports, but the latifundios failed to bring about a broader prosperity. Urban Argentina grew dramatically, but at a cost; as immigrants streamed into Argentina from Spain, Italy, Britain, Russia, and other European countries, a growing gap between rich and poor intensified social tensions. In 1913, Buenos Aires became the first South American city to open a subway system, but in poorer neighborhoods large families squeezed into *conventillos* (tenements) and struggled on subsistence wages. Conflicts exploded into the open—in 1909, following police repression of a May Day demonstration, anarchist immigrant Simón Radowitzky killed police chief Ramón Falcón with a bomb, and in 1919, President Hipólito Yrigoyen ordered the army to crush a metalworkers' strike during what is now recalled as *La Semana Trágica* (The Tragic Week).

Yrigoyen, ironically enough, pardoned Radowitzky a decade later at the beginning of the Great Depression. His second administration, though, was the first to suffer one of repeated military coups that plagued the country for most of the 20th century. This opened the way for the ascendancy of Juan and Eva Perón, simultaneously the most loved and loathed figures in modern Argentine politics.

THE PERÓNS AND THEIR LEGACY

Unlike most of the military caste, Juan Domingo Perón (1895–1974) came from relatively humble origins in the provincial Buenos Aires town of Lobos, about 100 kilometers southwest of the capital. During his youth, Argentina was a prosperous country, but certain sectors—most notably the *oligarquía terrateniente* (landed elite)—were far more prosperous than others. Many Argentines attributed the maldistribution of wealth to foreign "liberal" sectors, especially the

© WAYNE BERNHARDSON

Peronists honor Evita at Recoleta Cemetery on the 50th anniversary of her death, July 26, 2002.

British, who used Argentina as a source of raw commodities but prevented industrialization that would bring a broader-based prosperity.

Opportunistically or not, Perón shared this outlook. In the course of his military travels, he got to know most of Argentina (as well as Fascist Italy) first-hand, but his career was undistinguished until 1944, when he turned a moribund labor department into a power base as the Secretaría de Trabajo y Bienestar Social (Secretariat for Labor and Social Welfare). Ideologically, he appealed to labor bosses and their clientele (whom he co-opted with extravagant benefits), radical intellectuals (who distrusted foreign capital), and conservative nationalists (who distrusted foreigners, period).

Thanks partly to his wife Eva, whose charismatic populism exceeded even his own, the demagogic Perón managed to convince both left- and right-wing extremists that he was their champion—even as they trained their rifle sights on each other. After the loss of his post and a brief imprisonment, he won the presidency in 1946 and 1952, and used his power to raise wages and pensions, improve working conditions, and guarantee job security. While Perón and his allies threatened their critics, "Evita" Perón capriciously dispensed favors to their supporters through her own private foundation until her death, from cancer, in 1952.

At the same time, Perón's administration expanded the state bureaucracy and splurged on pharaonic works projects, heavy and heavily subsidized industry, and unsustainable social spending that squandered the country's post–World War II surpluses. By 1955, amidst growing social disorder and economy disarray, General Pedro Aramburu's so-called Revolución Libertadora (really a coup) commenced three disastrous decades of dictatorships, punctuated by brief periods of civilian rule.

With Perón in Spanish exile and his "Justicialist" party banned, the downward spiral continued. By the early 1970s, several guerrilla groups (inspired by Fidel Castro's Argentine ally Ernesto "Che" Guevara) had begun operations in the northwestern sierras, the pro-Peronist left-wing Montoneros had become an urban guerrilla movement, and bank robberies, political kidnappings, and assassinations were almost everyday events. From Madrid the aging Perón, with the help of right-wing spiritualist José López Rega (known as *El Brujo*, "The Witch"), cynically manipulated leftist sympathizers (whom he later called "callow and stupid") in Argentina.

After winning the presidency in 1973, Perón's stand-in Hector Cámpora permitted the caudillo's return on the chaotic night of June 20, when hundreds may have died in clashes between right-wing Peronists and leftist Montoneros on the road to Ezeiza airport. Perón won the presidency again in September of that year, but lived less than a year. His successor was his hapless "running mate" María Estela "Isabelita" Martínez de Perón, an exotic dancer whom he had met and married (after Evita's death) while in exile. Meanwhile, López Rega's sinister, secretive Alianza Anticomunista Argentina (AAA, "Argentine Anticommunist Alliance") battled the Montoneros and other "subversive" organizations and individuals.

THE DIRTY WAR AND ITS AFTERMATH

Continued political instability emerged into almost-open warfare until 1976, when the military ousted Isabelita in a bloodless coup that became the most systematic and bloodiest reign of terror in Argentine history. General Jorge Rafael Videla headed a three-man junta that imposed a ferocious military discipline on the entire country.

Under its euphemistically named Proceso de Reorganización Nacional (Process of National Reorganization), the military's *Guerra Sucia* (Dirty War) claimed the lives of as many as 30,000 Argentines, ranging from leftist urban and rural guerrillas to suspected sympathizers and large numbers of innocent bystanders whose links to armed opposition groups were tenuous at best. Many more were imprisoned and tortured, or sent (or escaped) into exile. Only a few courageous individuals and groups, such as Nobel Peace Prize winner Adolfo Pérez Esquivel and the famous Madres de Plaza de Mayo, who marched around Buenos Aires's central plaza in quiet defiance, dared to risk public opposition.

One rationale for taking power was the corruption of civilian politicians, but the military and their civilian collaborators were just as adept in diverting international loans to demolish vibrant but neglected neighborhoods and create worthless public works like freeways that went nowhere. Much of the money found its way into offshore bank accounts. The horror ended only after the military underestimated the response to their 1982 invasion of the British-ruled Falkland (Malvinas) Islands; after a decisive defeat, the military meekly ceded control to civilians. The main coup plotters and human-rights violators even went to prison—an unprecedented occurrence in Latin America (though they were later pardoned).

Following a 1983 return to constitutional government, Argentina underwent several years of hyperinflation in which President Raúl Alfonsín's Radical-party government squandered an enormous amount of good will. President Carlos Menem's succeeding Peronist administration overcame hyperinflation by pegging the peso at par with the U.S. dollar through a "currency basket" that ensured it would print no more pesos than it had hard currency reserves to back.

Menem's strategy—really the brainchild of Economy Minister Domingo Cavallo—brought a decade of economic stability during which foreign investment flowed into Argentina. Privatization of inefficient state-run monopolies, which had had thousands of so-called *ñoquis* ("ghost employees"—who may or may not actually work for their paychecks) on the payroll, brought major improvements in telecommunications, transportation, and other sectors. The financial and service sectors flourished, giving many Argentines a sense of optimism through most of the 1990s.

The boom had a dark side, though, in the form of "crony capitalism" in which the president's associates enriched themselves through favorable privatization contracts. At the same time, reform barely brushed the provinces, which maintained large public payrolls for patronage, and even printed their own *bonos* (bonds), "funny money" that further reduced the confidence of international investors. The Menem years also saw still-unsolved incidents of terrorism in the deadly bombings of Buenos Aires's Israeli Embassy in 1992 and AMIA Jewish cultural center in 1994 (In August 2003, Britain arrested the former Iranian ambassador to Argentina, Hade Soleimanpour, in connection with the AMIA bombing but refused to extradite him to Buenos Aires).

Even before the partial debt default of late 2001, the economy contracted and Argentines began to suffer. After the resignation of Menem's luckless successor Fernando de la Rúa in December, the country had a series of caretaker presidents before the congress chose Peronist Eduardo Duhalde (whom De la Rúa had defeated two years earlier) to serve until elections in late 2003. In a controversial move, Duhalde ended Cavallo's convertibility policy and devalued the peso, which lost nearly 75 percent of its value within a few months. At the same time, he continued the De la Rúa administration's *corralito* policy, which restricted bank withdrawals to maintain hard currency reserves, but also strangled the country's economy.

As the economy stagnated and unemployment rose, homelessness also rose and scavengers became a common sight even in prosperous neighborhoods. Strikes, strident pickets blocking bridges and highways, and frustration with politicians and institutions like the International Monetary Fund (IMF) contributed to the mood of *bronca* (aggravation). Under pressure, the ambitious Duhalde advanced presidential elections to early 2003, but also manipulated Peronist primary rules to favor his chosen successor, Santa Cruz governor Néstor Kirchner, over his political nemesis Carlos Menem. (*Buenos Aires Herald* columnist Martín Gambarotta characterized the political maneuvers of Duhalde and Menem as "two men playing a chess match with boxing gloves.")

Government and Politics

Argentine politics are often contentious, with little consensus, but since the end of the 1976–83 military dictatorship it has been remarkably stable and peaceful. The major exception was the storm of political and economic protest that led to the deaths of five demonstrators in Buenos Aires's Plaza de Mayo on December 20, 2001, and brought the resignation of President Fernando de la Rúa. The country then had three provisional presidents in two weeks before Buenos Aires Province Senator Eduardo Duhalde, who had lost the 1999 presidential election to De la Rúa, assumed the office in an extra-constitutional congressional vote.

Argentines' lack of faith in institutions, though, has led to barrio activism through spontaneous *asambleas populares* (popular assemblies) and less-constructive practices such as *escrache*, in which groups of citizens loudly and publicly demonstrate against politicians, judges, bankers, or representatives of other institutions at their homes or work places. *Escraches,* which began after a series of pardons and other measures limited prosecutions of alleged torturers and murderers of the military dictatorship, often deteriorate into shouting matches.

Another questionable form of political protest has been the emergence of *piquetes* (pickets), which block roads and highways to pressure politicians for assistance or handouts to the unemployed. With unemployment exceeding 20 percent, this is a legitimate issue, but picket leaders claim the right to dispense this assistance as patronage for their loyal followers. Surveys show that Argentines are, overwhelmingly, fed up with picket abuses.

Unlike 1970s Argentina, though, early 21st-century Argentina appears to be imploding rather than exploding, and the villains are less obvious than they once were. Political analyst James Neilson of the *Buenos Aires Herald* suggests that, despite vocal protests, inertia rather than genuine activism characterizes the country's politics.

ORGANIZATION

Formally in force but often ignored in practice, the Constitution of 1853 created a checks-and-balances system of executive, legislative, and judicial branches resembling that of the United States. The bicameral Congreso Nacional (National Congress—the legislative branch) consists of a 257-member Cámara de Diputados (Chamber of Deputies) and a 72-member Senado (Senate), whose members represent 23 provinces and the Ciudad Autónoma de Buenos Aires (Autonomous City of Buenos Aires). The Cámara de Diputados is subject to redistricting following each decennial census.

In reality, however, the president wields great discretionary powers, often governs by decree, and frequently intervenes in provincial affairs. A 1994 constitutional amendment reduced the executive's term from six years to four, but also allowed him or her to run for immediate reelection to a second term. The same amendment abolished a provision that required the president to be Roman Catholic.

Argentina's constitution is federal, and each province and the city of Buenos Aires has its own autonomous government. Argentine federalism is one-sided, though, as the federal government funds provincial governments through revenue-sharing; in practice, this is a burden, as fiscally irresponsible provinces can blame revenue shortages on Buenos Aires. La Rioja, for instance, collects only 10 percent of its budget in local tax revenue.

In addition to the city of Buenos Aires and 23 provinces, Argentina claims the Islas del Atlántico Sur (including the British-ruled Falkland/Malvinas Islands and South Georgia) and Antártida Argentina (an Antarctic wedge below 60° S latitude between 25° and 74° W longitude). While Argentina is persistent and vocal in its claims to the Falklands and South Georgia, it acknowledges that Antarctic claims are on hold by international treaty.

POLITICAL PARTIES

For all its factionalism, the Partido Justicialista (PJ, the Peronist or Justicialist party) is the country's largest and most cohesive political entity. For most of the past century, the next most important has been the misnamed Unión Cívica Radical (UCR), a middle-class party that seems to function better in opposition than in power. Since the collapse of the Radical president Fernando de la Rúa's administration in 2001, though, the party has almost dropped off the map; the two top vote-getters in the 2003 presidential election were Peronists Néstor Kirchner and Carlos Menem, while the UCR candidate drew less than five percent.

The Peronists, Radicals, and similar entities, though, are barely parties in the European or North American sense—in some ways, it might be more accurate to call them movements. When ex-Radicals Ricardo López Murphy and Elisa Carrió ran in the 2003 primary, they did so at the heads of their own hastily created parties—the conservative López Murphy (who finished a strong third) for the Movimiento Federal Recrear and the populist anticorruption campaigner Carrió (a weak fourth) for her Alternativa por una República de Iguales (ARI, Alternative for a Republic of Equals).

As of late 2003, the Peronists held a majority in the Senado, with 40 seats, while there were 15 Radicals; 10 other parties shared the remaining 17. In the Cámara de Diputados, the Peronists held 116 seats and the Radicals 61; none of the other 30 parties occupied more than 11 seats (in a triumph of Argentine individualism, 17 of these parties held one seat only, including the appropriately named Partido Unipersonal). The Peronists hold 16 of 24 provincial governorships.

Historically, many officeholders have used their supporters for political intimidation instead of dialogue. Voters, for that matter, cannot vote directly for candidates, but only for lists chosen by party bosses. More often than not, the parties serve as patronage machines that, after mobilizing their most militant members for elections, reward them with well-paid public posts that may or may not actually involve working for their paychecks. Such "ghost employees" are called *ñoquis* (gnocchi) after the inexpensive potato pasta traditionally served the 29th of each month in restaurants and cash-strapped households—the insinuation is that they start showing up at the office just in time to collect their salary on the first of the following month.

Many Argentines have assumed a "plague on all your houses" attitude toward politicians in general, but the Peronists in particular have managed to dominate the even-more-divided opposition parties in most of the country. In Buenos Aires, though, the most important political force is the Alianza, an alliance of the Radicals and the slightly left-of-center Frente de País Solidario (Frepaso, National Solidarity Front).

ELECTIONS

Dating from 1853 and amended in 1994, Argentina's constitution now stipulates a four-year presidential term; no president may serve more than two consecutive terms. There are no limits on number of terms for senators, whose terms are six years, or deputies, who serve four years.

Elections and dates are ostensibly fixed, but military coups, other political crises, and simple expediency have often disrupted orderly transitions. In 1989, for instance, economic chaos forced the resignation of Radical president Raúl Alfonsín, and newly elected Carlos Menem took office early. The late-2002 collapse of Radical president Fernando de la Rúa's administration led to five caretakers within two weeks.

Likewise, in early 2003, caretaker president Eduardo Duhalde stage-managed the elections so that his chosen successor Néstor Kirchner would not have to face former president Menem (whose constitutional eligibility was questionable, in any event) in a Peronist primary; he also advanced the general-election date by more than six months. Menem and Kirchner were the first-round leaders, but when Menem withdrew because unfavorable polls made his defeat look inevitable (though he claimed otherwise), the runoff never took place.

JUDICIAL AND PENAL SYSTEMS

According to the constitution the courts act independently, but in practice they are subject to political influence and even whim. When former president Carlos Menem encountered judicial opposition to administrative reforms, for instance, he managed to expand the Supreme Court from five to nine members, with one of the new appointees being his former tennis coach. This gave Menem a so-called "automatic majority" for his projects, and insurance against political scandals such as an illegal arms sale to Croatia.

When the political winds shifted, though, congressional allies of new president Néstor Kirchner managed to force the resignation of Chief Justice Julio Nazareno and Justice Guillermo López. They also successfully impeached Justice Eduardo Moliné O'Connor, who will now have more free time for the tennis courts. Some observers have questioned whether Kirchner's new appointees will be the best legal scholars or simply more political cronies.

Meanwhile, important cases in the lower courts drag on for years and even decades due to inefficiency or political influence. The most high-profile example is the investigation into the 1994 bombing of the AMIA Jewish cultural center in Buenos Aires's Once neighborhood, which killed 87 people. The government of president Néstor Kirchner has pledged to pursue the matter—in which both former Iranian diplomats and Buenos Aires provincial police have been implicated—with greater diligence.

Justice may also vary according to social class. The military caste, for instance, escaped judgment for their Dirty War crimes with almost complete impunity except for a handful of top officers (all of whom were later pardoned by Menem, though he himself had been imprisoned during the dictatorship). Rich and powerful civilians have avoided detention even when

the charges have been murder, but petty thieves can count on jail time.

BUREAUCRACY

The government institutions most travelers are likely to come into contact with are immigration, customs, and police. Immigration and customs generally treat foreigners fairly, but Argentine police are notoriously corrupt. The capital's Policía Federal is generally better than provincial forces, particularly the Buenos Aires provincial police—a "mafia with badges;" its members are infamous for shaking down motorists for bribes for minor equipment violations.

The politicized administrative bureaucracy remains one of Argentina's most intractable problems, thanks to the continuing presence of *ñoquis,* or ghost employees, at the federal, provincial, and municipal levels. While abuses are less extreme than they were in the past, when individuals often drew multiple paychecks without performing any work whatsoever, bloated state payrolls are still cause for concern.

While the privatizations of the 1990s reduced federal-sector employment by nearly two-thirds, they had little impact on the provinces. Provincial payrolls still include nearly 1.4 million Argentines in what, for the most part, might be more accurately called positions rather than jobs. For the tourist, it may be gratifying to find an obscure museum open 60 hours per week, staffed by three people, but the cumulative economic impact of such practices has been catastrophic.

In practical terms, the absence of a professional civil service means a lack of continuity, as officials lose their jobs with every change of administration; continuing political influence means an abundance of uninterested and often ill-qualified officials who take their time dealing with any but the most routine matter. It also, of course, means nepotism and corruption—Transparency International consistently ranks Argentina among the world's worst offenders in its annual survey of perceived corruption. In 2003, Argentina was 90th of 133 countries surveyed; on the South American continent, only

Venezuela (100), Bolivia (106), Ecuador (113), and Paraguay (129) ranked lower.

THE MILITARY

Thanks to repeated coups in the 20th century and the vicious dictatorship of the 1976–83 "Dirty War," the Argentine military earned a reputation as one of the worst even on a continent infamous for armed repression. Its ignominious collapse in the 1982 Falkland Islands War, followed by public revelations of state terrorism and the conviction of the top generals and admirals responsible for kidnapping, torture, and murder helped overcome the worst aspects of its traditional impunity.

Since the 1983 return to constitutional rule, civilian governments have eliminated conscription, the military budget has declined to barely one percent of GDP (less than half that of neighboring Chile), and Argentine forces have undertaken more strictly military operations such as peacekeeping in the Balkans. While periods of political disorder such as 2001–02 always bring coup rumors, the military appears to have little or no interest in taking the reins of government.

The size of the military services has also been reduced. As of 2001, for instance, the navy had only 27,000 personnel, heavily weighted toward noncommissioned officers. It has about 50 ships, including three submarines.

Nevertheless, there remains an ugly reminder of military fanaticism in the person of retired colonel Mohamed Alí Seineldín, who mounted a rebellion against the constitutional government in 1989 and received a 2003 pardon from outgoing president Eduardo Duhalde from a life term in a military prison. Seineldín, who despite his name is a fundamentalist Catholic, has taken to making bizarre public statements regarding oral and anal sex, and asserting that the CIA and the Fuerzas Armadas Revolucionarias de Colombia (FARC, the Colombian guerrilla army) are conspiring to destabilize Argentina—as if Argentines were incapable of doing so themselves.

Despite the country's reputation for dictatorial bellicosity, two Argentines have won Nobel Peace Prizes: foreign minister Carlos Saavedra Lamas (1936) for mediating a Chaco War settlement between Paraguay and Bolivia, and Adolfo Pérez Esquivel (1984) for publicizing the 1976–83 military dictatorship's human rights atrocities.

Economy

To most foreign observers, Argentina's economy is an enigma. Rich in natural resources, with a well-educated populace and modern infrastructure, for most of seven decades it has lurched from crisis to crisis, with the notable exception of the stable, prosperous 1990s. In late 2001, it stunned the world and even many Argentines by defaulting on part of its US$141 billion foreign debt, triggering a political and economic meltdown comparable to the Great Depression of the 1930s. In the first quarter of 2002, the economy shrank 16.3 percent, marking 14 consecutive quarters of contraction.

Argentina actually emerged from World War II in an enviable position, but the government of the charismatic General Juan Domingo Perón and its successors squandered

enormous budget surpluses from agricultural exports on bloated state enterprises which, in collusion with corrupt labor leaders, became industrial dinosaurs impossible to reform. Then, during the 1970s and 1980s, large loans destined for massive public works projects filled the pockets—or Swiss bank accounts—of the nefarious generals and their civilian collaborators who ruled the country.

Corruption and deficit spending resulted in hyperinflation that reached levels of 30 percent or more *per month.* Shortly after taking power in 1989, President Carlos Menem's administration became the first Argentine government in recent memory to tackle the inflation problem through Economy Minister Domingo Cavallo's "convertibility" policy; this "currency basket" fixed the value of the Argentine peso at par with the U.S. dollar, and required the government to back every peso printed with a dollar or other hard currency.

Selling off unprofitable state enterprises such as Aerolíneas Argentinas, the state telecommunications enterprise Entel, and most of the extensive railroad networks made convertibility possible. Inflation dropped to zero and, after an initial glitch, there was steady economic growth, but the Mexican crisis of 1995 followed by a Brazilian devaluation that reduced Argentine competitiveness led to increasing unemployment and recession. After a brief recovery, convertibility proved to be an economic straitjacket that, by the second year of the De la Rúa administration, was unsustainable.

In a desperation move, De la Rúa reappointed Cavallo to the Economy Ministry, but a run on bank deposits brought severe restrictions on withdrawals, known collectively as the *corralito* (literally, "little fence"), whose unpopularity triggered Cavallo's resignation and De la Rúa's downfall. De la Rúa's successor Eduardo Duhalde, though, made things even worse by eliminating convertibility, pesifying dollar savings accounts at a 1:1.4 rate, and floating the local currency so that those accounts soon lost most of their value. At the same time, in a classic case of Argentine "crony capitalism," the new president pesified dollar debts at a rate of 1:1, benefiting the large industrialists who were his political base.

With devaluation, according to the Economist Intelligence Unit, in less than a year Buenos Aires went from the world's 22nd most expensive city (of 131 surveyed) to the 120th. As the dollar-to-peso ratio plummeted from 1:1 to 1:3.5 in only a few months, citizens with the discipline to save saw their frozen wealth evaporate; those who had accumulated large debts saw their burdens reduced. Devaluation also meant the return of inflation—about 25 percent for 2002—though it failed to reach the nightmarish level of the 1980s because banking restrictions limited cash in circulation. It dropped to about four percent in 2003, but as the economy recovers inflation could be a renewed concern.

In theory, a devalued peso should make Argentine exports more competitive, but this has not yet happened—partly because the Duhalde administration also slapped an export tax on all profits over US$5 million. Banks have taken the brunt of criticism for not repaying their depositors, but even though some are solvent enough to do so, government restrictions prevent this.

In 2002 Argentine GDP contracted by more than 11 percent, but in 2003 it rebounded to a seven percent increase (from an admittedly low base), with only three percent inflation. Still, the country's monstrous US$185 billion debt—a figure that equals 143 percent of GDP—is worrisome. It's not that Argentines don't have money, but much of it is not in Argentina—by some accounts they hold more than US$100 billion overseas, with another US$20 billion in the country but "beneath the mattress."

Foreign and Argentine investors considered the late-2002 appointment of 37-year-old Alfonso Prat Gay, a onetime J.P. Morgan investment banker, to the presidency of the Banco Central as a positive development. Still, some consider the political pressure on all Argentine appointees a troubling sign.

In the long run, economists such as Arturo Porczeanski believe the only way to stabilize prices is to adopt the dollar as Argentina's currency, as "any effort to convince Argentines that the peso is worth anything are in vain. They only have faith in the dollar." In a similar vein, Cavallo remarked that "forcing Argentines to save in pesos would be as difficult as forcing them to learn to speak Chinese instead of Spanish."

This, of course, has long been the case—for many decades, Argentines have speculated on the dollar in times of crisis. In the 1970s, when Montoneros guerrillas headed by Rodolfo Galimberti kidnapped empresario Jorge Born, they demanded and got a ransom of US$60 million—at a time when that was *real* money. In an only-in-Argentina scenario, the pardoned Galimberti later became the business partner of the man he abducted.

EMPLOYMENT, UNEMPLOYMENT, AND UNDEREMPLOYMENT

Through four years of recession, Argentine unemployment rose dramatically—the official figure for 2002 exceeded 20 percent and it was 15.6 percent at the end of 2003. The real figure is likely higher and underemployment is also rampant. These figures are probably not quite so bad in Buenos Aires as in the provinces, but street, bus, and subway vendors are far more numerous than in the past, and the numbers of people rummaging through garbage for recyclables has shocked even Argentines.

During the crisis of early 2002, many unemployed individuals spent the night in line to buy dollars at Banco de la Nación and private exchange houses in hopes of selling their spot to those who had sufficient pesos to purchase dollars. Similarly, individuals waited outside the Italian consulate and other European missions to sell their place in line for passports and visas. Now, though, there is an increasingly militant sector of publicly protesting *piquetes* (pickets) who have put enormous pressure on the government for remedial action and, some would argue, handouts for graft.

AGRICULTURE

Since the 19th century, the Argentine pampas have developed from the meat locker and wool-shed of the world to one of its main granaries, growing corn, wheat, oats, sorghum, and soybeans, among other crops. The country's agriculture has diversified, though, to include vegetables such as potatoes, onions, carrots, squash, beans, and tomatoes, and to fruit crops like apples, pears, and grapes—the latter of which help make Argentina the world's fifth-largest wine producer.

Other commercial crops include subtropical cultigens such as sugar cane, olives, tea, yerba mate, and tobacco, mostly in provinces to the north and west of the capital. Agriculture accounts for roughly 10 percent of GDP but about 31.6 percent of exports, or about US$8 billion per year.

INDUSTRY

Argentina's industrial heyday was the immediate post–World War II period, when Juan Domingo Perón invested vast sums in manufacturing products such as steel, chemicals, and petrochemicals; the military controlled large parts of the economy, including its own weapons-manufacture and support industries.

Despite the privatizations of the 1990s, much Argentine industry is still inefficient and unable to compete without state assistance—or cronyism. In the aftermath of the 2002 economic meltdown, frustrated unemployed workers occupied some factories that had closed, and began to run them as cooperatives. Some were successful, at least in the short term, and others were not. In the absence of capital investment, the long-term prognosis for low-productivity installations was not good.

Accounting for about 32 percent of GDP, industry includes food processing, motor vehicles, consumer durables, textiles, printing, metallurgy, and steel. Much of this activity is concentrated in the southern Buenos Aires suburbs of Avellaneda and Quilmes, across the Riachuelo, and in large cities like Rosario, Córdoba, and Mendoza.

DISTRIBUTION OF WEALTH

The gap between rich and poor, once an issue of the landed and the landless, is more complex today. When giant *estancias* and wheat farms ruled the rural landscape, land meant power, but this is less true in contemporary Argentina's highly urbanized society.

More important is the difference between hereditary wealth and a nouveau-riche plutocracy on the one hand, and a struggling working class on the other. Over the past three decades, the gap between rich and poor has increased, especially during the past five years of recession or, some would say, depression.

Historically, the disparity between rich and poor has been far less extreme than in other Latin American countries, but the meltdown of 2001–02, with its devastating impact on the middle class, has resurrected the issue. As of

2002, 55 percent of all Argentines were considered to fall beneath the poverty line, and about six million (one-sixth of the population) were considered indigent.

According to World Bank figures from the calendar year 2000, with the Argentine peso at par with the U.S. dollar, the country's per capita income was US$7,460, while in 2002 it fell to US$4,080. In practice, purchasing power was higher than that would suggest, but there is no doubt it has fallen more for the lower middle classes than for the well-to-do. White-collar crime (fraud and tax evasion) by the rich are also common.

In Buenos Aires, according to a study of official statistics, the income of the richest 10 percent (which totaled 37.5 percent of total income) of the population was 17.9 times that of the poorest 10 percent (which totaled 2.1 percent of total income) in the year 1974. Today, though, that gap has increased tenfold.

The gap between rich and poor has geographical as well as social dimensions. Poverty affects nearly 20 percent of *porteños,* primarily in the city's run-down southern neighborhoods, while the northern barrios and areas beyond them in the province of Buenos Aires are relatively wealthy.

EDUCATION

Argentina's formal literacy rate of nearly 97 percent is one of the highest in the Americas, but that statistic disguises some serious problems. Education is free through high school and compulsory to age 12, and the curriculum is rigid; more importantly, though, many schools are disorderly and continual teachers' strikes have meant that students often only get half a year, or less, of instruction.

There are also widely varying standards. The level of public schools in rural areas can be low, but other public secondary schools, most notably the Colegio Nacional Buenos Aires, are even more prestigious than some of their private bilingual counterparts in the capital.

Public universities like the capital's Universidad de Buenos Aires and the Universidad Nacional de La Plata, in the provincial capital, are generally superior to private universities. Public university education is free of charge, but has generated a surplus of high-status degrees in fields like law and intellectually stimulating but less obviously practical subjects like psychology and sociology—and not enough in hands-on disciplines like engineering and computer science. Some activists insist on open admissions to careers such as medicine, and claim that any rejection is discriminatory.

Schoolteachers generally do not receive university degrees, but attend special teachers' colleges. There is vocational and technical training as well, but these skills enjoy little respect even when those jobs pay more than white-collar positions or office work.

Several Argentine scientists have won Nobel Prizes, including Bernardo Houssay (Medicine, 1946), Luis Federico Leloir (Chemistry, 1972), and the recently deceased César Milstein (Medicine, 1984). One continual concern is the "brain drain" of educated Argentines overseas; Milstein, for instance, spent his most productive years in England because political pressures at Argentine universities made research impossible. Many talented individuals, though, have left simply because the economy has failed them.

TOURISM

Both international tourism (which accounts for about 10 percent of Argentine exports) and domestic travel are significant factors in the economy. In the aftermath of the 2001 terrorist attacks on the United States and Argentina's own domestic instability, long-distance tourist traffic probably diminished in the short run, but visitors from neighboring countries immediately appreciated the bargains that devaluation had wrought. Budget travelers soon streamed into a country that had been intolerably expensive for more than a decade, and more affluent long-distance travelers started to return in greater numbers than before.

Just before the 2004 summer season, the Secretaría de Turismo de la Nación announced that international air traffic had risen by 35 percent over the 2002 numbers, and anticipated that the number of foreign visitors would rise by more than 40 percent over the previous years. According to INDEC, the state statistical agency, the number of foreign visitors in 2000 (the last year for which complete statistics have been released) exceeded 2.9 million. Total tourism revenues for the year were about US$3 billion.

Most visitors, though, came from other South American countries, mainly Chile (567,967 in 1999), Paraguay (499,831), Uruguay (488,007), Brazil (466,016), and Bolivia (95,109). These figures may be even more misleading, as many such visits involve short shopping trips across the border.

Visitors from the United States numbered 280,833, while those from Europe totaled 353,983. Long-distance visitors spent substantially more money on travel-related expenses such as accommodations, food, and transportation—US$121 per day for U.S. visitors, US$94 per day for Europeans—than did other South Americans except for Brazilians, who averaged US$132 per day. Chileans spent only US$87, Uruguayans only US$81, and Bolivians only US$45.

The 634,816 American and European travelers who came to Argentina accounted for only about 20 percent of visitors to the country but they spent more than US$1 billion, about 38 percent of total tourism income. Their stays tended to be longer—about two weeks for U.S. citizens and nearly three weeks for Europeans—than those of visitors from neighboring countries, who averaged about a week.

As Argentina's main gateway, Buenos Aires benefits more than any other locality from the tourist trade, with more than two million foreign visitors per annum. Many other visitors to the city, of course, come from elsewhere in the country; in 1999, 7.2 million Argentines spent a total of US$2.7 billion on visits to the capital.

The People

According to the 2001 census, Argentina has 36,223,947 inhabitants, an increase of about 3.6 million over 1991 figures.

POPULATION GEOGRAPHY

Nearly a third of all Argentines live in the Capital Federal (2,768,772) and the 24 counties of Gran Buenos Aires (8,684,953), for a total of 11,453,725. Most of the rest are also city dwellers, in population centers such as Rosario, Córdoba, Mar del Plata, Mendoza, Salta, and other provincial capitals and cities. The southern Patagonian provinces of Chubut, Santa Cruz, and Tierra del Fuego are very thinly populated, as are the hot northern provinces of Chaco and Formosa.

Indigenous Peoples

Argentina has the smallest indigenous population of any South American country except Uruguay, but certain provinces and regions have substantial concentrations. The most numerous are the Kollas (Quechuas) of northwestern Argentina and the Mapuches of Patagonia, who reside mostly in La Pampa, Neuquén, and Río Negro. There are also significant numbers of Guaraní in the northeast, and Mataco, Mocoví, and Toba in Santa Fe and the Gran Chaco.

There are no definitive statistics on native peoples, though the 2001 census questionnaire asked whether "there is in this household any person who considers himself or herself a member or descendent of an indigenous group." Until the census agency INDEC releases complete figures on this subject, the best estimates are that there exist 170,000 to 500,000 Kollas (many of them Bolivian immigrants), 40,000 to 90,000 Mapuches, and substantially smaller populations of the others.

Ethnic Minorities

Argentina is a country of immigrants, both recent and not-so-recent, and the capital reflects that history. Spaniards, of course first colonized what is now Argentina, but a 19th-century tidal wave

THE AFRO-ARGENTINES AND THEIR "DEMISE"

In a country of immigrants, the heritage of many Argentines is often conspicuous. According to some accounts, even more Argentines have Italian surnames than Spanish ones. Anglo-Argentines are prominent and have their own daily newspaper, and German-Argentines still support a weekly. Buenos Aires has numerous Jewish community landmarks, and so-called *Turcos* of Middle Eastern descent, such as former President Carlos Menem, have made their mark in politics.

Yet an Afro-Argentine population that by official statistics once comprised nearly a third of Buenos Aires's population has been nearly invisible. When the revolutionary government of 1810 tentatively banned the slave trade three years later, almost a third of 32,000 *porteños* were of African origin. As late as 1838, the figure was nearly 15,000 of almost 63,000. Yet by 1887, there were only 8,000 among more than 430,000 city residents.

After the turn of the century, Afro-Argentines virtually fell off the city map. In the 1970s, newspaper and magazine articles even puzzled over the disappearance of a community that fought honorably in the 19th-century civil and regional wars, supported social and charitable organizations, sponsored a lively local press, and contributed to the arts. How and why this could have happened was, seemingly, an enigma.

Two plausible hypotheses were widely accepted. One was that Afro-Argentines were frontline cannon fodder, particularly in the Paraguayan war, where they suffered disproportionate casualties. Another was that the 19th-century yellow-fever epidemics in San Telmo, where many Afro-Argentines lived, decimated their numbers as wealthier criollos moved to higher, healthier ground in the northern suburbs.

Historian George Reid Andrews argued that there was slim evidence for either hypothesis and, moreover, little for the disappearance of the community itself. What he did learn, by examining archival materials and the capital's Afro-Argentine press, was that the community itself was unconcerned with demographic decline but clearly worried about its socioeconomic status.

As the slave trade ended by the mid-19th century and massive European immigration transformed the city a couple of decades later, Afro-Argentines were clearly a declining *percentage* of the population, but that does not explain their plunging absolute numbers. Andrews, though, found that Argentine authorities and opinion-makers consciously excised the Afro-Argentine presence to help promote the country as a European outpost in the Americas.

Some of this, certainly, owed its origins to a racism that was present from early independence times. Political opponents of Bernardino Rivadavia, a presumed mulatto who served as president in 1826–27 before his forced resignation, stigmatized him with the epithet "Dr. Chocolate." Argentine school children are taught proudly that their country abolished slavery early, in 1813, but these measures were so half-hearted that the institution lingered for nearly another half-century.

More insidiously, though, census-takers systematically undercounted Afro-Argentines by equally half-hearted efforts that sometimes even avoided their neighborhoods. When summarizing the data, they minimized the black presence by creating vague racial categories such as *trigueño* (wheat-colored), and incorporating individuals with African background into them. Eventually, in Andrews's words, Buenos Aires's Afro-Argentines were "forgotten, but not gone."

Even as more and more European immigrants streamed into Argentina, Afro-Argentines kept alive institutions such as the Shimmy Club, a social organization that sponsored dances only half a block off Avenida Corrientes, into the 1970s. Here rhythmic drum-based *malambo, milonga,* and *zamba* filled the hall and, on occasion, spilled out into the street.

Andrews thought that Argentine society was absorbing blacks and, indeed, defining them as whites in accordance with an unspoken ideology, even as their contributions to society survived.

continued on next page

Know Argentina

THE AFRO-ARGENTINES AND THEIR "DEMISE" (cont'd)

In recent years, though, there's been a small but complex revival of black culture in Buenos Aires that involves Afro-Argentines (now estimated at about 3,000) but also Afro-Uruguayans, Afro-Brazilians, Cape Verde Portuguese (perhaps 8,000), Cubans, and Africans. This has not always been convivial, as the remaining Afro-Argentines clearly distinguish themselves from latecomers even as they share some cultural features.

Still, Argentine society's continued refusal to acknowledge their presence and its own African heritage may be their greatest adversary. Created in 1996, the Fundación Africa Vive (Africa Lives Foundation) claims there are more than two million Argentines of African descent; according to director María Magdalena Lamadrid, "A single drop of blood is enough" to define an Afro-Argentine.

Yet when, in 2002, Lamadrid herself attempted to fly to Panama to participate in a conference on Dr. Martin Luther King Jr.'s life, immigration officials detained her on suspicion of carrying a false passport. One allegedly said, "she can't be black and Argentine."

of Italians, Basques, English, Irish, Welsh, Ukrainians and other nationalities made Buenos Aires a mosaic of immigrants; Italo-Argentines even came to outnumber Argentines of Spanish origin.

Some immigrant groups retain a high visibility, most notably a Jewish community that numbers at least 200,000 and is historically concentrated in the Once district of Buenos Aires. Since the onset of the 2001–02 economic crisis, though, many have needed assistance from Jewish community organizations, and some Argentine Jews have emigrated or considered emigrating to Israel despite the insecurity there. It's worth mentioning that still-unsolved terrorist incidents in Buenos Aires killed 29 people in Retiro's Israeli Embassy, and 87 people in Once's Asociación Mutua Israelita Argentina (AMIA), a Jewish cultural center, in 1994; most Jewish community landmarks are well fortified.

Middle Eastern immigrants are less numerous, but have occupied high-profile positions—the most notable being former president Carlos

Menem, of Syrian descent. Palermo's new Islamic Center, funded by Saudi Arabia, is nevertheless disproportionately large compared to the capital's Muslim population. Argentines misleadingly refer to anyone of Middle Eastern descent as *turcos* (Turks), a legacy of the initial immigration from the region.

In recent years, Asian faces have become more common. There has long been a community of about 30,000 Japanese-Argentines, concentrated in the capital and the Greater Buenos Aires suburb of Escobar, but Belgrano also has a modest Chinatown near the Barrancas. Many Koreans work in Once and live in the southern barrio of Nueva Pompeya.

Other South Americans, mostly Bolivians, Paraguayans, and Peruvians, flocked to Argentina during the early-1990s boom. They generally work at menial jobs, and many have returned home since the economic meltdown of 2001–02. They are mostly concentrated in certain Buenos Aires neighborhoods—Peruvians in Congreso, Paraguayans in Constitución, and Bolivians in Nueva Pompeya.

THE PROMISED LAND OF THE SOUTH

Argentina's Jewish community of about 200,000 is Latin America's greatest and the world's sixth-largest. Still, it draws little international attention except when it literally explodes onto the news—as in 1992 when a car bomb destroyed Buenos Aires's Israeli embassy and in 1994 when a similar event leveled the city's main Jewish cultural center. Ever since the first Jews arrived in the mid-19th century, though, the community has endured a cycle of ups and downs in both the capital and the countryside.

In the mid-19th century, Buenos Aires's first Jews were individual professionals who arrived as representatives of British, French, and German exporters; about 50 of these formed the first Congregación Israelita de la República Argentina in 1862. The first Moroccan Jews arrived in the early 1880s, but the main impetus for organized immigration began in 1881, when President Julio Argentino Roca appointed an honorary agent in Paris, with special attention to Jewish refugees from Tsarist pogroms.

Still, nearly eight years passed before the first 120 farming families arrived, but their welcome was less than even lukewarm—an immigration inspector separated them for two days and nearly sent them back on the steamer that brought them. Finally admitted as *colonos* who had purchased property from Rafael Hernández (brother of the author of the epic *gauchesco* poem *Martín Fierro*), they never received their property, as Hernández reneged on the deal due to an increase in prices.

Many Jews settled in Buenos Aires, of course, but the French baron Maurice de Hirsch responded to Hernández's duplicity by sponsoring a program to settle the *colonos* in Santa Fe Province, where they created the Colonia Agrícola Moisesville. Riding like gauchos and introducing new crops such as rice and sunflowers, the new settlers prospered in a community (population about 2,000) that still, today, has four synagogues (only one of which remains open, however).

In all, between 1888 and 1938, about 200,000–250,000 Jewish immigrants entered Argentina;

another 10,000 or so were Holocaust survivors who arrived after WWII. As birthrates fell after 1960, the young preferred the cities, and upwards of 30,000 emigrated to Israel through 1983, the community's profile began to change.

Traditionally middle-class, the Jewish population suffered along with the rest of Argentina in the economic meltdown of 2001–02, and about 20 percent now live below the poverty line. Despite assistance from overseas organizations, the situation is dire enough that some have chosen to emigrate to Israel—preferring the political uncertainties of a war zone to jobless futility in the country of their birth. By some estimates, up to 10 percent of the population could leave for Israel, where new immigrants receive jobs and government subsidies to get started.

Moisesville, for its part, retains much of its identity, even though only about 15 percent of the remaining population is Jewish—the town shuts down for Jewish holidays even though the majority is now Roman Catholic. With the movement to the cities, many Jewish landowners now lease their properties to Gentile farmers.

Coincidentally, Jewish themes appear in Argentine literature and, more recently, the cinema (though not so prominently as in Hollywood). Russian immigrant Alberto Gerchunoff (1884–1950) left a series of vignettes recently republished as *The Jewish Gauchos of the Pampas* (University of New Mexico Press, 1998), while Nina Barragan has reconstructed the Moisesville experience in *Losers and Keepers in Argentina* (University of New Mexico Press, 2001).

A version of Gerchunoff's *Los Gauchos Judíos* made it to the screen in the early 1970s. More recently, director Antonio Ottone made the early colony the setting for *Un Amor en Moisesville* (2000), known in English as *Divided Hearts*. The well-known actors Federico Luppi and Norma Aleandro appeared in director Eduardo Mignogna's *Sol de Otoño* (1996), a Buenos Aires–based comedy/drama about a love affair between an older couple, a non-Jew and a Jew.

Culture

RELIGION

Roman Catholicism remains Argentina's official and dominant religion, though church membership is no longer a requirement for the presidency. Evangelical Protestantism, with its street preachers and storefront churches, is growing even in sophisticated Buenos Aires, mostly but not exclusively among working-class people. Other religions have fewer adherents.

Catholicism in particular has left the country with many of its greatest landmarks, ranging from the colonial chapels, churches, and cathedrals of Córdoba and the northwest, to the neoclassical dignity of Buenos Aires's Catedral Metropolitana. Immigrant Protestant communities are responsible for Buenos Aires landmarks like the Danish and Swedish churches of San Telmo and the impressive Russian Orthodox dome opposite Parque Lezama, also in San Telmo.

Roman Catholicism

Starting with the famous Dominican Bartolomé de las Casas in Mexico, factions in the Catholic Church have wrestled with the contradictions between its official mission of recruiting and saving souls and its duty to alleviate the misery of those who have experienced secular injustice and persecution. Argentina is no exception—figures such as the late cardinal Antonio Quarracino were outright apologists for the vicious military dictatorship of 1976–83, but others lobbied against its excesses and in favor of a return to democracy. Some more-militant clergy worked in the slums under the influence of "liberation theology," and some lost their lives in the aftermath of the 1976 coup.

Folk Catholicism, including spiritualist practices, often diverges from Church orthodoxy in the veneration of unofficial saints such as San Juan's Difunta Correa and Corrientes's Gaucho Antonio Gil, and even historical figures like Juan and Evita Perón, tango legend Carlos Gardel, and healer Madre María, all of whose tombs are in Buenos Aires's landmark cemeteries Recoleta and Chacarita. Novelist Tomás Eloy Martínez

The trinity of Argentine folk heroes--tango singer Carlos Gardel, Evita Perón, and soccer star Diego Maradona--salute the audience at La Boca's Teatro Catalinas Sur.

© WAYNE BERNHARDSON

has sardonically labeled his countrymen as "cadaver cultists" for their devotion to the dead.

Protestantism

Anglicans were the original bearers of Protestantism in Argentina, but Scandinavian communities were numerous enough to justify construction of Danish and Swedish churches. More-recent Protestant denominations are often shrill evangelicals; nearby Uruguay's capital city of Montevideo is one of the centers of Reverend Sun Myung Moon's cultish Unification Church (no relation to Moon Handbooks!).

Other Religions

The Argentine constitution guarantees freedom of religion, and adherents of non-Christian faiths are not rare, if not exactly numerous. The largest and most conspicuous of these is Judaism, as the capital's Jewish community is at least 200,000 strong (a planned community census may well reveal a larger number). The government of Saudi Arabia sponsored the construction of Palermo's Centro Islámico Rey Fahd, whose vastness overshadows the capital's relatively small community of observant Muslims.

LANGUAGE

Spanish is Argentina's official language, but English is widely spoken at tourist offices, airlines, travel agencies, upscale hotels, and in business settings. In the provinces it's less common, though its use is spreading, especially in the travel and tourism sector. Foreign-language use is also vigorous among ethnic communities such as Italo-Argentines, Anglo-Argentines, and German-Argentines. The Anglo-Argentine and business communities even support a daily tabloid, *The Buenos Aires Herald*, while the German-Argentine community has the weekly *Argentinisches Tageblatt*. Welsh is making a comeback in Chubut Province.

Buenos Aires also has its own distinctive street slang, known as *lunfardo*, which owes its origins to working-class immigrant communities. Many lunfardo words have worked their way into everyday Argentine speech even though they may be

VOSEO

Along with Uruguayans, Paraguayans, and some Central Americans, Argentines commonly use the distinctive second-person familiar form of address known as *voseo* (use of the pronoun *vos*). Spaniards and most other Latin Americans, by contrast, employ the *tuteo* (use of the pronoun *tú*) in most circumstances.

Use of the *voseo*, a somewhat archaic form that dates from the 16th and 17th centuries, involves different verb endings for all regular and most irregular verbs. This means adding a last-syllable accent for stress—instead of *tú hablas*, for instance, Argentines will say *vos hablás*. Likewise, with an irregular verb such as *decir* (to say), Argentines will also say *vos decís* rather than *tú dices*.

In the imperative form, there are also differences—instead of *ven* (come), Argentines say *vení*. Negative imperatives, however, are the same in both the *tuteo* and the *voseo*, e.g. *no vengas* (don't come). Some very common verbs, such as *ir* (to go) and *estar* (to be) are similarly irregular in both the *voseo* and the *tuteo*, but others are not. In the *voseo*, for instance, *tú eres . . .* becomes *vos sos. . . .*

Despite the differing verb forms, Argentines still use the possessive article *tu* and the reflexive or conjunctive object pronoun *te* (*¿te vas?*). Alert travelers will quickly recognize the differences, but they may wish to refrain from using the form, considered substandard in some contexts, unless absolutely certain that it is appropriate. The *tuteo* is never considered incorrect, though it may sound quaint in some contexts.

unintelligible at first to those who have learned Spanish elsewhere. Some are fairly obvious in context, such as *laburar* instead of *trabajar* for work or labor, but others are obscure.

While many of its idioms are crude by standards of formal Spanish, *lunfardo* has acquired a certain legitimacy among Argentine scholars. There is even an academy for the study of *porteño* slang, the Academia Porteña del Lunfardo (Estados Unidos 1379, Monserrat, Buenos Aires, tel. 011/4383-2393).

Recreation

Argentina offers exciting options for hiking, climbing, and mountain biking in the Andes; birdwatching in the high lakes of the northern puna, the rivers, and wetlands of Mesopotamia, the long Atlantic shoreline, and the fjords of the southern rainforests; and sightings of marine mammals ranging from seals, sea lions, and dolphins to orcas and the great right whales of Patagonia.

On the eastern Andean slopes, the runoff permits white-water rafting and kayaking almost from the Bolivian border in the north to Chubut Province in the south, and sea kayaking in the fjords and glacier-fed lakes of the south.

For suggestions as to possible operators, see Organized Tours later in this section.

NATIONAL PARKS AND OTHER PROTECTED AREAS

Argentina has an impressive roster of national parks, reserves and monuments, and some significant provincial reserves as well. In fact, Argentina and neighboring Chile were pioneers in setting aside land for conservation purposes, even if they haven't always backed up legislation with sufficient funding, and have sometimes given way to commercial pressures. Some provinces, most notably in Patagonia, have also set aside key areas.

Argentina's main conservation agency is the Administración de Parques Nacionales (APN, Avenida Santa Fe 690, Retiro, Buenos Aires, tel. 011/4311-0303, www.parquesnacionales.gov.ar). While its selection of brochures on national parks and other protected areas is improving, the staff themselves are best informed on the country's most high-profile destinations, such as Parque Nacional Iguazú and Parque Nacional Los Glaciares. Hours are 10 A.M.–5 P.M. weekdays only. The APN also maintains branch offices in cities such as Salta, San Martín de los Andes, San Carlos de Bariloche, El Calafate, and Ushuaia, while rangers staff information offices at many of its parks and reserves.

Moreno Glacier, Parque Nacional Los Glaciares, Santa Cruz Province

© WAYNE BERNHARDSON

Argentina has three main categories of protected areas: *parques nacionales* (national parks), *reservas nacionales* (national preserves), and *monumentos naturales* (natural monuments), though the practical distinctions among them are not always clear. According to law, the national parks are "areas to be preserved in their natural state, which are representative of a biogeographical region and have natural beauty or scientific interest." Often contiguous with national parks, national reserves may be buffers that permit "conservation of ecological systems . . . or the creation of independent conservation zones."

Natural monuments are "places, things, and live animal or plant species, of aesthetic, historic or scientific interest, to which is granted absolute protection." They usually have one outstanding feature, such as the petrified forest of Santa Cruz Province, but may also consist of a rare or endangered species such as the southern right whale and the *huemul* (Andean deer).

The following paragraphs summarize the APN's most important units by region but omit some of the less accessible ones. Also included are provincial reserves.

The Pampas

On the south bank of the Paraná, in Buenos Aires Province northwest of the capital, **Reserva Natural Estricta Otamendi** protects 2,600 hectares of gallery forest and wetlands.

In southwestern Buenos Aires Province, the 6,700-hectare **Parque Provincial Ernesto Tornquist** encompasses much of the Sierra de la Ventana, the highest peaks in the pampas.

Rich in wildlife and endemic plants, the granitic summits of 9,901-hectare **Parque Nacional Lihué Calel** rise like islands above the arid ocean of the western pampas. It was also one of the last Mapuche hideaways during General Roca's brutal war of the 1880s.

Mesopotamia and the Chaco

Along the Paraguayan border, Formosa Province's 47,754-hectare **Parque Nacional Río Pilcomayo** is an internationally recognized wetland with stretches of palm savanna and abundant wildlife. The animals are harder to spot in the

15,000 hectares of Chaco Province's densely forested **Parque Nacional Chaco,** which has smaller sectors of marshes and palm savannas.

One of the country's greatest sights is the thundering mists of the *cataratas* at **Parque Nacional Iguazú,** which has much more to offer in its 67,000 hectares of subtropical rain forest in Misiones Province, along the Brazilian border.

Even better, perhaps the best wildlife-watching sites on the continent, are two vastly underrated wetland units in Corrientes Province's Iberá marshes, the 15,060-hectare **Parque Nacional Mburucuyá** and the sprawling **Reserva Provincial Esteros del Iberá**.

Along the Río Uruguay, in Entre Ríos Province, the 8,500-hectare **Parque Nacional El Palmar** embraces the largest intact stands of the grazing-sensitive *yatay* palm savanna. Also in Entre Ríos, near the town of Diamante, the gallery forests of the 2,458-hectare **Parque Nacional Pre-Delta** mark the transition to the Paraná Delta proper.

The Andean Northwest

In the puna of Jujuy Province, the 15,000-hectare **Monumento Natural Laguna de los Pozuelos** is a shallow, high-altitude lake with three species of flamingos and many other birds.

Northwestern Argentina has three parks primarily protecting the subtropical rainforest known as *yungas,* though there are other ecosystems within them. These include Jujuy's 76,306-hectare **Parque Nacional Calilegua,** northern Salta Province's nearly inaccessible 72,000-hectare **Parque Nacional Baritú,** and eastern Salta's 44,162-hectare **Parque Nacional Finca El Rey.**

In the high puna west of the city of Salta, the 65,000-hectare **Parque Nacional Los Cardones** takes its name from the *cardón* cactus whose woody trunk once served as a building material. In western La Rioja Province, 215,000-hectare **Parque Nacional Talampaya** is a scenic desert badlands also notable for its geology, fossils, and archaeological riches.

In the rolling highlands of western Córdoba Province, the 37,000 hectares of **Parque Nacional Quebrada del Condorito** are the Andean condor's easternmost natural habitat.

Cuyo

In northwestern San Luis Province, the red sandstone canyons of the 150,000-hectare **Parque Nacional Sierra de la Quijadas** is one of the world's dinosaur hotspots, with San Juan's 63,000-hectare **Parque Provincial Ischigualasto** a paleontological contender.

Mendoza Province has set aside two high Andean refuges, including the 6,962-meter "Roof of the Americas" in 71,000-hectare **Parque Provincial Aconcagua,** a target of trekkers and climbers from around the world. The other is **Parque Provincial Tupungato,** whose namesake 6,650-meter summit is a more demanding technical climb.

Southern Mendoza Province has several more reserves, most notably the limestone cave of **Reserva Natural Caverna de las Brujas,** the shallow wetlands of 40,000-hectare **Reserva Natural Laguna de Llancanelo,** and the volcanic badlands of 442,996-hectare **Reserva Natural La Payunia.**

Patagonia and Tierra del Fuego

In northern Neuquén Province, black-necked swans float on the waters of the 11,250-hectare **Parque Nacional Laguna Blanca,** whose namesake lake formed when lava flows dammed a desert stream. Hugging the Chilean border to the southwest, 412,000-hectare **Parque Nacional Lanín** takes its name from the slightly lopsided snow-covered cone that straddles the Chilean border above extensive monkey-puzzle (Araucaria) woodlands.

Pioneer conservationist Francisco P. Moreno spurred the creation of Argentina's first national park, the contiguous 750,000-hectare **Parque Nacional Nahuel Huapi** in Río Negro Province, by donating his own land at the west end of the glacial Lago Nahuel Huapi. On a peninsula jutting into the lake's north shore in Neuquén, the 1,753-hectare **Parque Nacional Los Arrayanes** is a separate unit protecting pure forests of the cinnamon-barked *arrayán* tree, a myrtle relative.

In western Chubut Province, south of El Bolsón, **Parque Nacional Lago Puelo** comprises 27,675 hectares of its namesake lake, with its transparently blue-green waters, and forested Andean slopes that give way to treeless fell fields. West of Esquel, the 263,000-hectare **Parque Nacional Los Alerces** is most notable for its humid Valdivian forest, which includes the long-lived, redwoodlike *alerce* (false larch).

In eastern Chubut, the Atlantic-coastal **Reserva Provincial Península Valdés** is one of the country's major attractions for its diverse wildlife, including whales, sea lions, elephant seals, Magellanic penguins, and other seabirds. Southeast of Trelew, **Reserva Provincial Punta Tombo** is the largest penguin-nesting site, but there are several other reserves along or near southbound RN 3.

Argentina honored its greatest conservationist's name with the creation of northwestern Santa Cruz Province's **Parque Nacional Perito Moreno,** an isolated 115,000-hectare park with aquamarine lakes, alpine peaks, and Andean-Patagonian woodlands.

In addition to the world-famous Glaciar Moreno, southwestern Santa Cruz's 600,000-hectare **Parque Nacional Los Glaciares** has snow- and ice-covered pinnacles to match or surpass Chile's Torres del Paine.

On northern Santa Cruz's Province's Patagonian steppe, scattered specimens of fossil *Proaraucaria* trees litter the grounds of the 13,700-hectare **Monumento Natural Bosques Petrificados.** Thanks to a public-private initiative, the 60,000-hectare **Parque Nacional Monte León,** near the town of Piedrabuena, has become Argentina's second coastal national park. Its only predecessor was the 63,000-hectare **Parque Nacional Tierra del Fuego,** which stretches from the wildlife-rich Beagle Channel coastline through Patagonian forests to the needles of the Andean uplands.

Chilean National Parks

Several Chilean national parks fall within the coverage of this guidebook, starting with the remote, gigantic 3,525,901-hectare **Parque Nacional Bernardo O'Higgins** in Region XII (Magallanes). The contiguous, 181,414-hectare **Parque Nacional Torres del Paine** is far more famous for its soaring granite towers.

Cuernos del Paine, Parque Nacional Torres del Paine, Chile

To its south, the 189-hectare **Monumento Natural Cueva del Milodón** was once inhabited by the late-Pleistocene ground sloth and, later, by early humans. To the southeast, along the border, the cave dwellings at the 5,030-hectare **Parque Nacional Pali Aike** constitute a major archaeological site, and the park is home to guanaco and other wildlife.

Several reserves are in the vicinity of the city of Punta Arenas, including two scenic forest reserves: the 13,500-hectare **Reserva Nacional Magallanes** in the hills only a short distance west of town, and the 18,000-hectare **Reserva Nacional Laguna Parillar,** which also features wetlands. The 97-hectare **Monumento Natural Los Pingüinos** consists of Isla Magdalena, a huge Magellanic penguin colony in the Strait of Magellan. Across the strait, just north of the town of Porvenir, the 25-hectare **Monumento Natural Laguna de los Cisnes** is a seasonal wetland.

Several huge units occupy nearly the entirety of archipelagic Magallanes: the 1,097,975-hectare

Reserva Nacional Las Guaitecas, 2,313,875-hectare **Reserva Nacional Alacalufes,** the 1,460,000-hectare **Parque Nacional Alberto de Agostini,** and the 63,903-hectare **Parque Nacional Cabo de Hornos.**

HIKING

Argentina has plenty of ideal hiking terrain, but only a few parks and reserves have integrated and well-maintained trail systems. Instituto Geográfico Militar maps at a scale of 1:50,000 are available for parts of the country, but for the most part don't expect to find trails with clearly signposted junctions—multiple tracks are the rule. If necessary, try to contract a local guide.

The prime hiking and backpacking areas are the Andes west of Mendoza toward the Chilean border; the national parks of the northern Patagonian lake district, particularly Nahuel and to a lesser degree Lanín; and the northern Chaltén Sector of Parque Nacional Los Glaciares. The season is short there, however; for year-round hiking, try the Sierras de Córdoba and adjacent parts of San Luis Province, and Buenos Aires Province's Sierra de la Ventana and Sierras de Tandil.

The northwestern subtropical and desert provinces of Tucumán, Salta, and Jujuy also offer good options, and enjoy their dry season in the winter months of June, July, and August. Parts of these provinces, though, are high-altitude desert where nights get *very* cold.

CLIMBING

Argentina's thousands of miles of Andean cordillera make it a climber's buffet and, for some, a mecca. The biggest single attraction—literally so—is 6,962-meter Cerro Aconcagua, the highest summit in the Americas. For serious technical climbers, though, this strenuous walkup is a lesser draw than the vertical spires of the Fitz Roy range in the Chaltén Sector of Parque Nacional Los Glaciares, or even Parque Nacional Nahuel Huapi's ice-covered 3,478-meter Monte Tronador.

Note that while the standard route up Aconcagua requires more stamina than technical

Know Argentina

skill, the altitude and ferocious weather often combine to make it a dangerous climb; even experienced mountaineers in prime condition have died here. On more technical routes in the Fitz Roy range and elsewhere, these warnings apply equally if not more.

In addition to these areas, there are many other options, including the rest of Parque Nacional Nahuel Huapi in the vicinity of Bariloche, the 3,776-meter Volcán Lanín near Junín de los Andes, and the northwestern high country of Salta and Jujuy Provinces. The Sierras de Córdoba are popular with climbers there, and even Buenos Aires Province has possibilities in the low granite ranges of Tandil and Sierra de la Ventana. Summer thunderstorms are a potential hazard, except in Patagonia (where frontal storms from the Pacific are the rule).

For general information on mountaineering in Argentina, try the **Centro Andino Buenos Aires** (Rivadavia 1255, Oficinas 2/3, tel. 011/4381-1566, www.caba.org.ar). There are also numerous local and provincial mountaineering clubs, which appear under the corresponding geographical entries.

CYCLING AND MOUNTAIN BIKING

Both long-distance riders and recreational mountain bikers will find Argentina's spectacular landscapes appealing and its rugged terrain challenging. Because many roads have dirt or gravel surfaces, and because paved roads are often so narrow that riding on the shoulder is essential, a mountain bike is the best alternative. Riders without their own bikes will find them readily available in tourist towns like Bariloche, Salta, and the like, but their condition varies widely—check brakes, tires, and everything else before renting.

In some parts of the country, cycling may be a seasonal activity, but in the northwest (where water may be scarce) and northeast the weather is suitable all year. If touring, carry rain gear, a tent, and supplementary camping gear, especially since some of the most enjoyable riding areas have almost no services.

Possible touring routes are countless, but the most popular area is the scenic northern Patagonian lake district. Increasing numbers of cyclists, some of them through-riders from Alaska to Tierra del Fuego, are braving the dusty southern Patagonia section of RN 40, between Esquel and El Calafate, nearly all of which is a rugged gravel surface requiring a sturdy mountain bike, a knowledge of bicycle repairs, and a good tent—services are few and far between. It also requires tremendous stamina and balance, as the powerful winds can either stop progress to a crawl or bowl a rider over. Feasible as early as October, it's probably best from December to April.

HORSEBACK RIDING

Argentina was born on horseback, and recreational riding is common even in and around Buenos Aires. It's most interesting in the provinces, though, and especially the northern Patagonian lake district.

SKIING

Since the seasons are reversed in southern South America, Argentina's Andean slopes reach their peak in August. While its international and regional ski resorts may not have the reputation of Chile's best, the mountains near Bariloche have long drawn skiers from around the continent and the world. Southern Mendoza Province's self-contained Las Leñas is the top Argentine resort, but there are also options west of the city of Mendoza, and at San Martín de los Andes, Villa la Angostura, Esquel, and even Ushuaia.

BIRD-WATCHING

Argentina's diverse natural environments—ranging from nearly waterless deserts to lush marshes, subtropical rainforests, riverine gallery forests, temperate Andean woodlands, and an Atlantic coastline that stretches from the midlatitudes to the sub-Antarctic—means a chance to add lots of new species to your life list. The finest bird-watching areas are the high northwestern puna and subtropical *yungas* forest, the spectacular Iberá wetlands of Corrientes Province, Misiones Province's Parque Nacional Iguazú, the Río Paraná Delta, the grasslands of the pampas, the Atlantic littoral, and the temperate Andean woodlands.

For bird-watching suggestions, contact the **Sociedad Ornitológica del Plata** (25 de Mayo 749, 2nd floor, Buenos Aires, tel. 011/4312-8958, info@avesargentinas.org.ar, www.avesargentinas.org.ar).

WATER SPORTS

Argentines have traditionally flocked to the country's Atlantic beaches, riversides, and southern lakes, but have only recently begun to enjoy active water sports like surfing, sea kayaking, white-water rafting, and kayaking.

White-Water Rafting and Kayaking

Descending from the rain-shadow side of the Andes, Argentine rivers mostly lack the tremendous spring snowmelt that turns Chilean rivers into white water, but there are commercially viable rivers from Salta in the north to Esquel in the south, and the number is growing. In subtropical Salta, the Class III–IV Río Juramento is a year-round river because of controlled releases from the Cabra Corral dam.

Most other runnable rivers are to the south, though, and depend on seasonal runoff; the Río Mendoza, for instance, can be a torrent of high waves in December but has no rapids to speak of until water levels drop later in the season. The country's top river is the Class IV Río Manso, south of Bariloche.

Diving

Diving is less common in Argentina than one might expect, but in summer the Chubut provincial city of Puerto Madryn has a cluster of diving outfitters and operators for the warm shallow waters of the Golfo Nuevo.

Surfing and Windsurfing

The good news is that, with a long coastline and a relatively small population of dedicated surfers, there's little competition for waves; the bad news is that the Atlantic surf is generally tamer than the Pacific. The best surfing areas, such as Mar del Plata, are saturated with nonsurfers in the summer months of January and February, and often on weekends as well. Shallow waters and wide tidal ranges may be further deterrents.

Buenos Aires provincial beach resorts like Mar del Plata and Miramar are the main areas, but parts of Patagonia like desolate Cabo Raso (where competition is zero) are suitable. The waters of the Golfo Nuevo, at Puerto Madryn, are too sheltered for big waves, but the blustery Patagonian winds make it a godsend for windsurfers.

Fishing

Argentina is a favorite destination for fly-fishing enthusiasts eager to test their skill on lakes, rivers, and fjords from the central Patagonian lake district to the southernmost tip of Tierra del Fuego. In the Paraná Delta and the upper reaches of Argentine Mesopotamia, though, there are big fighting fish.

SPECTATOR SPORTS

As in most of the rest of Latin America, *fútbol* (soccer) is by far the most popular spectator sport. For a country born on horseback, equestrian sports like horse racing, polo, and the gaucho-derived *pato* all enjoy popularity.

Argentina has had an international boxing presence ever since Luis Angel Firpo (1894–1960), the "Wild Bull of the Pampas," nearly won the world heavyweight championship from Jack Dempsey in New York in 1923. Although the sport has declined since then, it may be making a comeback.

Argentine tennis has long enjoyed an international reputation, with stars like Guillermo Vilas and Gabriela Sabatini. In 2002, David Nalbandian, of Córdoba Province, became the first Argentine to reach the 2002 men's finals at Wimbledon before losing to Lleyton Hewitt of Australia.

Argentine basketball, for the most part, lacks a high international profile, but the NBA success of San Antonio's 6.5-foot (1.98-meter) Emanuel Ginóbili is spurring interest in the sport, which now has a nationwide league.

Rugby is an amateur endeavor here, but Los Pumas, the national team, has earned a global reputation.

Soccer

Argentina is a perpetual soccer power—having won the World Cup in 1978 and 1986—and the birthplace of Diego Armando Maradona, one of the sport's all-time legends. As of mid-2004, the international soccer authority FIFA ranked the national team fifth-best in the world, behind only Brazil, France, Spain, and Mexico.

What its English creators like to call "the beautiful game," though, often falls short of its billing; the *Buenos Aires Herald* may have said it best with the headline "Another Boring 0–0 Tie." Still, Argentina is a soccer-mad country, with six first-division teams in Buenos Aires, another six in its suburbs, and the rest of the country not far behind. The season runs March–December; for current information, check the Asociación de Fútbol Argentina's website (www.afa.org.ar), which appears in both English and Spanish.

Arts and Entertainment

In the midst of Argentina's ongoing economic crisis, one sector of Argentine society that truly showed resilience was arts and entertainment. After Tucumán native Tomás Eloy Martínez, a professor of Spanish at Rutgers, won the Spanish Alfaguara literary prize (US$175,000) for *El Vuelo de la Reina,* a novel about crime and corruption, he remarked that "One of Argentina's riches is forgotten but it is the quality, the leadership of our culture. [In that field] we can speak as equals to the U.S. or France."

Ever since independence, Argentina's impact on the arts has been remarkable for a geographically remote land with a relatively small population. Many Argentines have been eloquent writers and even more are voracious readers. In the visual arts, particularly modern art, they have been innovative, and their architecture has often been

grand even if derivative of Europe. Classical music has always held a place in Argentine culture, but Buenos Aires has one of the most vigorous rock music scenes since 1960s London or San Francisco. Likewise, Argentine cinema, theater, and dance have all been influential beyond the country's borders.

LITERATURE

In the 19th century, even as the free-roaming gaucho was becoming a wage laborer on the *estancias* of the pampas, Argentine literature enshrined his most positive qualities in José Hernández's epic poem *Martín Fierro* (1872 and 1879), available in many editions and in English translation. This so-called *gauchesco* (gauchesque) tradition has never completely disappeared, and is most memorable in Ricardo Güiraldes's novel *Don Segundo Sombra* (1926). Translated into many languages, Güiraldes's romanticized fiction is widely available.

Born of U.S. immigrant parents in Buenos Aires Province, William Henry Hudson (1841–1922) left Argentina for London at the age of 33, but his memoir *Long Ago and Far Away* (1922) is a staple of Argentine public education. An accomplished amateur naturalist, he also wrote *Idle Days in Patagonia* (1893) about his bird-watching explorations, plus short stories and even a novel, *Green Mansions* (1904), set in the Venezuelan rain forest. Argentines know him as Guillermo Enrique Hudson.

A more critical assessment of Argentina and its rural heritage came from the educator and politician Domingo F. Sarmiento. His *Life in the Argentine Republic in the Days of the Tyrants* (1845), an eloquent tirade against rural caudillos despite his own provincial origins, has become a staple of Latin American history courses in English-speaking countries.

No Argentine author has ever won a Nobel Prize for Literature, but three have won the Premio Cervantes, the Spanish-speaking world's most important literary honor: essayist, poet, and short-story writer Jorge Luis Borges (1979), novelist Ernesto Sábato (1984), and novelist Adolfo Bioy Casares (1990). Other noteworthy writers include Julio Cortázar, Victoria Ocampo, Manuel Puig, and Osvaldo Soriano, much of whose work is available in English translation. Publication dates below indicate the Spanish-language original, unless otherwise noted.

Globally, the most prominent is Borges (1899–1986), often mentioned but never chosen for the Nobel. Ironically enough for an urbane figure with a classical education, who loathed Perón and Peronism, his short stories, poetry, and essays often focus on urban lowlifes and rural themes, including gaucho violence. Borges never wrote a novel; his most frequently read works are collections of obscure and even surrealistic stories such as those in *Labyrinths* (1970, in English). More recently, Eliot Wineberger has edited a wide-ranging collection of the author's short pieces, many of them previously untranslated, in *Jorge Luis Borges: Selected Non-Fictions* (New York: Viking, 1999).

Sábato (born 1911) has acquired renown in the English-speaking world as the coordinator of *Nunca Más,* an official account of the brutalities of the 1976–83 military dictatorship. Born in Buenos Aires Province but long resident in the capital, his best work may be the engrossing psychological novel *On Heroes and Tombs* (1961; New York: Ballantine, 1991), which credibly depicts places and examines people in the city; its subsection "Report on the Blind," capable of standing alone, is truly extraordinary. Sábato's novella *The Tunnel* (1950; New York: Ballantine, 1988), about artistic obsession, is equally absorbing but less conspicuously *porteño* in its approach.

Borges's close friend Bioy Casares (1914–1999) collaborated with the older man on detective stories under the pseudonym Honorario Bustos Domecq, but his own fantastical novella *The Invention of Morel* (University of Texas Press, 1985) is a purposefully disorienting work that director Eliseo Subiela transformed into the award-winning film *Man Facing Southeast*. Bioy's *Diary of the War of the Pig* (New York: McGraw Hill, 1972) takes place in the barrio of Palermo, mostly within the area popularly referred to as "Villa Freud." His *The Dream of Heroes* (New York: Dutton, 1987) paints an otherworldly portrait of the late 1920s, a time when Carnaval flourished in Buenos Aires.

Son of a diplomatic family, the Belgian-born Cortázar (1914–1984) was a short-story writer, experimental novelist, and committed leftist who went into Parisian exile after losing his university post in a Peronist purge. Michelangelo Antonioni turned one of Cortázar's short stories into the famous film *Blow-Up*, but the author is also known for the novels *Hopscotch* (1963; New York: Random House, 1966), about a failed Francophile poet in Buenos Aires, and *62: A Model Kit* (1968; New York: Random House, 1972).

Enthralled with popular culture, particularly the movies, Manuel Puig (1932–1990) authored a series of novels including *Betrayed by Rita Hayworth* (1968); the detective novel *The Buenos*

Aires Affair (New York: Dutton, 1968); and *Kiss of the Spider Woman* (New York: Vintage, 1991), which Brazilian director Héctor Babenco made into an award-winning English-language film starring William Hurt and Raúl Julia. Puig wrote the original version of *Eternal Curse on the Reader of These Pages* (English; New York: Random House, 1982), about an amnesiac victim of the dictatorship, in English, later translating it into Spanish.

Journalist and novelist Osvaldo Soriano (1943–1997) wrote satirical fiction such as *A Funny Dirty Little War* (Columbia, Louisiana, and London: Readers International, 1989), depicting the consequences of national upheaval in a small community, and *Winter Quarters* (same publisher and year). His *Shadows* (New York: Knopf, 1993), which takes its Spanish title *Una Sombra Ya Pronto Serás* from a classic tango, became a disorienting road movie under Héctor Olivera's direction.

Essayist Victoria Ocampo (1891–1979), whose poetess sister Silvina (1909–1994) was Bioy Casares's wife, founded the literary magazine *Sur;* some of her essays appear in Doris Meyer's biography *Victoria Ocampo: Against the Wind and the Tide* (University of Texas Press, 1990). Borges was one of her collaborators at *Sur,* which became a prestigious publishing house that brought works by Aldous Huxley, D.H. Lawrence, and even Jack Kerouac to Spanish-speaking readers.

Tomás Eloy Martínez, quoted earlier on Argentina's cultural resilience and vitality, is author of several novels dealing the Argentine condition through fictionalized biography, most notably *The Perón Novel* (New York: Pantheon Books, 1988)—based partly on his own interviews with the late caudillo. *Santa Evita* (New York: Knopf, 1996), by contrast, can only be called post-biographical, as it traces the odyssey of Evita's embalmed body to Italy, Spain, and back to Buenos Aires.

Novelist Federico Andahazi, who is also a psychiatrist, outraged industrialist heiress Amalia Fortabat when an independent jury awarded him her self-anointed literary prize for *The Anatomist* (New York: Doubleday, 1998), a sexually explicit (but far from erotic) tale set in medieval Italy.

VISUAL ARTS

With its small, dispersed settlements, Argentina lacked the great tradition of colonial religious art of the populous central Andean highlands, which developed their own "schools" of painting and sculpture in Peru and Bolivia. In colonial times, according to *porteño* art critic Jorge Glusberg, "Buenos Aires was practically devoid of any cultural life." Glusberg has even argued that the colonial period, "characterized by subordination to the European models currently in vogue," lasted until after World War II.

Glusberg may underrate the work of some earlier figures, but many innovative Argentine painters and sculptors have flourished artistically, if not always financially, since then—in both figurative and abstract modes. His English-language book *Art in Argentina* (Milan: Giancarlo Politi Editore, 1986), is a readable and well-illustrated introduction to contemporary Argentine art, though it needs an update. The same is true of Rafael Squirru's Spanish-only *Arte Argentino Hoy* (Buenos Aires: Ediciones de Arte Gaglianone, 1983), with color displays of 48 different 20th-century painters and sculptors.

Painting

One of Argentina's first notable artists, European-trained Prilidiano Pueyrredón (1823–1870) painted landscapes and people of rural Buenos Aires. Other early painters included Eduardo Sívori (1847–1918) and Ernesto de la Cárcova (1866–1927), who both displayed concern with social causes such as poverty and hunger.

One of Argentine art's extraordinary stories is Cándido López (1840–1902), a junior army officer who lost his right forearm to gangrene after being struck by a grenade in battle against Paraguay. Remarkably, López painted over 50 oils of war scenes with his left hand; even more remarkably, his paintings were not romanticized scenes of combat heroism, but vivid landscapes depicting routine activities—ordinary encampments and river crossings, for instance—in addition to the occasional battle.

Benito Quinquela Martín (1890–1977) chronicled immigrant factory workers and stevedores in his vivid oils of La Boca. One of modern Argentine art's pioneers was Borges's friend Xul Solar (1887–1963; real name, Alejandro Schulz Solari), who dealt with esoteric and mystical themes in his watercolors.

One of Argentina's best-known modern artists is the versatile Antonio Berni (1905–1981), who worked in painting, drawing, engraving, collage, and sculpture. His socially conscious canvases, such as *Juanito Laguna Bañándose entre Latas* (Juanito Laguna Bathing in the Trash), have fetched astronomical prices in international auctions. His *Monstruos* (Monsters) is a series of three-dimensional works (1964–71) from the nightmares of Ramona Montiel, a prostitute who dreams of war, death, and destruction.

In conjunction with other artists, including Lino Spilimbergo (1896–1964), Juan Carlos Castagnino (1908–1972), Galician-born Manuel Colmeiro (1901–1999), and Demetrio Urruchúa (1902–1978), Berni was part of the politically conscious Nuevo Realismo (New Realism) movement, whose greatest public legacy is the ceiling murals in Buenos Aires's recycled Galerías Pacífico shopping center, under the influence of the famed Mexican David Alfaro Siqueiros.

When not collaborating in such projects, Spilimbergo specialized in geometric forms, still lifes, and lighted landscapes. Castagnino specialized in rural, even gauchesque, landscapes, while Colmeiro and Urruchúa were both socially oriented painters and muralists.

Influenced by pop art, self-taught Jorge de la Vega (1930–1971) alternated figurative and abstract geometrical work; in his series of *Monstruos* or *Bestiario,* he attached external objects such as coins, sticks, and especially mirrors to his canvases, deforming both the subject and the viewer.

One of the rising modern painters is Guillermo Kuitca (born 1960), of Russian-Jewish immigrant origins. Kuitca contrasts small figures with large environments, transforms everyday abstractions such as floor plans and road maps, and creates abstract visual expressions of popular music themes like the anti-lynching classic "Strange Fruit" and the Rolling Stones's "Gimme Shelter."

Sculpture

Buenos Aires is a city of monuments. Unfortunately, many if not most of them are pretentious busts of ostensible statesmen and colossal equestrian statues of military men like national icon José de San Martín, caudillo Justo José Urquiza, and Patagonian invader Julio Argentino Roca. The Rodin-influenced Rogelio Yrurtia (1879–1950), though he did create President Bernardino

Porteño sculptor León Ferrari created *La Civilización Cristiana y Occidental* (Christian and Western Civilization) to protest the bombing of Vietnam in 1964.

Rivadavia's mausoleum, displayed his talents better in statues like the larger-than-life-size *The Boxers,* at his house and museum in the capital's barrio of Belgrano; even better is his working-class tribute *Canto al Trabajo* (Ode to Labor), on San Telmo's Plazoleta Olazábal.

Those who followed Yrurtia have been far more daring. León Ferrari (born 1920) created the prescient *La Civilización Occidental y Cristiana* (Western and Christian Civilization, 1965), a sardonic Vietnam-era work that portrays Christ crucified on a diving F-105. Similarly, Juan Carlos Distéfano (born 1933) blends sculpture and painting in works like *El Rey y La Reina* (1977), a disturbingly lifelike representation of a couple shot to death in an automobile; in context, it was a thinly disguised portrayal of extrajudicial executions carried out by death squads after the military coup of 1976. Remarkably, the work was shown publicly, on the Florida pedestrian mall, shortly thereafter.

Alberto Heredia (1924–2000) mocked the pomposity of monumental public art in works such as *El Caballero de la Máscara* (The Masked Horseman). The title is misleading, as this headless parody of an equestrian statue is a collage that ridicules 19th-century strongmen and their contemporary counterparts. Heredia originally titled it *El Montonero,* a reference to the early Federalist cavalry, but could not exhibit the piece under that name because the leftist guerrilla group Montoneros was a hot-button issue at the time.

ARCHITECTURE

Because Buenos Aires languished as a backwater of the Spanish colonial empire until the creation of the Viceroyalty of the River Plate in the late 18th century, little remains of its precarious early architecture. The northwestern provinces of Jujuy, Salta, Tucumán, and Córdoba, though, retain significant colonial constructions both in their capital cities and in the countryside. Many of these are ecclesiastical constructions, ranging from modest chapels in the Quebrada de Humahuaca to full-fledged cathedrals in Córdoba.

For most of the 19th century, *porteño* architecture evolved from its Spanish colonial origins to an Italianate style but, from the early 20th century, the reigning architectural fashion was a Beaux Arts academicism, both for public buildings and landowning oligarchy's ornate *palacetes* (mansions). Many French professionals, including landscape architect Charles Thays, worked on *porteño* projects in what has been called, perhaps with some exaggeration, the Paris of the South. These architectural styles spread to many other cities, and figures like Thays also designed public parks elsewhere, most notably in the Andean city of Mendoza.

From the 1930s, the capital developed greater residential and commercial density with buildings such as the Edificio Kavanagh, a 30-story Deco highrise on Plaza San Martín that was the first structure in the country to have air-conditioning. The late 20th century saw some hideous developments, such as Italian-born Clorindo Testa's brutalist Biblioteca Nacional (National Library) in Palermo (in fairness, the building's interior is more attractive, and practical, than it appears from outside). One positive development is the recycling of historical structures, such as the Galerías Pacífico and the Mercado del Abasto into contemporary shopping centers, and the former brick warehouses at Puerto Madero into fashionable restaurants and residential lofts.

Architect Alejandro Bustillo, who designed many luxurious *porteño* buildings, also created a magnificent northern Patagonian style with Bariloche's landmark Centro Cívico. His many imitators, though, have failed to achieve the same harmony of nature and culture.

It would be misleading to ignore vernacular architecture styles, ranging from the adobes of the Andes to the distinctive *casa chorizo,* a long narrow construction sometimes barely wider than an adult's armspan, on deep lots in Buenos Aires. The traditional bright primary colors of the wood-frame, metal-clad houses of La Boca derive from the fact that early residents scavenged their paint from ships on the Riachuelo. Houses in the Río Paraná Delta sit atop stilts to avoid flooding.

MUSIC

Argentines are musical people, their interests ranging from folk, pop, rock, and blues to classical. Argentine popular music takes many forms, from the folk tradition of the Andean northwest to the accordion-based immigrant *chamamé* of the northeastern lowlands and the hard-nosed *rock nacional* of Buenos Aires. Both instrumentally and with lyrics, the signature sound and dance is the plaintive, melancholy tango, the Argentine blues. In their musical interests, Argentine performers are versatile and un–self-conscious about crossing boundaries—traditional folksinger Mercedes Sosa, for instance, sometimes performs with erratic rock musician Charly García, and many classical composers and performers have incorporated tango into their repertoire.

Classical Music and Dance

Since its completion in 1908, Buenos Aires's Teatro Colón has been the continent's preeminent high-culture venue. Thanks to the presence of the Colón, the Teatro Avenida, and other classical venues, early-20th-century Argentina produced an abundance of classical composers, particularly in opera and ballet.

Among the notable early figures were Héctor Panizza (1875–1967); Constantino Gaito (1878–1945), who produced *gauchesco* ballet such as *La Flor del Irupé* (The Flower of Irupé); Felipe Boero (1884–1958); and Italian-born Pascual de Rogatis (1880–1980). Possibly the most distinguished, though, was Juan José Castro (1895–1968), whose career suffered because of his outspoken opposition to the military government of 1943 and the subsequent Perón regime. Castro's ballets included *Mekhano* and *Offenbachiana*.

Interestingly enough, the Spanish composer Manuel de Falla (1876–1946) spent the last seven years of his life in Alta Gracia, a provincial Córdoba town that was also the boyhood home of Ernesto "Che" Guevara, following the victory of Perón's ally Francisco Franco in the Spanish Civil War. Franco's regime had executed Falla's friend, playwright Federico García Lorca.

One of ballet's outstanding figures was Roberto García Morillo (1911–1996), whose works included *Usher* and *Harrild*. Arnaldo D'Espósito (1897–1945), Luis Gianneo (1897–1968), and Alberto Ginastera (1916–1983) were his contemporaries. A later generation of opera composers includes Valdo Sciamarella (born 1924), Mario Perusso (born 1936), and Gerardo Gandini (born 1936).

Contemporary Argentine classical music can boast figures like Daniel Barenboim (born 1942), a pianist and conductor who has held posts at the Orchestre de Paris, the Chicago Symphony Orchestra, and the Deutsche Staatsoper Berlin. Barenboim is a versatile figure who has, among other achievements, recorded tango and other popular music (also an Israeli citizen, he has played the West Bank in defiance of that government's objections). He also performed at the Colón during the 2002 economic crisis, when the theater could not afford to pay high-profile international acts.

Though she lives in Brussels, pianist Martha Argerich (born 1941) has sponsored competitions in Buenos Aires. She has drawn rave reviews for her Carnegie Hall concerts from *The New York Times,* and has won a Grammy for best instrumental soloist.

United States–based Osvaldo Golijov (born 1960) is responsible for classical works like *The St. Mark Passion,* but is flexible enough to work on movie soundtracks (for British director Sally Potter's widely panned *The Man Who Cried*) and even rock bands like Mexico's Café Tacuba.

Rosario-born but Europe-based tenor José Cura (born 1962) has drawn attention as a credible successor to Luciano Pavarotti on the international opera scene. Among ballet performers, the most significant is Julio Bocca (born 1967), a prodigy who has performed in New York, Paris, and elsewhere. He has formed his own company, the Ballet Argentino, and continues to perform in Argentina even during the economic crisis.

Tango

Tango overlaps the categories of music and dance, and even within those categories there are distinctions. As music, the tango can be instrumental, but it gained its initial popularity and international reputation through the *tango canción* (tango song) of the legendary Carlos Gardel and, to a lesser degree, others. One *porteño* songwriter has described the tango as "a sad feeling that is danced," and there is no doubt that it appeals to nostalgia for things lost—whether they be an old flame or the old neighborhood.

The charismatic Gardel, whose birthdate and birthplace are both topics of controversy, attained immortality after dying young in an aviation accident in Medellín, Colombia in 1935. According to his die-hard admirers, "Gardel sings better every day." Uruguayan-born Julio Sosa (1926–1964), who also died young in a car accident, was nearly as important; at a time when Peronism was outlawed, his subtle smile and gestures on stage evoked the exiled caudillo.

As opposed to the *tango canción,* orchestral tango music is the legacy of bandleaders and composers like Osvaldo Pugliese (1905–1995), Aníbal "Pichuco" Troilo (1914–1975), and especially Astor Piazzola (1921–1992), whose jazz influences were palpable. Important lyricists included Enrique Santos Discépolo (1908–1992), also a composer, and Homero Manzi (1907–1951).

Practiced by skilled and sexy dancers in nightclubs, the tango floor show is popular with tourists, but that tells only part of the story. The tango is not exclusive to the young and lithe—in fact, one could easily argue that its nostalgia lends it to older individuals with longer memories—and a recent revival has made it just as popular with mixed-age audiences at *milongas* (informal dance clubs).

Tango remains a daily presence in the lives of *porteños,* with both a 24-hour FM radio station (FM 92.7) and a cable TV channel, Sólo Tango. Contemporary performers of note include several women, such as Eladia Blásquez (born 1931), Susana Rinaldi (born 1935), and Adriana Varela (born 1958). Pop singers such as Sandro and Cacho Castaña (born 1942) have also sung tango, while the much younger Omar Giammarco produces tango-flavored music using accordion instead of bandoneón. La Chicana is a tango-song group that adds a flute to the traditional instrumental mix, and even works with rock musicians.

Folk

Tango may be an urban folk music, but Argentina's true folk tradition stems from *payadores,* gauchos who sang verses with guitar accompaniment; in dance, it can take the form of *malambo,* a competitive male-only affair that, despite its identification with the rural pampas, contains echoes of flamenco. An older current derives from the northwestern Andean provinces and their link to the Bolivian and Peruvian highlands, featuring the *zampoña* (panpipes) and *charango,* a tiny stringed instrument that uses an armadillo shell as its sound box.

Born in Buenos Aires Province, the late Atahualpa Yupanqui (1908–1992) belongs to these purist traditions, as does the Salta-based group Los Chalchaleros, an institution for over half a century. Tucumán native Mercedes Sosa (born 1935) also comes from this tradition, but is less a purist, having even performed with the brilliant rock musician Charly García. Their contemporary León Gieco (born 1951) crosses the line into folk-rock and even rap.

Tomás Lipán, an Aymará Indian from the northwestern village of Purmamarca, in Jujuy Province, embodies the region's Andean folk roots, but adds urban touches like the bandoneón to create an Argentine hybrid. Soledad Pastorutti (born 1980), who goes by her first name only as a performer, is a self-conscious folkie who sings and dresses in *gauchesco* style.

Immigrant communities have left their mark in accordion-based *chamamé,* typical of the humid lowland provinces along the Río Paraná and Río Uruguay, north of Buenos Aires to the Brazilian and Paraguayan borders. Among the notable performers are Antonio Tárragó Ros and Chango Spasiuk (born 1968), from a Ukrainian community in Misiones Province.

Rock and Pop

It may be no exaggeration to say that Buenos Aires, like London or San Francisco in the mid- to late 1960s, has one of the most vigorous rock scenes ever. Despite the handicap of trying to fit a multisyllabic language into a monosyllabic musical idiom, the practitioners of *rock nacional* have had remarkable success.

In terms of live music, there's something almost every night. The down side to this is that some of the top bands have a small but pugnacious hard core of fans who tend to crowd the stage; most visitors unaccustomed to the scene may prefer to stand back a bit.

Argentine rock's pioneer is Roberto Sánchez (born 1945), better known by his stage name Sandro. As an early rocker who became a movie idol, with a domineering manager, Sandro draws obvious comparisons with Elvis Presley, but "El Maestro" is also a credible tango singer and was the first Argentine to appear at Madison Square Garden. A surprisingly unpretentious individual, he is also the honoree of *Tributo a Sandro: Un Disco de Rock,* an exceptional tribute album by Argentine, Chilean, Colombian, and Mexican bands.

Charly García (born 1951) transcends generations—many of his fans are in their twenties and often younger. García, who sings and plays mostly keyboards, incorporates women into his backing bands even as lead guitarists and saxophonists; he displays a sense of history in adapting his own Spanish-language lyrics to classics like Eddie Cochran's "Summertime Blues," the Byrds' "I'll Feel a Whole Lot Better," Neil Young's "Don't Let It Bring You Down," and even the obscure Small Faces gem "Tin Soldier."

Nearly as revered as Charly is the Dylanesque León Gieco (also born 1951); his album *Bandidos Rurales* (2002) bears thematic resemblance to Dylan's *John Wesley Harding*. He does an utterly brilliant cover of Sandro's "Si Yo Fuera Carpintero," itself a brilliant Spanish-language adaptation of Tim Hardin's "If I Were a Carpenter."

Fito Páez (born 1963) and García protegé Andrés Calamaro (born 1961) also have major solo careers, but many acts in the *rock nacional* idiom have a stronger group than individual identity. Among them are Attaque 77, Babasónicos, Los Divididos (a branch of the earlier Sumo and famous for their versions of the Mexican folk song "Cielito Lindo" and the Doors' "Light My Fire"), Las Pelotas (the other faction of Sumo), Los Pi-

ojos, the Stones-influenced Los Ratones Paranóicos, and Patricio Rey y Sus Redonditos de Ricota. Almafuerte and the power trio A.N.I.M.A.L are the leading heavy-metal bands.

Grammy winners Los Fabulosos Cadillacs (best alternative Latin rock group in 1998) have toured North America, playing salsa- and reggae-influenced rock at venues like San Francisco's legendary Fillmore Auditorium. Others in this idiom include Los Auténticos Decadentes, Los Cafres, and especially the band-of-the-moment Bersuit Vergarabat.

Buenos Aires has a robust blues scene, thanks to individuals like the guitarist Pappo and groups like La Mississippi and Memphis La Blusera, who have even taken their act to the stage of the Teatro Colón (to the disgust of classical music critics, it must be added). The female vocal trio Las Blacanblus treats blues standards in a distinctive style with minimal accompaniment, only guitar and piano. International blues figures such as B.B. King, and many less-famous but still credible foreign artists, have also played in BA.

In a category of their own are Les Luthiers, an eclectic bunch that makes its own unique instruments (which defy description) and caricatures Argentine society's most authoritarian and bourgeois sectors. While musically sophisticated, the band's shows are as much theater as concert.

Jazz

Both traditional and free-form jazz play a part in Argentina's musical history. A fixture in the former idiom is Buenos Aires's Fénix Jazz Band, whose vocalist Ernesto "Cachi" Carrizo says he can't sing blues in Spanish because "the blues in Spanish seems to me as absurd as tango in English."

Better known beyond strictly Argentine circles is saxophonist Gato Barbieri (born 1932), also composer of the soundtrack for *The Last Tango in Paris*. Famous for TV and movie soundtracks like *Bullitt, Cool Hand Luke,* and *Mission Impossible,* Hollywood regular Lalo Schifrin (also born 1932) originally moved to the United States to play piano with Dizzy Gillespie. Schifrin, who also writes classical music, makes a brief onscreen appearance as an orchestra conductor in the opening sequence of the Hannibal Lecter gorefest *Red Dragon* (2002); his father, Luis, was concertmaster of the Teatro Colón's orchestra.

CINEMA

Given the country's political and economic instability, it's surprising that Argentine cinema has been as productive and successful as it has. In the year 2000, for instance, Argentine directors managed to make 30 full-length features and four documentaries. In October 2002, the American Cinemateque showed a dozen new films in the three-day New Argentine Cinema 2002 in Hollywood's Egyptian Theater, with attendance by Argentine directors and actors.

Special effects are generally limited and Argentine films, like those in Europe, tend to be more character- than plot-driven. There are plenty of outstanding directors and actors, though and quite a few films from the last 20 years–plus are available on video.

Not only have Argentines made good films, but foreign directors have found Argentina an appealing location—all the more so now that the peso's collapse has made it inexpensive to shoot here. Readers who know Spanish should look for film critic Diego Curubeto's *Babilonia Gaucha* (Editorial Planeta, Buenos Aires, 1993), on the Argentina-Hollywood relationship; Curubeto also wrote *Cine Bizarro* (Editorial Sudamericana, Buenos Aires, 1996), on idiosyncratic films from Argentina and elsewhere.

Argentine Directors, Movies, and Actors

In its earliest years, Argentine cinema dealt almost exclusively with *porteño* topics such as Carnaval, but it's startling to see Argentine actors in blackface even given the capital's Afro-American traditions. Later, tango legend Carlos Gardel worked in Hollywood as well as Buenos Aires, leaving films such as *El Día Que Me Quieras* (The Day You Love Me, 1935).

Over the years, several Argentine films have made respectable showings at the Oscars. Director Sergio Renán's *La Tregua* (The Truce, 1975) was the first nominated for best foreign-language film; based on a story by the Uruguayan Mario Benedetti, it lost to the tough competition of Federico Fellini's *Amarcord*.

María Luisa Bemberg (1922–1995), astonishingly enough, made her first feature at the age of 58, but made up for lost time with films like the 1984 nominee *Camila,* based on the true story of 19th-century heiress Camila O'Gorman, her Jesuit lover, the self-serving politicization of their plight by Unitarists and Federalists, and their persecution by the Rosas dictatorship. Among its virtues, the film does an excellent job of representing the country's Afro-Argentine population of the time.

In 1985, director Luis Puenzo's *The Official Story* won the Oscar for his treatment of the controversial issue of military adoptions of "disappeared" parents' babies during the 1976–83 Dirty War; it stars Norma Aleandro, a highly respected theater actress and director as well. Puenzo also drew scorn, though, for implying that some Argentines, at least, were unaware of extrajudicial tortures and murders.

Based partly on Adolfo Bioy Casares's novella *The Invention of Morel,* Eliseo Subiela's *Man Facing Southeast* won a nomination in 1986; the plot of the 2001 Hollywood production *K-Pax,* starring Kevin Spacey and Jeff Bridges, bears a remarkable resemblance to Subiela's work. Most recently, in 2002, Juan José Campanella's maudlin *Hijo de la Novia* (Son of the Bride) received a nomination; Ricardo Darín plays the title role, a type-A *porteño* restaurateur whose father (Héctor Alterio) wants to give Darín's Alzheimer's-stricken mother (Aleandro) a church wedding.

The Oscars, though, showcase only a small percentage of Argentine films and are not necessarily representative. Often subtly and sometimes overtly political, they may be eloquent and passionate but also introspective—partly due, perhaps, to the popularity of psychoanalysis.

Subiela's *The Dark Side of the Heart* (1992), an erotic love story with both humor and pathos, takes place in Buenos Aires and Montevideo; based loosely on *porteño* poet Oliverio Girondo's life, it features a cameo by Uruguayan poet Mario Benedetti. Puenzo (born 1946) used San Telmo, La Boca, and Palermo as settings for his adaptation of

Albert Camus's *The Plague* (1992), with William Hurt, Raúl Juliá, and Robert Duvall; filmed in English, the French/Argentine production uses disease as a metaphor for dictatorship.

Bemberg also made the English-language *Miss Mary* (1986), the tale of an English governess on an Argentine *estancia*, with Julie Christie; and *I Don't Want to Talk About It* (1992), a truly peculiar romance starring the late Marcelo Mastroianni and set in a conservative provincial town (the filming took place in the Uruguayan city of Colonia, across the river from Buenos Aires).

Adolfo Aristarain (born 1943) directed the versatile Federico Luppi in the Spanish-language thriller *Time of Revenge* (1981), a labor drama available on video, and also directed Luppi in *A Place in the World* (1992), a socially conscious film disqualified for an Oscar because it was unclear whether it was an Uruguayan, Argentine, or Spanish production (most of the filming took place in Argentina's scenic San Luis Province). Aristarain also directed the English-language film *The Stranger* (1986), a psychological thriller with Peter Riegert, Bonnie Bedelia, and a cast of Argentine cameos, but its ingenious structure can't compensate for a plot full of holes.

Other films have gotten less international recognition but are worth seeing, such as Bruno Stagnaro's and Adrián Caetano's low-budget *Pizza, Birra, Faso* (1997), an unsentimental story of *porteño* lowlifes trying to get by. Darín shares the lead with Gastón Pauls in Fabián Bielinsky's *Nine Queens* (2001), the twist-filled noirish tale of *porteño* con-men who strike up a partnership in crisis-racked Buenos Aires; according to reports, Mel Gibson has bought the rights to an English-language remake.

Politically committed director Fernando "Pino" Solanas (born 1936), a left-wing Peronist, dealt with the theme of expatriation in *The Exile of Gardel* (1985). Tango legend Astor Piazzola wrote the soundtrack and also appears in the film which, appropriately enough for a film whose title figure may have been born in France, takes place in Paris.

The prolific Leopoldo Torre Nilsson (1924–78), who shot nearly 30 features in his relatively short lifetime, adapted Manuel Puig's novel *Boquitas*

Pintadas (Painted Lips), a story of hypocrisy and petty jealousies in a small provincial town, to the screen in 1974. Torre Nilsson also filmed *La Guerra del Cerdo* (War of the Pigs, 1975); set in Palermo, it's a discomforting adaptation of Adolfo Bioy Casares's story of generational conflict and political polarization in the immediate pre-coup years. Argentine jazz legend Gato Barbieri wrote the soundtrack.

Fans of the offbeat can look for director Emilio Vieyra's *Sangre de Vírgenes* (Blood of the Virgins, 1967), presumably the finest vampire flick ever filmed in Bariloche. Available on DVD through the British distributor Mondo Macabro (www.mondomacabro.co.uk), it also includes a documentary short on Argentine exploitation films starring Isabel (Coca) Sarli, an international figure in the 1960s and 1970s.

Director Héctor Olivera (born 1931) has turned two of Osvaldo Soriano's satirical novels into movies: *A Funny Dirty Little War* (1983), depicting the comic consequences of a military coup in a provincial town (it has nothing to do, directly at least, with the dictatorship of 1976–83); and *Una Sombra Ya Pronto Serás* (Shadows, 1994), a road movie with no landmarks. Luppi appeared in the former.

Starting with a bungled robbery in Buenos Aires, Marcelo Piñeyro's *Wild Horses* (1995) becomes a road romance that ends with a chase in the Patagonian province of Chubut. Héctor Alterio, who plays opposite Norma Aleandro in *Hijo de la Novia,* plays a hostage who goes along for the ride.

Gustavo Mosquera directed the innovative *Moebius* (1996), really a collaborative film-school project set mostly in a Borgesian Buenos Aires subway; a disappearing train, audible but not visible, serves as a metaphor for the victims of the 1976–83 Dirty War. Displaying great creativity and technical proficiency on a shoestring budget, its anachronisms—antique dial telephones alongside cell phones, for instance—imply an unsettling continuity despite the return to representative government.

In addition to the Argentine films above, Federico Luppi (born 1936) has appeared in two outstanding films by Mexican director Guillermo del Toro: the sci-fi thriller *Cronos* (1992) and the politically charged ghost story *The Devil's Backbone,* set during the Spanish Civil War. Luppi also played the lead role of a socially committed physician in U.S. director John Sayles's *Men with Guns* (1997), an eloquent parable on political violence in Latin America.

Norma Aleandro (born 1936), best known overseas for *The Official Story,* has won many international acting awards. She has also appeared opposite Anthony Hopkins in Sergio Toledo's *One Man's War,* a human-rights drama set in Paraguay.

Cecilia Roth (born 1958), who appeared with Luppi in *A Place in the World,* has worked frequently with maverick Spanish director Pedro Almodóvar, most recently in *All About My Mother* (1999).

THEATER

Argentines, especially *porteños,* are avid theatergoers. The theater tradition dates from late colonial times, when creation of the Viceroyalty of the River Plate gave the capital a certain legitimacy and pretensions, at least, to high culture. Over the 19th century, it developed through institutions like the *sainete,* a humorous performance dealing with immigrant issues.

Formal theater dates from the late 19th century, thanks to the patronage of the Montevideo-born Podestá family, who built theaters in Buenos Aires and La Plata. Influential early playwrights included Montevideo-born Florencio Sánchez (1875–1910), who wrote *sainetes* but drew much of his inspiration from Ibsen; Gregorio de Laferrere (1867–1913), who wrote comic plays; and Roberto Payró (1867–1928), also a novelist.

Twentieth-century European dramatists such as Federico García Lorca and Jean Cocteau found the Buenos Aires theater scene justified the long trip across the Atlantic in the days before jets. Among Argentina's best-loved 20th-century performers are comedian Luis Sandrini (1905–1980) and Lola Membrives (1888–1969); the best-known contemporary playwright is Juan Carlos Gené. Norma Aleandro,

Omar Gasparini created the public Mural Escenográfico for La Boca's Catalinas Sur theater group.

while primarily known for her films, is active as a theater director.

Buenos Aires's Avenida Corrientes is the traditional locus of live theater, but the last few years of economic hardship have taken the luster off many of its venues and it's worth seeking out "off-Corrientes" alternatives. Especially worthwhile are community groups like La Boca's imaginative, politically committed Teatro Catalinas Sur.

Ranging from vulgar burlesque with elaborate stage shows to Shakespearean and avantgarde drama, the Buenos Aires theater scene is busiest June–August. The difference between traditional theaters and shoestring venues is not so much the quality of acting as the production budget, which allows much more elaborate sets at larger venues. The biggest productions can even

THE REBIRTH OF FILETE

The flamboyant folk art called *filete* began with Sicilian immigrants whose horsecarts were truly "art on wheels." Their symmetrical ornamental lines, enriched by elaborate calligraphy, simulated the moldings and wrought-iron ornamentation on late 19th- and early 20th-century buildings of Buenos Aires—the word *filete* derives from the Italian *filetto*, meaning a strip that separates moldings.

Gradually, the capital's *fileteadores* made their craft the standard for commercial sign-painting, as it drew attention to fixed businesses like restaurants, cafés, and a variety of other services. It suffered, though, during the dark days of the Proceso dictatorship (1976–83), when the generals banned it from public transportation for its alleged unreadability. Since the return to representative government, though, *filete* has made a comeback, and skilled *fileteadores* can make a handsome living.

For readymade decorative plaques, visit Plaza Dorrego's Sunday Feria de San Pedro Telmo, where typical themes and subjects are tango (and tango legend Carlos Gardel), plus skillfully drawn dragons, flowers, and fruits. Many of these plaques display *piropos*, aphorisms, or proverbs.

Perhaps typical of contemporary *fileteadores*

Filete artist Martiniano Arce of San Telmo has decorated his own casket-- and his wife's.

is Martiniano Arce, whose San Telmo studio is literally a memorial to his craft—he has already chosen and painted his and his wife's coffins, and keeps them on display in his house. He does not shy away from commercial work, saying that his art is incomplete until someone owns it—in addition to the cover for the rock band Fabulosos Cadillacs' *Fabulosos Calavera* CD, he has commemorated the McDonald's tenth anniversary in Argentina in a custom design, and even painted a symbolic bottle for Coca Cola.

Arce and several of his colleagues will produce custom work on commission; a typical plaque of about 20 by 30 centimeters (8 by 12 inches) costs around US$100. Most of their houses proclaim their craft conspicuously, but it's best to phone for an appointment unless you just want to admire their studios from the outside. Arce is at Perú 1089, 1st floor (tel. 011/4362-2739, elfileteador@martinianoarce.com, www.martinianoarce.com).

Other artists include **Adrián Clara** (tel. 011/4381-2676); **Jorge Muscia** (Carlos Calvo 370, tel. 011/4361-5942); and **Mabel Matto** (Estados Unidos 510, 1st floor). **Eduardo Genovese** (tel. 011/4581-0798, www.fileteado.com.ar) teaches classes at various cultural centers around Buenos Aires.

move intact to the Atlantic beach resort of Mar del Plata for the summer, but even small provincial towns may have surprisingly professional companies.

ARTS AND CRAFTS

Argentina's artisanal heritage is not so immediately evident as, say, the indigenous textile traditions of the Peruvian or Guatemalan highlands, but both the city and the countryside have characteristic crafts. The most truly urban expression of folk art is *filete,* the elaborate rainbow signage that, in the hands of its most skilled practitioners, approaches the finest calligraphy.

Befitting their origins on the Río de la Plata (literally, "River of Silver"), Argentine silversmiths create truly intricate jewelry, as well as adornments such as the *facón* (knife) and *espuelas* (spurs) that accompany traditional gaucho clothing. The major center for skilled silverwork is the Buenos Aires provincial town of San Antonio de Areco.

Expert leatherworkers, in turn, produce gaucho-style clothing and horse gear such as *rastras* (belts), reins, and saddles. Both these traditions come together in the production of paraphernalia for *mate,* the herbal "Paraguayan tea" whose consumption is a cultural bellwether in the region. Traditionally, *mate* (the herb) is sipped with a silver *bombilla* (straw) from a *mate* (gourd, in a different context), which may be mounted in a leather holder.

In the northwestern provinces of Salta and Jujuy, indigenous Andean weaving traditions are apparent in blankets, ponchos, sweaters, and similar garments. The Huarpe styles of Cuyo and the Mapuche of northern Patagonia differ in their approaches to such goods.

ENTERTAINMENT

Argentines in general and *porteños* in particular are night people—discos and dance clubs, for instance, may not even *open* until 1 A.M. or so, and stay open until dawn. That said, not everything of interest takes place at those hours.

All the Buenos Aires dailies have thorough event listings, especially in their end-of-the-week supplements, and the larger provincial newspapers do as well. For discount tickets to certain events, including tango shows, cinemas, and live theater, Buenos Aires, Mar del Plata and other large cities have *carteleras,* consolidator agencies with last-minute specials.

Bars, Clubs, and Discos

Buenos Aires's Recoleta and Palermo neighborhoods have the largest numbers of places to dance and drink; rock and techno, but also Latin styles like salsa, are the music of choice. Buenos Aires has some cavernous dance clubs (*boliches*) with state-of-the-art sound systems and recorded techno, but the more interesting venues are smaller ones with live folk, rock, and even jazz.

The distinction between cafés and bars is not always obvious—in fact, it's often more a continuum than a dichotomy. Some of the more stylish (or pretentious) bars often go by the English word "pub," pronounced as in English, though many call themselves Irish. Likewise, live music venues that most foreigners would consider clubs may be simple bars at certain hours and lively nightspots at others.

Some provincial cities also have clustered nightlife areas, such as Salta's Calle Balcarce area near the old railroad station, Córdoba's Nueva Córdoba zone, and Mendoza's Arístides de Villanueva and outlying Chacras de Coria.

Cinemas

Buenos Aires is the only Argentine city that still has a real downtown cinema district, but even there many venues have consolidated into multiplexes that specialize in first-run Hollywood fare; there are also suburban-style multiplexes in shopping centers like Buenos Aires's Patio Bullrich. In some provincial cities, the central cinemas have closed but multiplexes have opened in suburban areas. Buenos Aires is the only city with a substantial art house or repertory circuit, but cultural centers and universities in regional capitals often reprise classics or show less-commercial movies.

Most imported films appear in the original language, with Spanish subtitles. The major exceptions are animated and children's films, which are invariably dubbed into Spanish.

HOLIDAYS, FESTIVALS, AND EVENTS

Argentina observes the typical national holidays and quite a few special events on top of that. The summer months of January and February, when most Argentines leave on vacation, are generally a quiet time; things pick up after school starts in early March.

January

January 1 is **Año Nuevo** (New Year's Day), an official holiday.

February or March

Dates for the pre-Lenten **Carnaval** (Carnival) vary from year to year but most celebrations take place on weekends rather than during the week. While unlikely ever to match the spectacle of Brazilian festivities, Carnaval is enjoying a revival, especially in Buenos Aires neighborhoods and Mesopotamian cities like Gualeguaychú.

March/April

Semana Santa (Holy Week) is widely observed in Catholic Argentina, though only the days from **Viernes Santo** (Good Friday) through **Pascua** (Easter) are official holidays. Many Argentines, though, use the long weekend for a minivacation.

May

May 1 is **Día del Trabajador** (International Labor Day), an official holiday. On May 25, Argentines observe the **Revolución de Mayo** (May Revolution of 1810), when *porteños* made their

first move toward independence by declaring the viceroy illegitimate. This is not, however, the major independence celebration, which takes place July 9.

June

June 10 is **Día de las Malvinas** (Malvinas Day), an official holiday celebrating Argentina's claim to the British-governed Falkland Islands. June 20, also an official holiday, is **Día de la Bandera** (Flag Day).

July

July 9, **Día de la Independencia,** celebrates the formal declaration of Argentine independence at the northwestern city of Tucumán in 1816. Later in the month, when school lets out, many Argentines take **Vacaciones de Invierno** (Winter Holidays), when flights and even buses out of the capital fill up fast.

August

August 17 is **Día de San Martín,** the official observance of the death (not the birth) of Argentina's independence hero.

October

October 12 is **Día de la Raza** (equivalent to Columbus Day), an official holiday.

November

November 2's **Día de los Muertos** (Day of the Dead) is the occasion for Argentines to visit the graves of their loved ones, though this is not the colorful event it is in Mexico or Guatemala.

December

December 25 is **Navidad** (Christmas Day), an official holiday.

Accommodations

Argentina has an abundance of accommodations in all categories, from campgrounds to youth-hostel dormitories to extravagant luxury suites and everything in between. National and municipal tourist officials offer accommodations lists and brochures, but these frequently exclude budget options and may even omit some midrange and high-end places.

Prices, especially since the devaluation of 2001–02, are often negotiable; do not assume the *tarifa mostrador* (rack rate) is etched in stone. Visitors also should not take hotel ratings too seriously, as they often represent an ideal rather than a reality, and some one- or two-star places are better than others that theoretically rank higher.

Prices in Buenos Aires proper often fall during the peak summer season of January and February, as business travel slows to a crawl; for excursion destinations, though, prices usually rise as *porteños* flee the capital for sand, sun, and sex on the beach. The same is true for popular provincial destinations like San Antonio de Areco. Other peak seasons, when prices may rise, are Semana Santa (Holy Week) and July's winter school vacations, which coincide with patriotic holidays.

Note also that Argentine hotels levy 21 percent in Impuesto de Valor Agregado, or IVA (Value Added Tax or VAT). Unless otherwise indicated, rates in this book include IVA, but if there's any question at the front desk, ask for clarification to avoid unpleasant surprises when paying the bill.

CAMPING

Organized camping is common throughout Argentina; campgrounds are generally spacious, with shade, clean toilets, and bathrooms with hot showers, and even groceries and restaurants. They are often surprisingly central, and they are almost always cheap, rarely more than a couple of dollars per person. Devaluation, though, has made modest hotels more than competitive with them.

In the peak summer season and on weekends, the best sites can be crowded and noisy, as families on a budget take advantage of bargain prices.

It's usually possible to find a quiet—but less desirable—site on the periphery. But remember that Argentines stay up late—very late—for their barbecues.

HOSTELS

For youthful and budget travel, Argentina has growing hostel networks and many independent hostels as well, where bunks start at around US$5 pp. Since the devaluation of 2002, these are no longer the only budget options, but they do offer an opportunity to get together with like-minded travelers. Many of them offer more-expensive private rooms, in addition to the customary dormitory accommodations, for individuals and couples.

For up-to-the-minute information on official Argentine hostels, contact **Hostelling International Argentina** (Florida 835, 3rd floor, Oficina 319-B, tel. 11/4511-8712, fax 11/4312-0089, raaj@hostels.org.ar, www.hostels.org.ar). The competing but rather torpid **Asociación Argentina de Albergues de la Juventud** (AAAJ, Talcahuano 214, tel./fax 11/4372-7094, info@aaaj.org.ar, www.hostelling-aaaj.org.ar) has a smaller network of affiliates, though there is some overlap. There is also the **Argentina Hostels Club** (ahc@argentinahostels.com, www.argentinahostels.com), a growing confederation that's strongest in the Andean northwest, Mesopotamia, Buenos Aires, and Patagonia.

Note that most Argentine hostels have begun to avoid the term *albergue;* in Argentine Spanish, an *albergue transitorio* means a by-the-hour hotel. Many have adapted the English word "hostel," or Hispanicized it into *hostal* (a term more common in Chile, where it's a step above an *hospedaje*).

OTHER BUDGET ACCOMMODATIONS

Budget accommodations in Argentina can cost as little as US$5 pp; they go by a variety of names

A DAY (OR MORE) IN THE COUNTRY

Over the past decade-plus, facing economic reality, many of Argentina's great rural estates have opened themselves to the tourist trade. From the subtropical north to the sub-Antarctic south, diversification has become the word for owners of *estancias,* some of which earn more income from hosting visitors than they do growing grain or raising livestock. For many visitors, staying at an *estancia* is their entire vacation.

Figures suggest the scale of the phenomenon. According to the Buenos Aires–based Red Argentina de Turismo Rural (Ratur), more than 1,000 *estancias* are open to the public, rural tourism has grown 70 percent since 1997—about 200,000 people every month spend some time in the countryside—and the figure should grow more with devaluation. For 45 percent of farms, tourism comprises 10 percent of their income; for 17 percent, it represents half of their income; and for eight percent, it represents 95 percent of their income. In Patagonia, where *estancia* visits are growing at 10 percent annually, tourist revenue can be the equivalent of 10,000 kilograms of wool; in Santa Cruz Province, where 40 percent of wool *estancias* have failed in recent years, it represents 15 percent of income from the wool clip.

Throughout the country, some *estancias* are reasonably priced places with limited services, but others are magnificent properties with castlelike *cascos* (big houses), elaborate service that includes gourmet meals, and recreational activities such as horseback riding, tennis, and swimming. Some *estancias* aim at day-trippers—weekending in the countryside of Buenos Aires Province has become an increasingly popular option for escaping the capital—but most of them prefer overnight guests.

Many *estancias* get detailed individual coverage in this book, but various others are open to the public. Several groups of them have formed networks to promote themselves as tourist destinations.

Affiliated with the Sociedad Rural Argentina, the traditionally powerful landowners' organization, the **Red Argentina de Turismo Rural** (Ratur, Florida 460, 4th floor, Buenos Aires, tel. 011/4328-0499, fax 011/4328-0878, ratur@infovia.com.ar, www.raturestancias.com.ar) represents *estancias* in northern and southern Buenos Aires Province, as well as the northwestern provinces, Mesopotamia, and even some in Patagonia.

Estancias Argentinas (Diagonal Roque Sáenz Peña 616, 3rd floor, Buenos Aires, tel. 011/4343-2366, fax 4343-9568, reservas@estanciasargentinas.com, www.estanciasargentinas.com) operates primarily in Buenos Aires Province, with a few affiliates in Córdoba and the northeastern Mesopotamian provinces.

The best-organized provincial group is **Estancias de Santa Cruz** (Suipacha 1120, Retiro, Buenos Aires, tel./fax 011/4325-3098 or 011/4325-3102, info@estanciasdesantacruz.com, www.estanciasdesantacruz.com). Most of its affiliates are in the southwestern corner of its home province, but there are also a few members on the Argentine side of Tierra del Fuego.

La Pampa Province has recently created its own network, **Red de Estancias Turísticas de La Pampa** (Suipacha 346, Buenos Aires, tel. 011/4326-5111, lapampaestancias@argentina.com, www.lapampaestancias.com.ar).

---

that may camouflage their quality—they can range from dingy fleabags with mattresses that sag like hammocks to simple but cheerful and tidy places with firm new beds.

An *hospedaje* is generally a family-run lodging with a few spare rooms; *pensiones* and *casas de huéspedes* are comparable, nearly interchangeable

terms. All may often have long-term residents as well as overnight guests. *Residenciales* (singular *residencial*) are generally buildings constructed with short-stay accommodations in mind, but they may also have semipermanent inhabitants. All of these places may even go by the term *hotel,* though usually that belongs to a more-formal category.

That said, there are some exceptionally good values in all these categories. Many will have shared bath and toilet (*baño general* or *baño compartido*), or offer a choice between shared and private bath *baño privado;* bathtubs are unusual. In some cases, they will have ceiling fans and even cable TV, but there is often an extra charge for cable and almost always a surcharge for air-conditioning.

Travelers intending to stay at budget accommodations should bring their own towels, though some provide them. Many, but by no means all, include breakfast in their rates; ask to be certain.

MIDRANGE ACCOMMODATIONS

Midrange hotels generally offer larger, more-comfortable, and better-furnished rooms, almost always with private bath, than even the best budget places. Ceiling fans, cable TV, and even a/c are common, but they may not have on-site parking. Some have restaurants. Rates can range from US$25 up to US$100 d; some are better values than their high-end counterparts.

HIGH-END ACCOMMODATIONS

Luxury hotels with top-flight service, which can range well upward of US$100 per night, are few outside the capital and major resort areas. In the capital, these will usually offer amenities like restaurants, swimming pools, gym facilities, business centers, Internet connections, and conference rooms; outside the capital, these are mostly resort hotels and will lack the business facilities. Invariably they will offer secure parking.

Some of the best options in this category are country-inn resorts on *estancias,* offering traditional hospitality and ambience with style unmatchable at other high-end places. Again, prices may be upward of US$100, often substantially upward.

Food and Drink

Food and drink range from the economical and ordinary to the truly elegant and everything in between. For most of the 1990s, eating well at restaurants was financially challenging except for cheap cafeteria lunches and *tenedor libre* (literally, "free fork") buffets, but the peso collapse of 2002 has made it possible to eat diverse and imaginative food for a fraction of its former price—at least for visitors with dollars or Euros in their wallets.

Stereotypically, the Argentine diet consists of beef and more beef. This common perception is not entirely mistaken, but the local diet has always had a Spanish touch and, for more than a century, a marked Italian influence with pizza and pasta. Over the past decade, though, the restaurant scene has become far more cosmopolitan, adventurous, and nuanced, with Brazilian, Japanese, Thai, Vietnamese, and many other once exotic cuisines—not to mention high-quality variations on Argentine regional dishes. Certain Buenos Aires neighborhoods, such as Palermo Viejo and Las Cañitas, seem to have sprouted stylish and sophisticated new eateries on every corner and in between.

WHERE TO EAT

Places to eat range from hole-in-the-wall *comedores* (eateries) or fast-food *bares* (unavoidably but misleadingly translated as "bars", with no formal menu, in bus and train stations, to *cafés, confiterías* (teahouses) and elegant *restaurantes* in Buenos Aires and other major tourist centers. A bar, of course, can also be a drinking establishment; this is usually obvious in context. A café is both more and less than its English-language equivalent would suggest, though it does serve food.

RESTAURANT TERMINOLOGY

The term *restaurante* (occasionally *restorán* or, more fashionably, *restó*) usually refers to places

DINING VOCABULARY AND ETIQUETTE

Restaurant vocabulary is mostly straightforward. The usual term for menu is *la carta; el menú* is almost equally common, but can also mean a fixed-price lunch or dinner. The bill is *la cuenta. Cubiertos* are silverware, while a *plato* is a plate and a *vaso* a glass. A *plato principal* is a main dish or entrée.

Note that one might ask for a *vaso de agua* (glass of water), but never for a *vaso de vino* (literally but incorrectly, a glass of wine); rather, ask for a *copa de vino*. When speaking English, native Spanish-speakers frequently make a comparable error in requesting "a cup of wine."

Many but not all Argentine restaurants assess a small *cubierto* (cover charge) for dishes, silverware, and bread. This is not a *propina* (tip); generally, a 10 percent tip is the norm, but Argentines themselves often ignore this, especially in times of economic crisis. Women in a group will often tip little or nothing, but a good rule of thumb is that anyone able to afford a restaurant meal can afford a tip.

It's worth emphasizing that the occupation of waiter is traditionally male and professional, rather than a short-term expedient for university students or aspiring actors, but this is changing in the new, stylish restaurants, where servers are just as likely to be young and female. Note that *mozo*, a common and innocuous term for a waiter here, implies an insulting servility in neighboring Chile (parts of which are covered in this book). When in doubt, use *mesero* or *jóven*, even if the individual in question is not particularly young; for a female, use *señorita* unless the individual is of at least late middle-age.

Know Argentina

with sit-down service, but within this definition there can be great diversity. Most often, the term refers to a locale with a printed menu and table service, but it can range from any place with a basic beef and pasta menu to truly elegant settings with complex cuisine, elaborate wine lists, and professional waiters.

The usually international fast-food villains have franchises here, but the best cheap food comes from *rotiserías* (delicatessens), which serve excellent takeaway fare and may have basic seating. Likewise, supermarkets like Coto and Disco have budget *cafeterías* that are excellent options for budget visitors.

Bares and *comedores* are no-frills eateries, with indifferent service, offering *minutas* (short orders); the term *comedor* can also mean a hotel breakfast nook or dining room. A *café*, by contrast, is a place whose patrons may dawdle over coffee and croissants, but its de facto purpose is to promote social interaction in personal affairs, business deals and other transactions—even though it also serves snacks, *minutas,* and alcoholic drinks (beer, wine, and hard liquor).

Confiterías, by contrast, serve breakfast, light meals like sandwiches, snacks like cakes and other desserts, and coffee-based drinks. Generally more formal than cafés, some of them prestigious, they are suitable for afternoon tea; some have full-scale restaurant menus, often in a separate sector.

WHAT TO EAT

Argentina is famous for beef—in abundance—and grains, but fresh fruit, vegetables, and an underrated wealth of seafood add diversity to the country's cuisine. While the stereotypical diet of beef and more beef may have serious shortcomings, visitors will easily find alternatives, especially in Buenos Aires.

According to historian John C. Super, whatever the negative consequences of the Spanish invasion, it actually improved a diet that was, by some accounts, nutritionally deficient (often protein-poor) in late pre-Columbian times. In Super's opinion,

The combination of European and American foods created diversified, nutritionally rich diets. Crop yields were higher than those in Europe, and longer or staggered

growing seasons made fresh food available during much of the year. The potential for one of the best diets in the history of the world was evident soon after discovery of the New World. For Europeans, the introduction of livestock and wheat was an essential step in creating that diet.

When Europeans first set foot in South America, in the densely populated Andean region, the staples were beans, squash, and a variety of potatoes and other tubers, but the diet was low in animal protein—only the llama, alpaca, guinea pig, and wild game were readily available, and not in all areas. Spanish introductions like wheat and barley, which yielded only a four-to-one harvest ratio in Europe, reached at least two to three times that in the Americas.

The Spanish introductions blended with the indigenous base to create many of the edibles found on Argentine tables today. The abundance of seafood, combined with European animal protein and high-productivity European fruits like apples, apricots, grapes, pears, and many others, resulted in a diverse food production and consumption system which, however, is changing today.

Consumption of red meat, the hallmark of the diet, may be decreasing among more-affluent Argentines but it remains the entrée of choice among lower classes. Thanks to the Italian-immigrant influence, an assortment of pastas is available almost everywhere.

Cereals

Trigo (wheat), a Spanish introduction, is most common in *pan* (bread), but also appears in the form of pasta. *Arroz* (rice) is a common *guarnición* (side order).

Maíz (maize or corn) is a main ingredient in many dishes, including the Italian-derived polenta. Maize leaves often serve as a wrapping for traditional dishes like *humitas,* the northwestern Argentine equivalent of Mexican tamales.

Legumes, Vegetables, and Tubers

Salads are almost invariably safe, and all but the most sensitive stomachs probably need not be concerned with bugs from greens washed in tap water. In restaurants, green salads are usually large enough for two diners.

Porotos (beans of all sorts except green beans) are traditional in families of Spanish descent. Other common legumes include *chauchas* (green beans), *arvejas* (peas), *lentejas* (lentils), and *habas* (fava beans).

In many varieties, *zapallo* (squash) is part of the traditional diet, as is the *tomate* (tomato). Other Old World vegetables include *acelga* (chard), *berenjena* (eggplant), *coliflor* (cauliflower), *lechuga* (lettuce), and *repollo* (cabbage). *Chiles* (peppers) are relatively uncommon; Argentine cuisine is rarely *picante* (spicy) except in the Andean Northwest, and even those dishes rarely challenge palates accustomed to Mexican or Thai cuisine.

Native to the central Andes, *papas* (potatoes) grow in well-drained soils at higher elevations in northwestern Argentina; *papas fritas* (French fries) are almost universal, but spuds also appear as *purée* (mashed potatoes) and in Italian dishes such as *ñoquis* (gnocchi). Other common tubers include *zanahorias* (carrots) and *rábanos* (radishes).

Vegetarianism

While vegetarian restaurants are fairly few except in Buenos Aires proper, the ingredients for quality vegetarian meals are easy to obtain, and many eateries prepare dishes such as pasta and salads which are easily adapted into a vegetarian format. Before ordering any pasta dish, verify whether it comes with a meat sauce—*carne* means "beef" here, and waiters or waitresses may consider chicken, pork, and similar items as part of another category—sometimes called *carne blanca* (literally, "white meat"). Faced with a reticent cook, you can always claim *alergia* (allergy).

Fruits

As its seasons are reversed from those in the Northern Hemisphere, temperate Argentina produces many of the same fruits as the north, often available as fresh juices. Items like *manzana* (apple), *pera* (pear), *naranja* (orange), *ciruela* (plum), *sandía* (watermelon), *membrillo* (quince), *durazno* (peach), *frambuesa* (raspberry), and *frutilla* (strawberry) will be familiar to almost everyone. When requesting *jugo de naranja* (orange juice), be sure it comes *exprimido* (fresh-squeezed) rather than out of a can or box.

Also widely available, mostly through import, are tropical and subtropical fruits like banana and *ananá* (pineapple). Mango, *maracuyá* (passion fruit), and similar tropical fruits are less common but not unknown.

The *palta* (avocado), a Central American domesticate known as *aguacate* in its area of origin, often appears in Argentine salads.

Meats and Poultry

Prior to the Spaniards, South America's only domesticated animals were the *cuy* (guinea pig, rare in what is now Argentina), the llama and alpaca, and the dog, sometimes used for food. The Spaniards enriched the American diet with their domestic animals, including cattle, sheep, pigs, and poultry (chickens and ducks).

Carne, often modified as *carne de vacuno,* or *bife* (beef) is the most common menu item, and comes in a variety of cuts. Among them are *bife de chorizo* (sirloin or rump steak), *bife de lomo* (tenderloin), *asado de tira* (rib roast), and *matambre* (rolled flank steak). *Milanesa* is a breaded cutlet or chicken-fried steak that, at cheaper restaurants, can be intolerably greasy.

The widest selection is usually available in the *parrillada* or *asado,* a mixed grill that includes prime cuts but also *achuras,* a broad term that encompasses offal such as *chinchulines* (small intestines), *mollejas* (sweetbreads), *criadillas*

CATTLE CULTURE AND THE ARGENTINE DIET

From his hotel room on the Avenida de Mayo in Buenos Aires, American poet Robert Lowell once wrote that he could hear "the bulky, beefy breathing of the herds." Ever since feral livestock changed the face of the pampas in the 16th century, displacing the native guanaco and rhea, cattle have been a symbol of wealth and the foundation of the Argentine diet. Riding across the pampas, Charles Darwin found the reliance on beef remarkable:

I had now been several days without tasting any thing besides meat: I did not at all dislike this new regimen; but I felt as if it would only have agreed with me with hard exercise. I have heard that patients in England, when desired to confine themselves exclusively to an animal diet, even with the hope of life before their eyes, have scarce been able to endure it. Yet the Gaucho in the Pampas, for months together, touches nothing but beef. . . . It is, perhaps, from their meat regimen that the Gauchos, like other carnivorous animals, can abstain long from food. I was told that at Tandeel, some troops voluntarily pursued a party of Indians for three days, without eating or drinking.

Recent research has suggested that this diet has not been quite so universal as once imagined—urban archaeologist Daniel Schávelzon has unearthed evidence that, for instance, fish consumption was much greater in colonial Buenos Aires than once thought—but there is no doubt that the *parrilla* is a culinary institution. Beef may not be healthy in the quantities that some Argentines enjoy, and many of them will even admit it. But few can bypass traditional restaurants, where flamboyantly clad urban gauchos stir the glowing coals beneath grilled meat on a vertical spit, without craving that savory beef.

For most Argentines, *bien cocido* (well done) is the standard for steak, but *jugoso* (rare) and *a punto* (medium) are not uncommon.

(testicles), *morcilla* (blood sausage), and *riñones* (kidneys). *Asado* can also mean a simple roast. *Chimichurri* is a garlic-based sauce that often accompanies the *parrillada.*

Sausages such as the slight spicy *chorizo* may also form part of the *asado;* in a hot-dog bun, it becomes *choripán. Panchos* are basic hot dogs, while *fiambres* are processed meats.

Cordero (lamb), often roasted on a spit over an open fire, is more common in Patagonia. *Cerdo* (pork) appears in many forms, ranging from simple *jamón* (ham) to *chuletas* (chops) to *lomito* (loin) and *matambre de cerdo. Chivo* (goat) or *chivito* (the diminutive) is a western-Argentine specialty that sometimes appears on menus in the capital; note that the Uruguayan *chivito* is very different, a steak sandwich or plate slathered with eggs, fries, and other high-calorie extras.

Stews and casseroles include *carbonada* (beef, rice, potatoes, sweet potatoes, corn, squash, and fruit like apples and peaches), and *puchero* (beef, chicken, bacon, sausage, morcilla, cabbage, corn, garbanzos, peppers, tomatoes, onions, squash, and sweet potatoes). Broth-cooked rice serves as a garnish.

Ave (poultry) most often means *pollo* (chicken), which sometimes appears on menus as *gallina* (literally, hen) in a casserole or stew; eggs are *huevos. Pavo* (turkey) is becoming more common.

Fish and Seafood

Argentine fish and seafood may not have the international reputation of its beef, but the long coastline, territorial seas and huge freshwater rivers and lakes provide abundant options. Buenos Aires, Mar del Plata, and other coastal cities have fine seafood restaurants, but these are less common in the interior.

Seafood, among the most abundant animal-protein sources in pre-Columbian times, includes both *pescado* (fish) and *mariscos* (shellfish and crustaceans). The most common fish are *congrio* (conger eel, covering a variety of species), sometimes called *abadejo; lenguado* (sole or flounder); *merluza* (hake); and *trucha* (trout). *Salmón* (salmon) normally comes from fish farms in Patagonia and in Chile.

Note that the cheapest restaurants often ruin perfectly good fish by preparing it *frito* (deep-fried), but on request almost all will prepare it *a la plancha* (grilled, usually with a dab of butter) or *al vapor* (steamed). Higher-priced restaurants will add elaborate sauces, often including shellfish.

Among the shellfish, visitors will recognize the relatively commonplace *almejas* (clams), *calamares* (squid), *camarones* (shrimp), *cangrejo* (crab), *centolla* (king crab), and *mejillones* (mussels), *ostiones* or *callos* (scallops, but beware—the latter word can also mean tripe), *ostras* (oysters), and *pulpo* (octopus). Spanish restaurants normally serve the greatest variety of fish and shellfish.

"Fast Food" Snacks

Ignoring the invasion of international franchises, Argentina has some of the continent's best snack food. The best of the best is the empanada, a flaky dough turnover most frequently filled with ground beef, hard-boiled egg, and olive, but it may also come with ham and cheese, chicken, onion, and (rarely) tuna or fish. The spicier ground-beef *salteña* comes from northwestern Argentina but is available in Buenos Aires; the tangy *empanada árabe* (lamb with a touch of lemon juice) is more difficult to find. Empanadas *al horno* (oven-baked) are lighter than *fritas* (fried, sometimes in heavy oil).

Argentine pizza is also exceptional, though less diverse in terms of toppings than in North America. For slices, try the cheeseless *fugazza* with Vidalia-sweet onions or its cousin *fugazzeta,* enhanced with ham and mozzarella. Argentines embellish their slices with *fainá,* a baked chickpea dough that fits neatly atop.

Desserts

Many Argentines have a sweet tooth. At home, the favorite *postre* is fresh fruit, ranging from grapes (most single-family homes have their own arbors) to apples, pears, and oranges. In restaurants, this becomes *ensalada de frutas* (fruit salad) or, somewhat more elaborately, *macedonia. Postre vigilante,* consisting of cheese and *membrillo* (quince) or *batata* (sweet potato) preserves, is another fruit-based dessert; it also goes by the name *queso y dulce.*

Arroz con leche (rice pudding) and *flan* (egg custard, often topped with whipped cream) are also good choices, as is the Spanish custard known as *natillas*. An acquired taste is *dulce de leche*, which one international travel magazine referred to as "its own major food group." Argentines devour this sickly sweet caramelized milk, spread on just about anything and often spooned out of the jar in private homes, in prodigious quantities.

Though it stems from the Italian tradition, Argentine ice cream lacks the high international profile of gelato—when a pair of *porteños* opened an ice creamery in Oakland, California, they chose the compromise name of Tango Gelato, stressing its Italian origins without suppressing its Buenos Aires way station. Argentina has a remarkable number of high-quality ice creameries and a remarkable diversity of flavors, ranging from the standard vanilla and chocolate (with multiple variations on those standards, including white chocolate and bittersweet chocolate) to lemon mousse, *sambayón* (resembling eggnog), the Argentine staple *dulce de leche* (caramelized milk), and countless others.

International and Ethnic Food

Buenos Aires has the greatest variety of international food, though some tourist-oriented areas also have good selections. Italian and Spanish are probably the most common foreign cuisines, but French and Chinese venues are also numerous. Brazilian, Mexican, and Middle Eastern cuisine are less common; some popular world food cuisines, such as Japanese, Thai, and Vietnamese, have made significant inroads.

MEALS AND MEALTIMES

Despite some regional differences, Argentine food is relatively uniform throughout the country, except in Buenos Aires, where diverse ethnic and international cuisine is abundant; the Andean northwest, where some dishes resemble those of highland Bolivia and Peru; and Patagonia, where game dishes are not unusual (most of this, such as venison, is farmed).

By North American and European standards, Argentines are late eaters except for *desayuno* (breakfast). *Almuerzo* (lunch) usually starts around 1 P.M., *cena* (dinner) around 9 P.M. or later–sometimes much later. *Porteños* often bide their time between lunch and dinner with a late-afternoon *té* (afternoon tea) that consists of a sandwich or some sort of pastry or dessert; it can be very substantial.

Since Argentines often eat *after* the theater or a movie, around 11 P.M. or even later on weekends, anyone entering a restaurant before 9 P.M. may well dine alone. One advantage of an early lunch and dinner is that fewer customers means fewer smokers; this is not foolproof, but statistically things are on your side.

Breakfast and Brunch

Most Argentines eat a light breakfast of coffee or tea and *pan tostado* (toast, occasionally with ham and/or cheese), *medialunas* (croissants), or *facturas* (pastries, also eaten for afternoon tea); *medialunas* may be either *de manteca* (buttery and sweet) or *salada* (saltier, baked with oil). *Mermelada* (jam) usually accompanies plain *tostados.*

As a side dish, eggs may be either *fritos* (fried) or *revueltos* (scrambled), or sometimes *duros* (hardboiled). In some fashionable restaurant zones, a more elaborate Sunday brunch has become an option.

Lunch

Lunch is often the day's main meal, usually including an *entrada* (appetizer), followed by a *plato principal* (entrée), accompanied by a *guarnición* (side dish) and a *bebida* (soft drink) or *agua mineral* (mineral water), and followed by *postre* (dessert).

Upscale restaurants often offer fixed-priced lunches that make it possible to eat well and stylishly without busting the budget. It's also possible to find local fast-food items like *hamburguesas* (hamburgers), sandwiches, pizza, and pasta, without resorting to international franchises.

Té

Té, the fourth meal of the typical Argentine day, can range from a late-afternoon sandwich to the

Know Argentina

THE RITE OF *MATE*

It's rarely on the menu, but the single most important social drink in Argentina and most of the River Plate region—including Uruguay, Paraguay, and southern Brazil—is *mate*, made from the dried, shredded leaf of *Ilex paraguayensis.*

Espresso, in its many forms, may dominate café society, but the *mate* infusion transcends commercialism. Its production is a major industry, but its consumption belongs to home and hearth. Native to the forests of the upper Río Paraná Delta, a relative of the everyday holly, *yerba mate* became a commercial crop in plantations on colonial Jesuit missions.

Mate gear can be works of art even for those who don't drink Argentina's traditional bitter herbal tea.

© WAYNE BERNHARDSON

Transplanted Europeans took to it—the Austrian Jesuit Martin Dobrizhoffer asserted that *mate* "speedily counteracts the languor arising from the burning climate, and assuages both hunger and thirst"—but, unlike coffee and tea, it never really established markets across the Atlantic or even elsewhere in the Americas, except for parts of Chile.

Production diminished with the Jesuits' expulsion from the Americas in 1767, but the so-called "Paraguayan tea" kept its place in humble households and privileged palaces alike. According to the English sailor Emeric Essex Vidal, who visited Buenos Aires in the 1820s,

> Mate *is in every house all day long, and the compliment of the country is to hand the* mate *cup to every visitor, the same cup and tube serving for all, and an attendant being kept in waiting to replenish for each person. Throughout the provinces, the weary traveler, let him stop at what hovel soever he may, is sure to be presented with the hospitable* mate-*cup, which, unless his prejudices are very strong indeed, will be found a great refreshment.*

equivalent of afternoon tea, with elaborate cakes and cookies, and is often a social occasion as well. Presumably intended to tide people over until their relatively late dinnertime, it often becomes larger and more elaborate than its name would imply.

Dinner

Dinner resembles lunch, but in formal restaurants it may be substantially more elaborate (and more expensive), and it can be a major social occasion. Argentines dine late—9 P.M. is early, and anything before that will likely earn incredulous "What are you doing here?" stares

from waiters. The exception to this rule is at tourist-oriented areas like BA's Puerto Madero complex, where restaurateurs have become accustomed to North Americans and Europeans who, lodged at nearby luxury hotels, often can't wait any later than 7 P.M.

BUYING GROCERIES

Abundant across Buenos Aires, North American-style supermarkets such as Coto and Disco carry a wide selection of processed foods but often a lesser variety (and quality) of fresh produce than is available in produce markets. Many

In fact, the purpose of *mate* is hospitality; preparing and serving it is a ritual. It is also an equalizer, as everyone sips in turn from the same *bombilla* (metallic tube or straw), placed in the same *yerba*-stuffed *mate* (a term which also means "gourd"), filled with slightly below-boiling water by the *cebador* (brewer). It is customary to drink the gourd dry, and then return it to the *cebador*, who will pass it clockwise around the group. Note that, in this context, to say *gracias* (thank you) means that you want no more.

Not all rituals are equal, though, and *mate*'s material culture can differ dramatically among classes. While the servant whose sole job was to prepare and serve it is a thing of the past, upper-class households own far more elaborate paraphernalia than working-class families—just as British peers have more ornate tea sets than the untitled. While simple gourds might be plain calabashes or even plastic, others might be elaborately carved wood set in silver or even gold; the *bombilla*, likewise, can range from utilitarian aluminum to ceremonial silver.

Most Argentines prefer *mate amargo* (bitter, i.e. without sugar), but northerners often take it *dulce,* with sugar and fragrant herbs known as *yuyos* (literally, "weeds"). While it's a mostly homebound custom in Argentina, Uruguayans (who consume even more than Argentines) make it a public affair as they walk the streets with leather-encased gourds and enormous Thermoses. In the ferocious Paraguayan summer, street vendors sell ice-cold *yerba* in the form of *tereré*.

Supermarkets sell *yerba* in bulk packages with engaging designs that look half a century old. It's also available in tea bags as *mate cocido,* which is weaker, and may be more palatable to neophytes, than the first bitter swallows from the freshly prepared gourd. Do not confuse it, however, with *mate de coca,* another innocuous infusion but made from the leaf of the notorious coca plant.

Fortunately for its Argentine aficionados, *mate* is inexpensive. No one really has to worry any more, as did Dobrizhoffer, that,

If many topers in Europe waste their substance by an immoderate use of wine and other intoxicating liquors, there are no fewer in America who drink away their fortunes in potations of the herb of Paraguay.

of them also have cheap cafeterias with surprisingly good food.

In areas where supermarkets are fewer, almost all neighborhoods have corner shops where basic groceries and fresh produce are available, usually within just a few minutes' walk. Butchers are numerous, fishmongers somewhat less so.

BEVERAGES
Coffee, Tea, and Chocolate
Unreconstructed caffeine addicts will feel at home in Argentina, where espresso is the norm even in small provincial towns. *Café chico* is a dark viscous brew in a miniature cup, supplemented with enough sugar packets to make it overflow onto the saucer. A *cortado* comes diluted with milk—for a larger portion request a *cortado doble*—and follows lunch or dinner. *Café con leche,* equivalent to a latte, is a breakfast drink; ordering it after lunch or dinner is a serious *faux pas.*

Té negro (black tea) usually comes in bags and is insipid by most standards. Visitors wanting British-style tea with milk should ask for tea first and milk later; otherwise, they may get a tea bag immersed in lukewarm milk. Herbal teas range from the nearly universal *manzanilla* (chamomile) and *rosa mosqueta* (rose hips) to *mate de coca* (coca leaf), but *yerba mate,* the so-called "Paraguayan tea," is one of the country's most deeply embedded customs.

Chocolate-lovers will enjoy the *submarino,* a bar of semisweet chocolate that dissolves smoothly in steamed milk from the espresso machine. Powdered chocolate is also available, but less flavorful.

Water, Juices, and Soft Drinks

Argentine tap water is potable almost everywhere except in some of the northerly tropical deserts; ask for *agua de la canilla.* For ice, request it *con hielo.* Visitors with truly sensitive stomachs might consider bottled water, which is widely available. Ask for *agua pura* or *agua mineral;* some brands, such as Eco de los Andes and Villavicencio, are spring water, while others are purified. For carbonated water, add *con gas* or ask for the even cheaper *soda,* which comes in large siphon bottles.

Gaseosas (singular *gaseosa*) are sweetened bottled soft drinks (including most of the major transnational brands but also local versions such as the tonic water Paso de los Toros).

Fresh-squeezed *jugos* (fruit juices) are good though limited in their diversity. *Naranja* (orange) is the standard; to ensure freshness, ask for *jugo de naranja exprimido.*

Alcoholic Drinks

Argentina is less famous for its wines than Chile is, perhaps because domestic consumption overshadows exports, but it's the world's fifth-largest wine producer. Most production takes place in the western and northwestern provinces of Mendoza, San Juan, and Salta, but it's increasing in the southerly Patagonian province of Río Negro.

Tinto is red wine, while *blanco* is white. Good wine is almost always reasonably priced, even during times of high inflation. The best restaurants have a wide selection, usually in full bottles though sometimes it's possible to get a *media botella* (half bottle) or, increasingly frequently, wine by the glass. Argentines often mix their table wines—even reds—with soda water or ice.

An increasing number of wine bars also offer Spanish tapas, sushi, and other light meals. Keep an eye out for Torrontés, a unique Argentine variety from the vineyards around Cafayate, in Salta Province. Wine tourism is popular here and in the Cuyo provinces of Mendoza and San Juan.

For more information on Southern Cone wines and wineries, look for Christopher Fielden's *The Wines of Argentina, Chile, and Latin America* (New York: Faber and Faber, 2001), though it doesn't account for some recent developments. Harm de Blij's *Wine Regions of the Southern Hemisphere* (Rowman and Littlefield, 1985) is a more intellectually sophisticated overview.

While Argentine wines are more than worthwhile, Argentines themselves are leaning more toward beer, which tastes best as *chopp,* direct from the tap, rather than from bottles or cans. The most widely available beer is Quilmes, produced in its namesake suburb across the Riachuelo from La Boca.

Hard liquor is not quite so popular, but whiskey, gin, and the like are readily available. *Ginebra bols* (differing from gin) and *caña* (cane alcohol) are local specialties.

Argentina's legal drinking age is 18.

Getting There

Most overseas visitors arrive in Argentina by air, mostly at Buenos Aires, but smaller regional airports get some of this traffic. Many also arrive overland from Chile, Bolivia, Uruguay, Paraguay, and Brazil. Almost all of the latter arrive by bus or private vehicle; there is no international rail service. There are ferry connections to Uruguay.

BY AIR

Buenos Aires has regular air links with North America, Europe, and Australia/New Zealand, plus less frequent routes from southern Africa across the Atlantic (some via Brazil). It is, however, a relatively expensive destination during peak periods such as the Christmas/New Year's and Holy Week holidays; an Advance Purchase Excursion (Apex) fare can reduce the bite considerably, but may have minimum- and maximum-stay requirements, allow no stopovers, and impose financial penalties for any changes. Economy-class (Y) tickets, valid for 12 months, are more expensive but allow maximum flexibility. Travelers staying more than a year, though, have to cough up the difference for any interim price increases.

Discount ticket agents known as consolidators in the United States and "bucket shops" in Britain may offer the best deals through so-called "bulk fares," but they often have other drawbacks—they may not, for instance, allow mileage credit for frequent-flyer programs. Courier flights, on which passengers surrender some or all of their baggage allowance to a company sending equipment or documents to overseas affiliates or customers may be even cheaper, but are less common to Latin America than to other parts of the world. They are available for short periods only, and often leave on short notice.

Other options include Round the World (RTW) and Circle Pacific routes that permit numerous stopovers over the course of much longer multicontinental trips, but putting these itineraries together requires some effort. Two useful resources for researching airfares and many other aspects of international travel are the third edition of Edward Hasbrouck's *The Practical Nomad* (Avalon Travel Publishing, 2004) and the same author's *The Practical Nomad Guide to the Online Marketplace* (Avalon Travel Publishing, 2001).

Many airlines reduced their services to Argentina after the economic collapse of 2001–02, as debt default and devaluation meant far fewer Argentines could splurge on overseas travel. Some, however, are restoring and even expanding services as devaluation has made the country a travel bargain for foreigners. Likewise, the Argentine market had been less attractive to foreign business travelers, but this also is changing.

From North America

Miami; Washington, D.C. (Dulles); New York; Chicago; Dallas; and Los Angeles are the main gateways to Buenos Aires; Canadian passengers may also use Toronto.

Aerolíneas Argentinas is the traditional carrier, but other options include American Airlines, Copa, LanChile, Lloyd Aéreo Boliviano, Mexicana, Southern Winds, Transportes Aéreos Mercosur (TAM), United Airlines, and Varig. Aerolíneas Argentinas, American, and United have the only nonstop or direct services; others require changing planes elsewhere in Central or South America.

Air Canada has recently begun flights from Toronto to Buenos Aires, three or four times per week, which for non-Canadians avoids the hassle of getting a U.S. visa just for transit purposes.

From Mexico, Central America, and the Caribbean

Mexicana flies daily except Sunday from Mexico City. Lloyd Aéreo Boliviano and Varig also fly to and from Mexico, but less directly.

Cubana flies daily from Havana, while Avianca has connections to the Caribbean, Central America, and Mexico via Bogotá.

Copa flies daily from Panama, with connections throughout the region.

INTERNATIONAL AIRLINES IN BUENOS AIRES

Unless otherwise indicated, the addresses below are in the Microcentro and vicinity.

Aerolíneas Argentinas: Perú 2, Monserrat, tel. 011/4340-7777

AeroMéxico: Esmeralda 1063, 9th floor, Retiro, tel. 011/4315-1936

AeroSur: Avenida Santa Fe 851, 1st floor, tel. 011/4516-0999

Air Canada: Avenida Córdoba 656, tel. 011/4327-3640

Air France: San Martín 344, 23rd floor, tel. 011/4317-4700

Air New Zealand: Marcelo T. de Alvear 590, 10th floor, Retiro, tel. 011/4315-5494

Alitalia: Suipacha 1111, 28th floor, Retiro, tel. 011/4310-9999

American Airlines: Avenida Santa Fe 881, Retiro, tel. 011/4318-1111

American Falcon: Avenida Santa Fe 963, 4th floor, Retiro, tel. 011/4393-5700

Avianca: Carlos Pellegrini 1163, 4th floor, Retiro, tel. 011/4394-5990

British Airways: Carlos Pellegrini 1163, tel. 011/4320-6600

Copa/Continental: Carlos Pellegrini 989, 2nd floor, Retiro, tel. 011/4132-3535

Cubana de Aviación: Sarmiento 552, 11th floor, tel. 011/4326-5291

Delta: Reconquista 737, 3rd floor, tel. 011/4312-1200

Iberia: Carlos Pellegrini 1163, 1st floor, Retiro, tel. 011/4131-1000

KLM: Suipacha 268, 9th floor, tel. 011/4326-8422

LanChile: Cerrito 866, Retiro, tel. 011/4378-2200

Lloyd Aéreo Boliviano (LAB): Carlos Pellegrini 141, 2nd floor, tel. 011/4323-1900

Lufthansa: Marcelo T. de Alvear 636, Retiro, tel. 011/4319-0600

Mexicana: Avenida Córdoba 755, 1st floor, Retiro, tel. 011/4000-6300

Pluna: Florida 1, tel. 011/4342-4420

Qantas: Avenida Córdoba 673, 13th floor, Retiro, tel. 011/4514-4726

South African Airways: Carlos Pellegrini 1141, 5th floor, Retiro, tel. 011/5556-6666

Southern Winds: Avenida Santa Fe 784, Retiro, 011/4515-8600

Swiss International: Avenida Santa Fe 846, 1st floor, Retiro, tel. 011/4319-0000

Taca: Carlos Pellegrini 1275, Retiro, tel. 011/4325-8222

Transportes Aéreos de Mercosur (TAM): Cerrito 1026, Retiro, tel. 011/4819-4800

United Airlines: Avenida Eduardo Madero 900, 9th floor, Retiro, tel. 0810/777-8648

Varig: Avenida Córdoba 972, 3rd floor, Retiro, tel. 011/4329-9211

From Europe

From Europe, there are direct services to Buenos Aires with Aerolíneas Argentinas (from Rome and Madrid); Air Europa (from Madrid); Air France (from Paris); Alitalia (from Milan and Rome); British Airways (from London); Iberia (from Barcelona and Madrid); KLM (from Amsterdam); Lufthansa (from Frankfurt via São Paulo); Southern Winds (from Madrid); and Swiss International (from Geneva and Zurich). TAM has connections from Paris via São Paulo.

From Asia, Africa, and the Pacific

The most direct service from the Pacific is Aerolíneas Argentinas's twice-weekly service from Sydney via Auckland. From Australia, Qantas links up with LanChile flights via Tahiti, Easter Island, and Santiago, or with LanChile via Los Angeles. Air New Zealand also links up with LanChile. From Japan, it's easiest to make connections via Los Angeles.

South African Airways flies five times weekly from Johannesburg to São Paulo, where TAM and Varig offer connections to Buenos Aires.

Within South America

Buenos Aires has connections to neighboring republics of Uruguay, Brazil, Paraguay, Bolivia, and Chile, and elsewhere on the continent as well. There are no flights to the Guyanas, however.

Some major international airlines fly to and from Ezeiza to Montevideo, Uruguay, but most flights to the Uruguayan capital leave from close-in Aeroparque. There are also flights from Aeroparque to Punta del Este, Uruguay's popular summer resort and weekend getaway. Aerolíneas Argentinas and Pluna are the main carriers, but American Falcon and Aerovip also have a few flights.

To Brazil, the main destinations are São Paulo and Rio de Janeiro, but there are also flights to Florianópolis and Porto Alegre, with connections to other cities. The main carriers are Aerolíneas Argentinas, TAM, and Varig.

Paraguay-bound flights go mostly to the capital city of Asunción, with Aerolíneas Argenti-

nas, TAM, and Varig; some TAM flights go to Ciudad del Este, however, and on to Brazil.

Lloyd Aéreo Boliviano flies to the lowland Bolivian city of Santa Cruz de la Sierra and on to the highland capital of La Paz, while AeroSur flies three times weekly to Santa Cruz, Cochabamba, and La Paz. Aerolíneas also flies to Santa Cruz, while TAM has connections to Santa Cruz and Cochabamba via Asunción.

Discounted fares are less common in Latin America than North America; the main exception is the highly competitive Buenos Aires–Santiago de Chile route, where European carriers like Air France and Lufthansa try to fill empty seats between Chile and the Argentine capital, where most trans-Atlantic passengers board or disembark. This has kept fares low on competitors like Aerolíneas Argentinas and LanChile as well.

LanChile also has flights to Mendoza, Córdoba, and Rosario, and to the northern Patagonian city of Bariloche. American Falcon may begin flights from Santiago to Mendoza.

Flights to Peru, Ecuador, Colombia, and Venezuela are all via capital cities, though some carriers stop elsewhere en route. Aerolíneas Argentinas goes to Lima and Caracas, Grupo Taca to Lima en route to Mexico City, and Avianca to Bogotá.

OVERLAND
From North America, Mexico, and Central America

Overland travel from North America or elsewhere is problematic because Panama's Darien Gap to Colombia is impassable for motor vehicles, time-consuming, and very difficult and potentially dangerous even for those on foot. The route passes through areas controlled by drug smugglers, guerrillas, and/or brutal Colombian paramilitaries.

Those visiting other parts of the continent and remaining for an extended period may want to consider shipping a vehicle. To locate a shipper, check the Yellow Pages of your local phone directory under Automobile Transporters, who are normally freight consolidators rather than the company that owns the ship, which will charge higher container rates. Since many more people ship vehicles to Europe than to South America, finding the right shipper may take patience; one reliable U.S. consolidator is **McClary, Swift & Co.** (360 Swift Avenue, South San Francisco, CA 94080, tel. 650/872-2121, mcclaryswift @unitedshipping.com, www.unitedshipping .com/offices/partners/mcclary.php), which has affiliates at many U.S. ports.

Argentine bureaucracy has improved in recent years, and clearing customs with a vehicle is simpler than it used to be. Vehicles arrive at the **Estación Marítima Buenos Aires** (Dársena B, Avenida Ramón Castillo y Avenida Maipú, Retiro, tel. 011/4311-0692, 011/4317-0675, or 011/4312-8677); here it is necessary to present your passport, vehicle title, and the original *conocimiento de embarque* (bill of lading), and to fill out a customs application. You will then obtain an appointment with a customs inspector to retrieve the vehicle, which will cost about US$300 for port costs and another US$200 for the shipper; if the vehicle has been in port longer than five days, there will be additional charges. The vehicle can remain in Argentina legally for eight months, with an eight-month extension possible; any visit to a neighboring country restarts the clock. In event of any difficulty, consult a private *despachante de aduana* (customs broker), such as **José Angel Vidal Labra** (tel. 011/4345-7887, vidla@sinectis.com.ar).

Another possibility is Chile, whose ports are less bureaucratic and safer for the vehicle than those of Argentina. The most probable ports of entry are San Antonio, southwest of Santiago, and Valparaíso, northwest of the capital. It does pay to be there within a couple of days of the vehicle's arrival, or storage charges can mount up. Leave the gas tank as nearly empty as possible (for safety's sake) and leave no valuables, including tools, inside.

To arrange a shipment from San Antonio or Valparaíso, contact the Santiago consolidator **Ultramar** (Moneda 970, 18th floor, Santiago Centro, tel. 2/63001817, fax 2/6986552, italia @ultramar.cl). For a trustworthy customs agent to handle the paperwork, contact the office of **Juan Alarcón Rojas** (Fidel Oteíza 1921, 12th floor,

Providencia, Santiago, tel. 02/2252780, fax 02/2045302, alrcon@entelchile.net); Chile's country code is 56.

Bicycles, of course, can be partially dismantled, packaged, and easily shipped aboard airplanes, sometimes for no additional charge. Except that there is rarely any additional paperwork for bringing a bike into the country, many of the same cautions apply as to any other overland travel.

From Neighboring South American Countries

Argentina has numerous border crossings with Chile, a few with Bolivia and Paraguay, many with Brazil, and a few with Uruguay. Relatively few of the Chilean crossings have scheduled public transportation, nor do those with Bolivia, but the Paraguayan, Brazilian, and Uruguayan borders are heavily transited.

International bus service is available from the neighboring republics, and also from more-distant destinations such as Peru, Ecuador, and Colombia.

Both international and domestic bus services normally have comfortable reclining seats (with every passenger guaranteed a seat), clean toilets, a/c, and meals and refreshments served on board, at least on the longest trips. If not, they make regular meal stops. Between Santiago and Mendoza, there are *taxi colectivos,* shared taxis that are slightly more expensive but faster than full-size buses.

From the settlements of San Pedro de Atacama and Calama in Northern Chile, there are buses to Salta and Jujuy via the Paso de Jama, which is smoothly paved on the Chilean side and should be completed on the Argentine side before the next edition of this book. The busiest crossing, though, is the Los Libertadores tunnel between Mendoza and Santiago. There are summer buses only from Talca to Malargüe over the 2,553-meter Paso del Maule (also known as the Paso Pehuenche).

In northern Patagonia, there are buses from Temuco to Neuquén over the 1,884-meter Paso de Pino Hachado via Curacautín and Lonquimay; the alternative 1,298-meter Paso de Icalma is slightly to the south. There is also a regular bus service from Temuco to San Martín de los Andes via the Paso de Mamuil Malal (Paso Tromen to Argentines); a bus-boat combination from Panguipulli to San Martín de los Andes via the 659-meter Paso Huahum and Lago Pirehueico; a paved highway from Osorno to Bariloche via the Paso de Cardenal Samoré that's the second-busiest crossing between the two countries; and the scenic bus-boat shuttle from Puerto Montt and Puerto Varas to Bariloche.

There are many southern Patagonian crossings, but the roads are often bad and only a few have public transportation. Those served by scheduled transport include the mostly gravel road from Futaleufú, Chile, to Esquel (local buses only); Coyhaique to Comodoro Rivadavia on a mostly paved road via Río Mayo on comfortable long-distance coaches; Chile Chico to Los Antiguos to Los Antiguos (shuttles with onward connections in either direction; Puerto Natales to El Calafate via Río Turbio on a steadily improving but mostly gravel route; Punta Arenas to Río Gallegos via an almost entirely paved highway with one brutal stretch on the Argentine side; and Punta Arenas to Ushuaia and Río Grande.

In addition, many border crossings are suitable for private motor vehicles and mountain bikes, and a few by foot.

There are three major crossings to Bolivia in northernmost Argentina, the most important of which is the walk-across from Villazón to La Quiaca, on RN 9 in Jujuy Province. The other two are in Salta Province, at Aguas Blancas (on RN 50 from Tarija, Bolivia) and Pocitos (from Yacuiba and Santa Cruz de la Sierra), on RN 34.

At the confluence of the Río Pilcomayo and the Río Paraguay, the Formosa Province border town of Clorinda sits directly across from Asunción, the capital of Paraguay. There are several minor border crossings along the Río Paraguay and the Río Paraná, but the only other major

one is the Misiones provincial capital of Posadas, opposite the smaller Paraguayan city of Encarnación. In both major crossings, bridges connect the two countries.

One of the continent's most important border zones is the controversial *Triple Frontera* at the confluence of the Río Paraná and the Río Iguazú, where Argentina, Brazil, and Paraguay converge in northernmost Misiones Province. A bridge connects Argentina's Puerto Iguazú with Foz do Iguaçu in 7   In addition to several minor river crossings, there are two major highway bridges over the Río Uruguay in Corrientes Province: between Santo Tomé and the Brazilian town of São Borja, and between Paso de los Libres and the larger Brazilian city of Uruguaiana.

From Uruguay, there are three highway bridges over the Río Uruguay into Entre Ríos Province: between Gualeguaychú and the Uruguayan town of Fray Bentos, between Colón and the Uruguayan city of Paysandú, and between Concordia and the Uruguayan city of Salto.

BY BOAT

From Buenos Aires, there are ferry connections across the river to the Uruguayan capital of Montevideo, but also to the resort town of Piriápolis (in summer only) and to the charming 18th-century town of Colonia. From the suburban river port of Tigre, there are launches to the Uruguayan river ports of Carmelo and Nueva Palmira.

In addition, there is the popular and scenic but increasingly expensive bus-boat-bus route between Bariloche and the Chilean city of Puerto Montt, and a relatively short cruise (three days plus) that carries passengers between Punta Arenas (Chile) and Ushuaia.

Getting Around

BY AIR

In addition to international air service, Argentina has a wide network of domestic airports and a handful of airlines centered on Buenos Aires; indeed, to fly between Argentine cities, more often than not it's unavoidable to change planes in BA. Most of these use Aeroparque Jorge Newbery, the city airport, but some use the international airport at Ezeiza.

Aerolíneas Argentinas has domestic as well as international flights, while its affiliate Austral (the distinction between the two is dubious) serves exclusively Argentine destinations from Jujuy and Puerto Iguazú in the north to Ushuaia in Tierra del Fuego.

Other domestic airlines come and go, with the exception of Líneas Aéreas del Estado (LADE, www.lade.com.ar), the air force's heavily subsidized commercial-aviation branch. Miraculously surviving budget crises and privatizations, it flies to southern Buenos Aires Province and out-of-the-way Patagonian destinations on a wing and a prayer.

Other private airlines have consistently failed. At the moment, the most viable alternative airline is Southern Winds (www.sw.com.ar), which serves destinations ranging from Puerto Iguazú and Salta in the north to Mendoza in the west to Neuquén, Bariloche, and El Calafate in the south.

American Falcon (www.americanfalcon.com.ar) flies from Aeroparque to Salta, Tucumán, Puerto Iguazú, and the Patagonian resort of Bariloche. Aerovip flies 19-seater planes from its Aeroparque hub to Mar del Plata, Tandil, Rosario, and Paraná.

Fares

Air fares fell with the devaluation of 2002 and have remained reasonable, though foreigners are not eligible for discount fares available to Argentine citizens and residents. This means, in effect, that foreigners are paying full Y-class fares, but this also means greater flexibility in purchasing one-way *cabotaje* tickets and "open jaws"

routes that land at one city and return from another, and to mix and match airlines. There are also "Visit Argentina" air passes.

Sample Aerolíneas Argentinas/Austral destinations, with one-way fares from Aeroparque, include Bariloche (US$127), Córdoba (US$71), El Calafate (US$92), Puerto Iguazú (US$91), Mar del Plata (US$50), Mendoza (US$92), Salta (US$111), Trelew (US$85), and Ushuaia (US$107). These fares do not include airport taxes (about US$5 per ticket), nor the 10.5 percent Value-Added Tax (IVA) on domestic flights.

Available only in conjunction with international travel to Buenos Aires, Aerolíneas Argentinas's "Visit Argentina" pass includes three coupons, each valid for one numbered flight. If the international travel is with Aerolíneas, the cost is US$300, with additional coupons for US$125 each; with other international airlines, the cost is US$400, plus US$165 for each additional coupon. Only foreigners and nonresident Argentines are eligible for these passes, which require considerable planning to eke out maximum advantage.

Southern Winds has slightly lower fares, with no discount fares for Argentines. LADE, which flies smaller, older planes and makes many stops, is known for bargain-basement fares; from Buenos Aires, for instance, Mar del Plata costs only US$40, Bariloche US$94. It is also known, though, for unreliability in making and honoring reservations and keeping to its schedules.

BY BUS

Buses along the principal highways, and those connecting other main cities and resorts, are frequent and almost invariably spacious and comfortable, sometimes even luxurious. A few on backroad routes are only a little better than Central American "chicken buses," and they may be infrequent, but distances are relatively short.

So-called Pullman buses have reclining seats, and for short to medium runs, say up to seven hours, they're more than adequate. Seats are guaranteed. For truly long distances, some travelers prefer the more spacious *servicio diferencial* or *coche cama* service, which provides greater leg room in seats that recline almost horizontally. Fares are very reasonable by international standards—the 16-hour trip from Buenos Aires to Puerto Iguazú costs only about US$30 in *coche cama,* including onboard and/or roadside meal service. A comparable fare for the 23-hour trip to Bariloche, in northern Patagonia, is less than US$50.

Most cities have a central *terminal de buses* (bus terminal), but in a few places there are multiple terminals for long-distance, regional, and rural services, or for individual companies. Some companies also have separate ticket offices in more-central locations than the terminals themselves.

Bus services are so frequent that reservations are rarely necessary except for a few infrequently traveled routes and some international services, or during holiday periods like *Semana Santa* (Holy Week), Christmas/New Year's, and occasionally during the January/February summer vacation season. Note also that fares rise and fall with demand, depending on the season.

BY TRAIN

Once the primary mode of interurban transportation, domestic rail service is now limited to a handful of long-distance domestic services, mostly to the Atlantic beach resorts of southern Buenos Aires Province but also to Rosario, Tucumán, and Posadas. There is also service between the Río Negro provincial capital of Viedma and the resort city of Bariloche.

Schedules, though, are infrequent, the trains are mostly slow, and high demand from impoverished Argentines makes reservations essential, often far in advance. Fares are low—only US$7–10 pp for the 404 kilometers from Constitución to Mar del Plata, for instance, and US$12–21 pp for the 1,200 kilometers from Retiro (Buenos Aires) to Tucumán.

The best long-distance line is the one between Constitución (Buenos Aires) and Mar del Plata. This route, perhaps the only line in the country that could be justified on economic grounds, may see a high-speed upgrade.

In addition to regular passenger trains, there are also tourist excursions, including Salta's popular Tren a las Nubes (Train to the Clouds) and the narrow-gauge La Trochita, in Río Negro and Chubut Provinces; the latter was immortalized in Paul Theroux's overrated bestseller *The Old Patagonian Express.*

See Local Transportation later in this section for information on suburban and long-distance trains.

BY CAR OR MOTORYCLE

Driving in Argentina, especially in Buenos Aires, is not for the timid. In the words of *Buenos Aires Herald* columnist Martín Gambarotta, this is a country "where pedestrians and not cars have to stop at a zebra crossing." According to United Nations statistics, the traffic death rate of 25 per 100,000 is South America's highest, nearly twice that of Chile and the United States, and almost three times that of Germany.

According to another *Herald* article, "Argentines' penchant for speed—evident in many urban drivers who weave in and out of fast-moving city traffic for no evident reasons, and in the yearly death toll that makes their roads among the most dangerous in the world—is reflected by their veneration of Formula One race car drivers like the legendary Juan Manuel Fangio and Carlos Reutemann, the former governor of Santa Fe." In 2002, Buenos Aires provincial governor Felipe Solá named RN 2, the Buenos Aires–Mar del Plata freeway, in honor of Fangio, and the YPF oil company has named its highest-octane fuel for the famous racer.

Argentine highways are divided into *rutas nacionales* (abbreviated here as RN, for which the federal government is responsible), and *rutas provincials* (RP, which each province maintains). Generally, but not necessarily, the federal highways are better maintained; the exception is prosperous provinces like Santa Cruz, which has large royalty revenues from oil.

Speed limits on most highways are generally around 100 km/hour, but 120 km/hour on four-lane divided roads. Officially, helmets are obligatory for motorcyclists, but enforcement is lax, especially in the cities. The most thickheaded riders appear to believe their skulls are strong enough, but emergency-room statistics have proved them wrong.

Vehicle Documents, Driver's License, and Equipment

Most South American countries, including Argentina, Chile, Uruguay, and Brazil, have dispensed with the cumbersome *Carnet de Passage en Douanes* that required depositing a large bond in order to import a motor vehicle. Officials at the port of arrival or border post will usually issue a 90-day permit on presentation of the vehicle title, registration, bill of lading (if the vehicle is being shipped), and your passport. For shipped vehicles, there are some fairly substantial port charges (which rise rapidly if the vehicle has been stored more than a few days).

Before traveling to Argentina, obtain an International or Interamerican Driving Permit (visitors to Uruguay should note that that country officially recognizes only the latter, though in practice they appear more flexible). These permits are available through the American Automobile Association, (AAA) or its counterpart in your home country, and are normally valid for one calendar year from date of issue. Strictly speaking, they are not valid without a state or national driver's license, but Argentine police usually ignore the latter. Legally, another form of identification, such as national ID card or passport, is also necessary.

The police, though, pay close attention to vehicle documents—*tarjeta verde* ("green card") registration for Argentine vehicles, customs permission for foreign ones—and liability insurance (though many Argentines drive without it, it is reasonably priced from the Automóvil Club Argentino, the national automobile club, and other insurers). Vehicles without registration may be impounded on the spot. Argentine vehicles should have proof of a *verificación técnica* (safety inspection).

At roadside checkpoints, the police are also rigid about obligatory equipment such as headrests for the driver and each passenger, *valizas*

(triangular emergency reflectors), and *matafuegos* (one-kilo fire extinguishers). Headrests are imperative for the driver and each passenger. In any instance of document irregularity or minor equipment violation, provincial police in particular may threaten fines while really soliciting *coimas* (bribes). A firm but calm suggestion that you intend to call your consulate may help overcome any difficulty.

Road Hazards

Argentine traffic is fast and ruthless, many roads are narrow with little or no shoulder, and others are poorly surfaced or potholed. Heavy truck traffic can make all these routes dangerous, and not just because of excess speed—impatient Argentine drivers will often try to pass in dangerous situations, and head-on crashes are disturbingly common, even between passenger buses.

Porteño drivers in the city and stray cattle in the provinces might seem to be enough to deal with, but the economic crisis of 2001–02 led to a major increase of *piquetes* (roadblocks) of demonstrators protesting unemployment and other issues. *Piqueteros* (pickets), though they tend to focus on stopping commercial traffic, manage to slow down everything else as well; never try to run one of these roadblocks, which can raise the wrath of the pickets. Rather, try to show solidarity and, in all likelihood, you'll pass without incident. The poor northern provinces of Jujuy and Salta were hotbeds of picket activity.

Note that members of the American Automobile Association (AAA), Britain's Automobile Association (AA), and similar foreign automobile clubs are often eligible for limited roadside assistance and towing through the Automóvil Club Argentina (www.aca.org.ar), which has affiliates in most major cities and many smaller ones.

Unleaded fuel is available everywhere, though some older vehicles still use leaded. In remote areas where gas stations are few, carry additional fuel.

Expenses

Prior to devaluation, Argentina had some of the most expensive gasoline in the Americas except for Uruguay, but prices have fallen in dollar terms—

at least temporarily, even as they rose in peso terms. Buenos Aires prices are about US$.58 per liter for regular, US$.64 for super, and US$.67 for Fangio. *Gasoil* (diesel) is typically cheaper than gasoline, about US$.46 per liter, but the differential is shrinking. Because gasoline prices are unregulated, they may rise quickly.

Note, however, that so-called "Patagonian prices" south of Sierra Grande on RN 3 and El Bolsón on RN 40 are more than one-third cheaper for gasoline; there is no price differential, though, for diesel.

Repairs are cheap in terms of labor, but can be expensive in terms of parts, many of which must be imported. Fortunately, Argentine mechanics are skilled at rehabilitating virtually any salvageable part.

Car Rental

Aggressive drivers, traffic congestion, and lack of parking make driving in Buenos Aires inadvisable, but beyond the capital a vehicle can be very useful, especially in the wide-open spaces of northwestern Argentina or Patagonia. To rent a car, you must show a valid driver's license and credit card, and be at least 21 years old.

Both local and international agencies maintain offices in Buenos Aires, where rental costs are typically lower than elsewhere in the country but higher than in North America. Since the devaluation of 2002, prices are more volatile, but they usually involve a fixed daily amount plus a per-kilometer charge; unlimited-mileage deals are normally for weekly or longer periods. Insurance is additional.

It is also possible to rent camper vehicles and motorhomes in Buenos Aires and Patagonia through **Gaibu Motorhome Time** (Florida 716, 6° A, Buenos Aires, tel. 011/4322-0075, fax 011/4393/ 8649, informes@gaibu.com, www.gaibu.com).

BY BICYCLE

For the physically fit or those intending to become physically fit, cycling can be an ideal way to see the country. Because so many roads are unpaved in the most scenic areas, a *todo terreno* (mountain bike) is a much better choice than a

touring bike. Cyclists should know basic mechanics, though the increasing availability of mountain bikes within the country means that parts and mechanics are easier to find than they once were. In an emergency, it's easy to put a bicycle onboard a bus.

Some cyclists dislike the main Argentine highways because their narrowness, coupled with fast drivers and the lack of shoulders, can make them unsafe. There are many alternative routes with less traffic, though, and some really interesting ones, such as RN 9 between Salta and Jujuy, and RP 52 from Uspallata to Mendoza. Patagonian roads, such as coastal RN 3 and the interior RN 40, can be difficult because of high winds.

BY ORGANIZED TOUR

Because of Argentina's complex travel logistics, organized tours can be a useful option for visitors with limited time, and many reputable U.S. and Argentine operators offer and even coordinate tours. Sometimes these take in sights in neighboring countries, usually Chile but sometimes Uruguay or Brazil. Within each category, the companies listed here appear in alphabetical order.

United States–Based Operators

The **American Geographical Society** (P.O. Box 938, 47 Main St., Suite One, Walpole NH 03608-0938, tel. 888/805-0884, fax 603/756-2922, agstravl@sover.net, www.amergeog.org) operates a 17-day luxury cruise through southernmost Patagonia and Tierra del Fuego and on to the Falkland Islands; its only Argentine stop is at Ushuaia, but it visits several other areas covered in this book, primarily in Chile. Rates start at US$6,285 pp, based on double occupancy, including airfare from Miami.

Primarily but not exclusively for cyclists, **Backroads** (801 Cedar St, Berkeley, CA 94710, 510/ 527-1555 or 800/462-2848, fax 510/527-1444, www.backroads.com) offers an 11-day "Chile & Argentina Hiking" tour that takes in Bariloche and vicinity, along with Chile's Lago Llanquihue area, for US$3,998 pp. Their nine-day "Patagonian Walking" trip includes stays at luxury lodgings in Chile's Parque Nacional Torres del Paine and Argentina's Parque Nacional Los Glaciares; rates are US$5,298 pp.

For travelers at least 55 years of age, **Elderhostel** (11 Avenue de Lafayette, Boston, MA 02111, tel. 877/426-8056, registration@elderhostel.org, www.elderhostel.org), operates a variety of two-week trips to Patagonia, the Argentine and Chilean wine country, and the Iguazú Falls area of Argentina and Brazil, as well as parts of Uruguay and Paraguay.

Nature Expeditions International (7860 Peters Road, Suite F-103, Plantation, FL 33324, 954/693-8852 or 800/869-0639, fax 954/693-8854, naturexp@aol.com, www.naturexp.com) operates upscale "soft adventure" and culture-oriented tours to the Southern Cone countries of Argentina and Chile, among other destinations. A 16-day Chilean trip taking in Santiago, Valparaíso, Puerto Varas, Bariloche, El Calafate, and Buenos Aires starts at US$4,425 pp, while a 21-day Brazil/Argentina trip includes Manaus, Rio de Janeiro, Paratí, Iguazú Falls, Buenos Aires, El Calafate, and Bariloche.

Orvis (1711 Blue Hills Drive, Roanoke VA 24012-8613, tel. 888/235-9783, fax 540/343-7053, vacations@orvis.com, www.orvis.com) arranges fishing holidays in the vicinity of northern Patagonia's Junín de los Andes, southern Patagonia's Río Gallegos, and the Argentine side of Tierra del Fuego.

Powderquest Tours (7108 Pinetree Rd., Richmond, VA 23229, 804/285-4961 or 888/565-7158, fax 240/209-4312, info@powderquest.com, www.powderquest.com) runs five or six nine- to 13-day Southern Cone ski tours annually. Las Leñas, Chapelco, Cerro Bayo, and Cerro Catedral (Ladera Sur) are the Argentine resorts included; on the Chilean side, stops may include Portillo, Valle Nevado, and Termas de Chillán.

REI Adventures (P.O. Box 1938, Sumner, WA 98390-1938, tel. 800/622-2236, travel@rei.com, www.rei.com) offers a 10-day multisport tour of the Argentine and Chilean lake district for US$2,095 pp; it also works in Torres del Paine on the Chilean side.

Affiliated with the Smithsonian Institution, **Smithsonian Journeys** (P.O. Box 23293, Washington, D.C. 20026-3293, 202/357-4700 or 877/338-8687, reservations@smithsonianjourneys.org, www.smithsonianjourneys.org) offers a 13-day "Patagonian Andes" excursion, about equally split between Argentina and Chile, for US$4,995 pp. It also does a 14-day trip, "From the Vineyards of Mendoza to the Atacama Desert," via northwestern Argentina and across the Andes to Chile's San Pedro de Atacama (US$5,675 pp).

Wilderness Travel (1102 Ninth Street, Berkeley, CA 94710, 510/558-2488 or 800/368-2794, fax 510/558-2849, www.wildernesstravel.com) offers a variety of trips focused primarily on Patagonia, including the 16-day "In Patagonia" excursion that focuses mostly on Argentina but also visits Torres del Paine, starting at US$4,295 pp; and the 15-day "Peaks of Patagonia" that takes in Torres del Paine and Argentina's Glaciar Moreno and Fitz Roy areas starting at US$3,595 pp.

Wildland Adventures (3516 NE 155th St, Seattle, WA 98155, 800/345-4453, fax 206/363-6615, info@wildland.com, www.wildland.com) operates small group tours (two to eight persons) through locally based guides. In Argentina, their 10-day "Best of Patagonia" takes in Glaciar Moreno and other sights via Buenos Aires for US$2,325 pp. The 14-day "In the Wake of Magellan" trip (from US$4,290) includes both Torres del Paine and a segment of the scenic luxury cruise between Punta Arenas and Ushuaia, as well as Argentina's Glaciar Moreno.

UK-Based Operators

Explore Worldwide (1 Frederick St., Aldershot, Hants. GU11 1LQ, tel. 01252/760000, info @exploreworldwide.com, www.exploreworldwide.com) organizes 16- to 22-day tours primarily to Patagonia and the lake district of Argentina and Chile.

Journey Latin America (12/13 Heathfield Terrace, Chiswick, London W4 2JU, tel. 020/8747-3108, fax 020/8742-1312, www.journeylatinamerica.co.uk) specializes in small-group tours throughout Latin America, including Argentina.

Australia-Based Operators

Peregrine Adventures (258 Lonsdale St., Melbourne, Victoria 3000, tel. 03/9662-2700, fax 03/9662-2422, websales@peregrineadventures.com, www.peregrineadventures.com) organizes tours to the lake district and southern Patagonia.

World Expeditions (71 York St., Level 5, Sydney, NSW 2000, tel. 02/9279-0188, fax 02/9279-1974, enquiries@worldexpeditions.com.au, www.worldexpeditions.com.au), one of Australia's biggest operators, has a variety of tours to Patagonia and elsewhere in Argentina. It also has branches in Melbourne (393 Little Bourke St., Melbourne, Victoria 3000, tel. 03/9670-8400, fax 03/9670-7474, travel@worldexpeditions.com.au) and Brisbane (36 Agnes Street, Shop 2, Fortitude Valley, Queensland 4006 (tel. 07/3216-0823, fax 07/3216-0827, adventure@worldexpeditions.com.au).

Argentina-Based Operators

The operators below invariably have English-speaking personnel and have services in many parts of Argentina. Many locally focused operators, though, have very good services as well.

The Buenos Aires-based **Asatej Group** (Florida 835, Oficina 205, tel. 011/4114-7600, www.asatej.com) is Argentina's youth- and budget-oriented operator, which has refocused on incoming tourism since the peso collapse of early 2002.

Salta-based **Clark Expediciones** (Caseros 121, Salta, tel. 0387/421-5390, clark@clarkexpediciones.com, www.clarkexpediciones.com) is a bird-watching specialist but also does more-general natural history and hiking tours.

Bariloche-based **Meridies** (info@meridies.com.ar, www.meridies.com.ar) is primarily an adventure-oriented climbing company that does strenuous trips like Volcán Lanín and Cerro Aconcagua, but it also does a week-long driving and hiking trip along the southern portion of RN 40 ("La Cuarenta") in Patagonia.

Buenos Aires–based **Sendero Sur** (Perú 359, Oficina 608, Monserrat, tel./fax 011/4343-1571, www.senderosur.com.ar) does a series of activity-oriented trips that include cycling in the Argentine and Chilean lake districts, visits to Patagonian *estancias,* and hiking in and around Parque Nacional Los Glaciares and Ushuaia.

Chile-Based Operators

Several Chilean-based operators figure in Chilean Patagonia and Tierra del Fuego, and some of them also work the Argentine side of the border. Chile's country code is 56.

Big Foot Adventure Patagonia (Bories 206, Puerto Natales, tel. 061/414611, fax 061/414276, explore@bigfootpatagonia.com, www.bigfootpatagonia.com) operates activities-oriented trips to Patagonia, mostly but not exclusively in Parque Nacional Torres del Paine, where it has concessions for activities like ice hiking, kayaking, and mountaineering. It offers a diverse set of packages ranging from four days/three nights to 13 days/12 nights for US$690 to US$1,900 pp, depending on the number of passengers. Its U.S. affiliate is **Americas Travel** (348 Hayes St., San Francisco, CA 94102-4421, tel. 415/703-9955, fax 415/703-9959, info@americastravel.net, www.americastravel.net).

From October to April, **Cruceros Australis** (Avenida Bosque Norte 0440, 11th floor, Las Condes, Santiago, tel. 02/4423110, fax 02/2035173, www.australis.com), offers three-, four-, and seven-day cruises through the fjords of southern Tierra del Fuego and Cape Horn on its luxury liner *Mare Australis.* Rates vary throughout the season, which runs from October through April. Cruceros Australis also has offices in Buenos Aires (Carlos Pellegrini 989, Retiro, tel. 011/4325-8400, fax 011/4325-6600) and in Miami (4014 Chase Ave. Suite 202, Miami Beach, FL 33140, 305/695-9618 or 877/678-3772, fax 305/534-9276). For more information see The Fjords of Fuegia section in the Tierra del Fuego and Chilean Patagonia chapter.

Explora Hotels (Américo Vespucio Sur 80, 5th floor, Las Condes, Santiago, tel. 56/2-2066060, fax 56/2284655, reservexplora@explora-chile.cl, www.explora.com) offers very expensive, all-inclusive packages, ranging from three days to a week, at its magnificently sited hotel in Parque Nacional Torres del Paine.

Cruceros Australis's sister company **Navimag** (Avenida El Bosque Norte 0440, Las Condes,

11th floor, tel. 2/4423120, fax 2/2035025, www
.navimag.com) sails between the Patagonian
town of Puerto Natales and the mainland city
of Puerto Montt. While these are not cruises in
the traditional sense of the word, they are more
than just utilitarian transportation as they pass
through the spectacular fjordlands of archipelagic Chile.

Puerto Williams–based, German-run **Sea &
Ice & Mountains Adventures Unlimited,**
(tel./fax 061/621150, 621227, coiron@simltd
.com, www.simltd.com) operates yacht tours
through Tierra del Fuego and Cape Horn in the
summer months.

LOCAL TRANSPORTATION

Even as cars clog the streets of Buenos Aires and
other cities, most Argentines still rely on public
transportation to get around. Services in the capital and Gran Buenos Aires are frequent and reasonably well but not perfectly integrated.

entrance to Subte Línea A, at Plaza de Mayo,
Buenos Aires

Underground

Buenos Aires has the country's only subway system, popularly known as the Subte (www.metro-
vias.com.ar). Though it dates from 1913, it
moves city residents efficiently and is expanding to underserved neighborhoods; for details,
see the Buenos Aires chapter.

Colectivos (Buses)

Even small cities and towns are fairly well-served
by local buses, which often run 24/7. Fares are
mostly in the US$.35 range, but vary according
to distance. In Buenos Aires and some other localities, *colectivos* have fare boxes that make
change, but in others they require *fichas* (tokens)
or magnetic cards.

Trains

With a few exceptions, suburban trains are less
useful to short-term visitors than they are to
commuters who live in Buenos Aires Province.
They are very cheap and, while they may be improving, most are not improving nearly so fast as
the Subte.

Taxis and Remises

Buenos Aires and other cities have abundant
fleets of taxis, painted black with yellow roofs.
Since a spate of robberies that began some years
ago, nearly all of them are now so-called *radio
taxis* and some people prefer the security of phoning for a cab, but many if not most *porteños* still
flag them down in the street. If in doubt, lock the
back doors so that no one can enter the cab by
surprise.

All regular cabs have digital meters. In Buenos
Aires, it costs about US$.45 to **bajar la bandera**
("drop the flag," i.e. switch on the meter) and
another US$.04 per 100 meters; provincial cities
tend to be a little cheaper. Verify that the meter is
set at zero.

Drivers do not expect tips; sometimes, to avoid
having to make change, they will even round
the fare *down*. It's best to carry small bills rather
than have to rely on the driver's making change,
especially if he has just come on shift. Since there
is a handful of dishonest drivers, before handing over the bill you may want to ask if he has the

proper change for a large note, stating the amount that you're handing over.

Remises are radio taxis that charge an agreed-upon rate based on distance; the dispatcher will let you know the fare when you call, based on the pickup and drop-off points.

Hotels, restaurants, and other businesses will gladly ring radio taxis and *remises* for customers and clients, especially when the hour is late.

Bicycles

Cycling may not be the safest way of navigating Argentina's chaotic traffic, but the number of cyclists is growing rapidly with the economic crisis. If riding around Buenos Aires or other Argentine cities, side streets may be safer than fast-moving avenues, but they are also narrower, with less room to maneuver. Weekend traffic is not so wild as on weekdays, and parts of downtown are virtually deserted on Sunday. There are few dedicated bike paths, most of which go through city parklands.

Walking

Most Argentine cities are compact enough that walking suffices for sightseeing and other activities, but the first rule of pedestrian safety is that that you are invisible—for an overwhelming majority of Argentine drivers, crosswalks appear to be merely decorative. While making turns, drivers weave among pedestrians rather than slowing or stopping to let them pass. Jaywalking is endemic, perhaps because it's not much more hazardous than crossing at the corner with the light.

Despite the hazards, in congested areas pedestrians can often move faster than automobiles. Much of the country has hot, humid summers, so carry and consume plenty of fluids. Frequent thunderstorms in the humid pampas and Mesopotamia make an umbrella advisable.

Visas and Officialdom

Citizens of neighboring countries—Bolivians, Brazilians, Uruguayans, and Paraguayans—need only national identity cards, but most other nationalities needs passports. U.S. and Canadian citizens, along with those of the European Community and Scandinavian countries, Switzerland, Israel, Australia, New Zealand, and other Latin American countries need passports but not advance visas. Citizens of nearly every African and Asian country, with the exceptions of South Africa and Japan, need advance visas.

Regulations change, however, and it may be helpful to check the visa page of Argentina's **Ministerio de Relaciones Exteriores** (Foreign Relations Ministry, www.mrecic.gov.ar/consulares/pagcon.html). See the accompanying sidebar for contact information of the most important Argentine embassies and consulates overseas.

Argentina routinely grants 90-day entry permits to foreign visitors, in the form of a tourist card. Theoretically, this card must be surrendered on departure; in practice, it's the passport stamp that counts. For US$100, the entry is renewable for 90 days at the **Dirección Nacional de Migraciones** (Avenida Argentina 1355, Retiro, Buenos Aires, tel. 011/4317-0237, 8 A.M.– 1 P.M. weekdays only).

In the provinces, renewal can be done at any office of the Policía Federal (Federal Police), but in smaller towns the police may not be accustomed to providing the service. Buenos Aires visitors may find it cheaper and simpler to take a ferry trip to Colonia, Uruguay.

Formally, arriving visitors must have a return or onward ticket, but enforcement is inconsistent— if you have a Latin American, North American, or Western European passport, for instance, it is unlikely you will be asked to show the return ticket (in the Western Hemisphere, only Cubans need a visa to enter Argentina). The author has entered Argentina dozens of times over many years, at Buenos Aires's international airport and some of the most remote border posts, without ever having been asked for either.

Airlines, though, may feel differently and not permit a passenger without a round-trip ticket to board a flight to Argentina. Likewise, if the arriving passenger presents an Eastern European, Asian,

Know Argentina

ARGENTINE CONSULATES IN OTHER COUNTRIES

Argentina has wide diplomatic representation throughout the world, even though economic difficulties have reduced this presence over the past couple of decades. In capital cities, embassies and consulates are often, though not always, at the same address; intending visitors should go to consulates, rather than embassies, for visas or other inquiries.

Australia: John McEwen House, 2nd Floor, 7 National Circuit, Barton ACT, tel. 02/6273-9111

Consulate: 44 Market Street, 20th floor, Sydney NSW, tel. 02/9262-2933

Bolivia: Sánchez Lima 2103, La Paz, tel. 2/241-7737

Brazil: Praia Botafogo 228, Entreloja, Rio de Janeiro, tel. 21/2533-1646

Avenida Paulista 1106, Sobreloja, São Paulo, tel. 11/3897-9522

Canada: 90 Sparks St., Suite 910, Ottawa, Ontario K1P 514, tel. 613/236-2351

5001 Yonge St., 1st floor, Toronto, Ontario M2N 6P6, tel. 416/955-9075

2000 Peel St, Montréal, Québec H3A 2W5, tel. 514/842-6582

Chile: Vicuña Mackenna 41, Santiago, tel. 2/222-8977

Pedro Mont 160, Puerto Montt, tel. 65/253966

21 de Mayo 1878, Punta Arenas, tel. 56/261532

France: 6 Rue Cimarosa, Paris, tel. 1/4434-2200

Germany: Dorotheenstraße 89, 3rd Floor, Berlin, tel. 30/226-8924

Lyonerstraße 34, Frankfurt am Main, tel. 69/972-0030

Mexico: Blvd. Manuel Ávila Camacho 1, 7th Floor, Colonia Lomas de Chapultepec, México D.F., tel. 55/5395-9251

New Zealand: 142 Lambton Quay, 14th Floor, Wellington, tel. 4/472-8330

Paraguay: Palma 319, 1st Floor, Asunción, tel. 21/498582

Artigas 960, Encarnación, tel. 71/201067

Switzerland: Jungfraustraße 1, Bern, tel. 31/356-4350

United Kingdom: 27 Three Kings Yard, London W1Y 1FL, tel. 20/7318-1340

United States: 1811 Q St. NW, Washington, D.C. 20009, 202/238-6460

5550 Wilshire Blvd., Ste. 210, Los Angeles, CA 90036, 323/954-9155

800 Brickell Ave., Penthouse 1, Miami, FL 33131, 305/373-1889

245 Peachtree Center Ave., Ste. 2101, Atlanta, GA 30303, 404/880-0805

205 N. Michigan Ave., Ste. 4209, Chicago, IL 60601, 312/819-2610

12 W. 56th St., New York, NY 10019, 212/603-0400

3050 Post Oak Blvd., Ste. 1625, Houston, TX 77056, 713/871-8935

Uruguay: Wilson Ferreira Aldunate 1281, Montevideo, tel. 2/902-8623

Avenida General Flores 209, Colonia, tel. 52/22093

Edificio Espigón Gorlero, Avenida Gorlero and Calle 19 (Comodoro Gorlero), Sala H, Punta del Este, tel. 42/441632

FOREIGN CONSULATES IN BUENOS AIRES

As a major world capital, Buenos Aires has a full complement of embassies and consulates that provide citizen services. Where the embassy and consulate are not in the same location, the list below provides the latter's address, as consulates are primarily responsible for dealing with individuals traveling for either business or pleasure.

Unless otherwise indicated, addresses below are in the Microcentro and vicinity.

Australia: Villanueva 1400, Palermo, tel. 011/4777-6580

Belgium: Defensa 113, 8th floor, Monserrat, tel. 011/4331-0066

Bolivia: Avenida Belgrano 1670, 1st floor, Monserrat, tel. 011/4381-0539

Brazil: 5th floor, Carlos Pellegrini 1363, Retiro, tel. 4515-6500

Canada: Tagle 2828, Palermo, tel. 011/4805-3032

Chile: San Martín 439, 9th floor, tel. 011/4394-6582

Denmark: Leandro N. Alem 1074, 9th floor, Retiro, 011/4312-6901

France: Santa Fe 846, 3rd floor, Retiro, tel. 011/4312-2409

Germany: Villanueva 1055, Palermo, tel. 011/4778-2500

Ireland: Avenida del Libertador 1068, 6th floor, Recoleta, tel. 011/5787-0801

Israel: 10th floor, Avenida de Mayo 701, Monserrat, tel. 011/4338-2500

Italy: Marcelo T. de Alvear 1125, Retiro, tel. 011/4816-6132

Japan: Bouchard 547, 17th floor, tel. 011/4318-8200

Mexico: Arcos 1650, Belgrano, tel. 011/4789-8826

Netherlands: Olga Cossentini 831, 3rd floor, Edificio Porteño Plaza 2, Puerto Madero, tel. 011/4338-0050

New Zealand: Carlos Pellegrini 1427, 5th floor, tel. 011/4328-0747

Norway: Esmeralda 909, 3rd floor, Retiro, tel. 011/4312-2204

Paraguay: Viamonte 1851, Balvanera, tel. 011/4815-9801

Peru: Florida 165, 2nd floor, tel. 011/4334-0970

Spain: Guido 1760, Recoleta, tel. 011/4811-0070

Sweden: Tacuarí 147, 6th floor, Monserrat, tel. 011/4342-1422

Switzerland: Santa Fe 846, 10th floor, Retiro, tel. 011/4311-6491

United Kingdom: Dr. Luis Agote 2412, Recoleta, tel. 011/4803-7070

United States of America: Colombia 4300, Palermo, tel. 011/5777-4533

Uruguay: Avenida Las Heras 1915, Recoleta, tel. 011/4807-3040

or African passport, he or she may well be asked for proof of return transport. Immigration officials have a great deal of discretion in these matters.

Always carry identification, since either the federal or provincial police can request it at any moment, though they rarely do so without some reason. Passports are also necessary for routine transactions like checking into hotels, cashing travelers checks, or even payment by credit card.

Dependent children under age 14 traveling without both parents presumably need notarized parental consent, but the author's now-teenage daughter has visited Argentina many times with only one parent, and has never been asked for such a document.

Argentine-born individuals, even if their parents were not Argentines or if they have been naturalized elsewhere, sometimes attract unwanted attention from immigration officials. Generally, they may enter the country for no more than 60 days on a non-Argentine document. Argentine passports renewed outside the country expire on reentry, making it necessary to renew them with the Policía Federal, which can be a bothersome and time-consuming process on a short trip.

LOST OR STOLEN PASSPORTS

Visitors who suffer a lost or stolen passport must obtain a replacement at their own embassy or consulate. After obtaining a replacement passport, it's necessary to visit the Dirección Nacional de Migraciones to replace the tourist card.

CUSTOMS

Traditionally notorious for truly flagrant corruption, Argentine customs has improved from the days of the so-called *aduana paralela* (parallel customs) and normally presents no obstacle to tourists. Short-term visitors may import personal effects including clothing, jewelry, medicine, sporting gear, camping equipment and accessories, photographic and video equipment, personal computers, and the like, as well as 400 cigarettes, two liters of wine or alcoholic beverages (adults over 18 only), and up to US$300 of new merchandise.

Customs inspections are usually routine, but at Buenos Aires's international airports, river ports, and some land borders, incoming checked baggage may have to pass through X-rays; do not put photographic film in checked baggage. Fresh food will be confiscated at any port of entry.

At some remote border posts, the Gendarmería Nacional (Border Guards) handles all formalities, from immigration to customs to agricultural inspections. Visitors arriving from drug-producing countries like Colombia, Peru, and Bolivia may get special attention at all border posts, as may those from Paraguay, with its thriving contraband economy.

POLICE AND MILITARY

Argentina is notorious for police corruption. For this reason, *porteños* and other Argentines scornfully call both federal and provincial police *la cana*—an insult that should never be used to their face.

The Policía Federal (Federal Police) are more professional than provincial forces like that of Buenos Aires Province; the latter is almost universally detested for harassing motorists for minor equipment violations and, even worse, for their *gatillo fácil* (hair-trigger) response to minor criminal offenses. In fairness, many police officers have died at the hands of well-armed criminals (who are sometimes police officers themselves, however).

Nevertheless, police officers often solicit *coimas* (bribes) at routine traffic stops. To avoid paying a bribe, either state your intention to contact your consulate, or use broken Spanish even if you understand the language well. Either one may frustrate a corrupt official sufficiently to give up the effort.

Since the end of the 1976–83 military dictatorship, the Argentine military has lost prestige and appears to have acknowledged its inability to run the country, despite occasional clamor for a coup by fringe figures. Still, security is heavy around military bases and photography is taboo—though mostly a thing of the past, signs proclaiming that "the sentry will shoot" are sometimes posted.

Conduct and Customs

Argentines, and especially *porteños* (like New Yorkers), have a stereotyped reputation for brusqueness and some of them complain that, especially in the current crisis, "nobody respects anybody here any more."

Still, politeness goes a long way with officials, shopkeepers, and others with whom you may have contact. It is always good form to offer the appropriate polite greeting: *buenos días* (good morning), *buenas tardes* (good afternoon), or *buenas noches* (good evening or good night).

In terms of general conduct, both women and men should dress conservatively and inconspicuously when visiting churches, chapels, and sacred sites. This, again, is an issue of respect for local customs, even if Argentines themselves don't always observe it.

GENDER ROLES

Like other Latin American societies, Argentina has a strong *machista* (chauvinist) element. Argentine women are traditionally mothers, homemakers, and children's caregivers, while men are providers and decision-makers, although there are increasing numbers of professionals and other working women.

Many Argentine men view foreign women as sexually available, but this is not necessarily discriminatory—they view Argentine women the same way. Harassment often takes the form of *piropos,* sexist comments which are often innocuous and can even be poetic, but are just as likely to be vulgar. It is best to ignore verbal comments, which are obvious by tone of voice even if you don't understand them; if they're persistent, seek refuge in a café or *confitería.*

Despite challenges, women have acquired political prominence. The most prominent and notorious, of course, was Evita Perón, but her rise to the top was an unconventional one. The highest-profile females in current politics are first lady Cristina Fernández—a senator from Santa Cruz Province—and former legislator and presidential candidate Elisa Carrió, a vociferous anticorruption campaigner who, unfortunately, is better at identifying problems than offering solutions.

GAYS AND LESBIANS

Despite its conspicuous Catholicism, Argentina is a fairly tolerant country for both gays and lesbians, and public displays of affection—men kissing on the cheek, women holding hands—are relatively common even among heterosexuals.

In 2002, the capital's legislature established domestic-partner regulations applicable to gay couples (and to other unmarried couples as well), with regard to health insurance and pension rights. There was opposition from the Catholic Church and from the Buenos Aires Bar Association (the latter on a legal technicality that only the federal government could establish such legislation).

The Buenos Aires–based **Comunidad Homosexual Argentina** (CHA, Tomás Liberti 1080, La Boca, tel. 11/4361-6352), the country's foremost gay-rights organization, was instrumental in lobbying for the legislation.

Certain districts in Buenos Aires, most notably Recoleta, Barrio Norte, and Palermo, have a number of openly gay entertainment venues. Outlying areas like the Paraná Delta are also remarkably tolerant, and other large cities have their enclaves as well. When in doubt, though, discretion is advisable.

PHOTOGRAPHIC ETIQUETTE

Unlike some countries with large indigenous populations, Argentines are not exactly camera-shy, though an in-your-face approach is not necessarily appropriate either. Especially when inclusion of people is incidental to, say, a landscape, it's not a problem. However, if a person is the photograph's primary subject, try to establish a rapport before asking permission to photograph, if you can manage Spanish or have another language in common. Photographers should be particularly respectful of the indigenous peoples of northwestern Argentina and of Patagonia.

Tips for Travelers

Know Argentina

OPPORTUNITIES FOR STUDY AND EMPLOYMENT

In an imploding economy with upward of 20 percent unemployment, remunerative work is hard to come by even for legal residents, let alone visitors on tourist or student visas. Nevertheless, foreigners have found work teaching English or another foreign language, working in the tourist industry, or performing casual labor in bars or restaurants. The problem with such jobs is that they either require time to build up a clientele (in the case of teaching), may be seasonal (in the case of tourism), and can be poorly paid (in the case of restaurants, except in a handful of places where tips are high). Language teachers may find, in any event, that few Argentines can afford the luxury of one-on-one lessons.

Ideally, obtaining a work permit from an Argentine consulate is better than attempting to obtain one in-country, as employment may not begin until the permit is actually granted. No matter what, the process requires submitting documents and takes some time.

BUSINESS TRAVEL

There are few legal restrictions on foreign businesses operating in Argentina, but the recent business climate, due largely to the government's debt default and banking restrictions, has not been conducive to investment. In country risk assessments, featured like sports scores on the front page of many newspapers, Argentina ranks among the world's highest—by mid-2002, this key statistic had soared over 6,000 compared to 1,200 for its beleaguered neighbor Uruguay and only 150 for Chile. In September 2003, after more than a year of relative stability, it had only fallen to 5,100.

Corruption remains an issue, as a Transparency International survey for 2002 ranked Argentina 92nd of 133 countries evaluated, on par with Albania, Ethiopia, and Pakistan. Political officeholders have an unfortunate reputation for shaking down foreign companies for bribes, and customs procedures can be trying despite efforts at professionalizing the service. Intellectual-property rights for computer software, CD and cassette recordings, and DVDs and videotapes are problematic.

Good background sources on business, at least for those who read Spanish, are the businesses dailies mentioned under Media later in this section, and the magazine *Mercado* (www.mercado.com.ar). The most accessible English-language source is the U.S. State Department's Country Commercial Guide service (www.usatrade.gov/website/CCG.nsf), though it often lags behind events. Its best bets for investment include travel and tourism services, computer equipment and software, management consulting, medical equipment, energy technology, building materials and supplies, and biotechnology. It is questionable, though, whether the economy will be able to support imports in its present state.

Nevertheless, some investors are convinced that Argentine businesses may offer high yields on investments because devaluation has depressed prices in dollar terms. Residential real estate, for instance, has been a bargain, and sellers are showing increased willingness to offer properties. In any event, before signing any business deal, consult a local lawyer recommended by your embassy, consulate, or a truly trusted friend.

Business Etiquette

Conducting business is as much a personal and social activity as an economic one; even though initial contacts may be formal, with appointments arranged well in advance, topics such as family and sports are often part of the conversation. Formality in dress and appearance is not so rigid as it once was, but in sectors like banking it's still the rule.

An ability to speak Spanish well is a plus, even though many Argentine business figures speak English well (and more than a few have been educated in English-speaking countries). The best months for business travel are April–November; in January and February, when school lets out and Argentines take their summer vacations, Buenos Aires can seem almost deserted. Many people also leave for winter holidays, the last two weeks of July.

Useful Organizations

Nearly all important business-oriented organizations are in Buenos Aires. One critically important and unavoidable contact is the national customs headquarters, the **Administración Nacional de Aduanas** (Azopardo 350, Monserrat, tel. 011/4338-6400, fax 011/4338-6555). If importing equipment for permanent use, it's essential to deal with them through a *despachante de aduanas* (private customs broker).

U.S. citizens can get advice at the **Cámara de Comercio de los Estados Unidos en Argentina** (U.S. Chamber of Commerce, Viamonte 1133, 8th floor, Microcentro, tel. 11/4371-4500, fax 11/4371-8400, amcham@amchamar.com.ar, www.amchamar.com.ar).

Their Argentine counterpart is the **Cámara Argentina de Comercio** (Argentine Chamber of Commerce, Avenida Leandro N. Alem 36, Planta Baja, Microcentro, tel. 11/5300-9000, fax 11/5300-9058, centroservicios@cac.com.ar, www.cac.com.ar).

Importers may want to consult with the **Cámara de Importadores de la República Argentina** (Argentine Chamber of Importers, Avenida Belgrano 427, 7th floor, Monserrat, tel./fax 011/4342-1101/0523, cira@cira.org.ar, www.cira.org.ar).

Argentina's main stock exchange is the **Bolsa de Comercio de Buenos Aires** (Sarmiento 299, 1st floor, Microcentro, tel. 011/4316-7000, saber @bolsar.com, www.bcba.sba.com.ar).

For agricultural contacts, visit the **Sociedad Rural Argentina** (Argentine Agricultural Association, Florida 460, Microcentro, tel. 011/4324-4700, sra@rural.org.ar, www.ruralarg.org.ar).

TRAVELERS WITH DISABILITIES

For people with disabilities, Argentina can be a problematic country. The narrow, uneven sidewalks in many cities, not to mention the fast-moving traffic, are unkind to people with disabilities, especially those who need wheelchairs.

Public transportation can rarely accommodate passengers with disabilities, though the capital's newer Subte stations have elevators and others are being retrofitted. Avis has recently introduced rental vehicles with hand controls.

Few older buildings are specifically equipped for handicapped people, but many of these are low and can often accommodate people with disabilities. Newer hotels are often high-rises, and disabled access is obligatory.

TRAVELING WITH CHILDREN

In most ways, Argentina is a child-friendly country and Buenos Aires is a child-friendly city. In fact, since many Argentines enjoy large extended families, they may feel little in common with people in their late twenties and older who do *not* have children, and traveling with kids can open doors.

Many of the country's parks and plazas have playground equipment, and it's easy to mix with Argentine families there. What foreign parents may find unusual is that even toddlers may be out on the swings and slides with their families at 11 P.M. or even later. Likewise, kids are off across the street, around the neighborhood and even on the buses and Subte at ages when nervous North American parents are driving their kids three blocks to school and waiting until the doors close behind them.

On public transportation, strangers may spontaneously but gently touch small children and even set them on their laps. While this may be disconcerting to non-Argentines, it's not necessarily inappropriate in cultural context.

Many cultural activities are child-oriented, particularly during late July's winter school holidays.

WOMEN TRAVELERS

Like many other parts of Latin America, Argentine society has strong *machista* (male chauvinist) elements. Though nearly everybody visits and leaves Argentina without experiencing any unpleasantness, women are certainly not exempt from harassment and, rarely, violence. The most common form of harassment is the *piropo*, a sexist remark that can range from clever and humorous to crude and insulting.

If you do receive unwanted attention, the best strategy is to ignore it, and the odds are that the problem will just go away. If not, the next best option is to return to your hotel, enter a restaurant, or find some other public place where harassment will be more conspicuous and you're likely to find support. Some women have suggested wearing a bogus wedding ring, but truly persistent suitors might see this simply as a challenge.

GAY AND LESBIAN TRAVELERS

Argentine public opinion in general, and that of Buenos Aires in particular, has turned remarkably tolerant of homosexuals, if not necessarily of public homosexual behavior. Buenos Aires has an active gay scene that revolves around Avenida Santa Fe, in Barrio Norte, and there are enclaves elsewhere. Within the city limits of Mar del Plata, for instance, there recently opened a gay-oriented resort area known as Calu Beach.

Early November's Marcha de Orgullo Gay (Gay Pride Parade) leads from BA's Plaza de Mayo to Congreso.

Demonstrative contact such as kissing between males (on the cheek, at least) and holding hands for females does not have the same connotations as it might in North America or some European countries, and is common among heterosexuals. This does not mean that homosexuals can always behave as they wish in public, however—the police, never society's most enlightened sector, have beaten and jailed individuals who have offended their sense of propriety. If in doubt, be circumspect.

Health and Safety

Midlatitude Buenos Aires and vicinity offer no major health risks beyond those associated with any large city; public health standards are good and tap water is potable. In some parts of northernmost subtropical Argentina, though, there's a small risk of malaria or similar tropical diseases.

A good general source on foreign health matters is Dr. Richard Dawood's *Travelers' Health* (New York: Random House, 1994), a small encyclopedia on the topic. Dr. Stuart R. Rose's *International Travel Health Guide* (Northampton, MA: Travel Medicine Inc., 2000) is updated annually and regionally focused. Try also the fifth edition of Dirk G. Schroeder's *Staying Healthy in Asia, Africa, and Latin America* (Avalon Travel Publishing, 2000).

For up-to-date information on health issues in Argentina and elsewhere in the Southern Cone, visit the U.S. Centers for Disease Control (CDC) Temperate South America regional page (www.cdc.gov/travel/temsam.htm), covering Chile, Argentina, Uruguay, and the Falkland Islands. Another good source is the United Kingdom's Department of Health (www.doh.gov.uk/traveladvice/index.htm), which provides a chart of recommended prophylaxis by country.

Note that at present, thanks to devaluation of the peso, quality medical care is so cheap that in some cases it might justify a trip to Buenos Aires. For instance, one might pay US$100 for a magnetic resonance image (MRI) that might have cost ten times that in the United States. A half-hour visit with a top orthopedist costs US$10, and a series of X-rays less than US$20. Such favorable prices may not continue as the peso recovers, but it's worth consideration.

Visitors considering medical care, however, should choose private hospitals and clinics, especially since the economic crisis has strained the resources of public hospitals. One outstanding choice is **Clínica Fleni** (Montañeses 2325, Belgrano, tel. 011/5777-3200, www.fleni .org.ar), whose focus is pediatrics and neurology but which also has outstanding orthopedics specialists. Another possibility is the **Fundación Favaloro** (Avenida Belgrano 1746, Monserrat, tel. 011/4378-1200, www.fundacionfavaloro.org), whose specialty is cardiology. Nearly all the doctors at both are English-speaking.

BEFORE YOU GO

Theoretically, Argentina demands no proof of vaccinations, but if you are coming from a tropical country where yellow fever is endemic, authorities could ask for a vaccination certificate.

Traveling to Argentina or elsewhere without adequate medical insurance is risky. Before leaving your home country, obtain medical insurance that includes evacuation in case of serious emergency. Foreign health insurance may not be accepted in Argentina, so you may be required to pay out of your own pocket for later reimbursement. Often, however, private medical providers accept international credit cards in return for services.

Numerous carriers provide medical and evacuation coverage; an extensive list, including Internet links, is available at the U.S. State Department's website (www.travel.state.gov/medical.html).

GENERAL HEALTH MAINTENANCE

Common-sense precautions can reduce the possibility of illness considerably. Washing the hands frequently with soap and water and drinking only bottled, boiled, or carbonated water will help diminish the likelihood of contagion for short-term visitors—though Argentine tap water is potable almost everywhere.

Where purified water is impossible to obtain, such as backcountry streams where there may be livestock or problems with human waste, pass drinking water through a one-micron filter and purify it further with iodine drops or tablets (but avoid prolonged consumption of iodine-purified water). Nonpasteurized dairy products, such as goat cheese, can be problematic and are best avoided.

FOOD- OR WATER-BORNE DISEASES

While relatively few visitors to Argentina run into problems of this sort, contaminated food and drink are not unheard of. In many cases, it's simply exposure to different sorts of bugs to which your body soon becomes accustomed, but if symptoms persist the problem may be more serious.

Traveler's Diarrhea

Colloquially known as *turista* in Latin America, the classic traveler's diarrhea (TD) usually lasts only a few days and almost always less than a week. Besides "the runs," symptoms include nausea, vomiting, bloating, and general weakness. The usual cause is the notorious *Escherichia coli* bacterium from contaminated food or water; in rare cases *E. coli* infections can be fatal.

Fluids, including fruit juices, and small amounts of bland foods such as freshly cooked rice or soda crackers, may relieve symptoms and help regain strength. Dehydration can be a serious problem, especially for children, who may need to be treated with an oral rehydration solution (ORS) of carbohydrates and salt.

Over-the-counter remedies like Pepto-Bismol, Lomotil, and Immodium may relieve symptoms but can also cause problems. Prescription drugs such as doxycyline and trimethoprim/sulfamethoxazole can also shorten the cycle. These may not, however, be suitable for children, and it's better for everyone to avoid them if at all possible.

Continuing and worsening symptoms, including bloody stools, may mean dysentery, a much more serious ailment that requires a physician's attention.

Dysentery

Bacterial dysentery, resembling a more intense form of TD, responds well to antibiotics, but amoebic dysentery is far more serious, sometimes leading to intestinal perforation, peritonitis, and liver abscesses. Like diarrhea, its symptoms include soft and even bloody stools, but some people may be asymptomatic even as they pass on *Entamoeba hystolica* through unsanitary toilet and food-preparation practices. Metronidazole, known by the brand names Flagyl or Protostat, is an effective treatment, but a physician's diagnosis is advisable.

Cholera

Resulting from poor hygiene, inadequate sewage disposal, and contaminated food, contemporary cholera is less devastating than its historic antecedents, which produced rapid dehydration, watery diarrhea, and imminent death without almost equally rapid rehydration. While today's cholera strains are highly infectious, most carriers do not even come down with symptoms. Existing vaccinations are ineffective, so international health authorities now recommend against them.

Treatment can only relieve symptoms. On average, about five percent of victims die, but those who recover are immune. It's not a common problem in Argentina, but it's not unheard of either, especially in northern subtropical areas.

Hepatitis A

Usually passed by fecal-oral contact under conditions of poor hygiene and overcrowding, hepatitis A is a virus. The traditional gamma globulin prophylaxis has limited efficacy and wears off in just a few months. New hepatitis A vaccines, though, are more effective and last longer.

Typhoid

Typhoid is a serious disease common under unsanitary conditions, but the recommended vaccination is an effective prophylaxis.

INSECT-BORNE DISEASES

Argentina is not quite malaria-free but there is none in or around Buenos Aires; a few other insect-borne diseases may be present if not exactly prevalent.

Dengue Fever

Like malaria, dengue is a mosquito-borne disease of the lowland tropics, but it's less common than malaria and only rarely fatal. Often debilitating in the short term, its symptoms include fever, headache, severe joint pain, and skin rashes, but most people recover fairly quickly though there is no treatment. Uncommon but often fatal, the more severe dengue hemorrhagic fever sometimes occurs in children, particularly those who have suffered from the disease previously.

Eradicated in Argentina in 1963, the mosquito vector *Aedes egypti* is once again present as far south as Buenos Aires. There were several hundred confirmed cases of dengue in lowland subtropical areas of Salta Province in 1997, and health authorities believe outbreaks are possible in Buenos Aires. The best prophylaxis is to avoid mosquito bites by covering exposed parts of the body with insect repellent or appropriate clothing.

Chagas' Disease

Also known as South American trypanosomiasis, Chagas' disease is most common in Brazil but affects about 18 million people between Mexico and Argentina; 50,000 people die from it every year. Not a tropical disease per se, it has a discontinuous distribution—Panamá and Costa Rica, for instance, are Chagas'-free.

Since it is spread by the bite of the night-feeding cone-nose or assassin bug, which lives in adobe structures, avoid such structures (these still exist in the countryside); if it's impossible to do so, sleep away from the walls. Insect repellents carrying DEET offer some protection. Chickens, dogs, and opossums may carry the disease.

Chagas' initial form is a swollen bite often accompanied by fever, which soon subsides. In the long run, though, it may cause heart damage leading to sudden death, intestinal constipation, and difficulty in swallowing; there is no cure. Charles Darwin may have been a chronic sufferer.

HANTAVIRUS

Hantavirus is an uncommon but deadly disease contracted by breathing, touching, or ingesting feces or urine of the long-tailed rat. Primarily a rural phenomenon and most prevalent in southerly Patagonia, the virus thrives in enclosed areas; when exposed to sunlight or fresh air, it normally loses its potency. Avoid places frequented by rodents, particularly abandoned buildings, but note that there have been apparent cases in which hikers and farm workers have contracted the disease in open spaces.

It is not a serious problem in urban Buenos Aires, but in July 2002 a veterinarian contracted the disease near the provincial capital of La Plata and later died.

RABIES

Rabies, a virus transmitted through bites or scratches by domestic animals (like dogs and cats) and wild mammals (like bats), is a concern; many domestic animals in Argentina go unvaccinated, especially in rural areas. Human prophylactic vaccination is possible, but may be incompatible with malaria medication.

Untreated rabies can cause an agonizingly painful death. In case of an animal bite or scratch, clean the affected area immediately with soap and running water, and then with antiseptic substances like iodine or 40 percent–plus alcohol. If possible, try to capture the animal for diagnosis, but not at the risk of further bites; in areas where rabies is endemic, painful post-exposure vaccination may be unavoidable.

SNAKEBITE

The federal capital does not have poisonous snakes, but the aggressive and highly venomous pit viper *yarará* (*Bothrops neuwiedi*) is found in parts of Buenos Aires Province and elsewhere in the country. The timid but even more venomous coral snake (*Micrurus coralinus*) is found is humid areas such as the Paraná Delta.

The *yarará,* whose venom paralyzes the nervous system, is responsible for most of the country's snakebite incidents, but strikes are not common. Death is not instantaneous and antivenins are available, but the wisest tactic is to be alert and avoid confrontation. If bitten, get to medical facilities as quickly as possible, but avoid excessive movement that helps the venom circulate.

ALTITUDE SICKNESS

At the highest elevations, above about 3,000 meters in the northern and the central Andes, *apunamiento* or *soroche* can be an annoyance and even a danger, of particular concern to older people or those with respiratory problems. Even among young, robust individuals, a quick rise from sea level to the *puna* in the space of a couple of hours can cause intense headaches, vertigo, either drowsiness or insomnia, shortness of breath, and other symptoms. Combined with hypothermia, it can easily be life-threatening.

For most people, rest and relaxation will help relieve these symptoms as the body gradually adapts to the reduced oxygen at higher altitudes; aspirin or a comparable painkiller will combat headache. Should symptoms persist or worsen, moving to a lower elevation will usually have the desired effect. Some individuals have died at elevations above 4,000 meters; it is better to stay at an intermediate altitude than to climb to these very high elevations from sea level on the same day. Do not overeat, avoid or limit alcohol consumption, and drink extra fluids.

Stephen Bezruchka's *Altitude Illness, Prevention & Treatment* (Seattle: The Mountaineers, 1994) deals with the topic in great detail; the fifth edition of James A. Wilkerson's edited collection *Medicine for Mountaineering & Other Wilderness Activities* (Seattle: The Mountaineers, 2001) discusses other potential problems as well.

HYPOTHERMIA

Hypothermia is a dangerously quick loss of body heat, most common in cold and damp weather at high altitudes or high latitudes—be particularly careful in areas with major temperature variations between day and night. Symptoms include shivering, disorientation, loss of motor functions, skin numbness, and physical exhaustion. The best remedy is warmth, shelter, and food; unlike cottons, woolen clothing retains warmth even when wet. Avoid falling asleep if at all possible; in truly hazardous conditions, it's possible you will not regain consciousness. Carry drinking water and high-energy snacks.

SUNBURN

Since Buenos Aires and vicinity lie within temperate latitudes comparable to those in the Northern Hemisphere, sunburn is not quite the serious problem it is in subtropical northern Argentina, where nearly vertical solar rays are far more intense, or southernmost Patagonia and Tierra del Fuego, where ozone-destroying aerosols have increased the entry of ultraviolet radiation and caused skin problems for people and even for livestock like cattle and sheep.

Still, Argentine-sun worshippers put themselves at risk whenever the sun breaks through the clouds. If you dress for the beach, use a heavy sunblock; on city streets, walk in the shade whenever possible.

SEXUALLY TRANSMITTED DISEASES

While life-threatening AIDS (SIDA in Spanish) is by far the most hazardous of sexually transmitted diseases (STDs) and certainly gets the most press, other STDs are far more prevalent and also serious if left untreated. All are spread by unprotected sexual conduct; the use of latex condoms can greatly reduce the possibility of contracting sexually transmitted diseases, but not necessarily eliminate it.

Most STDs, including gonorrhea, chlamydia, and syphilis, are treatable with antibiotics, but some strains have developed immunity to penicillin and alternative treatments. If taking antibiotics, be sure to complete the prescribed course, since an interrupted treatment may not kill the infection and could even help it develop immunity.

The most common of STDs is **gonorrhea,** characterized by a burning sensation during urination, and penile or vaginal discharge; it may cause infertility. **Chlamydia** has milder symptoms but similar complications. **Syphilis,** the only major disease that apparently spread to Europe from its American origins in the aftermath of the Spanish invasion, begins with ulcer and rash symptoms that soon disappear; long-term complications, however, can include cardiovascular problems and even mental derangement.

Herpes, a virus that causes small but irritating ulcers in the genital area, has no effective treatment. It is likely to recur, spreads easily when active, and can contribute to cervical cancer. **Hepatitis B,** though not exclusively a sexually transmitted disease, can spread through the mixing of bodily fluids such as saliva, semen, and menstrual and vaginal secretions. It can also spread through insufficiently sanitary medical procedures, inadequately sterilized or shared syringes, during body piercing, and under similar circumstances. Like Hepatitis A, it can lead to liver damage but is more serious; vaccination is advisable for high-risk individuals, but it is expensive.

HIV/AIDS

As in most countries, HIV/AIDS is an issue of increasing concern. According to Argentina's Health Ministry, there are more than 24,000 full-blown AIDS cases and 150,000 HIV-infected individuals, but concerns are that the figure may be substantially higher—many carriers are probably unaware they are infected.

HIV/AIDS is not exclusively a sexually transmitted disease (IV drug users can get it by sharing needles), but unprotected sexual activity is a common means of transmission; the use of latex condoms can reduce the possibility of infection.

Buenos Aires has two AIDS-support organizations: **Cooperación, Información y Ayuda al Enfermo de SIDA** (Coinsida, Finocchieto 74, Constitución, tel. 011/4304-6664); and **Línea SIDA** (Zuviría 64, Parque Chacabuco, tel. 011/4922-1617).

SMOKING

Approximately 40 percent of Argentines smoke, including nearly half the male population; tobacco directly causes 40,000 deaths per annum. According to one survey, three of every 10 Argentine *cardiologists* smoke, and few of those make any recommendation to their own patients on the subject. Three of 10 students between the ages of 13 and 15 are smokers.

In a sense, nonsmokers are like pedestrians and smokers are like Argentine drivers—the former risk their lives if they follow their convictions. Still, there is widespread recognition that the habit is unhealthy, and effective smoking restrictions are in force on public transportation and a few other settings. If faced with secondhand smoke in one of the few places where it's prohibited, such as buses or taxis, it's easiest to appeal to courtesy with a white lie such as "*soy asmático*" (I'm asthmatic).

Many businesses have eliminated or reduced smoking on their premises, and there's a growing movement to educate and to limit public consumption of tobacco. **Sin Pucho** (Tucumán 3527, Buenos Aires, tel. 011/4862-6913, sinpucho@infovia.com.ar) is an ex-smokers' support group. There's also **Fumadores Anónimos** (Smokers Anonymous, tel. 011/4788-1653, averbuj2000@yahoo.com.ar).

LOCAL DOCTORS

Top-quality medical services, with the latest technology, are readily available in Buenos Aires. Foreign embassies sometimes maintain lists of English-speaking doctors, who may have overseas training and are numerous in the capital and other large cities.

It is possible, though, that the economic crisis may make it impossible to keep technology up to date, as devaluation has nearly tripled the cost of imported equipment in dollar terms.

PHARMACIES

Pharmacies serve an important public-health role, but also carry certain risks. Pharmacists may provide drugs on the basis of symptoms that they don't completely comprehend, especially if there is a language barrier; while the cumulative societal impact may be positive, individual recommendations may be erroneous.

Note that many medications available by prescription only in North America or Europe may be sold over the counter in Argentine pharmacies. Travelers should be cautious about self-medication even when such drugs are available; check expiration dates, as out-of-date drugs sometimes remain on the shelf.

In large cities and even some smaller towns, pharmacies remain open all night for emergency prescription service on a rotating basis. The *farmacia de turno* and its address will usually be posted in the windows of other pharmacies, or advertised in the newspaper.

CRIME

Though many Argentines believe assaults, rapes, homicide, and crimes against property are increasing, Argentina is a safe country by most standards. Because *porteños* and other Argentines keep late hours, there are plenty of people on the street at most times, and rarely will you find yourself walking alone down a dark alleyway.

Still, certain precautions almost go without saying—most crimes are crimes of opportunity. Never leave luggage unattended, store valuables in a hotel safe, keep close watch on your belongings at sidewalk cafés, and carry a photocopy of your passport with the date of entry into the country. Do not carry large amounts of cash (money belts or leg pouches are good alternatives for hiding cash), do leave valuable jewelry at home, and do keep conspicuous items such as photo and video cameras out of sight as much as possible. Do not presume that any area is totally secure.

If you should be accosted by anyone with a firearm or other potentially lethal weapon, do not resist. While guns are uncommon—knives are the weapon of choice—and truly violent crime against tourists is unusual, consequences of a misjudgment can be lethal. Certain barrios are more crime-prone than others.

One phenomenon that has disturbed Argentines in recent years is the so-called *secuestro exprés* (express kidnapping), in which criminals hold an individual for a small ransom or, alternatively, force someone to withdraw money from an ATM. Far more common in Buenos Aires Province than in the capital or elsewhere in the country, these crimes have *not* targeted tourists—rather, they appear to concentrate on individuals whose movements are familiar to the lawbreaker.

More common is the crime of distraction, in which an individual bumps into the victim and spills a substance like ice cream or mustard; while the perpetrator apologizes profusely, his or her accomplice surreptitiously lifts items of value. Pickpocketing is also common on crowded public transportation; carry wallets and other items of value in a front trouser pocket or, even better, an interior jacket pocket.

Information and Services

MONEY

While traveling in Argentina, it makes sense to have a variety of money alternatives. International credit cards are widely accepted, and foreign ATM cards work almost everywhere. Because ATMs are open 24 hours, many visitors prefer this alternative, but economic instability and occasional regulations that limit cash withdrawals for Argentines have made Argentine ATMs iffy at times; it makes sense to have a cash reserve in U.S. dollars (rather than Euros; though the European currency is gaining credibility, it's not an everyday item, especially outside Buenos Aires). Travelers checks may be the safest way to carry money, since they're usually refundable in case of loss or theft, but changing them outside Buenos Aires can be a frustrating experience even when stability reigns.

If carrying an emergency cash reserve, use an inconspicuous leg pouch or money belt—not the bulky kind that fits around the waist, which thieves or robbers easily recognize, but a zippered leather belt that looks like any other.

Currency

Throughout the 1990s, money was a simple matter. The Argentine peso (Ar$) was at par with the U.S. dollar, which circulated almost interchangeably alongside it, but the economic collapse of late 2001 has complicated matters. Many merchants still accept cash dollars, but exchange rates vary and any change will come in pesos.

Banknotes exist in denominations of 5, 10, 20, 50, and 100 pesos. Coins exist in denominations of 1, 5, 10, 25 and 50 centavos, but one-centavo coins have nearly disappeared and most businesses generally round off prices to the nearest five or 10 centavos.

Fortunately *bonos* (bonds issued by provincial governments in lieu of cash for salaries and other obligations) are also disappearing. Known as *patacones* (in Buenos Aires Province), *lecop* (in many provinces), *lecor* (in Córdoba Province), and by other names as well, these bonds have circulated alongside the peso but many businesses and services do not accept them. Other things being equal, insist on pesos.

Counterfeiting of both U.S. and foreign currency appears to be increasing. Merchants will often refuse a U.S. banknote with the smallest tear or writing on it; at the same that they will accept any peso note that is not flagrantly *trucho* (bogus). On any Argentine banknote, look for the conspicuous watermark with the initials of the historical figure depicted on it—J.S.M. for José de San Martín on the five-peso note, for instance.

Exchange Rates

Following the debt default of early 2002, the government of caretaker president Eduardo Duhalde devalued the peso from 1 to 1.4 per dollar but, when that proved unsustainable, the president floated the currency in mid-February of 2002. By midyear, the peso had fallen to 3.5 to the dollar before stabilizing, and by early 2004 it had recovered to the 2.8–2.9 range.

For the most up-to-date exchange rates, consult the business section of your daily newspaper or an online currency converter such as www.oanda.com.

The exchange rate is front-page news on virtually every Argentine daily. The best sources on exchange-rate trends are the financial dailies *Ambito Financiero* and *Buenos Aires Económico*.

Changing Money

During the 1990s, when the peso was at par with the dollar, changing money was a nonissue, as the two were virtually interchangeable. The floating of the peso in early 2002, however, made banks, *casas de cambio* (exchange houses), and surreptitious exchanges relevant again.

ATMs, abundant and becoming universal except in a few remote areas, match the best bank rates and are accessible 24/7. Unfortunately, in the aftermath of devaluation and a run on deposits, the government declared bank holidays on which was difficult or impossible to withdraw cash; there is no guarantee this will not happen again, but exchange rates have been fairly steady since early 2003, with the peso gradually gaining strength against the dollar.

Foreign ATM-cardholders were not subject to the banking controls known as the *corralito,* which limited withdrawals from Argentine accounts. Many banks, though, have limited hours and access because of protests known as *escraches,* and some have covered their doors and windows with plywood and even sheet metal.

During bank holidays, or when exchange-rate policies create an active black market, street changers known as *arbolitos* (little trees, because they are planted in one spot) are a common sight in the Buenos Aires's financial district, known as La City, along Calle San Martín.

Most ATMs, unfortunately, dispense large banknotes, often of Ar$100 and rarely smaller than Ar$50. One way around this problem is to punch in an odd amount, such as Ar$290, in order to ensure getting some smaller notes.

Travelers Checks and Refunds

Despite their safeguards, travelers checks have many drawbacks here. In addition to the time-consuming bureaucracy of changing them at banks and exchange houses, they often carry a substantial penalty in terms of commission—up to three percent or even more in some cases. Businesses other than exchange houses rarely accept them under any circumstances and, in out-of-the-way places, nobody will. Travelers checks, unfortunately, should be a last-resort means of carrying and changing money here; cash (despite the risks) and ATM cards are better options.

Bank Transfers

Many Argentine exchange houses, post offices, and other businesses are affiliated with Western Union, making it relatively straightforward to send or receive money from overseas. For a list of Western Union affiliates in Argentina, visit the company's website (www.westernunion.com). The American Express Money Gram is another alternative; AmEx has a large headquarters in Retiro, Buenos Aires, and affiliates throughout the country.

In an emergency, it's possible to forward money to U.S. citizens via the U.S. embassy in Buenos Aires by establishing a Department of State trust account through its **Overseas Citizens Services** (Washington, D.C., tel. 202/647-5225); there is a US$20 service charge for setting up the account. It is possible to arrange this as a wire or overnight mail transfer through Western Union (tel. 800/325-6000 in the United States); for details, visit the State Department's website (www.travel.state.gov).

Credit and Debit Cards

Credit cards have been common currency for

many years and, in the aftermath of the 2002 peso crisis, when Argentines could not withdraw their savings, their use became even more widespread. Visa and MasterCard are most widely accepted, but there are inconsistencies—a significant number of businesses prefer American Express, sometimes to the exclusion of the others, or even Diner's Club. Debit cards are also widely accepted, at least those with Visa or MasterCard affiliation.

There are possible drawbacks to using credit cards, though. During the 1990s boom years, Argentine merchants generally refrained from the *recargo,* a surcharge on credit card purchases because of slow bank payments; many have reinstituted the *recargo,* which can be up to 10 percent, to cut their losses due to the peso's loss of value between the customer's payment and the bank's reimbursement. Note that hotels in particular may offer discounts for payments in cash.

Fluctuating exchange rates may also affect the charge that eventually appears on your overseas account. If the rate has changed in the interim between your payment in Buenos Aires and its posting to the home account, it may be either greater or smaller in terms of dollars (or other foreign currency), depending on the peso's performance.

Note that, in general, *propinas* (gratuities) may *not* be added to charged restaurant meals. Keep some cash, either dollars or pesos, for tips.

To deal with lost or stolen cards, the major international credit card companies have Buenos Aires representatives: **American Express** (Arenales 707, Retiro, tel. 011/4310-3000); **Diner's Club** (Avenida Santa Fe 1148, Retiro, tel. 011/4814-5627); **MasterCard** (Perú 143, Monserrat, tel. 011/4331-2088 or 0800/555-0507); and **Visa** (Avenida Corrientes 1437, 3rd floor, tel. 011/4379-3300).

Costs

For most of the 1990s, Argentina was South America's most expensive country, so much so that even North Americans and Europeans found it costly. Wealthy Argentines, for their part, par-

THE RISING COSTS OF THE SOUTHERN CONE

Shortly after completion of this book's manuscript, tourism sector prices in parts of Argentina and in Chile underwent notable increases in dollar terms, primarily in accommodations and, to a lesser degree, food. The reasons and degree of increases were different in each country, however.

Argentina's peso gained against the dollar, but even more significant was the rejuvenated tourist economy in the capital city of Buenos Aires and, especially, in popular Patagonian destinations like San Carlos de Bariloche, San Martín de los Andes, Puerto Madryn, El Calafate, and Ushuaia.

The reason for price pressures in Argentina, though, was not so much the peso's strength and the economy at large as increased domestic demand—for the most part, Argentines could still not afford to travel beyond their own borders, and thus spent their pesos at home. At the same time, foreigners flocked to Argentina as their dollars and Euros bought far more than in the days of dollar-peso parity. Fortunately, there has been no return to the hyperinflation of the 1970s and 1980s, and prices have not skyrocketed anywhere close to their pre-devaluation levels. Still, travelers should be prepared for steadily rising prices for food, accommodations, and transportation.

In Chile, thanks to booming copper prices, the local peso strengthened nearly 20 percent against the U.S. dollar before subsiding slightly. Visitors should probably count on dollar prices some 15 to 20 percent above those listed in this book, except in transportation, which has remained fairly stable. Domestic inflation remains near zero, but prices in South America's most stable economy are, on the whole, higher than in Argentina.

tied in Miami, Madrid, Rome, and other "inexpensive" destinations.

This anomaly was a function of former economy minister Domingo Cavallo's fixed exchange rate, which reduced previous hyperinflation to near zero. Cavallo's "convertibility" policy, though, also froze prices at a relatively high but unsustainable level that eventually made Argentine exports noncompetitive and contributed to the default of late 2001.

After the peso float of February 2002 and subsequent banking restrictions that limited the amount of money in circulation, Argentina became a bargain for visitors with dollars or other hard currency. According to the Economist Intelligence Unit, Buenos Aires fell from being the 22nd most-expensive city in the world (of 131 surveyed) to the 120th. A crippling four-year recession, with unemployment exceeding 20 percent, has kept prices from skyrocketing in spite of devaluation. Businesses such as restaurants have had to keep prices relatively low, attempting to sell more at a lower margin.

Though the peso has gained strength since early 2003, travel in Argentina is inexpensive by global standards, but much depends on the traveler's expectations. There are suitable services for everyone from barebones budget backpackers to pampered international business travelers. Budget travelers will still find hotel rooms for less than US$10 pp and some excellent values for only a little more money. Hotels and resorts of international stature, like the Hyatt and Sheraton chains and their local equivalents, normally charge international prices, but even these have had to lower their rates during the crisis.

Likewise, meals range from a couple of dollars or even less at the simplest *comedores,* but restaurants with sophisticated international cuisine can charge a lot more; even the latter, though, often serve moderately priced lunchtime specials.

As of press time, shoestring travelers could get along on US$20 per day or conceivably even less for accommodations and food. For US$50 per day it's possible to live comfortably and eat well, and a budget of US$100 can seem extravagant. It's worth adding, though, that economic volatility—hyperinflation was a recurrent phenome-

non in the late 20th century—makes it impossible to guarantee that prices will not rise.

Taxes

Argentina imposes a 21 percent *impuesto de valor agregado* (IVA, value-added tax or VAT) on all goods and services, though this is normally included in the advertised price; if in doubt, ask (*¿Incluye los impuestos?*). Tax evasion is a national sport, though, and hotel owners often ignore the tax for cash payments.

Tourists, however, may request IVA refunds for purchases of Argentine products valued more than about US$25 from shops that display a "Global Refund" decal on their windows. Always double-check, however, that the decal is not out of date.

When making any such purchase, request an invoice and other appropriate forms. Then, on leaving the country, present these forms to Argentine customs; customs will then authorize payment to be cashed at Banco de la Nación branches at the main international airport at Ezeiza, Aeroparque Jorge Newbery (for flights to some neighboring countries), or at Dársena Norte (for ferry trips to Uruguay). Refunds can also be assigned to your credit card.

At smaller border crossings, however, do not expect officials to be prepared to deal with tax refunds. Some crossings do not even have separate customs officials, but rather are staffed by the Gendarmería (Border Guards), a branch of the armed forces.

Tipping

In restaurants with table service, a 10 percent gratuity is customary, but in smaller family-run eateries the practice is rare. Taxi drivers are customarily not tipped, but rounding off the fare to the next-highest convenient number is appropriate. Where there is no meter, this is not an issue.

Bargaining

Bargaining is not the way of life in Argentina that it is in some Latin American countries, but in flea or crafts markets the vendor may start at a higher price than he or she expects to receive—

avoid insultingly low offers or such a high offer that the vendor will think you a fool. Depending on your language and bargaining skills, you should be able to achieve a compromise that satisfies everybody.

Even in some upscale Buenos Aires shops, prices for items like leather jackets may be open to negotiation.

Student Discounts

Student discounts are relatively few, and prices are so low for most services that it's rarely worth arguing the point. Students, though, may be eligible for discount international airfares.

COMMUNICATIONS

Postal Services

Since the privatization of Correo Argentino, the Argentine post office, service has been more reliable than in the past, but there's some uncertainty now that the government of newly elected President Néstor Kirchner has canceled their contracts because of reported failure to meet payments. Domestic services remain generally cheap, international services more expensive. Major international couriers provide fast, reliable services at premium prices.

General delivery at Argentine post offices is *lista de correos,* literally a list arranged in alphabetical order. There is a small charge for each item addressed to you.

Note that, in Spanish-language street addresses, the number follows rather than precedes the name; instead of "1343 Washington Avenue," for example, a comparable Argentine address would read "Avenida Callao 272." Argentines and other Spanish speakers normally omit the word *calle* (street) from addresses; where an English speaker might write "499 Jones Street," an Argentine would simply use "Tucumán 272," for example. It is not unusual for street addresses to lack a number, as indicated by *s/n* (*sin número,* without a number), especially in small provincial towns.

Telephone and Fax

Argentina has two major telephone companies,

Telecom (north of Avenida Córdoba in Buenos Aires) and **Telefónica** (south of Avenida Córdoba). The country code is 54; the *característica* (area code) for the Capital Federal and Gran Buenos Aires is 011, but there is a bewildering number of area codes for individual cities, smaller cities and towns, and rural areas. All telephone numbers in the Capital Federal and Gran Buenos Aires have eight digits, while those in other provincial cities and rural areas vary. When calling out of the area code, it's necessary to dial zero first.

Cellular phone numbers in Buenos Aires all have eight digits, prefixed by 15. In addition, certain toll-free and other specialty numbers have six or seven digits with a three-digit prefix.

Public telephones are abundant; some of them operate with coins only, but most also accept magnetic card phones or rechargeable-account cards. The basic local phone rate is Ar$.25 (about US$.09) for five minutes or so; domestic long-distance is considerably more expensive. Phone cards are convenient for in-country calls but less useful for more-expensive overseas calls.

For long distance and overseas calls, as well as for fax services, it's simplest to use *locutorios* (call centers), which are abundant in both Buenos Aires and the provinces. Prices are increasingly competitive, and now tend to be much cheaper than placing *cobro revertido* (collect) or *tarjeta de crédito* (credit card) calls to the United States or any other country. Calls are more expensive during peak hours, 8 A.M.–8 P.M. weekdays and 8 A.M.–1 P.M. Saturday.

It's also possible to make home-country credit card calls through overseas operators. There are contact numbers for Australia (tel. 800/555-6100); Canada (tel. 800/222-1004 or 800/888-3868); France (tel. 800/555-3300); Germany (tel. 800/555-4900); Italy (tel. 800/555-3900); United Kingdom (British Telecom) (tel. 800/555-4402); USA (AT&T tel. 800/222-1288 or 800/555-4288; MCI tel. 800/555-1002 from Telecom, tel. 800/222-6249 from Telefónica; and Sprint tel. 800/222-1003).

Travelers interested in having a **cell phone** to use while in Argentina will find that opening an account without a permanent Argentine address is something of a nuisance. But rental phones are available from **Nolitel** (tel. 011/4311-3500, reservas@nolitelgroup.com) in Buenos Aires.

Internet Access

In the last few years, public Internet access has become both abundant and so cheap that, if price trends continue, providers will soon be paying customers to use their services. Rarely does access cost more than US$1 per hour, and it's often even cheaper. Many *locutorios* offer access, but there are also numerous Internet cafés. Some Internet service providers, most notably AOL, Compuserve, and Earthlink, have local dial-up numbers, but these often collect a surcharge.

MEDIA

Newspapers

Historically, freedom of the press has been tenuous, as Argentine governments have controlled the supply of newsprint and withheld official advertising from newspapers and magazines that have published items not to their liking. Nevertheless, since the end of the 1976–83 dictatorship, the trend has been largely positive for liberty of expression. Many of the newspapers and periodicals mentioned below have websites, listed in the Internet Resources in the back of this book.

Buenos Aires papers are also, some to a greater degree than others, national papers sold widely throughout the provinces. The middle-of-the-road tabloid *Clarín,* the Spanish-speaking world's largest-circulation daily, sells nearly 600,000 copies weekdays and more than a million Sundays, but its circulation is more sensitive to hard economic times than papers with a steadier niche clientele. Part of a consortium that includes TV and radio outlets, it also publishes *¡Ole!,* a sports daily.

According to Anglo-Argentine journalist Andrew Graham-Yooll, until your obituary appears in *La Nación,* you are not really dead—a comment that reflects the social standing of the capital's most venerable (1870) and center-right daily. With a circulation of about 200,000— twice that on Sundays when it has an exceptional

 © WAYNE BERNHARDSON

Know Argentina

Many *porteños* get their daily newspapers and magazines at corner kiosks.

cultural section—the paper was the creation of Bartolomé Mitre, who later became president.

Página 12 is a the tabloid voice of Argentina's intellectual left and, while its outspokenness its admirable, it would benefit from more rigorous editing—many articles are far too long and err on the side of hyperanalysis. The paper's political columnist Horacio Verbitsky is one of the country's most famous and capable journalists, however.

The capital has three financial newspapers, which publish weekdays only: the morning *Ambito Financiero,* which also publishes an outstanding arts and entertainment section; the afternoon *El Cronista,* and *Buenos Aires Económico.*

With a circulation of only about 8,000, Graham-Yooll's own *Buenos Aires Herald* is an English-language daily that has suffered from the drop in tourist and business travel, as its niche market correlates highly with hotel occupancy. It stresses commerce and finance, but also produces intelligent analyses of political and economic developments; its thicker Sunday edition includes

PROVINCIAL AND MUNICIPAL TOURIST OFFICES

Every Argentine province and a number of municipalities maintain tourist representatives in Buenos Aires. The area code for all of them is 011.

Buenos Aires: Avenida Callao 235, San Nicolás, tel. 4371-7045, turismo@casaprov.gba.gov.ar, www.gba.gov.ar/turismo

Catamarca: Avenida Córdoba 2080, Balvanera, tel. 4374-6891, www.catamarca.gov.ar

Chaco: Avenida Callao 322, Balvanera, tel. 4372-5209, casadelchaco@velocom.com.ar

Chubut: Sarmiento 1172, San Nicolás, tel. 4383-7458, chubuturbue@chubutur.gov.ar, www.chubutur.gov.ar

Córdoba: Avenida Callao 332, Balvanera, tel. 4373-4277, agencia.turismo@cba.gov.ar, www.cba.gov.ar

Corrientes: San Martín 333, 4th floor, Microcentro (San Nicolás), tel. 4394-7418, fabitoq@netizen.com.ar, www.corrientes.gov.ar

Entre Ríos: Suipacha 844, Retiro, tel. 4326-2573, casadeentrerios@vivientrerios.com, www.vivientrerios.com

Formosa: Hipólito Yrigoyen 1429, Monserrat, tel. 4381-7048, info@casadeformosa.gov.ar

Jujuy: Avenida Santa Fe 967, Retiro, tel. 4393-6096, casadejujuy@yahoo.com, www.jujuy.gov.ar

La Pampa: Suipacha 346, Microcentro (San Nicolás), tel. 4326-0511, hcapital@lapampa.gov.ar, www.turismolapampa.gov.ar

La Rioja: Avenida Callao 745, San Nicolás, tel. 4815-1929, larioja@infovia.com.ar, www.larioja.gov.ar

Mar del Plata (municipal): Avenida Corrientes 1660, Local 16, San Nicolás, tel. 4384-5658, casamdop@mardelplata.gov.ar, www.mardelplata.gov.ar

Mendoza: Avenida Callao 445, San Nicolás, tel. 4371-7301, turismo@mendoza.gov.ar, www.mendoza.gov.ar

---

material from the *The New York Times* and several British papers including *The Independent.*

The German-language *Argentinisches Tageblatt* began as a daily in 1889 but is now a Saturday weekly, with a circulation of about 10,000.

Magazines and Newsletters

Noticias is the Argentine counterpart to English-language weeklies like *Time* and *Newsweek. Trespuntos* and *Veintitres,* though, are more critical and innovative. *La Maga* (www.lamaga.com.ar) is an arts-oriented monthly.

Radio and Television

What was once a state broadcast monopoly is now far more diverse, thanks to privatization and the advent of cable, but conglomerates like the Clarín and El Cronista groups control much of the content. Both radio and TV tend to stress entertainment at the expense of journalism.

Radio Rivadavia, Argentina's most popular station (AM 630), plays popular music and also hosts talk programs. Radio Mitre (AM 790) is the voice of the Clarín group. Buenos Aires's FM Tango 92.7 plays all tango, all the time, while Radio Folclorísimo (AM 1410) plays folk music 24/7.

Clarín and El Cronista also control TV stations and some cable service (where overseas media like CNN, ESPN, BBC, Deutsche Welle, and others are available). TV news coverage, though, can be surprisingly good, and there is even a 24-hour cable Tango channel.

MAPS AND TOURIST INFORMATION

Maps

The Automóvil Club Argentino (ACA, Argentine Automobile Club, Avenida del Libertador 1850, Palermo, tel. 011/4808-4000, www.aca.org.ar) publishes the most-comprehensive series of highway maps (including major city plans) of all Argentine provinces. Members of overseas affiliate automobile clubs like the AAA in the United States and the AA in Britain can buy these maps

Know Argentina

Misiones: Avenida Santa Fe 989, tel. 4322-0686, infomisiones@datamarkets.com.ar, www.misiones.gov.ar

Neuquén: Perón 687, Microcentro, tel. 4327-2454, casanqn_turismo@neuquen.gov.ar, www.neuquen.gov.ar

Pinamar (municipal): Florida 930, 5th floor, Retiro, tel. 4315-2680, www.pinamar.gov.ar

Río Negro: Tucumán 1916, Balvanera, tel. 4371-5599, casaderionegro@infovia.com.ar, www.rionegro.gov.ar

Salta: Diagonal Norte (Roque Sáenz Peña) 933, Microcentro, tel. 4326-1314

San Juan: Sarmiento 1251, Microcentro, tel. 4382-9241, www.turismo.sanjuan.gov.ar

San Luis: Azcuénaga 1083, Recoleta, tel. 4823-9413, www.sanluis.gov.ar

Santa Cruz: Suipacha 1120, Retiro, tel. 4325-3098 or 4325-3102, infosantacruz@infovia.com.ar, www.santacruz.gov.ar

Santa Fe: Montevideo 373, 2nd floor, San Nicolás, tel. 4375-4570, delegacionsantafe@ciudad.gov.ar

Santiago del Estero: Florida 274, Microcentro, tel. 4326-9418

Tierra del Fuego (Instituto Fueguino de Turismo): Marcelo T. de Alvear 790, Retiro, tel. 4311-0233, infuebue@arnet.com.ar

Tucumán: Suipacha 140, Microcentro, tel. 4322-0565, turismo@tucuman.gov.ar, www.tucuman.gov.ar

Villa Carlos Paz (municipal): Lavalle 623, Oficinas 38/39, Microcentro, tel. 4322-0053, casacarlospaz@carlospaz.gov.ar, www.carlospaz.gov.ar

Villa Gesell (municipal): Bartolomé Mitre 1702, San Nicolás, tel./fax 4374-5199

---

at discount prices. ACA has offices in all provincial capitals and many smaller cities as well.

For topographic maps, visit the **Instituto Geográfico Militar** (Avenida Cabildo 301, Palermo, Buenos Aires, tel. 011/4576-5576, www.igm.gov.ar).

Tourist Offices

The **Secretaría Nacional de Turismo** (www.turismo.gov.ar), the national tourism service, has its main office in Buenos Aires, but every Argentine province also maintains a tourist information representative in the capital.

Each province also operates an information office in its own capital, and often in specific tourist destinations as well. Almost every other locality has its own tourist office—even in very small towns; these normally keep long summer hours but may be limited the rest of the year.

FILM AND PHOTOGRAPHY

Color print film is widely available, color slide film less reliably so. In any event, film tends to be cheaper in North America and Europe, so it's best to bring as much as possible. If purchasing film in Argentina, check the expiration date to make sure it's current, especially in out-of-the-way places. In the capital and larger tourist centers, competent print-film processing is readily available and moderately priced, but it's better to hold slide film until your return to your home country if possible (but store it under cool, dark, and dry conditions).

Environmental conditions can affect the quality of your shots and the type of film you should use. Bright sun can wash out photographs; in these circumstances, it's best to use a relatively slow film, around ASA 64 or 100, and a polarizing filter to reduce glare. A polarizing filter also improves contrast, dramatizing the sky and clouds, but can result in a dark foreground if you're not careful.

WEIGHTS AND MEASURES

Time

Argentina is three hours behind GMT for most

PHOTOGRAPHIC ETIQUETTE—AND A WARNING

Most Argentines, especially *porteños*, are not exactly camera-shy, but visitors should be cautious about photographing political protests—the police are notorious for cataloguing dissidents, so protestors may be suspicious of people with cameras. Likewise, avoid photography near military installations, although The Sentry Will Shoot signs are mostly a thing of past.

Generally, if a person's presence in a photograph is incidental, as in a townscape, it's unnecessary to ask permission, but avoid the in-your-face approach. If in doubt, ask; if rejected, don't insist. If you're purchasing something from a market vendor, he or she will almost certainly agree to be photographed.

There is one absolute no-no, however—without express permission, do not even think about photographing Israeli or Jewish community sites anywhere in Argentina. Since car-bomb attacks on Retiro's Israeli Embassy in 1992 and Once's Jewish cultural center in 1994, federal police are stationed outside all these sites. They will politely or, if necessary, not-so-politely, discourage would-be photographers.

of the year, and does not observe daylight savings (summer time). When the U.S. Eastern Time Zone is on daylight savings (during the Northern-Hemisphere summer) and Argentina is on standard time, Buenos Aires is one hour ahead of New York; the rest of the year, there is a two-hour difference.

Electricity

Throughout the country, nearly all outlets are 220 volts, 50 cycles, so converters are necessary for North American appliances like computers, electric razors, and the like. Traditional plugs have two rounded prongs, but more-recent ones have three flat blades that form,

roughly, an isosceles triangle; cheap adapters are widely available.

Adequately powered converters, though, are hard to find, so it's better to bring one from overseas.

Measurements

The metric system is official, but this doesn't completely eliminate the variety of vernacular measures that Argentines use in everyday life. Rural folk often use the Spanish *legua* (league) of about five kilometers as a measure of distance, and the *quintal* of 46 kilos is also widely used, especially in wholesale markets and agricultural statistics.

Glossary

acequia—irrigation canal, especially in the Cuyo provinces

aduana—customs

aduana paralela—"parallel customs;" corrupt customs officials

agua de la canilla—tap water; in adjacent Chile, this is *agua de la llave*

albergue juvenil—youth hostel

albergue transitorio—a by-the-hour-hotel, frequently used by young and not-so-young couples in search of privacy

altiplano—high steppe of northern Argentine Andes; synonymous with puna

andén—platform at a train station or bus terminal

anexo—telephone extension

arbolito—street money-changer, so called because they are planted in one spot

argentinidad—nebulous notion of Argentine nationalism, often associated with the gaucho

arrabales—geographically and socially peripheral parts of Buenos Aires, identified with immigrants and the rise of the tango

asambleas populares—neighborhood assemblies of protestors and activists frustrated with Argentine institutions

autopista—freeway

avenida—avenue

balneario—bathing or beach resort

baño compartido—shared bath (in a hotel or other accommodations)

baño general—shared or general bath (in a hotel or other accommodations)

baño privado—private bath

barrancas—natural levee on the original banks of the Río de Plata, now far inland in San Telmo, Belgrano, and other parts of Buenos Aires because of continual landfill

barras bravas—"soccer hooligans," violent gangs affiliated with soccer teams

barrio—borough or neighborhood

bis—used to modify addresses, bus routes, and the like that have the same number; Paseo 110 and Paseo 110 bis, for example, are similar to 110 Paseo and 110-A Paseo in English

boleadoras—rounded stones, tied together with leather thong, used for hunting by Pampas and Patagonian Indians; also known as *bolas*

boliche—dance club

bono—bond, a provincial letter of credit serving as a parallel currency equivalent to the peso. If at all possible, visitors should avoid accepting *bonos,* which are being phased out.

bronca—a singularly *porteño* combination of aggravation and frustration; there is no precise English equivalent, the closest being "wrath" or, in Britain, "aggro"

cabildo—colonial governing council

cabotaje—full-fare domestic airline ticket

cacique—indigenous chief or headman

cajero automático—automatic teller machine (ATM)

calle—street

camarote—sleeper berth on a train

camioneta—pickup truck

campo—countryside

candombe—music and dance of Afro-Argentine *porteños,* of whom few remain

característica—telephone area code

carne—beef; other kinds of meat are *carne blanca* (literally, "white meat")

carretera—highway

cartelera—discount ticket agency

cartonero—a scavenger who picks recyclables from the garbage on Buenos Aires streets; synonymous with *ciruja* (literally, "surgeon")

casa chorizo—"sausage house," a narrow residence on a deep lot

casa de cambio—official money-exchange facility, often just "cambio"

casco—"big house" of an *estancia*

casilla—post office box

caudillo—in early independence times, a provincial warlord, though the term is often used for any populist leader, such as Juan Domingo Perón

cerro—hill

chamamé—accordion-based folk music of northeastern Argentine littoral

chopp—draft beer

cobro revertido—collect or reverse-charge telephone call

coche cama—spacious, fully reclining, long-distance bus seat

cocoliche—pidgin blend of Italian and Spanish spoken by Mediterranean European immigrants

coima—bribe

colectivo—a city bus

comedor—simple eatery or dining room

confitería—a restaurant/café with a menu of *minutas* (short orders)

conventillo—tenement, often an abandoned mansion taken over by squatters

corralito—unpopular banking restrictions imposed by the Argentine government during the debt default and devaluation of 2001–02

cospel—bus token, still used in some provincial cities (pl. *cospeles*)

costanera—any road along a seashore, lakeshore, or riverside

criollo—in colonial times, an Argentine-born Spaniard; in the present, normally a descriptive term meaning "traditionally" Argentine

desaparecido—"disappeared one," victim of the military dictatorship of 1976–83

descamisados—"shirtless ones," working-class followers of Juan and Evita Perón

día de campo—"day in the countryside" on a tourist *estancia*

dique—deep water basin dredged in the harbor of Buenos Aires

doble tracción—four-wheel drive, also known as *cuatro por cuatro* (the latter written as "4X4")

edificio—building

embalsado—"floating island" in the marshes of Iberá

encomienda—in colonial times, a grant of Indian labor within a given geographical area; the *encomendero* (holder of the *encomienda*) incurred the reciprocal obligation to provide instruction in the Spanish language and Catholic religion, though such obligations were rarely honored

escrache—public demonstration, originally identifying human-rights violators at their residences, but since extended to perceived corrupt officials and institutions

estancia—cattle or sheep ranch controlling large extents of land, often with an absentee owner, dominant manager, and resident employees

estanciero—owner of an *estancia*

estatuas vivas—"living statues," mimes in touristed areas of Buenos Aires

estero—estuary

facón—gaucho knife

farmacia de turno—pharmacy remaining open all night for emergencies, on a rotating basis

feria—artisans' market

ficha—token, formerly used on Buenos Aires subway and still used on city buses in some parts of the country

filete—traditional art of *porteño* sign painters, in a calligraphic style

fileteador—*filete* artist

gasoil—diesel fuel

gauchesco—adjective describing romantic art or literature about, as opposed to by, gauchos

golfo—gulf

golpe de estado—coup d'etat

Gran Aldea—"great village," Buenos Aires prior to the influx of 20th-century immigrants

heladería—ice creamery

hipódromo—horserace track

hospedaje—family-run lodging

indígena—indigenous person

indigenista—adjective describing romantically pro-Indian literature, music, and art

infracción—traffic violation

ingenio—industrial sugar mill of northwestern Argentina

intendencia—park headquarters

isla—island

islote—islet

istmo—isthmus

IVA—*impuesto de valor agregado,* or value-added tax (VAT)

lago—lake

laguna—lagoon

latifundio—large landholding, usually an *estancia*

local—numbered office or locale, at a given street address

locutorio—telephone call center

lunfardo—*porteño* street slang that developed in working-class immigrant barrios like La Boca but is now more widely used in Argentine Spanish, though not in formal situations

machista—male chauvinist

malevo—street bully

media pensión—half board, at a hotel or guesthouse

menú—menu; also, a fixed-price meal

meseta—Patagonian steppe

mestizo—individual of mixed indigenous and Spanish ancestry

milonga—informal neighborhood dance club, which often includes tango as a participant rather than spectator activity

minuta—a short-order meal like pasta

mirador—overlook or viewpoint

mozo—term of address for a restaurant waiter; note that in neighboring Chile, this would be extremely rude

museo—museum

ñoqui—"ghost employee," collecting a state salary despite performing little or no work

oligarquía terrateniente—traditional land-owning "aristocracy" of the pampas

onces—Chilean afternoon tea

palacete—mansion

pampa—broad, flat expanse in and around Buenos Aires Province

pampero—southwesterly cold front on the Argentine pampas

parada—bus stop

parque nacional—national park

partido—administrative subdivision of an Argentine province, equivalent to a county

pasarela—catwalk in wet or marshy area

paseaperros—professional dog walker

payador—spontaneous gaucho singer

peaje—toll booth

peatonal—pedestrian mall

pensión—family-run accommodation

pensión completa—full board, at a hotel or guesthouse

picante—spicy-hot; the Argentine tolerance for spicy food is very low, however, and most visitors may find foods labeled spicy relatively bland

pingüinera—penguin colony

piquete—protestors' roadblock

piropo—sexist remark, ranging from humorous and innocuous to truly vulgar; also, on *filete,* an aphorism

playa—beach

polideportivo—sports club

porteño—native or resident of Buenos Aires

propina—tip, as at a restaurant

puente—bridge

puerto—port

Pullman—first-class bus, with reclining seats and luggage storage underneath

pulpería—general store, often the only retail outlet in a rural area

puna—high steppe of northern Argentine Andes; synonymous with altiplano

Puntano—native of the province of San Luis

quebrada—canyon

quinta—country estate

ramal—branch of a bus or rail line

rastra—studded gaucho belt

recargo—surcharge on credit card purchases

reducción—colonial settlement where missionaries concentrated indigenous population for catechization

remise—meterless radiotaxi charging a fixed rate within a given zone

reserva nacional—national reserve

residencial—permanent budget accommodations, often also called hotel

restó—fashionable, even pretentious, term for a restaurant, especially in Buenos Aires

río—river

rotisería—delicatessen

ruca—Mapuche plank house, with thatched roof

ruta—route or highway

ruta nacional—federal highway

ruta provincial—provincial highway

saladero—meat-salting plant of late-colonial and early-republican times

s/n—*sin número,* a street address without a number

sudestada—cold wind out of the southeast

tango canción—"tango song," with music and lyrics expressing nostalgia

tanguero—tango dancer

tarifa mostrador—hotel "rack rate," from which there are often discounts

tenedor libre—literally "free fork," all-you-can-eat restaurant

toldo—tent of animal skins, inhabited by mobile Pampas Indians in pre-Columbian times

trasnoche—late-night cinema, often starting at 1 A.M. or later

trucho—bogus

turco—Argentine of Middle Eastern descent

ventanilla—ticket window at a bus terminal or train station

villa miseria—urban shantytown

viveza criolla—"artful deception," ranging from small-scale cheating to audacious chutzpah

voseo—use of the second-person-singular pronoun *vos* and its distinct verb forms in Argentina, Uruguay, Paraguay, and some other countries; most others, though, use the *tuteo* (the pronoun *tú* and its forms)

yungas—subtropical cloud forest of northwestern Argentina

zafra—sugar harvest of northwestern Argentina

ABBREVIATIONS

4WD—four-wheel-drive

ACA—Automóvil Club Argentino

APN—Administration de Parques Nacionales (National Parks Administration)

BA—Buenos Aires

int.—*interno,* like ext. (extension) in English

IVA—Impuesto de Valor Agregado (Value-Added Tax)

RN—Ruta Nacional (National Highway)

RP—Ruta Provincial (Provincial Highway)

Spanish Phrasebook

Spanish is Argentina's official language, but the stereotypical *porteño* intonation—equivalent to a Bronx accent in New York—is unmistakably different from any other variant. Argentine Spanish in general is distinctive, often Italian-inflected, most notable for pronouncing the "ll" diphthong and "y" as "zh." "Llegar" (to arrive), for example, is pronounced "zhe-gar," while "yo" (I) is pronounced "zho."

Another distinguishing feature is the use of the familiar pronoun "vos" instead of "tú." Verb forms of the *voseo* differ from those of the *tuteo,* although Argentines will always understand speakers who use "tú." In the western Cuyo provinces, it's not unusual to hear the *tuteo.* See the sidebar "El Voseo" earlier in this section for more information.

Visitors spending any length of time in Buenos Aires, especially students and business people, should look for Tino Rodríguez's *Primer Diccionario de Sinónimos del Lunfardo* (Buenos Aires: Editorial Atlántida, 1987), which defines *porteño* street slang—some of whose usage requires *great* caution for those unaware of their every meaning.

PRONUNCIATION GUIDE

Spanish is a more phonetic language than English, but there are still occasional variations in pronunciation, especially in Argentina.

Consonants

c — as 'c' in "cat," before 'a,' 'o,' or 'u'; like 's' before 'e' or 'i'

d — as 'd' in "dog," except between vowels, then like 'th' in "that"

g — before 'e' or 'i,' like the 'ch' in Scottish "loch"; elsewhere like 'g' in "get"

h — always silent

j — like the English 'h' in "hotel," but stronger

ll — like the 'z' in "azure"

ñ — like the 'ni' in "onion"

r — always pronounced as strong 'r'

rr — trilled 'r'

v — similar to the 'b' in "boy" (not as English 'v')

y — like "ll," it sounds like the "z" in azure. When standing alone, it's pronounced like the 'e' in "me."

z — like 's' in "same" b, f, k, l, m, n, p, q, s, t, w, x as in English

Vowels

a — as in "father," but shorter

e — as in "hen"

i — as in "machine"

o — as in "phone"

u — usually as in "rule"; when it follows a 'q' the 'u' is silent; when it follows an 'h' or 'g,' it's pronounced like 'w,' except when it comes between 'g' and 'e' or 'i,' when it's also silent (unless it has an umlaut, when it again pronounced as English 'w'

Stress

Native English speakers frequently make pronunciation errors by ignoring stress—all Spanish vowels—a, e, i, o and u—may carry accents that determine which syllable of a word gets emphasis. Often, stress seems unnatural to nonnative speakers—the surname Chávez, for instance, is stressed on the first syllable—but failure to observe this rule may mean that native speakers may not understand you.

NUMBERS

zero — *cero*

one — *uno (masculine)*

one — *una (feminine)*

two — *dos*

three — *tres*

four — *cuatro*

five — *cinco*

six — *seis*

seven — *siete*

eight — *ocho*

nine — *nueve*

10 — *diez*

11 — *once*

12 — *doce*

13 — *trece*

14 — *catorce*

15 — *quince*

16 — *diez y seis*

17 — *diez y siete*

18 — *diez y ocho*

19 — *diez y nueve*

20 — *veinte*

21 — *veinte y uno*

30 — *treinta*

40 — *cuarenta*

50 — *cincuenta*

60 — *sesenta*

70 — *setenta*

80 — *ochenta*

90 — *noventa*

100 — *cien*

101 — *ciento y uno*

200 — *doscientos*

1,000 — *mil*

10,000 — *diez mil*

1,000,000 — *un millón*

DAYS OF THE WEEK

Sunday — *domingo*

Monday — *lunes*

Tuesday — *martes*

Wednesday — *miércoles*

Thursday — *jueves*

Friday — *viernes*

Saturday — *sábado*

TIME

While Argentines normally use the 12-hour clock (A.M. and P.M.), they sometimes use the 24-hour clock, usually associated with plane or bus schedules,. Under the 24-hour clock, for example, *las diez de la noche* (10 P.M.) would be *las 22 horas* (2200 hours).

What time is it? — *¿Qué hora es?*

It's o'clock — *Es la una.*

It's o'clock — *Son las dos.*

It's two o'clock — *A las dos.*

It's ten to three — *Son tres menos diez.*

It's ten past three — *Son tres y diez.*

It's three fifteen — *Son las tres y cuarto.*

It's two forty five — *Son tres menos cuarto.*

It's two thirty — *Son las dos y media.*

It's six A.M. — *Son las seis de la mañana.*

It's six P.M. — *Son las seis de la tarde.*

It's ten P.M. — *Son las diez de la noche.*

Today — *hoy*

Tomorrow — *mañana*

Morning — *la mañana*

Know Argentina

Tomorrow morning — *mañana por la mañana*
Yesterday — *ayer*
Week — *la semana*
Month — *mes*
Year — *año*
Last night — *anoche*
The next day — *el día siguiente*

USEFUL WORDS AND PHRASES

Argentines and other Spanish-speaking people consider formalities important. Whenever approaching anyone for information or some other reason, do not forget the appropriate salutation—good morning, good evening, etc. Standing alone, the greeting *hola* (hello) can sound brusque.

Note that most of the words below are fairly standard, common to all Spanish-speaking countries. Many, however, have more idiomatic Argentine equivalents; refer to the Glossary for these.

Hello. — *Hola.*
Good morning. — *Buenos días.*
Good afternoon. — *Buenas tardes.*
Good evening. — *Buenas noches.*
How are you? — *¿Cómo está?*
Fine. — *Muy bien.*
And you? — *¿Y usted?*
So-so. — *Más o menos.*
Thank you. — *Gracias.*
Thank you very much. — *Muchas gracias.*
You're very kind. — *Muy amable.*
You're welcome — *De nada (literally, "It's nothing.")*
Yes — *sí*
No — *no*
I don't know. — *No sé.*
It's fine; okay — *Está bien.*
Good; okay — *Bueno.*
Please — *por favor*
Pleased to meet you. — *Mucho gusto.*
Excuse me (physical) — *Perdóneme.*
Excuse me (speech) — *Discúlpeme.*
I'm sorry. — *Lo siento.*
Goodbye — *adiós*

See you later — *hasta luego (literally, "until later")*
More — *más*
Less — *menos*
Better — *mejor*
Much, a lot — *mucho*
A little — *un poco*
Large — *grande*
Small — *pequeño, chico*
Quick, fast — *rápido*
Slowly — *despacio*
Bad — *malo*
Difficult — *difícil*
Easy — *fácil*
He/She/It is gone; as in "She left," "He's gone" — *Ya se fue.*
I don't speak Spanish well. — *No hablo bien el español.*
I don't understand. — *No entiendo.*
How do you say . . . in Spanish? — *¿Cómo se dice . . . en español?*
Do you understand English? — *¿Entiende el inglés?*
Is English spoken here? (Does anyone here speak English?) — *¿Se habla inglés aquí?*

TERMS OF ADDRESS

When in doubt, use the formal *usted* (you) as a form of address. If you wish to dispense with formality and feel that the desire is mutual, you can say *Me podés tutear* (you can call me "tu") even though Argentines use the slightly different verb forms that correlate with the familiar pronoun "vos."

I — *yo*
You (formal) — *usted*
you (familiar) — *vos*
He/him — *él*
She/her — *ella*
We/us — *nosotros*
You (plural) — *ustedes*
They/them (all males or mixed gender) — *ellos*
They/them (all females) — *ellas*
Mr., sir — *señor*
Mrs., madam — *señora*
Miss, young lady — *señorita*
Wife — *esposa*

Husband — *marido or esposo*
Friend — *amigo (male), amiga (female)*
Sweetheart — *novio (male), novia (female)*
Son, daughter — *hijo, hija*
Brother, sister — *hermano, hermana*
Father, mother — *padre, madre*
Grandfather, grandmother — *abuelo, abuela*

GETTING AROUND

Where is . . . ? — *¿Dónde está . . . ?*
How far is it to . . . ? — *¿A cuanto está . . . ?*
from . . . to . . . — *de . . . a . . .*
Highway — *la carretera*
Road — *el camino*
Street — *la calle*
Block — *la cuadra*
Kilometer — *kilómetro*
North — *norte*
South — *sur*
West — *oeste; poniente*
East — *este; oriente*
Straight ahead — *derecho; adelante*
To the right — *a la derecha*
To the left — *a la izquierda*

ACCOMMODATIONS

¿Hay habitación? — Is there a room?
May I (we) see it? — *¿Puedo (podemos) verla?*
What is the rate? — *¿Cuál es el precio?*
Is that your best rate? — *¿Es su mejor precio?*
Is there something cheaper? — *¿Hay algo más económico?*
Single room — *un sencillo*
Double room — *un doble*
Room for a couple — *matrimonial*
Key — *llave*
With private bath — *con baño privado*
With shared bath — *con baño general; con baño compartido*
Hot water — *agua caliente*
Cold water — *agua fría*
Shower — *ducha*
electric shower — *ducha eléctrica*
Towel — *toalla*
Soap — *jabón*
Toilet paper — *papel higiénico*

Air conditioning — *aire acondicionado*
Fan — *ventilador*
Blanket — *frazada; manta*
Sheets — *sábanas*

PUBLIC TRANSPORT

Bus stop — *la parada*
Bus terminal — *terminal de buses*
Airport — *el aeropuerto*
Launch — *lancha*
Dock — *muelle*
I want a ticket to . . . — *Quiero un pasaje a . . .*
I want to get off at . . . — *Quiero bajar en . . .*
Here, please. — *Aquí, por favor.*
Where is this bus going? — *¿Adónde va este autobús?*
Roundtrip — *ida y vuelta*
What do I owe? — *¿Cuánto le debo?*

FOOD

Menu — *la carta, el menú*
Glass — *vaso*
Fork — *tenedor*
Knife — *cuchillo*
Spoon — *cuchara*
Napkin — *servilleta*
Soft drink — *agua fresca*
Coffee — *café*
Cream — *crema*
Tea — *té*
Sugar — *azúcar*
Drinking water — *agua pura, agua potable*
Bottled carbonated water — *agua mineral con gas*
Bottled uncarbonated water — *agua sin gas*
Beer — *cerveza*
Wine — *vino*
Milk — *leche*
Juice — *jugo*
Eggs — *huevos*
Bread — *pan*
Watermelon — *sandía*
Banana — *banana*
Apple — *manzana*
Orange — *naranja*
Peach — *durazno*

Pineapple — *ananá*
Meat (without) — *carne (sin)*
Beef — *carne de res*
Chicken — *pollo; gallina*
Fish — *pescado*
Shellfish — *mariscos*
Shrimp — *camarones*
Fried — *frito*
Roasted — *asado*
Barbecued — *a la parrilla*
Breakfast — *desayuno*
Lunch — *almuerzo*
Dinner, or a late night snack — *cena*
The check, or bill — *la cuenta*

MAKING PURCHASES

I need . . . — *Necesito . . .*
I want . . . — *Deseo . . . or Quiero . . .*
I would like . . . (more polite) — *Quisiera . . .*
How much does it cost? — *¿Cuánto cuesta?*
What's the exchange rate? — *¿Cuál es el tipo de cambio?*

May I see . . . ? — *¿Puedo ver . . . ?*
This one — *ésta/ésto*
Expensive — *caro*
Cheap — *barato*
Cheaper — *más barato*
Too much — *demasiado*

HEALTH

Help me please. — *Ayúdeme por favor.*
I am ill. — *Estoy enfermo.*
Me duele. — *It hurts.*
Pain — *dolor*
Fever — *fiebre*
Stomach ache — *dolor de estómago*
Headache — *dolor de cabeza*
Vomiting — *vomitar*
Diarrhea — *diarrhea*
Drugstore — *farmacia*
Medicine — *medicina*
Pill, tablet — *pastilla*
Birth control pills — *pastillas anticonceptivas*
Condom — *condón, preservativo*

Suggested Reading

ARCHAEOLOGY, ETHNOGRAPHY, AND ETHNOHISTORY

McEwan, Colin, Luis A. Borrero and Alfredo Prieto, eds. *Patagonia: Natural History, Prehistory and Ethnography at the Uttermost End of the Earth.* Princeton: Princeton University Press, 1997. First published under the auspices of the British Museum, this is a collection of learned but accessible essays on topics ranging from Patagonia's natural environment to early human occupation, first encounters between Europeans and indigenes, the origins of the Patagonian "giants," and even Patagonian travel literature.

Schávelzon, Daniel. *Historia del Comer y del Beber en Buenos Aires.* Buenos Aires: Aguilar, 2000. Urban archaeologist Schávelzon chronicles the evolution of the *porteño* diet

through salvage excavations in the city, finding among other surprises that beef consumption was not always so great as some have assumed.

GUIDEBOOKS AND TRAVELOGUES

Crouch, Gregory. *Enduring Patagonia.* New York: Random House, 2001. Details one mountaineer's experiences on Fitz Roy and Cerro Torre in Parque Nacional Los Glaciares.

Darwin, Charles. *Voyage of the Beagle* (many editions). Perhaps the greatest travel book ever written, Darwin's narrative of his 19th-century journey bursts with insights on the people, places, and even politics he saw while collecting the plants and animals that led to his revolutionary theories. The great scientist observed the city of Buenos Aires, the surrounding pampas and Patagonia, and met key figures in the country's history, including the dictator Rosas.

France, Miranda. *Bad Times in Buenos Aires.* Hopewell, N.J.: The Ecco Press, 1998. A timeless title, perhaps, but it refers to the author's sardonic analysis of her early 1990s residence in the Argentine capital.

Green, Toby. *Saddled with Darwin.* London: Phoenix, 1999. An audacious if uneven account by a young, talented writer of his attempt to retrace the hoofprints—not the footsteps—of Darwin's travels through Uruguay, Argentina, and Chile. Self-effacing but still serious, the author manages to compare Darwin's experience with his own, reflect on contemporary distortions of the great scientist's theories, and stay almost completely off the gringo trail.

Guevara, Ernesto. *The Motorcycle Diaries: A Journey around South America.* New York and London: Verso, 1995. Translated by Ann Wright, this is an account of an Argentine drifter's progress from Buenos Aires across the Andes and up the Chilean coast by motorcycle and, when it broke down, by any means necessary. The author is better known by his nickname "Che," a common Argentine interjection.

Head, Francis Bond. *Journeys Across the Pampas & Among the Andes.* Carbondale: Southern Illinois University Press, 1967. Nearly a decade before Darwin, "Galloping Head" rode across the Argentine plains and over the Andes into Chile, in the early years of Argentine independence. Originally published in 1826, some of Head's observations on the gaucho's abilities and adaptability resemble Darwin's, but Head detested Buenos Aires itself.

Moreno, Francisco Pascasio. *Perito Moreno's Travel Journal: a Personal Reminiscence.* Buenos Aires: Elefante Blanco, 2002. Absorbing translation of the great Patagonian explorer's northern Patagonian letters and journals, including his thrilling escape down the Río Limay from his indigenous captors.

Naipaul, V.S. *The Return of Eva Perón.* New York: Knopf, 1980. The great but controversial British Nobel author's acerbic observations on Argentine society, in the context of his visit during the vicious 1976–83 dictatorship.

Petrina, Alberto, ed. *Buenos Aires: Guía de Arquitectura.* Buenos Aires and Seville: Municipalidad de la Ciudad de Buenos Aires and Junta de Andalucía, 1994. Outstanding architectural guide with eight walking tours of the city, embellished with architectural sketches and photographs.

Roosevelt, Theodore. *A Book Lover's Holiday in the Open.* New York: Scribner's, 1916. After retiring from politics, the still vigorous U.S. president undertook numerous overseas adventures; among other stories, this collection retells his crossing of the Andes from Chile into the lake district of northern Argentine Patagonia, and his meeting with legends like Perito Moreno.

Symmes, Patrick. *Chasing Che: A Motorcycle Journey in Search of the Guevara Legend.* New York: Vintage, 2000. Symmes follows the tiremarks of Che's legendary trip from Buenos Aires through Argentina and Chile in the early 1950s.

Vidal, Emeric Essex. *Buenos Aires and Montevideo in a Series of Picturesque Illustrations Taken on the Spot.* Buenos Aires: Mitchell's English Book-Store, 1944. Originally published in London in 1820: this British naval officer's remarkable travelogue literally paints a picture—with full-color illustrations to complement his text descriptions—of Buenos Aires in the early independence years.

Willis, Bailey. *A Yanqui in Patagonia.* Stanford: Stanford University Press, 1947. Out of print but well worth seeking, this U.S. geologist's memoir is a vivid account of the northern Patagonian frontier in the early 20th century. It's also fascinating for his assessment of the region's potential, and for his account of intrigues within the Argentine governments of the day.

Wilson, Jason. *Buenos Aires: a Cultural and Literary Companion.* New York: Interlink, 2000. Part of the "Cities of the Imagination" series, this is a breathlessly thorough summary of what *porteño,* other Argentine, and foreign authors have written about the capital. It's particularly good at providing a sense of what untranslated Argentine authors have written about the city.

HISTORY

Andrews, George Reid. *The Afro-Argentines of Buenos Aires, 1800–1900.* Madison: University of Wisconsin Press, 1980. Pathbreaking research on the so-called "disappearance" of the capital's Afro-Argentine community, which once comprised nearly a third of its total population.

Crow, John A. *The Epic of Latin America,* 3rd ed. Berkeley: University of California Press, 1980. A comprehensive history of the region, told more through narrative than analysis, in an immensely readable manner. Several chapters deal with Argentina.

Cushner, Nicholas P. *Jesuit Ranches and the Agrarian Development of Colonial Argentina, 1650–1767.* Albany, NY: SUNY Press, 1982. A workmanlike account of the Argentine Jesuit missions.

Cutolo, Vicente Osvaldo. *Buenos Aires: Historia de las Calles y sus Nombres.* Buenos Aires: Editorial Elche, 1988, 2 vols. This weighty two-volume set details the history not just of nearly every street in the city, but also the story behind the name.

De la Fuente, Ariel. *Children of Facundo.* Duke University Press, 2000. Still a relevant topic inn provincial politics, this is a detailed account of the rise of caudillos, with loyal gaucho support, in 19th-century La Rioja.

Dujovne Ortiz, Alicia. *Eva Perón.* New York: St. Martin's Press, 1996. Filled with controversial assertions, this nevertheless absorbing biography is at its most eloquent in describing the transformation of a poor provincial girl into a powerful international figure through a relentless and bitterly ruthless ambition, blended with a genuine concern for the truly destitute. Shawn Fields's translation to English, unfortunately, is awkward.

Eidt, Robert. *Pioneer Settlement in Northeast Argentina.* University of Wisconsin, 1971. Transformation of natural and cultural landscapes in the province of Misiones, from colonial times to the present.

Goñi, Uki. *The Real Odessa.* New York and London: Granta, 2002. A remarkable account of the controversial links between the Juan Perón government and the shadowy organization that spirited Nazi war criminals from Europe to Argentina. Employing a variety of archival sources on a topic that most often relies on rumor, Goñi implicates the Vatican and its Argentine branch as go-betweens in negotiations with the remnants of the Nazi regime.

Guillermoprieto, Alma. *Looking for History: Dispatches from Latin America.* New York: Vintage Books, 2001. This collection of essays from the talented Mexican journalist includes illuminating pieces on Eva Perón and Che Guevara.

Guy, Donna J. *Sex and Danger in Buenos Aires.* Lincoln: University of Nebraska Press, 1991. An academic account of the seamier side of immigration, relating it to sexual imbalance in the population, homosexuality, prostitution, the rise of the tango, and even Peronism.

Lynch, John. *Spanish-American Revolutions, 1808–1826,* 2nd ed. New York: W. W. Norton, 1986. Comprehensive account of the independence movements in Spanish America.

Moya, José C. *Cousins and Strangers: Spanish Immigrants in Buenos Aires, 1850–1930.* Berkeley:

University of California Press, 1998. An account of the capital's, and the country's, ambivalent relationship with immigrants often disparaged as *Gallegos* (Galicians).

Nouzeilles, Gabriela, and Gabriela Montaldo, eds. *The Argentina Reader: History, Culture, Politics.* Durham, NC: Duke University Press, 2002. Too big and heavy to carry along on the road, but this diverse collection of essays and extracts is an excellent introduction to the country through the eyes of Argentines, and visitors to Argentina, since colonial times.

Parry, J. H. *The Discovery of South America.* London: Paul Elek, 1979. A well-illustrated account of early voyages and overland explorations on the continent.

Rock, David. *Argentina 1516–1987: from Spanish Colonization to the Falklands War and Alfonsín.* London: I.B. Taurus, 1987. A comprehensive narrative and analysis of Argentine history prior to Carlos Menem's presidency.

Rock, David. *Authoritarian Argentina: the Nationalist Movement, Its History and Its Impact.* Berkeley: University of California Press, 1993. Building on the author's earlier work, Rock examines the durability of right-wing nationalism that led to the 1976–83 "Dirty War," even as comparable nationalisms were failing in Spain, Portugal, Mexico, and other countries.

Scobie, James R. *Buenos Aires: From Plaza to Suburb, 1870–1910.* New York: Oxford University Press, 1974. A classic account of the city's explosive growth of the late 19th century, and the transition from "Gran Aldea" to "Paris of the South."

Shumway, Norman. *The Invention of Argentina.* Berkeley: University of California Press, 1991. An intellectual history of Argentina's founding myths, and the degree to which elitist debate excluded entire sectors of society from participation and resulted in frequent ungovernability.

Slatta, Richard. *Cowboys of the Americas.* New Haven and London: Yale University Press, 1990. A spectacularly illustrated comparative analysis of New World horsemen, including both Argentine gauchos and Chilean *huasos.*

GOVERNMENT AND POLITICS

Castañeda, Jorge G. *Utopia Unarmed: the Latin American Left After the Cold War.* New York: Knopf, 1993. A former academic and Mexican foreign minister makes Argentina the starting point in his analysis of the democratization of Latin America's revolutionary left, with a particularly good analysis of the Montoneros urban guerrilla movement.

Caviedes, César. *The Southern Cone: Realities of the Authoritarian State.* Totowa, NJ: Rowman & Allanheld, 1984. A comparative study of the military dictatorships of Chile, Argentina, Uruguay, and Brazil of the 1970s and 1980s.

Verbitsky, Horacio. *The Flight: Confessions of an Argentine Dirty Warrior.* New York: The New Press, 1996. Account of the worst excesses of the military dictatorship of 1976–83, based on interviews with Francisco Scilingo, a self-confessed torturer and murderer who shoved political prisoners out of airplanes over the South Atlantic. Scilingo was the first Argentine military officer to break the silence over human-rights violations.

LITERATURE AND LITERARY CRITICISM

For more suggestions on Argentine literature, see Literature under Arts and Entertainment earlier in this section.

Aira, César. *The Hare.* London and New York: Serpent's Tail, 1998. Touching the dangerous territory of magical realism, Aira's novel of Rosas, the Mapuche, and a wandering English naturalist on the pampas is a complex tale that ties up neatly at the end.

Fuentes, Carlos. *The Campaign.* New York: Farrar Straus Giroux, 1991. He's not an Argentine himself, but Mexico's great contemporary novelist has managed to express the epic contradictions of the independence era through the character of a criollo from Buenos Aires.

Gerchunoff, Alberto. *Jewish Gauchos of the Pampas.* Albuquerque: University of New Mexico Press, 1998. Evocative vignettes of life in the Jewish agricultural colonies of Entre Ríos, some of them romanticized but others portraying violence and deceit on the frontier.

Martínez, Tomás Eloy. *Santa Evita.* New York: Knopf, 1996. One of Argentina's leading contemporary writers tackles the Evita myth in a fictionalized version of her post-mortem odyssey from Argentina to Italy, Spain, and back to Buenos Aires.

Martínez, Tomás Eloy. *The Perón Novel.* New York: Pantheon Books, 1988. Based on the author's own lengthy interviews with the exiled caudillo, for which fiction seemed the appropriate outlet. According to Jorge Castañeda, "Whether Perón ever actually uttered these words is in the last analysis irrelevant: he could have, he would have, and he probably did."

Meyer, Doris. *Victoria Ocampo: Against the Wind and the Tide.* Austin: University of Texas Press, 1990. Biography of the woman who led Argentina's equivalent to Britain's "Bloomsbury Group," through her literary magazine *Sur.* Her peers and friendships included Jorge Luis Borges, Adolfo Bioy Casares (married to her sister Silvina, also a writer), and international figures such as Andre Malraux, José Ortega y Gasset, and Rabindranath Tagore. The volume includes 15 of Victoria's own essays.

Vásquez Montalbán, Manuel. *The Buenos Aires Quintet.* London: Serpent's Tail, 2003. In this seemingly disjointed but ultimately coherent and insightful novel, first published in 1997, the late Spanish journalist sent his fictional gourmet detective Pepe Carvalho to Buenos Aires to track down a returned Dirty War exile.

Wilson, Jason. *Traveler's Literary Companion: South & Central America, Including Mexico.* Lincolnwood, Illinois: Passport Books, 1995. An edited collection of excerpts from literature, including fiction, poetry, and essays, that illuminates aspects of the countries from the Río Grande to the tip of Tierra del Fuego, including Argentina, Buenos Aires, and Chile.

Woodall, James. *Borges: a Life.* New York: Basic Books, 1997. An analytical—in the Freudian sense—biography of Argentina's most prominent literary figure. Originally appeared in Britain under the title *The Man in the Mirror of the Book* (London: Hodder & Stoughton, 1996).

Valenzuela, Luisa. *Bedside Manners.* London, Serpent's Tail, 1995. Surrealistically disorienting account of an exile's return to a country that is too familiar and at the same time unrecognizable.

ENVIRONMENT AND NATURAL HISTORY

Hudson, William Henry. *The Bird Biographies of W.H. Hudson.* Santa Barbara, California: Capra Press, 1988. A partial reprint of the romantic naturalist's detailed description of the birds he knew growing up in Buenos Aires Province, with illustrations.

Internet Resources

WEBSITES

Aerolíneas Argentinas
www.aerolineas.com.ar
Home page for Argentina's struggling flagship airline.

Aconcagua
www.aconcagua.com.ar
Clearing house for climbers and hikers on
the highest peak in the Americas.

Administración de Parques Nacionales
www.parquesnacionales.gov.ar
Primary government agency in charge of national parks and other conservation areas.

Aeropuertos Argentinos 2000
www.aa2000.com.ar
Private concessionaire operating most of Argentina's international and domestic airports,
including Buenos Aires's Ezeiza and Aeroparque; in English and Spanish.

Ambitoweb
www.ambitoweb.com
Online version of *porteño* financial daily *Ambito Financiero.*

American Falcon
www.americanfalcon.com.ar
Domestic airline with small planes and limited
routes, but due to begin flights to Chile.

AmeriSpan
www.amerispan.com
Information on language instruction throughout the Americas, including Argentina.

Argentina Business
www.invertir.com/index.html
Guide to business and investment in
Argentina.

Argentina Travel Net
www.argentinatravelnet.com
Portal for Argentine travel sites, though not
nearly all of the links are closely related to
travel; in Spanish and English.

Argentine Wines
www.argentinewines.com
Close-to-comprehensive introduction to Argentine wines and wine regions; in Spanish
and English.

**Asociación Argentina de Albergues de la Ju-
ventud (AAAJ)**
www.hostelling-aaaj.org.ar
Argentine hostelling organization, with limited facilities throughout the country.

Asociación de Fútbol Argentina
www.afa.org.ar
Argentina's professional soccer league; in English and Spanish.

Asociación Ornitológica del Plata
www.avesargentinas.org.ar
Buenos Aires–based bird-watching and conservation organization.

Automóvil Club Argentino (ACA)
www.aca.org.ar
Argentine automobile association, useful for
both information and up-to-date road maps.
Offers discounts for members of affiliated
clubs, such as AAA in the United States and
the AA in Britain.

B y T Argentina
www.bytargentina.com/ecentro.htm
Short-term apartment rentals and other information on Buenos Aires; in English and
Spanish.

Buenos Aires Herald
www.buenosairesherald.com
Abbreviated version of the capital's venerable

English-language daily, worthwhile for its editorials alone.

Centers for Disease Control
www.cdc.gov
   U.S. government page with travel health advisories.

CIA Factbook
www.odci.gov/cia/publications/factbook/
geos/ar.html
   The world's most notorious spooks perform at least one admirable public service in their annual encyclopedia of the world's countries, which appears complete online.

Ciudad Autónoma de Buenos Aires
www.buenosaires.gov.ar
   Comprehensive city government site, which includes tourist information in English and Portuguese as well as Spanish.

Clarín
www.clarin.com
   Outstanding online version of the capital's tabloid daily, the largest-circulation newspaper in the Spanish-speaking world.

Country Commercial Guide
www.usatrade.gov/website/CCG.nsf
   U.S. State Department's detailed summary of business climate and possibilities in Argentina and other foreign countries.

Currency Converter
www.oanda.com
   Present and historic exchange rate information.

Department of Health
www.doh.gov.uk/traveladvice/index.htm
   British government agency with country-by-country health advice.

Department of State
www.travel.state.gov
   Travel information and advisories from U.S. government; while it has a great deal of useful material, its warnings are often exaggerated.

Feria del Libro
www.el-libro.com/index.html
   Buenos Aires's heavily attended annual book fair.

Festival Buenos Aires Tango
www.festivaldetango.com.ar
   The capital's increasingly popular series of autumn (Feb.–Mar.) tango events, following Brazilian Carnaval.

Fondo Nacional de las Artes
www.fnartes.gov.ar
   Official federal government site with information on performing arts, architecture, cinema, and related fields.

Fundación Vida Silvestre Argentina
www.vidasilvestre.org.ar
   Nongovernmental wildlife and habitat advocates.

Gay in Buenos Aires
www.gayinbuenosaires.com.ar
   Portal to articles and services of interest to homosexual residents and visitors.

Greenpeace
www.greenpeace.org.ar
   Argentine affiliate of the international conservation organization.

Hostelling International Argentina
www.hostels.org.ar
   Argentine Hostelling International affiliate, with information on travel and activities throughout the country.

Instituto Geográfico Militar
www.igm.gov.ar
   Military geographical institute, preparing and selling maps of the country.

Instituto Nacional de Estadísticas y Censos (INDEC)
www.indec.mecon.ar
   Homepage for federal government statistical agency.

Interpatagonia
www.interpatagonia.com
Probably the most complete site for content and services on both the Argentine and Chilean sides of the Southern Cone's southernmost region.

La Nación
www.lanacion.com.ar
Major *porteño* daily, with an excellent Sunday cultural section.

La Plata
www.laplata.gov.ar/index.htm
Portal of the capital city of Buenos Aires Province.

Latin American Network Information Center (LANIC)
http://lanic.utexas.edu
Organized by the University of Texas, this site has a huge collection of quality links to Argentina and other Latin American countries.

Líneas Aéreas del Estado (LADE)
www.lade.com.ar
Commercial passenger arm of the Argentine air force.

Mercopress News Agency
www.falkland-malvinas.com
Montevideo-based Internet news agency covering politics and business in the Mercosur common market countries of Argentina, Brazil, Uruguay, and Paraguay, as well as Chile and the Falkland/Malvinas Islands; in English and Spanish.

Metrovías
www.metrovias.com.ar
Details on Buenos Aires subway system.

Ministerio de Relaciones Exteriores
www.mrecic.gov.ar/consulares/pagcon.html
Argentine foreign ministry, with information on visas and consulates; in English and Spanish.

Páginas Amarillas
www.paginasamarillas.com.ar
Yellow Pages for the entire country.

Página 12
www.pagina12.com
Outspoken left-of-center Buenos Aires daily, which has shifted from reporting toward opinion but features some of the country's best writers.

Secretaría Nacional de Turismo
www.turismo.gov.ar
National tourism authority, with information in Spanish and English.

Southern Winds
www.sw.com.ar
More-or-less viable domestic airline competitor to Aerolíneas Argentinas.

Trespuntos
www.3puntos.com
Investigative weekly newsmagazine.

UkiNet
www.ukinet.com
Freelancer's human-rights-oriented website, with an archive of his best work from Britain's Guardian and other sources.

USENET DISCUSSION GROUPS

Soc.culture.argentina
No-holds-barred discussion group that touches on many other issues besides travel.

Rec.travel.latin-america
Regional discussion group dealing with all Latin American countries, with a steady number of postings on Argentina.

Index

Estancias

Gauchos

bolas: 119
Casa de Museo: 133
clothing: 626
Día de la Tradición: 493
diet: 633
Festival del Puestero: 392
Fiesta de la Tradición: 134
gauchesco literature: 133, 614–615
Gil, Antonio: 186, 275, 606
history: 37, 118, 122, 137, 589
in art: 46–47
Jewish gauchos: 605
Museo de Motivos Argentinos José Hernán-
    dez: 76, 79–80
Museo Gauchesco del Pintor Gasparini:
    133–134
Museo Histórico Nacional: 61
Museo Histórico Provincial: 357
of the pampas: 130
payadores music: 620
Pulpería La Blanqueada: 133
San Antonio de Areco: 132, 133

Glaciers

Avenida de los Glaciares: 550
Glaciar Balmaceda: 565
Glaciar D'Agostini: 550
Glaciar Grey: 569, 572
Glaciar Martial: 519, 524
Glaciar Moreno: 416, 442, 480, 486, 487, 488–489
Glaciar Pía: 551
Glaciar Serrano: 550
Glaciar Torre: 492
Glaciar Upsala: 489–490
Glaciar Viedma: 491–492
Parque Nacional Los Glaciares: 487–493

H

hantavirus: 660–661
health and safety: 658–664
heladerías (ice creameries): 103
hepatitis: 660
hiking: 611; Parque Nacional Torres del Paine 567–569; Parque Provincial Aconcagua 258
Hill Station (Estancia Los Pozos): 478
history: 586–594; 14-day history tour 17–19
holidays: 627
horseback riding: 612; Buenos Aires 96; *see also specific place*
horse racing: 96
Humahuaca: 315–317
hypothermia: 661

I

ice creameries (*heladerías*): 103
indigenous peoples: 602
industry: 600
information and services: 664–672
Inka Empire: 587
insect-borne diseases: 660
Internet access: 669
invertebrates: 582
Iruya: 317–318
Isla Martín García: 115–117
itineraries: art and architecture 20–22; history 17–19; introductory tour 12–13; nature-lover's tour 25–27; top-to-tip tour 14–16; wine country tour 23–24

JKL

Jáchal: 275
Jesús: 196–197
Jewish population: 605
judicial and penal systems: 597
Jujuy Province: 288–322
Junín de los Andes: 392–394
kayaking: 613
Kimiri Aike: 555
La Boca: 61–63
La Cuarenta: 496–497
La Falda: 367–369
Lago Blanco: 534
Lago del Desierto: 492
Lago Fagnano (Kami): 530–531
Lago Lácar: 401
Lago Lolog: 401
Lago Nahuel Huapi: 417–418
Lago Posadas: 501
Lago Roca: 490
La Hoya: 430
Lake District, The: 390–424
La Leona: 497–498
language: 607; glossary 673; Spanish phrasebook 676
La Pampa Province: 163–168
La Plata: 123–129
La Posta de Hornillos: 312
La Quiaca: 318
La Rioja (city): 342–345
La Rioja Province: 336–349
Las Leñas: 266–267
La Trochita: 426, 427
literature: 614–616
Loreto: 197
Los Antiguos: 503–504
Los Molles: 265–266
Los Penitentes: 255
luggage: 6
Luján: 130–132

M

Magallanes Region (Chile): 4, 535–572
Magellanic penguin colonies: 450–451, 452, 472
Maimará: 312
Malargüe: 263–265
maps: 670–671
Mar del Plata: 144–155
marine wildlife: 578–579
mate (drink): 636–637

Must-Sees

Tango

U.S.~Metric Conversion

1 inch	=	2.54 centimeters (cm)
1 foot	=	.304 meters (m)
1 yard	=	0.914 meters
1 mile	=	1.6093 kilometers (km)
1 km	=	.6214 miles
1 fathom	=	1.8288 m
1 chain	=	20.1168 m
1 furlong	=	201.168 m
1 acre	=	.4047 hectares
1 sq km	=	100 hectares
1 sq mile	=	2.59 square km
1 ounce	=	28.35 grams
1 pound	=	.4536 kilograms
1 short ton	=	.90718 metric ton
1 short ton	=	2000 pounds
1 long ton	=	1.016 metric tons
1 long ton	=	2240 pounds
1 metric ton	=	1000 kilograms
1 quart	=	.94635 liters
1 US gallon	=	3.7854 liters
1 Imperial gallon	=	4.5459 liters
1 nautical mile	=	1.852 km

To compute Celsius temperatures, subtract 32 from Fahrenheit and divide by 1.8. To go the other way, multiply Celsius by 1.8 and add 32.

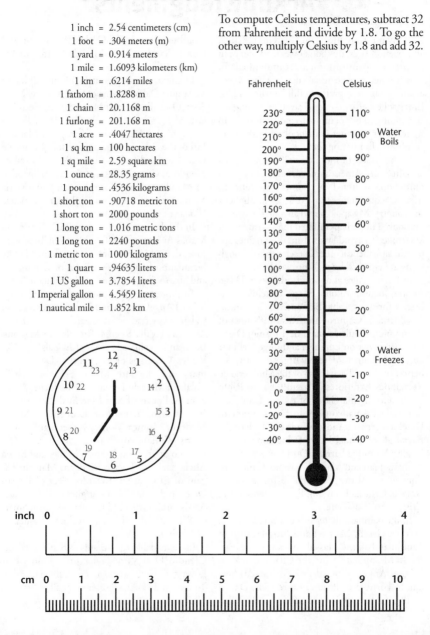

Acknowledgments

Like my previous efforts on Guatemala, Chile, and Buenos Aires, this book owes its existence in its present form to numerous individuals in North America, Argentina, and elsewhere. Once again, the highest praise to Bill Newlin and his Emeryville staff at Avalon Travel Publishing for continuing to offer author-friendly contracts to writers even as other guidebook publishers are ruthlessly eliminating them.

In the course of more than 20 years' experience in South America, more than half that as a guidebook writer, I owe enormous debts to friends, acquaintances, and officials throughout the country. My apologies to anyone I may have overlooked or perhaps omitted through an errant keystroke. To avoid favoritism, their names appear in alphabetical order in each region, though some are grouped by workplace.

In Buenos Aires and vicinity, thanks to Diego Allolio; Joaquín Allolio; Mario Banchik of Librerías Turísticas; Pablo Blay and Mariana Travacio; Mirta S. Capurro and Ricardo Sangla of the municipal Subsecretaría de Turismo; Diego Curubeto; Marion Eppinger and Jorge Helft for keeping me up to date on Argentine art; Alberto Fernández Basavilbaso of the Ministerio de Relaciones Exteriores; Martín Chaves, Pablo Fisch, and Silvina Garay of Asatej; León Ferrari; Rafael Amadeo Gentili; Josh Goodman; Derek Foster and Andrew Graham-Yooll of the *Buenos Aires Herald;* Harry S. Ingham; Nicolás Kugler; Monique Larraín; Dori Lieberman; my nephews Juan and Manuel Massolo; Carlos Enrique Meyer of the Secretaría de Turismo de la Nación; Cristina Paravano; Ernesto Semán; and Cristián Soler of Tigre.

In the pampas, my regards to Mónica García of Villa Gesell; Michael and Judy Hutton of Tandil; and all my Massolo in-laws of Olavarría. In Mesopotamia and the Chaco, thanks to Miguel Angel Allou of Foz do Iguaçu; Fernando Fornero of Paraná, Entre Ríos; Daniel Aníbal Garcés of Roque Sáenz Peña; Pedro Noailles of Colonia Carlos Pellegrini; and Charly Sandoval and Micaela Steffen of Yacutinga Lodge, Misiones.

In Cuyo, thanks go out to Johnny Albino of Malargüe; Daniel Cadile of Campo Base, Mendoza; Oscar Femenía of Mendoza; Gabriela Furlotti of Mendoza; Marcelo Gavirati of Puerto Madryn; Raphaël Joliat of San Juan; Mariana Juri of the Subsecretaría de Turismo, Mendoza; David Rivarola of San Luis; Pedro Rosell of Mendoza; Gabriela Testa of the Municipalidad de Mendoza; Hugo Torres of San Juan; María Marta Seijo of Mendoza; and María Graciela Viollaz of Malargüe.

In the Andean northwest, special mention to Matías Avenali and Alfredo Bolsi of Tucumán; José María Lucero of Salta; Frank and Heike Neumann of Salta; César Perea of Catamarca; and Sixto Vásquez (Toqo) of Humahuaca, Jujuy.

In Argentine Patagonia, the list is long: Miguel Angel Alonso and Leslie Scovenna of El Calafate; my traditional research assistant Laura Alvarez of Villa Regina, Río Negro; Mariano Besio and Cecilia Scarafoni of El Calafate; Alejandro Caparrós of El Chaltén; Dany Feldman and the late Mario Feldman of El Calafate; Marcelo Ferrante of Bariloche; Asunción Gallardo of San Martín de los Andes; Juan Carlos Lamas of Ecocentro Puerto Madryn; Mónica Montes Roberts and Estela Maris Williams of Entretur, Trelew; Charly Moreno of Trevelin; Herman Müller and María Alicia Sacks of Puerto Madryn; Marcelo Pagani of El Chaltén; Ricardo Pérez of Puerto Deseado; María Elisa Rodríguez of El Calafate; Alexis Simunovic of El Calafate; Agustín Smart of Estancia Menelik; and Rubén Vasquez of El Chaltén.

In Tierra del Fuego, regards to Barrie O'Byrne, Claudio Don Vito, Javier Jury, Julio César Lovece, and Sebastián Mair of Ushuaia, and to Tommy and Natalie Prosser Goodall of Estancia Harberton.

In Chilean Patagonia, thanks to Miguel Angel Muñoz and Andrea Lagunas Flores of Sernatur, Punta Arenas; Ivette Martínez of Punta Arenas; Alfonso López Rosas of Path@gone, Puerto Natales; Edmundo Martínez G. of Puerto Natales; Werner and Cecilia Ruf-Chaura of Casa Cecilia, Puerto Natales; Hernán Jofré of Concepto Indigo, Puerto Natales; and Wolf Kloss of Puerto Williams.

Stateside, thanks to Dan Buck of Washington, D.C.; Leandro Fernández Suárez of the Argentine consulate in Los Angeles; and Patricio Rubalcaba and Misty Pinson of LanChile, Miami. A special mention goes to Diana Page, now at the U.S. Embassy in Mexico City.

And finally, thanks to my wife María Laura Massolo; my daughter Clio Bernhardson-Massolo; my Alaskan Malamute Gardel, who slept at my feet through most of the process of writing this up, while patiently awaiting his next walk around the neighborhood; and Gardel's adopted Akita brother Sandro, who reminds me when I need to take a nap.

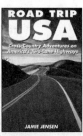

PERU

ECUADOR

CHILE

BOLIVIA

BRAZIL

ARGENTINA

EXPLORING THE *South* OF THE WORLD

INTRODUCING LANCHILE VACATIONS
Uniquely Customized Land Adventures

LanChile now offers **LanChile Vacations**, an array of customized packages for a complete travel experience. You can create a vacation tailored exactly to your clients' specifications, whether they are traveling alone or in a small group, and whether they choose from the modules outlined in our programs, or create a unique itinerary crafted around their individual interests and desire for adventure. So while your clients enjoy unforgettable cultural and natural adventures, you can relax knowing they will experience travel in its most perfect form. LanChile's 72 years of travel expertise will stand behind your clients every step of the way. Enjoy the complete experience of travel with **LanChile Vacations**.

All LanChile Vacations are commissionable.

LANCHILE
VACATIONS

For reservations and information, please call LanChile Vacations
at 1-877-219-0345 or visit us at www.lanchilevacations.com

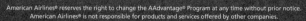

Keeping Current

Although we strive to produce the most up-to-date guidebook humanly possible, change is unavoidable. Between the time this book goes to print and the moment you read it, a handful of the businesses noted in these pages will undoubtedly change prices, move, or even close their doors forever. Other worthy attractions will open for the first time. If you have a favorite gem you'd like to see included in the next edition, or see anything that needs updating, clarification, or correction, please drop us a line. Send your comments via email to atpfeedback@avalonpub.com, or use the address below.

Moon Handbooks Argentina
Avalon Travel Publishing
1400 65th Street, Suite 250
Emeryville, CA 94608, USA
www.moon.com

Avalon Travel Publishing
An Imprint of
Avalon Publishing Group, Inc.

AVALON
publishing group incorporated

Editor: Amy Scott
Series Manager: Kevin McLain
Acquisitions Editor: Rebecca K. Browning
Copy Editor: Candace English
Graphics Coordinator: Deb Dutcher
Production Coordinator: Jacob Goolkasian
Cover Designer: Kari Gim
Interior Designers: Amber Pirker, Alvaro
    Villanueva, Kelly Pendragon
Map Editors: Naomi Adler Dancis, Olivia Solís
Cartographers: Suzanne Service, Kat
    Kalamaras, and Mike Morgenfeld
Indexers: Marie S. Nichols, Peter Brigaitis

ISBN: 1-56691-509-0
ISSN: 1550-2627

Printing History
1st Edition—November 2004
5 4 3 2 1

Text © 2004 by Wayne Bernhardson.
Maps © 2004 by Avalon Travel Publishing, Inc.
All rights reserved.